DATE DUE			
May 22 78			

Inorganic Chemistry

AN ADVANCED TEXTBOOK

THERALD MOELLER
Associate Professor of Chemistry
University of Illinois

New York · JOHN WILEY & SONS, *Inc.*
London · CHAPMAN & HALL, *Limited*

Library of Congress Catalog Card Number: 52-7487

PRINTED IN THE UNITED STATES OF AMERICA

Preface

Emphasis upon the various phases of chemistry has proved to be quite generally cyclic in nature. In the early days of modern chemistry, inorganic materials received primary attention. This period was followed by the development of physical chemistry and organic chemistry, and, subsequent to the First World War, organic chemistry was strongly emphasized and attained a position of well-deserved eminence. More recently, however, the pendulum has begun another swing toward inorganic chemistry, with emphasis upon its physico-chemical aspects rather than upon its treatment in a purely descriptive fashion. The remarkable theoretical and technical advances which have been made and continue to be made are again raising inorganic chemistry to the position that it so richly merits.

Unfortunately, however, instruction in inorganic chemistry has not expanded in a completely comparable fashion. Too often, college and university students have made their only contacts with the subject in their freshman general chemistry and sophomore analytical chemistry courses. These contacts have been insufficient to acquaint the students with the modern aspects of inorganic chemistry and to appraise them of its scope and possibilities. Too often, they have felt that all that is to be done in the field has long since been done. Too often, they have concluded that no opportunities exist either in research or in technology. Sober reflection shows the fallacies in such statements. Sober reflection also shows the need for more complete instruction in modern and advanced inorganic chemistry.

For a number of years, the University of Illinois has offered a one-semester lecture course in advanced inorganic chemistry which surveys the field from a modern point of view and acquaints students with existing problems and current investigations. This course admits advanced undergraduate students and beginning graduate students. At the graduate level, the course provides the foundation material upon which the more advanced and specialized courses in inorganic chemistry are based. Student interest has always been high, and enrollments are consistently large.

Those who have taught this course have been plagued by the lack of suitable textbooks to delineate the pattern which is desired. As a consequence, they have drawn material from a variety of books and have supplemented this information by other material drawn from widely scattered original literature sources. The difficulties inherent in such a procedure are apparent to teacher and student alike. This textbook of mine has resulted from an attempt to remedy this situation by bringing together in a single volume those selected portions of the tremendous body of available information which seem essential to a comprehensive understanding of inorganic chemistry. It is designed primarily for a course of the type outlined, but I hope that it will be of use to all those who are interested in the subject.

Mechanically, this book is divided into two broad parts. In Part I the various principles required in systematic inorganic chemistry are outlined. These principles are taken up in a logical order, which permits a principle once developed to be used in the development of another. A considerable volume of factual material is included to implement the discussions. In Part II the chemical elements and their compounds are discussed from the modern point of view and with the thought of applying, wherever possible, the principles developed in Part I. Part II is not encyclopedic in nature, but it does contain much descriptive matter and many tabulations and systematizations which, it is hoped, will be useful. The approach in Part II is by families arranged by types of elements. The order followed is unconventional, but it is logical and teachable.

Every attempt has been made to keep the discussions up to date and to document thoroughly all important items. To these ends, the literature has been covered by references to original publications reasonably well through 1950. The reader will recognize, of course, the impossibility of including accounts of the very latest researches and will appreciate that a certain obsoleteness characterizes any scientific report. I hope, however, that except for such revisions as are essential in the light of continuing investigations the fundamental approach will be adequate.

I am fully aware that neither this book nor any other can satisfy all the needs and all the desires of all interested individuals. The order of topics may not appeal to everyone; the choice of topics may not be in accord with the desires of every person; the amount of emphasis given each topic may not reflect the views of every reader; the inclusion of certain topics, nucleonics, for example, may be regarded as of questionable value; the essentially non-mathematical treatment of the subject may be considered a deficiency. It is my feeling at present that the topics covered and the order and fashion in which they are covered can do much toward providing an individual with needed knowledge of inorganic chemistry. To this end I have attempted to strike a reasonable balance between theoretical and descriptive approaches. I will very much appreciate comments, criticisms, suggestions, and indications of errors.

To acknowledge all the assistance received in the compilation of this book would be impossible, for help was received from innumerable individuals over a period of years. I am deeply grateful to all those with whom I have discussed the content of this book and who have made suggestions regarding it. I wish to acknowledge in particular the assistance given me by my colleagues, Professors L. F. Audrieth, J. C. Bailar, Jr., and B S. Hopkins, and to express appreciation to my wife, Ellyn, for her understanding and her help in handling proof. I am grateful also to Messrs. R. H. Marshall, F. L. Pundsack, F. A. J. Moss, V. Ramaniah, and M. Tecotzky for their assistance in checking final proof.

THERALD MOELLER

University of Illinois
June, 1952

Contents

PART ONE. PRINCIPLES

CHAPTER

1. Introduction 3
2. Atomic Nuclei and Properties Related Thereto 16
3. The Extranuclear Structures of the Atoms 79
4. The Periodic Classification of the Elements 109
5. Characteristics Dependent upon the Extranuclear Structures—I. General 127
6. Characteristics Dependent upon the Extranuclear Structures—II. Valency and the Chemical Bond 171
7. Complex Ions and Coordination Compounds 227
8. Oxidation-Reduction—Oxidation Potentials 280
9. Acids and Bases 306
10. Non-aqueous Solvents 337

PART TWO. THE CHEMICAL ELEMENTS

11. The Inert Gas Elements 373
12. Hydrogen 386
13. Periodic Group VIIb—The Halogens 417
14. Periodic Group VIb—The Oxygen Family 481
15. Periodic Group Vb—The Nitrogen Family 556
16. Periodic Group IVb—The Carbon Family 661
17. Periodic Group IIIb—The Boron Family 734
18. Periodic Group I—The Alkali and Coinage Metals 818
19. Periodic Group II—The Alkaline Earth and Zinc Family Elements 845
20. The Transition Elements 868
21. The Inner Transition Elements 891

Appendix I. Characteristics of the Naturally Occurring Isotopes 911

Appendix II. Members of the Disintegration Series 917

Author Index 919

Subject Index 939

PART ONE
Principles

CHAPTER 1

Introduction

Inorganic chemistry is not general chemistry. To some, this may appear as an obvious statement of fact. To others, it may appear as a contradiction of accepted opinion. As opposed to organic chemistry, inorganic chemistry is properly a study of all chemical materials other than the hydrocarbons and their derivatives. Not only does inorganic chemistry embrace the properties and modes of preparation of such materials, but it goes beyond and seeks to account for and explain specific characteristics and observed similarities, differences, and trends in observed behaviors. Modern inorganic chemistry, unlike classical inorganic chemistry, is more than a descriptive science. It attempts to relate the properties of chemical substances to their structures, which in turn are related to the ultimate structures of the particles which combined to make those substances. Modern inorganic chemistry employs, therefore, both the experimental and theoretical approaches and requires familiarity with each. It is concerned with all the elements and with all the combinations in which these elements are found. Since it embraces a study of a variety of different individual materials, bonds, and behaviors, it is inherently more involved than organic chemistry. Organic chemistry, though concerned with more individual compounds, involves a limited number of bond types and, therefore, a more restricted number of behavior types. It is no exaggeration to state that the phenomena of organic chemistry will receive adequate theoretical interpretation long before those of inorganic chemistry.

Inorganic chemistry is not general chemistry. General chemistry is properly introductory chemistry and embraces only broad interpretations of the behaviors of chemical materials while providing the necessary bases for the further, more detailed studies involved in specific phases of chemistry. General chemistry amounts essentially to a combination of the elements of theoretical chemistry, analytical chemistry, organic chemistry, and inorganic chemistry. That many of the examples studied are inorganic in nature provides no real basis for terming it inorganic chemistry. Emphasis on these materials is merely essential to an understanding of the periodic system as a whole. The unfortunate concept of synonymity has been maintained too long. It were well to discard it and then to develop the subject clearly and without preconceived views.

Classical inorganic chemistry was essentially purely descriptive. As such, it was the dominant phase of chemistry throughout the major portion of the nineteenth century. With the advent of ideas on atomic structure in the early years of the twentieth century, emphasis changed, and the resulting trend toward accounting for observed properties and behaviors rather than accepting and tabulating them as such has increased as more and more knowledge about the fundamental character of matter has been accumulated. This was the genesis of modern inorganic chemistry. Its growth during the twentieth century has been largely along such lines, although necessary emphasis upon descriptive chemistry has been retained to provide data for systematic studies. The lines of demarcation between inorganic chemistry and other phases of chemistry have become less well defined. As a result, one finds in modern inorganic chemistry considerations of crystal structures, radioactivity, color, analytical methods, oxidation-reduction phenomena, acid-base phenomena, physical measurements of a number of types, and a host of other things. To fit these into a logical picture which will then describe the scope of the entire subject is the primary purpose of the first part of this book.

Because so much of modern development in inorganic chemistry either involves atomic structure directly or is concerned with interpretations based upon atomic structures, it seems wise to base the general treatment of the subject upon the concepts of atomic structure. From these views, then, other concepts can be developed logically. In this chapter, significant developments which have led to modern views on atomic structure are outlined. In the next two chapters, the natures, implications, and applications of modern views are discussed. Subsequent chapters are devoted to the development of inorganic chemistry in the light of these views, and in Part II the principles developed in Part I are applied to specific inorganic materials.

THE ATOMIC NATURE OF MATTER

The concept that matter is built up of tiny discrete particles probably originated with the early Greek philosophers. In fact, the designation *atom* for such a particle stems from the Greek meaning "not divided." However, it was not until about 1802–1803 that the rather nebulous ideas of the early thinkers were given the more quantitative interpretation necessary to modern development. At that time, John Dalton, the father of modern atomic theory, suggested that:

1. Matter is composed of tiny real particles called atoms.
2. Atoms of any pure substance can be neither subdivided nor changed one into another.
3. Atoms are incapable of being destroyed or created.
4. Atoms of any pure substance are identical with each other in weight, size, and other properties.
5. Atoms of one pure substance differ in weight and other characteristics from those of other substances.
6. Chemical combination amounts to the union of atoms in definite numerical proportions.

The fundamental importance of these thoughts cannot be minimized, even though some are no longer true in substance. Dalton's hypotheses were incapable of direct verification, but they were in accord with experimental fact and influenced chemical thought for over a century. It should be mentioned also that Dalton supplemented his general concepts with values for atomic sizes and weights. These values are without real significance.

Developments subsequent to Dalton's proposals amounted to expansions of the atomic theory and more comprehensive explanations of its tenets. Thus Prout (in 1815) proposed that the weights of all atoms were simple multiples of the weight of the hydrogen atom and that hydrogen was thus the fundamental material out of which all other elements were constructed. Although fundamentally incorrect (p. 36), Prout's hypothesis does contain the ideas that atoms themselves are complex and that certain even more simple particles may exist. As the nineteenth century progressed, this thought grew in stature, particularly after the work of Michael Faraday (in 1833) showed matter to be electrical in nature and demonstrated equivalences between electrical energy and chemical change.

The complexity of the atom became increasingly apparent with discovery of the electron, of x-radiation and other types of radiation, of radioactivity, of nuclear reactions, and of a number of subatomic particles. The inescapable conclusion based upon the wealth of accumulated data is that a number of *particles* are essential to the construction of the atom. These particles may now be considered in detail.

Fundamental components of atoms

It is convenient to consider atoms as being composed of several types of ultimate particles. Some of these are of sufficient stability to be capable of independent existence outside an atom. Others are so unstable by comparison as to exist only momentarily outside the atom or to possess only transient existence within the atom itself. Most of these particles are simple in nature, although some composite particles are known as well. However, there is little or no positive evidence that any composite particle plays a real role in the construction of an atom. Only the salient features of these particles need be considered here. For more detailed consideration, reference should be made to such a comprehensive text as that by Stranathan.[1]

Stable Particles. Only three such particles are recognized, namely, the negative electron, the proton, and the neutron.

THE NEGATIVE ELECTRON, ELECTRON, OR NEGATRON (e^-, ${}_{-1}^{0}e$, β^-).* The term electron was first employed in 1874 by Stoney, who used it for the unit charge on a monovalent negative ion. Because of errors, however, the currently accepted magnitude of this charge is some sixteen times Stoney's value. In 1879, Sir William Crookes showed that in highly evacuated discharge tubes so-called cathode rays streamed from the negative poles when high potentials were applied. Regardless of the natures of the negative poles used or the natures of the residual gases in such tubes, these cathode rays were found to possess the following characteristics:

1. Travel in straight lines from the negative pole (cathode).
2. Cast shadows when targets are placed in their paths.
3. Produce mechanical motion in pinwheels.
4. Produce fluorescence in glass walls of the tubes.
5. Heat thin metal foils to incandescence.
6. Impart negative charges to objects in their paths.
7. Suffer deflection in applied electrostatic or magnetic fields.

Later, it was also shown that they cause ionization in gases, expose photographic plates, and yield penetrating x-radiation when directed against suitable targets. These characteristics suggest that such

[1] J. D. Stranathan: *The "Particles" of Modern Physics.* The Blakiston Company, Philadelphia (1942).

* Among physicists, the term *negatron* is preferred, and the term *electron* is applied to both negative and positive particles. Among chemists, however, the term *electron* is used universally to characterize the negative particle, and this is the usage which will be followed in this book.

rays are made up of small but energetic negative particles. This was proved in 1897 by Sir J. J. Thomson. These particles are called *electrons*.

Although independent evidences for the existence of electrons in matter were obtained through the production of identical particles by thermionic and photoelectric emission and as a result of radioactive decay, perhaps the most significant studies were made with cathode rays. Using tubes in which a collimated beam of cathode rays could be deflected by the simultaneous application of magnetic and electrostatic fields arranged perpendicular to each other, Thomson[2] evaluated the ratio of charge to mass ($e:m$) for the electron by measuring the magnitudes of the two fields required to produce no deflection in the electron beam. Although the value obtained by Thomson has been revised upward by more precise measurement, his observation that the ratio $e:m$ is the same regardless of the nature of the cathode or residual gas has been shown to be valid. This leads to the conclusion that all electrons are identical. Evaluation of the electronic charge was first effected by Millikan[3, 4] by use of the classic oil-drop experiment, in which the rate of fall of a tiny charged oil droplet due to gravity was exactly balanced by an electrostatic field of measured intensity. Millikan's value was accepted as exact for many years, and only recently have more precise measurements necessitated revision of it. The numerical characteristics given in Table 1·1 represent the most generally accepted values at the present time. The reader will understand that literally hundreds of experiments in addition to those described have been involved in the complete characterization of the electron.

It should be pointed out that, although the electron has been characterized as a finite particle and is most usefully so considered by the chemist, it does possess wave properties. Although it is beyond the scope of this book to explore this view, such properties as reflection and diffraction can best be explained by means of such considerations. These views on the wave properties of an apparently particulate material were first advanced by de Broglie[5] and have since formed the basis for theoretical views on the extranuclear structures of the atoms. Their treatment lies properly in the realm of theoretical physics.

THE PROTON (p, ${}_1^1p$, P, ${}_1^1$H). Detailed experiments with discharge tubes of the cathode ray type showed the presence of beams of positive

[2] J. J. Thomson: *Phil. Mag.* [5], **44**, 293 (1897).
[3] R. A. Millikan: *Phil. Mag.* [6], **19**, 209 (1910).
[4] R. A. Millikan: *Phys. Rev.* [1], **32**, 349 (1911); **2**, 109 (1913).
[5] L. de Broglie: *Ann. phys.*, **3**, 22 (1925).

particles (positive rays or canal rays), which unlike the electrons of cathode rays depended for their charges and masses upon the natures of the residual gases in the tubes. Some of the results obtained for the positive rays will be explored in the next chapter (pp. 21–25). However, it was found that unipositive particles with maximum ratio of charge to mass were obtained when the residual gas was hydrogen. These particles, called *protons*, were found to be identical with hydrogen atoms from which the single electrons had been removed. The appearance of protons as products in a variety of nuclear reactions has led to the general feeling that their presence in all atomic species is likely (pp. 66–71). The general characteristics of the proton are summarized in Table 1·1.

THE NEUTRON (n, ${}_0^1n$, N). Existence of a neutral particle common to most atomic species was predicted around 1920, but the difficulties associated with detecting a particle which could neither ionize other materials except by direct collision nor be deflected by magnetic or electrostatic fields were so great that proof of its existence was long in coming. The discovery of the neutron was foreshadowed by an observation by Bothe and Becker[6] that bombardment of certain of the lighter elements (e.g., Li, Be, B) with alpha particles yielded a penetrating radiation, an observation which was checked by others but attributed to gamma radiation (p. 57). In 1932, Chadwick[7] showed definitely that such radiation was due to neutral particles of approximately unit mass (Table 1·1) generated by nuclear reactions such as

$${}_4^9\text{Be} + {}_2^4\text{He} \rightarrow {}_6^{12}\text{C} + {}_0^1n$$

(see p. 26 for explanation of notation used). Although similar reactions are difficult to effect with the heavier elements, evidences from a variety of nuclear reactions, especially those of the fission type (pp. 72–77), support the view of the nearly universal occurrence of neutrons.

Unstable Particles. Among such particles are the positron, the neutrino and antineutrino, and the meson.

THE POSITIVE ELECTRON OR POSITRON (e^+, ${}_1^0e$, β^+). The positive counterpart of the electron was discovered more or less accidentally by Anderson[8] in 1932, when, during studies on the effects of magnetic fields upon particles ejected from atomic nuclei by absorption of cosmic

[6] W. Bothe and H. Becker: *Z. Physik,* **66,** 289 (1930).
[7] J. Chadwick: *Proc. Roy. Soc.* (*London*), **A136,** 692 (1932).
[8] C. D. Anderson: *Phys. Rev.,* **41,** 405 (1932); **43,** 491 (1933).

rays, he noticed fog tracks* exactly like those given by electrons but deflected in the opposite direction. Particles responsible for these tracks were called *positrons.* They apparently resulted from cosmic radiation through the creation of electron-positron pairs. They are also noted in the decay of certain radioactive substances (p. 54). However, their stable existence under any circumstance appears highly unlikely since electrons and positrons mutually annihilate each other with the production of gamma radiation (p. 57). Characteristics of the positron are summarized in Table 1·1.

THE NEUTRINO AND ANTI-NEUTRINO (ν). These are particles of small mass and zero charge the existence of which has been postulated to account for energy changes during the radioactive emission of electrons and positrons (p. 54). The neutrino is supposedly associated with and shares the energy of the electron, whereas the anti-neutrino occupies the same position with respect to the positron. Although these particles seem very probable, no concrete evidence for the existence of either has been obtained.

THE MESON (FORMERLY MESOTRON). To account for nuclear binding energies (p. 18), Yukawa[10] postulated the existence of a particle (the meson) of mass intermediate between the electron and the proton. Mesons were discovered first in cosmic ray studies, resulting doubtless from the effects of cosmic radiation on matter. Recent work in ultrahigh energy ranges with the cyclotron has led to the creation of mesons in the laboratory. Mesons are of two types, designated π and μ, the former being somewhat heavier than the latter (Table 1·1). Both π and μ mesons are unstable and are believed to decay as

$$\pi^{\pm} \rightarrow \mu^{\pm} + \nu \qquad 10^{-8} \text{ sec.}$$

$$\mu^{\pm} \rightarrow e^{\pm} + 2\nu \qquad 2 \times 10^{-6} \text{ sec.}$$

Apparently, both types of mesons may be either positively or negatively charged as indicated. An interesting summary of the characteristics of mesons is given by Keller.[11]

Composite Particles. The only composite particles which are of importance are the deuteron and the alpha particle.

* When an energetic particle passes through a gas, ions result. If at the same time this gas is rendered supersaturated with water vapor, condensation results upon these ions, and the path of the particle becomes visible as a track of tiny water droplets. This phenomenon was first used by Wilson[9] in the study of such particles. The familiar Wilson cloud chamber employs this phenomenon.

[9] C. T. R. Wilson: *Proc. Roy. Soc. (London)*, **A85**, 285 (1911); **A87**, 277 (1912).

[10] H. Yukawa: *Proc. Phys.-Math. Soc. Japan* [3], **17**, 48 (1935).

[11] J. M. Keller: *Am. J. Phys.*, **17**, 356 (1949).

THE DEUTERON (d, ${}^2_1d$, ${}^2_1\mathrm{H}$, ${}^2_1\mathrm{D}$). The deuteron is a deuterium (heavy hydrogen) nucleus and bears the same relation to heavy hydrogen that the proton does to ordinary hydrogen. Although useful as a bombarding particle (p. 70), it plays no role in the ultimate composition of matter.

THE ALPHA PARTICLE (α, ${}^4_2\mathrm{He}$). The alpha particle is a doubly charged helium nucleus. Its appearance as a product of radioactive decay (p. 57) and the fact that the masses of many comparatively stable atomic nuclei are multiples of its mass (p. 28) suggest its importance as a fundamental atomic constituent. Actually, there is little or no evidence to support this view.

Suggestions as to other particles, namely anti-protons, anti-neutrons, and various other types of mesons, must still be regarded as tentative and in need of experimental verification. The general characteristics of the particles described above are summarized in Table 1·1.

TABLE 1·1
CHARACTERISTICS OF ELEMENTARY PARTICLES

Particle	Designation	Mass, AMU*	Charge, esu × 10^{10}†	Relative Charge
Electron	e^-, ${}^{\ 0}_{-1}e$, β^-	0.0005486	−4.8029 (= e)	$-e$
Proton	p, ${}^1_1p$, ${}^1_1\mathrm{H}$	1.00757	+4.8029	$+e$
Neutron	n, ${}^1_0n$	1.00893	0	0
Positron	e^+, ${}^0_1e$, β^+	0.0005486	+4.8029	$+e$
Neutrino	ν	....	0	0
Anti-neutrino	....	....	0	0
Meson	π	0.156‡	±4.8029	$\pm e$
	μ	0.118§	±4.8029	$\pm e$
Deuteron	d, ${}^2_1d$, ${}^2_1\mathrm{D}$	2.01416	+4.8029	$+e$
Alpha	α, ${}^4_2\mathrm{He}$	4.00279	+9.6058	$+2e$

* AMU, atomic mass units, are the units of the physical atomic weight scale (p. 33); 1 AMU = 1.6603×10^{-24} g.

† esu, electrostatic units, are the fundamental units of electrical charges.

‡ Equivalent to 285 electron masses.

§ Equivalent to 216 electron masses.

The development of modern atomic theory

Modern atomic theory has developed largely since about 1898. This development has amounted to a series of discoveries involving the elementary particles just described and the phenomena associated with them, followed by logical expansions of theoretical views to accomodate these observations. The picture is not complete, nor is it conceivable that a complete picture will be obtained for many years to come. The developing picture has assumed more and more of a mathematical character, and less and less opportunity to use models, formerly so common, remains. The story of these developments is a fascinating one. Here, however, only a few of the more outstanding contributions to a picture useful to chemists and physicists alike can be described. In the next two chapters, these basic observations are expanded and supplemented.

The first attempt to depict an atom from an electrical point of view was apparently made in 1904 by Thomson.[12] He pictured a jelly-like atom made up of positive and negative electricity, with the positive charge distributed uniformly throughout a sphere representing the atom. Inasmuch as atomic diameters had been shown to be of the order of 10^{-8} cm. (1 A), the positive portion of such an atom would necessarily extend through a region of this size. It soon became apparent, however, that the relatively high energies associated with alpha particles ejected from radioactive atoms would require the existence of a positive charge concentrated in a region of diameter somewhat less than 10^{-8} cm. As a result, Thomson's views could not be correct.

Modern views accept a nuclear atom. These stem from experiments carried out by Rutherford[13] on the scattering of alpha particles by thin metal foils. In a detailed investigation, Rutherford allowed collimated beams of alpha particles from radium-C (p. 65) to pass through thin foils (ca. 0.0004 cm.) of gold, platinum, silver, and copper and noted the deflection suffered by such particles by allowing them to strike a zinc sulfide fluorescent screen, where they could be observed. Although the majority of the particles passed through the foils undeflected, a limited number were deflected through much larger angles than could be accounted for only by attractions between heavy alpha particles and light electrons. To account for such deflections, Rutherford proposed that an atom is largely space occupied by widely separated electrons, with the mass concentrated in a tiny, centrally located, positively charged nucleus. On this basis, observed alpha particle deflections might be considered as having arisen in the manner shown diagrammatically in Figure 1·1. Indeed from the measured angles of deflection and the assumption that an alpha particle and a nucleus repel each other according to the inverse square law, it was possible to evaluate the nuclear charges (Ze) of the atoms of the elements used as foils. The validities of this assumption and the basic premise of a

[12] J. J. Thomson: *The Corpuscular Theory of Matter*, Ch. VI, VII. Archibald Constable & Co., Ltd., London (1907).

[13] E. Rutherford: *Phil. Mag.* [6], **21,** 669 (1911).

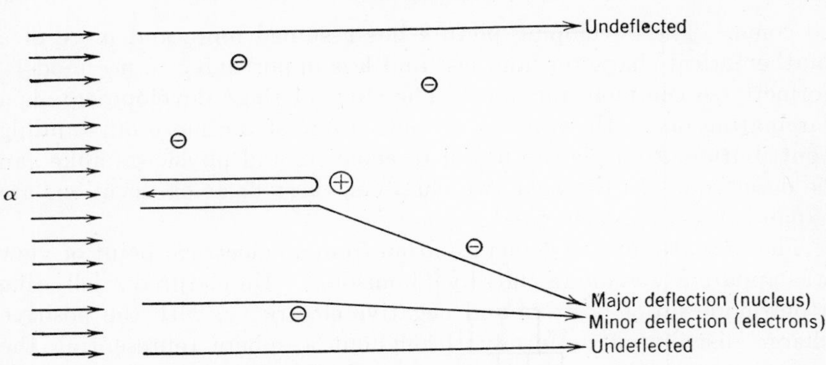

FIG. 1·1. Schematic representation of scattering of alpha particles by an atom.

nuclear atom are shown by calculated nuclear charges of 78 (±5%) for gold, 29.3 (±0.5) for copper, etc.[14]

The other really significant development essential to the appearance of modern views was due to work by Moseley.[15] Röntgen had shown in 1895[16] that bombardment of a target with cathode rays (electrons) yielded a very penetrating radiation of short wavelength, which he called x-rays. Such radiation is now believed to be due to the energy released when inner electrons in atoms are displaced and other electrons then drop back into the vacated spaces (pp. 81–83). It was soon shown that x-rays could be diffracted into spectra somewhat similar to those obtained with longer wavelength radiation (p. 80), provided a grating of sufficiently close spacings, such as a natural or synthetic crystal, were employed. Such a spectrum consisted of series of lines which, in the order of increasing wavelength or decreasing frequency, were called *K*, *L*, *M*, etc., series. Lines of the *K* series were observed for all elements, those of the *L* series only with zinc and elements of larger atomic weight, and those of the *M* series only with the heaviest elements. Moseley prepared x-ray tubes in which targets made either from elements of regularly increasing position in the periodic system or from their compounds were bombarded. The resultant radiations were diffracted by appropriate crystals, and the spectra produced were recorded photographically. When these spectra were compared, it was noted that, if for a given series of lines (for instance, *K*) a line of particular frequency (for instance, the highest) was selected, this line was displaced regularly toward shorter wave lengths as atomic weight of the target material

[14] H. Geiger and E. Marsden: *Phil. Mag.* [6], **25,** 604 (1913).
[15] H. G. J. Moseley: *Phil. Mag.* [6], **26,** 1024 (1913); [6], **27,** 703 (1914).
[16] W. C. Röntgen: *Ann. Physik,* **64,** 1 (1898). Reprint of an earlier paper.

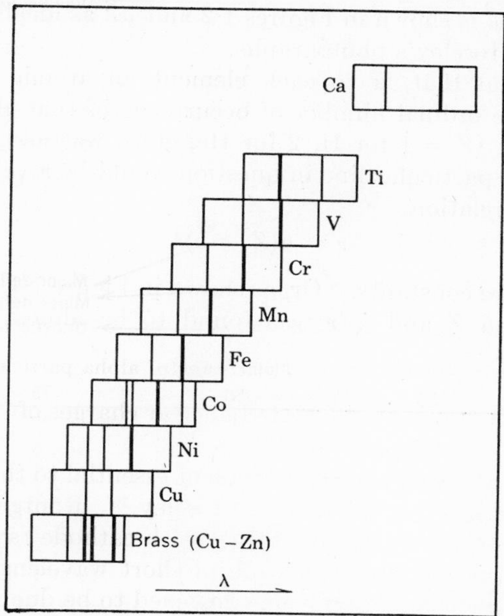

FIG. 1·2. Graphic adaptation of Moseley's x-ray spectra for *K* series for lighter elements.

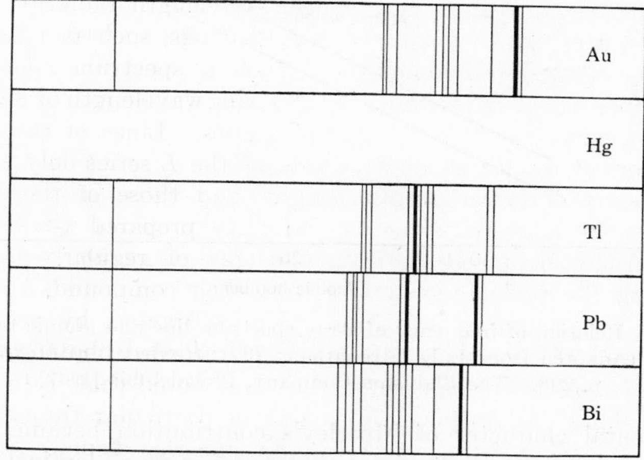

FIG. 1·3. Graphic adaptation of Moseley's x-ray spectra for *L* series for heavier elements.

increased. This is shown in Figures 1·2 and 1·3 as idealized drawings adapted from Moseley's photographs.

Moseley found that, if to each element an atomic number (Z), representing the ordinal number of occurrence of that element in the periodic system ($Z = 1$ for H, 2 for He, etc.), was assigned, the frequency ν of the particular line in question would be given very nearly exactly by the relation

$$\nu = a(Z - b)^2 \qquad (1\cdot1)$$

where a and b are constants. Or, as shown in Figure 1·4, the graphical relation between Z and $\sqrt{\nu}$ was found to be almost linear. The

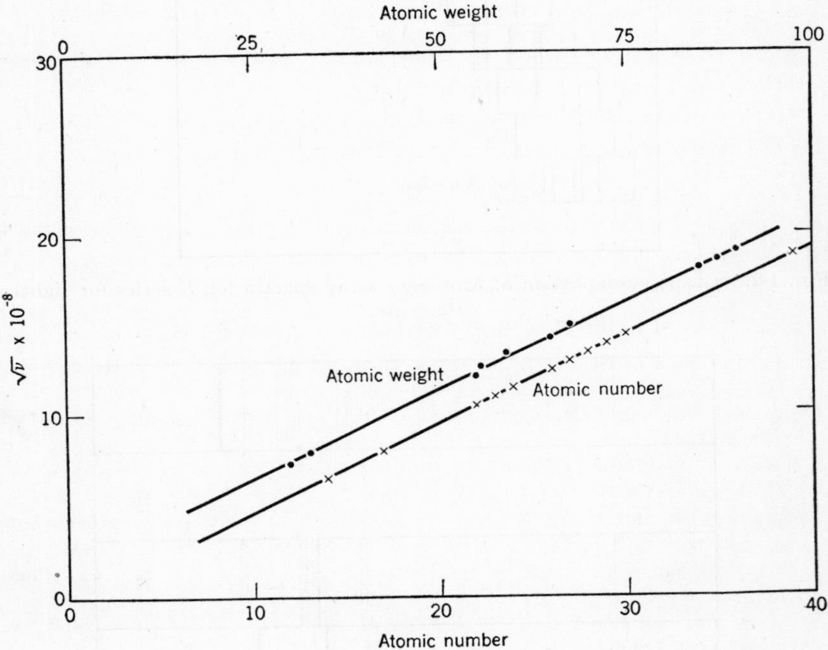

Fig. 1·4. Relation of frequency of x-ray spectrum line and atomic number and weight. (Adapted from J. D. Stranathan: *The "Particles" of Modern Physics*, p. 298. The Blakiston Company, Philadelphia [1942].)

fundamental character of Moseley's contribution became apparent when it was shown that his atomic number was identical with the nuclear charge as deduced from Rutherford-type scattering experiments. The atomic number was interpreted as giving the number of electrons within the atom.

The observations of Rutherford and Moseley provide the foundations of present-day atomic theory. They have, of course, been supplemented by a variety of important and profound developments, among them the discovery of isotopes, Bohr's theory of electronic arrangements and the subsequent considerations of Sommerfeld and the quantum mechanics, the discovery of nuclear transformations, the discovery of other fundamental particles, the discovery of nuclear fission, and a host of others. Many of these are considered in the two subsequent chapters.

The essentials of modern atomic theory

From experimental observation and theoretical consideration, it is believed that the atom consists essentially of two parts, namely:

1. A positively charged nucleus which is small in size (diameter $\sim 10^{-12}$ cm.) and comparatively heavy.
2. An extranuclear arrangement of electrons which is comparatively large (diameter $\sim 10^{-8}$ cm.) and diffuse in character.

The nucleus may be regarded as a physical factor governing many of the physical characteristics of the atom, whereas the extranuclear structure is a chemical factor determining its chemical behavior. It is now necessary to explore each factor in greater detail.

SUGGESTED SUPPLEMENTARY REFERENCES

H. T. Briscoe: *The Structure and Properties of Matter*, Ch. I, II. McGraw-Hill Book Co., New York (1935).

F. Daniels: *Outlines of Physical Chemistry*, Ch. XXI. John Wiley and Sons, New York (1948).

S. Glasstone: *Textbook of Physical Chemistry*, Ch. I, II. D. Van Nostrand Co., New York (1946).

A. W. Stewart and C. L. Wilson: *Recent Advances in Physical and Inorganic Chemistry*, 7th Ed., Ch. I. Longmans, Green and Co., London (1944).

J. D. Stranathan: *The "Particles" of Modern Physics*. The Blakiston Co., Philadelphia (1942).

S. Glasstone: *Sourcebook on Atomic Energy*, Ch. I, II. D. Van Nostrand Co., New York (1950).

CHAPTER 2

Atomic Nuclei and Properties Related Thereto

Some detailed considerations on atomic structure may now be offered. Of the two general regions into which the structure of the atom has been divided, that involving the nucleus will be discussed first since it bears less relationship to the majority of the topics to be considered in this book than does the extranuclear region. Although it may be argued that discussions of atomic nuclei lie more properly in the fields of applied and theoretical physics, the line of demarcation between physics and chemistry has become so indistinct in recent years that neither of these branches of physical science can any longer be considered independent of the other. If the chemist is to employ the outer architecture of the atom to best advantage in solving his problems, he must be conversant with the inner architecture as well and with those properties which are dependent upon it.

Although knowledge relative to atomic nuclei has increased tremendously in the past few years, it must be admitted that surprisingly little is known in comparison with what remains to be learned. This is particularly true of theoretical considerations. Much of what is offered in a theoretical way to account for the constituents of atoms and their behaviors amounts more exactly to restatement of observed fact and cannot be used for further predictions. This is due largely to the lack of adherence of particles of nuclear and subnuclear dimensions to classical behavior. However, much useful information concerning the behaviors of nuclei, their syntheses, their stabilities, the release of energy from them, and their general properties can be presented. If such fundamental points as the exact compositions of atomic nuclei and the true natures of the binding forces which render them stable remain unsettled, they should be regarded as goals for future achievement.

In the discussion which follows, no attempt has been made to cover more than the real essentials. The treatment is non-mathematical and, where possible, modular in character. More comprehensive treatments as indicated in the cited references may be consulted with profit by the interested individual.

THE COMPOSITIONS OF ATOMIC NUCLEI

A number of combinations of the fundamental particles discussed in Chapter 1 lead to nuclei with the requisite mass numbers (A)* and positive charges (Z). Among the more important nuclear pictures which have been offered are those which are described here.

The Proton-Electron Concept. Offered shortly after development of the nuclear atom concept, this view, in spite of its weaknesses, was quite generally held until the discovery of the neutron in 1932. The nucleus was considered to contain sufficient protons (A) to account for its mass and sufficient electrons ($A - Z$) to neutralize the proton charges in excess of those indicated by the atomic number (Z). Both nuclear protons and electrons were regarded as essentially free, and a distinction between extranuclear and nuclear electrons was always necessary. The improbability of the coexistence of oppositely charged particles within the small element of space (sphere of diameter 10^{-12} cm.) encompassed by the atomic nucleus caused many to question the proton-electron concept and led both Harkins and Rutherford to postulate the existence of the neutron as early as 1919. The improbability of such a charge combination must be regarded as the strongest argument in support of the ultimate rejection of this view.

The Proton-Neutron Concept. Discovery of the neutron was followed logically by an alteration of the nuclear picture to accomodate this neutral particle. Since the neutron was regarded as a close combination of an electron with a proton, the nucleus was considered to contain protons equal in number to the atomic number (Z) and neutrons (N) equal in number to the mass number (A) minus the atomic number. The proton-neutron concept is the most consistent in accounting for the majority of the properties of atomic nuclei and is the most widely held at the present time. Nevertheless, it is far from perfect. It is difficult, for example, to conceive of the stable packing together of numbers of positive particles in the small element of volume that is the nucleus. Nor in the usual sense can one conceive of sizable attractive forces between neutrons and protons. Although it is perhaps wrong to visualize the nucleus as a mere grouping of neutrons and protons, such a view is qualitatively useful. To regard a neutron as being a combination of a proton and an electron is probably equally in error, but it is again of qualitative use.

* The mass number is the whole number closest in magnitude to the actual weight (in AMU) of the species in question.

The Positron-Neutron Concept. Alternatively, the nucleus may be considered to contain positrons equal in number to the atomic number (Z) and neutrons equal in number to the mass number (A). In a broad sense, then, the proton would represent an intimate combination between a positron and a neutron. Although such a concept is attractive in accounting for positron emission in decay processes (p. 54), there is little evidence that it is a true one. Nothing is gained by adopting this view in preference to the proton-neutron concept.

In the discussions which follow, the neutron-proton model is used exclusively. Inasmuch as the neutron and proton differ by a unit charge, one may write

$$\text{neutron} + \text{positive charge} \rightleftharpoons \text{proton} \tag{2·1}$$

and

$$\text{proton} + \text{negative charge} \rightleftharpoons \text{neutron} \tag{2·2}$$

For practical purposes, particularly in accounting for changes in nuclear charges during radioactive decay processes (pp. 62–66), this positive charge may be regarded as a positron (e^+) and this negative charge as an electron (e^-). The neutron and proton can then be formally related as

$$\text{neutron} \underset{+e^-}{\overset{+e^+}{\rightleftharpoons}} \text{proton} \tag{2·3}$$

The true state, however, is less simple. It is believed that attractive forces between neutron and proton are due to transformation of one into the other by means of electronic charges, such transformations being referred to as exchange or resonance processes. The small masses of the electron and positron forbid their functioning in such processes. Mesons with their larger masses, however, can so function, and it is believed that they are responsible for nuclear forces. According to Serber[1] nuclear forces arise from the creation and annihilation of π mesons (p. 9) by nuclear particles (nucleons). He proposes the following scheme of nuclear process:

$$p \rightleftharpoons n + \pi^+ \tag{2·4}$$

$$\pi^\pm \rightarrow \mu^\pm + \nu \tag{2·5}$$

$$\mu^\pm \rightarrow e^\pm + 2\nu \tag{2·6}$$

$$\mu^- + p \rightarrow n + \nu \tag{2·7}$$

[1] R. Serber: *Phys. Rev.*, **75**, 1459 (1949).

which show the relation of proton to neutron in terms of π and μ mesons and the neutrino (ν). This view appears acceptable in the light of most recent evidences.

Many attempts have been made to reduce observed nuclear compositions to a series of types which are more or less periodic in character. It is beyond the scope of this treatment to discuss this subject in detail. The interested reader will find the comprehensive account by Kurbatov[2] to be worth study. It is of interest to point out, however, that nuclei with 2, 8, 20, 28, 50, 82, or 126 neutrons or protons are especially stable. These so-called magic numbers are conceived to represent closed shells of nucleons.[3,4]

ISOTOPES

Of the postulates of Dalton's atomic theory (p. 5), only the one suggesting that all atoms of a given element are identical to one another and equal in weight has been proved to be seriously in error. Actually, if identity is taken to mean identity in chemical characteristics, only the idea of equality in weight need be seriously altered. Such a postulation, although incapable of proof in Dalton's time, seemed so logical that even the many fractional atomic weights found during attempts to prove Prout's hypothesis (p. 5) failed to shake faith in it. That fractional atomic weights necessitate the assumption that atoms themselves must have fractional weights for acceptance of this phase of Dalton's theory apparently troubled few, if any, investigators.

This general concept was first questioned in 1886 by Sir William Crookes. The following quotation from Crookes's original publication[5] summarizes his views: "I conceive that when we say the atomic weight of, for instance, calcium is 40, we really express the fact that, while the majority of calcium atoms have an actual weight of 40, there are not a few which are represented by 39 or 41, a less number by 38 or 42, and so on." When one realizes that this statement was based upon no physical or chemical evidence, one is struck by Crookes's almost prophetic insight into the nature of matter. Yet this concept was not destined for acceptance for some time. Shortly after this proposal, Crookes separated the earth yttria (p. 891) into a number of components with similar chemical properties but different phosphorescence spectra.[6] These he regarded as containing the same element

[2] J. D. Kurbatov: *J. Phys. Chem.*, **49**, 110 (1945).
[3] M. G. Mayer: *Phys. Rev.*, **74**, 235 (1948); **75**, 1969 (1949); **78**, 16, 22 (1950).
[4] R. A. Brightsen: *Nucleonics*, **6**, No. 4, 14 (1950).
[5] W. Crookes: *Nature*, **34**, 423 (1886).
[6] W. Crookes: *Trans. Chem. Soc.*, **53**, 487 (1888); **55**, 257 (1889).

but with differing atomic weights. Subsequent work by others showed his postulated *meta-elements* to be different elements, and the concept of variability in atomic weight was abandoned.

More conclusive evidence of the truth of Crookes's early speculations was presented shortly after the discovery of radioactivity. In 1906, Boltwood[7] discovered a new radioactive element, which he called ionium and which he found to have chemical properties so similar to those of thorium as to render its compounds chemically inseparable from those of thorium. Further work by others showed differences in mass and radioactive properties which proved ionium and thorium to be different materials. Yet even the arc spectra of the two were identical.[8] The chemical identities of mesothorium-I with radium and of radium-D with lead were established at about the same time, and Soddy suggested[9] that "chemical homogeneity is no longer a guarantee that any supposed element is not a mixture of several different atomic weights, or that any atomic weight is not merely a mean number."

Final evidence was presented in 1913, when it was shown by positive ray analysis[10] (p. 21) that neon contains atoms of mass numbers 20 and 22, those of the latter type constituting much the smaller fraction of the whole. At the same time, Soddy, in considering the radioactive elements, suggested the term *isotope* (Greek, equal places) in the following words:[11] "The same algebraic sum of the positive and negative charges in the nucleus when the arithmetical sum is different gives what I call 'isotopes' or 'isotopic elements' because they occupy the same place in the periodic table. They are chemically identical, and save only as regards the relatively few physical properties which depend upon atomic mass directly, physically identical also."

Subsequent investigations have shown that the occurrence of elements as mixtures of isotopes is the rule rather than the exception. Isotopes may be defined as atoms the nuclei of which contain the same number of protons but different numbers of neutrons. It follows, therefore, that all isotopes of a given species contain the same number of electrons, and, since these electrons are identically arranged (Ch. 3), it is not surprising that essential identity in chemical characteristics should result. Such differences in properties as are due to mass

7 B. B. Boltwood: *Am. J. Sci.* [4], **22, 537** (1906); [4], **24**, 370 (1907).

8 A. S. Russell and R. Rossi: *Proc. Roy. Soc.* (*London*), **A77**, 478 (1912).

9 F. Soddy: *Ann. Reports*, **7**, 286 (1910).

10 J. J. Thomson: *Proc. Roy. Soc.* (*London*), **A89**, 1 (1914).

11 F. Soddy: *Report of the British Association for the Advancement of Science*, p. 445 (1913).

differences can be large only with the lightest elements because it is only with them that percentage differences in mass are appreciable.

The detection and study of isotopes

One of the most important experimental approaches to the study of isotopes has involved positive ray analysis. Although discovered in 1886 by Goldstein[12] as luminous paths behind a perforated cathode in a discharge tube, positive rays were not examined systematically until much later, when their production was shown to be a common phenomenon and their natures to depend upon the type of residual gas present in the tube[13] (p. 8).

Like electrons, positive rays are deflected by electrostatic and magnetic fields, and the extents of such deflections in fields of known strength may be used for the evaluation of charge to mass ($e:m$) ratios. The parabola method devised by Thomson[13] was the first used for accurate studies. In this procedure, a narrow beam of positive particles, obtained by passage through a small hole in the cathode of a discharge tube, was passed through electrostatic and magnetic fields of known strengths applied simultaneously and colinearly. Deflections were measured by recording the position of the emergent beam upon a photographic plate. It can be shown[13] that under such conditions all particles of the same charge to mass ratio but of differing velocities will fall along a parabolic path recorded on the film. In an actual experiment, a variety of parabolic paths, each characteristic of a particular positive ion species, is obtained. From the constants of a given parabola and the known field strengths, the characteristic charge to mass ratio can be evaluated.

Exact interpretation of experimentally determined positive ray parabolas is complicated by a number of factors. Thus every ionizable material in the discharge tube will yield at least one parabola, and careful account of the purity of the sample must be taken. Furthermore, a single material will commonly yield more than a single ionization product. For example, an analysis of carbon dioxide[13] gave parabolas corresponding to the species CO_2^+, CO^+, C^+, C^{+2}, O^+, and O^{+2}. Each parabola requires careful characterization.

In spite of these difficulties, positive ray parabolas may be used to show the existence of isotopes and to evaluate their mass numbers. In 1913, Thomson[10] first ascribed particles of mass 22 found in the analysis of neon to an element of similar properties occurring in the

[12] E. Goldstein: *Ber. Preuss. Akad. Wiss.*, **39**, 691 (1886).

[13] J. J. Thomson: *Rays of Positive Electricity and Their Application to Chemical Analyses*, 2nd Ed. Longmans, Green and Co., London (1921).

neighborhood of neon, but these observations were soon shown to be due to a neon isotope of this mass number (p. 20).

Nearly simultaneously, both Dempster[14] and Aston[15] adapted positive ray procedures to the study of mass spectra. Both procedures differed from Thomson's essentially in the application of the magnetic field perpendicular to the electric field in order to effect focusing of all particles of a given charge to mass ratio. The fundamentals of Dempster's apparatus are shown in Figure 2·1. Positive ions from a heated filament F were accelerated by an electric field

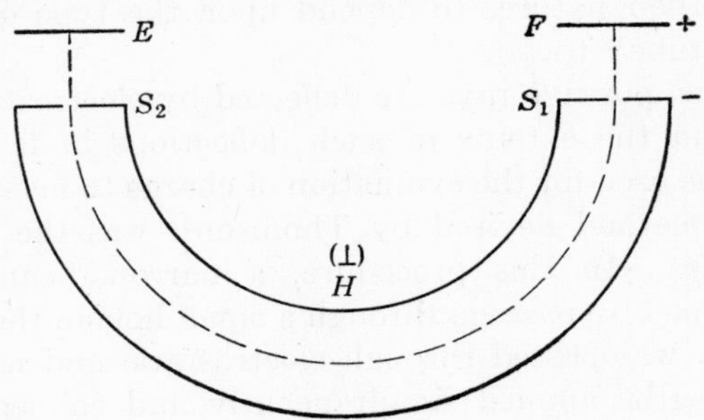

Fig. 2·1. Principles of Dempster's apparatus.

applied between this source and a slit S_1, and then bent by a magnetic field H applied perpendicular to the plane of the drawing. Those passing through a second slit S_2 were then measured as a positive ion current with an electroscope at E. Since it can be shown that the masses of the positive ions reaching the electroscope are dependent upon the accelerating potential and since the measured positive ion current is proportional to the number of positive ions striking the electroscope, Dempster's procedure amounted to varying the accelerating potential and recording a positive ion current at each potential. Plots of positive ion current against mass number then yielded peaks indicating isotopes at definite mass numbers, the heights of these peaks being proportional to the relative abundances of the isotopes. Typical of Dempster's early results are data given in Figure 2·2 for magnesium, where the existence of magnesium isotopes of mass numbers 24, 25, and 26 is clearly shown.[16] From the relative heights of the peaks the average mass was determined to be 24.34.

Dempster's apparatus used the focusing action of the magnetic

[14] A. J. Dempster: *Phys. Rev.*, **11**, 316 (1918).

[15] F. W. Aston: *Proc. Camb. Phil. Soc.*, **19**, 317 (1919); *Phil. Mag.* [6], **38**, 707 (1919).

[16] A. J. Dempster: *Science*, **52**, 559 (1920); *Phys. Rev.*, **18**, 415 (1921).

field to bring together particles having the same velocity but differing in direction. Aston's apparatus,[15] however, brought together at one spot all positive ions having the same direction and the same charge to mass ratio, regardless of their velocities. The essential details of Aston's apparatus are indicated in Figure 2·3. A narrow bundle of

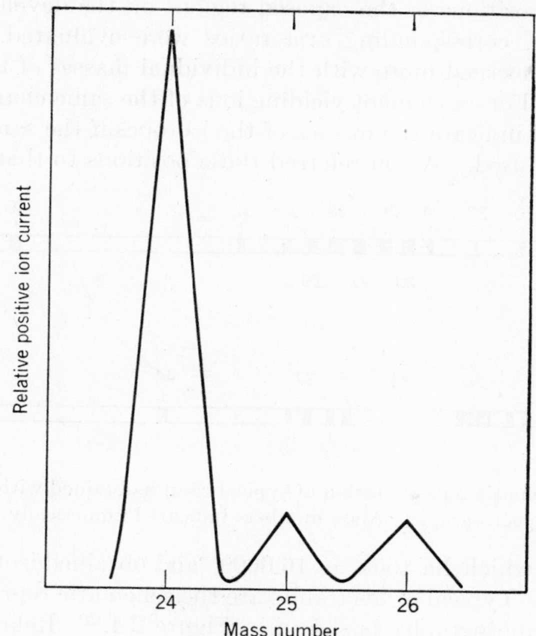

FIG. 2·2. Analysis of magnesium by Dempster's method.

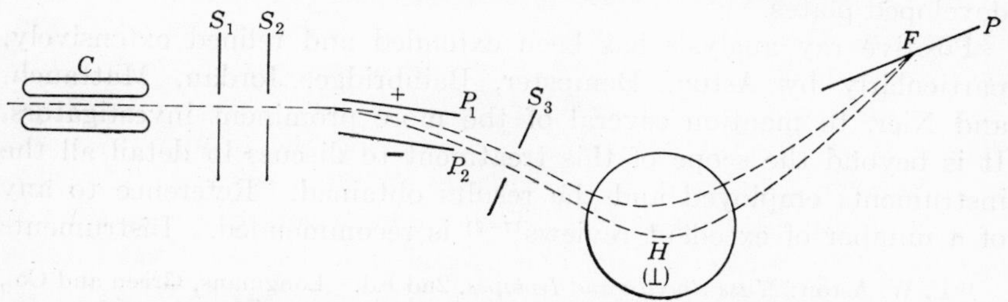

FIG. 2·3. Principles of Aston's mass spectrograph.

positive rays admitted through a hole in the cathode C was collimated by the slit system S_1 and S_2 and passed between charged plates P_1 and P_2, P_1 being positively charged. The resulting angles of deflection were dependent upon the ion velocities, the slower ions being deflected through greater angles than the faster ones. After passage through a third slit S_3 the divergent beam was passed through a magnetic field H, so applied as to produce deflections opposite to those obtained in the electric field. Ultimately, all particles of the same $e:m$ ratio were brought to a focus at a given point on the photographic plate P. This apparatus is called a mass spectrograph.

From the positions of the exposed regions on the developed photographic plate, corresponding $e:m$ ratios were evaluated. Actually, Aston was concerned more with the individual masses of the particles themselves. For an element yielding ions of the same charge, exposed regions would indicate the masses of the isotopes if the same reference standard was used. Aston referred these positions to that of oxygen,

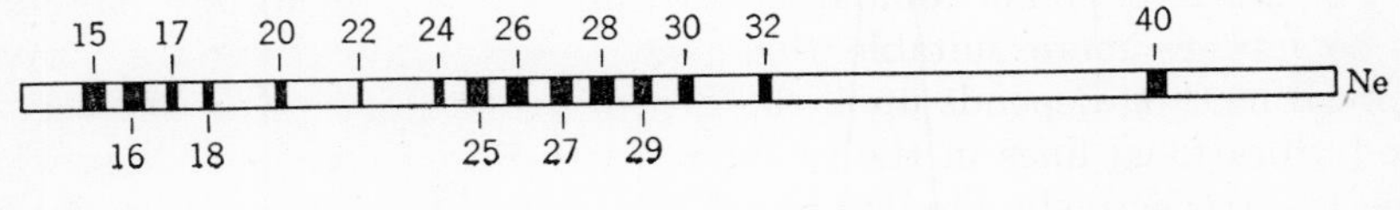

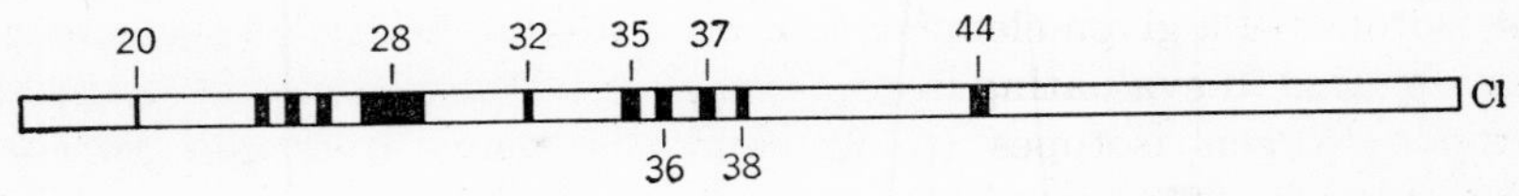

FIG. 2·4. Schematic representation of typical results obtained with Aston's mass spectrograph. Mass numbers indicated numerically.

the mass of which he took as 16.0000, and obtained isotopic masses accordingly. Typical of his results are the schematic reproductions of some of his photographs as shown in Figure 2·4.[17] Relative isotopic abundances were evaluated from the intensities of the lines on the developed plates.

Positive ray analysis has been extended and refined extensively, particularly by Aston, Dempster, Bainbridge, Jordan, Mattauch, and Nier, to mention several of the more prominent investigators. It is beyond the scope of this treatment to discuss in detail all the instruments employed and the results obtained. Reference to any of a number of excellent reviews[17–21] is recommended. Instruments

[17] F. W. Aston: *Mass Spectra and Isotopes*, 2nd Ed. Longmans, Green and Co., London (1942).

[18] J. D. Stranathan: *The "Particles" of Modern Physics*, Ch. 5. The Blakiston Co., Philadelphia (1942).

[19] E. B. Jordan and L. B. Young: *J. Applied Phys.*, **13**, 526 (1942).

[20] N. D. Coggeshall and J. A. Hipple: J. Alexander's *Colloid Chemistry, Theoretical and Applied*, Vol. VI, pp. 39–107. Reinhold Publishing Corp., New York (1946).

[21] J. Mattauch: *Angew. Chem.*, **A59**, 37 (1947).

used may be described as either mass spectrometers or mass spectrographs. Mass spectrometers are devices which measure the intensities of positive ion beams, usually electrically, and which are employed to establish the abundances of the isotopes. These may be classified[19] as radian spectrometers, magnetic lens spectrometers, crossed-field spectrometers, and sector spectrometers depending upon the mode of operation. Mass spectrographs, on the other hand, are devices which correlate the positions of positive ion beams, usually photographically, with ion masses and which are used to evaluate the masses of isotopes. Mass spectra are being used for ordinary analytical purposes increasingly often.

For the detection of comparatively rare isotopes, the optical method is sometimes more suitable than the positive ray procedure. The optical method depends upon the fact that the positions of rotational and vibrational lines in the far and near infrared regions of emission spectra, respectively, are influenced by the masses of the species which produce them. Slight line displacements, therefore, characterize the isotopes of a given element, and the extents of these displacements may be used in evaluating isotopic masses. The existence of both the heavier oxygen isotopes (p. 32) and the heavy hydrogen isotope, deuterium (p. 387), was indicated by optical data.

Data used in compiling the table of isotopic compositions of the elements given in Appendix I (pp. 913–916) are from a variety of sources.[22]

Generalizations relative to atomic nuclei

Examination of the table in Appendix I indicates a number of items of importance. In the range of nuclear charges from 0 through 83, stable isotopes of all mass numbers except 5 and 8 are known. Some 274 stable isotopes have been recognized, and of the elements listed only 23 are simple (i.e., non-isotopic or pure elements). Nuclei of the same mass number but differing charge, the so-called *isobars*, are not particularly uncommon; but, in a given set of isobars, only one member is normally abundant. The only exception is that of the $A = 40$ isotopes of argon and calcium, both of which are abundant. The existence of stable isobars of adjacent elements appears to be limited to the pairs $^{113}_{48}Cd$- $^{113}_{49}In$,* $^{123}_{51}Sb$- $^{123}_{52}Te$, and $^{138}_{56}Ba$- $^{138}_{57}La$- $^{138}_{58}Ce$.

[22] G. T. Seaborg and I. Perlman: *Revs. Modern Phys.*, **20**, 585 (1948).

* A variety of methods of indicating mass number and nuclear charge have been employed. In this book the notation recommended by the International Union of Chemistry is employed as being most nearly free from ambiguity. For

Such a condition is apparently one of instability or its incidence would be more common (p. 55). In addition to the unstable nuclei characterizing all nuclear charges above 83, similar species are known for all other charges. In total, nuclei with charges from 0 through 98 and mass numbers from 1 through at least 246 have been characterized.

Other generalizations may be summarized in terms of the so-called rules of Harkins. These "rules" appeared originally as a series of periodic properties listed by Harkins[23] in a treatment of the proton-electron nucleus, but in a slightly different form they are equally applicable to the proton-neutron nucleus. Modified, these rules are:

1. *No common nucleus except hydrogen contains fewer neutrons than protons.* No stable nucleus except those of $^{1}_{1}H$ and $^{3}_{2}He$ has a mass less than twice its charge. Among the more common and more stable species, the mass number is commonly twice the charge, indicating a tendency toward equality in the numbers of neutrons and protons. Neutron to proton ratios never exceed 1.6, and those nuclei with neutron to proton ratios exceeding 1.2 are very uncommon in nature. The general variation of this ratio with nuclear charge for the more abundant natural isotopes is shown in Figure 2·5.

2. *Elements with even nuclear charges are more abundant, more stable, and richer in isotopes than those with odd charges.* Data in Appendix I indicate that elements with odd nuclear charges never have more than two stable isotopes and that elements with even nuclear charges are uniformly richer in isotopes than their odd-numbered neighbors. All stable elements having odd charges consist primarily of one nuclide. Among the lighter elements, those with even charges are often more abundant than their odd-charged neighbors. All those elements the existence of which in nature has been questioned have odd charges, e.g., 43, 61. The half-lives of radioactive isotopes indicate the even-

---

any symbol X, this notation becomes

$$\begin{matrix} a & & c \\ & X & \\ b & & d \end{matrix}$$

where a is mass number (A), b is nuclear charge (Z), c is ionic charge if any, and d is the number of atoms of X present. American practice commonly records a and b as

$$\begin{matrix} & a \\ X & \\ & b \end{matrix}$$

[23] W. D. Harkins: *Chem. Revs.*, **5**, 371 (1928).

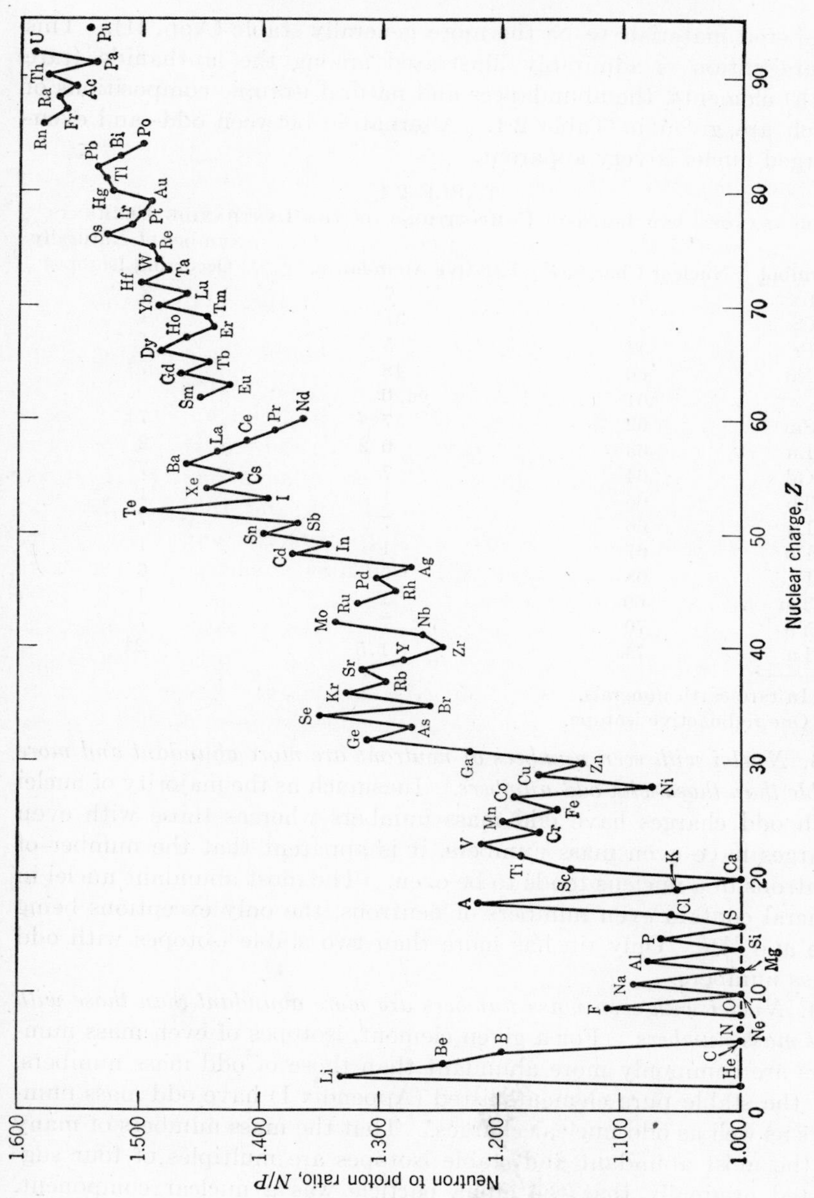

Fig. 2.5. Neutron to proton ratios for most abundant isotopes.

numbered materials to be the more generally stable (App. II). This generalization is admirably illustrated among the lanthanide (rare earth) elements, the abundances and natural isotopic compositions of which are given in Table 2·1. Alternation between odd- and even-charged nuclei is very apparent.

TABLE 2·1

Abundances and Isotopic Compositions of the Lanthanide Elements

Symbol	Nuclear Charge, Z	Relative Abundance,* %	Number of Naturally Occurring Isotopes
La	57	7	2
Ce	58	31	4
Pr	59	5	1
Nd	60	18	7†
	61	ca. 0	..
Sm	62	7	7†
Eu	63	0.2	2
Gd	64	7	7
Tb	65	1	1
Dy	66	7	7
Ho	67	1	1
Er	68	6	6
Tm	69	1	1
Yb	70	7	7
Lu	71	1.5	2†

* In rare earth minerals.

† One radioactive isotope.

3. *Nuclei with even numbers of neutrons are more abundant and more stable than those with odd numbers.* Inasmuch as the majority of nuclei with odd charges have odd mass numbers whereas those with even charges have even mass numbers, it is apparent that the number of neutrons in a nucleus tends to be even. The most abundant nuclei in general contain even numbers of neutrons, the only exceptions being ${}^{9}_{4}Be$ and ${}^{14}_{7}N$. Only tin has more than two stable isotopes with odd mass numbers.

4. *Nuclei with even mass numbers are more abundant than those with odd mass numbers.* For a given element, isotopes of even mass numbers are commonly more abundant than those of odd mass numbers. All the stable pure elements listed (Appendix I) have odd mass numbers as well as odd nuclear charges. That the mass numbers of many of the most abundant and stable isotopes are multiples of four suggested originally that the alpha particle was a nuclear component. It is more probably the result of neutron-proton pairing. Some 87% of the nuclei in the crust of the earth have even mass numbers.

Nuclei are commonly classified in terms of whether they contain even or odd numbers of protons (Z) and neutrons (N). Four such combinations are possible. As shown in Table 2·2, the most common arrangement is *even-even* and the least common *odd-odd*. It appears

TABLE 2·2
TYPES OF ATOMIC NUCLEI

Type	Designation	Number of Stable Examples
Z even, N even	even-even	163
Z even, N odd	even-odd	56
Z odd, N even	odd-even	50
Z odd, N odd	odd-odd	5

to make but little difference whether the arrangement is *even-odd* or *odd-even*. For further information on such systematics, summaries on nuclear physics should be consulted.[3, 4, 24]

References to the relative abundances of the elements in the foregoing discussions suggest the advisability of a more comprehensive treatment of the general topic of abundances at this point. The eminent geochemist V. M. Goldschmidt considered the earth to have resulted from the condensation of a gaseous material into an iron core, an intermediate sulfide-oxide zone, a siliceous envelope, and an atmosphere.[25] During condensation, the elements were believed to concentrate in these zones. Based upon the zone in which they concentrated, the elements were then classified as siderophilic (core), chalcophilic (intermediate), lithophilic (crust), and atmophilic (atmosphere). Siderophilic elements embrace the Periodic Group VIIa and VIII elements and gold. Chalcophilic elements include those in Periodic Groups Ib (except gold), IIb, IIIb, IVb (except carbon and silicon), Vb (except nitrogen), and VIb (except oxygen). Lithophilic elements include hydrogen and those in Periodic Groups Ia, IIa, IIIa, IVa, Va, and VIa. Carbon, silicon, nitrogen, oxygen, the halogens, and the inert gases are included in the lithophilic-atmophilic class.

It is of course exceedingly difficult to arrive at the absolute abundances of all the elements in the earth as a whole. However, exacting analyses of large numbers of minerals and rocks so chosen as to be representative do give reasonably accurate indications of the abundances of the elements in the igneous rocks of the crust of the earth. The excellent studies of Clarke, Washington, Goldschmidt, and many others on this problem have been summarized ably by Rankama and Sahama.[26] It is from this source that the data given in Table 2·3 have been summarized.

[24] J. Mattauch and S. Fluegge: *Nuclear Physics Tables and an Introduction to Nuclear Physics*, pp. 97–104. Interscience Publishers, New York (1946).

[25] D. T. Gibson: *Quart. Revs.*, **3**, 263 (1949). Excellent and timely review.

[26] K. Rankama and Th. G. Sahama: *Geochemistry*, Ch. 2. University of Chicago Press, Chicago (1950).

TABLE 2·3

ABUNDANCES OF THE ELEMENTS IN THE IGNEOUS ROCKS OF THE CRUST OF THE EARTH

Atomic Number	Symbol	Abundance		
		Grams/Metric Ton	Atoms/100 Atoms Si	Per Cent
1	H	present		
2	He	0.003	0.0000076	3×10^{-7}
3	Li	65	0.091	6.5×10^{-3}
4	Be	6	0.0067	6×10^{-4}
5	B	3⁻	0.0028	3×10^{-4}
6	C	320⁻	0.27	0.032
7	N	46.3	0.033	4.6×10^{-3}
8	O	466,000	296	46.6
9	F	600–900	0.32–0.48	0.06–0.09
10	Ne	0.00007	0.000000035	7×10^{-9}
11	Na	28,300	12.4	2.83
12	Mg	20,900	8.76	2.09
13	Al	81,300	30.5	8.13
14	Si	277,200	100	27.72
15	P	1,180	0.38	0.118
16	S	520	0.16	0.052
17	Cl	314	0.09	0.0314
18	A	0.04	0.00001	4×10^{-6}
19	K	25,900	4.42	2.59
20	Ca	36,300	9.17	3.63
21	Sc	5	0.0011	5×10^{-4}
22	Ti	4,400	0.92	0.44
23	V	150	0.030	0.015
24	Cr	200	0.039	0.02
25	Mn	1,000	0.18	0.1
26	Fe	50,000	9.13	5.0
27	Co	23	0.004	2.3×10^{-3}
28	Ni	80	0.014	8.0×10^{-3}
29	Cu	70	0.011	7.0×10^{-3}
30	Zn	132	0.020	0.0132
31	Ga	15	0.0022	1.5×10^{-3}
32	Ge	7	0.00095	7×10^{-4}
33	As	5	0.00067	5×10^{-4}
34	Se	0.09	0.000012	9×10^{-6}
35	Br	1.62	0.00020	1.6×10^{-4}
36	Kr	....	....	....
37	Rb	310	0.036	0.031
38	Sr	300	0.035	0.030
39	Y	28.1	0.00307	2.81×10^{-3}
40	Zr	220	0.026	0.022
41	Nb	24	0.0026	2.4×10^{-3}

TABLE 2·3 (*Continued*)

Atomic Number	Symbol	Abundance		
		Grams/Metric Ton	Atoms/100 Atoms Si	Per Cent
42	Mo	2.5–15	0.0003–0.0016	$2.5\text{–}15 \times 10^{-4}$
43	Tc			
44	Ru	present	....	....
45	Rh	0.001	0.0000001	1×10^{-7}
46	Pd	0.010	0.0000009	1×10^{-6}
47	Ag	0.10	0.000009	1×10^{-5}
48	Cd	0.15	0.000013	1.5×10^{-5}
49	In	0.1	0.000007	1×10^{-5}
50	Sn	40	0.00343	4×10^{-3}
51	Sb	1	0.000083	1×10^{-4}
52	Te	0.0018(?)	....	1.8×10^{-7}
53	I	0.3	0.000024	3×10^{-5}
54	Xe	....	....	....
55	Cs	7	0.00053	7×10^{-4}
56	Ba	250	0.018	0.025
57	La	18.3	0.00128	1.83×10^{-3}
58	Ce	46.1	0.00321	4.61×10^{-3}
59	Pr	5.53	0.000389	5.53×10^{-4}
60	Nd	23.9	0.00162	2.39×10^{-3}
61	....	....	....	....
62	Sm	6.47	0.000419	6.47×10^{-4}
63	Eu	1.06	0.000068	1.06×10^{-4}
64	Gd	6.36	0.000394	6.36×10^{-4}
65	Tb	0.91	0.000056	9.1×10^{-5}
66	Dy	4.47	0.000269	4.47×10^{-4}
67	Ho	1.15	0.000068	1.15×10^{-4}
68	Er	2.47	0.000144	2.47×10^{-4}
69	Tm	0.20	0.0000115	2.0×10^{-5}
70	Yb	2.66	0.000149	2.66×10^{-4}
71	Lu	0.75	0.000037	7.5×10^{-5}
72	Hf	4.5	0.00030	4.5×10^{-4}
73	Ta	2.1	0.00012	2.1×10^{-4}
74	W	1.5–69	0.000082–0.0038	$1.5\text{–}69 \times 10^{-4}$
75	Re	0.001	0.000000054	1×10^{-7}
76	Os	present	....	....
77	Ir	0.001	0.00000005	1×10^{-7}
78	Pt	0.005	0.00000027	5×10^{-7}
79	Au	0.005	0.00000026	5×10^{-7}
80	Hg	0.077–0.5	0.0000039–0.000025	$7.7\text{–}50 \times 10^{-6}$
81	Tl	0.3–3	0.000015 –0.00015	$3\text{–}30 \times 10^{-5}$
82	Pb	16	0.00080	1.6×10^{-3}
83	Bi	0.2	0.000009	2×10^{-5}
84	Po	0.0000000003	14×10^{-15}	3×10^{-14}

TABLE 2·3 (*Continued*)

Atomic Number	Symbol	Abundance		
		Grams/Metric Ton	Atoms/100 Atoms Si	Per Cent
85	At	present	....	....
86	Rn	present	....	....
87	Fr	present	....	....
88	Ra	0.0000013	58×10^{-12}	1.3×10^{-10}
89	Ac	0.0000000003	13×10^{-15}	3×10^{-14}
90	Th	11.5	0.00050	1.15×10^{-3}
91	Pa	0.0000008	35×10^{-12}	8×10^{-11}
92	U	4	0.00016	4×10^{-4}
93	Np	probably present	....	....
94	Pu	present	....	....
95	Am	probably present	....	....
96	Cm	probably present	....	....
97	Bk	?	....	....
98	Cf	?	....	....

The masses of atoms and atomic nuclei

The mass of an electron relative to that of either a proton or a neutron is so small that even in atoms containing the largest numbers of electrons the total mass contribution by the electrons is effectively negligible in comparison with the combined contributions by the nucleons. However, even though the nucleus is the governing factor relative to the mass of an atom, all methods of measuring the masses of atoms yield values which include the electron masses as well. The term isotopic weight may be used to characterize such a mass when it is compared with that of some arbitrarily chosen standard, normally oxygen. The weighted average of the isotopic weights for a particular element is the atomic weight of that element. Although in a general way this makes the existence of fractional atomic weights fairly obvious, certain refinements in explanation are essential to a complete understanding of the subject.

Aston's early mass spectrographic data on hydrogen yielded an atomic weight of 1.007775, based upon the assumption that ordinary oxygen is not an isotopic mixture and has a weight of 16.0000. This value was in good agreement with the chemical observation that 1.00778 grams of hydrogen combine with 8 grams of oxygen. Subsequent proof (p. 33) that oxygen is a mixture of isotopes of mass numbers 16, 17, and 18 necessitated a revision in Aston's mass determinations and the establishment of a new basis for mass spectrographic values. As a result, two atomic weight scales, the physical and the chemical, are in use. The rather fortuitous agreement between the values for hydrogen is due to the existence in just the correct proportions of a hydrogen isotope of mass number 2 (p. 387), a fact which was unknown to Aston.

Physical atomic weights are referred to the mass of the 16-isotope of oxygen taken as 16.00000. Chemical atomic weights are referred to the average mass of the natural mixture of oxygen isotopes taken as 16.00000. The two scales can be related to each other by considering the relative abundances of the oxygen isotopes. Inasmuch as the composition of natural oxygen is $^{16}O(99.757\%)$, $^{17}O(0.039\%)$, and $^{18}O(0.204\%)$, it is apparent that the true mass of the isotopic mixture is

$$(16 \times 0.99757) + (17 \times 0.00039) + (18 \times 0.00204) = 16.00447$$

Since this is the value which is taken chemically as 16.00000, physical atomic weights will always be larger than the chemical values by the ratio 16.00447:16.00000, or 1.00028 (the Mecke-Childs factor).

Chemical atomic weights are employed universally for the evaluation of chemical processes. The physical values, however, are employed to describe any process or property which relates to atomic nuclei. Thus, they are the values which are involved in evaluating the energy changes associated with nuclear processes (p. 59). Isotopic masses or weights are expressed on the physical scale.

It seems appropriate to discuss briefly the experimental evaluation of atomic and isotopic weights. Physical values for the individual isotopes can be determined by means of mass spectrographic measurements (p. 24). If a physical atomic weight of the element in question is desired, it can then be calculated from the masses and abundances of the various isotopes. The probable errors in refined measurements of this sort amount to only a few parts in 100,000. Isotopic masses can be evaluated independently from packing fraction (p. 38) and nuclear reaction (p. 69) data. Values so obtained agree almost exactly with those obtained by mass spectrographic means.

Although chemical atomic weights are based upon oxygen, it is not always convenient or desirable to determine the value for an element by direct comparison with oxygen. The indirect procedures which are necessary, therefore, must be chosen carefully and must be carried out with great precision to insure accurate results. Chemically determined values may always be checked if physical values are available. Indeed it has become common practice to evaluate the physical values first and use them to calculate chemical values.

Classically, an important method of determining chemical atomic weights involved the law of Dulong and Petit, a rough generalization indicating that the product of the atomic specific heat of a solid element by its atomic weight is constant at 6.2 to 6.4. Evaluation of atomic heat capacity thus leads to a rough value for the atomic weight. This was rendered more nearly exact by comparing the rough value obtained with the equivalent weight of the same element to determine its oxidation state (p. 179) and then calculating the atomic weight from the product of equivalent weight by oxidation number (p. 179). The limitations of such a procedure are obvious.

More accurate results are obtained by the actual analysis of compounds of known compositions. Among the most useful of procedures of this type are those involving determination of the ratios metal halide:silver and metal halide:silver halide. This general method was used by Stas in his pioneer work on atomic weights, but it is to Richards and his students that we are indebted for the refinements which made the method one of precision. Accounts of these researches may be consulted with profit by anyone interested in improved experimental techniques.[27] In more recent times, extensive accurate chemical work has been done largely by Baxter and Hönigschmid.

Use of the ratios mentioned above necessitates accurate knowledge of the chemical atomic weight of silver and of the ratios Ag:Cl and Ag:Br. The ratios have been determined repeatedly with great accuracy. Exact evaluation of the atomic weight of silver requires establishment, directly or indirectly, of the Ag:O ratio. This ratio may be determined directly by measuring such ratios as $KClO_3$:KCl:Ag:3O or $Ba(ClO_4)_2$:$BaCl_2$:2Ag:8O, the general procedure involving conversion of a weighed quantity of the oxy compound to chloride, followed by precipitation with silver nitrate and determination of the silver chloride by a nephelometric method. Use of quartz apparatus, bottling and weighing *in vacuo*, dehydration in dry hydrogen chloride, and use of closed systems for all operations are essential to accurate results.

Indirectly, the silver to oxygen ratio has been established by synthesis of silver nitrate from a weighed quantity of pure silver. The ratio Ag:$AgNO_3$ is then dependent upon the chemical atomic weight of nitrogen, which is obtained by independent means. Other indirect determinations have employed such ratios as $NaNO_3$:NaCl:Ag, Ag:AgCl; Ag_2SO_4:2AgCl:2Ag, N:S; NH_4Cl:Ag, $AgNO_3$:Ag, AgCl:Ag. Agreement between direct and indirect methods is indicated by the

[27] T. W. Richards and G. S. Forbes: *Carnegie Inst. Wash. Publ.*, **69**, 47 (1907); *Z. anorg. Chem.*, **55**, 34 (1907).

fact that both the barium perchlorate procedure[28] and the silver-silver nitrate method[27] yielded a value of 107.880 for the chemical atomic weight of silver.

The atomic weight of a metal is then determined by analyzing a weighed quantity of its anhydrous chloride or bromide for halide by the silver nitrate procedure and calculating back. Because of uncertainties in the nephelometric method ordinarily employed, dry reactions such as the reduction of silver nitrate to silver with hydrogen[29] seem particularly promising.

For the lighter non-metals such as carbon and fluorine, determination of atomic weights by gas density measurements is of particular value. The method depends upon the fact that at constant pressure the buoyancy effects of the several gases are directly proportional to their densities (and thus to their molecular weights). For a number of gases, therefore, the same buoyancy effect may be achieved by suitable alterations of gas pressures. Accordingly, a suitable gas-density microbalance is balanced about a suitable reference point, using some reference gas (for instance, oxygen) at a measured pressure. A gas containing the element in question is then admitted, and the pressure required to obtain the same balance is measured. From compressibility data for the two gases, the molecular weight of the second can then be evaluated and the desired atomic weight calculated. Thus a determination of the chemical atomic weight of carbon, using carbon monoxide, carbon dioxide, and ethylene, yielded a value of 12.0108,[30] which is in accord with band spectroscopic evidence that carbon normally contains about 1% of the 13 isotope.

The atomic weights of the elements show a remarkable constancy in magnitudes, indicating general lack of variability in the isotopic compositions of the various elements. This is not unexpected in view of the fact that natural mixing processes spread over the geological ages would tend on the average to destroy any original differences. This constancy is not limited to our own planet but appears to be more or less universal. Thus chlorine, nickel, and iron from meteorites show the same atomic weights as those from earthly sources. However, natural isotopic fractionation processes (pp. 38–52) do effect slight alterations in isotopic abundances and produce minor variations in atomic weights. The classic recorded example is with boron,[31] minerals from Tuscany, Asia Minor, and California containing boron

[28] O. Hönigschmid and R. Sachtleben: *Z. anorg. allgem. Chem.*, **178**, 1 (1929).
[29] O. Hönigschmid and R. Schlee: *Angew. Chem.*, **49**, 464 (1936).
[30] M. Woodhead and R. Whytlaw-Gray: *J. Chem. Soc.*, **1933**, 846.
[31] H. V. A. Briscoe et al.: *J. Chem. Soc.*, **127**, 696 (1925); **1926**, 70; **1927**, 282.

with atomic weights 10.823, 10.818, and 10.841, respectively. Other instances reported among the lighter elements show the heavier isotopes of oxygen to be slightly more abundant in atmospheric oxygen than in oxygen obtained from water, the lighter potassium isotope (^{39}K) to be preferentially concentrated by land plants, the lighter carbon isotope (^{12}C) to be preferentially concentrated by plants, and the heavier (^{13}C) by limestone, etc. Variations in atomic weights among the heavy elements are due to their radioactive origins (p. 63).

Mass defects in atomic nuclei

Although the difficulties imposed by fractional atomic weights (p. 19) were largely resolved by the discovery of isotopes, isotopic masses were found to deviate slightly but significantly from whole numbers. The attractive hypothesis that such masses are multiples of the mass of some fundamental particle (the whole number rule) can no longer be entertained, although the closeness with which isotopic masses do approach whole numbers makes such mass numbers particularly useful in characterizing isotopes. Neither are isotopic masses given by a summation of the masses of their constituent particles.

Such isotopic masses as are known are tabulated in Appendix I. Among the lightest ($A < 20$) and heaviest elements ($A > 180$) these isotopic masses are greater than the corresponding mass numbers, whereas among the intermediate elements the reverse is true. The difference between the isotopic mass (M) and the mass number (A) is known as the *mass defect* or the *mass* excess (Δ), as shown by the relation

$$\Delta = M - A \tag{2·8}$$

Positive mass defects thus characterize the lightest and heaviest elements, whereas those for the other elements are negative. Harkins and Aston attributed mass defects to the packing of nuclear particles into tiny elements of volume—the "packing effect." In preference to the actual mass defect for a given isotope, Aston employed the fractional mass deviation or *packing fraction* (f), which is defined as

$$f = \frac{M - A}{A} = \frac{\Delta}{A} \tag{2·9}$$

The packing fraction may be regarded, therefore, as indicating the average mass gain or loss per nucleon for the isotope in question as compared with the condition existing in the ^{16}O nucleus. Because of the interrelation of mass and energy, nuclei with positive packing fractions may be regarded as possessing excess energy and tending toward instability, whereas nuclei with negative packing fractions

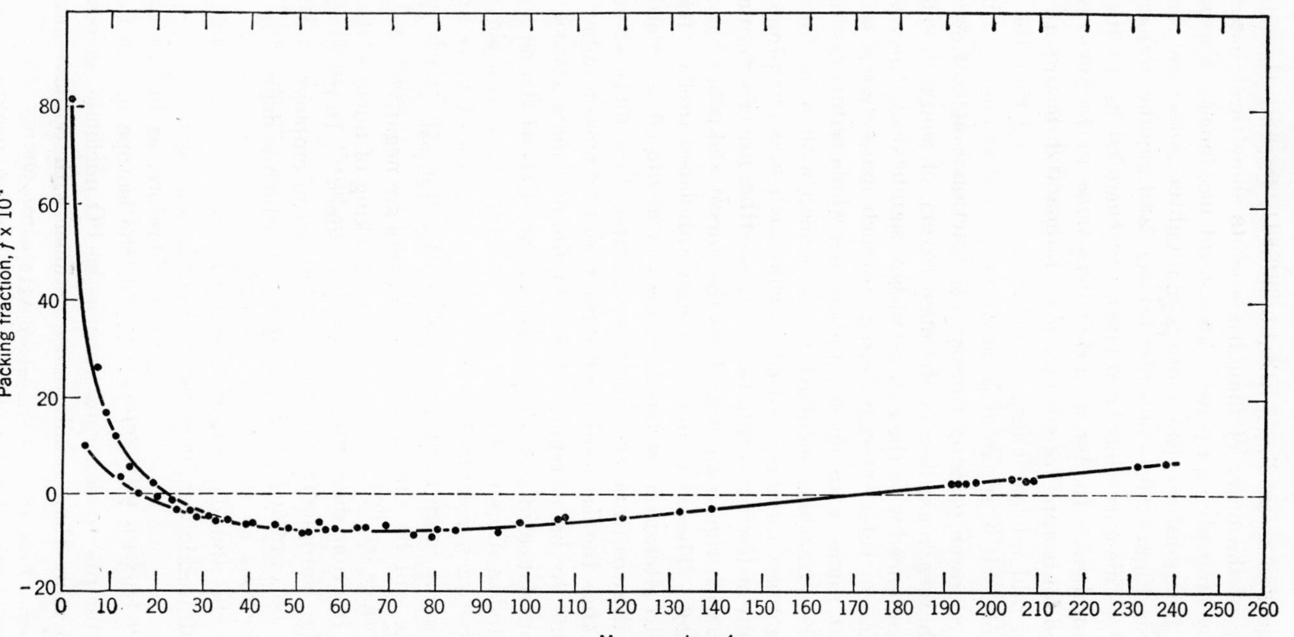

FIG. 2·6. Packing fraction curve for most abundant isotopes.

may be regarded as tending toward stability. Packing fractions are numerically of the order of magnitude of 10^{-4} and are customarily expressed by multiplying by 10^4. This has been done in Appendix I.

Packing fractions for the more abundant isotopes are recorded graphically in Figure 2·6. This plot is essentially similar to that given by Aston.[32] This curve has been given two branches in the region of low mass numbers. In Aston's original treatment, the lower branch was reserved for isotopes of even nuclear charges and the upper branch for those of odd nuclear charges, the inference being that the latter are less stable. It is apparent from Appendix I that nuclei with even charges have lower packing fractions than those neighboring nuclei with odd charges, regardless of the mass region, although the effect is somewhat enhanced with the lightest elements. This is in accord with the abundance rules already cited (pp. 26–29). Later studies[33] showed that nuclei with mass numbers which are multiples of four have packing fractions significantly smaller than those for other neighboring mass numbers, an effect which is especially pronounced in the region of low mass numbers. It seems fitting to characterize such nuclei with the lower branch of the curve. This has been done in Figure 2·6. The well-known resistance of such nuclei (^{4}He, ^{12}C, ^{16}O, ^{20}Ne) to alteration by bombardment is in complete accord with inferences drawn from the packing fraction curve. It should be mentioned that the flat minimum in the region of mass number 50–60 suggests this to be a region of maximum nuclear stability. The extreme abundance of iron and nickel in the earth taken as a whole has been cited in support of this view. It is obvious that a plot of the difference between calculated and actual mass against mass number would represent more accurately the characteristics of each nuclear species. As will be shown later, such a curve also reflects nuclear binding energies (p. 60).

Packing fraction data may be used to evaluate atomic weights. Thus, if the isotopic masses are evaluated roughly, exact isotopic masses can be obtained by applying a correction determined by the packing fractions as read from the packing fraction curve. Combined with the abundances of the isotopes, these masses then yield the physical atomic weight of the element in question.

The concentration and separation of isotopes

Early attempts to separate isotopes met with little success and effected no more than small concentrations of individual materials.

[32] F. W. Aston: *Proc. Roy. Soc. (London)*, **A115**, 487 (1927).
[33] H. E. Duckworth: *Phys. Rev.*, **62**, 19 (1942).

The improved methods of later years, particularly since 1939, however, have permitted the separation in high states of purity of many isotopes and the concentration of many others. The literature on the subject has expanded so considerably, that it is manifestly impossible in a book of this type to cover it completely. Some of the many excellent summaries which have appeared[34–43] should be consulted for comprehensive accounts.

The marked similarities in both chemical and physical properties among the isotopes of a given element render separations, or even concentrations, exceedingly difficult. The obvious procedures are physical in character, for mass differences impart greater differences in physical properties than in chemical. Chemical procedures are dependent upon differences in the rates of particular reactions rather than upon inherently different chemical behaviors. In spite of the experimental difficulties, however, the demands for isotopes as tracers and the desirable properties which some of them possess have led to practical separational procedures.

Of fundamental importance in any separation process is the so-called separation, or fractionation, factor s. If, before the mixture is subjected to the separation procedure, it contains n_1 atoms of the lighter isotope and n_2 atoms of the heavier (for instance, per gram of mixture) and if, after application of the procedure, the numbers of atoms of lighter and heavier species are, respectively, n_1' and n_2', the separation factor is then given by the expression

$$s = \frac{n_1'/n_2'}{n_1/n_2} \tag{2·10}$$

The separation factor may characterize a single stage in a multiple procedure, or it may be applied to the entire process as an overall

[34] F. W. Aston: *Mass Spectra and Isotopes*, 2nd Ed., Ch. XVI. Longman's, Green and Co., London (1942).

[35] J. D. Stranathan: *The "Particles" of Modern Physics*, Ch. 5. The Blakiston Co., Philadelphia (1942).

[36] H. S. Taylor and S. Glasstone: *A Treatise on Physical Chemistry*, 3rd Ed., Vol. I, pp. 54–76. D. Van Nostrand Co., New York (1942).

[37] H. C. Urey: in *Recent Advances in Surface Chemistry and Chemical Physics*, pp. 73–87. The Science Press, Lancaster, Pa. (1939).

[38] O. J. Walker: *Ann. Reports*, **35**, 134 (1938).

[39] H. D. Smyth: *Atomic Energy for Military Purposes*. Princeton University Press, Princeton, N. J. (1945).

[40] A. J. E. Welch: *Ann. Reports*, **41**, 87 (1944).

[41] A. M. Squires: *J. Chem. Education*, **23**, 538 (1946).

[42] D. W. Stewart: *Nucleonics*, **1** (No. 2), 18 (1947).

[43] W. Groth: *Z. Elektrochem.*, **54**, 5 (1950).

factor. If x single stages are involved, an overall enrichment factor S is given as

$$S = s^x \tag{2·11}$$

The efficiency of the process is determined by the magnitude of its enrichment factor. Because in many procedures separation factors are only slightly greater than unity, it is common to run them in cascade[44] to amplify the enrichment achieved in a single stage. Such procedures are more properly called fractionation procedures rather than separation procedures, for they effect stepwise enrichments in particular components. The only procedure of those to be described which is not a fractionation procedure is the one employing electromagnetic methods.

Methods Involving Physical Characteristics. Such procedures must, of necessity, be dependent upon mass differences among the several isotopes involved. Some of the more important ones are now described.

ELECTROMAGNETIC METHODS. The collecting of an ion beam containing only particles of a given mass using an appropriately designed mass spectrograph or spectrometer should provide a theoretically ideal procedure for the clean-cut separation of the isotopes of a given element. The principle of this procedure, which is essentially that of the Dempster mass spectrograph (p. 22), is shown in Figure 2·7. Such a method should be limited only by the precision with which the ion beam can be focused and should yield absolutely pure isotopic materials. Practically, the small ion beams (10^{-8} amp. or less) which characterize most mass spectrographs and spectrometers limit sharply the quantities of materials which can be collected. However, by use of high-intensity instruments, microgram quantities of several isotopes, particularly those of lithium, potassium, and rubidium, were obtained. In fact proof that the radioactivities of the latter two elements are due, respectively, to ^{40}K and ^{87}Rb was obtained by use of these separated isotopes.

Considerable interest has been focused upon the electromagnetic separation of the uranium isotopes. Nier was able to separate sufficient $^{235}_{92}U$ in this fashion to prove it to be the fissionable isotope (p. 73), but his apparatus could separate only somewhat less than a microgram a day. Under auspices of the Manhattan District Project, electromagnetic separators employing very large magnetic fields were developed and found useful for the separation of $^{235}_{92}U$. The first such apparatus used the magnet from the 37-in. University of California cyclotron; it was called, therefore, the calutron. In later

[44] K. Cohen: *Nucleonics*, **2** (No. 6), 3 (1948).

installations, much larger magnets were employed, and other magnetic separators using extended ion sources and beams rather than one-dimensional systems produced by the slit arrangement of the calutron were studied. The general details of this subject are covered by

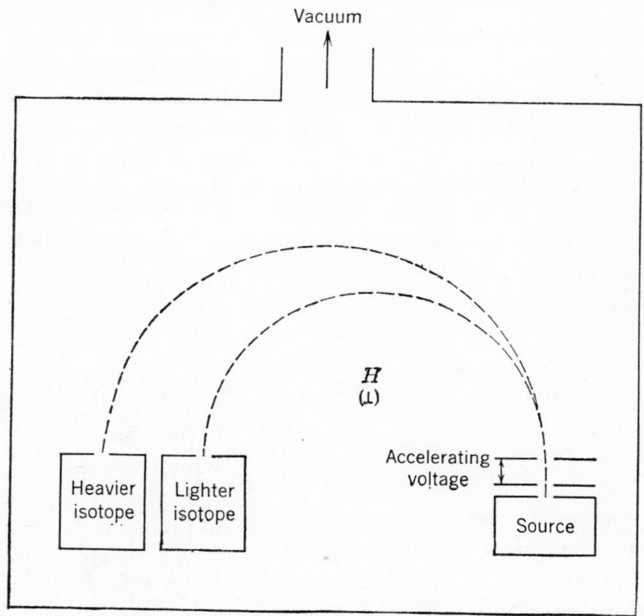

FIG. 2·7. Principles of electromagnetic separation of isotopes.

Smyth.[39] Since December 1945, the electromagnetic separators at Oak Ridge have been used also for concentrating a wide variety of stable isotopes.[45, 46] Many such isotopes are now available for research purposes.

GASEOUS DIFFUSION METHODS. In terms of Graham's law, the rate at which a gas diffuses through an aperture which is small in comparison with the mean free path of its molecules is inversely proportional to the square root of its density or molecular weight. The diffusion of a gas mixture the components of which differ in molecular weight must, therefore, alter the composition of that mixture. Obviously, if the molecules owe their mass differences to differences in isotopic contents, an alteration in isotopic ratio must also result. If m_h and m_l represent the masses of the heavier and lighter isotopes (or compounds

[45] C. P. Keim: *Chem. Eng. News*, **25**, 2624 (1947).
[46] L. P. Smith, W. E. Parkins, and A. T. Forrester: *Phys. Rev.*, **72**, 989 (1947).

containing them), respectively, one might expect a separation proportional to $\sqrt{m_l/m_h}$. Rayleigh's treatment of the problem, however, shows that, even under conditions where mixing is perfect and there is no accumulation of the less diffusible gas at the surface of the diffuser, the enrichment of the undiffused residue in the heavier component is given with reasonable accuracy by

$$\text{enrichment} = \sqrt[\frac{m_h+m_l}{m_h-m_l}]{\frac{\text{initial volume}}{\text{final volume}}} \tag{2·12}$$

Since the mass difference, $m_h - m_l$, will always be comparatively small (except for the hydrogen isotopes), it is obvious that a single-stage diffuser cannot concentrate isotopes. It is also apparent that the greatest success would be expected with the lighter elements.

Even before the isotopic complexity of neon had been established definitely, Aston separated ordinary neon of mass 20.2 into fractions of masses 20.28 and 20.15 by fractional diffusion. The classical researches, however, on gas diffusion are those on hydrogen chloride carried out by Harkins.[47, 48] Over a period of years (1915 on), Harkins and his coworkers diffused hydrogen chloride through porous porcelain at atmospheric pressure, absorbed the undiffused gas in sodium hydrogen carbonate, regenerated hydrogen chloride (now slightly enriched in $^{37}_{17}$Cl), and recycled the material. After reduction of some 19,000 liters of initial gas to a few milliliters, a material containing chlorine of mass 35.512 was obtained. That this represents only a very slight enrichment over the initial material of mass 35.457 is unimportant in comparison with the proof obtained that the procedure would function.

Many of the difficulties inherent in the Harkins procedure have been overcome in the low-pressure, multiple-diffusion method of Hertz.[49] In this procedure a series of connected diffusion units, each consisting of some material through which the gas must pass by diffusion, is employed. The general details of such an arrangement are shown in Figure 2·8. Gas from container V_L is passed through the diffuser D_1, where a portion diffuses through a clay pipe. The diffused gas, slightly enriched in the lighter isotope, is returned to V_L by a pump P_1, whereas the undiffused gas, slightly enriched in the heavier isotope, is passed on to a second diffuser D_2. The diffused gas from D_2 is then returned to D_1 by way of P_1 and V_L. This procedure is

[47] W. D. Harkins and A. Hayes: *J. Am. Chem. Soc.*, **43**, 1803 (1921).
[48] W. D. Harkins and F. A. Jenkins: *J. Am. Chem. Soc.*, **48**, 58 (1926).
[49] G. Hertz: *Z. Physik*, **79**, 108, 700 (1932).

repeated in the various units of the apparatus in such fashion that from the nth unit the lighter isotope is always returned to the $n - 1$ unit, whereas the heavier is passed on to the $n + 1$. It is apparent that once a steady state is established the heavier isotope will concentrate in V_H and the lighter in V_L. Jets of mercury vapor used instead of porous tubes as diffusion barriers increase the efficiency of the process.

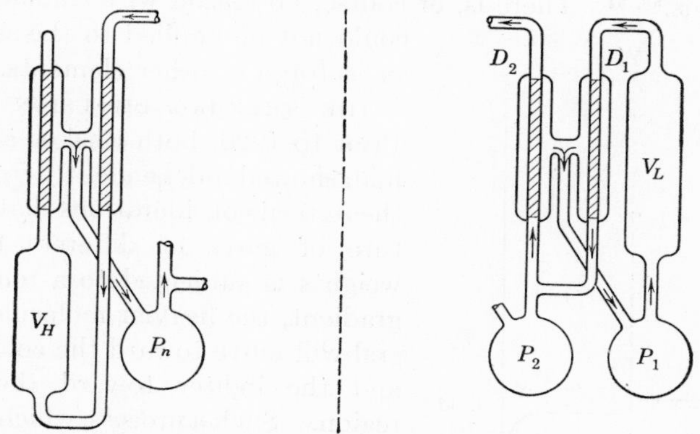

FIG. 2·8. Principles of the Hertz multiple diffusion apparatus.

Some truly remarkable concentrations and separations have been achieved by the Hertz procedure. Thus, ${}^{2}_{1}H$ has been obtained spectroscopically pure from the natural mixture, the neon isotopes have been obtained in high states of purity, and sizable concentrations of the heavy isotopes of carbon and nitrogen have been realized. However, the low pressures essential to efficient separation seriously limit the quantities of materials which can be prepared. A practical limitation on this otherwise effective process is thereby imposed.

Fractional diffusion through a porous barrier from a region of higher pressure to a region of lower pressure is used for the large-scale concentration of the 235-isotope of uranium at the Oak Ridge K-25 installation. In this plant, several thousand diffusion stages are operated in cascade. Uranium(VI) fluoride gas, prepared from natural uranium, is fed by a blower into an intermediate diffuser unit containing several square feet of porous barrier. Part of the gas is diffused into a lower pressure region maintained by another blower. The diffused gas, enriched in ^{235}U, is passed on to another diffuser, and the undiffused gas is cycled to another stage in the opposite direction. Although the ideal separation factor for $^{238}UF_6$ and $^{235}UF_6$ is 1.0043, it is said that each $^{235}UF_6$ molecule is diffused some 2,000,000 times before emerging in the product.[41] The design and construction of such a plant were complicated by the corrosive character of the gaseous fluoride and by the necessity for operating at reduced pressures. The barriers employed must of necessity be corrosion resistant, mechanically strong, and uniform in pore size, the pores being only a few millionths of a millimeter in diameter. Engineering problems surmounted in the construction and operation of this plant were tremendous.[50, 51] There is, of course, no reason why similar methods could not be applied to the separation of isotopes of other elements.

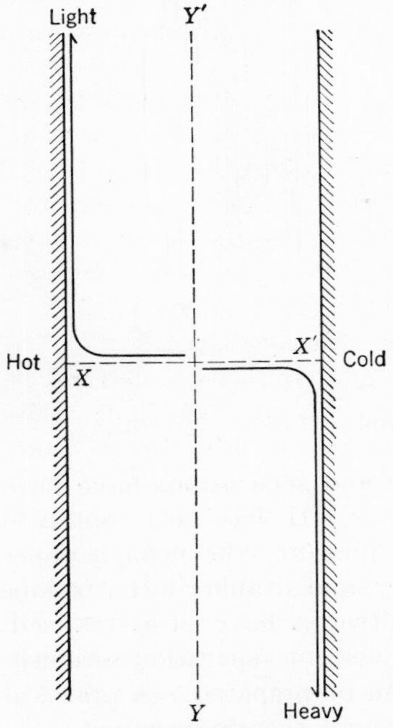

FIG. 2·9. Principle of isotope separation by thermal diffusion.

THE THERMAL DIFFUSION METHOD. Prior to 1920, both Enskog and Chapman showed independently from purely theoretical considerations that, if a mixture of gases of different molecular weights is subjected to a temperature gradient, the heavier molecules in general will move toward the colder region and the lighter toward the warmer region. Such a process, which is wholly independent of the kinetic properties of the gases, will continue until balanced by the ordinary kinetic diffusion of the gas molecules. Chapman and Dootson confirmed these predictions by studies of mixtures of carbon dioxide and hydrogen, but the first application to isotope separations was made many years later.[52] The method suggested by Clusius and Dickel amounts to enhancing the thermal diffusion effect by the use of convection currents; it is illustrated simply by the diagram in Figure 2·9. If a gaseous mixture is placed between two plates arranged vertically, a concentration gradient along the axis XX' is produced by thermal diffusion, molecules containing the heavier isotope moving toward the

[50] J. F. Hogerton: *Chem. & Met. Eng.*, **52** (No. 12), 98 (1945).

[51] M. Benedict and C. Williams: *Engineering Developments in the Gaseous Diffusion Process*, Div. II, Vol. 6, National Nuclear Energy Series. McGraw-Hill Book Co., New York (1949).

[52] K. Clusius and G. Dickel: *Naturwissenschaften*, **26**, 546 (1938); **27**, 148, 487 (1939).

cooler surface. At the same time, convection currents establish a concentration gradient along the axis YY', and the net effect is transportation of the lighter material toward the top and the heavier toward the bottom. If the vertical axis is made long in comparison with the horizontal, even slight concentration changes produced by thermal effects can be magnified tremendously by convection. In practice, this has been accomplished by using long vertical tubes (e.g., 10 mm. diameter glass) cooled externally and containing electrically heated wires (e.g., nichrome) as hot elements or by employing concentric tubes with inner heating and external cooling. Comprehensive discussions of the process have appeared.[53, 54]

The preliminary studies of Clusius and Dickel were followed by their separation of the isotopes of chlorine[55] in an apparatus consisting of several individual columns 6 to 9 meters in length, connected in series and employing hydrogen chloride gas. Heating was effected by axial wires of platinum maintained at 690°C. After some 37 days of operation, this apparatus produced about 8 ml. of hydrogen chloride gas containing chlorine of physical atomic weight 36.98 (i.e., 99.4% $H^{37}Cl$). With partially enriched hydrogen chloride (Cl = 35.17), the same apparatus yielded daily 16 ml. of gas containing chlorine of isotopic mass 34.979 (99.6% $H^{35}Cl$) after 14 days of operation. Efficiency, based on energy imput, amounted to only 9×10^{-9}. Numerous other equally effective separations have been achieved by this method, among them the oxygen isotopes (99.5% ^{18}O)[56] and helium.[57]

Since thermal diffusion is a continuous process, it is well suited to large-scale operations. The process is being used technically for the concentration of ^{13}C. Methane is the carrier gas in tall columns of iron pipe which contain an insulated axial heating wire and are cooled externally with water.[58] The yield of ^{13}C has been increased markedly, and the cost has been reduced correspondingly by new developments. Thermal diffusion effects also exist in liquids. Some preliminary concentration of ^{235}U was effected by this means at Oak Ridge.[39, 41]

CENTRIFUGAL METHODS. Centrifugal methods are closely allied to the diffusion methods already discussed because in a sense they are dependent upon diffusion of heterogeneous particles in an enhanced

[53] A. J. E. Welch: *Ann. Reports*, **37**, 153 (1940).

[54] R. C. Jones and W. H. Furry: *Revs. Modern Phys.*, **18**, 151 (1946).

[55] K. Clusius and G. Dickel: *Z. physik. Chem.*, **44B**, 397, 451 (1939).

[56] K. Clusius and G. Dickel: *Z. physik. Chem.*, **193**, 274 (1944).

[57] B. B. McInteer, L. T. Aldrich, and A. O. Nier: *Phys. Rev.*, **72**, 510 (1947); **74**, 946 (1948).

[58] Anon.: *Chem. Eng. News*, **24**, 394, 488 (1946).

gravitational field. This is in effect a type of pressure diffusion. The possibility of separating isotopes by such gravitation effects was suggested in 1919 by Lindemann and Aston and developed theoretically in 1922 by Mulliken. In an applied centrifugal field, the theoretical separation factor S (i.e., the ratio of the isotopes at the center over the corresponding ratio at the periphery) is given by

$$S = e^{V^2(M_2-M_1)/2RT} \tag{2·13}$$

where V is the peripheral velocity, M_2 and M_1 the molecular weights of the materials containing the isotopes in question, R the gas constant, and T the absolute temperature. It is apparent that at constant temperature and velocity, the extent of the separation is dependent upon the *mass difference* between the isotopes in question. Such a procedure, therefore, should be as effective with the heavier elements as with the lighter, a characteristic which is particularly desirable since other physical approaches depend rather upon the *relative masses* of the isotopes and become decreasingly effective with the heavier elements.

Early attempts at separation by centrifugal means failed because attainable peripheral velocities were insufficient. With the development of high-velocity gas-driven centrifuges by Beams and his coworkers, isotopic concentrations by this means became practical. With equipment of this type, appreciable concentrations of the chlorine isotopes (as carbon tetrachloride[59] and as hydrogen chloride[60]) and of the bromine isotopes[61] have been effected.

Separation in the liquid phase is less effective. As a consequence, the so-called evaporative centrifuge technique is employed. This technique, in brief, consists of condensing a gas in the periphery of the centrifuge and allowing the liquid to evaporate slowly while the centrifuge is spinning at high velocity, the resulting light fractions being drawn off gradually from the center by reduction in pressure. Results obtained are in accord with the predictions of Mulliken's theory. In the light of equation 2·13, enhanced separations might be expected as temperature is decreased.

Appreciable concentrations of the uranium isotopes have been effected by using tall cylindrical centrifuges in which gaseous uranium(VI) fluoride is passed downward at the periphery and upward at the center or axis. By this means, a constant diffusion of molecules from one current to another is established by the centrifugal field, and

[59] J. W. Beams and C. Skarstrom: *Phys. Rev.*, **56**, 266 (1939).
[60] H. C. Pollack: *Phys. Rev.*, **57**, 935 (1940).
[61] R. F. Humphreys: *Phys. Rev.*, **56**, 684 (1939).

a net concentration of the lighter isotope results at the axis and of the heavier at the periphery.[39, 41]

DISTILLATION METHODS. Theoretical considerations offered by Lindemann in 1919 indicated that, since the rates of escape of atoms or molecules from a liquid surface are in general inversely proportional to the square roots of their masses, isotopic concentrations could be effected by distillation. Although Aston's early attempts to concentrate the neon isotopes by this means were unsuccessful, use of an elaborate fractionating column operating at low pressures and at near the triple point enabled Keesom and van Dijk[62] to alter the mass of neon from the ordinary value of 20.183 to 20.091 and 21.157 for light and heavy fractions, respectively. Similarly, evaporation of liquid hydrogen at its triple point was used to concentrate the isotope ${}^{2}_{1}H$ to the point where it could be detected spectroscopically (p. 387).

Fractional distillation of water concentrates both the hydrogen and oxygen isotopes, but the changes effected are small. With columns employing either alternate stationary and rotating plates or gauze packing to improve contact between down-flowing liquid and up-flowing vapor, the $H_2^{18}O$ concentration has been increased some five-fold. Preliminary concentrations of ${}^{2}_{1}H$ have been effected in this manner. Applications and limitations of the procedure have been treated by Urey.[37]

A somewhat different approach involves unidirectional evaporation from a liquid surface. This amounts to complete condensation of all material which enters the vapor state and the avoidance of a distillation equilibrium. Under such conditions, the quantities of materials removed from the liquid under given conditions are entirely dependent upon relative molecular velocities (and therefore upon relative masses). Best results have been obtained with mercury. In initial studies, Brønsted and von Hevesy[63] evaporated mercury in a vacuum at 40 to 60°C. and condensed essentially all the escaping vapors on a surface cooled with liquid air and placed 1 to 2 cm. above the mercury surface. This distance roughly equals the mean free path of mercury atoms and ensures the absence of collisions between mercury atoms in the free state. After numerous fractional repetitions of the processes in which the initial volume of 2700 ml. was reduced by a factor of about 100,000 in each direction, light and heavy fractions with specific gravities of 0.99974 and 1.00023, respectively, as compared with ordinary mercury, were obtained. By the same procedure, Hönig-

[62] W. H. Keesom and H. van Dijk: *Proc. Koninkl. Nederland. Akad. Wetenschap.*, **34**, 42 (1931); **37**, 615 (1934); **38**, 809 (1935).

[63] J. N. Brønsted and G. von Hevesy: *Phil. Mag.*, **43**, 31 (1922).

schmid and Birkenbach[64] obtained fractions with chemical atomic weights of 200.564 ± 0.006 and 200.632 ± 0.007, as compared with an original value of 200.61 ± 0.006, and Harkins and his associates[65] obtained 100-gram samples of mercury differing in atomic mass by 0.189. An interesting improvement on this molecular distillation procedure[66, 67] involves combination of a number of individual units into a single arrangement by a series of containers arranged in a stair-step fashion. Above each cell is a sloping roof so arranged that material condensing above the cell flows down and drips into the next higher cell in the stair. Constant liquid level is maintained in each cell by an overflow device permitting liquid to flow to the next lower cell in the stair. The arrangement is thus completely automatic, with the lighter isotope concentrating in the top cell and the heavier in the bottom one. Striking concentrations of the mercury isotopes have apparently been obtained, but the procedure does not appear to be an especially practical one.

ION MIGRATION METHODS. In 1921, Lindemann suggested that ions of different masses should migrate with different velocities. Thus, ion migration should effect isotopic concentrations, although early negative results indicate such rate differences to be small. Studies at the Bureau of Standards have shown, however, that, if ion migration in an electric field is balanced against counterflowing electrolyte, using a packing (e.g., of 100-mesh sand), definite alterations in the natural abundance ratios of the potassium,[68–70] chlorine,[71] and copper[72] isotopes can be effected. For example, with potassium the ratio of $^{39}K:^{41}K$ was increased from 14.2 to 24 in about 500 hours, with a separation factor of 0.385×10^{-2}. In no case, however, were major concentrations obtained.

Electrolytic ion migration in fused melts has been shown to effect enrichment of the heavy isotopes of silver[73] and of lithium and potassium.[74] Again the concentrations are not striking.

[64] O. Hönigschmid and L. Birkenbach: *Ber.*, **56**, 1219 (1923).

[65] W. D. Harkins and B. Mortimer: *Phil. Mag.* [7], **6**, 601 (1928).

[66] Anon.: *Chem. Eng. News*, **25**, 1510 (1947).

[67] Anon.: *J. Chem. Education*, **25**, 170 (1948).

[68] A. K. Brewer, S. L. Madorsky, and J. W. Westhaver: *Science*, **104**, 156 (1946).

[69] A. K. Brewer, S. L. Madorsky, J. K. Taylor, V. H. Dibeler, P. Bradt, O. L. Parham, R. J. Britten, and J. G. Reid, Jr.: *J. Research Natl. Bur. Standards*, **38**, 137 (1947).

[70] J. W. Westhaver: *J. Research Natl. Bur. Standards*, **38**, 169 (1947).

[71] S. L. Madorsky and S. Straus: *J. Research Natl. Bur. Standards*, **38**, 185 (1947).

[72] S. L. Madorsky and S. Straus: *J. Research Natl. Bur. Standards*, **41**, 41 (1948).

[73] A. Klemm: *Z. Naturforsch.*, **2a**, 9 (1947).

[74] A. Klemm, H. Hintenberger, and P. Hoernes: *Z. Naturforsch.*, **2a**, 245 (1947).

MISCELLANEOUS METHODS. A number of miscellaneous but quite generally unsuccessful procedures have been described. Among the most interesting of those of a very specific nature is the reported alteration in the natural ratio of the helium isotopes by super-fluid flow below the λ-point (p. 376).[75,76] Enrichment of ^3He in material not passing as a surface film, although slight, was measurable, suggesting that this isotope lacks super-fluid properties.

Methods Involving Chemical Characteristics. The isotopes of a given element are chemically identical in that they react in the same fashion with a given reagent. However, they do not, in general, react at the same rate, and it is upon this fact that chemical methods for isotopic concentration and separation are based. Differences in reaction rates are dependent upon differences in zero point energy, i.e., energy at absolute zero. These differences are small; so rate differences are correspondingly small, and any separations based upon them are of necessity fractional in character.

THE ELECTROLYTIC METHOD. Electrolysis was first suggested as a means of isotope separation by Kendall and Crittenden in 1923 but received no confirmation until Washburn and Urey[77] observed the quantity of ^2_1H to be greater in the residual water in electrolytic hydrogen cells than in ordinary water. Exploitation of this observation and details of the electrolytic separation of deuterium (^2_1H) are considered in Chapter 12 (pp. 387–389). The procedure has not proved particularly successful with elements other than hydrogen.

EXCHANGE REACTION METHODS. Studies with deuterium (pp. 390–391) showed that it often exchanged with the light hydrogen isotope in chemical reactions and suggested that isotopes of other elements might exhibit similar behaviors. The subject was treated theoretically by Urey and Greiff,[78] who evaluated equilibrium constants for a number of systems of potential value by statistical means. Representative systems from their paper are summarized in Table 2·4.

Reactions listed in Table 2·4 involve equilibria between liquid and gas phases. This is the type of reaction studied most extensively by Urey and his students.[37] For any such system, the following features are desirable: rapid establishment of the equilibrium, intimate contact between the phases, and ready conversion of the gaseous

[75] J. G. Daunt, R. E. Probst, H. L. Johnston, L. T. Aldrich, and A. O. Nier: *Phys. Rev.*, **72**, 502 (1947).

[76] J. G. Daunt, R. E. Probst, and H. L. Johnston: *J. Chem. Phys.*, **15**, 759 (1947).

[77] E. W. Washburn and H. C. Urey: *Proc. Natl. Acad. Sci.*, **18**, 496 (1932).

[78] H. C. Urey and L. J. Greiff: *J. Am. Chem. Soc.*, **57**, 321 (1935).

TABLE 2·4
EQUILIBRIUM CONSTANTS FOR EXCHANGE REACTIONS

Equilibrium System	Equilibrium Constant		
	273.1°K.	298.1°K.	600°K.
$S^{16}O_2(g) + 2H_2{}^{18}O(l) \rightleftharpoons S^{18}O_2(g) + 2H_2{}^{16}O(l)$	1.040	1.028	......
$C^{16}O_2(g) + 2H_2{}^{18}O(l) \rightleftharpoons C^{18}O_2(g) + 2H_2{}^{16}O(l)$	1.097	1.080	......
$C^{16}O_2(g) + 2H_2{}^{18}O(g) \rightleftharpoons C^{18}O_2(g) + 2H_2{}^{16}O(g)$	1.128	1.110	1.028
$2{}^{18}O_2(g) + S^{16}O_4{}^{-2}(soln.) \rightleftharpoons 2{}^{16}O_2(g) + S^{18}O_4{}^{-2}(soln.)$	1.051	1.036	0.993
${}^{13}CO_2(g) + {}^{12}CO_3{}^{-2}(soln.) \rightleftharpoons {}^{12}CO_2(g) + {}^{13}CO_3{}^{-2}(soln.)$	1.015	1.012	0.997
${}^{35}Cl_2(g) + 2H^{37}Cl(soln.) \rightleftharpoons {}^{37}Cl_2(g) + 2H^{35}Cl(soln.)$	1.007	1.006	1.0003

component containing the desired element into the liquid component, and vice versa, to render the process continuous. These points are illustrated admirably in the concentration of the ${}^{15}_{7}N$ isotope by use of the equilibrium[79]

$${}^{15}NH_3(g) + {}^{14}NH_4{}^+(soln.) \rightleftharpoons {}^{15}NH_4{}^+(soln.) + {}^{14}NH_3(g) \quad K = 1.023$$

Equilibrium is established by flowing an ammonium salt solution down a suitable column countercurrent to a stream of ammonia gas. At the bottom of the column, ammonia is regenerated from the ammonium salt by the action of sodium hydroxide and continuously returned to the system. As indicated by the equilibrium constant for the system as written, the ammonium salt solution is continually enriched in ${}^{15}N$, and the gas stream is depleted in it. Use of columns containing large numbers of theoretical plates renders this process quite efficient, and it is employed for the large-scale commercial concentration of the heavy nitrogen isotope.[80, 81]

Notable successes have been achieved in other gas-liquid exchange reactions. Among them are[37]

$${}^{13}CO_2(g) + H^{12}CO_3{}^-(soln.) \rightleftharpoons H^{13}CO_3{}^-(soln.) + {}^{12}CO_2(g)$$

$$H^{12}CN(g) + {}^{13}CN^-(soln.) \rightleftharpoons {}^{12}CN^-(soln.) + H^{13}CN(g) \quad K = 1.026$$

$${}^{34}SO_2(g) + H^{32}SO_3{}^-(soln.) \rightleftharpoons H^{34}SO_3{}^-(soln.) + {}^{32}SO_2(g)$$

Of particular importance also is the fact that if hydrogen gas and liquid water are equilibrated in the presence of a suitable catalyst the deuterium concentration in the liquid phase amounts to about three

[79] H. C. Urey, J. R. Huffman, H. G. Thode, and M. Fox: *J. Chem. Phys.*, **5**, 856 (1937).

[80] E. W. Becker and H. Baumgärtel: *Angew. Chem.*, **A59**, 88 (1947).

[81] Anon.: *Chem. Eng. News*, **27**, 87 (1949).

times that in the gas phase. Concentration of the heavy hydrogen isotope by this means has been effected (p. 391).

Solid-liquid systems involving natural and synthetic zeolites as cation exchangers have been investigated also. When a sodium zeolite (say NaZ, where Z is the zeolite anion) is treated with a metal salt solution, the sodium and metal (M^{+n}) ions exchange according to the equation

$$M^{+n}(\text{soln.}) + n\text{NaZ(s)} \rightleftharpoons M(\text{Z})_n(\text{s}) + n\text{Na}^+(\text{soln.})$$

Reversal of the reaction by addition of a sodium salt then regenerates the original materials. It is conceivable that not all the isotopes of the metal M would exchange at the same rate. Although no practical results have been obtained, slight alterations in the isotopic compositions of lithium[82] and of potassium[83] have been effected in this fashion. For example, the ^{6}Li isotope is taken up more readily by the zeolite and released less readily than the ^{7}Li isotope.

A procedure often described as an exchange in a liquid-liquid system but which is more probably dependent upon slight differences in electrode potentials between the lithium isotopes is that in which small droplets of lithium amalgam were allowed to drop through a methanol solution of lithium chloride in a tall column.[84] Under these conditions, the equilibrium

$$^7\text{Li(amalg.)} + {}^6\text{Li}^+(\text{alc.}) \rightleftharpoons {}^6\text{Li(amalg.)} + {}^7\text{Li}^+(\text{alc.})$$

was established, the lighter isotope concentrating in the amalgam. By rendering the process continuous the ^{6}Li:^{7}Li ratio was altered from 1:11.6 to 1:5.1. The procedure lacks practicality.

More recently, exchange reactions in gas-gas systems have been shown to be useful. For example, the equilibrium

$$^{15}\text{NO(g)} + {}^{14}\text{NO}_2\text{(g)} \rightleftharpoons {}^{14}\text{NO(g)} + {}^{15}\text{NO}_2\text{(g)}$$

established in a thermal diffusion column effects sizable alterations in the isotopic composition of nitrogen.[85] Correspondingly, a countercurrent gaseous process based upon the equilibrium

$$^{12}\text{CO}_2\text{(g)} + {}^{13}\text{CO(g)} \rightleftharpoons {}^{13}\text{CO}_2\text{(g)} + {}^{12}\text{CO(g)}$$

has been used to concentrate the ^{13}C isotope.[86]

[82] T. I. Taylor and H. C. Urey: *J. Chem. Phys.*, **5**, 597 (1937).
[83] T. I. Taylor and H. C. Urey: *J. Chem. Phys.*, **6**, 429 (1938).
[84] G. N. Lewis and R. T. MacDonald: *J. Am. Chem. Soc.*, **58**, 2519 (1936).
[85] T. I. Taylor and W. Spindel: *J. Chem. Phys.*, **16**, 635 (1948).
[86] R. B. Bernstein and T. I. Taylor: *J. Chem. Phys.*, **16**, 903 (1948).

Exchange reactions are particularly advantageous in that they can be cascaded without difficulty to increase separation factors remarkably. Slight separations achieved in single-phase operations can thus be magnified, and large-scale installations become practical. Reviews[37, 87] should be consulted for further details.

MISCELLANEOUS CHEMICAL METHODS. Certain chemical reactions appear to produce slight alterations in isotopic ratios although significant differences have not been demonstrated. Among such reactions are: preferential liberation of $^{1}_{1}H$ as the free element or gaseous hydride when water, acidic solutions, or alkaline solutions are treated with certain metals, metal carbides, or metal sulfides; differences in ease of liberation of the oxygen isotopes when hydrogen peroxide is decomposed on colloidal platinum; preferential reaction of $^{35}_{17}Cl$ when carbon tetrachloride is heated with sodium amalgam; and differences in the rate of liberation of the chlorine isotopes when carbonyl chloride is decomposed photochemically.

THE STABILITIES OF ATOMIC NUCLEI

Nuclear instability

Inasmuch as many nuclei are stable, attractive forces must exist between neutrons and protons. Although the natures of these forces are not completely understood (p. 18), they appear to amount to energy exchanges *via* mesons. At the same time, coulombic repulsive forces among the protons must also exist.

If only the attractive forces between neutrons and protons are considered, it is apparent that any energy exchange between these particles would be at a maximum when equal numbers of neutrons and protons were present. Nuclear neutron to proton ratios ($N:P$), on this basis, should then approach unity. However, since the protons mutually repel each other, there will also be a tendency toward reduction of these forces through reduction in the number of protons. Such an effect should increase as the number of protons increases. The actual neutron to proton ratio characterizing a nucleus will then be such that a balance exists between the tendency toward neutron-proton equalization and the tendency toward proton reduction. With nuclei containing but few protons (low Z), the first tendency will predominate ($N:P = 1$); but with nuclei containing many protons, the second will become increasingly important, and the neutron to proton ratio will increase slowly. In Figure 2·5, such ratios increased from 1 to 1.6 for the naturally occurring nuclei.

[87] A. L. G. Rees: *Ann. Reports,* **38,** 83 (1941).

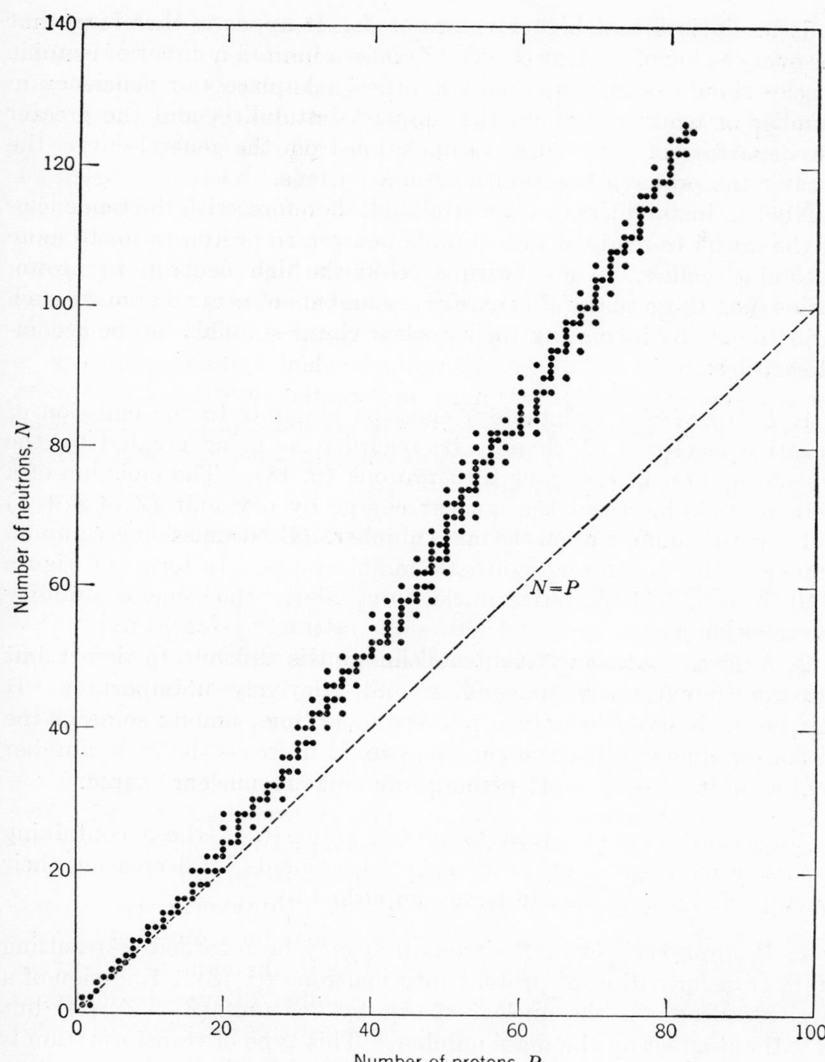

FIG. 2·10. Relations between numbers of neutrons and protons in stable naturally occurring nuclei.

In Figure 2·10, the numbers of neutrons in stable naturally occurring nuclei are plotted against the numbers of protons. An average curve drawn through these points represents the neutron-proton conditions for greatest potential nuclear stability. Its coincidence with the dotted curve for the condition $N = P$ is apparent at low values of Z, as is its deviation at higher values of Z. It appears, therefore, that for every value of nuclear charge (Z) only a limited number of isotopic species should possess marked stabilities. An excess or deficiency in number of neutrons should then impart instability, and the greater the departure of the nuclear composition from the general curve, the greater the probable instability of that nucleus.

Nuclear instabilities can be correlated, therefore, with the tendencies of the nuclei to readjust unfavorable neutron to proton ratios to more favorable values. Nuclei with excessively high neutron to proton ratios (i.e., those containing excessive numbers of neutrons) make such adjustments by increasing their nuclear charges. This can be accomplished by:

1. *Beta emission.* Beta (β^-) emission amounts to the emission of negative electrons which may be regarded as being created by the transformation of neutrons into protons (p. 18). The emission of a beta particle increases the nuclear charge by one unit ($Z \rightarrow Z + 1$) but is without effect upon the mass number. Beta emission is common among both natural and synthetic radioisotopes. In terms of Figure 2·10, it would characterize nuclei lying above the general stability curve as shown.
2. *Neutron emission.* Neutron emission is difficult to detect but apparently extremely uncommon and relatively unimportant. It has been observed in only a few instances, e.g., among some of the fission products. Neutron emission would decrease the mass number by one unit ($A \rightarrow A - 1$) without affecting the nuclear charge.

Nuclei with low neutron to proton ratios (i.e., those containing excessive numbers of protons) make adjustments by decreasing their nuclear charges. This can be accomplished by:

1. *Positron emission.* Positrons (β^+) may be regarded as resulting from transformation of protons into neutrons (p. 18). Emission of a positron decreases the nuclear charge by one unit ($Z \rightarrow Z - 1$) but is without effect on the mass number. This type of transformation is known only among the synthetic radioisotopes.
2. *Orbital electron capture.* As an alternative to positron emission, a nucleus may capture an orbital electron, thereby converting a proton to a neutron and giving the same mass and charge effects. Since the electron captured is normally one of those closest to the nucleus, i.e., a K electron (p. 87), the process is usually termed K-electron capture, or more simply K-capture. To fill the vacancy so created, an electron from a higher energy level drops into the K-shell, and characteristic

x-radiation is emitted. *K*-electron capture is rather uncommon and is usually found only among the synthetic radioisotopes.

3. *Proton emission.* Proton emission may be regarded as a possible means of increasing neutron to proton ratios, but it is highly unlikely and of no importance.

In terms of Figure 2·10, these processes would characterize nuclei lying below the general stability curve as shown.

In general, whether a nucleus will attain stability through beta emission or through positron emission or *K*-electron capture can be predicted by application of the stable isobar rule of Mattauch.[88] This empirical generalization states that stable isobar pairs do not exist where nuclear charges differ by only one unit. Although a few apparent exceptions are known (p. 25), the lack of more exceptions indicates its validity. It is not improbable that each of the known exceptions is characterized by one unstable isotope of long half-life and feeble activity. A nucleus, therefore, ordinarily decays to a stable isobaric nucleus. Thus unstable $^{24}_{11}Na$ decays to stable $^{24}_{12}Mg$ by beta emission; unstable $^{13}_{7}N$ decays to stable $^{13}_{6}C$ by positron emission; unstable $^{49}_{23}V$ decays to stable $^{49}_{22}Ti$ by *K*-electron capture, etc. The absence of stable naturally occurring isotopes of charges 43 and 61 is associated with the existence of stable isotopes of all mass numbers in these charge regions. It is presumed, therefore, that only radioactive isotopes of these elements can exist.

It may be inferred from the foregoing discussion that there can be but one arrangement of neutrons and protons in a particular nuclear species and that if such a species is unstable it can decay, therefore, in but one fashion. Although this is generally true, there is abundant evidence that the nucleons may be present in more than one energy condition, or in other words that nuclear energy levels may exist in much the same fashion as do extranuclear electronic levels (pp. 81–86). Such levels are metastable with respect to the one of lowest energy content, but sometimes their stabilities are such that a given nucleus (fixed Z and A) may exist in more than one level and thus possess different properties. This gives rise to the phenomenon of nuclear isomerism.

Decay processes are complicated by nuclear isomerism. This is shown in a general way in Figure 2·11. The unstable nucleus X may exist in any one of several energy levels A, A', or A''. A and A' are

[88] J. Mattauch and S. Fluegge: *Nuclear Physics Tables and an Introduction to Nuclear Physics*, p. 97. Interscience Publishers, New York (1946). *Z. Physik*, **91**, 361 (1934).

metastable with respect to A''. Such a nucleus could gain stability by losing energy through transition from A or A' to A'', a process known as isomeric transition (I.T.). No mass or charge alteration occurs, but energy is lost either as short wavelength or gamma (γ) radiation or by transfer to orbital electrons. The latter may cause one or more orbital electrons to be emitted from the atom in question. Such electrons are called internal conversion electrons (e^-), and their emission is accompanied by x-radiation as with K-electron capture.

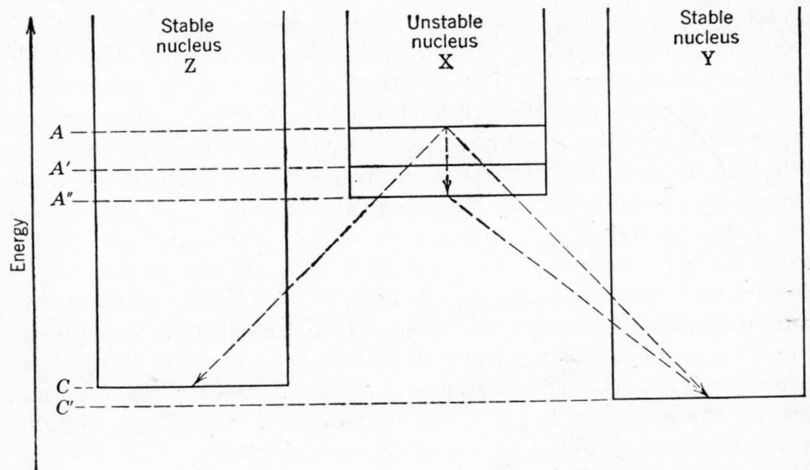

FIG. 2·11. Diagrammatic representation of nuclear isomerism.

The unstable nucleus X (Figure 2·11) may decay to the stable nucleus Y of energy C' by alternative paths. If the isomeric transition from A to A'' requires an appreciable time interval, decay may proceed by the path A–A''–C' as well as by the direct path A–C'. The same type of decay but with two half-life periods (p. 58) would result. In some instances, however, nuclear isomerism may lead to two different decay types and products. Thus nucleus X (Figure 2·11) might decay to nucleus Y by the path A–C' and to another nucleus Z of energy C by the path A–C. Obviously, such a situation could exist only if C' and C were nearly identical and nuclei Y and Z were stable isobars of X. Examples of both nuclear isomerism effects are known. Thus $^{60}_{27}Co$ decays to $^{60}_{28}Ni$ by beta emission, but two decay paths are noted, one involving direct β^- decay followed by an isomeric transition and the other successively an isomeric transition, a β^- emission, and two isomeric transitions. On the other hand, $^{106}_{47}Ag$ decays by β^- activity to $^{106}_{48}Cd$ and by β^+ activity to $^{106}_{46}Pd$. Both β^- and α

activity are shown by certain naturally occurring isotopes, among them RaC, AcC, and ThC.

Gamma radiation associated with the above processes is penetrating electromagnetic radiation of somewhat shorter wavelength than x-radiation. Its emission is associated with energy changes within the nucleus and is not associated with mass or charge changes. Gamma radiation results from a secondary energy release mechanism.

One other instability factor requires consideration. This is the sheer mass of the nucleus. Nuclei possessing excessive masses are spontaneously unstable. Thus no nuclei of mass numbers above 209

TABLE 2·5
NUCLEAR DECAY PROCESSES

Process	Designation	Change in Z	Change in A	Examples
Beta emission	β^-	+1	0	${}^{14}_{6}C \xrightarrow{5100\ y.} {}^{14}_{7}N$
				${}^{234}_{90}UX_1 \xrightarrow{24.1\ d.} {}^{234}_{91}UX_2$
Positron emission	β^+	−1	0	${}^{19}_{10}Ne \xrightarrow{20.3\ s.} {}^{19}_{9}F$
				${}^{23}_{12}Mg \xrightarrow{11.6\ s.} {}^{23}_{11}Na$
K-electron capture	K	−1	0	${}^{55}_{26}Fe \xrightarrow{4\ y.} {}^{55}_{25}Mn$
				${}^{73}_{33}As \xrightarrow{90\ d.} {}^{73}_{32}Ge$
Isomeric transition	I.T.	0	0	${}^{52}_{25}Mn \xrightarrow{21\ m.} {}^{52}_{25}Mn$
				${}^{60}_{27}Co \xrightarrow{10.7\ m.} {}^{60}_{27}Co$
Alpha emission	α	−2	−4	${}^{238}_{92}UI \xrightarrow{4.5 \times 10^9\ y.} {}^{234}_{90}UX_1$
				${}^{226}_{88}Ra \xrightarrow{1590\ y.} {}^{222}_{86}Rn$

(at ${}^{209}_{83}Bi$) are stable. Such nuclei readjust themselves to the stable range by following down the curve in Figure 2·10 through emission of alpha (α) particles. Emission of an alpha particle (p. 10) decreases the mass number by four units ($A \rightarrow A - 4$) and the nuclear charge by two ($Z \rightarrow Z - 2$). The emission of a particle of such large mass and charge requires a comparatively energetic parent nucleus. With but few exceptions only the heaviest nuclei possess these energies. Emission of alpha particles by light nuclei is most uncommon.

The general attempt of nuclei to attain stability through emission of energy due to the readjustments described above gives rise to the phenomenon of radioactivity. The various processes involved in radioactive decay are summarized in Table 2·5. The energies associated with such processes are commonly expressed in millions of electron volts (Mev).

Radioactive decay

Radioactive decay is essentially random in character and is kinetically a first-order process, i.e., one in which the rate depends only upon the number of decaying atoms present. Each decay process is thus governed by the expression

$$-\frac{dn}{dt} = \lambda n \tag{2·14}$$

where n is the number of atoms of the species present and λ is a constant characteristic of that species. Integration of this expression and evaluation of the time necessary for one-half of the atoms present initially to decompose (i.e., the half-life period) give

$$t_{1/2} = \frac{0.6932}{\lambda} \tag{2·15}$$

Each radioactive species is characterized by its half-life period. Such periods range from 10^{-7} sec. to 10^{14} years.

Although decay of a particular species commonly gives a stable product in a single step, examples of chain decay are known. In the production of synthetic radioisotopes by bombardment (p. 71) or fission (p. 72), products with large excesses of neutrons result. A number of successive beta emissions is thereby essential before the stability curve (Figure 2·10) can be approached. Among the heavy nuclei, on the other hand, successive alpha emissions lead to a general following down of the stability curve, but the curve drops more steeply than simple alpha emissions would predict. Hence nuclei with excessive numbers of neutrons result, and periodic beta emissions are noted. This is characteristic of the various heavy element decay series (pp. 64–65).

If a given radioisotope decays to a second active material, the activity of the first material will decrease with time while that of the second will increase in the reverse order. Eventually, a state of apparent equilibrium between the two will be reached, a state in which the decrease in activity of the first will be balanced by the increase in activity of the second. In chain decay, all the members will be involved, and the general equilibrium will be governed by the long half-life of the parent element. It follows from Equation 2·14 that such an equilibrium is characterized by the expression

$$n_1\lambda_1 = n_2\lambda_2 = n_3\lambda_3 = \cdots = n_n\lambda_n \tag{2·16}$$

where the subscripts refer to the various species involved.

Binding energies and nuclear stabilities

Nuclear stabilities have been related to packing fractions and mass defects (pp. 36–38). This is possible because in the synthesis of any nucleus from its component particles a certain quantity of mass disappears by transformation into energy in terms of the Einstein relation

$$E = mc^2 \tag{2·17}$$

The energy-equivalent of this mass loss is known as the binding energy of the nucleus, and its magnitude is a measure of the stability of that nucleus. Indeed, it is much more exacting to characterize a species in terms of its binding energy than in terms of either packing fraction or mass defect, for the binding energy is determined by the true mass loss and does not involve the more indeterminate mass number.

Binding energies may be calculated readily from nuclear compositions. Thus for the deuteron, which is composed of one neutron and one proton, the calculated mass is (p. 10)

$$1.00893 + 1.00757 = 2.01650 \text{ AMU}$$

The mass of the deuteron is that of the deuterium atom (2.01471) less one electron mass (0.00055), or 2.01416 AMU. The mass loss in the synthesis of the deuteron, 0.00234 AMU, corresponds, in terms of Equation 2·17, to an energy of 2.18 Mev.* Similarly, the binding energy of the $^{16}_{8}O$ isotope can be calculated. Since this atom contains eight neutrons, eight protons, and eight electrons, its mass should be that of eight neutrons (8×1.00893) and eight hydrogen atoms (8×1.00812), or 16.13640 AMU. The actual mass is 16.00000 AMU; so the mass loss of 0.1364 AMU corresponds to a binding energy of 127 Mev.

In a similar way, binding energies can be calculated for other species. In comparing these, it is most common to evaluate the binding energy per nucleon (e.g., 7.9 Mev for $^{16}_{8}O$). Values of this type are summarized in Appendix I and plotted in Figure 2·12. It is apparent that this curve is essentially the reciprocal of the packing fraction

* Substitution in Equation 2·17 of $m = 1.661 \times 10^{-24}$ gram for 1 AMU and $c = 2.998 \times 10^{10}$ cm./sec. gives an energy $E = 1.493 \times 10^{-3}$ erg. However, since 1 electron volt (ev) $= 1.602 \times 10^{-12}$ erg or 1 Mev $= 1.602 \times 10^{-6}$ erg, substitution shows 1 AMU to be equivalent to 931 Mev. Correspondingly, 1 electron mass is equivalent to 0.5107 Mev.

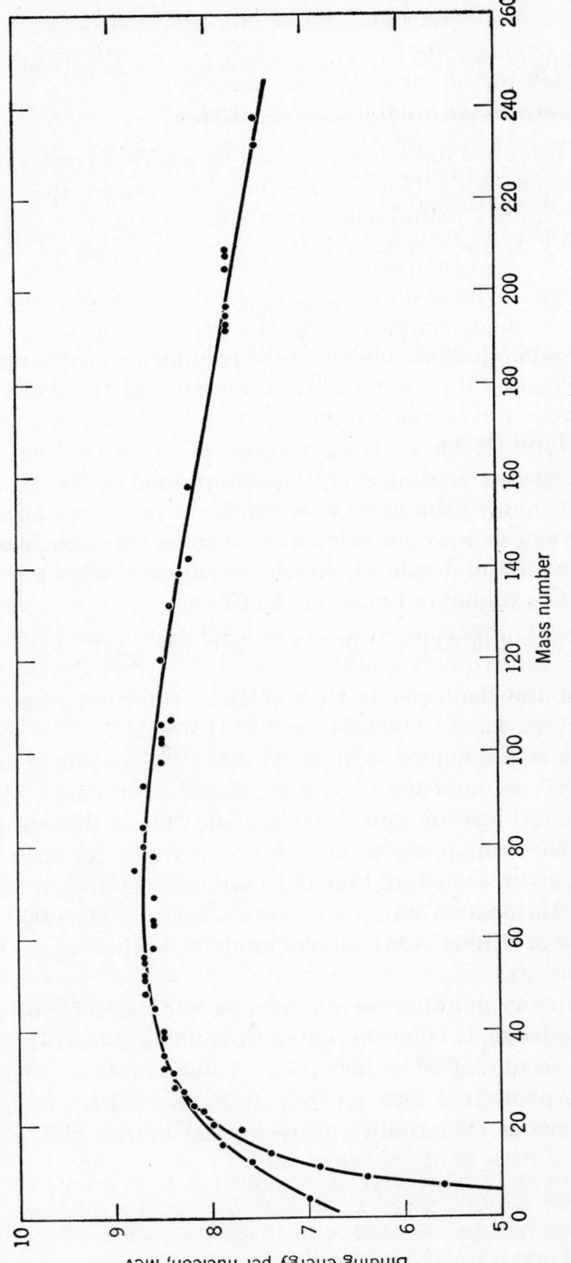

FIG. 2·12. Nuclear binding energy curve.

curve (Figure 2·6). Except for the lightest nuclei, binding energies per nucleon average about 6 to 8 Mev. A maximum of some 8.7 Mev is reached in the vicinity of mass number 55 (i.e., at iron), with decreases at low mass numbers being more abrupt and irregular than at high ones. It follows that maximum nuclear stability toward natural decay or toward alteration by bombardment would characterize those species with highest binding energies. Thus the synthesis of $^{4}_{2}He$ from hydrogen atoms, a highly energetic and potentially useful process (p. 68), is accompanied by increased stability due to increased binding energy. The abundance of iron (p. 885) is associated with the same factor. The decomposition of the heavy elements, either naturally or by fission (p. 69), occurs because lighter nuclei have greater binding energies.

Natural radioactivity

The discovery of radioactivity among the naturally occurring elements was a more or less accidental result of attempts by Henri Becquerel to relate x-radiation to fluorescence. Among the materials studied was a uranium salt which fluoresced brilliantly when exposed to ultraviolet radiation. However, when this substance was wrapped in black paper and placed adjacent to a photographic plate, the plate was fogged. Subsequent studies showed the property of affecting a photographic plate to be common to all uranium compounds and to be independent of fluorescence, phosphorescence, or physical state.[89] Further work was assigned to Marie Curie, who in collaboration with Pierre Curie soon found the phenomenon to be more pronounced with the natural uranium ore pitchblende than with pure uranium compounds of the same uranium content. From such source, the new and highly radioactive elements polonium[90] and radium[91] were extracted. Subsequent studies by the Curies and others revealed radioactive properties among all the heaviest elements.

Early investigations on radioactive materials were concerned primarily with their spontaneous release of energy and were carried out without knowledge of their relation to atomic structures. In fact, information accumulated in this way provided the foundations for much of present atomic theory as has been indicated. In the light of present knowledge, the results obtained by early investigators must be regarded as little short of remarkable.

Most of the naturally occurring radioactive isotopes are those of

[89] H. Becquerel: *Compt. rend.*, **122**, 420, 501, 559, 689, 762, 1086 (1896).
[90] P. Curie and M. Curie: *Compt. rend.*, **127**, 175 (1898).
[91] P. Curie, M. Curie, and G. Bémont: *Compt. rend.*, **127**, 1215 (1898).

high nuclear charges and mass numbers. All nuclei with charges greater than 83 are radioactive, and in addition certain nuclei of charges 81 (thallium isotopes), 82 (lead isotopes), and 83 (bismuth isotopes) are also unstable. Only a few naturally occurring isotopes of lower nuclear charges have been shown to be radioactive. These are summarized in Table 2·6. These isotopes are all characterized by

TABLE 2·6
NATURALLY RADIOACTIVE ISOTOPES OF LIGHTER ELEMENTS

Nucleus	Decay	Product	Half-life, years	Energy of Radiation, Mev
$^{3}_{1}H$	β^-	$^{3}_{2}He$	12.4	0.0179
$^{14}_{6}C$	β^-	$^{14}_{7}N$	5×10^3	0.145
$^{40}_{19}K$	β^-, γ	$^{40}_{20}Ca$	1.8×10^9	1.9(β^-) 1.5(γ)
$^{87}_{37}Rb$	β^-, γ, e^-	$^{87}_{38}Sr$	6.3×10^{10}	0.13(β^-) 0.13(γ)
$^{115}_{49}In$	β^-	$^{115}_{50}Sn$	6×10^{14}	0.63
$^{150}_{60}Nd$	β^-	$^{150}_{61}$	ca. 5×10^{10}	0.011
$^{152}_{62}Sm$	α	$^{148}_{60}Nd$	1.0×10^{12}	2.0
$^{176}_{71}Lu$	β^-, γ (33%) K (67%)	$^{176}_{72}Hf$ $^{176}_{70}Yb$	2.4×10^{10}	0.4(β^-) 0.26(γ)
$^{187}_{75}Re$	β^-	$^{187}_{76}Os$	4×10^{12}	0.043

long half-lives (except $^{3}_{1}H$) and comparatively feeble activities. It is conceivable that, as the sensitivities of detecting instruments increase, other examples will be found. Certainly one wonders whether the apparent exceptions to Mattauch's rule (pp. 25, 55) will not each be characterized by an unstable but long-lived species.

The heavy radioactive isotopes may be grouped into so-called disintegration or decay series, of which there are three for the naturally occurring elements and one for a number of materials arising from synthetically obtained heavy isotopes.[92, 93, 94] These series are referred to as $4n$ (or thorium), $4n + 1$ (or neptunium), $4n + 2$ (or uranium), and $4n + 3$ (or actinium) series, the numerical designation indicating whether the mass numbers of the members are exactly divisible by *4* or

[92] F. Hagemann, L. I. Katzin, M. H. Studier, A. Ghiorso, and G. T. Seaborg: *Phys. Rev.*, **72,** 252 (1947).

[93] A. C. English, T. E. Cranshaw, P. Demers, J. A. Harvey, E. P. Hincks, J. V. Jelley, and A. N. May: *Phys. Rev.*, **72,** 253 (1947).

[94] G. T. Seaborg: *Chem. Eng. News*, **26,** 1902 (1948).

divisible by 4 with remainders of 1, 2, or 3. Each series is characterized by a parent of long half-life and a series of decay processes which lead ultimately to a stable end product. With the three natural series, the end products are isotopes of lead; with the $4n + 1$ series a bismuth isotope results.

The general characteristics of the disintegration series are indicated in Table 2·7. Included in this table are data indicating that lead

TABLE 2·7
CHARACTERISTICS OF THE DISINTEGRATION SERIES

Series		Parent	Half-life of Parent, years	Stable End Product	Particles Lost		Mass of Lead from Minerals
					α	β^-	
$4n$	Th	$^{232}_{90}$Th	1.39×10^{10}	$^{208}_{82}$ThD	6	5	207.9
$4n + 1$	Np	$^{237}_{93}$Np	2.25×10^{6}	$^{209}_{83}$Bi	7	4	......
$4n + 2$	U	$^{238}_{92}$UI	4.51×10^{9}	$^{206}_{82}$RaG	8	7	206.03
$4n + 3$	Ac	$^{235}_{92}$AcU	7.07×10^{8}	$^{207}_{82}$AcD	7	5	207

samples isolated from thorium, uranium, and actinium minerals agree in mass with values calculated from the disintegration series and suggesting that such lead was produced by these disintegrations. The lead-uranium and lead-thorium ratios in minerals, coupled with knowledge of the various half-life periods in the appropriate series, indicate the age of the earth to be some 2000 to 3000 million years.

Specific details concerning the disintegration series are summarized in Appendix II (pp. 917–918). In this tabulation each radioisotope in general decays to the one placed immediately under it. Exceptional are the cases of nuclear isomerism where two decay paths lead to chain branchings. Wherever chain branching occurs, merger again results in a subsequent step. The last material given for each series is the stable end product. The names characterizing the various isotopes were given, in general, as the series were worked out. It will be noted that the system used has some regularity.

Successive transformations in the natural disintegration series were first systematized by comparisons of the chemical properties of the various isotopes. Using such information, Rutherford, Soddy, and Fajans formulated the so-called displacement laws. These may be stated as:

1. When an element emits an alpha particle, the product has the properties of an element two places to the left of the parent in the periodic table.

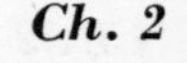

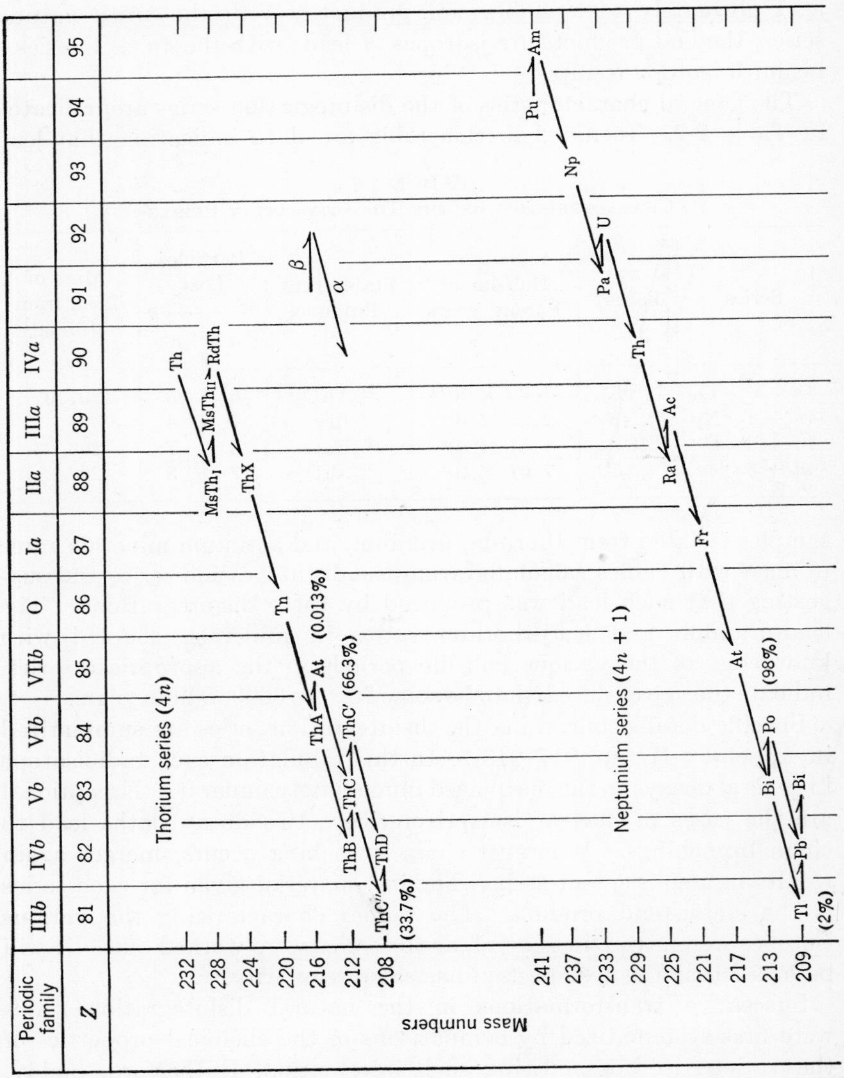

Periodic family	IIIb	IVb	Vb	VIb	VIIb	O	Ia	IIa	IIIa	IVa					
Z	81	82	83	84	85	86	87	88	89	90	91	92	93	94	95

Mass numbers

Thorium series ($4n$): 232, 228, 224, 220, 216, 212, 208

Th, $MsTh_I$, $MsTh_{II}$, RdTh, ThX, Tn, ThA, At (0.013%), ThB, ThC, ThC' (66.3%), ThC'' (33.7%), ThD

β α

Neptunium series ($4n + 1$): 241, 237, 233, 229, 225, 221, 217, 213, 209

Am, Pu, Np, U, Pa, Th, Ac, Ra, Fr, At, Po (98%), Bi, Tl (2%), Pb, Bi

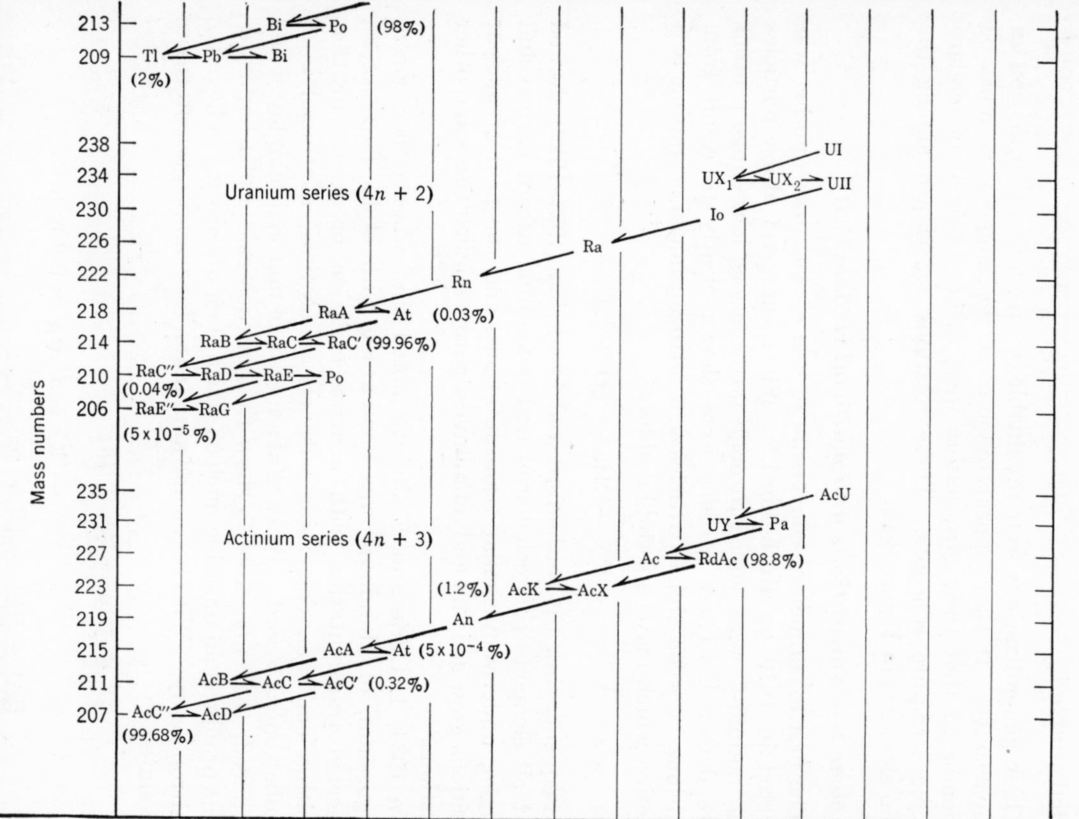

Fig. 2·13. Periodic relations among members of the disintegration series.

2. When an element emits a beta particle, the product has the properties of an element one place to the right of the parent in the periodic table.

These generalizations were invaluable in correlating information on radioactivity. If they appear obvious at the moment, it must be remembered that their formulators were without benefit of modern atomic structure concepts. These relations are shown among the radio elements in Figure 2·13.

Nuclear transmutations and artificial radioactivity

The first experimental conversion of one nucleus into another was effected in 1919 by Rutherford.[95] When energetic alpha particles from radium-C were passed through nitrogen gas, long-range protons were detected. These protons were shown clearly to result from collisions between alpha particles and nitrogen nuclei according to a reaction which may be formulated as

$$^{14}_{7}\text{N} + {}^{4}_{2}\text{He} \rightarrow {}^{17}_{8}\text{O} + {}^{1}_{1}\text{H}$$

Subsequent work by Rutherford and Chadwick (1921–1922) showed that all elements between boron and potassium, except carbon and oxygen, underwent similar transmutations, and the field of nuclear reactions grew as more and more investigators studied these and other reactions.

In 1934, I. Curie and F. Joliot[96] noted that when either boron, magnesium, or aluminum was bombarded with alpha particles an expected transmutation with neutron emission occurred but that positron emission, decreasing with elapse of time, continued after bombardment ceased. By careful analyses of materials employed and produced, they were able to show that in each case alpha bombardment produced an unstable nucleus which then underwent radioactive positron decay. With boron and aluminum, for example, the processes amounted to

$$^{10}_{5}\text{B} + {}^{4}_{2}\text{He} \rightarrow {}^{13}_{7}\text{N} + {}^{1}_{0}n$$
$$\qquad\qquad {}^{13}_{7}\text{N} \rightarrow {}^{13}_{6}\text{C} + \beta^{+} \ (t_{1/2} = 9.9 \text{ min.})$$
$$^{27}_{13}\text{Al} + {}^{4}_{2}\text{He} \rightarrow {}^{30}_{15}\text{P} + {}^{1}_{0}n$$
$$\qquad\qquad {}^{30}_{15}\text{P} \rightarrow {}^{30}_{14}\text{Si} + \beta^{+} \ (t_{1/2} = 2.55 \text{ min.})$$

Such was the discovery of artificial radioactivity.

[95] E. Rutherford: *Phil. Mag.* [6], **37,** 581 (1919).

[96] I. Curie and F. Joliot: *Compt. rend.*, **198,** 254 (1934).

There is no real distinction between a nuclear reaction leading to stable products and one leading to unstable products. In terms of Bohr's approach[97] bombardment of a nucleus amounts first to absorption of the bombarding particle to produce an unstable compound nucleus. In a second step this compound nucleus decomposes within a short time interval (10^{-12} to 10^{-14} sec.) to a set of products. These products may be stable or they may be unstable and undergo decomposition with periods which are long in comparison with the life of the compound nucleus.

Because atomic nuclei differ but little in size from the bombarding particles, they present tiny targets. The probability of a collision is described in terms of the *cross-section* (σ) of the nucleus. Nuclear cross-section is defined by the equation

$$\sigma = N/Inx \tag{2·18}$$

where N is the number of processes occurring in the target, I the number of incident particles, n the number of target nuclei per cubic centimeter of target, and x the target thickness in centimeters. Nuclear cross-sections have magnitudes of the order of 10^{-24} cm.^{2} (= 1 barn). The situation is further complicated by the facts that positive bombarding particles are strongly repelled by nuclei and that binding energies are such that only the most energetic of particles are effective in producing rupture. Only recently have the experimental means become available for effecting nuclear reactions on any but minute scales.

Nuclear reactions may be carried out by bombardment with alpha particles, deuterons, protons, neutrons, x-radiation, gamma radiation (photons), or electrons. The magnitudes of the energy barriers which must be surmounted render positive particles comparatively inefficient, particularly against nuclei with large charges. In a measure, this is compensated for by rendering the positive particles more energetic. Neutrons, on the other hand, have no energy barriers to overcome and are very effective. Even neutrons of low energies (slow or thermal neutrons) enter nuclei and produce many important reactions. Gamma- and x-ray-induced reactions are comparatively rare. Those involving electrons have become important only since the development of electron accelerators such as the betatron.

In discussing nuclear reactions, it is customary to employ the notation

$$\mathrm{M}(a,b)\mathrm{M}'$$

[97] N. Bohr: *Naturwissenschaften,* **24,** 241 (1936); *Nature,* **137,** 344 (1936).

where M and M′ are, respectively, the target and product species, a is the bombarding agent, and b is the emitted particle or photon (if any). Thus, the reactions mentioned above (p. 66) may be written ${}^{10}_{5}B(\alpha,n){}^{13}_{7}N$ and ${}^{27}_{13}Al(\alpha,n){}^{30}_{15}P$.

It must be emphasized that equations describing nuclear reactions, like those describing chemical reactions, must balance as to mass numbers and charges. Nuclear reactions, like their chemical counterparts, are characterized by the absorption or release of energy. This may be indicated by including an energy term Q in the equation as, for example,

$${}^{14}_{7}N + {}^{4}_{2}He \rightarrow {}^{17}_{8}O + {}^{1}_{1}H + Q$$

Obviously Q may be positive (exoergic reaction) or negative (endoergic reaction). Values of Q are commonly expressed per nucleus reacting and are much larger than corresponding chemical values. For the ${}^{14}_{7}N(\alpha,p){}^{17}_{8}O$ reaction 1.13 Mev of energy is absorbed ($Q = -1.13$ Mev), corresponding to 4.33×10^{-17} kcal. per atom. For a gram atom, then, 6.02×10^{23} times as much energy, or $2.61 \times 10^{+7}$ kcal., would be required. Ordinary chemical reactions seldom produce or require more than 1 to 2×10^{2} kcal. of energy.

The energetics of nuclear reactions are of course associated with the mass changes which characterize them (p. 59). Mass changes may be used to evaluate the energies of nuclear reactions in terms of Equation 2·17, or conversely observed energy changes may be used to evaluate masses and therefore physical atomic weights (p. 33). As typical of the evaluation of a nuclear reaction, the conversion of hydrogen into helium may be considered. This reaction may take any one of a number of courses, but for simplicity let us assume the reaction to be represented by

$$2{}^{1}_{1}H + 2{}^{1}_{0}n \rightarrow {}^{4}_{2}He + Q$$

The total mass of the reactants $(2 \times 1.00812) + (2 \times 1.00893)$, or 4.03410 AMU, when compared with the mass of ${}^{4}_{2}He$, 4.00390 AMU, shows the reaction to be characterized by a mass loss of 0.0302 AMU. This is equivalent to a release of 28.12 Mev of energy per helium atom produced or 6.45×10^{8} kcal. per gram atom of helium. Comparable thermonuclear (or fusion) reactions involving tritium appear to be even more highly exothermic. It is little wonder that the conversion of hydrogen to helium should produce such tremendous solar temperatures or that it should be of interest as a source of energy.

The energy associated with a nuclear reaction may be used to evaluate the isotopic mass of one of the reactants or products, provided the isotopic masses of the other materials involved are known. This is possible because of the mass equivalence of energy. It is apparent that physical atomic weights may be evaluated from such data, provided isotopic abundances are known.

Types of nuclear reactions

Nuclear reactions may be classified either in terms of the overall transformation which occurs or in terms of the nature of the bombarding particle. Using the first method, one can distinguish the following types of reactions:

1. *Capture reactions.* The bombarding particle is absorbed with or without the emission of gamma radiation, but no massive particle other than the product nucleus is produced. Neutron capture is common.
2. *Particle-particle reactions.* In addition to the product nucleus, a massive particle (proton, neutron, etc.) is produced. Such reactions are commonly encountered.
3. *Fission reactions.* A heavy nucleus, created by bombardment, breaks into two or more fragments, with masses roughly half that of the original. The process produces large amounts of energy and usually several neutrons. Although neutron-induced fission involving $^{235}_{92}U$ and $^{239}_{94}Pu$ has been most widely investigated, fission of other thorium, protactinium, and uranium isotopes with neutrons, protons, deuterons, alpha particles, and gamma rays has been effected as well as fission of isotopes of lighter elements such as tantalum, platinum, thallium, lead, and bismuth with high energy deuterons and alpha particles. Neutron-induced fission is discussed in detail on pp. 72–77.
4. *Spallation reactions.* In addition to products of the normal type, large numbers of light fragments corresponding to decreases in mass number up to 30 units and in charge up to 14 units result. Such reactions occur only when the bombarding particles are very highly energetic and are of rather recent discovery. They are of considerable potential importance.
5. *Fusion reactions.* Certain light nuclei may fuse together to produce heavier nuclei, e.g., in the formation of helium from hydrogen (p. 68). Such reactions are exothermic and of considerable interest as potential sources of energy. It appears that triggering such reactions by high initial temperatures may be essential to their continuation on large scales.

TABLE 2·8

TYPES OF NUCLEAR REACTIONS

Reaction Type	Type of Activity Produced in Product	Examples
1. Alpha-induced reactions		
(α,n)	stable or β^+	${}^{9}_{4}Be(\alpha,n){}^{12}_{6}C$ ${}^{27}_{13}Al(\alpha,n){}^{30}_{15}P$
(α,p)	stable	${}^{14}_{7}N(\alpha,p){}^{17}_{8}O$ ${}^{27}_{13}Al(\alpha,p){}^{30}_{14}Si$
2. Proton-induced reactions		
(p,γ)	β^+	${}^{14}_{7}N(p,\gamma){}^{15}_{8}O$ ${}^{12}_{6}C(p,\gamma){}^{13}_{7}N$
(p,n)	β^+	${}^{11}_{5}B(p,n){}^{11}_{6}C$ ${}^{18}_{8}O(p,n){}^{18}_{9}F$
(p,d)	....	${}^{9}_{4}Be(p,d){}^{8}_{4}Be$
(p,α)	stable or β^+	${}^{14}_{7}N(p,\alpha){}^{11}_{6}C$ ${}^{27}_{13}Al(p,\alpha){}^{24}_{12}Mg$
3. Deuteron-induced reactions		
(d,p)	β^-	${}^{23}_{11}Na(d,p){}^{24}_{11}Na$ ${}^{37}_{17}Cl(d,p){}^{38}_{17}Cl$
(d,n)	stable or β^+	${}^{12}_{6}C(d,n){}^{13}_{7}N$ ${}^{37}_{17}Cl(d,n){}^{38}_{18}A$
$(d,2n)$	....	${}^{37}_{17}Cl(d,2n){}^{37}_{18}A$
(d,α)	stable or β^-	${}^{16}_{8}O(d,\alpha){}^{14}_{7}N$ ${}^{37}_{17}Cl(d,\alpha){}^{35}_{16}S$
4. Gamma-induced reactions		
(γ,n)	β^+	${}^{9}_{4}Be(\gamma,n){}^{8}_{4}Be$
5. Neutron-induced reactions		
(n,γ)	β^-	${}^{79}_{35}Br(n,\gamma){}^{80}_{35}Br$ ${}^{238}_{92}U(n,\gamma){}^{239}_{92}U$
(n,p)	β^-	${}^{14}_{7}N(n,p){}^{14}_{6}C$ ${}^{85}_{37}Rb(n,p){}^{85}_{36}Kr$
(n,α)	β^-	${}^{19}_{9}F(n,\alpha){}^{16}_{7}N$ ${}^{85}_{37}Rb(n,\alpha){}^{82}_{35}Br$
$(n,2n)$	β^+	${}^{14}_{7}N(n,2n){}^{13}_{7}N$ ${}^{85}_{37}Rb(n,2n){}^{84}_{37}Rb$
$(n,\text{fission})$	β^-	${}^{235}_{92}U(n,\text{fission})$ fission products ${}^{232}_{90}Th(n,\text{fission})$ fission products ${}^{239}_{94}Pu(n,\text{fission})$ fission products

Classification of nuclear reactions in terms of the bombarding agent gives the types summarized, together with appropriate examples, in Table 2·8.[98, 99] Each of these may now be considered in some detail.

1. *Alpha-induced reactions.* Because of large coulombic repulsions, reactions of this type are comparatively inefficient for any but the lightest nuclei. The reaction ${}^{9}_{4}Be(\alpha,n){}^{12}_{6}C$ provides a convenient source of neutrons and is commonly effected by use of powdered beryllium and radon in a sealed cylinder. Information on (α,p) and (α,n) reactions has already been given (pp. 66–69).

2. *Proton-induced reactions.* Although coulombic repulsions are less with protons than with alpha particles, the smaller mass of the proton renders it difficult for the proton to surmount or penetrate the nuclear energy barrier unless it is highly energized. Proton reactions commonly yield positron emitters because of unfavorable increases in nuclear charge.

3. *Deuteron-induced reactions.* Deuterons are perhaps the most effective of the positively charged particles. Because of a comparatively large mass defect, the deuteron is inherently energetic. Further increases in energy may be supplied by cyclotron acceleration. Although barrier effects permit perhaps only one deuteron in 10^6 to enter a nucleus, the availability of the deuteron in a measure overcomes this difficulty. A (d,p) reaction amounts essentially to capture of a neutron from the deuteron and is thus similar to a simple (n,γ) reaction. It is believed that in this reaction the deuteron is broken up outside the target nucleus, with only the neutron then entering. This explanation was first given by Oppenheimer and Phillips.[100] Hence such a process is referred to as an Oppenheimer-Phillips (O-P) process. Certain (d,n) reactions, notably ${}^{2}_{1}H(d,n){}^{3}_{2}He$, ${}^{9}_{4}Be(d,n){}^{10}_{5}B$, ${}^{12}_{6}C(d,n){}^{13}_{7}N$, are excellent neutron sources.

4. *Gamma-induced reactions.* Gamma and x-radiation are extremely inefficient in effecting nuclear transformations. The reaction ${}^{9}_{4}Be(\gamma,n){}^{8}_{4}Be$ is an excellent neutron source. Nuclei are sometimes energized by gamma radiation, energy loss by isomeric transition then occurring. An example is ${}^{115}_{49}In(\gamma,\gamma){}^{115}_{49}In$, the product showing a 4.1-hour gamma activity.

5. *Neutron-induced reactions.* In the absence of coulombic repulsions, neutron reactions are dependent only upon the energy of the bombarding particle and the cross section of the nucleus in question.

[98] E. C. Pollard and W. L. Davidson: *Applied Nuclear Physics.* 2nd Ed., John Wiley and Sons, New York (1951).

[99] R. R. Williams, Jr.: *J. Chem. Education,* **23,** 423 (1946).

[100] J. R. Oppenheimer and M. Phillips, *Phys. Rev.,* **48,** 500 (1935).

Probability of collision is enhanced by use of thermal neutrons, i.e., neutrons which have been slowed by passage through a moderator such as graphite or heavy water. All elements except helium (specifically, ^4_2He) have been transmuted by neutron bombardment.

Until recently, neutron reactions have been limited by the lack of larger neutron sources. Since neutrons have no independent existence, they must always result from other nuclear reactions. With the development of the chain-reacting pile, an unlimited neutron source has become available, and large-scale neutron-induced reactions are now carried out in routine fashion.

Simple neutron capture, (n,γ), is an effective means of increasing the mass number of an atomic species and, through consequent increase in neutron to proton ratio, of producing β^- active radioisotopes. Many isotopes now available from the Oak Ridge National Laboratory result in this fashion. Neutron capture can occur only if neutrons of comparatively low energy content are employed.

Perhaps the most interesting of the neutron reactions are those resulting in fission. Shortly after the discovery of the neutron, Fermi found neutron bombardments to be followed by β^- activity in many cases. Since β^- decay increases nuclear charge, Fermi reasoned that neutron bombardment of uranium might lead to transuranium elements. When uranium was so bombarded, four β^- activities, which could be assigned to no element in the region $Z = 86$–92, were found.[101] Since part of the activity concentrated with manganese, added as a carrier and recovered, it was concluded that a congener of manganese with charge 93 had been produced. Further studies suggested the presence of elements of even higher atomic numbers.[101] Extended studies by Hahn, Meitner, and Strassmann[102] indicated at least nine different beta activities in the products, and elements with charges through 97 were necessary to account for them. However, that all such products should have arisen by stepwise beta decay of uranium after neutron capture seemed unlikely because of the improbability of such instability as a result of the absorption of a single neutron.

The true explanation was narrowly missed by Curie and Savitch,[103] who found among the reaction products a material of 3.5-hour activity which was precipitated with a lanthanum carrier, but they concluded it to be an actinium isotope. Subsequent events have shown that the material was in reality a lanthanum isotope.

[101] E. Fermi, E. Amaldi, O. D'Agostino, F. Rasetti, and E. Segrè: *Proc. Roy. Soc.* (*London*), **A146**, 483 (1934).

[102] O. Hahn, L. Meitner, and F. Strassmann: *Ber.*, **70B**, 1374 (1937).

[103] I. Curie and P. Savitch: *Compt. rend.*, **206**, 906, 1643 (1938).

Ultimate simplification of the perplexing array of information on the neutron bombardment of uranium was provided by Hahn and Strassmann.[104] Materials precipitating with barium and lanthanum ions as carriers were found and assumed at first to be radium and actinium isotopes, even though no alpha emissions which might yield such isotopes were noted. Subsequent tests narrowed one set of activities to either barium or radium isotopes. Accordingly, barium and mesothorium-I (a radium isotope) were added and the mixture fractionated. The activity in question concentrated with barium and was thus due to a barium isotope. Subsequently, lanthanum was also clearly identified as well as isotopes of strontium, yttrium, an inert gas (Xe or Kr), and an alkali metal (Cs or Rb). Meitner concluded that neutron capture was followed by the complete rupture of the uranium nucleus.

Nuclear fission was announced in the United States by Niels Bohr in an impromptu statement before the American Philosophical Society. Its nature was verified almost immediately in a number of laboratories, and a number of reports concerning it appeared in 1939. The veil of secrecy which was soon placed over further investigations was lifted only in 1945 with the announcement of the bombings of Hiroshima and Nagasaki and the publication of the Smyth Report.[39] Prior to this account, only a few scattered reviews had appeared.[105–107]

The fission process can be pictured conveniently in terms of the "liquid-drop" approach of Bohr and Wheeler.[108] Attractive forces within a nucleus may be regarded as causing that nucleus to assume a spherical shape, in much the same fashion as do the cohesive forces within a drop of liquid, whereas repulsive forces may promote elongation of the "droplet." Nuclear stability may then be expected when the attractive forces counterbalance the repulsive. As nuclear charge increases, the repulsive forces increase, and it has been calculated that nuclei with charges in excess of perhaps 100 would elongate and spontaneously subdivide into smaller nuclei. Each nucleus possesses a critical energy which must be exceeded before such elongation and subdivision can occur. If this energy is not too large, excitation resulting from neutron capture may be sufficient for elongation and fission. Thermal neutrons impart sufficient energy to fission nuclei such as $^{235}_{92}U$ and $^{239}_{94}Pu$, but high-energy neutrons are required for

[104] O. Hahn and F. Strassmann: *Naturwissenschaften*, **27**, 11, 89 (1939).
[105] O. R. Frisch: *Ann. Reports*, **36**, 7 (1939); **37**, 7 (1940).
[106] L. A. Turner: *Revs. Modern Phys.*, **12**, 1 (1940).
[107] K. K. Darrow: *Bell System Tech. J.*, **19**, 267 (1940).
[108] N. Bohr and J. A. Wheeler: *Phys. Rev.*, **56**, 426 (1939).

$^{238}_{92}U$, $^{231}_{91}Pa$, and $^{232}_{90}Th$. Fission in natural uranium is due to the 235-isotope.

Subsequent studies under auspices of the Manhattan District have demonstrated the presence of a variety of lighter elements in the products of the neutron-induced fission of $^{235}_{92}U$.[109] As shown by the fission yield curve given in Figure 2·14, isotopes with mass numbers

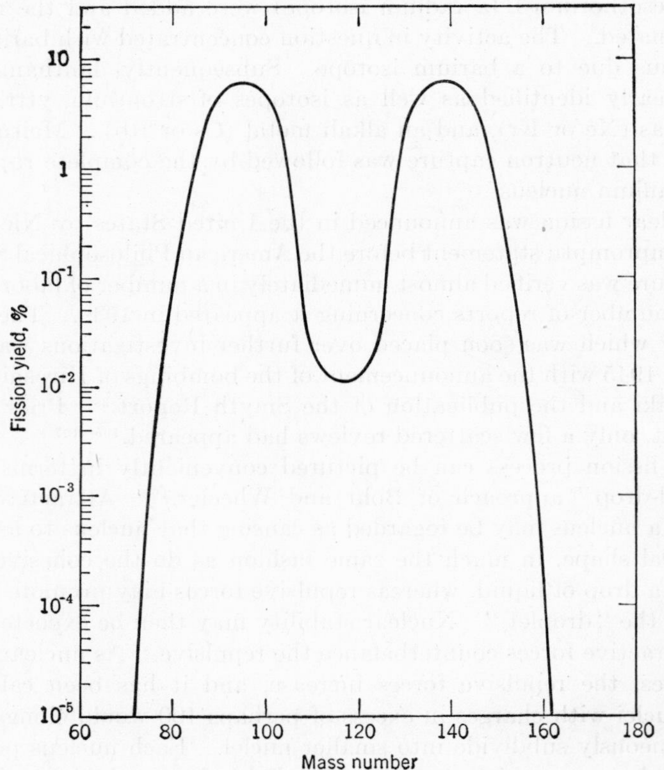

Fig. 2·14. Yields in slow neutron fission of $^{235}_{92}U$.

ca. 72 to 162 result, maximum yields being at mass numbers 95 and 139 and a minimum yield at 117. Maximum fission yields are, therefore, in the charge regions of roughly 40 to 42 and 56 to 58. Because of neutron excesses, many fission products are $\beta-$ active.

Primary interest in nuclear fission has centered in the tremendous release of energy which accompanies it. The summed-up masses of

[109] *Plutonium Project*, J. M. Siegel (Ed.): *J. Am. Chem. Soc.*, **68**, 2411 (1946).

the fission products and the 1 to 3 neutrons* accompanying each fission are always somewhat less than those of the original uranium and the bombarding neutron. The resulting energy equivalent of the mass loss is some 200 Mev per gram atom of $^{235}_{92}U$, most of this energy appearing as kinetic energy of the products. Even in the early stages of investigation, the possibility of a self-perpetuating chain reaction maintained by product neutrons was considered as a

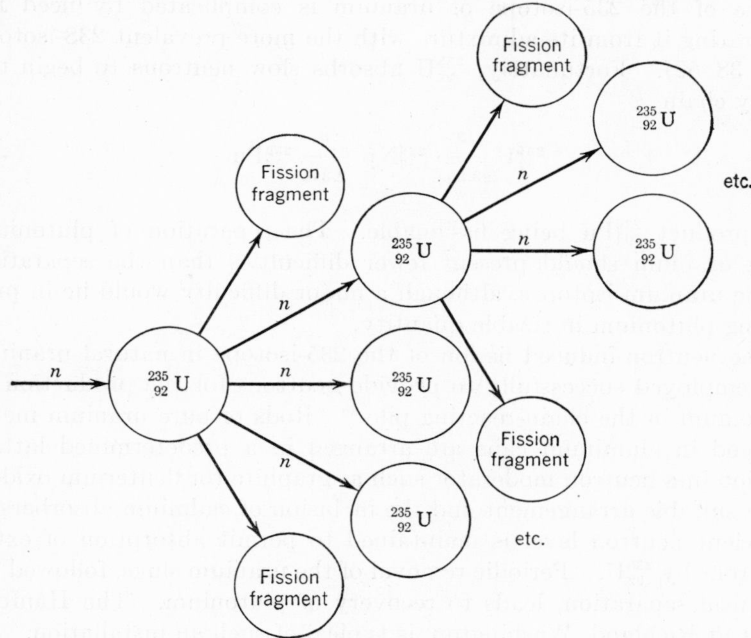

Fig. 2·15. Schematic representation of chain process in nuclear fission.

source of unbelievably large amounts of energy. Its attainment and control must be regarded as one of the outstanding technical advancements of all time.

Probability considerations show that a self-sustaining chain reaction can occur only if the total mass of the fissionable material is such that product neutrons may be absorbed and thus serve as ignitor neutrons for subsequent fissions. The exact magnitude of this "critical mass" is still a closely guarded secret. When it is exceeded, chain propagation occurs in an expanding fashion and with extreme rapidity in much the fashion shown in Figure 2·15 and, in the absence of any

* Declassified information indicates that on the average 2.5 ± 0.1 neutrons result for every atom of uranium-235 undergoing thermal neutron fission.

other neutron absorbers, results in an explosion. In the presence of an efficient neutron absorber such as cadmium, chain propagation can be so controlled that the number of neutrons builds up to some constant level without increasing indefinitely. A controlled chain reaction is thus achieved, as in the chain-reacting piles. The applications and implications of explosive fission are sufficiently well known to require no further discussion.

Use of the 235-isotope of uranium is complicated by need for separating it from its admixture with the more prevalent 238-isotope (pp. 38–52). Fortunately, $^{238}_{92}U$ absorbs slow neutrons to begin the decay chain

$$^{239}_{92}U \xrightarrow[23.5 \text{ m.}]{-\beta^-} {}^{239}_{93}Np \xrightarrow[2.3 \text{ d.}]{-\beta^-} {}^{239}_{94}Pu$$

the product $^{239}_{94}Pu$ being fissionable. The separation of plutonium from uranium should present fewer difficulties than the separation of the uranium isotopes, although a major difficulty would lie in producing plutonium in sizable quantity.

The neutron-induced fission of the 235-isotope in natural uranium was employed successfully to provide neutrons for the production of plutonium in the chain-reacting pile.[39] Rods of pure uranium metal encased in aluminum cans are arranged in a predetermined lattice fashion in a neutron moderator such as graphite (or deuterium oxide). By a suitable arrangement and the inclusion of cadmium absorbers, a sufficient neutron level is maintained to permit absorption of extra neutrons by $^{238}_{92}U$. Periodic removal of the uranium slugs, followed by chemical separation, leads to recovery of plutonium. The Hanford plant at Richland, Washington, is typical of such an installation.

Only a few of the aspects of fission have been presented. The tremendous radioactivities resulting from fission make the large-scale process hazardous even when controlled. Every precaution must be taken by workers who deal with these materials. Chain-reacting piles generate much thermal energy and must be cooled. Use of energy transferred through a coolant for power is being explored.[110] Piles are also tremendous neutron sources and are used as such for the production of radioisotopes in quantity.

Essentially as a result of investigations involving fission and related subjects, a new phase of chemical physics dealing with nuclear processes has been developed. This is called aptly *nucleonics*. It must be pointed out also that the chemistry of the transuranium ele-

[110] F. Daniels: *Chem. Eng. News*, **24**, 1514 (1946).

ments is associated irrevocably with nuclear fission. More information on these materials is presented later (pp. 104, 891–901).

Applications of induced radioactivity

Many uses of synthetic radioisotopes in addition to those indicated above are possible. Certain of these have been summarized by Seaborg.[111] Many depend upon the indicator or tracer properties of radioisotopes. Studies on reaction mechanisms, behaviors of materials in small concentrations, efficiencies of analytical separations, diffusion processes, and metabolism among both plants and animals (especially those involving $^{14}_{6}C$) are of this type. The medicinal use of radioisotopes in the treatment of malignancies and technical application of gamma radiation in radiography represent other uses, depending upon specific characteristics.

Of extreme interest are investigations of the chemistries of new elements in terms of their synthetic radioisotopes. The extreme sensitivities of methods of detecting radioactivity make such studies possible even though the materials are present in subweighable (e.g., 10^{-6} gram) quantities. Thus the chemistry of element 43 (technetium) has been elucidated[112, 113] through use of several isotopes produced by the reaction $^{A}_{42}Mo(d,n)^{A+1}_{43}Tc$. Similarly, the chemistry of element 85 (astatine) has been studied[114] by use of a 7.5-hour isotope produced by the reaction $^{209}_{83}Bi(\alpha,2n)^{211}_{85}At$. The chemistries of the transuranium elements (pp. 891–901) were determined in like fashion before the elements were isolated in weighable quantities. These are exemplified by studies on $^{239}_{93}Np$.[115] Information on element 61 has been obtained from the fission-produced 147-isotope.[116]

SUGGESTED SUPPLEMENTARY REFERENCES

H. A. Bethe: *Elementary Nuclear Theory,* John Wiley and Sons, New York (1947).

G. Friedlander and J. W. Kennedy: *Introduction to Radiochemistry,* John Wiley and Sons, New York (1949).

J. D. Stranathan: *The "Particles" of Modern Physics,* the Blakiston Co., Philadelphia (1942).

A. W. Stewart and C. L. Wilson: *Recent Advances in Physical and Inorganic Chemistry,* 7th Ed. Longmans, Green and Co., London (1944).

---

[111] G. T. Seaborg: *Chem. Revs.,* **27,** 199 (1940).

[112] C. Perrier and E. Segrè: *J. Chem. Phys.,* **5,** 712 (1937); **7,** 155 (1939).

[113] E. Segrè: *Nature,* **143,** 460 (1939).

[114] D. R. Corson, K. R. MacKenzie, and E. Segrè: *Phys. Rev.,* **57,** 459, 1087 (1940).

[115] E. McMillan and P. H. Abelson: *Phys. Rev.,* **57,** 1185 (1940).

[116] J. A. Marinsky, L. E. Glendenin, and C. D. Coryell: *J. Am. Chem. Soc.,* **69,** 2781 (1947).

H. D. Smyth: *Atomic Energy for Military Purposes*, Princeton University Press, Princeton, N. J. (1945).

E. C. Pollard and W. L. Davidson: *Applied Nuclear Physics*, 2nd Ed. John Wiley and Sons, New York (1951).

S. Fluegge: *An Introduction to Nuclear Physics*, Interscience Publishers, New York (1946).

R. Stoops (Ed.): *Rapports et Discussions sur les Isotopes*, Septième Conseil de Chimie, Institut International de Chimie Solvay. Coudenberg, Bruxelles (1948).

G. T. Seaborg and I. Perlman: "Table of Isotopes," *Revs. Modern Phys.*, **20**, 585 (1948).

C. D. Coryell: "The Scientific Importance of the Nuclear Power Projects," *J. Chem. Education*, **23**, 395 (1946).

G. Volkoff: "The Fundamentals of Nuclear Energy," *J. Chem. Education*, **24**, 538 (1947).

E. U. Condon: "Physics Gives Us-Nuclear Engineering," *Westinghouse Engineer* (November 1945).

Anon.: "Types of Radioactive Decay," *Chem. Eng. News*, **25**, 3073 (1947).

O. Hönigschmid: "Thirty Years of Chemical Atomic Weight Determinations," *Angew. Chem.*, **53**, 177 (1940).

I. Perlman: "Alpha Radioactivity and the Stability of Heavy Nuclei," *Nucleonics*, **7** (No. 2), 3 (1950).

A. C. Wahl and N. A. Bonner: *Radioactivity Applied to Chemistry*, John Wiley and Sons, New York (1951).

K. Way, L. Fano, M. R. Scott, and K. Thew (Compilers): *Nuclear Data.* NBS Circular 499. U. S. Government Printing Office, Washington (1950).

S. Glasstone: *Sourcebook on Atomic Energy.* D. Van Nostrand Co., New York (1950).

CHAPTER 3

The Extranuclear Structures of the Atoms

All modern theory of atomic structure is based upon the nuclear atom of Rutherford (p. 11). Although the fundamental concept of extranuclear electrons has been retained, many modifications of Rutherford's original views as to their positions and behaviors have been made necessary by various experimental observations. To account for the fact that these electrons do not in time fall into the positively charged nucleus as a result of purely electrostatic attraction, Rutherford was forced to postulate their extremely rapid motion about the nucleus with the resultant centrifugal force exactly balancing the inward attractive force. Such a situation would be formally analogous to that involving revolution of the planets about a central sun, but it differs in the important respect that within the atom the particles involved bear opposite electrical charges. As a consequence, regardless of the rapidity with which the electron moved, it would always be accelerated toward the nucleus and should, therefore, describe a spiral path of steadily decreasing curvature until eventually it entered the nucleus. In this process, the electron would lose energy continuously, and this energy should appear as continuous radiation without any sharp breaks. That such a process does not occur and that radiation emitted by atoms is discontinuous, as is evidenced by the appearance of definite spectral lines, are, of course, well known.

It was to overcome such difficulties that Bohr proposed his theory of the structure of the hydrogen atom in 1913. Since Bohr's theory and subsequent modifications of it are based upon Planck's quantum theory and the interpretation of atomic spectra, a brief consideration of these two items should serve as a suitable preface to further discussions.

Prior to 1900, it had been assumed quite generally that although radiation emitted from a perfect radiator (i.e., a so-called black body) is not uniform, it must be radiated continuously. In 1900, however, Planck reached the important conclusion that radiation can neither be emitted nor absorbed continuously but rather only in definite quantities which are multiples of some fundamental factor, namely, the frequency* characteristic of the material in question. Thus radiant energy could be thought of as being highly discontinuous and made up of definite numbers of units which Planck termed *quanta.* This fundamental postulate forms the basis of the so-called *quantum theory,* which has been so helpful in giving new interpretation and understanding to physics and chemistry and which has permitted more complete characterizations of particles of atomic dimensions which do not obey the classical laws which are applicable to macroscopic particles. According to Planck, the energy (E) of the quantum amounts to

$$E = h\nu \tag{3·1}$$

where ν is the frequency of the radiator (or absorber) and h is a universal action constant, known as Planck's constant, with the dimensions of energy multiplied by time (numerically 6.624×10^{-27} erg-sec.).

Radiant energy is commonly encountered as it is manifested in spectra of various types. Whereas x-ray spectra have been discussed already (pp. 12–14) as related to the innermost electrons within atoms, the longer wavelength optical spectra of the ultraviolet, visible, and infrared regions are most commonly employed in describing the extranuclear electrons since they are related to the outermost electrons. Such spectra arise when gases or vapors of chemical substances are heated to elevated temperatures, commonly by means of electric sparks or arcs, although occasionally even by the Bunsen flame. When resolved by means of a suitable grating or prism in a spectroscope, such spectra amount to series of lines of well-defined wavelengths or frequencies. The positions which these lines occupy in the recorded spectrum correspond, in terms of Planck's theory, to definite energy changes, and these energy changes in turn correspond to certain transitions of electrons among various positions in the extranuclear arrangements. Atomic spectra are normally exceedingly complex because, under the conditions employed to excite spectra, lines due not only to neutral atoms but to the various positive ions produced by loss of electrons from the neutral atoms are all present together.

* Radiation is often characterized in terms of its wavelength (λ). The ratio of the velocity of light (c) to the wavelength gives the frequency (ν) of the radiation, which, if the units are correctly chosen, might be regarded as the number of vibrations per unit of time (usually the second). The simple reciprocal of the wavelength gives another characteristic called the wave number ($\bar{\nu}$), i.e., the number of wavelengths per unit length (usually the centimeter).

However, careful analyses of these patterns are of invaluable assistance in elucidating electronic configurations.

THE BOHR THEORY OF THE HYDROGEN ATOM

The optical spectrum of hydrogen, the simplest of elements, consists of several series of lines which are described as to spectral region as

Lyman series	ultraviolet
Balmer series	visible
Paschen series	near infrared
Brackett series	far infrared
Pfund series	far infrared

The wavelengths (λ) of the lines characterizing the Lyman, Balmer, and Paschen series had been shown some years before Bohr's proposals were advanced to be determined by the more or less empirical relation

$$\frac{1}{\lambda} = \bar{\nu} = R_{\mathrm{H}}\left(\frac{1}{n_1^2} - \frac{1}{n_2^2}\right) \tag{3·2}$$

where λ is the wavelength; $\bar{\nu}$ is the wave number; n_1 and n_2 are integers, with n_2 being larger than n_1; and R_{H} is a constant known as the Rydberg constant and having the value 109,737.303 cm.$^{-1}$ Lines in the more recently discovered Brackett and Pfund series are related to the same expression, and each series is characterized by a particular value for n_1. The optical spectra of other elements are similar as regards series of lines, but they are vastly more complex because of the larger numbers of electrons present and the resultant increases in numbers of possible electronic transitions.

In 1913, Bohr[1] proposed an interpretation of the spectrum of hydrogen based upon the concept that the electron in the hydrogen atom always described a circular orbit about the nucleus but that the electron might be found in any one of a limited number of these orbits. Such orbits, named *stationary states* by Bohr, may be thought of in the pictorial sense as differing from each other in radius. They have the same significance as the *energy levels* of modern parlance. According to Bohr, the number of such orbits or states is limited by the condition that the angular momentum* of the electron in its path about the nucleus must always be an integral multiple of $h/2$. This amounts to quantization of the angular momentum, and in Bohr's time it represented a new concept offered without essential support. More

[1] N. Bohr: *Phil. Mag.* [6], **26**, 1, 476, 857 (1913).

* The momentum of an electron moving in some orbit can be resolved into two vectorial factors, one along the radius and the other at right angles. The latter is referred to as the angular momentum of the electron.

recent work, however, has shown that the momentum of a particle of mass m moving in a circular path of radius r and at a constant velocity v is given by mvr. It follows, therefore, that the possible Bohr orbits are determined by

$$mvr = n\frac{h}{2\pi} \tag{3·3}$$

where n is an integer, termed a quantum number, characterizing the orbit. Since r increases with n in this expression, values of n should then indicate the order of the orbits of increasing size from the nucleus out.

Equally fundamental was Bohr's further postulate that as long as the electron remains in a given orbit it neither radiates nor absorbs energy. As already indicated, this view was in direct opposition to the concepts of classical theory. Movement of the electron from one orbit to another, however, was considered to involve the absorption or the emission of a definite quantity of energy, depending upon whether the electron moved from a lower state to a higher or vice versa. This energy is manifested as radiation. The frequency of such radiation, and therefore the position of any spectral line which it might produce if it were emitted, was then related to the energies of the electron in the two orbits, E_2 and E_1, as

$$E_2 - E_1 = h\nu \tag{3·4}$$

According to Bohr, therefore, lines in the spectrum of hydrogen result from the dropping of electrons excited to higher stationary states or orbits back to lower, less energetic states. Each line was ascribed to a transfer of the electron from an orbit of some n value to an orbit of some lower n value. Using this concept, Bohr was able to account for the observed wavelengths of the lines in the Lyman, Balmer, and Paschen series by assigning n_1 values (Equation 3·2) of 1, 2, and 3, respectively, to these series. Later extensions to include n_1 values of 4 and 5 permit equally good interpretations of the Brackett and Pfund series.

Thus lines in the five spectral series for hydrogen arise from the transitions

Lyman	from $n = 2, 3, 4 \cdots$ to $n = 1$
Balmer	from $n = 3, 4, 5 \cdots$ to $n = 2$
Paschen	from $n = 4, 5, 6 \cdots$ to $n = 3$
Brackett	from $n = 5, 6, 7 \cdots$ to $n = 4$
Pfund	from $n = 6, 7 \cdots$ to $n = 5$

These relationships are shown diagrammatically in Figure 3·1, where the circles represent the permitted orbits in their approximate positions relative to the nucleus and the arrows the characteristic electronic transitions.

The success achieved by the fundamental Bohr theory in explaining the origin and significance of the hydrogen spectrum prompted its

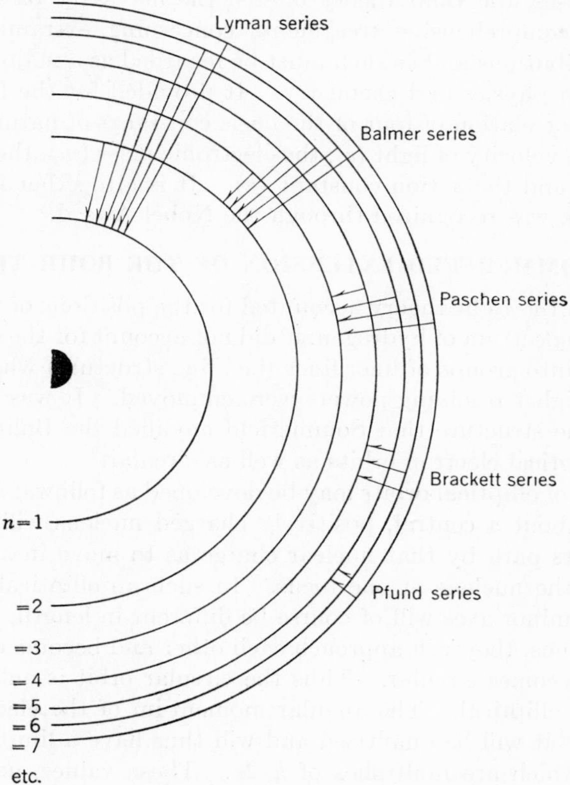

FIG. 3·1. Diagrammatic representation of the origin of the hydrogen spectrum.

extension to other systems. Although it achieved some success in accounting for the spectra of such hydrogen-like species as single ionized helium (He^+), doubly ionized lithium (Li^{+2}), and triply ionized beryllium (Be^{+3}), it failed completely when applied on a quantitative basis to materials containing more than a single electron.

This lack of applicability is traceable to the attempt of the Bohr theory to depict extranuclear structures pictorially rather than to any fundamental error in conceiving of electrons as occupying certain energy states (orbits) relative to the nucleus. The properties of the electron were inadequately described through its characterization only in terms of the quantum number n_1, or the size of the orbit. The uncertainty of knowing exactly both the position of the orbit and the velocity of the electron within it (Heisenberg's principle of uncertainty) renders the Bohr description of these orbits inexact. However, despite its weaknesses, the Bohr theory offered the necessary basis for later and more comprehensive treatments concerning extranuclear electronic distributions and as such must be regarded as a major contribution to both physics and chemistry. It provided for the first time a successful correlation of four of the basic constants of natural science, namely, the velocity of light (c), the electronic mass (m), the electronic charge (e), and the action constant (h). It is altogether fitting that Bohr's work was recognized through the Nobel Award.

THE SOMMERFELD EXTENSION OF THE BOHR THEORY

Although the Bohr theory accounted for the positions of the lines in the optical spectrum of hydrogen, it did not account for the splitting of these lines into groups of finer lines (i.e., fine structure) when spectroscopes of higher resolving powers were employed. It was to account for such fine structure that Sommerfeld modified the Bohr theory to include elliptical electron orbits as well as circular.[2]

The idea of elliptical orbits may be developed as follows: An electron revolving about a central, positively charged nucleus will be so disturbed in its path by that nuclear charge as to move in an elliptical path with the nucleus at one focus. In such an elliptical orbit, the major and minor axes will of course be different in length, but, as the orbit broadens, they will approach each other and become equal when the orbit becomes circular. Thus the circular orbit is only a special case of the elliptical. The angular momentum of the electron in an elliptical orbit will be quantized and will thus have a limited number of values which are multiplies of $h/2\pi$. These values, according to Sommerfeld, may amount to $kh/2\pi$, where k is an integer known as the *azimuthal quantum number*.

The orbit designation n, as used by Bohr and now referred to as the *principal quantum number*, and k are related as

$$\frac{n}{k} = \frac{\text{length of major axis}}{\text{length of minor axis}} \tag{3.5}$$

from which it is apparent that for any given value of n except 1, k may have more than a single value. When k and n are equal, a circular

[2] A. Sommerfeld: *Phys. Z.*, **17**, 491 (1916); *Ann. Physik* [4], **51**, 1 (1916).

orbit results, but as k becomes smaller and smaller with respect to n, elliptical orbits of greater and greater eccentricites develop. To illustrate, the fourth Bohr orbit ($n = 4$) would be subdivided into four orbits of increasing eccentricities as characterized by k values of 4, 3, 2, and 1. These orbits are shown diagrammatically in Figure 3·2, the notation n_k, expressed numerically, being used to describe them or, perhaps more exactly, the electrons occupying them.

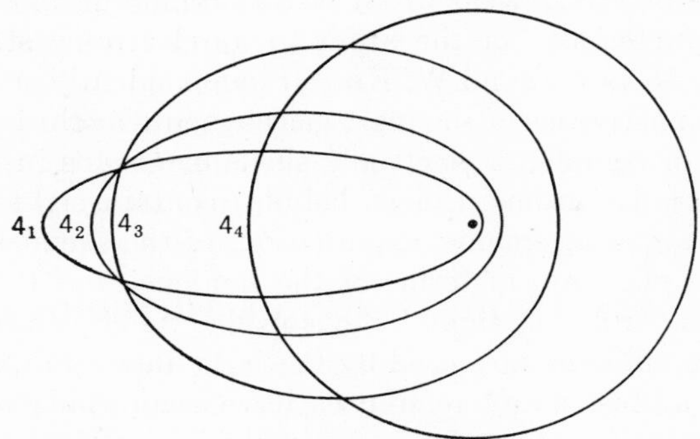

FIG. 3·2. Sommerfeld orbits where $n = 4$.

The velocity of an electron moving in an elliptical orbit will be greatest when the electron approaches closest to the nucleus and least when it is farthest removed from the nucleus. This variability in velocity coupled with a relativity effect of change in mass with change in velocity will result in a net displacement of the orbit each time the electron moves through it. As a result, the entire orbit will move, or precess, around the nucleus. This precessional movement will result in small energy differences, depending on the position of the orbit, and will be reflected as fine structure in the spectrum. The explanation of this phenomenon in the hydrogen spectrum is a notable achievement of Sommerfeld's modification.

Perhaps the greatest single contribution of the Sommerfeld concept, however, lies in its subdivision of the original Bohr stationary states into several substates or levels of slightly differing energies as characterized by differences in orbit shapes. This is the basis of modern concepts of electronic configurations. Inherent also in the idea of elliptical orbits is the concept of penetrating orbits. That certain electrons may penetrate closer to the nucleus than others is of importance in accounting for differences in their properties and in the properties of atoms or ions dependent upon their presence. Like the Bohr theory, the Sommerfeld extension does not apply with mathematical exactness to atoms containing more than a single electron. It is useful, however, in giving qualitative pictures of the structures of the more complicated atoms. Perhaps its major fault is the inaccurate values for angular momentum which it gives. This is referred to later.

ELECTRONIC DISTRIBUTIONS IN ATOMS IN TERMS OF THE BOHR-SOMMERFELD THEORY

Acceptance of the nuclear atom was tantamount to ascribing the chemical characteristics of the atom to its electronic structure. In 1916, both G. N. Lewis[3] and W. Kossel[4] independently suggested that the chemical inactivities of the inert gas elements might be ascribed to the presence of completed electronic shells or groups in their atoms. Since the inert gas atoms, except helium, contain eight electrons in their outermost arrangements, explanations of the chemical characteristics of other elements in terms of the tendencies of their atoms to approach this "rule of eight" developed. As a consequence and because of the cubic models used by Lewis to illustrate the combining capacities of atoms, many references have been made to the Lewis theory of the atom. Actually, neither Lewis nor Kossel offered any new concept of atomic structure beyond the fundamental ideas of Bohr and Sommerfeld. They were interested in the chemical characteristics of atoms, and any models which they may have used were only valence models which emphasized the importances of certain electronic groups (pp. 173–174).

The concept of completed electronic groupings among atoms of the inert gas elements was extended by Langmuir[5] to the first comprehensive picture of electronic arrangements. Since the atomic numbers of the inert gases are, respectively, 2, 10, 18, 36, 54, and 86, these numbers of electrons were taken as representing completions of the various electronic levels. The net capacities of individual levels for electrons were then obtained by subtracting from each total the number of electrons in the preceding inert gas. These capacities amount to 2, 8, 8, 18, 18, 32, and represent, of course, the numbers of elements in the various horizontal series of the periodic classification (p. 122). Langmuir conceived of the building up of the structures of elements with increasing atomic number as amounting to the successive filling of these groups to completion. By this means, he was able to ascribe similar electronic configurations to elements of similar properties, but his assumption that a new electron must always enter an incompleted

[3] G. N. Lewis: *J. Am. Chem. Soc.*, **38,** 762 (1916).

[4] W. Kossel: *Ann. Physik* [4], **49,** 229 (1916).

[5] I. Langmuir: *J. Am. Chem. Soc.*, **41,** 868, 1543 (1919).

group and could not enter a new group until other groups were completed was not in accordance with observed fact. As a consequence, the Langmuir theory did not reflect electronic arrangements with complete accuracy. Furthermore, to account for stabilities in structures in the vicinities of nickel, palladium, and platinum, some rather unlikely arrangements had to be proposed.

In a measure, some of the difficulties inherent in the Langmuir approach were resolved by Bury's postulation[6] that the maximum numbers of electrons in the various shells are 2, 8, 18, 32. According to Bury, the outermost shell in an atom can contain no more than eight electrons, and no shell can contain more than eight electrons unless another shell farther removed from the nucleus is being formed. This concept permitted logical explanations for the configurations of the transition and inner transition elements in terms of the phenomenon of inner building, i.e., the filling up of inner electronic levels, while the outermost ones remain constant (pp. 103–106). This is admirably illustrated in the lanthanide or rare earth series. Langmuir would have depicted the configuration of the lanthanum ($Z = 57$) atom as 2, 8, 8, 18, 18, 3, whereas Bury gave it the arrangement 2, 8, 18, 18, 9, 2. The Bury concept thus predicted that the lanthanide series should end with element 71; the unmodified Langmuir approach extended this series through element 72. Discovery of element 72 in association with zirconium and its characterization as a congener of zirconium[7] may be cited in support of Bury's ideas. The filling of electron shells in terms of the Bury approach may be illustrated by the inert gas atom configurations given in Table 3·1. Electron shells in this table are

TABLE 3·1
ELECTRONIC CONFIGURATIONS OF INERT GAS ATOMS

Symbol	Atomic Number, Z	Number of Electrons					
		K	L	M	N	O	P
He	2	2					
Ne	10	2	8				
A	18	2	8	8			
Kr	36	2	8	18	8		
Xe	54	2	8	18	18	8	
Rn	86	2	8	18	32	18	8

designated in order K, L, M, N, etc., as they become farther and farther removed from the nucleus (p. 12).

Further spectroscopic studies led Bohr to almost the same conclusion relative to the building up of electronic groups[8] and suggested

[6] C. R. Bury: *J. Am. Chem. Soc.*, **43**, 1602 (1921).
[7] D. Coster and G. von Hevesy: *Nature*, **111**, 79, 182, 252 (1923).
[8] N. Bohr: *Z. Physik*, **9**, 1 (1922).

that electrons in the second, third, and fourth levels be subdivided, respectively, as 4, 4; 6, 6, 6; and 8, 8, 8, 8. This concept of subdivision of main electronic groups inherent in the Sommerfeld ideas was placed upon a sound basis in 1924, when both Stoner[9] and Main Smith[10] arrived at the correct distributions of electrons within the various groups as being 2 (for $n = 1$); 2, 2, 4 ($n = 2$); 2, 2, 4, 4, 6 ($n = 3$); and 2, 2, 4, 4, 6, 6, 8 ($n = 4$). However, their results were based upon nothing more than logical extensions of the Bohr-Sommerfeld theory, although by that time everyone was agreed that this theory applied rigidly only to atoms containing but a single electron. The configurations of the inert gas elements as written by Main Smith are instructive in indicating how the electronic arrangements he proposed were described in terms of the quantum numbers n and k. These configurations[10] are given in Table 3·2.

TABLE 3·2

Main Smith Notation for Inert Gas Atom Configurations

			Electronic Distribution					
		n	1	2	3	4	5	6
Symbol	Atomic Number, Z	k	1	112	11223	1122334	11223	1122
He	2		2					
Ne	10		2	224				
A	18		2	224	224			
Kr	36		2	224	22446	224		
Xe	54		2	224	22446	22446	224	
Rn	86		2	224	22446	2244668	22446	224

QUANTUM DESIGNATIONS FOR ELECTRONS

The concept of electrons revolving about atomic nuclei in orbits of limited and well-defined shapes, which characterizes the Bohr-Sommerfeld treatment of extranuclear structure, can be regarded as no more than a rough pictorial view. Modern concepts based upon wave mechanics are concerned primarily with the comparative densities of electronic charges at given points within the atom and have probability as their basis. Since even in terms of this view, electrons will tend to group themselves in certain series of positions relative to the nucleus, it is convenient to think of the electrons as occupying energy levels with respect to the nucleus. The Bohr orbits may, therefore, be considered equivalent to energy regions in which the probability of electron occupancy is high. Such energy levels may be regarded as discrete in character, and electronic transitions are permitted only

[9] E. C. Stoner: *Phil. Mag.* [6], **48,** 719 (1924).

[10] J. D. Main Smith: *Chem. & Ind.*, **43,** 323 (1924). See also *Chemistry and Atomic Structure*, Ch. XII, XIII, XIV. Ernest Benn, Ltd., London (1924).

between these levels. These transitions account for spectral lines, and, as with the Bohr theory, the relative positions of these spectral lines permit descriptions of the properties of the electrons.

Electrons are best described in terms of four so-called *quantum numbers*. Two of these numbers may be thought of in much the same sense as those described in the preceding section. Two others are added to permit more detailed and precise interpretations of atomic spectra. By use of these four quantum numbers, the electrons which make up a given atom may be characterized completely, and a more exact understanding of the characteristics of the atom as determined by its electronic arrangement or configuration may be obtained.

If the electrons are considered as occupying a number of energy levels, these levels may be distinguished from each other in terms of values of the *principal quantum number n*. The exact significance of n may be determined from the relation

$$W = \frac{-2\pi^2 Z^2 e^4 \mu}{h^2}\left(\frac{1}{n^2}\right) \tag{3·6}$$

where W represents the energy of the electron in a particular level of a hydrogen-like atom, Z the total number of electrons (i.e., atomic number), e the electronic charge, μ the mass, and h Planck's constant. Although in terms of the older concepts, n might be regarded as the ordinal number of the particular orbit in which the electron is found, it must now be thought of as indicating only the position of the energy level with respect to the nucleus. Crudely, this amounts to a designation of the mean distance of the electron from the nucleus since, for example, electrons of principal quantum number 2 will be more energetic and thus, on the average, farther from the nucleus than those of principal quantum number 1. The principal quantum number may have any integer value from unity to infinity, an infinite value corresponding, of course, to the complete removal of the electron from the atom and the production of a positive ion. For convenience, the energy levels may still be regarded as electron shells and the older shell notation employed. We have then $n = 1$ for the K shell, $n = 2$ for the L shell, $n = 3$ for the M shell, and so on.

Although the general energy positions of the electrons are described by the principal quantum numbers, these alone do not account for all the spectral lines. To account for all, it is necessary to describe more clearly the energies of individual electrons through the use of other quantum numbers. That part of the energy due to orbital motion about the nucleus is described by the *subsidiary* or *azimuthal quantum number l*, the magnitude of which is a measure of the orbital angular momentum of the electron. Orbital angular momentum again has no true meaning in terms of non-existent orbits but may be thought of as a vector quantity

$$\frac{h\sqrt{l(l+1)}}{2\pi} \tag{3·7}$$

If the Bohr-Sommerfeld orbits were real representations of electron paths, their shapes or eccentricities would be expressed in terms of values of l. The values which l may have embrace n values from zero to $n - 1$. Thus the electrons in each principal energy or quantum level may be regarded as being distributed through n subsidiary levels. Although electrons may be described in terms of numerical values for l, custom dictates the use of equivalent letter designations, the first four of which come from the old spectral terms, sharp, principal, diffuse, and fundamental. Thus electrons for which $l = 0$ are named s electrons; for $l = 1$, p electrons; for $l = 2$, d electrons; and for $l = 3$, f electrons. For larger l values, the letters g, h, etc., are employed, although in actual considerations of known neutral atoms only s, p, d, and f electrons are involved. A wave function associated with the orbital motion of an electron is referred to as an *orbital*. It is customary to refer to s, p, d, and f orbitals in describing the configurations and properties of atoms.

The observed splitting of certain spectral lines when the source which emits them is placed in a magnetic field (Zeeman effect) necessitates a further refinement in electronic designations. Under the influence of the magnetic field, the vector quantity describing the orbital angular momentum undergoes a precessional movement and describes a cone about an axis in the direction of the magnetic field. The possible positions which this vector may assume in space are limited, and the magnitude of its component in the direction of the magnetic field is given in terms of the *magnetic quantum number* m_l by the expression

$$m_l\left(\frac{h}{2\pi}\right) \tag{3·8}$$

The magnetic quantum number may have any integral value and zero from $-l$ to $+l$, there being $2l + 1$ possible orientations in space of the angular momentum vector. Thus, for an s electron, $l = 0$ and $m_l = 0$; for a p electron, $l = 1$ and $m_l = -1, 0, +1$; for a d electron, $l = 2$ and $m_l = -2, -1, 0, +1, +2$; and for an f electron, $l = 3$ and $m_l = -3, -2, -1, 0, +1, +2, +3$. Positive values of m_l describe orbital angular momentum components in the direction of the applied field; negative values refer to components in the opposite direction.

One other characteristic of electrons requires description, namely their spin or rotation about their own axes. Because of its spin, each electron has an added angular momentum amounting to

$$\frac{h\sqrt{s(s+1)}}{2\pi} \tag{3·9}$$

where the spin s is given by ½. In an applied magnetic field, therefore, the vector representing this spin momentum can also orient itself so that its component m_s (the *spin quantum number*) is either in the direction of the field or opposed to it, that is, has a value of either $+\frac{1}{2}$ or $-\frac{1}{2}$. In a more utilitarian fashion, this amounts to saying that for each possible combination of the other three quantum numbers (n, l, m_l), two electrons differing from each other only in spin are possible. Or, putting it another way, two electrons differing in spin may exist for each value of m_l. Each orbital may accomodate such a pair of electrons.

The electrons within any atom may be discussed in terms of the magnitudes to the four quantum numbers. It is an observed fact, however, that no two electrons within the same atom can have the same values for the four quantum numbers. This generalization is known as the Pauli exclusion principle and is tantamount to a statement that each electron differs from every other electron in a given atom in its total energy. The smallest such difference will, of course, be between two electrons which differ from each other in spin alone.

Electrons within a given quantum level

The total number of electrons within a given quantum level and the distribution of these electrons as governed by the permitted values of the subsidiary quantum number l may be determined by evaluation of the various quantum numbers and application of the Pauli exclusion principle. Thus for the K shell, the principal quantum number n equals one, and l can, of necessity, have only a zero value. The magnetic quantum number m_l must also be zero, indicating the possibility of but a single orbital, and application of the idea of electron spin as embodied in the spin quantum number m_s shows the presence of a maximum of two electrons. These electrons are of the s type. In a similar fashion, it can be shown that the maximum numbers of electrons possible in the L, M, N, O, etc., shells are, respectively, 8, 18, 32, 50, etc. Determination of these values and the corresponding electron distributions are summarized in Table 3·3.

TABLE 3·3

Distribution of Electrons among the Quantum Levels

Shell	n	l	m_l	Number of Electrons Distributed	Total
K	1	0(s)	0	2	2
L	2	0(s)	0	2	8
		1(p)	+1, 0, −1	6	
M	3	0(s)	0	2	18
		1(p)	+1, 0, −1	6	
		2(d)	+2, +1, 0, −1, −2	10	
N	4	0(s)	0	2	32
		1(p)	+1, 0, −1	6	
		2(d)	+2, +1, 0, −1, −2	10	
		3(f)	+3, +2, +1, 0, −1, −2, −3	14	
O	5	0(s)	0	2	50
		1(p)	+1, 0, −1	6	
		2(d)	+2, +1, 0, −1, −2	10	
		3(f)	+3, +2, +1, 0, −1, −2, −3	14	
		4(g)	+4, +3, +2, +1, 0, −1, −2, −3, −4	18	

Electronic configurations of atoms of the elements

The electronic configurations of atoms of the various elements are conveniently expressed in terms of the quantum numbers. It is customary to refer to the various electrons in terms of the notation

$$nl^x$$

where n is expressed numerically as 1, 2, 3, 4, etc., l is expressed as its equivalent letter value s, p, d, f, etc., and x is expressed numerically as the number of electrons present in the orbital or orbitals characterized by l. If all the electronic levels of the atom are designated in this fashion, a summation of the x values represents the atomic number Z.

In arriving at the electronic configurations of atoms of the various elements, it is convenient to consider the positions which electrons would take if these atoms were built up in order, beginning with hydrogen, by the successive addition of individual electrons with corresponding increases in balancing nuclear charges. In terms of such an approach, each new electron, as it enters, will tend to occupy the available orbital of lowest energy, and addition to higher energy orbitals will be expected only after lower orbitals have been filled to capacity. The electronic configuration of each atom may then be expressed in terms of those orbitals (designated by the foregoing notation) which are occupied either partially or completely. These are arranged in order of increasing values of the principal quantum number. The result represents the configuration of the atom in its lowest energy or *ground* state.

One other point is of importance. When electrons enter a level of fixed n and l values, available orbitals are occupied singly until each orbital is so occupied before any electron pairing occurs.[11] This is known as the principle of maximum multiplicity. It is of no consequence among s orbitals because the second electron must always and of necessity pair with the first. Among the p, d, and f orbitals, however, the concept is of importance, particularly as it is useful in accounting for the presence of unpaired electrons and of properties dependent upon them (pp. 166–167). Thus, to use an example, the electronic configuration of the phosphorus atom, although usually written $1s^22s^22p^63s^23p^3$, is actually $1s^22s^22p^63s^23p^13p^13p^1$, with three unpaired electrons in the $3p$ level. The chemical characteristics of phosphorus and its compounds are in accord with this arrangement (pp. 558–559). For convenience, Pauling[11] has suggested separate designations of the various orbitals in a given level, np_x, np_y, np_z, etc.

Knowledge of the exact order in which atomic orbitals are occupied is based upon interpretations of atomic spectra in terms of how lines of particular wavelengths result from permitted electronic transitions. Such interpretations are complicated by the complexities of the spectral patterns among the elements and by the overlaps occurring among systems of the same general type. These situations are particularly acute among the complicated atoms of the heavier elements. Although the exact order of occupancy is well established among the lighter elements, it is not known with complete certainty for all the heaviest elements. Furthermore, among the higher quantum levels, energies associated with orbitals of different l values are very nearly the same. As a consequence, it is difficult to say that one orbital will always be occupied before another of nearly the same energy. Exact agreement among published summaries is not found for materials in this region.

Although it is impossible to depict the energy levels exactly, an approximate representation is given by an energy level diagram of the type used by Pauling[11] and others.[12,13] Such a diagram, modified somewhat in the region of higher principal quantum numbers in the light of later observations, is given in Figure 3·3. Each subsidiary quantum level is designated by a horizontal line indicating a relative energy content on the vertical energy scale, and each available orbital (i.e., space for two electrons) is indicated by a small circle. Levels of

[11] L. Pauling: *The Nature of the Chemical Bond*, 2nd Ed., pp. 25–26. Cornell University Press, Ithaca, N. Y. (1940).

[12] T. H. Hazelhurst: *J. Chem. Education*, **18**, 580 (1941).

[13] W. F. Luder: *J. Chem. Education*, **20**, 24 (1943).

approximately the same energy content are connected by vertical lines at the right of the diagram. Such arrangements are called valence shells. Their relation to the chemical behaviors of the ele-

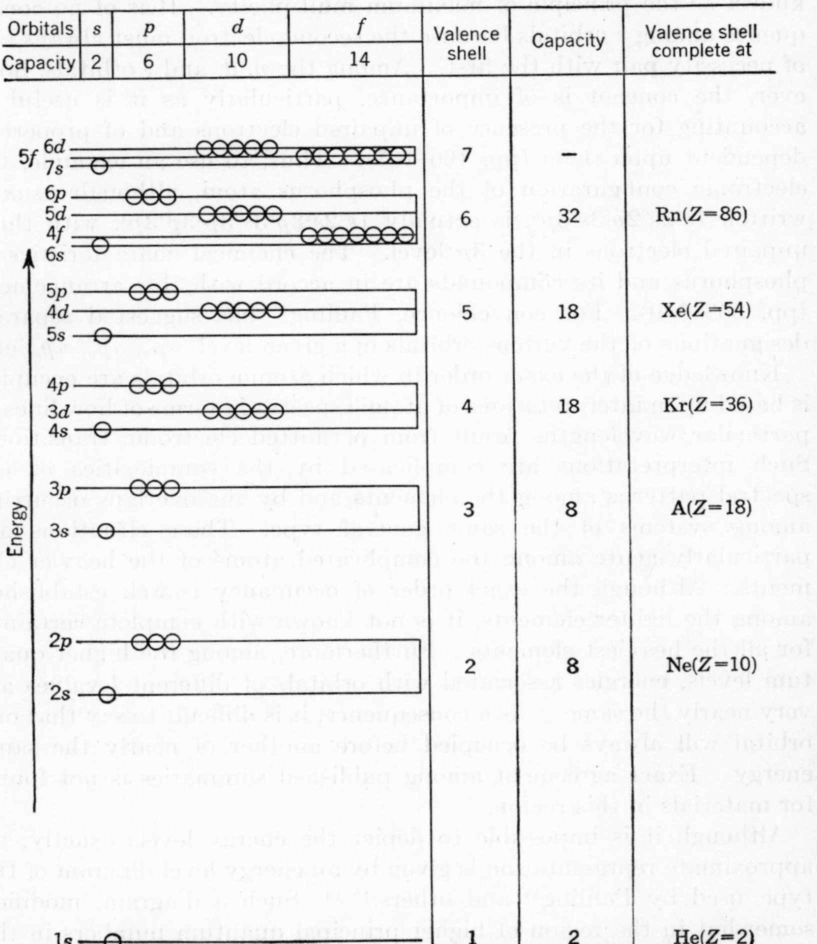

Orbitals	s	p	d	f
Capacity	2	6	10	14

Energy (orbitals)	Valence shell	Capacity	Valence shell complete at
5f, 6d, 7s	7	—	
6p, 5d, 4f, 6s	6	32	Rn(Z=86)
5p, 4d, 5s	5	18	Xe(Z=54)
4p, 3d, 4s	4	18	Kr(Z=36)
3p, 3s	3	8	A(Z=18)
2p, 2s	2	8	Ne(Z=10)
1s	1	2	He(Z=2)

Fig. 3·3. Energy level diagram for atomic orbitals. (Adapted with some modifications from T. H. Hazlehurst: *J. Chem. Education*, **18**, 580 [1941].)

ments is considered later (Ch. 6). In general, electrons may be expected to occupy the orbitals in order as they appear, beginning at the bottom of the diagram, each set of orbitals (of given n and l) being filled before electrons enter the next set.

Strictly speaking, such is not the case. The arrangement given in

Figure 3·3 characterizes elements of low atomic numbers only. As atomic number increases, the relative energies of many of the levels change somewhat, but not all change to the same degree. The result is a slightly altered arrangement for elements of high atomic numbers.

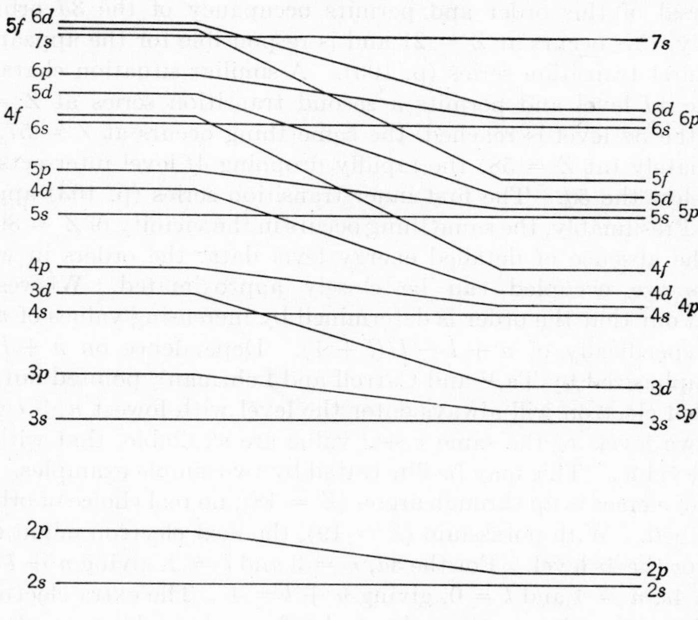

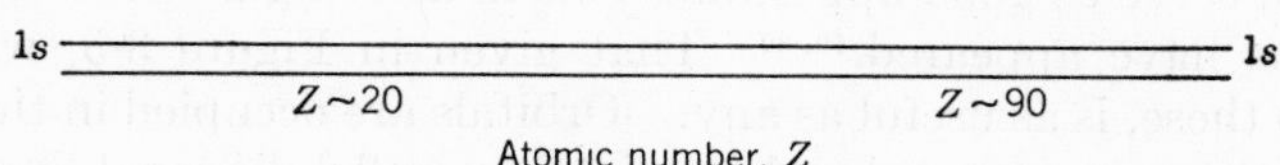

FIG. 3·4. Variations in energy levels with atomic number.

These changes are shown very completely and comprehensively in the graphs presented by DeVault[14] and, more schematically, although none the less effectively, in the diagram given by Herzberg.[15] The general details of the Herzberg diagram are given in Figure 3·4.

[14] D. DeVault: *J. Chem. Education*, **21,** 526, 575 (1944).

[15] G. Herzberg: *Atomic Spectra and Atomic Structure*, p. 148. Dover Publications, New York (1944).

Although the p levels are influenced somewhat, their relative positioning remains unchanged. On the other hand, the d and f levels change rather profoundly. Thus, at low atomic numbers ($Z < 20$), the $3d$ orbitals lie above the $4s$. However, increase in atomic number effects a reversal of this order and permits occupancy of the $3d$ orbitals. Actually, this occurs at $Z = 21$ and is responsible for the appearance of the first transition series (p. 103). A similiar situation characterizes the $4d$ level and permits a second transition series at $Z = 39$. When the $5d$ level is reached, the same thing occurs at $Z = 57$, but immediately (at $Z = 58$) the rapidly dropping $4f$ level intersects and falls below the $5d$. The first inner transition series (p. 103) appears here. Presumably, the same thing occurs in the vicinity of $Z = 89–91$.

In the absence of detailed energy level data, the orders in which orbitals are occupied can be closely approximated. Wiswesser[16] pointed out that the order is determined by increasing values of $n + l$ (more specifically of $n + l - l/(l + 1)$. Dependence on $n + l$ was also emphasized by Ta,[17] and Carroll and Lehrman[18] pointed out that an added electron will always enter the level with lowest $n + l$ value or, if two levels of the same $n + l$ value are available, that with the lower n value. This may be illustrated by two simple examples. For atoms of elements up through argon ($Z = 18$), no real choice of orbitals is involved. With potassium ($Z = 19$), the next electron might enter the $3d$ or the $4s$ level. For the $3d$, $n = 3$ and $l = 2$, giving $n + l = 5$; for the $4s$, $n = 4$ and $l = 0$, giving $n + l = 4$. The extra electron in potassium, therefore, enters the $4s$ level, as does the next electron characterizing calcium. With scandium ($Z = 21$), the choice is $3d$ or $4p$. Calculation shows $n + l$ to be 5 for both; so the electron goes to the level of lower n value, namely, the $3d$. The order is thus: $1s2s2p3s3p4s3d4p5s4d5p6s4f5d6p7s5f6d7p8s$.

Various mnemonic devices which reflect this dependence on $n + l$ and which serve as good approximations in arriving at electronic configurations have appeared.[19, 20] That given in Figure 3·5, which is similar to these, is as useful as any. Orbitals are occupied in the order in which they are struck by the series of parallel diagonal lines. An exception is found where a single $5d$ electron is added before any $4f$ orbitals are occupied, the remainder of the $5d$ electrons then appearing

[16] W. J. Wiswesser: *J. Chem. Education*, **22**, 314 (1945).
[17] Y. Ta: *Ann. phys.* [12], **1**, 88 (1946).
[18] B. Carroll and A. Lehrman: *J. Chem. Education*, **25**, 662 (1948).
[19] Pao-Fang Yi: *J. Chem. Education*, **24**, 567 (1947).
[20] L. M. Simmons: *J. Chem. Education*, **25**, 698 (1948).

after completion of the $4f$ level. In a parallel fashion, one or more $6d$ electrons should appear before any of the $5f$ type.

The electronic configurations of the neutral atoms in their ground states are summarized in Table 3·4. Discrepancies between recorded

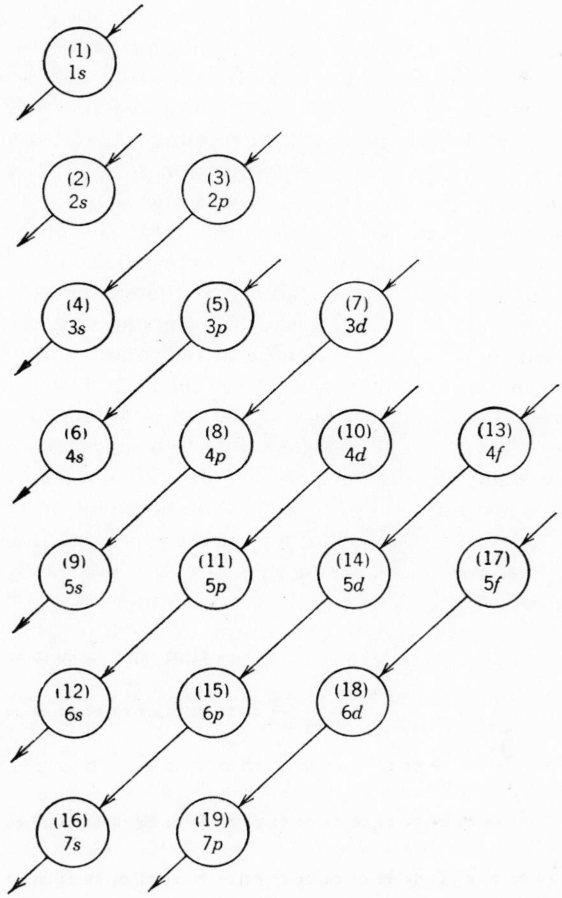

FIG. 3·5. Order of occupancy of atomic orbitals.

configurations and those deduced in the light of the above considerations are not numerous and occur only when the energy levels involved approach each other very closely. Such situations are without significant effects upon overall chemical behavior. Hence, in the absence of specific information as to the exact configuration of a given

TABLE 3·4

THE ELECTRONIC CONFIGURATIONS OF THE ATOMS OF THE ELEMENTS

Symbol	Atomic Number, *Z*	Number and Distribution of Electrons																		
		1s	2s	2p	3s	3p	3d	4s	4p	4d	4f	5s	5p	5d	5f	6s	6p	6d	6f	7s
H	1	1																		
He	2	2																		
Li	3	2	1																	
Be	4	2	2																	
B	5	2	2	1																
C	6	2	2	2																
N	7	2	2	3																
O	8	2	2	4																
F	9	2	2	5																
Ne	10	2	2	6																
Na	11	2	2	6	1															
Mg	12	2	2	6	2															
Al	13	2	2	6	2	1														
Si	14	2	2	6	2	2														
P	15	2	2	6	2	3														
S	16	2	2	6	2	4														
Cl	17	2	2	6	2	5														
A	18	2	2	6	2	6														
K	19	2	2	6	2	6		1												
Ca	20	2	2	6	2	6		2												
Sc	21	2	2	6	2	6	1	2												
Ti	22	2	2	6	2	6	2	2												
V	23	2	2	6	2	6	3	2												
Cr	24	2	2	6	2	6	5	1												
Mn	25	2	2	6	2	6	5	2												
Fe	26	2	2	6	2	6	6	2												

Co	27	2	2	6	2	6	7	2								
Ni	28	2	2	6	2	6	8	2								
Cu	29	2	2	6	2	6	10	1								
Zn	30	2	2	6	2	6	10	2								
Ga	31	2	2	6	2	6	10	2	1							
Ge	32	2	2	6	2	6	10	2	2							
As	33	2	2	6	2	6	10	2	3							
Se	34	2	2	6	2	6	10	2	4							
Br	35	2	2	6	2	6	10	2	5							
Kr	36	2	2	6	2	6	10	2	6							
Rb	37	2	2	6	2	6	10	2	6			1				
Sr	38	2	2	6	2	6	10	2	6			2				
Y	39	2	2	6	2	6	10	2	6	1		2				
Zr	40	2	2	6	2	6	10	2	6	2		2				
Nb	41	2	2	6	2	6	10	2	6	4		1				
Mo	42	2	2	6	2	6	10	2	6	5		1				
Tc	43	2	2	6	2	6	10	2	6	6		1				
Ru	44	2	2	6	2	6	10	2	6	7		1				
Rh	45	2	2	6	2	6	10	2	6	8		1				
Pd	46	2	2	6	2	6	10	2	6	10						
Ag	47	2	2	6	2	6	10	2	6	10		1				
Cd	48	2	2	6	2	6	10	2	6	10		2				
In	49	2	2	6	2	6	10	2	6	10		2	1			
Sn	50	2	2	6	2	6	10	2	6	10		2	2			
Sb	51	2	2	6	2	6	10	2	6	10		2	3			
Te	52	2	2	6	2	6	10	2	6	10		2	4			
I	53	2	2	6	2	6	10	2	6	10		2	5			
Xe	54	2	2	6	2	6	10	2	6	10		2	6			
Cs	55	2	2	6	2	6	10	2	6	10		2	6			1
Ba	56	2	2	6	2	6	10	2	6	10		2	6			2
La	57	2	2	6	2	6	10	2	6	10		2	6	1		2

TABLE 3·4 (*Continued*)

Symbol	Atomic Number, *Z*	Number and Distribution of Electrons																	
		1*s*	2*s*	2*p*	3*s*	3*p*	3*d*	4*s*	4*p*	4*d*	4*f*	5*s*	5*p*	5*d*	5*f*	6*s*	6*p*	6*d*	6*f*	7*s*
Ce*	58	2	2	6	2	6	10	2	6	10	2	2	6			2				
Pr*	59	2	2	6	2	6	10	2	6	10	3	2	6			2				
Nd*	60	2	2	6	2	6	10	2	6	10	4	2	6			2				
*	61	2	2	6	2	6	10	2	6	10	5	2	6			2				
Sm*	62	2	2	6	2	6	10	2	6	10	6	2	6			2				
Eu*	63	2	2	6	2	6	10	2	6	10	7	2	6			2				
Gd*	64	2	2	6	2	6	10	2	6	10	7	2	6	1		2				
Tb*	65	2	2	6	2	6	10	2	6	10	9	2	6			2				
Dy*	66	2	2	6	2	6	10	2	6	10	10	2	6			2				
Ho*	67	2	2	6	2	6	10	2	6	10	11	2	6			2				
Er*	68	2	2	6	2	6	10	2	6	10	12	2	6			2				
Tm*	69	2	2	6	2	6	10	2	6	10	13	2	6			2				
Yb*	70	2	2	6	2	6	10	2	6	10	14	2	6			2				
Lu*	71	2	2	6	2	6	10	2	6	10	14	2	6	1		2				
Hf	72	2	2	6	2	6	10	2	6	10	14	2	6	2		2				
Ta	73	2	2	6	2	6	10	2	6	10	14	2	6	3		2				
W	74	2	2	6	2	6	10	2	6	10	14	2	6	4		2				
Re	75	2	2	6	2	6	10	2	6	10	14	2	6	5		2				
Os	76	2	2	6	2	6	10	2	6	10	14	2	6	6		2				
Ir	77	2	2	6	2	6	10	2	6	10	14	2	6	9						
Pt	78	2	2	6	2	6	10	2	6	10	14	2	6	9		1				
Au	79	2	2	6	2	6	10	2	6	10	14	2	6	10		1				
Hg	80	2	2	6	2	6	10	2	6	10	14	2	6	10		2				
Tl	81	2	2	6	2	6	10	2	6	10	14	2	6	10		2	1			
Pb	82	2	2	6	2	6	10	2	6	10	14	2	6	10		2	2			
Bi	83	2	2	6	2	6	10	2	6	10	14	2	6	10		2	3			
Po	84	2	2	6	2	6	10	2	6	10	14	2	6	10		2	4			

At	85	2	2	6	2	6	10	2	6	10	14	2	6	10		2	5		
Rn	86	2	2	6	2	6	10	2	6	10	14	2	6	10		2	6		
Fr	87	2	2	6	2	6	10	2	6	10	14	2	6	10		2	6		1
Ra	88	2	2	6	2	6	10	2	6	10	14	2	6	10		2	6		2
Ac	89	2	2	6	2	6	10	2	6	10	14	2	6	10		2	6	1	2
Th*	90	2	2	6	2	6	10	2	6	10	14	2	6	10		2	6	2	2
Pa*	91	2	2	6	2	6	10	2	6	10	14	2	6	10	2	2	6	1	2
U*	92	2	2	6	2	6	10	2	6	10	14	2	6	10	3	2	6	1	2
Np*	93	2	2	6	2	6	10	2	6	10	14	2	6	10	4	2	6	1	2
Pu*	94	2	2	6	2	6	10	2	6	10	14	2	6	10	5	2	6	1	2
Am*	95	2	2	6	2	6	10	2	6	10	14	2	6	10	6	2	6	1	2
Cm*	96	2	2	6	2	6	10	2	6	10	14	2	6	10	7	2	6	1	2
(Bk	97	2	2	6	2	6	10	2	6	10	14	2	6	10	8	2	6	1	2)
(Cf	98	2	2	6	2	6	10	2	6	10	14	2	6	10	9	2	6	1	2)

* Probable configurations as given by W. F. Meggars: *Science*, **105**, 514 (1947).

atom, a configuration deduced as outlined above is generally acceptable and useful. It will be noted that for elements in the region $Z = 91\text{–}98$ configurations involving f electrons have been given. Evidence in support of this usage appears later in this chapter (pp. 104–105).

Types of elements based upon electronic configurations of their atoms

In terms of similarities and differences in electronic configurations, four essentially different types of atoms may be distinguished in Table 3·4. For purposes of classification and discussion, elements characterized by atoms of these types may be grouped as *inert gas elements, representative elements, transition elements,* and *inner transition elements.* Although the detailed characteristics of each of these groups of elements will be discussed in Part II of this book, some general distinctions may be outlined briefly.

Inert Gas Elements. Elements of this type are characterized by atoms in which all subsidiary quantum levels that are present* are filled to capacity. Except for helium, where the configuration is $1s^2$, each atom of this type has in its level of maximum principal quantum number (n) the arrangement ns^2np^6. The inert gas elements have, in effect, completed electronic groups and may be regarded as the end members of series of elements in which the individual quantum groups are being filled. Their inertness toward chemical reactions may be ascribed to this fact. The inert gas elements embrace helium, neon, argon, krypton, xenon, and radon (including actinon and thoron).

Representative Elements. Elements of this type are characterized by atoms in which the levels of maximum principal quantum number are incompletely filled, all underlying levels present being filled to capacity. This type of configuration is somewhat broader in scope than that characterizing the inert gas elements and embraces, in a given quantum level, anything from ns^1 through ns^2np^5. Elements of this type include those with atomic numbers from *seven* less through *two* more than that of a given inert gas element. All the non-metallic elements and the metallic elements from Periodic Groups Ia and IIa and the *b*-families are classed as representative elements. Since many of these elements are abundant in nature (Table 2·3), compounds containing representative elements are commonly encountered. The proximities of these elements to the inert gas elements and the stabilities of the configurations of the atoms of the latter contribute to the

* *Presence* is used in the sense of actual occupancy in these discussions.

tendencies of the representative elements to react by electron loss or gain to achieve inert gas arrangements (pp. 175–178).

Transition Elements. Elements of this type are characterized by atoms in which an inner d level is present but is not filled to capacity. Atoms of elements of this type have configurations which in general amount to $(n-1)d^{1-9}ns^2$, although rigid adherence to two electrons in the ns level is not required since examples are known (Table 3·4) where the arrangement is ns^1 or even ns^0. Four transition series appear among the elements, corresponding respectively to occupancy of 3d, 4d, 5d, and 6d orbitals. All such series begin with Periodic Group IIIa elements, namely, scandium ($Z = 21$), yttrium ($Z = 39$), lanthanum ($Z = 57$), and actinium ($Z = 89$). By definition, the first three transition series end at nickel ($Z = 28$), palladium ($Z = 46$), and platinum ($Z = 78$), respectively, the fourth series being limited in membership only by the number of known elements. In terms of the rigid definitions here employed, elements from Periodic Groups Ib (copper family) and IIb (zinc family) are classified as representative rather than transition elements. Because of the carry-over in properties, elements in these families have many characteristics which render them quite analogous to the transition elements, and for this reason some authors prefer to classify them with the latter elements. The exact position which they are given is largely a matter of choice.

All the transition elements are metals. Although many are rare a number are abundant (Table 2·3), and many are common either alone (e.g., iron) or in alloys (e.g., manganese, vanadium, tungsten) in technical products of strength and durability. Elements of this type resemble each other strikingly, particularly in physical characteristics. Detailed discussions of their physical and chemical properties in relation to electronic configurations will be found in later sections of this book (pp. 169–170, 868–876).

Inner Transition Elements. Elements of this type are, strictly speaking, transition elements, although they may be so distinguished electronically from the regular transition elements as to be literally members of transition series within transition series. Hence the term *inner transition.* Atoms of elements of the inner transition type contain not only incompletely filled d levels but incompletely filled f levels as well. Best-characterized elements of this type are the rare earth elements (or *lanthanide* series elements) in which the distinguishing electrons occupy the 4f orbitals. This series begins with cerium ($Z = 58$). The electronic configurations given in Table 3·4 are the most probable as listed by Meggars (*loc. cit.*) and indicate not only the absence of 5d electrons in the majority of cases but also completion of the $4f$ level at ytterbium ($Z = 70$). In discussing these elements, it has been customary to adopt the more approximate general configuration $4f^{1-13}5s^2 5p^6 5d^1 6s^2$ for the series and to consider that a regular filling of the $4f$ orbitals occurs from cerium ($4f^1$) through lutetium ($4f^{14}$). There appears to be no real reason for departing from this procedure here. By rigid definition, both lanthanum ($Z = 57$, $4f^0$) lutetium ($Z = 71$, $4f^{14}$) would be excluded from this series. However, the similarities in chemical and physical characteristics existing between these and the other elements commonly justify their inclusion.

The appearance of a second inner transition series among the heavier elements has been speculated upon many times in the past.[21] Only recently, however, has any concrete evidence in support of such contentions been produced. The marked similarities in properties existing among the transuranium elements (p. 891), the increasing stability of the +3 oxidation state with atomic number among these elements, apparent similarities to some of the rare earth elements, and complete lack of similarities to rhenium, osmium, etc., led Seaborg[22] to postulate that they are members of such a series (called the *actinide series*), beginning in the neighborhood of thorium. This implies, of course, that thorium, protactinium, and uranium are not electronic congeners of hafnium, tantalum, and tungsten, as had been proposed. Detailed considerations of the properties of the heavy elements and their compounds in comparison with those of corresponding lanthanide materials strongly support the inclusion of these elements in a second inner transition series.[23, 24]

Unfortunately, the emission spectra of the heavy elements (Th, Pa, U, Np, Pu, Am, and presumably Cm, Bk, and Cf) are so complex that they have not been completely analyzed. They do bear striking resemblances, however, to the emission spectra of the lighter lanthanide elements,[25] suggesting similarities in electronic arrangements. Fairly complete analysis of the emission spectrum of uranium[26] indicates definitely the presence of at least *three* $5f$ electrons in the neutral atoms and mono-positive ions. The spectrum of mono-positive americium suggests[25] strongly the presence of *seven* $5f$ electrons. It may be

[21] L. L. Quill: *Chem. Revs.*, **23,** 87 (1938). General review.

[22] G. T. Seaborg: *Chem. Eng. News*, **23,** 2190 (1945).

[23] G. T. Seaborg: *Nucleonics*, **5** (No. 5), 16 (1949).

[24] Z. Szabó: *Phys. Rev.*, **76,** 147 (1949).

[25] F. S. Tomkins and M. Fred: *J. Opt. Soc. Am.*, **39,** 357 (1949).

[26] C. C. Kiess, C. J. Humphreys, and D. D. Laun: *J. Opt. Soc. Am.*, **36,** 357 (1946); *J. Research Natl. Bur. Standards*, **37,** 57 (1946).

Outer / Inner	Element	Inert gas	Representative							Transition									Inner transition												
	Electrons		*s*		*p*					*d*									*f*												
	Disting. *n*	0	1	2	1	2	3	4	5	1	2	3	4	5	6	7	8	9	1	2	3	4	5	6	7	8	9	10	11	12	13
	1		H																												
$1s^2$	2	He	Li	Be	B	C	N	O	F																						
$2s^2\ 2p^6$	3	Ne	Na	Mg	Al	Si	P	S	Cl																						
$3s^2\ 3p^6$	4	A	K	Ca																											
	(3)									Sc	Ti	V	Cr	Mn	Fe	Co	Ni														
$3s^2\ 3p^6\ 3d^{10}$	4		Cu	Zn	Ga	Ge	As	Se	Br																						
$4s^2\ 4p^6$	5	Kr	Rb	Sr																											
	(4)									Y	Zr	Nb	Mo	Tc	Ru	Rh	Pd														
$4s^2\ 4p^6\ 4d^{10}$	5		Ag	Cd	In	Sn	Sb	Te	I																						
$5s^2\ 5p^6$	6	Xe	Cs	Ba																											
	(5)									La																					
	(5,4)																		Ce	Pr	Nd		Sm	Eu	Gd	Tb	Dy	Ho	Er	Tm	Yb
$4f^{14}\ 5s^2\ 5p^6$	(5)									Lu	Hf	Ta	W	Re	Os	Ir	Pt														
$5s^2\ 5p^6\ 5d^{10}$	6		Au	Hg	Tl	Pb	Bi	Po	At																						
$6s^2\ 6p^6$	7	Rn	Fr	Ra																											
	(6)									Ac																					
	(6,5)																		Th	Pa	U	Np	Pu	Am	Cm	Bk	Cf				

FIG. 3·6. Classification of elements by electronic configurations.

concluded then that the 5*f* level begins to fill somewhere below uranium in the atomic number sequence. The configurations given in Table 3·4 are not necessarily exact but appear to be the most probable ones.

The first 5*f* electron is shown in this table for protactinium ($Z = 91$). By analogy with the lanthanide series, it might be expected at thorium ($Z = 90$). In Seaborg's opinion,[27] however, whether or not this electron appears with thorium is of much less consequence in arriving at the series than is the probable presence of *seven* 5*f* electrons in the curium ($Z = 96$) atom, the formal analog of gadolinium ($Z = 64$). Since the 5*f* and 6*d* levels are so nearly identical energetically, shifts between these two levels might well lie within the bonds of chemical binding energies, and the appearance of the 5*f* orbitals might be delayed further than the appearance of the 4*f* level in the first inner transition series. In any event, one would depart but little from the actual state of affairs in considering that the electronic configurations of atoms of elements of atomic numbers 90–98 amount to $5f^{1-9}6s^2 6p^6 6d^1 7s^2$.

The four types of elements distinguished above are presented in summary fashion in Figure 3·6. This diagrammatic representation is adapted from the similar one presented originally by Gardner[28] and doubtless used by Luder[29] and Babor[30] as a model for their periodic tables (pp. 123, 125). The types of elements are classified in terms of the distinguishing outer electronic arrangements in their atoms, with the immediately underlying completed shells being given at the extreme left. The arrangement is idealistic in that it does not bring out the minor variations in orbital occupancy previously discussed, but it is useful in bringing together materials of the same general types and in defining the limits of existence of the various types of elements. In the sense that it lists together elements of similar electronic configurations, it may be regarded as a type of periodic table.

The directional characteristics of atomic orbitals

It is apparent from the preceding discussions that the various orbitals characterizing an atom differ from each other in terms of the distance *r* of the electron from the nucleus. This, it will be recalled, was a primary consideration of the Bohr theory. The orbitals are also described by their angular distribution in space relative to the

[27] G. T. Seaborg: *Science*, **104**, 379 (1946)
[28] R. Gardner: *Nature*, **125**, 146 (1930).
[29] W. F. Luder: *J. Chem. Education*, **20**, 21 (1943).
[30] J. A. Babor: *J. Chem. Education*, **21**, 25 (1944).

nucleus (p. 90), and this distribution is characteristic of a particular orbital type regardless of the magnitude of the principal quantum number. For the hydrogen atom, with its single 1*s* electron, it can be shown that the probability of finding the electron in any spherical shell of radius *r* is a maximum when *r* is identical with the radius of the orbit of this electron as given by the Bohr theory. This electron,

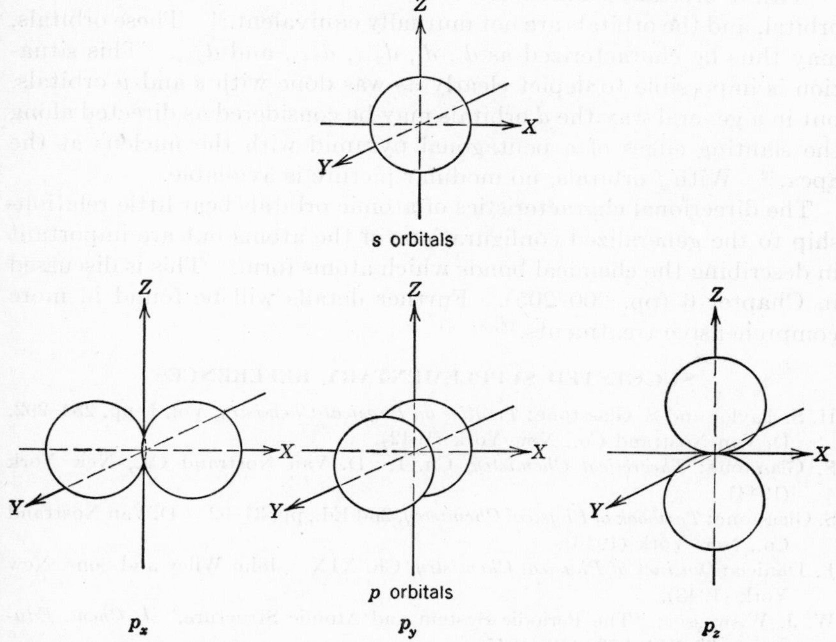

FIG. 3·7. Spatial distribution of *s* and *p* orbitals. (Adapted from L. Pauling: *The Nature of the Chemical Bond*, 2nd Ed., p. 77. Cornell University Press, Ithaca [1940].)

and any other *s* electron, has its most probable location in a spherical surface with the nucleus as a center, as shown in Figure 3·7. Orbitals of the *s* type are said, therefore, to be spherically symmetrical and without directional characteristics.

With *p*, *d*, and *f* orbitals, the situation becomes increasingly complex. These orbitals are found in sets of three, five, and seven. Although it is impossible to determine the direction of any one orbital in a given set, the axes (with the nucleus at their crossing) along which the orbitals in a given set lie are at definite angles to each other in space. Thus, with *p* orbitals, the three in each set are mutually at right angles to each other and lie along three Cartesian coordinates with the nucleus at the center,[31] as shown in Figure 3·7. Designation of p orbitals as p_x, p_y, and p_z (p. 93) emphasizes this directional character. Because of the fact that orbital angular momentum components may lie either in the direction of the applied field or in the opposite direction, each orbital of the p type has both positive and negative components (Figure 3·7).

With d orbitals maxima are attained in four directions with each orbital, and the orbitals are not mutually equivalent.[31] These orbitals, may thus be characterized as d_x, d_z, d_{x+y}, d_{x+z}, and d_{y+z}. This situation is impossible to depict clearly as was done with s and p orbitals, but in a general way the d orbitals may be considered as directed along the slanting edges of a pentagonal pyramid with the nucleus at the apex.[32] With f orbitals, no modular picture is available.

The directional characteristics of atomic orbitals bear little relationship to the generalized configurations of the atoms but are important in describing the chemical bonds which atoms form. This is discussed in Chapter 6 (pp. 200–205). Further details will be found in more comprehensive treatments.[16, 31–34]

SUGGESTED SUPPLEMENTARY REFERENCES

H. S. Taylor and S. Glasstone: *Treatise on Physical Chemistry*, Vol. I, pp. 284–292. D. Van Nostrand Co., New York (1942).

S. Glasstone: *Theoretical Chemistry*, Ch. I. D. Van Nostrand Co., New York (1944).

S. Glasstone: *Textbook of Physical Chemistry*, 2nd Ed., pp. 31–92. D. Van Nostrand Co., New York (1946).

F. Daniels: *Outlines of Physical Chemistry*, Ch. XIX. John Wiley and Sons, New York (1948).

W. J. Wiswasser: "The Periodic System and Atomic Structure," *J. Chem. Education*, **22**, 314, 370, 418 (1945).

D. DeVault: "A Method of Teaching the Electronic Structure of the Atom," *J. Chem. Education*, **21**, 526, 575 (1944).

C. H. D. Clark: *The Electronic Structure and Properties of Matter*, Ch. II. Chapman and Hall, Ltd., London (1934).

---

[31] L. Pauling: *J. Am. Chem. Soc.*, **53**, 1367 (1931).
[32] G. E. Kimball: *J. Chem. Phys.*, **8**, 188 (1940).
[33] W. J. Wiswesser: *J. Chem. Education*, **22**, 370, 418 (1945).
[34] E. J. Bowen: *Ann. Reports*, **40**, 12 (1943).

CHAPTER 4

The Periodic Classification of the Elements

Examination of the electronic configurations of the atoms of the various elements (pp. 98–101) reveals periodic recurrences of particular types of configurations as one proceeds regularly through the series of atomic numbers. In the light of present knowledge as to the roles played by the electronic arrangements in determining the properties of the elements, it is, therefore, quite obvious that the elements may be arranged in some regular fashion which will reflect resulting periodic similarities in properties. Hence it may appear that the periodic classification is merely a consequence of investigations of atomic structure and is only a convenient means for expressing these results. Such is not the case, however, for development of the periodic classification preceded the elucidation of modern atomic theory. Indeed, periodic classifications derived as results of meticulous observations on the properties of the elements and their compounds served as fundamental bases for the very evaluations of electronic configurations which ultimately supported them and placed them upon sound theoretical foundations.

Because the periodic arrangement is so obvious in the light of our present knowledge, some tendencies to overlook its origins and to accept it at face value without further inquiry may exist. It is, therefore, of importance to examine in roughly chronological order some of the more significant developments leading to such a classification before attempting to explore modern concepts relating to it. The brief summary presented here may be supplemented by reference to the numerous comprehensive accounts which are available.[1–5]

[1] F. P. Venable: *The Development of the Periodic Law*, Chemical Publishing Co., Easton, Pa. (1896).

[2] J. D. Main Smith: *Chemistry and Atomic Structure*, Ch. VI. Ernest Benn,

SIGNIFICANT DEVELOPMENTS LEADING TO THE SYSTEMATIC CLASSIFICATION OF THE ELEMENTS

Although it is conceivable that early investigators may have attempted to classify known elements shortly after their discovery and recognition as fundamental substances, all modern effort may be traced directly or indirectly to the atomic theory proposed by John Dalton (p. 5). Dalton's theory in itself contained nothing relative to such a systematic grouping, but it did provoke thought and speculation as to whether atoms of the various elements, although apparently different in properties, might be composed of the same fundamental substance and whether the marked similarities among certain elements might be traceable to their atoms.

The first of these considerations was expressed in Prout's hypothesis in 1815 (p. 5), but the second was not elucidated adequately until many years later. Fundamental as was Prout's hypothesis, it was discredited by experimentally observed deviations of atomic weights from whole numbers, and in 1860 the precise atomic weight determinations of Stas lead to its complete abandonment. It has been only within recent years that the true significance of this hypothesis has been realized (p. 36).

In 1817 Döbereiner noted that within a group of elements closely related to each other in chemical properties atomic weights are either nearly the same or else the atomic weight of the middle element is approximately the arithmetic mean of those of the other two. Thus the atomic weights of iron, cobalt, and nickel are nearly the same, whereas in the series chlorine, bromine, and iodine, the mean of the atomic weights of chlorine (35) and iodine (127), i.e., 81, is nearly the same as the atomic weight of bromine (80). These *triads* of Döbereiner represent the first reported attempt at classification.

Various modifications of Döbereiner's ideas appeared in the early part of the nineteenth century. In 1850, Pettenkofer suggested that among chemically similar elements successive differences in atomic weights amount to either some constant or to a multiple of some constant. This is, in fact, a statement that among such elements atomic weights can be derived from a modified arithmetical progres-

---

Ltd., London (1924).

[3] G. N. Quam and M. B. Quam: *J. Chem. Education*, **11**, 27, 217, 288 (1934).

[4] B. S. Hopkins: *Chapters in the Chemistry of the Less Familiar Elements*, Ch. I. Stipes Publishing Co., Champaign, Ill. (1939).

[5] M. E. Weeks: *The Discovery of the Elements*, 4th Ed., Ch. XXI. Journal of Chemical Education, Easton, Pa. (1939).

sion involving the lowest atomic weight and multiples of an integer. Thus in the series oxygen (16), sulfur (32), selenium (80), and tellurium (128), the difference between the first two is 16 and between any other two is 48, or 3 × 16. This general concept is also implicit in Cooke's statement in 1854 that triads were merely parts of series, the members of each series following an algebraic law in increase in atomic weight.

In 1857, Odling arranged the known elements into thirteen groups on the basis of similarities in chemical and physical properties, the members of each group being listed in order of atomic weights. Although this scheme placed the most closely related elements together, it showed no relationships between atomic weights and chemical characteristics. Odling's arrangement most closely resembles present-day groupings in qualitative analysis, since elements forming compounds of similar solubilities were placed together. Although probably fundamental in character, such an arrangement reflected no periodicity in properties and bore no relation to later-determined electronic configurations.

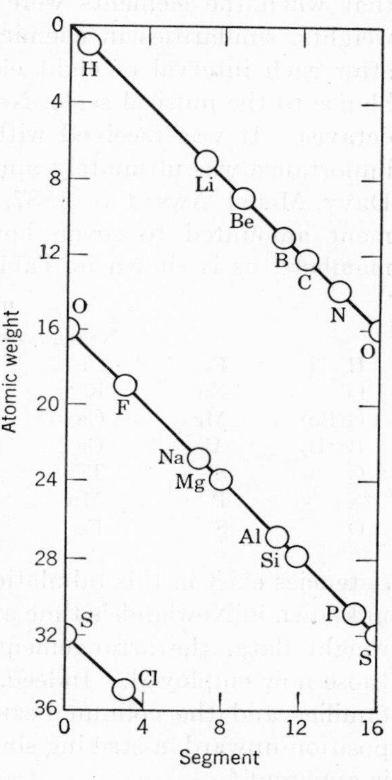

Fig. 4·1. The Telluric Screw of de Chancourtois.

The first real periodic classification, in the sense in which the term is now used, was the *Telluric Screw* proposed by de Chancourtois in 1862. Using a cylinder as a base, de Chancourtois divided its surface into sixteen equal segments (because the atomic weight of oxygen was taken as 16) and plotted atomic weights as ordinates on the genetrix. Through these atomic weight values, he drew a helix on the surface at a 45° angle to the axis. This helix crossed a given genetrix at distances from the base which were multiples of 16, and elements the atomic weights of which differed from each other by sixteen units thus fell along the same perpendicular lines. This is apparent in the portion of the Telluric Screw reproduced as a flat surface in Figure 4·1. The great similarities existing among elements lying on the same genetrix was apparent to de Chancourtois. In pointing out this periodic recurrence of properties, he stated that "properties of substances are the properties of numbers."

Of equal importance as a forerunner of modern classifications is the arrangement proposed in 1864–1866 by Newlands. Newlands noted that when the elements were placed in order of increasing atomic weights, similarities in chemical and physical properties reappeared after each interval of eight elements. Because of a fancied resemblance to the musical scale, Newlands termed this concept the law of octaves. It was received with ridicule. However, its fundamental importance was ultimately appreciated and finally recognized by the Davy Medal Award in 1887. Specifically, the Newlands arrangement amounted to seven horizontal series, each containing eight members, as is shown in Table 4·1. Although some marked inconsistencies exist in this tabulation because of the discovery of elements unknown in Newlands's time and because of inaccuracies in his atomic weight data, the arrangement bears a recognizable resemblance to those now employed. Indeed, if the table is rearranged into vertical families and the column beginning with hydrogen is displaced one position upward, a striking similarity to the Mendeléeff table (p. 116) is apparent.[6]

TABLE 4·1
NEWLANDS'S LAW OF OCTAVES

H	F	Cl	Co, Ni	Br	I	Pt, Ir
Li	Na	K	Cu	Rb	Cs	Os
G(Be)	Mg	Ca	Zn	Sr	Ba, V	Hg
Bo(B)	Al	Cr	Y	Ce, La	Ta	Tl
C	Si	Ti	In	Zr	W	Pb
N	P	Mn	As	Di, Mo	Nb	Bi
O	S	Fe	Se	Ro(Rh), Ru	Au	Th

Final evolution of the periodic classification came in 1869 as a result of the apparently independent efforts of Dimitri Mendeléeff and Lothar Meyer. Mendeléeff's approach to classification of the elements was based largely on considerations of their chemical properties whereas that of Lothar Meyer stressed their physical characteristics. Yet each developed a tabulation surprisingly similar to that of the other, and both emphasized the law of periodicity of properties with atomic weight. In clarity of presentation and in fundamental understanding of the importance of this periodicity, of the significances of odd and even series of elements, and of the transition elements, Mendeléeff went considerably beyond Lothar Meyer, and as a result the greater

[6] W. H. Taylor: *J. Chem. Education,* **26,** 491 (1949).

proportion of the credit due for such a development is usually given to him. The publications of Mendeléeff and Lothar Meyer were communicated in March[7] and December[8] of 1869, respectively.

As a consequence of periodic variations noted when such properties as atomic volume, melting point, boiling point, malleability, etc., were plotted against atomic weights, Lothar Meyer arrived at the tabulation of the elements reproduced in Figure 4·2. This arrangement of fifty-five elements into groups and subgroups is remarkably similar to the Mendeléeff arrangement shown in Figure 4·4. Lothar Meyer is probably better remembered for his atomic volume curve than for his periodic table because of the importance which atomic volumes have played in the development of chemical thought. Corrections in atomic weights and change of emphasis from atomic weight to atomic number as the criterion for the position of an element have had but little effect in altering the general shape of the curve. The complete curve based upon the latest data as given in Chapter 5 (pp. 130–131) has the same basic appearance and illustrates the same points as Lothar Meyer's original.

The proposals offered by Mendeléeff merit more detailed consideration because of their importance in influencing subsequent chemical progress. The original Mendéeleff table is reproduced in Figure 4·3. In subsequent publications, the vertical form of the original table was altered to that shown in Figure 4·4, and it is this latter form, modified only to the extent of adding a Group 0 to accommodate the inert gas elements and of including elements discovered since it was published, which has been so common and which still appears in many textbooks and reference works. The resemblances between the vertical table given in Figure 4·3 and the "long" forms now in common use should be apparent to the reader.

The breadth of Mendeléeff's understanding is remarkable in the light of the inaccuracies existent in information available to him. This is at once apparent from a consideration of the following statements, which are summarized from his early publications.[7, 9] Periodicity of properties is brought out by the arrangement; the arrangement corresponds with the valencies of the elements; the characteristics of the elements are determined by the magnitudes of their atomic weights; known atomic weights may be corrected from the positions which the elements occupy in the table; elements with very similar chemical properties have atomic weights which are nearly the same

[7] D. Mendeléeff: *J. Russ. Phys.-Chem. Soc.*, **1**, 60 (1869); *Z. Chem.*, **5**, 405 (1869).
[8] L. Meyer: *Ann.*, Supplementband **VII**, 354 (1870).
[9] D. Mendeléeff: *Ann.*, Supplementband **VIII**, 133 (1871).

I	II	III	IV	V	VI	VII	VIII	IX
	B = 11.0	Al = 27.3				?In = 113.4		Tl = 202.7
	C = 11.97	Si = 28	Ti = 48		Zr = 89.7	Sn = 117.8		Pb = 206.4
	N = 14.01	P = 30.9	V = 51.2	As = 74.9	Nb = 93.7	Sb = 122.1	Ta = 182.2	Bi = 207.5
	O = 15.96	S = 31.98	Cr = 52.4	Se = 78	Mo = 95.6	Te = 128?	W = 183.5	
	F = 19.1	Cl = 35.38		Br = 79.75		I = 126.5		
			Mn = 54.8		Ru = 103.5		Os = 198.6?	
			Fe = 55.9		Rh = 104.1		Ir = 196.7	
			Co = Ni = 58.6		Pd = 106.2		Pt = 196.7	
Li = 7.01	Na = 22.99	K = 39.04		Rb = 85.2		Cs = 132.7		
			Cu = 63.3		Ag = 107.66		Au = 196.2	
?Be = 9.3	Mg = 23.9	Ca = 39.9		Sr = 87.0		Ba = 136.8		
			Zn = 64.9		Cd = 111.6		Hg = 199.8	

Fig. 4-2. Lothar Meyer's chart of the elements.

(e.g., Os, Ir, and Pt) or which increase regularly (e.g., Li, Na, and K); the most widely diffused elements in nature are those with small atomic weights. Perhaps even more striking was Mendeléeff's boldness in predicting the existence of elements not yet discovered and in summarizing the properties which these elements should possess, all on the basis of unoccupied positions in his table. In every case, these predictions were verified exactly by subsequent researches. Thus his ekaaluminum became the gallium discovered by de Boisbaudran in 1875, his ekaboron the scandium discovered by Nilson in 1879, and his ekasilicon the germanium discovered by Winkler in 1886.

I	II	III	IV	V	VI
			Ti = 50	Zr = 90	? = 180
			V = 51	Nb = 94	Ta = 182
			Cr = 52	Mo = 96	W = 186
			Mn = 55	Rh = 104.4	Pt = 197.4
			Fe = 56	Ru = 104.4	Ir = 198
			Ni = Co = 59	Pd = 106.6	Os = 199
H = 1			Cu = 53.4	Ag = 108	Hg = 200
	Be = 9.4	Mg = 24	Zn = 65.2	Cd = 112	
	B = 11	Al = 27.4	? = 68	Ur = 116	Au = 197?
	C = 12	Si = 28	? = 70	Sn = 118	
	N = 14	P = 31	As = 75	Sb = 122	Bi = 210
	O = 16	S = 32	Se = 79.4	Te = 128	
	F = 19	Cl = 35.5	Br = 80	I = 127	
Li = 7	Na = 23	K = 39	Rb = 85.4	Cs = 133	Tl = 204
		Ca = 40	Sr = 87.6	Ba = 137	Pb = 207
		? = 45	Ce = 92		
		?Er = 56	La = 94		
		?Yt = 60	Di = 95		
		?In = 75.6	Th = 118?		

FIG. 4·3. Mendeléeff's original table of the elements.

The comparison of predicted and measured properties for the last of these as summarized in Table 4·2 is particularly revealing of Mendeléeff's grasp of the relationships existing among the elements.

Acceptance of the Mendeléeff classification may be regarded as the beginning of a true renaissance in chemical thought. For the first time variations among the properties of the elements and their compounds were fitted into a logical pattern, and it was no longer necessary to treat an element as an individual completely detached from and unrelated to its neighbors. The bases for all modern developments in chemistry were laid in the period following Mendeléeff's proposal, and the developments in atomic structure already discussed

Series	Group I — R_2O	Group II — RO	Group III — R_2O_3	Group IV RH_4 RO_2	Group V RH_3 R_2O_5	Group VI RH_2 RO_3	Group VII RH R_2O_7	Group VIII — RO_4
1	H = 1							
2	Li = 7	Be = 9.4	B = 11	C = 12	N = 14	O = 16	F = 19	
3	Na = 23	Mg = 24	Al = 27.3	Si = 28	P = 31	S = 32	Cl = 35.5	
4	K = 39	Ca = 40	= 44	Ti = 48	V = 51	Cr = 52	Mn = 55	Fe = 56, Co = 59, Ni = 59, Cu = 63
5	(Cu = 63)	Zn = 65	= 68	= 72	As = 75	Se = 78	Br = 80	
6	Rb = 85	Sr = 87	?Yt = 88	Zr = 90	Nb = 94	Mo = 96	= 100	Ru = 104, Rh = 104, Pd = 106, Ag = 108
7	(Ag = 108)	Cd = 112	In = 113	Sn = 118	Sb = 122	Te = 125	I = 127	
8	Cs = 133	Ba = 137	?Di = 138	?Ce = 140				
9								
10			?Er = 178	?La = 180	Ta = 182	W = 184		Os = 195, Ir = 197, Pt = 198, Au = 199
11	(Au = 199)	Hg = 200	Tl = 204	Pb = 207	Bi = 208			
12				Th = 231		U = 240		

FIG. 4·4. Mendeléeff's table of 1872.

in Chapters 2 and 3 resulted directly or indirectly from consideration of the regularities existing among the elements and made apparent by the periodic classification.

Subsequent developments in the classification of the elements centered largely in extensions, expansions, and only slight modifications of the Mendeléeff table with atomic weights as a basis for tabulation. Although such a basis imposed certain difficulties, among them the reversed orders in the pairs argon-potassium, cobalt-nickel,

TABLE 4·2

COMPARISON OF PREDICTED WITH MEASURED PROPERTIES

Predicted for Ekasilicon (Es) (1871)	Property	Found for Germanium (Ge) (1886)
72	Atomic weight	72.32
5.5	Specific gravity	5.47 (20°C.)
13 cc.	Atomic volume	13.22 cc.
Dirty gray	Color	Grayish white
0.073	Specific heat	0.076
White EsO_2	Heating in air	White GeO_2
Slight	Action of acids	None by HCl
EsO_2 with Na K_2EsF_6 with Na	Preparation	GeO_2 with C K_2GeF_6 with Na
Refractory, sp. gr. 4.7, mol. vol. 22 cc.	Dioxide	Refractory, sp. gr. 4.703, mol. vol. 22.16 cc.
B.p. 100°C., sp. gr. 1.9, mol. vol. 113 cc.	Tetrachloride	B.p. 86°C., sp. gr. 1.887, mol. vol. 113.35 cc.
B.p. 160°C., sp. gr. 0.96	Tetraethyl derivative	B.p. 160°C., sp. gr. < 1.00

and tellurium-iodine, it was not until Moseley's development of the atomic number concept (p. 12) and subsequent realization that the properties of the elements are dependent upon the number and arrangement of the electrons within their atoms that a true basis for systematic arrangement became apparent. The modern periodic system is, of course, based upon such a concept, but the steps leading to its development have been both interesting and illustrative of the trends in chemical thinking.

BASES OF A PERIODIC CLASSIFICATION

By its very nature, a periodic system reflects periodic variations in properties as a function of some arbitrarily selected base. Originally, this base was atomic weight since atomic weight was the one property known at that time which reflected Dalton's atomic theory. The fallacy in retaining atomic weight as a base is of course apparent from the considerations offered in Chapters 2 and 3, for atomic weight, being a nuclear property, has but little effect upon chemical characteristics. Atomic number, on the other hand, measures the number of electrons, and, since chemical and physical properties are ordinarily governed by electrons, these properties as well. The energy demands relative to the filling of quantum levels (p. 93) of course produce periodic recurrences of type configurations and account for periodicity when atomic number is used as a basis.

If periodicity in properties is a function of electronic configurations rather than mass, one may well ask why a periodic table based upon atomic weights could ever have been devised. The answer to this lies in the regularities in the building up of atoms of greater and greater complexities as already discussed (p. 52). As protons are added (increasing the charge), neutrons must also be added (increasing the mass) in order to produce nuclei of maximum stabilities. Of course the rate of increase in mass is greater than the rate of increase of charge because of the increasingly larger numbers of neutrons required to impart stabilities to nuclei containing larger numbers of protons, but the two properties change in the same direction except in the isolated cases where the excessive abundances of heavier isotopes produce unimportant reversals in average atomic weights. It is apparent, therefore, that atomic weight and number bases lead to the same result.

Since the periodic system is a reflection of variations in properties, it is of interest to note what properties do show such variations. It is apparent from the preceding discussion that only those characteristics which are related to the actual *arrangement* of the electrons can vary periodically with atomic numbers. Properties which depend only on the total *number* of electrons can show no such variations. The vast majority of the chemical and physical properties are dependent upon electronic configurations, and only comparatively few, such as x-ray spectra (p. 12), are dependent upon numbers of electrons alone. Among the properties which are periodic in character are atomic volume, atomic radius, ionic radius, ionization potential, electron affinity, electronegativity, standard oxidation potential of the free element, oxidation state or number, ion mobility, melting point, boiling point, compressibility, optical spectrum, magnetic behavior, heat of formation of a given compound type, parachor, hardness, and refractive index. Certain of these are considered in detail in subsequent chapters. The comprehensive discussion given by Harkins and Hall[10] may be consulted with profit in this connection.

One may well wonder whether any predictions as to the magnitudes of periodic variations can be made. In terms of our present state of knowledge, it is manifestly impossible for one to make exact predic-

[10] W. D. Harkins and R. E. Hall: *J. Am. Chem. Soc.*, **38**, 169 (1916).

tions as to such magnitudes, but it is possible to approach them rather closely. In an extremely interesting and searching article, Hsueh and Chiang[11] consider any periodic property to consist of two factors, one a periodic factor determining the periodicity and the other an amplitude factor causing numerical change in the property within a given family of elements. The periodicity factor is, in turn, a function of valency or outermost electronic configuration, and the amplitude factor is a function of energy state and atomic radius. The periodicity function may be either a maximum at the center of a period or a minimum at the center. Periodic properties of the increasing class embrace atomic frequency, melting point, boiling point, etc., whereas those of the decreasing class are atomic volume, atomic radius, atomic parachor, etc. Correspondingly, the amplitude function may amount to either parallel or crossing combination, that is, the amplitudes for the sixteen periodic families may simultaneously increase or decrease or they may change in reverse order for positive and negative elements. Properties involving parallel combination are such ones as atomic volume, atomic radius, ionic radius, and ionization potentials, whereas those involving crossing combination are such ones as melting point, boiling point, and hardness. Periodic properties may therefore be classified, according to Hsueh and Chiang, into the four general types: parallel amplitude, increasing periodicity; parallel amplitude, decreasing periodicity; crossing amplitude, increasing periodicity; and crossing amplitude, decreasing periodicity.

By combining periodicity and amplitude functions, Hsueh and Chiang derive a property equation

$$P = k\frac{Z^\alpha}{n^\beta}\left[\int V\,dZ\right]^\gamma \tag{4.1}$$

from which the numerical magnitude of a property P is related to the atomic number Z of the element in question in terms of valence V, a function of the periodic factor γ, the principal quantum number n, and two parameters α and β, which are constants for a given family of elements but different for different families. By means of this equation and a consideration of the types of periodic properties already mentioned, theoretical variations in properties are evaluated and found to be in reasonably good agreement with observed variations. Certainly curves plotted from theoretical values so calculated against atomic number agree closely with similar ones drawn from measured values.

[11] Chin-Fang Hsueh and Ming-Chien Chiang: *J. Chinese Chem. Soc.*, **5**, 263 (1937). (In English.)

ESSENTIALS OF A PERIODIC CLASSIFICATION

Although the Mendeléeff arrangement served well and contributed to many significant developments, its geometry imposed many weaknesses and so-called defects, and a number of changes designed to circumvent these difficulties have been proposed. The major objection offered to the Mendeléeff tabulation centers in the inability of that arrangement to reflect the electronic configurations of the atoms of the elements. Inconsistences in oxidation state predictions, marked differences in the properties of elements placed in the same group (e.g., Mn vs. Cl, or Na vs. Cu), dissimilarities between subgroups within a given group in general, incompleteness in the separation of metals from non-metals, and inconsistencies in the grouping of materials giving colorless and diamagnetic ions as opposed to those giving colored and paramagnetic ions all depend upon the absence of exact electronic configuration relationships. Difficulties in the inclusion of hydrogen, the lanthanides and actinides, and the transition elements as a group stem from the same source. Much discussion has been devoted to those "defects" and to suggestions for remedying them.[12, 13]

The ideal periodic arrangement, therefore, should be one based upon electronic configurations. It should be of such form that not only are these configurations shown clearly and correctly but also the characteristics of the elements which are dependent upon these configurations are presented with equal clarity. Although it is manifestly easy to record electronic configurations concisely and correctly, it is equally difficult to devise a geometrical figure which will satisfy both the criteria listed with equal exactness. Naturally, geometrical arrangements which are planar are preferred because they are easily visualized from a printed page or chart; so a further limitation as to dimension is also imposed. Any working modification of the Mendeléeff chart must embrace these principles.

MODERN TRENDS IN PERIODIC CLASSIFICATION

The literature is replete with suggested (and discarded) modifications of the Mendeléeff periodic table.[14] In fact so many modifications have appeared that one is tempted to conclude that practically every author has his own concept of what a workable arrangement

[12] E. W. Zmaczynski: *J. Chem. Education*, **14**, 232 (1937).

[13] W. F. Luder: *J. Chem. Education*, **20**, 21 (1943).

[14] G. N. Quam and M. B. Quam: *J. Chem. Education*, **11**, 27, 217, 288 (1934). Also innumerable references subsequent to 1934, particularly in the *Journal of Chemical Education*.

must be. Unfortunately, the majority of the tabulations proposed are either unwieldy or utterly worthless, and only a few valuable suggestions have been made. Geometry does not permit of an arrangement which is sufficiently ideal to serve all the required purposes equally well. Thus the many three-dimensional models, embracing globes, helices, cones, prisms, castles, etc., are interesting but lacking in utility. To a lesser extent, the more involved two-dimensional arrangements do little toward solving the difficulty, and essentially the only suggestions as to modifications which are truly constructive are those centering in reflection of electronic configurations.

Certainly the most useful of these modifications, and at the same time one of the earliest to be proposed, is the so-called long or Bohr table, a modern version of which is given in Figure 4·5. Properly speaking, the term "long" is preferred because, although the table as constructed reflects the Bohr theory of electronic arrangements, it was not devised as such by Bohr himself. In fact, so many people have contributed to its development that no single person can or should receive sole credit. The table was used in simple form by Rang in 1893 and by Werner in 1905 and has since been championed by Bury and many others.

Mechanically, the long form is derived from the original Mendeléeff form by merely extending each of the long periods and breaking the short periods to accomodate the transition series in the long periods. When this is done, electronic arrangements are then reflected since, as one proceeds from left to right, electrons are added successively and a regular order is preserved. Placing the inert gas elements at the extreme right then gives a logical completion for each series of s and p electrons. Furthermore, a logical separation of subgroups is also effected, and the elements found in any vertical column in this tabulation are true analogs of each other.

The advantages of the "long" form are legion.[15] Not only does it relate the position of an element to the electronic arrangement in its atoms, but it also reflects similarities, differences, and trends in chemical properties more clearly than its predecessor. It is an easy chart to remember and to reproduce. It avoids the erroneous interpretations often resulting from the Mendeléeff system. In short, it provides a clearer means of correlating the mass of information which has accumulated about the elements and their compounds. Frequent reference to the "long" form is made in subsequent chapters of this book, and the discussions of properties in Chapters 5 and 6 illustrate its applications.

[15] L. S. Foster: *J. Chem. Education,* **16,** 409 (1939).

Period \ Group	Ia	IIa	IIIa	IVa	Va	VIa	VIIa	VIII			Ib	IIb	IIIb	IVb	Vb	VIb	VIIb	0
1 1s	1 H																1 H	2 He
2 2s2p	3 Li	4 Be											5 B	6 C	7 N	8 O	9 F	10 Ne
3 3s3p	11 Na	12 Mg											13 Al	14 Si	15 P	16 S	17 Cl	18 A
4 4s3d 4p	19 K	20 Ca	21 Sc	22 Ti	23 V	24 Cr	25 Mn	26 Fe	27 Co	28 Ni	29 Cu	30 Zn	31 Ga	32 Ge	33 As	34 Se	35 Br	36 Kr
5 5s4d 5p	37 Rb	38 Sr	39 Y	40 Zr	41 Nb	42 Mo	43 Tc	44 Ru	45 Rh	46 Pd	47 Ag	48 Cd	49 In	50 Sn	51 Sb	52 Te	53 I	54 Xe
6 6s (4f) 5d 6p	55 Cs	56 Ba	57 * La	72 Hf	73 Ta	74 W	75 Re	76 Os	77 Ir	78 Pt	79 Au	80 Hg	81 Tl	82 Pb	83 Bi	84 Po	85 At	86 Rn
7 7s (5f) 6d	87 Fr	88 Ra	89 ** Ac															

* Lanthanide Series 4f	58 Ce	59 Pr	60 Nd	61	62 Sm	63 Eu	64 Gd	65 Tb	66 Dy	67 Ho	68 Er	69 Tm	70 Yb	71 Lu
** Actinide Series 5f	90 Th	91 Pa	92 U	93 Np	94 Pu	95 Am	96 Cm	97 Bk	98 Cf					

FIG. 4·5. Conventional long form of the periodic system.

In spite of its usefulness, the "long" form of the periodic table is not free from defect.[13] It suffers from its inability to reflect exact distribution of electrons among all the orbitals (*s*, *p*, *d*, *f*, etc.). It suggests no absolutely clean-cut position for hydrogen. It is mechanically incapable, as drawn, of including elements of the inner transition type. In Figure 4·5, the last two of these difficulties have been only incompletely resolved. Hydrogen is placed with both the alkali metals (Group Ia) and the halogens (Group VIIb), a dual positioning which reflects both its ability to lose an electron and its electronic structure as being one electron short of an inert gas arrangement. The inner transition elements are placed in two series (lanthanide and actinide) at the bottom of the table, the elements lanthanum and actinium being given places as analogs of scandium and yttrium in the sixth and seventh periods. Admittedly, these are unsatisfactory compromises.

Certain proposed modifications of the long form which are designed to overcome at least some of these difficulties may be mentioned. For example, Luder[13] has described in detail what amounts to a modern extension of Gardner's chart (Figure 3·6, p. 105). In such an arrangement, the position given an element is determined by the quantum position assumed by the electron which distinguishes that element from the element of atomic number one unit less. This electron Luder calls the "differentiating" electron. In effect, such a procedure groups like elements together by its emphasis upon electronic configurations, but in its original form it does so at the expense of preserving a sequence of atomic numbers. By means of a slight rearrangement, amounting only to writing symbols for elements beyond the third period on more than a single line, Babor[16] has resolved this difficulty. The Luder-Babor chart in its final form approximates the Gardner arrangement mentioned above. It is debatable whether such a chart is really a periodic table in the strict sense of the word. Its major advantages embrace separation of the elements into types and inclusion in a logical fashion of the inner transition elements.

In a measure, the "long" form may be expanded by merely spreading the elements out to accomplish the same end. This has been done in a variety of ways, for example, in the conical chart of Zmaczynski[12] and the triangular chart of Wagner and Booth.[17] It is obvious that two-dimensional geometry seriously hampers this sort of approach and that only a limited number of useful arrangements of this type could ever be practical.

[16] J. A. Babor: *J. Chem. Education*, **21**, 25 (1944).

[17] H. A. Wagner and H. S. Booth: *J. Chem. Education*, **22**, 128 (1945).

f														d										p						s		Electron Subgroup	Period
1	2	3	4	5	6	7	8	9	10	11	12	13	14	1	2	3	4	5	6	7	8	9	10	1	2	3	4	5	6	1	2		
																														1 H	2 He	s	1
																														3 Li	4 Be	s	2
																								5 B	6 C	7 N	8 O	9 F	10 Ne	11 Na	12 Mg	sp	3
																								13 Al	14 Si	15 P	16 S	17 Cl	18 A	19 K	20 Ca	sp	4
														21 Sc	22 Ti	23 V	24 Cr	25 Mn	26 Fe	27 Co	28 Ni	29 Cu	30 Zn	31 Ga	32 Ge	33 As	34 Se	35 Br	36 Kr	37 Rb	38 Sr	spd	5
														39 Y	40 Zr	41 Nb	42 Mo	43 Tc	44 Ru	45 Rh	46 Pd	47 Ag	48 Cd	49 In	50 Sn	51 Sb	52 Te	53 I	54 Xe	55 Cs	56 Ba	spd	6
57 La	58 Ce	59 Pr	60 Nd	61	62 Sm	63 Eu	64 Gd	65 Tb	66 Dy	67 Ho	68 Er	69 Tm	70 Yb	71 Lu	72 Hf	73 Ta	74 W	75 Re	76 Os	77 Ir	78 Pt	79 Au	80 Hg	81 Tl	82 Pb	83 Bi	84 Po	85 At	86 Rn	87 Fr	88 Ra	spdf	7
89 Ac	90 Th	91 Pa	92 U	93 Np	94 Pu	95 Am	96 Cm	97 Bk	98 Cf																							f	8
Inner Transition Elements														Transition Elements								Coinage and Volatile Metals		p-valencied Metals				Non-metals	Inert Gases	Alkaline Metals		Types of Elements	

FIG. 4·6. Periodic system according to Simmons.

An unconventional and even more extensive effort toward solving the problem of electronic configurations has been made by Simmons.[18] In effect, the Simmons arrangement, as reproduced in composite form in Figure 4·6, amounts to a reversed Gardner-Luder-Babor arrangement, with the metals of Group IIa occupying the end positions at the extreme right in accordance with the completion of *ns* orbitals. Such a tabulation is advantageous in that the atomic number sequence is preserved and that elements of like structures and properties are grouped together. Its advantages are largely those of the Luder-Babor arrangement, and its disadvantages are largely those imposed by the unusual reversed order. It is, however, quite useful in predicting the electronic configurations of the atoms of almost any chosen element.

The reader will recognize that in none of these cases has the exact order of electronic arrangements (Table 3·4, p. 98) been reflected. This is of course due to the closeness with which the various quantum sublevels approach each other among the heavier elements and to the fact that the energies of such levels do not decrease in an exactly parallel fashion as atomic numbers increase. Thus irregular configurations which no arrangement can predict or accomodate arise. In the last analysis, this seems unimportant since the small differences in energy which cause these irregularities are insufficient to alter the characteristics of the elements (p. 97). Surely positioning of the element to indicate its relationship to its immediate neighbors is of greater significance, and to this end there seems to be but little reason for utilizing the involved modifications mentioned above in preference to the simpler "long" form. As Wiswesser points out, arguments relative to ideal arrangements are inconclusive.[19]

CONVENTIONS RELATIVE TO PERIODIC CLASSIFICATIONS

For many years, it has been customary to divide the elements into nine periodic groups and to subdivide all these groups except 0 (the inert gas group) and VIII (the ferrous and platinum metal group) into subgroups or families. The families have ordinarily been designated as "A" and "B." A certain lack of consistency in the designation of A and B families characterizes all except those in Groups I and II. Certain authorities have preferred to extend the A families through the transition series to Group VIII and then include all elements after Group VIII in a given period in the B families. Others have preferred to place the transition, copper group, and zinc group elements in B

[18] L. M. Simmons: *J. Chem. Education*, **24**, 588 (1947); **25**, 658 (1948).

[19] W. J. Wiswesser: *J. Chem. Education*, **22**, 314 (1945).

families and all others in A families. The first of these conventions is the more widely accepted and is the one followed in this book. Actually what one does in this connection is of but little real importance, for one should use more precise family designations than family numbers when discussing the elements.

By common agreement, periodic arrangements are broken up into horizontal *periods*. Each period is characterized by a principal quantum number which describes the s and p levels filled when that period is completed with an inert gas element. Thus, in the second period, the $2s$ and $2p$ orbitals are completely occupied, in the third period, the $3s$ and $3p$, and so on. The older term *series* was applied to the short Mendeléeff form, short and long series being used to distinguish between 8-element and 18- or 32-element arrangements.

IN CONCLUSION

It will be obvious that no attempt has been made in this chapter to discuss comprehensively the wide variety of periodic tables which have been described. The attempt has been, on the contrary, to present something of the mechanics and bases of the periodic classification and to indicate its general utility. Specific applications and illustrations of what can be done with the table will be found in subsequent chapters.

SUGGESTED SUPPLEMENTARY REFERENCES

H. T. Briscoe: *The Structure and Properties of Matter*, Ch. III. McGraw-Hill Book Co., New York (1935).

K. Seubert (Ed.): *Das natürliche System der chemischen Elemente*, Vol. 68 of Ostwald's *Klassiker der exakten Wissenschaften*. Verlag von Wilhelm Englemann, Leipzig (1895). Collection of reprints of papers by Lothar Meyer (1864–1869) and Dimitri Mendeléeff (1869–1871).

F. P. Venable: *The Development of the Periodic Law*, Chemical Publishing Co., Easton, Pa. (1896).

J. D. Main Smith: *Chemistry and Atomic Structure*, Ch. VI. Ernest Benn, Ltd., London (1924).

G. N. Quam and M. B. Quam: *J. Chem. Education*, **11**, 27, 217, 288 (1934).

B. S. Hopkins: *Chapters in the Chemistry of the Less Familiar Elements*, Ch. I. Stipes Publishing Co., Champaign, Ill. (1939).

M. E. Weeks: *The Discovery of the Elements*, 4th Ed., Ch. XXI. Journal of Chemical Education, Easton, Pa. (1939).

CHAPTER 5

Characteristics Dependent upon the Extranuclear Structures

I. General

The chemical characteristics of the elements and their compounds, and in a large measure the physical characteristics as well, are determined by the extranuclear structures of the atoms and ions from which they are derived. More specifically, these characteristics are determined largely by the electrons in the highest quantum levels (i.e., the "outermost" electrons) since electrons in lower ("underlying") levels ordinarily are not directly involved and exert no more than modifying effects. It follows then that a particular set of properties will characterize all elements (or compounds), the atoms (ions or molecules) of which possess a given type of electronic arrangement. While this is true in substance, it is not true in exact detail. Admittedly, the characteristics of pure substances of similar electronic arrangements are closely parallel, but there are significant differences and variations in properties which require explanation on other bases.

Although a complete understanding of all such deviations and variations is desirable, information of such a comprehensive nature is beyond the scope of this presentation. There are, however, certain factors such as size relationships, attraction for and repulsion of electrons, and magnetic behaviors which can be approached with profit in providing a foundation for such an understanding. It is the purpose of this chapter to discuss such topics. In subsequent chapters, the utilities of the concepts developed will be considered in some detail.

SIZE RELATIONSHIPS

An inevitable consequence of the development of the atomic theory was the assignment of sizes to atomic and ionic particles. The early view that such particles be considered as rigid spheres in contact with each other in solid substances led logically to the concept that each particle has a definite volume, diameter, and radius. On this basis, it was then possible to develop systematic crystal chemistry and to relate many properties to differences in the sizes of such rigid spheres.

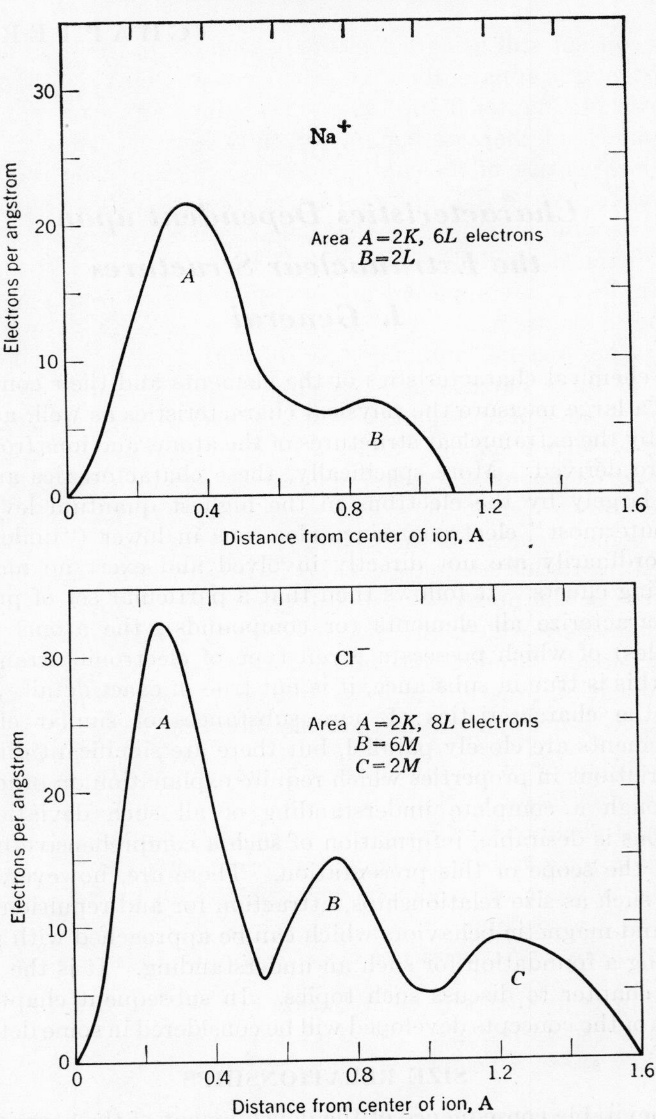

FIG. 5·1. Radial distribution curves for sodium and chloride ions in sodium chloride.

This concept still has great utility, although, in the light of present knowledge, it is apparently a pictorial concept which is far from exact. As shown in Chapter 3 (pp. 88–91), it is impossible to represent the electronic cloud characterizing an atom or ion accurately in terms of any model because of the continuously varying intensity of the cloud. However, it is true that the average electron density in such a cloud reaches maximum values at rather definite distances from the nucleus. These distances, which correspond to the positions of the principal quantum levels, are apparent in radial distribution curves of the type included in Figure 5·1.[1] The concept of distance from the nucleus is then a rather real one, and, if one considers the electron cloud about an atomic or ionic particle as a sphere of influence, one may readily develop the idea of an atomic or ionic radius as a means of expressing the size of such a sphere. Indeed, he may even extend this concept to the development of crystal models in terms of balls of various relative sizes. Yet it must be recognized that such an approach carries some element of artificiality, and it cannot, therefore, be expected to provide adequate answers for all problems which may arise.

Because of the presence of fluctuating electron clouds and because of the influences which external conditions have upon the intensities of such clouds, atomic and ionic dimensions will vary with both environment and method of measurement. Among the factors upon which such dimensions depend are the following:[2]

1. Multiplicity of the bond, i.e., whether the bond is single, double, or triple, if covalent in character.
2. Relative amounts of covalent and ionic bonding.
3. Oxidation numbers of the materials concerned.
4. The number of neighbors with which the particle under consideration is associated.
5. Repulsion of particles not directly bonded to each other.

It is apparent that any combination of these factors may produce significant size variations. Although such variations are numerically small, they are of considerable relative importance.

Atomic and molecular volumes

Certainly one of the earliest approaches to assignment of sizes lay in the concept of *atomic* and *molecular volumes*. By definition, the atomic volume is given by the ratio of gram atomic weight to density and the molecular volume by the ratio of gram molecular (or formula)

[1] R. J. Havighurst: *Phys. Rev.*, **29**, 1 (1927).

[2] J. A. Campbell: *J. Chem. Education*, **23**, 525 (1946).

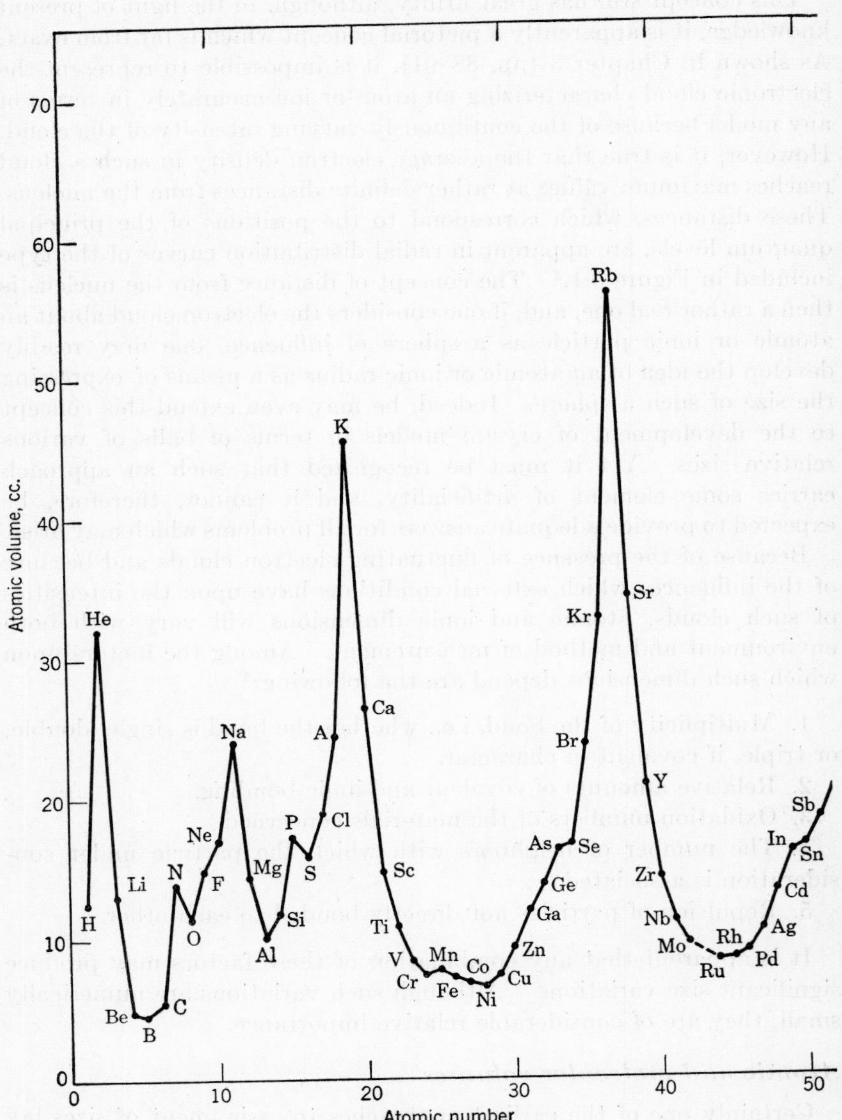

FIG. 5.2. The atomic volumes of the elements.

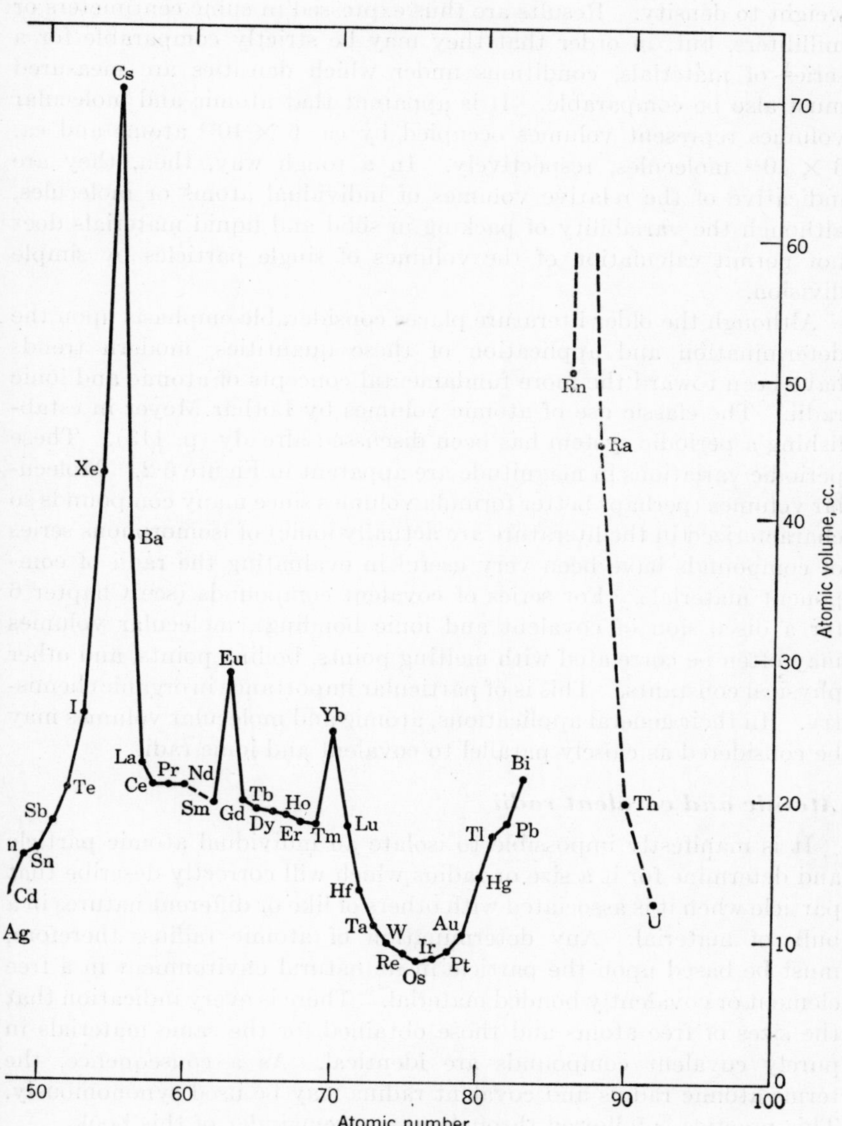

FIG. 5·2 (*Continued*).

weight to density. Results are thus expressed in cubic centimeters or milliliters, but, in order that they may be strictly comparable for a series of materials, conditions under which densities are measured must also be comparable. It is apparent that atomic and molecular volumes represent volumes occupied by ca. 6×10^{23} atoms and ca. 6×10^{23} molecules, respectively. In a rough way, then, they are indicative of the relative volumes of individual atoms or molecules, although the variability of packing in solid and liquid materials does not permit calculation of the volumes of single particles by simple division.

Although the older literature places considerable emphasis upon the determination and application of these quantities, modern trends have been toward the more fundamental concepts of atomic and ionic radii. The classic use of atomic volumes by Lothar Meyer in establishing a periodic system has been discussed already (p. 113). These periodic variations in magnitude are apparent in Figure 5·2. Molecular volumes (perhaps better formula volumes since many compounds so characterized in the literature are actually ionic) of isomorphous series of compounds have been very useful in evaluating the radii of component materials. For series of covalent compounds (see Chapter 6 for a discussion of covalent and ionic bonding), molecular volumes may often be correlated with melting points, boiling points, and other physical constants. This is of particular importance in organic chemistry. In their general applications, atomic and molecular volumes may be considered as closely parallel to covalent and ionic radii.

Atomic and covalent radii

It is manifestly impossible to isolate an individual atomic particle and determine for it a size or radius which will correctly describe that particle when it is associated with others of like or different natures in a bulk of material. Any determination of atomic radius, therefore, must be based upon the particle in its natural environment in a free element or covalently bonded material. There is every indication that the sizes of free atoms and those obtained for the same materials in purely covalent compounds are identical. As a consequence, the terms atomic radius and covalent radius may be used synonomously. This practice is followed throughout the remainder of this book.

The methods of x-ray, electron, and neutron diffraction and of band spectroscopy provide data for interatomic distances in free elements and in covalent molecules. If it is then assumed that the atoms involved are effective spheres which just contact each other in the solid state, such measured interatomic distances may be apportioned between any two atoms involved and atomic or covalent radii determined. In applying such considerations to covalent materials containing unlike atoms, some predetermined radius which may be used for comparison is essential. Thus Huggins,[3] in deriving the first published set of atomic or covalent radii, assumed the radius of the sulfur atom to be 1.05 A and used this value to determine other radii from measured interatomic distances in covalent crystals of the zinc sulfide type.* For a free element or a material containing like atoms, half the measured interatomic distance provides the desired radius.

Experiment shows a remarkable constancy in covalent radius for a particular element, provided the multiplicity of the bond remains the same. For example, the single-bond carbon to carbon distance in the diamond is 1.542 A (radius of carbon = 0.771 A) whereas in a large number of saturated hydrocarbons it varies between 1.52 and 1.55 A.[4] Similarly, values for other materials are in like agreement. It appears, furthermore, that the assumption of additivity among such radii is also valid. Thus Pauling points out that, since the carbon to carbon distance in diamond is 1.542 A and the silicon to silicon distance in the free element is 2.34 A, the carbon to silicon distance in materials containing both elements should be 1.94 A.[5] Experimentally, it is 1.93 A in tetramethyl silane. This additivity also characterizes materials possessing some ionic character (p. 205), but strictly speaking it is best applied only in cases of pure covalent bonding.

The general characteristics of covalent radii and the influence of various factors on their magnitudes have been considered in detail by Pauling and Huggins.[6] A shortening of interatomic distance and concomitant decrease in radius accompany change from single bond to double bond to triple bond. This is particularly apparent with carbon where values for double- and triple-bond radii of 0.665 and 0.602 A, respectively, are to be compared with 0.771 A for a single bond. As is pointed out in the next chapter (pp. 192–215), covalent bonds associated with individual atoms differ both in number and in dis-

[3] M. L. Huggins: *Phys. Rev.*, **21**, 205 (1923); **28**, 1086 (1926).

* In the zinc sulfide mineral wurtzite, each atom is surrounded tetrahedrally by four other atoms. This arrangement, which is common to a wide variety of materials, is one of the basic crystallographic arrangements. It is referred to as the zinc sulfide, or wurtzite structure. The diamond and sphalerite structures are very similar.

[4] L. Pauling: *The Nature of the Chemical Bond*, 2nd Ed., p. 161. Cornell University Press, Ithaca (1940).

[5] *Ibid.*, p. 163.

[6] L. Pauling and M. L. Huggins: *Z. Krist.*, **87**, 205 (1934).

tribution in space. These factors are reflected in the magnitudes of atomic radii, different sets of values being necessary for tetrahedral, square, octahedral, etc., types of arrangements. For non-metal atoms, so-called normal valence radii are commonly employed. These are the radii associated with atoms in compounds where the number of covalent bonds for the species in question is given by the usual negative oxidation number (1 for the halogens, 2 for oxygen, etc.). Such radii are often tetrahedral radii, although significant deviation from the tetrahedral is sometimes noted. A comparison of radii such as that made in Table 5·1 emphasizes these points.

TABLE 5·1

COMPARISON OF MAGNITUDES OF VARIOUS TYPES OF COVALENT RADII

						B	C	N	O	F
Tetrahedral						0.89	0.77	0.74	0.74	0.72
Normal valence						0.89	0.77	0.74	0.74	0.72
						Al	Si	P	S	Cl
Tetrahedral						1.26	1.17	1.10	1.04	0.99
Normal valence							1.17	1.10	1.04	0.99
	Fe^{II}	Co^{II}	Ni^{II}	Cu	Zn	Ga	Ge	As	Se	Br
Tetrahedral				1.35	1.31	1.26	1.22	1.18	1.14	1.11
Normal valence							1.22	1.21	1.17	1.14
Square				1.32(II)						
Octahedral	1.23	1.32	1.39							
	Ru^{II}	Rh^{II}	Pd^{II}	Ag	Cd	In	Sn	Sb	Te	I
Tetrahedral				1.53	1.48	1.44	1.40	1.36	1.32	1.28
Normal valence							1.40	1.41	1.37	1.33
Octahedral	1.33	1.43	1.50	1.49(III)						
	Os^{II}	Ir^{II}	Pt^{II}	Au	Hg	Tl	Pb	Bi		
Tetrahedral				1.50	1.48	1.47	1.46	1.46		
Normal valence							1.46	1.51		
Square				1.31(III)						
Octahedral	1.33	1.43	1.50	1.49(III)						

In a table of atomic radii which is useful for the entire group of elements, values for metals and non-metals must be strictly compatible. For many of the metals, covalent compounds are difficult to find, and the use of values based upon interatomic distances in any other type of compound is questionable practice. However, Pauling[7, 8] has shown that metallic and covalent radii are so closely related that they

[7] L. Pauling: *Phys. Rev.*, **54**, 899 (1938).

[8] L. Pauling: *J. Am. Chem. Soc.*, **69**, 542 (1947).

Ia	IIa	IIIa	IVa	Va	VIa	VIIa	VIII	VIII	VIII	Ib	IIb	IIIb	IVb	Vb	VIb	VIIb	0
1 H																1 H	2 He
3 Li 1.225	4 Be 0.889											5 B 0.80	6 C 0.771	7 N 0.74	8 O 0.74	9 F 0.72	10 Ne
11 Na 1.572	12 Mg 1.364											13 Al 1.248	14 Si 1.173	15 P 1.10	16 S 1.04	17 Cl 0.994	18 A
19 K 2.025	20 Ca 1.736	21 Sc 1.439	22 Ti 1.324	23 V 1.224	24 Cr 1.172	25 Mn 1.168	26 Fe 1.165	27 Co 1.157	28 Ni 1.149	29 Cu 1.173	30 Zn 1.249	31 Ga 1.245	32 Ge 1.223	33 As 1.21	34 Se 1.17	35 Br 1.142	36 Kr
37 Rb 2.16	38 Sr 1.914	39 Y 1.616	40 Zr 1.454	41 Nb 1.342	42 Mo 1.291	43 Tc	44 Ru 1.241	45 Rh 1.247	46 Pd 1.278	47 Ag 1.339	48 Cd 1.413	49 In 1.497	50 Sn 1.412	51 Sb 1.41	52 Te 1.37	53 I 1.334	54 Xe
55 Cs 2.35	56 Ba 1.981	57 La 1.690	72 Hf 1.442	73 Ta 1.343	74 W 1.299	75 Re 1.278	76 Os 1.255	77 Ir 1.260	78 Pt 1.290	79 Au 1.336	80 Hg 1.440	81 Tl 1.549	82 Pb 1.538	83 Bi 1.52	84 Po 1.53	85 At	86 Rn
87 Fr	88 Ra	89 Ac															

58 Ce 1.646	59 Pr 1.648	60 Nd 1.642	61	62 Sm 1.66	63 Eu 1.850	64 Gd 1.614	65 Tb 1.592	66 Dy 1.589	67 Ho 1.580	68 Er 1.567	69 Tm 1.562	70 Yb 1.699	71 Lu 1.557
90 Th 1.652	91 Pa	92 U 1.421	93 Np	94 Pu	95 Am	96 Cm	97 Bk	98 Cf					

0 1 2 3 A

Fig. 5·3. Chart of covalent radii of the elements.

may be used interchangeably. Accordingly, a set of compatible values obtained for metals or for covalent crystals may be compiled. In Figure 5·3, such a set[8] is presented both numerically and graphically (using circles of suitable sizes) in terms of the periodic system after the scheme of modular presentation used so effectively by Campbell.[2] It must be emphasized that these are radii characterizing the elements in the solid state.

For more extensive treatments of the subject of atomic or covalent radii, various standard references should be consulted.[9–11]

Ionic radii

By means of x-ray diffraction techniques, the interionic distances in many ionic crystals (for discussion of ionic vs. covalent or molecular crystals, see pp. 225–226) have been evaluated. Such distances may be correlated with each other and reduced to more useful terms by assuming that each ion involved has a definite radius and that the sum of such radii gives the measured distance. It is apparent that the magnitudes of individual ionic radii are thereby dependent upon the method used to apportion observed interionic distances between the ions in question. The procedure normally followed necessitates adoption of some independently determined ionic radius as a standard and assumption that this radius remains unchanged in all ionic crystals containing that species. From this fixed radius, then, others can be evaluated from experimentally determined interionic distances in binary compounds and an assumed packing of ions as rigid spheres. This is the "substitutional" procedure, first utilized by Bragg[12] but employed very extensively by subsequent investigators in the field. Obviously, it can be no more accurate than its selected base value and its assumptions. Its application is limited to materials which are truly ionic in the solid state.

Certain other approaches embodying modifications of Bragg's procedure are worthy of mention. In 1920, Landé[13] obtained a set of absolute ionic radii by the same general procedure, using as a basis the assumption that in a crystal of lithium iodide the comparatively large iodide ions contact each other, the interionic distance thus being

[9] L. Pauling: *The Nature of the Chemical Bond*, 2nd Ed., Chapter V. Cornell University Press, Ithaca (1940).

[10] O. K. Rice: *Electronic Structure and Chemical Bonding*, pp. 319–332. McGraw-Hill Book Co., New York (1940).

[11] C. W. Stillwell: *Crystal Chemistry*, Ch. II. McGraw-Hill Book Co., New York (1938).

[12] W. L. Bragg: *Phil. Mag.* [6], **40,** 169 (1920).

[13] A. Landé: *Z. Physik*, **1,** 191 (1920).

twice the iodide radius. Other ionic radii obtained by substitution are in excellent agreement with the present-day values. Using molecular refraction data, Wasastjerna[14] evaluated a corresponding set of ionic radii, individual values in which are nominally within 0.10 A of those now accepted. Using Wasastjerna's values for fluoride and oxide radii (1.33 and 1.32 A, respectively), Goldschmidt[15] determined empirical radii from measured interionic distances in ionic crystals by Bragg's procedure. Goldschmidt's values, although differing significantly in some cases from those now used, provided bases for modern crystal chemistry and the introduction of size relationships into the interpretation of properties in inorganic chemistry.

The apportionment of interionic distances has been approached theoretically by Pauling,[16] who has emphasized repeatedly that useful values for ionic radii are those which, when added together with such suitable corrections as are necessary, give the equilibrium interionic distances in crystals. Because such equilibrium distances are dependent not only upon the types of electron distributions in the ions involved but also upon the structure of the crystal in question and the ratio of cation to anion radius (radius ratio, ρ), it was necessary that Pauling base his treatment upon certain so-called standard crystals. These crystals, namely, sodium fluoride, potassium chloride, rubidium bromide, and cesium iodide, with interionic distances of 2.31, 3.14, 3.43, and 3.85 A, respectively, were selected because they possess about equal ionic character, have the same sodium chloride structure,* have essentially the same radius ratio ($\rho = 0.75$), and contain, in each case, two ions of the same inert gas type although with different nuclear charges.

Since for such isoelectronic ions radii are determined by the distributions of electrons, which in turn vary inversely with *effective* nuclear charges, evaluation of radii is dependent upon correct assignment of effective nuclear charges. This Pauling did by deducting

[14] J. A. Wasastjerna: *Z. physik. Chem.*, **101**, 193 (1922); *Soc. Sci. Fennica, Comm. Phys.-Math.*, **1** (No. 38), (1923).

[15] V. M. Goldschmidt: *Skrifter Norske Videnskaps-Akad. Oslo*, No. 2 (1926); No. 8 (1927); *Trans. Faraday Soc.*, **25**, 253 (1929).

[16] L. Pauling: *J. Am. Chem. Soc.*, **49**, 765 (1927); *Proc. Roy. Soc. (London)*, **A114**, 181 (1927); *The Nature of the Chemical Bond*, 2nd Ed., pp. 343–350, Cornell University Press, Ithaca (1940).

* The sodium chloride structure, i.e., a face-centered cubic in which each cation is surrounded octahedrally by six equally spaced anions and each anion by six equally spaced cations, is actually characteristic of all but cesium iodide. However, Pauling was able to correct the measured cesium to iodide distance to what it would be were the structure of the sodium chloride type.

from the actual nuclear charge a screening correction to take into account the modifying effects of other electrons upon those outermost in the ion. Exact calculations necessary to the evaluation of such screening constants are beyond the scope of this book but were based upon treatment of refraction data and x-ray term values. For a given crystal containing isoelectronic ions, the measured interionic distance was then apportioned between the two ions in the inverse ratio of the effective nuclear charges. Values were thus obtained for Na^+ (0.95 A), K^+ (1.33 A), Rb^+ (1.48 A), Cs^+ (1.69 A), F^- (1.36 A), Cl^- (1.81 A), Br^- (1.95 A), and I^- (2.16 A). Utilization of these values in conjunction with measured interionic distances in other crystals led to a series of values for other ions with inert gas atom arrangements. Thus the radius of the lithium ion (= 0.60 A) was calculated from a combination of the 2.00 A distance in lithium oxide with the 1.40 A oxide ion radius. In a sense, many of the values so calculated are for psuedo-ions since highly charged types such as S^{+6}, Cl^{+7}, N^{+5}, etc., have no actual existence as ionic species (p. 179). Extension of these calculations also led to radii for ions of the pseudo-inert gas (18-electron) type.

Radii so calculated are relative to those of alkali metal and halide ions but are not absolute in the sense that their sums do not always give observed interionic distances. For multivalent ions, such radii are actually those which these ions would possess if they were to keep their individual electronic distributions but behave in coulombic attraction as if they were univalent. More properly, therefore, such radii are termed *univalent radii.* Pauling has shown that *crystal radii,* which when added do express interionic distances, can be calculated from univalent radii by multiplication by an appropriate correction factor in terms of the equation

$$R_x = R_1 Z^{-2/(n'-1)} \tag{5·1}$$

where R_x and R_1 are, respectively, crystal and univalent radii, Z is the ionic charge, and n' is a repulsion exponent which is related to the repulsive forces arising from interpenetration of the two ions. For each inert gas or pseudo-inert gas type, n' has a particular value (n' = 5 for He, 7 for Ne, 9 for A or Cu^+, 10 for Kr or Ag^+, 11 for Xe or Au^+). Comparative values for univalent and crystal radii as calculated by Pauling are summarized in Figure 5·4. The close parallel between Pauling's calculated crystal radii and those determined empirically as shown in Table 5·2 is indicative of the accuracy of Pauling's considerations.

Legend: Ion / Cryst. / Univ.

	Ia	IIa	IIIa	IVa	Va	VIa	VIIa	VIII	VIII	VIII	Ib	IIb	IIIb	IVb	Vb	VIb	VIIb	0
1	H^{+1}																H^{-1} 2.08 2.08	He^{0} 0.93
2	Li^{+1} 0.60 0.60	Be^{+2} 0.31 0.44											B^{+3} 0.20 0.35	C^{+4} 0.15 0.29; C^{-4} 2.60 4.14	N^{+5} 0.11 0.25; N^{-3} 1.71 2.47	O^{+6} 0.09 0.22; O^{-2} 1.40 1.76	F^{+7} 0.07 0.19; F^{-1} 1.36 1.36	Ne^{0} 1.12
3	Na^{+1} 0.95 0.95	Mg^{+2} 0.65 0.82											Al^{+3} 0.50 0.72	Si^{+4} 0.41 0.65; Si^{-4} 2.71 3.84	P^{+5} 0.34 0.59; P^{-3} 2.12 2.79	S^{+6} 0.29 0.53; S^{-2} 1.84 2.19	Cl^{+7} 0.26 0.49; Cl^{-1} 1.81 1.81	A^{0} 1.54
4	K^{+1} 1.33 1.33	Ca^{+2} 0.99 1.18	Sc^{+3} 0.81 1.06	Ti^{+4} 0.68 0.96	V^{+5} 0.59 0.88	Cr^{+6} 0.52 0.81	Mn^{+7} 0.46 0.75				Cu^{+1} 0.96 0.96	Zn^{+2} 0.74 0.88	Ga^{+3} 0.62 0.81	Ge^{+4} 0.53 0.76; Ge^{-4} 2.72 3.71	As^{+5} 0.47 0.71; As^{-3} 2.22 2.85	Se^{+6} 0.42 0.66; Se^{-2} 1.98 2.32	Br^{+7} 0.39 0.62; Br^{-1} 1.95 1.95	Kr^{0} 1.69
5	Rb^{+1} 1.48 1.48	Sr^{+2} 1.13 1.32	Y^{+3} 0.93 1.20	Zr^{+4} 0.80 1.09	Nb^{+5} 0.70 1.00	Mo^{+6} 0.62 0.93					Ag^{+1} 1.26 1.26	Cd^{+2} 0.97 1.14	In^{+3} 0.81 1.04	Sn^{+4} 0.71 0.96; Sn^{-4} 2.94 3.70	Sb^{+5} 0.62 0.89; Sb^{-3} 2.45 2.95	Te^{+6} 0.56 0.82; Te^{-2} 2.21 2.50	I^{+7} 0.50 0.77; I^{-1} 2.16 2.16	Xe^{0} 1.90
6	Cs^{+1} 1.69 1.69	Ba^{+2} 1.35 1.53	La^{+3} 1.15 1.39								Au^{+1} 1.37 1.37	Hg^{+2} 1.10 1.25	Tl^{+3} 0.95 1.15	Pb^{+4} 0.84 1.06	Bi^{+5} 0.74 0.98			
7																		
						Ce^{+4} 1.01 1.27												

FIG. 5·4. Chart of univalent and crystal radii for inert gas and pseudo-inert gas type ions.

TABLE 5·2

VALUES FOR IONIC (CRYSTAL) RADII FOR C.N. 6

Symbol	Atomic Number	Ionic Species	Ionic Radius, A Empirical[18]	Calculated[16]
H	1	H^+		
		H^-		2.08
He	2			
Li	3	Li^+	0.78	0.60
Be	4	Be^{+2}	0.34	0.31
B	5	B^{+3}		0.20
C	6	C^{+4}	0.20	0.15
		C^{-4}		2.60
N	7	N^{+5}	0.1–0.2	0.11
		N^{-3}		1.71
O	8	O^{+6}		0.09
		O^{-2}		1.40
F	9	F^{+7}		0.07
		F^-		1.36
Ne	10			
Na	11	Na^+	0.98	0.95
Mg	12	Mg^{+2}	0.78	0.65
Al	13	Al^{+3}	0.57	0.50
Si	14	Si^{+4}	0.39	0.41
		Si^{-4}	1.98	2.71
P	15	P^{+5}	0.3–0.4	0.34
		P^{-3}		2.12
S	16	S^{+6}	0.34	0.29
		S^{-2}	1.74	1.84
Cl	17	Cl^{+7}		0.26
		Cl^-	1.81	1.81
A	18			
K	19	K^+	1.33	1.33
Ca	20	Ca^{+2}	1.06	0.99
Sc	21	Sc^{+3}	0.83	0.81
Ti	22	Ti^{+4}	0.64	0.68
V	23	V^{+4}	0.61	
		V^{+5}	0.4	0.59
Cr	24	Cr^{+3}	0.65	
		Cr^{+6}	0.34–0.4	0.52
Mn	25	Mn^{+2}	0.91	
		Mn^{+4}	0.52	
		Mn^{+7}		0.46
Fe	26	Fe^{+2}	0.83	
		Fe^{+3}	0.67	
Co	27	Co^{+2}	0.82	
		Co^{+3}	0.65*	
Ni	28	Ni^{+2}	0.78	
Cu	29	Cu^+		0.96
Zn	30	Zn^{+2}	0.83	0.74
Ga	31	Ga^{+3}	0.62	0.62

TABLE 5·2 (*Continued*)

Symbol	Atomic Number	Ionic Species	Ionic Radius, A Empirical[18]	Ionic Radius, A Calculated[16]
Ge	32	Ge^{+4}	0.44	0.53
		Ge^{-4}		2.72
As	33	As^{+5}		0.47
		As^{-3}		2.22
Se	34	Se^{+6}	0.3–0.4	0.42
		Se^{-2}	1.91	1.98
Br	35	Br^{+7}		0.39
		Br^{-}	1.96	1.95
Kr	36			
Rb	37	Rb^{+}	1.49	1.48
Sr	38	Sr^{+2}	1.27	1.13
Y	39	Y^{+3}	1.06	0.93
Zr	40	Zr^{+4}	0.87	0.80
Nb	41	Nb^{+5}		0.70
Mo	42	Mo^{+6}		0.62
		Mo^{+4}	0.68	
Tc	43			
Ru	44	Ru^{+4}	0.65	
Rh	45	Rh^{+3}	0.69	
Pd	46	Pd^{+2}	0.50*	
Ag	47	Ag^{+}	1.13	1.26
Cd	48	Cd^{+2}	1.03	0.97
In	49	In^{+3}	0.92	0.81
Sn	50	Sn^{+4}	0.74	0.71
		Sn^{-4}		2.94
Sb	51	Sb^{+5}		0.62
		Sb^{-3}		2.45
Te	52	Te^{+6}		0.56
		Te^{+4}	0.89	
		Te^{-2}		2.21
I	53	I^{+7}		0.50
		I^{+5}	0.94	
		I^{-}		2.16
Xe	54			
Cs	55	Cs^{+}	1.65	1.69
Ba	56	Ba^{+2}	1.43	1.35
La	57	La^{+3}	1.22	1.15
Ce	58	Ce^{+4}	1.02	1.01
		Ce^{+3}	1.18	
Pr	59	Pr^{+4}	1.00	
		Pr^{+3}	1.16	
Nd	60	Nd^{+3}	1.15	
	61			
Sm	62	Sm^{+3}	1.13	
Eu	63	Eu^{+3}	1.13	
Gd	64	Gd^{+3}	1.11	
Tb	65	Tb^{+3}	1.09	

TABLE 5·2 (*Continued*)

Symbol	Atomic Number	Ionic Species	Ionic Radius, A Empirical[18]	Calculated[16]
Dy	66	Dy^{+3}	1 07	
Ho	67	Ho^{+3}	1.05	
Er	68	Er^{+3}	1.04	
Tm	69	Tm^{+3}	1.04	
Yb	70	Yb^{+3}	1.00	
Lu	71	Lu^{+3}	0.99	
Hf	72	Hf^{+4}	0.86	
Ta	73	Ta^{+5}	0.73	
W	74	W^{+6}	0.68 (?)	
		W^{+4}	0.68	0.66
Re	75	Re^{+7}		
Os	76	Os^{+4}	0.67	
Ir	77	Ir^{+4}	0.66	
Pt	78	Pt^{+4}		
		Pt^{+2}	0.52	
Au	79	Au^{+}		1.37
Hg	80	Hg^{+2}	1.12	1.10
Tl	81	Tl^{+3}	1.05	0.95
		Tl^{+}	1.49	
Pb	82	Pb^{+4}	0.84	0.84
		Pb^{+2}	1.32	
		Pb^{-4}		2.15
Bi	83	Bi^{+5}		0.74
		Bi^{+3}	1.20*	
Po	84			
At	85			
Rn	86			
Fr	87			
Ra	88	Ra^{+2}	1.52*	
Ac	89	Ac^{+3}		1.11†
Th	90	Th^{+4}	1.10	0.95†
Pa	91	Pa^{+4}		0.91†
		Pa^{+3}		1.06†
U	92	U^{+4}	1.05	0.89†
		U^{+3}		1.03†
Np	93	Np^{+4}		0.88†
		Np^{+3}		1.02†
Pu	94	Pu^{+4}		0.86†
		Pu^{+3}		1.01†
Am	95	Am^{+4}		0.85†
		Am^{+3}		1.00†
Cm	96			
(Bk	97			)
(Cf	98			)

* Largely from R. W. G. Wyckoff: *The Structure of Crystals*, The Chemical Catalog Co., New York (1924).

† W. H. Zachariasen: *Phys. Rev.*, **73**, 1104 (1948).

It must not be assumed that a given ionic radius is constant in any and all crystals. A number of factors influence the magnitudes of crystal radii. Thus a decrease in the coordination number* of a particular ion is accompanied by a decrease in interionic distance or radius.[17] Goldschmidt[18] recognized this effect in his data and suggested correction factors of 1.03 and 0.93 to 0.95 for changing from coordination number 6 to 8 and 6 to 4, respectively. Pauling[16] has suggested values of similar magnitudes. It is imperative, therefore, that crystal radii be described in terms of particular coordination numbers. Since *six* is probably the most common coordination number, values are commonly given for this condition. This practice is followed in Table 5·2.

Variation in crystal radius is also produced because of the oxidation states or valences (p. 179) of the neighboring ions. Although Goldschmidt made no allowance for this effect in his data, measured interionic distance may be so corrected by multiplying by $\sqrt[n'-1]{Z_1 Z_2}$, Z_1 and Z_2 being the ionic charges in a binary compound and n' having the same significance as before (p. 138).

The effects of radius ratio (p. 137) on interionic distances and radii are more obscure and have been elucidated clearly only for the alkali metal halides.[19] In a crystal built up by a packing of rigid spheres, it can be shown that the exact arrangements which the ions assume are determined by radius ratio, as indicated in Table 5·3. For the

TABLE 5·3

CRYSTAL ARRANGEMENTS OF RIGID SPHERES *A* ABOUT SPHERE *C*

Number of *A*'s (= C.N. of *C*)	Arrangement of *A*'s	Radius Ratio, $R_C:R_A$
2	linear	up to 0.15
3	triangular	0.15 to 0.22
4	tetrahedral	0.22 to 0.41
4	planar	0.41 to 0.73
6	octahedral	0.41 to 0.73
8	cubic	0.73 and above

* Coordination number (C.N.), in the crystallographic sense, implies the number of nearest neighbors associated with the species under consideration in the crystal itself. In Chapter 7, the term coordination number is used in a chemical sense to indicate the number of groups associated through electron pair bonding with a central metal ion in a coordination compound. The two usages should always be clarified by definition and not confused.

[17] W. H. Zachariasen: *Z. Krist.*, **80**, 137 (1931).

[18] V. M. Goldschmidt: *Geochemische Verteilungsgesetze der Elemente*, **8**, 69 (1926); *Ber.*, **60**, 1263 (1927).

[19] L. Pauling: *J. Am. Chem. Soc.*, **50**, 1036 (1928); *The Nature of the Chemical Bond*, 2nd Ed., pp. 351–363, Cornell University Press, Ithaca (1940).

alkali metal halides, then, where the sodium chloride structure (C.N. = 6) persists above radius ratio 0.73, there are fewer anions than normal (6 vs. 8) packed around the cation, and there is less than the normal anion repulsion. Interionic distances are, therefore, somewhat less than would be expected in the absence of such an effect. On the other hand, as the radius ratio decreases, anions become more crowded around the cations, and mutual anion repulsion becomes important. This prevents closeness of approach and increases

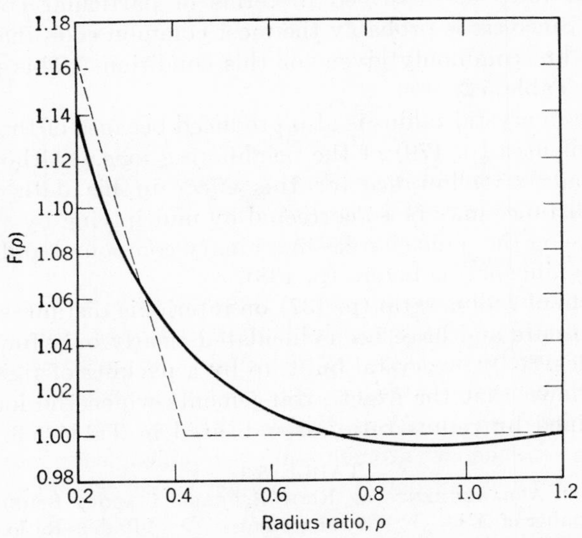

Fig. 5·5. Radius ratio correction chart. (Adapted from L. Pauling: *The Nature of the Chemical Bond*, 2nd Ed., p. 357. Cornell University Press, Ithaca [1940].)

interionic distances. Such a situation is of particular importance among lithium salts because the excessively small size of the lithium ion permits anion-anion ($\rho < 0.414$) contact in all halides but the fluoride. Even in lithium fluoride ($\rho = 0.44$) anion approach is sufficient to increase crystal distances. It is necessary, therefore, that a radius ratio correction be applied.[19] A graphic interpretation of this effect is given in Figure 5·5.[19] For more comprehensive treatments of these and other phases of the subject of ionic radii, works by Pauling[4] (Ch. X), Rice[10] (Ch. XIV), and Stillwell[11] (Ch. II) should be consulted.

Data summarized in Table 5·2 represent values for ionic radii as calculated by Pauling,[16] Goldschmidt,[15] and Zachariasen,[17] values in the latter two series having been brought up to date in terms of more recent observations. It must be emphasized that all these values apply only to ions as they are found in ionic crystals. They do not apply rigidly to solvated ions which exist in electrolytic solutions. It might be expected, as a first approximation, that the same trends would appear in solution as in the crystal lattice, but such analogies should be limited. Complete sets of solvated ionic radii are lacking.

It is sometimes convenient to be able to approximate an ionic radius. For this purpose, a number of empirical procedures have been suggested. As useful as any is that of Li and Sun[20] in which the ionic radius, R_x, is calculated from the atomic number Z, the oxidation number of the ion V, and the principal quantum number of the outer electrons n by the relation

$$R_x = 0.42Z^{-1}V^{1/3}n^3 \tag{5·2}$$

Rather good agreement is obtained, particularly if in the region lithium-fluorine n^2 is used instead of n^3.

Van der Waals radii

The non-metallic elements exist in the solid state as aggregations of molecules (p. 217). Although the bonding within a given non-metal molecule is largely covalent in character, individual molecules are held to each other by so-called van der Waals forces (p. 215) and assume equilibrium positions within the crystalline solids. Half the distance between two atoms within two molecules so located would be referred to as a van der Waals radius. Van der Waals radii are essentially non-bonded types of radii. In numerical magnitudes, they approximate ionic radii of the same elements since atoms so held present essentially the same electronic arrangements away from the bonds as do their negative ions. This is apparent if one compares values for van der Waals radii as summarized in Table 5·4[21] with

TABLE 5·4

Van der Waals Radii of Non-metals, in Angstroms*

				H	1.2
N	1.5	O	1.40	F	1.35
P	1.9	S	1.85	Cl	1.80
As	2.0	Se	2.00	Br	1.95
Sb	2.2	Te	2.20	I	2.15

* Data from L. Pauling.[21]

corresponding ionic radii listed in Table 5·2. Although van der Waals radii are somewhat variable in magnitudes, they are useful in con-

[20] S.-T. Li and C. E. Sun: *J. Chinese Chem. Soc.*, **7**, 73 (1940).

siderations of non-metal structures and those of certain organic compounds.[21, 22]

Variations and trends in size relationships

A number of significant trends in values for both covalent and ionic radii are apparent in the summaries given in Figures 5·3, 5·4, and 5·6[23] and in Table 5·2. Within any given periodic family, sizes increase with atomic number for species of comparable electronic arrangements because of the addition of extra electronic shells. Although the compensating effect of parallel increase in nuclear charge is insufficient to overcome such expansion, it is more significant among the transition elements and those which immediately follow the transition series than among other elements. As a consequence, size increases with atomic number within families containing such elements are less pronounced.

Within a given horizontal period where atomic number is increasing from family to family, there is a general decrease in the sizes of comparable species. This arises from the effects of increasing nuclear charge without addition of new electron shells. Within the transition series, size decreases of this type are especially small because added differentiating electrons (p. 123) enter inner d levels. After each transition series, there is an increase in size due to the involvement of higher quantum levels, but the sizes of materials in this region (with underlying 18-electron shells) never approach those of comparable materials with underlying 8-electron shells (compare, e.g., Ag^+, $r = 1.26$ A, with Rb^+, $r = 1.48$ A). Enhanced nuclear charges produce contracting effects upon the populous 18-electron arrangements which prevent increased size.

Parallel decreases in size with increasing nuclear charge are of particular importance among the inner transition series. In the lanthanide series, it will be recalled (p. 104) that an increase of fourteen units in nuclear charge is accompanied by the filling up of the $4f$ quantum level without alteration in the outer arrangement of $5s^2 5p^6 5d^{0 \text{ or } 1} 6s^2$ for the neutral atoms. A parallel decrease in size is thus indicated since there is no compensation for increased nuclear charge. This size decrease is known as the *lanthanide contraction.* It is apparent not only in atomic radii but also in the radii of ions of

[21] L. Pauling: *The Nature of the Chemical Bond*, 2nd Ed., pp. 187–193. Cornell University Press, Ithaca (1940).

[22] W. H. Rodebush: Abstracts of papers presented at 110th Meeting of the American Chemical Society, p. 9P. September 1946.

[23] T. Moeller: *J. Chem. Education*, **19**, 428 (1942).

TABLE 5·5
SIZE RELATIONSHIPS AMONG THE GROUP IIIA ELEMENTS

Symbol	Z	Atomic Volume, cc.	Atomic* Radius, A	Molecular Volumes, cc.				Radius of R^{+3} in A	
				$R_2(SO_4)_3 \cdot 8H_2O$	R_2O_3				
					A Type	*B* Type	*C* Type	Empirical	Calculated
Sc	21	14.79	1.439				35.53	0.83	0.681†
Y	39	20.46	1.616	240.8			45.13	1.06	0.827
La	57	22.43	1.690		50.28		(47 ca.)	1.22	1.004†
Ce	58	20.70	1.646		47.89			1.18	0.939†
Pr	59	20.79	1.648	253.9	46.65			1.16	0.910
Nd	60	20.62	1.642	252.4	46.55	(51 ca.)		1.15	0.900
Sm	62	21.70	1.66	247.9		46.9	48.38	1.13	0.872
Eu	63	29.00	1.850	247.3		46.5	48.28	1.13	0.870
Gd	64	19.79	1.614	246.4		(43 ca.)	47.58	1.11	0.862
Tb	65	19.11	1.592				46.38	1.09	0.845†
Dy	66	18.97	1.589	242.8			45.49	1.07	0.836
Ho	67	18.65	1.580	241.1			44.89	1.05	0.826
Er	68	18.29	1.567	239.3			44.38	1.04	0.818
Tm	69	18.12	1.562				44.11	1.04	0.812†
Yb	70	24.76	1.699	235.1			42.5	1.00	0.790
Lu	71	17.96	1.557	234.7			42.25	0.99	0.787

* Data from Pauling.[8]
† Based upon oxides only.

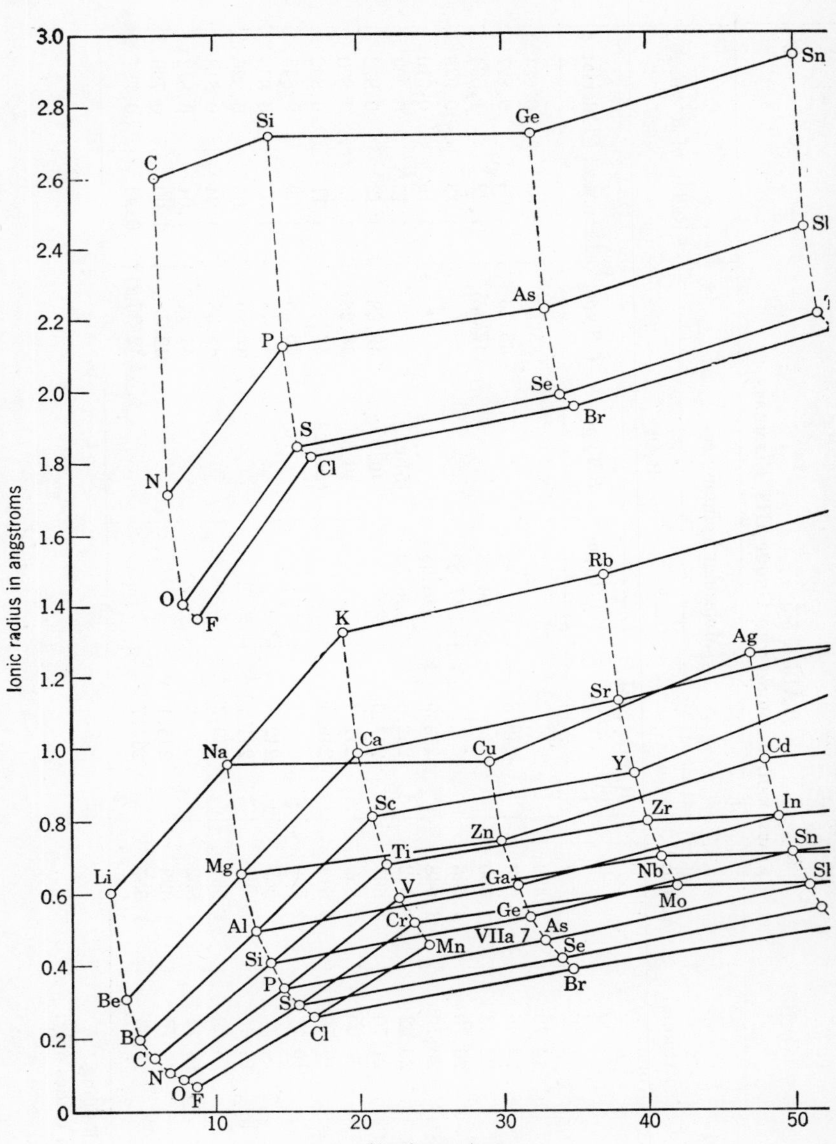

FIG. 5·6. Graphic representation of ionic radii. (Redrawn from T. Moeller: *J. Chem. Education*, **19**, 428 [1942].)

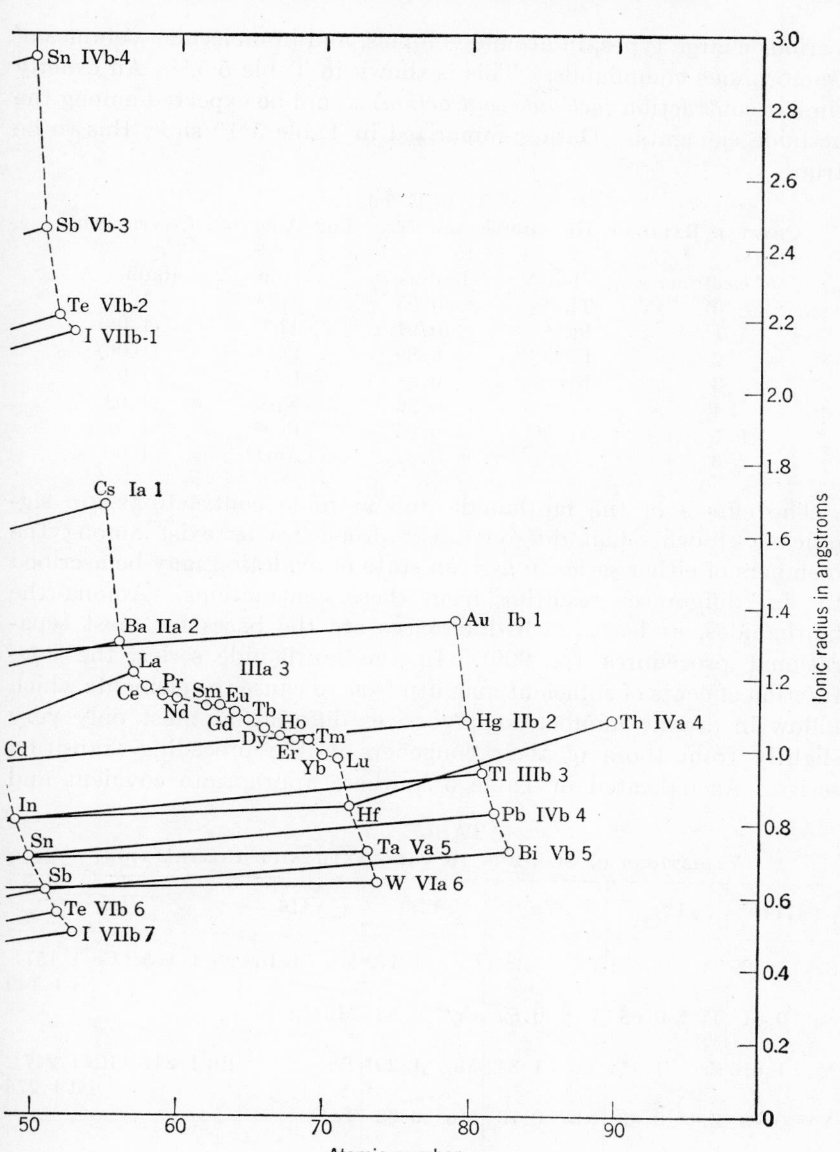

FIG. 5·6 (*Continued*).

various charge types, in atomic volumes, and in molecular volumes of isomorphous compounds. This is shown in Table 5·5.[24] An exactly similar contraction (*actinide contraction*) would be expected among the actinide elements. Data summarized in Table 5·6[25] show this to be true.

TABLE 5·6

CRYSTAL RADII OF HEAVIER ELEMENTS. THE ACTINIDE CONTRACTION

	+4		+3	
5f electrons	Ion	Radius, A	Ion	Radius, A
0	Th^{+4}	0.95	Ac^{+3}	1.11
1	Pa^{+4}	(0.91)	Th^{+3}	(1.08)
2	U^{+4}	0.89	Pa^{+3}	(1.06)
3	Np^{+4}	0.88	U^{+3}	1.04
4	Pu^{+4}	0.86	Np^{+3}	1.02
5	Am^{+4}	0.85	Pu^{+3}	1.01
6	.....	......	Am^{+3}	1.00

The effects of the lanthanide and actinide contractions are significant. Such small differences in properties as exist among the members of either series in a given state of oxidation may be ascribed to size differences resulting from these contractions. Among the lanthanides, at least, such differences are the bases for most separational procedures (p. 906). In the lanthanide series, the contraction effect is of sufficient magnitude as to cause the elements which follow in atomic number to have sizes differing at most only very slightly from those of their congeners in the preceding transition series. As indicated in Table 5·7, where appropriate covalent and

TABLE 5·7

VARIATIONS IN SIZE DUE TO THE LANTHANIDE CONTRACTION

IIIa	IVa	Va	VIa	VIIa	VIII	
Sc 1.439	Ti 1.324	V 1.224	Cr 1.172	Mn 1.168	Fe 1.165	Co 1.157 Ni 1.149
Sc^{+3} 0.81	Ti^{+4} 0.68	V^{+5} 0.59	Cr^{+6} 0.52	Mn^{+7} 0.46		
Y 1.616	Zr 1.454	Nb 1.342	Mo 1.291	Tc	Ru 1.241	Rh 1.247 Pd 1.278
Y^{+3} 0.93	Zr^{+4} 0.80	Nb^{+5} 0.70	Mo^{+6} 0.62	Tc^{+7}		
La 1.690	Hf 1.442	Ta 1.343	W 1.299	Re 1.278	Os 1.255	Ir 1.260 Pt 1.290
La^{+3} 1.15	Hf^{+4} (0.86)	Ta^{+5} (0.73)	W^{+6} (0.68)	Re^{+7}		

[24] T. Moeller and H. E. Kremers: *Chem. Revs.*, **37**, 97 (1945).
[25] W. H. Zachariasen: *Phys. Rev.*, **73**, 1104 (1948).

crystal radii are summarized, the normal size increase characterizing the family Sc-Y-La vanishes after the lanthanide series, and such pairs as Zr-Hf, Nb-Ta, W-Mo, etc., possess nearly identical sizes. The marked similarities in properties within such pairs and the attendant difficulties in chemical separation are thus direct results of the lanthanide contraction. It may be pointed out, also, that contraction is sufficient among the lanthanides that atomic and ionic radii drop below corresponding values for yttrium, a member of the preceding transition series. Inasmuch as the sizes of yttrium materials are roughly equaled by dysprosium and holmium materials, it is not surprising to find these elements (as well as their immediate neighbors) occurring with yttrium in nature. Nor is it surprising that separation of these elements from yttrium is exceedingly difficult.

The magnitudes of ionic radii are dependent upon the numbers of electrons lost or gained in ion formation. A cation is always smaller than its parent neutral atom, and conversely an anion is always larger than the neutral atom from which it is derived. Correspondingly, if several oxidation states are distinguishable for a given element, the higher the positive oxidation number (p. 179) or the lower the negative oxidation number the smaller the ion. The following radii data for lead are typical and illustrate these variations: Pb^0, 1.538 A; Pb^{+2}, 1.32 A; Pb^{+4}, 0.84 A; Pb^{-4}, 2.15 A.

Applications of size relationships

A detailed consideration of the applications of size relationships seems inappropriate at this point since it is essential that a number of other concepts be presented before such applications achieve their true meanings. However, in anticipation of future discussions some of the more important applications may be summarized, together with references to chapters and pages where they are treated. Among these are the following:

1. Electron attraction and repulsion (Ch. 5, pp. 152–164).
2. Valency and bond type (Ch. 6, pp. 178–215).
3. Acid-base character and salt hydrolysis (Ch. 9, pp. 312–321).
4. Stereochemical considerations (Ch. 6, pp. 178–180; Ch. 7, pp. 253–270).
5. Compound stability (Ch. 6, pp. 181–186).
6. Coordinating tendencies of ions and molecules (Ch. 7, pp. 235–236).
7. Oxidizing and reducing properties (Ch. 8, pp. 293–297).
8. Geochemistry.

Since the last of these topics is not treated as such in any subsequent chapter but is handled only by spot references, it might be mentioned that Goldschmidt[26] postulated that materials of similar ionic radii and preferably, though not necessarily, the same ionic charges will replace each other in minerals. The occurrences of apparently unrelated elements within the same mineral are often accounted for in this fashion. Goldschmidt's table as reproduced in Table 5·8 indicates at

TABLE 5·8

SPECIES OCCURRING TOGETHER IN MINERALS

Ionic Radius	Ionic Species
0.1–0.3	B^{+3}, C^{+4}, N^{+5}, S^{+6}
0.3–0.5	Be^{+2}, Si^{+4}, P^{+5}, V^{+5}
0.5–0.7	Li^{+1}, Mg^{+2}, Al^{+3}, Ga^{+3}, Fe^{+3}, Cr^{+3}, V^{+3}, Ti^{+4}, Ge^{+4}, Mo^{+6}, W^{+6}
0.7–0.9	Ni^{+2}, Co^{+2}, Fe^{+2}, Zn^{+2}, Sc^{+3}, In^{+3}, Zr^{+4}, Hf^{+4}, Sn^{+4}, Nb^{+5}, Ta^{+5}
0.9–1.1	Na^{+1}, Ca^{+2}, Cd^{+2}, Y^{+3}, Gd^{+3} to Lu^{+3}, Ce^{+4}, Th^{+4}, U^{+4}
1.1–1.4	K^{+1}, Sr^{+2}, La^{+3} to Eu^{+3}
1.4–1.7	Rb^{+1}, Cs^{+1}, Tl^{+1}, Ba^{+2}, Ra^{+2}

least some combinations which may be expected and which are thus justifiable.

In conclusion, one must point out the fact that independent consideration of size without allowance for nuclear and ionic charge effects is dangerous. It will be apparent that many of the applications of the size principle relate to electron attraction. It is further apparent that, whereas enhanced attraction of this sort is favored by small atom or ion size, it is also favored by large nuclear or cationic charge. This approach will be developed in more detail in the next chapter (pp. 208–211).

IONIZATION POTENTIALS

The promotion of electrons to higher energy levels as a result of the absorption of energy has been discussed in connection with the origin and interpretation of spectra (p. 82). It follows, of course, that the absorption of sufficient energy will result in the complete removal of an electron (or electrons) from the sphere of influence of the positive nucleus of an atom with the production of a positive ion. The amount of energy necessary to effect such a removal of the most loosely bound electron from an isolated gaseous atom of an element in its lowest energy state is called the *ionization potential*, or perhaps, more rigidly, the *firstio nization potential* of that element. Correspondingly, the energy associated with the removal of the most loosely bound electron from the ion produced by the loss of one electron, again

[26] V. M. Goldschmidt: *Ber.*, **60**, 1263 (1927).

in its lowest energy state, is referred to as the *second ionization potential.* In like fashion, *third, fourth, etc., ionization potentials* may be defined.[27] The term ionization potential when used without modification is understood to mean the first ionization potential.

The concept of ionization potential may be illustrated graphically in terms of the hydrogen atom. As indicated in Figure 5·7, the input of progressively larger amounts of energy promotes the single electron

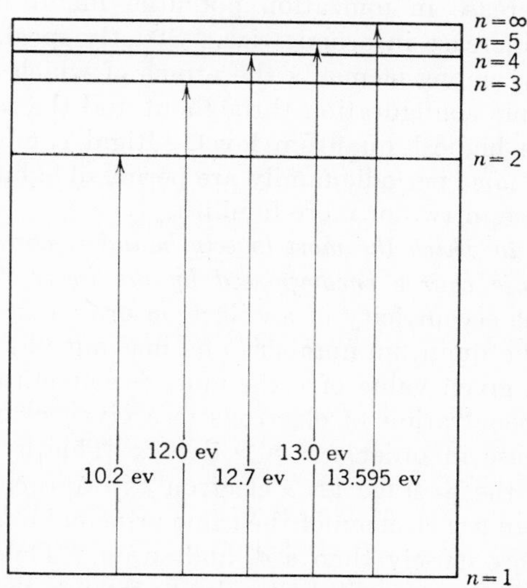

Fig. 5·7. Graphic representation of energy levels in the hydrogen atom.

from its normal position in the first quantum level ($n = 1$) to successively higher levels ($n = 2$, 3, etc.) until ultimately the electron is raised to an infinite level and is, thereby, completely removed. The situation is much the same with more complicated atoms except that with these systems some one electron will be easier to promote to higher levels than the others.

The numerical magnitudes of ionization potentials are influenced by a number of factors. Among the more obvious of these factors are the following:[28]

1. *The charge upon the atomic nucleus.* In general, as the nuclear charge increases among atoms with similar outer electronic arrangements, ionization potential will increase because of the enhanced attraction of the nucleus for electrons.

[27] J. Sherman: *Chem. Revs.,* **11,** 93 (1932).

[28] H. H. Sisler and C. A. Vander Werf: *J. Chem. Education,* **22,** 390 (1945).

2. *The shielding effect of inner electronic shells.* The attractive force exerted by the nucleus on the most loosely held electrons is at least partially counterbalanced by the repulsive forces exerted by the inner electrons. The electron to be removed is thus shielded from the nucleus by these inner shells, and some decrease in ionization potential results.

3. *The atomic radius.* In terms of what has already been said (pp. 146–152), a decrease in ionization potential might be expected to accompany an increase in atomic size. Strictly speaking, of course, this is true only among elements the atoms of which have the same types of electronic configuration throughout and the same number of electrons in the highest quantum level. Rigid comparisons among members of the *same* periodic family are permissible but not comparisons among those in two or more families.

4. *The extent to which the most loosely bound electron penetrates the cloud of electronic charge encompassed by the inner electronic shells.* Inasmuch as the eccentricity of an electron orbit is measured by the magnitude of the quantum number l and inasmuch as the smaller the value of l for a given value of n the more eccentric the orbit (p. 90), the degree of penetration of electrons in a given principal quantum level will decrease in order $s > p > d > f$. This is tantamount to saying that on the average an s electron will approach the nucleus more closely than a p electron of the same principal quantum number, a p electron more closely than a d, and so on. Thus, other factors being equal, an s electron will be harder to remove than a p electron, a p electron harder to remove than a d electron, and a d electron harder to remove than an f electron, and ionization potentials will decrease in this order.

Of course the measured ionization potential for an element is determined by a combination of all these factors, and it is not always possible to ascribe a greater influence to one factor than to any of the others. Thus, for example, although an electron may be shielded from the nucleus by inner electron shells, as soon as it penetrates close to the nucleus, this shielding disappears and attractive forces on the electron increase.

Numerically, ionization potentials are expressed in electron volts (p. 59). The values tabulated for the various elements in Table 5·9 are so expressed.[27, 29] It should be pointed out that many of these potentials are incapable of being attained by the energies

[29] C. E. Moore: *Atomic Energy Levels.* Circular of National Bureau of Standards, No. 467, June 15, 1949.

released in chemical reactions alone and are achievable only in discharge tubes. In a very general way, values of above about 15 electron volts are difficult to reach by chemical means alone. Hence the formation of highly charged cations in chemical processes is highly unlikely. This is in general accord with observed fact that simple cations with charges greater than two are most uncommon, but as will be shown later (Ch. 6) the formation of gaseous ions as measured by the ionization potential is not always the controlling step in compound formation. The stabilities of the inert gas and, to lesser extents, the pseudo-inert gas arrangements are indicated in Table 5·9 both by the large values of ionization potentials characterizing these elements and by the tremendous jumps in ionization potentials accompanying any penetration into an inert gas or pseudo-inert gas arrangement (stair-step arrangements in Table 5·9). Increases in magnitude from first to second to third, etc., ionization potentials for any given elements are due to the fact that it is always more difficult to remove electrons from a positive ion than from a neutral atom.

Periodic variations of first ionization potentials with atomic numbers are indicated in Figure 5·8. The inert gas elements occupy maximum positions. The sharp drop to a minimum value for an alkali metal after each inert gas is associated with the addition of a single *s* electron to the next higher quantum level, this *s* electron being proportionately better shielded than *s* electrons in lower arrangements. The general increase from alkali metal through halogen in each series of elements is due largely to the effects of increased nuclear charge, since size variations in these regions are not large. Omitting the transition series, we note significant drops in ionization potential at the Group IIIb elements, B, Al, Ga, In, and Tl. With each of these elements, the first *p* electron in the *n*th quantum level appears, and, since this electron is less penetrating than previously added *s* electrons, it is better shielded and thus easier to remove. These discontinuities increase in magnitude with increasing atomic number, paralleling increases in the complexities of the underlying electronic arrangements. Similar irregularities are apparent with the Group VIb elements, O, S, Se, and (to a much reduced extent) Te, but their origins are obscure. These discontinuities are characteristic of the first ionization potential only.

Within the transition and inner transition series, essential constancy in ionization potential is associated with constancy in outermost electronic arrangement and only rather slight changes in atomic size. A general increase in potential, paralleling decrease in size, characterizes each such series, and as might be expected this increase is less

TABLE 5·9

IONIZATION POTENTIALS OF THE ELEMENTS

Atomic Number	Symbol	Valence Configuration	Ionization Potential, ev I	II	III	IV	V	VI	VII	VIII
1	H	$1s^1$	13.595							
2	He	$1s^2$	24.580	54.40						
3	Li	$2s^1$	5.390	75.6193	122.420					
4	Be	$2s^2$	9.320	18.206	153.850	217.657				
5	B	$2s^22p^1$	8.296	25.149	37.920	259.298	340.127			
6	C	$2s^22p^2$	11.264	24.376	47.864	64.476	391.986	489.84		
7	N	$2s^22p^3$	14.54	29.605	47.426	77.450	97.863	551.925	666.83	
8	O	$2s^22p^4$	13.614	35.146	54.934	77.394	113.873	138.080	739.114	871.12
9	F	$2s^22p^5$	17.42	34.98	62.646	87.23	114.214	157.117	185.139	953.60
10	Ne	$2s^22p^6$	21.559	41.07	64	97.16	126.4	157.91		
11	Na	$3s^1$	5.138	47.29	71.65	98.88	138.60	172.36	208.44	264.155
12	Mg	$3s^2$	7.644	15.03	80.12	109.29	141.23	186.86	225.31	265.97
13	Al	$3s^23p^1$	5.984	18.823	28.44	119.96	153.77	190.42	241.93	285.13
14	Si	$3s^23p^2$	8.149	16.34	33.46	45.13	166.73	205.11	246.41	303.87
15	P	$3s^23p^3$	11.0	19.65	30.156	51.354	65.007	220.414	263.31	309.26
16	S	$3s^23p^4$	10.357	23.4	35.0	47.29	72.5	88.029	280.99	328.80
17	Cl	$3s^23p^5$	13.01	23.80	39.90	53.5	67.80	96.7	114.27	348.3
18	A	$3s^23p^6$	15.755	27.62	40.90	59.79	75.0	91.3	124.0	143.46
19	K	$4s^1$	4.339	31.81	46	60.90		99.7	118	155
20	Ca	$4s^2$	6.111	11.87	51.21	67	84.39		128	147
21	Sc	$3d^14s^2$	6.56	12.89	24.75	73.9	92	111.1		159
22	Ti	$3d^24s^2$	6.83	13.63	28.14	43.24	99.8	120	140.8	

23	V	$3d^3 4s^2$	6.74	14.2	29.7	48	65.2	128.9	151	173.7
24	Cr	$3d^5 4s^1$	6.76	16.6	(31)*	(50.4)	(72.8)			
25	Mn	$3d^5 4s^2$	7.432	15.70	(32)	(52)	(75.7)			
26	Fe	$3d^6 4s^2$	7.896	16.16						
27	Co	$3d^7 4s^2$	7.86	17.3						
28	Ni	$3d^8 4s^2$	7.633	18.2						
29	Cu	$3d^{10} 4s^1$	7.723	20.34	29.5					
30	Zn	$3d^{10} 4s^2$	9.391	17.89	40.0					
31	Ga	$4s^2 4p^1$	6.00	20.43	30.6	63.8				
32	Ge	$4s^2 4p^2$	8.13	15.86	34.07	45.5	93.0			
33	As	$4s^2 4p^3$	10 ±	20.1	28.0	49.9	62.5			
34	Se	$4s^2 4p^4$	9.750	21.3	33.9	42.72	72.8	81.4		
35	Br	$4s^2 4p^5$	11.84	19.1	25.7	(50)				
36	Kr	$4s^2 4p^6$	13.996	26.4	36.8	(68)				
37	Rb	$5s^1$	4.176	27.36	(47)	(80)				
38	Sr	$5s^2$	5.692	10.98						
39	Y	$4d^1 5s^2$	6.6	12.3	20.4					
40	Zr	$4d^2 5s^2$	6.95	13.97	24.00	33.8				
41	Nb	$4d^4 5s^1$	6.77		24.2					
42	Mo	$4d^5 5s^1$	7.18							
43	Tc	$4d^6 5s^1$								
44	Ru	$4d^7 5s^1$	7.5							
45	Rh	$4d^8 5s^1$	7.7							
46	Pd	$4d^{10}$	8.33	19.8						
47	Ag	$4d^{10} 5s^1$	7.574	21.4	35.9					

* Doubtful values in parentheses.

All first ionization potentials and all other potentials for elements through vanadium from C. E. Moore.[29] All other values from J. Sherman.[27]

TABLE 5·9 (*Continued*)

Atomic Number	Symbol	Valence Configuration	Ionization Potential, ev I	II	III	IV	V	VI	VII	VIII
48	Cd	$4d^{10}5s^2$	8.991	16.84	38.0					
49	In	$5s^25p^1$	5.785	18.79	27.9	57.8				
50	Sn	$5s^25p^2$	7.332	14.5	30.5	39.4	80.7			
51	Sb	$5s^25p^3$	8.64	(18)	24.7	44.0	55.5			
52	Te	$5s^25p^4$	9.01		30.5	37.7	60.0	(72)		
53	I	$5s^25p^5$	10.44	19.4						
54	Xe	$5s^25p^6$	12.127	(21.1)	32.0	(46)	(76)			
55	Cs	$6s^1$	3.893	23.4	(35)	(51)	(58)			
56	Ba	$6s^2$	5.210	9.95						
57	La	$5d^16s^2$	5.61	11.4	(20.4)					
58	Ce	$4f^26s^2$	(6.91)	14.8						
59	Pr	$4f^36s^2$	(5.76)							
60	Nd	$4f^46s^2$	(6.31)							
61		$4f^56s^2$								
62	Sm	$4f^66s^2$	5.6	11.4						
63	Eu	$4f^76s^2$	5.67	11.4						
64	Gd	$4f^75d^16s^2$	6.16							
65	Tb	$4f^96s^2$	(6.74)							
66	Dy	$4f^{10}6s^2$	(6.82)							
67	Ho	$4f^{11}6s^2$								
68	Er	$4f^{12}6s^2$								
69	Tm	$4f^{13}6s^2$								
70	Yb	$4f^{14}6s^2$	6.2							
71	Lu	$4f^{14}5d^16s^2$	5.0							
72	Hf	$5d^26s^2$	5.5 ±	(14.8)						

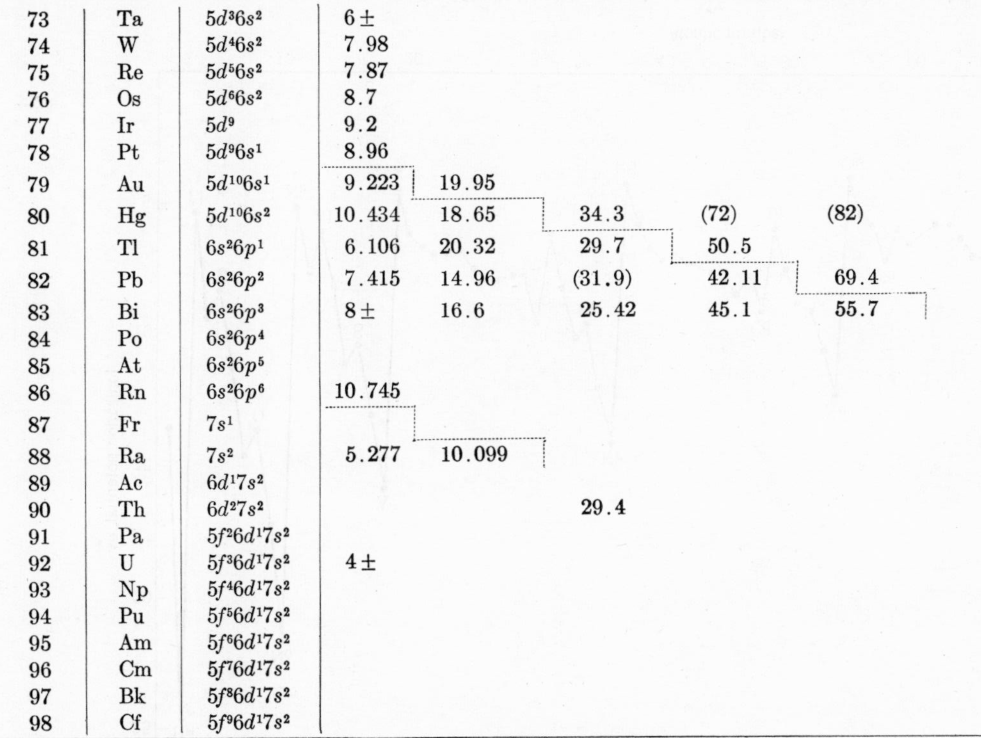

73	Ta	$5d^36s^2$	6±				
74	W	$5d^46s^2$	7.98				
75	Re	$5d^56s^2$	7.87				
76	Os	$5d^66s^2$	8.7				
77	Ir	$5d^9$	9.2				
78	Pt	$5d^96s^1$	8.96				
79	Au	$5d^{10}6s^1$	9.223	19.95			
80	Hg	$5d^{10}6s^2$	10.434	18.65	34.3	(72)	(82)
81	Tl	$6s^26p^1$	6.106	20.32	29.7	50.5	
82	Pb	$6s^26p^2$	7.415	14.96	(31.9)	42.11	69.4
83	Bi	$6s^26p^3$	8±	16.6	25.42	45.1	55.7
84	Po	$6s^26p^4$					
85	At	$6s^26p^5$					
86	Rn	$6s^26p^6$	10.745				
87	Fr	$7s^1$					
88	Ra	$7s^2$	5.277	10.099			
89	Ac	$6d^17s^2$					
90	Th	$6d^27s^2$			29.4		
91	Pa	$5f^26d^17s^2$					
92	U	$5f^36d^17s^2$	4±				
93	Np	$5f^46d^17s^2$					
94	Pu	$5f^56d^17s^2$					
95	Am	$5f^66d^17s^2$					
96	Cm	$5f^76d^17s^2$					
97	Bk	$5f^86d^17s^2$					
98	Cf	$5f^96d^17s^2$					

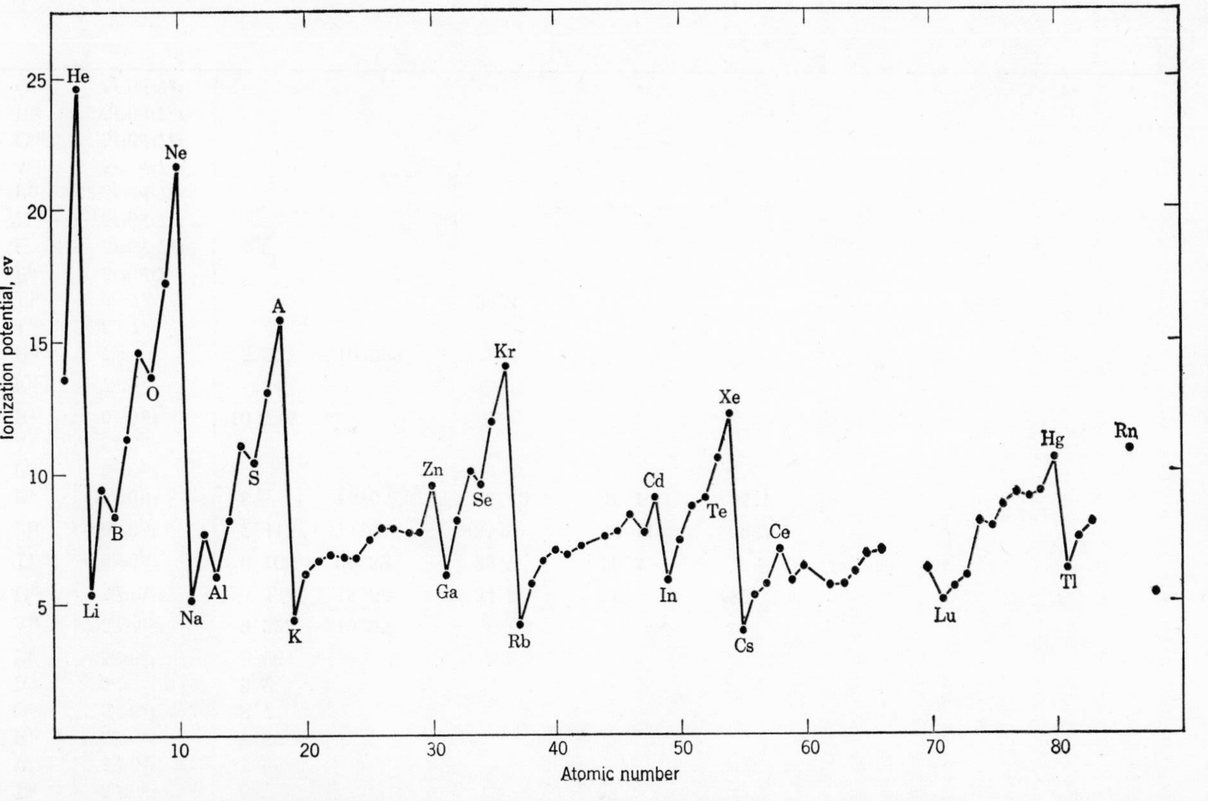

FIG. 5·8. Variations in first ionization potentials with atomic number.

pronounced with an inner transition series than with a transition series alone.

As far as individual families of elements are concerned, ionization potentials generally decrease with increase in atomic number. This trend is best associated with increase in size while maintaining the same type of electronic arrangement, since the combined effects of adding removable electrons to higher and higher energy levels and shielding due to the presence of underlying shells usually more than counterbalance the effect of increased nuclear charge. One cardinal exception may be cited, however. Elements immediately following the lanthanides in atomic number (Hf through Pb) have higher ionization potentials than the corresponding elements in the preceding series. This is merely another effect of the comparatively large increase in nuclear charge without expansion to higher electron shells which characterizes the lanthanide region. The greater nuclear attraction and decreased size which result thus decrease the ease with which electrons can be removed. This effect becomes less pronounced as atomic number continues to increase and apparently disappears at bismuth. The fact that ionization potentials of the elements in the B family of a particular periodic group are higher than those of the elements of corresponding electronic configurations in the A family is also worthy of note. Penetration effects are more pronounced with underlying 18-electron arrangements than with 8-electron arrangements, and these combine with increased nuclear charge to render electron removal more difficult.

Applications of the ionization potential concept are legion. Since ionization potentials measure ease of ion formation, most applications center in the behaviors of the free elements as reducing agents or in the natures of linkages in the compounds which they form. As such, they will be discussed in subsequent chapters (Ch. 6 and 8).

ELECTRON AFFINITIES

Although the energy required to remove an electron (or electrons) from a neutral atom can be evaluated experimentally with considerable accuracy, the energy associated with the addition of an electron (or electrons) to a neutral atom can be arrived at only indirectly and seldom with great accuracy. The energy released when an electron is added to a neutral gaseous atom in its lowest energy state is termed the *electron affinity*. By analogy, second, third, etc., electron affinities might be expected. However, these would involve the input of energy rather than its loss since the addition of an electron to a negative ion would be opposed by coulombic repulsion. Only the electron affinities of the most electronegative elements have been evaluated, and these have been calculated from thermodynamic data for ionic compounds by use of the Born-Haber cycle (p. 184). Values so obtained are summarized in Table 5·10.[30]

TABLE 5·10
ELECTRON AFFINITIES OF CERTAIN ELEMENTS

Symbol	Electron Affinity kcal.	Electron Affinity ev
F	98.5	4.27
Cl	92.5	4.01
Br	87.1	3.78
I	79.2	3.43
H	16.4	0.71
O	−168*	−7.28*
S	−79.4*	−3.44*
Se	−97*	−4.21*
Li-Cs	0	0

* For two electrons.

The electron affinity of an element is essentially the ionization energy of its uninegative ion with sign reversed. The greater its magnitude, the greater the tendency of the element to gain an electron, or the greater its oxidizing power. Applications will be considered later in conjunction with those of ionization potentials.

ELECTRONEGATIVITIES OF THE ELEMENTS

Both ionization potentials and electron affinities may be regarded as more or less quantitative expressions of a general property of the elements which the chemist terms electronegativity, that is, the tendency of an atom to attract electrons to itself. In a general way, it is apparent that small atoms have greater attractions for electrons than large ones and are, therefore, more electronegative. It is also apparent that higher electronegativities would be expected for atoms the orbitals of which are nearly filled than for those the orbitals of which are sparsely occupied. However, a uniform quantitative mode of expressing electronegativities is desirable.

Fortunately, Pauling[31] has derived a useful scale of electronegativities through consideration of variations in the difference Δ between the actual energy of a bond between two atoms A and B and the energy expected for a normal covalent bond (p. 192) between

[30] L. Pauling: *The Nature of the Chemical Bond*, 2nd Ed., pp. 66, 341. Cornell University Press, Ithaca (1940).

[31] L. Pauling: *J. Am. Chem. Soc.*, **54,** 3570 (1932); *The Nature of the Chemical Bond*, 2nd Ed., pp. 58–69, Cornell University Press, Ithaca (1940).

these atoms. Values of Δ increase as the electronegativity difference between the two atoms increases, but these values do not satisfy any relationship amounting to a difference between numerical properties of the atoms concerned. Pauling has found, however, that the square roots of the Δ values do approach such a relation and has evaluated the term $0.208\sqrt{\Delta}$ for a number of bonds, this relation being derived from the conversion of Δ values from kilogram calories to electron volts by the ratio Δ:23.06. To each element, a numerical value of electronegativity was then assigned, these values being so chosen that their differences are approximately equal to the square roots of the Δ values in electron volts. In order to bring the electronegativities of the elements C to F up to 2.5 to 4.0, an arbitrary constant of 2.05 was added to the original values. Such a procedure was suited to evaluation of electronegativities for the elements H, C, N, O, F, Si, P, S, Cl, Ge, As, Se, Br, and I, but values for other elements had to be calculated from thermochemical data for compounds containing the elements in question and one of the elements mentioned above.

TABLE 5·11

Pauling's Scale of Electronegativities

Element	Electronegativity	Element	Electronegativity
F	4.0	Sn	1.7
O	3.5	Ti	1.6
Cl	3.0	Zr	1.6
N	3.0	Al	1.5
Br	2.8	Be	1.5
S	2.5	Sc	1.3
C	2.5	Y	1.3
I	2.4	Mg	1.2
Se	2.4	Ca	1.0
Te	2.1	Li	1.0
P	2.1	Sr	1.0
H	2.1	Na	0.9
As	2.0	Ba	0.9
B	2.0	K	0.8
Si	1.8	Rb	0.8
Sb	1.8	Cs	0.7
Ge	1.7		

Numerical values for electronegativities as given by Pauling[31] are summarized in Table 5·11, and periodic variations in their magnitudes are shown graphically in Figure 5·9. Electronegativities are highest for the smallest elements, as might be expected, and decrease with increase in size in any particular family. In a given series of elements, they also decrease with decreasing numbers of outer electrons. Use of the electronegativity concept in determining bond character will be discussed in a subsequent chapter (Ch. 6, pp. 205–208), but in a very general way it should be apparent that the most highly ionic compounds will result between elements of the most widely divergent electronegativities. The electronegativities of the elements are also useful in approximating bond energies and in establishing qualitatively the thermal stabilities of compounds.

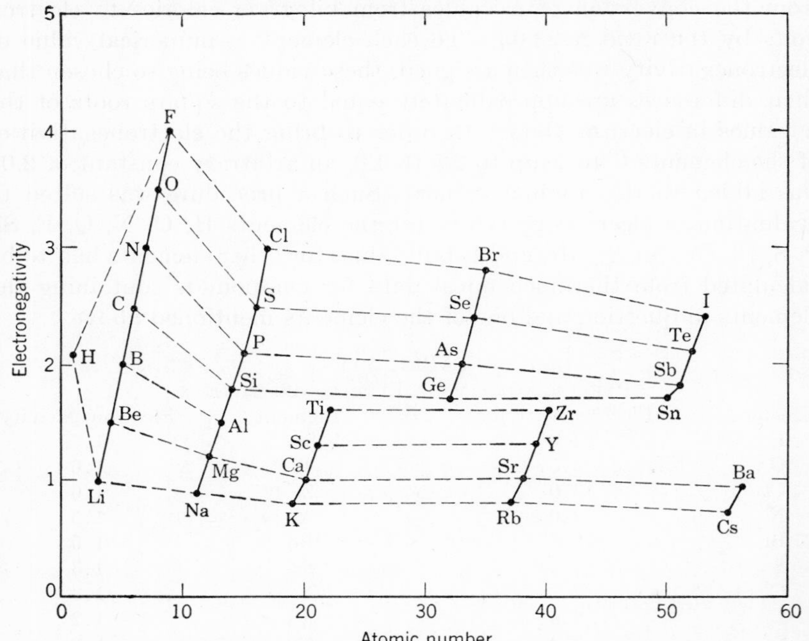

Fig. 5·9. Periodic variations in the electronegativities of the elements.

The qualitative relation between electronegativity and electron loss or gain has been pointed out. There is, however, a somewhat more quantitative relation between this property and the electron affinity and ionization potential. Mulliken,[32] for example, has pointed out that the average of the first ionization potential and the electron affinity should measure electronegativity. Strictly speaking, this is a straightforward relation only for univalent atoms. If the electron affinities of the alkali metals are assumed to be zero, the sum of ionization potential (in kilocalories) and electron affinity (in kilocalories) divided by 130 gives values which deviate but slightly from the numerical electronegativity values summarized in Table 5·11 for the halogens, alkali metals, and hydrogen.[32]

[32] R. S. Mulliken: *J. Chem. Phys.*, **2**, 782 (1934); **3**, 573 (1935).

MAGNETIC PROPERTIES

It is well known that the movement of an electric charge produces a magnetic effect. It is to be expected, therefore, that the spin and orbital motions of electrons in atoms, molecules, and ions will be responsible for the observed magnetic moments* of these materials. Each electron, in fact, may be regarded as an individual micromagnet, and the total moment exhibited by the material as such may then be regarded as the resultant of the moments of all the individual electrons.

All materials exhibit some degree of polarization or orientation when placed in a magnetic field, but two kinds of behavior may be distinguished. Thus a substance may be less permeable to the magnetic lines of force than a vacuum and as a result may tend to move from the stronger part of the field to the weaker part. The field

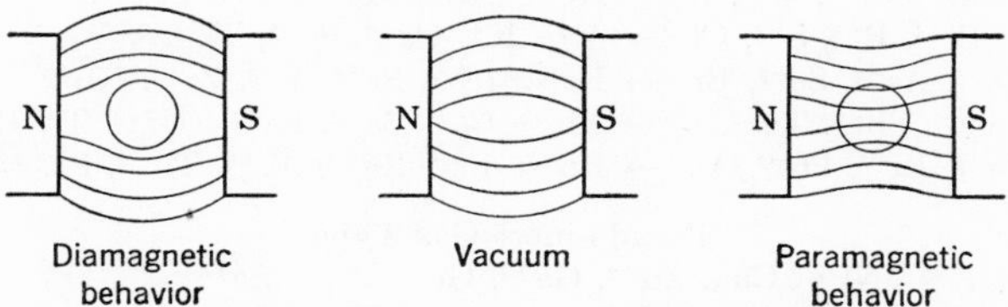

FIG. 5·10. Changes in magnetic lines of force when materials are introduced into a magnetic field.

induced in it is in effect opposite to the external field, and the material is literally repelled. Such a substance is said to be *diamagnetic*. On the other hand, a substance may exhibit exactly the opposite behavior and be attracted to the magnetic field. Such a substance is *paramagnetic*. The relationship between diamagnetic and paramagnetic materials is shown in Figure 5·10. In a few instances, the fields within materials are increased tremendously (perhaps a millionfold or more). Substances exhibiting this behavior are *ferromagnetic* and are comparatively rare. Diamagnetic and paramagnetic behavior, however, are of especial interest in conjunction with the structures of compounds and the types of binding present. They will be discussed in detail.

The modifying effects of an applied magnetic field upon the motion of electrons render all substances diamagnetic. Even paramagnetic materials also exhibit diamagnetism, and corrections for this characteristic must be made in precise measurements of permanent magnetic

* In a simple bar magnet, the magnetic moment is given by the pole strength multiplied by the distance between the poles. Magnetic moments due to electron motion may be thought of in the same fashion.

moments. Diamagnetism is a function of the distribution of electron density within an atom, molecule, or ion and arises from the interaction of the applied field with filled electron orbits. In diamagnetic materials, the effects of the individual electrons are mutually neutralized. Among molecular materials, it is characteristic of all substances in which electrons are completely paired, especially the organic compounds. It is always characteristic of those species possessing inert gas (8-electron), pseudo-inert gas (18-electron) or pseudo-inert gas + 2 (18 + 2-electron) arrangements. Materials of these types are summarized in Table 5·12.[33] As a first criterion of diamagnetism one

TABLE 5·12

DIAMAGNETIC IONIC AND PSEUDO-IONIC SPECIES

Inert Gas Type

$H^- \rightarrow He \leftarrow Li^+, Be^{+2}, B^{+3}, C^{+4}, N^{+5}$

$C^{-4}, N^{-3}, O^{-2}, F^- \rightarrow Ne \leftarrow Na^+, Mg^{+2}, Al^{+3}, Si^{+4}, P^{+5}$

$Si^{-4}, P^{-3}, S^{-2}, Cl^- \rightarrow A \leftarrow K^+, Ca^{+2}, Sc^{+3}, Ti^{+4}, V^{+5}$

$Ge^{-4}, As^{-3}, Se^{-2}, Br^- \rightarrow Kr \leftarrow Rb^+, Sr^{+2}, Y^{+3}, Zr^{+4}, Nb^{+5}$

$Sn^{-4}, Sb^{-3}, Te^{-2}, I^- \rightarrow Xe \leftarrow Cs^+, Ba^{+2}, La^{+3}, (Hf^{+4}, Ta^{+5})$

$Pb^{-4}, Bi^{-3}, Po^{-2}, At^- \rightarrow Rn \leftarrow Fr^+, Ra^{+2}, Ac^{+3}, Th^{+4}, Pa^{+5}$

Pseudo-inert Gas Type

$Ni \leftarrow Cu^+, Zn^{+2}, Ga^{+3}, Ge^{+4}, As^{+5}, Se^{+6}$

$Pd \leftarrow Ag^+, Cd^{+2}, In^{+3}, Sn^{+4}, Sb^{+5}, Te^{+6}, I^{+7}$

$Pt \leftarrow Au^+, Hg^{+2}, Tl^{+3}, Pb^{+4}, Bi^{+5}$

Pseudo-inert Gas + 2 Type

Ni + 2 electrons $\leftarrow Ga^+, Ge^{+2}, As^{+3}, Se^{+4}, Br^{+5}$

Pd + 2 electrons $\leftarrow In^+, Sn^{+2}, Sb^{+3}, Te^{+4}, I^{+5}$

Pt + 2 electrons $\leftarrow Tl^+, Pb^{+2}, Bi^{+3}$

may use the presence of an even number of electrons, although as shown below this is not always a true criterion.

Paramagnetic behavior is shown when the magnetic effects of the individual electrons are not mutually neutralized and is associated with the presence of either unpaired electrons or an incompleted electronic level. The permanent moments characterizing paramagnetic materials are of sufficient magnitudes that their diamagnetic properties become unimportant. Unlike diamagnetism, paramagnetism is dependent upon temperature since it is associated with orientation of dipoles (p. 186) in a field. Although the presence of an odd number of electrons is commonly characteristic of paramagnetic substances, lack of electron pairing may occur when an even number of electrons is present if the principle of maximum multiplicity, or single occupancy of available orbitals, is obeyed (p. 93). Paramagnetism is common to many ions derived from the transition and inner transition metals, to

[33] R. F. Robey and W. M. Dix: *J. Chem. Education*, **14**, 414 (1937).

molecules containing odd numbers of electrons, to a few molecules containing even numbers of electrons but unpaired electron spins (e.g., O_2), and to many complex ions (p. 261). It is often a property of considerable importance and utility.

It has been pointed out that both the spin and the orbital motion of an electron are sources of magnetic moment. The total magnetic moment of a material is then made up of two components, the so-called *spin* and *orbital contributions.* Both these contributions are due to the presence of unpaired electrons, but in many instances these unpaired electrons are in effect the outermost ones in the species under consideration and are not screened by other electrons. In such cases, the spin contribution becomes important, and the orbital contribution may be neglected. This amounts to a cancellation of the greater portion of the orbital contribution by the interaction of these materials with other ions in solution or in the crystalline state. The most common examples embrace ions of the transition metals. On the other hand, when the unpaired electrons lie well within the ions and are screened by outer electrons, as is true among ions derived from the inner transition metals, the orbital contribution cannot be neglected and must be combined with the spin contribution to give the total moment.

When a substance is placed in a magnetic field of H gausses or oersteds,* the total magnetic flux B in the substance is given by the relation

$$B = H + 4\pi I \tag{5·3}$$

where I is the intensity of magnetization. The so-called *magnetic susceptibility* per unit volume (κ) is then

$$\kappa = I/H \tag{5·4}$$

and per unit mass κ/ϱ or $I/H\varrho$, where ϱ is the density. It is common to express magnetic susceptibility per gram of material by χ and per gram mole by χ_M. It is apparent that

$$\chi_M = M\kappa/\varrho \tag{5·5}$$

where M is the molecular weight. The *magnetic permeability* of the material, μ, is defined by the relation

$$\mu = B/H \tag{5·6}$$

whence Equation 5·3 then reduces to

$$\mu = 1 + 4\pi\kappa \tag{5·7}$$

* A field of one *gauss* or one *oersted* is a field of such intensity that a unit magnetic pole is acted upon with a force of one dyne.

The susceptibility (χ) of a diamagnetic material has a small negative value, whereas that of a paramagnetic substance has a positive value of somewhat larger magnitude. Variation in susceptibility with temperature is given, empirically, by the Curie law

$$\chi = C/T \tag{5·8}$$

or the Curie-Weiss law

$$\chi = C/(T - \Delta) \tag{5·9}$$

C being a constant, and Δ the Curie point. More exact expressions derived from the quantum mechanics may be found in more comprehensive treatments than this one.[34, 35]

The permanent magnetic moment of a material, μ_B, is of more importance in describing the properties of a paramagnetic substance. Numerically, this is expressed in Bohr magnetons, the Bohr magneton, μ_e, having the magnitude 5564 gauss-cm. per gram mole and being given by the expression

$$\mu_e = \frac{he}{4\pi mc} \tag{5·10}$$

where h is the Planck constant, e the electronic charge, c the velocity of light, and m the electron mass. The magnetic moment is related to the mole susceptibility by the Langevin expression

$$\chi_M = \frac{N\mu_B^2}{3kT} \tag{5·11}$$

where N is Avogadro's number, k the Boltzmann constant, and T the absolute temperature, or by some modification thereof.

For many cases, the permanent moment is given by the expression

$$\mu_B = \sqrt{4S(S + 1) + L(L + 1)} \tag{5·12}$$

where S is the resultant spin angular momentum and L the resultant orbital angular momentum (see Ch. 3). For those cases where the orbital contribution is small and can be neglected, the moment then becomes

$$\mu_B = \sqrt{4S(S + 1)} = 2\sqrt{S(S + 1)} \tag{5·13}$$

and since the number of unpaired electrons (**n**) equals $2S$, the moment may be related directly to the number of such unpaired electrons by the expression

[34] J. H. Van Vleck: *Theory of Electric and Magnetic Susceptibilities.* Oxford University Press, London (1932).

[35] P. W. Selwood: *Magnetochemistry.* Interscience Publishers, New York (1943).

$$\mu_B = \sqrt{n(n+2)} \tag{5·14}$$

Thus the expected moment for one unpaired electron would be the $\sqrt{3}$ or 1.73, for two the $\sqrt{8}$ or 2.83, and so on to values of 3.87, 4.90, 5.92, and 6.93 for 3, 4, 5, and 6 unpaired electrons, respectively. As a

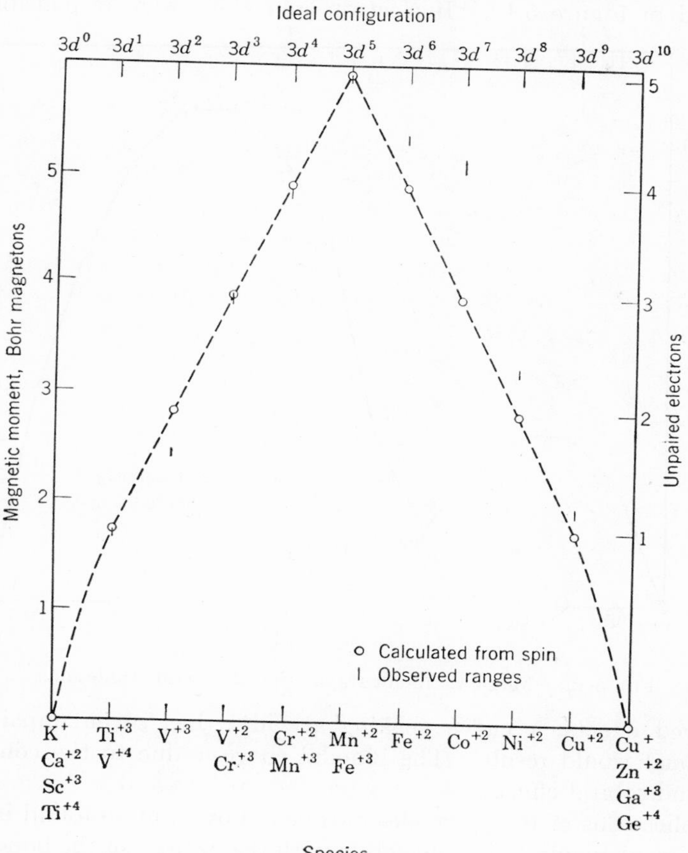

FIG. 5·11. Magnetic moments of ions of elements in first transition series and beyond.

first approximation, then, the moment of a material may be calculated if the number of unpaired electrons is known, or conversely the observed moment may be used to indicate the number of unpaired electrons present. That such a procedure is well adapted to derivatives of the transition metals is shown by the comparison between calculated and observed moments summarized in Figure 5·11 for ions from the first transition series and those immediately following. The principle of maximum multiplicity (p. 93) is thereby confirmed.

In cases where orbital contribution must be considered, the situation is so complicated as to be beyond the scope of this book. As an example, one may cite values for the tripositive lanthanides summarized in Figure 5·12. If electron spin alone were responsible for

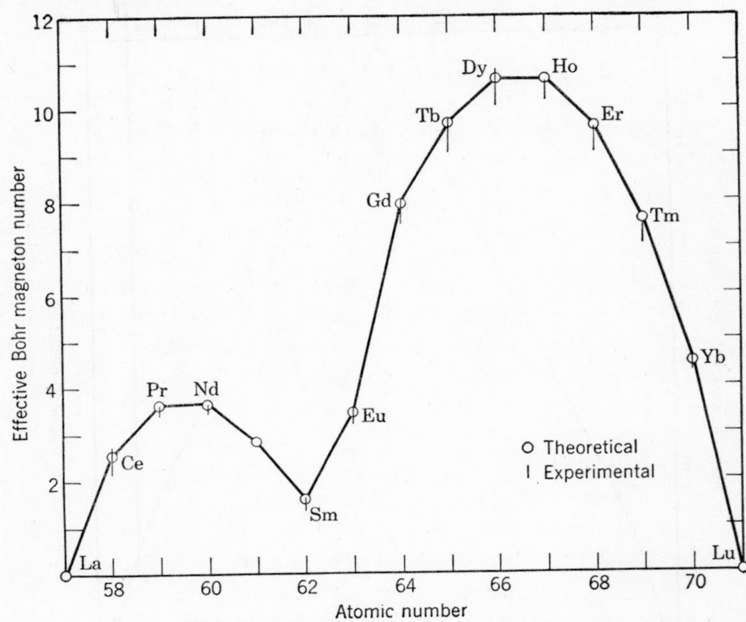

FIG. 5·12. Magnetic moments of tripositive lanthanide ions.

observed effects, a curve peaking at Gd^{+3} (i.e., seven unpaired 4*f* electrons) would result. The binodal curve is due to the combined spin and orbital effects.

Applications of the principles outlined above will be found in later chapters, particularly in connection with the natures of the bonding in coordination compounds (pp. 256–261). For specific details about the relation of magnetic properties to problems in inorganic chemistry, the text by Selwood should be consulted.[35]

SUGGESTED SUPPLEMENTARY REFERENCES

C. H. D. Clark: *The Electronic Structure and Properties of Matter*, Ch. VII, VIII, X. Chapman and Hall, Ltd., London (1934).

F. O. Rice and E. Teller: *The Structure of Matter*. John Wiley and Sons, New York (1949).

P. W. Selwood: *Magnetochemistry*. Interscience Publishers, New York (1943).

CHAPTER 6

Characteristics Dependent upon the Extranuclear Structures
II. Valency and the Chemical Bond

Valency is a term which has had many meanings. In its broadest sense, it is a term used to describe the power or ability which elements possess to combine with one another. In this sense, it has an intangible quality which requires more adequate and rigid definition. A chemical bond, on the other hand, is more definite in that it may be regarded as the force which actually holds two chemical entities together. It is apparent from the discussions in previous chapters that the fundamental abilities of elements to combine with each other are related to the extranuclear structures of their atoms. It is the purpose of this chapter to explore this relation in some detail and to point out, in terms of the extranuclear structures and other characteristics dependent upon them, what types of bonds may be expected and what their properties may be. As will be shown, these bonds are in general either electrostatic or non-electrostatic in character.

The development of modern views on valency and bond formation has, of necessity, paralleled closely the development of the theory of atomic structure. In order that the picture may be complete and that current views may be appreciated more completely, it is of interest to begin our discussion with a brief summary of the more significant developments which have influenced current electronic theories.

DEVELOPMENT OF THE ELECTRONIC THEORY OF VALENCY

Only a few of the more significant contributions need be considered here. For more comprehensive treatments available reference works[1,2] should be consulted. After the development of Dalton's

[1] N. V. Sidgwick: *The Electronic Theory of Valency*, Ch. IV. Clarendon Press, Oxford (1927).

[2] W. G. Palmer: *Valency, Classical and Modern*, Ch. I, II. Cambridge University Press, London (1944).

atomic theory (p. 5), Berzelius (in 1812) assumed the attractive forces between atoms in chemical compounds to be purely electrostatic in character and thereby provided the first really significant ideas in terms of modern thought. Although the views of Berzelius were strongly supported by Faraday's statement (in 1834) of the laws of electrochemical equivalence and by the phenomena of electrolysis in general, they were discarded as being universally applicable after the discovery of such organic reactions as the replacement of positive hydrogen by negative chlorine without profound alteration in properties. A rival theory, based largely upon structural views and free from any assumptions as to the natures of forces between atoms, thus arose and, because of its widespread applicability to organic compounds, soon superseded the theory of Berzelius. Of course with the development of Arrhenius's views on electrolytic dissociation, attention was directed again toward electrostatic attractions, and it became apparent that two types of valency, ionizable and non-ionizable, exist. That more attention was not directed to this difference is due doubtless to deplorable lack of cooperation and understanding between the inorganic and organic chemists in whose hands investigations of the properties of compounds lay. The views of Werner (pp. 229–230) did much to resolve the difficulty.

TABLE 6·1

Abegg's Table of Maximum Valencies and Contravalencies

Periodic group	0	I	II	III	IV	V	VI	VII
Normal valency	0	+1	+2	+3	±4	−3	−2	−1
Contravalency	0	(−7)*	(−6)	(−5)		+5	+6	+7

* Values in parentheses not observed.

With the discovery of the electron (p. 7), developments came rapidly. Thomson himself felt that valency must be associated with electrons and suggested that electrostatic attractions resulting from the transfer of electrons from one atom to another were possible. In developing his periodic table, Mendeléeff had indicated a relation between valence number and the group in which the element was placed (p. 113). In 1904, Abegg[3] expanded this concept into a so-called rule-of-eight by ascribing to each element both maximum positive and negative valence numbers such that the numerical sum (signs not considered) is eight, the positive valence number being equal to the periodic group number. Abegg's views are summarized in Table 6·1. It is at once apparent that the type formulas for

[3] R. Abegg: *Z. anorg. Chem.*, **39**, 330 (1904).

hydrides and oxides characterizing so many early periodic tables are expressions of this rule of eight. The significance of Abegg's views was aptly summarized and put into essentially modern terminology by Drude, who stated[4] that "Abegg's positive valency number v signifies the number of loosely attached negative electrons in the atom; his negative valency number v' means that the atom has the power of removing v' negative electrons from other atoms, or at least of attaching them more firmly to itself."

The significance of this observation was not apparent until after the elucidation of atomic numbers by Moseley in 1913 (pp. 12–14). All modern views may be traced to two important and independent papers published by Kossel[5] and Lewis[6] in 1916. Inherent in both papers are views on the stabilities of the 8-electron outer arrangements in the inert gas elements (plus the 2-electron arrangement in helium) and the tendencies of elements with atomic numbers close to those of the inert gas elements to achieve these structures through involvement of the outermost electrons in their atoms.

Kossel[5] directed attention to the strongly electropositive characteristics of elements just following the inert gas elements in atomic numbers and the tendencies of these elements to possess positive valence numbers. Likewise, he pointed out the strongly electronegative characteristics of the elements just preceding the inert gas elements in atomic numbers and their corresponding tendencies to show negative valence numbers. On this basis, he proposed that the atoms of such elements lose or gain sufficient electrons to achieve the structures of inert gas atoms when they enter into chemical combination with each other and that the compounds so formed consist of ions. The ionic charge or the number of electrons lost or gained thus became the valence number. In support of these views, Kossel presented a diagram, like Figure 6·1, in which the constancy of the total number of electrons present in ions derived from a number of elements of adjacent atomic numbers is shown. It is apparent that the inert gas configurations are either achieved or closely approached in a significantly large number of cases. It is also apparent that other configurations, notably the nickel group structures where 28, 46, and 78 electrons are present (i.e., the psuedo-inert gas structures), are also achieved with considerable frequency. Kossel's views clearly provide the basis for modern concepts of ion formation by electron transfer (pp. 178–181) and have been of inestimable value in systematizing

[4] P. Drude: *Ann. Physik* [4], **14,** 677 (1904).
[5] W. Kossel: *Ann. Physik,* [4], **49,** 229 (1916).
[6] G. N. Lewis: *J. Am. Chem. Soc.,* **38,** 762 (1916).

ionic (electrovalent) compounds. Kossel himself recognized, however, that many compounds could not be fitted into this concept, a very important class being those in which decision as to which element is positive and which negative is difficult.

This difficulty was overcome, in large measure, by the postulates of Lewis.[6] The views of Lewis, although agreeing with those of Kossel

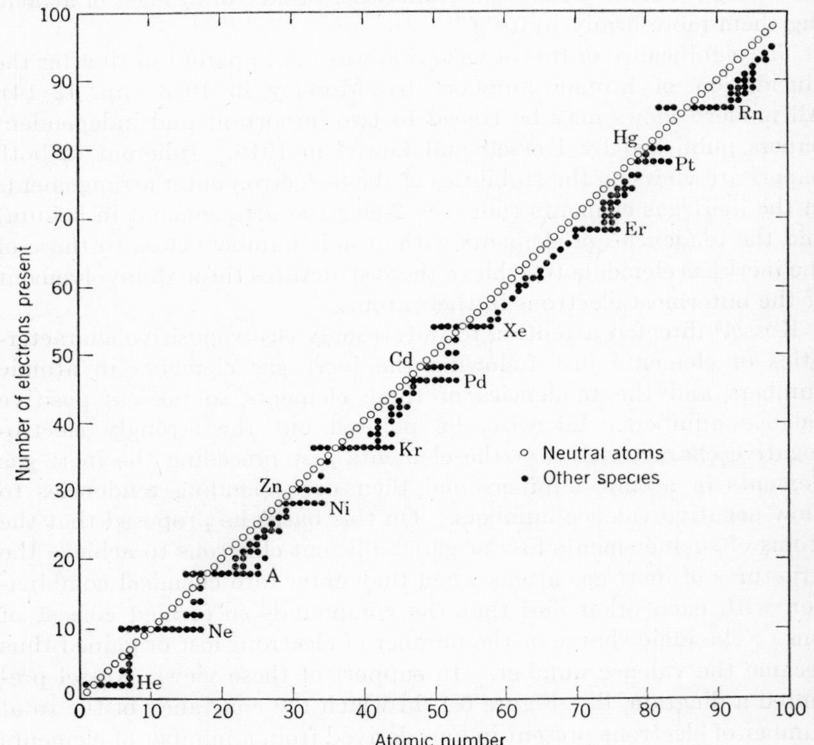

FIG. 6·1. Oxidation states of the elements on a Kossel type plot.

as regards the stability of the inert gas electron arrangements, differed significantly in that approach to these arrangements was thought of as resulting from the sharing of electrons between atoms. Using the now familiar cubic atomic models, Lewis pictured the structures of many simple molecules, the shared electrons between any two atoms being considered as belonging to both atoms and contributing to inert gas atom structures for both. Compounds so described were non-ionic in character, the essential opposites of those treated by Kossel. Lewis's views were adopted by Langmuir and were considerably extended by him. It was Langmuir[7] who suggested the term *covalence* to describe the sharing of electrons as opposed to *electrovalence* to describe electron transfer.

It was perhaps logical that the cumbersome cubic models be replaced by the mere symbols for the elements associated with sufficient dots, crosses, etc., to represent the valence electrons (i.e., those in the highest quantum level or levels). The familiar symbolism expressed by such notations as

$$Na^+ \qquad :\ddot{\underset{..}{Cl}}:^- \qquad H:\ddot{\underset{..}{Cl}}:$$

is a direct consequence of the cubic Lewis valence model of the atom.

Subsequent developments have centered largely in extensions and modifications of the Kossel and Lewis concepts and in their incorporation into modern quantum theory. The significance of the electron pair became apparent more or less empirically before its necessity was predicted theoretically. Its incorporation into electronic formulas followed and did much to simplify the systematization of chemical compounds. Such electronic formulas based upon these concepts remain useful and should continue to be so for many years to come.

Much of modern development has been concerned not so much with the facts that electrons may be lost, gained, or shared as with explaining why they may be and what the mechanisms of such involvement are. Development of the concept of the chemical bond as a force holding groups together has made it apparent that a variety of such forces may exist, those of the Kossel and Lewis types being only two of the most common. Those which we may consider may be classified conveniently as:

1. Electrostatic bonds and attractions.
   a. Ionic or electrovalent bonds.
   b. Miscellaneous electrostatic attractions.
   c. Hydrogen and hydroxyl bonds.
2. Non-electrostatic bonds and attractions.
   a. Non-ionic or covalent bonds.
   b. Miscellaneous non-electrostatic attractions.
3. Metallic bonds.

IMPORTANCE AND LIMITATIONS OF THE "RULE OF EIGHT"

Emphasis upon the 8-electron arrangement (rule of eight or octet) as governing the chemical behaviors of the elements has been so general

[7] I. Langmuir: *J. Am. Chem. Soc.*, **41,** 868 (1919).

since its elucidation by Kossel and Lewis that this arrangement is often thought of as being the only possible one or as controlling all chemical characteristics. Much of this emphasis is undoubtedly due to the rigidity with which the rule does apply to most organic compounds and to the fact that the properties of the majority of the more common elements can be explained adequately in terms of it. Actually, of course, there is no magic in the octet concept, and its application is limited to those elements the atomic numbers of which differ by no more than three or four units from those of the inert gas elements.

The inert gas arrangement (ns^2np^6) is undeniably one of stability. This is evidenced by the breaks in energy level diagrams at the inert gas configurations (p. 94) and by the high ionization potentials associated with penetration into these arrangements (pp. 155–159). This stability is due to the presence of closed shell configurations which cause both the resultant spin momentum and the resultant orbital angular momentum (p. 90) to be zero and thus render interaction with electrons in other atoms negligible. Although this is true in neutral atoms, it is not in ions which have achieved the same configurations because of the electrostatic forces which such ions may exert upon other bodies. It is not surprising that atoms of elements close to the inert gases in atomic numbers should achieve these structures. However, the demands of high ionization potentials and low electron affinities are such for elements which are several places removed from the inert gases in atomic numbers that they cannot achieve inert gas arrangements. Overemphasis on the octet must, therefore, be avoided.

That a variety of ionic configurations may result is indicated by the summary given by Foster.[8] In brief, the following ionic structures may be distinguished:

1. Regular configurations
   a. No electrons:
   H^+, D^+, T^+
   b. Two electrons (helium structure):
   $H^- \rightarrow He \leftarrow Li^+, Be^{+2}$
   c. Eight electrons (inert gas structures):

$$N^{-3}, O^{-2}, F^- \rightarrow Ne \leftarrow Na^+, Mg^{+2}, Al^{+3}$$

$$S^{-2}, Cl^- \rightarrow A \leftarrow K^+, Ca^{+2}, Sc^{+3}$$

$$Se^{-2}, Br^- \rightarrow Kr \leftarrow Rb^+, Sr^{+2}, Y^{+3}, Zr^{+4}$$

[8] L. S. Foster: *J. Chem. Education*, **16**, 409 (1939).

$Te^{-2}, I^- \rightarrow Xe \leftarrow Cs^+, Ba^{+2}, La^{+3}, Ce^{+4}$

$At^- \rightarrow Rn \leftarrow Fr^+, Ra^{+2}, Ac^{+3}, Th^{+4}$

d. Eighteen electrons (nickel group structures):

$Ni \leftarrow Cu^+, Zn^{+2}, Ga^{+3}$

$Pd \leftarrow Ag^+, Cd^{+2}, In^{+3}$

$Pt \leftarrow Au^+, Hg^{+2}, Tl^{+3}$

e. Eighteen plus two electrons (zinc group structures):

$Zn \leftarrow Ga^+, Ge^{+2}, As^{+3}$

$Cd \leftarrow In^+, Sn^{+2}, Sb^{+3}$

$Hg \leftarrow Tl^+, Pb^{+2}, Bi^{+3}$

2. Irregular configurations

a. Ions such as Hg_2^{+2}

b. Many ions derived from transition metals, e.g., V^{+2}, V^{+3}, Cr^{+2}, etc.

c. Ions derived from inner transition metals, e.g., Nd^{+3}, Gd^{+3}, Eu^{+2}, Am^{+3}, Cm^{+3}, etc.

The majority of these configurations are in accord with those one would expect from the arrangements of electrons in the neutral atoms (pp. 98–101). In the "eighteen plus two" structures, an individual electron pair which is available for combination is not involved. This is the "inert pair" of Sidgwick.[9] It amounts to a pair of *s* electrons in the *n*th quantum level for which sufficient energy to cause unpairing (p. 196) has not been supplied.

The octet concept shows a similar lack of universal applicability among materials containing covalent linkages. Although compounds of many of the elements, especially carbon, are treated adequately by this generalization, many others are not.[10] Typical of these are many halides (e.g., $BeCl_2$, BCl_3, $AlCl_3$, PF_5, SF_6, WCl_6, OsF_8), many coordination compounds (Ch. 7), metal carbonyls (pp. 700–717) and nitrosyls (pp. 598–605), etc. It is apparent that Foster's classification may be expanded to include covalent materials as well.

Although the octet is a definitely useful concept, its applications are limited, and it should not receive the universal attention normally

[9] N. V. Sidgwick: *The Electronic Theory of Valency*, p. 179, Clarendon Press, Oxford (1927); *Ann. Reports*, **30**, 120 (1933).

[10] W. F. Luder: *J. Chem. Education*, **22**, 221 (1945).

focused upon it. It is much more important that attention be directed to the important phenomenon of electron pairing (p. 175). The concept that electrons seek to pair with each other is nearly universal in application and is always useful as a first approximation in predicting chemical behavior. This "rule of two"[10] is far more fundamental than the "rule of eight."

ELECTROSTATIC BONDS AND ATTRACTIONS

Ionic or electrovalent linkages

The ability of atoms of an element to lose electrons is measured by the various ionization potentials characterizing that element. Conversely, the ability to gain electrons is measured by the electron affinity or the electronegativity. It would follow, therefore, that ionic linkages resulting from electron transfer should occur most commonly between elements with comparatively low ionization potentials and elements with comparatively high electron affinites. Under such conditions, although the amount of energy available from the electron affinity is not ordinarily sufficient to supply that required for electron loss, sufficient energy becomes available through the electrostatic attractions between ions of unlike charges in crystals of the resulting compound to permit anion and cation formation. As the ionization potential increases, more and more energy must be supplied to render the product ionic, and the net result is the formation of a covalent linkage unless the energy of solvation of the ions (p. 294) or the lattice energy (p. 181) is particularly large. In the crystalline condition, such compounds consist of orderly geometrical arrangements of ions held in fixed positions by balanced coulombic forces. When fused, these compounds retain their ionic characteristics, although the ions become mobile. Even in the vapor state, there are evidences for the existence of ion pairs. In truly ionic compounds, therefore, no molecules are present—only aggregations of charged particles. The chemical formulas characterizing ionic compounds represent the stoichiometries necessary to algebraic balances of ionic charges and have no molecular implications. Likewise, the term molecular weight is not strictly a correct one. Formula weight is preferred.

The orderly arrangements of ions in ionic crystals have been mentioned in connection with the discussion of ionic radii (pp. 136–145). Crystals of non-ionic materials are equally orderly. The general subject of crystal chemistry as such has no real place in this book; no attempt, therefore, will be made to discuss crystals in a comprehensive way. However, a summation of some of the principal types of crystal arrangements will aid in clarifying subsequent discussions. The more important crystal types are summarized in Table 6·2, and

TABLE 6·2
THE CRYSTAL SYSTEMS

System	Lengths of Crystal Axes*	Arrangement of Crystal Axes*	Examples
Cubic or regular	$a = b = c$	$\alpha = \beta = \gamma = 90°$	$NaCl$, $CsCl$, CaO, Cu
Tetragonal	$a = b \neq c$	$\alpha = \beta = \gamma = 90°$	SnO_2, K_2PtCl_4, Sn
Orthorhombic	$a \neq b \neq c$	$\alpha = \beta = \gamma = 90°$	$HgCl_2$, K_2SO_4, I_2
Monoclinic	$a \neq b \neq c$	$\beta = \gamma = 90°$ $\alpha \neq 90°$	$KClO_3$, $K_3Fe(CN)_6$, S
Triclinic	$a \neq b \neq c$	$\alpha \neq \beta \neq \gamma \neq 90°$	$CuSO_4 \cdot 5H_2O$, $K_2S_2O_8$
Rhombohedral	$a = b = c$	$\alpha = \beta = \gamma \neq 90°$	Al_2O_3, As, Bi
Hexagonal	$a = b \neq c$	$\alpha = \beta = 90°$ $\gamma = 120°$	SiO_2 (quartz), AgI, Zn

* Crystal axes lie along coordinates in space, the lengths being a, b, and c and the angles between them α, β, and γ.

these are shown pictorially in terms of arrangements of constituent ions in the unit cells in Figure 6·2. For more detailed discussions, standard works[11–14] on crystal chemistry should be consulted.

The magnitudes of ionic charges, or the *oxidation numbers** of the elements in electrovalent compounds, are limited. Consideration of ionization potential data (pp. 156–159) indicates highly charged cations to be energetically incapable of existence except under such extreme conditions as those existing in arcs or discharge tubes or in hot stars. In crystalline compounds, cations with charges greater than *two* are uncommon, whereas cations with charges greater than *three* probably never exist except with the heaviest elements (e.g., Th^{+4}). Correspondingly, the addition of more than *two* electrons to form *simple* anions is energetically impossible except perhaps with nitrogen

[11] C. W. Stillwell: *Crystal Chemistry*, McGraw-Hill Book Co., New York (1938).

[12] R. C. Evans: *An Introduction to Crystal Chemistry*, Cambridge University Press, London (1939).

[13] A. F. Wells: *Structural Inorganic Chemistry*, 2nd Ed. Clarendon Press, Oxford (1950).

[14] A. E. van Arkel: *Molecules and Crystals in Inorganic Chemistry*, Interscience Publishers, New York (1949).

* Oxidation number signifies, if positive, the number of electrons which must be added to a cation to give a neutral atom or, if negative, the number of electrons which must be removed from an anion to give a neutral atom. It follows that compound ions or radical ions such as ammonium and carbonate must also have characteristic oxidation numbers. The oxidation number concept may be applied also to materials held by covalent linkages (p. 211). As a means of indicating the charge or effective charge associated with an element without making any commitment as to the type of bonding involved, the term *oxidation state* is employed.

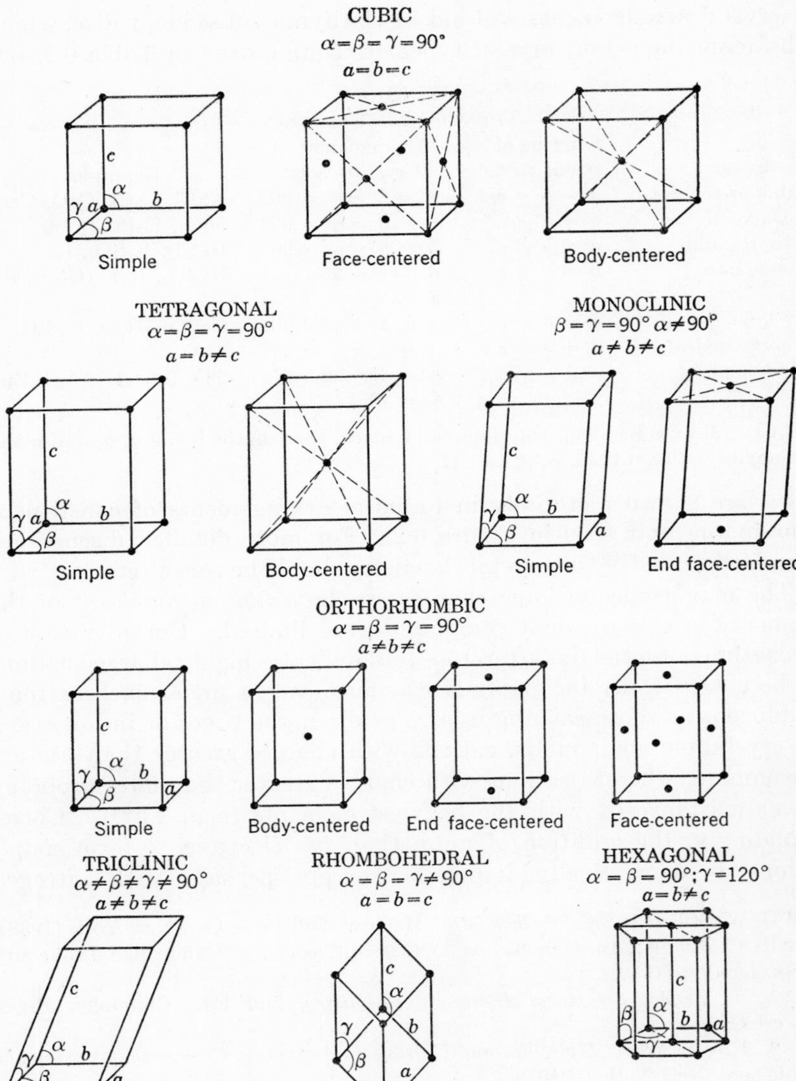

FIG. 6·2. Unit cells in the crystal systems.

(p. 558). Simple anionic species are thus limited to H^-, F^-, Cl^-, Br^-, I^-, At^-(?), O^{-2}, S^{-2}, Se^{-2}, Te^{-2}, Po^{-2}(?), N^{-3}. On the other hand, complex cations and anions with larger charges are not uncommon. In polar solvents, solvation effects often permit the existence of highly charged ions.

Compounds containing ionic linkages are characterized by rather well-defined sets of properties. Among these are the following:

1. Electrical conductance, with material transfer, just below the melting point, in the fused condition, and in solution in polar solvents. This is due, of course, to ions.
2. Comparatively high melting and boiling points. In both fusion and vaporization, the expenditures of rather large amounts of energy are essential in overcoming electrostatic forces of attraction. Melting points are useful but not absolute criteria, since they are also influenced by such factors as crystal structures.
3. Solubility in associated or polar solvents with high dielectric constants. This subject is considered in more detail in Chapter 10.

Possession of these general characteristics may be taken as a first criterion in determining the presence of ionic linkages. This fact is made apparent for a group of metal chlorides by the data summarized in Table 6·3. It must be pointed out, however, that only in a limited number of cases does one encounter pure ionic bonding. The majority of the known inorganic compounds occupy intermediate positions between the extremes of pure electrovalence and pure covalence.

Many of the characteristics of the ionic linkage are related to the formation and destruction of ionic crystals. Such properties are dependent upon the forces existing within these crystals and are related to ionic size, to oxidation state, and to electronic configuration. Among such properties are heat of formation, heat of sublimation, heat of combustion, heat of solvation, compressibility, hardness, melting point, boiling point, solubility, tendency toward solvolysis, acidity, and basicity. It is instructive to determine whether these are related to crystal stabilities in a quantitative way, or whether the relationships can be no more than qualitative in nature.

Such relations as do exist are dependent upon the *crystal* or *lattice energies* of the compounds. The crystal or lattice energy of an ionic crystal is the energy released when a large number of positive and negative gaseous ions (representing a mole of the material), separated from each other by infinite distances, are brought together into a crystal lattice which is characterized by definite interatomic distances. When such a process occurs, one must consider not only the attractive

TABLE 6·3

PHYSICAL CONSTANTS FOR CERTAIN ANHYDROUS CHLORIDES

Compound	Melting Point, °C.	Boiling Point, °C.	Equivalent Conductance,* ohm^{-1}	Compound	Melting Point, °C.	Boiling Point, °C.	Equivalent Conductance,* ohm^{-1}	Compound	Melting Point, °C.	Boiling Point, °C.	Equivalent Conductance,* ohm^{-1}
HCl	−114	−85	10^{-6}								
LiCl	606	1337	166	$BeCl_2$	405	(500)	0.066	BCl_3	−107	12.6	0
NaCl	800	1442	134	$MgCl_2$	712	1000	29	$AlCl_3$	subl.	183	15×10^{-6}
KCl	776	1415	104	$CaCl_2$	772	1100	52	$GaCl_3$	75.5	205	10^{-7}
RbCl	715	1388	78	$SrCl_2$	872	1250	56	$InCl_3$	subl.	600(?)	14.7
CsCl	645	1289	67	$BaCl_2$	960	1350	65	$TlCl_3$	25(?)	dec.	10^{-3}
				$RaCl_2$	ca. 1000	....	.....				
							ionic	covalent			

* At melting point.

forces existing between ions of opposite charges but also the repulsive forces of ions of like charge as these ions approach each other in forming the crystal. Inasmuch as the crystal is three-dimensional, the lattice energy for a particular compound cannot be obtained directly by considering the attractive and repulsive forces alone or in combination unless correction for crystal geometry is made. It can be shown that the lattice energy may be calculated, using the relation

$$U_0 = \frac{e^2 z^2 N A}{r_0}\left(1 - \frac{1}{n'}\right) \tag{6·1}$$

where U_0 is the lattice energy, e is the unit of electrical charge, z is the highest common factor of the oxidation numbers of the two ions, N is the Avogadro constant, r_0 is the interionic distance, n' is a constant called the Born exponent (p. 138), and A is a constant called the Madelung constant.[15] The Madelung constant is the geometrical correction factor, its numerical magnitude being determined by the type of crystal lattice. Typical Madelung constants for a variety of crystal types are summarized in Table 6·4.[15]

TABLE 6·4
VALUES OF MADELUNG CONSTANTS

Crystal Type	Madelung Constant
Sodium chloride	1.747558
Cesium chloride	1.762670
Sphalerite	1.63806
Wurtzite	1.641
Fluorite	5.03878
Cuprite	4.11552
Rutile	4.816
Anatase	4.800
Cadmium iodide	4.71
β-Quartz	4.4394
Corundum	25.0312

The magnitude of the lattice energy is thus determined by a number of factors, of which oxidation state is obviously the most important. Any decrease in either cation or anion radius or in both will increase the lattice energy. In general, a large value for the lattice energy is indicative of considerable crystal stability since it means that only those processes which supply relatively large amounts of energy can disrupt the lattice.

In the majority of cases, direct evaluation of lattice energy is either impossible or exceedingly difficult because of the absence of sufficient essential data. However, lattice energy may be related to ordinary

[15] J. Sherman: *Chem. Revs.*, **11**, 93 (1932).

thermochemical quantities by means of the so-called Born-Haber cycle.[16, 17] This is an approach based upon the assumption that the formation of an ionic crystal may occur either by direct combination of the elements or by an alternative process in which the reactants are vaporized, the gaseous atoms are converted into ions, and the gaseous ions are combined to give the product. For a simple substance such as an alkali metal halide (MX), such a process might be formulated

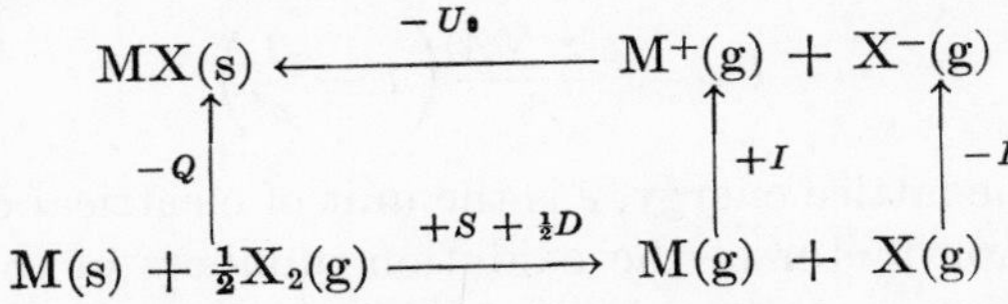

$$
\begin{array}{ccc}
MX(s) & \xleftarrow{\quad -U_0 \quad} & M^+(g) + X^-(g) \\
\uparrow {\scriptstyle -Q} & & \uparrow {\scriptstyle +I} \qquad \uparrow {\scriptstyle -E} \\
M(s) + \tfrac{1}{2}X_2(g) & \xrightarrow{\; +S + \frac{1}{2}D \;} & M(g) + X(g)
\end{array}
$$

each step being denoted by an energy quantity. These have the following significances:

U_0 = lattice energy of crystal MX.
I = ionization potential of metal M.
E = electron affinity of halogen X.
S = sublimation energy of metal M.
D = dissociation energy of molecular halogen X_2.
Q = ordinary thermochemical heat of formation of solid MX.

A negative sign associated with an energy quantity indicates evolution of energy; a positive sign indicates absorption of energy. Inasmuch as the same product is obtained from the same reactants by either path, the total energy changes must be equal in the two paths. It follows that

$$-Q = S + \tfrac{1}{2}D + I - E - U_0 \tag{6·2}$$

or, solving for U_0, that

$$U_0 = Q + S + \tfrac{1}{2}D + I - E \tag{6·3}$$

Thus lattice energies can be calculated if other thermochemical quantities are known. In early practice, however, lattice energies as calculated by Equation 6·1 were employed to evaluate electron affinities. The relations among these quantities for a few typical ionic compounds are shown in Table 6·5.

Inasmuch as the thermal stabilities of compounds are often characterized in terms of their heats of formation, it is of interest to examine this quantity in more detail. As shown by Equation 6·2, the heat of formation of a crystalline ionic compound amounts to a combination

[16] M. Born: *Verhandl. deut. physik. Ges.*, **21**, 13 (1919).
[17] F. Haber: *Verhandl. deut. physik. Ges.*, **21**, 750 (1919).

TABLE 6·5

BORN-HABER CYCLE DATA FOR CERTAIN IONIC COMPOUNDS

Compound	Q, kcal.	S, kcal.	$\frac{1}{2}D$, kcal.	I, kcal.	E, kcal.	U, kcal.
LiF	144.7	38.3	32.2	123.8	98.9	240.1
NaF	136.6	26.0	32.2	118.0	97.8	215.0
KF	134.5	21.7	32.2	99.6	97.6	190.4
RbF	132.8	19.9	32.2	95.9	99.0	181.8
CsF	131.5	19.1	32.2	89.4	99.4	172.8
LiCl	97.5	38.3	28.9	123.8	95.2	193.3
NaCl	98.2	26.0	28.9	118.0	90.7	180.4
KCl	104.9	21.7	28.9	99.6	90.7	164.4
RbCl	104.9	19.9	28.9	95.9	90.7	158.9
CsCl	106.6	19.1	28.9	89.4	95.1	148.9
LiBr	83.7	38.3	26.9	123.8	89.6	183.1
NaBr	86.3	26.0	26.9	118.0	85.6	171.7
KBr	94.2	21.7	26.9	99.6	84.6	157.8
RbBr	96.1	19.9	26.9	95.9	86.3	152.5
CsBr	97.5	19.1	26.9	89.4	89.4	143.5
LiI	65.0	38.3	25.4	123.8	81.8	170.7
NaI	69.5	26.0	25.4	118.0	78.1	160.8
KI	78.9	21.7	25.4	99.6	76.6	149.0
RbI	80.8	19.9	25.4	95.9	77.8	144.2
CsI	83.9	19.1	25.4	89.4	81.7	136.1
MgO	146	36.5	59.2	520.6	−178	940.3
CaO	151.7	47.5	59.2	412.9	−171	842.3
SrO	141	39.7	59.2	383.8	−167	790.7
BaO	133	49.1	59.2	349.0	−157	747.3
MgS	82.2	36.5	66.6	520.6	−72.4	778.3
CaS	114	47.5	66.6	412.9	−80.8	721.8
SrS	113	39.7	66.6	383.8	−84.3	687.4
BaS	111	49.1	66.6	349.0	−80.2	655.9

of a number of energy terms. It is apparent that changes in its magnitude will result from alterations in any of these terms. Two compounds are best compared, therefore, by taking into account all the steps summarized in the Born-Haber cycle. When this is done, the relative effects of individual steps become obvious, and a more nearly correct picture of the stabilities of the compounds is obtained. For example, it is apparent from such data as are given in Table 6·5 that the heats of formation of the alkali metal fluorides decrease with increasing size of the metal ion whereas with the other halides the reverse is true. This condition is due primarily to the proportionally larger lattice energies resulting from the closeness of approach of small metal and fluoride ions.

Other applications of the concept of lattice energy and the Born-Haber cycle will appear in subsequent discussions, particularly in those dealing with solubilities (pp. 342–344), with polyhalides (pp. 454–455), and with ionic compounds of the alkali (pp. 831–832) and alkaline earth (pp. 856–859) metals.

Miscellaneous electrostatic attractions

A number of electrostatic attractions which are uniformly weaker than those noted in strictly ionic compounds may be distinguished. These invariably involve *dipoles.* A chemical dipole arises when an unequal charge distribution exists between two atoms within a molecule. This condition may result in a diatomic molecule because of differences in the electronegativities of the two atoms or in an angular polyatomic molecule where a similar electronegativity difference occurs. A dipole is in effect then a non-ionic material in which one end bears a positive or a negative charge with respect to the other. The magnitude of this charge difference is expressed in terms of the *dipole moment* (μ), that is, of the product of charge by the distance between the charge centers. Dipole moments have magnitudes of the order of 10^{-18} electrostatic unit (1×10^{-18} esu $= 1$ Debye or 1 D).

Thus simple molecules such as those of the hydrogen halides have dipole moments. As might be expected, the numerical magnitude of the dipole moment increases wih increasing electronegativity of the halogen in this series (from 0.4×10^{-18} for HI to 1.9×10^{-18} for HF). On the other hand, a carbon dioxide molecule has zero dipole moment, even though carbon and oxygen differ markedly in electronegativities (p. 163). Since each C—O bond must possess a dipole moment, the obvious conclusion is that the atoms must lie in a straight line (O—C—O) for the individual dipoles to be opposed and to neutralize each other mutually. Water, however, has a dipole moment of the order of 1.71–1.97×10^{-18} esu, indicating that the molecule must be angular in arrangement. Experiment shows this to be true, the HOH angle being about 104°40′. Since negative charge resides in the oxygen and positive charges in the hydrogens, the dipole here is essentially a resultant as shown by

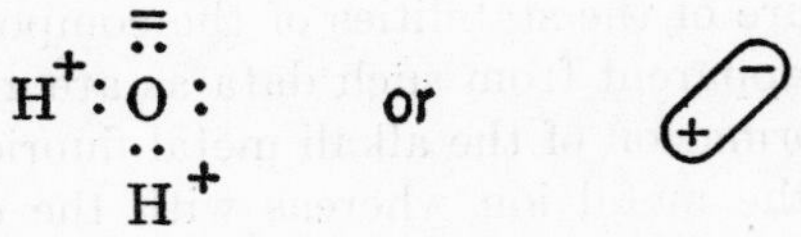

$$\mathrm{H^{+}}:\overset{=}{\underset{\cdot\cdot}{\ddot{\mathrm{O}}}}: \quad \text{or} \quad (+\ \ -)$$
$$\mathrm{H^{+}}$$

The existence of dipoles permits apparently neutral molecules to attract ions and other such molecules and results in combinations which, although often apparently stoichiometric, are not related to electron transfer or sharing. Among such attractions are the following:

1. *Dipole-dipole attractions.* Two dipoles will of course attract each other, leading to an alignment of molecular particles such as one finds in many associated liquids of the polar type (p. 339). Although such attractions are not large, they are of sufficient magnitude to alter profoundly such properties as vapor pressure and boiling point.
2. *Ion-dipole attractions.* Strong dipoles such as water are strongly attracted to both positive and negative ions. The solvation of ions and the related phenomenon of the dissolution of an ionic substance in a polar solvent (p. 339) are thus dependent upon ion-dipole attractions. It is probable that many so-called coordination compounds (Ch. 7) exist because of attraction of this type.
3. *Ion-induced dipole attractions.* Strongly negative or strongly positive ions, when brought in the neighborhood of molecules the electrons of which are comparatively far from centers of positive attraction, disturb these electronic arrangements sufficiently so that induced dipoles result. An attraction will then exist between the ion and the induced dipole. Again, certain complex ions, e.g., the triiodide (I_3^-), apparently form in this way.
4. *Dipole-induced dipole attractions.* Strong dipoles may induce dipoles in materials with easily deformable electronic arrangements in the same fashion as do ions. The resulting attractive forces would be expected to be somewhat weaker on the average than those characterizing the ion-induced dipole types. A few instances of such combination, among them the inert gas element hydrates (p. 381), are known.
5. *Induced dipole-induced dipole attractions.* Such attractions are extremely weak, but they do exist between certain neutral atoms or molecules as a result of the fluctuating dipoles produced by continuous changes in the intensities of charge concentrations in electron atmospheres. The liquefaction of the inert gas elements is apparently due to such attractions (p. 376).

The hydrogen bond

That the hydrogen atom may under appropriate conditions be attracted simultaneously to two more electronegative atoms, instead of only one, and thereby act as a bridge or bond between the two, is well known. Originally conceived of as a situation involving covalently linked hydrogen, the hydrogen bond is now recognized as being primarily electrostatic in character. The hydrogen atom, with its single 1*s* orbital, is incapable of forming more than a single covalent bond; therefore, formulations which require addition of an extra pair of electrons to the hydrogen atom cannot be given credence. Nor can it always be said that the hydrogen atom involved shifts tautomerically from one electronegative atom to the other.

The hydrogen bond was probably first recognized as being of common occurrence and of considerable importance by Latimer and Rodebush,[18] although some years earlier its existence between nitrogen and oxygen in trimethyl ammonium hydroxide had been postulated,[19] and it had been used to account for the reduced acidities of phenolic hydrogens ortho to carbonyl groups in benzenoid compounds.[20] Latimer and Rodebush used the concept to account for association in water and liquid hydrogen fluoride, for existence of high dielectric constants among these materials, for the slight ionization of aqueous ammonia, and for association of acetic acid into dimeric species. Subsequently, numbers of examples of hydrogen bonding have been found.

Hydrogen bonds are noted only between highly electronegative atoms such as fluorine, oxygen, chlorine, and nitrogen, although there are evidences that carbon which has been highly substituted with negative groups (e.g., $CHCl_3$, HCN) also enters into hydrogen bonding. Such bonds as FHF, OHF, NHF, OHO, NHO, CHO, NHN, CHN, and OHCl may be distinguished. These bonds are comparatively weak, their energies being only of the order of 5 kcal. (6.7 kcal. for FHF, 4.5 kcal. for OHO, 1.3 kcal. for NHN) as compared with roughly 100 kcal. for ionic or covalent linkages. It follows, therefore, that such bonds are not only easily ruptured but they are also formed with equal ease. When appropriate materials are combined at ordinary temperatures, hydrogen bonds form.

Not only are the strengths of hydrogen bonds greatest with the most electronegative elements, but also increases in the electronegativity of a particular element result in increased hydrogen bonding ability. Thus phenols form stronger hydrogen bonds than aliphatic alcohols, substituted ammonium ions (e.g., R_3NH^+) form stronger hydrogen bonds than the ammonium ion itself, etc. However, a given electronegativity cannot alone account for the hydrogen bonding tendencies of a series of non-metals, for, although nitrogen and chlorine have the

[18] W. M. Latimer and W. H. Rodebush: *J. Am. Chem. Soc.*, **42,** 1419 (1920).
[19] T. S. Moore and T. F. Winmill: *J. Chem. Soc.*, **101,** 1635 (1912).
[20] P. Pfeiffer: *Ann.*, **398,** 137 (1913).

same electronegativity, chlorine is by far the poorer hydrogen bonding agent. Small size in the electronegative element is also necessary.

It appears that when a hydrogen is bonded to one electronegative element, the strong pull which an atom of that element exerts upon the bonding electrons leaves an effective positive charge on the hydrogen atom which is sufficient, because of the absence of any screening electrons, to cause attraction for the second electronegative atom. That more than two such materials cannot be held by a single hydrogen is doubtless due to the restricted space around the comparatively tiny hydrogen atom. Although the majority of the groups so attracted have in their structures non-metal atoms with unshared electron pairs, these electron pairs are not directly involved.

Examples of hydrogen bonding are numerous, particularly among organic compounds. Some instances of importance among inorganic substances are the following:

1. *Association among simple hydrides.* The hydrides HF, H_2O, and NH_3 are characterized by melting points, boiling points, and molar heats of vaporization which are abnormally high in comparison with those noted for hydrides of similar and related elements. On the other hand, corresponding values for the electronically saturated methane are low and comparable to those for related hydrides. For the simple carbon family hydrides, as well as among the inert gas elements where interatomic attractions are at a minimum, such constants increase rather regularly with molecular weight. For the simple fluorine, oxygen, and nitrogen family hydrides, however, high initial values are followed by minima for the second members and then by increases with molecular weights. These trends are apparent in Figures 6·3 and 6·4. Molecules of the hydrides of fluorine, oxygen, and nitrogen are held together and built into aggregates by hydrogen bonding, whereas those of other hydrides are not.

2. *Association among other hydrogen compounds.* Similar situations are found with liquid hydrogen cyanide, hydrogen peroxide, certain alcohols, carboxylic acids, etc.

3. *Anion solvation.* Certain oxygenated anions appear to hydrate both in solution and in crystal lattices. Such anion water (p. 498) is apparently held by OHO bonds. Thus, in $CuSO_4 \cdot 5H_2O$, four water molecules are associated with the copper(II) ion, but the remaining one is associated with the sulfate ion (p. 499). The existence of acid fluoride ions of the types HF_2^-, $H_2F_3^-$, and $H_3F_4^-$ (p. 428) may be explained in terms of attractions between fluoride ions and hydrogen fluoride molecules through FHF bonds.

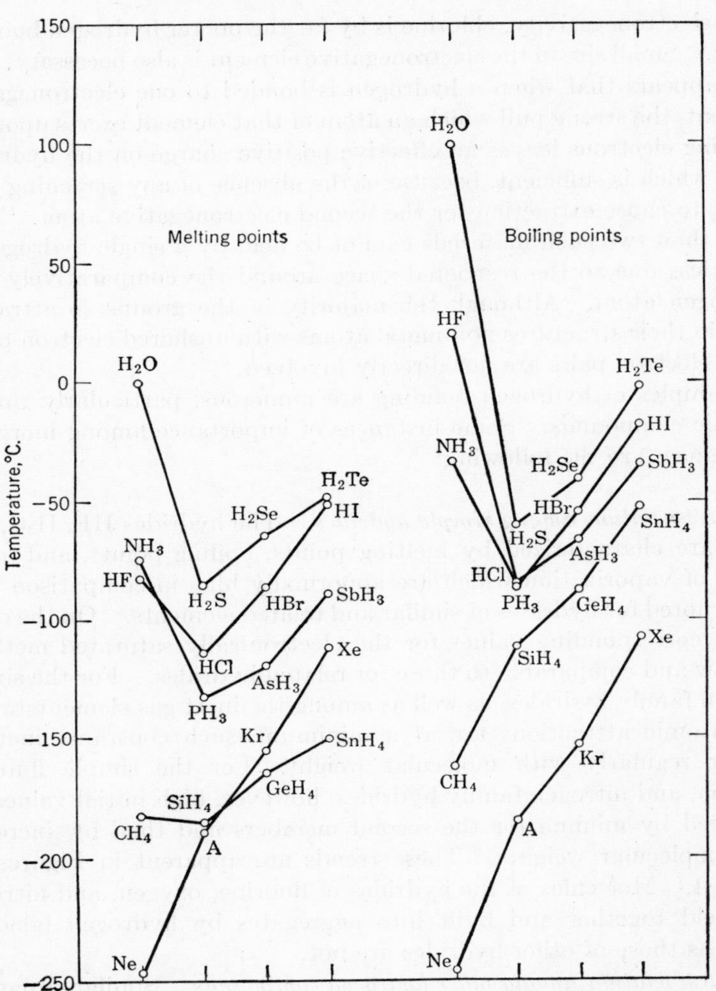

FIG. 6·3. Melting and boiling points of the simple hydrides. (Inert gas elements included for comparisons.)

4. *Abnormal solubility relations.* The uniformly greater solvent power of materials such as $CHCl_3$ or $CHCl_2F$ over closely related compounds such as CCl_4 or CCl_3F for compounds containing functional oxygen or nitrogen groups is logically ascribed to their abilities to hydrogen bond to the solute molecules. These solutes and many acid halides liberate energy when dissolved in chloroform but not in carbon

tetrachloride.[21] This is further proof of the formation of hydrogen bonds.

It is apparent that absolute distinction between the hydrogen bond and certain dipole attractions may be difficult. Unlike such attractions in general, the hydrogen bond appears to have some directional

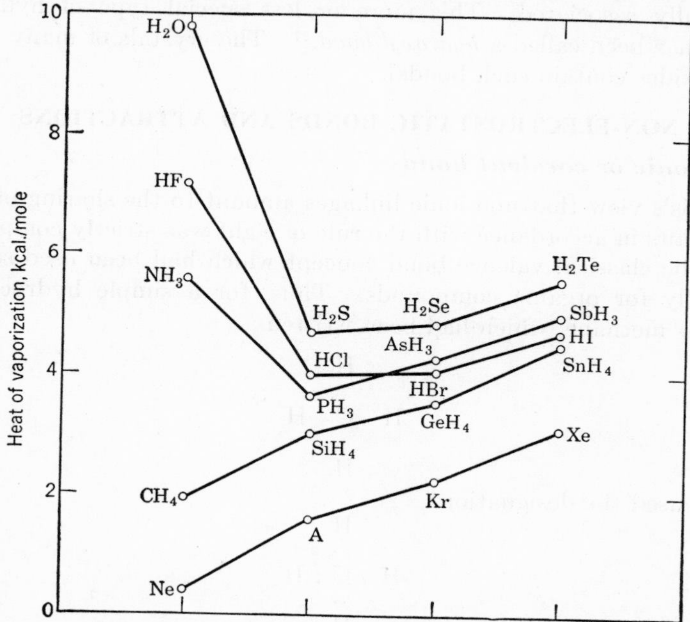

FIG. 6·4. Heats of vaporization of the simple hydrides. (Inert gas elements included for comparisons.)

characteristics. Numerous experimental approaches, among them solubility determinations, heat of mixing measurements, dielectric constant determinations, and infrared spectroscopic studies, have been used to establish hydrogen bond formation. Certain references[22–26] may be consulted with profit for further information.

[21] L. F. Audrieth and R. Steinman: *J. Am. Chem. Soc.*, **63,** 2115 (1941).

[22] L. Pauling: *The Nature of the Chemical Bond*, 2nd Ed., Ch. IX. Cornell University Press, Ithaca (1940).

[23] W. H. Rodebush: *Advances in Nuclear Chemistry and Theoretical Organic Chemistry* (edited by R. E. Burk and O. Grummitt), pp. 137–161. Interscience Publishers, New York (1945).

[24] A. F. Wells: *Structural Inorganic Chemistry*, 2nd Ed., pp. 235–258. Clarendon Press, Oxford (1950).

[25] M. Davies: *Ann. Reports*, **43,** 5 (1946).

[26] L. Hunter: *Ann. Reports*, **43,** 141 (1946).

The hydroxyl bond

Hydroxyl groups form bonds involving hydrogen bridges in a variety of compounds. These bonds are often somewhat longer than other hydrogen bonds, and it appears that in each of them the hydrogen remains covalently attached to the oxygen with which it was originally associated. This more or less special type of hydrogen bond has been called a *hydroxyl bond*.[27] The crystals of many metal hydroxides contain such bonds.

NON-ELECTROSTATIC BONDS AND ATTRACTIONS

Non-ionic or covalent bonds

Lewis's view that non-ionic linkages amount to the sharing of electron pairs in accordance with the rule of eight was strictly compatible with the classical valence bond concept which had been used so successfully for organic compounds. Thus, for a simple hydrocarbon such as methane, which had been written

$$\begin{array}{c} \text{H} \\ | \\ \text{H—C—H} \\ | \\ \text{H} \end{array}$$

Lewis used the designation

$$\begin{array}{c} \text{H} \\ \cdot\cdot \\ \text{H : C : H} \\ \cdot\cdot \\ \text{H} \end{array}$$

Correspondingly, double and triple bonds were considered to involve the sharing of two and three pairs of electrons,* respectively, as

$$\dot{\underset{\cdot}{\text{C}}}::\dot{\underset{\cdot}{\text{C}}} \quad \text{and} \quad \cdot\,\text{C}:::\text{C}\,\cdot$$

[27] J. D. Bernal and H. D. Megaw: *Proc. Roy. Soc.* (*London*), **A151**, 384 (1935).

* Some prefer a notation which distinguishes between the origins of the electrons. Thus methane would be written as

$$\begin{array}{c} \text{H} \\ \cdot\times \\ \text{H} \overset{\times}{\cdot} \text{C} \overset{\cdot}{\times} \text{H} \\ \times\cdot \\ \text{H} \end{array}$$

the electrons associated originally with the carbon being designated by crosses and those with the four hydrogens by dots. Such an approach is merely a convenience, for once such a bond has formed both electrons in the pair are equivalent and cannot be distinguished from each other.

Among the hydrocarbons and among many inorganic compounds, each bonded atom was regarded as contributing a single electron to the pair. It soon became apparent, however, that in certain compounds the octet concept could be preserved only if some bonds resulted from the donation of both electrons by a single atom. A classical example is an amine oxide, R_3NO, which could then be formulated as

$$\begin{array}{ccccc} & & \mathrm{R} & & \\ & & \cdot\cdot & & \cdot\cdot \\ \mathrm{R} & : & \mathrm{N} & : & \mathrm{O}\,: \\ & & \cdot\cdot & & \cdot\cdot \\ & & \mathrm{R} & & \end{array}$$

the nitrogen atom having supplied both electrons to the N—O bond. This type of linkage was termed *semi-polar* by Lowry[28] because of the resulting inequality of charge distribution, the electron pair donor becoming positive and the acceptor negative. In formulas, the use of an arrow to indicate the direction of donation or the actual use of charges directly is common. Thus an amine oxide may be written variously as

$$\begin{array}{ccc} & \mathrm{R} & \\ & | & \\ \mathrm{R}- & \mathrm{N} & \rightarrow \mathrm{O} \\ & | & \\ & \mathrm{R} & \end{array} \qquad \text{or} \qquad \begin{array}{ccccc} & & \mathrm{R} & & \\ & & \cdot\cdot^{+} & & \cdot\cdot^{-} \\ \mathrm{R} & : & \mathrm{N} & : & \mathrm{O}\,: \\ & & \cdot\cdot & & \cdot\cdot \\ & & \mathrm{R} & & \end{array}$$

Sidgwick's preference[29] for the term *coordinate covalent linkage* in view of its commonness among the Werner complexes (Ch. 7) has received wider acceptance. In effect a coordinate covalent bond amounts to a type of charged double bond.

The emphasis placed by Lewis on the importance of the electron pair[30] is truly striking. It must be pointed out that these views were advanced before the development of the quantum mechanical concept of the double occupancy of electronic orbitals, based upon the pairing of electron spins (pp. 91, 93). Although covalent linkages commonly require electron pairs, this is not invariably true. Thus evidences for the existence of limited numbers of 1-electron and 3-electron covalent

[28] T. M. Lowry: *Trans. Faraday Soc.*, **18,** 285 (1923).

[29] N. V. Sidgwick: *The Electronic Theory of Valency*, p. 60. Clarendon Press, Oxford (1927).

[30] G. N. Lewis: *Valence and the Structure of Atoms and Molecules.* The Chemical Catalog Co., New York (1923).

bonds have been obtained. They are discussed later. Classical treatments of the covalent bond have been given by Sidgwick,[31, 32] more modern treatment by Pauling.[33]

The Concept of Resonance in Covalent Bonds. Before attempting an evaluation of the nature of the covalent bond, it is essential that the principles of resonance[34] are presented at least qualitatively. Chemical systems may exist in a variety of quantum mechanical energy states, the state having the lowest energy being called the *normal state* and the others, in general, *excited states.* Quantum mechanics then tells us that of all conceivable structures which might exist for a given material in its normal state, the actual structure is that imparting maximum stability to the system.

For a given system then which may possess two structures, say I and II in the normal state, energy considerations may show that maximum stability is obtained for one structure to the exclusion of the other or that both structures are of more nearly equivalent stabilities. In the latter case, the normal state will then involve both structures I and II, and the system will resonate between the two. However, even if structures I and II are exactly equivalent, the actual structure will not be exactly intermediate between the two because the total energy of the system will seek a minimum value which will lie below that for either I or II as a consequence of interaction between the two. An extra stability, measured in terms of the so-called *resonance energy,* relative to either I or II results. The situation is analogous if more than two structures are conceivable.

When applied to covalently bonded materials, the theory of resonance is often useful in accounting for the remarkable bond strengths that are commonly observed. For many such materials, more than a single structure involving variations in the distributions of valence electrons may be written. The actual structure is then regarded as involving resonance among the possible structures by the exchange or rearrangement of electrons among them. This may be illustrated by specific examples. Thus, for the neutral hydrogen molecule with its electron pair bond, the following structures involving electrons designated respectively as · and $\times$ may be written:

[31] N. V. Sidgwick: *The Electronic Theory of Valency,* Ch. VI. Clarendon Press Oxford (1927).

[32] N. V. Sidgwick: *Some Physical Properties of the Covalent Link in Chemistry.* Cornell University Press, Ithaca (1933).

[33] L. Pauling: *The Nature of the Chemical Bond,* 2nd Ed., Ch. I–VIII, incl. Cornell University Press, Ithaca (1940).

[34] *Ibid.,* pp. 8–12.

$$\begin{array}{ll} H^{\times}\!—\!\cdot H & \text{I} \\ H^{\cdot}\!—\!{\times}H & \text{II} \\ H^{+}\!—\!:\!{\times}H^{-} & \text{III} \\ H{\times}\!:^{-}\!—\!H^{+} & \text{IV} \end{array}$$

Inasmuch as the two hydrogen atoms are characterized by identical ionization potentials and electron affinities, structures III and IV are highly unlikely. Calculation shows them to be energetically improbable. Hence the structure of the hydrogen molecule must involve resonance primarily between structures I and II. Again, to consider a more complicated case, the structure of the carbon dioxide molecule is described as involving resonance among the structures

$$\underset{\text{I}}{:\overset{..}{O}::C::\underset{..}{O}:} \qquad \underset{\text{II}}{:\overset{-\,..}{O}:C:::\overset{+}{O}:} \qquad \underset{\text{III}}{:\overset{+}{O}:::C:\overset{..\,-}{\underset{..}{O}}:}$$

each making approximately the same contribution.

Formally, resonance amounts to an effective rearrangement of electrons among two or more structures. It can occur only among those structures in which the same number of unpaired electrons is present. Although this concept would indicate a possible equilibrium among the resonance structures for a given material, none of the individual resonance structures has any actual physical existence by itself and is important only in its contribution to the structure as a whole. The important aspect of resonance is in the gain in stability resulting from resonance energy.

The existence of resonating structures may sometimes be deduced from measured bond distances. For example, in the sulfate ion the measured S—O bond distance is 1.51 A, as compared with the radius sum value (p. 133) of 1.78 A for a single covalent bond. A certain amount of double bond character due to resonance is thus indicated. Other similar situations can be distinguished.[35]

The Nature of the Covalent Bond. Theoretical treatment of the covalent bond is far more difficult than treatment of the electrovalent bond. Lewis's emphasis on the importance of the electron pair provided no explanation of why it is important, but rather reflected observed fact. Indeed, it was not until development of the quantum mechanics (1927 and since) that any reasonable hypotheses as to the stabilities of unions resulting from the sharing of electrons could be offered. Several such treatments have been advanced, notably those of Heitler and London, of Hund and Mulliken, and of Pauling and

[35] L. E. Sutton: *Ann. Reports*, **37**, 36 (1940).

Slater. They are based either upon involvement of electrons in terms of atomic orbitals (pp. 92–102) or upon the molecules as a whole in terms of molecular orbitals. The significant postulates characterizing these theories may be considered with profit, although it must be emphasized that such concepts are rigidly applicable to only the simplest structures. The complexities of the mathematical approaches to any of these presentations preclude more than elementary and qualitative discussions in this book.

THE HEITLER-LONDON THEORY. The Heitler-London views[36] are based upon the pairing and resultant neutralization of opposed electron spins. As two simple like atoms, say, hydrogen atoms, approach each other, the very weak attractive forces existing at large interatomic distances become smaller and are ultimately replaced by strong repulsive forces. Union of the two atoms into a stable molecule would be precluded were it not for the fact that the two possible molecular structures are equivalent (p. 195), and resonance permits a normal state of lower energy in the resulting molecule. Inasmuch as each of the two electrons in this case may with equal probability be found with either atom, the interaction which results depends only upon the spin quantum numbers of the electrons. If the spins are opposed, attractive forces result since the available orbital in each atom may then be doubly occupied without violation of the Pauli exclusion principle. A similar approach may be made in other cases. The importance of the Lewis electron pair thus becomes apparent.

The significance of unpaired electrons is at once obvious. In order for an atom to enter into chemical combination, it must possess one or more electrons which can pair with those in another atom through the canceling of electron spins. The valency of a species is thus determined by the number of unpaired electrons which it possesses. Although participation in bond formations by electrons which are already paired is formally ruled out, such electrons may be involved if they can be unpaired without the expenditure of excessive energy. In a general way, this may occur if no change in the total principal quantum number (n) of that electron is required. Thus nitrogen with an outer configuration of $2s^2 2p_x^1 2p_y^1 2p_z^1$ shares its $2p$ electrons with fluorine in the formation of nitrogen trifluoride (NF_3) but cannot form a pentafluoride because no more orbitals in the $n = 2$ level are available to accomodate one of the unpaired $2s$ electrons. With phosphorus, on the other hand, the configuration $3s^2 3p_x^1 3p_y^1 3p_z^1$ does permit the formation of a pentafluoride since $3d$ orbitals are presumably available.

As a first approximation, the Heitler-London concept is a very useful

[36] W. Heitler and F. London: *Z. Physik*, **44**, 455 (1927).

one, for many cases of covalent bond formation can be treated in terms of it. Like the Lewis theory, it embraces three fundamental ideas, namely:

1. Each atom in a molecule tends to assume a structure containing a closed shell of electrons.
2. A chemical bond results when two electrons are paired (in spin).
3. The pair of electrons is localized between the two bonded atoms.

Inherent differences arise, however. For example, for a material such as phosphorus pentafluoride a considerable amount of energy will presumably be required to pass the inert gas structure characterizing the trifluoride, and an assumption of entry of electrons into $3d$ orbitals will violate the first principle above. Furthermore, implicit in the Heitler-London theory is the assumption that the electrons in a shared pair come from different atoms. The coordinate linkage is thus ruled out. Maximum covalency is limited as indicated above, but the spin theory fails to account for such apparent anomalies as the lack of existence of perbromates. Odd molecules (p. 212) are likewise incapable of explanation.

THE HUND-MULLIKEN THEORY. The Heitler-London spin theory assumes that atomic orbitals remain unchanged when a molecule is formed. Inasmuch as the electron fields around each of the combining atoms will undergo mutual interaction, such an assumption is not warranted. Hund[37] and Mulliken[38] have developed an approach to bond formation which is based upon the effects of the various electron fields upon each other and which employs molecular orbitals rather than atomic orbitals. Each such orbital, characterizing the molecule as a whole, is described by a definite combination of quantum numbers and possesses a relative energy value. Molecular configurations are then built up by feeding electrons into these orbitals, the atomic nuclei involved being separated by fixed equilibrium distances. Each entering electron will, within the limits of the Pauli exclusion principle, seek the lowest possible quantum state. As these molecular orbitals are occupied, series of closed electronic groups are built up in much the same fashion as those which arise in the building up of the extranuclear structures in isolated atoms. In such a concept, the quantum numbers n and l have but little significance, especially in comparison with those describing the component λ of orbital angular momentum along an axis joining the atomic centers. Corresponding to the designations s, p, d, etc., for electrons in isolated atoms where $l = 0$, 1, or 2 are the designations σ, π, δ, etc., where $\lambda = 0$, ± 1, or ± 2. Since

[37] F. Hund: *Z. Physik*, **51**, 788, 793 (1928); *Z. Elektrochem.*, **34**, 437 (1928).
[38] R. S. Mulliken: *Chem. Revs.*, **9**, 347 (1931); *Revs. Modern Phys.*, **4**, 1 (1932).

electron spin gives two possible electrons for each λ value, the numbers of permissible electrons of each type are readily obtained. These values are summarized in Table 6·6.

TABLE 6·6
ATOMIC VS. MOLECULAR ORBITALS

Complete Electron Shells in Isolated Atoms	Values of l	Values of λ	Complete Electron Groups in Molecules		
s^2	0	0	σ^2		
p^6	1	$+1, 0, -1$	σ^2	π^4	
d^{10}	2	$+2, +1, 0, -1, -2$	σ^2	π^4	δ^4

When a molecule is formed from atoms, electrons may sometimes be promoted to a higher energy level for lack of space for them in the given level or because of the limitations of the Pauli principle. Such electrons in the resulting molecule occupy excited levels; they are called *anti-bonding* electrons. Electrons which do not occupy excited states are called *bonding* electrons; those which are not involved in molecule formation are called *non-bonding* electrons. Since molecule formation results only if the total energy of the system decreases, it will occur at the equilibrium internuclear distances if in the resulting configuration the number of bonding electrons exceeds the number of anti-bonding ones. In general, half the difference between the numbers of bonding (n_b) and anti-bonding (n_a) electrons gives the number of electron pair bonds in the molecule.

Further consideration of these views is somewhat beyond the scope of this treatment. More detailed works[39–43] should be consulted. However, the electronic behaviors in the formation of a few simple diatomic molecules have been summarized in Table 6·7. In these examples the K's which appear inside the brackets mean merely that the K shells are present but not involved. The Hund-Mulliken theory is advantageous in that it does not require electron spins for covalent bonds, and it is applicable to many simple molecules. However, since decision as to which electrons are bonding or anti-bonding in complex molecules is difficult, its application to them is extremely involved.

[39] R. deL. Kronig: *Optical Basis of the Theory of Valency*, Ch. IV, V. Cambridge University Press, London (1935).

[40] J. H. van Vleck and A. Sherman: *Revs. Mod. Phys.*, **7**, 168 (1935).

[41] W. G. Palmer: *Valency, Classical and Modern*, pp. 179–208. Cambridge University Press, London (1944).

[42] P. Ray: *The Theory of Valency and the Structure of Chemical Compounds*, pp. 29–38. Calcutta (1946).

[43] C. A. Coulson: *Quart. Revs.*, **1**, 144 (1947).

THE PAULING-SLATER THEORY. Pauling[44] and Slater[45] have developed what amounts to a logical extension of the Heitler-London theory to account for directional characteristics in covalent bonds. This extremely important characteristic of non-ionic linkages is considered in the next section. It is important, however, to consider some of the more useful concepts of the theory. Regardless of approach, it is apparent that an atom can form an electron-pair bond

TABLE 6·7

SIMPLE DIATOMIC MOLECULES IN TERMS OF THE CONCEPT OF MOLECULAR ORBITALS

Reactants	Product	Electron Pair Bonds
$2F(1s^22s^22p^5)$	$F_2[KK(z\sigma)_b{}^2(y\sigma)_a{}^2(x\sigma)_b{}^2(w\pi)_b{}^4(v\pi)_a{}^4]$	$\frac{n_b - n_a}{2} = 1$
$2O(1s^22s^22p^4)$	$O_2[KK(z\sigma)_b{}^2(y\sigma)_a{}^2(x\sigma)_b{}^2(w\pi)_b{}^4(v\pi)_a{}^2]$	$= 2$
$2N(1s^22s^22p^3)$	$N_2[KK(z\sigma)_b{}^2(y\sigma)_a{}^2(w\pi)_b{}^4(x\sigma)_b{}^2]$	$= 3$
$N(1s^22s^22p^3) + O(1s^22s^22p^4)$	$NO[KK(z\sigma)_b{}^2(y\sigma)_a{}^2(x\sigma)_b{}^2(w\pi)_b{}^4(v\pi)_a{}^1]$	$= 2.5$
$C(1s^22s^22p^2) + O(1s^22s^22p^4)$	$CO[KK(z\sigma)_b{}^2(y\sigma)_a{}^2(w\pi)_b{}^4(x\sigma)_b{}^2]$	$= 3$

a = anti-bonding electrons. b = bonding electrons.

for each stable orbital. Such a bond will in general owe its stability to resonance. This means that for each such bond two electrons of opposed spins and a stable orbital in each atom are essential. It appears furthermore that the formation of each additional electron-pair bond within a molecule renders that molecule even more stable so that structures of greatest stability result when all the stable orbitals in an atom are used either in forming bonds or in holding unshared electrons.

As might be expected, covalency is related to the position occupied by the element in question in the periodic system. Hydrogen, with but a single orbital, can form only *one* covalent bond. Elements in the first row of the periodic table are limited to *four* such bonds since the L shell contains but four orbitals (i.e., $2s$, $2p_x$, $2p_y$, $2p_z$). The octet concept is also generally applicable to elements in the second row since, although the M shell contains an extra *five* $3d$ orbitals, these are somewhat less stable than the $3s$ and $3p$ orbitals and are filled last. Cases in which $3d$ orbitals are involved embrace PF_5, PF_6^-, SiF_6^{-2}, etc., but are not common. No examples are known where all *nine* of the M-shell orbitals are involved. With the third-row representative elements, four covalent bonds are also characteristic, but increased covalence is permitted by the more ready availability of other orbitals and the decreased energy differences among them. The same trend

[44] L. Pauling: *J. Am. Chem. Soc.*, **53**, 1367 (1931); *Phys. Rev.*, **40**, 891 (1932).

[45] J. C. Slater: *Phys. Rev.*, **37**, 481 (1931); **38**, 1109 (1931).

continues in an enhanced fashion among representative elements in subsequent periodic series. Among the transition elements, increased covalencies are permitted by use of $(n - 1)d$ orbitals as well as the ns and np types. According to Sidgwick[46] maximum observed covalences are Li–F, 4; Na–Br, 6; Rb–, 8.

The Directional Characteristics of Covalent Bonds. It has been pointed out in Chapter 3 (pp. 106–108) that the distributions of the charge intensities of electrons in various orbitals are geometrical in character, s orbitals being spherically symmetrical, the three p orbitals lying along axes which are mutually at right angles, etc. It follows that bonds involving these orbitals must be similarly directed. To take this into account and to relate structural chemistry to the covalent bond, the Pauling-Slater extension of the Heitler-London theory suggests that the strongest covalent bonds result where maximum overlapping of atomic orbitals occurs, that is, where there is maximum interpenetration of the charge densities of the electrons involved in bond formation. The bond formed by a given orbital will then lie in the direction in which that orbital has its maximum value.[47] Covalent bonds are thus directed bonds.

To illustrate, suppose one considers the directional distributions of the bonds in the simple hydrides water and ammonia. The oxygen atom with the structure $1s^22s^22p_x^22p_y^12p_z^1$ has two unpaired p electrons. When combination with hydrogen occurs, these electrons are paired with s electrons from two hydrogen atoms. Since the p_y and p_z orbitals are at right angles to each other, a structure of the type

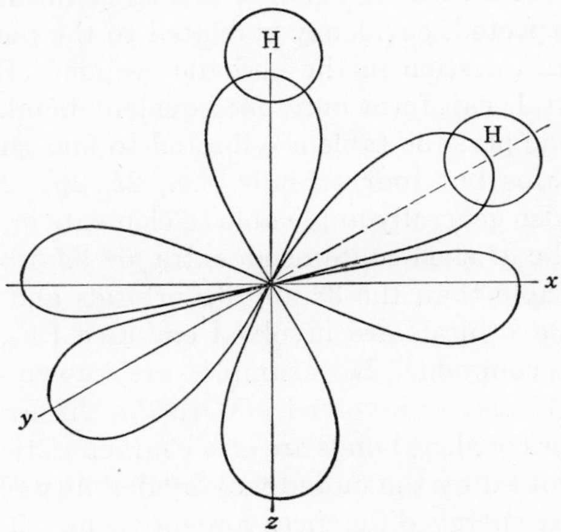

[46] N. V. Sidgwick: *Ann. Reports*, **30**, 110 (1933).

[47] L. Pauling: *The Nature of the Chemical Bond*, 2nd Ed., Ch. III. Cornell University Press, Ithaca (1940). A complete and comprehensive explanation.

with two O—H bonds at 90° to each other would be expected. With the nitrogen atom ($1s^2 2s^2 2p_x{}^1 2p_y{}^1 2p_z{}^1$), three unpaired $2p$ electrons are present; so by analogy one would expect the structure

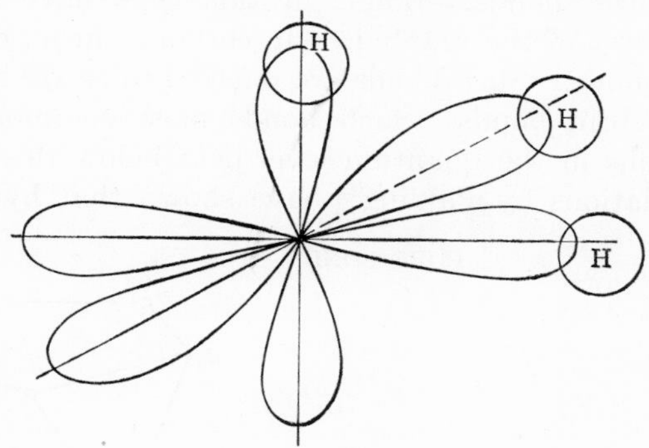

with the three N—H bonds at 90° angles in a pyramid arrangement. Hydrogen interactions and partial ionic character (p. 205) distort these arrangements so that the actual bond angles are ca. 105° and 108° for water and ammonia, respectively, but the principle is clear.

The case with carbon ($1s^2 2s^2 2p_x{}^1 2p_y{}^1$) is somewhat more complex since the prediction of three bonds at right angles and one essentially undirected is at variance with the observed tetrahedral character of the carbon atom. However, Pauling[47] points out that if each of the four bonds results from a linear combination of s and p orbitals, greater bond strength will result than if these orbitals are used alone and that the resulting bond strengths are of such magnitude that the bonds must lie at tetrahedral angles (109°28′) to each other. Such combinations of orbitals are referred to as *hybrid bond orbitals*, and the general phenomenon is termed *hybridization of orbitals*. One may have not only hybrids involving s and p orbitals but also those involving d orbitals as well. The latter are of particular importance in describing the bonding in coordination compounds of the transition metals (pp. 256–261).

The directional characteristics of the more important covalent bonds may be summarized as follows:

1. *Bonds derived from pure orbitals.*
   a. s bonds. Pure s bonds are not directional because they occur singly and because s orbitals are spherically symmetrical.
   b. p bonds. Pure p bonds lie in three planes which are mutually perpendicular. In compounds where they are present, bond angles are of the order of 90°.

c. d bonds. Pure *d* bonds are rare but appear to be directed along the slant edges of a pentagonal pyramid.

2. *Bonds derived from hybrid orbitals.*

a. sp hybrid bonds. Bonds of this type have a tetrahedral symmetry of the type noted in carbon, silicon, or germanium compounds. Such bonds are referred to as sp^3 bonds.

b. spd hybrid bonds. Such bonds most commonly involve *d* electrons in the quantum level next below the valence shell. Calculations by Pauling[47] have shown that hybrid bonds of

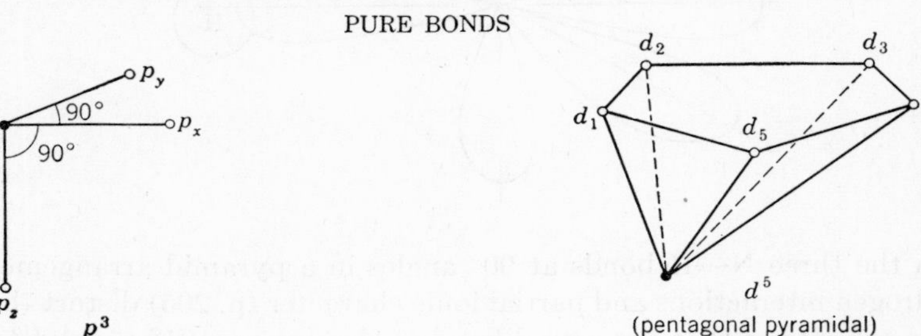

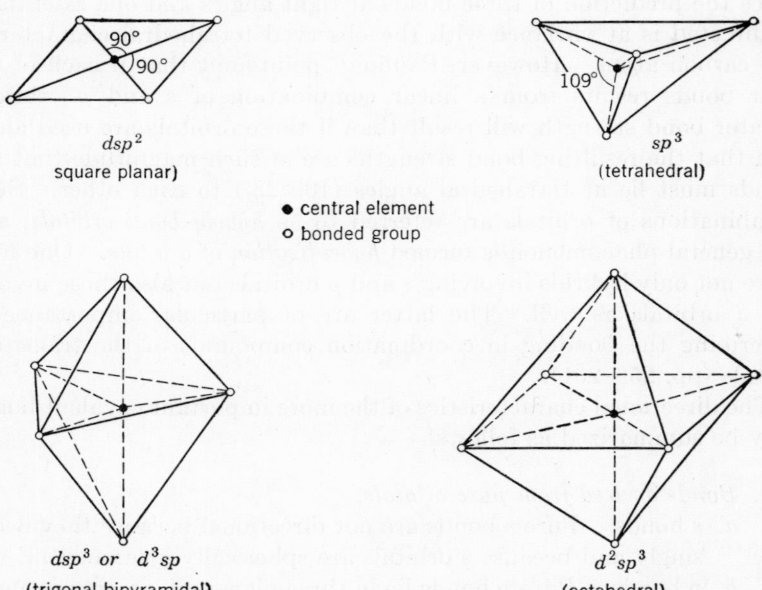

FIG. 6·5. Directional characteristics of various types of covalent bonds.

considerable stability may result under such circumstances. If, as in the case of Ni^{+2}, but a single $(n-1)d$ orbital is available, together with ns and np orbitals, hybridization of the type dsp^2 will result. This condition gives covalent bonds lying in a plane and directed toward the corners of a square. If, as in the case of Co^{+3}, two $(n-1)d$ orbitals are available, together with the ns and np orbitals, hybridization of the type d^2sp^3 will result. This gives six covalent bonds which are directed toward the corners of a regular octahedron. These types of dsp hybridization are discussed in detail in Chapter 7.

Graphically, the natures of such directed bonds are summarized in Figure 6·5.

The directional characteristics of many possible bond types have been summarized by Kimball,[48] as indicated in Table 6·8. Although

TABLE 6·8
DIRECTIONAL CHARACTERISTICS OF COVALENT BONDS

Covalence	Bond Type	Spatial Arrangement
2	sp or dp	linear (straight line)
	p^2, ds, or d^2	angular
3	sp^2, dp^2, d^2s, or d^3	trigonal plane
	dsp	unsymmetrical plane
	p^3 or d^2p	trigonal pyramid
4	sp^3 or d^3s	tetrahedron
	dsp^2 or d^2p^2	tetragonal plane
	d^2sp, dp^3, or d^3p	irregular tetrahedron
	d^4	tetragonal pyramid
5	dsp^3 or d^3sp	bi-pyramid
	d^2sp^2, d^4s, d^2p^3, or d^4p	tetragonal pyramid
	d^3p^2	pentagonal plane
	d^5	pentagonal pyramid
6	d^2sp^3	octahedron
	d^4sp or d^5p	trigonal prism
	d^3p^3	trigonal antiprism
	d^3sp^2, d^5s, d^4p^2	mixed
7	d^3sp^3, d^5sp	ZrF_7^{-3} (face-centered octahedron)
	d^4sp^2, d^4p^3, d^5p^2	TaF_7^{-2} (face-centered trigonal prism)
8	d^4sp^3	dodecahedron
	d^5p^3	antiprism
	d^5sp^2	face-centered prism

many of these arrangements are unknown, they all possess directional properties. That more types are not known is probably related at least to some extent to differences in *bond strengths,* the strongest bonds forming preferentially. Pauling[47] refers to the strength of a

[48] G. E. Kimball: *J. Chem. Phys.*, **8**, 188 (1940).

bond involving only *s* orbitals as unity and compares other bond strengths with this on a relative basis. The maximum attainable bond strength is 3, which is closely approached in d^2sp^3 bonds. Values assigned to common bond types are summarized in Table 6·9. It

TABLE 6·9
RELATIVE BOND STRENGTHS

Bond Type	Number of Bonds	Direction	Relative Bond Strength
s	1	non-directional	1
p	3	right angles	1.732
d	5	pentagonal pyramid	2.236
sp^3	4	tetrahedron	2
dsp^2	4	square plane	2.694
d^2sp^3	6	octahedron	2.923

should be emphasized that in all these bonds no distinction is made as to whether the necessary electrons are provided by both atoms or by only one. Thus there is no real difference between normal and coordinate covalence.

In evaluating the spatial arrangements in simple molecules, Helferich[49] arrived at some more or less empirical, but none the less useful, generalizations, which may be called Helferich's rules. These rules may be summarized as follows:

1. Molecules or ions of the type AX_2 (X = same or different atoms) have straight-line structures if the central atom (A) has no unshared electrons, and angular structures if the central atom has one or more unshared electron pairs. Thus CO_2, CS_2, N_2O, and N_3^- all possess straight-line structures in accordance with the electronic formulas

```
..    ..    ..    ..    ..    ..    ..    ..-
O::C::O     S::C::S     N::N::O     N::N::N
..    ..    ..    ..    ..    ..    ..    ..
```

whereas H_2O, H_2S, and NO_2^- are angular in accordance with the formulas

```
    ..        ..        .. ..-
H : O :   H : S :     : O : N
    ..        ..        .. ..
    H         H            : O :
                             ..
```

2. Molecules or ions of the type AX_3 (X = same or different atoms) have planar structures if the central atom (A) has no unshared electrons, and pyramidal structures with A at the apices if the central

[49] B. Helferich: *Z. Naturforsch.*, **1**, 666 (1946).

atom has an unshared pair of electrons. Thus, CO_3^{-2}, NO_3^-, and BF_3 are planar in accordance with the formulas

```
      ..                    ..                 ..
    : O :                 : O :              : F :
   ..  ..  .. -2      ..  ..  .. -       ..  ..  ..
  O : : C : O :     : O : N : : O      : F : B : F :
  ..      ..          ..      ..         ..      ..
```

whereas NH_3, SO_3^{-2}, H_3O^+, and ClO_3^- are pyramidal in accordance with the formulas

```
                    ..                                 ..
   H              : O :             H                : O :
   ..           ..  ..  .. -2       ..     +       ..  ..  .. -
H : N : H     : O : S : O :     H : O : H        : O : Cl : O :
   ..           ..  ..  ..          ..             ..  ..   ..
```

3. Molecules or ions of the type AX_4 have tetrahedral structures if the central atom (A) has no unshared electrons in its outer shell and if this shell is of the inert gas type and planar structures if the outer shell is not of the inert gas type. Examples illustrating this rule are not well defined.

These rules are useful as first approximations in arriving at the directed natures of covalent bonds. The importance of unshared electron pairs in fixing geometry merely emphasizes the fact that such a pair may be directed in the same sense that a covalent bond is. Examples will be discussed later among the halogen compounds (p. 445).

Partial Ionic Character in Covalent Bonds. The discussion presented thus far leads to the conclusion that chemical bonds involving electrons are either electrovalent or covalent in character. In practice, this is probably never absolutely true and is closely approached in only a limited number of cases. Ionic bonds are favored in combinations in which the elements differ markedly from each other in electronegativity. As such differences become less pronounced, bonds become increasingly covalent in character, and in unions involving atoms of the same electronegativity the greatest degree of covalency is shown. The breaks are not sharp, however, and as electronegativities change there appears to be a more or less gradual transition from essentially ionic to essentially covalent character. Even in combinations between identical atoms, equal sharing of electrons may not occur. Thus the bond in the hydrogen molecule possesses about 2% of ionic character because of small contributions to the total structure made by the ionic resonance structures (p. 195). Similar situations exist in other comparable cases. It is possible, therefore, to describe each covalent bond in terms of its partial ionic character.[50]

It is convenient to refer to covalent linkages possessing appreciable ionic character as *polar linkages** and to those possessing only very slight ionic character as *non-polar linkages.*[51] In a general way, then, the sharing of the electron pair may be regarded as approaching equality in a non-polar bond but deviating to a greater or lesser extent from equality in a polar linkage. The degree of this displacement or the degree of polarity may often be measured by the magnitude of the dipole moment (pp. 186–187). Zero dipole moment ($\mu = 0$) thus indicates equality of electron distribution in a simple diatomic molecule or complete symmetry of bond distribution in a more complex molecule containing a number of bonds each of which possesses dipole character (e.g., in CCl_4). Increasing polarity would then be indicated in the following cases:

	H_2, F_2, Cl_2, Br_2, I_2	HI	HBr	HCl	HF
$\mu(\times 10^{18})$	0	0.4	0.8	1.0	1.9
		H_2Te	H_2Se	H_2S	H_2O
$\mu(\times 10^{18})$		0	. . .	1.10	1.85

paralleling, of course, increased electronegativity on the part of the element combined with hydrogen. In fact, dipole moment data may be used to evaluate an electronegativity scale which differs only insignificantly from that given on p. 163.

Exact evaluation of the percentage of ionic character in a bond is difficult. By evaluating the ratios of observed dipole moments for the hydrogen halides to those obtained for completely ionic structures for these compounds through multiplication of the unit charge by the internuclear distances, Pauling[50] determined the ionic fraction of each bond. His values of 17% for HCl, 11% for HBr, and 5% for HI were supplemented by an estimate of 60% for HF in the absence of dipole moment data for this last compound. Using these values and the relation

$$\text{amount of ionic character} = 1 - e^{-\frac{1}{4}(x_A - x_B)^2} \qquad (6 \cdot 4)$$

where x_A and x_B are, respectively, the electronegativities of the elements A and B in a bond A—B, Pauling then related amount of ionic

[50] L. Pauling: *The Nature of the Chemical Bond*, 2nd Ed., Ch. II. Cornell University Press, Ithaca (1940).

* An unfortunate confusion in terminology exists, since in the literature ionic and polar linkages are often considered to be the same. It is more in keeping with modern practice to divide linkages broadly into ionic and covalent and to subdivide the latter into polar and non-polar.[51]

[51] S. J. French: *J. Chem. Education*, **13**, 122 (1936).

character to electronegativity difference ($x_A - x_B$) by means of an empirical graph of the type shown in Figure 6·6. Such a curve is admittedly lacking in complete accuracy, but it does reflect at least the approximate ionic characters of bonds. It is apparent that all bonds for which the electronegativity difference is above 1.7 are more than 50% ionic. Such bonds are commonly termed ionic.

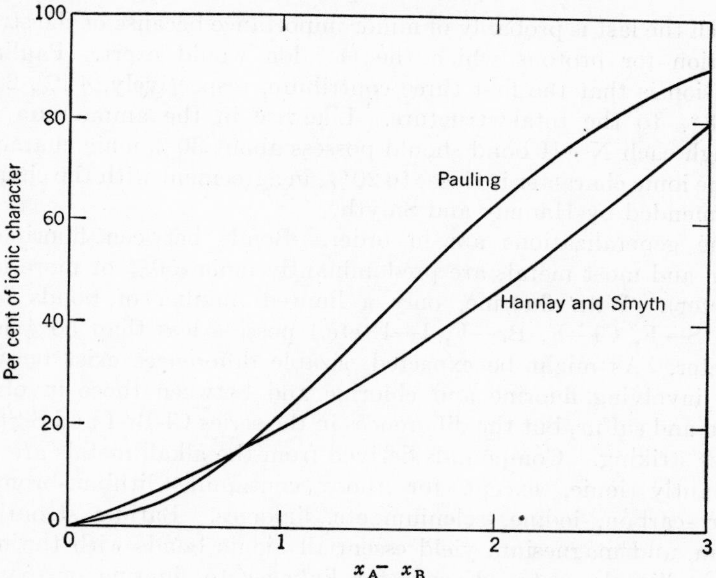

FIG. 6·6. Relation of amount of ionic character in a bond A—B to the electronegativities of the bonded atoms.

Recent measurements[52] have shown that the bond in hydrogen fluoride is 43% ionic, rather than 60% as assumed by Pauling. This necessitates revision of Pauling's curve relating percent ionic character to electronegativity as shown in Figure 6.6. Bonds possessing 50% or greater ionic character could then form only if the electronegativity difference is 2.1 or more. A revision of Equation 6.4 to

$$\text{amount of ionic character} = 0.16(x_A - x_B) + 0.035(x_A - x_B)^2 \quad (6.5)$$

then permits more exact calculations.

Of course, in molecules containing a number of bonds the picture is more complex. For water, the electronegativity difference is 1.4, corresponding, according to Pauling's treatment, to 39% ionic charac-

[52] N. B. Hannay and C. P. Smyth: *J. Am. Chem. Soc.*, **68**, 171 (1946).

ter in the O—H bond. However, the water molecule may possess four resonance structures as

$$\begin{array}{cccc}
\text{H} & \text{H}^+ & \text{H} & \text{H}^+ \\
\cdot\cdot & {}^{-}\cdot\cdot & \cdot\cdot{}^{-} & \cdot\cdot{}^{=} \\
:\text{O}:\text{H} & :\text{O}:\text{H} & :\text{O}:\text{H}^+ & :\text{O}:\text{H}^+ \\
\cdot\cdot & \cdot\cdot & \cdot\cdot & \cdot\cdot
\end{array}$$

of which the last is probably of minor importance because of the strong attraction for protons which the O^{-2} ion would exert. Pauling's conclusion is that the first three contribute, respectively, 44%, 28%, and 28% to the total structure. Likewise in the ammonium ion, although each N—H bond should possess about 30% ionic character, the true ionic character is closer to 20%, in agreement with the changes recommended by Hannay and Smyth.

Some generalizations are in order. Bonds between fluorine or oxygen and most metals are predominantly ionic (50% or more ionic character). With fluorine, only a limited number of bonds (e.g., C—F, S—F, Cl—F, Br—F, I—F etc.) possess less than 50% ionic character. As might be expected, sizable differences exist between bonds involving fluorine and chlorine and between those involving oxygen and sulfur, but the differences in the series Cl-Br-I and S-Se-Te are less striking. Compounds derived from the alkali metals are predominantly ionic, except for those containing lithium-bromine, -sulfur, -carbon, -iodine, -selenium, etc., linkages. Barium, strontium, calcium, and magnesium yield essentially ionic bonds with the more non-metallic elements. Except for linkages to fluorine or oxygen, beryllium forms predominantly covalent bonds. Aluminum resembles beryllium very closely, and the only boron linkages which are more than 50% ionic are to fluorine. Carbon bonds are all predominantly covalent. With silicon, the Si—F bond is predominantly ionic, all others being predominantly covalent. Other examples may be worked out from the table of electronegativities previously given (p. 163).

A somewhat less quantitative, but nevertheless useful, approach to the problem of transitions between electrovalence and covalence is based upon ion deformation or polarization.[53, 54] When ions approach each other closely, the attraction of the cation for the electron atmosphere of the anion and the simultaneous repulsion of the nucleus of the anion result in deformation, distortion, or polarization of the anion. This is shown crudely in the diagram:

[53] K. Fajans: *Naturwissenschaften*, **11**, 165 (1923).
[54] K. Fajans and G. Joos: *Z. Physik*, **23**, 1 (1924).

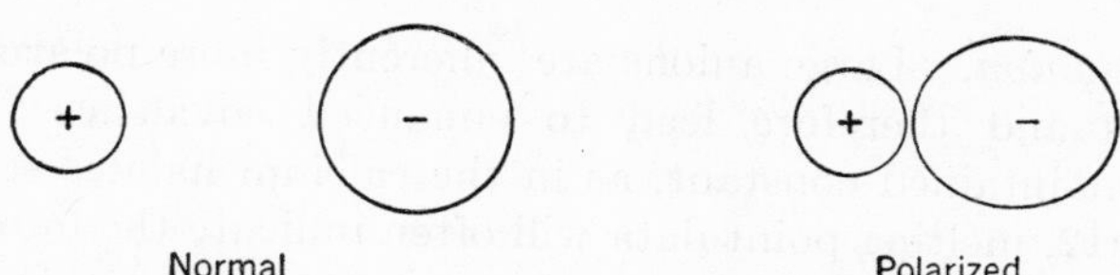

The cation would be similarly polarized by the anion, but the effect would be less pronounced because of the smaller cation size. The net effect of ion polarization is an increase in the degree to which electrons are shared, or an increase in covalent character.

Ion deformation is favored by a number of factors. These are summarized in a series of generalizations known as Fajans's rules. Thus increased covalence is favored by:

1. *Large charge upon either cation or anion.* The enhanced forces of attraction resulting from high ion charges cause increased polarization and increasing covalence. Although strict comparisons illustrating this point would require series of compounds of rather similar elements of constant size, the data on melting points of anhydrous chlorides summarized in Table 6·10 indicate the general trend, subject of course to the limitations of melting point data (p. 181).

TABLE 6·10

Effect of Cation Charge upon Covalent Character

Cation	Cation Radius, *A*	Melting Point of Anhydrous Chloride, °C.
Na^{+}	0.95	800
Ca^{+2}	0.99	772
Mg^{+2}	0.65	712
Al^{+3}	0.50	subl.

2. *Small cation.* Because of its greater concentration of positive charge, a small cation has an inherently greater polarizing effect upon an anion than a large cation. Again strict comparisons are valid only if other factors, notably cation charge, are maintained constant. The decrease in melting points of the anhydrous chlorides of the Group IIa elements with decreasing cation size, as shown in Table 6·11, illustrates this generalization.

TABLE 6·11

Effect of Cation Size upon Covalent Character

Cation	Cation Radius, *A*	Melting Point of Anhydrous Chloride, °C.
Be^{+2}	0.31	405
Mg^{+2}	0.65	712
Ca^{+2}	0.99	772
Sr^{+2}	1.13	872
Ba^{+2}	1.35	960
Ra^{+2}	....	ca. 1000

3. *Large anion.* Large anions are inherently more polarizable than small ones and therefore lead to enhanced covalence. Again, if charge is maintained constant, as in the calcium halides summarized in Table 6·12, melting point data will often indicate the importance of this factor.

TABLE 6·12

EFFECT OF ANION SIZE UPON COVALENT CHARACTER

Compound	Anion Radius, A	Melting Point, °C.
CaF_2	1.36	1392
$CaCl_2$	1.81	772
$CaBr_2$	1.95	730
CaI_2	2.16	575

4. *Cation with non-inert gas atom structure.* Cations with 18-electron structures appear to effect greater anion deformation than those with 8-electron arrangements even if charge and size are maintained constant. Thus the fact that the melting points of the anhydrous chlorides of the unipositive coinage metals are lower than those of the alkali metals (Table 6·13) indicates increased covalence among these materials.

TABLE 6·13

EFFECT OF UNDERLYING ARRANGEMENT UPON COVALENT CHARACTER

Eight-Electron Shell			Eighteen-Electron Shell		
Cation	Cation Radius, A	Melting Point of Anhydrous Chloride, °C.	Cation	Cation Radius, A	Melting Point of Anhydrous Chloride, °C.
Na^+	0.95	800	Cu^+	0.96	422
K^+	1.33	776	Ag^+	1.26	455
Rb^+	1.48	715	Au^+	1.37	170(dec.)

Although it is manifestly impossible to divorce one factor from all others in every case, these rules are very helpful in making approximate comparisons. It is apparent that in general they predict increasing covalence with increasing atomic number in families containing non-metals and the reverse in families containing metals.

The extents to which anions are polarized increase with increasing cation charge and decreasing cation radius. Often it is impossible to speak of one of these without mentioning the other, and it would be desirable to combine the two in some fashion. This has been done empirically by Cartledge [55] in terms of the *ionic potential* (ϕ), which is

[55] G. H. Cartledge: *J. Am. Chem. Soc.*, **50**, 2855, 2863 (1928); **52**, 3076 (1930).

defined by the relation

$$\phi = \frac{\text{cation charge}}{\text{cation radius}} \tag{6·6}$$

Inasmuch as the magnitude of the ionic potential increases with both increasing cation charge and decreasing size, large ionic potentials are associated with strong polarizing effects or increased covalence. Empirically, it is found that, if $\sqrt{\phi} < 2.2$ for anhydrous halides, they will be ionic and conduct electricity in the fused state, whereas, if $\sqrt{\phi} > 2.2$, they will be non-ionic and non-conductors. Ion hydration (p. 342), complex ion formation (p. 236), and acid-base behaviors among oxygen-hydrogen compounds (p. 319) may be correlated with ionic potential data.

Transition from ionic to covalent binding is accompanied by reductions in electrical conductances, melting points, and boiling points. It is interesting also that deviation of the color of a solid compound from the colors of its components may be taken as an indication of covalence.[56] This is especially true among anhydrous metal halides, where transitions from solid white chlorides (e.g., $SnCl_4$, $SbCl_3$, AgCl, $HgCl_2$) to comparatively highly colored solid iodides (e.g., red SnI_4, red SbI_3, yellow AgI, red HgI_2) are not uncommon. Color here results from highly polarized anions and is to be contrasted with that due to unpaired electrons in transition and inner transition metal ions (pp. 874, 899).

The unequal distribution of shared electrons when atoms of different electronegativities combine justifies extension of the *oxidation number* concept (p. 179) to covalent bonds. Thus, in a compound such as hydrogen chloride, the more electronegative chlorine may be regarded as acquiring a greater share in the shared electron pair than the hydrogen and may be assigned an oxidation number of -1. The hydrogen then has an oxidation number of $+1$. Similarly, in an ion such as chlorate for which the structure

```
          ..
        : O :
   ..     ..    .. -
 : O  :  Cl  :  O :
   ..     ..    ..
```

may be written, the more electronegative oxygens may be regarded as effectively acquiring electrons from the chlorine, giving chlorine an oxidation number of $+5$ and oxygen a value of -2. Here one oxygen atom has of course obtained one electron from the metal which

[56] K. S. Pitzer and J. H. Hildebrand: *J. Am. Chem. Soc.*, **63**, 2472 (1941).

yielded the balancing cation. On the other hand, in molecules of free elements, e.g., H_2, Cl_2, etc., where the atoms are identical, each would be assigned an oxidation number of zero.

One-Electron and Three-Electron Covalent Bonds. That materials containing 1- and 3-electron bonds are limited in number is further evidence for the importance of electron pairing in the formation of covalent linkages. An outstanding example of a 1-electron bond is found in the hydrogen molecule-ion, H_2^+, a species which although found only spectroscopically is nevertheless characterized by a bond energy of 61 kcal. per mole.[57] The hydrogen molecule-ion may be described as a combination of the two resonance forms

$$\mathrm{H}\cdot \quad \mathrm{H}^+ \qquad \text{and} \qquad \mathrm{H}^+ \quad \cdot\mathrm{H}$$

which structures account for some 50 kcal. of the bond energy. The equilibrium bond distance is 1.06 A. Such 1-electron bonds are possible only between two like atoms or atoms of nearly identical electronegativities because only then can two resonance structures of essentially equal stabilities result.

There exist also a limited number of molecules which contain odd numbers of electrons. These are called *odd molecules,* and their stabilities are apparently due to the presence of 3-electron bonds.[58] If three bonding electrons are available, a structure involving two atoms A and B might, without violation of the Pauli principle, amount to

$$\mathrm{A}: \quad \cdot\mathrm{B} \qquad \text{and} \qquad \mathrm{A}\cdot \quad :\mathrm{B}$$

Neither structure above would be energetically feasible, but, if A and B were sufficiently alike, the two structures might then possess essentially, the same energies, and resonance between them might stabilize a bond which in effect involves three electrons, i.e., A · · · B. Such a bond has about half the strength of an electron-pair bond and forms between like atoms or those differing by not much more than 0.5 in electronegativity. Thus three electron bonds might characterize linkages in the pairs oxygen-fluorine, nitrogen-oxygen, nitrogen-chlorine, and chlorine-oxygen. Important 3-electron bonds are found in the species NO $(:\mathrm{N}\overset{\cdots}{=\!=}\mathrm{O}:)$, NO_2 $(:\ddot{\mathrm{O}}\overset{\cdots}{—}\mathrm{N}{=}\ddot{\mathrm{O}}:)$, OF $(:\ddot{\mathrm{O}}\overset{\cdots}{—}\ddot{\mathrm{F}}:)$, ClO_2 $(:\ddot{\underset{\cdot\cdot}{\mathrm{O}}}—\ddot{\mathrm{Cl}}\overset{\cdots}{—}\ddot{\mathrm{O}}:)$, O_2^- $(:\ddot{\mathrm{O}}\overset{\cdots}{—}\ddot{\mathrm{O}}:^-)$, O_2 $(:\mathrm{O}\overset{\cdots}{\underset{\cdots}{—}}\mathrm{O}:)$,

[57] L. Pauling: *The Nature of the Chemical Bond,* 2nd Ed., pp. 13–19. Cornell University Press, Ithaca (1940).

[58] *Ibid.*, pp. 264–276.

$ON(SO_3)_2^-$ (: $\ddot{O}\overset{\cdots}{—}N(SO_3)_2^-$), and He_2^+ (He · · · He^+). These materials are discussed individually in later chapters. If a regular electron-pair bond is present in addition to the 3-electron bond, e.g. $A\overset{\cdots}{—}B$, the energy of the structure is close to that of the dimeric arrangement : A—B—B—A :. Sometimes the dimer may be the more stable (e.g., NO_2 gives N_2O_4), and sometimes the reverse may be true (e.g., NO does not dimerize except at very low temperatures).

Atomic Crystals or Giant Molecules. In a solid such as the diamond, silicon carbide, boron nitride, or aluminum nitride, complete electron-pair covalent bonding links all atoms together in all directions in space. As a consequence, it is impossible to distinguish individual molecular groups, and any particle of the material may be regarded as a molecule. Such solids are characterized as *atomic crystals* or *giant molecules.* Because of the comparatively large numbers of bonds which would have to be broken to produce rupture of any type, such substances are characterized by extreme hardnesses, low solubilities in all solvents, high melting points, and high boiling points. They are, of course, non-conductors.

Electron-Deficient Covalent Structures. In some instances, elements with fewer valence electrons than valence shell orbitals (e.g., boron, aluminum, platinum) form covalent compounds in which there are insufficient electrons present to account for electron pair bonds among all the atoms present. Typical of these compounds are the boron hydrides such as B_2H_6 and B_4H_{10} (pp. 774–795); the dimeric aluminum alkyls such as $[Al(CH_3)_3]_2$ (p. 743); the tetrameric platinum tetra alkyls such as $[Pt(CH_3)_4]_4$; and certain interstitial compounds (p. 221). Such materials are called *electron deficient* and present interesting problems concerning structures and bond types.[59–63]

Early views relating the structures of certain of these compounds to resonance forms involving 1-electron and electron-pair bonds appear less tenable than postulations requiring bridge structures. The natures of such bridges and their origins, however, are in some question. Pitzer[59] considers the boron hydrides to contain double bonds in which protons are imbedded (protonated double bonds), a concept which has met with considerable favor[61] (pp. 790, 793). On the other hand, the dimeric aluminum alkyls are apparently bonded by electrostatic attractions between positive aluminum and negative carbon

[59] K. S. Pitzer: *J. Am. Chem. Soc.*, **67**, 1126 (1945).
[60] K. S. Pitzer and H. S. Gutowsky: *J. Am. Chem. Soc.*, **68**, 2204 (1946).
[61] H. C. Longuet-Higgins: *J. Chem. Soc.*, **1946**, 139.
[62] R. E. Rundle: *J. Am. Chem. Soc.*, **69**, 1327 (1947).
[63] R. E. Rundle: *J. Chem. Phys.*, **17**, 671 (1949).

atoms[60] (pp. 743–744). Rundle[62, 63] points out that in all compounds which possess electron-deficient structures, a metal with more low energy orbitals than valence electrons is combined with atoms or groups containing no unshared electron pairs. On this basis, it is postulated that electron-deficient bonding involves a tendency to use all low-energy orbitals and amounts to use of one normal bond (electron-pair) and one unused excess low-energy orbital per bond. A complete evaluation of the relative merits of these proposals is beyond the scope of the discussion in this book. For details, the original papers should be consulted.

Isosterism and Isosteric Groups. In 1919, Langmuir[64] pointed out that in molecules or ions containing the same number of atoms and

TABLE 6·14
PHYSICAL CONSTANTS OF ISOSTERIC MOLECULES

Property	Isosteric Molecules			
	N_2	CO	N_2O	CO_2
Critical temperature, °C.	−127	−122	35.4	31.9
Critical pressure, atm.	33	35	75	77
Density of liquid, gram/ml.	0.796	0.793	0.856(10°C.)	0.858(10°C.)
Viscosity, poise (× 10⁶), 20°C.	166	163	148	148
Magnetic susceptibility, Bohr magnetons (× 10⁶) at 40 atm., 16°C.	......	......	0.12	0.12
Thermal conductivity at 100°C.	0.0566	0.0543	0.0506	0.0506
Refractive index of liquid, D line, 16°C.	......	......	1.193	1.190
Dielectric constant of liquid at 0°C.	......	......	1.598	1.582
Solubility in water, at 0°C.	2.4	3.5	1.305	1.780
Hydrate	......	......	$N_2O{\cdot}6H_2O$	$CO_2{\cdot}6H_2O$
Heat of formation of hydrate, kcal./mole	......	......	14.9	15.0

the same total number of electrons the electrons might be expected to arrange themselves in a similar fashion. Groups of this type were called *isosteric groups* or, more simply, *isosteres.* Although general similarities might be expected among all isosteric groups, much greater similarities in physical properties would characterize those isosteres which have the same electrical charge. That this is strikingly true is shown by the data summarized in Table 6·14 for the pairs N_2-CO

[64] I. Langmuir: *J. Am. Chem. Soc.,* **41,** 1543 (1919).

and N_2O-CO_2. Comparable similarities may be expected in other like pairs, although the majority of the groups listed by Langmuir and summarized in Table 6·15 possess charge differences. Many cases of isomorphism can be reconciled in terms of isosterism.

TABLE 6·15

ISOSTERES ACCORDING TO LANGMUIR

Isosteric Groups	Isosteric Groups
H^-, He, Li^+	NO_3^-, CO_3^{-2}
O^{-2}, F^-, Ne, Na^+, Mg^{+2}, Al^{+3}	NO_2^-, O_3
S^{-2}, Cl^-, A, K^+, Ca^{+2}, (Sc^{+3})*	HF, OH^-
(Se^{-2}), Br^-, Kr, Rb^+, Sr^{+2}, (Y^{+3})	ClO_4^-, SO_4^{-2}, PO_4^{-3}(SiO_4^{-4})
(Te^{-2}), I^-, Xe, Cs^+, Ba^{+2}, (La^{+3})	ClO_3^-, SO_3^{-2}
(At^-, Rn, Fr^+, Ra^{+2}, Ac^{+3})	SO_3, PO_3^-
Cu^+, Zn^{+2}, (Ga^{+3}, etc.)	$S_2O_6^{-2}$, $P_2O_6^{-4}$
Ag^+, Cd^{+2}, (In^{+3}, etc.)	$S_2O_7^{-2}$, $P_2O_7^{-4}$
(Au^+, Hg^{+2}, Tl^{+3}, etc.)	SiH_4, PH_4^+
N_2, CO, CN^-	MnO_4^-, CrO_4^{-2}
CH_4, NH_4^+	SeO_4^{-2}, AsO_4^{-3}
CO_2, N_2O, N_3^-, CNO^-(ONC^-, OCN^-)	(IO_6^{-5}, TeO_6^{-6})

* Materials in parentheses not in Langmuir's paper.

The concept of isosterism as outlined by Langmuir is still commonly used by inorganic chemists, but others have extended and modified it somewhat.[65] Thus, Grimm[66] considered all molecules or groups containing the same number of valence electrons to be isosteric, regardless of the number of atoms involved, and used isomorphism as a criterion. These views were extended by Erlenmeyer and his coworkers,[67] who concluded that only the outermost or boundary electrons should be considered in determining isosterism. It is in this form that the concept has been of particular use in accounting for similarities among the properties of apparently unrelated organic structures.

Miscellaneous non-electrostatic attractions

Substances consisting of non-polar molecules with completed electronic groups solidify at low temperatures to what are called molecular crystals. The forces holding such crystals together apparently arise from electronic interactions (perhaps fluctuating dipoles, p. 187) and have magnitudes of the order of 1 kcal. per mole. They are the nonspecific van der Waals forces.

[65] H. L. Bradlow, C. A. Vander Werf, and J. Kleinberg: *J. Chem. Education*, **24**, 433 (1947).

[66] H. G. Grimm: *Z. Elektrochem.*, **31**, 474 (1925); *Naturwissenschaften*, **17**, 535 (1929).

[67] H. Erlenmeyer, E. Berger, and M. Leo: *Helv. Chim. Acta*, **16**, 733 (1933).

THE METALLIC BOND. NATURE OF THE METALLIC STATE

The metallic elements are generally described as those which by virtue of the presence of comparatively few electrons in the valence levels of their atoms tend to be electropositive in character. This is an adequate description as far as chemical characteristics are concerned, but it is not useful in indicating the natures of the forces which exist within a solid metal. This metallic bond is probably better approached through a consideration of physical characteristics and how these may be interpreted in terms of a logical concept.[68]

Among the physical properties which are characteristic of the type of aggregation which we call the metallic state are the following:

1. *Conduction phenomena.* Metallic materials in general show high electrical conductivity without material transfer and high thermal conductivity. Electrical conductivity is a periodic function of atomic number, being highest (per atom) for univalent metals, less for divalent metals, and at minimum values for multiple electron metals. In general, it decreases with increasing temperature and resultant increase in the frequencies of atomic vibrations. Thermal conductivity has been less thoroughly studied.

2. *Optical characteristics.* Metals are uniformly lustrous, and all but copper and gold are silvery or grayish. It is apparent, except with copper and gold, that metals must absorb light of all frequencies and immediately radiate it.

3. *Mechanical characteristics.* Metals are characterized by such mechanical properties as ductility, malleability, and flow upon application of stress. Although there is little resistance to deformation, there is ample evidence for the existence of strong cohesive forces which resist the complete fracture or disruption of the object.

4. *Emission phenomena.* Many metals when exposed to radiation of short wavelength or when heated to sufficiently high temperatures emit electrons. These are, respectively, the phenomena of photoelectric and thermionic emission. In photoelectric emission, there is always a limiting or threshold frequency below which no emission occurs. It is evident, then, that an electron must be given a certain liminal amount of energy before it can escape from the metal. Photoelectric emission is temperature-independent up to the point at which thermionic emission begins. Above this temperature electrons are then emitted as a result of thermal energy.

[68] W. C. Fernelius and R. F. Robey: *J. Chem. Education*, **12**, 53 (1935).

5. *Structural characteristics.* Unlike the solid non-metallic elements which are made up of aggregations of discrete molecules and are comparatively open and with low densities, metals possess close-packed structures in which each atomic particle is associated with a number of close neighbors. Comparatively high densities thus result.

Although these are properties which are thought of as characterizing all metallic substances, it must be emphasized that there are many borderline cases where an element possesses some metallic properties and some non-metallic ones. Such elements as antimony, germanium, and tellurium are cases in point.

Any reasonable explanation of metallic structure or formulation of a metallic bond must be reconcilable with the foregoing characteristics. It is evident that in some fashion such a bond must involve the electron since many of these phenomena are dependent upon electrons or can be accounted for in terms of electrons. According to Bernal,[69] a metallic bond should possess the following characteristics:

1. Ability to act between identical metallic atoms and at the same time between widely different metallic atoms.
2. Lack of direction, as shown by retention of properties in the liquid state, and of saturation to permit large numbers of close neighbors.
3. Attractive force varying inversely as some high power of the internuclear distance.
4. Equilibrium repulsive force which is atomic in nature.
5. Ability to permit electron transfer from atom to atom.

These characteristics are inherent in modern electronic theories.

Electronic theories of the metallic bond

Modern views are based upon a combination of investigative and theoretical approaches. Experimental evaluation of the physical properties summarized above, plus additional study of conduction phenomena using solutions of alkali and alkaline earth metals in liquid ammonia, indicate clearly the presence of comparatively free electrons in metals. Emission and conduction phenomena may be explained logically in this fashion, as may also optical characteristics if it is assumed that immediate radiation of absorbed light energy is rendered essential by rapidly moving electrons. With regard to solutions of metals in liquid ammonia, it is found that metals which lose electrons very readily often dissolve extensively (and reversibly) in

[69] J. D. Bernal: *Trans. Faraday Soc.*, **25**, 367 (1929).

liquid ammonia to yield solutions which possess bronze colors if concentrated and blue colors if dilute (pp. 347–349). The bronze solutions exhibit the high electrical conductances characteristic of solid metals whereas more dilute solutions show electrolytic conductance.

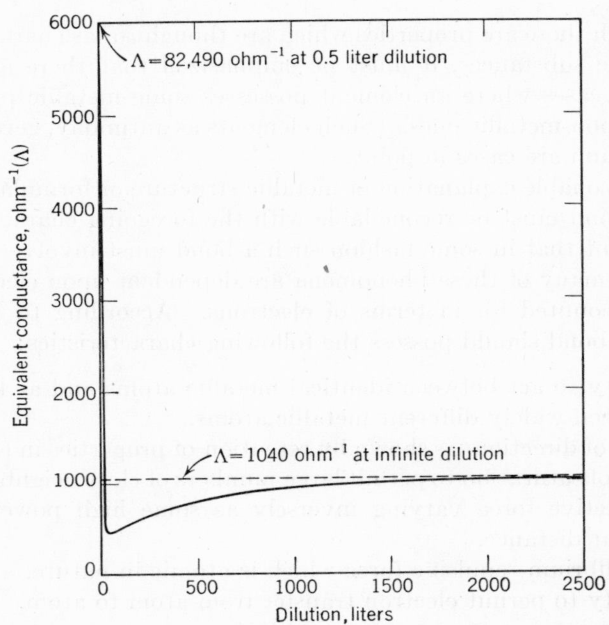

FIG. 6·7. Effect of concentration on conductances of solutions of sodium in liquid ammonia.

This is shown in Figure 6·7.[70] The properties of such solutions are best accounted for in terms of the equilibrium (using an alkali metal as typical)

$$M + (x + y)NH_3 \rightleftharpoons M(NH_3)_x^+ + e^-(NH_3)_y$$

The ammonated electron is blue in color (p. 348). That electrons may be removed from metals by ammonia is indirect evidence of their original presence in those metals in comparatively free states.

Modern electronic theory of the metallic bond may be traced to Drude,[71] who envisioned metals as containing numbers of free electrons moving in spaces among atoms like the molecules of the ideal

[70] C. A. Kraus and W. W. Lucasse: *J. Am. Chem. Soc.*, **44**, 1941 (1922).
[71] P. Drude: *Ann. Physik* [4], **1**, 566 (1900); [4], **3**, 369 (1900).

kinetic theory gas. Subsequent expansions of this concept brought Lorentz[72] to the belief that solid metals consist of lattices of rigid cation spheres with free electrons moving in the interstices. These electrons are the ordinary valence electrons associated with individual atoms. With the development of quantum mechanics and enunciation of the Pauli exclusion principle (p. 91), this view was modified to this extent: although electrons within a certain piece of metal might be considered free, they actually are held by all the atoms in the aggregated structure and occupy a large number of discrete energy states each of which can hold no more than two electrons. These electrons may thus be regarded as occupying limited bands within the bulk of the material. Although a detailed treatment of the subject is beyond the scope of this presentation, it can be shown that electrons in these bands (Brillouin zones) may be transferred from one energy state to another without the expenditure of excessive amounts of energy. It is because this can occur that electrons within metals are comparatively mobile. As a working concept, therefore, we may regard a metal as consisting of a mass of positive ions immersed in a sea of electrons. Since there are not enough such electrons to give stable electronic groups around all materials, individual electrons may be considered as holding more than two ions together in the lattice. This produces an essentially dynamic electron lattice, but these electrons are restricted to certain energy zones and can move from one such zone to another only under specialized energy conditions. For a more comprehensive summary of the quantum mechanical view of the metallic bond, the reader may consult any of the numerous excellent summaries which are available.[73–77]

An alternative view of the metallic bond, which is somewhat easier to visualize, has been offered by Pauling.[78–81] It pictures a metal as a structure in which 1-electron and electron-pair bonds resonate among a

[72] H. A. Lorentz: *The Theory of Electrons*, G. E. Stechert and Co., New York (1923).

[73] F. Seitz: *Modern Theory of Solids.* McGraw-Hill Book Co., New York (1940).

[74] F. Seitz and R. P. Johnson: *J. Applied Phys.*, **8**, 84, 186, 246 (1937).

[75] J. C. Slater: *Revs. Mod. Phys.*, **6**, 209 (1934).

[76] C. W. Stillwell: *Crystal Chemistry*, Ch. III. McGraw-Hill Book Co., New York (1938).

[77] H. J. Emeléus and J. S. Anderson: *Modern Aspects of Inorganic Chemistry*, Ch. XIII. D. Van Nostrand Company, New York (1938).

[78] L. Pauling: *The Nature of the Chemical Bond*, 2nd Ed., Ch. XI. Cornell University Press, Ithaca (1940).

[79] L. Pauling: *J. Am. Chem. Soc.*, **69**, 542 (1947).

[80] L. Pauling: *Proc. Roy. Soc.* (*London*), **A196**, 343 (1949).

[81] L. Pauling: *Physica*, **15**, 23 (1949).

number of positions. This concept is in agreement with observed interatomic distances in many metals and with the close packing and maximum crystal coordination numbers (p. 143) which characterize metal structures and thus promote increasing numbers of possible bond positions. Other characteristics of metals may also be accounted for in terms of this concept.[78] Metals have the mechanical properties of ductility and malleability because the numbers and directions of bonds which individual atoms can form are not restricted, and bonds remaining after deformation are as strong as those existing before.

It is apparent that the metallic bond possesses characteristics of both ionic and covalent bonds but is at the same time somewhat distinct from each. Just as there are intermediates between truly ionic and truly covalent bonds, so also there are intermediates between ionic and metallic bonds and between covalent and metallic bonds. In fact, there are many species other than the pure metals which possess metallic properties to greater or lesser degrees. Among them are the following: concentrated solutions of metals in liquid ammonia (p. 348), solid metal ammonates such as $Ca(NH_3)_6$ (p. 351), certain free radicals such as $(CH_3)_4N$ which yield amalgams, certain alkyls such as C_2H_5Hg which are conductors, sulfidic minerals such as FeS_2 and PbS, compounds containing homatomic anions such as polystannides and polyplumbides (p. 732), and the alloys and intermetallic compounds.

The natures and compositions of alloys

Alloys in general are of the following types:

1. *Simple mixtures,* where the component metals are mutually insoluble in each other in the solid state.

2. *Solid solutions,* where the atoms of one component fit themselves into the crystal lattice of the other. Such solid solutions are of two different kinds:

a. Substitutional solid solutions, in which atoms of one element can occupy positions in the crystal lattice of a second element that were occupied originally by atoms of that second element. Solid solubility of this sort is governed by the comparative sizes of the atoms of the two elements. If the atomic radii are identical or nearly so (e.g., Cu = 1.275 A and Ni = 1.243 A), complete solid solubility will result. If the radii are somewhat divergent (e.g., Sn = 1.50 A and Pb = 1.746 A), only limited solid solubility will occur. Solid solubility is also favored by lack of electronegativity differences between the two materials.

b. Interstitial solid solutions, in which very small atoms of non-metallic elements (e.g., H, B, C, N) occupy positions in the interstices of the metal lattices. In general, the structures of the metals are preserved, though often distorted, and the stoichiometry of combination is determined by solubility. According to Hägg,[82] interstitial solid solutions result only if the ratio of the atomic radius of the non-metal to that of the metal is less than 0.59. Subsequent discussions will cover interstitial hydrides (p. 411), nitrides (p. 579), carbides (p. 699), and borides (p. 769).

3. *Intermetallic compounds or intermediate phases,* where atoms of more than one metal appear in apparently stoichiometric proportions although in no relation to ordinary valence rules. Observed compositions are rather those necessary for greatest crystal stabilities and metallic bond strengths.

The intermediate phases merit further treatment. That they are not valence compounds in the ordinary sense is evidenced by such typical compositions as $AuMg_3$, $Cd_{11}K$, and BiTe. Their metallic properties indicate lack of complete utilization of all valence electrons. In general, such intermediate phases seldom involve metals of the same periodic group and never metals of the same periodic subgroup or family. Furthermore, it appears that a given metal either combines with all the members of a particular subgroup or with none.

In many binary systems, the addition of a metal of higher inherent oxidation number (M′) to a metal of lower inherent oxidation number (M) gives the same general succession of alloy phases. This phenomenon may be indicated roughly as

α	$\alpha + \beta$	β	$\beta + \gamma$	γ	$\gamma + \epsilon$	ϵ	$\epsilon + \eta$	η

M COMPOSITION M′

where α and η are simple substitutional solid solutions and β, γ, ϵ are intermediate phases. These intermediate phases, which are characterized by maximum melting points, have, respectively, body-centered cubic, cubic with many atoms to the unit cell, and hexagonal close-packed structures. Portions of such successions of phases are shown for three alloy systems in Figure 6·8. Typical β, γ, and ϵ structure compositions are summarized in Table 6·16.

In an attempt to reduce such observations to common ground and to systematize the variety of formulations characterizing β-phase alloys,

[82] G. Hägg: *Z. physik. Chem.*, **B12,** 33 (1931).

Hume-Rothery[83] pointed out that for this phase the ratio of total valence electrons to total atoms is constant at 3:2 (or 21:14). If the valence electrons are taken as those in the highest principal quantum level, and the Group VIII elements are assumed to have no valence electrons, this generalization applies to many β-phase compositions (Table 6·16). This principle was extended[84] to the γ-phase, where the corresponding ratio is 21:13, and to the ϵ-phase,[85] where the ratio is 7:4 (or 21:12). These ratios are commonly called the Hume-Rothery

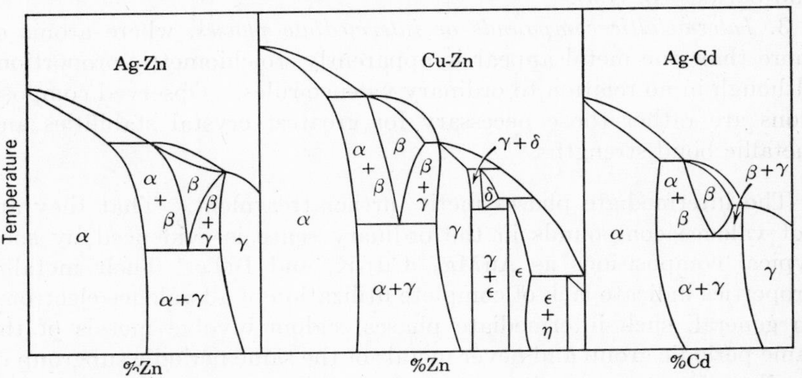

FIG. 6·8. Phase diagrams for some typical binary alloy systems. (Not drawn accurately or exactly to scale.)

ratios. They have been of considerable value in relating apparently unrelated structures, although the many known exceptions (among them the ones given in Table 6·16) show that they are not invariable.

In spite of these exceptions, the Hume-Rothery ratios apply in such a number of cases that they must have some theoretical significance. According to Jones,[86, 87] when electrons are fed into the lattice of a metal in its formation, the last electrons to enter a given Brillouin zone (p. 219) may either overflow into the next permitted zone or the lattice may change to accomodate more electronic states within the first zone, i.e., a new phase may result. The numbers of electrons required per atom to fill the necessary Brillouin zones are: for the β-phase, 1.480, and for the γ-phase, 1.538. The experimental Hume-

[83] W. Hume-Rothery: *J. Inst. Metals,* **35,** 295 (1926).

[84] A. J. Bradley and J. Thewlis: *Proc. Roy. Soc.* (*London*), **A112,** 678 (1926).

[85] A. F. Westgren and G. Phragmén: *Metallwirtschaft,* **7,** 700 (1928); *Trans. Faraday Soc.,* **25,** 379 (1929).

[86] H. Jones: *Proc. Roy. Soc.* (*London*), **A144,** 225 (1934); **A147,** 396 (1934).

[87] N. F. Mott and H. Jones: *Theory of the Properties of Metals and Alloys,* pp. 170–174. Clarendon Press, Oxford (1936).

Rothery ratios of 1.50 and 1.615, respectively, are thus in quite good agreement with the calculated, especially since each phase may cover a considerable range of compositions (e.g., with Cu-Zn, the γ-phase embraces ratios from 1.58 to 1.66). It is also pointed out[86, 87] that phase transformations might be expected at ratios slightly greater than the theoretical ones because occupation of a few more energy states than those representing a filled zone may be essential to the production of a change in crystal structure.

TABLE 6·16
TYPICAL BINARY INTERMEDIATE PHASES

β-Structures		γ-Structures		ε-Structures	
Example	Valence Electrons: Atoms	Example	Valence Electrons: Atoms	Example	Valence Electrons: Atoms
CuZn	3:2	Cu_5Zn_8	21:13	$CuZn_3$	7:4
AgZn	3:2	Ag_5Zn_8	21:13	$AuZn_3$	7:4
Cu_3Al	3:2	Cu_9Al_4	21:13	$AgCd_3$	7:4
Cu_5Sn	3:2	$Cu_{31}Sn_8$	21:13	Ag_5Al_3	7:4
FeAl	3:2	$Na_{31}Pb_8$	21:13	Cu_3Sn	7:4
Ag_3Al	3:2	Co_5Zn_{21}	21:13	$CuBe_3$	7:4
Cu_5Si	3:2	Cu_9Ga_4	21:13	Cu_3Ge	7:4
$CoZn_3$	3:2	Ni_5Zn_{21}	21:13	$FeZn_7$	7:4
LiAg	2:2	$Li_{10}Pb_3$	22:13		
LiTl	4:2	$Li_{10}Ag_3$	13:13		
MgTl	5:2				
AlNd	6:2				
TlSb	8:2				

As an alternative, Pauling and Ewing[88] suggest that the stabilization of such intermediate phases results in part from the valence electron-atom ratio and in part from the filling of Brillouin polyhedra. For a typical Brillouin arrangement, a certain number of electrons per unit cell is required, and this number is provided by appropriate stoichiometric combinations of metals in terms of their metallic valences.[79–81] For more details, the original paper should be consulted.

CLATHRATE COMPOUNDS

Certain solid molecular compounds have been prepared in which a molecule of one component is completely enclosed by one or more molecules of a second component in such a way that its escape is prevented unless the forces which bind its surroundings together are

[88] L. Pauling and F. J. Ewing: *Revs. Mod. Phys.*, **20**, 112 (1948).

overcome. Such cage compounds have been called *clathrate* compounds[89] (Latin *clathratus*, enclosed by cross bars of a grating). In general, they occur when mixtures of the components are crystallized under optimum conditions. Their properties are roughly those of the enclosing material. Such compounds are stable at ordinary temperatures with respect to decomposition into their components, but melting or dissolution permits the enclosed component to escape. Examples are hydroquinone compounds which approach the composition $(C_6H_6O_2)_3 \cdot X (X = HCl, HBr, H_2S, CH_3OH, SO_2, CO_2, HCN,$ etc.); amine compounds containing sulfurous acid, e.g. $(p\text{-}H_2NC_6H_4\text{-}NH_2)_9 \cdot H_2SO_3$; phenol compounds, e.g. $(C_6H_6O)_4 \cdot SO_2$, $(C_6H_6O)_5 \cdot SO_2$, $(C_6H_6O)_8 \cdot CO_2$; and certain compounds of the inert gas elements (pp. 382–383).

It is obvious that the conditions under which clathrate compounds can form are limited and highly specific. Among those of importance are:

1. An open crystal structure in the enclosing component. This necessitates directed linkages holding the molecule and crystal together, sufficient extension of the groups to form a cavity of suitable size, and a rigid structure.
2. Small access holes to the enclosed cavity. This may result from either proper disposition of groups in the formation of the crystal or sufficient surface area in the enclosing groups.
3. Ready availability of the trapped component at the time when the cavity is closed.

Such compounds are of considerable theoretical interest but are lacking in practical importance. Information on possible arrangements in clathrate compounds and the structures which lead to them is to be found in Powell's discussions.[89]

NON-STOICHIOMETRIC COMPOUNDS

The law of definite proportions is one of the basic tenets of chemistry. Its validity is indicated by the restrictions imposed upon bond formation where electrons are involved as already outlined, and its application is generally the assumed basis for any type of chemical combination. There are, however, many instances of apparent departure from this rule among *solid* compounds. Such compounds do not possess the exact compositions which are predicted from electronic considerations alone and are commonly referred to as Berthollide or non-stoichiomet-

[89] H. M. Powell: *J. Chem. Soc.*, **1948**, 61; *Endeavour*, **9**, 154 (1950); *Research*, **1**, 353 (1947–1948).

ric compounds as opposed to the normal Daltonide or stoichiometric compounds. As examples, one may cite certain metallic hydrides such as $VH_{0.56}$, $CeH_{2.69}$ (p. 411); certain oxides such as $TiO_{1.7-1.8}$, $FeO_{1.055}$, $WO_{2.88-2.92}$; such sulfides, selenides, and tellurides as $Cu_{1.7}S$, $Cu_{1.6}Se$, $Cu_{1.65}Te$, $CuFeS_{1.94}$; the tungsten bronzes, Na_xWO_3; etc. Combinations of these types are particularly common among minerals.

Lack of true stoichiometry of this type is associated with so-called *defect crystal lattices.* Defects in a crystal lattice amount to variations from the regularity which characterizes the material as a whole. They are of two types:

1. *Frenkel defects,* in which certain atoms or ions have migrated to interstitial positions some distance removed from the "holes" which they vacated.
2. *Schottky defects,* in which "holes" are left in random fashion throughout the crystal because of migration of atoms or ions to the surface of the material.

Although both types of defect probably characterize crystals of non-stoichiometric compounds, the Schottky defects are the more important. Obviously detectable departure from true stoichiometric composition can result only if serious defects are present. It would follow, therefore, that many apparently stoichiometric compounds are not truly so. If excess metal is present in a crystal, it may also result from partial reduction of high-valent cations; whereas if excess non-metal is present, higher valent cations or lower valent anions than those normally present may be responsible. Many instances are known of multiple oxidation number in a single crystal. Non-stoichiometric compounds often show semi-conductivity, fluorescence, and centers of color. For a comprehensive discussion of this rather complex subject, a detailed review[90] should be consulted.

SUMMARY OF BOND TYPES

The important linkages which hold together the components of crystalline solids and their general characteristics may be summarized as follows:

1. *Ionic linkages,* in which the crystals are made up of regular geometrical arrangements of positive and negative ions. Such solids tend to possess high melting and boiling points, are hard and difficult to deform, and tend to be soluble in polar solvents. When dissolved in such solvents or fused, they are excellent conductors. Crystals

[90] J. S. Anderson: *Ann. Reports,* **43,** 104 (1946).

characterized by such linkages are called ionic crystals. The salts are examples.

2. *Covalent linkages*, in which the crystals are made up of molecules produced by the sharing of electrons, usually in pairs, between atoms of the elements involved. Such solids possess properties essentially opposite from those outlined for ionic crystals, although the partial ionic characters of many covalent bonds effect corresponding modifications. The following types of covalent crystalline solids may be distinguished:

a. Non-polar molecular crystals, where weak attractive forces resulting from electronic motion are responsible for crystal stability. Such crystals are soft and easily melted or vaporized. Solid hydrogen, solid helium, and solid carbon tetrachloride are examples.

b. Polar molecular crystals, where orientation of dipoles results in somewhat greater attractive forces and consequent increases in crystal stability. Although such materials are non-conductors, they do have enhanced melting points, boiling points, and solubilities in polar solvents over strictly non-polar crystals. Solid water, solid hydrogen chloride, etc., are examples.

c. Atomic crystals, where three dimensional covalent bonding results in giant molecules. Such crystals are resistant to deformation and are often harder and higher melting than ionic crystals. Diamond, silicon carbide, etc., are examples.

3. *Metallic linkages*, in which mobile electrons provide the necessary forces for crystal stability. Such solids are characterized by toughness, malleability, ductility, high conductivity, luster, and insolubility in liquids other than molten metals. Any metal would be an example.

A useful summary of this general type has been given by Sisler.[91]

SUGGESTED SUPPLEMENTARY REFERENCES

L. Pauling: *The Nature of the Chemical Bond*, 2nd Ed. Cornell University Press, Ithaca (1940).

O. K. Rice: *Electronic Structure and Chemical Binding*, Ch. XI–XVIII. Mc-Graw-Hill Book Co., New York (1940).

Y. K. Syrkin and M. E. Dyatkina (translated by M. A. Partridge and D. O. Jordan): *Structure of Molecules and the Chemical Bond*, Interscience Publishers, New York (1950).

W. Hückel (translated by L. H. Long): *Structural Chemistry of Inorganic Compounds*, Ch. II. Elsevier Publishing Co., New York (1950).

A. F. Wells: *Structural Inorganic Chemistry*, 2nd Ed., Ch. I–V. Clarendon Press, Oxford (1950).

---

[91] H. H. Sisler: *J. Chem. Education*, **25**, 562 (1948).

CHAPTER 7

Complex Ions and Coordination Compounds

An abundance of information has been accumulated about so-called *molecular* or *addition* compounds, i.e., compounds formed by combinations of apparently saturated materials which are capable of independent existence. Such substances vary widely in their inherent stabilities and other properties. Some appear to exist only in crystal lattices and undergo decomposition into their components when these lattices are disrupted by dissolution or other treatment. Others retain their identities as molecules or ions when dissolved and can be recovered from solution as such. With some, the physical and chemical properties appear to be essentially those of the components; with others, they are completely different. In some, the binding is ionic in character; in others, it is covalent. Yet it is convenient to discuss all of these methods as a broad class because the methods of preparation and many other characteristics are the same.

Molecular compounds of these types are referred to broadly as *complex* compounds or *coordination* compounds, and the corresponding ions are usually called *complex* ions. Sometimes they are called *Werner complexes* because of Werner's elucidation of their structures and properties (pp. 229–230). Those which possess sufficient stabilities to retain their identities in solution have been called *penetration complexes*.[1] These are indistinguishable in general from ordinary covalent compounds, although in some cases the bonding in them is apparently more nearly ionic than covalent (p. 261). Correspondingly, those which are reversibly dissociated in solution into their components are called *normal complexes*. These are predominantly ionic in character. Thus ions such as $Fe(CN)_6^{-4}$ or $Co(NH_3)_6^{+3}$ could be called penetration complexes, whereas ions such as $Cd(CN)_4^{-2}$ or $Co(NH_3)_6^{+2}$ could be called normal complexes. The classification is more one of convenience than of fundamental importance.

[1] W. Biltz: *Z. anorg. allgem. Chem.*, **164**, 245 (1927).

SYSTEMATIC APPROACH TO COMPLEX SUBSTANCES

The systematic study and explanation of the natures of these complex materials may be approached by citing some experimental observations of long standing and then determining in what fashion they may be reconciled and explained. As typical of those on the so-called penetration complexes, let us consider data relative to ammonia-containing compounds derived from cobalt (III) chloride. Treatment of aqueous cobalt(II) chloride solutions with excess ammonia, followed by oxidation, yields solutions from which a variety of compounds can be isolated. Among those of importance are:

1. *Luteocobaltic chloride*, $CoCl_3 \cdot 6NH_3$, an orange-yellow crystalline compound. Treatment of this compound in the solid state with sulfuric acid liberates all the chlorine as hydrogen chloride and leaves a sulfate, $Co_2(SO_4)_3 \cdot 12NH_3$. Treatment of the solid with hydrochloric acid even at 100°C. effects no removal of ammonia. Conductance measurements on aqueous solutions of the compound indicate the presence of *four* ions (p. 232), and treatment of such solutions with silver nitrate precipitates all the chlorines immediately. Similarly, treatment of the solid with moist silver oxide gives a water-soluble, strongly basic compound of composition $CoOOH \cdot 6NH_3$, which, on addition of acids, reforms salts of the type $CoX_3 \cdot 6NH_3$. Stable bonding between cobalt and ammonia is indicated.

2. *Roseocobaltic chloride*, $CoCl_3 \cdot 5NH_3 \cdot H_2O$, a pink crystalline compound. The water present in this compound is firmly held at room temperature and is lost only at 100°C. or above, when the new compound $CoCl_3 \cdot 5NH_3$ results. Conductance measurements again show the presence of *four* ions, and again all the chlorines are immediately precipitated by silver ion and are thus ionic in character. Even though this compound contains less ammonia than the luteo chloride (above), its properties are closely comparable, suggesting an essential equivalence between water and ammonia in its structure.

3. *Purpureocobaltic chloride*, $CoCl_3 \cdot 5NH_3$, a violet-colored compound. When treated with sulfuric acid, this compound loses only *two* chlorines as hydrogen chloride, leaving as product $CoClSO_4 \cdot 5NH_3$, a compound which in aqueous solution yields no immediate precipitate with silver ion. Conductance measurements on solutions of the purpureo chloride show the presence of *three* ions, and from such solutions only *two* chlorines are precipitated immediately by silver ion. The third chlorine is precipitated only slowly and after long standing or boiling. A difference in chlorine bonding is thus indicated.

In addition, two related compounds, one violet in color (*violeocobaltic chloride*) and the other green (*praseocobaltic chloride*), but both having the composition $CoCl_3 \cdot 4NH_3$, can be prepared. The conductances of solutions of these compounds show the presence of only *two* ions, and from them only *one* chlorine is immediately precipitated by silver ion. Yet the chemical behaviors of these two compounds are quite different.

This information, together with a tremendous amount of similar data on corresponding platinum, palladium, chromium, etc., compounds, was accumulated before any information on electronic structures and chemical bonding was available. Obviously, some theory which not only could account for the existence of such compounds but also could at the same time explain the striking changes in properties produced by small changes in composition (e.g., alteration of ammonia content in the foregoing series) was essential. Early interesting but wholly unsuccessful explanations offered by Blomstrand, Jörgensen, and others[2, 3] are of no more than historical importance and need not be discussed. Modern theory may be traced to the work of Alfred Werner, to whom complete credit must be given not only for advancing a correct explanation for the characteristics of these compounds but also for producing a theory which anticipated later developments in structural chemistry and was sufficiently flexible to accommodate them without essential alteration.

Werner's original interests in organic compounds and valency in general led him to consider the molecular compounds mentioned above. In 1893, these considerations were crystallized in a dream into a comprehensive theory. It is said that by noon of the day following this dream, Werner had completed the revolutionary paper[4] which summarized these views on structures and properties and opened an entirely new field for investigation. In the subsequent twenty years, Werner devoted himself to proving the postulates of his original theory and produced a truly classical series of publications. It is significant that every postulate was verified experimentally not only by Werner but by many others working independently. The Nobel Award was a fitting recognition of Werner's contributions.

The fundamental postulates of Werner's theory may be summarized as follows:

[2] R. Schwarz (translated by L. W. Bass): *The Chemistry of the Inorganic Complex Compounds*. John Wiley and Sons, New York (1923).

[3] A. Werner: *Neuere Anschauungen auf dem Gebiete der anorganischen Chemie*, Vierte Auflage. T. Viewig u. Sohn, Braunschweig (1920).

[4] A. Werner: *Z. anorg. Chem.*, **3**, 267 (1893).

1. Metals possess two types of valency, so-called primary (principal) or ionizable valency and secondary or non-ionizable valency.

2. Every metal has a fixed number of secondary valencies, or coordination number (see footnote, p. 143). Thus, for example, cobalt(III) and platinum(IV) were recognized as having six such valencies (coordination number = 6), whereas copper(II) has four (coordination number = 4).

3. Primary valencies are satisfied by negative ions whereas secondary valencies may be satisfied by either negative groups or neutral molecules. In certain instances, a given negative group may satisfy both, but in every case fulfillment of the coordination number of the metal appears essential. Modern studies have shown that a limited number of positive groups may also occupy coordination positions.

4. The secondary valencies are directed in space about the central metal ion. Thus six such valencies were regarded as directed to the apices of a regular octahedron circumscribed about the metal ion whereas four such bonds might be arranged in either a planar or a tetrahedral manner. This postulate predicted a variety of types of isomerism and was the most difficult to prove. Indeed, it was not until nineteen years had elapsed before Werner obtained conclusive proof through the actual resolution of a strictly inorganic compound into its predicted optical isomers (p. 265).

Application of these views to the ammonia derivatives of cobalt(III) chloride already mentioned above will illustrate the utility of Werner's views. If, following Werner, primary valencies are designated by solid lines and secondary valencies by dotted lines, these compounds may be formulated as

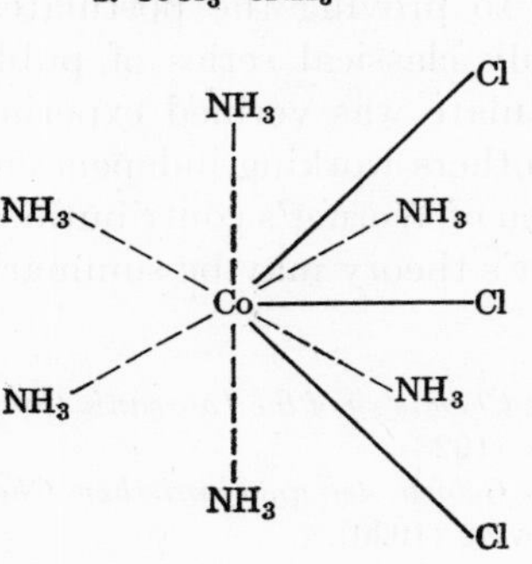

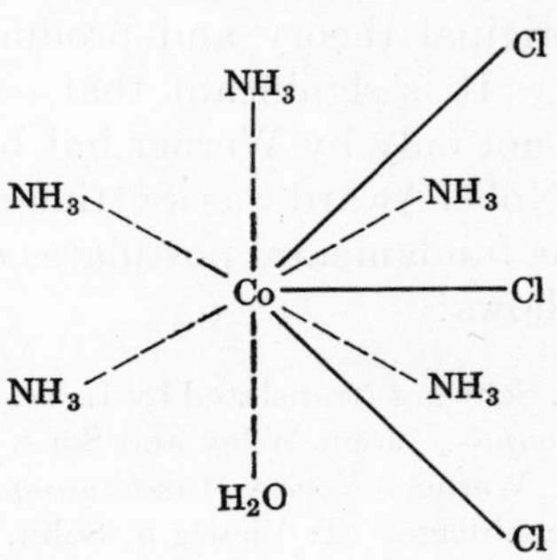

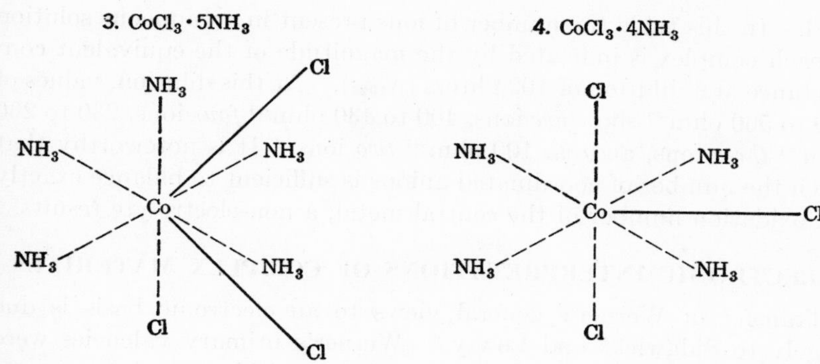

Satisfaction of six secondary valencies is characteristic of each. These formulations predict the correct number of ions in each case (pp. 228–229) as well as firm association of chlorine with cobalt in the last two cases. The existence of two forms of $CoCl_3 \cdot 4NH_3$ (p. 229) is due to differing three-dimensional arrangements of the four ammonias and two chlorines about the central cobalt(III) ion (p. 262).

In order to designate materials held by secondary valencies (i.e., so-called coordinated materials), it has become customary to enclose the metal ion and all such materials in square brackets when writing formulas. Thus the compounds just considered are written as

$$[Co(NH_3)_6]Cl_3, [Co(NH_3)_5(H_2O)]Cl_3, [Co(NH_3)_5Cl]Cl_2, [Co(NH_3)_4Cl_2]Cl$$

the entire material within brackets functioning as an ion in each case and everything outside the brackets also being ionic in character. The portion so enclosed is called the *coordination sphere.* Use of this notation, satisfaction of the coordination number of the metal in question, effect of entry of anions into the coordination sphere upon the oxidation number of the complex, and alteration in number of ions due to such entry are summarized for some platinum (IV) compounds in Table 7·1. These may be regarded as typical of the entire

TABLE 7·1

SOME DATA ON COORDINATION COMPOUNDS OF PLATINUM(IV)

Formula	Λ_{1024}, ohm^{-1}	Ions Indicated
$[Pt(NH_3)_6]Cl_4$	523	5
$[Pt(NH_3)_5Cl]Cl_3$	404	4
$[Pt(NH_3)_4Cl_2]Cl_2$	229	3
$[Pt(NH_3)_3Cl_3]Cl$	97	2
$[Pt(NH_3)_2Cl_4]$	0	0
$K[Pt(NH_3)Cl_5]$	108.5	2
$K_2[PtCl_6]$	256	3

field. In this table the number of ions present in an aqueous solution of each complex is indicated by the magnitude of the equivalent conductance at a dilution of 1024 liters (Λ_{1024}). At this dilution, values of 520 to 560 ohm^{-1} show *five* ions, 400 to 430 ohm^{-1} *four* ions, 230 to 260 ohm^{-1} *three* ions, and ca. 100 ohm^{-1} *two* ions. It is noteworthy that when the number of coordinated anions is sufficient to balance exactly the oxidation number of the central metal, a non-electrolyte results.

ELECTRONIC INTERPRETATIONS OF COMPLEX MATERIALS

Transfer of Werner's general views to an electronic basis is due largely to Sidgwick[5] and Lowry.[6] Werner's primary valencies were regarded as amounting to electron transfer and his secondary or non-ionic valencies to electron pair sharing. Inasmuch as the majority of the groups which coordinate to metal ions have in their structures atoms with unshared electron pairs, these covalent bonds were considered to arise by the donation of electron pairs to the central metal by these groups. Bonds of this type have been characterized as coordinate bonds, (p. 193), although the term *semi-polar* is sometimes applied. Because the coordinating groups act as donors, bonds of this type have often been indicated by arrows. Thus the $[Co(NH_3)_6]^{+3}$ ion may be written

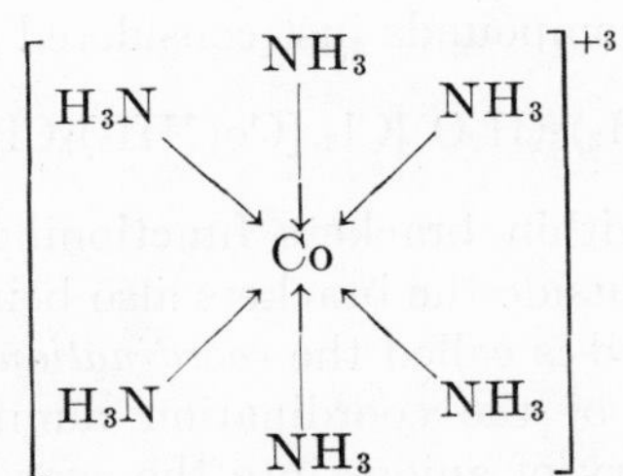

The concept of direct donation of electron pairs to a central cation is open to question. Such a concept involves the rather improbable accumulation of negative charge on a normally electropositive material. Thus, in an ion such as $[Co(NH_3)_6]^{+3}$, donation of an electron pair by the nitrogen in each ammonia requires that the cobalt actually become negative with respect to the ammonias. Such a condition is manifestly unlikely. Furthermore, the lone pairs of electrons spoken of as being donated are in many instances (e.g., with water, ammonia, the amines, etc.) *s* electron pairs which have no bonding characteristics (p. 196). Certainly excitation of one such electron to some higher level

[5] N. V. Sidgwick: *J. Chem. Soc.*, **123**, 725 (1923).
[6] T. M. Lowry: *J. Soc. Chem. Ind.*, **42**, 316 (1923).

where it might have bonding character requires more energy than is available through bond formation and does not appear as a likely solution to the problem.

Various alternative explanations have been offered in attempts to overcome these objections but still preserve the essentials of the Sidgwick theory. Perhaps the most significant of these is based upon the metal ion acting as both an electron donor and acceptor. This preserves the expected charge balance, but in unmodified form the concept is difficult to interpret. However, Pauling's views on the hybridization of orbitals[7] (pp. 201–204) not only embrace this concept in a logical fashion but also overcome the objection of bonding by nonbonding electrons. Because of the only very slight energy differences among $(n - 1)d$ and ns or np orbitals among the transition metal ions in particular, a redistribution of electrons among these orbitals to give hybrid bonds is possible and several (normally *four* or *six*) bonds become available. In this process, it is probable that certain orbitals are first vacated and then reoccupied. Change from paramagnetism to diamagnetism during complex formation in many instances suggests this to be true. Further and more detailed discussions will be found later in connection with material on stereoisomerism (pp. 256–261).

The concept of hybrid bonds requires that all bonds be covalent in character. Although it might be highly desirable to group all so-called coordination compounds and complex ions under this single valency type, the properties of these compounds (p. 227) do not warrant such an all-inclusive classification. Not only are the extremes of covalent and ionic bonding represented but also all intermediate cases as well as many in which attractions of the ion-dipole type are important. Thus, to cite an example, the ion $[Co(C_2O_4)_3]^{-3}$ can be resolved into optically active isomers whereas the formally similar ion $[Al(C_2O_4)_3]^{-3}$ apparently cannot, an indication that the covalent bonding present in the cobalt complex does not characterize the aluminum one (p. 266). No attempt should be made to limit complexes in general through a rigid valence theory. The true worth of studying such materials lies not in adapting them to a rigid pattern but in using them to illustrate a variety of approaches.

In an attempt to systematize known coordination numbers, Sidgwick[5,8] devised the concept of effective atomic number (abbreviated

[7] L. Pauling: *The Nature of the Chemical Bond*, 2nd Ed., Ch. III. Cornell University Press, Ithaca (1940).

[8] N. V. Sidgwick: *The Electronic Theory of Valency*, Ch. X. Clarendon Press, Oxford (1927).

E. A. N. in the literature). The effective atomic number of a metal in a complex is derived by deducting from the atomic number of that metal the number of electrons lost in ion formation and then adding the number of electrons gained by coordination (two for each coordinated group in general). In many cases, the effective atomic number so calculated is equal to the atomic number of the next heavier inert gas element, as shown in Table 7·2. Sidgwick and, particularly,

TABLE 7·2
THE EFFECTIVE ATOMIC NUMBER CONCEPT

Metal Ion	Atomic Number of Metal	Coordination Number	Electrons Lost in Ion Formation	Electrons Added by Coordination	E. A. N.
Fe^{+2}	26	6	2	12	36(Kr)
Co^{+3}	27	6	3	12	36(Kr)
Cu^{+}	29	4	1	8	36(Kr)
Pd^{+4}	46	6	4	12	54(Xe)
Ir^{+3}	77	6	3	12	86(Rn)
Pt^{+4}	78	6	4	12	86(Rn)
Cr^{+3}	24	6	3	12	33
Fe^{+3}	26	6	3	12	35
Ni^{+2}	28	6	2	12	38
Ni^{+2}	28	4	2	8	34
Pd^{+2}	46	4	2	8	52
Ir^{+4}	77	6	4	12	85
Pt^{+2}	78	4	2	8	84

Blanchard[9] have laid considerable emphasis upon such equalities as indicating the coordinating tendencies of the various metal ions and in predicting the probable compositions of various complexes. However, there are sufficient important exceptions to this generality (Table 7·2) to indicate its utility as a first approximation but not as a basis for complete prediction.

FACTORS INFLUENCING THE FORMATION OF COMPLEX IONS AND COORDINATION COMPOUNDS

The formation of complex ions and coordination compounds is affected by many physical and chemical factors. Some of the more important of these factors may be summarized as follows.

1. *Environmental Factors.* Temperature and pressure are often important. Thus compounds containing coordinating groups which

[9] A. A. Blanchard: *Chem. Revs.*, **21,** 3 (1937); **26,** 409 (1940).

are volatile (e.g., water, ammonia, and ethylenediamine) are uniformly less stable at elevated temperatures and commonly undergo decomposition when heated. This is exemplified by the equation

$$[Cr(en)_3]Cl_3 \xrightarrow{210°C.} [Cr(en)_2Cl_2]Cl + en$$

(en = ethylenediamine). In like manner, reduction in pressure above a compound often results in loss of a volatile component, a situation common among hydrated metal salts. Photochemical sensitivity has been less thoroughly characterized.

2. *Concentration Factors.* The stabilities and even existence of complex ions in solution are markedly influenced by concentration changes. In many of the cases where complexes existing in the solid state are destroyed upon dissolution, solvent molecules apparently have greater tendencies to associate themselves with metal ions than the other groups present and thus destroy the original complexes. In some instances, however, addition of the original complexing agent in sufficient amount may regenerate the complex in measurable quantity. A case in point involves double copper(II)–alkali metal chlorides. In the solid state, yellow species of the type $[CuCl_4]^{-2}$ appear to exist, but, on dissolution in water, the characteristic pale blue of the hydrated copper(II) ion appears. Addition of excess chloride ion (as HCl, LiCl, or other very soluble chloride) causes appearance of a green color, suggesting the existence of an equilibrium of the type

$$\underset{\text{blue}}{[Cu(H_2O)_x]^{+2}} + 4Cl^- \rightleftharpoons \underset{\text{yellow}}{[CuCl_4]^{-2}} + xH_2O$$

Correspondingly, pink hydrated cobalt(II) ion is converted in aqueous solution to blue complexes by addition of chloride, bromide, or thiocyanate, but upon dilution the hydrated ion is regenerated.

On the other hand, concentration effects are often important where the species involved are inherently more stable. For example, aqueous chromium(III) chloride solutions slowly change from green to violet upon dilution, presumably because of displacement of an equilibrium of the type

$$\underset{\text{green}}{[Cr(H_2O)_5Cl]^{+2}} + H_2O \rightleftharpoons \underset{\text{violet}}{[Cr(H_2O)_6]^{+3}} + Cl^-$$

Although most common in reactions involving water, where the term *aquation* is applied, the phenomenon is a general one, applying to many other materials as well.

3. *Nature of the Metal Ion.* This is of primary importance. The most stable complexes result from cations derived from the transition

metals and the metals immediately following the transition elements, although as the charts given by Bailar[10] show, the formation of coordination compounds is by no means limited to these materials. In a very general way, the metals from which the majority of the best-characterized complexes are derived may be summarized as

V	Cr	Mn	Fe	Co	Ni	Cu	Zn
	Mo	—	Ru	Rh	Pd	Ag	Cd
	W	Re	Os	Ir	Pt	Au	Hg
	(U)						

Cobalt, chromium, and the platinum metals have been the most extensively investigated. Noteworthy by their absence are the alkali, alkaline earth, and lanthanide metals. It is apparent that those cations which serve best as centers for coordination are the ones with comparatively small sizes and high nuclear or ionic charges (pp. 210–211). If one accepts the opinion that coordination results from the acceptance of electron pairs by the cation or from ion-dipole attractions, it is only logical that such electron-attracting characteristics should be important. However, the absence of any absolutely direct relation between stability of product and size or charge (or both) of the central cation indicates that other factors also must be of importance. In terms of the Pauling concept of hybridization of orbitals (p. 201), the preponderance of complexes among a limited group of cations is apparent, for it is only among these materials that the necessary orbitals are available without the imposition of excessive energy requirements.

4. *Nature of the Coordinating Group.* Almost any group (ion or molecule) having in its structure an atom with an unshared electron pair may act as a coordinating agent, although there are marked differences in the ease with which such groups attach and in the stabilities of the resulting products. Among simple coordinating

TABLE 7·3

TRENDS IN STABILITIES AS RELATED TO COORDINATED GROUPS

Decreasing Stability →

NH_3, RNH_2, R_2NH, R_3N
H_2O, ROH, R_2O, RCOR, RCHO
R_3As, R_3P, R_2S, PX_3
CO, NO
CN^-, SCN^-, F^-, OH^-, Cl^-, Br^-, I^-

(R = alkyl or aryl radical)
(X = halide group)

[10] J. C. Bailar, Jr.: *Chem. Revs.*, **23**, 65 (1938).

groups, the general trends noted in Table 7·3 can be distinguished. That these are not absolute is indicated by such facts as the stabilities of pyridine complexes as opposed to the instabilities of most complexes containing tertiary amines and reversals in the order of stabilities of halide complexes from fluoride > iodide in some cases to iodide > fluoride in others. In general, a more strongly coordinating group will replace a more weakly coordinating one to produce a product of enhanced stability.

In addition to groups which may be regarded as electron pair donors, ethylene and other organic materials containing ethylenic linkages form stable compounds with certain metal ions, particularly platinum. These compounds have been reviewed by Keller,[11] but their natures are not completely understood. It has become common to consider them as possessing *metallated double bonds,* the bonding electrons in the ethylenic linkages being assumed to associate with the metal ions as well.[12]

5. *Nature of the Ion Outside the Coordination Sphere.* The thermal stabilities of coordination compounds are often affected by the tendencies of external ions to enter the coordination sphere. Thus ions such as CN^-, SCN^-, Cl^-, Br^-, $C_2O_4^{-2}$, and NO_2^- have pronounced tendencies to do this and may sometimes do so at the expense of materials already coordinated to the metal. On the other hand, ions such as NO_3^- and, particularly, ClO_4^- show little or no such tendency. Complete absence of coordinating reactions is generally assured in perchlorate solutions, which are commonly used when no complexing is desired.

6. *Ring Formation.* Ring formation, resulting when a given coordinating agent can occupy simultaneously more than a single coordination position, is commonly of greater importance than any of the other factors already listed. Such ring-forming groups are referred to as *polydentate* groups, the most common being the *bidentate* groups or those which can occupy two positions. Morgan and Drew[13] have referred to the bidentate groups as *chelating* groups (from the Greek χηλή, crab's claw) and to the resulting ring structures as *chelate* rings. Ordinarily, such rings are most stable, presumably because of reduced strain, when they contain five or six members, including the metal ion. The extensive review by Diehl[14] lists many types of structures, most of them organic in nature, which yield chelate rings

[11] R. N. Keller: *Chem. Revs.,* **28,** 229 (1941).
[12] A. D. Walsh: *J. Chem. Soc.,* **1947,** 89.
[13] G. T. Morgan and H. D. K. Drew: *J. Chem. Soc.,* **117,** 1456 (1920).
[14] H. Diehl: *Chem. Revs.,* **21,** 39 (1937).

TABLE 7·4
TYPICAL CHELATE STRUCTURES (BIDENTATE GROUPS)

Chelating Group: Classification[14]	Chelating Group: Examples	Typical Chelates
1. Two acidic groups:		
Inorganic dibasic acids	CO_3^{-2}, SO_3^{-2}, SO_4^{-2}	$[Co(NH_3)_4CO_3]X$
Organic dicarboxylic acids	$C_2O_4^{-2}$, phthalate	$M_3^{I}[M^{III}(C_2O_4)_3]$
Organic disulfonic acids	$CH_2(SO_3)_2^{-2}$	$[Coen_2\{CH_2(SO_3)_2\}]Br$
α-Hydroxy carboxylic acids	glycolate, salicylate	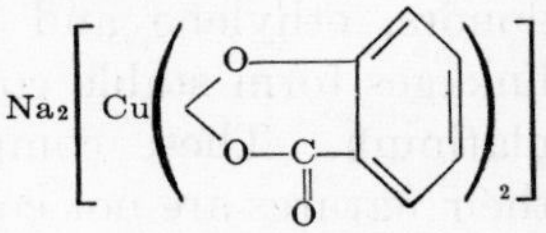 $Na_2[Cu(O—, O—C=O)_2]$
Organic diamides	$NH(CONH_2)_2$, $(CONH_2)_2$	$K_2[Cu\{(NHCO)_2NH\}_2]$
Acidic dihydroxy compounds	glycols, pyrocatechol	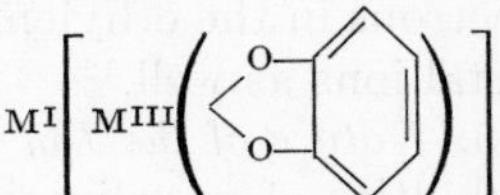 $M^{I}[M^{III}(O—, O—)_2]$
α-Hydroxy oximes	α-acyloin oximes	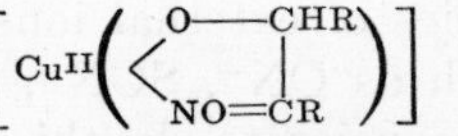 $[Cu^{II}(O—CHR, NO=CR)]$
Inorganic acid amides	$(NH_2)_2SO_2$	$Na[Rh(H_2O)_2\{(HN)_2SO_2\}_2]$
2. One acidic group, one coordinating group		
α-Amino carboxylic acids	$R_2C(NH_2)CO_2^-$	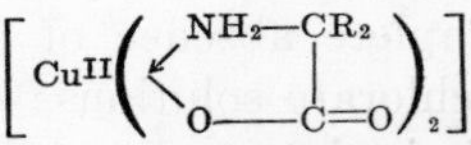 $[Cu^{II}(NH_2—CR_2, O—C=O)_2]$
α-Hydroxy carboxylic acids	lactate, glycolate	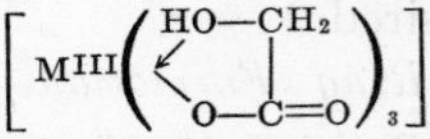 $[M^{III}(HO—CH_2, O—C=O)_3]$
Certain dihydroxy compounds	biphenol	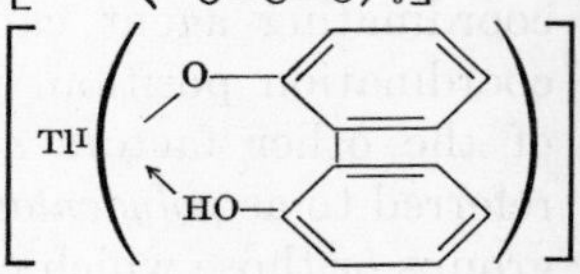 $[Tl^{I}(O—, HO—)]$
β-Hydroxy carbonyl compounds	β-diketones o-hydroxyaldehydes o-hydroxyphenones	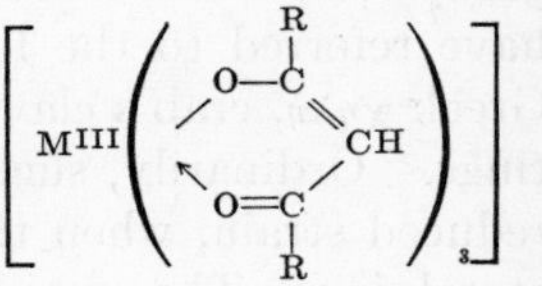 $[M^{III}(O—C(R), CH, O=C(R))_3]$
Hydroxyl amines	ethanolamines o-aminophenol	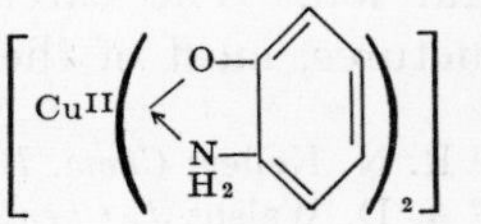 $[Cu^{II}(O—, NH_2)_2]$

TABLE 7·4 (*Continued*)

Chelating Group		Typical Chelates
Classification[14]	**Examples**	
Hydroxy azo compounds	*o*-hydroxyazobenzene *p*-nitrobenzeneazo-resorcinol	$[M^{II}(O\text{—}C_6H_4\text{—}N{=}N\text{—}R)_2]$
8-Quinolinols	8-quinolinol 5,7-dihalo-8-quinolinol	$[Ga^{III}(O\text{—}C_9H_6N)_3]$
α-Hydroxyl oximes	α-benzoin oximes salicylaldoxime	$[Ni^{II}(O{=}N{=}C(C_6H_5)\text{—}C(H)(C_6H_5)\text{—}O(H))_2]$
Ketoximes	benzil oxime *o*-nitrosophenol	$[Fe^{II}(O{=}N{=}C(C_6H_5)\text{—}C(C_6H_5){=}O)_2]$
Glyoximes	dimethylglyoxime(anti)	$[Ni^{II}(O{=}N{=}C(CH_3)\text{—}C(CH_3){=}N\text{—}OH)_2]$
B. Two coordinating groups		
Diamines	ethylenediamine propylenediamine	$[Coen_3]Cl_3$
	α,α′-dipyridyl *o*-phenanthroline	$[Fe^{II}(C_5H_4N\text{—}C_5H_4N)_3]X_2$
Amino pyridyls	α-pyridylhydrazine	$[Fe^{II}(C_5H_4N\text{—}NH\text{—}NH_2)_2]Cl_2$

TABLE 7·4 (*Continued*)

Chelating Group		Typical Chelates
Classification[14]	Examples	
Dihydroxyl compounds	1,2-glycols pinacol glycerol	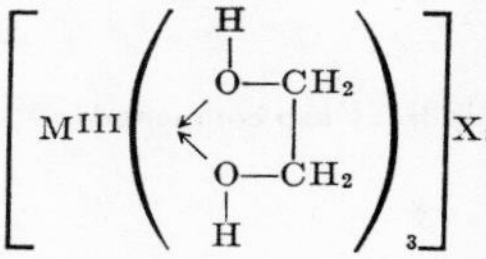 $\left[M^{III}\left(\begin{matrix}H\text{—}O\text{—}CH_2\\ H\text{—}O\text{—}CH_2\end{matrix}\right)_3\right]X_3$
α-Hydroxy oximes	α-benzoin oxime	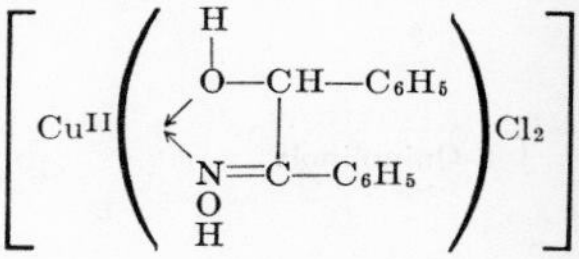 $\left[Cu^{II}\left(\begin{matrix}H\text{—}O\text{—}CH\text{—}C_6H_5\\ HO\text{—}N{=}C\text{—}C_6H_5\end{matrix}\right)\right]Cl_2$
Organic disulfides	dithioethers	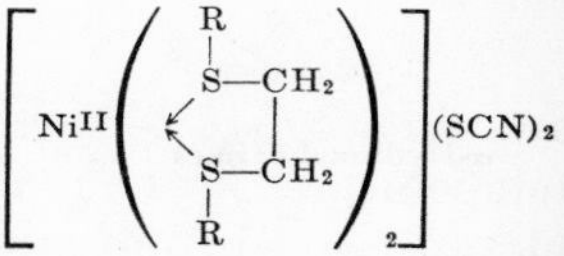 $\left[Ni^{II}\left(\begin{matrix}R\text{—}S\text{—}CH_2\\ R\text{—}S\text{—}CH_2\end{matrix}\right)_2\right](SCN)_2$
Glyoximes	dimethylglyoxime	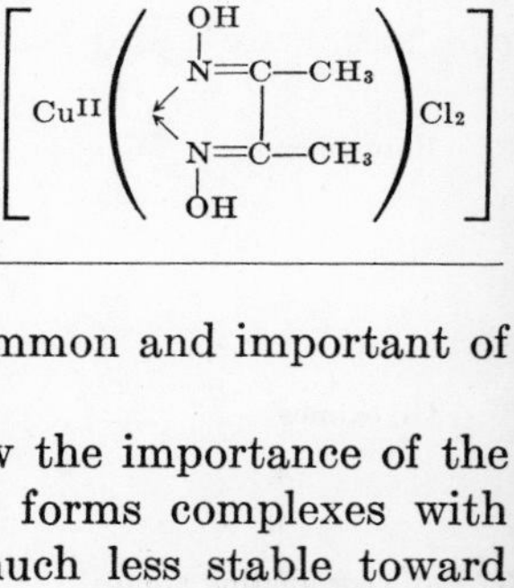 $\left[Cu^{II}\left(\begin{matrix}HO\text{—}N{=}C\text{—}CH_3\\ HO\text{—}N{=}C\text{—}CH_3\end{matrix}\right)\right]Cl_2$

containing metal ions. Some of the more common and important of these structures are summarized in Table 7·4.

A few examples may be considered to show the importance of the phenomenon. Thus, ethylamine, $C_2H_5NH_2$, forms complexes with cobalt(III) and chromium(III) which are much less stable toward other reagents or toward heat than those formed by ethylenediamine, $H_2NCH_2CH_2NH_2$, a molecule which yields five-membered chelate rings. Neither phenol, C_6H_5—OH, nor benzaldehyde, C_6H_5—CHO, gives particularly stable coordination compounds, but combination of the two structures into salicylaldehyde, o-HOC_6H_4—CHO, gives a material which forms many stable chelated complexes. These complexes may be formulated as

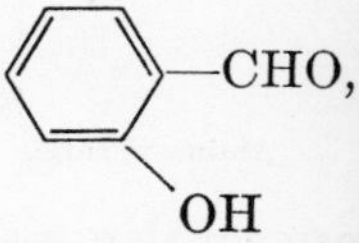

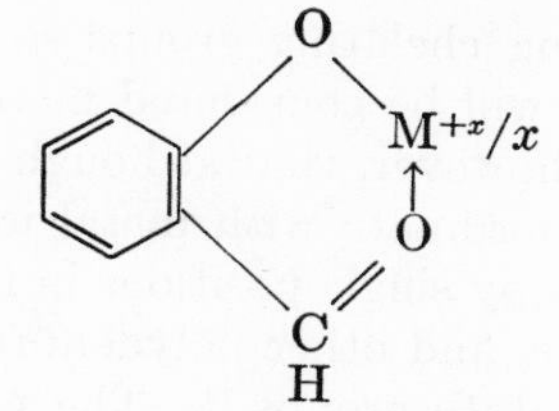

O ⟶ M^{+x}/x ← O = CH (salicylaldehyde chelate)

Correspondingly, although complexes derived from acetone,

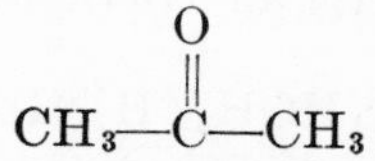

$$CH_3{-}\overset{\overset{\displaystyle O}{\|}}{C}{-}CH_3$$

are unimportant, those derived from acetylacetone,

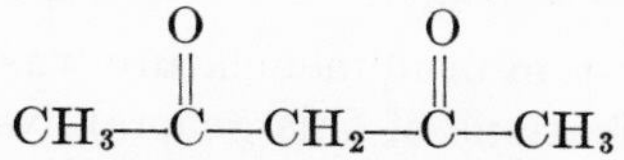

$$CH_3{-}\overset{\overset{\displaystyle O}{\|}}{C}{-}CH_2{-}\overset{\overset{\displaystyle O}{\|}}{C}{-}CH_3$$

are often so stable thermally that they can be volatilized at elevated temperatures without decomposition. In these and in similar complexes derived from other β-diketones, chelation probably involves an *enol* structure[15] and may be formulated as

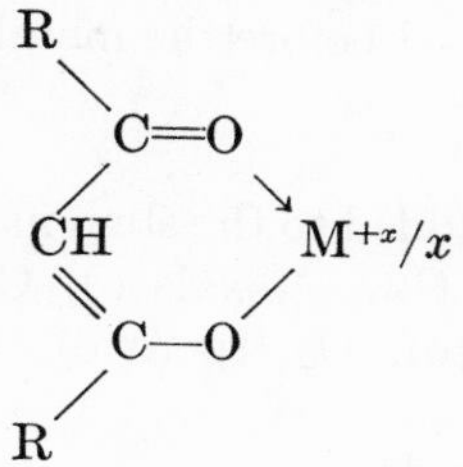

R—C=O → M^{+x}/x ← O—C(R)=CH (ring: C=O, CH, C—O)

$R = CH_3,\ C_2H_5,\ C_6H_5$, etc.

In like manner, acetates such as the copper(II) compound are salt-like in character, whereas the corresponding amino acetates, such as

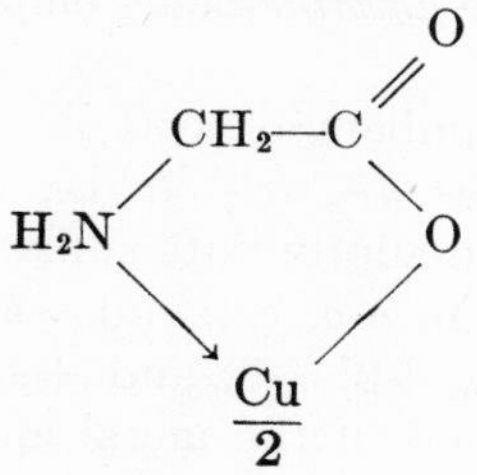

H_2N—CH_2—C(=O)—O—$\frac{Cu}{2}$ ($H_2N \rightarrow \frac{Cu}{2}$)

are covalent in character.

[15] L. E. Marchi: *Inorganic Syntheses*, Vol. II, p. **10**. McGraw-Hill Book Co., New York (1946).

Compounds containing chelating groups such as ethylenediamine, oxalate, and carbonate will be considered more extensively later. It should be pointed out, however, that although most dinegative anions (e.g., $C_2O_4^{-2}$, CO_3^{-2}) coordinate with metal ions by chelation, some, notably the sulfate, occupy single positions in the coordination sphere. Tridentate, tetradentate, and other polydentate groups are much less common than the bidentate groups.[14] The majority of those which have been studied are polyamines such as diethylenetriamine, $H_2NCH_2CH_2NHCH_2CH_2NH_2$, or triethylenetetramine,

$$H_2NCH_2CH_2NHCH_2CH_2NHCH_2CH_2NH_2.$$

THE NOMENCLATURE OF COORDINATION COMPOUNDS

A comprehensive system of nomenclature was devised by Werner.[16] Although some modifications of this general system have been found necessary and other modifications have been proposed, all modern systems still contain sufficient of the Werner approach to make its consideration profitable.

According to the Werner system, cation and anion are named in order as with simple compounds. In naming an ion containing coordinating groups, these groups are mentioned before the metal which is present, and in the following order:

1. Negative groups, the suffix *-o* being added to the stem name of the group. E.g., Cl^-(chloro), NO_2^-(nitro), $C_2O_4^{-2}$(oxalato), CO_3^{-2}(carbonato), CN^-(cyano), SCN^-(thiocyanato), O_2^{-2}(peroxo), O^{-2}(oxo), OH^-(hydroxo), etc.
2. Water, the name *aquo* being employed.
3. Derivatives of ammonia, the amine names being employed directly.
4. Ammonia, the name *ammine* being employed.

In each case, the numbers of coordinating groups present are indicated by the prefixes *di-*, *tri-*, *tetra-*, etc. The metal is then named as the *stem* plus an appropriate suffix. If the metal appears in the cation, the suffixes *−a*, *−o*, *−i*, and *−e* are employed to indicate that the metal is in +1, +2, +3, and +4 oxidation states, respectively. On the other hand, if the metal appears in the anion, these single letter suffixes plus the ending *−ate* are added to the metal stems.

[16] A. Werner: *Neuere Anschauungen auf dem Gebiete der anorganischen Chemie*, Vierte Auflage, pp. 92–95. T. Viewig u. Sohn, Braunschweig (1920).

If the coordination compound is a non-electrolyte, the coordinated groups are named as indicated above, but the name of the metal is used as such without suffix. In *polynuclear complexes* (p. 272), that is, those containing more than a single ion of the metal, the name of the bridging coordinated group is prefixed by μ.

Although the value of this system in systematizing the chemistry of the coordination compounds cannot be minimized, it was often cumbersome and non-specific in its original form. In order to overcome certain of these difficulties, the Nomenclature Committee of the International Union of Chemistry (I.U.C.) suggested[17] what might be called a modified Werner system. The fundamental postulates offered may be summarized[18, 19] as follows:

1. The cation is named first, followed by the anion.
2. The names of all negative groups end in *–o*, whereas those of neutral groups have no characteristic ending. By way of exception and in deference to established practice, water is called *aquo*.
3. Coordinated groups are listed in order: negative groups, neutral groups.
4. The oxidation state of the central metallic element is designated by a Roman numeral placed in parentheses. With complex cations or neutral molecules, this numeral is placed immediately after the name of the element to which it relates, no alteration in the name of the metal being made. With complex anions, the Roman numeral is placed immediately after the name of the complex, which invariably ends in *–ate*.
5. The names of coordinated groups are not ordinarily separated by hyphens or parentheses.

It is apparent that these recommendation differ basically from those of Werner only in the mode of designating the oxidation state of the central element. Use of Roman numeral designation is admittedly more specific and less confusing than the original letter designation and has been rather uniformly adopted. Comparisons of the two systems are given by the examples tabulated in Table 7·5.

Useful as are the I. U. C. rules, they still have limitations. Fernelius et al.[19] have suggested a number of extensions which should

[17] W. P. Jorissen, H. Bassett, A. Damiens, F. Fichter, and H. Remy: *J. Am. Chem. Soc.*, **63,** 889 (1941).

[18] W. C. Fernelius: *Chem. Eng. News*, **26,** 161 (1948).

[19] W. C. Fernelius, E. M. Larsen, L. E. Marchi, and C. L. Rollinson: *Chem. Eng. News*, **26,** 520 (1948).

TABLE 7·5

NOMENCLATURE OF COORDINATION COMPOUNDS

Formula	Werner Name	I. U. C. Name	Modified I. U. C. Name
$[Co(NH_3)_6]Cl_3$	hexamminecobalti chloride	hexaamminecobalt(III) chloride	hexaamminecobalt(III) chloride
$[Co(NH_3)_4Cl_2]^+$	dichlorotetramminecobalti ion	dichlorotetraamminecobalt(III) ion	dichlorotetraamminecobalt(III) ion
$[Cr(en)_3]^{+3}$	triethylenediaminechromi ion	triethylenediamine-chromium(III) ion	tris(ethylenediamine)chromium(III) ion
$[Co(C_2O_4)_3]^{-3}$	trioxalatocobaltiate ion	trioxalatocobaltate(III) ion	trioxalatocobaltate(III) ion
$[Pt(NH_3)_2Cl_4]$	tetrachlorodiammineplatinum	tetrachlorodiammineplatinum	tetrachlorodiammineplatinum(IV)
$[Co(en)_2ClNH_3]^{+2}$	chlorodiethylenediamine-amminecobalti ion	chlorodiethylenediamine-amminecobalt(III) ion	chlorobis(ethylenediamine)-amminecobalt(III) ion
$[Cr(NH_3)_6][Co(CN)_6]$	hexamminechromihexacyano-cobaltiate	hexaamminechromium(III)-hexacyanocobaltate(III)	hexaamminechromium(III) hexacyanocobaltate(III)
$[(NH_3)_5Co—O_2—Co(NH_3)_5]^{+4}$	decammine-μ-peroxodicobalti ion	decaammine-μ-peroxodicobalt(III) ion	decaammine-μ-peroxodicobalt(III) ion
$[Co(en)_2(Cl)(NO_2)]^+$	chloronitrodiethylenediamine-cobalti ion	chloronitrodiethylenediamine-cobalt(III) ion	chloronitrobis(ethylenediamine)cobalt(III) ion
$[Pt(NH_3)_2Cl_2]$	dichlorodiammineplatinum	dichlorodiammineplatinum	dichlorodiammineplatinum(II)

increase the utility of the I. U. C. system. Among these extensions are the following:

1. The names of coordinated positive groups end in *-ium*.
2. Positive groups are listed last, after negative and neutral groups.
3. Groups of the same general nature (i.e., all negative, all neutral, all positive) are listed in alphabetical order without regard to any prefixes designating the numbers of such groups present.
4. Zero oxidation state for the central element is designated by the Arabic character O placed in parentheses.
5. Coordinated hydrogen salts are named as acids by dropping the word hydrogen and replacing the suffix *-ate* by *-ic*.
6. Oxidation state of the central element is designated in the usual manner even though the complex is a neutral molecule.
7. Use of prefixes such as *bis-*, *tris-*, and *tetrakis-*, followed by the name of the coordinated group set off by parentheses is preferred to that of the old designations *di-*, *tri-*, and *tetra-* to indicate numbers of coordinated groups if the names of those groups are complex.

These are logical suggestions and should be adopted. They are used in this book in subsequent discussions. Their usefulness is apparent in the examples given in Table 7·5 under the heading "modified I. U. C. name."

Even the modified I. U. C. system cannot accomodate all materials to advantage. Fernelius et al.[19] have suggested a series of additions, some (especially those pertaining to isomerism) of which have been employed for some time in a semi-empirical fashion, although others have not yet been accepted widely. Among the more important of these extensions are the following:

1. The designation μ to indicate bridging groups is retained from the Werner system, with the added recommendation that it be repeated before the name of each bridging group. Thus the

$$\left[(\mathrm{en})_2\mathrm{Co} \begin{matrix} \nearrow \mathrm{NH_2} \searrow \\ \searrow \mathrm{O_2} \nearrow \end{matrix} \mathrm{Co(en)_2}\right]^{+4} \text{ ion}$$

would then be called bis(ethylenediamine)cobalt(III)-μ-amido-μ-peroxobis(ethylenediamine)cobalt(IV) ion.

2. Designation of the point of attachment in an organic molecule is recommended if more than one atom in that molecule can act as a donor. Use of the symbols of the donor elements, placed after the

name of the coordinating group, is recommended, as exemplified by

$$\left[\begin{array}{l} \quad\quad\quad\quad\quad OH \\ CH_3—C{=}N \\ \quad\quad\quad\quad\quad\quad\searrow \\ \quad\quad\quad\quad\quad\quad\quad CoCl_2 \\ \quad\quad\quad\quad\quad\quad\nearrow \\ CH_3—C{=}N \\ \quad\quad\quad\quad\quad OH \end{array}\right]$$

dichloro(dimethylglyoxime-N,N′)cobalt(II).

3. In order to render the name of a material more descriptive of any isomerism present, it is suggested that:

a. The preceding rule be extended to cover cases of structural isomerism (p. 250). Thus thiocyanate coordinated through sulfur would be *thiocyanato-S-* and through nitrogen, *thiocyanato-N-*.

b. Geometrical isomers (pp. 253–264) be distinguished alternatively by the terms *cis-* and *trans-* or the numbers 1,2- and 1,3- for planar arrangements (p. 254) and 1,2- and 1,6- for octahedral arrangements (p. 262).

c. The sign of rotation in optical isomers (p. 265) be designated by *d-* or *l-* (and *meso*), separated from the name by a hyphen and preceding any designation of geometrical isomerism. Optically active coordinating groups should be so designated within the name of the compound. Thus, *d-cis-*$[Co(l\text{-pn})_2Cl_2]Cl$ would be termed *d-cis-*dichlorobis(*l*-propylenediamine)cobalt(III) chloride. Absolute configurations are to be denoted by the capitals D and L.

4. Coordination of doubled groups or situations in which two coordination centers are linked directly are designated by the prefix *bi-* placed before the name of the material inolved. Thus, H_4O_2 would be called *biaquo,* and a metal-metal linkage would be called *bi-platinum, bi-palladium,* etc., as the case might be.

5. The suffix *-yl* to designate oxy-ions is considered unnecessary because in such ions the oxygens are themselves coordinated to the metal ion. Thus, *dioxouranium*(VI) is preferred to *uranyl* as a name for the UO_2^{+2} group.

6. Abbreviations (e.g., en for ethylenediamine) should always be accompanied by a statement as to their exact meaning.

It will be recognized that the proposals pertaining to isomerism are in keeping with organic practice. Use of some of these, particularly as applied to cases of geometrical isomerism, will become apparent in the next section.

ISOMERISM AMONG COORDINATION COMPOUNDS

Isomerism is commonly considered to be characteristic only of organic compounds. However, isomerism is a phenomenon of position or arrangement and, as such, cannot be limited to the compounds of any one element or to any one class of compounds. Although many examples of isomerism are noted among various inorganic substances, the coordination compounds offer such a variety of examples and types of isomerism as to be placed in a class apart from all other substances, organic or inorganic. The variety of linkage types and the increased number of possible geometrical arrangements combine to produce more types of isomerism than are known among the compounds of carbon.

The classification of types of isomerism given by Werner[20] is still generally acceptable and is followed in this discussion. For more detailed accounts, the many excellent summaries which have appeared should be consulted.[2, 20–25]

Polymerization isomerism

Compounds are said to be polymerization isomers when, although they have the same stoichiometric composition, their actual molecular compositions are multiples of the simplest stoichiometric arrangement. The name used is a misnomer in that no actual polymerization of simple materials to more complex ones occurs. The differences among polymerization isomers are differences in arrangement, not in numbers of repeating groups.

Werner distinguished coordination polymers and nuclear polymers among the coordination compounds. Coordination polymerization may be illustrated by the series of compounds based upon trinitrotriamminecobalt(III) and dichlorodiammineplatinum(II) as summarized in Table 7·6. Other similar series are based, respectively, upon the compounds $[Cr(NH_3)_3(SCN)_3]$, $[Pt(NH_3)_2(CN)_2]$, $[Pt(NH_3)_2(SCN)_2]$, $[Pt(NH_3)_2Cl_4]$, and $[Ptpy_2Cl_2]$ (py = pyridine). Nuclear

[20] A. Werner: *Neuere Anschauungen auf dem Gebiete der anorganischen Chemie*, Vierte Auflage, pp. 327–386. T. Viewig u. Sohn, Braunschweig (1920).

[21] Gmelin's *Handbuch der anorganischen Chemie*, System-Nummer **58B**, pp. 5–8. Verlag Chemie G.m.b.h., Berlin (1930).

[22] P. Pfeiffer: in Freudenberg's *Stereochemie*, pp. 1200–1377. F. Deuticke, Leipzig u. Wien (1933).

[23] M. M. J. Sutherland: in Friend's *A Textbook of Inorganic Chemistry*, Vol. X, Ch. III. Charles Griffin and Co., Ltd., London (1928).

[24] W. C. Fernelius: *Chemical Architecture* (R. E. Burk and O. Grummitt, Eds.), Ch. III. Interscience Publishers, New York (1948).

[25] J. C. Bailar, Jr.: *Chem. Revs.*, **19**, 67 (1936).

TABLE 7·6

TYPICAL EXAMPLES OF COORDINATION POLYMERIZATION

Number of Stoichiometric Groups	Cobalt Series	Platinum Series
1	$[Co(NH_3)_3(NO_2)_3]$	$[Pt(NH_3)_2Cl_2]$
2	$[Co(NH_3)_6][Co(NO_2)_6]$	$[Pt(NH_3)_4][PtCl_4]$
	$[Co(NH_3)_4(NO_2)_2][Co(NH_3)_2(NO_2)_4]$	
3	$[Co(NH_3)_5NO_2][Co(NH_3)_2(NO_2)_4]_2$	$[Pt(NH_3)_4][Pt(NH_3)Cl_3]_2$
		$[Pt(NH_3)_3Cl]_2[PtCl_4]$
4	$[Co(NH_3)_6][Co(NH_3)_2(NO_2)_4]_3$	
	$[Co(NH_3)_4(NO_2)_2]_3[Co(NO_2)_6]$	
5	$[Co(NH_3)_5NO_2]_3[Co(NO_2)_6]_2$	

polymerization isomerism is less common and is perhaps best illustrated by the following examples:

$$\left[(H_3N)_3Co\begin{matrix}\diagup OH \searrow \\ —OH\rightarrow \\ \diagdown OH \nearrow\end{matrix}Co(NH_3)_3\right]X_3 \text{ and } \left[Co\left\{\begin{matrix}\swarrow HO \diagdown \\ \\ \nwarrow HO \diagup\end{matrix}Co(NH_3)_4\right\}_3\right]X_6$$

$$\left[(H_3N)_4Co\begin{matrix}\diagup OH \searrow \\ \\ \diagdown OH \nearrow\end{matrix}Co(NH_3)_4\right]Br_4\cdot 2H_2O \text{ and } [Co(NH_3)_4(OH)(H_2O)]Br_2$$

As is to be expected from the differences in arrangement within these polymerization isomers, sizable differences in physical and chemical properties exist among them.

Coordination isomerism

This type of isomerism results in compounds containing both coordinated cations and anions when differences in the distribution of the coordinating groups occur. If two different metal ions are involved, the donor groups may attach to give isomers of the types $[MA_x][M'B_x]$ or $[M'A_x][MB_x]$ or any intermediate between these extremes. Typical examples of this type of isomerism are

$[Co(en)_3][Cr(CN)_6]$ and $[Cr(en)_3][Co(CN)_6]$

$[Co(en)_2pn][Cr(CN)_6]$ and $[Cr(en)_2pn][Co(CN)_6]$

$[Co(NH_3)_6][Cr(C_2O_4)_3]$ and $[Cr(NH_3)_6][Co(C_2O_4)_3]$

$[Cu(NH_3)_4][PtCl_4]$ and $[Pt(NH_3)_4][CuCl_4]$

and the series $[Co(en)_3][Cr(C_2O_4)_3]$, $[Co(en)_2C_2O_4][Cr(en)(C_2O_4)_2]$, $[Cr(en)_2C_2O_4][Co(en)(C_2O_4)_2]$, and $[Cr(en)_3][Co(C_2O_4)_3]$.

On the other hand, if the same metal appears in both cation and anion either in the same oxidation state or in different oxidation states, coordination isomers will exist if donors are distributed between cation and anion. Examples in which there is no difference in oxidation state are

$[Cr(NH_3)_6][Cr(SCN)_6]$ and $[Cr(NH_3)_4(SCN)_2][Cr(NH_3)_2(SCN)_4]$
$[Pt(NH_3)_4][PtCl_4]$ and $[Pt(NH_3)_3Cl][Pt(NH_3)Cl_3]$
$[Cr(en)_3][Cr(C_2O_4)_3]$ and $[Cr(en)_2C_2O_4][Cr(en)(C_2O_4)_2]$
$[Cr(en)_2(H_2O)_2][Cr(C_2O_4)_3]\cdot 2H_2O$ and $[Cr(en)_2C_2O_4][Cr(H_2O)_2(C_2O_4)_2]\cdot 2H_2O$

Examples in which differences in oxidation state exist are

$\overset{II}{[Pt(NH_3)_4]}\overset{IV}{[PtCl_6]}$ and $\overset{IV}{[Pt(NH_3)_4Cl_2]}\overset{II}{[PtCl_4]}$

$\overset{II}{[Pt(py)_4]}\overset{IV}{[PtCl_6]}$ and $\overset{IV}{[Pt(py)_4Cl_2]}\overset{II}{[PtCl_4]}$

Coordination isomers show the same essential differences in properties as polymerization isomers, and for the same reason.

Hydrate isomerism

As is shown in a later chapter (pp. 497–500), water may appear in stoichiometric quantities in compounds in a variety of ways. Thus combined water may coordinate to metal ions in much the same fashion as ammonia, or it may appear in lattice positions without being closely associated with a given metal ion. These differences produce hydrate isomerism, a phenomenon which is probably best illustrated by the hydrated chromium(III) chlorides, $CrCl_3\cdot 6H_2O$. Three such chlorides have been prepared: $[Cr(H_2O)_6]Cl_3$, a violet-colored compound giving three ionic chlorines; $[Cr(H_2O)_5Cl]Cl_2\cdot H_2O$, a green compound giving two ionic chlorines; and $[Cr(H_2O)_4Cl_2]Cl\cdot 2H_2O$, a green compound giving only one ionic chlorine. Other examples of hydrate isomerism are

$[Co(NH_3)_4(H_2O)Cl]Cl_2$ and $[Co(NH_3)_4Cl_2]Cl\cdot H_2O$
$[Co(NH_3)_3(H_2O)_2Cl]Br_2$ and $[Co(NH_3)_3(H_2O)(Cl)Br]Br\cdot H_2O$
$[Co(NH_3)_4(H_2O)Cl]Br_2$ and $[Co(NH_3)_4Br_2]Cl\cdot H_2O$
$[Cr(py)_2(H_2O)_2Cl_2]Cl$ and $[Cr(py)_2(H_2O)Cl_3]\cdot H_2O$

Definite differences in physical and chemical properties as well as in color are noted among these compounds.

Ionization isomerism

Compounds which have the same stoichiometric composition but yield different ions in solution are called ionization isomers. This type of isomerism is illustrated classically by red-violet $[Co(NH_3)_5Br]SO_4$ and red $[Co(NH_3)_5SO_4]Br$, which yield sulfate and bromide, respectively, as anions. Other examples of ionization isomerism are

$[Co(NH_3)_5NO_3]SO_4$	and	$[Co(NH_3)_5SO_4]NO_3$
$[Co(NH_3)_5Br]C_2O_4$	and	$[Co(NH_3)_5C_2O_4]Br$
$[Co(NH_3)_4(Cl)(NO_2)]Cl$	and	$[Co(NH_3)_4Cl_2]NO_2$
$[Co(en)_2(Cl)(NO_2)]NO_2$	and	$[Co(en)_2(NO_2)_2]Cl$
$[Pt(NH_3)_4Cl_2]Br_2$	and	$[Pt(NH_3)_4Br_2]Cl_2$

and the series $[Co(en)_2(Cl)(NO_2)]SCN$, $[Co(en)_2(SCN)(NO_2)]Cl$, and $[Co(en)_2(SCN)(Cl)]NO_2$. The occurrence of materials in which dinegative anions occupy single coordination positions is noteworthy among isomers of this type.

Structural or salt isomerism

Isomerism of this type occurs when more than a single atom in a coordinated group may function as a donor. A number of groups might conceivably cause isomerism of this type. Thus, the thiocyanate radical with the structure $:\ddot{\underset{..}{S}}:\ddot{C}:\ddot{\underset{..}{N}}^-$ might coordinate through either the sulfur or the nitrogen, although only those compounds in which attachment is through the nitrogen have been characterized. Similarly, the thiosulfate ion,

$$\begin{array}{c} :\ddot{O}: \\ :\ddot{\underset{..}{S}}:\ddot{\underset{..}{S}}:\ddot{\underset{..}{O}}:^{-2} \\ :\underset{..}{O}: \end{array}$$

might attach through either sulfur or oxygen, although again only one type of compound, that with sulfur as donor, has been reported. Both carbon monoxide, $:C:::O:$, and the cyanide radical, $:C:::N:^-$, are other typical cases. Although these act as bridging groups, attachment to a single metal is apparently through carbon in each case.

The situation with the NO_2^- ion, $:\ddot{\underset{..}{O}}:\ddot{N}::\ddot{\underset{..}{O}}^-$, is somewhat more complex. Jörgensen[26] prepared two pentamminecobalt(III) chlor-

[26] S. M. Jörgensen: *Z. anorg. Chem.*, **5**, 147 (1893); **19**, 109 (1899).

ides, each containing a single coordinated NO_2^- group, one which was red and easily decomposed by acids and the other which was yellow-brown and stable to acids. The red compound, either in solution or in the solid state, underwent slow transformation into the yellow-brown one. The two materials were designated as

$$\underset{\substack{\text{nitritopentammine}\\ \text{red}}}{[Co(NH_3)_5(ONO)]Cl_2} \quad \text{and} \quad \underset{\substack{\text{nitropentammine}\\ \text{yellow-brown}}}{[Co(NH_3)_5(NO_2)]Cl_2}$$

because of the enhanced stability of the Co—N bond and because compounds containing six such bonds have yellow to brown colors whereas those containing five such bonds and a Co—O bond tend to be red. Werner[27] prepared the similar isomers

$$[Co(en)_2(ONO)_2]X \quad \text{and} \quad [Co(en)_2(NO_2)_2]X$$
$$[Co(NH_3)_2(py)_2(ONO)_2]X \quad \text{and} \quad [Co(NH_3)_2(py)_2(NO_2)_2]X$$

Recent kinetic studies on the conversion of the nitritopentammine to the nitropentammine, based upon changes in absorption spectra,[28] support the belief that two isomers exist. However, it is also reported[29] that the two materials yield identical Debye-Scherrer x-ray patterns and ultraviolet absorption spectra and nearly identical infra-red spectra. On this basis, it is proposed[29] that there is no isomerism and that only the nitro form exists. The red color is ascribed to unreacted starting material. Obviously, more work will be necessary before the problem can be considered solved.

Coordination position isomerism

In polynuclear complexes, coordination groups may be present in the same numbers but may arrange themselves differently with respect to the different metal ion nuclei present. This gives coordination position isomerism. The following examples are typical:

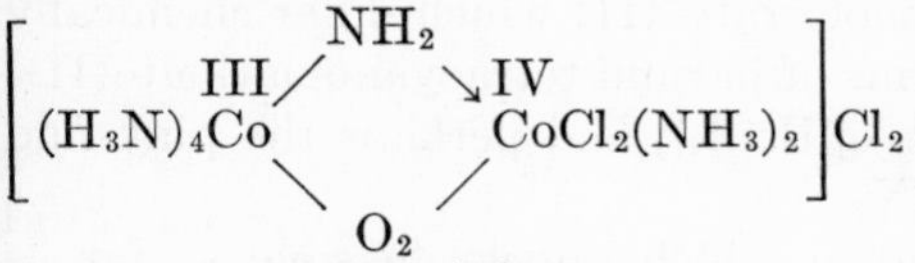

$$\left[(H_3N)_4\overset{III}{Co}\begin{matrix} \diagup NH_2 \searrow \\ \diagdown O_2 \diagup \end{matrix}\overset{IV}{Co}Cl_2(NH_3)_2 \right]Cl_2 \text{ and}$$

unsymmetrical

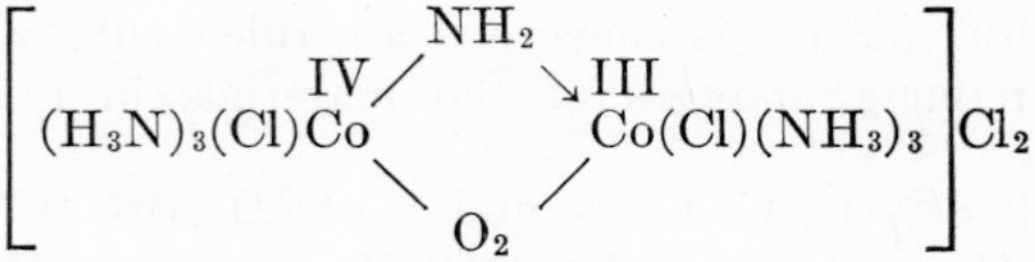

$$\left[(H_3N)_3(Cl)\overset{IV}{Co}\begin{matrix} \diagup NH_2 \searrow \\ \diagdown O_2 \diagup \end{matrix}\overset{III}{Co}(Cl)(NH_3)_3 \right]Cl_2$$

symmetrical

[27] A. Werner: *Ber.*, **40**, 765 (1907).

[28] B. Adell: *Svensk Kem. Tid.*, **56**, 318 (1944); **57**, 260 (1945); ***Z. anorg. Chem.***, **252**, 272 (1944).

[29] J. Lecomte and C. Duval: *Bull. soc. chim.* [5], **12**, 678 (1945).

The analogy between isomerism of this type and that existing between ethylene dichloride, $ClCH_2CH_2Cl$, and ethylidene chloride, CH_3CHCl_2, is apparent.

Valence isomerism

Werner applied this terminology to materials in which the same group may be held by different types of valence bonds (sometimes primary, sometimes secondary). Typical examples are

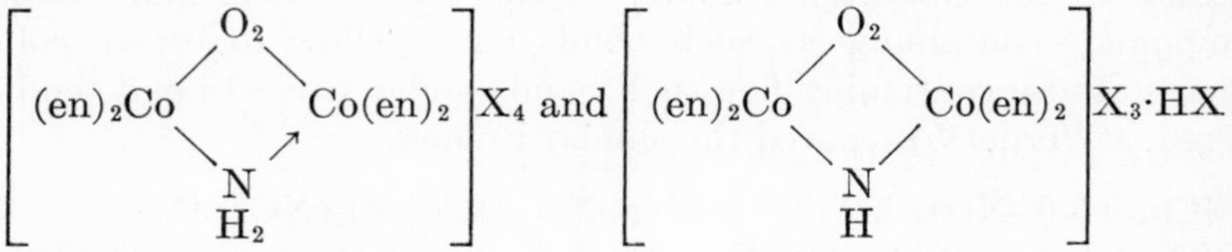

$$\left[\begin{array}{ccc} & O_2 & \\ & \diagup \quad \diagdown & \\ (en)_2Co & & Co(en)_2 \\ & \diagdown \quad \nearrow & \\ & N & \\ & H_2 & \end{array}\right]X_4 \text{ and } \left[\begin{array}{ccc} & O_2 & \\ & \diagup \quad \diagdown & \\ (en)_2Co & & Co(en)_2 \\ & \diagdown \quad \diagup & \\ & N & \\ & H & \end{array}\right]X_3 \cdot HX$$

and the rather similar

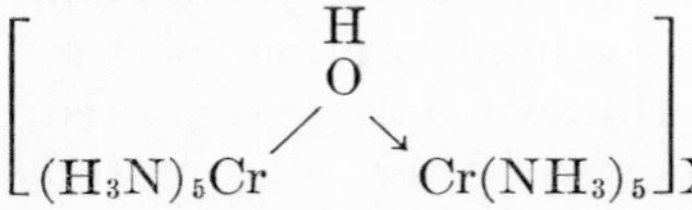

$$\left[\begin{array}{ccc} & H & \\ & O & \\ & \diagup \quad \searrow & \\ (H_3N)_5Cr & & Cr(NH_3)_5 \end{array}\right]X_5 \text{ and } [(H_3N)_5Cr—O—Cr(NH_3)_5]X_4 \cdot HX$$

Werner also considered the pink and black isomers characterized by the empirical formula $[Co(NH_3)_5(NO)]X_2$ to be examples of this type of isomerism, but more modern work, as recently summarized,[30] casts some doubt upon this assumption (pp. 599, 604).

Miscellaneous types of isomerism

Isomerism within a coordinating group may also occur. For example, one may obtain $[Co(en)_2(isopropylamine)Cl]^{+2}$ and $[Co(en)_2$-$(n$-$propylamine)Cl]^{+2}$ as isomeric cations. Among other cases of apparent but unexplained isomerism may be cited the following: two forms of potassium hexacyanoferrate(III) which differ chemically from each other; two similar forms of barium tetracyanoplatinate(II); red and green forms of $[Pt(NH_3)_4][PtCl_4]$; and perhaps the pink and black forms of $[Co(NH_3)_5(NO)]X_2$.

Certain other cases of isomerism which appear feasible as far as formulation is concerned are ruled out by the relative oxidizing and reducing powers of the materials in question. Among them are $[Co(NH_3)_5ClO_3]Br_2$ and $[Co(NH)_5BrO_3]ClBr$; $[\overset{IV}{Pt}(NH_3)_2(SO_3)_2]$ and $[\overset{II}{Pt}(NH_3)_2(S_2O_6)]$; and $\overset{IV}{Ce}[\overset{II}{Fe}(CN)_6]$ and $\overset{III}{Ce}[\overset{III}{Fe}(CN)_6]$.

[30] T. Moeller: *J. Chem. Education*, **23,** 542 (1946).

Geometrical or stereoisomerism

Stereoisomerism is by all odds the most interesting and important of the types of isomerism noted among the coordination compounds. It will be recalled (p. 230) that the existence of stereoisomerism was a fundamental postulate of Werner's theory. The preparation of predicted isomers and the evaluation of their properties may be regarded as among the most convincing arguments in favor of acceptance of Werner's views. Stereoisomerism among inorganic compounds is somewhat more involved than among organic materials because of the greater variety of spatial arrangements which can exist. Among organic compounds, the simple tetrahedron or the tetrahedron as it is distorted through multiple bonding is more simply treated.

Stereoisomerism may be considered most conveniently as it is related to the coordination number of the central metal ion or atom.[24] The variety of possible geometrical arrangements increases as the coordination number increases. Although arrangements for coordination numbers up through *six* have been well established, questions as to the true pictures with higher coordination numbers have not been answered completely. The stereochemical characteristics of the various coordination numbers are now considered.

Coordination Number 2. In compounds where this coordination number is exhibited, existence of stereoisomers is precluded by the impossibility of more than a single arrangement in space of the groups involved. Whether the groups lie in a straight line or are in an angular arrangement is of no consequence, since for a given material the arrangement is always the same. Such groups as $[Ag(NH_3)_2]^+$ and $[Ag(CN)_2]^-$ have no stereoisomers.

Coordination Number 3. Stereoisomers have not been obtained for materials in which this rather uncommon coordination number is exhibited. Although various geometrical arrangements are known, it appears that the arrangement in a given material is always the same, whether it is planar, trigonal-pyramidal, etc.

Coordination Number 4. By analogy to organic chemistry, the tetrahedral arrangement might be considered as characterizing materials showing this coordination number. However, the possibility of planar arrangements cannot be neglected. Decision as to which arrangement is correct for a particular material must be based upon the results of structural studies involving x-ray techniques or upon a comparison of the number of preparable isomers with the number predicted for each arrangement. Both spatial arrangements are found among coordination compounds of the metals.

Regardless of whether the arrangement were tetrahedral or planar, materials of the types $[Ma_4]$, $[Ma_3b]$, or $[Mab_3]$ (a and b are different groups, each occupying but a single position) should have no stereoisomers, for every conceivable spatial arrangement for each of these substances is exactly equivalent. On the other hand, for materials of the type $[Ma_2b_2]$, although no isomerism is predicted for a tetrahedral arrangement, *cis* and *trans* isomers are predicted for a planar one. This is apparent from the graphic formulations

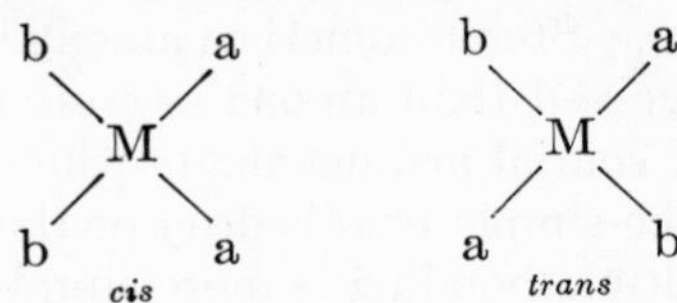

all materials lying in the same plane. Correspondingly, a difference exists between the predicted numbers of isomers for materials of the type [Mabcd], the tetrahedral arrangement giving mirror-image enantiomorphs

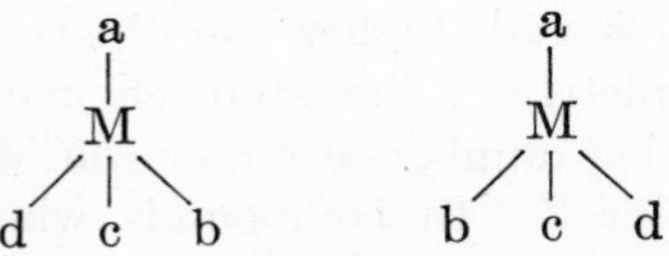

and the planar arrangement three isomers

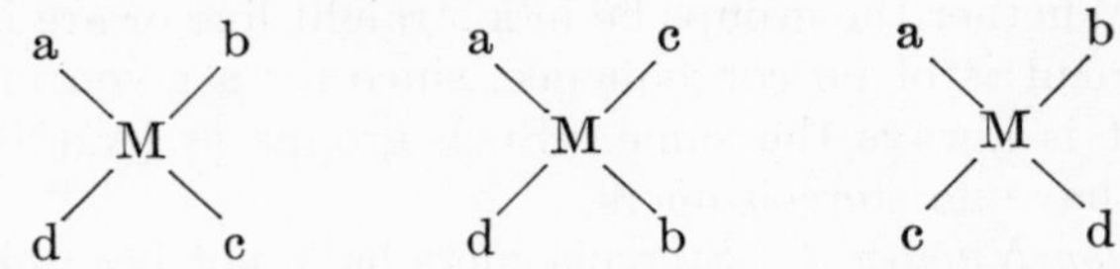

The utility of determining spatial arrangement through preparation of isomers is best illustrated with dipositive platinum. Treatment of potassium tetrachloroplatinate(II) with aqueous ammonia yields the so-called *beta* form of dichlorodiammineplatinum(II), $[Pt(NH_3)_2Cl_2]$. Treating tetrammineplatinum(II) chloride with hydrochloric acid gives another form (*alpha*) of the same compound, a form possessing different properties. It follows, therefore, that the configuration of platinum(II) is planar. This is confirmed by the existence of other compounds of the type $[Pta_2b_2]$, e.g., $[Pt(NH_3)_2py_2]Cl_2$, $K_2[PtCl_2(NH_2SO_3)_2]$, in two isomeric forms. Further experimental proof of the correctness of the planar configuration is given by the preparation of three isomers each of the ion $[Pt(NH_3)(py)(NH_2OH)(NO_2)]^+$ [31]

[31] I. I. Tscherniaev: *Ann. inst. platine*, **6**, 55 (1928).

and the compounds $[Pt(C_2H_4)(NH_3)(Cl)(Br)]$[32] and $[Pt(NH_3)(py)(Cl)(Br)]$.[33] In addition, Mills and Quibell[34] succeeded in resolving into optical isomers an isobutylenediaminestilbenediamineplatinum(II) complex. As shown below, if the arrangement of the coordinating groups is coplanar with the platinum, no plane of symmetry is present, and the existence of optical isomers would be expected. On the other hand, if the arrangement is tetrahedral, there is a plane of symmetry. This gives convincing proof for the planar arrangement.

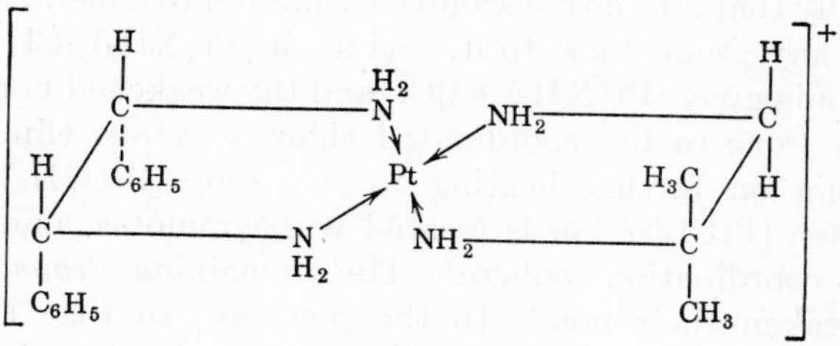

coplanar

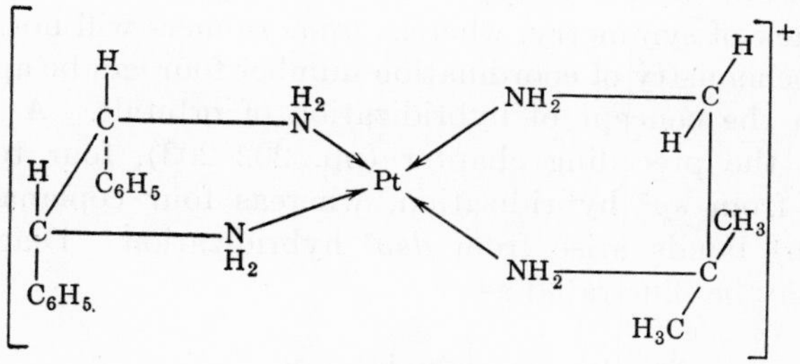

tetrahedral

Decision as to which isomer is *cis* and which *trans* in planar materials of the type $[Ma_2b_2]$ may be reached by experimental means. If $[Pt(NH_3)_2Cl_2]$ is again taken as an example, the following approach may be outlined. Werner[35] prepared the materials $[Pt(NH_3)_2(py)_2]Cl_2$ by reacting the alpha and beta forms with pyridine, and he noted what substances were eliminated when these were heated. On the assumption that thermally eliminated groups should be *trans* to each other, formation of two moles of ammonia or two moles of pyridine would indicate a *trans* structure in $[Pt(NH_3)_2(py)_2]Cl_2$ and

[32] A. D. Gel'man and E. Gorushkina: *Compt. rend. acad. sci. U. R. S. S.*, **55**, 33 (1947).

[33] A. D. Gel'man, E. F. Karandashova, and L. N. Essen: *Doklady Akad. Nauk. S. S. S. R.*, **63**, 37 (1948).

[34] W. H. Mills and T. H. H. Quibell: *J. Chem. Soc.*, **1935**, 839.

[35] A. Werner: *Z. anorg. Chem.*, **3** 267 (1893).

presumably a *trans* structure in the original compound, whereas elimination of only one mole of pyridine or ammonia would indicate a *cis* structure. The *alpha* compound was thus shown to be *trans*. Furthermore, reactions involving oxalic acid are different, the *beta* isomer leading to a complex of composition $[Pt(NH_3)_2(C_2O_4]$, which, because bidentate groups must always occupy *cis* positions, indicates a *cis* arrangement in the original *beta* compound. The so-called *trans-effect* of Tscherniaev (Chernaev)[36] may also be used. It is observed experimentally that a negative group coordinated to a metal ion loosens the bond of any group *trans* to it. Thus, if $[Pt(NH_3)_4]Cl_2$ is heated, loss of ammonia gives $[Pt(NH_3)_3Cl]Cl$, and the weakened bond holding an ammonia *trans* to the coordinated chlorine causes elimination of that ammonia on further heating to give *trans*-$[Pt(NH_3)_2Cl_2]$ (i.e., *alpha*). When $[PtCl_4]^{-2}$ ion is treated with ammonia, one ammonia enters the coordination sphere. The remaining *trans* chlorines mutually weaken their bonds to the platinum so that the second ammonia must enter *cis* to the first, giving the *beta* isomer. In general, *cis* isomers of this type will have dipole moments (p. 186) because of lack of symmetry, whereas *trans* isomers will not.

The stereochemistry of coordination number four can be approached also through the concept of hybridization of orbitals. As has been discussed in the preceding chapter (pp. 202–203), four tetrahedral bonds arise from sp^3 hybridization, whereas four coplanar (square configuration) bonds arise from dsp^2 hybridization. Diagrammatically, this may be illustrated as

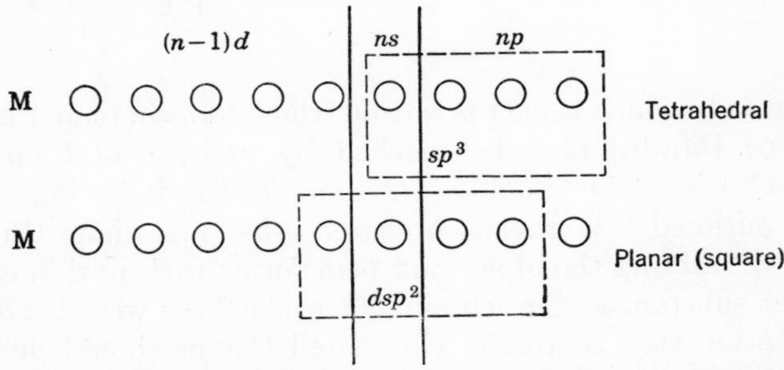

the orbitals being designated by circles and those involved in bonding being enclosed by dotted lines. This concept has been applied with particular success to the complexes of nickel(II). Thus, keeping in mind the fact that in the dipositive nickel ion there are 26 electrons, one might formulate a four-coordinate complex such as $[Ni(CN)_4]^{-2}$ in either of two ways:

[36] I. I. Tscherniaev: *Ann. inst. platine*, **4**, 243 (1926).

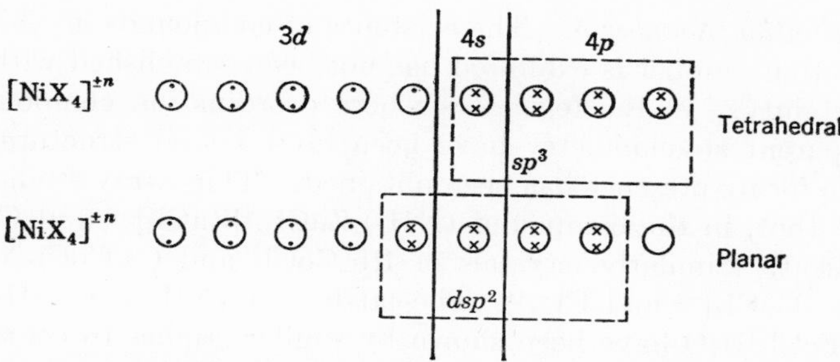

The number of electrons within each orbital is indicated by dots or crosses. In the tetrahedral arrangement, the $3d$ orbitals are unaffected and contain two unpaired electrons. Tetrahedral nickel complexes would be expected, therefore, to exhibit the same paramagnetism as the simple nickel(II) ion. With the planar arrangement, diamagnetism would be expected. That the ion $[Ni(CN)_4]^{-2}$ is actually diamagnetic shows clearly that it possesses a planar structure.

Since dsp^2 bonds are stronger than sp^3 bonds,[7] the planar arrangement would be the preferred one for nickel(II). Similar situations would exist for complexes of platinum(II) and palladium(II). It is true, however, that there are certain paramagnetic nickel(II) complexes, e.g., $[Ni(NH_3)_4]SO_4$, $[Ni(N_2H_4)_2]SO_3$, $[Ni(N_2H_4)_2](NO_2)_2$, the magnetic moments of which suggest sp^3 bonding.

The situation with dipositive copper is of interest since this ion contains one more electron than nickel(II). Although the electronic configuration of copper(II), as usually given,

3d | 4s | 4p

Cu^{+2} ⊙ ⊙ ⊙ ⊙ ⊙ | ○ | ○ ○ ○

suggests that sp^3 bonding must result, Pauling points out[7] that placing the unpaired electron in a $4p$ orbital requires no loss in energy. Hence the stronger dsp^2 bonding might result. Obviously magnetic data would be of no value in this case. X-ray studies do indicate,[37] however, that copper(II) complexes are planar in arrangement. The electronically similar silver(II) complexes are also planar.[38]

Where no d orbitals are available, tetrahedral complexes will result. This is the case with beryllium(II), zinc(II), cadmium(II), mercury(II), etc. For further general information on square complexes, a review by Mellor[39] is suggested.

[37] E. G. Cox and K. C. Webster: *J. Chem. Soc.*, **1935**, 731.
[38] E. G. Cox, W. Wardlaw, and K. C. Webster: *J. Chem. Soc.*, **1936**, 775.
[39] D. P. Mellor: *Chem. Revs.*, **33**, 137 (1943).

Coordination Number 5. The existence of compounds in which this coordination number is exhibited has not been established with absolute certainty. In the few cases where coordination compounds of this apparent stoichiometry have been investigated structurally, no evidence for its presence has been obtained. Thus x-ray studies have shown[40] that, in the compound $(NH_4)_3ZnCl_5$, $[ZnCl_4]^{-2}$ and Cl^- ions are present. Similarly, crystals of Rb_3CoCl_5 and Cs_3CoCl_5 contain the ions $[CoCl_4]^{-2}$ and Cl^-.[41] The lattices of $(NH_4)_2InCl_5 \cdot H_2O$ and $(NH_4)_2FeCl_5 \cdot H_2O$ have been shown by similar studies to contain the octahedral species $[InCl_5(H_2O)]^{-2}$ [42] and $[FeCl_5(H_2O)]^{-2}$, [43] respectively. Such simple molecules as $Fe(CO)_5$, TaX_5, NbX_5, $MoCl_5$, etc., which contain five groups attached to a central element, possess trigonal bipyramid arrangements in the solid state.

Coordination Number 6. This is the commonest, and therefore most widely studied, of the coordination numbers. Since several geometrical arrangements are possible, decision as to what arrangements are to be expected is necessary. Six coordinated groups may be arranged about a central atom or ion (M) in a plane, at the apices of a circumscribed trigonal prism, or at the apices of a circumscribed regular octahedron. These arrangements, together with numbers designating substitution positions, may be indicated as follows:

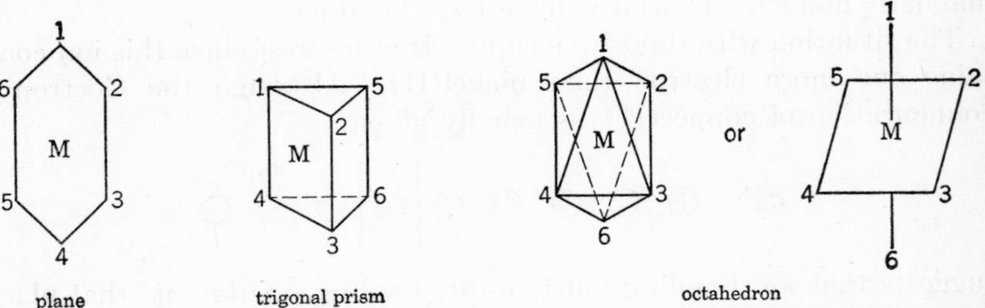

In each of these arrangements, all positions are equivalent. Therefore, but a single isomer is predicted by each for materials of the types $[Ma_6]$, $[Ma_5b]$, and $[Mab_5]$. However, significant differences do exist for materials of the types $[Ma_4b_2]$ and $[Ma_2b_4]$. Both the plane and the trigonal prism predict three isomers, namely, with (1,2), (1,3), and (1,4) arrangements, whereas the octahedron predicts only two,

[40] H. P. Klug and L. Alexander: *J. Am. Chem. Soc.*, **66**, 1056 (1944).
[41] H. M. Powell and A. F. Wells: *J. Chem. Soc.*, **1935**, 359.
[42] H. P. Klug, E. Kummer, and L. Alexander: *J. Am. Chem. Soc.*, **70**, 3064 (1948).
[43] I. Lindqvist: *Arkiv Kemi Mineral. Geol.*, **24A**, 1 (1947).

namely, (1,2) and (1,6).* Experimentally, no more than two isomers have ever been isolated for compounds of this type regardless of the metal present. Werner concluded, therefore, that the arrangement about the metal in 6-coordinate complexes is always octahedral, a conclusion which has been supported by the experimentally determined crystal structures of numerous compounds, the existence of optical isomers predictable on the basis of this arrangement, (pp. 264–267), and theoretical evaluation of the directional characteristics of the covalent bond.

As previously pointed out (pp. 201–204), hybridization[7] of d, s, and p orbitals gives stronger covalent bonds than those involving s and p orbitals alone. When this hybridization is of the d^2sp^3 type, six covalent bonds directed to the apices of a regular octahedron result. Since this hybridization is more probable for the majority of materials than the d^4sp or d^5p types essential to a trigonal prism arrangement (p. 203), the octahedral arrangement is the important one. Because of the availability of d orbitals among transition metal ions, d^2sp^3 hybridization is common to many of them. The preponderance of 6-coordinate complexes derived from such ions is thus obvious.

Some examples may be cited to show the application of this concept. Thus, iron(II) and iron(III) ions have the outer electronic arrangements

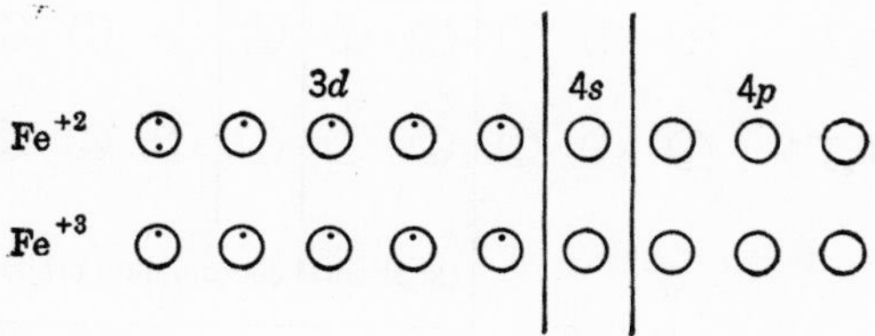

In the formation of cyano complexes involving these ions, rearrangement of electrons occurs in the d orbitals, and addition of twelve electrons from six cyanide ions in each case gives the hybrid arrangement $3d^24s4p^3$. This may be shown as

* It is suggested that models be used to illustrate these and other stereochemical arrangements. Equivalences and differences in position and arrangement which are not readily apparent on paper are obvious when considered in terms of three-dimensional models. Thus, in the octahedral structure, all adjacent positions are identical, so that (1,4), (1,5), (2,3), (3,4), (4,5), etc., arrangements are the same as (1,2), and (2,4) and (3,5) arrangements are the same as (1,6). In practice, the first substituent is considered to occupy the 1 position, and others are referred to it as simply as possible.

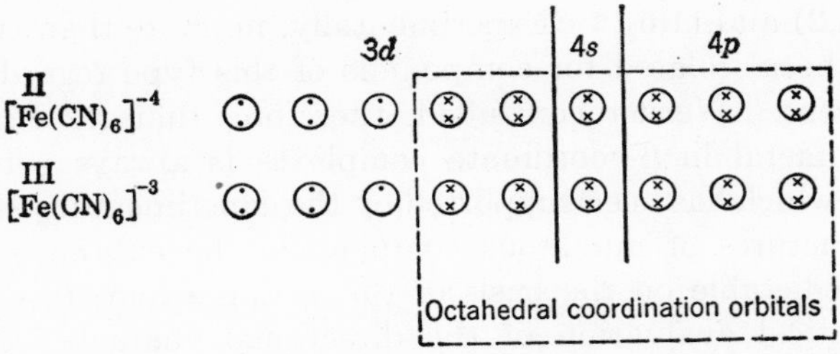

3*d* 4*s* 4*p*

II $[Fe(CN)_6]^{-4}$

III $[Fe(CN)_6]^{-3}$

Octahedral coordination orbitals

The presence of the unpaired electron renders the hexacyanoferrate(III) ion paramagnetic, in agreement with experimental observation.

Extension of the concept to cobalt(II) and cobalt(III) gives for the simple ions

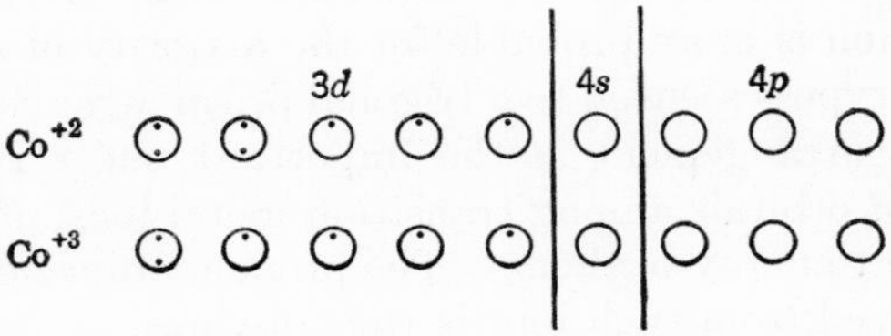

3*d* 4*s* 4*p*

Co^{+2}

Co^{+3}

and for complexes such as the hexacyano or hexammine derivatives

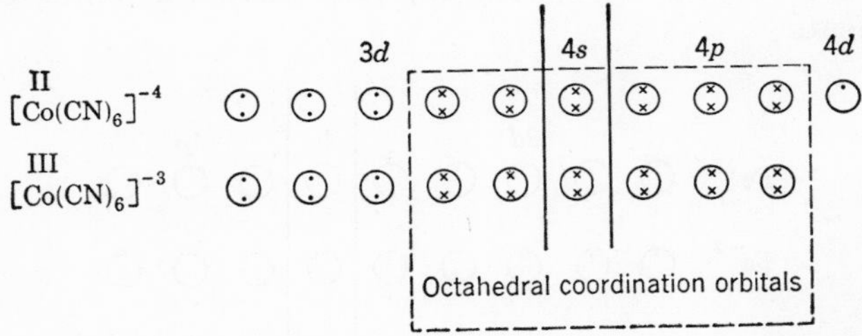

In hexacoordinated cobalt(II) materials, promotion of the extra electron to a 4*d* orbital is necessary to permit d^2sp^3 bonding. Such an electron would be loosely held.[7] Its ready removal is indicated by the ease with which cobalt(II) complexes can be oxidized and by the stabilities of the cobalt(III) compounds.

Comparable situations involving other materials are summarized in Table 7·7. For ions derived from non-transition metals, use of *d* orbitals in the valence shell doubtless occurs, an octahedral geometry again resulting. Then, however, the *d* orbitals involved must be those of the same principal quantum number as the *s* and *p* orbitals rather than one less. Such cases are much less common than those involving transition metal ions, but they are sometimes encountered among the IIb, IIIb, IVb, Vb, VIb, and VIIb Periodic Families.

It should be pointed out that the bonding in 6-coordinated complexes may be ionic rather than covalent. Magnetic data often serve to distinguish between the two types of bonding. Thus, although the magnetic moment of the ion $[Fe(CN)_6]^{-3}$ indicates the presence of but one unpaired electron, that of the ion $[FeF_6]^{-3}$ indicates the

TABLE 7.7

OCTAHEDRAL BONDING IN 6-COORDINATE MATERIALS

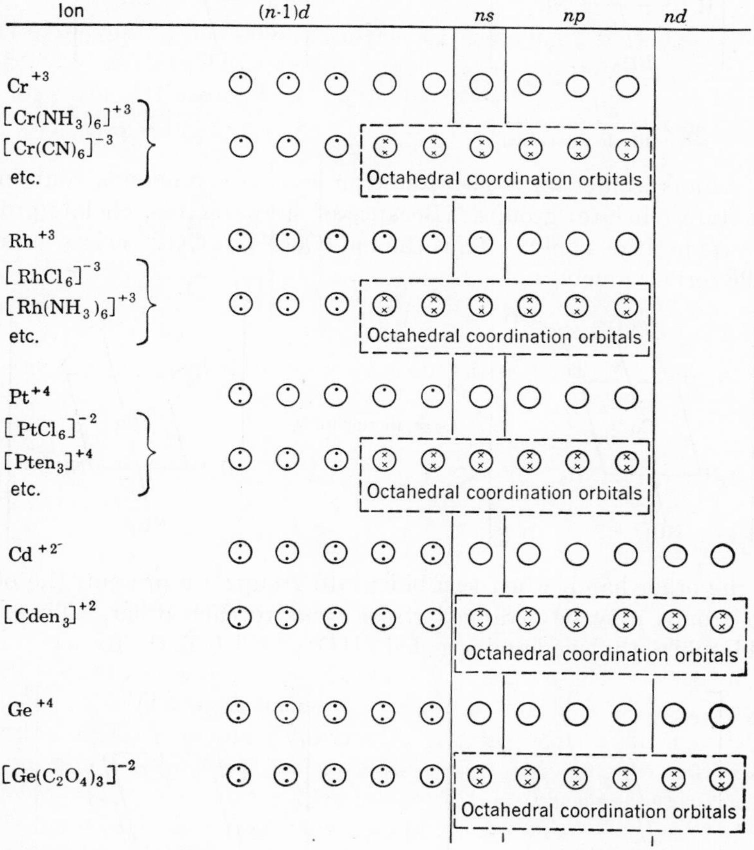

Ion	(n-1)d					ns	np			nd	
Cr^{+3}	(·)	(·)	(·)	○	○	○	○	○	○		
$[Cr(NH_3)_6]^{+3}$, $[Cr(CN)_6]^{-3}$, etc.	(·)	(·)	(·)	(×)	(×)	(×)	(×)	(×)	(×)		
				Octahedral coordination orbitals							
Rh^{+3}	(:)	(·)	(·)	(·)	(·)	○	○	○	○		
$[RhCl_6]^{-3}$, $[Rh(NH_3)_6]^{+3}$, etc.	(:)	(:)	(:)	(×)	(×)	(×)	(×)	(×)	(×)		
				Octahedral coordination orbitals							
Pt^{+4}	(:)	(·)	(·)	(·)	(·)	○	○	○	○		
$[PtCl_6]^{-2}$, $[Pten_3]^{+4}$, etc.	(:)	(:)	(:)	(×)	(×)	(×)	(×)	(×)	(×)		
				Octahedral coordination orbitals							
Cd^{+2}	(:)	(:)	(:)	(:)	(:)	○	○	○	○	○	○
$[Cden_3]^{+2}$	(:)	(:)	(:)	(:)	(:)	(×)	(×)	(×)	(×)	(×)	(×)
						Octahedral coordination orbitals					
Ge^{+4}	(:)	(:)	(:)	(:)	(:)	○	○	○	○	○	○
$[Ge(C_2O_4)_3]^{-2}$	(:)	(:)	(:)	(:)	(:)	(×)	(×)	(×)	(×)	(×)	(×)
						Octahedral coordination orbitals					

presence of *five* such electrons and is the same as that for the uncomplexed iron(III) ion.[7] Bonding in the second complex is, therefore, ionic. In such a case, no geometrical distribution of valence bonds about the central metal is noted.

CIS-TRANS ISOMERISM. In terms of an octahedral distribution of coordinated groups, the existence of two forms of the compound

$[Co(NH_3)_4Cl_2]Cl$ (p. 229) presents no problem. These may be formulated as *cis* and *trans* isomers as*

cis–
or 1,2-dichlorotetrammine
cobalt (III) chloride (violet)

and

trans–
or 1,6-dichlorotetrammine
cobalt (III) chloride (green)

Cis-trans isomerism is also found in certain compounds containing bidentate (chelate) groups. Because of steric factors, chelate groups span *cis* positions only. Thus the ion $[Co(NH_3)_4CO_3]^+$ exists in but a single form, namely,

or, more simply,

On the other hand, when two bidentate groups are present, the other two groups may be arranged *cis* or *trans* to each other. Thus, the dichlorobis(ethylenediamine)cobalt(III) ion exists in the forms

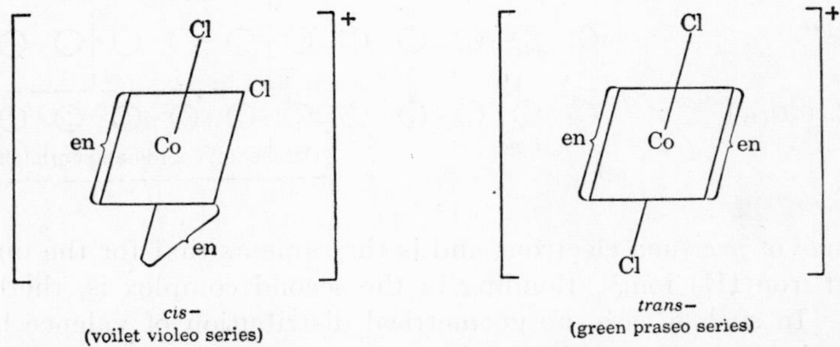

cis–
(voilet violeo series)

trans–
(green praseo series)

* Many authors prefer to omit any uncoordinated material, e.g., Cl^- in the examples discussed above, and also to omit the symbol for the metal ion at the center of the octahedron. In this discussion, ions outside the coordination sphere

Identity in either the mono- or bidentate groups is not a criterion for this type of isomerism. Thus ions such as $[Co(en)_2(NO_2)Cl]^+$ and $[Co(en)(C_2O_4)Cl_2]^-$ should, theoretically at least, exist in *cis* and *trans* forms.

When a bidentate group is replaced by two monodentate groups, such groups may be assumed to enter *cis* to each other. Rearrangement to the more symmetrical, and therefore more generally stable, *trans* configuration can then occur. This is exemplified by the following scheme of reactions:

$$\underset{\text{red}}{[Co(NH_3)_4CO_3]^+} \xrightarrow{\text{HCl}} \textit{cis}\text{-}\underset{\text{violet}}{[Co(NH_3)_4Cl_2]^+} \xrightarrow[\text{or boil}]{\text{let stand}} \textit{trans}\text{-}\underset{\text{green}}{[Co(NH_3)_4Cl_2]^+}$$

both *cis* and *trans* forms being capable of isolation. Substitution of hydrobromic acid for hydrochloric acid gives the green *trans* dibromo compound directly without any apparent formation of the *cis*. The greater size of the bromide ion undoubtedly accounts for its reluctance to enter a *cis* arrangement.

For a given material, decision as to which form is *cis* or *trans* must be based originally upon a study of reactions resulting in the conver-

TABLE 7·8

EVALUATION OF CONFIGURATIONS IN DICHLOROTETRAMMINECOBALT(III) SALTS

$[Co(NH_3)_4CO_3]Cl \xrightarrow{\text{dil. HCl}} [Co(NH_3)_4(H_2O)Cl]Cl_2$

$[Co(NH_3)_4CO_3]Cl \xrightarrow{\text{dil. } H_2SO_4} [Co(NH_3)_4(H_2O)_2]_2(SO_4)_3$

$[Co(NH_3)_4(H_2O)Cl]Cl_2 \xrightarrow{H_2SO_4 + HCl} [Co(NH_3)_4Cl_2]HSO_4$

$[Co(NH_3)_4(H_2O)_2]_2(SO_4)_3 \xrightarrow{\text{conc. } H_2SO_4 + HCl} [Co(NH_3)_4Cl_2]HSO_4$

$[Co(NH_3)_4(H_2O)_2]_2(SO_4)_3 \xrightarrow{NH_3} [Co(NH_3)_4(H_2O)(OH)]SO_4$

$[Co(NH_3)_4Cl_2]HSO_4 \xrightarrow{BaCl_2} [Co(NH_3)_4Cl_2]Cl$ green *trans* (praseo) series

$[Co(NH_3)_4(H_2O)(OH)]SO_4 \xrightarrow{\text{heat at } 100°} [(NH_3)_4Co(OH)_2Co(NH_3)_4](SO_4)_2$

$[(NH_3)_4Co(OH)_2Co(NH_3)_4](SO_4)_2 \xrightarrow{\text{conc. HCl, } -12°} [Co(NH_3)_4(H_2O)_2]Cl_3 + [Co(NH_3)_4Cl_2]Cl$ violet *cis* (violeo) series

$[Co(NH_3)_4CO_3]Cl \xrightarrow{\text{conc. HCl}} [Co(NH_3)_4Cl_2]Cl$ violet *cis* (violeo) series

$[Co(NH_3)_4Cl_2]Cl$ (violet *cis*) $\xrightarrow{\text{conc. HCl, slowly}} [Co(NH_3)_4Cl_2]Cl$ green *trans* (praseo) series

$[Co(NH_3)_4Cl_2]Cl$ (violet *cis*) $\xrightarrow{H_2O} [Co(NH_3)_4(H_2O)Cl]Cl_2$

---

are omitted, except where the entire compound is being discussed, but the symbol for the central element is retained for purposes of clarity. Any ionic charge is designated in the conventional manner.

sion of a material of known configuration into the desired substance. As illustrative of this general method of approach, consider the preparation of the dichlorotetramminecobalt(III) compounds as summarized in Table 7·8. These reactions are self-explanatory. Similar series have been worked out for other materials. Thus it can be shown in a similar fashion that the reddish-orange and yellow-orange compounds of composition $[Cren_2(NCS)_2]NCS$ resulting from treatment of $K_3[Cr(NCS)_3]$ with ethylenediamine are, respectively, the *cis* and *trans* isomers.

OPTICAL ISOMERISM. Consideration of models of the dichlorobis(ethylenediamine)cobalt(III) ion shows a plane of symmetry (through the ethylenediamine groups) in the *trans* form but no plane of symmetry in the *cis* form. The *cis* form would be expected then, by analogy to organic compounds, to exist as two optical isomers (enantiomorphs). The *d* and *l* forms are not superimposable and bear a mirror-image relationship to each other as

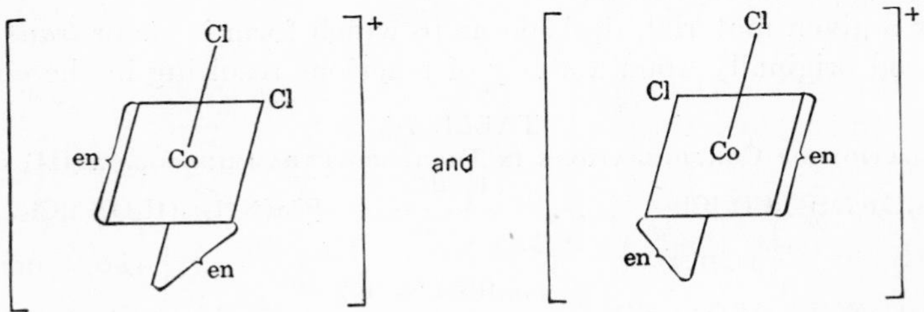

Obviously, the assymetry of the *cis* form of this ion is induced by the bidentate ethylenediamine group. Optical isomerism would be expected in all materials of the type $[M(AA)_2a_2]^{\pm n}$, where AA represents a bidentate group, but obviously it could not characterize materials of the type $[Ma_4b_2]^{\pm n}$. Three bidentate groups also cause assymetry and lead to optical isomerism. This is apparent, for example, in the tris(ethylenediamine)platinum(IV) ion, the *d* and *l* forms of which may be represented as

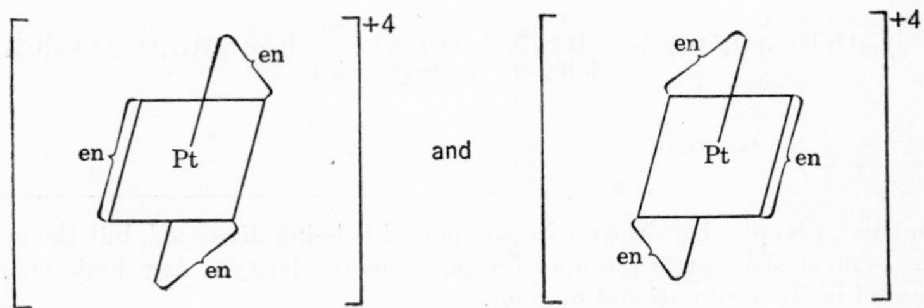

Werner's theory predicted optical isomerism among the 6-coordinate materials, but experimental proof of its existence was difficult to obtain. In 1911, Werner[44] succeeded in resolving the *cis* forms of the $[\mathrm{Coen_2(NH_3)X}]^{+2}$ ions (X = Cl, Br) into *dextro-* and *laevo-*rotatory forms (specific rotation = ±43° for the bromide salt) by crystallization of the *d*-bromocamphorsulfonates. Although this seemed to be convincing proof of the validity of Werner's postulations, the belief that optical activity centered in carbon atoms was so firmly established that many argued that the ethylenediamine molecules themselves were responsible (even though they are optically inactive themselves). As final proof of his argument that optical activity in these compounds lay in the metal ion, Werner[45] effected the resolution of the

$$\left[\mathrm{Co}\left\{\begin{matrix}\mathrm{HO} \\ \\ \mathrm{HO}\end{matrix}\!\!>\!\mathrm{Co(NH_3)_4}\right\}_3\right]^{+6}$$

ion, a purely inorganic material, into forms of high rotatory power (molecular rotation = ±47,600°).* The only other truly inorganic material to be separated into its *d* and *l* forms is the $[\mathrm{Rh\{(HN)_2SO_2\}_2(H_2O)_2}]^-$ ion. This was resolved by crystallization of the α-phenylethylamine derivatives.[46]

By methods of crystallization involving optically active organic cations or anions, many coordination compounds containing organic chelating groups have been resolved. Thus Werner resolved the *cis*-$[\mathrm{Co(en)_2Cl_2}]^+$ (violeo) and *cis*-$[\mathrm{Co(en)_2(NO_2)_2}]^+$ (flavo) ions. Ions of the types $[\mathrm{M(en)_3}]^{+n}$ [where M = Co(III), Cr(III), Pt(IV), Rh(III), Ir(III), Zn(II), Cd(II)] and $[\mathrm{M(C_2O_4)_3}]^{+n-6}$ [where M = Co(III), Cr(III), Rh(III), Ir(III), Pt(IV)] may be cited as other examples. As illustrative of the general technique involved, reference may be made to the use of *d*-α-bromocamphor-π-sulfonate in the resolution of *cis*-$[\mathrm{Co(en)_2Cl_2}]^+$.[47] Selective adsorption of *d* or *l* forms on inert optically active materials such as quartz[48] and differences in the rates

[44] A. Werner: *Ber.*, **44,** 1887 (1911).

[45] A. Werner: *Ber.*, **47,** 3087 (1914).

* Optically active materials are characterized in terms of *specific rotation* or *molecular rotation.* The specific rotation, $[\alpha]^t_\lambda$, at a temperature t and wave length λ, is defined by the relation $[\alpha]^t_\lambda = r/cl$, where r is the observed rotation in degrees, c is the concentration in grams per milliliter, and l is the length of the cell in decimeters. The molecular rotation is obtained by multiplying the specific rotation by the molecular weight.

[46] F. G. Mann: *J. Chem. Soc.*, **1933,** 412.

[47] J. C. Bailar, Jr.: *Inorganic Syntheses*, Vol. II, p. 224. McGraw-Hill Book Co., New York (1946).

[48] R. Tsuchida, M. Kobayashi, and A. Nakamura: *J. Chem. Soc. Japan*, **56,** 1339 (1935); *Bull. Chem. Soc. Japan*, **11,** 38 (1936).

with which certain diastereoisomers* react with a few coordinating agents[49] have yielded partial resolutions but have not proved to be extremely effective.

That a material may be resolved is in itself indication that directed covalent bonds are present. Lack of racemization in a resolved material gives further evidence for stable covalent linkages. It is only when coordinated groups are so attached that optical isomerism is possible. If the groups are free to move, as they would be if they were ionically attached, no such isomerism is possible. These differences are well illustrated among the trioxalato complexes of several tripositive ions. The ions $[Co(C_2O_4)_3]^{-3}$ and $[Cr(C_2O_4)_3]^{-3}$ are comparatively easy to resolve, but apparently no resolution is obtained with the formally similar $[Al(C_2O_4)_3]^{-3}$ and $[Fe(C_2O_4)_3]^{-3}$ ions (p. 233). The bonding is, therefore, covalent in the first two but ionic in the second two. This view is supported by the observation[50] that the last two undergo rapid exchange with added oxalate ion containing radiocarbon ($^{14}_{6}C$) whereas the first two do not. Obviously the oxalato groups are much less firmly held in the aluminum and iron(III) compounds than in the others.

Optical activity is not limited to mononuclear complexes. In 1913, for example, Werner[51] separated the polynuclear ion

$$\left[en_2Co \begin{smallmatrix} NH_2 \\ \swarrow \quad \searrow \\ \nwarrow \quad \nearrow \\ NO_2 \end{smallmatrix} Coen_2\right]^{+4}$$

into three forms by crystallization of the *d*-bromocamphorsulfonates. Two of these forms were optically active (*d* and *l*) forms, which may be formulated as

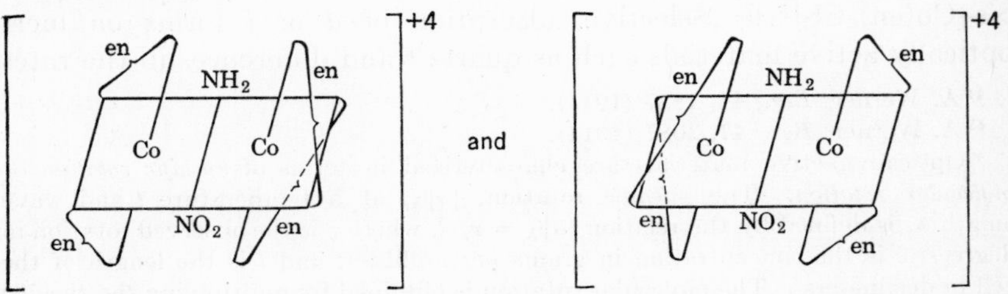

* Diastereoisomers are optical isomers which are not mirror images. Thus, the dextro (D) and laevo (L) rotatory forms of the $[Co(en)_2(d\text{-tart})]^+$ ion are diasterioisomers (*d*-tart being *d*-tartrate ion).

[49] H. B. Jonassen, J. C. Bailar, Jr., and E. H. Huffman: *J. Am. Chem. Soc.*, **70**, 756 (1948).

[50] F. A. Long: *J. Am. Chem. Soc.*, **63**, 1353 (1941).

[51] A. Werner: *Ber.*, **46**, 3674 (1913).

The other was an optically inactive, internally compensated (*meso*) form, which may be formulated as

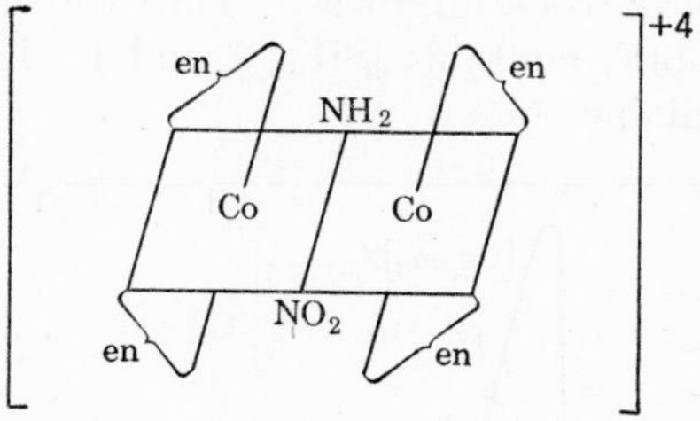

Both *d* and *l* forms revert to the *meso* when their solutions are heated.

A further analogy to optical activity among organic compounds is found in the example of the Walden inversion reported by Bailar and Auten.[52] The essentials of the conversion involved are apparent from the following scheme of reactions:

$$l\text{-}[Co(en)_2Cl_2]Cl \underset{HCl}{\overset{K_2CO_3}{\rightleftharpoons}} d\text{-}[Co(en)_2CO_3]_2CO_3$$

$$\downarrow Ag_2CO_3$$

$$l\text{-}[Co(en)_2CO_3]_2CO_3 \xrightarrow{HCl} d\text{-}[Co(en)_2Cl_2]Cl$$

Many coordination complexes are characterized by extremely high optical rotatory powers. Although this property is, in a measure, due to the special kind of molecular dissymmetry present in these materials, it is probably due to a greater extent to the fact that measurements have often been made at wavelengths in the vicinities of absorption bands. The rotatory powers of coordination compounds are markedly dependent upon the wavelength of the light used. In many cases, rotation may even undergo change in sign as the wavelength is altered to that of an absorption band. This is apparent in the rotatory dispersion curves obtained by Jaeger,[53] some of which are reproduced in Figure 7·1. It is apparent that designation of a material as *dextro* or *laevo* is thus purely formal and should always be accompanied by a wavelength indication.

Coordination Number 7. This coordination number is recognized in only a limited number of compounds and need not be considered in detail. An octahedron with one fluoride beyond the center of one face is said to characterize the $[ZrF_7]^{-3}$ ion in its ammonium and potassium salts,[54] and a trigonal prism with one fluoride beyond the center

[52] J. C. Bailar, Jr., and R. W. Auten: *J. Am. Chem. Soc.*, **56**, 774 (1934).

[53] F. M. Jaeger: *Optical Activity and High Temperature Measurement,* Pt. I. McGraw-Hill Book Co., New York (1930).

[54] G. C. Hampson and L. Pauling: *J. Am. Chem. Soc.*, **60**, 2702 (1938).

of one face is characteristic of the $[NbF_7]^{-2}$ and $[TaF_7]^{-2}$ ions.[55] As with coordination number five, some compounds of appropriate stoichiometry appear to be mixtures. Thus the crystal lattice of the compound $(NH_4)_3SiF_7$ contains $[SiF_6]^{-2}$ and F^- ions.[56] No data on isomerism are available.

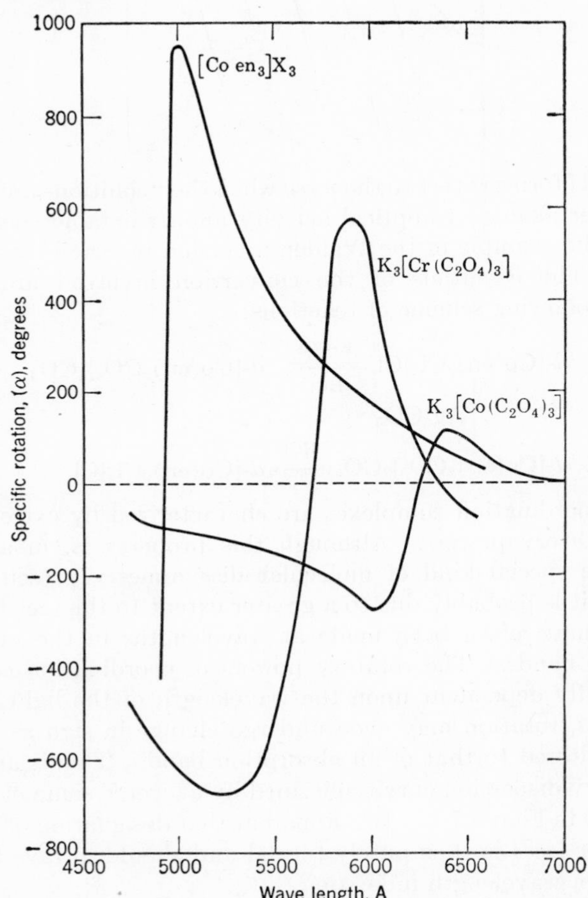

Fig. 7·1. Typical rotatory dispersion curves for some complexes in aqueous solution.

Coordination Number 8. Although the number of examples of this coordination number is limited, materials of the following types have been studied: fluorides such as $[OsF_8]$, $[TaF_8]^{-3}$; acetylacetonates of tetrapositive metals such as thorium, hafnium, cerium; 8-quinolinol

[55] J. L. Hoard: *J. Am. Chem. Soc.*, **61,** 1252 (1939).

[56] J. L. Hoard and M. B. Williams: *J. Am. Chem. Soc.*, **64,** 633 (1942).

Tetrahedral, 4-coordinate

Square planar, 4-coordinate

Octahedral, 6-coordinate

H																H	He
Li	Be *c*											B	C	N	O	F	Ne
Na	Mg *a c*											Al	Si	P *d*	S	Cl	A
K	Ca *c*	Sc *d*	Ti	V	Cr *c*	Mn	Fe *c*	Co	Ni *b*	Cu	Zn *c*	Ga *a*	Ge	As	Se	Br	Kr
Rb	Sr	Y *d*	Zr	Nb	Mo	Tc	Ru	Rh	Pd *b*	Ag	Cd *c*	In *a*	Sn *c*	Sb *a c*	Te	I	Xe
Cs	Ba *c*	R.E. *d*	Hf *d*	Ta	W	Re	Os	Ir	Pt *b*	Au	Hg *c*	Tl	Pb	Bi	Po	At	Rn
Fr	Ra	Ac *d*															

a · Tetrahedral only in MgTe, GaAs, GaSb, InN
b · Tetrahedral only in forced configurations except for $Ni(CO)_4$, $Pt(CH_3)_3Cl$
c · Planar only in phthalocyanins
d · Octahedral configuration probable

FIG. 7·2. Stereochemistries of the various elements.

chelates of tetrapositive metals; cyano complexes such as $[Mo(CN)_8]^{-4}$ and $[W(CN)_8]^{-4}$; and oxalato complexes such as $[U(C_2O_4)_4]^{-4}$. A variety of structural arrangements depending upon different types of bonding have been suggested. Thus, d^3fsp^3 or d^3f^4s bonding (unlikely because of use of f orbitals) should give a cubic structure; d^5p^3 or d^4sp^3 bonding should give an Archimedes antiprism (found for $[TaF_8]^{-3}$); d^4sp^3 bonding should give a dodecahedron (found for $[Mo(CN)_8]^{-4}$); and d^5sp^2 bonding should give a rectangular face-centered trigonal prism (probable for $[OsF_8]$.).

All these arrangements predict such a variety of isomers that the problems of geometrical and optical isomerism have not been solved. A promising start, made with the $[U(C_2O_4)_4]^{-4}$ ion,[57–59] showed the number of isomers which were isolated to rule out the cubic and trigonal prism arrangements but not to distinguish between the other possible configurations for this material.

The stereochemical characteristics of the various elements in a variety of compounds are summarized in Figure 7·2.[24]

SOME SPECIAL TYPES OF COORDINATION COMPOUNDS

Discussions in preceding sections do not embrace a number of more or less specific types of coordination compounds. Many such materials are so specific in character (e.g., carbonyls, nitrosyls, and hydroxo complexes) that they are better discussed in appropriate chapters in Part II of this book. Others which are of a somewhat more general character may be considered here.

Inner complexes

Certain organic substances, because of the presence in their structures of both normal salt-forming groups and neutral donor groups, can through chelation satisfy simultaneously both the oxidation numbers and the coordination numbers of many metal ions. The β-diketones, discussed on p. 241, may be cited as typical of such substances, as may also 8-quinolinol and its derivatives, the various dioximes, salicylaldehyde and its derivatives, lake-forming reagents such as alizarin, etc. Taking 8-quinolinol as representative, the structures of chelates formed by a dipositive, 4-coordinate metal ion (e.g., Cu^{+2}) and a tripositive, 6-coordinate metal ion (e.g., Fe^{+3}) may be depicted, respectively, as

[57] L. E. Marchi, W. C. Fernelius, and J. P. McReynolds: *J. Am. Chem. Soc.*, **65**, 329 (1943).

[58] L. E. Marchi and J. P. McReynolds: *J. Am. Chem. Soc.*, **65**, 333 (1943).

[59] L. E. Marchi: *J. Am. Chem. Soc.*, **65**, 2257 (1943).

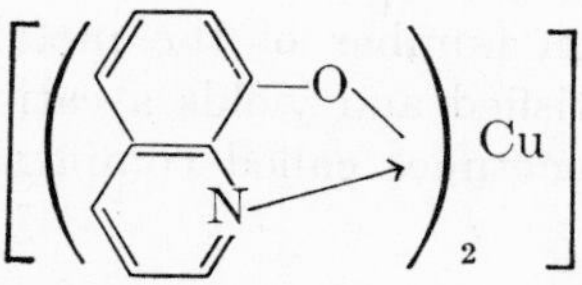

$$\left[\left(C_9H_6N{-}O\right)_2 Cu\right] \quad \text{and} \quad \left[\left(C_9H_6N{-}O\right)_3 Fe\right]$$

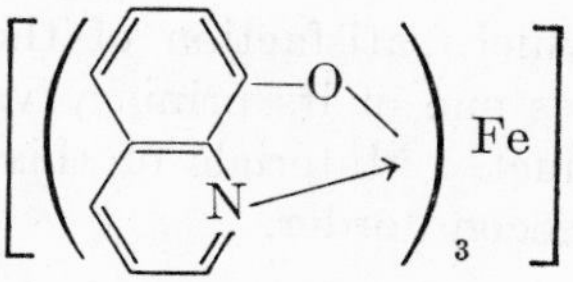

Compounds of this type show but little tendency to give ions in solution and commonly behave as non-electrolytes. They are referred to as *inner complexes*[14,60] or complexes of the first order. Because of their non-ionic character, many inner complexes can be extracted into organic solvents. Inner complex formation is thus useful in effecting separations among the metal ions. Furthermore, the intense colors characteristic of many inner complexes render these compounds useful for qualitative detections of metal ions and quantitative colorimetric determinations.

It should be pointed out that an organic molecule may react with a metal ion to form an inner complex structure of the type outlined and still possess overall anionic character.[60] This is true, for example, with the alizarin derivative of iron(III) which may exist as an anion of the structure

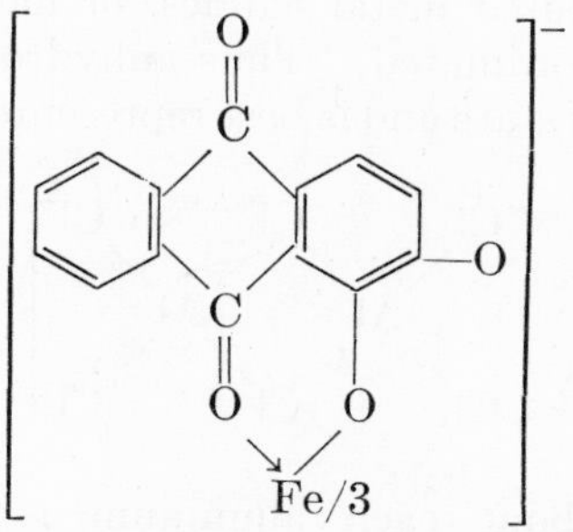

O, C, C, O, O, O, Fe/3

Furthermore, if the coordination number is not twice the oxidation number, reagents which normally form non-electrolytes will give ionic products. Thus titanium(IV) has a coordination number of six. When this material combines with a β-diketone, there results a structure such as

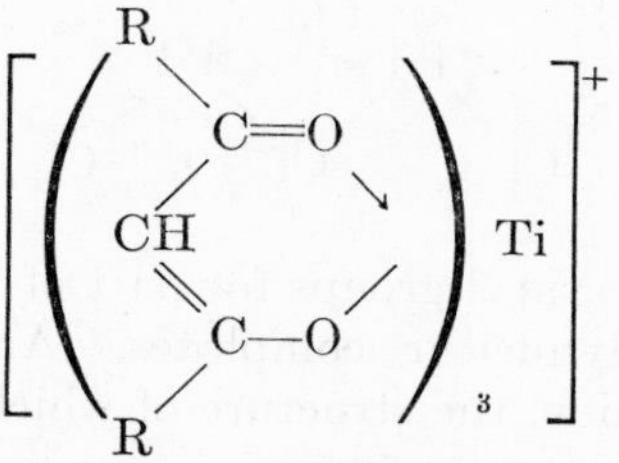

R, C=O, CH, C—O, R, Ti, 3

[60] H. A. Liebhafsky: *J. Chem. Education*, **23**, 341 (1946).

in which satisfaction of the coordination number of the metal ion leaves one of its primary valences unsatisfied and yields a cation as product. Materials of this type are sometimes called complexes of the second order.

Polynuclear complexes

Several references have been made (pp. 243, 266) to polynuclear complexes, that is, complexes containing more than a single center of coordination. Those derived from 6-coordinate metal ions have been studied extensively; they commonly contain such bridging groups as —OH, —O—, $—O_2—$, $—NH_2$, —NH—, and $—NO_2$. One, two, or three such groups are common to both coordination spheres. Less well-known are materials in which halogens act as bridging groups. Among well-characterized examples are the ions $[Tl_2Cl_9]^{-3}$ and $[W_2Cl_9]^{-3}$, in each of which three chlorines are common to two octahedra arranged about the metal ions.

Among 4-coordinate materials, halogen bridges in polynuclear complexes are frequently found.[61] These may characterize either metal halides, substituted metal halides, or halides to which certain other groups have coordinated. Thus anhydrous aluminum chloride is dimeric in the vapor state and is best represented as

```
⎡Cl        Cl        Cl⎤
   \      /  ↘      /
     Al          Al
   /   ↖      /     \
⎣Cl        Cl        Cl⎦
```

The arrangement about each aluminum is tetrahedral. Similar formulations may be given for such halides as Al_2Br_6, Au_2Br_6, and Fe_2Cl_6. Discrete molecules may even be lacking as, for example, in palladium(II) chloride, which is made up of long chains of the type

```
⎡        Cl        Cl        Cl        Cl⎤
       /    ↘    /    ↘    /    ↘    /
     Pd        Pd        Pd        Pd
    /    ↖    /    ↖    /    ↖    /
⎣Cl        Cl        Cl        Cl        ⎦
```

Substitution of alkyl or aryl groups for part of the halogen in a metal halide may give polynuclear complexes. An example is dimeric diethylgold(III) bromide, the structure of which corresponds to

[61] F. G. Mann: *Ann. Reports*, **35**, 148 (1938).

```
┌C2H5          Br          C2H5┐
│    \       /    ↘      /     │
│     Au             Au        │
│    /      ↖      /    \      │
└C2H5          Br          C2H5┘
```

Similarly, the addition of coordinated groups sometimes gives polynuclear halides. Thus a series of compounds of general formula $PtCl_2{\cdot}A$, where $A = PR_3$, AsR_3, CO, C_2H_4, PCl_3, $P(OCH_3)_3$, etc., has been characterized. These materials have polynuclear structures corresponding to the formulation

```
┌A          Cl          Cl┐
│  ↘      /    ↘      /   │
│    Pt           Pt      │
│  /      ↖      /    ↖   │
└Cl         Cl          A ┘
```

The arrangement around each platinum is planar. Comparable compounds are known for palladium, zinc, cadmium, mercury, copper, etc. The molybdenum "dihalides," $[Mo_6Cl_8]Cl_4$ and $[Mo_6Br_8]Br_4$, are also characteristic examples. Instead of halogens as bridges, pseudohalogens (pp. 463–480), such as cyanide, may be present.

The poly acids and their salts

One can distinguish a large group of oxygen-containing acids (and derived salts), in which apparent condensation of numbers of simple acid molecules has given materials containing more than a single mole of acid anhydride. Such acids are called *poly acids*. If but a single type of anhydride is involved, the acid is an *isopoly* acid, whereas if more than a single type of anhydride is present, the acid is a *heteropoly* acid. The polychromic acids, $H_2O{\cdot}yCrO_3$ ($y > 1$), may be cited as examples of the first class, and the polymolybdophosphoric acids, $mH_2O{\cdot}P_2O_5{\cdot}yMoO_3$ ($y = 12$ or 24, most commonly), as examples of the second. Acids of these types are most characteristic of molybdenum and tungsten (and to a lesser extent vanadium) and are of such extreme complexities that only in a limited number of cases have their structures been determined. Although they differ markedly in properties from the other types of coordination compounds discussed in preceding sections of this chapter, they are properly considered as compounds of this general type and best discussed here. Because of limitations of space, no more than a general account of their characteristics and probable structures can be given here.[62]

[62] A. R. Middleton: *J. Chem. Education*, **10**, 726 (1933).

1. *The Heteropoly Acids.* Although formally more involved than the isopoly acids, the heteropoly acids are probably the better understood of the two types and may, therefore, be considered first. Empirically, they ordinarily contain an atom of an element such as boron, silicon, phosphorus, or arsenic in combination with a number of atoms of another element (commonly molybdenum or tungsten, although a few others may be present) and comparatively large numbers of atoms of oxygen and hydrogen. Thus a molybdophosphoric acid might be formulated $H_wP_xMo_yO_z \cdot mH_2O$, and similar formulations might be given for other combinations.

Compounds have been prepared in which $y/x = 6$, $6 < y/x < 12$, and $y/x = 12$. Of these, the most common and best-known compounds are those in which $y/x = 6$ or 12. These are known, respectively, as 6- and 12-acids. The commonness of these ratios and the uniform success of Werner's theory in explaining other complex compounds prompted Miolati and Rosenheim[63] to suggest that added anhydride molecules are held to the central atom of a parent acid by coordinate linkages. For each non-metallic element (X), a parent

TABLE 7·9

HETEROPOLY ACIDS ACCORDING TO MIOLATI AND ROSENHEIM

Central Atom, X*	Oxidation State, n	Parent Acid	Limiting Heteropoly Acids†	Known Compounds
B	+3	$H_9[BO_6]$	$H_9[B(Mo_2O_7)_6]$	
Si	+4	$H_8[SiO_6]$	$H_8[Si(W_2O_7)_6]$	$H_4SiW_{12}O_{40}$
P	+5	$H_7[PO_6]$	$H_7[P(W_2O_7)_6]$	$H_3PW_{12}O_{40}$
Te	+6	$H_6[TeO_6]$	$H_6[Te(MoO_4)_6]$	
I	+7	$H_5[IO_6]$	$H_5[I(MoO_4)_6]$	

* 6-acids known where X = I, Te, Fe, Cr, Al, Co, Ni, Rh, Cu, Mn. 12-acids known where X = B, Si, P, As, Ti, Ge, Sn, Zr, Hf, Th, Ce.

† An indeterminate amount of water may be present also.

acid was regarded as resulting from sufficient hydration of the anhydride to give *six* oxygens coordinated to the central atom, i.e., a material of formula $H_{12-n}[XO_6]$, n being the oxidation state of X. Heteropoly acids then result from partial or complete substitution of these oxygens by equivalent simple groups such as MoO_4^{-2}, WO_4^{-2}, or VO_3^- or hypothetical doubled groups such as $Mo_2O_7^{-2}$, $W_2O_7^{-2}$, or $V_2O_6^{-2}$ or by coordination of the anhydride molecules MoO_3, WO_3, or $V_2O_5/2$ to these oxygens. In this fashion, limiting series of 6- and 12-acids were

[63] For an excellent summary, see A. Rosenheim in Abegg's *Handbuch der anorganischen Chemie*, Vol. 4, Pt. I, ii. pp. 977–1065. Verlag von S. Hirzel, Leipzig (1921).

derived as indicated in Table 7·9, a fixed coordination number of six being implied for all central atoms.

Although a number of heteropoly acids (and salts) can be fitted into such a concept, there are certain unreconciled difficulties which preclude current acceptance of this theory. Thus, high basicities are predicted, but they are seldom realized in practice. This means that the common salts of the heteropoly acids can be accomodated by the Miolati-Rosenheim formulation only if they are considered to be acid salts. That all of these compounds are highly hydrated suggests strongly that a portion of the hydrogen regarded as acidic is actually present as water. Furthermore, groups such as $Mo_2O_7^{-2}$ and $W_2O_7^{-2}$ are entirely hypothetical and have no independent existence. Difficulties are encountered in attempting to accommodate examples other than the 6- and 12-materials. Thus a polynuclear formulation such as

$$K_6H_6\left[\begin{matrix} O & & O \\ & As\text{–}Mo_2O_7\text{–}As & \\ (Mo_2O_7)_4 & & (Mo_2O_7)_4 \end{matrix}\right]$$

would be required for the compound of stoichiometric composition, $K_6H_6As_2Mo_{18}O_{65}$. Last, but of extreme importance, is the fact that where structural data have been obtained they are not in accord with these simple formulations. The Miolati-Rosenheim approach, therefore, may be regarded as giving useful first approximations but little more.

As an alternative, Pfeiffer[64] suggested that in adding to the hypothetical $H_{12-n}[XO_6]$ parent, the MoO_3 or WO_3 molecules might be coordinated around a central XO_6 anion in a second shell, giving, for instance, $H_{12-n}[XO_6(WO_3)_{12}]$. This view may be regarded as a forerunner of Pauling's and Keggin's concepts of the crystal arrangements in the 12-heteropoly acids. From x-ray data, Pauling[65] concluded that, since sufficient room exists around either molybdenum(VI) or tungsten(VI) for an octahedron of oxide ions, the 12-acids are made up of twelve such MoO_6 or WO_6 octahedra linked to each other by the mutual sharing of three corners. The three unshared corners then accommodate hydrogen ions to give stable neutral groups such as $Mo_{12}O_{18}(OH)_{36}$ or $W_{12}O_{18}(OH)_{36}$. In the center of this arrangement the tetrahedral ion XO_4 is placed, giving an arrangement which may be shown schematically as

[64] P. Pfeiffer: *Z. anorg. allgem. Chem.*, **105**, 26 (1918).
[65] L. Pauling: *J. Am. Chem. Soc.*, **51**, 2868 (1929).

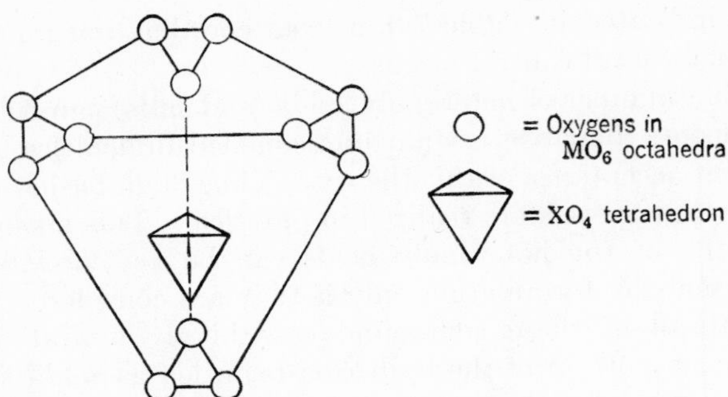

and which predicts a basicity of 8-*n* for the acid. Thus no acid containing less than eighteen moles of water should be stable, a prediction which is not supported by the existence of anhydrous acids $H_w[XMo_{12}O_{40}]$ (X = P, Si, Ti).

Keggin,[66] on the other hand, proposed the existence of a central XO_4 tetrahedron surrounded by twelve MoO_6 or WO_6 octahedra, each corner of the tetrahedron being shared with three octahedra, each of which in turn shares one oxygen atom with each of its neighbors. The four resulting Mo_3O_{13} or W_3O_{13} groups are then linked by sharing corners to give ultimately the groups $[XMo_{12}O_{40}]^{8-n}$ and $[XW_{12}O_{40}]^{8-n}$. Large resulting spaces in the crystals can then accommodate the numerous water molecules characteristic of the compounds. Keggin's views have been verified by x-ray studies on a number of materials and may be regarded as being valid for the crystalline materials. Unfortunately, however, data on the compositions of materials in solution do not agree. Nor is there an adequate explanation for the structures of the 6-acids.

The heteropoly acids and their salts result in general from direct combination of the components, followed by crystallization, precipitation, or extraction as a means of separation.

2. *The Isopoly Acids.* The situation with the isopoly acids is much more confused than with the heteropoly acids. Copaux and Miolati[63] proposed that they be regarded as derived from a hypothetical aquate $H_{10}[H_2O_6]$ by substitution of, for instance, MoO_4^{-2} or WO_4^{-2} or coordination of MoO_3 or WO_3. This would again lead to limiting 6- and 12-series, but the polymolybdates and polytungstates seldom correspond to these simple formulations. Depending upon the *p*H of the solution, a variety of such materials can be prepared. As a normal molybdate solution, for example, is treated with successively increasing quantities of acid, aggregation occurs with the formation of a number

[66] J. F. Keggin: *Proc. Roy. Soc.* (*London*), **144A,** 75 (1934).

of increasingly complex polyanions. These phenomena have been investigated by Jander and coworkers[67] in terms of the ionic weights, diffusion coefficients, and conductivities of the solutions as functions of *p*H. Their data are consistent with these transformations (*p*H values by the arrows):

$$MoO_4^{-2} \overset{6.5}{\rightleftharpoons} Mo_3O_{11}^{-4} \overset{4.5}{\rightleftharpoons} HMo_6O_{21}^{-5} \xrightleftharpoons{2.9\text{-}1.5} H_3Mo_6O_{21}^{-3}$$

$$\Big\updownarrow 1.25$$

$$MoO_3{\cdot}aq \overset{1.0}{\leftrightharpoons} H_7Mo_{24}O_{78}^{-5} \overset{1.0}{\leftrightharpoons} H_7Mo_{12}O_{41}$$

Similar studies have been made on tungstate and vanadate systems and with analogous results.

Data of this type have been difficult to reconcile with the results of direct analysis and have not been supported by structural determinations on solid compounds. Some of the difficulties characteristic of those encountered for all these materials may be outlined for the paramolybdates. Direct analysis does not permit an unambiguous decision between the compositions $3M_2O{\cdot}7MoO_3{\cdot}aq$ and $5M_2O{\cdot}12MoO_3{\cdot}aq$ because of small differences in $M_2O:MoO_3$ ratios. Although Rosenheim preferred the second composition and formulated the ammonium salt as $(NH_4)_5H_5[H_2(MoO_4)_6]{\cdot}7H_2O$, crystallographic density and cell dimension data[68] indicate clearly that the formula of this salt is $(NH_4)_6[Mo_7O_{24}]{\cdot}4H_2O$. The similarity of the paramolybdates to the 6-heteropolymolybdo acids suggests strongly that one molybdenum acts as a central atom in the anion and that the other six molybdenums surround it as MoO_6 octahedra, giving an ion $[Mo(Mo_6O_{24})]^{-6}$. However, this is only speculative, and confirmation of this and other points mentioned above is highly desirable.

DETECTION OF COMPLEX IONS IN SOLUTION

As has already been indicated (p. 227), complex species which exist in the solid state are not necessarily the same as those which exist in solution. In certain cases, there is evidence that complex ions are present in solution, although it is impossible to prepare solid compounds containing them. Study of such materials is limited to the application of physical methods which yield data on the compositions and stabilities of the species. Detailed considerations of these procedures are somewhat beyond the scope of this book, but among the most commonly employed approaches are the following:

[67] G. Jander, K. F. Jahr, and W. Henkeshoven: *Z. anorg. allgem. Chem.*, **194**, 383 (1930).

[68] J. H. Sturdivant: *J. Am. Chem. Soc.*, **59**, 630 (1937).

1. Absorption spectra measurements.
2. Raman spectra measurements.
3. Refractive index studies.
4. Conductance measurements.
5. Transference studies.
6. Electromotive force and polarographic measurements.
7. Amperometric titration studies.
8. *p*H and *p*H titration studies.
9. Freezing point depression measurements.
10. Dialysis studies.
11. Solubility studies.
12. Magnetic moment evaluations.
13. Distribution studies involving immiscible solvents.

CONCLUSION

The importance of coordination compounds and the concepts regarding their formation and constitution cannot be overemphasized. It will be apparent from subsequent discussions of specific topics in Part II of this book that the views developed in this chapter can be extended to almost every phase of inorganic chemistry. In fact, such approaches are so tempting that they have been overemphasized by many individuals. However, it may be of interest to summarize rather broadly a number of general fields in which knowledge and application of coordination compounds have proved of value.[69] Among them are:

1. The mineral world, many minerals being coordination compounds.
2. The plant world, compounds such as chlorophyll being derived from metal ions by addition of coordinating groups.
3. The animal world, the coloring materials in blood (hemin, hemocyanin), for example, being coordination compounds.
4. The arts and sciences, the most notable useful coordination compounds being the metal phathalocyanins (pigments); the metal lakes (dyeing); and the cyano complexes (metallurgy, electrodeposition).
5. Analytical chemistry, many qualitative and quantitative operations being based upon the formation or properties of coordinated derivatives of the metal ions.

SUGGESTED SUPPLEMENTARY REFERENCES

A. Werner: *Neuere Anschauungen auf dem Gebiete der anorganischen Chemie*, Vierte Auflage. T. Viewig u. Sohn, Braunschweig (1920).

[69] G. T. Morgan and F. H. Burstall: *Inorganic Chemistry. A Survey of Modern Developments*, Ch. XIII. W. Heffer and Sons, Ltd., Cambridge (1936).

R. Schwarz (translated by L. W. Bass): *The Chemistry of the Inorganic Complex Compounds.* John Wiley and Sons, New York (1923).

R. Weinland: *Einführung in die Chemie der Komplex-Verbindungen,* 2nd Ed. Verlag von F. Enke, Stuttgart (1924).

G. T. Morgan and F. H. Burstall: *Inorganic Chemistry. A Survey of Modern Developments,* Ch. XIII. W. Heffer and Sons, Ltd., Cambridge (1936). (Most of the book.)

M. M. J. Sutherland: in Friend's *A Textbook of Inorganic Chemistry,* Vol. X. Charles Griffin and Co., Ltd., London (1928).

H. J. Emeléus and J. S. Anderson: *Modern Aspects of Inorganic Chemistry,* Ch. IV. D. Van Nostrand Co., New York (1938).

A. E. Martell and M. Calvin: *Chemistry of the Metal Chelate Compounds.* Prentice-Hall, New York (1952).

W. C. Fernelius: *Chemical Architecture* (R. E. Burk and O. Grummitt, Ed.), Ch. III. Interscience Publishers, New York (1948).

R. N. Keller: "The Coordination Theory and Coordination Compounds of the Platinum Group Metals," *J. Chem. Education,* **18,** 134 (1941).

R. Gilchrist: "The Platinum Metals," *Chem. Revs.,* **32,** 277 (1943).

R. S. Nyholm: "Recent Stereochemistry of the Group VIII Elements," *Quart. Revs.,* **4,** 321 (1949).

J. Bjerrum: "On the Tendency of Metal Ions toward Complex Formation," *Chem. Revs.,* **46,** 381 (1950).

Symposia on Complex Inorganic Compounds, *Chem. Revs.,* **19,** 55–100 (1936); **21,** 1–128 (1937).

Papers published in honor of the seventy-fifth birthday of P. Pfeiffer: *Angew. Chem.,* **62,** 201–254 (1950).

I. Lindqvist: "Some New Aspects of the Polymolybdates," *Nova Acta Regiae Soc. Sci. Upsaliensis* [IV], **15,** No. 1 (1950).

CHAPTER 8

Oxidation-Reduction Oxidation Potentials

Oxidation is a term used originally to characterize those reactions in which the element oxygen combined or reacted with some other chemical substance. In the sense that *oxidation* implied the addition of oxygen, the term *reduction* was used to characterize those reactions in which oxygen was removed from its compounds, usually through use of hydrogen. It is still not uncommon to see references to the oxidizing power of a molecule or ion expressed in terms of its oxygen content or references to reducing power in terms of hydrogen content.

The limitations of such definitions became apparent even before the dependence of chemical behaviors upon electrons was pointed out, for the inherent similarities between the combination of, for instance, a metal such as copper with oxygen and with sulfur or with chlorine could not be denied. Nor could the similarities between reactions of metal oxides with hydrogen and with other metals or metal salts in general with other metals be overlooked. Consideration of all such reactions in terms of the electrons which are involved renders these similarities apparent and provides a basis for their logical classification. Thus an element is combined with oxygen because of the removal of electrons from that element by the more electronegative oxygen, whereas oxygen is "removed" from a compound by hydrogen because hydrogen provides electrons to the element which had originally lost them to oxygen. Similar reactions involving other elements can be explained similarly. Therefore, the terms oxidation and reduction can be extended logically to all reactions in which materials may give up or acquire electrons. In a broad way, then, oxidation is synonymous with electron loss, and reduction with electron gain.

The terms *electron loss* and *electron gain* merit closer scrutiny.[1, 2]

[1] C. A. Vander Werf, A. W. Davidson, and H. H. Sisler: *J. Chem. Education*, **22,** 450 (1945).

[2] C. A. Vander Werf: *J. Chem. Education*, **25,** 547 (1948).

In some reactions, such as, for example, the reaction of sodium with chlorine to give ionic sodium chloride, there can be no argument as to their meanings; it is obvious that one element (here sodium) loses electrons and is oxidized while the other element (here chlorine) gains electrons and is reduced. On the other hand, when hydrogen reacts with chlorine to form hydrogen chloride, there is no electron gain or loss in the same sense because the bond in the resulting molecule is covalent in character. The situation becomes even more complex in reactions such as that in which permanganate is converted to manganese(II) ion by iron(II) ion in acidic solution, for although by common consent the permanganate is reduced the manner in which electrons are added is not immediately obvious. It has usually been sufficient to consider that redistribution of electrons causes the observed changes even though the actual mechanism may be somewhat obscure.

Some solution to this apparent dilemma lies in application of electronegativity concepts to covalent bonds and in use of the oxidation numbers or states so indicated (p. 211). Thus, in the hydrogen-chlorine reaction, the greater electronegativity of the chlorine renders it effectively negative with respect to hydrogen in the polar bond joining the two. If chlorine is then said to be in a -1 state of oxidation and hydrogen in a $+1$ state, chlorine is reduced and hydrogen oxidized, and the reaction involves oxidation-reduction. Similarly, in the permanganate ion, manganese is in a $+7$ state of oxidation due to electronegativity differences, and its conversion to manganese(II) must then involve addition of electrons or reduction. The artificiality of this concept is obvious; yet it is a useful concept and one widely applicable to inorganic reactions. Perhaps it would be less artificial to consider as oxidation any process resulting in increase (in a positive direction) in oxidation state and as reduction any process resulting in decrease in oxidation state.[2]

ION-ELECTRON HALF-REACTIONS

Many of the oxidation-reduction processes involving inorganic materials take place in solution (usually aqueous) and depend upon ions to a greater or lesser degree. Such ionic reactions are commonly described by completed ionic equations balanced by conventional procedures. Thus the equations*

* In the discussions in this and subsequent chapters, strong protonic acids (p. 314) will be indicated in ionic equations by use of the unsolvated proton, H^+. It is well known, of course, that the existence of unsolvated protons in any solvent of even mildly basic character is highly unlikely, if not impossible (pp. 315, 400). However, inasmuch as all ions will be solvated to greater or lesser extent in such solvents, the exact degree of solvation being always indeterminate, it seems more

$$3Cu + 8H^+ + 2NO_3^- \rightleftharpoons 3Cu^{+2} + 2NO + 4H_2O$$

and

$$6Fe^{+2} + 14H^+ + Cr_2O_7^{-2} \rightleftharpoons 6Fe^{+3} + 2Cr^{+3} + 7H_2O$$

describe reactions typical of those commonly encountered.

Completed equations so written are free of any arbitrary assumptions as to the mechanisms of the reactions which they describe, but their balancing must of necessity require such assumptions. Although it is apparent that dissolution of copper in nitric acid (first equation above) proceeds by the loss of two electrons per atom of the metal, the mechanism by which electrons convert nitrate ion to nitrogen(II) oxide is much less obvious. The same may be said of the second reaction described above, where loss of a single electron readily accounts for the oxidation of the iron(II) ion, but difficulties attend description of reduction of the dichromate ion. Of course the usual explanation suggests transfer of sufficient electrons from the reducing agent to the oxidizing agent to effect observed changes in oxidation state, but this is tantamount to saying that in the examples cited, for example, nitrogen(V) and chromium(VI), or perhaps N^{+5} and Cr^{+6}, are the oxidizing agents. That the nitrate and dichromate ions are the species actually involved and that the reactions described occur only in acidic solutions are thus completely ignored. Although one may admit that such considerations are of no especial consequence in balancing operations alone, he must certainly recognize the desirability of a more fundamental treatment.

Oxidation-reduction reactions may be thought of as occurring in two parts, one embracing oxidation and the other reduction, This consideration is justified by the fact that many such reactions can be duplicated in appropriate electrochemical cells as summations of individual anode and cathode reactions. Partial reactions of these types are referred to as *ion-electron half-reactions*, since they involve ions and the requisite numbers of electrons. Expression of these half-reactions in equation form gives ion-electron equations. They include only those materials actually involved in or produced by the process. To illustrate, the oxidation of copper by nitric acid (above) may be formulated in terms of the equations

$$Cu \rightleftharpoons Cu^{+2} + 2e^- \qquad \text{(oxidation)}$$

---

consistent to recognize the existence of solvation and then write *all* ions as unsolvated than to solvate the proton arbitrarily and leave all other ions unsolvated. The inclusion of H_3O^+ in equations for reactions in aqueous solutions adds no especial element of correctness and has the disadvantage of rendering such equations cumbersome.

and

$$NO_3^- + 4H^+ + 3e^- \rightleftharpoons NO + 2H_2O \qquad \text{(reduction)}$$

whereas reduction of dichromate by iron(II) ion may be described by the equations

$$Fe^{+2} \rightleftharpoons Fe^{+3} + e^- \qquad \text{(oxidation)}$$

and

$$Cr_2O_7^{-2} + 14H^+ + 6e^- \rightleftharpoons 2Cr^{+3} + 7H_2O \qquad \text{(reduction)}$$

In any case, then, the completed equation is obtained by the algebraic summation of the half-equations after equalization of the numbers of electrons involved.

Treatment of oxidation-reduction processes in terms of ion-electron half-reactions has the advantages of indicating clearly the oxidizing and reducing agents and outlining the conditions under which they react. Electron changes are clearly indicated, and arbitrary hypotheses involving improbable species (e.g., N^{+5}, Cr^{+6}) are thus avoided. Furthermore, these processes are quite generally reproducible as electrode processes in appropriate electrochemical cells. That oxidation-reduction processes do proceed *via* ion-electron half-reactions seems highly probable, therefore.

Certain conventions are observed in the formulation of equations of the ion-electron type. The inclusion of materials which have no existence in fact under the conditions of the reaction at hand is precluded. Thus the N(V)–N(II) couple cannot be stated simply as $N^{+5} + 3e^- \rightarrow N^{+2}$, because the materials involved are actually NO_3^- and NO. Furthermore, since these reactions occur in aqueous solutions, water and the hydrogen ion or the hydroxyl ion may be involved. In acidic solutions, the proton (H^+) does not enter into reactions involving conversion of an atom into a simple ion which can be effected directly by electron loss or gain. In alkaline solutions, however, because of the insolubilities or amphoteric properties of many hydroxides,* inclusion of hydroxyl ion is often necessary. On the other hand, in reactions involving oxy anions, inclusion of hydrogen or hydroxyl ion, depending on the pH of the medium, is essential. These conventions are apparent in the comparative equations summarized in Table 8·1 for various couples. Although all these equations have been written with the electrons on the same side of the double arrow, it is

* In this discussion and in others appearing in this chapter, the term *hydroxide* is non-definitive as to the exact constitution of the material. If a substance obtained by interaction of metal and hydroxyl ions is water insoluble, it will be formulated as a hydroxide regardless of its true composition. Exact distinctions in compositions are discussed later (pp. 500–502).

TABLE 8·1

ION-ELECTRON EQUATIONS FOR TYPICAL REACTIONS

Couple	Acidic Solution	Alkaline Solution
Na(0)–Na(I)	$Na \rightleftharpoons Na^+ + e^-$	$Na \rightleftharpoons Na^+ + e^-$
Fe(0)–Fe(II)	$Fe \rightleftharpoons Fe^{+2} + 2e^-$	$Fe + 2OH^- \rightleftharpoons Fe(OH)_2 + 2e^-$
Fe(II)–Fe(III)	$Fe^{+2} \rightleftharpoons Fe^{+3} + e^-$	$Fe(OH)_2 + OH^- \rightleftharpoons Fe(OH)_3 + e^-$
Al(0)–Al(III)	$Al \rightleftharpoons Al^{+3} + 3e^-$	$Al + 4OH^- \rightleftharpoons AlO_2^- + 2H_2O + 3e^-$
Cr(III)–Cr(VI)	$2Cr^{+3} + 7H_2O \rightleftharpoons Cr_2O_7^{-2} + 14H^+ + 6e^-$	$CrO_2^- + 4OH^- \rightleftharpoons CrO_4^{-2} + 2H_2O + 3e^-$
Cl(0)–Cl(V)	$\frac{1}{2}Cl_2 + 3H_2O \rightleftharpoons ClO_3^- + 6H^+ + 5e^-$	$\frac{1}{2}Cl_2 + 6OH^- \rightleftharpoons ClO_3^- + 3H_2O + 5e^-$

immaterial on which side they appear as long as they are associated with the oxidant. Use of the double arrow emphasizes the equilibrium characteristics of such reactions.

OXIDATION POTENTIALS

That any chemical reaction proceeds at all is due to the inherent tendency of the system to approach equilibrium conditions. Such conditions may result under almost any concentration circumstances, but for practical purposes we often limit considerations of reactions to those circumstances under which equilibria are sufficiently displaced to give us measurable quantities of reaction products. Although the driving forces leading to the establishment of such equilibria depend upon the reaction type, they are always governed, in the thermodynamic sense, by the tendency of the *free energy** of the system in question to decrease until at equilibrium the free energies of the products equal those of the remaining reactants. Alteration in free energy in oxidation-reduction systems is associated with the tendency of the reductant to lose electrons and the oxidant to gain electrons.

Inherent tendency toward electron gain or loss in a particular system can be measured as an electrical driving force and expressed as a potential value. Since it is quite impossible to obtain absolute values for such potentials, they are best and most commonly expressed relative to some arbitrarily selected standard. By this means, each ion-electron half-reaction may be described quantitatively in terms of its characteristic potential value. Such potentials may be called oxida-

* Free energy is a thermodynamic quantity which measures the maximum available work which can be obtained in going from an initial state to a final state. The free energy change in a reaction amounts to the sum of the free energies of formation of the products in the reaction less the sum of the free energies of formation of the reactants. In order that a reaction should be spontaneous or even energetically possible, a decrease in free energy must occur. In other words, the change in free energy in any spontaneous process must be negative.

tion-reduction potentials, but they are usually characterized merely as *oxidation potentials* since their magnitudes measure the relative ease with which the reductants appearing in the various half-reactions oxidize.

As bases for absolute comparison, so-called *standard* oxidation potentials (E^0) are employed.[3] Standard oxidation potentials are those characterizing half-reactions at 25°C. (298°K.), in which all metals are considered as solids, all gases are taken to be at one atmosphere pressure, and all ions are measured at unit activity.* As a standard of reference, the reaction summarized by the equation

$$\tfrac{1}{2}H_2(1 \text{ atm.}) \rightleftharpoons H^+(a = 1) + e^- \qquad (8\cdot2)$$

is assumed to have a potential value of zero at 25°C. (i.e., $E^0_{298} =$ 0.000 volt), and all other potentials (standard or otherwise) are referred to this value.

Summarized in Tables 8·2 and 8·3, respectively, are standard potentials for many of the more common inorganic couples in acidic and alkaline media. These values are those given by Latimer.[3] In tabulating these potentials (and in their subsequent use in this book), the conventions employed by Latimer[3] have been followed. Thus in each equation, the reductant has been placed on the left and the oxidant, together with the requisite number of electrons, on the right. To distinguish between reductants more powerful than hydrogen gas and those which are less powerful, positive and negative potential values are given.† If the potential is positive, the reductant in the

[3] W. M. Latimer: *The Oxidation States of the Elements and Their Potentials in Aqueous Solutions*. Prentice-Hall, New York (1938).

* Activity (a) may be regarded as an effective or thermodynamic concentration. It has the dimensions of ordinary molal (m) concentrations but is related to them by the expression

$$a = \gamma m \qquad (8\cdot1)$$

where γ is a correction factor known as an *activity coefficient*. Activities are used because most ionic substances depart from expressed molalities in their behaviors in aqueous solutions as a result of interionic attraction effects. Deviations between activities and molalities decrease with decreasing concentrations. They are also least with compounds of the 1:1 type (i.e., NaCl, $MgSO_4$, etc.) but become increasingly large with departures from the 1:1 type.

† Although the sign convention of Latimer is employed throughout this book, it is only fair to indicate that many authors, particularly those interested in polarography (e.g., Heyrovsky, Kolthoff), prefer exactly the opposite convention. This stems from the fact that reductants characterized by positive potentials in Tables 8·2 and 8·3 are actually negatively charged when combined with various oxidants to give voltaic cells. In the opinion of the author, the sign convention employed is of far less importance than a statement indicating which convention is used. Too often such statements are omitted in literature discussions.

TABLE 8·2
STANDARD OXIDATION POTENTIALS IN ACIDIC SOLUTION

Couple	Equation	E^0_{298}, volts
Li(0)–Li(I)	$Li \rightleftharpoons Li^+ + e^-$	+3.02
Cs(0)–Cs(I)	$Cs \rightleftharpoons Cs^+ + e^-$	3.02
Rb(0)–Rb(I)	$Rb \rightleftharpoons Rb^+ + e^-$	2.99
K(0)–K(I)	$K \rightleftharpoons K^+ + e^-$	2.922
Ba(0)–Ba(II)	$Ba \rightleftharpoons Ba^{+2} + 2e^-$	2.90
Sr(0)–Sr(II)	$Sr \rightleftharpoons Sr^{+2} + 2e^-$	2.89
Ca(0)–Ca(II)	$Ca \rightleftharpoons Ca^{+2} + 2e^-$	2.87
Na(0)–Na(I)	$Na \rightleftharpoons Na^+ + e^-$	2.712
La(0)–La(III)	$La \rightleftharpoons La^{+3} + 3e^-$	2.37
Mg(0)–Mg(II)	$Mg \rightleftharpoons Mg^{+2} + 2e^-$	2.34
H(–I)–H(0)	$H^- \rightleftharpoons \frac{1}{2}H_2 + e^-$	2.23
Th(0)–Th(IV)	$Th + 2H_2O \rightleftharpoons ThO_2 + 4H^+ + 4e^-$	1.80
Be(0)–Be(II)	$Be \rightleftharpoons Be^{+2} + 2e^-$	1.70
Hf(0)–Hf(IV)	$Hf + H_2O \rightleftharpoons HfO^{+2} + 2H^+ + 4e^-$	1.68
Al(0)–Al(III)	$Al \rightleftharpoons Al^{+3} + 3e^-$	1.67
Zr(0)–Zr(IV)	$Zr + 2H_2O \rightleftharpoons ZrO_2 + 4H^+ + 4e^-$	1.43
Mn(0)–Mn(II)	$Mn \rightleftharpoons Mn^{+2} + 2e^-$	1.05
Ti(0)–Ti(IV)	$Ti + 2H_2O \rightleftharpoons TiO_2 + 4H^+ + 4e^-$	0.95
Si(0)–Si(IV)	$Si + 2H_2O \rightleftharpoons SiO_2 + 4H^+ + 4e^-$	0.84
U(0)–U(VI)	$U + 2H_2O \rightleftharpoons UO_2^{+2} + 4H^+ + 6e^-$	0.82
Zn(0)–Zn(II)	$Zn \rightleftharpoons Zn^{+2} + 2e^-$	0.7620
B(0)–B(III)	$B + 3H_2O \rightleftharpoons H_3BO_3 + 3H^+ + 3e^-$	0.73
Ta(0)–Ta(V)	$2Ta + 5H_2O \rightleftharpoons Ta_2O_5 + 10H^+ + 10e^-$	0.71
Cr(0)–Cr(III)	$Cr \rightleftharpoons Cr^{+3} + 3e^-$	0.71
Te(–II)–Te(0)	$H_2Te(aq) \rightleftharpoons Te + 2H^+ + 2e^-$	0.69
Nb(0)–Nb(V)	$2Nb + 5H_2O \rightleftharpoons Nb_2O_5 + 10H^+ + 10e^-$	0.62
P(I)–P(III)	$H_3PO_2 + H_2O \rightleftharpoons H_3PO_3 + 2H^+ + 2e^-$	0.59
As(–III)–As(0)	$AsH_3 \rightleftharpoons As + 3H^+ + 3e^-$	0.54
Ga(0)–Ga(III)	$Ga \rightleftharpoons Ga^{+3} + 3e^-$	0.52
P(0)–P(III)	$P + 3H_2O \rightleftharpoons H_3PO_3 + 3H^+ + 3e^-$	0.49
Fe(0)–Fe(II)	$Fe \rightleftharpoons Fe^{+2} + 2e^-$	0.440
Eu(II)–Eu(III)	$Eu^{+2} \rightleftharpoons Eu^{+3} + e^-$	0.43
Cr(II)–Cr(III)	$Cr^{+2} \rightleftharpoons Cr^{+3} + e^-$	0.41
Cd(0)–Cd(II)	$Cd \rightleftharpoons Cd^{+2} + 2e^-$	0.402
Se(–II)–Se(0)	$H_2Se(aq) \rightleftharpoons Se + 2H^+ + 2e^-$	0.36
In(0)–In(III)	$In \rightleftharpoons In^{+3} + 3e^-$	0.340
Tl(0)–Tl(I)	$Tl \rightleftharpoons Tl^+ + e^-$	0.3363
P(0)–P(I)	$P + 2H_2O \rightleftharpoons H_3PO_2 + H^+ + e^-$	0.29
Co(0)–Co(II)	$Co \rightleftharpoons Co^{+2} + 2e^-$	0.277
Ni(0)–Ni(II)	$Ni \rightleftharpoons Ni^{+2} + 2e^-$	0.250
V(II)–V(III)	$V^{+2} \rightleftharpoons V^{+3} + e^-$	0.20
P(III)–P(V)	$H_3PO_3 + H_2O \rightleftharpoons H_3PO_4 + 2H^+ + 2e^-$	0.20
Sn(0)–Sn(II)	$Sn \rightleftharpoons Sn^{+2} + 2e^-$	0.136
Pb(0)–Pb(II)	$Pb \rightleftharpoons Pb^{+2} + 2e^-$	0.126
P(–III)–P(0)	$PH_3(g) \rightleftharpoons P + 3H^+ + 3e^-$	0.04
Fe(0)–Fe(III)	$Fe \rightleftharpoons Fe^{+3} + 3e^-$	0.036
D(0)–D(I)	$\frac{1}{2}D_2 \rightleftharpoons D^+ + e^-$	0.0034
H(0)–H(I)	$\frac{1}{2}H_2 \rightleftharpoons H^+ + e^-$	0.0000
S(–II)–S(0)	$H_2S(aq) \rightleftharpoons S + 2H^+ + 2e^-$	–0.141
Re(0)–Re(VII)	$Re + 4H_2O \rightleftharpoons ReO_4^- + 8H^+ + 7e^-$	–0.15
Sn(II)–Sn(IV)	$Sn^{+2} \rightleftharpoons Sn^{+4} + 2e^-$	–0.15
Cu(I)–Cu(II)	$Cu^+ \rightleftharpoons Cu^{+2} + e^-$	–0.167
S(IV)–S(VI)	$H_2SO_3 + H_2O \rightleftharpoons SO_4^{-2} + 4H^+ + 2e^-$	–0.20

TABLE 8·2 (*Continued*)

Couple	Equation	E^0_{298}, volts
Sb(0)–Sb(III)	$Sb + H_2O \rightleftharpoons SbO^+ + 2H^+ + 3e^-$	−0.212
As(0)–As(III)	$As + 2H_2O \rightleftharpoons HAsO_2 + 3H^+ + 3e^-$	−0.2475
V(III)–V(IV)	$V^{+3} + H_2O \rightleftharpoons VO^{+2} + 2H^+ + e^-$	−0.314
Bi(0)–Bi(III)	$Bi + H_2O \rightleftharpoons BiO^+ + 2H^+ + 3e^-$	−0.32
Cu(0)–Cu(II)	$Cu \rightleftharpoons Cu^{+2} + 2e^-$	−0.3448
S(0)–S(IV)	$S + 3H_2O \rightleftharpoons H_2SO_3 + 4H^+ + 4e^-$	−0.45
Cu(0)–Cu(I)	$Cu \rightleftharpoons Cu^+ + e^-$	−0.522
Te(0)–Te(IV)	$Te + 2H_2O \rightleftharpoons TeO_2(s) + 4H^+ + 4e^-$	−0.529
I(−I)–I(0)	$I^- \rightleftharpoons \frac{1}{2}I_2 + e^-$	−0.5345
As(III)–As(V)	$HAsO_2 + 2H_2O \rightleftharpoons H_3AsO_4 + 2H^+ + 2e^-$	−0.559
Sb(III)–Sb(V)	$2SbO^+ + 3H_2O \rightleftharpoons Sb_2O_5(s) + 6H^+ + 4e^-$	−0.64
O(−I)–O(0)	$H_2O_2 \rightleftharpoons O_2 + 2H^+ + 2e^-$	−0.682
Se(0)–Se(IV)	$Se + 3H_2O \rightleftharpoons H_2SeO_3 + 4H^+ + 4e^-$	−0.740
Fe(II)–Fe(III)	$Fe^{+2} \rightleftharpoons Fe^{+3} + e^-$	−0.771
Hg(0)–Hg(I)	$Hg \rightleftharpoons \frac{1}{2}Hg_2^{+2} + e^-$	−0.7986
Ag(0)–Ag(I)	$Ag \rightleftharpoons Ag^+ + e^-$	−0.7995
N(I)–N(III)	$H_2N_2O_2 + 2H_2O \rightleftharpoons 2HNO_2 + 4H^+ + 4e^-$	−0.80
N(IV)–N(V)	$N_2O_4 + 2H_2O \rightleftharpoons 2NO_3^- + 4H^+ + 2e^-$	−0.81
O(−II)–O(0)	$H_2O \rightleftharpoons \frac{1}{2}O_2 + 2H^+(10^{-7}\ m) + 2e^-$	−0.815
Pd(0)–Pd(II)	$Pd \rightleftharpoons Pd^{+2} + 2e^-$	−0.83
Os(0)–Os(VIII)	$Os + 4H_2O \rightleftharpoons OsO_4 + 8H^+ + 8e^-$	−0.85
Hg(0)–Hg(II)	$Hg \rightleftharpoons Hg^{+2} + 2e^-$	−0.854
Hg(I)–Hg(II)	$Hg_2^{+2} \rightleftharpoons 2Hg^{+2} + 2e^-$	−0.910
N(III)–N(V)	$HNO_2 + H_2O \rightleftharpoons NO_3^- + 3H^+ + 2e^-$	−0.94
N(II)–N(V)	$NO + 2H_2O \rightleftharpoons NO_3^- + 4H^+ + 3e^-$	−0.96
N(II)–N(III)	$NO + H_2O \rightleftharpoons HNO_2 + H^+ + e^-$	−0.99
I(−I)–I(I)	$I^- + H_2O \rightleftharpoons HIO + H^+ + 2e^-$	−0.99
V(IV)–V(V)	$VO^{+2} + 3H_2O \rightleftharpoons V(OH)_4^+ + 2H^+ + e^-$	−1.00
Cl(V)–Cl(VII)	$ClO_3^- + H_2O \rightleftharpoons ClO_4^- + 2H^+ + 2e^-$	−1.00
Te(IV)–Te(VI)	$TeO_2(s) + 4H_2O \rightleftharpoons H_6TeO_6(s) + 2H^+ + 2e^-$	−1.02
N(II)–N(IV)	$2NO + 2H_2O \rightleftharpoons N_2O_4 + 4H^+ + 4e^-$	−1.03
Br(−I)–Br(0)	$2Br^- \rightleftharpoons Br_2(l) + 2e^-$	−1.0652
N(III)–N(IV)	$2HNO_2 \rightleftharpoons N_2O_4 + 2H^+ + 2e^-$	−1.07
I(−I)–I(V)	$I^- + 3H_2O \rightleftharpoons IO_3^- + 6H^+ + 6e^-$	−1.085
Br(−I)–Br(0)	$2Br^- \rightleftharpoons Br_2(aq) + 2e^-$	−1.087
Se(IV)–Se(VI)	$H_2SeO_3 + H_2O \rightleftharpoons SeO_4^{-2} + 4H^+ + 2e^-$	−1.15
I(0)–I(V)	$\frac{1}{2}I_2 + 3H_2O \rightleftharpoons IO_3^- + 6H^+ + 5e^-$	−1.195
Pt(0)–Pt(II)	$Pt \rightleftharpoons Pt^{+2} + 2e^-$	ca. −1.2
O(−II)–O(0)	$H_2O \rightleftharpoons \frac{1}{2}O_2 + 2H^+ + 2e^-$	−1.229
Cl(III)–Cl(V)	$HClO_2 + H_2O \rightleftharpoons ClO_3^- + 3H^+ + 2e^-$	−1.23
Tl(I)–Tl(III)	$Tl^+ \rightleftharpoons Tl^{+3} + 2e^-$	−1.25
Mn(II)–Mn(IV)	$Mn^{+2} + 2H_2O \rightleftharpoons MnO_2 + 4H^+ + 2e^-$	−1.28
N(I)–N(III)	$N_2O + 3H_2O \rightleftharpoons 2HNO_2 + 4H^+ + 4e^-$	−1.29
Au(I)–Au(III)	$Au^+ \rightleftharpoons Au^{+3} + 2e^-$	ca. −1.29
Br(−I)–Br(I)	$Br^- + H_2O \rightleftharpoons HBrO + H^+ + 2e^-$	−1.33
Cl(0)–Cl(VII)	$\frac{1}{2}Cl_2 + 4H_2O \rightleftharpoons ClO_4^- + 8H^+ + 7e^-$	−1.34
Cl(−I)–Cl(0)	$Cl^- \rightleftharpoons \frac{1}{2}Cl_2 + e^-$	−1.3583
Cr(III)–Cr(VI)	$2Cr^{+3} + 7H_2O \rightleftharpoons Cr_2O_7^{-2} + 14H^+ + 6e^-$	−1.36
Au(0)–Au(III)	$Au \rightleftharpoons Au^{+3} + 3e^-$	−1.42
Br(−I)–Br(V)	$Br^- + 3H_2O \rightleftharpoons BrO_3^- + 6H^+ + 6e^-$	−1.44
I(0)–I(I)	$\frac{1}{2}I_2 + H_2O \rightleftharpoons HIO + H^+ + e^-$	−1.45
Cl(−I)–Cl(V)	$Cl^- + 3H_2O \rightleftharpoons ClO_3^- + 6H^+ + 6e^-$	−1.45
Pb(II)–Pb(IV)	$Pb^{+2} + 2H_2O \rightleftharpoons PbO_2 + 4H^+ + 2e^-$	−1.456
Cl(0)–Cl(V)	$\frac{1}{2}Cl_2 + 3H_2O \rightleftharpoons ClO_3^- + 6H^+ + 5e^-$	−1.47

TABLE 8·2 (*Continued*)

Couple	Equation	$\overset{0}{E}_{298}$, volts
Cl(−I)–Cl(I)	$Cl^- + H_2O \rightleftharpoons HClO + H^+ + 2e^-$	−1.49
Mn(II)–Mn(III)	$Mn^{+2} \rightleftharpoons Mn^{+3} + e^-$	−1.51
Br(0)–Br(V)	$\frac{1}{2}Br_2 + 3H_2O \rightleftharpoons BrO_3^- + 6H^+ + 5e^-$	−1.52
Mn(II)–Mn(VII)	$Mn^{+2} + 4H_2O \rightleftharpoons MnO_4^- + 8H^+ + 5e^-$	−1.52
Cl(−I)–Cl(III)	$Cl^- + 2H_2O \rightleftharpoons HClO_2 + 3H^+ + 4e^-$	−1.56
Br(0)–Br(I)	$\frac{1}{2}Br_2 + H_2O \rightleftharpoons HBrO + H^+ + e^-$	−1.59
N(I)–N(II)	$N_2O + H_2O \rightleftharpoons 2NO + 2H^+ + 2e^-$	−1.59
Ce(III)–Ce(IV)	$Ce^{+3} \rightleftharpoons Ce^{+4} + e^-$	−1.61
Cl(0)–Cl(I)	$\frac{1}{2}Cl_2 + H_2O \rightleftharpoons HClO + H^+ + e^-$	−1.63
Cl(0)–Cl(III)	$\frac{1}{2}Cl_2 + 2H_2O \rightleftharpoons HClO_2 + 3H^+ + 3e^-$	−1.63
Mn(IV)–Mn(VII)	$MnO_2 + 2H_2O \rightleftharpoons MnO_4^- + 4H^+ + 3e^-$	−1.67
Au(0)–Au(I)	$Au \rightleftharpoons Au^+ + e^-$	−1.68
I(V)–I(VII)	$IO_3^- + 3H_2O \rightleftharpoons H_5IO_6 + H^+ + 2e^-$	ca. −1.7
Ni(II)–Ni(IV)	$Ni^{+2} + 2H_2O \rightleftharpoons NiO_2 + 4H^+ + 2e^-$	−1.75
O(−II)–O(−I)	$2H_2O \rightleftharpoons H_2O_2 + 2H^+ + 2e^-$	−1.77
N(0)–N(I)	$N_2 + H_2O \rightleftharpoons N_2O + 2H^+ + 2e^-$	−1.77
Co(II)–Co(III)	$Co^{+2} \rightleftharpoons Co^{+3} + e^-$	−1.84
Ag(I)–Ag(II)	$Ag^+ \rightleftharpoons Ag^{+2} + e^-$	−1.98
	$2SO_4^{-2} \rightleftharpoons S_2O_8^{-2} + 2e^-$	−2.05
	$O_2 + H_2O \rightleftharpoons O_3 + 2H^+ + 2e^-$	−2.07
O(−II)–O(II)	$H_2O + 2F^- \rightleftharpoons F_2O + 2H^+ + 4e^-$	−2.1
O(−II)–O(0)	$H_2O \rightleftharpoons O(g) + 2H^+ + 2e^-$	−2.42
F(−I)–F(0)	$F^- \rightleftharpoons \frac{1}{2}F_2 + e^-$	−2.85
F(−I)–F(0)	$HF \rightleftharpoons \frac{1}{2}F_2 + H^+ + e^-$	−3.03

TABLE 8·3

STANDARD OXIDATION POTENTIALS IN ALKALINE SOLUTION

Couple	Equation	$\overset{0}{E}_{298}$, volts
Li(0)–Li(I)	$Li \rightleftharpoons Li^+ + e^-$	+3.02
Cs(0)–Cs(I)	$Cs \rightleftharpoons Cs^+ + e^-$	3.02
Ca(0)–Ca(II)	$Ca + 2OH^- \rightleftharpoons Ca(OH)_2 + 2e^-$	3.02
Sr(0)–Sr(II)	$Sr + 2OH^- + 8H_2O \rightleftharpoons Sr(OH)_2{\cdot}8H_2O + 2e^-$	2.99
Rb(0)–Rb(I)	$Rb \rightleftharpoons Rb^+ + e^-$	2.99
Ba(0)–Ba(II)	$Ba + 2OH^- + 8H_2O \rightleftharpoons Ba(OH)_2{\cdot}8H_2O + 2e^-$	2.97
K(0)–K(I)	$K \rightleftharpoons K^+ + e^-$	2.922
La(0)–La(III)	$La + 3OH^- \rightleftharpoons La(OH)_3 + 3e^-$	2.76
Na(0)–Na(I)	$Na \rightleftharpoons Na^+ + e^-$	2.712
Mg(0)–Mg(II)	$Mg + 2OH^- \rightleftharpoons Mg(OH)_2 + 2e^-$	2.67
Th(0)–Th(IV)	$Th + 4OH^- \rightleftharpoons ThO_2 + 2H_2O + 4e^-$	2.64
Hf(0)–Hf(IV)	$Hf + 4OH^- \rightleftharpoons HfO(OH)_2 + H_2O + 4e^-$	2.60
B(0)–B(III)	$B + 4OH^- \rightleftharpoons H_2BO_3^- + H_2O + 3e^-$	2.5
Al(0)–Al(III)	$Al + 4OH^- \rightleftharpoons H_2AlO_3^- + H_2O + 3e^-$	2.35
Zr(0)–Zr(IV)	$Zr + 4OH^- \rightleftharpoons ZrO(OH)_2 + H_2O + 4e^-$	2.32
Be(0)–Be(II)	$2Be + 6OH^- \rightleftharpoons Be_2O_3^{-2} + 3H_2O + 4e^-$	2.28
P(0)–P(I)	$P + 2OH^- \rightleftharpoons H_2PO_2^- + e^-$	1.82
Si(0)–Si(IV)	$Si + 6OH^- \rightleftharpoons SiO_3^{-2} + 3H_2O + 4e^-$	1.73
P(0)–P(III)	$P + 5OH^- \rightleftharpoons HPO_3^{-2} + 2H_2O + 3e^-$	1.71
P(I)–P(III)	$H_2PO_2^- + 3OH^- \rightleftharpoons HPO_3^{-2} + 2H_2O + 2e^-$	1.65
Mn(0)–Mn(II)	$Mn + 2OH^- \rightleftharpoons Mn(OH)_2$	1.47

TABLE 8·3 (*Continued*)

Couple	Equation	E^0_{298}, volts
Cr(0)–Cr(III)	$Cr + 3OH^- \rightleftharpoons Cr(OH)_3 + 3e^-$	1.3
Ga(0)–Ga(III)	$Ga + 4OH^- \rightleftharpoons H_2GaO_3^- + H_2O + 3e^-$	1.22
Zn(0)–Zn(II)	$Zn + 4OH^- \rightleftharpoons ZnO_2^{-2} + 2H_2O + 2e^-$	1.216
Cr(0)–Cr(III)	$Cr + 4OH^- \rightleftharpoons CrO_2^- + 2H_2O + 3e^-$	1.2
P(III)–P(V)	$HPO_3^{-2} + 3OH^- \rightleftharpoons PO_4^{-3} + 2H_2O + 2e^-$	1.05
Sn(II)–Sn(IV)	$HSnO_2^- + 3OH^- + H_2O \rightleftharpoons Sn(OH)_6^{-2} + 2e^-$	0.96
Te(–II)–Te(0)	$Te^{-2} \rightleftharpoons Te + 2e^-$	0.92
S(IV)–S(VI)	$SO_3^{-2} + 2OH^- \rightleftharpoons SO_4^{-2} + H_2O + 2e^-$	0.90
Fe(0)–Fe(II)	$Fe + 2OH^- \rightleftharpoons Fe(OH)_2 + 2e^-$	0.877
P(–III)–P(0)	$PH_3(g) + 3OH^- \rightleftharpoons P + 3H_2O + 3e^-$	0.87
N(IV)–N(V)	$N_2O_4 + 4OH^- \rightleftharpoons 2NO_3^- + 2H_2O + 2e^-$	0.85
H(0)–H(I)	$H_2 + 2OH^- \rightleftharpoons 2H_2O + 2e^-$	0.828
Cd(0)–Cd(II)	$Cd + 2OH^- \rightleftharpoons Cd(OH)_2 + 2e^-$	0.815
Re(0)–Re(VII)	$Re + 8OH^- \rightleftharpoons ReO_4^- + 4H_2O + 7e^-$	0.81
Sn(0)–Sn(II)	$Sn + 3OH^- \rightleftharpoons HSnO_2^- + H_2O + 2e^-$	0.79
Se(–II)–Se(0)	$Se^{-2} \rightleftharpoons Se + 2e^-$	0.78
Co(0)–Co(II)	$Co + 2OH^- \rightleftharpoons Co(OH)_2 + 2e^-$	0.73
As(III)–As(V)	$AsO_2^- + 4OH^- \rightleftharpoons AsO_4^{-3} + 2H_2O + 2e^-$	0.71
As(0)–As(III)	$As + 4OH^- \rightleftharpoons AsO_2^- + 2H_2O + 3e^-$	0.68
Sb(0)–Sb(III)	$Sb + 4OH^- \rightleftharpoons SbO_2^- + 2H_2O + 3e^-$	0.66
Ni(0)–Ni(II)	$Ni + 2OH^- \rightleftharpoons Ni(OH)_2 + 2e^-$	0.66
Pb(0)–Pb(II)	$Pb + 2OH^- \rightleftharpoons PbO + H_2O + 2e^-$	0.578
Fe(II)–Fe(III)	$Fe(OH)_2 + OH^- \rightleftharpoons Fe(OH)_3 + e^-$	0.56
Pb(0)–Pb(II)	$Pb + 3OH^- \rightleftharpoons HPbO_2^- + H_2O + 2e^-$	0.54
S(–II)–S(0)	$S^{-2} \rightleftharpoons S + 2e^-$	0.508
S(–II)–S(0)	$HS^- + OH^- \rightleftharpoons S + H_2O + 2e^-$	0.478
N(II)–N(III)	$NO + 2OH^- \rightleftharpoons NO_2^- + H_2O + e^-$	0.46
Bi(0)–Bi(III)	$Bi + 3OH^- \rightleftharpoons BiOOH + H_2O + 3e^-$	0.46
Mn(II)–Mn(III)	$Mn(OH)_2 + OH^- \rightleftharpoons Mn(OH)_3 + e^-$	0.40
Cu(0)–Cu(I)	$2Cu + 2OH^- \rightleftharpoons Cu_2O + H_2O + 2e^-$	0.361
Se(0)–Se(IV)	$Se + 6OH^- \rightleftharpoons SeO_3^{-2} + 3H_2O + 4e^-$	0.35
Tl(0)–Tl(I)	$Tl + OH^- \rightleftharpoons TlOH + e^-$	0.3445
Cu(0)–Cu(II)	$Cu + 2OH^- \rightleftharpoons Cu(OH)_2 + 2e^-$	0.224
N(I)–N(III)	$N_2O_2^{-2} + 4OH^- \rightleftharpoons 2NO_2^- + 2H_2O + 4e^-$	0.18
Cr(III)–Cr(VI)	$Cr(OH)_3 + 5OH^- \rightleftharpoons CrO_4^{-2} + 4H_2O + 3e^-$	0.12
Cu(I)–Cu(II)	$Cu_2O + 2OH^- + H_2O \rightleftharpoons 2Cu(OH)_2 + 2e^-$	0.09
O(–I)–O(0)	$HO_2^- + OH^- \rightleftharpoons O_2 + H_2O + 2e^-$	0.076
Tl(I)–Tl(III)	$TlOH + 2OH^- \rightleftharpoons Tl(OH)_3 + 2e^-$	0.05
Te(0)–Te(IV)	$Te + 6OH^- \rightleftharpoons TeO_3^{-2} + 2H_2O + 4e^-$	0.02
N(III)–N(V)	$NO_2^- + 2OH^- \rightleftharpoons NO_3^- + H_2O + 2e^-$	–0.01
Se(IV)–Se(VI)	$SeO_3^{-2} + 2OH^- \rightleftharpoons SeO_4^{-2} + H_2O + 2e^-$	–0.03
Hg(0)–Hg(II)	$Hg + 2OH^- \rightleftharpoons HgO(r) + H_2O + 2e^-$	–0.0984
Pd(0)–Pd(II)	$Pd + 2OH^- \rightleftharpoons Pd(OH)_2 + 2e^-$	–0.1
Ir(0)–Ir(III)	$2Ir + 6OH^- \rightleftharpoons Ir_2O_3 + 3H_2O + 6e^-$	–0.1
N(I)–N(II)	$N_2O_2^{-2} \rightleftharpoons 2NO + 2e^-$	–0.10
Hg(0)–Hg(I)	$2Hg + 2OH^- \rightleftharpoons Hg_2O + H_2O + 2e^-$	–0.123
N(I)–N(III)	$N_2O + 6OH^- \rightleftharpoons 2NO_2^- + 3H_2O + 4e^-$	–0.15
Pt(0)–Pt(II)	$Pt + 2OH^- \rightleftharpoons Pt(OH)_2 + 2e^-$	–0.16
Cl(V)–Cl(VII)	$ClO_3^- + 2OH^- \rightleftharpoons ClO_4^- + H_2O + 2e^-$	–0.17
Co(II)–Co(III)	$Co(OH)_2 + OH^- \rightleftharpoons Co(OH)_3 + e^-$	–0.2
I(–I)–I(V)	$I^- + 6OH^- \rightleftharpoons IO_3^- + 3H_2O + 6e^-$	–0.26
Ag(0)–Ag(I)	$2Ag + 2OH^- \rightleftharpoons Ag_2O + H_2O + 2e^-$	–0.344
Cl(III)–Cl(V)	$ClO_2^- + 2OH^- \rightleftharpoons ClO_3^- + H_2O + 2e^-$	–0.35
O(–II)–O(0)	$4OH^- \rightleftharpoons O_2 + 2H_2O + 4e^-$	–0.401

TABLE 8·3 (*Continued*)

Couple	Equation	E^0_{298}, volts
Ni(II)–Ni(IV)	$Ni(OH)_2 + 2OH^- \rightleftharpoons NiO_2 + 2H_2O + 2e^-$	−0.49
I(−I)–I(I)	$I^- + 2OH^- \rightleftharpoons IO^- + H_2O + 2e^-$	−0.49
Mn(VI)–Mn(VII)	$MnO_4^{-2} \rightleftharpoons MnO_4^- + e^-$	−0.54
I(I)–I(V)	$IO^- + 4OH^- \rightleftharpoons IO_3^- + 2H_2O + 4e^-$	−0.56
Mn(IV)–Mn(VII)	$MnO_2 + 4OH^- \rightleftharpoons MnO_4^- + 2H_2O + 3e^-$	−0.57
Ag(I)–Ag(II)	$Ag_2O + 2OH^- \rightleftharpoons 2AgO + H_2O + 2e^-$	−0.57
Mn(IV)–Mn(VI)	$MnO_2 + 4OH^- \rightleftharpoons MnO_4^{-2} + 2H_2O + 2e^-$	−0.58
Cl(I)–Cl(III)	$ClO^- + 2OH^- \rightleftharpoons ClO_2^- + H_2O + 2e^-$	−0.59
Br(−I)–Br(V)	$Br^- + 6OH^- \rightleftharpoons BrO_3^- + 3H_2O + 6e^-$	−0.61
Cl(−I)–Cl(V)	$Cl^- + 6OH^- \rightleftharpoons ClO_3^- + 3H_2O + 6e^-$	−0.62
I(V)–I(VII)	$IO_3^- + 3OH^- \rightleftharpoons H_3IO_6^{-2} + 2e^-$	ca. −0.70
Ag(II)–Ag(III)	$2AgO + 2OH^- \rightleftharpoons Ag_2O_3 + H_2O + 2e^-$	−0.74
Cl(−I)–Cl(III)	$Cl^- + 4OH^- \rightleftharpoons ClO_2^- + 2H_2O + 4e^-$	−0.76
N(I)–N(II)	$N_2O + 2OH^- \rightleftharpoons 2NO + H_2O + 2e^-$	−0.76
Br(−I)–Br(I)	$Br^- + 2OH^- \rightleftharpoons BrO^- + H_2O + 2e^-$	−0.76
O(−II)–O(−I)	$3OH^- \rightleftharpoons HO_2^- + H_2O + 2e^-$	−0.87
N(III)–N(IV)	$2NO_2^- \rightleftharpoons N_2O_4 + 2e^-$	−0.88
Cl(−I)–Cl(I)	$Cl^- + 2OH^- \rightleftharpoons ClO^- + H_2O + 2e^-$	−0.94
Cl(III)–Cl(IV)	$ClO_2^- \rightleftharpoons ClO_2 + e^-$	−1.15
	$O_2 + 2OH^- \rightleftharpoons O_3 + H_2O + 2e^-$	−1.24
O(−II)–O(−I)	$OH^- \rightleftharpoons OH + e^-$	−1.4

half-reaction under consideration is a better reducing agent than hydrogen gas and should reduce hydrogen ion to hydrogen gas. Conversely, if the potential is negative, the oxidant in the half-reaction is a better oxidizing agent than hydrogen ion and should oxidize hydrogen gas to hydrogen ion. Thus, since

$$Fe \rightleftharpoons Fe^{+2} + 2e^- \qquad E^0_{298} = 0.440 \text{ volt}$$

iron is readily oxidized by hydrogen ion and liberates hydrogen gas from aqueous protonic acids. However, since

$$Fe^{+2} \rightleftharpoons Fe^{+3} + e^- \qquad E^0_{298} = -0.771 \text{ volt}$$

iron(II) ion cannot be oxidized by hydrogen ion to iron(III), the reverse reaction being favored. Liberation of hydrogen gas accompanied by oxidation of iron(0) to iron(III) is thus impossible.

Numerical magnitude of the oxidation potential

Data in Tables 8·2 and 8·3 embrace the potential range from −3.03 volts to +3.02 volts, the spread in acidic solutions being larger because of the generally more positive values noted for most systems in alkaline solution (p. 292). In a very general way, those half-reactions characterized by the largest positive potential values contain the most powerful reductants, whereas those characterized by the largest negative potential values contain the most powerful oxidants. Although the qualifications of unit activities, etc., are implicit in these statements, rough comparisons of reducing or oxidizing power can be made in terms of standard potential values.

Alteration in effective concentration (activity for an ion, pressure for a gas) profoundly affects the oxidation potential of a system, and standard potential values must be corrected, therefore, for such changes before they can be applied rigidly to usually encountered experimental conditions. Corrections of this type are made by means of the relation

$$E = E^0 - \frac{RT}{n\mathfrak{F}} \ln Q \qquad (8\cdot3)$$

where E is the potential under the conditions of the reaction, E^0 is the standard potential for the system in question, R is the gas constant (8.3118 joules per degree per mole), T is the absolute temperature (°K.), n is the number of electrons involved in the process, $\mathfrak{F}$ is the Faraday constant (96,494 coulombs), and Q is the activity quotient for the reaction. The activity quotient is the product of the activities (pressures) of the reaction products divided by the product of the activities of the reactants, each quantity being raised to a power indicated by the corresponding coefficient in the equation for the reaction. It is, therefore, a thermodynamic equilibrium constant. All pure solids and liquids are considered to have unit activities. If E^0 values are expressed at 25°C., substitution for the constants and conversion to ordinary logarithms (base 10) converts Equation 8·3 to

$$E = E^0 - \frac{0.0591}{n} \log Q \qquad (8\cdot4)$$

which form is then simple to use. Obviously, if all materials are at unit activity, Q is one, and $E = E^0$.

The general effects of concentration changes may be illustrated by some examples. Alteration of the potential characterizing Equation 8·2 is of fundamental importance. If the activity of hydrogen ion is reduced to 10^{-7} m (i.e., to the value in pure water), the pressure of gaseous hydrogen remaining at one atmosphere, the resulting potential may be calculated as

$$E = E^0 - \frac{0.0591}{n} \log \frac{a_{H^+}}{p_{H_2}} \qquad (8\cdot5)$$

$$= 0 - \frac{0.0591}{1} \log \frac{10^{-7}}{1}$$

$$= +0.414 \text{ volt}$$

Correspondingly, still further reduction of hydrogen ion activity as the alkaline range is entered causes the potential to become even more positive. This is of course a fundamental reason for the generally higher positive magnitudes for potentials in alkaline medium as compared with acidic medium.

To carry these considerations farther, consider the system

$$Mn^{+2} + 4H_2O \rightleftharpoons MnO_4^- + 8H^+ + 5e^-$$

for which

$$E = E^0_{298} - \frac{0.0591}{n} \log \frac{a_{MnO_4^-} \times a_{H^+}^8}{a_{Mn^{+2}}} \qquad (8\cdot6)$$

$$E = -1.52 - \frac{0.0591}{5} \log \frac{a_{MnO_4^-} \times a_{H^+}^8}{a_{Mn^{+2}}}$$

If the activities of all the ionic species are altered to 0.1, substitution gives

$$E = -1.52 - \frac{0.0591}{5} \log \frac{0.1 \times 0.1^8}{0.1}$$

which reduces to

$$E = -1.43 \text{ volts}$$

Here it is obvious that the activity of the hydrogen ion is the controlling factor in determining the potential because of the high power to which it is raised.

The dependence of potential values upon hydrogen ion activity (concentration) is of considerable importance. Strictly speaking, of course, only those potentials which characterize reactions involving water and its ions are affected. Thus the standard potential for the Na(O)–Na(I) couple remains constant over the entire pH range because neither hydrogen nor hydroxyl ion is involved in the half-reaction. On the other hand, the standard potential for the Fe(II)–Fe(III) couple remains constant only over that pH range in which hydrous hydroxide precipitation does not occur. Once this pH is exceeded, the couple measured amounts to

$$Fe(OH)_2 + OH^- \rightleftharpoons Fe(OH)_3 + e^-$$

and the influence of the hydrogen ion activity (or hydroxyl ion activity) becomes apparent. Since in a system of this type the two hydroxides possess different basicities and precipitate at different pH values (pp. 502–503), there is no continuous transition in potential value from the highly acidic to the highly alkaline range. For more involved couples, e.g., Mn(II)–Mn(VII), dependence of potentials upon hydrogen ion activity is obvious from the characteristic equations. The variations obtained for a number of typical couples are summarized in Figure 8·1. Here values are plotted against hydrogen ion concentration instead of

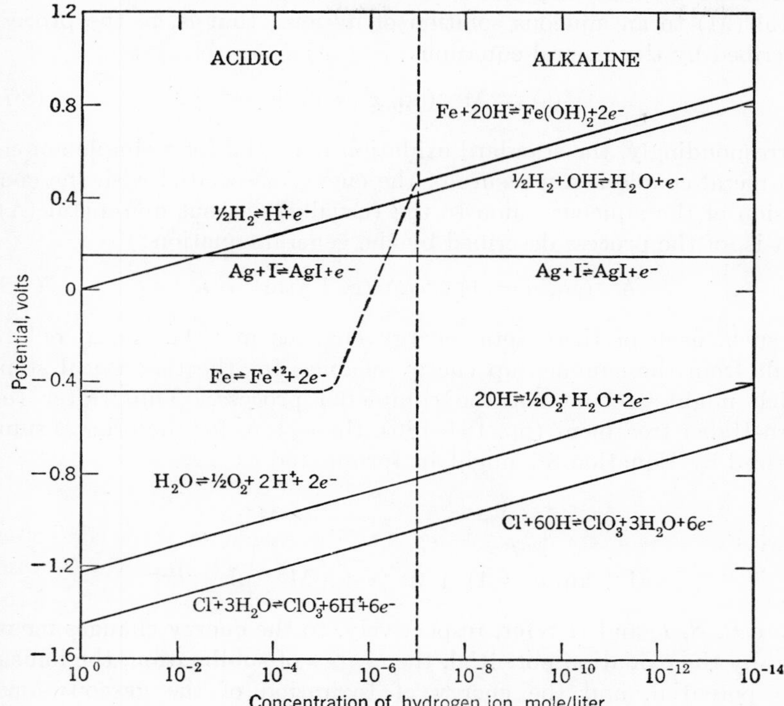

FIG. 8·1. Variation of potentials of particular couples with hydrogen ion concentration.

activity for convenience. In a general way, substitution of concentrations for activities will indicate identical trends for most couples.

Factors which determine the magnitude of the standard potential

The relative reducing powers of metals and oxidizing powers of nonmetals as revealed by the magnitudes of their standard oxidation potentials are associated qualitatively with differences in electropositive and electronegative character, respectively. Thus the most electropositive element (cesium, neglecting francium) is characterized by the largest positive potential value, and the most electronegative element (fluorine) by the largest negative potential value. However, in certain cases factors other than these may be of considerable importance.

The standard oxidation potential for a metal-metal cation couple is a measure of the energy associated with the conversion of a solid metal (M) to an aqueous solution of its ions, that is, of the process described by the general equation

$$M(s) \rightleftharpoons M^{+n}(aq, a = 1) + ne^- \tag{8·7}$$

Correspondingly, the standard oxidation potential for a simple anion–non-metal couple is a measure of the energy associated with the conversion of the aqueous anion to the (usually) gaseous non-metal (A), that is, of the process described by the general equation

$$A^{-n}(aq, a = 1) \rightleftharpoons \tfrac{1}{2}A_2(g, 1 \text{ atm}) + ne^- \tag{8·8}$$

As such, each of these total energy changes may be considered to result from the summed-up energy changes for the theoretical steps which might account for the completed process. Thus, after the Born-Haber treatment (pp. 184–186), these steps for the process summarized by Equation 8·7 might be formulated as

$$\begin{array}{ccc} M(s) & \xrightarrow{+S} & M(g) \\ \uparrow \pm P & & \downarrow +I \\ M^{n+}(aq, a = 1) + ne^- & \xleftarrow{-H} & M^{n+}(g) + ne^- \end{array}$$

where P, S, I, and H refer, respectively, to the energy changes measured by the oxidation potential, the energy of sublimation, the ionization potential, and the energy of hydration of the gaseous ions. Exothermic quantities are indicated as negative and endothermic quantities as positive. Inasmuch as energy must be conserved in the entire cyclic process, it follows that

$$\pm P = S + I - H \tag{8·9}$$

all terms being expressed in comparable units.* Apparently, then, the energy change expressed by the oxidation potential is determined by the relative magnitudes of the energies put in to sublime and ionize the metal as compared with the energy recovered through hydration of the gaseous ions. Since the latter two quantities are often large compared with the first, their relative values will commonly determine the magnitude of the potential.

* Since S, I, and H are commonly expressed in kilogram calories per gram mole (or gram ion), conversion of P to volts must involve use of the equivalence 1 volt = 23,066 gcal. = 23.066 kcal.

In the same fashion, the change shown in Equation 8·8 may be formulated cyclically as

$$\begin{array}{ccc} \frac{1}{2}A_2(g) & \xrightarrow{+D} & A(g) \\ \pm P\uparrow & & \downarrow -E \\ A^{-n}(aq,\ a = 1) & \xleftarrow{-H} & A^{-n}(g) \end{array}$$

where D and E refer, respectively, to the energy changes measured by the dissociation energy of the gaseous molecules and the electron affinity of the gaseous ions. Again, by conservation of energy

$$\pm P = D - E - H \tag{8·10}$$

and the magnitude of the oxidation potential will be determined by all three factors.

If all the energy changes indicated in Equations 8·9 and 8·10 were known accurately, potential values could be calculated directly from them. These energy changes are actually the free energy changes for the processes described and can be evaluated from experimentally determined heats of sublimation, heats of dissociation, etc., only if the corresponding *entropy* changes are also known.* Lack of complete data prevents anything beyond rough potential calculations for a majority of the known reactions. However, certain generalizations based upon data which are known are instructive.

Equation 8·9 indicates that decreased reducing power (or enhanced nobility) in a metal is favored by large values for ionization potential and sublimation energy and a small value for the hydration energy. Inasmuch as the sublimation energy is somewhat dependent upon the boiling point, metals with excessively high boiling points (e.g., the platinum metals) would be expected to be quite noble. To illustrate the effects of these factors, let us compare potassium ($E^0_{298} = +2.922$ volts) with silver ($E^0_{298} = -0.7995$ volt). The stepwise energy changes (not free energy changes) are:

	K	Ag
$M(s) \rightleftharpoons M(g)$	21.7 kcal.	67 kcal.
$M(g) \rightleftharpoons M^+(g) + e^-(g)$	100.0	175
$M^+(g) \rightleftharpoons M^+(aq)$	−77	−113
$M(s) \rightleftharpoons M^+(aq) + e^-(g)$	44.3	128

* Entropy (S) is a thermodynamic quantity which measures the disorder in a system. When multiplied by the absolute temperature (T), it gives the energy required to restore a system to its original state when it has been transferred from that state to another. The change in entropy (ΔS) is related to the change in free energy (ΔF) and the change in heat content or *enthalpy* (ΔH) by the relation

$$\Delta F = \Delta H - T\,\Delta S.$$

Thus potassium is the more electropositive element because the energies associated with its sublimation and subsequent ionization are much smaller than the corresponding values for silver whereas the difference in hydration energies is proportionately much less.

Of particular interest are variations in the standard oxidation potentials of the alkali metals (Table 8·2). Helpful data of aid in accounting for these variations may be summarized as:

	Li	Na	K	Rb	Cs
$M(s) \rightleftharpoons M(g)$	38.3 kcal.	26.0 kcal.	21.7 kcal.	19.9 kcal.	19.1
$M(g) \rightleftharpoons M^+(g) + e^-(g)$	124.5	118.5	100.0	96.3	89.8
$M^+(g) \rightleftharpoons M^+(aq)$	−123	−97	−77	−70	−63
$M(s) \rightleftharpoons M^+(aq) + e^-(g)$	39.1	47	44.3	45.8	45.5

Although these data do not give exact measures of potential values, they do indicate qualitatively that the increase in reducing power from sodium to cesium is in accord with decrease in ionization potential augmented by decrease in sublimation energy, the decrease in hydrational energy being insufficient to overcome the combined effects of the other two. The apparently anomalously high oxidation potential for lithium, however, is due to the fact that the very large energy of hydration associated with the small lithium ion completely overbalances the increased energy input due to larger values of sublimation and ionization energies. In contact with aqueous solutions, therefore, lithium is as strong a reducing agent as cesium. In the absence of water, it is not. It should be pointed out that exact calculations based upon free energy and entropy changes do yield potential values in good agreement with the experimental values for these elements.[4]

Equation 8·10 indicates decreased oxidizing power of a non-metal to be favored by high dissociation energy, low electron affinity, and low energy of hydration of the negative ion. Trends in the halogen family may be indicated qualitatively by the following summary:

	F	Cl	Br	I
$\frac{1}{2}X_2(g) \rightleftharpoons X(g)$	32.2 kcal.	28.9 kcal.	26.9 kcal.	25.4 kcal.
$X(g) + e^-(g) \rightleftharpoons X^-(g)$	−98.5	−92.5	−87.1	−79.2
$X^-(g) \rightleftharpoons X^-(aq)$	−117	−85	−78	−68
$\frac{1}{2}X_2(g) \rightleftharpoons X^-(aq) + e^-(g)$	−183.3	−148.6	−138.2	−121.8

Decrease in oxidizing power among the halogens with increasing atomic weight is due primarily to decrease in hydrational energy combined with decrease in electron affinity, the changes in dissociation energy being insignificant by comparison.

More complicated half-reactions may also be reduced to theoretical steps, but the energy quantities associated with such steps are unknown

[4] W. M. Latimer: *The Oxidation States of the Elements and Their Potentials in Aqueous Solutions*, pp. 283–285. Prentice-Hall, New York (1938).

and are incapable of evaluation in most instances. For other details, Latimer's book should be consulted.[3]

Applications of oxidation potential data

Use of oxidation potential data permits quantitative treatment of oxidation-reduction processes. A few general applications may be considered at this point to provide the necessary background for the specific uses discussed in subsequent chapters (particularly in Part II).

Reaction Predictions. In general, the oxidized form in any couple will oxidize the reduced form in any couple of higher positive potential. Thus, having given

$$H_2S \rightleftharpoons 2H^+ + S + 2e^- \qquad E^0_{298} = -0.141 \text{ volt}$$

and

$$2Cr^{+3} + 7H_2O \rightleftharpoons Cr_2O_7^{-2} + 14H^+ + 6e^- \qquad E^0_{298} = -1.36 \text{ volts}$$

one would predict (and correctly) that dichromate will oxidize hydrogen sulfide in acidic solution, the complete equation for the process being the summation of the two given. The same considerations would apply to other similar combinations.

Predictions of this sort, although useful, are sometimes more theoretical than practical in character. Oxidation potentials measure energy differences only and bear no relation to reaction kinetics. Many reactions which are energetically possible are not actually observed because they proceed too slowly to be followed. Thus direct reductions of many cations (e.g., Cu^{+2}) with hydrogen gas which might be expected from potential data are not observed because of unfavorable kinetics. Certain other reactions which appear to be energetically possible are not observed because of unfavorable mechanisms. Thus, although direct oxidation of iron(0) to iron(III) has a standard potential of +0.04, the reaction between iron and hydrogen ion always yields iron(II) rather than iron(III) (p. 290). Oxidation to iron(II) occurs preferentially ($E^0_{298} = +0.440$ volt), and iron(II) cannot then be oxidized further by hydrogen ion.

Strictly speaking, oxidation potential values refer only to equilibrium systems, and many reactions are encountered in which such conditions do not exist. Although potential data are useful in predicting reactions, they must be employed judiciously.

Combinations of Half-Reactions. The method of evaluating a potential value for a reaction described by the summation of equations for two half-reactions depends upon whether a completed reaction or another half-reaction is produced.

If the combination of two half-reactions results in a completed reaction, the half-reaction potentials are additive algebraically. Thus, if it is desired to combine

$$\mathrm{Cu} \rightleftharpoons \mathrm{Cu}^{+2} + 2e^- \qquad E^0_{298} = -0.345 \text{ volt}$$

with

$$\mathrm{Al} \rightleftharpoons \mathrm{Al}^{+3} + 3e^- \qquad E^0_{298} = +1.67 \text{ volts}$$

to give

$$2\mathrm{Al} + 3\mathrm{Cu}^{+2} \rightleftharpoons 2\mathrm{Al}^{+3} + 3\mathrm{Cu}$$

by subtraction of the first from the second, the potential is determined to be +2.015 volts.* Combinations of this type are of particular importance in considerations involving voltaic cells. If the calculated potential has a positive value, the reaction will proceed from left to right as shown in the equation. If the potential has a negative value, the reaction will proceed spontaneously in the reverse direction unless the quantity of energy indicated by the potential is supplied from an external source.

If the combination of two half-reactions yields a third half-reaction, the free energy changes characterizing the reactions, not the potentials, are additive. The final oxidation potential characterizing the third half-reaction must then be calculated from the free energy change so obtained. Change in standard free energy (ΔF^0_{298}) is related to the standard potential as

$$\Delta F^0_{298} = -nE^0_{298}\mathfrak{F} \tag{8·11}$$

where n is the number of electrons involved in the half-reaction and $\mathfrak{F}$ in the Faraday constant (23,066 cal. per volt, since free energy changes are commonly expressed in calories). In the majority of calculations, complete numerical evaluation of free energy changes is unnecessary, for the Faraday constant may be carried along as such and canceled at the end. Thus combination of

$$\mathrm{Mn}^{+2} + 2\mathrm{H_2O} \rightleftharpoons \mathrm{MnO_2} + 4\mathrm{H}^+ + 2e^- \qquad E^0_{298} = -1.28 \text{ volts}$$

with

$$\mathrm{Mn}^{+2} \rightleftharpoons \mathrm{Mn}^{+3} + e^- \qquad E^0_{298} = -1.51 \text{ volts}$$

* Although it is necessary to balance the chemical quantities in the equation and to equalize the electron loss and gain, no such adjustment is made in the potential values. Potential values measure losses of certain numbers of electrons per atom or ion and are independent of the total number of atoms or ions of that species present. In the example cited, combination could have been effected by reversing the first reaction and adding. Turning an ion-electron equation around reverses the sign of its potential.

by subtraction of the second from the first, yields

$$Mn^{+3} + 2H_2O \rightleftharpoons MnO_2 + 4H^+ + e^-$$

for the Mn(III)–Mn(IV) couple. The corresponding changes in free energy amount to

$$\text{Mn(II)–Mn(IV)} \qquad \Delta F^0_{298} = -(2)(-1.28)(\mathfrak{F}) = 2.56\mathfrak{F}$$

$$\text{Mn(II)–Mn(III)} \qquad \Delta F^0_{298} = -(1)(-1.51)(\mathfrak{F}) = 1.51\mathfrak{F}$$

from which ΔF^0_{298} for Mn(III)–Mn(IV) becomes $+1.05\mathfrak{F}$. Since for the third couple $n = 1$,

$$E_{298} = -1.05\mathfrak{F}/1\mathfrak{F} = -1.05 \text{ volts}$$

Other combination swould be handled similarly.

Evaluation of Equilibrium Constants. The standard free energy change (ΔF^0) in a reaction may be expressed either by Equation 8·11 or by the expression

$$\Delta F^0 = -RT \ln K \tag{8·12}$$

where K is the equilibrium constant for the reaction, activities being employed. Equating Equations 8·11 and 8·12, converting to common logarithms, and solving gives

$$\log K = \frac{nE^0\mathfrak{F}}{2.303RT} \tag{8·13}$$

Introduction of values for R and $\mathfrak{F}$ and evaluation at 298°K reduces Equation 8·13 to

$$\log K_{298} = 16.92nE^0_{298} \tag{8·14}$$

Equation 8·14 then provides a means of evaluating an equilibrium constant from a standard potential or of evaluating a potential from an equilibrium constant.

The utility of Equation 8·14 may be made more apparent by its application to some specific reactions. Thus the calculated potential (at 298°K) for the reaction expressed by the completed equation

$$Cd + 2Ag^+ \rightleftharpoons Cd^{+2} + 2Ag$$

is + 1.2015 volts. Hence,

$$\log K_{298} = \log a_{Cd^{+2}}/a_{Ag^+}{}^2 = 16.92 \times 2 \times 1.2015 = 40.66$$

from which

$$K_{298} = a_{Cd^{+2}}/a_{Ag^+}{}^2 = 4.6 \times 10^{40}$$

The magnitude of the equilibrium constant is such that for all practical purposes the reaction is displaced completely to cadmium ion and silver.

By way of contrast, consider

$$Hg + Hg^{+2} \rightleftharpoons Hg_2^{+2} \qquad E^0_{298} = +0.056 \text{ volt}$$

for which

$$\log K_{298} = \log a_{Hg_2^{+2}}/a_{Hg^{+2}} = 16.92 \times 2 \times 0.056 = 1.895$$

or

$$K_{298} = a_{Hg_2^{+2}}/a_{Hg^{+2}} = 79$$

Here, at equilibrium, the activity (in effect the concentration) of the mercury(I) ion is only 79 times that of the mercury (II) ion. As a consequence, the addition of any material (e.g., sulfide ion, hydroxyl ion, and ammonia and chloride ion) which forms a mercury(II) compound which is much less soluble than the corresponding mercury(I) compound will convert mercury(I) to mercury(0) and mercury(II) (pp. 853–855).

Specific types of equilibrium constants such as instability constants and solubility product constants can be evaluated in the same general manner. As an illustration, consider the evaluation of the solubility product constant for silver bromide at 25°C. The half-reactions

$$Br^- + Ag \rightleftharpoons AgBr + e^- \qquad E^0_{298} = -0.073 \text{ volt}$$

and

$$Ag \rightleftharpoons Ag^+ + e^- \qquad E^0_{298} = -0.7995 \text{ volt}$$

may be combined algebraically to give

$$Ag^+ + Br^- \rightleftharpoons AgBr \qquad E^0_{298} = +0.7265 \text{ volt}$$

for which

$$\log \frac{1}{K_{298}} = 16.92 \times 0.7265 = 12.292$$

or

$$K_{298} = 5.1 \times 10^{-13}$$

Other examples may be handled in similar fashions.

Stabilization of Oxidation States. In the preceding chapter many of the coordination compounds discussed contained tripositive cobalt. That this is not a stable oxidation state in simple cobalt compounds is shown by the half-reaction

$$Co^{+2}(aq) \rightleftharpoons Co^{+3}(aq) + e^- \qquad E^0_{298} = -1.842 \text{ volts}$$

the large negative potential indicating that simple cobalt(III) ion is capable of oxidizing not only many common anions but water as well. However, in the presence of many coordinating groups, cobalt(III) compounds often form at the expense of cobalt(II) compounds. Correspondingly, the manganese(III) ion is such a powerful oxidizing agent that its soluble salts are incapable of existence in contact with water, whereas such complexes as hexacyanomanganate(III), $[Mn(CN)_6]^{-3}$, are stable and easy to prepare. Such a compound as copper(II) iodide or hypophosphite cannot be obtained because of the reducing power of the anion, but bis(ethylenediamine)copper(II) salts containing these anions show no evidences of reduction of the copper. By the same token, although simple copper(I) salts containing oxidizing anions such as nitrate cannot be prepared, coordination of the copper(I) ion with acetonitrile renders them stable. Silver(II) is known for its powerful oxidizing properties, yet coordination with pyridine markedly decreases this oxidizing power, and a number of comparatively stable tetrapyridinesilver(II) compounds have been prepared. These and many similar examples where coordination has markedly altered the oxidizing or reducing power of a metal ion have been discussed in considerable detail by various authors. [5–8]

Many examples of elements in apparently unusual oxidation states in difficulty soluble compounds are also known. Thus cobalt(III) hydroxide is readily obtained by air or peroxide oxidation of the cobalt(II) compound. Manganese(III) orthophosphate is precipitated after oxidation of manganese(II) with nitric acid in the presence of phosphate even though nitric acid is not ordinarily a sufficiently powerful oxidant to effect the manganese(II)–manganese(III) conversion. The same factors apparently account also for the fact that the ease with which metals can be oxidized to even common oxidation states increases if an anion is present to precipitate the product.

The extents to which oxidation states can be stabilized due to the formation of complexes or difficultly soluble compounds may be measured in terms of the magnitudes of appropriate oxidation potentials. Unfortunately, oxidation potential data are available only for comparatively few systems. Some of the values which are available[3] for various systems are summarized in Tables 8·4, 8·5, and 8·6. For comparison in each series, the standard potential for the simple couple

[5] H. J. Emeléus and J. S. Anderson: *Modern Aspects of Inorganic Chemistry*, pp. 151–153. D. Van Nostrand Co., New York (1938).

[6] M. J. Copley, L. S. Foster, and J. C. Bailar, Jr.: *Chem. Revs.*, **30**, 227 (1942).

[7] A. A. Blanchard: *J. Chem. Education*, **20**, 454 (1943).

[8] J. C. Bailar, Jr.: *J. Chem. Education*, **21**, 523 (1944).

in acid solution is included. These are values for systems free of complexing or precipitating groups. Use of the term aq in association with metal ions in half-reactions for these couples is dictated by lack of knowledge as to the degrees of hydration of the various species.

TABLE 8·4

OXIDATION POTENTIALS FOR COBALT AND IRON COUPLES

Couple	Half-Reaction	E^0_{298}, volts
Co(0)–Co(II)	$Co + xH_2O \rightleftharpoons Co^{+2}(aq) + 2e^-$	+0.277
	$Co + 6NH_3(aq) \rightleftharpoons [Co(NH_3)_6]^{+2} + 2e^-$	+0.422
	$Co + CO_3^{-2} \rightleftharpoons CoCO_3 + 2e^-$	+0.632
	$Co + 2OH^- \rightleftharpoons Co(OH)_2 + 2e^-$	+0.73
	$Co + S^{-2} \rightleftharpoons CoS(\beta) + 2e^-$	+1.07
Co(II)–Co(III)	$Co^{+2}(aq) \rightleftharpoons Co^{+3}(aq) + e^-$	−1.842
	$Co(OH)_2 + OH^- \rightleftharpoons Co(OH)_3 + e^-$	−0.2
	$[Co(NH_3)_6]^{+2} \rightleftharpoons [Co(NH_3)_6]^{+3} + e^-$	−0.1
	$[Co(CN)_6]^{-4} \rightleftharpoons [Co(CN)_6]^{-3} + e^-$	+0.83
Fe(0)–Fe(II)	$Fe + xH_2O \rightleftharpoons Fe^{+2}(aq) + 2e^-$	+0.440
	$Fe + CO_3^{-2} \rightleftharpoons FeCO_3 + 2e^-$	+0.755
	$Fe + 2OH^- \rightleftharpoons Fe(OH)_2 + 2e^-$	+0.877
	$Fe + S^{-2} \rightleftharpoons FeS + 2e^-$	+1.00
	$Fe + 6CN^- \rightleftharpoons [Fe(CN)_6]^{-4} + 2e^-$	ca. +1.5
Fe(II)–Fe(III)	$Fe^{+2}(aq) \rightleftharpoons Fe^{+3}(aq) + e^-$	−0.771
	$2FeS + S^{-2} \rightleftharpoons Fe_2S_3 + 2e^-$	+0.7
	$Fe(OH)_2 + CH^- \rightleftharpoons Fe(OH)_3 + e^-$	+0.56
	$Fe^{+2} + 6F^- \rightleftharpoons [FeF_6]^{-3} + e^-$	> −0.4
	$[Fe(CN)_6]^{-4} \rightleftharpoons [Fe(CN)_6]^{-3} + e^-$	−0.36
	$[Fe(dipy)_3]^{+2} \rightleftharpoons [Fe(dipy)_3]^{+3} + e^-$	ca. −1.1
	$[Fe(ophen)_3]^{+2} \rightleftharpoons [Fe(ophen)_3]^{+3} + e^-$	−1.14
	$[Fe(NO_2\text{–}ophen)_3]^{+2} \rightleftharpoons [Fe(NO_2\text{–}ophen)_3]^{+3} + e^-$	−1.25

dipy = dipyridyl, ophen = orthophenanthroline, NO_2-ophen = nitro-orthophenanthroline.

Data summarized in Table 8·4 indicate clearly that oxidation of cobalt(0) to cobalt(II) is much easier to effect in the presence of precipitating or complexing groups than in their absence. These differences are even more striking with the cobalt(II)–cobalt(III) couples. Addition of either hydroxyl ion or ammonia so reduces the oxidizing power of cobalt(III) that oxidation to the tripositive state may be effected with atmospheric oxygen (for $H_2O \rightleftharpoons 2H^+ + \frac{1}{2}O_2 + 2e^-$, $E^0_{298} = -1.229$ volts). In the presence of cyanide, stabilization is so pronounced that the cobalt(II) compound is oxidized by water and has no stable existence in aqueous solution. Among the iron(II)–iron(III) couples listed, examples of the stabilization of both oxidation states appear, but as with cobalt the oxidation of elemental iron is uniformly easier in the presence of groups which precipitate or complex the oxidation product than in their absence.

TABLE 8·5
OXIDATION POTENTIALS FOR COPPER COUPLES

Couple	Half-Reaction	E^0_{298}, volts
Cu(0)–Cu(I)	$Cu + xH_2O \rightleftharpoons Cu^+(aq) + e^-$	−0.522
	$Cu + 2Cl^- \rightleftharpoons [CuCl_2]^- + e^-$	−0.19
	$Cu + Cl^- \rightleftharpoons CuCl + e^-$	−0.124
	$Cu + 2Br^- \rightleftharpoons [CuBr_2]^- + e^-$	−0.05
	$Cu + Br^- \rightleftharpoons CuBr + e^-$	−0.03
	$Cu + 2I^- \rightleftharpoons [CuI_2]^- + e^-$	0.00
	$Cu + 2NH_3 \rightleftharpoons [Cu(NH_3)_2]^+ + e^-$	+0.11
	$Cu + I^- \rightleftharpoons CuI + e^-$	+0.19
	$Cu + SCN^- \rightleftharpoons CuSCN + e^-$	ca. +0.27
	$2Cu + 2OH^- \rightleftharpoons Cu_2O + H_2O + 2e^-$	+0.361
	$Cu + 2CN^- \rightleftharpoons [Cu(CN)_2]^- + e^-$	ca. +0.43
	$2Cu + S^{-2} \rightleftharpoons Cu_2S + 2e^-$	+0.95
Cu(0)–Cu(II)	$Cu + xH_2O \rightleftharpoons Cu^{+2}(aq) + 2e^-$	−0.3448
	$Cu + CO_3^{-2} \rightleftharpoons CuCO_3 + 2e^-$	−0.053
	$Cu + 4NH_3 \rightleftharpoons [Cu(NH_3)_4]^{+2} + 2e^-$	+0.05
	$Cu + 2OH^- \rightleftharpoons Cu(OH)_2 + 2e^-$	+0.224
	$Cu + S^{-2} \rightleftharpoons CuS + 2e^-$	+0.76
Cu(I)–Cu(II)	$Cu^+(aq) \rightleftharpoons Cu^{+2}(aq) + e^-$	−0.167
	$CuCl \rightleftharpoons Cu^{+2} + Cl^- + e^-$	−0.566
	$CuBr \rightleftharpoons Cu^{+2} + Br^- + e^-$	−0.657
	$CuI \rightleftharpoons Cu^{+2} + I^- + e^-$	−0.877
	$[Cu(CN)_2]^- \rightleftharpoons Cu^{+2}(aq) + 2CN^- + e^-$	ca. −1.12
	$[Cu(NH_3)_2]^+ + 2NH_3 \rightleftharpoons [Cu(NH_3)_4]^{+2} + e^-$	0.0
	$Cu_2S + S^{-2} \rightleftharpoons 2CuS + 2e^-$	+0.58

Data in Tables 8·5 and 8·6 indicate the same trends for oxidation of copper(0) and silver(0), respectively. It follows that in any of these series conversion of one oxidation product to another in a reaction characterized by a higher positive potential will occur readily, but the reverse conversions can be effected only in those cases where the oxidation potential values are sufficiently close to each other to permit sufficient alterations by concentration (activity) control.

These and other oxidation state stabilizations probably cannot be reduced to a common simple explanation. However, some general insight into the effects of precipitation and complex formation on oxidation potential values can be gained by a consideration of activity (concentration) effects as indicated by Equation 8·4. It is apparent that reduction in activities (concentrations) of the products in any given couple without corresponding reductions in the activities of the reactants will correct the standard potential in a positive direction to a new value. Correspondingly, reductions in activities (concentrations) of the reactants without balancing alterations for the products will render the true potential more negative than the standard value.

TABLE 8·6

OXIDATION POTENTIALS FOR AG(0)–AG(I) COUPLES

Half-Reaction	E^0_{298}, volts
$Ag + xH_2O \rightleftharpoons Ag^+(aq) + e^-$	−0.7995
$2Ag + SO_4^{-2} \rightleftharpoons Ag_2SO_4 + 2e^-$	−0.65
$Ag + C_2H_3O_2^- \rightleftharpoons AgC_2H_3O_2 + e^-$	−0.64
$Ag + NO_2^- \rightleftharpoons AgNO_2 + e^-$	−0.59
$Ag + BrO_3^- \rightleftharpoons AgBrO_3 + e^-$	−0.55
$2Ag + C_2O_4^{-2} \rightleftharpoons Ag_2C_2O_4 + 2e^-$	−0.47
$2Ag + CO_3^{-2} \rightleftharpoons Ag_2CO_3 + 2e^-$	−0.46
$2Ag + CrO_4^{-2} \rightleftharpoons Ag_2CrO_4 + 2e^-$	−0.45
$Ag + 2NH_3 \rightleftharpoons [Ag(NH_3)_2]^+ + e^-$	−0.37
$Ag + IO_3^- \rightleftharpoons AgIO_3 + e^-$	−0.37
$2Ag + 2OH^- \rightleftharpoons Ag_2O + H_2O + 2e^-$	−0.344
$Ag + Cl^- \rightleftharpoons AgCl + e^-$	−0.222
$4Ag + Fe(CN)_6^{-4} \rightleftharpoons Ag_4Fe(CN)_6 + 4e^-$	−0.19
$Ag + SCN^- \rightleftharpoons AgSCN + e^-$	−0.09
$Ag + Br^- \rightleftharpoons AgBr + e^-$	−0.073
$Ag + 2S_2O_3^{-2} \rightleftharpoons [Ag(S_2O_3)_2]^{-3} + e^-$	−0.01
$Ag + CN^- \rightleftharpoons AgCN + e^-$	+0.04
$Ag + I^- \rightleftharpoons AgI + e^-$	+0.15
$Ag + 2CN^- \rightleftharpoons [Ag(CN)_2]^- + e^-$	+0.29
$2Ag + S^{-2} \rightleftharpoons Ag_2S + 2e^-$	+0.71

Both precipitation and complex ion formation effect reductions in ion activities. For a given couple, a given reagent seldom if ever causes the same reduction in activities for both oxidation states. If it is assumed, therefore, that any couple containing a precipitate or a complex ion is only a variation of the simple couple involving the free ions; then its potential may be regarded as a corrected value based upon the standard potential of the simple reaction. This concept is admittedly not completely valid, but it serves as a useful approximation. The direction in which this correction is made, as reflected by the potential for the second couple, will then reflect the relative effect of the precipitating or complexing agent in removing reactant or product ions.

To illustrate, consider the couples

$$Co^{+2}(aq) \rightleftharpoons Co^{+3}(aq) + e^- \qquad E^0_{298} = -1.842 \text{ volts}$$

and

$$[Co(NH_3)_6]^{+2} \rightleftharpoons [Co(NH_3)_6]^{+3} + e^- \qquad E^0_{298} = -0.1 \text{ volt}$$

Here the actual potential for the second couple may be related roughly to that of the first as

$$E = -1.842 - \frac{0.059}{1} \log a_{Co^{+3}}/a_{Co^{+2}} \qquad (8{\cdot}15)$$

The fact that the potential for the second couple is much less negative than that for the first would be interpreted in terms of Equation 8·15 as being due to a reduction in the activity of the cobalt(III) ion without corresponding alteration in that for the cobalt(II) ion. This is in agreement with experimental observation that hexamminecobalt(III) ion is very much less dissociated into its components than is its cobalt(II) analog.

Similar considerations may be applied to other reactions of the types summarized in Tables 8·4, 8·5, and 8·6. Thus oxidation of copper(I) to copper(II) in the presence of chloride ion is more difficult to effect than in the case of the aqueous ions alone because of the insolubility of copper(I) chloride and consequent reduction in the activity (concentration) of copper(I) ion. On the other hand, in the presence of sulfide ion, the reverse is true because the copper(II) compound is less soluble than the copper(I) compound. Furthermore, in Table 8·6, the potentials as arranged in order of increasing positive character indicate a parallel decrease in activity (concentration) of silver ion.

Such considerations are essentially approximate in character, but they are useful in describing trends among a series of related materials. For convenience in these and other approximations, concentrations may be employed instead of activities.

SUGGESTED SUPPLEMENTARY REFERENCES

S. Glasstone: "Oxidation Numbers and Valence," *J. Chem. Education*, **25**, 278 (1948).

W. M. Latimer: *The Oxidation States of the Elements and Their Potentials in Aqueous Solutions*. Prentice-Hall, New York (1938).

P. Delahay, M. Pourbaix, and P. van Rysselberghe: "Potential-*p*H Diagrams," *J. Chem. Education*, **27**, 683 (1950).

A. A. Frost: "Oxidation Potential-Free Energy Diagrams," *J. Am. Chem. Soc.*, **73**, 2680 (1951).

CHAPTER 9

Acids and Bases

Few subjects in chemistry have excited more interest and more resultant controversy than the subjects of acids and bases. Althoug the terms *acid* and *base* are so common in chemical parlance as to b acceptable almost without question or definition under most circum stances, more careful consideration will show how indefinite they hav become in much of our thinking. One may well ask what is an acid o what is a base? These questions have usually been answered i terms of one or more of several theoretical approaches, but, funda mentally, they should be answered in terms of the satisfaction of certai experimental facts. Thus, we have come to regard acids and bases a mutual opposites which in general lose their defining properties whe brought in contact with each other. Acids have been characterize by their tastes, by their effects upon indicators, and by their catalyti effects upon certain reactions. Such properties must be satisfactoril accounted for by any theoretical concept of acid constitutions. N theory which has been advanced or is likely to be advanced is usefu unless the experimental behaviors are considered, and much of th confusion and controversy which have resulted from the varied moder approaches to acid-base behavior disappear when these approache are considered from the factual point of view.

The trend toward experimental justification of theoretical point of view is emphasized by Lewis,[1] who has listed the following phenom nological criteria of acid-base behavior:

1. "When an acid and a base can combine, the process of combin tion, or neutralization, is a rapid one.
2. "An acid or a base will replace a weaker acid or base from i compounds.
3. "Acids and bases may be titrated against one another by the u of substances, usually colored, known as indicators.
4. "Both acids and bases play an extremely important part in pr moting chemical processes through their action as catalysts."

[1] G. N. Lewis: *J. Franklin Inst.*, **226**, 293 (1938).

Such criteria as these should be used in the evaluation of the various approaches to be presented in this discussion.

SIGNIFICANT DEVELOPMENTS IN THE HISTORY OF THE ACID-BASE CONCEPT

It is instructive to preface modern acid-base concepts with a brief review of some of the more important developments which have led to them. These developments illustrate significant changes in thinking which have been brought about by changes in the understanding of chemical principles. This general subject has been ably discussed in great detail by Walden.[2]

There is evidence that certain salts were recognized in the thirteenth century, but the formulation of theories about acids and bases was slow through the alchemical periods of the thirteenth to seventeenth centuries. It remained for Boyle in 1680 to characterize acids as dissolving many substances, as precipitating sulfur from its solutions in alkalies, as changing blue plant dyes to red, and as losing all these properties on contact with alkalies.

Concepts in the eighteenth century centered around sour taste, reaction with limestone, the turning of syrup of violet to red, and production of neutral materials with alkalies as characteristics of acids. These concepts culminated in 1787 with Lavoisier's statement that acids are binary compounds, one element in which is oxygen and the other the basic principle.

The acidifying character of oxygen was acceptable until Davy, in 1811, upon analyzing muriatic acid could find no oxygen. His conclusion that hydrogen represented the fundamental acidifying principle may be regarded as the forerunner of many of our present-day ideas, although it is significant that in 1814 Davy stated further that acidity does not depend upon any one elementary substance but rather upon a peculiar combination of various substances.

In spite of vigorous defense of the oxygen theory by many chemists, among them Berzelius, it was doomed by the more fundamental ideas of Davy and certain of his contemporaries. Thus Gay-Lussac in 1814 concluded that an acid was any body neutralizing alkalinity and that acids and bases could be defined only in terms of each other. This idea, in conjunction with Davy's rather similar concept, must be regarded as fundamental to much modern thought.

Further support of the hydrogen theory of acidity was advanced in 1838 by Liebig, who regarded acids as compounds containing hydrogen

[2] P. Walden: *Salts, Acids, and Bases*. McGraw-Hill Book Co., New York (1929).

which could be replaced by metals. The labile character of such hydrogen was acceptable as a criterion for acidity for many subsequent years, and Liebig's rather clear insight into the properties of acids (especially organic acids) has become increasingly apparent.

One other development should be cited to promote a clear appreciation of modern concepts. The recognition by Faraday in 1834 that electrolytic conductance is due to charged particles (ions) and his characterization of acids, bases, and salts as electrolytes laid much of the foundation for later developments.

SEMI-MODERN AND MODERN APPROACHES TO THE ACID-BASE CONCEPT

Much that characterizes present-day views on acids and bases is traceable to the theory of electrolytic dissociation proposed in 1884 by Arrhenius and developed later by Ostwald. Modern concepts have grown in scope from those following directly from the Arrhenius theory to embrace more and more types of materials as acids and bases.[3] This is apparent in the discussion which follows, where the arrangement is chosen to emphasize this trend.

The water-ion or Arrhenius concept

On the basis of the Arrhenius theory, an acid is definable as any hydrogen-containing compound which yields hydrogen ions in water solution and a base as any hydroxy compound which yields hydroxyl ions in water solution. The process of neutralization then amounts to the combination of hydrogen and hydroxyl ions to form water.

This concept has been invaluable in elucidating the characteristics of aqueous solutions, and most of our views on the quantitative aspects of neutralization, hydrolysis, acid and base strength, etc., have grown up around it. Although the approach is limited in scope by its very definitions, it is still extremely useful and certainly should not be discarded as some have suggested. With slight modifications, it often does more to clarify the behaviors of aqueous solutions than some of the more complex views.

Since the general implications of the water-ion theory are quite familiar, no expansion beyond the citing of objections which have been raised to it need be given here. Serious among these objections is that basic and amphoteric characters are limited to hydroxy compounds, although many ions possess basic properties comparable to those of the hydroxyl ion, and amphoterism is well characterized among many oxides, sulfides, halides, etc., as well as among hydroxides

[3] N. F. Hall: *J. Chem. Education*, **17**, 124 (1940).

Perhaps an equally serious objection involves the limitation of the neutralization process to reactions occurring in aqueous solutions, although reactions involving salt formation occur in many other solvents and even in the absence of solvent. The objection that hydrogen ions cannot exist as such in aqueous solutions because of their high hydrational energy (ca. 250 kcal. per mole) cannot be regarded as serious, for the theory is sufficiently flexible to admit the hydrated hydrogen ion as the acidifying principle. Nor can the limitation of acid strength to a function of the solvent water be considered too serious a defect since acids are most often compared in aqueous solution. The approach is necessarily a limited one but thoroughly useful within its limitations.

The protonic concept

As a logical extension of the water-ion theory, the protonic concept of acidity was advanced nearly simultaneously by Brønsted[4] and Lowry[5] in 1923. Inasmuch as the treatment given by Brønsted is the more comprehensive and inasmuch as Lowry has done but little by comparison to extend the theory, the theory usually bears Brønsted's name.

In terms of this approach, acids and bases are characterized and interrelated by the equation

$$\text{acid (A)} \rightleftharpoons \text{base (B)} + \text{proton } (H^+) \tag{9·1}$$

It follows then that an acid is any hydrogen-containing molecule or ion which is capable of releasing a proton (i.e., of acting as a proton donor) whereas a base is any molecule or ion which is capable of combining with a proton (i.e., of acting as a proton acceptor), By definition, acids and bases are thus made independent of a solvent and bear no relationship to salts. Salts are to be regarded as mere aggregations of positive and negative ions which may be only indirectly related to acids and bases. It is implied further that materials may be inherently acidic or basic without necessarily exhibiting the property.

Although a material can be inherently an acid, it can function as such only when it is in contact with some base other than that derived directly from itself through the loss of a proton. Similarly, an inherently basic substance will function as an actual base only when brought in contact with some proton donor. In practice, therefore, acid-base reactions reduce fundamentally to competitions for protons expressi-

[4] J. N. Brønsted: *Rec. trav. chim.*, **42,** 718 (1923).
[5] T. M. Lowry: *Chem. and Ind.*, **42,** 43 (1923); *Trans. Faraday Soc.*, **20,** 13 (1924).

ble as equilibria of the type

$$\text{acid}_1 + \text{base}_2 \rightleftharpoons \text{acid}_2 + \text{base}_1 \quad (9\cdot2)$$

such equilibria being displaced in the direction of the weaker acid and base. In such an equilibrium, *base*$_1$ may be regarded as derived from *acid*$_1$ by the loss of a proton by the latter, and it is called the corresponding or *conjugate base* of that acid. It follows that in like fashion one may refer to the *conjugate acid* of some particular base. These equilibria indicate further that neutralization as defined in terms of salt formation has no place in this theory. One can, however, conveniently consider the transfer of a proton from an acid to a base as amounting to a neutralization process.

Acids and Bases in Aqueous Solutions. The Brønsted-Lowry concept has proved particularly advantageous in the treatment of aqueous solutions. In a measure, this success is due to recognition of the dualistic role played by water in acid-base processes. Thus water can function as an acid in the presence of bases stronger than itself. This is exemplified by its donation of protons to such bases as ammonia and the carbonate ion as

$$H_2O + NH_3 \rightleftharpoons NH_4^+ + OH^-$$
$$H_2O + CO_3^{-2} \rightleftharpoons HCO_3^- + OH^-$$

Furthermore, water can function as a base in the presence of acids stronger than itself. This is exemplified by its acceptance of protons from such acids as hydrogen chloride, the acid sulfate ion, and the hydrated aluminum ion as

$$HCl + H_2O \rightleftharpoons H_3O^+ + Cl^-$$
$$HSO_4^- + H_2O \rightleftharpoons H_3O^+ + SO_4^{-2}$$
$$Al(H_2O)_x^{+3} + H_2O \rightleftharpoons H_3O^+ + Al(H_2O)_{x-1}(OH)^{+2}$$

In terms of such behavior, the acids characteristic of the water-ion approach are readily systematized, and the role of water as an acid-base solvent becomes apparent.

It follows that in water solutions acids and bases may be molecular, cationic, or anionic in character, the molecular acids and the anionic bases being the commonest representatives. The recognition of this generalization and the consequent systematic classification of a large number of otherwise apparently unrelated materials represent truly important contributions of the protonic theory. The scope of the approach is indicated by the typical acids and bases listed in Table 9·1

In addition to broadening the scope of acid-base relationships in aqueous solutions by pointing out the acidic and basic properties of a variety of materials, the protonic concept is perhaps most useful in accounting logically for the hydrolysis of salt solutions. When a salt is dissolved in water, an unbalance in the concentrations of solvent cation (H_3O^+) and anion (OH^-) will result if the salt cation and anion differ in their proton donor and acceptor properties toward water. Thus a solution of ammonium chloride has a *p*H somewhat less than 7 because the proton donor ability of the ammonium ion exceeds the proton acceptor ability of the chloride ion, and a measurable excess of hydronium ions appears in the solution. Correspondingly, a solution of sodium carbonate is alkaline in character because the carbonate ion

TABLE 9·1

Brønsted Acids and Bases in Aqueous Solution

Type	Typical Acids	Typical Bases
Molecular	HI, HBr, HCl, HF, HNO_3, H_2SO_4, $HClO_4$, H_3PO_4, H_2S, H_2O	NH_3, N_2H_4, NH_2OH, aliphatic amines, aromatic amines, H_2O
Cationic	$Al(H_2O)_x^{+3}$, NH_4^+, $Fe(H_2O)_x^{+3}$, $Cu(H_2O)_x^{+2}$	$Al(H_2O)_{x-1}(OH)^{+2}$, $Cu(H_2O)_{x-1}(OH)^+$
Anionic	HSO_4^-, $H_2PO_4^-$, HCO_3^-, HS^-	I^-, Br^-, Cl^-, F^-, HSO_4^-, SO_4^{-2}, HPO_4^{-2}, CN^-, HCO_3^-, CO_3^{-2}, OH^-, O^{-2}

shows proton acceptor tendencies exceeding the proton donor properties of the hydrated sodium ion. On the other hand, a solution of aluminum chloride reacts acidic because the hydrated aluminum ion shows marked proton donor characteristics whereas the chloride ion is too weak a base to accept protons from water to a significant extent. Such a salt as sodium chloride yields an essentially neutral solution because neither ion shows acidic or basic tendencies toward water. The comparative proton donor abilities of hydrated cations and further information useful to the understanding of salt hydrolysis will be presented later in conjunction with a discussion of acid and base strengths (pp. 314–315; 321).

Acids and Bases in Non-aqueous Solutions. The versatility of the protonic approach is demonstrated by its ready extension to relationships in non-aqueous solvents. Acidic and basic properties of solutes are markedly influenced by the relative proton donor and acceptor properties of the solvent itself. On the basis of such characteristics, a number of types of solvents are distinguishable,[6] the most important of which[7] are summarized in Table 9·2.

[6] J. N. Brønsted: *Ber.*, **61,** 2049 (1928).

[7] N. F. Hall: *Chem. Revs.*, **8,** 191 (1931).

TABLE 9·2

TYPES OF PROTONIC SOLVENTS

Solvent Type	Characteristics	Examples
Acidic	tendency to release protons	HF, H_2SO_4, CH_3COOH, HCOOH, HCN, C_6H_5OH
Basic	tendency to accept protons	NH_3, N_2H_4, NH_2OH, amines
Amphiprotic	tendency either to release or to accept protons	H_2O, alcohols
Aprotic	tendency neither to release nor to accept protons	C_6H_6, $CHCl_3$, $C_2H_4Cl_2$

The effect of solvent type upon the acid-base character of the solute may be profound. Thus urea behaves as an acid when dissolved in liquid ammonia (a basic solvent) but as a strong base in anhydrous formic acid (an acidic solvent). The reactions occurring can be formulated as

$$\mathrm{CO(NH_2)_2} + \mathrm{NH_3} \rightleftharpoons \mathrm{CO(NH^-)(NH_2)} + \mathrm{NH_4^+}$$

$$\underset{\text{acid}}{\mathrm{HCOOH}} + \underset{\text{base}}{\mathrm{CO(NH_2)_2}} \rightleftharpoons \underset{\text{base}}{\mathrm{HCOO^-}} + \underset{\text{acid}}{\mathrm{CO(NH_3^+)(NH_2)}}$$

Correspondingly, to cite another example, the material which we call nitric acid on the basis of its properties in aqueous solutions apparently behaves as a proton acceptor in liquid hydrogen fluoride,[8]

$$HNO_3 + HF \rightleftharpoons H_2NO_3^+ + F^-$$

As a general rule, materials which are weakly basic in the amphiprotic solvent water become more strongly basic in highly acidic solvents[9–13] such as acetic and formic acids, and are often titratable therein. Correspondingly, acidic strength is enhanced in a basic solvent.

The Strengths of Acids and Bases. Several non-definitive references have been made to acid strength and to base strength. In a purely qualitative fashion, one can say that acid strength is measured by the

[8] J. H. Simons: *Chem. Revs.*, **8**, 213 (1931).
[9] N. F. Hall and T. H. Werner: *J. Am. Chem. Soc.*, **50**, 2367 (1928).
[10] J. B. Conant and T. H. Werner: *J. Am. Chem. Soc.*, **52**, 4436 (1930).
[11] N. F. Hall: *J. Am. Chem. Soc.*, **52**, 5115 (1930).
[12] L. P. Hammett and N. Dietz: *J. Am. Chem. Soc.*, **52**, 4795 (1930).
[13] L. P. Hammett: *Chem. Revs.*, **13**, 61 (1933).

extent to which protons are released and base strength by the extent to which they are accepted. One can point out further that the conjugate base of a strong acid is necessarily weak and of a weak acid necessarily strong. In a more quantitative fashion, however, strengths should be expressed in terms of the equilibrium constants for Equation 9·1, that is, for acid strength by

$$K_A = a_B a_{H^+}/a_A \qquad (9\cdot3)$$

and for base strength by

$$K_B = a_A/a_B a_{H^+}, \qquad (9\cdot4)$$

where the appropriate activities (p. 285) are designated by *a*'s.

As has been shown, however, such simple equilibria as indicated by Equation 9·1 are not attainable in practice, and the observed equilibria are always of the type indicated in Equation 9·2, that is, of the type

$$A_1 + B_2 \rightleftharpoons A_2 + B_1 \qquad (9\cdot5)$$

for which

$$K = a_{A_2}a_{B_1}/a_{A_1}a_{B_2} \qquad (9\cdot6)$$

Such equilibria as these can be used for the evaluation of relative acid and base strengths in a series of materials if one acid-base pair is common to all the equilibria. For comparisons in water solution, such a condition is maintained, and one may write

$$A + H_2O \rightleftharpoons H_3O^+ + B \qquad (9\cdot7)$$

for which

$$K' = a_{H_3O^+} \cdot a_B/a_A a_{H_2O} \qquad (9\cdot8)$$

Since the activity of the water in dilute solutions may be regarded as constant, we then have, employing a new constant which includes the activity of the water,

$$K_A' = a_{H_3O^+} \cdot a_B/a_A \qquad (9\cdot9)$$

and

$$K_B' = a_A/a_{H_3O^+}a_B \qquad (9\cdot10)$$

where the magnitudes of K_A' and K_B' indicate the strengths of the acid A and the base B, respectively.

Inasmuch as it is quite impossible to evaluate accurately (if at all) the activities of the materials involved in such equilibria, the characteristic constants (k_A' and k_B') usually given are based upon concentrations rather than activities. These constants are identical with the K_A' and K_B' of Equations 9·9 and 9·10 only at infinite dilution. Summarized in Table 9·3 are constants (k_A') for a number of representative

TABLE 9·3

RELATIVE STRENGTHS OF ACIDS IN WATER SOLUTION

Acid	Conjugate Base	k_A'	pk_A'	Temperature, °C.
$HClO_4$	ClO_4^-	?	highly neg.	..
HCl	Cl^-	$\sim 10^{+7}$	~ -7	25
HNO_3	NO_3^-	?	neg.	..
H_2SO_4	HSO_4^-	?	neg.	..
H_3O^+	H_2O	55.5	−1.74	25
HIO_3	IO_3^-	1.9×10^{-1}	0.72	25
$H_4P_2O_7$	$H_3P_2O_7^-$	1.4×10^{-1}	0.85	25
$H_2C_2O_4$	$HC_2O_4^-$	5.9×10^{-2}	1.23	25
H_3PO_3	$H_2PO_3^-$	5×10^{-2}	1.30	25
H_5IO_6	$H_4IO_6^-$	2.3×10^{-2}	1.64	25
HSO_4^-	SO_4^{-2}	2×10^{-2}	1.70	18
H_2SO_3	HSO_3^-	1.7×10^{-2}	1.77	25
$H_3P_2O_7^-$	$H_2P_2O_7^{-2}$	1.1×10^{-2}	1.96	18
H_3PO_2	$H_2PO_2^-$	1×10^{-2}	2.00	25
$HClO_2$	ClO_2^-	10^{-2}	2	25
H_3PO_4	$H_2PO_4^-$	7.5×10^{-3}	2.12	18
$Fe(H_2O)_x^{+3}$	$Fe(H_2O)_{x-1}(OH)^{+2}$	6.3×10^{-3}	2.20	18
H_3AsO_4	$H_2AsO_4^-$	4.8×10^{-3}	2.32	25
H_2SeO_3	$HSeO_3^-$	3×10^{-3}	2.52	25
H_2Te	HTe^-	2.3×10^{-3}	2.64	25
HF	F^-	7.2×10^{-4}	3.14	25
HNO_2	NO_2^-	4.5×10^{-4}	3.35	25
HCO_2H	HCO_2^-	1.8×10^{-4}	3.74	18
H_2Se	HSe^-	1.7×10^{-4}	3.77	25
$HOCN$	OCN^-	1.2×10^{-4}	3.92	18
$HSCN$	SCN^-	10^{-4}	4	18
$Cr(H_2O)_x^{+3}$	$Cr(H_2O)_{x-1}(OH)^{+2}$	10^{-4}	4	25
$HC_2O_4^-$	$C_2O_4^{-2}$	6.4×10^{-5}	4.19	25
$H_2PO_3^-$	HPO_3^{-2}	2×10^{-5}	4.70	25
HN_3	N_3^-	1.9×10^{-5}	4.72	25
$HC_2H_3O_2$	$C_2H_3O_2^-$	1.9×10^{-5}	4.72	25
$Al(H_2O)_x^{+3}$	$Al(H_2O)_{x-1}(OH)^{+2}$	1.3×10^{-5}	4.89	18
HTe^-	Te^{-2}	1×10^{-5}	5.00	25
$H_4IO_6^-$	$H_3IO_6^{-2}$	1×10^{-6}	6.00	25
H_2CO_3	HCO_3^-	3.5×10^{-7}	6.46	25
$H_2P_2O_7^{-2}$	$HP_2O_7^{-3}$	2.9×10^{-7}	6.54	18
H_2S	HS^-	9.1×10^{-8}	7.04	18
$H_2N_2O_2$	$HN_2O_2^-$	9×10^{-8}	7.05	25
HSO_3^-	SO_3^{-2}	6.24×10^{-8}	7.20	25
$H_2PO_4^-$	HPO_4^{-2}	5.9×10^{-8}	7.23	18
$HOCl$	OCl^-	3.7×10^{-8}	7.43	18
$HP_2O_7^{-3}$	$P_2O_7^{-4}$	3.6×10^{-9}	8.44	18
HCN	CN^-	7.2×10^{-10}	9.14	25

TABLE 9·3 (*Continued*)

Acid	Conjugate Base	k_A'	pk_A'	Temperature, °C.
$HAsO_2$	AsO_2^-	6×10^{-10}	9.22	25
H_3BO_3	$H_2BO_3^-$	5.8×10^{-10}	9.24	25
NH_4^+	NH_3	3.3×10^{-10}	9.48	18
HSe^-	Se^{-2}	10^{-10}	10	25
HCO_3^-	CO_3^{-2}	6×10^{-11}	10.22	25
HIO	IO^-	1×10^{-11}	11.00	25
$HN_2O_2^-$	$N_2O_2^{-2}$	1×10^{-11}	11.00	25
H_2O_2	HO_2^-	2.4×10^{-12}	11.62	25
H_3AlO_3	$H_2AlO_3^-$	6.3×10^{-13}	12.20	25
HPO_4^{-2}	PO_4^{-3}	3.6×10^{-13}	12.44	18
$Ca(H_2O)_x^{+2}$	$Ca(H_2O)_{x-1}(OH)^+$	10^{-13}	13	25
HS^-	S^{-2}	1.2×10^{-15}	14.92	18
H_2O	OH^-	1.07×10^{-16}	15.97	18
OH^-	O^{-2}	$< 10^{-36}$	> 36	25

acids. Given also are the negative logarithms, or pk_A' values. The latter are somewhat more useful for comparisons than the former.

Although the relative strengths of many acids are clearly indicated by such data, an uncertainty appears for the strongest acids. This uncertainty is ascribable to the basic properties of the solvent, water. Really, the strength of no acid stronger than the hydronium ion can be evaluated in aqueous solution because of the immediate and quantitative conversion of such an acid to hydronium ion. The same condition applies to bases, for the acidic properties of water are such that all bases stronger than the hydroxyl ion are immediately converted to that ion on contact with water. The net result is that all the strongest acids appear to be of about the same strength in water solution, and, to a somewhat lesser extent, the same is true of the strongest bases. Water, therefore, may be regarded as exerting a leveling effect upon acid and base strength. In a similar fashion, any solvent with basic properties will level the strengths of acids, and any solvent with acidic properties will level the strengths of bases.

Some indication, however, that the individual strengths of the very strong acids are manifested in sufficiently concentrated aqueous solutions is given in studies upon the catalytic effects of various acids upon the inversion of sucrose.[14] The relative effects of several acids studied upon the rate of inversion, as shown in Figure 9·1, are indicative of increases in intrinsic strength in the series CCl_3CO_2H, HNO_3, HCl, HBr, $HClO_4$, in agreement with predicted trends (pp. 318–321).

[14] A. Hantzsch and A. Weissberger: *Z. physik. Chem.*, **125**, 251 (1927).

A true evaluation of acid (or base) strength independent of the solvent is desirable. Whether universal strength scales applicable to any and all solvents and transferable from one solvent to another can ever be devised is questionable in view of the many complicating factors involved. However, a number of attempts to establish such scales through the use of solvents which exert little or no leveling effects have been made. Such solvents may be called *differentiating* in character since they tend to bring out inherent differences among materials.

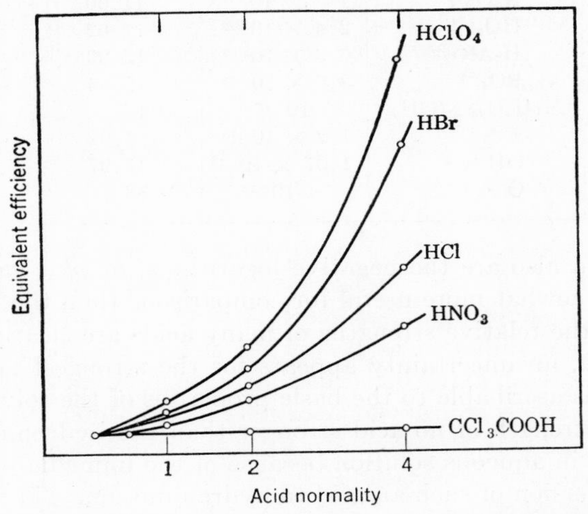

Fig. 9·1. Relative strengths of various acids in aqueous solution as shown by their efficiencies in catalyzing the inversion of sucrose.

Perhaps the most useful of the differentiating solvents are those which are aprotic, since they can impose no limitations upon acidic or basic properties through tendencies toward proton loss or gain. In such solvents, acid-base systems can be established only through the introduction of a second base or acid. For purposes of measurement and comparison, the second base or acid can conveniently be an indicator, and through the proper choice of indicators any desired range of acid or base strength can be investigated in the solvent in question.

Thus, if HA and B represent respectively some acid and one form of an indicator, the equilibrium

$$HA + B \rightleftharpoons HB + A \tag{9·11}$$

will be established between the acid and the indicator. For this equilibrium,

$$K = \frac{K_{HA}}{K_{HB}} = \frac{c_{HB}}{c_B} \cdot \frac{c_A}{c_{HA}} \qquad (9\cdot12)$$

where the magnitude of K measures acidity and depends upon the comparative strengths of the two acids HA and HB, and concentrations (c) are employed. Since the two forms of the indicator, B and HB, possess different colors, adjustment of the relative amounts of HA and its conjugate base A to produce a given indicator color (i.e., a certain ratio of c_{HB} to c_B) and an evaluation of the ratio of c_A to c_{HA} should give a measure of the acid strength of HA as compared with the indicator. Repetition for a series of acids should then indicate the relative strengths of these acids.

Such procedures have been rather extensively employed with the aprotic benzene as solvent. Brønsted[15] determined the relative strengths of twenty-four acids (most of them organic) under these conditions and found the qualitative order of strength to be much the same as in water, with hydrogen chloride being the strongest acid investigated. Others[16, 17] have extended these observations, and the entire general subject has been discussed in detail by Hall.[7]

Of particular importance in this connection are the measurements made by Hantzsch and Voigt[18] of relative acid strength in chloroform and ether. Using equi-molar solutions of the dimethyl yellow salts of a number of acids, these investigators determined the dilutions (with solvent) necessary to cause the indicator to change color. At these dilutions, the reactions

$$\underset{\text{salt}}{BH^+X^-} \rightarrow \underset{\text{indicator}}{B} + \underset{\text{acid}}{HX} \qquad (9\cdot13)$$

were assumed to be complete, with the amount of dilution necessary then being a measure of the stability of the dimethyl yellow salt, or the acid strength of HX. For a series of organic acids in dry chloroform, relative dilutions varied from 1 for acetic acid to 95,000 for trichloroacetic acid, whereas in aqueous solution there is only an 11,000-fold increase in dissociation constants between these two. Studies of the same series of acids in dry ether indicated less pronounced differences because of the enhanced basicity of the solvent. In moist chloroform, observed differences were also less because of the leveling effect of the water.

[15] J. N. Brønsted: *Ber.*, **61B**, 2049 (1928).
[16] V. K. LaMer and H. C. Downes: *J. Am. Chem. Soc.*, **55**, 1840 (1933).
[17] V. K. LaMer and H. C. Downes: *Chem. Revs.*, **13**, 47 (1933).
[18] A. Hantzsch and W. Voigt: *Ber.*, **62B**, 975 (1929).

Extension of these observations to the strongest inorganic acids indicated that in dry chloroform necessary dilutions were too high to be measurable significantly. However, under more basic conditions, for example, in moist chloroform or in a mixture of ether with chloroform (dry or moist), significant and measurable differences were noted, with apparent intrinsic strength decreasing in the series $HClO_4$, HBr, HCl, HNO_3. Although values for HI were not given, it is reasonable to assume that this acid would be stronger than HBr but weaker than $HClO_4$.

A similar differentiation in acid strength results when a highly acidic solvent is employed. Thus in acetic acid, displacement of a reaction such as

$$HX + HC_2H_3O_2 \rightleftharpoons H_2C_2H_3O_2^+ + X^-$$

toward the ionic materials is a direct indication of the acid strength of the material HX since acetic acid is in itself very weakly basic.

The general subject of strength among protonic acids has been discussed theoretically in an excellent paper by Hammett.[19] Apparently puzzling anomalies between acid strength as shown by indicator studies in non-ionic systems and by hydrogen ion activity determinations in ionic systems are rendered more logical when considered in relation to the relative dielectric constants (p. 339) of the media involved. Although comparisons of any type within a given solvent need not involve dielectric constant considerations, comparisons of acidities or basicities among several solvents should take into account differences in both solvent basicity and dielectric behavior. It is for this reason that the development of universal strength scales is questionable.

Trends and Regularities in Strengths of Protonic Acids in Aqueous Solutions. The acids listed in Table 9·3 are of three general types, hydro acids (e.g., HCl, H_2S, HS^-), oxy acids (e.g., H_2SO_4, HCO_3^-), or solvated ions (e.g., $Al(H_2O)_x^{+3}$, $Ca(H_2O)_x^{+2}$, NH_4^+). Consideration of the pk_A' values tabulated and the general remarks made in the preceding section indicate the existence of important trends in acidic strengths among these materials.

Among the hydro acids characterizing the elements in any particular periodic family, there is a general increase in acid strength with increasing molecular weight or increasing size of the more electronegative element. This may seem contrary at first glance, to what is expected since it is the reverse of changes in ionic character. Thus, in the series H_2O-H_2S-H_2Se-H_2Te the last compound is at the same time

[19] L. P. Hammett: *J. Am. Chem. Soc.*, **50**, 2666 (1928).

the most strongly acidic and the least ionic. It must be recalled, however, that acid strength is measured by the ease with which a proton can be removed from the other material with which it is combined. The weakening of this bond due to increased size of the non-metal more than compensates for any decrease in ionic character and gives correspondingly increased acidity. On the other hand, in any horizontal series in the periodic system, acid strength increases with the electronegativity of the non-metal present. An example is the increase in the series H_3N-H_2O-HF. Here size changes are proportionally small and are without appreciable effects.

Among the oxy acids, strength is again determined by both the electronegativity and the size of the central element, although the first of these factors is commonly the more important. Such acids all contain the fundamental structure (X = any element)

$$:\ddot{\underset{..}{X}}:\ddot{\underset{..}{O}}:H$$

from which it is apparent that the more electronegative and the smaller the element X the more strongly electrons associated with oxygen will be pulled toward X and the more readily the proton can be removed by a suitable base. If X is a small, highly electronegative element (non-metal), acidic properties will result, but as the size of X increases and its electronegativity decreases, amphoteric behavior will appear and will be followed by completely basic character. According to Gallais,[20] basic character predominates in such compounds when the electronegativity of X is less than 1.7, and acidic character predominates when the electronegativity of X is greater than 1.7. It follows that, as the electronegativity departs more and more from this mean value, basic or acidic strength is enhanced. The presence of additional oxygens attached to X renders X smaller and more positive, thus increasing the acid strength of the compound.

Some examples may be considered with profit. Thus ClOH is an acid, but NaOH gives strongly basic hydroxyl ions in solution. Both H_2SO_3 and H_2SeO_3 are acids, but the former is the stronger. In the series HClO-$HClO_2$-$HClO_3$-$HClO_4$, acid strength increases markedly. All these effects are illustrated admirably among the oxygen-hydrogen compounds of certain transition metals. Thus the manganese(II) compound is basic, the manganese(IV) compound is amphoteric, and the manganese(VI) and manganese(VII) compounds are strongly acidic.

[20] F. Gallais: *Bull. soc. chim. France* [5], **14,** 425 (1947).

The strengths of individual oxy acids as measured by k_A' values show certain regularities. Pauling[21] points out that such strengths can be expressed by two rules:

1. The magnitudes of the successive constants k_1', k_2', k_3' · · · stand in the ratios $1:10^{-5}:10^{-10}$. This generalization is quite generally applicable, as shown by the data in Table 9·3.

2. The magnitude of the first ionization constant (k_1') is dependent upon the value of m in the formula $XO_m(OH)_n$. If $m = 0$, as in $B(OH)_3$, the acid is very weak ($k_1' \geqq 10^{-7}$); if $m = 1$, the acid is weak ($k_1' \cong 10^{-2}$); if $m = 2$, the acid is strong ($k_1' \cong 10^3$); if $m = 3$, the acid is very strong ($k_1' \cong 10^8$). Reference to Table 9·3 again shows the applicability of the generalization.

These rules are invaluable in giving qualitative indications of acid strengths in the absence of tabulations of k_A' or pk_A' values. Pauling's second rule is given in substance by the summary presented by Ricci.[22]

Regularities in k_A' values suggest that such constants might be calculated theoretically. In an important paper, Kossiakoff and Harker[23] calculated many constants very effectively by means of an approach based upon the assumptions that:

1. The value of k_A' is determined by the free energy (p. 284) of transfer of a proton from an OH group to the surrounding water.

2. This free energy depends upon the formal charge of the central atom of the acid, the number of non-hydroxyl oxygens in the acid ion available for attachment of the proton, the number of equivalent acidic hydrogens, and the actual structure of the acid as determined crystallographically.

These are, of course, the items considered above in the qualitative discussion of acid strength. Although the mechanics of the calculations employed need not be considered here, the results obtained are in general good agreement with experimentally determined values. Ricci[22] points out that of the assumptions made by Kossiakoff and Harker only those relating energy to formal charge and number of non-hydroxyl oxygens are essential to the empirical correlation of k_A' values. Both these papers should be consulted for more details. The generalizations given by Gallais[20]

[21] L. Pauling: *General Chemistry*, p. 394. W. H. Freeman and Co., San Francisco (1947).

[22] J. E. Ricci: *J. Am. Chem. Soc.*, **70**, 109 (1948).

[23] A. Kossiakoff and D. Harker: *J. Am. Chem. Soc.*, **60**, 2047 (1938).

$$pk_A' = 8.3 + 4.2(x_H - x_X) \quad \text{for } m = 0 \tag{9·14}$$

and

$$pk_A' = 2 + 2.2(x_H - x_X) \quad \text{for } m \neq 0 \tag{9·15}$$

where x_H and x_X are, respectively, the electronegativities of H and X, although less involved, do not give completely accurate results.

Acid strength among hydrated ions is measured by the displacement of Brønsted equilibria of the type

$$M(H_2O)_x^{+n} + H_2O \rightleftharpoons M(H_2O)_{x-1}OH^{+n-1} + H_3O^+$$

Thus, the ease with which a proton is lost is determined by the extent to which an O—H bond in a coordinated water molecule is weakened by the central metal ion. If this ion is small and has a high positive charge [e.g., iron(III)], a general displacement of electrons toward it might be expected, and a proton should be capable of fairly ready removal by a base. Large cations with comparatively low charges (e.g., those of the alkali and alkaline earth metals) are, therefore, only weakly acidic. Amphoterism would be expected among intermediate materials (e.g., aluminum ion).

Although the protonic concept of acid-base behavior is admittedly superior to the water-ion approach, it suffers from its excessive emphasis upon the proton. It is true that most of the common acids are protonic in nature, but there are many which are not. Furthermore, there are numerous reactions, particularly those occurring in the absence of solvent and at high temperatures, which have the characteristics of acid-base reactions but involve no protons. Such reactions illustrate the limitations of the concept.

The Lux-Flood concept

Lack of applicability of the protonic concept to oxide systems where acid-base behavior is well recognized led Lux[24] to suggest that in such systems a base is any material which gives up oxide ions and an acid is any material which gains oxide ions. This is indicated by the equations

$$\text{base} \rightleftharpoons \text{acid} + xO^{-2}$$
$$CaO \rightleftharpoons Ca^{+2} + O^{-2}$$
$$SO_4^{-2} \rightleftharpoons SO_3 + O^{-2}$$

The limitations of such a concept are obvious. It will be apparent that, like the protonic approach, this view can be reduced to one part

[24] H. Lux: *Z. Electrochem.*, **45**, 303 (1939).

of the more general theories of Lewis (pp. 326–329) and Usanovich (pp. 329–230).

Flood and his coworkers[25, 26] have extended the Lux concept to a number of systems and have pointed out that in such systems acid strengths may be compared by comparing the magnitudes of equilibrium constants defined as

$$K = a_{\text{acid}} a_{\text{O}^{-2}} / a_{\text{base}} \tag{9·16}$$

Thus acid strength is found to increase in the series TiO_3^{-2}, SiO_3^{-2}, BO_2^-, PO_3^-.

The general theory of solvent systems

That water is not unique in its ability to act as an ionizing solvent and as a medium for acid-base behavior still surprises many people. Yet evidence for similar behavior of other solvents was presented many years ago. Franklin[27] pointed out the acidic characteristics of ammonium salts and the basic characteristics of metal amides, imides, and nitrides in liquid ammonia and incorporated this information into his ammono system of acids, bases, and salts.[28, 29] Similar considerations have shown that such protonic solvents as liquid hydrogen sulfide, hydrazine, hydroxylamine, and glacial acetic acid can also function as solvents in which acid-base behaviors may exist and can be regarded as parents for systems of acids and bases. Extension of these views, to some extent through analogy, to non-protonic solvents has enlarged the concept of acid-base systems to include such materials as liquid sulfur dioxide, carbonyl chloride, selenium oxychloride, bromine trifluoride, and dinitrogen(IV) oxide.

Analogies among these solvents become apparent when one considers the autoionization characteristic of each. Although such ionization is ordinarily comparatively small, conductance measurements have shown its existence in a variety of instances. One cannot, of course, state with certainty the exact natures of all the ionic species present, for the ions (especially the cations) are undoubtedly solvated to a greater or lesser extent. In the comparative summary given in Table 9·4, both solvated and unsolvated cations are listed, with no claim being laid to the accuracy of either formulation.

[25] H. Flood and T. Förland: *Acta Chem. Scand.*, **1**, 592, 781 (1947).
[26] H. Flood, T. Förland, and B. Roald: *Acta Chem. Scand.*, **1**, 790 (1947).
[27] E. C. Franklin: *J. Am. Chem. Soc.*, **27**, 820 (1905).
[28] E. C. Franklin: *Am. Chem. J.*, **47**, 285 (1912).
[29] E. C. Franklin: *The Nitrogen System of Compounds.* Reinhold Publishing Corp., New York (1935).

Based upon such considerations, several definitions for acids and bases have been advanced in terms of a parent solvent.[30–32] They may be combined to admit as an acid any material giving, either by direct dissociation or by interaction with the solvent, the cation characteristic of the solvent and as a base any material giving the anion characteristic of the solvent. A salt is regarded as any material giving solutions in the solvent of greater conductivity than the pure solvent and yielding at least one ion different from those characterizing the solvent. Acids may be derived directly from the solvent or bear no relation to the solvent except in terms of cation. Thus hydrazoic

TABLE 9·4

AUTOIONIZATION OF VARIOUS SOLVENTS

Solvent	Dissociation Reaction				
H_2O	H_2O	$+ H_2O$	$\rightleftharpoons H_3O^+$	$+ OH^-$	(or $H^+ + OH^-$)
NH_3	NH_3	$+ NH_3$	$\rightleftharpoons NH_4^+$	$+ NH_2^-$	(or $H^+ + NH_2^-$)
$HC_2H_3O_2$	$HC_2H_3O_2$	$+ HC_2H_3O_2$	$\rightleftharpoons H_2C_2H_3O_2^+$	$+ C_2H_3O_2^-$	(or $H^+ + C_2H_3O_2^-$)
NH_2OH	NH_2OH	$+ NH_2OH$	$\rightleftharpoons NH_3OH^+$	$+ NHOH^-$	(or $H^+ + NHOH^-$)
SO_2	SO_2	$+ 2SO_2$	$\rightleftharpoons SO \cdot SO_2^{+2}$	$+ SO_3^{-2}$	(or $SO^{+2} + SO_3^{-2}$)
$COCl_2$	$COCl_2$	$+ COCl_2$	$\rightleftharpoons COCl \cdot COCl_2^+$	$+ Cl^-$	(or $COCl^+ + Cl^-$)
$SeOCl_2$	$SeOCl_2$	$+ SeOCl_2$	$\rightleftharpoons SeOCl \cdot SeOCl_2^+$	$+ Cl^-$	(or $SeOCl^+ + Cl^-$)
N_2O_4	N_2O_4	$+ 2N_2O_4$	$\rightleftharpoons 2NO \cdot NO_2^+$	$+ 2NO_3^-$	(or $NO^+ + NO_3^-$)
BrF_3	BrF_3	$+ BrF_3$	$\rightleftharpoons BrF_2^+$	$+ BrF_4^-$	

acid, HN_3, behaves as an acid in liquid ammonia and is a true ammono acid since it is derived from ammonia, whereas nitric acid, HNO_3, although also an acid in liquid ammonia, is not an ammono acid.

Neutralization, in terms of the general theory of solvent systems, amounts to combination of the solvent cation with the solvent anion to produce the solvent. Analogies to the familiar interaction of hydrogen (hydronium) and hydroxyl ions in aqueous solutions are apparent from the typical neutralizations listed in Table 9·5.

Extension of acid-base behavior from water to other protonic solvents in terms of this approach appears logical and requires no explanation. The inclusion of non-protonic systems, however, needs justification in terms of experimental evidence since it represents a radical departure from the views considered thus far.[33]

Germann[31, 34] has shown that dissolution of anhydrous aluminum chloride in pure phosgene ($COCl_2$) increases the conductivity of the latter by some one hundred thousand times. The resulting solutions upon electrolysis yield carbon monoxide at the cathode and chlorine

[30] E. C. Franklin: *J. Am. Chem. Soc.*, **46**, 2137 (1924).

[31] A. F. O. Germann: *Science*, **61**, 71 (1925); *J. Am. Chem. Soc.*, **47**, 2461 (1925).

[32] H. P. Cady and H. M. Elsey: *Science*, **56**, 27 (1922); *J. Chem. Education*, **5**, 1425 (1928).

[33] J. P. McReynolds: *J. Chem. Education*, **17**, 116 (1940).

[34] A. F. O. Germann and C. R. Timpany: *J. Am. Chem. Soc.*, **47**, 2275 (1925).

at the anode, corresponding to the evolution of hydrogen and oxygen from, for instance, aqueous sulfuric acid. Furthermore, these solutions dissolve many metals, with the production of carbon monoxide and crystallizable metal salts, react with carbonates, liberating carbon dioxide, and neutralize phosgene solutions of chlorides such as calcium chloride. These behaviors are best accounted for by considering that carbonyl chloride undergoes autoionization to chloride and to $COCl^+$ or CO^{+2} ions and that solutions of aluminum chloride in this solvent contain the comparatively weak acid $COClAlCl_4$ or $COAl_2Cl_8$. On these bases, analogies to aqueous solutions become apparent.

TABLE 9·5
NEUTRALIZATION REACTIONS IN VARIOUS SOLVENTS

Solvent	Acid Ion	Base Ion	Typical Neutralization Acid	+ Base	→ Salt	+ Solvent
H_2O	$H_3O^+(H^+)$	OH^-	HCl	$NaOH$	$NaCl$	H_2O
NH_3	$NH_4^+(H^+)$	NH_2^-	NH_4Cl	$NaNH_2$	$NaCl$	$2NH_3$
NH_2OH	$NH_3OH^+(H^+)$	$NHOH^-$	$NH_2OH \cdot HCl$	$KNHOH$	KCl	$2NH_2OH$
$HC_2H_3O_2$	$H_2C_2H_3O_2^+(H^+)$	$C_2H_3O_2^-$	$HClO_4$	$NaC_2H_3O_2$	$NaClO_4$	$HC_2H_3O_2$
$COCl_2$	$COCl^+$	Cl^-	$2COClAlCl_4$	$CaCl_2$	$Ca(AlCl_4)_2$	$2COCl_2$
SO_2	SO^{+2}	SO_3^{-2}	$SOCl_2$	Cs_2SO_3	$2CsCl$	$2SO_2$
$SeOCl_2$	$SeOCl^+$	Cl^-	$(SeOCl)_2SnCl_6$	$2KCl$	K_2SnCl_6	$2SeOCl_2$
N_2O_4	NO^+	NO_3^-	$NOCl$	$AgNO_3$	$AgCl$	N_2O_4
BrF_3	BrF_2^+	BrF_4^-	BrF_2SbF_6	$AgBrF_4$	$AgSbF_6$	$2BrF_3$

Liquid sulfur dioxide was apparently suggested as an acid-base solvent by Cady and Elsey,[32] but most of the investigative work on such systems has been carried out by Jander and his school.[35] Only a few lines of evidence in support of including them need be cited. Thus solutions of thionyl chloride and cesium sulfite can be titrated to a conductimetric end point in liquid sulfur dioxide (see Table 9·5). Such a reaction is of course entirely analogous to the neutralization of hydrochloric acid by sodium hydroxide in aqueous solution or of ammonium nitrate by sodamide in liquid ammonia. Furthermore, one may cite the amphoteric behavior of aluminum sulfite in liquid sulfur dioxide which parallels closely the amphoteric behavior of aluminum hydroxide in water. Using aluminum chloride and tetramethylammonium sulfite solutions, one can precipitate aluminum sulfite first as

$$2Al^{+3} + 3SO_3^{-2} \rightarrow Al_2(SO_3)_3(s)$$

[35] G. Jander and K. Wickert: *Z. physik. Chem.*, **A178**, 57 (1936). See also subsequent papers by Jander et al., e.g., those listed by McReynolds.[33]

and redissolve it in excess sulfite ion as

$$Al_2(SO_3)_3(s) + 3SO_3^{-2} \rightarrow 2[Al(SO_3)_3]^{-3}$$

By treating the resulting solution with the acid thionyl chloride, one can then reprecipitate aluminum sulfite as

$$2[Al(SO_3)_3]^{-3} + 3SO^{+2} \rightarrow Al_2(SO_3)_3(s) + 6SO_2$$

Investigations of acid-base behavior in selenium oxychloride have been due largely to Smith,[36] who has shown that solutions of stannic chloride in this solvent have acidic properties and can be titrated conductimetrically with solutions of such bases as potassium chloride, calcium chloride, and pyridine. As an extension of the theory of solvent systems, Smith proposes that an acid represent an electron pair acceptor toward the molecule or ion of the solvent and a base represent an electron pair donor toward the solvent. This scheme offers a link between the theory of solvent systems and the electronic theories to be considered next.

Work done in 1948 and 1949[37–39] showed that comparable acid-base reactions can take place in liquid dinitrogen(IV) oxide. Nitrosyl chloride, NOCl, is neutralized by silver nitrate (Table 9·5), and solutions of nitrosyl chloride in dinitrogen tetroxide react readily with metals such as iron, zinc, and tin to yield insoluble metal chlorides or salts of the type $(NO)_xMCl_y$ and nitrogen(II) oxide. Comparable direct reactions with the solvent are limited to the most electropositive metals because of the low concentration of NO^+ ions in the solvent. Amphoterism, comparable with that noted in aqueous solutions or in ammonia, is also apparent in reactions described by the equations

$$Zn + x(C_2H_5)_2NH_2NO_3 + N_2O_4 \rightarrow [(C_2H_5)_2NH_2]_x[\text{nitrato zincate complex}] + NO$$

$$Zn(NO_3)_2 + x(C_2H_5)_2NH_2NO_3 \rightarrow [(C_2H_5)_2NH_2]_x[\text{nitrato zincate complex}]$$

The complex produced is soluble but uncharacterized.

Another interesting acid-base solvent is liquid bromine trifluoride (p. 366). The comparatively high specific conductance (8.0×10^{-3}

[36] G. B. L. Smith: *Chem. Revs.*, **23**, 165 (1938).

[37] C. C. Addison and R. Thompson: *Nature*, **162**, 369 (1948).

[38] C. C. Addison and R. Thompson: *J. Chem. Soc.*, **1949**, 211, 218 (Supplementary Issue No. 1).

[39] W. R. Angus, R. W. Jones, and G. O. Phillips: *Nature*, **164**, 433 (1949).

ohm^{-1} cm^{-1} at 25°C)[40] of this solvent is indicative of its dissociation into BrF_2^+ and BrF_4^- ions. The conductance of the solvent is increased by addition of compounds such as BrF_2SbF_6 and $(BrF_2)_2SnF_6$ or $KBrF_4$ and $AgBrF_4$. These materials behave, respectively, as acids and bases in the solvent.[41] Titration of BrF_2SbF_6 with $AgBrF_4$ yields a sharp conductimetric end point at the 1:1 equivalence indicated by the equation

$$BrF_2SbF_6 + AgBrF_4 \rightarrow AgSbF_6 + 2BrF_3$$

The general theory of solvent systems possesses the obvious advantage of relating acid-base behavior in numerous solvents, both protonic and non-protonic in nature. However, it suffers from its restriction of such behavior to solvents and its emphasis on the dependence of the behavior upon the solvent. Any acid-base reaction occurring in the absence of a solvent has no place in this treatment. Furthermore, this approach places an overemphasis upon the ionic character of neutralization processes. Certainly many neutralizations occur without the formation or interaction of ions. In addition, the practical importance of many of the solvent systems best considered by this concept is slight, and this is sometimes cited as a further objection. In spite of its utility under certain circumstances, the general theory of solvent systems has received but little attention in recent years.

The Lewis electronic theory

The fundamentals of this concept were first stated in 1923 by G. N. Lewis,[42] but the general ideas apparently lay dormant until revived in 1938 by Lewis[1] and extended by him and his students. The fundamental postulates and extensions of the theory have been ably reviewed by Luder.[43, 44]

In terms of this approach, an acid is regarded as any molecule, radical, or ion in which the normal electronic grouping (often eight) about some atom is incomplete; the atom can then accept an electron pair or pairs. Correspondingly, a base is regarded as any structure containing an atom which is capable of donating an electron pair.

[40] A. A. Banks, H. J. Emeléus, and A. A. Woolf: *J. Chem. Soc.*, **1949**, 2861.

[41] A. A. Woolf and H. J. Emeléus: *J. Chem. Soc.*, **1949**, 2865.

[42] G. N. Lewis: *Valence and the Structure of Atoms and Molecules.* The Chemical Catalog Co., New York (1923).

[43] W. F. Luder: *Chem. Revs.*, **27**, 547 (1940).

[44] W. F. Luder and S. Zuffanti: *The Electronic Theory of Acids and Bases*, John Wiley and Sons, New York (1946).

Acids are thus the electron pair acceptors of Sidgwick,[45] and bases the electron pair donors. Neutralization then amounts to the formation of a coordinate bond (p. 193) between the base and the acid, the resulting product undergoing rearrangement, dissociation, or no change as necessitated by stability requirements. The metathetical processes characterizing the Brønsted-Lowry view are therefore without necessary significance in this concept.

Some idea as to the scope of this interpretation can be gained from the examples listed in Table 9·6. It is apparent from these examples

TABLE 9·6

EXAMPLES ILLUSTRATING THE LEWIS THEORY

Acid	Base	Neutralization Product
HCl	H_2O	$H_2O \rightarrow HCl$ $(H_3O^+ + Cl^-)$
H_2O	NH_3	$H_3N \rightarrow HOH$ $(NH_4^+ + OH^-)$
SO_3	CaO	$CaO \rightarrow SO_3$ $(Ca^{+2} + SO_4^{-2})$
HNO_3	R_3N	$R_3N \rightarrow HNO_3$ $(R_3NH^+ + NO_3^-)$
BF_3	R_2O	$R_2O \rightarrow BF_3$
$SnCl_4$	Cl^-	Cl $\searrow$ $SnCl_4^{-2}$ (i.e., $SnCl_6^{-2}$) $\nearrow$ Cl
H_2O	CN^-	$NC^- \rightarrow HOH$ $(HCN + OH^-)$
Cu^{+2}	NH_3	$(H_3N\rightarrow)_4Cu^{+2}$ (i.e., $Cu(NH_3)_4^{+2}$)
Co^{+3}	NH_3 Cl^-	$(H_3N\rightarrow)_4Co(\leftarrow Cl)_2^+$ (i.e., $Co(NH_3)_4Cl_2^+$)
$AlCl_3$	$COCl_2$	Cl $/ \quad \searrow$ $OC \qquad AlCl_3$ $(COCl^+ + AlCl_4^-)$ $\diagdown$ Cl
SO^{+2}	SO_3^{-2}	$O_3S \rightarrow SO$ $(2SO_2)$

that every type of acid or base characterized by any of the theoretical approaches already discussed is correctly defined by the Lewis theory. Furthermore, it is apparent that acid-base behavior is not made dependent upon any one element, upon any given combination of elements, upon the presence of ions, or upon the presence or absence of a solvent. This lack of arbitrary limitation may be considered a strong argument in favor of the Lewis concept.

That the Lewis concept represents an essential interpretation of experimental fact rather than a mere theoretical approach is brought out when it is considered in the light of Lewis's "phenomenological criteria" (p. 306).[1] From the many examples and illustrations which

[45] N. V. Sidgwick: *The Electronic Theory of Valency.* Oxford University Press, New York (1927).

have been given,[43, 44, 46, 47] the following may be cited as representative and typical:

1. *Rapidity of neutralization.* Neutralization is conceived by Lewis to occur with such rapidity that activational energies are unnecessary. Such a conclusion is supported by the well-known reactions $H_3O^+ + OH^-$ and $HCl + NH_3$ as well as by such reactions as $Cu^{+2} + NH_3$ and $BCl_3 + (C_2H_5)_3N$, all of which are Lewis neutralizations.

2. *Displacement of weaker acid or base.* The hydrogen ion displaces the copper(II) ion from $Cu(NH_3)_4{}^{+2}$ because it is a stronger acid than the copper(II) ion. Correspondingly, hydroxyl ion displaces acetate ion from acetic acid because it is the stronger base.

3. *Titration, using indicators.* Using methyl violet as a typical indicator, one can titrate the acid HCl with the base NH_3 in aqueous medium, the acid BCl_3 with the base phthalic anhydride in chlorobenzene, or the acid $AlCl_3$ with the base C_5H_5N in chloroform, the color change in each instance being from yellow in the presence of excess acid to violet in the presence of excess base.

4. *Catalysis.* The well-known acidic catalytic effects of sulfuric acid, hydrofluoric acid, boron trifluoride, aluminum trichloride, etc., and the basic catalytic effects of organic amines, amides, etc., are entirely systematized by the Lewis view. They are treated in more detail in a later section (pp. 334–335).

In spite of the many apparent advantages of this interpretation, several objections can be cited. Inasmuch as neutralization involves the donation and the acceptance of an electron pair, it is obvious that any case of coordination must represent acid-base behavior. Although this may be desirable, it does bring many seemingly unrelated reactions into the realm of neutralization. To some extent, these difficulties are resolved by Bjerrum's correlation of the Brønsted and Lewis approaches[48] in terms of the definitions:

base = proton acceptor or electron pair donor

acid = proton donor

antibase = base acceptor or electron pair acceptor.

Perhaps a more fundamental objection is the lack of any uniform scale of acid or base strength. Instead, acid and base strengths are

[46] W. F. Luder, W. S. McGuire, and S. Zuffanti: *J. Chem. Education*, **20**, 344 (1943).

[47] W. F. Luder: *J. Chem. Education*, **22**, 301 (1945).

[48] J. Bjerrum: *Acta Chem. Scand.*, **1**, 528 (1947); *Tids. Kjemi, bergvesen Met.*, **8**, 129 (1948).

made variable and dependent upon the reaction chosen. Although it is true that strengths relative to some reference material can be evaluated readily, the resulting values are more or less specific in nature. One other objection centers in the exclusion of the displacement of hydrogen by metals from acid-base phenomena. Such a reaction, as far as the Lewis approach is concerned, is an oxidation-reduction reaction which, although related to acid-base reactions (see p. 307), is nevertheless distinct from them. Were it to be included, any other oxidation-reduction reaction might justifiably be treated similarly.

Such objections as those given above are not fundamentally serious and do not detract materially from the general utility of the theory. The Lewis electronic view has done much to interrelate the diametrically opposed views encountered when one attempts to tie the other approaches thus far discussed into a unified whole. It has the further advantage of explaining readily the long-accepted basic properties of metal oxides and the acidic properties of non-metal oxides and of permitting the inclusion of many gas phase and high-temperature, non-solvent reactions as neutralization processes.

The Usanovich concept

The most comprehensive of all acid-base theories is due to Usanovich.[49] In an attempt to cover all recognized phases of the field, Usanovich has defined an acid as any material which forms salts with bases through neutralization, gives up cations, or combines with anions or electrons. In like manner, he has considered as bases materials which neutralize acids, give up anions or electrons, or combine with cations. Underlying the theory is a fundamental concept of salt formation which is made apparent by the examples given in Table 9·7.

Here, apparently, is an approach which includes every example of acid-base behavior explained by any of the theories thus far considered, and includes in addition all oxidation-reduction processes as representative of one phase of acid-base character. Although the theory is based primarily upon the positive and negative traits of acids and bases, some stress is also placed upon coordinate unsaturation, acid function being determined by the presence of coordinately unsaturated positive particles, and basic function by the presence of similarly saturated negative particles. Although in general acidity is promoted by highly charged positive particles (compare the highly basic Na_2O with the less basic Al_2O_3) and basicity by highly charged negative

[49] M. Usanovich: *J. Gen. Chem.* (*U.S.S.R.*), **9**, 182 (1939).

particles (compare the high basicity of Na_2O with the lesser value for NaCl), exact consideration of size as well as charge relationships is necessary to explain many trends (such as the increasing basicity in the series BeO to RaO).

TABLE 9·7

ACID-BASE RELATIONSHIPS IN THE USANOVICH SENSE

Acid	+ Base	→ Salt	Justification
SO_3	Na_2O	Na_2SO_4	Na_2O yields O^{-2} SO_3 combines with O^{-2}
$Fe(CN)_2$	KCN	$K_4Fe(CN)_6$	KCN yields CN^- $Fe(CN)_2$ combines with CN^-
Sb_2S_5	$(NH_4)_2S$	$(NH_4)_3SbS_4$	$(NH_4)_2S$ gives up S^{-2} Sb_2S_5 gains S^{-2}
Cl_2	Na	NaCl	Na loses an electron Cl gains an electron

The Usanovich theory is particularly advantageous in classifying together all examples of acidity and basicity, but it suffers from its very generality in including many reactions which are perhaps better considered from other points of view. This fault is particularly true of oxidation-reduction phenomena. For specific problems, the Usanovich approach is likely to be of extreme value; but for general considerations, it is undoubtedly too broad to be of wide utility.

It seems proper to conclude this section in a recapitulatory fashion. Six concepts of acid-base behavior have been summarized, and something of the utility and limitations of each has been indicated. In some instances, one point of view overlaps another, and the views have been considered in the general order of increasing comprehensiveness. It is only natural for one to wonder what the true picture is and what one should really know about acid-base theory. Actually, each approach is correct as far as it goes, and no conflict exists among them. One should be conversant with each point of view and should adapt his thinking to the particular problem at hand. In some cases (for example, the titration of hydrochloric acid with sodium hydroxide in aqueous solution) one need go no further than the Arrhenius approach for an adequate and workable explanation. On the other hand, a similar reaction in a non-protonic system might better be treated in terms of the general theory of solvent systems. Furthermore, for reactions occurring between solids, an electronic approach would be the most reasonable. And so on for other situations. No single point of view should be regarded as adequate for all circumstances. Each has its own field of special applicability, and knowledge of the fundamentals of all is essential.

SOME APPLICATIONS OF ACID-BASE THEORY

The basicities of metallic elements and their compounds

Although the term *basicity*, as applied to the metallic elements and their compounds, has been employed to cover a variety of phenomena, from the ease with which the free elements lose electrons under oxidizing conditions through the extent to which metal salts hydrolyze in aqueous solution to the ease with which oxygen-containing salts decompose when heated, all such phenomena are reducible, directly or indirectly, to relative attractions (or lack of attractions) for anions or electrons. In this respect, they are, therefore, all manifestations of acid-base behavior in terms of the broad electronic concept offered by Usanovich.

Since basicity involves the loss of anions or electrons, any property which measures the tendency of an element to lose electrons or which measures the lack of attraction which an ion has for electrons or anions in turn measures the basicity of that element or ion. There is, therefore, no ambiguity in referring to such a variety of phenomena as mentioned above as measures of basicities. A broad generalization of this sort would be impossible in terms of older approaches to acid-base character, and in this respect the Usanovich interpretation does much to clarify an otherwise confused situation.

Relation of acid-base behavior to oxidation-reduction

Only a formalized relationship exists between acid-base behavior and oxidation-reduction in terms of the Brønsted-Lowry concept. This is apparent from the defining equations

$$\text{acid} \rightleftharpoons \text{base} + \text{proton} \tag{9·17}$$

$$\text{reductant} \rightleftharpoons \text{oxidant} + \text{electron} \tag{9·18}$$

and the characteristic equilibria

$$\text{acid}_1 + \text{base}_2 \rightleftharpoons \text{base}_1 + \text{acid}_2 \tag{9·19}$$

$$\text{red.}_1 + \text{oxid.}_2 \rightleftharpoons \text{oxid.}_1 + \text{red.}_2 \tag{9·20}$$

Acid-base behavior amounts to proton transfer, and oxidation-reduction to electron transfer. Such a formalized similarity leads to similarities in thermodynamic treatment but represents little more than an analogy.

In terms of the Lewis treatment, however, the relation is much more definite.[43, 50] Although acid-base reactions involve a coordinate shar-

[50] W. F. Luder: *J. Chem. Education*, **19**, 24 (1942).

ing of electron pairs, oxidation-reduction reactions involve an essentially complete transfer of electrons (pp. 280–284). Any differences between the two types of phenomena then beome differences of degree rather than of kind. Acidity and oxidizing power may be regarded as different manifestations of *electrophilic* character, since acids attract shares in electrons and oxidizing agents attract electrons completely. In like manner, basicity and reducing power represent different manifestations of *electrodotic* character, since bases donate shares in electrons and reducing agents donate electrons completely. This fact can be made more apparent by some examples. Silver ion, for instance, behaves as an acid in the presence of a base such as ammonia and as an oxidant in the presence of a reductant such as zinc. In both cases, silver ion is exhibiting an attraction for electrons. Furthermore, sulfide ion behaves as a base when reacting with water but as a reductant when reacting with an oxidant such as the permanganate ion. Yet both behaviors represent electron donor character on the part of the sulfide ion.

An even more pronounced relationship is of course inherent in the Usanovich treatment. Actually, oxidation-reduction occupies no unique position in terms of this approach. Rather, it is a phase of acid-base behavior.

Acid-base relationships at elevated temperatures

Although much emphasis has been placed upon acid-base behavior at room and somewhat lower temperatures, only recently[51] has there been any attempt to extend any of the theoretical approaches systematically to reactions occurring at higher temperatures.

The acidic properties of "onium" salts in their parent solvents suggest their behaviors as acids at elevated temperatures.[52] Much information upon the acidic properties of such materials is available. For instance, fused ammonium nitrate dissolves many metal oxides, hydroxides, and carbonates and oxidizes many metals in the same fashion as aqueous nitric acid. It may, in fact, be regarded as a high-temperature nitric acid. A combination of fused ammonium nitrate and ammonium chloride shows the properties of high-temperature aqua regia; and the acidic properties of ammonium chloride in soldering fluxes, in the dehydration of hydrated metal chlorides which might otherwise hydrolyze, and in the preparation of non-volatile anhydrous chlorides (particularly of the rare earth elements) by reaction with metal oxides are well recognized. The acidic properties of other

[51] L. F. Audrieth and T. Moeller: *J. Chem. Education*, **20**, 219 (1943).
[52] L. F. Audrieth and M. T. Schmidt: *Proc. Natl. Acad. Sci.*, **20**, 221 (1934).

ammonium salts and of pyridinium salts at elevated temperatures, together with the rather wide use of the former in the opening up of certain types of ores, are other examples. That acidity should characterize such materials is apparent from the Brønsted-Lowry concept, and their consideration as acids is nothing but a logical extension of this concept.

There are many high-temperature acid-base reactions which are not amenable to treatment in terms of the Brønsted-Lowry theory because protonic materials are absent. However, many such reactions, some involving fusion and some apparently occurring directly between solids, can be considered conveniently in terms of the Lewis approach. Summarized in Table 9·8 are a few general examples[51] chosen at random from the fields of ceramics and metallurgy.

TABLE 9·8
HIGH-TEMPERATURE ACID-BASE REACTIONS BASED UPON THE LEWIS THEORY

Base	Acid	Neutralization Product	Applications
O^{-2} (from MO, MOH, MCO_3, MSO_4)	SiO_2 Al_2O_3 B_2O_3	SiO_3^{-2}, SiO_4^{-4} AlO_2^-, AlO_3^{-3} BO_2^-, BO_3^{-3}	Manufacture of glass, cement, and ceramic products—slag formation
O^{-2} (from MO)	$BO_2^-(B_2O_3)$ PO_3^-	BO_3^{-3} PO_4^{-3}	Borax bead tests Phosphate bead tests
O^{-2} (from MO, etc.)	$S_2O_7^{-2}$ HSO_4^-	SO_4^{-2} SO_4^{-2}	Opening up of ores
S^{-2} (from Na_2S)	FeS Cu_2S	FeS_2^{-2} CuS^-	Orford process for nickel concentration
F^- (from alkali fluorides)	BeF_2 AlF_3 TaF_5	BeF_4^{-2} AlF_6^{-3} TaF_7^{-2}	Electrolytic melts

In each instance, the reaction outlined represents an interaction between an electron pair donor (base) and an electron pair acceptor (acid). The bases selected are simple electronically saturated anions, the structures of which may be represented as

$$:\ddot{\underset{\cdot\cdot}{O}}:^{-2},\ :\ddot{\underset{\cdot\cdot}{S}}:^{-2},\ \text{and}\ :\ddot{\underset{\cdot\cdot}{F}}:^{-}.$$

Each of the acids is a coordinatively unsaturated ion or molecule containing an atom capable of accepting an electron pair.

Although the reactions cited are given simple formulations, they may well be more complicated. An acidic oxide such as silica exists as a giant molecule which must undergo depolymerization or degradation before the simple ions given in Table 9·8 can form. Such a degradation is probably effected by strong anion bases at elevated temperatures through the formation of intermediate polyanionic complexes in much the same fashion as isopoly acids are degraded in aqueous solution to simple anions by increasing the *p*H (p. 277). A similar situation doubtless exists in the metaphosphate reactions, since the existence of discrete metaphosphate ions under any circumstance appears improbable (p. 649). Rather, it is more probable that the metaphosphate ion is a polymeric aggregate which reacts with basic oxides to form a whole series of intermediate polyphosphates of indefinite compositions.

Numerous examples of high-temperature acid-base reactions in addition to those cited are known.[51] In general, they have often been encountered in technical practice, but, as yet, they have received little systematic physico-chemical attention. Fundamental investigations of such reactions should open new fields to the theoretical chemist, to the preparative chemist, to the ceramist, and to the metallurgist.

Acid-base reactions in the gas phase

The general concepts outlined in the preceding section may be extended to cover many reactions which occur in the gas phase. Reaction of a gaseous hydrogen halide with gaseous ammonia or any comparable reaction is obviously a proton transfer reaction and is described clearly by the Brønsted-Lowry approach. Many other reactions which involve gases are acid-base reactions from the Lewis point of view. For example, the reversible gas-phase reactions between trimethyl boron and ammonia and various amines have been studied from this basis.[53, 54]

Acid-base catalysis

The catalytic properties of acids and bases represent an important phase of acid-base behavior, and reference has already been made to catalysis as a phenomenological criterion (p. 306). In spite of early recognition of the catalytic properties of hydrogen acids and metal hydroxides in aqueous solution, only since the introduction of modern theoretical concepts have other materials reacting under other conditions been recognized as acid and base catalysts.

[53] H. C. Brown, M. D. Taylor, and M. Gerstein: *J. Am. Chem. Soc.*, **66**, 431 (1944).

[54] H. C. Brown, H. Bartholomay, Jr., and M. D. Taylor: *J. Am. Chem. Soc.*, **66**, 435 (1944).

The importance of acid-base catalysis may be inferred from the extensive literature which has accumulated concerning it.[44, 55] There is room in this discussion to point out only a few general considerations. The original literature should be consulted for a comprehensive discussion.

Although the Brønsted-Lowry definitions have served to emphasize the importance of protonic materials as acid catalysts in both aqueous and non-aqueous media (compare, for example, the hydrolysis of esters as catalyzed by acids such as hydrochloric in aqueous medium with the ammonolysis of esters as catalyzed by ammonium salts in liquid ammonia), perhaps the most fruitful generalizations have come from applications of the Lewis electronic theory. In terms of this theory it is often possible to show how a known acid or base catalyst may form an unstable intermediate by acceptance or donation of an electron pair. Many examples of the type reactions summarized in Table 9·9 have been considered in detail in an interesting review paper.[56]

TABLE 9·9

ACID AND BASE CATALYSIS IN TERMS OF THE LEWIS THEORY

Reaction Type	Typical Catalysts
1. Acid-catalyzed reactions	
Friedel-Crafts	BF_3, $AlCl_3$, H_2SO_4, P_2O_5, HF
Cannizzaro	$Al(OR)_3$
Semi-carbazone	HX
Halogenation	$FeBr_3$, $SbCl_5$, $ZnCl_2$, $SnCl_4$
Hydrolysis	Hg^{+2}
Sulfonation, nitration	BF_3
2. Base-catalyzed reactions	
Cannizzaro	OH^-
Claisen	$OC_2H_5^-$
Aldol condensation	$C_2H_3O_2^-$, CO_3^{-2}, pyridine, amines
Benzoin condensation	CN^-
Perkin	$C_2H_3O_2^-$, CO_3^{-2}, SO_3^{-2}, PO_4^{-3}, pyridine, quinoline, $(C_2H_5)_3N$

SUGGESTED SUPPLEMENTARY REFERENCES

N. F. Hall et al.: *Acids and Bases*. Journal of Chemical Education, Easton, Pa. (1941). General discussions of modern views.

D. Davidson et al.: *More Acids and Bases*. Journal of Chemical Education, Easton, Pa. (1944). General discussions of modern views.

N. F. Hall: "Modern Conceptions of Acids and Bases," *J. Chem. Education*, **7**, 782 (1930).

R. P. Bell: "Acids and Bases," *Ann. Reports*, **31**, 71 (1934).

N. Bjerrum: "Acids, Salts, and Bases," *Chem. Revs.*, **16**, 287 (1935).

[55] R. P. Bell: *Acid-Base Catalysis*, Oxford University Press, London (1941).

[56] W. F. Luder and S. Zuffanti: *Chem. Revs.*, **34**, 345 (1944).

K. Wickert: "General Considerations on Solvents, Acids, Bases and Salts," *Z. physik. Chem.*, **A178**, 361 (1937).

I. M. Kolthoff: "The Lewis and Brønsted-Lowry Definitions of Acids and Bases," *J. Phys. Chem.*, **48**, 51 (1944).

W. F. Luder: "Contemporary Acid-Base Theory," *J. Chem. Education*, **25**, 555 (1948).

L. F. Audrieth: *Acids, Bases, and Non-Aqueous Systems.* Twenty-third annual Priestley Lectures, Pennsylvania State College, 1949. University Lithoprinters, Ypsilanti, Michigan (1949).

R. P. Bell: "The Use of the Terms Acid and Base," *Quart. Revs.*, **1**, 113 (1947).

L. Ebert and N. Konopik: "Acidity and Basicity," *Osterr. Chem.-Ztg.*, **50**, 184 (1949).

W. F. Luder and S. Zuffanti: *The Electronic Theory of Acids and Bases*, John Wiley and Sons, New York (1946).

R. S. Bradley: "Note on the Symmetry between Electron and Proton Transfer," *J. Chem. Education*, **27**, 208 (1950).

CHAPTER 10

Non-aqueous Solvents

The ability of water to dissolve materials of a wide variety of types, structures, and compositions has often led to the very general assumption that water is unique in its solvent characteristics. Historically, such properties of water as its availability, its convenience in handling, its long liquid range, and its ability to form solvates have undoubtedly combined with its solvent properties to direct attention to it as opposed to other solvents. The Arrhenius views of electrolytic dissociation as being limited to aqueous solutions probably did much to foster this attention. Indeed, in 1893, Ostwald was convinced that in so far as its abilities to form electrolytic solutions or to bring about ionization were concerned, water stood in a class by itself, a position "which is not even approximately simulated by any other substance."[1] Although it is to be admitted that subsequent researches have failed to reveal another solvent entirely approaching water in behavior, they have demonstrated that differences among solvents are differences of degree rather than of kind and that all the effects produced by water are also produced by many other solvent materials. Realization that water is not unique in its characteristics has done much toward developing the fundamental concepts of solution chemistry so necessary to a comprehensive understanding of inorganic and physical chemistry.

From a historical point of view, investigations of solvents and solvent properties may be grouped roughly into three broad periods. In the five-to-seven-year interval subsequent to 1892, attention was directed to such organic compounds as alcohols, esters, and ketones as electrolytic solvents for inorganic substances. Results obtained were usually essentially qualitative in nature and of but little real scientific value since the electrolytes studied were usually selected because of their solubilities rather than for their suitabilities to conductance measurements. Furthermore, such data as were reported usually embraced rather narrow concentration ranges, thus permitting only

[1] W. Ostwald: *Lehrbuch der allgemeinen Chemie*, Vol. II, Pt. 1, p. 705. Verlag von W. Engelmann, Leipzig (1893).

approximate extrapolations to infinite dilution, and often were of doubtful accuracy because of uncertainties in solvent and solute purities.

A second period, beginning with the liquid ammonia studies of Cady in 1897 and embracing both continuance of these studies in subsequent years by Franklin, Kraus, and others and the pioneer investigations of Walden on the solvent character of liquid sulfur dioxide, may be regarded as introducing the third period, that of modern study in the twentieth century. During this last period, a variety of solvents have been investigated from both the practical and the theoretical points of view. With refinements in technique have come particularly rapid developments along theoretical lines.

It is manifestly impossible to divorce any consideration of solvents from acid-base behavior since such a large proportion of the interest in non-aqueous media has stemmed from the acid-base reactions which characterize them. As a consequence, the views summarized in Chapter 9 on reactions in such solvents should be used to implement and supplement the considerations applying to other behaviors as presented in this chapter.

That current interest in non-aqueous solvents has become particularly widespread is evidenced by both the literature which is accumulating and the symposia which have been conducted for its consideration. A number of general references may be consulted with profit as indicating the scope of such interest and the variety of investigations which are being and have been carried out.[2–10] Of these, the work by Walden[4] may be regarded as a classic and may be cited as a general reference for information on all types of non-aqueous systems.

CLASSIFICATIONS OF SOLVENTS

Solvents may be classified in a number of ways. Perhaps the most obvious of these classifications, the one based upon chemical constitu-

[2] P. Walden: *Z. anorg. Chem.*, **29**, 371 (1902).

[3] C. A. Kraus: *The Properties of Electrically Conducting Systems.* Chemical Catalog Co., New York (1922).

[4] P. Walden: *Elektrochemie nichtwässriger Lösungen.* Verlag J. A. Barth, Leipzig (1924).

[5] P. Walden: *Salts, Acids, and Bases.* McGraw-Hill Book Co., New York (1929). Translated by L. F. Audrieth.

[6] E. C. Franklin: *The Nitrogen System of Compounds.* Reinhold Publishing Corp., New York (1935).

[7] "Symposium on Non-aqueous Solvents," *Chem. Revs.*, **8**, 167–352 (1931).

[8] "Symposium on Liquid Ammonia," *Chem. Revs.*, **26**, 1–104 (1940).

[9] H. J. Emeléus: *Ann. Reports*, **36**, 135 (1939).

[10] G. Jander: *Naturwissenschaften*, **32**, 169 (1944).

tion, is at the same time of least value since it can do no more than bring together materials with generally similar solvent characteristics. Although this may be desirable under certain circumstances, knowledge derived from it is ordinarily more qualitative than quantitative in character.

A more convenient basis for classification lies in the electrolytic characteristics of the solvent. Solvents which are themselves polar in nature behave in general as ionizing solvents either because of the attractions which such polar groups have for ions already existent in solutes or because of the tendencies which such materials have to rupture polar covalent linkages present in non-ionic compounds such as the hydrogen acids (p. 400). In a very general way, the electrolytic behavior of the solvent is thus related to its dielectric constant,* solvents with high dielectric constants behaving as better electrolytic solvents than those with lower dielectric constants.[11] This is apparent from the familiar relation

$$F = \frac{1}{\varepsilon} \cdot \frac{e_1 e_2}{(r_1 + r_2)} \qquad (10\cdot1)$$

in which the energy F necessary to separate two ions of charges e_1 and e_2 and radii r_1 and r_2 is related to the dielectric constant ε of the medium in which such separation occurs. The data[12] summarized in Table 10·1 may be cited as indicative of a general decrease in apparent degree of dissociation (α) with decrease in dielectric constant of the solvent, other factors remaining constant. Solvents with high dielectric constants such as formic acid, nitromethane, hydrogen cyanide, acetonitrile, methyl thiocyanate, ammonia, ethylene glycol, methanol, and water should and do behave as our best ionizing solvents; those with low dielectric constants, such as the hydrocarbons and halogenated hydrocarbons, are the poorest.

The concept of leveling and differentiating solvents which has proved so useful in conjunction with the Brønsted-Lowry theory (p. 315) may be applied with profit to electrolytic solvents in general. Leveling solvents, that is, those in which most soluble electrolytes

* The dielectric constant (ε) of a medium is defined in terms of the expression

$$F = \frac{qq_1}{\varepsilon r^2}$$

where F is the force of attraction between two charges q and q_1 separated in that medium by a distance r. The dielectric constant for a vacuum is unity.

[11] P. Walden: *Elektrochemie nichtwässriger Lösungen*, pp. 40–49. Verlag J. A. Barth, Leipzig (1924).

[12] P. Walden and E. J. Birr: *Z. physik. Chem.*, **A153**, 1 (1931).

TABLE 10·1

EFFECT OF DIELECTRIC CONSTANT ON ELECTROLYTIC BEHAVIOR

Solvent	Dielectric Constant	α at 2000 Liters Dilution for		
		$(C_2H_5)_4NPi$*	$(C_2H_5)_2NH_2Pi$*	$(C_2H_5)_2NH_2Cl$
H_2O	81.1 (18°)	0.99	0.97	0.97
CH_3OH	35.4 (13°)	0.95	.....	0.92
C_2H_5OH	25.4 (25°)	0.89	.....	0.88
CH_3CN	36.4 (20°)	0.95	0.90	0.31
$(CH_3)_2CO$	20.7 (20°)	0.88	0.76	0.10
C_5H_5N	12.4 (21°)	0.74	0.53	0.04
$C_2H_4Cl_2$	10.9 (0°)	0.47	0.005	ca. 0.0

* Pi = picrate.

appear strong, embrace the highly polar materials such as water, ammonia, and the lower alcohols. Differentiating solvents, that is, those in which electrolytes often vary widely in strength with changes in the solvent, embrace less polar materials such as certain amines and halogenated hydrocarbons.

Classification of solvents as protonic and non-protonic is intimately related to acid-base phenomena and has been considered from that point of view in the preceding chapter (p. 322). As far as non acid-base behavior is concerned, such a classification has but little utility.

A final classification based upon analogies derived from the concept that each solvent acts as a parent for a system of compounds has proved to be extremely useful. To some extent, this point of view has been discussed already in conjunction with the general theory of solvent systems as applied to acids and bases (p. 322). However, its utility extends much farther, and much of the chemistry of many water-like solvents has been evaluated by this means. Solvents, therefore, may be considered in terms of formally equivalent groups as indicated in Table 10·2, each solvent then serving as a parent for many compounds

TABLE 10·2

FORMALLY EQUIVALENT GROUPS AMONG SOLVENTS

Solvent	Equivalent Group or Ion		
H_2O	H_3O^+	OH^-	O^{-2}
H_2S	H_3S^+ (?)	SH^-	S^{-2}
NH_3	NH_4^+	NH_2^-	NH^{-2} or N^{-3}
N_2H_4	$N_2H_5^+$	$NHNH_2^-$	NNH_2^{-2}
NH_2OH	NH_3OH^+	$NHOH^-$	NOH^{-2}
SO_2	SO^{++}		SO_3^{-2}
$COCl_2$	$COCl^+$		
N_2O_4	NO^+	NO_3^-	
$(CH_3CO)_2O$	CH_3CO^+	$CH_3CO_2^-$	

TABLE 10·3
Physical Constants for Water and Certain Water-Like Solvent

Physical Constant	H_2O	NH_3	NH_2OH	N_2H_4	CH_3NH_2	CH_3OH	CH_3CO_2H	$(CH_3CO)_2O$	H_2S	HCN	HF	SO_2
Molecular weight	18.016	17.032	33.032	32.048	31.058	32.042	60.052	102.09	34.09	27.03	20.008	64.06
Density (grams/ml.)	0.958 (100°)	0.683 (−33.4°)	1.204 (33°)	1.0114 (15°)	0.7691 (−70°)	0.793 (20°)	1.049 (20°)	1.082 (20°)	0.950 (−61.3°)	0.681 (25.6°)	0.991 (19.5°)	1.46 (−10°)
Molecular volume (ml.)	18.8	24.9	27.4	31.7	40.4	40.5	57.3	109.1	35.9	39.7	20.8	44
Melting point (°C.)	0	−77.7	33	1.8	−92.5	−97.8	16.6	−73.1	−85.60	−13.4	−83.1	−75.46
Boiling point (°C.)	100	−33.4	58 (22 mm.)	113.5	−6.5	64.65	118.1	140	−60.75	25.6	19.54	−10.02
Critical temperature (°C.)	374.1	132.4		380	156.9	240.0	321.6	296	100.4	183.5	230.2	157.2
Critical pressure (atm.)	217.7	112		145	73.6	78.7	57.2	46	89	55		77.7
Heat of fusion (kcal./mole)	1.435	1.43				0.525	2.684		0.568	2.009	1.094	1.769
Heat of vapn. (kcal./mole)	9.719	5.64		10.2 (23.1°)		8.42	5.81	6.76	4.463	6.027	7.24	5.96
Equiv. cond. (ohm^{-1})	6×10^{-8} (25°)	5×10^{-9} (−33.4°)						$2\text{–}5 \times 10^{-7}$ (25°)	3.7×10^{-11} (−78.3°)	4.5×10^{-7} (0°)	1.4×10^{-5}	1×10^{-7} (0°)
Dielectric constant (ε)	81.1 (18°)	22 (−34°)		53 (22°)		35.4 (13°)	9.7 (18°)	20.5 (20°)	10.2 (−60°)	123 (15.6°)	83.6 (0°)	13.8 (14.5°)
Viscosity (dyne sec./cm^2.)	0.00959 (25°)	0.00265 (−33.5°)						0.008511 (25°)	0.00432 (−60.75°)	0.00201 (20.2°)		0.0039 (0°)
Molecular f.p. constant (°C./1000 grams)	1.859	0.97							3.85	1.805		
Molecular b.p. constant (°C./1000 grams)	0.51	0.34						2.83	0.67	0.85		1.45
Dipole moment ($D \times 10^{18}$)	1.85	1.47		1.83		1.68			1.10	2.8	1.9	1.61

and compound types. Compounds containing the formally equivalent groups listed in this table, when dissolved in their parent solvents, might then be expected to exhibit strikingly similar characteristics. That this expectation is borne out by experimental data will become apparent from subsequent discussions in this chapter.

Much attention has been directed to "water-like" solvents,[10] particularly by way of the analogies just indicated. These are the solvents possessing physical properties which compare closely with those of water. In Table 10·3, the physical constants for a number of the more common solvents of this type have been summarized. Reference to these data should be helpful in conjunction with the material on various solvents to be considered later.

SOLUBILITY IN POLAR SOLVENTS

Ionic compounds are most soluble in polar solvents. The dissolution of an ionic crystal may be regarded as proceeding because the polar solvent molecules possess sufficient attractions for the ions to pull them away from their positions in the crystal lattice. Such an attraction implies that the ions must become solvated in the process. Because molecules of non-polar solvents are incapable of such solvation effects such solvents do not affect ionic compounds. The dissolution of an ionic compound in a polar solvent occurs, therefore, if the attraction between solvent molecules and ions exceeds the attractions among the ions in the crystal lattice, or in other words if the energy of solvation (p. 294) of the ions exceeds the lattice energy (p. 181) of the crystal. Solubility in a particular solvent is thus a measure of the strength of bonding in the crystal or of the stability of the crystal.

It is difficult to obtain exact values for the solvation and lattice energies of all materials. However, useful information relative to solubilities can be made through a cyclic approach of the Born-Haber type (p. 184). Thus,

$$\begin{array}{ccc} MX(s) & \xrightarrow{U_0} & M^+(g) + X^-(g) \\ {\scriptstyle \pm L}\searrow & & \swarrow{\scriptstyle -H} \\ & M^+(solv.) + X^-(solv.) & \end{array}$$

where U_0 is the lattice energy, H the solvation energy of the gaseous ions, and L the observed heat of solution at infinite dilution. Since the total energy change is the same by either path, it follows that

$$\pm L = U_0 - H \tag{10·2}$$

positive quantities being endothermic and negative quantities being exothermic. The solvation energies of positive and negative ions are additive since at infinite dilution anion and cation are without effect upon each other.

Dissolution of an ionic compound is also affected by the weakening of interionic attractions in the lattice when a solvent with a high dielectric constant is employed. This is apparent from Equation 10·1, since the forces between the ions vary inversely with the dielectric constant. It follows that solvents characterized by high dielectric constants dissolve a given ionic compound most readily and dissolve a greater variety of ionic compounds. Water ($\varepsilon = 81.1$) is a cardinal example. Dielectric constant and the solvation energy for a given ion may be related by the Born equation

$$H = \frac{e^2}{2r}\left(1 - \frac{1}{\varepsilon}\right) \qquad (10\cdot3)$$

where the terms have the same connotations as in Equations 10·1 and 10·2. An increase in the magnitude of the dielectric constant thus increases the solvation energy and the solubility. In many instances, therefore, the dielectric constant is a factor of governing importance.

It is of interest to examine solubility trends in the light of this discussion. Inasmuch as both solvation energy and lattice energy are increased by decreases in cation and anion size, it is difficult to relate solubility trends to size relationships alone. However, the two opposing changes are not often of the same magnitude, and, in a general way, other factors being equal, solubility increases with increase in cation or anion size. With increasing cation or anion charge, however, the lattice energy increases much more rapidly than the solvation energy. It is not surprising, therefore, that parallel sharp decreases in solubility are observed. The electronic arrangements in the ions are also of importance because of the polarizing effects exerted by cations upon anions (p. 208). If the anion is more readily polarized by the cation than is the solvent, the lattice energy will increase more than the solvation energy, and solubility will decrease. If the solvent is more readily polarized, solubility will increase. This is admirably illustrated by the cations in the A and B families in a particular periodic group. The B family cations normally exert greater polarizing effects than the A family cations, and thus yield generally less soluble compounds. Tables of solubilities provide useful data confirming these trends. Specific examples are cited in later chapters of this book. It must be emphasized, however, that rigid comparisons are permitted only among compounds of the same type and containing closely similar ions.

LIQUID AMMONIA AS A SOLVENT

One of the most water-like, and certainly one of the most comprehensively studied, of the non-aqueous solvents is liquid ammonia. Early interest in reactions in this medium has been continued until the literature has become extremely voluminous and complex. References already cited[6–9] should be supplemented by the excellent yearly reviews compiled for the period 1933–1940 under the general guidance of Watt.[13–16]

The water-like character of ammonia is reflected particularly by a comparison of the properties given in Table 10·3. Liquid ammonia, like water, is associated through hydrogen bonding (p. 189). However, since the NHN bond is somewhat weaker than the OHO bond (p. 188), such properties as are dependent upon association are less pronounced with ammonia than with water. Since the dielectric constant of ammonia is lower than that of water, ammonia is the poorer electrolytic solvent (p. 343). However, the lower viscosity of liquid ammonia might be expected to promote greater ionic mobilities and thereby overcome, to some extent, the dielectric constant effect. Although experimental studies involving ammonia are usually carried out at the boiling temperature or below, the ease with which ammonia can be liquefied by pressure alone permits investigations at room temperatures or slightly below in closed systems under pressure.

Solubilities in liquid ammonia

Inasmuch as the solubilities of materials in liquid ammonia are often markedly different from the corresponding solubilities in water and inasmuch as the reactions solutes undergo are often functions of their solubilities, a general summary of solubilities is desirable. Perhaps the outstanding difference between ammonia and water is the ability of ammonia to dissolve, without chemical reaction, free metals which are strongly reducing in character (p. 218). Thus the alkali metals dissolve readily to yield characteristic blue solutions from which the free metals can be recovered by evaporation of the solvent. The alkaline earth metals (calcium, strontium, and barium) show similar

[13] G. W. Watt: *J. Chem. Education*, **11,** 339 (1934); **12,** 171 (1935).

[14] N. O. Cappel and G. W. Watt: *J. Chem. Education*, **13,** 231 (1936); **14,** 174 (1937).

[15] G. W. Watt and N. O. Cappel: *J. Chem. Education*, **15,** 133 (1938); **16,** 219 (1939); **17,** 274 (1940).

[16] G. W. Watt and W. B. Leslie: *J. Chem. Education*, **18,** 210 (1941).

behaviors, although their solubilities are not as large and evaporation of ammonia yields, as first solid phases, rather unstable metal ammonates of composition $M(NH_3)_6$. Magnesium exhibits a slight, though measurable, solubility, as does aluminum,[17, 18] and the same is apparently true to lesser degrees of beryllium, zinc, gallium, lanthanum, cerium, and manganese.

Non-metals such as iodine, sulfur, selenium, and phosphorus are somewhat soluble in liquid ammonia. With sulfur, and perhaps with the others as well, this solubility is due, at least in part, to reaction with the solvent. The solubilities of inorganic salts show trends markedly different from those noted in water. As might be expected, those salts which are most readily and extensively solvated are the most soluble. With ammonia, the nature of the anion appears to play an even more important role than with water, the nature of the cation being comparatively unimportant except that a number of ammonium salts are soluble irrespective of anion. Among the halides, solubility increases markedly from fluoride to iodide, essentially all fluorides being insoluble and even such iodides as that of silver being very soluble. The only chlorides which are really soluble are ammonium and beryllium chlorides. Soluble inorganic salts ordinarily contain such anions as iodide, perchlorate, nitrate, thiocyanate, cyanide, or nitrite, whereas salts containing carbonate, oxalate, sulfate, sulfite, sulfide, arsenate, phosphate, hydroxide, or oxide ions are uniformly insoluble.

Representative solubility data for substances of an inorganic nature are summarized in Table 10·4. The solubilities of organic materials appear to depend upon the natures of the functional groups which are present. In a very general way, the solubilities of these substances in liquid ammonia parallel those in the lower alcohols.

The theoretical implications of solubilities in liquid ammonia have been summarized by Hildebrand.[19] Interpretation of observed results is complicated by the combination in ammonia of such properties as high dielectric constant, high dipole moment, high basicity, ability to hydrogen bond, high dispersion forces, and comparatively small molecular volume. Operation of all these factors renders application of a simple theory quite impossible, but it is possible to account for certain observed phenomena if a single factor predominates in its

[17] A. W. Davidson, J. Kleinberg, W. E. Bennett, and A. D. McElroy: *J. Am. Chem. Soc.*, **71**, 377 (1949).

[18] A. D. McElroy, J. Kleinberg, and A. W. Davidson: *J. Am. Chem. Soc.*, **72**, 5178 (1950).

[19] J. H. Hildebrand: *J. Chem. Education*, **25**, 74 (1948).

influence. Thus the magnitude of the dielectric constant appears to govern the solubilities of highly ionic compounds. The fact that ammonia functions as a poorer electrolytic solvent than water is apparent from the previous discussion on solubility (pp. 342–344).

TABLE 10·4
SOME REPRESENTATIVE SOLUBILITIES IN LIQUID AMMONIA

Solute	Solubility, grams solute/100 grams NH_3	Temperature, °C.	Solute	Solubility, grams solute/100 grams NH_3	Temperature, °C.
Li	11.3	−33	$LiNO_3$	243.66	25
Na	24.6	−33	$NaNO_3$	97.60	25
K	49.0	−33	KNO_3	10.4	25
S	21	30	NH_4NO_3	390.0	25
NaF	0.35	25	$Ca(NO_3)_2$	80.22	25
NaCl	3.02	25	$Sr(NO_3)_2$	87.08	25
NaBr	137.95	25	$Ba(NO_3)_2$	97.22	25
NaI	161.90	25	$AgNO_3$	86.04	25
KCl	0.04	25	NaSCN	205.50	25
KBr	13.50	25	NH_4SCN	312.0	25
KI	182.0	25	KOCN	1.70	25
NH_4Cl	102.5	25	Li_2SO_4	0	25
NH_4Br	237.9	25	Na_2SO_4	0	25
NH_4I	368.5	25	K_2SO_4	0	25
$BaCl_2$	0	25	$KClO_3$	2.52	25
MnI_2	0.02	25	$KBrO_3$	0.002	25
AgCl	0.83	25	KIO_3	0	25
AgBr	5.92	25	NH_4ClO_4	137.93	25
AgI	206.84	25	$NH_4C_2H_3O_2$	253.16	25
ZnI_2	0.10	25	NH_4HCO_3	0	25
$NaNH_2$	0.004	25	$(NH_4)_2CO_3$	0	25
KNH_2	3.6	25	$(NH_4)_2HPO_4$	0	25
K_2CO_3	0	25	$(NH_4)_2S$	120.0	25
H_3BO_3	1.92	25	ZnO	0	25

Data taken largely from H. Hunt: *J. Am. Chem. Soc.*, **54**, 3509 (1932); H. Hunt and L. Boncyk: *J. Am. Chem. Soc.*, **55**, 3528 (1933).

Hydrogen bonding between ammonia and a solute will quite obviously increase the solubility of the latter. In a sense, the ability to hydrogen bond is associated with the basic character of ammonia in either the Brønsted-Lowry or G. N. Lewis sense. Ammonia is the most basic of all common solvents except perhaps methylamine or ethylenediamine. As a consequence, it functions as a useful solvent for a variety of acidic substances, both inorganic and organic. Dispersion forces relate to the attractions which molecules that do not react exert upon each other by virtue of the moving electrons which they contain. If sufficient electrons are present to render the molecule highly polarizable (p. 187), this effect may overcome orientation effects due to dipole moment. With water, the attractive effect toward other materials is due mainly to dipole character, but with ammonia dispersion and dipole effects are nearly equal. Ammonia, therefore, is not as good a solvent as water for strong dipoles, but it is better for non-polar substances (e.g., many organic compounds) and for molecules containing many electrons (e.g., iodine compounds).

In terms of Hildebrand's discussion,[19] solubility increases in, for instance, the series NaF, NaCl, NaBr, NaI are associated with decreases in melting point and lattice energy. In addition, the iodide is extremely soluble because the solid phase is an ammonate, $NaI{\cdot}4NH_3$. Decreases in solubility from lithium halides to cesium halides are in accord with a corresponding decrease in tendency to ammonate. Dissolution of free metals seems to be favored by the almost negligible ionization of pure ammonia, the resistance of ammonia to reduction by free electrons, and the ability of ammonia to solvate metal ions. Solubilities of the alkali metals apparently vary because of variations in the magnitude of factors which oppose dissolution, such as sublimation energy of the free metal and ionization energy of the gaseous metal atom, and in the magnitude of factors which favor dissolution, such as solvation energy of the gaseous metal ion, solvation of the electron, and alteration in entropy values (p. 295). Lack of exact values for the last three factors precludes any exact evaluation of these variations.

Nature of solution of metals in liquid ammonia

Although the general behavior of metals in liquid ammonia has been treated in conjunction with the discussion of the nature of the metallic state (p. 212), a more comprehensive examination of their characteristics appears warranted. Of the many published summaries which describe such systems, those given by Johnson and Meyer[20] and by Fernelius and Watt[21] are perhaps the best for consultation because of their completeness and of their comprehensive coverage of the original literature. Of interest too are several less technical discussions.[22]

The alkali metals are readily soluble without appreciable thermal

[20] W. C. Johnson and A. W. Meyer: *Chem. Revs.*, **8**, 273 (1931).

[21] W. C. Fernelius and G. W. Watt: *Chem. Revs.*, **20**, 195 (1937).

[22] W. C. Johnson and W. C. Fernelius: *J. Chem. Education*, **5**, 664, 828 (1928); **6**, 20, 441 (1929); **7**, 981 (1930).

effects and without chemical reaction [in the absence of such catalysts as iron, iron(III) oxide, or platinum or of light of wavelength 2150–2550 A which favor amide formation] to give blue solutions which possess identical absorption spectra at given dilutions, conduct the electric current, show strongly paramagnetic behaviors, and have densities less than the density of pure ammonia. Although the alkaline earth metals yield ammonates, their solutions in liquid ammonia have many of the characteristics of the solutions of the alkali metals.

It is noteworthy that marked solubility among the metals is limited to those metals which readily lose electrons (p. 217). This gives a clue to the generally accepted theory of the constitution of these solutions as proposed by Kraus.[23] Metal atoms are assumed to be in equilibrium with metal ions and free electrons as

$$M \rightleftharpoons M^+ + e^-$$

the ammonia molecules then solvating these ions and electrons reversibly as

$$M^+ + xNH_3 \rightleftharpoons M(NH_3)_x{}^+$$
$$e^- + yNH_3 \rightleftharpoons e^-(NH_3)_y$$

Such a view is supported by a variety of experimental evidences. The transition of conductance from values approaching those for free metals in concentrated solutions to values approaching those for electrolytic salt solutions as the quantity of ammonia is increased has been discussed earlier (p. 218). This behavior is rendered reasonable if one considers that successive additions of ammonia convert more and more metal atoms to ammonated metal ions and electrons. Conductance measurements show further that the anion is the same regardless of the metal dissolved, differences in equivalent conductance values being those predictable on the basis of known values for the cations. Inasmuch as the mobility of the ammonated electron appears to be somewhat less than that of the free electron, conductance in dilute solutions becomes electrolytic in character while in the absence of excessive ammonation in concentrated solutions, it is metallic in nature.

The strongly reducing properties shown by solutions of metals in liquid ammonia are in accord with such a view. In effect, such solutions may be regarded as abundant sources of free electrons which may then add to any reducible ion or compound present. The wide spread use of liquid ammonia solutions of sodium etc. in organic

[23] C. A. Kraus: *J. Am. Chem. Soc.*, **30**, 1323 (1908); **43**, 749 (1921).

reductions may be cited as a case in point.[24, 25] Many inorganic reductions are also of importance.[26]

The more recently expressed views of Ogg[27] are also in essential agreement with this general concept except that the colored components are considered to amount to single electrons and electron pairs trapped in cavities which they create in the liquid rather than to solvated electrons. These single electrons and electron pairs are postulated to be in equilibrium with each other, the point of the equilibrium being influenced by both temperature and concentration. The polarographic studies of Laitinen and Nyman[28] may be regarded as offering independent support of the concept of existence of free electrons. Proposals that metal solutions in liquid ammonia are colloidal in nature[29] appear to be untenable.[21]

Reactions in liquid ammonia

Chemical reactions which take place in liquid ammonia solutions may be discussed conveniently under the headings (1) reduction reactions, (2) acid-base reactions, (3) metathesis reactions in which acid-base character is not exhibited, (4) ammonation reactions, and (5) ammonolysis reactions. Comprehensive information on all these types of reactions may be obtained from published summaries[9, 21, 30–32] to supplement the brief summary presented here.

Reduction Reactions. The availability of free electrons in solutions of metals in liquid ammonia permits of a variety of reductions in such systems. Furthermore, the resistance of ammonia itself to further reduction provides a medium in which highly reduced states are stable. These factors combine to permit many reactions not observed in other media to take place.

Reduction reactions involving inorganic materials may be classified[21, 26] under the headings ammonium salts, free elements, hydrides, halides and cyanides, oxides, sulfides, nitrides and imides, and ternary compounds. Reactions with inorganic substances usually amount to the formation of binary compounds or to the liberation of free elements.

[24] A. J. Birch: *Quart. Revs.*, **4,** 69 (1950).
[25] G. W. Watt: *Chem. Revs.*, **46,** 317 (1950).
[26] *Ibid.*, 289.
[27] R. A. Ogg: *J. Chem. Phys.*, **13,** 533 (1945); **14,** 114, 295, 399 (1946). *Phys. Rev.*, **69,** 243, 544, 668 (1946).
[28] H. A. Laitinen and C. J. Nyman: *J. Am. Chem. Soc.*, **70,** 3002 (1948).
[29] J. F. Chittum and H. Hunt: *J. Phys. Chem.*, **40,** 581 (1936).
[30] C. A. Kraus: *Chem. Revs.*, **8,** 251 (1931); **26,** 95 (1940).
[31] W. C. Fernelius and G. B. Bowman: *Chem. Revs.*, **26,** 3 (1940).
[32] W. M. Burgess and E. H. Smoker: *Chem. Revs.*, **8,** 265 (1931).

Such reactions doubtless involve primary reduction by free electrons. Reactions summarized in Table 10·5 may be regarded as typical of inorganic materials. Organic reductions are also covered by Fernelius and Watt[21] and by Watt[25] but they have no place in this discussion.

TABLE 10·5
TYPICAL REDUCTION REACTIONS PRODUCED BY METALS IN LIQUID AMMONIA

Substance	Metal Employed	Products	Substance	Metal Employed	Products
NH_4Cl	Ca	$CaCl_2$	GeH_4	Na	$NaGeH_3$
$(NH_4)_2S$	Li	Li_2S	CO	Li	LiCO
$NH_4C_2H_3O_2$	Na	$NaC_2H_3O_2$	CO_2	Na	$NaCO_2H$
O_2	Na	Na_2O_2, NaOH, $NaNH_2$, $NaNO_2$	N_2O	K	N_2, KOH, KNH_2, KN_3
S	Na	Na_2S, Na_2S_x	NO	Na	NaNO
Se	K	K_2Se, K_2Se_x	NO_2	Ba	BaN_2O_2
P	Na	$Na_3P{\cdot}3NH_3$	Ag_2O	K	Ag
Sb	Li	$Li_3Sb{\cdot}NH_3$	CuO	K	Cu_2O
Pb	Na	Na_4Pb_9	GeS	Na	Ge
Hg	Na	$NaHg_8$	$Co(NO_3)_2$	Na	Co
CuI	Na	Cu	SCN^-	Ca	S^{-2}
AgCN	Ca	Ag			
$Zn(CN)_2$	Na	$NaZn_4$			
PbI_2	Na	Na_4Pb_9			
$ThBr_4$	K	$Th(NH)_2{\cdot}KNH_2$			
MnI_2	Na	Mn			

Acid-Base Reactions. In terms of the Brønsted-Lowry concept (p. 309), ammonium ion behaves as an acid in liquid ammonia, and amide, imide, and nitride ions behave as bases. Typical neutralizations involving ammonium salts and both soluble and insoluble amides, imides, and nitrides occur in this solvent. Furthermore, solutions of ammonium salts oxidize active metals, with the evolution of hydrogen, as do aqueous solutions of acids. Amphoterism is also noted, zinc amide, for example, dissolving in a solution of potassium amide in liquid ammonia to yield the ion $[Zn(NH_2)_4]^{-2}$, the ammono analog of the hydroxozincate ion $[Zn(OH)_4]^{-2}$. In like fashion, ammonobasic salts, such as $PbNH_2I$, are easily obtained, and bear the same relation to ammonia as do the aquobasic salts to water. In addition many ammono and aquoammono compounds derived from such non-metals as carbon, silicon, phosphorus, and sulfur exhibit acid-base behavior in liquid ammonia. Certain of these compounds are discussed later (pp. 570–573).

Metathesis Reactions Not Involving Acid-Base Behavior. The courses which such reactions follow are determined by the solubilities of the products. As has been indicated (p. 345), such solubilities in ammonia are often sufficiently different from the corresponding values in water to cause reactions to take entirely different courses. A case in point involves precipitation of ammonated barium bromide, $BaBr_2{\cdot}8NH_3$, when ammonia solutions of silver bromide and barium nitrate are mixed. In water, the exact reverse reaction occurs. On the other hand, many sulfides may be precipitated by ammonium sulfide from ammonia as well as from water. The general solubility variations already noted may be used to predict the courses of such reactions. Many metathesis reactions in liquid ammonia are of preparative significance, particularly where the desired products are more resistant to ammonolysis than to hydrolysis.

Ammonation Reactions. Reactions involving the direct addition of ammonia to another material are called ammonation reactions. Reactions leading to the formation of metal ammonates such as $Ba(NH_3)_6$ and to salt ammonates such as $BaBr_2{\cdot}8NH_3$ or $[Cr(NH_3)_6]Cl_3$ are characteristic examples. This type of reaction is of little importance in comparison with other types.

Ammonolysis Reactions. Ammonolysis, or ammonolytic, reactions are metathetical reactions in which ammonia is a reactant. Like hydrolysis or hydrolytic reactions, these are protolytic equilibria and are, therefore, related to acid-base behavior. They are considered separately, however, because they involve ammonia itself rather than solutes which might exhibit acidic or basic properties when dissolved in ammonia. Ammonolytic reactions are ordinarily less extensive than corresponding hydrolytic reactions because of the lower degree of self-dissociation with ammonia. This is reflected in the ion product of 1.9×10^{-33} (at $-50°C.$) for ammonia as compared with that of 1×10^{-14} (at 25°C.) for water.[31] As might be expected, ammonolysis reactions may involve either gaseous or liquid ammonia, the major disadvantage of the latter being the low temperature involved and the consequent reduction in reaction rate.

Ammonolysis reactions involving both inorganic and organic substances have been reviewed comprehensively by Fernelius and Bowman.[31] A few typical examples of the inorganic type are summarized in Table 10·6. For other examples, particularly of the organic type, the indicated reference[31] should be consulted. The catalytic effects of ammonium salts on the ammonolysis of esters may be regarded as analogous to the effects of aqueous acids on corresponding hydrolytic reactions.

TABLE 10·6
AMMONOLYSIS REACTIONS INVOLVING TYPICAL INORGANIC SUBSTANCES

Substance	Ammonolysis Product	Substance	Ammonolysis Product
$HgCl_2$	$HgNH_2Cl$	$SbCl_3$	SbN
HgI_2	Hg_2NI	$VOCl_3$	$VO(NH_2)_3$
BCl_3	$B(NH_2)_3$	$TaCl_5$	$Ta(NH_2)_2Cl_3 \cdot 3NH_3$
$SiCl_4$	$Si(NH_2)_4$	$TeBr_4$	Te_3N_4
$GeCl_4$	$Ge(NH)_2$	$MoCl_5$	$Mo(NH)_2NH_2$ or $Mo(NH_2)_4Cl$
SiH_3Cl	$(SiH_3)_3N$	Na_2O	$NaNH_2$
$TiCl_4$	$TiNCl \cdot xNH_3$	NaH	$NaNH_2$
$NOCl$	$NONH_2$	$N_2H_4 \cdot H_2SO_4$	$N_2H_4 + (NH_4)_2SO_4$
PCl_5	$P(NH)_2NH_2$	HX	NH_4X ($X = O, F, Cl, Br, I$)
PBr_3	$P(NH_2)_3$	PH_4I	PH_3

SUBSTITUTED AMMONIAS AS NON-AQUEOUS SOLVENTS

The striking similarities in solvent properties existent between ammonia and water suggest that certain substituted ammonias might also function as non-aqueous solvents for inorganic substances. On the basis of structural considerations alone, any such characteristics might be expected to be more pronounced with hydroxylamine, hydrazine, and the lower acid amides than with the primary, secondary, and tertiary amines. Since hydroxylamine and hydrazine are strictly inorganic in nature, they should also be of more interest than the substituted ammonias containing organic radicals. Hydroxylamine, containing as it does both the amide and the hydroxyl radicals, should show solvent properties corresponding to those of both ammonia and water. Although data on the physical constants of these two compounds are incomplete, the values summarized in Table 10·3 do support this point of view.

Early observations by Kohlschütter and Hofmann[33] indicated rather striking resemblances between hydroxylamine and water in solvent character, solvation, amphoteric behavior, and ability to oxidize active metals. Such work as has been done on this solvent supports these observations.

Detailed information on solubilities in hydroxylamine is lacking, but early work by de Bruyn[34] showed such materials as potassium iodide, bromide, and cyanide, barium hydroxide, and ammonia to be very soluble, with sodium and barium nitrates and sodium and potassium chlorides dissolving less readily. Solvolytic reactions doubtless

[33] V. Kohlschütter and K. A. Hofmann: *Ann.*, **307**, 314 (1899).

[34] C. A. Lobry de Bruyn: *Rec. trav. chim.*, **11**, 18 (1892).

accounted for the reactivity shown by anhydrous hydroxylamine toward many other substances. Preparation of compounds containing hydroxylamine of crystallization (i.e., hydroxylamates) and of hydroxylamino-basic salts such as those of mercury(II) has also been reported. It appears likely that solutions of inorganic salts in hydroxylamine would show electrolytic behavior. Further, and much needed, investigations on the solvent properties of the material should be aided by the summary of considerations of hydroxylamine as a parent of a system of acids, bases, and salts as given by Audrieth.[35]

Early studies by de Bruyn[36] showed anhydrous hydrazine to dissolve such salts as sodium chloride and nitrate, potassium chloride, bromide, and nitrate, and barium nitrate, but the only comprehensive studies of the solvent properties of hydrazine appear to be those reported by Welsh.[37,38] Many of the trends noted with ammonia appear to characterize hydrazine as well. Thus ammonium salts were found to be fairly soluble as were many nitrates, and decreases in solubility from iodide to chloride characterized many salts containing a common cation. In addition, such inorganic compounds as oxides, sulfides, carbonates, sulfates, and phosphates appeared to be rather uniformly insoluble. In many instances, solubility of a salt was attended by precipitation of free metals or uncharacterized materials, and with ammonium salts ammonia was evolved. The alkali metals reacted vigorously with hydrazine, probably to form hydrazides of the type MN_2H_3, with evolution of hydrogen, but no evidences of dissolution as the free metals were reported. Sulfur and iodine dissolved readily, but with vigorous reaction with the solvent. Most of the observations reported were qualitative in nature.

The conductances of many inorganic substances dissolved in hydrazine were also determined qualitatively.[38] Ionic compounds, if soluble, appear to give solutions which are highly conducting; covalent compounds give solutions which are poor conductors. These observations are in accord with behavior predicted by the high dielectric constant of hydrazine (Table 10·3). Other conductance data supporting the contention that hydrazine is an electrolytic solvent have since been obtained for a number of compounds.[39]

As for reactions in hydrazine, Welsh and Broderson[38] showed that hydrazine solutions of hydrazine sulfide will precipitate cadmium and

[35] L. F. Audrieth: *Trans. Illinois State Acad. Sci.*, **22,** 385 (1929).
[36] C. A. Lobry de Bruyn: *Rec. trav. chim.*, **15,** 174 (1896).
[37] T. W. B. Welsh: *J. Am. Chem. Soc.*, **37,** 497 (1915).
[38] T. W. B. Welsh and H. J. Broderson: *J. Am. Chem. Soc.*, **37,** 816, 825 (1915).
[39] P. Walden and H. Hilgert: *Z. physik. Chem.*, **A165,** 241 (1933).

zinc sulfides from halide solutions and that in hydrazine sodium will liberate free metals from cadmium, zinc, and iron compounds. As might be expected, hydrazine hydrochloride and sulfate are acidic in hydrazine, dissolving free metals with liberation of hydrogen and neutralizing such a base as sodium hydrazide. Further studies in this medium should be implemented by considerations of the hydrazine system of compounds offered by Audrieth and Mohr.[40] A detailed summary of the solvent characteristics of anhydrous hydrazine is given by Audrieth and Ogg.[41]

Of the acid amides, only formamide and acetamide have been studied extensively. Formamide was shown by Walden[42] to resemble water closely as an electrolytic solvent, and its use as a medium for electrodeposition reactions has been explored also (p. 368). The solvent properties of fused acetamide at 100°C. have also been shown to resemble those of water.[43] Acetamide solutions of salts are excellent conductors and lend themselves to electrolysis and metathesis reactions. Furthermore, solvates containing acetamide are readily obtained. The high dielectric constant of acetamide (59.2) favors its electrolytic solvent behavior.

The lower aliphatic amines show many of the solvent properties of ammonia, but, as the number of organic substituents or the sizes of such substituents increase, the amines become more organic in character and lose their abilities to dissolve ionic substances. Thus, although methyl amine is an excellent solvent for many salts and salt-like compounds,[44] particularly nitrates and halides and lithium salts in general, other amines show reduced solvent power for such materials paralleling decreases in dielectric constant. The reduced acidity of methylamine as compared with ammonia renders solutions of the alkali metals in this medium particularly stable and, consequently, very useful for reduction reactions. Although the alkali metals dissolve readily in anhydrous methylamine, as in liquid ammonia, and have measurable solubilities in ethylamine, they are apparently practically insoluble in other primary amines and in all secondary and tertiary amines.[30, 45] The ethanolamines appear to be excellent electrolytic solvents for a variety of inorganic substances. The properties

[40] L. F. Audrieth and P. H. Mohr: *Chem. Eng. News*, **26**, 3746 (1948).

[41] L. F. Audrieth and B. A. Ogg: *The Chemistry of Hydrazine*, Ch. 10. John Wiley and Sons, New York (1951).

[42] P. Walden: *Z. physik. Chem.*, **46**, 103 (1903); **54**, 129 (1905); **55**, 207, 683 (1905); **59**, 385 (1907); **75**, 555 (1910). Classic papers on organic solvent systems.

[43] O. F. Stafford: *J. Am. Chem. Soc.*, **55**, 3987 (1934).

[44] H. D. Gibbs: *J. Am. Chem. Soc.*, **28**, 1395 (1906).

[45] C. A. Kraus: *J. Am. Chem. Soc.*, **29**, 1557 (1907).

of anhydrous ethylenediamine as an electolytic solvent have been evaluated also.[46]

ORGANIC LIQUIDS AS NON-AQUEOUS SOLVENTS

Differences in bond character and structure between inorganic and organic compounds suggest that organic liquids should not, in general be suitable solvents for inorganic substances unless these substances are covalent in character. The generally low dielectric constants characterizing organic liquids support this view and indicate that, even if materials are measurably soluble, the resulting solutions will exhibit electrolytic properties only to limited degrees. Because little is to be gained from a consideration of all types of organic solvents, only those showing reasonable dielectric behavior are discussed here.

The alcohols may be compared to both water and the primary amines. In general, they are less polar than water but more polar than the corresponding amines, and as a result they exhibit solvent properties intermediate between those of water and the amines. As the length and complexity of the organic radical increase, the solvent power of alcohols for salts and salt-like compounds is reduced, but their ability to dissolve covalent and highly complexed substances is increased. Methanol, in particular, and ethanol and isopropanol, to a lesser extent, dissolve a variety of inorganic salts and yield conducting solutions, whereas the higher alcohols have but little solvent effect on these substances. On the other hand, alcohols immiscible or only slightly miscible with water are useful for extracting non-salt-like compounds from water or as direct solvents for those substances. Salts which are most soluble in water or tend to hydrate to the greatest extent are commonly most soluble in the lower alcohols. The electrolytic behavior of many salts in methanol parallels the behavior in water quite closely and supports the view that methanol is a "water-like" solvent.[47]

Ethers are less polar than alcohols and show reduced solvent power toward salts and salt-like compounds. On the other hand, they are often excellent solvents for highly covalent and complex substances. The ease with which diethyl ether extracts iron(III) and gallium(III) from aqueous chloride solutions containing hydrochloric acid or uranium(VI) from aqueous uranyl nitrate solutions may be cited as representative. Diethyl ether appears to be the only compound of this type to be studied extensively in relation to inorganic substances, although the diisopropyl homolog appears to have some advantages.

[46] G. L. Putnam and K. A. Kobe: *Trans. Electrochem. Soc.*, **74**, 609 (1938).
[47] J. W. Williams: *Chem. Revs.*, **8**, 303 (1931).

Of the ketones, acetone is the most readily available and consequently the best characterized. The moderately high dielectric constant of acetone (20.7 at 20°) suggests its ability to function as an electrolytic solvent, and its solvent properties are indicated by its polar nature. Naumann[48] has given qualitative solubility data for dozens of inorganic compounds which are to be supplemented by the quantitative data summarized by Walden.[49] In general, compounds which are soluble in water are also soluble in acetone although cardinal exceptions are found in such materials as sodium and ammonium chlorides, sodium and potassium carbonates, copper(II) and iron(II and III) sulfates, potassium hydroxide, and barium nitrate. Reactions occurring in acetone appear to parallel those in aqueous solutions,[50] and electrolytic behavior characterizes solutions of salts. The higher homologs of acetone exhibit similar solvent properties, solvent power toward covalent materials increasing with increasing complexity of the organic groups. Certain of the higher homologs are useful for extraction of materials from aqueous medium.

The lower aliphatic acids have been studied extensively as solvents for inorganic substances. These compounds, because of their acidic nature, are particularly good solvents for basic materials, and most reported accounts of their solvent properties have been from the acid-base point of view (p. 312). Although formic acid has been investigated as a medium for potentiometric titration of bases, such as urea, which are weak in aqueous solution,[51] more attention has been directed to solutions in glacial acetic acid[52, 53] (p. 312). Materials readily soluble in glacial acetic acid embrace acetates [except of calcium, zinc, iron(III), and silver], nitrates, halides[54] (especially iodides), cyanides, and thiocyanates; acids such as perchloric, sulfuric, orthophosphoric, hydrochloric, and hydrosulfuric; and basic compounds such as water and ammonia. On the other hand, most metal sulfates and sulfides and compounds which are difficultly soluble in water are insoluble in acetic acid. Quantitative solubility data are available for many acetates,[52] the highest solubilities again characterizing materials which solvate most readily and extensively. Although the dielectric constant is fairly low (9.7 at 18°C.), salt solutions in acetic acid are con-

[48] A. Naumann: *Ber.*, **37,** 4328 (1904).

[49] P. Walden: *Elektrochemie nichtwässriger Lösungen*, pp. 456–458. Verlag J. A. Barth, Leipzig (1924).

[50] A. Naumann: *Ber.*, **32,** 999 (1899).

[51] L. P. Hammett and N. Dietz: *J. Am. Chem. Soc.*, **52,** 4795 (1930).

[52] A. W. Davidson: *Chem. Revs.*, **8,** 175 (1931).

[53] N. F. Hall: *Chem. Revs.*, **8,** 191 (1931).

[54] A. W. Davidson and W. Chappell: *J. Am. Chem. Soc.*, **60,** 2043 (1938).

ductors and undergo neutralization, metathesis, and electrodeposition reactions. Neutralizations in acetic acid have been discussed in the previous chapter.

Of the acid anhydrides, only acetic anhydride has been investigated extensively as a solvent. The "water-like" character of acetic anhydride is evident from a comparison of physical constants as listed in Table 10·3, and the material functions as a better electrolytic solvent than glacial acetic acid. Although the conductance of the pure compound is low, there is ample evidence[55–57] for autodissociation into acetyl (CH_3CO^+) and acetate (CH_3COO^-) ions through solvolysis reactions of the type

$$MX + (CH_3CO)_2O \rightarrow CH_3COX + CH_3COOM$$

and neutralization reactions of the type

$$CH_3COCl + CH_3COOK \rightarrow KCl + (CH_3CO)_2O$$

Reactions of the latter type can be followed conductimetrically. Electrolytic behavior is apparent in the observation that compounds such as antimony(III) chloride and bromide and arsenic(III) chloride may be electrolyzed in this medium in accordance with Faraday's law.[58] The solubilities of many materials have been evaluated more or less qualitatively.[57] The most soluble compounds are acetyl derivatives, acetates of the alkali metals and Group IVb elements, and various acid halides. Alkali metal halides, heavy metal acetates, silver salts, and metal sulfides are among the least soluble materials.

Two potentially useful organic solvents are acetonitrile and nitromethane, the dielectric constants of which are, respectively, 36.4 and 40.4 at 20°C. Some solubilities of inorganic salts in these media have been evaluated, and a few conductance values have been reported, but no really comprehensive studies have been made.

LIQUID HYDROGEN FLUORIDE AS A SOLVENT

One of the most "water-like" of all non-aqueous solvents is hydrogen fluoride. Although liquid hydrogen fluoride has a rather low specific conductance, its high dielectric constant indicates that it is an excellent electrolytic solvent. Many inorganic substances are soluble in

[55] M. Usanovich and K. Yatsimirskiĭ: *J. Gen. Chem. (U.S.S.R.)*, **11,** 954, 959 (1941).

[56] H. Schmidt, C. Blohm, and G. Jander: *Angew. Chem.*, **A59,** 233 (1947).

[57] G. Jander, E. Rüsberg, and H. Schmidt: *Z. anorg. Chem.*, **255,** 238 (1948).

[58] H. Schmidt, I. Wittkopf, and G. Jander: *Z. anorg. Chem.*, **256,** 113 (1948).

this material, and interest in solutions of this type is evident from the abundant literature which has accumulated.[9, 59, 60]

The versatility of liquid hydrogen fluoride as a solvent is shown by the summary in Table 10·7.[59] Organic substances appear to be less

TABLE 10·7
SOLUBILITIES OF INORGANIC SUBSTANCES IN HYDROGEN FLUORIDE

Very Soluble	Slightly Soluble	Not Appreciably Soluble	Soluble with Reaction	Reaction Product Insoluble	Insoluble and Unreactive
H_2O	MgF_2	AlF_3	KCN	$AlCl_3$	$ZnCl_2$
NH_4F	CaF_2	ZnF_2	NaN_3	$FeCl_2$	$SnCl_2$
LiF	SrF_2	FeF_3	K_2SiF_6	$MnCl_2$	$NiCl_2$
NaF	BaF_2	PbF_2	$KClO_3$	$CeCl_3$	$CdCl_2$
KF	$CaSO_4$	CuF_2	$Ba(ClO_3)_2$	MgO	$CuCl_2$
RbF	$KClO_4$	HgF_2	Hydroxides	CaO	HgI_2
CsF	H_2S	HCl	Alkali and alkaline earth metal halides	SrO	AgCl
TlF	CO	HBr		BaO	AgBr
AgF	CO_2	HI		PbO	AgI
$Hg(CN)_2$		SiF_4		BaO_2	HgO
KNO_3		$Cu(NO_3)_2$		Al_2O_3	PbO_2
$NaNO_3$		$Bi(NO_3)_3$		CuO	MnO_2
$AgNO_3$		$Pb(NO_3)_2$			SnO_2
K_2SO_4		$Co(NO_3)_2$			Cr_2O_3
Na_2SO_4		$ZnSO_4$			WO_3
		$CdSO_4$			Mn_2O_3
		$CuSO_4$			
		Ag_2SO_4			

soluble in general than inorganic substances, and the use of liquid hydrogen fluoride as a medium for various types of organic reactions is probably more dependent upon its properties as an acid catalyst (p. 335) than upon its properties as a solvent.

Dissolution of inorganic materials in liquid hydrogen fluoride may take any one of a number of courses. According to Fredenhagen,[60] the following types of behavior may be distinguished:

1. *Dissolution with normal dissociation into ions.* Such behavior characterizes the dissolution of such materials as potassium fluoride. Although for many years it was believed that only fluorides dissolved in this fashion and that the only anion capable of existence in liquid hydrogen fluoride was the fluoride ion, more recent work[60] has shown that certain alkali metal iodates, periodates, perchlorates, and sulfates

[59] J. H. Simons: *Chem. Revs.*, **8**, 213 (1931).
[60] H. Fredenhagen: *Z. anorg. allgem. Chem.*, **242**, 23 (1939).

dissolve unchanged and undergo methathesis reactions in this medium to precipitate other salts of these anions. Precipitation of silver and thallium(I) chlorides by saturation of their fluoride solutions with dry hydrogen chloride suggests the momentary existence, at least, of chloride ion. In addition, certain non-metal fluorides (e.g., SbF_5, AsF_5, PF_5) have been found to give acidic solutions in liquid hydrogen fluoride.[61] Such solutions react with metal oxides and metals in the same fashion as do aqueous solutions of acids. It is presumed that reactions of these fluorides with the solvent yield protons (presumably solvated) and fluoanions (e.g., SbF_6^-, AsF_6^-, PF_6^-). Certain salts containing fluoanions (e.g., Na_3AlF_6, K_3CrF_6) also dissolve to give ionic solutions. These materials exhibit amphoterism.

2. *Dissolution with addition of hydrogen fluoride to the solute, followed by dissociation.* In effect, this type of behavior amounts to transfer of a proton to the solute and leads to the formation of a solvated proton and the fluoride ion. Water, nitric acid, and such soluble organic compounds as alcohols, aldehydes, ketones, ethers, acids, acid anhydrides, and carbohydrates behave in this fashion, the resulting solutions and the natures of the ionic species present having been studied by conductance and boiling point elevation procedures. Typical reactions of this type are indicated by the equations

$$H_2O + HF \rightleftharpoons H_3O^+ + F^-$$

$$CH_3OH + HF \rightleftharpoons CH_3OH\cdot HF \rightleftharpoons CH_3OH\cdot H^+ + F^-$$

$$(C_2H_5)_2O + HF \rightleftharpoons (C_2H_5)_2O\cdot H^+ + F^-$$

$$HNO_3 + HF \rightleftharpoons H_2NO_3^+ + F^-$$

$$KNO_3 + 2HF \rightleftharpoons H_2NO_3^+ + K^+ + 2F^-$$

The highly acidic nature of the solvent thus brings out basic properties even in materials like nitric acid, which are usually acidic (p. 312).

3. *Dissolution with reaction involving displacement of the acid radical of the solute by fluoride ion and liberation of the free acid.* This type of behavior is noted where the acid formed is insoluble in liquid hydrogen fluoride or will not add a proton, as in case 2 above. Thus alkali metal halides (except fluorides) and cyanides liberate the corresponding free hydrogen compounds as indicated by the equation

$$MX + HF \rightarrow M^+ + F^- + HX$$

where X = Cl, Br, I, or CN.

[61] A. F. Clifford: Doctoral Dissertation, University of Delaware (1949).

4. *Dissolution with reaction involving a more complete change in the solute.* Behavior of this sort is apparently determined largely by the nature of the anion in the salt employed. Thus sulfuric acid reacts to give fluosulfonic acid and water, the water in turn accepting a proton from the solvent. The complete reaction may then be represented as

$$H_2SO_4 + 2HF \rightarrow HSO_3F + H_3O^+ + F^-$$

On the other hand, chlorates yield chlorine dioxide, oxygen, hydronium ion, and fluoride ion; bromates give free bromine; permanganates and chromates yield volatile oxyfluorides of manganese and chromium, respectively; and carbonates give carbon dioxide.

MISCELLANEOUS PROTONIC SOLVENTS

It is manifestly impractical to cover all protonic solvents which have been studied in this presentation. Only a few of the more interesting and representative ones will be considered.

Liquid hydrogen sulfide

Although hydrogen sulfide might, at first glance, be thought analogous to water as a solvent, a comparison of physical constants (Table 10·3) indicates that this is far from the truth. Comprehensive studies have shown[62] that liquid hydrogen sulfide behaves more like an organic solvent than like water. Materials which are soluble without reaction embrace many organic compounds and only a few inorganic substances such as hydrogen chloride and bromide, zinc and aluminum chlorides, and a few sulfides. Other materials which are soluble are reactive because of their oxidizing power, the presence of an amine group, or their susceptibility to thiohydrolysis. In some few cases, metals and some oxidizing agents, for instance, reaction with the solvent without dissolution is noted, but many materials are both insoluble and unreactive, particularly most of the metal sulfides. Thiohydrolysis reactions characterize the behavior of the volatile chlorides of the fourth, fifth, and sixth periodic groups except those of carbon and silicon. Such reactions often yield sulfides (e.g., P_2S_3 from PCl_3) or thiochlorides (e.g., $PSCl_3$ from PCl_5), although reduction of the chloride may also occur. The conductances of materials dissolved in liquid hydrogen sulfide are uniformly low,[62] and the low conductance of the pure compound (Table 10.3) seems to preclude any appreciable self-dissociation and the development of a corresponding system of acids and bases.

[62] J. A. Wilkinson: *Chem. Revs.*, **8**, 237 (1931).

Liquid hydrogen cyanide

Another promising protonic solvent is liquid hydrogen cyanide.[63–66] This substance is especially "water-like" in its properties (Table 10·3) and has an exceptionally large dielectric constant. Its poisonous nature has doubtless limited previous studies upon its characteristics and will hamper its applications. Many organic substances, water, and covalent inorganic compounds such as the tin(IV) halides and the arsenic(III) halides, although soluble, give solutions which are poor conductors. On the other hand, salts such as potassium thiocyanate, permanganate, cyanate, iodide, and hexacyanoplatinate(IV) and materials such as sulfuric and hydrochloric acids and sulfur(VI) oxide dissolve to give highly conducting solutions. Most alkali metal, alkaline earth metal, silver, copper, and mercury salts studied are either difficultly soluble or insoluble. Evidence for autodissociation of the solvent into H_2CN^+ and CN^- ions is supported by neutralizations in this medium of cyanides with acids such as sulfuric or dichloracetic, neutralizations which can be followed conductimetrically. Solvolysis of salts such as silver sulfate and of acid chlorides such as acetyl chloride and amphoterism of materials such as iron(III) cyanide, as evidenced by its precipitation from iron(III) chloride with triethyl ammonium cyanide and subsequent dissolution in excess of the reagent to give $[(C_2H_5)_3NH]_3[Fe(CN)_6]$, may be cited as other points of similarity to behaviors in aqueous solutions. A number of organic compounds which serve as acid-base indicators in aqueous solutions show similar color changes in liquid hydrogen cyanide when acids or bases are added. In liquid hydrogen cyanide, acid strength decreases in the series $HClO_4$-H_2SO_4-HNO_3.

Anhydrous sulfuric acid

Early investigations by Hantzsch[67] on anhydrous sulfuric acid as a solvent and a reaction medium have been extended from the physicochemical point of view by Hammett and his students.[68–70] The high conductivity of the pure acid and the high concentration of hydrogen

[63] G. Jander and G. Scholz: *Z. physik. Chem.*, **A192**, 163 (1943).
[64] G. Jander and B. Grüttner with G. Scholz: *Chem. Ber.*, **80**, 279 (1947).
[65] G. Jander and B. Grüttner: *Chem. Ber.*, **81**, 102, 107, 114 (1948).
[66] J. Lange, J. Berga, and N. Konopik: *Monatsh.*, **80**, 708 (1949).
[67] A. Hantzsch: *Z. physik. Chem.*, **61**, 257 (1907); **62**, 626 (1908); **65**, 41 (1908); **68**, 204 (1909). *Ber.*, **B63**, 1782 (1930).
[68] L. P. Hammett and A. J. Deyrup: *J. Am. Chem. Soc.*, **55**, 1900 (1933).
[69] L. P. Hammett and F. A. Lowenheim: *J. Am. Chem. Soc.*, **56**, 2620 (1934).
[70] H. P. Treffers and L. P. Hammett: *J. Am. Chem. Soc.*, **59**, 1708 (1937).

sulfate ion in the pure substance indicate sizable autodissociation into either $H_3SO_4^+$ and HSO_4^- or H_3O^+, HSO_4^-, and SO_3. Furthermore, water and most oxygen-containing organic compounds are converted by the highly acidic solvent into ionized oxonium hydrogen sulfates, and salts containing any other anion are converted into hydrogen sulfates. High concentrations of added hydrogen sulfate ion so suppress the autodissociation of the solvent as to eliminate the complicating effects of interionic forces and ion association in electrolyte solutions. As a consequence, pure sulfuric acid under these conditions gives solutions which behave ideally with respect to freezing point, conductivity, and solubility phenomena. In fact, activity coefficients (p. 285) in such solutions are constant over wide concentration ranges. These observations have been confirmed by precision cryoscopic studies on sulfuric acid and on solutions in this solvent.[71–74]

Anhydrous nitric acid

The "water-like" character of anhydrous nitric acid has been pointed out by Jander and Wendt,[75] and some of its solvent properties have been evaluated. In certain respects, this solvent is somewhat like liquid hydrogen fluoride. Although alkaline earth metal nitrates are insoluble, alkali metal nitrates are quite soluble, and tetramethylammonium nitrate is extremely soluble. Most other soluble inorganic compounds are those which are already oxidized, e.g., sulfuric, perchloric, arsenic, and periodic acids and certain sulfates, peroxysulfates, and perchlorates. Many organic compounds are oxidized by this solvent, although nitrated and halogenated materials are more resistant to attack. Perchloric acid appears to be a stronger acid in this solvent than sulfuric acid. Many picrates, acetates, chromates, and acid chlorides undergo solvolysis to corresponding nitrates. Uranyl nitrate reacts with both perchloric acid and potassium or tetramethylammonium nitrate in nitric acid and is, therefore, amphoteric. Precision cryoscopic studies[76] show pure nitric acid to undergo dissociation according to the equation

$$2HNO_3 \rightleftharpoons NO_2^+ + NO_3^- + H_2O$$

and to act as an electrolytic solvent toward nitrogen pentoxide.

[71] R. J. Gillespie, E. D. Hughes, and C. K. Ingold: *J. Chem. Soc.*, **1950,** 2473.

[72] R. J. Gillespie: *J. Chem. Soc.*, **1950,** 2493, 2516, 2537, 2542.

[73] R. J. Gillespie, J. Graham, E. D. Hughes, C. K. Ingold, and E. R. A. Peeling: *J. Chem. Soc.*, **1950,** 2504.

[74] R. J. Gillespie and J. Graham: *J. Chem. Soc.*, **1950,** 2532.

[75] G. Jander and H. Wendt: *Z. anorg. Chem.*, **257,** 26 (1948); **258,** 1 (1949); **259,** 309 (1949).

[76] R. J. Gillespie, E. D. Hughes, and C. K. Ingold: *J. Chem. Soc.*, **1950,** 2552.

NON-PROTONIC COMPOUNDS AS NON-AQUEOUS SOLVENTS

Acid-base behavior in various non-protonic solvents has been discussed in Chapter 9. Although it is true that the greater part of the investigative effort which has been expended on such non-aqueous systems has dealt with acid-base behavior, other phases of their chemistries have received some attention as well. Some of these may be considered here. Only the more extensively studied solvents are included.

Liquid sulfur dioxide

Pioneer studies on this "water-like" solvent (Table 10·3) instituted by Walden[77] have been continued by Jander and his associates. The results of these studies have been reviewed repeatedly.[9, 78, 79] Jander's considerations have been based largely on the autodissociation of the solvent into thionyl (SO^{+2}) and sulfite (SO_3^{-2}) ions, around which concept an entire system of compounds has been developed.

Solubilities of inorganic substances in liquid sulfur dioxide vary widely. Many salts have solubilities of the order of 10^{-2} to 10^{-3} molar. Such compounds as oxides, chlorates, sulfates, sulfides, and hydroxides appear to be rather uniformly insoluble. Sulfites of the alkali metals, thallium(I), and ammonium are moderately soluble, whereas those of most of the other metals are essentially insoluble. Tetramethylammonium sulfite is very soluble and thus serves as a convenient source of sulfite ion in this medium. Alkali and alkaline earth metal iodides dissolve readily, but solubilities decrease rapidly through bromides and chlorides to fluorides. Compounds such as ammonium thiocyanate and acetate, thallous acetate, and antimony(III) chloride are also readily soluble, as are many organic compounds. High solubility is often associated with solvate formation, such compounds as $NaI \cdot 4SO_2$, $BaI_2 \cdot 2SO_2$, and $BaI_2 \cdot 4SO_2$ being easily formed and comparatively stable. Thionyl derivatives are soluble and free metals insoluble.

Solutions of many salts in liquid sulfur dioxide have specific conductances of the same orders of magnitude as those of aqueous solutions of acetic acid or ammonia of the same concentrations. Ionic mobilities in liquid sulfur dioxide are related as follows

$$SCN^- < Br^- < I^- < ClO_4^- < Cl^-$$

$$(CH_3)_4N^+ < K^+ < NH_4^+ < Rb^+$$

[77] P. Walden: *Ber.*, **32**, 2862 (1899).

[78] H. J. Emeléus and J. S. Anderson: *Modern Aspects of Inorganic Chemistry*, pp. 482–487. D. Van Nostrand Co., New York (1938).

[79] G. Jander: *Naturwissenschaften*, **26**, 779, 793 (1938).

Although most reactions which have been studied are of the acid-base type, metathesis reactions based upon the solubility relations in liquid sulfur dioxide may also be carried out. Thus thionyl bromide, thiocyanate, or acetate may be synthesized in liquid sulfur dioxide by treating the corresponding ammonium, silver, or potassium salt with thionyl chloride and removing the precipitated chloride. Ammonia and its organic derivatives react with the solvent according to the general equation

$$2\left[\gt\!\!-N\right] + 2SO_2 \rightleftharpoons \left[(\gt\!\!-N)_2SO\right]SO_3 \rightleftharpoons \left[(\gt\!\!-N)_2SO\right]^{+2} + SO_3^{-2}$$

the resulting products behaving as bases in the solvent.

Certain other reactions of rather general interest have been described. For example, amphoterism has been found to characterize the compound phosphorus(III) chloride.[80] Treatment of a sulfur dioxide solution of the compound with tetramethylammonium sulfite causes complete precipitation of phosphorus(III) oxide, which in turn is dissolved by excess tetramethylammonium sulfite to a material of composition $[(CH_3)_4N][PO_2SO_2]$. From such solutions, phosphorus(III) oxide is reprecipitated by addition of thionyl chloride. Other work has shown[81] that radicals such as RCO^+ (R = alkyl or aryl group) and NO^+ (p. 595) can exist in liquid sulfur dioxide. These result when the corresponding chlorides, RCOCl and NOCl, are treated in liquid sulfur dioxide with antimony(V) chloride. Solutions so obtained have the properties of solutions of strong electrolytes and undergo metathetical reactions. By such reactions, as followed by conductance changes or precipitation, compounds such as $(CH_3CO)ClO_4$, $(CH_3CO)_2SO_4$, $NOClO_4$, etc., can be prepared.

Although liquid sulfur dioxide does not itself behave as a reducing agent or as an oxidizing agent, it serves as a medium for oxidation-reduction reactions. Soluble iodides may be oxidized to iodine in this medium by reagents such as antimony(V) or iron(III) chloride. Conversely, free iodine may be reduced to iodide by sulfites such as $[\{(C_2H_5)_3N\}_2SO]SO_3$. Technically, liquid sulfur dioxide functions as an excellent solvent for organic reactions of the Friedel-Crafts, sulfation or sulfonation, bromination, or hydrogen bromide addition types.[82]

[80] G. Jander, H. Wendt, and H. Hecht: *Ber.*, **77B**, 698 (1945).

[81] F. Seel and H. Bauer: *Z. Naturforsch.*, **2b**, 397 (1947).

[82] J. Ross, J. H. Percy, R. L. Brandt, A. I. Gebhert, J. E. Mitchell, and S. Yolles: *Ind. Eng. Chem.*, **34**, 924 (1942).

Liquid carbonyl chloride

Treatment of solutions in liquid carbonyl chloride from the acid-base point of view has been discussed already (p. 324). The specific conductance of the pure compound is only of the order of 7×10^{-9} ohm^{-1}, but other evidences already cited appear sufficient to indicate its autodissociation into carbonyl (CO^{+2}) and chloride (Cl^-) ions or into $COCl \cdot COCl_2^+$ and Cl^- ions. Although aluminum chloride is the only solute which has been studied in detail, other covalent chlorides such as those of iodine(III), arsenic(III), antimony, and sulfur are also soluble.[83] Further studies on this solvent are indicated.

Selenium oxychloride

Early studies on selenium oxychloride by Lenher[84] and Ray[85] have been expanded by Smith[86] and fitted into his concept of selenium oxychloride as a parent for a system of chemical compounds. That selenium oxychloride has a measurable conductance (2×10^{-5} ohm^{-1} at 25°C.) and that it yields chlorine at the anode upon electrolysis have been cited as evidence for its autodissociation, probably into $[SeOCl \cdot SeOCl_2]^+$ and Cl^- ions.

Direct evidence for this mode of dissociation is lacking, but electrolysis of metal chloride solutions in selenium oxychloride yields chlorine at the anode and various cathode products, among them selenium(IV) oxide and selenium(I) chloride. Metals react with selenium oxychloride in a fashion which also supports this view, the reaction with copper being formulated as

$$3Cu + 6SeOCl^+ \rightarrow 3Cu^{+2} + Se_2Cl_2 + 2SeO_2 + 2SeOCl_2$$

$$3Cu^{+2} + 6Cl^- \rightarrow 3CuCl_2$$

The formation of solvates such as $MCl_4 \cdot 2SeOCl_2$ (M = Si, Ti, Sn) or $FeCl_3 \cdot 2SeOCl_2$ also supports this contention if such solvates are formulated as $(SeOCl)_2{}^{+2}[MCl_6]^{-2}$ or $(SeOCl)_2{}^{+2}[FeCl_5]^{-2}$. The sulfur(VI) oxide derivative has the characteristics of $(SeOCl)^+(SO_3Cl)^-$. Solvates with electron pair donors such as pyridine and quinoline appear to correspond to the formulations $(C_5H_5N{:}SeOCl)^+Cl^-$ and $(C_9H_7N{:}SeOCl)^+Cl^-$. Solutions of such solvates in selenium oxychloride are conductors, and reactions of the neutralization type between them may be followed conductimetrically.

[83] A. F. O. Germann: *J. Am. Chem. Soc.*, **47**, 2461 (1925).
[84] V. Lenher: *J. Am. Chem. Soc.*, **43**, 29 (1921); **44**, 1664 (1922).
[85] W. L. Ray: *J. Am. Chem. Soc.*, **45**, 2090 (1923).
[86] G. B. L. Smith: *Chem. Revs.*, **23**, 165 (1938).

Liquid nitrosyl chloride

The comparatively high dielectric constant (18.2 at 12°C.) of liquid nitrosyl chloride as well as evidences of at least potential ionic character in the compound (p. 597) suggest that it may function as an ionizing solvent. This is supported by its well-recognized tendency to form solvates with a variety of metal halides (p. 595). Not, however, until 1948 were the electrolytic solvent characteristics of liquid nitrosyl chloride investigated.[87] Certain solvates, behaving as mononitrosylium salts (p. 595), dissolve readily as strong electrolytes to give highly conducting solutions. Among them are $NOAlCl_4$, $NOFeCl_4$, and $NOSbCl_6$. Other such compounds, among them $(NO)_2SnCl_6$, $(NO)_2TiCl_6$, $NOHSO_4$, were found to be insoluble, and $(NO)_2S_2O_7$ behaved as a weak electrolyte. No indication of the stable existence of chloride ion (the base analog) has been obtained, and no acid-base reactions have been effected in this solvent. Further study is indicated.

Liquid bromine trifluoride

Studies on this most unusual solvent have been carried out from the acid-base point of view; they have been described in Chapter 9 (p. 326). They indicate that liquid bromine trifluoride is an ionizing solvent.

Liquid dinitrogen(IV) oxide

The solvent behavior of liquid dinitrogen(IV) oxide has been considered from the acid-base point of view (p. 325). Early consideration of this material as an electrolytic solvent[88] indicated that it has a very low specific conductivity (2×10^{-8} ohm^{-1} cm^{-1}) and dissolves only organic materials. Later studies,[89, 90] however, showed that certain nitrosyl compounds yield nitrosylium (NO^+) ions in the solvent and that nitrate ion may also exist. These views are supported by the acid-base behaviors already described (p. 325). Furthermore, solvolysis reactions occur in this medium, for example,

$$(C_2H_5)_2NH_2Cl + N_2O_4 \rightarrow NOCl + [(C_2H_5)_2NH_2]^+NO_3^-$$

The low conductance of liquid dinitrogen(IV) oxide, normal molecular weight in glacial acetic acid, and lack of decomposition by electrolysis

[87] A. B. Burg and G. W. Campbell, Jr.: *J. Am. Chem. Soc.*, **70**, 1964 (1948).
[88] P. F. Frankland and R. C. Farmer: *J. Chem. Soc.*, **79**, 1356 (1901).
[89] C. C. Addison and R. Thompson: *Nature*, **162**, 369 (1948).
[90] C. C. Addison and R. Thompson: *J. Chem. Soc.*, **1949**, 211, 218. (Supplementary issue No. 1.)

preclude any extensive autoionization process,[91] even though reactions in the solvent involve the solvent ions NO^+ and NO_3^-. It is believed[91] that the pure compound is polar and that dissociation into ions will occur only when highly polarizing groups are added. Careful measurements have indicated liquid dinitrogen(IV) oxide to have a specific conductivity of 1.3×10^{-12} ohm^{-1} cm^{-1} at 17°C., a dielectric constant of 2.42 at 18°C., and a molar polarization of 26.5 cc.[92, 93] Further studies again appear to be desirable. Anyone undertaking such studies should realize that this solvent is a very powerful oxidizing agent and is capable of reacting explosively with many reducing agents, particularly those of an organic nature.

Fused mercury(II) bromide

Although solvent characteristics are commonly limited to materials which are liquid at ordinary temperatures or slightly below, there is no fundamental reason for excluding higher melting substances. Studies conducted, for example, showed fused mercury(II) bromide to be markedly "water-like" in character.[94, 95] The measurable specific conductivity (1.45×10^{-4} ohm^{-1} cm.$^{-1}$ at 243°C.) is attributed to the autodissociation reaction

$$2HgBr_2 \rightleftharpoons HgBr^+ + HgBr_3^-$$

and many inorganic substances are soluble to give conducting systems. Neutralization reactions between acids such as mercury(II) sulfate and bases such as potassium or thallium(I) bromide can be followed conductimetrically, and many similar analogies to other solvent systems exist.

ELECTRODEPOSITION REACTIONS IN NON-AQUEOUS MEDIA

Several references have been made in the foregoing discussion to the electrodeposition of certain metals from specific nonaqueous solvents. At the present time practically no industrial importance has been attached to such reactions, but several of them are of sufficient potential importance to merit consideration. Electrodeposition from aqueous solutions is complicated by hydrogen discharge if salts of active metals are employed and by hydrolysis effects if compounds possessing covalent character are employed as solutes. Use of highly basic

[91] W. R. Angus, R. W. Jones, and G. O. Phillips: *Nature*, **164**, 433 (1949).
[92] C. C. Addison, J. Allen, H. C. Bolton, and J. Lewis: *J. Chem. Soc.*, **1951**, 1289.
[93] C. C. Addison, H. C. Bolton, and J. Lewis: *J. Chem. Soc.*, **1951**, 1294.
[94] G. Jander: *Angew. Chem.*, **62**, 264 (1950).
[95] G. Jander and K. Brodersen: *Z. anorg. Chem.*, **261**, 261 (1950); **262**, 33 (1950).

solvents avoids the first of these complications and permits the deposition of active metals which cannot exist in contact with water; use of highly acidic solvents avoids the second difficulty and permits the use of solutes which are themselves incapable of existence in aqueous media.

Many of the aspects of electrodeposition from a variety of non-aqueous solvents have been reviewed by Audrieth and Nelson,[96] and detailed studies on the use of specific solvents such as ammonia,[97] formamide[98, 99] and acetamide,[99, 100] glacial acetic acid,[101, 102] and acetic anhydride[58] have been reported. The stabilities of active metals in strongly basic solvents such as ammonia and the amines permit their deposition from such media. The deposition of lithium from lithium chloride solutions in anhydrous pyridine or propylamine and the deposition of metals such as aluminum and magnesium from solutions of their salts in ethanolamine are typical examples. It should be mentioned also that anhydrous ethylenediamine (dielectric constant = 16.0 at 18°C.) has proved to be an excellent medium for deposition of sodium and potassium.[46] The successful deposition of arsenic and antimony from acetic acid[101, 102] and acetic anhydride[58] and of certain of the rare earth metals as amalgams from ethanol solutions of their anhydrous chlorides[101, 103, 104] may also be cited as being of both theoretical and practical interest. Although some success has attended electrodeposition of beryllium from liquid ammonia and of aluminum from solvents such as ethyl bromide and ether, further researches on these important metals are indicated. A report[105] of the successful deposition of aluminum from an anhydrous mixture of aluminum chloride and ethyl pyridinium bromide in benzene or toluene seems very promising. It is only reasonable to conclude that any metal may be so deposited, provided a suitable solvent is employed.

[96] L. F. Audrieth, and H. W. Nelson: *Chem. Revs.*, **8**, 335 (1931).
[97] L. F. Audrieth, and L. F. Yntema: *J. Phys. Chem.*, **34**, 1903 (1930).
[98] H. Röhler: *Z. Elektrochem.*, **16**, 419 (1910).
[99] L. F. Audrieth, L. F. Yntema, and H. W. Nelson: *Trans. Illinois State Acad. Sci.*, **23**, 302 (1931).
[100] L. F. Yntema and L. F. Audrieth: *J. Am. Chem. Soc.*, **52**, 2693 (1930).
[101] L. F. Audrieth, R. E. Meints, and E. E. Jukkola: *Trans. Illinois State Acad. Sci.*, **24**, 248 (1931).
[102] C. W. Stillwell and L. F. Audrieth: *J. Am. Chem. Soc.*, **54**, 472 (1932).
[103] L. F. Audrieth, E. E. Jukkola, and R. E. Meints, with B S. Hopkins: *J. Am. Chem. Soc.*, **53**, 1805 (1931).
[104] E. E. Jukkola, with L. F. Audrieth and B S. Hopkins: *J. Am. Chem. Soc.*, **56**, 303 (1934).
[105] T. P. Wier and F. H. Hurley (to Rice Institute): U. S. Patent 2,446,349, Aug, 3, 1948.

SUGGESTED SUPPLEMENTARY REFERENCES

P. Walden: *Elektrochemie nichtwässriger Lösungen*, Verlag J. A. Barth, Leipzig (1924).

G. Jander: "Survey of Chemistry in Non-aqueous but 'Water-Like' Solvents," *Naturwissenschaften*, **32,** 169 (1944).

G. Jander and W. Klemm: *Die Chemie in wasserähnlichen Lösungsmitteln*, Springer-Verlag, Berlin (1949).

L. F. Audrieth: *Acids, Bases, and Non-aqueous Systems.* Twenty-third annual Priestley Lectures, Pennsylvania State College, 1949. University Lithoprinters, Ypsilanti, Michigan (1949).

PART TWO
The Chemical Elements

CHAPTER 11

The Inert Gas Elements

A systematic approach to the study of the chemical elements may take any of a number of courses. Regardless of the course which is followed, efforts must be made to bring out the overall relationships existing among the elements, the relationships existing within each family of elements, and the trends in properties characterizing these families. Not only is it important that this be done from the purely descriptive point of view, but it is equally important that some attempt be made, wherever possible, to associate trends and differences in properties with chemical principles, as developed in Part I of this book. The only approach which appears to offer an even reasonable promise in the successful achievement of such goals involves the atomic structures, or more exactly the electronic configurations, of the elements. The general classification of elements into inert gas, representative, transition, and inner transition types as discussed in Chapter 3 (p. 102), provides one basis for such an approach, and it is from this general point of view that material in Part II of this book is presented. Since the inert gas elements are chemically the simplest, it is convenient to discuss them first.

DEVELOPMENT OF THE CHEMISTRY OF THE INERT GAS ELEMENTS

Historical developments leading to present-day information on the inert gas elements are of general interest.[1–3] Information on these elements dates to an experiment performed by Cavendish in 1785 in which an electric spark was passed repeatedly through air containing excess added oxygen. After absorption of the product (NO_2) in an alkaline solution, Cavendish found a small residual volume of gas which was neither nitrogen (phlogisticated air) nor oxygen (dephlogisticated air) and which amounted, in his words, to "not more than $\frac{1}{120}$

[1] F. P. Gross: *J. Chem. Education*, **18**, 533 (1941).

[2] B S. Hopkins: *Chapters in the Chemistry of the Less Familiar Elements*, Ch. **22.** Stipes Publishing Co., Champaign, Illinois (1940).

[3] M. Schofield: *Science Progress*, **36**, 66 (1948).

part of the whole." What Cavendish had actually isolated was, of course, a mixture of the inert gases, but his observations were not considered in their true light until some one hundred years later. Interestingly enough, his figures are remarkably close to the volume contents of the inert gases in the atmosphere as we now know them.

The observation, by Janssen in 1868, of a new yellow line, differing in position from the D lines of sodium, in the solar spectrum during an eclipse caused Frankland and Lockyer to conclude that the sun contained a new element, which they called helium (Greek helios, the sun). Hillebrand actually obtained a sample of this gas in 1889 by heating the mineral cleveite (a variety of uraninite) but was unable to characterize it as something different from nitrogen. It remained for Ramsay in 1895 to show this material to be identical with Lockyer's helium.

Most developments in inert gas chemistry date from Lord Rayleigh's observation in 1894 that, although one liter of atmospheric nitrogen (freed from all known gaseous contaminants by chemical means) weighed 1.2572 grams, one liter of pure nitrogen (prepared by the decomposition of a nitrogen compound) weighed only 1.2506 grams under the same conditions. This difference caused Rayleigh to suspect the presence of a previously unidentified element in the atmosphere, and in collaboration with Ramsay he soon isolated a new gas, which was called argon (= inert). The detection of helium in the atmosphere in trace amounts by Kayser followed in 1895, and in 1898, Ramsay and Travers isolated another element, which they named neon (= new), by the fractional distillation of impure liquid argon. The less volatile fractions from liquid air were soon shown by the same workers to contain two other new elements, krypton (= hidden) and xenon (= stranger). The family was rendered complete by the discovery of radon (and its isotopes actinon and thoron) as a product of radioactive decay.

Two other significant developments in helium chemistry also merit attention. The identity of ionized helium and the alpha particle was established in 1903 by Ramsay and Soddy, and in 1907 Cady and McFarland reported the presence of up to 1.84% helium by volume in certain natural gases, particularly those from certain parts of Kansas.

The chemical inertness of these elements suggested to early workers that they be included in the Mendeléeff periodic table by an expansion of that table to include a Group O. Their classification in this fashion strengthened the Mendeléeff views by providing a logical transition between the highly electronegative halogens and the highly electropositive alkali metals.

PHYSICAL CHARACTERISTICS OF THE INERT GAS ELEMENTS

The numerical properties of the inert gas elements are summarized in Table 11·1. From many points of view, the trends in such values for this group of elements may be regarded as almost ideal. Nearly linear relationships are apparent between variations in many of these properties and variations in atomic number or weight. Such a situa-

TABLE 11·1
NUMERICAL CONSTANTS FOR INERT GAS ELEMENTS

Property	He	Ne	A	Kr	Xe	Rn
Atomic number	2	10	18	36	54	86
Atomic weight	4.003	20.183	39.944	83.7	131.3	222
Atomic radius (A)		1.60	1.91	2.00	2.2	
Density (g./ml.)(liq)	0.126	1.204	1.65(s)	2.6	3.06	4.4
Atomic volume (ml.)(liq)	31.77	16.76	24.21(s)	32.19	42.92	50.46
Melting point (°K.)	0.9?	24.43	83.9	104	133	202
Boiling point (°K.)	4.216	27.2	87.4	121.3	163.9	211.3
Heat of fusion (kcal./mole)	0.0033	0.080	0.280	0.341	0.549	
Heat of vaporization (kcal./mole)	0.025	0.405	1.600	2.240	3.100	3.600
Ionization potential (ev)						
first electron	24.58	21.559	15.755	13.996	12.127	10.745
second electron	54.40	41.07	27.62	26(ca.)	21(ca.)	
Ratio of specific heats (C_p:C_v)	1.65	1.64	1.65	1.69	1.67	
Water solubility (ml./l. at 20°C.)	13.8	14.7	37.9	73	110.9	
Critical temperature (°K.)	5.19	44.4	150.6	210.5	289.6	377.5
Critical pressure (atm.)	2.26	26.86	47.966	54.3	58.2	62.4
Gas density (g./l. at S.C.)	0.1785	0.9002	1.7809	3.708	5.851	9.73
Thermal conductivity at 0°C. ($K \times 10^6$)	343	111.2	38.2	21.2	12.4	

ion arises because each inert gas atom possesses a stable electronic arrangement which is only slightly altered by environmental conditions, and as a result interactions among adjacent atoms are at minima. Each atom behaves, therefore, as if it were effectively isolated, and complications in properties are avoided. The trend in a given property with the inert gas elements, as atomic number or weight is altered, is often considered sufficiently ideal as to act as a basis for comparison of similar trends among other families of elements (e.g., p. 190). Indicated increases in atomic radius, density, atomic volume, and melting and boiling points and decreases in ionization potential follow from the discussions in Chapter 5. It should be pointed out that the ratio of specific heats ($C_p:C_v$) deviates in each case only negligibly from the ideal value of 1.667 for a monatomic gas.

The boiling and melting points of the inert gas elements are very low in comparison with those of other materials of comparable atomic or molecular weights. That the inert gas elements liquefy or solidify at all is due only to the operation of van der Waals forces (p. 215), since all other types of attraction which might pull the atoms into comparatively fixed positions are absent. The fluctuating dipoles in the inert gas atoms, as produced by electronic motion, give only comparatively weak attractive forces which can actually become operative only when molecular activity is so slowed by excessive decreases in temperature as to permit close approach of the atoms. Such solid phases of these elements as have been examined have close-packed cubic structures.

Helium is unique among the elements in forming a true solid only under pressure, regardless of temperature. A minimum of some 25 atm. pressure is required, and the melting point recorded in Table 11·1 is an extrapolated value for this pressure. This condition doubtless arises from the very low van der Waals forces which would characterize an atom containing so few electrons and all in a completed quantum level. Liquid helium is also unique in that it exists in two forms, helium I and helium II. The phase relations existing with helium at low temperatures are indicated in Figure 11·1, transitions between the two liquid forms occurring along the so-called lambda (λ) line.

Helium I is a perfectly normal liquid, but the properties of helium II are so unusual that some investigators have characterized this form of the element as a fourth state of matter. When liquid helium I, which is boiling in a container, is cooled below the λ-point, boiling appears to cease, and the liquid becomes nearly invisible. The transition of helium I into helium II is accompanied by discontinuous changes in a number of physical properties, among them specific heat, viscosity, thermal conductivity, compressibility, and surface tension. Other properties, among them structure and molecular refractivity, do not change, but with some, among them density, vapor pressure, dielectric constant, and refractive index, changes in temperature coefficient occur at the λ point. Liquid helium II is characterized by a very low viscosity (ca. 0.001 that of hydrogen gas), by a very high thermal conductivity (ca. 800 times that of copper at room temperature), by peculiar flow phenomena which cause the levels of the liquid in two concentric vessels to equalize by flow in a superfluid film (Rollin film) up the walls of the more elevated container and over its top into the other, and by the so-called fountain effect in which the liquid sprays out of the end of a capillary when the lower end of the capillary is illuminated.

Liquid helium II has an open structure containing many atoms in low energy states (superfluid of no viscosity), among which a few atoms in higher energy states (gas) move. Its behavior is essentially that of a liquid with gas properties, that is, of a so-called degenerate

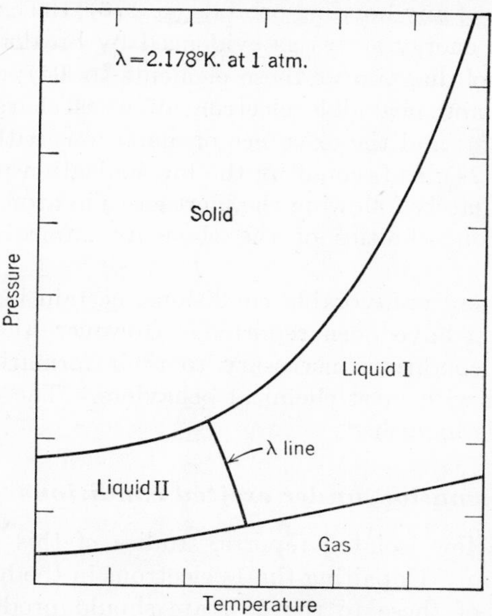

Fig. 11·1. Phase relations for helium at low temperatures. (Not drawn to scale.)

gas. In the superfluid the energies of atoms have been so reduced that thermal motion has ceased, yet the interatomic forces are insufficient to cause solidification. It is of interest that only the isotope with mass number *four* shows these characteristics.[4] This is associated with the presence of an uneven number of particles in the three-isotope. The concentration of the latter isotope by its lack of superfluid characteristics has been mentioned (p. 49). For further details on the characteristics and nature of helium II, reference to available monographs[5, 6] and reviews[7, 8] should be made.

[4] Anon.: *Chem. Eng. News*, **27**, 444 (1949).

[5] E. F. Burton, H. G. Smith, and J. O. Wilhelm: *Phenomena at the Temperature of Liquid Helium.* Reinhold Publishing Corp., New York (1940).

[6] N. H. Keesom: *Helium.* Elsevier, Amsterdam (1942).

[7] C. W. Hewlett: *Gen. Elec. Rev.*, **49** (No. 7), 42 (1946).

[8] S. A. Weissman: *J. Chem. Education*, **23**, 223 (1946).

CHEMICAL BEHAVIORS OF THE INERT GAS ELEMENTS

In the ordinary sense of the word, the inert gas elements are chemically inert. Every attempt to make them combine to give compounds of the usual types by treatment with oxidizing or reducing agents has met with failure. The comparative stability of the inert gas type of structure is suggested by the complete pairing of all electrons present and the absence of any bonding orbitals (p. 176); the existence of these atoms in stable energy states as evidenced by breaks in the Pauling type energy level diagram at these elements (p. 94); the peak ionization potentials and negligible electron affinities characterizing these elements (p. 155); and the existence of many ions with inert gas configurations (p. 174), as favored by the low ionization potentials of the elements immediately following the inert gases in atomic numbers and the high electron affinities of the elements immediately preceding them.

In spite of these unfavorable conditions, certain instances of compound formation have been reported. However, the products prepared and the conditions necessary to their formation are unusual when compared with most chemical behaviors. The following situations may be distinguished.

Compound formation under excited conditions

Except for a few isolated reports, studies of this type have been limited to helium. Unpairing the 1*s* electrons in the helium atom and promoting one of these to the 2*s* state should produce a condition giving chemical activity. This operation requires some 460 kcal. of energy per gram atom and can only be realized spectroscopically or under conditions of electric discharge or electron bombardment. Under such conditions, resonance effects (pp. 194–195) become sufficient so that attractive forces result. In discharge tubes the helium molecule ion, He_2^+, a three-electron bonded species (p. 213), and hydrogen helium combinations of the types HeH^+ and HeH_2^+ have been recognized. In a glow discharge a comparatively stable mercury helide ($HgHe_{10}$) has been formed,[9] and electron bombardment of tungsten in an atmosphere of helium has apparently yielded a tungsten helide, WHe_2.[10] Evidences for the formation of helides of elements such as bismuth, thallium, indium, zinc, sodium, potassium, rubidium

[9] J. J. Manley: *Nature*, **114**, 861 (1924); **115**, 947 (1925). *Phil. Mag.* [7], **4**, 699 (1927).

[10] E. H. Boomer: *Nature*, **115**, 16 (1925).

platinum, palladium, iron, uranium, iodine, sulfur, and phosphorus have also been presented.[10, 11] Such products are uniformly unstable.

Certain metals, when employed as electrodes in discharge tubes containing inert gases, appear to absorb apparently stoichiometric quantities of these gases, and thereby have their densities decreased and their solubilities in acids altered. Among the comparatively stable products reported are those the compositions of which are represented by the approximate formulas Pt_3He, FeHe, PdHe, BiHe, FeA, etc.[12–19] Of these, the material Pt_3He has been most thoroughly studied. This substance has a fixed decomposition temperature; gives an x-ray diffraction pattern characteristic of an amorphous substance; possesses a different density, acid solubility, and electrical resistance from platinum; and is not decomposed when its amalgam is attacked by nitric acid.

Compound formation by interstitial penetration

Although no data are available to support or deny this possibility, it is not unlikely that many or all of the "compounds" discussed in the preceding section are interstitial alloys comparable with the metallic hydrides (pp. 411–415).

Compound formation through coordination

Inasmuch as each inert gas atom possesses free electron pairs, such atoms might conceivably act as donors provided a sufficiently powerful electron pair acceptor is present. If such a condition did pertain, the largest inert gas atoms should show the property to the greatest extent. The only work lending any support to such a postulation is the thermal analysis study on the system argon-boron trifluoride carried out by Booth and Willson.[20] Freezing points, determined under pressures of up to 40 atm. for a variety of mixtures of known compositions, when plotted against the mole composition yielded a

[11] H. Krefft and R. Rompe: *Z. Physik*, **73**, 681 (1932).

[12] H. Damianovich: *Anales inst. invest. cient. y tecnol.*, **3–4**, 20 (1934).

[13] H. Damianovich and J. Piazzo: *Anales inst. invest. cient. y tecnol.*, **5–6**, 54, 62, 6 (1934–36).

[14] H. Damianovich: *Anales soc. cient. argentina*, **118**, 227 (1934); **120**, 98 (1935).

[15] H. Damianovich and J. Piazzo: *Anales soc. cient. argentina, Sección Santa Fé*, , 57, 59 (1936).

[16] H. Damianovich: *Anales asoc. quím. argentina*, **24**, 141 (1936); **26**, 249 (1938); **7**, 64 (1939).

[17] H. Damianovich: *Bull. soc. chim.* [5], **5**, 1085 (1938).

[18] H. Damianovich and G. Berraz: *Rev. brasil. chim.*, **6**, 71 (1938).

[19] H. Damianovich and C. Christer: *Rev. brasil. chim.*, **6**, 72 (1938).

[20] H. S. Booth and K. S. Willson: *J. Am. Chem. Soc.*, **57**, 2273, 2280 (1935).

curve with maxima corresponding to compounds containing 1, 2, 3, 6, 8, and 16 moles of boron trifluoride to 1 mole of argon. Compounds of the type $\mathrm{A \cdot}x\mathrm{BF_3}$ where $x = 1$, 2, or 3, were easily formulated by Booth and Willson in terms of the argon atom donating 1, 2, or 3 electron pairs, respectively. However, when $x = 6$, 8, or 16, it was necessary to postulate that fluorine in boron trifluoride might also serve as a donor to another boron, giving structures of the type

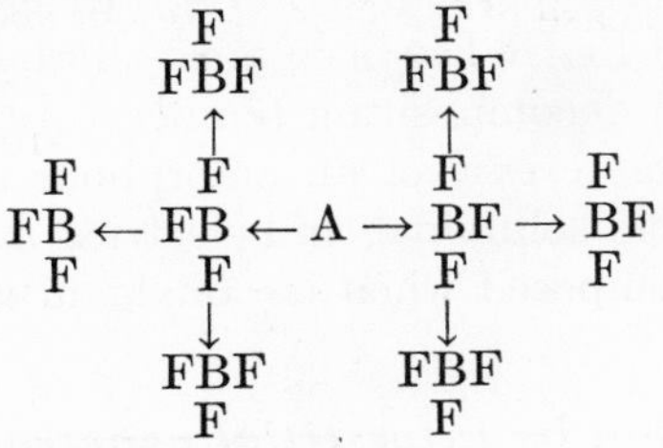

$$
\begin{array}{ccccccccc}
 & & \mathrm{F} & & & & \mathrm{F} & & \\
 & & \mathrm{FBF} & & & & \mathrm{FBF} & & \\
 & & \uparrow & & & & \uparrow & & \\
\mathrm{F} & & \mathrm{F} & & & & \mathrm{F} & & \mathrm{F} \\
\mathrm{FB} & \leftarrow & \mathrm{FB} & \leftarrow & \mathrm{A} & \rightarrow & \mathrm{BF} & \rightarrow & \mathrm{BF} \\
\mathrm{F} & & \mathrm{F} & & & & \mathrm{F} & & \mathrm{F} \\
 & & \downarrow & & & & \downarrow & & \\
 & & \mathrm{FBF} & & & & \mathrm{FBF} & & \\
 & & \mathrm{F} & & & & \mathrm{F} & &
\end{array}
$$

the material $\mathrm{A \cdot 8BF_3}$ being chosen as typical.

Such structures must be regarded with skepticism, particularly in view of the fact that pure boron trifluoride itself shows no tendency to polymerize regardless of temperature. The donor ability of the argon atom would be expected to be low even under optimum conditions. Since boron trifluoride has no permanent dipole moment attractions of the type discussed in the next section are also ruled out. Parallel studies on the krypton-boron trifluoride system[21] have given no evidences of compound formation, even though it might better be expected in this system. A reinvestigation of the argon-boron trifluoride system by the same authors[21] indicated complete immiscibility of the reactants under conditions comparable with those used by Booth and Willson and gave no evidences of any compound formation. What then do the maxima obtained by Booth and Willson indicate?

It should be pointed out that all these temperature variations lay in only a very narrow range (−127°C. to −133°C.) and that the use of high pressures rendered the system difficult to handle experimentally. Perhaps, as Wiberg and Karbe indicate, these maxima represent merely the freezing point of the boron trifluoride phase (f.p. of pure $\mathrm{BF_3}$ = −127.1°C.).

It is of interest that Wiberg and Karbe were unable to obtain evidences for compound formation between xenon and diborane, trimethyl boron, sulfur dioxide, hydrogen sulfide, dimethyl ether, or methanol.

[21] E. Wiberg and K. Karbe: *Z. anorg. Chem.*, **256**, 307 (1948).

Compound formation through dipole-induced dipole attraction

In the presence of a sufficiently strong dipole, an inert gas atom may become so polarized as to function as a dipole itself and thereby attract the original dipole (p. 187). Such forces are very weak, and any compounds formed in this fashion would be expected to be rather unstable, although perhaps more stable than those of the types mentioned above. Since ease of inducing a dipole would increase with the size of the inert gas atom, the heavier inert gases, particularly radon, would be expected to yield compounds of the greatest stabilities.

TABLE 11·2
STABILITIES OF INERT GAS HYDRATES AND DEUTEROHYDRATES

Inert Gas	Hydrate		Deuterohydrate Dissociation Pressure
	Formation	Dissociation Pressure, atm.	
He	None at several thousand atmospheres	....	....
Ne	None at 260 atm.	....	....
A	150 atm. at 0°C.	98.5 (0°C.) 210 (8°C.)	....
Kr	14.5 atm. at 0°C.	14.5 (0.1°C.)	1 (−25.1°C.)
Xe	1⁺ atm. at 0°C.	1.15 (0.1°C.)	1 (− 3.2°C.)
Rn	....	1 (0°C.)	....

The inert gas hydrates[22, 23] and deuterohydrates[24] are classic examples of this type of attraction. These compounds have the general formulas $G \cdot xH_2O$ and $G \cdot yD_2O$, with x and y approaching 6 but becoming equal to this number only with the heaviest inert gases. These compounds result when water (light or heavy) and the inert gas are brought together under pressure at low temperatures. They are crystalline compounds, the stabilities of which decrease rapidly from the radon compound down through the argon compound. As might be expected, the small and difficult to polarize neon and helium form no such compounds, at least under readily attainable conditions. The relative stabilities of the hydrates are indicated by the data in Table 11·2. The hydrates crystallize well in the presence of isomor-

[22] P. Villard: *Compt. rend.*, **123,** 377 (1896).
[23] R. de Forcrand: *Compt. rend.*, **135,** 959 (1902); **176,** 355 (1923); **181,** 15 (1925).
[24] M. Godchot, G. Cauquil, and R. Calas: *Compt. rend.*, **202,** 795 (1936).

phous sulfur(IV) oxide 6-hydrate ($SO_2 \cdot 6H_2O$),[25] and, by use of carefully controlled pressures, separation of the inert gases, especially radon and argon, has been effected through formation and decomposition of the hydrates.[26] The increase in water solubility with atomic number in this family of elements (Table 11·1) is apparent from these considerations.

Other instances of this type of attraction have been reported, the most striking being the formation of phenol derivatives, $Kr \cdot 2C_6H_5OH$, $Xe \cdot 2C_6H_5OH$, and $Rn \cdot 2C_6H_5OH$, isomorphous with the hydrogen sulfide derivative, $H_2S \cdot 2C_6H_5OH$.[27] The xenon and krypton compounds have dissociation pressures of 1 atm. at 4°C. and 6 to 10 atm. at 0°, but the radon compound melts at 50°C. Similar attempts to prepare radon compounds of the type $Rn \cdot AlCl_3$ or $Rn \cdot AlBr_3$ by formation of $H_2S \cdot AlCl_3$ and $H_2S \cdot AlBr_3$ in the presence of radon have been unsuccessful,[28] although the solid phases were found to contain very small percentages of radon. At low temperatures and pressures, crystals of hydrogen chloride, hydrogen bromide, hydrogen sulfide, sulfur(IV) oxide, carbon(IV) oxide, and acetone all collect radon in appreciable percentages.[27] The hydrogen chloride material is of sufficient stability to permit removal of radon from argon and neon through its formation. The work of Wiberg and Karbe[21] casts doubt upon conclusions that true compounds are formed under these conditions. It is of interest also that lithium ions tend to form clusters with inert gas atoms of the type $Li^+ \cdot nG$ ($n = 1$ or 2).[29] The stabilities of such aggregates and the quantities of gas held increase with increasing size of the inert gas atoms. Potassium ions do not exhibit comparable properties.

Compound formation by physical trapping

The formation of so-called clathrate compounds by the physical trapping of one component in the crystal lattice of the second during the formation of that lattice has been considered (pp. 223–224). Although no positive evidence is available in support or denial of the possibility, it is conceivable that at least some of the combinations described in the preceding section may be of this type.

Such cage compounds have been prepared by the crystallization of benzene or aqueous solutions of quinol which were subjected to high

[25] B. A. Nikitin: *Z. anorg. allgem. Chem.*, **227**, 81 (1936).
[26] B. A. Nikitin: *J. Gen. Chem.* (*U.S.S.R.*), **9**, 1176 (1936).
[27] B. A. Nikitin: *Compt. rend. acad. sci. U.R.S.S.*, **24**, 562 (1939).
[28] B. A. Nikitin and E. M. Joffe: *Doklady Akad. Nauk, S. S. S. R.*, **60**, 595 (1948)
[29] R. J. Munson and K. Hoselitz: *Proc. Roy. Soc.* (*London*), **A172**, 43 (1939).

pressures of argon, krypton, or xenon.[30, 31] With argon, crystallization under 40 atm. of argon pressure yielded a product containing about 9% argon by weight and corresponding to the composition 3 quinol·$A_{0.8}$. Corresponding krypton and xenon compounds contained 15.8% and 26%, respectively, of the inert gases by weight. These materials represent examples of a broad group of quinol clathrates of general formula ca. 3 quinol·X.

OCCURRENCE AND TECHNICAL RECOVERY OF THE INERT GAS ELEMENTS

The atmosphere is the only known source of all the inert gases (except radon). Some concept of the relative abundances of these components as compared with those of the commoner atmospheric gases may be gained from the data[1, 32] in Table 11·3. Helium is

TABLE 11·3
CHARACTERISTICS OF ATMOSPHERIC GASES

Gas	Composition of the Atmosphere		Boiling Point, °K.	Melting Point, °K.
	By Volume	By Weight		
N_2	78.03% (1:1.3)	1 lb. in 1.32 lb.	77.2	63
O_2	20.99% (1:4.8)	4.3 lb.	90.1	54.4
A	0.94% (1:106)	77 lb.	87.4	83.9
CO_2	0.031%* (1:3220)	....	....	217 (5.3 atm.)
H_2	0.01%* (1:10000)	7.18 tons	20.33	13.95
Ne	0.0015% (1:65000)	44 tons	27.2	24.43
He	0.0005% (1:200,000)	725 tons	4.216	0.9(?)
Ky	0.00011% (1:1,000,000)	173 tons	121.3	104
Xe	0.000009% (1:11,000,000)	1208 tons	163.9	133

* Variable.

found as a not too uncommon component of natural gases, particularly in some regions in the Southwest of the United States, where concentrations up to 7 to 8% have been reported. Its presence in such natural gases may be due to the entrapment of helium released by radio-active decay down through the ages. Certain minerals of a radioactive nature (e.g., pitchblende, cleveite, thorianite, monazite, fergusonite, carnotite, samarskite, and euxenite) also contain entrapped

[30] H. M. Powell and M. Guter: *Nature*, **164**, 240 (1949).
[31] H. M. Powell: *J. Chem. Soc.*, **1950**, 298, 300, 468.
[32] Anon.: *Chem. Eng.*, **54** (No. 3), 126 (1947).

helium. The presence of other inert gases in waters and minerals is believed to be due to contact with the atmosphere. Radon is produced in small amounts (because of short half-life) by radioactive decay of radium (pp. 65, 918).

The recovery of the inert gas elements from the atmosphere is based upon a complex liquefaction and rectification process.[1, 32] A comparison of boiling point data (Table 11·3) shows that the most volatile fractions will contain nitrogen, neon, and helium, whereas oxygen, argon, krypton, and xenon will concentrate in the residual liquid. A second fractionation of the less volatile portion yields argon of approximately 50% purity, which is then freed of residual oxygen by burning with hydrogen and passing over hot copper-copper oxide. Removal of nitrogen, oxygen, and water vapor then yields helium-neon and krypton-xenon mixtures. These may be separated further by continued fractionation or by selective adsorption on activated charcoal. The latter process takes advantage of the fact that, although at −190°C. neon, argon, kyrpton, and xenon are all adsorbed and helium and hydrogen are not, at −100°C. only argon, krypton, and xenon are adsorbed. Combinations of sorption and desorption at various temperatures are employed. Neon, argon, krypton, and xenon are all available commercially as products of the fractionation of liquid air.

Originally such helium as was recovered was obtained from minerals such as monazite either by heating directly to 1000 to 1200°C. in a vacuum system or by decomposing the mineral with sulfuric acid or potassium acid sulfate and then heating. Such a process was obviously inconvenient and very costly. Discovery of helium in natural gases was followed during World War I by a large-scale government-controlled (United States) development of methods of recovery. This program has been expanded until the yearly production of helium is measured in the tens of millions of cubic feet (e.g., over 63 million in 1946). The process employed[33] involves removal of carbon dioxide and then moisture and some of the higher hydrocarbons by chilling. Further reduction in temperature is then used to remove other hydrocarbons and nitrogen, and a final cooling to −190° under pressures of some 2500 lb. per in.^{2} liquefies the remainder of the nitrogen and permits withdrawal of helium of above 98% purity. Further purification is effected as desired.

Such small quantities of radon as are required for therapeutic purposes may be obtained by pumping the gas off acidified solutions of radium chloride and removing hydrogen and oxygen by explosion,

[33] A. Stewart: *U. S. Bur. Mines Inf. Circ.* **6745** (1933).

carbon dioxide and water by use of potassium hydroxide and phosphorus(V) oxide, and nitrogen and helium by freezing out the radon.[34]

APPLICATIONS OF THE INERT GAS ELEMENTS

Helium has been used most extensively in balloons and dirigibles where its non-inflammability makes it preferred to hydrogen. Because of its lesser solubility than nitrogen in the blood stream, helium has also been employed in admixture with oxygen by divers and others working under high pressures. Helium has also been employed to provide inert atmospheres for handling active metals and welding them, and it is of inestimable scientific value in attaining and maintaining extremely low temperatures. Neon is chiefly useful in discharge tubes used for illumination and decorative lighting. The familiar red color obtained when an electric discharge is passed through a tube filled with neon may be modified by the introduction of other inert gases or mercury and by the use of colored glass.[1] Neon-filled lamps have a variety of electrical uses, the familiar stroboscope being one. Argon is used extensively in gas-filled incandescent lamps, where its lower thermal conductivity and complete chemical inertness render it preferable to nitrogen in prolonging the life, and increasing the efficiencies of such bulbs. Argon is also used as a filler for other types of bulbs and display tubes and in providing inert atmospheres. Many Geiger counting tubes contain argon. Krypton and xenon, because of their rarity, have been used only to a limited extent. However, they are reported to be even more efficient than argon in incandescent lamp bulbs and would probably be better than argon in counting tubes. A krypton-xenon photographic flash tube has proved to be very successful for the taking of instantaneous exposures. Radon has been employed medicinally in the treatment of malignancies and also, because of its radioactivity, has shown some promise as a substitute for x-ray in industrial radiography.

SUGGESTED SUPPLEMENTARY REFERENCES

N. V. Sidgwick: *The Chemical Elements and Their Compounds*, pp. 1–10. Clarendon Press, Oxford (1950).

Gmelin's *Handbuch der anorganischen Chemie*, System-Nummer 1. Verlag Chemie G. m. b. h., Leipzig-Berlin (1926).

B S. Hopkins: *Chapters in the Chemistry of the Less Familiar Elements*, Ch. 22. Stipes Publishing Co., Champaign, Illinois (1940).

[34] J. A. T. Dawson: *J. Sci. Instruments*, **23**, 138 (1946).

CHAPTER 12

Hydrogen

In many respects hydrogen is unique among the elements. Like the atoms of the alkali metals, the hydrogen atom is characterized by a single valence electron; but, unlike the alkali metal atoms, it shows little tendency to lose this electron in chemical reactions and a great tendency to pair it to form molecules (e.g., H_2, HCl, etc.). Like the atoms of the halogens, the hydrogen atom lacks one electron of possessing a completed inert gas structure, but, unlike the halogen atoms, its electronegatively is so small that it can gain an electron only from the most electropositive metals. In many respects, hydrogen resembles the metallic elements, particularly in so far as the reactions of its solvated cation compare with those of other solvated cations; yet the majority of its properties and those of its compounds are properties of non-metallic materials. Although these apparent anomalities in behavior are reconcilable in terms of the unusual structure (single electron directly outside the nucleus) of the hydrogen atom and its small size, they have produced no end of difficulty in the systematic classification of hydrogen. Some periodic arrangements place hydrogen with the alkali metals; others with the halogens. The latter classification is the better because it agrees more nearly with the general properties of the element. Hydrogen, together with helium, is an introductory element to the entire periodic classification. On this basis, it might be better, even to consider these two elements apart from all the others and not to attempt to relate them closely to the others.

Because of the many unique aspects of hydrogen chemistry, it has probably been studied more thoroughly than any other single element. Accordingly, in this book a proportionally greater amount of space is devoted to it than to any other element, and a greater variety of topics are covered.

VARIETIES OF HYDROGEN

Hydrogen isotopes

Three isotopes of hydrogen are known. They have mass numbers of 1, 2, and 3, with corresponding atomic masses of 1.008123, 2.014708,

3.01707; they are called hydrogen (occasionally protium), deuterium (D), and tritium (T), respectively. Only the first two are found in detectable amounts in nature, the respective relative abundances being 99.9844% and 0.0156% (p. 911). Tritium is an unstable species which is produced by nuclear transformations (p. 394). Its presence in nature has been disputed, but more recent data[1,2] indicate the natural ratio of light hydrogen to tritium to be of the order of 10^{17-18} to 1.

Since ordinary hydrogen is almost entirely the isotope of mass number 1, its properties are essentially those of that isotope. The proportionally tremendous mass differences among the three hydrogen isotopes produce differences in both physical and chemical behaviors which are much more pronounced than those existing among isotopes of other elements (pp. 40–52). It is probably for this reason that the behaviors and characteristics of these materials have been explored so thoroughly.

Deuterium and Its Compounds. As has been indicated in Chapter 2 (p. 33), differences between chemical and physical atomic weight values for ordinary hydrogen led to prediction of the existence of an isotope of mass number 2. Although Allison and coworkers reported discovery of this isotope in 1930,[3,4] the apparently questionable validity of results obtained by the magneto-optic method used has caused credit to be withheld. Late in 1931, Urey, Brickwedde, and Murphy[5] found in the spectrum of the small amount of residue remaining after evaporation of a large volume of liquid hydrogen two faint lines, the wavelengths of which were in exact agreement with those calculated for Balmer series lines (p. 81) for a hydrogen isotope of mass number 2. This was undeniable evidence for the existence of the isotope.

Investigations relating to deuterium and its compounds were greatly accelerated by the discovery[6] that, when water is electrolyzed under suitable conditions, the lighter hydrogen isotope is liberated roughly six times more readily than the heavier one. In the hands of Lewis

[1] M. L. Eidinoff: *J. Chem. Education*, **25**, 31 (1948).

[2] A. V. Grosse, W. M. Johnston, R. L. Wolfgang, and W. F. Libby: *Science*, **113**, 1 (1951).

[3] F. Allison and E. J. Murphy: *J. Am. Chem. Soc.*, **52**, 3796 (1930).

[4] F. Allison, E. J. Murphy, E. R. Bishop, and A. L. Sommer: *Phys. Rev.*, **37**, 1178 (1931).

[5] H. C. Urey, F. G. Brickwedde, and G. M. Murphy: *Phys. Rev.*, **39**, 164, 864 (1932).

[6] E. W. Washburn, and H. C. Urey: *Proc. Natl. Acad. Sci.*, **18**, 496 (1932).

and MacDonald,[7] this procedure was soon shown to be very effective, and others obtained comparable results. Of the procedures applicable to the separation of deuterium as outlined in Chapter 2 (pp. 40–52), electrolysis remains the best.

The procedure, as it is commonly carried out, has been described in detail by Taylor, Eyring, and Frost.[8] Using as starting material water distilled from electrolyte which had accumulated in commercial electrolytic hydrogen cells (and had thereby been somewhat enriched), electrolysis was carried out in seven stages, using 0.5 *N* sodium hydroxide solutions and nickel electrodes. In the first stage, the total volume was reduced to about one-sixth the original. The alkali was then neutralized with carbon dioxide, and the water distilled, the distillate being added to a further group of cells where the composition was the same. After three successive electrolyses, the deuterium content of the water had increased to such an extent that the released gases contained appreciable quantities of the heavy isotope. Accordingly, such gases were burned, and the condensed products were returned to appropriate stages in the electrolysis. Deuterium content in residual samples of water was estimated from the specific gravity (p. 393). As representative of data obtained for such a seven-stage electrolysis, one may cite the figures given in Table 12·1. Large-scale

TABLE 12·1

CONCENTRATION OF DEUTERIUM BY ELECTROLYSIS[7]

Stage	Volume Electrolyzed (start)	Specific Gravity (d_4^{20}) of Residue	% D_2O in Residue
1	2310 liters*	0.998	. . .
2	340 liters	0.999	0.5
3	52 liters	1.001	2.5
4	10.15 liters	1.007	8.0
5	2 liters	1.031	30.0
6	420 ml.	1.098	93.0
7	83 ml.	1.104	99.0

* D:H about 1:3000 due to previous enrichment.

installations for the commercial preparation of either pure deuterium oxide or water enriched in deuterium oxide, such as those in Norway, employ the same general procedure.

The electrolytic separation of the hydrogen isotopes may be described in terms of a separation factor *s*, (p. 39), which is defined[9] as

[7] G. N. Lewis, and R. T. MacDonald: *J. Chem. Phys.*, **1**, 341 (1933).

[8] H. S. Taylor, H. Eyring, and A. A. Frost: *J. Chem. Phys.*, **1**, 823 (1933).

[9] A. Farkas: *Orthohydrogen, Parahydrogen, and Heavy Hydrogen*, p. 126. Cambridge University Press, London (1935).

$$s = [(\text{H})/(\text{D})]_{\text{gas}}/[(\text{H})/(\text{D})]_{\text{liquid}} \quad (12 \cdot 1)$$

where (H) and (D) are the respective concentrations of light and heavy hydrogen. The change in isotopic concentrations is related to the initial and final volumes of solution, V_0 and V, as[9]

$$\left[\frac{(\text{H})_0}{(\text{H})}\right]\left[\frac{(\text{D})}{(\text{D})_0}\right]^s = \left[\frac{V_0}{V}\right]^{s-1} \quad (12 \cdot 2)$$

where $(\text{H})_0$ and $(\text{D})_0$ are the initial concentrations and (H) and (D) the final ones. With a separation factor of 5, and an original normal deuterium content of about 0.02%, a reduction of some 130,000 volumes of water to 1 volume would be necessary to produce 99% D_2O.

Although the separation factor is essentially independent of deuterium concentration, it does vary markedly with the nature of the cathode employed and the *p*H of the electrolyte. Comparative studies[10] indicate higher values for a given cathode in alkaline media than in acidic. In alkaline solutions, values between 6 and 8 are obtained for lead, platinum, iron, and copper cathodes, efficiency decreasing roughly as Pb > Fe > Pt > Cu, etc.

The mechanism of the electrolytic process remains somewhat obscure.[11] It seems probable that differences in the rates of reduction of H_2O and D_2O combine with lower activational energy for the reaction $H + H \rightarrow H_2$ and with the exchange reaction $H_2O + HD \rightleftharpoons HDO + H_2$ to produce preferential liberation of the light isotope. It is significant that the electrolytic process concentrates tritium as well but is of no consequence in effecting other isotopic separations (p. 49).

As might be expected, the physical properties of deuterium are somewhat different from those of light hydrogen. A few of the commoner physical constants have been collected for comparative purposes in Table 12·2. Those applying to the molecular gas are for the normal forms and not for separated ortho and para forms (pp. 395–398). For more comprehensive treatments of physical properties and detailed references to sources, other accounts should be consulted.[12–14]

[10] B. Topley and H. Eyring: *J. Chem. Phys.*, **2,** 217 (1934).

[11] A. Farkas: *Orthohydrogen, Parahydrogen, and Heavy Hydrogen*, pp. 127, 131. Cambridge University Press, London (1935).

[12] *Ibid.*, pp. 142–175.

[13] E. B. Maxted: *Modern Advances in Inorganic Chemistry*, Ch. II. Clarendon Press, Oxford (1947).

[14] P. W. Selwood: *J. Chem. Education*, **18,** 515 (1941).

Chemically, deuterium enters into all the reactions characteristic of ordinary hydrogen and forms completely equivalent compounds. However, the large mass and zero point energy differences (p. 49) between the two isotopes render rates of equivalent reactions and the positions of equilibrium points in equivalent reactions considerably different. In general, deuterium reacts more slowly and less completely than its lighter analog, and these properties characterize the behaviors of corresponding compounds as well as the elements themselves.

TABLE 12·2

PHYSICAL CONSTANTS FOR HYDROGEN AND DEUTERIUM

Property	Hydrogen	Deuterium
Triple point, °K.	13.92	18.71
Boiling point, °K.	20.38	23.59
Latent heat of fusion, cal./mole	28.0	52.3
Latent heat of vaporization or sublimation,		
cal./mole at 18.58°K.	218.7 (liquid)	355.4 (solid)
at 13.92°K.	245.7 (solid)	340.8 (solid)
Vapor pressure, mm. Hg at		
13.92°K.	54	5.8
18.71°K.	458	130
20.38°K.	760	250
23.59°K.	1740	760
Zero point energy	6176 (for H_2)	4387 (D_2)

For example, deuterium is more slowly sorbed on metallic surfaces than hydrogen. In catalytic hydrogenation processes, deuterium reacts more slowly, although the general courses of the reactions are the same. With the halogens, e.g., bromine, reactions with deuterium possess somewhat higher energies of activation. Similar results are obtained for reactions with nitrogen. In the hydrolysis of aluminum carbide at 80°C., ordinary water forms methane very rapidly whereas deuterium oxide yields deuteromethane with striking slowness. The fermentation of glucose proceeds more slowly in heavy water than in light. Numerous other reactions yielding comparable results have been recorded.

By far the greatest amount of information on the chemical behavior of deuterium has come from a study of exchange reactions, i.e., reactions in which one or more deuterium atoms trade places with light hydrogen atoms in some ion or molecule. Gaseous molecular deuterium does not enter into such reactions particularly readily, but atomic deuterium will. Similarly, exchange will often occur in the presence of an hydrogenation catalyst. Usually, however, such reactions have been brought about by contact between the material and gaseous or liquid deuterium oxide. The literature of such exchange reactions is so complex[13, 15] that only a few systems need be treated here.

Atomic exchanges of the types

$$D + H_2 \rightleftharpoons H + HD$$

and

$$nD + H_nX \rightleftharpoons nH + D_nX$$

where H_nX is H_2O, NH_3, or CH_4, have been studied. Correspondingly, catalytic exchanges such as

$$D_2 + H_2O \rightleftharpoons D_2O + H_2$$

(see p. 51 as regards separation by this means) and

$$3D_2 + C_6H_6 \rightleftharpoons C_6D_6 + 3H_2$$

both in the presence of platinum black, have been recorded. On the other hand, a variety of hydrogen compounds undergo exchange when treated with deterium oxide (or HDO). Such reactions depend upon the presence of labile hydrogen and occur whenever the compound in question yields even a slight concentration of hydrogen ions in contact with the water solution or possesses a fair degree of polarity in bonds involving hydrogen. Thus ammonium salts undergo exchange in contact with deuterium oxide, presumably in stepwise fashion as

$$NH_4^+ \xrightarrow{D_2O} NH_3D^+ \xrightarrow{D_2O} NH_2D_2^+ \xrightarrow{D_2O} NHD_3^+ \xrightarrow{D_2O} ND_4^+$$

and organic substances such as alcohols, phenols, and carbohydrates exchange hydroxyl hydrogens for deuterium. A number of such cases are summarized in Table 12·3.[15] Although exchange reactions are equilibria, they are very useful in elucidating the mechanisms of reactions and in tracing the course of hydrogen in a variety of reactions because of the labeled character of deuterium.

Of the deuterium compounds, the oxide (D_2O or heavy water) has been the most extensively studied. In Table 12·4 a number of the physical constants of ordinary water and deuterium oxide are compared. Certain of these properties are fairly apparent; others require comment. On the basis of a lower value for dielectric constant, deuterium oxide would be expected to be the poorer electrolytic solvent. This appears to be true. The reduced ionic mobilities in deuterium oxide cited are typical as are the reduced solubilities. These differences are all differences of degree rather than of kind.

[15] A. Farkas: *Orthohydrogen, Parahydrogen, and Heavy Hydrogen*, pp. 176–201. Cambridge University Press, London (1935).

Like ordinary water, deuterium oxide adds to salts and other compounds to give materials of the hydrate type, i.e., deuterohydrates. Such examples as $CuSO_4 \cdot 5D_2O$, $Na_2SO_4 \cdot 10D_2O$, $CoCl_2 \cdot 6D_2O$, and $Kr \cdot 6D_2O$ (p. 381) may be cited to show comparisons with normal water. Deuterohydrates have slightly lower equilibrium vapor tensions than corresponding hydrates at the same temperatures and are characterized by somewhat lower heats of hydration. Otherwise they are comparable.

TABLE 12·3

Exchange Reactions Involving D_2O

Material	Observation	Comment
Benzene, C_6H_6	No exchange	
Glucose, Sucrose	Exchange of hydroxyl hydrogens	
Acetone, CH_3COCH_3; Acetylacetone, $CH_3CO \cdot CH_2CO \cdot CH_3$	Exchange of all hydrogens in alkaline medium	Due to enolization
Hydrogen peroxide, H_2O_2	Exchange of both hydrogens	
Ammonium salts, NH_4^+	Exchange of all hydrogens	
Hexammine cobalt(III) ion, $[Co(NH_3)_6]^{+3}$	Exchange of all hydrogens	
Hypophosphite ion, $H_2PO_2^-$	No exchange	Supports the structure $\left[\begin{array}{c} H \\ H : \ddot{\underset{..}{P}} : \ddot{\underset{..}{O}} : \\ : \ddot{\underset{..}{O}} : \end{array}\right]^-$
Acetate ion, $C_2H_3O_2^-$	No exchange	
Acetylene, C_2H_2	Exchange of both hydrogens in alkaline medium	Shows acidic nature of $\equiv C—H$

Deuterium oxide enters into all the reactions of ordinary water, and because of its normal ready availability is often useful in the preparation of other deuterium compounds. Thus metal deuteroxides (containing the —OD group) result from action of the corresponding oxides on deuterium oxide, whereas oxy-deuterium acids (e.g., D_2SO_4, D_3PO_4), may be prepared by treating the corresponding anhydrides with heavy water. Deuteroammonia may be obtained by exchange or by action of deuterium oxide on magnesium nitride, and deuteroacetylene (C_2D_2) by an analogous reaction involving calcium carbide. In like manner, deuterium sulfide results when anhydrous aluminum sulfide is treated with heavy water. Deuterium chloride has been obtained readily by reacting the oxide with benzoyl chloride. Once certain deuterium compounds have been obtained in this fashion, they may be used to prepare other derivatives. For example, volatile acids (as DNO_3) may be liberated from their salts with deuterosulfuric acid, and deuterium peroxide may be obtained from a peroxide and deuterosulfuric acid. These deuterium compounds resemble the corresponding hydrogen compounds closely but are characterized by

TABLE 12·4

Comparison of Physical Properties of H_2O, HDO, and D_2O

Property	H_2O	HDO	D_2O
Lattice constants of solid, A	a = 4.514		4.517
	c = 7.352		7.354
Specific gravity of solid at m.p.	0.917		1.017
Specific gravity at 20°C.	0.9982		1.1059
Molecular volume at 20°C., ml.	18.157		18.200
Freezing point, °C.	0		3.82
Boiling point, °C.	100	101.76	101.42
Vapor pressure at 20°C., mm.	17.535	16.27	15.2
Temperature of maximum density, °C.	4		11.6
Critical temperature, °C.	374.1		371.5
Critical pressure, atm.	217.7		218.6
Dielectric constant at 20°C.	82		80.5
Viscosity at 20°C., millipoises	10.09		12.6
Surface tension at 19°C., dynes/cm.	73.66		72.83
Magnetic susceptibility, $\chi \times 10^6$	0.72		0.65
Refractive index, n_D^{20}	1.33300		1.32844
Ion product (25°C.)	1×10^{-14}		0.3×10^{-14}
Molecular freezing point lowering, °C.	1.859		2.050
Latent heat of fusion at m.p., kcal./mole	1.435		1.522
Latent heat of vaporization at b.p., kcal./mole	9.719	9.849	9.960
Heat of formation at 25°C., kcal./mole	68.32		70.41
Ionic mobilities at 18°C.			
K^+	64.2		54.4
Cl^-	65.2		55.3
Representative solubilities at 25°C., grams/gram water			
NaCl	0.359		0.305
$BaCl_2$	0.357		0.289

decreased volatilities, increased densities, etc. The metal deuterides are strictly comparable with the hydrides (pp. 403–415). A comprehensive survey of references on deuterium compounds has been given by Kimball.[16]

The material HDO is of course intermediate in properties between water and deuterium oxide. It may be prepared by such exchange

[16] A. H. Kimball: *Bibliography of Research on Heavy Hydrogen Compounds.* National Nuclear Energy Series, Division III, Vol. 4C. McGraw-Hill Book Co., New York (1949).

reactions as

$$H_2O + D_2O \rightleftharpoons 2HDO$$

which occurs at elevated temperatures, in discharge tubes, or by photochemical activation, or

$$H_2O + HD \rightleftharpoons HDO + H_2$$

which occurs in the presence of appropriate catalysts. Certain of its properties are included in Table 12·4.

Tritium. After the discovery of deuterium, much effort was expended in searching for a hydrogen isotope of mass number 3. First positive evidence for the existence of this isotope in nature was probably obtained by Lozier, Smith, and Bleakney[17] from mass spectrometer studies on practically pure deuterium. Confirmatory evidence was soon offered through mass spectrometer data[18] for an ion of mass 5(DT^+) for a sample of water obtained by electrolyzing 75 metric tons of ordinary water down to 0.5 ml., a reduction in volume by a factor of 150 million. Since in this sample the D:T ratio was roughly 10^4:1, the original abundance of tritium was some 7 atoms in 10^{10}. Although these results have been questioned[1] (by Bleakney[19] himself, for example), it appears that there is good evidence[1, 2] for the natural existence of tritium. Thus exhaustive electrolyses of highly concentrated deuterium oxide samples have given residues in which tritium has been detected,[2] the quantities of the material being such that a natural ratio of some 10^{-18} atom of tritium per atom of light hydrogen was suggested. Natural tritium is believed to be formed by neutron bombardment of atmospheric nitrogen, the necessary neutrons resulting from the action of cosmic radiation on the atmospheric gases.

The results of nuclear studies are striking. Bombardment of deuterium compounds with high energy deuterons produces tritium and light hydrogen[20] according to the equation

$${}^2_1D + {}^2_1D \rightarrow {}^3_1T + {}^1_1H$$

Tritium has been obtained also by the action of slow neutrons on lithium[21]

$${}^6_3Li + {}^1_0n \rightarrow {}^3_1T + {}^4_2He$$

17 W. W. Lozier, P. T. Smith, and W. Bleakney: *Phys. Rev.*, **45**, 655 (1934).

18 P. W. Selwood, H. S. Taylor, W. W. Lozier, and W. Bleakney: *J. Am. Chem. Soc.*, **57**, 780 (1935).

19 R. Sherr, L. G. Smith, and W. Bleakney: *Phys. Rev.*, **54**, 388 (1938).

20 M. L. E. Oliphant, P. Harteck, and E. Rutherford: *Proc. Roy. Soc.* (*London*), **A144**, 692 (1934).

21 R. D. O'Neal and M. Goldhaber: *Phys. Rev.*, **57**, 1086 (1940); **58**, 574 (1940).

from the deuteron bombardment of beryllium[21]

$$^{9}_{4}Be + ^{2}_{1}D \rightarrow ^{3}_{1}T + ^{8}_{4}Be$$

or

$$^{9}_{4}Be + ^{2}_{1}D \rightarrow ^{3}_{1}T + 2^{4}_{2}He$$

and from a few related processes. The reaction Be(d,2α)T is a useful one for preparation of the material in sizable quantities.

Tritium is radioactive, undergoing a soft β^- decay of some 0.0179 Mev energy with a half-life of 12.4 years[2] and forming the three-isotope of helium. The isotope is a useful tracer and has potential uses in nuclear fusion processes (p. 68). The following physical constants have been determined:[22] triple point, 20.62°K.; pressure at triple point, 162.0 mm. Hg; normal boiling point, 25.04°K.; heat of sublimation at triple point, 393 cal. per mole; heat of vaporization at normal boiling point, 333 cal. per mole. All these constants are for normal molecular tritium and should be compared with those already given (Table 12·2) for light hydrogen and deuterium. Calculated values of 43.7°K. for the critical temperature and 20.8 atm. for the critical pressure are also available.[23]

Molecular hydrogen

Several types of hydrogen molecules are distinguishable, the most important of which are H_2, D_2, and HD. The last of these results from the equilibrium interaction of the molecules H_2 and D_2 at elevated temperatures and may be prepared either by the reaction of lithium hydride with deuterium oxide, by the reaction of lithium aluminum hydride with deuterium oxide,[24] or (in 85% concentration) by reaction of 82.8% aqueous sulfuric acid solution with deuterodiborane, B_2D_6.[25] In properties it is intermediate between the species H_2 and D_2. If tritium is considered, the molecular picture is complicated by the existence of mixed molecules such as HT or DT as well as simple T_2 molecules.

In 1927 Heisenberg[26] predicted from quantum mechanical considerations that because the spins of the two nuclei in the hydrogen molecule may be either parallel or opposed, as shown below, two more or less is isomeric forms of molecular hydrogen (*ortho* and *para*) should result. This supposition was confirmed by Bonhoeffer and Harteck,[27]

[22] E. R. Grilly: *J. Am. Chem. Soc.*, **73,** 843 (1951).
[23] E. F. Hammel: *J. Chem. Phys.*, **18,** 228 (1950).
[24] I. Wender, R. A. Friedel, and M. Orchin: *J. Am. Chem. Soc.*, **71,** 1140 (1949).
[25] F. J. Norton: *Science*, **111,** 202 (1950).
[26] W. Heisenberg: *Z. Physik*, **41,** 239 (1937).
[27] K. F. Bonhoeffer and P. Harteck: *Naturwissenschaften*, **17,** 182 (1929); *Z. physik. Chem.*, **B4,** 113 (1929).

who found that when ordinary hydrogen gas is cooled to liquid air or liquid hydrogen temperatures in the presence of activated charcoal, there appears a new modification (actually para) with markedly different properties. Similar complexities might be expected for all ele-

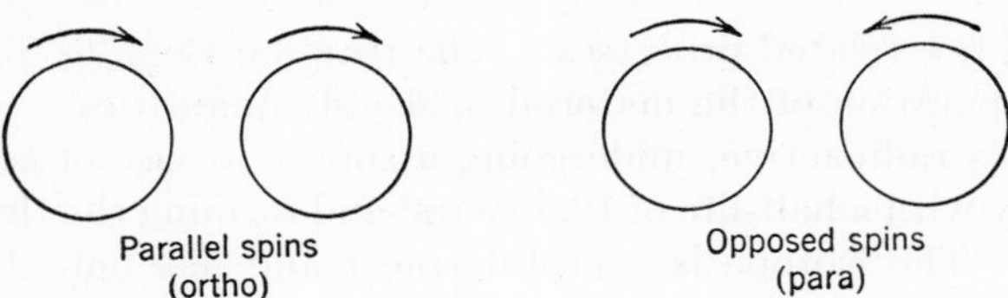

mentary diatomic molecules with nuclear spins, and indeed ortho and para forms are known not only for hydrogen but also for the molecules D_2, N_2, F_2, Cl_2, etc. Other factors preclude their existence for molecules such as HD and O_2.

With both hydrogen and deuterium, temperature-dependent equilibria between ortho and para forms exist. The equilibrium percentages of para hydrogen and ortho deuterium are shown as functions of temperature in Table 12·5. It is apparent that decreasing the

TABLE 12·5
ORTHO-PARA EQUILIBRIA FOR MOLECULAR HYDROGEN AND DEUTERIUM

Temperature, °K.	Percentage Para Hydrogen at Equilibrium	Percentage Ortho Deuterium at Equilibrium
0	100	100
25	99.00	95.29
50	76.80	79.19
100	38.46	67.82
160	......	66.72
200	25.95	.....
250	25.26	66.66
298	25.07	66.66
∞	25.00	66.67

temperature favors complete conversion to para hydrogen and ortho deuterium. These forms are the least energetic, the difference between the forms assumed by hydrogen and deuterium being due to the types of statistics obeyed by the materials.[13, 28] It follows that essentially para hydrogen or ortho deuterium may be prepared but that mixtures containing more than 75% ortho hydrogen or 33.33% para deuterium cannot be obtained.

Although these equilibria are temperature dependent, they are

[28] A. Farkas: *Orthohydrogen, Parahydrogen, and Heavy Hydrogen*, Pt. I, Ch. II, VI. Cambridge University Press, London (1935).

rather slowly attained. In the absence of catalysts ordinary hydrogen may be maintained at temperatures as low as 20°K. for appreciable periods without significant increase in the para hydrogen content. Correspondingly, para hydrogen prepared at low temperatures may be kept as long as a week in glass at ordinary temperatures with only slow conversion to the equilibrium mixture. Conversion of the equilibrium mixtures to para hydrogen or ortho deuterium at low temperatures is catalyzed by activated charcoal and certain metals such as tungsten or nickel. Reversion to the equilibrium mixture is favored for hydrogen by heating to 800°C. or more, presence of metallic catalysts (e.g., Pt or Fe), admixture with atomic hydrogen, electric discharge, and the presence of paramagnetic substances (e.g., O_2, NO, NO_2, Co^{+2}, Fe^{+2}) but not diamagnetic substances (e.g., N_2, N_2O, Zn^{+2}). Presumably similar situations would exist with deuterium. A detailed consideration of the kinetics of such conversions is given by Farkas.[29]

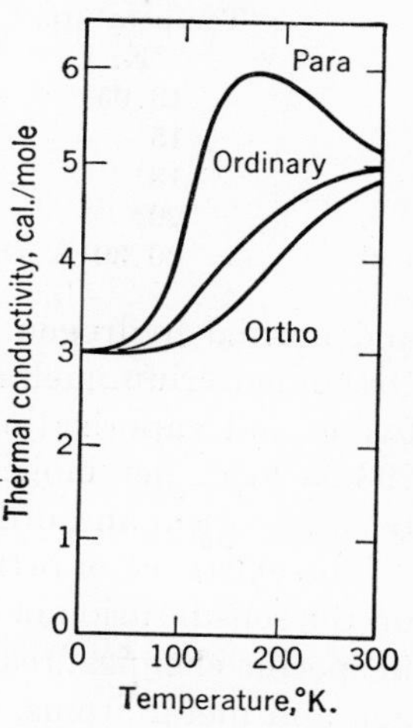

Fig. 12·1. Thermal conductivities of hydrogen molecules at low pressures. (Redrawn from A. Farkas: *Orthohydrogen, Parahydrogen, and Heavy Hydrogen*, p. 26. Cambridge University Press, London [1935].)

The properties of para hydrogen and ortho deuterium have been evaluated fairly completely, but those of ortho hydrogen and para deuterium are known only by extrapolation since the pure materials are not obtainable. Since para hydrogen possesses a lower internal energy than the ortho form, there are significant differences in band spectra intensities. The specific heats and thermal conductivities of para and normal hydrogen (hence ortho hydrogen) are markedly different especially at low pressures, so different in fact that the para content of a mixture is usually determined from the thermal conductivity of that mixture. This is apparent from the data given in Figure 12·1. Ortho hydrogen, for lack of neutralization of nuclear spins, has a magnetic moment, whereas para hydrogen does not. However, the contribution of nuclear spin to total magnetic moment is so small in comparison with the effects produced by electrons, that ordinary hydrogen is essentially diamagnetic. Para hydrogen melts at 13.82°K. and boils at 20.26°K. as compared to corresponding values of 13.95°K. and 20.39°K. for ordinary hydrogen. Accordingly, the vapor pressure

[29] *Ibid.*, Ch. IV.

of para hydrogen is slightly higher at a given temperature than for ordinary hydrogen, typical values being given in Table 12·6. It is interesting to note also that the thermal diffusion procedure of Clusius and Dickel (p. 44) has been reported to separate ortho hydrogen from para hydrogen.[30] Further details relating to differences between para

TABLE 12·6

Vapor Pressures of Normal and Para Hydrogen

Temperature, °K.	Vapor Pressure, mm. of Hg	
	Normal Hydrogen	Para Hydrogen
13.95	53.9	57.0
15	103.5	108.7
18	365.0	381.7
20	708.2	732.9
20.39	760.0	787.0

and normal hydrogen may be found in the monograph by Farkas.[31] Ortho deuterium melts at 18.63°K. and boils at 23.59°K., the heats of fusion and vaporization being, respectively, 47.07 kcal. per mole and 293.93 kcal. per mole.[32] Other similar differences may be expected between ortho and ordinary deuterium.

The existence of ortho and para forms has permitted measurements on the self-diffusion of hydrogen, on the hydrogen atom concentrations in specific chemical reactions, and on energy exchanges between hydrogen and metal atoms.

Atomic hydrogen

The dissociation of hydrogen according to the equation

$$H_2 \rightarrow H + H$$

is endothermic to the extent of some 98 to 101 kcal. per mole.* This is a sufficiently large energy quantity to preclude the existence of anything but very small quantities of atomic hydrogen by direct thermal dissociation except at very high temperatures. This fact is apparent from the data calculated by Langmuir[33] and summarized in Table 12·7. Although reduction in pressure increases the dissociation, the total quantity of material converted is of course reduced correspondingly.

[30] K. Schäfer and H. Corte: *Naturwissenschaften*, **33**, 92 (1946).

[31] A. Farkas: *Orthohydrogen, Parahydrogen, and Heavy Hydrogen*, Pt. I, Ch. III. Cambridge University Press, London (1935).

[32] E. C. Kerr, E. B. Rifkin, H. L. Johnston, and J. T. Clarke: *J. Am. Chem. Soc.*, **73**, 282 (1951).

* Values from 98 to 105 kcal. per mole have been recorded.

[33] I. Langmuir: *Gen. Elec. Rev.*, **29**, 153 (1926).

Three methods, all involving extremely energy-rich conditions, have been proposed for the production of atomic hydrogen. Langmuir[33] obtained the material by passing molecular hydrogen through an electric arc at high current density, a method which is employed currently in atomic hydrogen welding arrangements. A similar method based upon passing hydrogen at low pressures through a high-tension discharge tube was shown by Bonhoeffer[34] to yield atomic hydrogen.

TABLE 12·7

DISSOCIATION OF MOLECULAR HYDROGEN

Temperature, °K.	Dissociation, %
1000	0.000000371
2000	0.122
3000	9.03
4000	62.5
5000	94.69
6000	98.84
7000	99.69
8000	99.87
9000	99.93
10,000	99.96

Radiation of hydrogen with energy from a mercury vapor arc also gives atomic hydrogen.[35] As is expected, atomic hydrogen produced by any of these procedures is unstable with respect to the molecular form and must be used as generated if its properties are to be evaluated. The half-life, as estimated by Bonhoeffer, is some 0.3 sec. under the conditions of his experimental study. Reversion to the molecular form is catalyzed by metals such as Pt, Pd, W, Fe, Cr, Ag, Cu, Pd (in decreasing order of activity), the energy liberated being sufficient to heat many of these metals to incandescence or even to fusion. The efficiency of the atomic hydrogen torch is dependent upon this property.

Atomic hydrogen is an active reducing agent. Non-metals, such as sulfur, chlorine, bromine, or iodine, are converted rapidly to the corresponding hydrides. Metal oxides and chlorides, such as those of copper, lead, bismuth, silver, and mercury, are readily reduced to the free metals, as are the sulfides of cadmium, copper, and mercury. Oxides of aluminum, magnesium, chromium, and zinc, however, are unaffected. Many alkali metal salts, among them nitrates, nitrites, azides, cyanides, and thiocyanates, are reduced to the free metals, but the corresponding halides, sulfates, and phosphates are unaffected. Metals such as the alkali metals, antimony, and bismuth, are converted to hydrides. Ethylenic linkages are hydrogenated and azoxy groups

[34] K. F. Bonhoeffer: *Z. physik. Chem.*, **113**, 199 (1924).

[35] G. Cario and J. Franck: *Z. Physik*, **11**, 161 (1922).

reduced stepwise to amines. With oxygen, hydrogen peroxide is formed, Gieb and Harteck claiming[36] that at very low temperatures a form different from ordinary hydrogen peroxide, but reverting to it at $-115°C.$, results (p. 504). Carbon dioxide is reduced to formic acid. An excellent literature survey is given by Maxted.[13] There appears to be no real evidence that the so-called nascent hydrogen, so often postulated as a reactant in many reactions occurring in solution, is atomic hydrogen.[37]

Combined hydrogen

Combined hydrogen may be classified conveniently as covalent or anionic. Inasmuch as the ionization potential of hydrogen is so large (13.595 ev = 313.6 kcal. per gram atom), the production of truly cationic hydrogen in chemical combination is quite impossible. It is true that hydrogen often combines with more electronegative elements and is thereby assigned a positive oxidation number, but such compounds are polar rather than ionic. If the bonds in such compounds are sufficiently highly polar, they may be ruptured on contact with highly polar or basic solvents to yield solvated protons and whatever anion characterizes the original compound. As already discussed (pp. 310–312), this occurs in water, ammonia, hydrazine, etc. Because free protons can no more exist in these solvents than in pure compounds purely cationic hydrogen is limited in its existence to discharge tubes and nuclear reactions. Covalently bonded hydrogen is characteristic of the volatile (non-metal) hydrides (pp. 409–411). Anionic hydrogen, on the other hand, is not unexpected in view of the stability of the helium structure and the sizable electronegativity differences between hydrogen and certain of the metals. These differences, however, are sufficiently large to permit electron transfer to hydrogen only with very highly electropositive elements such as the alkali and alkaline earth metals. Binary compounds between hydrogen and such metals contain the negative hydride (H^-) ion (pp. 406–408). Since covalence greater than one is forbidden for hydrogen (p. 188), coordination to bonded hydrogen does not occur. The proton, however, may act as an acceptor toward a variety of bases (pp. 309–312).

THE GENERAL CHEMISTRY OF HYDROGEN

To a considerable extent, the general chemistry of hydrogen has been covered in preceding discussions. Many of the physical constants have been evaluated in this chapter in the discussions of atomic,

[36] K. H. Geib and P. Harteck: *Ber.*, **65B**, 1551 (1932).

[37] J. H. Reedy and E. D. Biggers: *J. Chem. Education*, **19**, 403 (1942).

molecular, and isotopic hydrogen; the hydrogen bond has been considered in Chapter 6 (pp. 187–191); the importance of the element in oxidation-reduction systems has been discussed in Chapter 8 (pp. 292–293); the acidic properties of the hydrogen ion have been summarized in Chapter 9 (pp. 308–321); the structure of the hydrogen atom has been discussed in Chapter 3 (pp. 81–86); the nuclear properties of hydrogen have been explored in Chapter 2 (pp. 70–71); and types of bonding have been considered both in Chapter 6 and in this chapter. The binary compounds of hydrogen are dealt with both in a later section of this chapter (pp. 403–415) and in subsequent chapters (e.g., Chapter 13 to 17, inclusive). Accordingly, the treatment of the general chemistry of hydrogen offered here is extremely brief.

Physical and chemical characteristics

Numerical properties of hydrogen are summarized in Table 12·2 and Table 12·8. The values in the latter table are for the ordinary isotopic mixture of hydrogen containing about one part of deuterium in 5000 and the ordinary ortho para mixture.

TABLE 12·8

NUMERICAL CONSTANTS OF HYDROGEN

Property	Numerical Value
Critical temperature, °K.	32
Critical pressure, atm.	20
Density of gas, gram/liter at 0°C., 1 atm.	0.08986
Density of liq., gram/ml. at	0.071
Solubility in H_2O, grams/100 grams at 25°C.	1.8

Chemically, hydrogen combines with most of the non-metallic elements and with many of the metals to produce compounds called hydrides. These are discussed in detail later (pp. 403–415). Hydrogen serves as a reducing agent toward many metal oxides and toward double and triple bonds involving carbon. Characteristic reactions of hydrogen, both molecular and atomic are summarized in Table 12·9. In general, these reactions are indicative of the tendency of hydrogen to bond by electron pair sharing, although bonds with highly electropositive elements are completely ionic (p. 406) and those with highly electronegative elements possess appreciable partial ionic character.

Preparation of hydrogen

Hydrogen is commonly prepared by reduction of the solvated (normally, hydrated) proton or oxidation of the negative hydride ion.

In general, metals or cations with positive standard potentials are capable of being oxidized by the proton (solvation implied but not stated) and will, under appropriate conditions, release hydrogen. The magnitude of the potential governs the conditions under which such reactions occur. Only the most highly electropositive metals can release hydrogen from water where the proton concentration is low; others require higher concentrations of protons such as are found in acidic solutions. Hydrogen is thus obtained in the laboratory by reactions of acids with metals such as iron or zinc. Anions, such as nitrate, which are stronger oxidizing agents than the proton must be

TABLE 12·9
COMMON REACTIONS OF HYDROGEN

Reaction	Examples, Limitations and Conditions
$H_2 + X_2 \rightarrow 2HX$	$X_2 = F_2, Cl_2, Br_2, I_2$. Catalyst necessary with I_2.
$H_2 + \frac{1}{2}O_2 \rightarrow H_2O$	Strongly exothermic. Proceeds with reduced vigor with S and practically not at all with Se or Te.
$3H_2 + N_2 \rightarrow 2NH_3$	Favored by catalyst at low temperature and high pressures. Corresponding reactions with P, As, Sb, Bi not known.
$xH_2 + 2M \rightarrow 2MH_x$	Where M = Li, Na, K, Rb, Cs, Ca, Sr, Ba, Ra to give saline hydrides. With many other metals to give metallic hydrides.
$yH_2 + M_xO_y \rightarrow xM + yH_2O$	With oxides of metals less active than iron.
$>C{=}C< + H_2 \rightarrow -\overset{\diagup\diagdown}{C}-\overset{\diagup\diagdown}{C}-$	Normally in presence of catalysts at elevated temperatures and under pressure.
$-C{\equiv}C- + 2H_2 \rightarrow -\overset{\diagup\diagdown}{C}-\overset{\diagup\diagdown}{C}-$	
$>C{=}O + H_2 \rightarrow -\overset{\diagup\diagdown}{C}-OH$	

absent since they will be reduced in preference to the proton. Low-valent cations such as Cr^{+2}, V^{+2}, and Ti^{+2} react similarly. In the presence of hydroxyl ion, amphoteric elements such as aluminum or silicon release hydrogen from water, although they are apparently unreactive in its absence. Such reactions proceed because of the more favorable oxidation potentials resulting from the stabilities of the resulting anions (AlO_2^-, SiO_3^{-2}) and the removal of normally insoluble oxidation products of the metals by hydroxyl ion. Reduction of protons by the electric current in both acidic or alkaline solutions and in neutral halide solutions is commonly employed as a technical preparative procedure. Oxidation of hydride ions is convenient because if water is used as the oxidant the quantity of hydrogen released is markedly increased (p. 408). Hydrides such as lithium aluminum hydride ($LiAlH_4$) and the simple lithium or calcium compound are commonly used (p. 408).

Industrial hydrogen is obtained by the reduction of water vapor at elevated temperatures with coke, lower hydrocarbons, or iron; from the cracking of hydrocarbons; from the destructive distillation of coal; by the electrolysis of aqueous solutions; or by action of hydrides on water.

Characteristics of the hydrogen ion

Although the existence of the free proton under any but extremely energy-rich conditions is precluded, it is still common practice to refer to reactions of the solvated proton as involving the hydrogen ion. This is entirely acceptable practice since solvation is normally neglected with other ions (p. 281). The hydrogen ion, because of its small size, represents a very effective concentration of positive charge and thus possesses properties which set it apart from other cations. These characteristics have been summarized in Chapter 9. The general chemistry of the hydrogen ion is associated with the half-reactions represented by the couples

$$\tfrac{1}{2}H_2 \rightleftharpoons H^+ + e^- \qquad E^0_{298} = 0.0000 \text{ volt}$$

in acidic solution and

$$\tfrac{1}{2}H_2 + OH^- \rightleftharpoons H_2O + e^- \qquad E^0_{298} = 0.83 \text{ volt}$$

in alkaline solution.

Technical applications of hydrogen

Perhaps the largest quantities of technical hydrogen are employed in the hydrogenation of materials such as nitrogen (to give ammonia), carbon monoxide (to give methanol and a variety of other useful organic products), coal and other organic products (to give hydrocarbons), and vegetable oils (to give edible fats). Applications of hydrogen as fuel in welding, as a lifting agent, etc., consume relatively smaller quantities of the element.

A SYSTEMATIC CONSIDERATION OF HYDRIDES

By direct or indirect means, binary combinations of hydrogen with a large number of the other elements can be prepared. By convention, such materials are referred to as hydrides, although this is not in strict keeping with common practice in nomenclature since combinations with elements which are more electronegative than hydrogen are probably even more common than those with elements which are less electronegative. Because of the variety of elements appearing in combination with hydrogen, the hydrides are characterized by a wide variety of properties and are thus representative of several types of bonding. Early interest in hydrogen compounds of the non-metals, particularly oxygen, the halogens, and carbon, led to Stock's classic researches[38] on the hydrides of boron and silicon, which in turn stimulated expanded investigations involving other elements. Undoubtedly, Paneth's systematic classification and discussion of the hydrides[39] provided a basis for modern trends in hydride chemistry.[40, 41] In this chapter, the hydrides are classified according to general properties and bond types, and the characteristics of each class are described. Detailed considerations of the specific properties of hydrides of the various non-metals appear in the next five chapters.

Classification of the hydrides

Paneth's original classification of the hydrides into *volatile* hydrides, *salt-like* hydrides, and *metal-like* hydrides on the basis of their comparative properties still appears reasonably adequate, although more detailed examination of the characteristics of specific members of each class has often indicated significant deviations from the general properties usually ascribed to the class as a whole and has suggested modifications. For instance, Gibb[41] prefers the classes *saline* or *salt-like* (possessing ionic crystal lattices), *volatile* (possessing covalent bonds in most cases), *polymeric* (containing two or more metal atoms linked by hydrogen bridges), and *metallic* (possessing the physical characteristics of metals). It appears more reasonable in view of the general properties of known hydrides to modify Paneth's classification less drastically and to consider the types *saline* or *salt-like, covalent or molecular* (usually volatile), and *metallic.*

The *saline* or *salt-like* hydrides are characterized by ionic lattices and attendant high melting points, high boiling points, and conductivity in the fused states (if stable). The *covalent* or *molecular* hydrides are characterized by molecular lattices made up of individual saturated covalent molecules and possess the attendant properties of

[38] A. Stock: *Hydrides of Boron and Silicon.* Cornell University Press, Ithaca, New York (1933).

[39] F. Paneth: *Radio Elements as Indicators and Other Selected Topics in Inorganic Chemistry,* pp. 91–122. McGraw-Hill Book Co., New York (1928).

[40] H. J. Emeléus and J. S. Anderson: *Modern Aspects of Inorganic Chemistry,* pp. 231–262. D. Van Nostrand Co., New York (1938).

[41] T. R. P. Gibb: *J. Chem. Education,* **25,** 577 (1948); *J. Electrochem. Soc.,* **93,** 188 (1948).

softness, low melting point, low boiling point, and lack of conductivity. Although the bonding within individual molecules is always covalent to some extent, it may show significant partial ionic character (e.g., with hydrogen fluoride). However, bonding never becomes strictly ionic, and these materials may be considered as a class apart from the *saline* class. The *metallic* hydrides are characterized by metallic

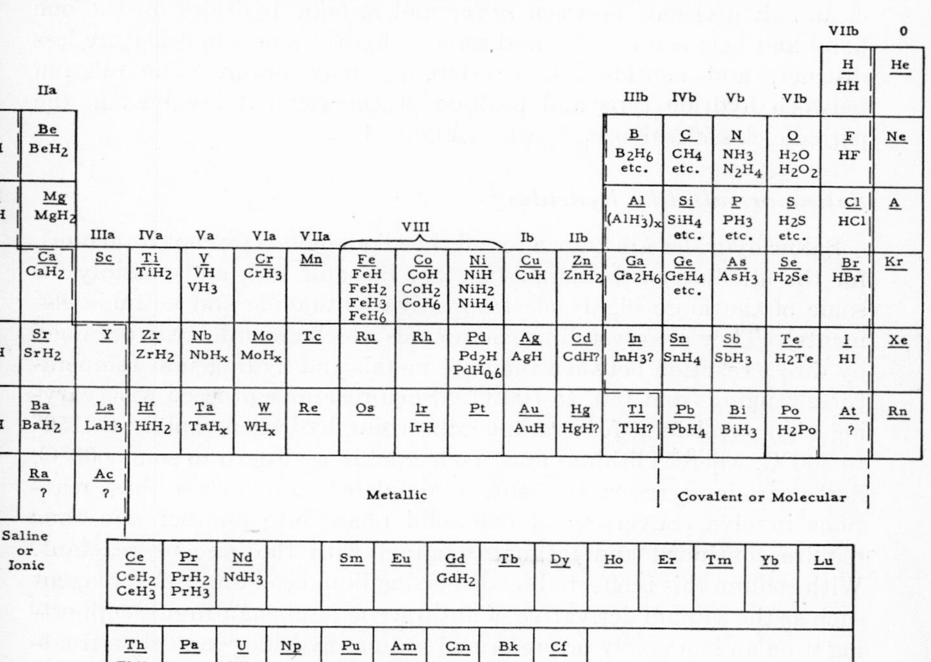

FIG. 12·2. Classification of hydrides.

structures and are alloy-like in most of their characteristics. They are in effect interstitial materials (p. 221) and lack the stoichiometry associated with true electronic bonding. Deuterium forms similar compounds.

The type of hydride which an element forms depends upon the electronegativity of that element. Only those elements with very low electronegativities (e.g., the alkali metals, the alkaline earth metals, and possibly the lanthanides and actinides) are sufficiently strong reducing agents to transfer electrons to the hydrogen atom and thereby form saline hydrides. On the other hand, only the most highly electronegative elements (e.g., the non-metals in Periodic Families IIIb, IVb, Vb, VIb, and VIIb) share electrons with hydrogen to form covalent hydrides. Here the electron attractions are insufficient to remove electrons from hydrogen atoms (p. 400). The remaining elements (e.g., the transition metals) yield only *metallic* hydrides if they show any tendency at all to combine with hydrogen. It should be apparent that, although the division between *saline* and *covalent* hydrides is clean-cut, divisions between *saline* and *metallic* hydrides on the one hand and between *metallic* and *covalent* hydrides on the other are less distinct, and considerable overlapping may occur. The relation between hydride type and position of the element involved in the periodic classification is shown in Figure 12·2.

Saline or salt-like hydrides

Saline hydrides are known for all the alkali metals (except francium), for the alkaline earth metals (Ca, Sr, Ba, and Ra), and possibly for some of the more highly electropositive lanthanide and actinide elements. They are crystalline compounds which are ordinarily obtained by direct reaction between the pure metals and hydrogen at temperatures ranging from 150° to 700°C. Such reactions proceed with varying vigors, calcium, for example, absorbing hydrogen rapidly at 150° to 300°C. whereas lithium must be heated in hydrogen to some 600°C. Some care is necessary to assure a complete reaction since these reactions involve conversion of one solid phase into another and thus require continued and intimate contact with the gaseous reactant. With sodium this is effected by dispersing liquid sodium with a reagent such as the sodium derivative of anthracene or phenanthrene, supporting it on an inert body or preformed sodium hydride,[42] and then treating with hydrogen at 250° to 300°C. under a pressure of one atmosphere.

The alkali metal hydrides possess cubic structures of the sodium chloride type (p. 137). The alkaline earth metal hydrides are structurally somewhat more complex, calcium hydride, for example, being hexagonal. It is rather definitely established that the lattices are ionic and contain negative hydride (H^-) ions formed by transfer of electrons from the metal atoms. Thus it has been shown that lithium hydride when fused or heated to insipient fusion conducts the electric current[43] and is thereby electrolytically decomposed with the deposition of lithium at the cathode[44] and hydrogen, in quantities in accord-

[42] V. L. Hansley and P. J. Carlisle: *Chem. Eng. News*, **23**, 1332 (1945).
[43] G. N. Lewis: *J. Am. Chem. Soc.*, **38**, 762 (1916). Note on p. 774.
[44] K. Moers: *Z. anorg. allgem. Chem.*, **113**, 179 (1920).

ance with Faraday's law, at the anode.[45] Similarly, calcium hydride, when dissolved in a molten lithium chloride-potassium chloride eutectic at 360°C. to avoid thermal decomposition, was found to liberate hydrogen at the anode during electrolysis in accordance with Faraday's law.[46] The alkali and alkaline earth metal hydrides have stoichiometric compositions.

Hydrides derived from the lanthanides (and presumably at least some of the actinides) present more difficult problems. Compositions such as $LaH_{2.76}$, $CeH_{2.69}$, $Pr_{2.85}$, and $ThH_{3.07}$ are characteristic and

TABLE 12·10

COMPARISON OF PROPERTIES OF HYDRIDES OF METALS

Hydride	Heat of Formation, kcal./mole of H_2	Change in Density on Formation, %
LiH	−43.2	+52.8
NaH	−33.2	+44
CaH_2	−46.6	+10
SrH_2	−42.2	......
BaH_2	−40.96	+20
$LaH_{2.76}$	−40.09	−12.8
$CeH_{2.69}$	−42.26	−17.5
$PrH_{2.85}$	−39.52	.....
$TaH_{0.76}$	slight	− 9.1
$VH_{0.56}$	− 9.28	− 6.7

might suggest that these hydrides are alloy-like in character However, these metals approach the alkali and alkaline earth metals in electropositive character, and the hydrides seem to possess at least some of the characteristics of saline compounds. Their heats of formation are very high and, as shown in Table 12·10,[47, 48] are of the same order of magnitude as values for the corresponding definitely ionic compounds. On the other hand, like the truly metallic hydrides, they are less dense than the parent metals whereas the truly saline hydrides are more dense (Table 12·10).[49] In the absence of further information, one may conclude that they represent transitions between the two classes.

The saline hydrides in general are insoluble in ordinary solvents at room temperatures unless reaction occurs, but they do dissolve without reaction in molten halides, and sodium hydride is soluble in molten

[45] K. Peters: *Z. anorg. allgem. Chem.*, **131,** 140 (1923).

[46] D. C. Bardwell: *J. Am. Chem. Soc.*, **44,** 2499 (1922).

[47] A. Sieverts and E. Roell: *Z. anorg. allgem. Chem.*, **153,** 289 (1926).

[48] A. Sieverts and A. Gotta: *Z. anorg. allgem. Chem.*, **187,** 155 (1930); **199,** 384 (1931).

[49] A. Sieverts and A. Gotta: *Z. Elektrochem.*, **32,** 105 (1926).

sodium hydroxide. The less stable hydrides cannot be fused under atmospheric pressure because of dissociation, but the more stable lithium hydride melts at 680°C. Chemically, the saline hydrides undergo thermal decomposition to metal and hydrogen at elevated temperatures, the alkali metal compounds (except LiH) decomposing in the range of 400° to 500°C. and the lithium and alkaline earth metal compounds decomposing at more elevated temperatures. At elevated temperatures, the saline hydrides are powerful reducing agents, and reductions such as refractory oxides to metals, carbon dioxide to formate, and metal sulfates to sulfides are easily carried out. Since at ordinary temperatures, corresponding reactions do not occur, it is conceivable that thermal dissociation of the hydride is essential to reduction. Many organic substances also undergo reduction at elevated temperatures.[42]

Lithium, calcium, and strontium hydrides are comparatively stable in dry air. The others may ignite spontaneously, although in perfectly dry air pure sodium hydride supposedly does not ignite below 230°C. The presence of traces of unreacted metal may lower the kindling temperature. In the presence of water all saline hydrides react vigorously according to the equation

$$H^- + H_2O \rightarrow H_2 + OH^-$$

the volume of hydrogen thus released being approximately twice that given by the corresponding metal. Solid saline hydrides, especially the lithium and calcium compounds, are thus excellent lightweight sources of hydrogen. Latimer[50] has estimated

$$H^- \rightleftharpoons \tfrac{1}{2}H_2 + e^- \qquad E^0_{298} = 2.23 \text{ volts}$$

by comparison of hydrides with fluorides. However, the excellent reducing properties thus predicted are obscured by the observed reduction of water. Saline hydrides are obviously excellent desiccants. Reactions with non-metals such as sulfur, nitrogen, phosphorus, and carbon to give the corresponding binary metal compounds and usually hydrogen have been reported.

Technically, lithium, sodium,[42] and calcium[51] hydrides are most commonly employed. Most common applications are those involving preparation of free metals, removal of scale on iron and steel objects with sodium hydride-sodium hydroxide mixtures, generation of hydrogen, and production of a variety of organic compounds.

[50] Latimer, W. M.: *The Oxidation States of the Elements and Their Potentials in Aqueous Solution*, p. 32. Prentice-Hall, New York (1938).

[51] Anon.: *Calcium Hydride*, Metal Hydrides, Inc., Beverly, Mass.

A series of closely related compounds is found in the borohydrides and aluminohydrides and the corresponding deuterium compounds, such as $LiBH_4$, $Be(BH_4)_2$, $Al(BH_4)_3$, $LiAlH_4$, $NaAlH_4$, and $LiAlD_4$. In many respects the reactions which these compounds undergo are comparable to those of the saline hydrides. However, since they are generically more closely related to the boron and aluminum hydrides, they are discussed later (Chapter 17, pp. 782–787).

The covalent or molecular hydrides

Covalent or molecular hydrides are known for all the truly non-metallic elements except the inert gases and for elements such as aluminum, gallium, tin, lead, antimony, and bismuth which are normally more metallic than non-metallic. Except for boron, aluminum, and gallium, each element listed in Figure 12·2 gives a simple mononuclear hydride of formula XH_{8-n}, where n is the number of valence electrons present in the neutral atom X. The simplest hydrides of boron and gallium are the dimeric materials B_2H_6 and Ga_2H_6, respectively, and the simplest hydride of aluminum is the polymeric $(AlH_3)_x$, all these compounds being electron deficient in character (p. 213). In addition to mononuclear hydrides, certain of the elements, notably all those except tin, lead, antimony, bismuth, tellurium, polonium (?), and the halogens, form polynuclear hydrides in which two or more atoms of the non-metal are directly attached to each other. This situation is of course most pronounced with carbon where an apparently infinite number of such combinations may result. Fluorine forms hydrides of the type H_xF_x, but these are composed of individual HF molecules joined by hydrogen bonds (p. 189) and are not polynuclear in the same sense.

The covalent hydrides may be prepared by a number of general methods. Among them are the following:

1. Direct combination of the free element with hydrogen, as with oxygen, nitrogen, or the halogens.
2. Reduction of certain compounds either with hydrogen (e.g., metal oxides give water) or under conditions where hydrogen is being generated (e.g., arsenic or antimony compounds with zinc and acid give arsine or stibine).
3. Hydrolysis of a metal (often magnesium) boride, silicide, carbide, etc., with water or with an acid in aqueous solution. This procedure often yields complex mixtures.
4. Treatment of a metal (often magnesium) silicide or germanide with a protonic acid in the absence of water. This procedure generally

gives less complex mixtures than the preceding one. As typical, one may cite the treatment of magnesium silicide with ammonium bromide in liquid ammonia to give silane[52] or with molten ethylamine hydrochloride or trimethylamine hydrochloride or ammonium bromide at elevated temperatures[53] to give mixtures of silicon hydrides.

5. Electrolytic reductions of solutions of compounds of the element in question. This procedure was employed by Paneth and Rabinowitsch[54] for the preparation of tin hydride (SnH_4) and amounted to electrolyzing a sulfuric acid solution of tin(II) sulfate containing dextrine or glucose with lead electrodes at temperatures below 50° to 60°C.

6. Reduction of the appropriate halide in ether solution with lithium aluminum hydride.[55] This procedure has been applied to the preparation of hydrides of silicon, germanium, and tin.

According to Hurd,[53] the hydrolytic procedures represented by methods 3 and 4 above are essentially ionic in nature, amounting to removal of cations from a crystal lattice and combination of anions left behind with protons. The natures of the resulting hydrides will then be dependent upon whether the non-metal atoms were present in the original crystal as discrete atoms or as molecular groups and upon whether the hydrolysis medium attacks the hydrides chemically. Specific details on the above procedures are considered in connection with later discussions (especially Chapters 16, 17).

The covalent hydrides exist in the same molecular form in all states of aggregation. In the solid state they are made up of molecular crystals of individual molecules held together by weak van der Waals attractions (p. 215). The comparatively low melting points of such solids and the low boiling points of the liquids resulting from them are thus not unreasonable. With ammonia, water, and hydrogen fluoride, hydrogen bonding produces anomalies in these properties (p. 189), but with these exceptions properties of this type increase more or less regularly with molecular weight for the hydrides of a particular type in a particular family. In general, all the covalent hydrides are volatile, although volatility is somewhat reduced in complicated polynuclear hydrides of high molecular weight. The covalent hydrides are non-conductors in the liquid state and when dissolved in non-polar solvents. Their chemical characteristics vary from one periodic family to another. They all undergo thermal decomposition to hydrogen and the other element, but the necessary conditions show

[52] W. C. Johnson and T. R. Hogness: *J. Am. Chem. Soc.*, **56**, 1252 (1934).

[53] D. T. Hurd: *J. Am. Chem. Soc.*, **69**, 1647 (1947).

[54] F. Paneth and E. Rabinowitsch: *Ber.*, **57**, 1877 (1924).

[55] A. E. Finholt, A. C. Bond, Jr., K. E. Wilzbach, and H. I. Schlesinger: *J. Am. Chem. Soc.*, **69**, 2692 (1947).

wide variability. In general, thermal instability increases with decreasing electronegativity of the non-metal, the hydrides of the heavier elements in any periodic family being less stable than those of the lighter elements.

The metallic hydrides

Instances of reversible absorption or occlusion of hydrogen by metals are well-known. Metals used as cathodes in the electrolysis of aqueous solutions often take up surprising quantities of hydrogen, as do metals which are cathodically deposited under conditions where reduction of protons can occur. A palladium cathode, for example, may take up one thousand times its volume of hydrogen, although some of this hydrogen is evolved rather violently when the current is turned off. Electrolytically deposited iron may contain one hundred times its volume of hydrogen. Similarly, many metals absorb hydrogen gas directly at moderate or elevated temperatures. For example, iron, palladium, and platinum are permeable to hydrogen at elevated temperatures whereas tantalum becomes brittle because of absorption of hydrogen. There is evidence too that those metals which are most efficient as hydrogenation catalysts (e.g., platinum, nickel) owe their efficiencies, at least in part, to their abilities to take up or combine with hydrogen. Hydrogen so absorbed can usually be removed by strong heating under vacuum conditions, but small amounts are often held very tenaciously.

The products obtained when metals take up hydrogen in these fashions are called metallic hydrides. Since they result from metals of widely differing characteristics (Figure 12·2), it is not surprising that their properties vary widely. It is impossible, therefore, to summarize any properties which are characteristic of all of them, but it is possible to offer some generalizations. In most cases, their properties are metallic and not markedly different from those of the parent metals. The quantity of hydrogen present ordinarily bears no exact stoichiometric relation to the metal, and formulas such as $ZrH_{1.92}$ and $TaH_{0.76}$, which are often given, probably represent no more than the conditions essential to saturation of the metal with hydrogen. In many cases, absorption of hydrogen results in no fundamental changes in the metal lattices, although density and X-ray determinations do show the lattices to be expanded and perhaps slightly distorted. There seems to be every evidence that in such cases hydrogen which has entered the metal lattice is occupying holes (interstices) between the metal atoms or ions and is thus held in solid solution. Accordingly, the terms interstitial solid solutions (p. 221) and interstitial compounds are often applied to the metallic hydrides. The strongly reducing properties of such hydrides (e.g., reduction of mercury compounds to the free metal) suggest that hydrogen is present in the atomic state, molecular hydrogen having undergone dissociation on entering the metal lattice.

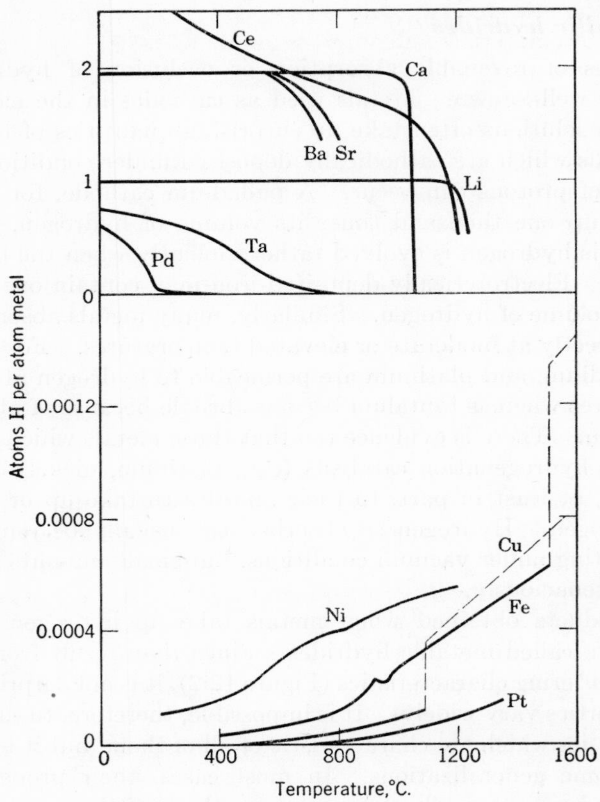

FIG. 12·3. Absorption of hydrogen by various metals.

The variations in individual properties among the metallic hydrides suggest more or less continuous transitions in the manner in which hydrogen is held according to the scheme

saline hydrides $\rightleftharpoons$ semi-metallic hydrides $\rightleftharpoons$ firmly bound interstitial hydrides $\rightleftharpoons$ loosely bound interstitial hydrides $\rightleftharpoons$ adsorption products with all materials except the saline hydrides being called alloylike or metallic. The semi-metallic hydrides represent transitions between true chemical binding and interstitial alloys and embrace hydrides derived from the metals in Periodic Groups IVa and Va. Hydrides of the lanthanide and actinide elements provide a direct transition between these materials and the true saline hydrides. In such materials, hydrogen may well be present both as such and bonded to the metal ions. Among the interstitial hydrides, the firmness with which hydrogen is held varies. It appears to reach maximum values with nickel, palladium, and platinum. In many cases where hydrogen is taken up in only comparatively small quantities, it is doubtful that penetration of the lattices occurs, and surface attraction is therefore the governing force.

Extensive studies by Sieverts[49] on densities and heats of formation (Table 12·10) indicate differences among metallic hydrides which are consistent with the foregoing pictures. Much effort has been expended in attempting to establish chemical formulas for metallic hydrides. Although a good deal of this work has been analytical, some of the most fruitful studies have involved measurements of hydrogen absorption as functions of pressure and temperature. Some typical curves for several metals at various temperatures are reproduced in Figure 12·3.[56] The true stoichiometries of the saline hydrides are apparent in the extended flat regions over broad temperature ranges and the sharp breaks at more elevated temperatures. With the other metals listed, hydrogen absorption drops with increasing temperature to rather constant values with palladium and tantalum, shows no constancy with cerium, resembles that in the saline hydrides with zirconium, and increases with iron, copper, and nickel. Evidences for true binding are thus not particularly strong, and differences in mode of attachment are apparent.

Perhaps the most extensively studied of the metallic hydrides is palladium hydride. Many of these studies have embraced measurements of the quantity of hydrogen taken up as a function of pressure at constant temperature. The results of determinations by Gillespie and coworkers,[57, 58] as summarized in Figure 12·4, are interpreted as indicating, at the two breaks on either side of flat portions, two solid solutions. One solid solution approaches the composition Pd_2H and separates in nearly pure form at more elevated temperatures. At lower temperatures, it dissolves increasing amounts of hydrogen, and

[56] G. Hüttig: *Z. angew. Chem.*, **39**, 67 (1926).

[57] L. J. Gillespie and F. P. Hall: *J. Am. Chem. Soc.*, **48**, 1207 (1926).

[58] L. J. Gillespie and L. S. Galstaun: *J. Am. Chem. Soc.*, **58**, 2565 (1936).

at room temperature the saturation value corresponds to the composition $PdH_{0.6}$. Similar studies with deuterium[59] show that, although deuterium absorption is less than hydrogen absorption at a given temperature and pressure, two solid solutions again result, the composition of the deuterium-poor-phase being Pd_2D at 200°C. The curves in Figure 12·4 show palladium hydride to be more or less semi-metallic in character and to be closer to a chemical compound than the hydrides of its immediate neighbors.

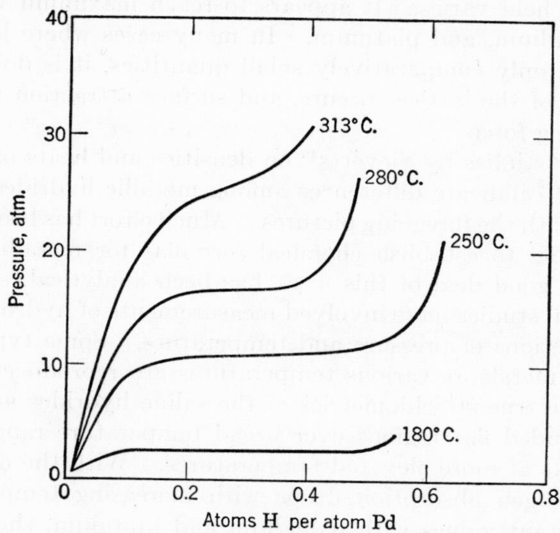

Fig. 12·4. Absorption of hydrogen by palladium.

Certain of the metallic hydrides do have exactly stoichiometric compositions. Perhaps the best known of these is copper hydride, CuH, which is obtained by reduction of copper(II) sulfate solution with sodium hypophosphite at 70°C.[60] This is an unstable reddish-brown solid which has a different crystal structure from copper metal. Above 60°C., it decomposes into copper and hydrogen. Its activity is also shown by its inflammability in chlorine and its release of hydrogen when treated with acid. Although its composition closely approaches CuH ($CuH_{0.96}$ is the highest value obtained),[61] it does not resemble the saline hydrides in properties, and its heat of formation (−5.12 kcal. per mole)[60] suggests it to be metallic rather than salt-like in

[59] L. J. Gillespie and W. R. Downs: *J. Am. Chem. Soc.*, **61**, 2496 (1939).
[60] A. Sieverts and A. Gotta: *Ann.*, **453**, 289 (1927).
[61] G. F. Hüttig and F. Brodkorb: *Z. anorg. allgem. Chem.*, **153**, 235 (1926).

character. Copper hydride appears to be of the same type as the hydrides NiH_2, CoH_2, FeH_2, FeH_6, and CrH_3 obtained by Weichselfelder[62] as insoluble products when ethereal solutions of phenyl magnesium bromide were treated with anhydrous metal chlorides and hydrogen, although Weichselfelder's work has been questioned.[63]

Uranium hydride, UH_3, and uranium deuteride, UD_3, are also representative of this class of materials. These compounds have been studied extensively as part of the general program of the Manhattan Project.[64] They result from direct action of hydrogen or deuterium on uranium and appear to be definitely stoichiometric compounds. The densities of the hydride and deuteride are 10.95 grams per cc. and 11.20 grams per cc., respectively, as compared with a density of 18.7 grams per cc. for uranium metal. Heats of formation are of the order of −30.4 kcal. per mole. The compounds are reducing agents toward heavy metal salts and certain organic compounds. Early structural determinations by Rundle[65] indicated cubic arrangements with eight uranium atoms per unit cell and suggested the presence of uranium-hydrogen (deuterium)-uranium bridges with one electron pair for the two bonds (p. 214). Metal-metal bonding appeared to be unimportant. Thus uranium hydride and deuteride are neither saline nor interstitial. The concept of hydrogen bridges is questionable, however, in the light of more recent neutron diffraction studies on the deuteride.[66]

Grimm's hydride displacement law

In view of the marked similarities between the physical properties of the Group IVb hydrides and those of following inert gases (e.g., CH_4 and Ne, etc.), Grimm suggested[67] that the addition of a proton to an atomic kernel should lead to much the same result as the expulsion of an electron from that kernel and that elements lying up to four places before each inert gas should, by the addition of hydrogen atoms, form "pseudo-atoms" resembling the normal atoms of adjacent elements. Thus the reaction $O^{-2} + H^+ \rightarrow OH^-$ should be comparable to $O^{-2} \rightarrow F^- + e^-$, and similarities between OH^- and F^- should be noted.

[62] T. Weichselfelder: *Ann.*, **447,** 64 (1926).

[63] M. D. Barnes and T. R. P. Gibb: Abstracts of Papers, p. 38P, 119th meeting of American Chemical Society, Cleveland, April 1951.

[64] F. H. Spedding, A. S. Newton, J. C. Warf, et al.: *Nucleonics*, **4;** (No. 1), 4; (No. 2), 17; (No. 3), 43 (1949).

[65] R. E. Rundle: *J. Am. Chem. Soc.*, **69,** 1719 (1947).

[66] R. E. Rundle: *J. Am. Chem. Soc.*, **73,** 4172 (1951).

[67] H. G. Grimm: *Z. Elektrochem.*, **31,** 474 (1925).

TABLE 12·11

GRIMM'S HYDRIDE DISPLACEMENT LAW

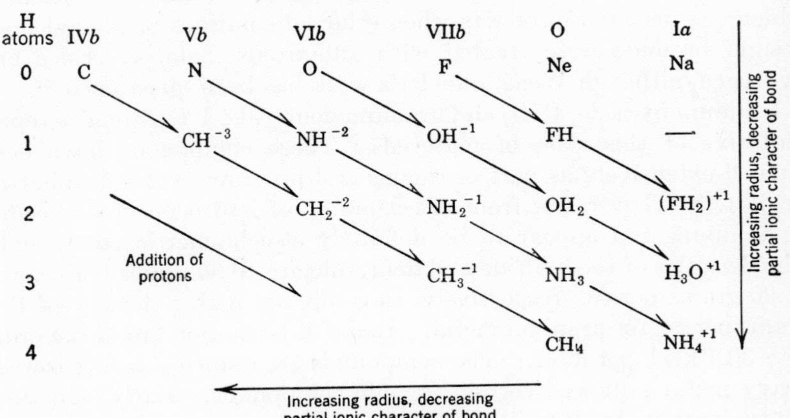

That such similarities do exist is indicated in Table 12·11, where materials placed in each vertical column do exhibit comparable properties. These properties are of course modified by the radii and partial ionic character trends indicated, but the classification is a useful one.

SUGGESTED SUPPLEMENTARY REFERENCES

N. V. Sidgwick: *The Chemical Elements and Their Compounds*, pp. 11–58. Clarendon Press, Oxford (1950).

A. Farkas: *Orthohydrogen, Parahydrogen, and Heavy Hydrogen*, Cambridge University Press, London (1935).

Gmelin's *Handbuch der anorganischen Chemie*, System-Nummer 2. Verlag Chemie G.m.b.h., Leipzig-Berlin (1927).

CHAPTER 13

Periodic Group VIIb
The Halogens

Having introduced the chemical elements by considering the inert gas elements and hydrogen, it is appropriate that we now direct our attention to the class of elements which has been called *representative* (p. 102). It will be recalled that this class embraces those elements in families one to seven places before and one to two places after the inert gas elements in the periodic arrangement. Since this class includes elements ranging in properties from strongly non-metallic to strongly metallic, no single discussion can cover the class adequately. Accordingly, each family is treated separately, beginning with the halogens. In discussing each family, emphasis is placed upon such trends, regularities, and differences in properties as are apparent from the considerations advanced in Part I of this book. In addition, such modern developments as have added to general understanding of the families are described, but no attempt is made to make the coverage of any family all-inclusive. Such supplementary material as is essential to such coverage can be obtained from the many available freshman textbooks and reference books.

The four halogens, fluorine, chlorine, bromine, and iodine, are comparatively familiar elements, their abundances in the igneous rocks of the crust of the earth being 0.06–0.09%, 0.031%, 0.00016%, and 0.00003%, respectively, with concentrated sources of each being readily available. The fifth halogen, now known as astatine,[1] apparently occurs in small quantities as short-lived isotopes of mass numbers 215, 216, and 218 resulting from beta decay branching of the three naturally occurring radioactive decay series at AcA, ThA, and RaA, respectively (pp. 64–65). Other isotopes are formed by alpha decay of francium isotopes.[2] However, most of the information now available on astatine has come from a study of the 211 isotope (α,

[1] D. R. Corson, K. R. Mackenzie, and E. Segrè: *Nature,* **159,** 24 (1947).

[2] G. T. Seaborg and I. Perlman: *Revs. Modern Phys.*, **20,** 585 (1948).

K-capture, $t_{1/2} = 7.5$ hours) first obtained by Corson, Mackenzie, and Segrè[3] as a result of alpha bombardment of bismuth. Although incompletely evaluated, the properties of astatine indicate halogen-like character but with a definite increase in metallic nature over iodine.

FAMILY RELATIONSHIPS AMONG THE HALOGENS

Numerical properties relating to the halogens are summarized in Table 13·1. Paralleling increases in atomic weight (or molecular weight, since the halogens exist as diatomic molecules) are increases in density, atomic volume, melting and boiling points, critical temperature and pressure, and heats of fusion and vaporization. These may be regarded as expected trends since there are no real differences in the types of materials compared or the bonds holding the individual molecules together in the bulk of the material. A general increase in size, both of the free atoms and ions derived from them, parallels the addition of more and more electrons.

Inasmuch as the outer electronic arrangements in the halogen atoms are all but one electron short of those characterizing atoms of the corresponding inert gas elements, it is not surprising that tendencies to approach the inert gas arrangements should be marked (p. 176). The large values of electron affinities and electro-negativities indicate the ease with which this is accomplished through negative halide ion formation. Correspondingly, the large heats of formation of the diatomic halogen molecules and their lack of marked dissociation even at elevated temperatures indicate further the ease with which inert gas arrangements are attained through electron pair sharing between like halogen atoms. Data appearing in subsequent sections of this chapter show the same to be true in other covalent linkages. Of course all such trends decrease as the size of the halogen atom increases because of resultant reduction in attraction for an electron. This is reflected in parallel decreases in electron affinity, electronegativity, and in standard potential for oxidation of halide ion to free halogen, $X^- \rightleftharpoons \frac{1}{2}X_2 + e^-$.

Data summarized in Table 13·1 give no definite information relative to positive oxidation states among the halogens, although the comparatively large values of the ionization potentials suggest that cationic species would be highly unlikely except possibly with iodine. On the other hand, the possibility of positive covalences resulting from the sharing of electrons with more electronegative elements cannot be

[3] R. D. Corson, K. R. Mackenzie, and E. Segrè: *Phys. Rev.*, **57**, 459, 1087 (1940); **58**, 672 (1940).

TABLE 13·1

NUMERICAL PROPERTIES OF HALOGENS

Property	Fluorine	Chlorine	Bromine	Iodine
Atomic number	9	17	35	53
Outer electron configuration	$2s^22p^5$	$3s^23p^5$	$4s^24p^5$	$5s^25p^5$
Molecular formula	F_2	Cl_2	Br_2	I_2
Atomic weight	19.00	35.457	79.916	126.92
Stable isotopes, mass numbers	19	35, 37	79, 81	127
Density of solid, gram/cc.	1.3	1.9	3.4	4.93
Atomic volume of solid, cc.	14.62	18.66	23.51	25.74
Melting point, °C.	−223	−102	−7.3	114
Boiling point, °C	−187	−34.6	58.78	183
Critical temperature, °C	−129	144	311	553
Critical pressure, atm.	55	76.1	102	......
Heat of fusion, kcal./mole	....	1.615	2.580	3.650
Heat of vaporization, kcal./mole	1.640	4.420	7.418	10.388
Dielectric constant of solid	....	2.0	3.2	4.0
Solubility in water, mole/liter at 20°C.	....	0.090(g)	0.210(l)	0.00133(s)
Dissociation of molecules				
Heat of dissociation, kcal./mole	37.7	56.9	45.2	35.4
Dissociation constant at 1000°C.	....	10^{-8}	8×10^{-3}	10^{-1}
Covalent radius, A	0.72	0.994	1.142	1.334
Ionization potential, ev	17.42	13.01	11.84	10.44
Electron affinity, ev	4.13	3.75	3.53	3.2
Electronegativity	4.0	3.0	2.8	2.5
Heat of hydration of X^-, kcal./gram ion	128	96.9	92.2	85.8
E^0_{298} for $X^- \rightleftharpoons \frac{1}{2}X_2 + e^-$, volts	−2.85	−1.358	−1.065	−0.535
Crystal radii, A				
X^{-1} in X^-	1.36	1.81	1.95	2.16
X^{+7} in XO_4^- (calc.)	0.07	0.26	0.39	0.50

overlooked. Actually, all the halogens except fluorine do form such linkages, and oxidation states of +1, +3, +5, and +7 are well recognized. Since there is no element more electronegative than fluorine, the existence of positive oxidation states involving that element appears unlikely (pp. 430, 437). The differences of two units among individual oxidation states of the halogens are understandable when one remembers that in a given halogen atom six of the seven valence electrons exist in pairs.

The shift in color of the vapor with increasing atomic number or weight is apparently due to a shift in wavelength of an absorption band. The absorption band, which removes only a small fraction of the blue light with fluorine (giving a yellow color), shifts gradually to longer wavelengths until with iodine only red and blue light are transmitted (giving a violet color). Iodine dissolves in solvents with low dielectric constants (e.g., chloroform, carbon tetrachloride) to give violet solutions but in solvents with higher dielectric constants (e.g., water, alcohol) to give brown solutions. Studies show that, although iodine is definitely diatomic in all solvents, it is in equilibrium with iodine bonded to the solvent by coordinate linkages in the brown solutions but essentially free in the violet solutions.[4] In the brown solutions, iodine is somewhat the more reactive.

CHEMICAL CHARACTERISTICS OF THE HALOGENS

The more important aspects of the chemical behaviors of the halogens are summarized in Table 13·2. It is apparent that many of

TABLE 13·2

CHEMICAL CHARACTERISTICS OF THE HALOGENS

General Equation*	Remarks
$nX_2 + 2M \rightarrow 2MX_n$	With practically all metals.
$3X_2 + 2P \rightarrow 2PX_3$	With excess P. Also with As, Sb, Bi.
$X_2 + PX_3 \rightarrow PX_5$	With excess X_2 but not with I_2. Also with As, Sb, using F_2, Cl_2.
$X_2 + H_2 \rightarrow 2HX$	With decreasing vigor in series F_2, Cl_2, Br_2, I_2.
$X_2 + H_2O \rightarrow 2M^+ + 2X^- + O_2$	Ditto.
$X_2 + H_2O \rightleftharpoons H^+ + X^- + HOX$	Not with F_2.
$X_2 + C_nH_{2n} \rightarrow C_nH_{2n}X_2$	With Cl_2, Br_2.
$X_2 + C_nH_y \rightarrow C_nH_{y-1}X + HX$	With Cl_2, Br_2 and many hydrocarbons.
$X_2 + 2C_nH_y \rightarrow 2nC + 2yHX$	With Cl_2 at elevated temperatures.
$X_2 + H_2S \rightarrow S + 2HX$	With Cl_2, Br_2, I_2.
$X_2 + CO \rightarrow COX_2$	With Cl_2, Br_2.
$X_2 + SO_2 \rightarrow SO_2X_2$	With F_2, Cl_2.
$3X_2 + 8NH_3 \rightarrow 6NH_4X + N_2$	With F_2, Cl_2, Br_2.
$X_2 + 2S \rightarrow S_2X_2$	With Cl_2, Br_2.
$2X_2 + S \rightarrow SX_4$	With Cl_2.
$X_2 + 2X'^- \rightarrow X_2' + 2X^-$	With halides.
$yX_2 + 2M_yO_z + 2zC \rightarrow 2MX_y + 2zCO$	With many metal oxides at elevated temperatures.
$X_2 + X_2' \rightarrow 2XX'$	With other halogens.
$X_2 + X'^- \rightarrow X'X_2^-$	With halides, especially I^-.

* $X_2 = F_2$, Cl_2, Br_2, or I_2.

the reactions of the halogens are related to their oxidizing abilities in terms of the ion-electron equation

$$X^- \rightleftharpoons \tfrac{1}{2}X_2 + e^-$$

[4] J. Kleinberg and A. W. Davidson: *Chem. Revs.*, **42**, 601 (1949).

standard potential values for which appear in Table 13·1. Thus the halogens oxidize a variety of metals, non-metals, and ionic species, including the halide ions. It is obvious that a free halogen will oxidize only those halide ions which are derived from less electronegative halogens.

Much of the chemistry of the halogens is centered in their behaviors in aqueous solutions. With water, two important reactions may occur, namely,

$$X_2 + H_2O \rightleftharpoons 2H^+ + 2X^- + \tfrac{1}{2}O_2 \qquad (1)$$
$$X_2 + H_2O \rightleftharpoons H^+ + X^- + HOX \qquad (2)$$

The relative reactivities of the halogens according to Equation 1 may be approximated from potentials calculated by combining the couples (p. 297)

$$X^- \rightleftharpoons \tfrac{1}{2}X_2 + e^-$$

and

$$2H_2O \rightleftharpoons O_2 + 4H^+ + 4e^- \qquad E^0_{298} = -0.815 \text{ volt}$$

This leads to the values 2.035 volts for fluorine, 0.545 volt for chlorine, 0.25 volt for bromine, and −0.28 volt for iodine. Thus fluorine reacts vigorously with water to evolve oxygen, but chlorine and bromine react with much less vigor. With iodine, the reverse reaction occurs. Reaction 2 is not noted with fluorine because of the vigor with which reaction 1 occurs. With the other halogens, equilibria result which are characterized at 25°C. by the equilibrium constants 4.8×10^{-4}, 5×10^{-9}, and 3×10^{-13} for chlorine, bromine, and iodine, respectively. Such equilibria involve hydrogen ion. As a consequence addition of acid favors oxidation of halide by hypohalite whereas addition of alkali favors hydrolysis of the halogen (p. 439).

The chemical behavior of fluorine often appears anomalous when compared with the corresponding behaviors of the other halogens because greater percentage differences in size, oxidizing power, and electronegativity exist between chlorine and fluorine than between even chlorine and iodine. Only within recent years have the pioneer researches of Moissan, Ruff, and others been extended sufficiently to permit a comparatively complete understanding of the chemical behavior of the element.[5–7] Much of our present knowledge stems from work done under the auspices of the Manhattan Project.[8]

[5] O. Ruff: *Angew. Chem.*, **46,** 739 (1933).

[6] H. J. Emeléus: *J. Chem. Soc.*, **1942,** 441.

[7] S. C. Ogburn: *J. Chem. Education*, **24,** 314 (1947).

[8] Much of this is summarized in a series of papers, *Ind. Eng. Chem.*, **39,** 236–433 (1947).

PREPARATION AND PRODUCTION OF ELEMENTAL HALOGENS

Sufficient differences exist between methods applicable to the preparation of the free halogens to warrant discussing the elements separately.

Fluorine

Although free fluorine was first isolated by Moissan in 1886 as a product of the electrolysis of anhydrous liquid hydrogen fluoride containing some potassium hydrogen fluoride (KHF_2),[9] modern developments may be traced to the introduction in 1919 of fused potassium acid fluoride as electrolyte.[10] Developments in the small-scale preparation of the element which followed[6, 11] led logically to large-scale operations and the production of fluorine in commercial quantities.[8, 12]

The electrolytic production of fluorine has been effected under three general sets of conditions,[12] namely:

1. Low temperatures (e.g., −33°C.), employing hydrogen fluoride containing less than 20% of potassium fluoride by weight.
2. Medium temperatures (ca. 100°C.), employing molten KF·2HF (m.p. 71.7°C.).
3. High temperatures (ca. 250°C.), employing molten KF·HF (m.p. 239°C.).

Because of the volatility of hydrogen fluoride, contamination of the product is difficult to avoid. This danger is reduced materially by the use of the fused potassium hydrogen fluorides over which the vapor pressure of hydrogen fluoride is comparatively low. As a consequence, only operations at medium and high temperatures have proved to be effective. Corrosion problems are reduced by use of such metals as nickel, copper, or Monel, all of which are soon covered with protective fluoride coatings, graphite, and unreactive plastics such as teflon. It is interesting that, although graphite is a suitable anode material at high temperatures, it disintegrates rapidly in the medium-temperature range. Compacted amorphous carbon can be used successfully in the latter range.

A number of successful commercial cells have been described.[8, 12] A typical one, employing an electrolyte approximately KF·2HF and

[9] H. Moissan: *Ann. chim. phys.* (6), **12**, 472 (1887).

[10] W. L. Argo, F. C. Mathers, B. Humiston, and C. O. Anderson: *Trans. Electrochem. Soc.*, **35**, 335 (1919).

[11] S. R. Carter and W. Wardlaw: *Ann. Reports*, **33**, 145 (1936).

[12] H. R. Leech: *Quart. Revs.*, **3**, 22 (1949).

containing a small amount of lithium fluoride, operates at 1500 amp. in the medium-temperature range. With steel cathodes separated by Monel screen diaphragms from copper-impregnated carbon anodes and periodic additions of hydrogen fluoride, such cells have been used continuously for over a year.[8, 13] Other similar installations have been employed by a number of commercial concerns. Wartime German developments[12, 14] centered in a 2000-amp. cell using approximately $KF \cdot 2.5HF$ at 75° to 85°C. and a 2000 to 2500-amp. cell operating at 245°C. Graphite anodes, silver cathodes, and diaphragm bells of magnesium alloy around the electrodes were found satisfactory in the high-temperature cells.

Electrolytic production of fluorine in the laboratory can be carried out successfully with modified cells of the commercial type or with small cells such as those described by a number of investigators.[15–18]

Preparation of fluorine by purely chemical means is not particularly successful because of the difficulty of oxidizing the fluoride ion. Numerous claims have been advanced for the liberation of fluorine as a result of thermal decomposition of high-valence metal fluorides, e.g., lead(IV), silver(II), manganese(III), but they lack unequivocal confirmation. It is true that compounds such as AgF_2, MnF_3, PbF_4, and CeF_4 are effective fluorinating agents, and they may release fluorine under appropriate conditions. However, they are usually prepared by reactions involving elemental fluorine so that their utilities as inexpensive sources would be limited.

Chlorine

On a laboratory scale, chlorine is normally prepared by the chemical oxidation of chloride ion, employing either hydrochloric acid or a metal chloride and sulfuric acid with a suitable oxidant such as manganese(IV) oxide, permanganate, etc. The bulk of the commercial chlorine, however, is produced by the electrolytic oxidation of chloride ion in aqueous sodium chloride solutions. The half-cell reactions involved are summarized by the equations

$$\text{anode:}\quad 2Cl^- \rightarrow Cl_2 + 2e^-$$
$$\text{cathode:}\quad 2H_2O + 2e^- \rightarrow 2OH^- + H_2$$

[13] Anon.: *Chem. Eng. News*, **24**, 2360 (1946).

[14] H. R. Neumark: *Trans. Electrochem. Soc.*, **91**, 367 (1947).

[15] L. M. Dennis, J. M. Veeder, and E. G. Rochow: *J. Am. Chem. Soc.*, **53**, 3263 (1931).

[16] W. C. Schumb and E. L. Gamble: *J. Am. Chem. Soc.*, **52**, 4302 (1930).

[17] P. Lebeau and A. Damiens: *Compt. rend.*, **181**, 917 (1925).

[18] G. H. Cady, D. A. Rogers, and C. A. Carlson: *Ind. Eng. Chem.*, **34**, 443(1942).

sodium hydroxide and hydrogen being obtained as by-products. Secondary oxidations and interaction of anode and cathode products are avoided by diaphragm separation of the electrodes in such equipment as the Nelson, Vorce, Hooker, etc., cells. Details of such cells may be found in any elementary chemistry textbook and need not be given here. Considerable improvement in cell operation and in the qualities of the products are obtained through use of mercury cathodes rather than steel. Because of the high overvoltage of hydrogen on mercury, hydrogen is not liberated at the cathode, but instead sodium ion is reduced to an amalgam as

$$\text{cathode:} \quad Na^+ + e^- + x\text{Hg} \rightarrow \text{Na(Hg)}x$$

The amalgam is then brought in contact with pure water, yielding hydrogen and sodium hydroxide, and the liberated mercury is recycled. In early Castner-Kellner cells, this was accomplished by rocking a compartmented cell, but in recent developments, particularly in wartime German cells,[19,20] flowing cathodes have been preferred.

The technical production of chlorine without caustic has received considerable attention, particularly in view of the early success of the direct oxidation of hydrogen chloride with gaseous oxygen at temperatures of 400° to 450°C. in the presence of a copper(II) chloride catalyst (Deacon process). Direct oxidation of solid sodium chloride with nitric acid accounts for the production of sizable quantities of chlorine. The gaseous mixture of nitric oxide, nitrosyl chloride, and chlorine is subjected to further vapor phase oxidation or to catalytic decomposition of the nitrosyl chloride, and the oxides of nitrogen are removed with sulfuric acid and recycled. Although oxidation of sodium chloride to chlorine with sulfur(VI) oxide has been studied extensively,[21] it has not proved practical. Chlorine is of course a by-product in the production of metals such as sodium, calcium, or magnesium by electrolytic reduction of their fused chlorides, some 8% of the chlorine produced technically in the United States in 1949, for example, having come from fused sodium chloride electrolysis.[20]

Bromine and iodine are normally prepared on a laboratory scale by methods comparable with those used for chlorine as well as by oxidation of the halide ion with chlorine. Oxidation of halide ions is used commercially for the production of both halogens. Bromine is recovered technically from sea water[22] by chlorination at pH 3.5 and

[19] R. M. Hunter: *Chem. Met. Eng.*, **52** (No. 10), 104 (1945).

[20] Anon.: *Chem. Eng. News*, **29**, 364 (1951).

[21] A. W. Hixon and A. H. Tenney: *Ind. Eng. Chem.*, **33**, 1472 (1941).

[22] L. C. Stewart: *Ind. Eng. Chem.*, **26**, 361 (1934).

removal with air. The bromine is then stripped from the air by absorption in sodium carbonate to give bromide plus bromate. Acidification then yields bromine which can be purified by distillation. Iodine is liberated from iodides in salt well brines by oxidation with nitrite and is removed by adsorption on charcoal.[23] Absorption in sodium hydroxide as hypoiodite and iodate is followed by liberation of the free halogen on addition of acid. Considerable iodine is also obtained from iodides concentrated in kelp and other sea plants as well as from iodates found in the sodium nitrate deposits in Chile. In the Chile deposits, reduction is effected with hydrogen sulfite ion according to the equation

$$2IO_3^- + 5HSO_3^- \rightarrow 3HSO_4^- + 2SO_4^{-2} + H_2O + I_2$$

COMPOUNDS OF THE HALOGENS

The halides

For purposes of discussion, the halides may be classified conveniently as

1. Ionic or salt-like halides.
2. Covalent or acid halides.
3. Complex halides.

Because of the wide differences in electronegativity among the halogens, it is obvious that such a classification is quite arbitrary. There is no real line of demarcation between the ionic and the covalent halides. One class often shades into the other when halides of a given element are considered. For this reason the discussion which follows is in no wise comprehensive or complete. For a detailed consideration of the halides, Ephraim's book[24] is recommended.

The Ionic or Salt-Like Halides. These halides exist in the solid state as ionic or semi-ionic crystals and are derived from the metals. As a class, they are characterized by comparatively high melting and boiling points, by solubility in associated or polar solvents, and by conductivity in such media or in the fused state. All variations in properties are found, however, as factors such as charge and size of the metal ion, electropositive character of the metal, and electronegative character of the halogen vary. Strictly speaking, true ionic character is probably limited to the halides of the alkali and alkaline earth elements and possibly the lanthanide and certain actinide elements. Halides

[23] G. R. Robertson: *Ind. Eng. Chem.*, **26,** 376 (1934).

[24] P. C. L. Thorne and E. R. Roberts: *Ephraim's Inorganic Chemistry*, 5th English Edition, Ch. 8, 9, 10, 12. Gurney and Jackson, London (1948).

of the other elements taken as a whole are doubtless more covalent than ionic in the anhydrous state, although they may dissolve in water to yield ionic solutions.

Increase in oxidation number and decrease in size on the part of the cation promote enhanced covalent character in the halide (p. 209). If one compares, for instance, the compounds KCl, $CaCl_2$, $ScCl_3$, and $TiCl_4$, he finds regular transition from a completely ionic structure to an essentially covalent structure. Correspondingly, covalent character increases with increasing size and decreasing electronegativity of the halogen. If one compares for instance, the compounds LiF, LiCl, LiBr, and LiI or CaF_2, $CaCl_2$, $CaBr_2$, and CaI_2, he finds corresponding decreases in melting point and changes in other properties which indicate ionic character. Fluorides of metallic elements are predominantly ionic; the other halides may or may not be. With a given metal which can exhibit more than a single oxidation state, ionic character in a given type of halide decreases markedly as oxidation number increases. For example, although uranium(IV) fluoride exhibits ionic behavior, uranium(VI) fluoride is volatile and covalent.

Salt-like halides vary widely in solubility. Although many fluorides are water soluble, those with extremely high lattice energies (p. 342), such as the lithium, alkaline earth, lanthanide, and actinide compounds, are insoluble. Chlorides, bromides, and iodides are commonly water soluble, with solubility increasing with the size of the halide ion. On the other hand, where covalent bonding is appreciable, the reverse is true. This is characteristic of the mercury(I), silver(I), lead(II), thallium(I), copper(I), etc., compounds.

The halide ions are capable of oxidation to free halogens as indicated by the potentials tabulated in Table 13·1. Increase in reducing character parallels increase in size as expected. Only the iodide is oxidized by atmospheric oxygen in acidic solution. Although the fluoride ion possesses some basic properties (p. 314), and is therefore somewhat hydrolyzed, the other halide ions are too weakly basic to accept protons from water.

The Covalent or Acid Halides. These halides exist in the pure condition as discrete molecules and are derived from either non-metals or metallic materials with large charge-size ratios. By convention, non-metal-halogen compounds containing oxygen, sulfur, or nitrogen as a third element, such as phosphorus(V) oxychloride ($POCl_3$), are included in this class. The covalent halides are characterized by volatility, by solubility in non-polar solvents, by solvolysis reactions in contact with polar solvents, and by lack of conductivity in the pure state. In a series of halides derived from some particular non-metal, melting point and boiling point commonly increase with molecular weight, a behavior which is usually characteristic of covalent materials (e.g., the hydrocarbons). It must be emphasized again that these properties describe only the limiting examples of such compounds.

Specific information on certain types of these halides is given in later sections of this chapter. Other compounds are discussed in subsequent chapters. The physical characteristics of those halides containing hydrogen are summarized in Table 13·3. The marked water

TABLE 13·3
PHYSICAL CHARACTERISTICS OF THE HYDROGEN HALIDES

Property	HF	HCl	HBr	HI
Melting point, °C.	−83.1	−114.8	−86.9	−50.7
Boiling point, °C.	19.54	−84.9	−66.8	−35.4
Critical temperature, °C.	230.2	51.3	91.0	150.5
Heat of fusion at m.p., kcal./mole	1.094	0.505	0.575	0.686
Heat of vaporization at b.p., kcal./mole	7.24	3.85	4.210	4.72
Density at b.p., grams/ml.	0.991	1.187	2.160	2.799
Surface tension at b.p., dyne/cm.	....	23.18	25.40	26.69
Heat of formation at 20°C., kcal./mole	64.4	21.9	7.3	1.32
Dissociation at 1000°C., %	....	0.014	0.5	33
Water solubility, grams/100 grams of solution at 20°C. and 1 atm.	35.3	42	49	57
Apparent dissociation in 0.1 N solution at 18°C., %	10	92.6	93	95
Dipole moment in gas, c.g.s. units $\times 10^{18}$	1.9	1.04	0.79	0.38
Partial ionic character, %	60	17	11	5
Internuclear distance, A	0.92	1.276	1.410	1.62
Dielectric constant of liquid	66	9	6	3
Magnetic susceptibility, $\chi_{mole} \times 10^6$ at 0°C.	−8.6	−22.1	−32.9	−47.7

solubilities of these covalent compounds are associated with their reactions with water in terms of the general equation

$$HX + H_2O \rightleftarrows H_3O^+ + X^-$$

The acidic properties of these materials have been considered in detail in a previous chapter (p. 318), and their reducing characteristics are related to the potentials already given. In addition to their formation by direct combination of the elements (p. 420), these halides can be prepared by treating a metal halide with a strong, non-volatile (and non-oxidizing, with bromide and iodide) acid, by hydrolyzing the halide of another non-metal (e.g., phosphorus), by reducing halides of noble metals (e.g., silver) with hydrogen, or by reducing a free halogen with a hydrogen compound (e.g., hydrocarbon, hydrogen sulfide).

Pure hydrogen fluoride differs in many ways from the other hydrogen halides because of its greater ionic character and its tendency to associate through hydrogen bonding (p. 189). In the solid state, hydrogen fluoride exists as infinite zig-zag chains of molecules

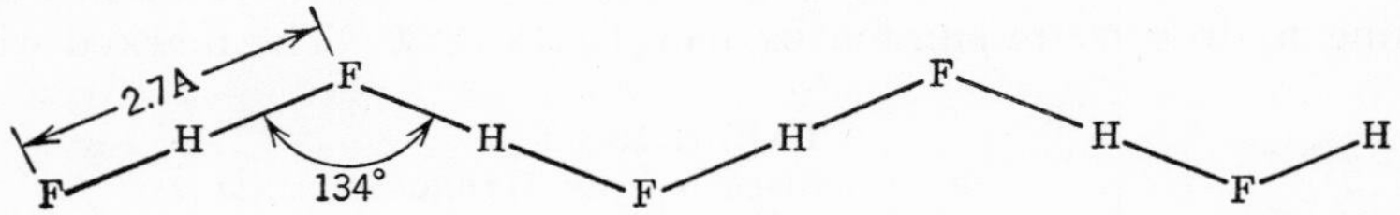

2.7 Å
F H F H F H F H F H
134°

Association also characterizes the liquid and continues into the vapor state. According to Simons and Hildebrand,[25] hexameric rings, $(HF)_6$, characterize the gaseous material inasmuch as in such rings structures of greatest stabilities are achieved. The electron diffraction data of Bauer, Beach, and Simons,[26] however, suggest chain configurations up to about $(HF)_5$, with an average F—H—F—H—F bond angle of about 140°. This appears to be a more acceptable structure. Formulation of the material as a dimer, $(HF)_2$, is not completely correct.

The tendency to hydrogen bond is sufficient so that metal fluorides are often solvated by hydrogen fluoride (p. 189), giving species of the types HF_2^-, $H_2F_3^-$, etc. Best characterized are the potassium compounds, KF·HF (m.p. 239°C.), KF·2HF (m.p. 71.7°C.), KF·3HF (m.p. 65.8°C.), and KF·4HF (m.p. 72°C.), which are so useful in the preparation of fluorine (pp. 422–423).

The fluorination of a variety of covalent halides has been studied extensively, particularly by H. S. Booth and his students.[27, 28] Treatment of many non-metal halides, e.g., $SiCl_4$, $PSBr_3$, BCl_3, with antimony(III) fluoride in the presence of antimony(V) chloride as catalyst (Swartz reaction) causes usually the successive replacement of chlorine or bromine by fluorine. Similar reactions may be effected with metal fluorides, such as the calcium compound, and hydrogen fluoride.[29]

The Complex Halides. Entry of a halide ion into the coordination sphere of a metal ion is not uncommon (p. 237). From one up to all of the available coordination positions may be occupied. Compounds of the latter type are of particular interest in connection with halides in general. Fluoride forms comparatively stable complexes with small

[25] J. H. Simons and J. H. Hildebrand: *J. Am. Chem. Soc.*, **46,** 2183 (1924).
[26] S. H. Bauer, J. Y. Beach, and J. H. Simons: *J. Am. Chem. Soc.*, **61,** 19 (1939).
[27] H. S. Booth and C. A. Seabright: *J. Am. Chem. Soc.*, **65,** 1834 (1943).
[28] H. S. Booth and S. G. Frary: *J. Am. Chem. Soc.*, **65,** 1836 (1943).
[29] M. M. Woyski: *J. Am. Chem. Soc.*, **72,** 919 (1950).

electropositive materials (e.g., B^{+3}, Al^{+3}, Si^{+4}) because of strong electrostatic attraction and high energies of the resulting bonds. On the other hand, the fluoride ion is not particularly polarizable and does not yield especially stable complexes with large cations. With large cations, the more polarizable chloride, bromide, and iodide yield complexes, the stabilities of which increase in this order (e.g., compare complexes of dipositive mercury). As is usual, halo complexes are most common with the transition metal ions. Because of size effects, fluoride is much the most likely to bring out the maximum coordination number in a metal ion.

Halo complexes are most commonly of the types $[MX_4]^{-4+n}$ and $[MX_6]^{-6+n}$, where n is the oxidation number of the metal M. Common examples are summarized in Table 13·4. Studies have shown

TABLE 13·4
COMMON HALO COMPLEX IONS

Type	Stereochemistry	n	Examples of Metals
$[MX_4]^{-4+n}$	tetrahedral or planar	+2	Be, Co, Cu, Cd, Zn, Hg, Pd, Pt
		+3	Au, Bi, In, Ga, Tl, V
$[MX_6]^{-6+n}$	octahedral	+3	Al, Ga, In, Tl, Mo, As, Rh, Sc, Ir
		+4	Ge, Hf, Zr, Ir, Os, Pd, Pt, Pb, Re, Sn, Ti
		+5	Nb, Ta, Sb, As, P

that many comparatively stable halo complexes exist in solution. It is not uncommon for metal ions to associate with successively increasing numbers of halide ions until their normal coordination numbers are completely satisfied by halide ions. Thus in the Cu^{+2}-Cl^- system, although $[CuCl_4]^{-2}$ is probably the most characteristic species, $[CuCl]^+$, $[CuCl_2]$, and $[CuCl_3]^-$ are undoubtedly present also.

Binary compounds with oxygen

Although the halogens do not combine directly with oxygen, binary compounds with oxygen can be prepared indirectly. Known compounds of this type are summarized in Table 13·5. The derivatives of chlorine, bromine, and iodine are properly called oxides, since oxygen

TABLE 13·5
BINARY HALOGEN–OXYGEN COMPOUNDS

Fluorine	Chlorine	Bromine	Iodine
OF_2	Cl_2O	Br_2O	I_2O_4
O_2F_2	ClO_2	Br_3O_8	I_4O_9
	Cl_2O_6	BrO_2	I_2O_5
	Cl_2O_7	Br_2O_7(?)	
	ClO_4(?)		

is more electronegative than any of these halogens. The fluorine compounds, however, are better called fluorides rather than oxides since fluorine is the more electronegative element. As might be expected, the fluorine-oxygen compounds are somewhat different from the others in their properties.

Fluorides of Oxygen. Oxygen difluoride, OF_2, is a colorless gas which condenses to a colorless liquid, boiling at −144.8°C. and freezing at −223.8°C. The liquid has a density of 1.90 grams per ml. at the melting point and 1.54 grams per ml. at the boiling point.[30] The O—F bond distance in the gas is 1.4 ± 0.1 A, and the F—O—F bond angle is 105 ± 5°.[31] The O—F single bond distance calculated from covalent radii is 1.46 A. It is apparent that the linkage is essentially covalent.

Chemically, oxygen difluoride is comparatively stable. Unlike its formula analog Cl_2O, it is not explosive. However, it is a potent oxidizing agent and reacts vigorously with metals, sulfur, phosphorus, the halogens, and hydrogen to form mixtures of fluorides and oxides.[30] Although it dissolves appreciably in water, the resulting solutions possess no acidic properties. This fact plus the observation that oxygen difluoride is converted by basic hydroxides to fluoride and oxygen indicates that the compound is not an acid anhydride. Aqueous solutions of the gas are strong oxidizing agents as indicated by the couple

$$H_2O + 2F^- \rightleftharpoons F_2O + 2H^+ + 2e^- \qquad E^0_{298} = -2.1 \text{ volts}$$

Oxygen difluoride was first detected in fluorine released by the electrolysis of moist potassium hydrogen fluoride,[32] but it is more conveniently prepared by the reaction of fluorine with sodium hydroxide solution[33] according to the equation

$$2F_2 + 2NaOH \rightarrow 2NaF + F_2O + H_2O$$

To avoid destruction of the product by the alkali, minimum contact between the two is necessary. Details of the procedure leading to a 70% yield are found in the original paper.[33] The compound is produced in other reactions involving elementary fluorine, for example, in its reaction with periodic acid.[34]

[30] O. Ruff and W. Menzel: *Z. anorg. allgem. Chem.*, **198**, 39 (1931).
[31] L. E. Sutton and L. O. Brockway: *J. Am. Chem. Soc.*, **57**, 473 (1935).
[32] P. LeBeau and A. Damiens: *Compt. rend.*, **185**, 652 (1927).
[33] P. LeBeau and A. Damiens: *Compt. rend.*, **188**, 1253 (1929).
[34] G. H. Rohrback and G. H. Cady: *J. Am. Chem. Soc.*, **70**, 2603 (1948).

Oxygen monofluoride, O_2F_2, is a red liquid which undergoes sufficient thermal decomposition at above −95°C. to prevent an accurate evaluation of its boiling point. It freezes at −160°C. to an orange solid.[35] The pale-brown vapor has a density corresponding to the composition O_2F_2 below −100°C. but undergoes thermal decomposition to a mixture of oxygen and fluorine at higher temperatures.[36] The density of the liquid at −156°C. is 1.734 grams per ml.[35] The chemical properties of the compound have not been evaluated. Oxygen monofluoride is prepared[35] by the action of a glow discharge on a mixture of oxygen and fluorine at liquid air temperatures and pressures of 15 to 20 mm.

Oxides of Chlorine. Of the four known oxides of chlorine, the compounds Cl_2O, ClO_2, and Cl_2O_7 have been known and studied extensively for some time. The hexoxide, Cl_2O_6, has been characterized more recently. Some data on the more characteristic physical properties of these compounds are summarized in Table 13·6.[37]

TABLE 13·6

PHYSICAL CONSTANTS OF CHLORINE OXIDES

Property	Cl_2O	ClO_2	Cl_2O_6	Cl_2O_7
Molecular weight	86.914	67.457	166.914	182.914
Melting point, °C.	−116	−59	3.5	−91.5
Boiling point, °C.	2	11.0	203 (calc.)	80
Heat of vaporization, kcal./mole	6.20	6.52	9.50	8.29
Vapor pressure, mm. at 0°C.	699	490	0.31	23.7
Density, grams/ml.	....	1.64 (0°C.)	2.02 (3.5°C.)	1.86 (0°C.)
Color (gas)	yellowish-red	yellow	red	....

Liquid chlorine monoxide, Cl_2O, explodes readily on contact with reducing agents but can be distilled without decomposition in their absence. The gas explodes on heating to a mixture of chlorine and oxygen. The gas is soluble in water to the extent of some 200 volumes to 1 of water at 0°C., forming an orange-yellow solution containing hypochlorous acid. This reaction is reversible. Electron diffraction data[31, 38] show the gas molecule to be angular, Cl—O—Cl bond angle 111°, with Cl—O and Cl—Cl bond distances of 1.71 A and 2.82 A, respectively.

[35] O. Ruff and W. Menzel: *Z. anorg. allgem. Chem.*, **211**, 204 (1933); **217**, 85 (1937).

[36] P. Frisch and H.-J. Schumacher: *Z. anorg. allgem. Chem.*, **229**, 423 (1936); *Z. physik. Chem.*, **B34**, 322 (1936).

[37] C. F. Goodeve and F. D. Richardson: *J. Chem. Soc.*, **1937**, 294.

[38] J. D. Dunitz and K. Hedberg: *J. Am. Chem. Soc.*, **72**, 3108 (1950).

The compound is best obtained by passing chlorine over freshly precipitated mercury(II) oxide, which has been dried previously at 300° to 400°C., according to the equation

$$2Cl_2 + 2HgO \rightarrow HgCl_2{\cdot}HgO + Cl_2O$$

The gaseous product is easily condensed to a liquid (Table 13·6).

Chlorine dioxide, ClO_2, although long more or less of a laboratory curiosity, has been developed recently into a commercial chemical because of its superior bleaching properties toward cellulosic materials, its excellent germicidal action in water purification, and its relation to the production of chlorites.[39–41] Electron diffraction data[38] show the gas molecule to be angular, O—Cl—O bond angle 116.5°, with a Cl—O bond distance of 1.49 A. This compound is an example of the class of materials known as odd molecules (p. 212). Like most such materials, it is extremely reactive. Pure gaseous chlorine dioxide explodes violently, as do mixtures of appreciable quantities of chlorine dioxide with reducing agents. The gas can be handled safely if diluted with carbon dioxide or air. Air–chlorine dioxide mixtures explode if the partial pressure of the chlorine dioxide exceeds 70 mm. of mercury, but partial pressures of 2 to 30 mm. appear safe.[40] Chlorine dioxide is a powerful oxidizing agent as indicated by the couple

$$Cl^- + 2H_2O \rightleftharpoons ClO_2 + 4H^+ + 5e^- \qquad E^0_{298} = -1.50 \text{ volts}$$

Mole for mole it will oxidize 2½ times as much material as elemental chlorine. It reacts with water or basic hydroxides to give mixtures of chlorites and chlorates, and with many metals[42] and metal peroxides[39, 40] to yield corresponding chlorites. Classically, the compound is prepared by reacting a chlorate with sulfuric acid at low temperatures, and distilling. Although this procedure is dangerous, it can be carried out successfully under rigidly controlled conditions.[42] Better results are obtained when oxalic acid is used, the carbon dioxide liberated in terms of the equation

$$2KClO_3 + 2H_2C_2O_4 \rightarrow 2ClO_2 + 2CO_2 + K_2C_2O_4 + 2H_2O$$

acting as a diluent. Technical methods[40] involve electrolysis, as

$$2NaCl + 2NaClO_2 + 2H_2O \xrightarrow{\text{elect.}} 2ClO_2 + 2NaCl + 2NaOH + H_2$$

[39] J. F. White, M. C. Taylor, and G. P. Vincent: *Ind. Eng. Chem.*, **34,** 782 (1942).

[40] E. R. Woodward: *Chem. Eng. News*, **22,** 1092 (1944).

[41] G. P. Vincent, E. G. Fenrich, J. F. Synan, and E. R. Woodward: *J. Chem. Education*, **22,** 283 (1945).

[42] M. Bigorgne: *Compt. rend.*, **225,** 527 (1947).

or preferably interaction of chlorite and chlorine diluted with air, as

$$2NaClO_2 + Cl_2 \xrightarrow{(H_2O)} 2NaCl + 2ClO_2$$

The latter process may be controlled by controlling the rate of flow of chlorine. The compound is best generated as it is used to avoid hazards. The reaction of silver chlorate with chlorine

$$2AgClO_3 + Cl_2 \xrightarrow{90^\circ} 2AgCl + 2ClO_2 + O_2$$

has been suggested as a safe method for laboratory preparations.[43]

The hexoxide, Cl_2O_6, has been studied recently in considerable detail.[37, 44, 45] The physical constants given in Table 13·6 suggest a greater degree of packing than in other chlorine oxides[37] and may be in accord with the non-planar arrangement

```
          ..      ..
         : O :   : O :
      ..   ..      ..  ..
     : O : Cl  :  Cl : O :
      ..   ..      ..  ..
         : O :   : O :
          ..      ..
```

The compound has a molecular weight in carbon tetrachloride corresponding to the composition Cl_2O_6.[37] Such a material is diamagnetic. However, in the liquid state and in aqueous solution, the compound exhibits paramagnetism. This may be interpreted as resulting from some decomposition to the odd molecule ClO_3 according to the equilibrium expression[46]

$$Cl_2O_6 + \text{heat} \rightleftharpoons 2ClO_3$$

The equilibrium constant over the range $-40°$ to 10°C. has a magnitude of the order of $3^+ \times 10^3$. Thermal decomposition into chlorine dioxide and oxygen, even at the melting point, is appreciable. The compound is sufficiently strongly oxidizing to react explosively with reducing agents such as ordinary stopcock grease. With alkali it yields a mixture of chlorate and perchlorate. Chlorine hexoxide is

[43] F. E. King and J. R. Partington: *J. Chem. Soc.*, **1926,** 925.

[44] M. Bodenstein, P. Harteck, and E. Padelt: *Z. anorg. allgem. Chem.*, **147,** 233 (1925).

[45] H.-J. Schumacher and G. Stieger: *Z. anorg. allgem. Chem.*, **184,** 272 (1929).

[46] J. Farquharson, C. F. Goodeve, and F. D. Richardson: *Trans. Faraday Soc.*, **32,** 790 (1936).

best prepared by the action of ozone on chlorine dioxide[37, 45] at 0° to 6°C., followed by fractionation, although irradiation of chlorine dioxide with ultraviolet also yields the material.[44, 47]

Chlorine heptoxide, Cl_2O_7, is more stable than either the monoxide or the dioxide, but detonates when heated or subjected to shock. As an oxidizing agent, it is also inferior to the lower oxides. With water, it forms perchloric acid. It may be obtained as a colorless, oily liquid by dehydrating perchloric acid with phosphorus(V) oxide at −10°C. and then distilling at 85°C.[48] Proper precautions are necessary to avoid explosions.

The existence of chlorine tetroxide, ClO_4, has been questioned.[49] The formation of this material in ether solution as a result of the reaction indicated by the equation

$$2AgClO_4 + I_2 \rightarrow 2AgI + 2ClO_4$$

has been postulated by Gomberg[50] because such solutions yield metal perchlorates when treated with metals and perchloric acid when treated with water. However, some perchloric acid always results in the silver perchlorate–iodine reaction. If the compound does exist, it is probably more a free radical than an oxide. Gomberg believed it to be a dimer, $(ClO_4)_2$.

Oxides of Bromine. All the oxides of bromine have been prepared and studied only comparatively recently. Bromine monoxide, Br_2O, is dark brown in both the solid and the liquid states. The solid melts at −17.5 ± 0.5°C., but neither the vapor pressure of the liquid nor its boiling point has been determined because of decomposition. Decomposition to bromine and oxygen occurs at any temperature above −40°C. Bromine monoxide dissolved in carbon tetrachloride is converted to hypobromite when shaken with alkali at 0°C.,[51] but, when the pure oxide is used, bromate results as well as hypobromite. Presumably, the oxide reacts with water to yield hyprobromous acid, but the latter decomposes very rapidly to give bromate. Bromine monoxide possesses oxidizing character, converting iodide to iodine, for example. The compound is prepared by passing bromine vapor over mercury(II) oxide obtained by precipitating a mercury(II)

[47] H. Booth and E. J. Bowen: *J. Chem. Soc.*, **127**, 510 (1925).

[48] C. F. Goodeve and J. Powney: *J. Chem. Soc.*, **1932**, 2078.

[49] C. F. Goodeve: *Trans. Faraday Soc.*, **30**, 30 (1934).

[50] M. Gomberg: *J. Am. Chem. Soc.*, **45**, 398 (1923).

[51] R. Schwarz and H. Wiele: *Naturwissenschaften*, **26**, 742 (1938); *J. prakt. Chem.*, **152**, 157 (1939).

chloride solution at 50°C. with sodium hydroxide and drying the product at 150°C.,[52] the optimum reaction temperature being 50° to 60°C.

An alternative procedure involves reaction of mercury(II) oxide with bromine dissolved in carbon tetrachloride.[53] Reaction first at 40° to 45°C., and then at 0° to −18°C. yielded 32 to 42% conversions. Bromine monoxide also results from the thermal decomposition of the dioxide in vacuum,[51, 54] and this procedure can be used to obtain the compound in the pure state.

The oxide Br_3O_8 exists in two solid modifications with a transition at −35 ± 3°C. It is stable at −80°C., but at higher temperatures it can be preserved only in the presence of ozone. With water, it gives a colorless solution possessing both acidic and oxidizing properties. Lewis and Schumacher[55] consider the primary product to be the substance $H_4Br_3O_{10}$, which undergoes immediate decomposition to hydrobromic acid, bromic acid, water, and oxygen. This oxide is obtained[55] by reaction of ozone with bromine vapor at −5° to 10°C., the product depositing as a white solid on the walls of the reaction chamber. The structure of this oxide should be of considerable interest.

Bromine dioxide, BrO_2, is formed as a yellow solid which is stable below −40°C. but decomposes at higher temperatures and under atmospheric pressure to bromine and oxygen. In a vacuum, it is decomposed to the monoxide and a white product which may be the heptoxide, Br_2O_7. It is less explosive than its chlorine analog. It is soluble in carbon tetrachloride and in water but reacts with water. With alkali, it gives bromate and bromide. It oxidizes iodide to iodine. Bromine dioxide is obtained by passing a mixture of oxygen and bromine at low pressures through a discharge tube, the lower portion of which is cooled by liquid air,[54] and distilling at −30°C. to remove unreacted bromine.

Oxides of Iodine. Although a number of binary oxygen-iodine compounds have been prepared, the only true oxide appears to be the pentoxide, I_2O_5. The other compounds, I_2O_4 and I_4O_9, appear to be salt-like in character and are more properly considered as iodine iodates. This is in keeping with other information which has accumulated on the basic nature of iodine (p. 460).[56]

[52] E. Zintl and G. Rienäcker: *Ber.*, **63B**, 1098 (1930).

[53] W. Brenschede and H.-J. Schumacher: *Z. physik. Chem.*, **B29**, 356 (1935); *Z. anorg. allgem. Chem.*, **226**, 370 (1936).

[54] R. Schwarz and M. Schmeisser: *Ber.*, **70B**, 1163 (1937).

[55] B. Lewis and H.-J. Schumacher: *Z. anorg. allgem. Chem.*, **182**, 182 (1929).

[56] I. Masson and C. Argument: *J. Chem. Soc.*, **1938**, 1702.

Iodine pentoxide, I_2O_5, is a white powder (sp. gr. 4.98) which may be fused without undergoing decomposition. At temperatures above 300°C., it decomposes to iodine and oxygen. It behaves as an oxidizing agent toward materials such as carbon monoxide, hydrogen sulfide, and hydrogen chloride and is reduced by them to iodine. With water, it yields iodic acid solutions. The oxide can be prepared by pyrolysis of either the compound I_2O_4 or the compound I_4O_9, by oxidation of iodine with concentrated nitric acid, or by dehydration of iodic acid at 200° to 240°C.

The compound I_2O_4 is normally regarded as an iodyl iodate, $(IO)IO_3$, rather than as a derivative of tetrapositive iodine, although no evaluations of its molecular complexity (I_2O_4 versus IO_2) or structure have appeared. It is a yellow, crystalline solid (sp. gr. 4.2) which is only slightly soluble in cold water and is insoluble in dry ether or glacial acetic acid. With hot water, it yields iodic acid and iodine, and with absolute ethanol largely iodine pentoxide.[57] With alkali, it yields iodate and iodide, whereas with hydrochloric acid it gives chlorine and iodine monochloride. Thermal decomposition to the pentoxide and iodine occurs above 85°C. and becomes rapid at 135°C.[58] The compound is formed[57–59] by warming iodic acid with concentrated sulfuric acid and is recovered by crystallizing over a period of some days, filtering, and drying, preferably[58] below 100°C.

The compound I_4O_9 is commonly regarded as a normal iodous or iodine(III) iodate, $I(IO_3)_3$. It is a light yellow, hygroscopic powder which decomposes at 75°C. or above to the pentoxide, iodine, and oxygen. With water, it yields iodine and iodic acid ultimately, the primary reaction to give the substance $I(OH)_3$ and iodic acid being followed by conversion of the former to iodic and hydriodic acids and their subsequent interaction.[58] The compound is prepared by reaction of ozone with iodine either in the vapor state or in solution in chloroform, carbon tetrachloride, or nitrobenzene.[58, 60] Alternatively, iodic acid can be treated with concentrated (sp. gr. 1.70) phosphoric acid to give the compound plus oxygen and iodine.[61]

The compounds I_2O_3 and I_2O do not exist in the free state. However, in the preparation of I_2O_4 a yellow iodyl sulfate, $(IO)_2SO_4$, which may be regarded as an acid-stabilized I_2O_3,[56] results. The same product is obtained by reacting iodine with iodine pentoxide in cold,

[57] M. M. P. Muir: *J. Chem. Soc.*, **95,** 656 (1909).
[58] R. K. Bahl and J. R. Partington: *J. Chem. Soc.*, **1935,** 1258.
[59] H. Kappeler: *Ber.*, **44,** 3496 (1911).
[60] F. Fichter and F. Rohner: *Ber.*, **42,** 4093 (1909).
[61] F. Fichter and H. Kappeler: *Z. anorg. Chem.*, **91,** 134 (1915).

92 to 98% sulfuric acid[62] or by heating iodic acid with sulfuric acid until iodine is evolved. In the presence of excess sulfur(VI) oxide, the yellow iodyl sulfate reverts to a normal solvated iodine(III) sulfate, $I_2(SO_4)_3 \cdot H_2SO_4$. Some evidence for an iodine(I) cation has been obtained by dissolving iodine and iodyl sulfate in concentrated sulfuric acid.[63] Further studies on these compounds should be profitable.

The oxy acids of the halogens and their salts

As indicated in the preceding section, certain of the halogen oxides may be regarded as anhydrides of oxygen-containing halogen acids. In such acids (or their salts) the halogen serves as a central atom to which one or more oxygen atoms are covalently bonded. Because of electronegativity differences, these bonds are more or less polar in character, with the halogen being electropositive. On this basis, such a series of fluorine compounds would be unexpected, a conclusion in keeping with the lack of acidic properties among the oxygen fluorides (p. 430). Reports do suggest, however, that salts derived from oxy-fluorine acids can be prepared. For example, fluorination of 50% potassium hydroxide solution at −50°C. yields a solution with oxidizing properties from which a solid can be obtained which shows oxidizing properties even after repeated fusions.[64] It is possible that either hypofluorite or fluorate is present. In like manner, electrolysis of a mixture of fused potassium hydroxide and fluoride yields a product which is precipitated by silver nitrate from nitric acid solution, presumably as a silver fluorate. The preparation of trifluoromethyl hypofluorite, CF_3OF, by fluorination of methanol and carbon monoxide in the presence of silver(II) fluoride has been described.[65] Further work appears indicated, but it is probable that such compounds cannot be considered as analogs of those of the other halogens.[66]

Sufficient differences exist among the oxy compounds of chlorine, bromine, and iodine to preclude generalizations embracing them all. With the oxy-chlorine compounds, however, the trends in properties summarized in Table 13·7 are well established. As a first hypothesis, these trends may be used in approaching the analogous bromine and iodine compounds.

Standard potential data essential to an understanding of variations

[62] P. Chrétien: *Compt. rend.*, **123,** 814 (1896); *Ann. chim. phys.* [7], **15,** 358 (1898)

[63] I. Masson: *J. Chem. Soc.*, **1938,** 1708.

[64] L. M. Dennis and E. G. Rochow: *J. Am. Chem. Soc.*, **55,** 2431 (1933).

[65] K. B. Kellogg and G. H. Cady: *J. Am. Chem. Soc.*, **70,** 3986 (1948).

[66] G. H. Cady: Abstracts of papers, 117th Meeting of American Chemical Society, Detroit, April 1950, p. 50–0.

TABLE 13·7

General Variations in Properties of Oxy Acids of Chlorine and Their Salts

	Acid		Salt	
Thermal stability increases. Oxidizing power decreases. Acid strength increases. ↓	HOCl		MOCl	Thermal stability increases. Oxidizing power decreases. Base strength of anion decreases. ↓
	HOClO		MOClO	
	$HOClO_2$		$MOClO_2$	
	$HOClO_3$	Thermal stability increases. → Oxidzing power decreases.	$MOClO_3$	

in oxidizing powers among these materials are summarized in Table 13·8. If reduction to the free halogen is considered, oxidizing power decreases with increase in oxidation number of the halogen for chlorine, bromine, or iodine. If reduction to the halide ion is considered, the same is generally true in alkaline solution. However, in acid solution

TABLE 13·8

Standard Potentials Characterizing Oxy Anions of the Halogens

Reaction	E^0_{298}, volts		
	X = Cl	Br	I
1. Reduction to X_2 in acid solution			
$\frac{1}{2}X_2 + H_2O \rightleftharpoons H^+ + HOX + e^-$	−1.63	−1.59	−1.45
$\frac{1}{2}X_2 + 2H_2O \rightleftharpoons 3H^+ + HOXO + 3e^-$	−1.63	......	....
$\frac{1}{2}X_2 + 3H_2O \rightleftharpoons 6H^+ + XO_3^- + 5e^-$	−1.47	−1.52	−1.195
$\frac{1}{2}X_2 + 4H_2O \rightleftharpoons 8H^+ + XO_4^- + 7e^-$	−1.34	......	−1.38(H_5IO_6)
2. Reduction to X^- in acid solution			
$X^- + H_2O \rightleftharpoons H^+ + HOX + 2e^-$	−1.49	−1.33	−0.99
$X^- + 2H_2O \rightleftharpoons 3H^+ + HOXO + 4e^-$	−1.56	......	....
$X^- + 3H_2O \rightleftharpoons 6H^+ + XO_3^- + 6e^-$	−1.45	−1.67	−1.09
$X^- + 4H_2O \rightleftharpoons 8H^+ + XO_4^- + 8e^-$	−1.34	......	−1.27(H_5IO_6)
3. Reduction to X^- in alkaline solution			
$X^- + 2OH^- \rightleftharpoons XO^- + H_2O + 2e^-$	−0.94	−0.76	−0.49
$X^- + 4OH^- \rightleftharpoons XO_2^- + 2H_2O + 4e^-$	−0.76	......	....
$X^- + 6OH^- \rightleftharpoons XO_3^- + 3H_2O + 6e^-$	−0.62	−0.61	−0.26
$X^- + 8OH^- \rightleftharpoons XO_4^- + 4H_2O + 8e^-$	−0.51	......	−0.38(IO_6^{-5})

the reverse is true with both bromine and iodine, and chlorous acid and hypochlorous acid occupy reversed positions among the chlorine materials. Inasmuch as reduction to halide is especially common, these trends are important. It must be pointed out also that periodate is always more strongly oxidizing than iodate whereas with chlorine the reverse is always true. Comparison of these potential values with those for reduction of free halogens to halide ions shows that the oxy acids are in general better oxidizing agents under comparable conditions. From a preparative point of view, these data are useful in indicating that chlorate in acid solution will oxidize iodine to iodate but not bromine to bromate and that bromate will convert chlorine to chlorate or iodine to iodate.

Hypohalous Acids and Hypohalites. Because of their thermal instabilities, the hypohalous acids are encountered in aqueous solution but not in the free condition, although a crystalline hydrate, $HOCl \cdot 2H_2O$, has been isolated[67] as the solid phase in equilibrium with concentrated hypochlorous acid solutions. In water, the acids are all weak, with acid strength decreasing with increasing size of the central halogen. At 25°C. pk_A' (p. 315) for hypochlorous acid is of the order of 8.[68] Hypohalites containing weakly acidic cations such as alkali metal ions are thus strongly hydrolyzed. Hypoiodous acid is somewhat amphoteric, as evidenced by its conversion to iodine monochloride by hydrochloric acid. Water solutions containing hypohalous acids are prepared by hydrolysis of the free halogens as

$$X_2 + H_2O \rightleftharpoons H^+ + X^- + HOX$$

the extent of the conversion decreasing in the series chlorine-bromine-iodine. A better general method of preparation involves shaking an aqueous suspension of mercury(II) oxide with the free halogen as

$$2X_2 + 2HgO + H_2O \rightarrow HgO \cdot HgX_2 + 2HOX$$

since direct reaction with water is reversible and yields halide as well. Aqueous hypochlorous acid may be concentrated by distillation although heat in general either causes liberation of the free halogen or conversion to halate and halide.

The free halogens react with cold dilute alkalies to give hypohalites as

$$X_2 + 2OH^- \rightarrow OX^- + X^- + H_2O$$

which on heating revert to halates and halides as

$$3OX^- \rightarrow XO_3^- + 2X^-$$

Of the hypohalites, the hypochlorites are the most common, being used technically as bleaching agents. Commercial aqueous hypochlorite is made by electrolysis of chloride solutions under conditions where anode and cathode products can mix. Calcium hypochlorite,

[67] C. H. Secoy and G. H. Cady: *J. Am. Chem. Soc.*, **63**, 1036 (1940).

[68] F. G. Soper: *J. Chem. Soc.*, **125**, 2227 (1924).

obtained by the interaction of chlorine with calcium hydroxide, and a mixed hypochlorite chloride, Ca(OCl)Cl, called bleaching powder, are common commercial bleaching agents.

Halous Acids and Halites. Neither chlorous, bromous, nor iodous acid can be isolated in the free form, nor is there any really clear evidence that the last two compounds exist even in aqueous solutions. Chlorites are well-characterized materials, but evidence for the existence of bromites and iodites is largely indirect. It may be that they result as unstable intermediates in the thermal decomposition of hypobromites and hypoiodites as

$$2XO^- \rightarrow XO_2^- + X^-$$

Chlorous acid has no true anhydride. However, as mentioned above (p. 432), it may be regarded as being derived from the mixed anhydride chlorine dioxide. Chlorine dioxide does not react directly with water to give chlorous acid, although it does yield chlorites (mixed with chlorates) with alkalies as

$$2ClO_2 + 2OH^- \rightarrow ClO_2^- + ClO_3^- + H_2O$$

However, an aqueous solution of chlorous acid can be prepared by reacting a suspension of barium chlorite with sulfuric acid and filtering. As previously indicated, such a solution is strongly oxidizing in character. The acid is only moderately weak with a pk_A' of the order of 2.

The chemistry of the chlorites has been reviewed extensively by White, Taylor, and Vincent[39] and by Vincent, Fenrich, Synan, and Woodward.[41] Interest in chlorites has stemmed from their explosive and bleaching characteristics. Although the heavy metal chlorites have been studied as detonators, they are probably too unpredictable to be useful. As bleaching agents toward cellulosic materials, however, the alkali metal chlorites are unsurpassed.[69] Chlorites appear to be comparatively stable in alkaline medium but undergo decomposition in acid solution, probably in terms of the equation

$$4HClO_2 \rightarrow 2ClO_2 + ClO_3^- + Cl^- + 2H^+ + H_2O.$$

When heated, they are converted to chlorates and chlorides. As previously mentioned, they react with chlorine to give chloride and chlorine dioxide. Methods of preparation involve reaction of alkalies with chlorine dioxide or, better, reaction of chlorine dioxide with peroxides as

$$Na_2O_2 + 2ClO_2 \rightarrow 2NaClO_2 + O_2$$

$$BaO_2 + 2ClO_2 \rightarrow Ba(ClO_2)_2 + O_2$$

[69] G. P. Vincent: *Chem. Eng. News*, **21**, 1176 (1943).

Direct reaction of chlorine dioxide with metals has been mentioned (p. 432).

Halic Acids and Halates. Chloric and bromic acids, although obtainable in solution, cannot be isolated as such because of decomposition. Iodic acid, however, is a stable white solid, which is readily obtained by oxidizing iodine with chloric acid solution, with concentrated nitric acid, with hydrogen peroxide, with ozone in the presence of water, or with chlorine in aqueous solution or by reaction of barium iodate with sulfuric acid. It forms colorless rhombic crystals which melt at 110°C. to give a solution plus solid $3I_2O_5 \cdot H_2O$. Chloric and bromic acid solutions are conveniently prepared by reacting the barium salts with sulfuric acid and filtering. All the halic acids are strong acids and powerful oxidizing agents. As such, they react with a variety of bases and reducing agents. Chloric acid solutions may yield oxygen and chloride, perchlorate and chloride, or chlorine dioxide and oxygen on decomposition.

The halates commonly result from the interaction of halogen with hot alkali as

$$3X_2 + 6OH^- \rightarrow XO_3^- + 5X^- + 3H_2O$$

or from the thermal decomposition of hypohalites. Commercially, electrolysis of hot halide solutions in the absence of a diaphragm is most often employed. Although most chlorates are water soluble, bromates are in general markedly less so, and many iodates, especially those of the heavy metals, are quantitatively insoluble. All halates undergo thermal decomposition. With chlorates, thermal decomposition leads to chloride and oxygen at high temperatures and to perchlorate and chloride at more moderate temperatures. With bromates, it leads to bromide and oxygen in some cases and to metal oxide, bromine, and oxygen or to metal oxide and bromide in others; but perbromate is never formed. With iodates, iodide and oxygen or oxide, iodine, and oxygen or periodate and iodide result. Iodates, unlike the others, show a marked tendency to crystallize with iodic acid, compounds such as $KIO_3 \cdot HIO_3$, $KIO_3 \cdot 2HIO_3$ being common. Iodic acid also adds to other compounds as well. Chlorates are useful in matches and pyrotechnics. Bromates and iodates are most commonly employed as analytical reagents.

Perhalic Acids and Perhalates. Neither perbromic acid nor its salts are known. The other materials are well characterized. However, the differences between the perchlorates and the periodates are sufficient to warrant discussion of these materials as two separate topics.

Perchloric acid, $HClO_4$, is commonly obtained in aqueous solution, although the pure anhydrous compound can be prepared by vacuum distillation as a colorless liquid, freezing at −112°C. and boiling with decomposition at 90°C. under one atmosphere of pressure. A number of hydrates, $HClO_4 \cdot nH_2O$, where $n = 1, 2, 2.5, 3, 3.5$, are known as crystalline compounds, the most characteristic being the 1-hydrate, which is called oxonium or hydronium perchlorate because of the analogy between its x-ray pattern and that of ammonium perchlorate.[70] This is a crystalline material melting at 50°C., and it is formed when potassium perchlorate is distilled with four times its weight of concentrated sulfuric acid. Commercial 72% perchloric acid contains only slightly more water than the 2-hydrate.

Perchloric acid is a very weak oxidizing agent when cold and dilute, but when hot and concentrated its oxidizing strength is so enhanced that it may react with explosive violence if an even reasonably strong reducing agent is present.[71] Many metals are oxidized by hydrogen ion in cold perchloric acid without reduction of the anion. On the other hand, in the hot acid, anion oxidations, such as Cr(0) to Cr(VI), are not uncommon. Solubility in perchloric acid is enhanced not only because the acid is the strongest of all acids but also because most perchlorates are water soluble. Combination of oxidizing effect, acidic strength, and solubility of its salts makes perchloric acid a valuable analytical reagent.[71] For analytical purposes, the acid is often mixed with sulfuric or nitric acid. Inasmuch as perchlorate ion has no measurable tendency to form complex ions with metal ions (p. 237), it is commonly employed in studies where the absence of complex ions must be assured.

Perchloric acid can be prepared by treating perchlorates with sulfuric acid and distilling. A modification, due to Willard,[72] involves reacting ammonium perchlorate with nitric and hydrochloric acids as

$$34NH_4ClO_4 + 36HNO_3 + 8HCl \rightarrow 34HClO_4 + 4Cl_2 + 35N_2O + 73H_2O$$

concentrating the dilute solution at 198° to 200°C. to eliminate unreacted hydrochloric and nitric acids, and distilling under vacuum. This procedure is of commercial importance. The electrolytic oxidation of chlorate to perchloric acid is also feasible.[73]

Perchlorates are obtained by neutralization of the acid, by reaction

[70] M. Volmer: *Ann.*, **440**, 200 (1924).

[71] G. F. Smith: *Perchloric Acid*, 2nd Ed., G. F. Smith Chemical Co., Columbus, Ohio (1951).

[72] H. H. Willard: *J. Am. Chem. Soc.*, **34**, 1480 (1912).

[73] K. C. Newnam and F. C. Mathers: *Trans. Electrochem. Soc.*, **75**, 271 (1939).

of the acid with metals, by thermal decomposition of chlorates under controlled conditions, or technically by electrolytic oxidation of chlorates. They bear many resemblances to permanganates and perrhenates and are often isomorphous with them. Cesium, rubidium, potassium, and, to a lesser extent, ammonium perchlorates have limited solubilities. The others are generally soluble. Silver perchlorate is unique in that it is soluble in either water or hydrocarbon solvents such as benzene. The perchlorates are weaker oxidizing agents than the acid, although at elevated temperatures they react vigorously. The anhydrous magnesium and barium compounds are widely used as excellent desiccants.[71]

A series of periodic acids is known, either as such or in the form of salts. These acids may be regarded as hydrates of a hypothetical iodine(VII) oxide and formulated as $I_2O_7 \cdot nH_2O$. The best known of these acids is the 5-hydrate, $I_2O_7 \cdot 5H_2O$ or H_5IO_6, so-called paraperiodic acid. It consists of colorless monoclinic crystals which melt at 140°C. with decomposition to iodic acid, water, and oxygen (plus some ozone). At 80°C. and under vacuum, this compound loses water to form the 2-hydrate, $I_2O_7 \cdot 2H_2O$ or $H_4I_2O_9$, dimesoperiodic acid, and at 100°C. the 1-hydrate, $I_2O_7 \cdot H_2O$ or HIO_4, metaperiodic acid, results. Salts of a hypothetical 3-hydrate, $I_2O_7 \cdot 3H_2O$ or H_3IO_5, mesoperiodic acid, are also known. The situation among these acids is comparable to the situations existing with such neighbors of iodine as antimony and tellurium. The enhanced size of iodine permits the iodine atom to surround itself with six oxygens in a stable arrangement, whereas the smaller chlorine can accommodate no more than four. The IO_6^{-5} group is octahedral, the IO_4^- group tetrahedral. In aqueous solutions in the pH range of 0 to 7, the species H_5IO_6, $H_4IO_6^-$, IO_4^-, and $H_3IO_6^{-2}$ and the equilibria involving them are sufficient to account completely for observed spectrophotometric and potentiometric behaviors.[74]

The periodic acids are both strong acids and strong oxidizing agents. As oxidizing agents, they resemble iodic acid but are somewhat more powerful (Table 13·8). Many metals, non-metals, and compounds, both inorganic and organic, are oxidized. In fact, the oxidizing properties of periodic acid form the bases for numerous useful analytical methods.[75] Although periodic acids and the periodates often liberate ozone when they react, they do not give hydrogen peroxide in acidic solution and are not obtained as a result of peroxide oxidation. As a

[74] C. E. Crouthamel, A. M. Hayes, and D. S. Martin: *J. Am. Chem. Soc.*, **73**, 82 (1951).

[75] G. F. Smith: *Analytical Applications of Periodic Acid and Iodic Acid and Their Salts*, 5th Ed. G. F. Smith Chemical Co., Columbus, Ohio (1950).

consequence they cannot be peroxy acids (p. 512). Periodic acids serve as parent acids for a series of poly acids containing molybdenum and tungsten (p. 274). Paraperiodic acid can be prepared by reacting the meso silver salt Ag_3IO_5 with chlorine and crystallizing the filtrate, but a better method[76] involves treatment of barium paraperiodate with concentrated nitric acid and crystallization after removal of precipitated barium nitrate. Commercially, the acid is prepared by the electrolytic oxidation of iodic acid.[75]

Salts of all the periodic acids are obtainable by direct or indirect means. Commonest among them are the paraperiodates. Like the acids, the periodates are powerful oxidizing agents and are used as such. In many ways they are more like the tellurates than the perchlorates. These compounds do not result, in general, from the thermal decomposition of iodates (compare chlorine). Quite the contrary, they are often decomposed themselves to the less strongly oxidizing iodates when heated. The acid salt $Na_3H_2IO_6$ is readily obtained by the oxidation of sodium iodate with chlorine or peroxydisulfate in sodium hydroxide solution.[77] This compound can be converted to the meta salt ($NaIO_4$) by treatment with excess concentrated nitric acid and crystallization as a 3-hydrate.[77] Chlorine oxidation of potassium iodate in alkaline medium yields insoluble potassium metaperiodate rather than the soluble para salt.[77] The barium compound is obtained as a precipitate when sodium paraperiodate solution is treated with barium ion.[77]

The fact that no perbromic acid or perbromate has been prepared is puzzling. Bromine shows a notable reluctance to form oxy compounds of any type, as is evidenced by the instabilities of the oxides (p. 434) and the oxy acids. Structurally, there is no logical reason for the non-existence of perbromic acid or its salts. It may well be that the absence of preparative procedures stems from lack of correct approach. That the bromine oxides have been prepared only recently (p. 434) lends some support to this argument.

Interhalogen compounds

The stabilities of the diatomic halogen molecules suggest that the sharing of electron pairs essential to their formation might also occur between atoms of different halogens. This would lead to molecules of the type XX′. Except for the iodine-fluorine compound, all possible examples of this type of interhalogen material have been prepared.

[76] H. H. Willard: *Inorganic Syntheses*, Vol. I, p. 172. McGraw-Hill Book Co., New York (1939).

[77] *Ibid.*, p. 168.

Interestingly enough, however, examples of more complicated compounds of general compositions XX_n', where $n = 3$, 5, or 7, are also known.[78] The structures of these compounds and the bond types characterizing them provide interesting problems.

The interhalogen compounds result either from the direct combination of two halogens or from the reaction of a lower interhalogen compound with a halogen. Such reactions proceed with varying vigor, depending upon the differences in electronegativities of the halogens which are involved. Although compounds containing three, five, or seven atoms of one halogen might appear, at first glance, to be addition compounds involving diatomic interhalogens and free halogen molecules, their properties are those of covalent compounds and are consistent with the assumption that they contain a central halogen atom surrounded by covalently bonded atoms of the other halogen. In such compounds, the smaller of the two halogens is invariably present in the larger quantity, the larger halogen then functioning as the central element. As the central halogen increases in size, its covalency, or its ability to accommodate atoms of the other halogen, increases. This is apparent, for example, in the series ClF_3, BrF_5, IF_7.

Although the simplest interhalogens, of necessity, possess linear structures, little is known about the structures of the higher ones. It is apparent from the formulas that all these compounds contain even numbers of electrons and that the central atoms must possess unshared electron pairs in molecules of all types except XX_7'. Since it is known that such unshared pairs sometimes influence the positions of other bonds formed by the element in question, they may perhaps be considered as occupying definite positions in space. Thus, in ICl_3 a trigonal bipyramid may result with the three chlorines in a plane about the iodine, the two unshared pairs being directed toward the apices. This would be in accord with d^2s or sp^2 bonding (p. 203). Similarly, in iodine pentafluoride, a square pyramid structure with four fluorines in a plane with the iodine and the other fluorine and the unshared electron pair occupying the fifth and sixth octahedral positions seems likely.[79] This would permit bonding such as d^2p^3 (p. 203). However, Raman data for chlorine trifluoride suggest that its structure is a symmetrical pyramid.[80] Similar data plus spectroscopic values indicate that the structure of iodine pentafluoride is a tetragonal pyramid,

[78] N. V. Sidgwick: *Ann. Reports*, **30**, 128 (1933).

[79] A. F. Wells: *Structural Inorganic Chemistry*, 2nd Ed., pp. 261–264. Clarendon Press, Oxford (1950).

[80] K. Schäfer and E. Wicke: *Z. Elektrochem.*, **52**, 205 (1948).

with four fluorines at the corners of the square base and the iodine and fifth fluorine on the fourfold axis normal to the base, and that the structure of iodine heptafluoride is a pentagonal bipyramid, with the iodine at the center of a regular pentagon formed by five fluorine atoms and the other two fluorines equally spaced above and below the plane.[81]

In accordance with accepted practice, all these compounds are named as halides of the less electronegative halogen. Although certain of them have been known for many years, much of our present knowledge has been derived from the researches of Ruff and Emeléus. Existing information on the interhalogens in general has been summarized by Sidgwick[78] and by Sharpe[82] and on the halogen fluorides in particular by Booth and Pinkston.[83]

Compounds of the Type XX′. These compounds are, in effect, still halogens, although electronegativity differences render them somewhat more polar in character than the molecular halogens themselves. In certain of their physical properties, however, they are intermediate between the two component halogens.[84] This is apparent in the boiling point and melting point data summarized in Table 13·9 and plotted against molecular weight in Figure 13·1. The regular trends in these constants are broken only at bromine monofluoride and iodine monochloride where electronegativity differences are enhanced and lead to higher values because of increased ionic character in the bonds. Such other physical constants as are available are also summarized in Table 13·9.

Chemically, these interhalogens are similar to the free halogens. They behave as oxidizing agents toward many metals and non-metals, yielding mixtures of the corresponding halides; they undergo hydrolysis, often according to the equation

$$XX' + H_2O \rightleftharpoons H^+ + X'^- + HOX,$$

X′ being the more electronegative halogen; they sometimes add to ethylenic double bonds; and they may unite with alkali metal halides to give polyhalides (p. 458). Unfortunately, most of the published information has summarized behaviors qualitatively without indicating the reaction products (e.g., with chlorine monofluoride).[85] In some respects, these interhalogen compounds appear to be even more reac-

[81] R. C. Lord, M. A. Lynch, W. C. Schumb, and E. J. Slowinski: *J. Am. Chem. Soc.*, **72**, 522 (1950).

[82] A. G. Sharpe: *Quart. Revs.*, **4**, 115 (1950).

[83] H. S. Booth and J. T. Pinkston: *Chem. Revs.*, **41**, 421 (1947).

[84] J. McMorris and D. M. Yost: *J. Am. Chem. Soc.*, **53**, 2625 (1931).

[85] O. Ruff and E. Ascher: *Z. anorg. allgem. Chem.*, **176**, 258 (1928).

TABLE 13·9

Physical Characteristics of Interhalogen Compounds

Compound	Molecular Weight	Melting point, °C.	Boiling Point, °C.	Vapor Pressure of Liquid, log p, (p = mm. Hg, T = °K.)	Density, grams/ml.	Heat of Formation, kcal./mole	Specific Conductance, ohm^{-1} cm.$^{-1}$	Trouton's Constant	Color
1. Type XX′									
ClF	54.457	−154	−100.8	$15.738 - 3109/T + 153800/T^2$		27.4			colorless(g)
BrF	98.916	−33*	−20*						red-brown(g)
BrCl	115.373	−66(ca.)	5(ca.)						....
ICl	162.377	27.2(α), 13.9(β)	97.4		3.10(l), (29°C.)	13.6(g)			red-brown(l)
IBr	206.836	36	116		3.7616(l), (42°C.)	1.5(g)			dark red(g)
2. Type XX_3'									
ClF_3	92.457	−83	12.0	$7.42 - 1292/T$	1.8853(l), (0°C.)		5×10^{-9}	20.8	pale green(l)
BrF_3	136.916	8.8	127.6	$8.41954 - 2220.2/T$	3.73(s) at m.p.; 2.843(l), at m.p.		8×10^{-3}	25.3	colorless(l)
ICl_3	233.291	101 (16 atm.)†	64 (subl.)†		3.1107(s), (15°C.)	28.3(s)			orange(s)
3. Type XX_5'									
BrF_5	174.916	−61.3	40.5	$8.0716 - 1627.7/T$	3.09(s) at m.p.			23.7	colorless(l)
IF_5	221.92	9.6	98	$8.83 - 2205/T$	3.75(s), (0°C.)	204.7(l)	1.5×10^{-5}		colorless(l)
4. Type XX_7'									
IF_7	259.92	5–6	4.5(subl.)	$9.6604 - 1602.6/T$‡	2.75(l) at m.p.			26.4	Colorless(l)

* Dec. by heat

† Sublimes even below 0°C. Dec. by heating to $ICl + Cl_2$.

‡ Solid

tive than the elements from which they are derived, probably because they are more readily dissociated than the halogens themselves.

Chlorine monofluoride may be prepared by direct combination of chlorine with fluorine in a copper container at 250°C.[85,86] The compound is also obtained by inducing the reaction by sparking at room temperature.[87] Bromine monofluoride is somewhat less stable than chlorine monofluoride and apparently when once prepared reverts spontaneously into other fluorides of bromine and free bromine.

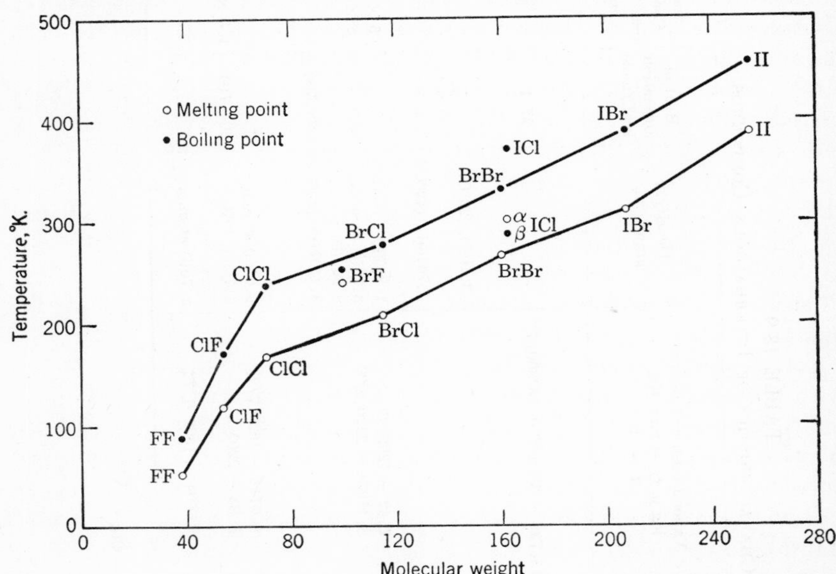

FIG. 13·1. Melting and boiling points of diatomic halogens and interhalogens.

Ruff and Braida[88] obtained a product estimated to contain 50% of the compound by reacting fluorine with bromine, diluted with nitrogen, at 10°C., and fractionally distilling under vacuum to separate the desired material from bromine and the tri- and pentabromides. The trend in decreased stability is apparently continued, for iodine monofluoride has not been prepared.

Bromine monochloride has not been obtained pure. Although phase rule studies on the system bromine-chlorine[89] give no indication of the formation of any bromine chlorides, spectroscopic and spectrophoto-

[86] L. Domange and J. Neudorffer: *Compt. rend.*, **226**, 920 (1948).
[87] K. Fredenhagen and O. T. Krefft: *Z. physik. Chem.*, **A141**, 221 (1929).
[88] O. Ruff and A. Braida: *Z. anorg. allgem. Chem.*, **214**, 91 (1933).
[89] B. J. Karsten: *Z. anorg. Chem.*, **53**, 365 (1907).

metric studies on bromine-chlorine mixtures either in the gaseous state or in carbon tetrachloride solution indicate the presence of a new absorption band at 3700 A, which is ascribed to the compound.[90] Similar observations lead to the conclusion that the system

$$Br_2 + Cl_2 \rightleftharpoons 2BrCl$$

has an equilibrium constant of about 5 at 20°C. and that the equilibrium mixture thus contains about 80% BrCl at this temperature.[91] Existence of bromine monochloride is also indicated by the fact that bromine-chlorine mixtures add to unsaturated acids more readily than either halogen alone, giving chlorobromo compounds.[92] The compound undergoes photochemical decomposition. Its instability is indicated by its small heat of formation, $+0.75 \pm 0.5$ kcal. per mole.[93] Iodine monochloride is prepared conveniently[94] by treating liquid chlorine with solid iodine in stoichiometric quantities and crystallizing by cooling the liquid product. It exists as unstable brownish-red tablets (β) which pass readily into ruby-red needles (α) on standing. Phase relations between the two forms are shown in Figure 13·2. Its uses in analytical chemistry are familar.

Iodine monobromide results from the direct combination of iodine with bromine, although much of the older evidence for its existence is indirect since bromine and iodine form a complete series of solid solutions with each other. Thermodynamic studies [95] of the equilibrium between iodine and bromine in the gaseous state and in solution in carbon tetrachloride show iodine monobromide to be slightly endothermic in character and to be dissociated to the extent of about 8% in the gaseous state and 9.5% in solution at 25°C.

Compounds of the Type XX_3'. Only three interhalogen compounds of this type have been characterized, namely, ClF_3, BrF_3, and ICl_3. Physical constants for these compounds are summarized in Table 13·9. The comparatively high boiling points and large values of Trouton's constant* for both the trifluorides indicate them to be

[90] S. Barratt and C. P. Stein: *Proc. Roy. Soc. (London)*, **A122,** 582 (1929).

[91] L. T. M. Gray and D. W. G. Style: *Proc. Roy. Soc. (London)*, **A126,** 602 (1930).

[92] N. W. Hanson and T. C. James: *J. Chem. Soc.*, **1928,** 1955, 2979.

[93] W. Jost: *Z. physik. Chem.*, **A153,** 143 (1931).

[94] J. Cornog and R. A. Karges: *Inorganic Syntheses*, Vol. I, p. 165. McGraw-Hill Book Co., New York (1939).

[95] D. M. Yost, T. F. Anderson, and F. Skoog: *J. Am. Chem. Soc.*, **55,** 552 (1933).

* Trouton's constant is the ratio of the molar heat of vaporization of a liquid to its boiling point expressed on the Kelvin scale. For normal (unassociated) liquids, its magnitude is about 21, but for associated liquids it is larger.

associated in the liquid state. The characteristics of bromine trifluoride as a non-aqueous, electrolytic solvent have been described in previous chapters (pp. 326, 366).

Both the trifluorides are extremely reactive chemically and behave as powerful fluorinating agents.[82] Chlorine trifluoride reacts with almost all elements except the inert gases, nitrogen, and a few metals. Its reactions with metals, like those of chlorine, are apparently cata-

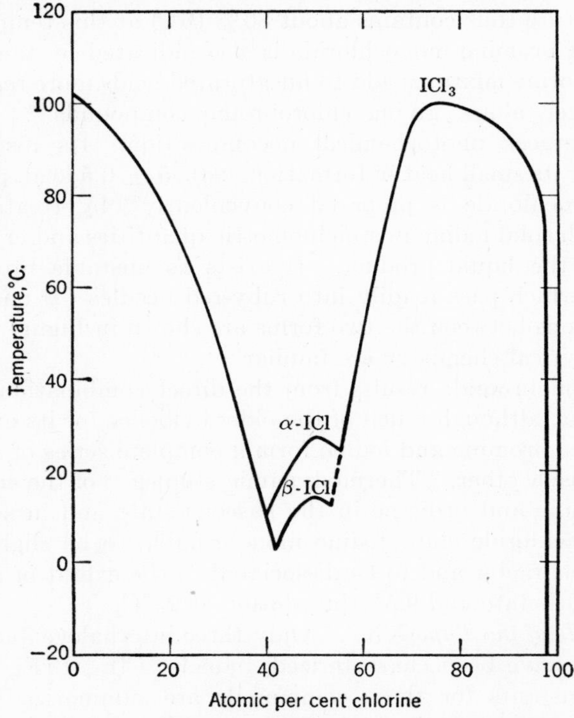

Fig. 13·2. Phase relations in the system iodine-chlorine.

lyzed by the presence of moisture. Dry chlorine trifluoride can be handled in glass and many metal containers. Nickel is unattacked up to 400°C. Bromine and iodine react with chlorine trifluoride to give, respectively, bromine trifluoride and iodine pentafluoride. Most inorganic compounds (except fluorides) and many organic compounds also react, many of the latter with combustion. Chlorine trifluoride was manufactured in quantity in Germany during the second World War as a potential incendiary agent. Bromine trifluoride is only slightly less reactive than chlorine trifluoride and shows many comparable reactions. Early work on the chemical behavior of chlorine trifluoride[96] and bromine trifluoride[97] was essentially qualitative in nature. More recent studies of bromine trifluoride[98–103] give data on the conversion of metal chlorides, bromides, and iodides to fluorides, on the formation of salts containing the BrF_4^- and BrF_2^+ groups, on reaction with water to give bromine, oxygen, and bromic and hydrofluoric acids, and on the conversion of many oxides to fluorides and oxyanions to fluoanions. Iodine trichloride is a much less reactive compound and is subject to ready thermal decomposition to the monochloride and chlorine. Phase relations are shown in Figure 13·2.

Chlorine trifluoride was first obtained[96] by reacting chlorine with excess fluorine. Both the mono- and trifluorides result, the proportions of the latter being increased markedly by raising the reaction temperature to around 250°C. Large-scale German production was based upon the same reaction run at 270° to 280°C.[104] in nickel reactor filled with metal turnings. The reaction is too slow below 270°C., and at temperatures above 280°C. thermal decomposition to fluorine and chlorine occurs. Bromine trifluoride was first obtained by Lebeau[105] by reacting fluorine with bromine at temperatures just above the melting point of the bromine. In the preparation of bromine monofluoride,[88] the trifluoride which also results is condensed in fractions collected at 10°C. It may then be purified by fractional distillation.[97] It is a product of the spontaneous decomposition of the monofluoride. Direct reaction of fluorine gas with liquid bromine is useful for laboratory preparations.[106] Iodine trichloride is ordinarily prepared by direct combination of the elements. A convenient procedure[107] involves treating excess liquid chlorine with powdered iodine and allowing the unused chlorine to evaporate from the flocculent, orange-colored solid trichloride.

[96] O. Ruff and H. Krug: *Z. anorg. allgem. Chem.*, **190**, 270 (1930).
[97] O. Ruff and A. Braida: *Z. anorg. allgem. Chem.*, **206**, 62 (1932).
[98] A. G. Sharpe and H. J. Emeléus: *J. Chem. Soc.*, **1948**, 2135.
[99] A. A. Woolf and H. J. Emeléus: *J. Chem. Soc.*, **1949**, 2865.
[100] H. J. Emeléus and A. A. Woolf: *J. Chem. Soc.*, **1950**, 164.
[101] V. Gutmann and H. J. Emeléus: *J. Chem. Soc.*, **1950**, 1046.
[102] A. A. Woolf and H. J. Emeléus: *J. Chem. Soc.*, **1950**, 1050.
[103] A. A. Woolf: *J. Chem. Soc.*, **1950**, 1053.
[104] Anon.: *Chem. Ind.*, **57**, 1084 (1945).
[105] P. Lebeau: *Compt. rend.*, **141**, 1018 (1905); *Bull. soc. chim.* [3], **35**, 148 (1906) *Ann. chim. phys.* [8], **9**, 241 (1906).
[106] J. H. Simons: *Inorganic Syntheses*, Vol. III, p. 184. McGraw-Hill Book Co., New York (1950).
[107] H. S. Booth and W. C. Morris: *Inorganic Syntheses*, Vol. I, p. 167. McGraw-Hill Book Co., New York (1939).

Compounds of the Type XX_5'. Only two interhalogen compounds of this type have been prepared, namely, BrF_5 and IF_5. Available physical constants for these materials are also summarized in Table 13·9. Bromine pentafluoride is comparable in chemical reactivity with chlorine trifluoride, reacting with all elements except nitrogen, oxygen, and the inert gases to yield fluorides and other uncharacterized products; with a variety of oxides, halides, hydrides; and with many organic compounds.[108] Many of these reactions are so violent as to be of little or no preparative value. Iodine pentafluoride is somewhat less reactive. For example, such elements as silver, copper, iron, chromium, hydrogen, oxygen, and iodine show little or no reaction, and even the alkali metals, sulfur, chlorine, and bromine react only when heated.[109] The compound is hydrolyzed to iodic and hydrofluoric acids and reacts with a variety of organic materials. Although the majority of the reactions reported have been but poorly characterized, iodine, rather than iodide, often appears as a reaction product. When heated to about 500°C., the compound decomposes to iodine and iodine heptafluoride. Boiling iodine pentafluoride dissolves potassium fluoride and converts it to the salt $K[IF_6]$.[110] Liquid iodine pentafluoride is an electrolytic solvent.[111]

Bromine pentafluoride is best prepared by reacting bromine diluted with nitrogen with excess fluorine in a copper vessel at 200°C.[108] Purification involves separation from the less volatile trifluoride, followed by distillation in quartz with the column maintained at 0°C. to reduce chemical attack. Iodine pentafluoride, although prepared by Gore[112] by treating silver(II) fluoride with iodine, is better obtained by a modification of Moissan's method[109] in which fluorine is reacted directly with iodine and the product removed by distillation as rapidly as it is formed,[113] and then redistilled to effect purification. An excess of iodine reduces the possibility of forming iodine heptafluoride.[114] Iodine pentafluoride also results when iodine pentoxide is treated with fluorine at 250°C.

Compounds of the Type XX_7'. The only known example of this type of compound is iodine heptafluoride, IF_7. This material is a colorless gas which may be condensed to a colorless liquid or a colorless crystalline solid. Such physical constants as have been evaluated are

[108] O. Ruff and W. Menzel: *Z. anorg. allgem. Chem.*, **202**, 49 (1931).

[109] H. Moissan: *Compt. rend.*, **135**, 563 (1902).

[110] H. J. Emeléus and A. G. Sharpe: *J. Chem. Soc.*, **1949**, 2206.

[111] A. A. Woolf: *J. Chem. Soc.*, **1950**, 3678.

[112] G. Gore: *Phil. Mag.* [4], **41**, 309 (1871); *Chem. News*, **24**, 291 (1871).

[113] O. Ruff and R. Keim: *Z. anorg. allgem. Chem.*, **193**, 176 (1930).

[114] O. Ruff and A. Braida: *Z. anorg. allgem. Chem.*, **220**, 43 (1934).

summarized in Table 13·9. Chemically, iodine heptafluoride appears to be comparable to chlorine trifluoride or bromine pentafluoride in activity, reacting with most metals, many non-metals including chlorine and iodine, water to yield periodate and fluoride ions, many inorganic compounds, and a variety of organic materials.[113] As with iodine pentafluoride, such reactions yield fluorides and often elemental iodine and are as yet of but little use in preparative chemistry.

Although iodine heptafluoride was probably first obtained (though not recognized) by Moissan[109] as a product of the thermal decomposition of the pentafluoride, Ruff and Keim[113] obtained the compound more conveniently and in better yields by heating iodine pentafluoride with fluorine. At 250° to 270°C. conversion of some 83% of the fluorine used was reported, the product being purified by pumping off silicon tetrafluoride at −90°C. and then fractionating at 0°C, with the receiver at −100°C. to remove unreacted iodine pentafluoride. Modification of this procedure gives iodine heptafluoride in nearly quantitative yields (based upon the iodine used).[115]

Vapor density measurements on interhalogens of all types support the formulas given. Values recorded for Trouton's constant suggest some degree of association for BrF_3, BrF_5, and IF_7 especially. The diatomic interhalogens, except ClF, appear to be associated to greater or lesser extents in the liquid state.

The polyhalides

The well-known enhanced solubility of iodine in solutions containing iodide ion is best explained[116] as involving the formation of triiodide ion according to the equilibrium expression

$$I^- + I_2 \rightleftharpoons I_3^-$$

This is not an isolated phenomenon.[82] The ability of halide ions, either in solution or in solid salts, to associate with molecular halogens or interhalogen compounds to yield univalent ions containing an abundance of halogen has been recognized for many years, particularly since the pioneering researches of Wells and his coworkers.[117–122]

[115] W. C. Schumb and M. A. Lynch: *Ind. Eng. Chem.*, **42,** 1383 (1950).
[116] G. Jones: *J. Phys. Chem.*, **34,** 673 (1930).
[117] H. L. Wells and S. L. Penfield: *Am. J. Sci.*, **43** [3], 17 (1892).
[118] H. L. Wells and S. L. Penfield: *Z. anorg. Chem.*, **1,** 85 (1892).
[119] H. L. Wells and H. L. Wheeler: *Am. J. Sci.*, **43** [3], 475 (1892).
[120] H. L. Wells and H. L. Wheeler: *Z. anorg. Chem.*, **1,** 442 (1892).
[121] H. L. Wells and H. L. Wheeler: *Am. J. Sci.*, **44** [3], 42 (1892).
[122] H. L. Wells and H. L. Wheeler: *Z. anorg. Chem.*, **2,** 255 (1892).

These species, which are referred to as polyhalides, appear to be of three types, namely, X_n^- (e.g., I_3^-), $XX_n'^-$ (e.g., ICl_4^-), and $XX'X_n''^-$ (e.g., $IBrCl^-$). The literature on this subject is complex, the best general reference being Gmelin's *Handbuch*.[123]

Polyhalide formation appears to be restricted to cases where a large cation, such as an alkali metal ion, an alkaline earth metal ion, a coordination complex such as $[Co(NH_3)_6]^{+3}$, or an organic base like an alkaloid or a quaternary ammonium ion is present, and it is more characteristic of iodides than of any of the other halides. These restrictions are of course more rigidly applicable to solid materials than to those

TABLE 13·10
TYPICAL SOLID POLYHALIDES

Type X_n^-	Type $XX_n'^-$	Type $XX'X_n''^-$
$NaI_3 \cdot 2H_2O$	NH_4IBr_2	CsFIBr
$KI_3 \cdot H_2O$	$KICl_2$	$RbFICl_3$
$NH_4I_3 \cdot 3H_2O$	$RbIBr_2$	$CsFICl_3$
RbI_3	$RbICl_2$	KClIBr
CsI_3	$RbBrCl_2$	RbClIBr
CsI_4	$CsICl_2$	CsClIBr
$NH_4I_5 \cdot H_2O$	$CsBrCl_2$	
$KI_7 \cdot H_2O$	$CsClBr_2$	
$RbI_7 \cdot H_2O$	$(CH_3)_3NHIBr_2$	
$RbBr_3$	$(CH_3)_4NIBr_2$	
$CsBr_3$	$C_5H_5NHIBr_2$	
$(CH_3)_4NI_9$	$C_5H_5NCH_3IBr_2$	
$(C_2H_5)_4NI_7$	$HICl_4 \cdot 4H_2O$	
$KI_9 \cdot 3C_6H_6$	KIF_6	
$RbI_9 \cdot 2C_6H_6$		
$CsI_9 \cdot 1\frac{1}{2}C_6H_6$		

existing in solution. As regards solid polyhalides, Grace[124] is of the opinion that in such ionic crystals the greatest thermal stability results when anion and cation approach each other in size. If polyiodides are considered, then, it is apparent only cations which are large in their own right, e.g., Cs^+ and $(C_2H_5)_4N^+$, or are made large by solvation, e.g., with water or benzene, should form stable compounds with ions such as I_3^- and I_7^-. That this is true is evidenced by the formulas for typical solid polyhalides given in Table 13·10.

If the formation of a polyhalide is assumed as a first hypothesis to involve interaction of a halide with a polarized neutral halogen or interhalogen molecule, the energy of polarization of that molecule must exceed the lattice energy of the halide in order for reaction to occur.

[123] Gmelin's *Handbuch der anorganischen Chemie*, System-Nummer **8**, pp. 403–431. Verlag Chemie, G.m.b.h., Berlin (1933).

[124] N. S. Grace: *J. Phys. Chem.*, **37**, 347 (1933).

The high lattice energies of the fluorides preclude their forming many stable polyhalides. On the other hand, chlorides form more such compounds, bromides form still more, and iodides commonly enter into polyhalide formation. In terms of this concept, then, polyhalide formation is increasingly easy with decreasing lattice energy in the original halide. Of the alkali metal halides, therefore, cesium iodide should be most likely to form such compounds. This is in accord with experimental observation, and is supported by thermal stability data of the type shown in Table 13·11.

TABLE 13·11
RELATIVE THERMAL STABILITIES OF SOME POLYHALIDES

Compound	Temperature at Which Dissociation Pressure Equals 760 mm., °C.
CsI_3	250
RbI_3	192
$CsBr_3$	147.5
$RbBr_3$	105.5
$CsBrI_2$	201.5
$CsBr_2I$	242.5
$RbBr_2I$	186.5
$CsCl_2I$	209
$RbCl_2I$	151
$CsClBr_2$	124
$RbClBr_2$	81
$CsCl_2Br$	138
$RbCl_2Br$	93

The structures of the polyhalides have not been elucidated completely. However, evidence which has been accumulated indicates that a large halogen atom (usually iodine) serves as a center around which other halogens are grouped. The ions I_3^-, ICl_2^-, IBr_2^-, and $IBrCl^-$ have all been shown by x-ray methods[125–128] to be linear, with the iodine atom in the center. As with the interhalogen compounds (p. 445), it is probable that the unshared electron pairs occupy spatial positions equivalent to those occupied by atoms, and it seems reasonable, therefore, that in these linear arrangements the central iodine is surrounded by three electron pairs and two other halogens are directed toward the apices of a circumscribed trigonal bipyramid. With the ion ICl_4^-, the four chlorines have been shown to be at the

[125] R. W. G. Wyckoff: *J. Am. Chem. Soc.*, **42,** 1100 (1920).
[126] G. L. Clark: *Proc. Natl. Acad. Sci.*, **9,** 117 (1923).
[127] R. M. Bozarth and L. Pauling: *J. Am. Chem. Soc.*, **47,** 1561 (1925).
[128] R. C. L. Mooney: *Z. Krist.*, **90,** 143 (1935); **98,** 324 (1938); **100,** 519 (1939).

corners of a square surrounding the central iodine.[129] This may be considered an octahedral arrangement, the two unshared electron pairs on the iodine being directed toward the two remaining apices of a circumscribed octahedron. No concrete evidences of isomerism among the polyhalides have been obtained.[128]

The polyhalides are characterized by low melting points. They are soluble in liquids of high dielectric constants, e.g., water, acetone, alcohols, but quite generally insoluble in liquids of low dielectric constant except the free halogens and interhalogens. Dissolution in water is often complicated by hydrolysis. Recrystallization from water is possible only if the polyhalide has a relatively low dissociation pressure. The compounds are commonly colored and range in color from yellow to blue-black. Their absorption spectra are characterized by bands in the regions of 2600 to 2900 A and 3400 to 3900 A.[130]

Outstanding among the chemical characteristics of the polyhalides are their tendencies to dissociate into simple halide plus halogen or interhalogen. In the absence of a solvent, such dissociation always yields the halide of largest lattice energy, that is, the one containing the most electronegative halogen.[131] For instance, dissociation of $CsICl_2$ yields $CsCl + ICl$ rather than $CsI + Cl_2$. Dissociation is readily effected by raising the temperature but is often appreciable at room temperature or below. Polyhalides containing one iodine atom are normally less dissociated than those containing no iodine or more than one iodine atom. Thermal stability for a given type of polyhalide appears always to increase in the series $Na^+ < K^+ < NH_4^+ < Rb^+ < Cs^+$. The most symmetrical polyhalides are also the least dissociated, stability increasing, for example, in the series $[BrII]^- < [FIBr]^- < [ClIBr]^- < [III]^- < [BrIBr]^- < [ClICl]^-$.[131] Among the substituted ammonium polyhalides, those containing even numbers of alkyl groups are more resistant to thermal dissociation than those with odd numbers of substituted groups. Sharpness of melting point is a criterion of thermal stability.[131]

It is difficult to classify all the reactions of all the polyhalides systematically. Cremer and Duncan[132] have examined many polyhalides in solution and prefer to classify the materials on the basis of observed behaviors as:

1. Those containing more than one iodine atom, which yield iodine by dissociation but do not undergo appreciable hydrolysis.

[129] R. C. L. Mooney: *Z. Krist.*, **98**, 377 (1938).
[130] F. L. Gilbert, R. R. Goldstein, and T. M. Lowry: *J. Chem. Soc.*, **1931**, 1092.
[131] H. W. Cremer and D. R. Duncan: *J. Chem. Soc.*, **1931**, 2243.
[132] H. W. Cremer and D. R. Duncan: *J. Chem. Soc.*, **1932**, 2031.

2. Those containing one iodine atom, which dissociate to yield iodine halides and hydrolyze to iodate, e.g., IBr_2^-, $IBrCl^-$, ICl_2^-, ICl_4^-.

3. Those containing no iodine, which yield bromine, chlorine, or bromine monochloride on dissociation and undergo appreciable hydrolysis, e.g., Br_3^-, $BrCl_2^-$, $ClBr_2^-$.

Cremer and Duncan[133] have also examined the behaviors of certain polyhalides in the absence of a solvent, particularly with gaseous reagents. Their conclusions as regard reactions with halogens may be summarized as follows:

1. A halogen may be replaced by a more electronegative one except that the central halogen atom is not replaceable. Thus chlorine replaces bromine in IBr_2^- to give ICl_2^- but will not replace iodine. Similarly, bromine converts I_3^- to IBr_2^- but not to Br_3^-.
2. A central electropositive halogen is not replaced by a more electropositive halogen except in the single case where Br_3^- is converted by iodine to IBr_2^-. This reaction is probably not a direct one.
3. The polyhalide may be converted to a monohalide, the halogen acting as an inert gas and sweeping out the other halogen.
4. A halogen or interhalogen formed by dissociation of the polyhalide may be replaced by another as in the reaction of $ClIBr^-$ with ICl to give ICl_2^-.
5. A halogen may be added directly to the polyhalide as in the reaction of ICl_2^- with chlorine to give ICl_4^-. Interhalogens do not so add.
6. The polyhalide may absorb halogen and dissolve in it. Recrystallization may then occur.

Although the compositions of solid polyhalides may be established by direct analysis, the best information on the natures of these solid phases has come from phase rule studies. Such studies have embraced either binary systems of metal halide and halogen or ternary systems involving metal halide, halogen, and solvent (e.g., water and benzene). Many such investigations have been carried out by Briggs and by Foote and their coworkers. As typical of the first type, one may cite studies of the cesium iodide–iodine system,[134] where the temperature-composition diagram shows the existence of the polyiodides CsI_4 and CsI_3, both melting incongruently, or of the system ammonium iodide–iodine,[135] where only NH_4I_3, melting incongruently at 175°C., is found.

[133] H. W. Cremer and D. R. Duncan: *J. Chem. Soc.*, **1933**, 181.
[134] T. R. Briggs: *J. Phys. Chem.*, **34**, 2260 (1930).
[135] T. R. Briggs and K. H. Ballard: *J. Phys. Chem.*, **44**, 322 (1940).

As typical of the second type, one may cite studies of the system rubidium iodide–iodine–benzene,[136] showing the existence of the solid polyiodides $RbI_7 \cdot 4C_6H_6$ and $RbI_8 \cdot 4C_6H_6$, or of the system ammonium iodide–iodine–water,[137] showing the existence of solid NH_4I_3 and $NH_4I_3 \cdot 3H_2O$ and probably $NH_4I_5 \cdot H_2O$.

The most comprehensive investigations of the preparation of polyhalides are those of Wells[117–122] and of Cremer and Duncan.[138] The methods most generally employed may be summarized as:

1. Direct addition of halogen to halide, e.g., CsI_3 from $CsI + I_2$, $KICl_4$ from $Cl_2 + KI$ in aqueous solution.
2. Direction addition of interhalogen to halide, e.g., $NaIBr_2$ from $NaBr + IBr$ vapor, NH_4IBr_2 from $NH_4Br + IBr$ in ethanol, $CsICl_4$ from $CsCl + ICl_3$ vapor.
3. Displacement of one halogen by another, e.g., $CsIBr_2$ from $CsBr_3 + I_2$.
4. Displacement of one interhalogen by another, e.g., $CsIBr_2$ from $CsICl_2 + IBr$.
5. Metathesis involving another polyhalide, e.g., $RbICl_2$ from $HICl_2 + RbCl$ solutions.

Original references should be consulted for details.

To conclude this section the various types of polyhalides are now discussed briefly.

Compounds Giving Ions of the Type X_n^-. Commonest of these are the trihalides, particularly the triiodides of which the cesium, rubidium, and ammonium compounds are well known in the anhydrous state. The situation with potassium has been of particular interest for many years, probably because of the widespread use of solutions of iodine in aqueous potassium iodide. Since such solutions definitely contain the I_3^- ion, e.g., the equilibrium constant for the equilibrium $I_2 + I^- \rightleftharpoons I_3^-$ having a definite value of 1.4×10^{-3} at 25°C.,[116] many attempts have been made to obtain the solid, KI_3. It is agreed, however, that an unsolvated potassium triiodide has no existence at room temperatures,[139, 140] particularly in view of the fact that the temperature-composition diagram of the system potassium iodide-iodine shows the

[136] H. W. Foote and M. Fleischer: *J. Phys. Chem.*, **44**, 633 (1940).

[137] T. R. Briggs, K. H. Ballard, F. R. Alrich, and J. P. Wikswo: *J. Phys. Chem.*, **44**, 325 (1940).

[138] H. W. Cremer and D. R. Duncan: *J. Chem. Soc.*, **1931**, 1857.

[139] N. S. Grace: *J. Chem. Soc.*, **1931**, 594.

[140] W. D. Bancroft, G. A. Scherer, and L. P. Gould: *J. Phys. Chem.*, **35**, 764 (1931).

only stable solids to be potassium iodide and iodine.[141] From aqueous solutions, however, the hydrated polyiodides $KI_3 \cdot H_2O$ and $KI_7 \cdot H_2O$ can be obtained,[134, 142] as may also two polymorphic modifications of $KI_3 \cdot 2H_2O$.

Less important materials of this type are $NaI_2 \cdot 3H_2O$,[143] stable at 0°C.; $NaI_4 \cdot 2H_2O$, also stable at 0°C; CsI_4 and $CsBr_4$; NH_4I_5; $2KBr_6 \cdot 3H_2O$,[144] stable at 0°C.; and miscellaneous materials such as $RbI_7 \cdot 4C_6H_6$ and $RbI_8 \cdot 4C_6H_6$ as mentioned above.[136]

Compounds Giving Ions of the Type $XX_n'^-$. These are probably the commonest of the polyhalides and the most stable in the non-solvated condition. First studied by Wells,[117–122] these materials were investigated later by Ephraim[145] and particularly by Cremer and Duncan.[131–133, 138] Numerous salts of the series IBr_2^-, ICl_2^-, $ClBr_2^-$, and $BrCl_2^-$ have been prepared and studied. In the series I_2Br^-, only the cesium compound has been obtained, and derivatives of I_2Cl^- have not been prepared. The general characteristics of these materials have been indicated already.

Of particular interest are compounds containing the group ICl_4^-. They are derived from the acid, which may be prepared as an orange-yellow crystalline hydrate, $HICl_4 \cdot 4H_2O$, either by dissolving iodine trichloride in hydrochloric acid and cooling in ice[138] or by adding chlorine to $HICl_2$ solution[138] or to iodine suspended in concentrated hydrochloric acid. Comparatively stable salts containing not only all the alkali metal ions but also many heavy metal ions[146] are well characterized. These are obtained as yellow or orange-yellow crystals as products of reactions of chlorides with iodine trichloride, iodides with chlorine, or iodates with hydrochloric acid. On heating, all evolve iodine trichloride ultimately and are converted to simple chlorides. In aqueous solution they undergo reversible hydrolysis according to the equation[132]

$$5ICl_4^- + 9H_2O \rightleftharpoons I_2 + 3IO_3^- + 20Cl^- + 18H^+$$

The compound KIF_6[110] appears to be the only reported example of materials containing the $XX_6'^-$ type of group. This compound loses

[141] T. R. Briggs and W. F. Geigle: *J. Phys. Chem.*, **34**, 2250 (1930).

[142] T. R. Briggs, K. D. G. Clack, K. H. Ballard, and W. A. Sassaman: *J. Phys. Chem.*, **44**, 350 (1940).

[143] G. H. Cheesman, D. R. Duncan, and I. W. H. Harris: *J. Chem. Soc.*, **1940**, 837.

[144] I. W. H. Harris: *J. Chem. Soc.*, **1932**, 1694.

[145] F. Ephraim: *Ber.*, **50**, 1069 (1917).

[146] R. F. Weinland and F. Schlegelmilch: *Z. anorg. Chem.*, **30**, 134 (1902).

iodine pentafluoride either at its melting point (ca. 200°C.) or under reduced pressures. Water hydrolyzes it to fluoride and iodate.

Compounds Giving Ions of the Type $XX'X_n''^-$. Although this group is represented by materials containing the $BrICl^-$ ion, it is perhaps more important in that the only known polyhalides containing fluorine belong to it. The absorption of iodine monobromide vapor by solid cesium fluoride to yield a yellow product is presumed to involve formation of CsBrIF.[131] Booth and his coworkers[147] have reported the preparation of $RbFICl_3$ (m.p. in closed tube 172°C., sp. gr. 3.159) and $CsFICl_3$ (m.p. in closed tube 194°C., sp. gr. 3.565) as orange-yellow crystalline compounds as products of (1) reaction of alkali metal fluoride with iodine and chlorine in aqueous solution, both in the presence or absence of hydrochloric acid; (2) reaction of solid alkali metal fluoride mixed with iodine with chlorine to constant weight; or (3) reaction of acidic metal fluoride solution with excess iodine trichloride. These compounds could be recrystallized, but they lose iodine trichloride on standing unless kept in a closed container or over iodine trichloride. The potassium and ammonium compounds were also prepared but were found to be less stable.

Electropositive characteristics of the halogens

In preceding sections, a number of instances have been mentioned in which the halogens bear formal electropositive charges toward each other or toward other more electronegative elements (especially oxygen). It is the purpose of this section to review other similar cases. With chlorine, electropositive character amounts to little more than measurable polarity in covalent bonds. The same is true but to a greater extent with the larger bromine. With iodine, however, electronegativity is so far reduced that definite cationic behavior either in simple or in complex compounds may be discerned. There is every reason to believe that the trend would continue to astatine. The general subject has been considered by Kleinberg.[148]

Compounds of Tripositive Iodine. The properties and preparation of iodine(III) iodates (p. 436), of iodine(III) sulfates (p. 436), and of tetrachloroiodate(III) compounds (p. 459) have been discussed. Oxidation of iodine with perchloric acid or with ozone and perchloric acid produces an iodine(III) perchlorate, $I(ClO_4)_3{\cdot}2H_2O$.[149] Oxidation of iodine with fuming nitric acid in the presence of acetic anhydride

[147] H. S. Booth, C. F. Swinehart, and W. C. Morris: *J. Am. Chem. Soc.*, **54**, 2561 (1932); *J. Phys. Chem.*, **36**, 2779 (1932).

[148] J. Kleinberg: *J. Chem. Education*, **23**, 559 (1946).

[149] F. Fichter and S. Stern: *Helv. Chim. Acta*, **11**, 1256 (1928).

yields the normal acetate, $I(C_2H_3O_2)_3$.[150] Inclusion of chlorinated or brominated acetic acids permits the preparation of compounds such as $I(CH_2ClCO_2)_3$, $I(CHCl_2CO_2)_3$, $I(CCl_3CO_2)_3$, $I(CH_2BrCO_2)_3 \cdot I(IO_3)_3$, whereas in the presence of phosphoric acid the normal phosphate, IPO_4, is formed.[149] These compounds decompose thermally and are readily hydrolyzed to iodine, iodic acid, and the corresponding other acid. That they contain cationic iodine is demonstrated by the fact that when iodine(III) acetate dissolved in acetic anhydride is electrolyzed, iodine is deposited on the cathode in accordance with the requirements of Faraday's law.[149] Halogenoid derivatives of both tri- and unipositive iodine have been described also (pp. 473–474).

Compounds of Unipositive Iodine, Bromine, and Chlorine. Although hypoiodous acid has been shown to exhibit basic properties (p. 439), it appears that coordination of the iodine with an amine such as pyridine (py) is essential to the formation of stable salts of unipositive iodine.[151–153] Compounds derived from the hypothetical bases I(py)OH and $I(py)_2OH$ have been obtained by treating the silver or mercury(I) salt of the appropriate acid with iodine and pyridine in a non-aqueous solvent, such as chloroform, according to the general equations.

$$AgA + py + I_2 \rightarrow I(py)A + AgI$$

$$Hg_2A_2 + 6py + 3I_2 \rightarrow 2I(py)A + 2Hg(py)_2I_2$$

Compounds prepared include $I(py)NO_3$, $I(py)_2NO_3$, $I(py)_2ClO_4$, $I(py)(C_2H_3O_2)$, and $I(py)^+$ derivatives of benzoic, phthalic, *p*-nitrobenzoic, and succinic acids. Spectrophotometric evidences for the existence of $I(py)^+$ and I_3^- ions in solutions of iodine in pyridine have been presented also.[154]

These compounds react with iodide ion to give free iodine as

$$I^+ + I^- \rightarrow I_2$$

They hydrolyze slowly to give iodine and iodate with either the compound I(py)OH or $I(py)_2OH$ as a presumable intermediate. With potassium chloride or bromide, they form the halides I(py)Cl or I(py)Br by metathesis. On being treated with sodium hydroxide,

[150] G. Fouque: *Chem. Ztg.*, **38**, 860 (1914); *Bull. soc. chim.* [4], **15**, 229 (1914).

[151] H. Carlsohn: *Über eine neue Klasse von Verbindungen des positiv einwertigen Iods.* Verlag J. Hirzel, Leipzig (1932).

[152] H. Carlsohn: *Angew. Chem.*, **46**, 747 (1933).

[153] H. Carlsohn: *Ber.*, **68B**, 2209 (1935).

[154] R. A. Zingaro, C. A. Vander Werf, and J. Kleinberg: *J. Am. Chem. Soc.*, **73**, 88 (1951).

they yield the hydroxides $I(py)OH$ and $I(py)_2OH$, which immediately revert to the stabilized anhydrides $(Ipy)_2O$ and $(Ipy_2)_2O$. Upon electrolysis in water-pyridine, methanol, or chloroform solution, the nitrate, $I(py)_2NO_3$, liberates iodine at the cathode. Treatment of the same compound in chloroform with metals showed iodine to be replaced even by platinum,[151] indicating unipositive iodine to be comparable to noble metal cations as an oxidizing agent.[155] According to Carlsohn, the dipyridine derivatives should be salt-like, corresponding to the structure $[I(py)_2]A$, whereas the monopyridine derivatives should not be, in accordance with the structure $[I(py)A]$. Conductance data for the nitrate in acetone or methanol are somewhat inconclusive, but with the benzoate the conductance of the monopyridine derivative is increased somewhat by the addition of pyridine. More work appears desirable before it can be concluded that these compounds agree rigidly with coordination theory.

Methyl-substituted pyridines such as β-picoline, 2,6-lutidine, 2,4-lutidine, and 2,4,6-collidine yield similar iodine(I) nitrates.[152] By corresponding procedures, bromine compounds, $Br(py)_2NO_3$ and $Br(py)_2ClO_4$, have been prepared also.[153, 156] Treatment of these compounds with potassium iodide in sodium hydroxide and subsequent addition of sulfuric acid liberate one mole of iodine per bromine atom,

$$Br^+ + 2I^- \rightarrow I_2 + Br^-$$

A similar chlorine compound, $Cl(py)_2NO_3$, has been reported also.[156] Some evidence for the existence of a unipositive bromine cation is given also by the enhanced brominating strength of bromide-free hypobromous acid solutions over free bromine[157] in acidic solutions. Such a cation is believed to result from reactions such as are represented by the equations

$$HOBr + H^+ \rightleftharpoons Br^+ + H_2O$$

and

$$HOBr + H^+ \rightleftharpoons Br(H_2O)^+$$

Electrodialysis experiments confirm the existence of cationic bromine in acidified hypobromous acid solutions.[158]

As is expected, fluorine does not fit into this series. However, a gaseous compound (b.p. −45.9°C.), the composition and vapor density

[155] W. Finkelstein: *Z. physik. Chem.*, **124**, 285 (1926).
[156] M. I. Uschakow and W. O. Tchistow: *Ber.*, **68B**, 824 (1935).
[157] D. H. Derbyshire and W. A. Waters: *Nature*, **164**, 446 (1949).
[158] K. Gonda-Hunwald, G. Gráf, and F. Körösy: *Nature*, **166**, 68 (1950).

of which are in agreement with the formula FNO_3, has been prepared either by bubbling fluorine through 3 *N* nitric acid at 0°C.[159, 160] or by reacting fluorine with solid potassium nitrate.[161] This rather unstable compound liberates iodine quantitatively from iodide, giving also fluoride and nitrate ions, and reacts with potassium hydroxide to give oxygen, fluoride, and nitrate. The presence of negative fluorine seems unlikely, therefore, although there is no information indicating it to be positive. Pauling and Brockway[162] suggest the following structure on the basis of electron diffraction data:

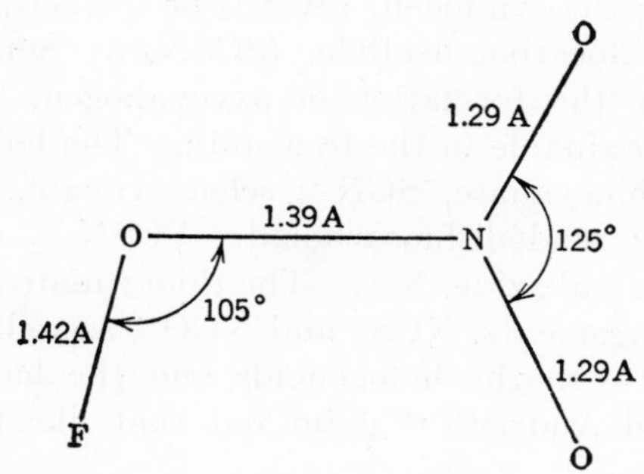

A similar perchlorate, $FClO_4$, has been obtained together with oxygen difluoride by the reaction of fluorine with concentrated perchloric acid.[163] It is an explosive gas condensing at −15.9°C. (755 mm.) to a liquid which freezes at −167.3°C.

Unipositive iodine and bromine characterize the polar interhalogens XX′ (pp. 446–449). In the cyanogen halides (pp. 471–473) it is probable that iodine is unipositive whereas the other halogens are negative.

The halogenoids or pseudo-halogens

A number of inorganic radicals are known which in the free state possess properties comparable to those of the elemental halogens and in the form of anions possess properties comparable to those of the halide ions. These materials have been called *halogenoids* by Browne and his coworkers[164] and *pseudo-halogens* by Birckenbach and Keller-

159 G. H. Cady: *J. Am. Chem. Soc.*, **56**, 2635 (1934).
160 O. Ruff and W. Kwasnik: *Angew. Chem.*, **48**, 238 (1935).
161 D. M. Yost and A. Beerbower: *J. Am. Chem. Soc.*, **57**, 782 (1935).
162 L. Pauling and L. O. Brockway: *J. Am. Chem. Soc.*, **59**, 13 (1937).
163 G. H. Rohrback and G. H. Cady: *J. Am. Chem. Soc.*, **69**, 677 (1947).
164 A. W. Browne, A. B. Hoel, G. B. L. Smith, and F. H. Swezey: *J. Am. Chem. Soc.*, **45**, 2541 (1923).

mann.[165] In their excellent review on these substances, Walden and Audrieth[166] define as a halogenoid "any univalent chemical aggregate composed of two or more electronegative atoms which shows in the free state certain characteristics of the halogens and which combines with hydrogen to form an acid and with silver to form a salt insoluble in water."

Chemically, the halogenoid materials embrace free molecular groups, which may be called free halogenoids, and anions, which may be called halogenoid ions. The free halogenoids which are definitely known are cyanogen, $(CN)_2$; thiocyanogen, $(SCN)_2$ or $(SCN)_x$; selenocyanogen, $(SeCN)_2$; and azidocarbondisulfide, $(SCSN_3)_2$. Some evidence also exists[116, 167, 168] for the formation of oxycyanogen, $(OCN)_2$, but the material is not obtainable in the free state. The halogenoid ions are cyanide, CN^-; thiocyanate, SCN^-; selenocyanate, $SeCN^-$; tellurocyanate, $TeCN^-$; azidodithiocarbonate, $SCSN_3^-$; cyanate, OCN^-; fulminate, ONC^-; and azide, N_3^-. The thiocyanate and cyanate may have the iso arrangements, NCS^- and NCO^-, as well.

Similarities between the halogenoids and the halogens are striking. Walden and Audrieth[166] point out that like the halogens the halogenoids:

1. Are usually (polymeric thiocyanogen is a glaring exception) quite volatile in the free condition.
2. Are often isomorphous when free and in the solid state.
3. Combine with many metals to give salts, the silver, mercury(I), and lead(II) compounds being insoluble in water.
4. Form hydracids with hydrogen, these acids being highly dissociated in water solution (hydrocyanic acid is very weak).
5. Form compounds with themselves, such as CNN_3, which are analogous to the interhalogen compounds (p. 444).
6. Form polyhalogenoid complexes, such as $Cs(SeCN)_3$, which are analogous to the polyhalide complexes (p. 453).
7. Form characteristic double and complex salts, such as $K_2[Hg(SCN)_4]$, $Na[Ag(CN)_2]$, which are comparable to corresponding halogen compounds.
8. May be prepared in the free condition either by chemical or electrolytic oxidation of the hydracids or their salts or by the thermal decomposition of higher valent compounds.

[165] L. Birckenbach and K. Kellermann: *Ber.*, **58B**, 786, 2377 (1925).

[166] P. Walden and L. F. Audrieth: *Chem. Revs.*, **5**, 339 (1928).

[167] A. P. Lidov: *J. Russ. Phys. Chem. Soc.*, **44**, 527, 529 (1912); *Comm. 8th Intern. Congr. Appl. Chem.*, **6**, 185, 191, 194 (1912).

[168] H. Hunt: *J. Am. Chem. Soc.*, **53**, 2111 (1931); **54**, 907 (1932).

These similarities may be supplemented by the following more specific comparisons between halogens and halogenoids:

1. Formation of compounds of similar compositions and properties, e.g., $COCl_2$ vs. $CO(N_3)_2$, SO_2Cl_2 vs. $SO_2(N_3)_2$, ICl vs. ICN, $SiCl_4$ vs. $Si(NCS)_4$.
2. Reaction of free groups with hydroxyl ion, e.g.:

$$Cl_2 + 2OH^- \rightarrow Cl^- + OCl^- + H_2O$$
$$(CN)_2 + 2OH^- \rightarrow CN^- + OCN^- + H_2O$$

3. Reaction of hydracids with oxidizing agents, e.g.:

$$MnO_2 + 4H^+ + 2Cl^- \rightarrow Mn^{+2} + 2H_2O + Cl_2$$
$$MnO_2 + 4H^+ + 2SCN^- \rightarrow Mn^{+2} + 2H_2O + (SCN)_2$$

4. Decomposition of lead(IV) compounds by heat, e.g.:

$$PbCl_4 \rightarrow PbCl_2 + Cl_2$$
$$Pb(SCN)_4 \rightarrow Pb(SCN)_2 + (SCN)_2$$

5. Addition of free groups to an ethylenic linkage, e.g.:

$$H_2C = CH_2 + Cl_2 \rightarrow H_2CCl{\cdot}CClH_2$$
$$H_2C = CH_2 + (SCN)_2 \rightarrow H_2CSCN{\cdot}CSCNH_2$$

On the basis of the conductivities of their salts in aqueous and alcoholic solutions, the halide and halogenoid ions may be arranged[165] in the following order of increasing reducing power: F^-, ONC^-, OCN^-, Cl^-, N_3^-, Br^-, CN^-, SCN^-, $SCSN_3^-$, I^-, $SeCN^-$, $TeCN^-$. However, the fact that iodine will oxidize azidodithiocarbonate ion to azidocarbondisulfide would indicate that the positions of $SCSN_3^-$ and I^- should be reversed. It would follow, according to this list, that oxidizing power among the free halogens and halogenoids should then decrease in the order:

$$F_2,\ Cl_2,\ Br_2,\ (CN)_2,\ (SCN)_2,\ I_2,\ (SCSN_3)_2,\ (SeCN)_2$$

Not much positive evidence can be supplied to support this arrangement, although bromine will oxidize thiocyanate to thiocyanogen, thiocyanogen will oxidize iodide to iodine, and iodine will oxidize selenocyanate to selenocyanogen, etc. Such couples as the following

$$SCSN_3^- \rightleftharpoons \tfrac{1}{2}(SCSN_3)_2 + e^- \qquad E^0_{298} = -0.275 \text{ volt}$$
$$I^- \rightleftharpoons \tfrac{1}{2}I_2 + e^- \qquad = -0.535$$
$$SCN^- \rightleftharpoons \tfrac{1}{2}(SCN)_2 + e^- \qquad = -0.77$$
$$Br^- \rightleftharpoons \tfrac{1}{2}Br_2 + e^- \qquad = -1.07$$

also support this order, although more comprehensive data are lacking.

The Free Halogenoids. These may be discussed best as individuals.

CYANOGEN. Probably the best-characterized of the free halogenoids is cyanogen. Cyanogen is a colorless, poisonous, water-soluble gas which is readily condensed to a liquid boiling at −21.17°C. and freezing at −27.9°C. These and other physical constants have been summarized by Cook and Robinson.[169] Chemically, cyanogen is characterized by a tendency to polymerize to insoluble paracyanogen, $(CN)_x$, at 500°C. and by a tendency to undergo hydrolysis slowly in water according to the scheme[166]

$$H_2N{-}\overset{\overset{O}{\|}}{C}{-}\overset{\overset{O}{\|}}{C}{-}NH_2 \xleftarrow{H_2O} (CN)_2 \xrightarrow{H_2O} HCN + HOCN$$

$$H_2N{-}CO{-}CO{-}NH_2 \xrightarrow{H_2O} (NH_4)_2C_2O_4 \text{ (ammonium oxalate)}$$

$$HCN \xrightarrow{H_2O} NH_4O\overset{\overset{O}{\|}}{C}{-}H \text{ (ammonium formate)}$$

$$HOCN \xrightarrow{H_2O} NH_4OCN \text{ (ammonium cyanate)} \xrightarrow{H_2O} CO(NH_2)_2 \text{ (urea)}$$

In alkaline medium it reacts readily to give cyanide and cyanate (p. 465). Hydrocyanic acid and cyanogen are related as

$$HCN \rightleftharpoons \tfrac{1}{2}(CN)_2 + H^+ + e^- \qquad E^0_{298} = -0.33 \text{ volt}$$

A number of structures have been proposed for cyanogen. From electron diffraction data, Brockway[170] suggested resonance involving the structures

$$:N:::C:C:::N: \qquad \text{I}$$
$$:\dot{N}::C::C::\dot{N}: \qquad \text{II}$$
$$:\overset{-}{\ddot{N}}::C::C::\overset{+}{N}: \qquad \text{III}$$
$$:\overset{+}{N}::C::C::\underset{..}{\overset{-}{N}}: \qquad \text{IV}$$

[169] R. P. Cook and P. L. Robinson: *J. Chem. Soc.*, **1935**, 1001.
[170] L. O. Brockway: *Proc. Natl. Acad. Sci.*, **19**, 868 (1933).

with structure I making the greatest contribution. Pauling, Springall, and Palmer[171] cite data agreeing with Brockway's structure and indicate bond distances to be C—N = 1.16 A and C—C = 1.37 A. The molecule is apparently linear. According to Kistiakowsky[172] the heat of dissociation of the cyanogen molecule according to the equation

$$(CN)_2(g) \rightleftharpoons 2CN(g)$$

is 77 ± 4 kcal. per mole, a value somewhat larger than that given for either fluorine or chlorine in Table 13·1.

Cyanogen may be liberated by heating the cyanides of inactive metals such as silver, mercury, or gold. Comparable reactions occur when halides of such metals are heated. Cyanogen is also liberated by the oxidation of cyanide ion in aqueous solutions by, for instance, Cu^{+2} ion, as

$$2Cu^{+2} + 6CN^- \rightarrow 2[Cu(CN)_2]^- + (CN)_2$$

(compare $Cu^{+2} + I^-$) or in fused cyanides by electrolytic means,[173] as

$$2CN^- \rightarrow (CN)_2 + 2e^-$$

THIOCYANOGEN. Thiocyanogen may be obtained by crystallization from concentrated solutions in ethyl chloride, ethyl bromide, or diethyl ether cooled to −70°C. When so prepared, it melts at −2° to −3°C. to a yellow oil which polymerizes irreversibly at room temperature to insoluble, brick-red parathiocyanogen, $(SCN)_x$. Cryoscopic measurements on bromoform solutions of thiocyanogen[174] give molecular weights corresponding to the formula $(SCN)_2$. However, in dilute solutions in carbon disulfide or hexane[175] at least partial dissociation to free SCN occurs. Polymeric thiocyanogen has been studied only incompletely.

A number of characteristic chemical reactions of thiocyanogen in solution have been studied.[166] The following are of some general interest in indicating the oxidizing power of the halogenoid and its halogen-like character:

[171] L. Pauling, H. D. Springall, and K. J. Palmer: *J. Am. Chem. Soc.*, **61**, 927 (1939).

[172] G. B. Kistiakowsky and H. Gershinowitz: *J. Chem. Phys.*, **1**, 432 (1933).

[173] M. Tzentnershrer and J. Szper: *Congr. intern. élec.*, Paris, Sec. 7, Rap. No. 4 (1932).

[174] H. Lecher and A. Goebel: *Ber.*, **54**, 2223 (1921).

[175] S. S. Bhatnagar, P. L. Kapur, and B. D. Khosla: *J. Indian Chem. Soc.*, **17**, 529 (1940).

$$(SCN)_2 + 2I^- \rightarrow 2SCN^- + I_2$$

$$(SCN)_2 + 2S_2O_3^{-2} \rightarrow 2SCN^- + S_4O_6^{-2}$$

$$(SCN)_2 + H_2S \rightarrow 2H^+ + 2SCN^- + S$$

$$(SCN)_2 + AsO_3^{-3} + H_2O \rightarrow 2SCN^- + 2H^+ + AsO_4^{-3}$$

$$(SCN)_2 + H_2O \rightarrow H^+ + SCN^- + HOSCN \xrightarrow{H_2O} H^+ + SO_4^{-2} + HCN$$

$$(SCN)_2 + 2CuSCN \rightarrow 2Cu^{+2} + 4SCN^-$$

$$(SCN)_2 + M \rightarrow M^{+2} + 2SCN^-$$

Like the iodine, thiocyanogen may be used as a titrimetric oxidizing agent[176] and for determining unsaturation in organic structures These reactions are perhaps better in accord with the structure

```
  ..
: S : C:::N :
  ..
: S : C:::N :
  ..
```

than with the structure

```
     ..
: S::S : C:::N :
     ..
     C:::N :
```

although an equilibrium between the two has been proposed. Th first of these structures is supported by the x-ray data of Strada.[17

Thiocyanogen in solution was first obtained by Söderbäck[178] by oxi dation of an ethereal suspension of silver thiocyanate with iodine o bromine. Such solutions may also be prepared in low yields by oxi dation of thiocyanic acid with manganese dioxide,[179] and electrolysi of thiocyanates in alcoholic solution[162] also yields the free halogenoid Treatment of lead(IV) acetate in ethereal solution with thiocyani acid[179] is cited as another preparational procedure. Lead(IV) thic cyanate is presumed to form and decompose, yielding $(SCN)_2$. convenient procedure yielding an acetic acid–acetic anhydride solutio

[176] H. P. Kaufmann and P. Gaertner: *Ber.*, **57B**, 928 (1924).

[177] M. Strada: *Gazz. chim. ital.*, **64**, 400 (1934).

[178] E. Söderbäck: *Ann.*, **419**, 217 (1919).

[179] H. P. Kaufmann and F. Kögler: *Ber.*, **58B**, 1553 (1925); **59B**, 178 (1926).

of reasonable stability involves oxidation of lead(II) thiocyanate by bromine in this medium.[180]

SELENOCYANOGEN. Selenocyanogen is obtained as a yellow powder which is fairly stable when dry and in vacuum but normally reverts to a red material. It is soluble in carbon tetrachloride, chloroform, benzene, and acetic acid, although its solutions in the last of these deposit selenium rather rapidly. Its molecular weight in benzene corresponds to the composition $(SeCN)_2$. Selenocyanogen is an oxidizing agent of slightly less strength than iodine. This is indicated by the fact that the equilibrium

$$2AgI + (SeCN)_2 \rightleftharpoons 2AgSeCN + I_2$$

is established when some 86% of the iodine is present as silver iodide. Hydrolysis converts selenocyanogen into selenious, hydrocyanic, and selenocyanic acids as

$$2(SeCN)_2 + 3H_2O \rightarrow H_2SeO_3 + 3HSeCN + HCN$$

Structurally, selenocyanogen is probably much like thiocyanogen, a linear formula being favored by Raman data.[181]

Selenocyanogen may be prepared in solution by electrolysis of potassium selenocyanate in methanol.[165] Better procedures[165] involve either treatment of excess silver selenocyanate with iodine in ether at temperatures below 10°C. or reaction of lead(IV) acetate in chloroform with potassium selenocyanate in anhydrous acetone.[179] Lead(IV) selenocyanate decomposes to the lead(II) compound and selenocyanogen.

AZIDOCARBONDISULFIDE. Azidocarbondisulfide is a white, crystalline solid which was first studied by Browne and his coworkers.[164] It is soluble in water to the extent of 3 parts in 10,000 at 25°C. Chemically, it is unstable and may decompose violently according to the equation

$$(SCSN_3)_2 \rightarrow 2N_2 + 2S + (SCN)_2$$

The decomposition is autocatalytic. The substance dissolves in aqueous alkali, presumably according to the equation

$$(SCSN_3)_2 + 2OH^- \rightarrow SCSN_3^- + OSCSN_3^- + H_2O$$

the analogy to the halogens being striking. There is some indication of the conversion of the ion $OSCSN_3^-$ to the ions $SCSN_3^-$ and $O_3SCSN_3^-$

[180] W. H. Gardner and H. Weinberger: *Inorganic Syntheses*, Vol. I, p. 84. McGraw-Hill Book Co., New York (1939).

[181] P. Spacu: *Bull. soc. chim.* [5], **3**, 2074 (1936).

by heat (compare $ClO^- \rightarrow Cl^- + ClO_3^-$). The formula $(SCSN_3)_2$ has been confirmed.[159] Azidocarbondisulfide is a weaker oxidizing agent than iodine.[182] Again, two equilibrium structures have been suggested

$$\mathrm{N{\equiv}N{=}N{-}\underset{\underset{\displaystyle S}{\|}}{C}{-}S{-}S{-}\overset{\overset{\displaystyle S}{\|}}{C}{-}N{=}N{\equiv}N}$$

and

$$\mathrm{N{\equiv}N{=}N{-}\overset{\overset{\displaystyle S}{\|}}{C}{-}\underset{\underset{\displaystyle S}{\|}}{S}{-}\overset{\overset{\displaystyle S}{\|}}{C}{-}N{=}N{\equiv}N}$$

but the first is believed to be the correct one.

Azidocarbondisulfide may be prepared by oxidizing potassium azidodithiocarbonate, $KSCSN_3$, with hydrogen peroxide, potassium iodate, potassium chromate, mercury(II) chloride, iron(III) chloride, chlorine, bromine, or iodine,[183] although the best procedure employs iodine. The product precipitates as it forms. Electrolytic oxidation of the potassium salt may also be used. The potassium compound is prepared by interaction of potassium azide with carbon disulfide at 40°C.

OXYCYANOGEN. Evidence for the existence of oxycyanogen is less complete than for the other free halogenoids. Lidov[167] claimed to have obtained the material as a gas, $(OCN)_2$, by oxidation of potassium cyanate with hydrogen peroxide, copper(II) oxide, or sodium hypobromite, by reduction of nitrogen(IV) oxide with carbon at 150°C., and by reaction of cyanogen bromide with silver oxide. These observations have not been confirmed.[168] Birckenbach and Kellermann,[165] were unable to isolate the compound as a result of electrolytic oxidation of potassium cyanate in methanol, but they did obtain a solution which liberated iodine from iodide and dissolved copper, zinc, and iron without the evolution of gases. This is indirect evidence that oxycyanogen was produced in solution. Formation of the compound as a result of reaction of iodine with silver cyanate has been reported also.[168]

Polyhalogenoids and Polyhalide-Halogenoids. A number of compounds which are direct analogs of the polyhalides (p. 453) have been prepared. These may contain only halogenoid groups or both halogen and halogenoid groups. Thus ammonium trithiocyanate, $NH_4(SCN)_3$,

[182] R. Ullman and G. B. L. Smith: *J. Am. Chem. Soc.*, **68**, 1479 (1946).
[183] F. Sommer: *Ber.*, **48**, 1833 (1915).

has been obtained as a crystalline substance which is stable below −6°C.[184] Correspondingly, the free thiocyanogen liberated during the electrolysis of cold, concentrated aqueous potassium thiocyanate solution is presumed to be present as trithiocyanate ion, $(SCN)_3^-$. The formation of this species may account for the reduction in the rate of hydrolysis of thiocyanogen when excess thiocyanate is present. Selenocyanogen is also more stable in selenocyanate solutions.[164] Electrometric titration of potassium selenocyanate solutions with iodine indicates the existence in solution of the unstable species $(SeCN)I_2^-$, $(SeCN)_2I^-$, and $(SeCN)_3^-$, all comparable with the polyiodide, I_3^-. Reaction of cyanogen iodide (below) with cesium iodide in aqueous solution yields a mixed compound, CsI_2CN.[185] It is only reasonable to assume that others should be formed as well.

Interhalogen-Halogenoids. The most extensively investigated of these interhalogen analogs are those containing the CN grouping in combination with a halogen, i.e., the so-called cyanogen halides of the type CNX (X = F, Cl, Br, I). The physical constants of these compounds are compared with those of cyanogen and hydrogen cyanide in Table 13·12. These constants should be compared with available

TABLE 13·12

Physical Constants for Cyanogen Halides

Property	$(CN)_2$	CNF	CNCl	CNBr	CNI	CNH
Molecular weight	52.036	45.018	61.475	105.934	152.938	27.026
Boiling point, °C.	−21.17	−72 (subl.)	12.6	61.3	....	25.7
Melting point, °C.	−27.9	....	−6.5	51.3	146	−14.0
Heat of vaporization at b.p., kcal./mole	5.778	7 (subl.)	6.358	....	....	6.760
Density of liquid at b.p., grams/ml.	0.9537	....	1.1963	1.8633	ca. 2.59	0.6820
Molecular volume at b.p., ml./mole	54.55	....	51.38	56.85	ca. 58.8	39.50
ΔF_{298} for formation, kcal./mole	69.1	....	35.5	ca. 40	46.75	....
C—X distance, A	....	....	1.67 ± 0.02	1.79 ± 0.02	1.97	....
C—N distance, A	....	....	1.13 ± 0.03	1.13 ± 0.04		

ones for the interhalogens of the same type (p. 447). Chemically, the cyanogen halides resemble both the free halogens and the free halogenoids. For example, hydrolysis of the chloride in the presence of alkali proceeds according to the equation

$$CNCl + 2OH^- \rightarrow OCN^- + Cl^- + H_2O$$

[184] H. Kerstein and R. Hoffmann: *Ber.*, **57B**, 491 (1924).

[185] C. H. Mathewson and H. L. Wells: *Am. Chem. J.*, **30**, 430 (1903).

Like the halogens, the cyanogen halides add to ethylenic linkages in certain organic compounds; and, like cyanogen and thiocyanogen, they undergo polymerization. Polymerization is favored by the presence of the corresponding hydrogen halide (HX) and thus is favored by the presence of moisture because of partial hydrolysis. It yields trimeric cyanuric compounds, $(CNX)_3$, which are believed to possess cyclic structures[186] as

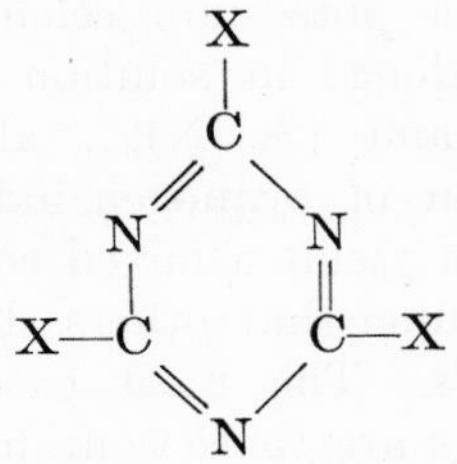

```
          X
          |
          C
        //  \
       N     N
       |     ||
    X—C      C—X
        \\  /
          N
```

The structures of the cyanogen halides have been explored rather extensively. Although a number of possible arrangements have been suggested, the most feasible suggestion,[187] based upon electron diffraction data for the chloride and bromide, involves the resonance structures

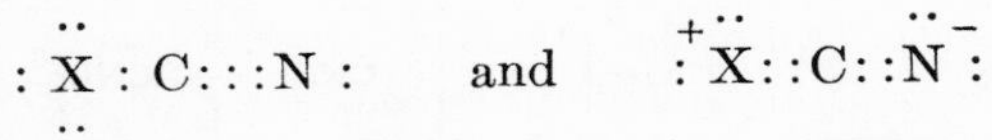

$$:\underset{\cdot\cdot}{\overset{\cdot\cdot}{X}}:C:::N: \quad \text{and} \quad \overset{+}{:}\overset{\cdot\cdot}{X}::C::\overset{\cdot\cdot}{N}:^{-}$$

(I) (II)

Structure II, because of the charge separation characterizing it, would be expected to be less satisfactory. Calculation shows this structure to contribute only 24% to the total structure in the chloride and 33% in the bromide, the difference being due to the greater electronegativity of the chlorine which would reduce its acceptance of a formal positive charge. The molecules are linear. The iodide has been treated similarly by Stevenson.[188] Crystal structure studies on cyanogen iodide[189] support these views as to resonance and indicate a molecular lattice in a rhombohedral structure with one molecule to the unit cell.

Cyanogen chloride and bromide can be prepared by treating hydrocyanic acid or an alkali metal cyanide with chlorine or bromine in aqueous solutions at low temperatures or in an inert medium such as

[186] J. Farquharson: *Trans. Faraday Soc.*, **32**, 219 (1936).
[187] J. Y. Beach and A. Turkevich: *J. Am. Chem. Soc.*, **61**, 299 (1939).
[188] D. P. Stevenson: *J. Chem. Phys.*, **7**, 171 (1939).
[189] J. A. A. Ketelaar and J. W. Zwartsenberg: *Rec. trav. chim.*, **58**, 449 (1939).

carbon tetrachloride or ethylenedichloride. The iodide is obtained by treating potassium or mercury(II) cyanide with iodine. Cyanogen fluoride is obtained in 20 to 25% yield as a gaseous product from the reaction of cyanogen iodide with silver fluoride at 220°C.[190]

Thiocyanogen halides have been less well characterized. The chloride results as a white solid from the direct action of chlorine on thiocyanogen in chloroform. This material is apparently polymeric, and even when prepared at −50° to −60°C. has the composition $(SCNCl)_3$.[191] A hexamer has also been reported.[192] Reaction of lead(II) thiocyanate in carbon tetrachloride-acetic acid medium with bromine to liberate thiocyanogen and then with iodine gives a solution of thiocyanogen iodide, SCNI.[193] A trichloride of thiocyanogen, $SCNCl_3$, boiling at 152° to 153°C. has been reported,[194] as has the bromide, $SCNBr_3$.[184] The compounds $I(SCN)_3$ and $I(OCN)_3$ are formed when the corresponding metal salts are treated with iodine monochloride.[195]

Other compounds of this general type are the explosive chlorazide, ClN_3,[196] bromazide, BrN_3,[197] and iodazide, IN_3.[198] Chlorazide has been studied comprehensively by Browne and his coworkers,[199, 200] who prepared the compound either by treating an ethereal suspension of silver azide with chlorine at room temperature or by adding acetic acid slowly to an equimolar mixture of sodium azide and sodium hypochlorite in aqueous solution and distilling.[196] The gaseous compound may be condensed to a yellow-orange liquid, which boils at around −15°C. and freezes to a yellow solid at around −100°C. It is a non-conductor and dissolves in butane, pentane, benzene, methanol, ethanol, ether, acetone, chloroform, carbon tetrachloride, and carbon disulfide. It reacts with ammonia to give the materials NH_4Cl and NH_2N_3 or the materials N_2, NH_4Cl, and NH_4N_3 if excess ammonia is present, with pentane to give the substances HN_3 and $C_5H_{11}Cl$, with

[190] V. E. Coslett: *Z. anorg. allgem. Chem.*, **201,** 75 (1931).

[191] A. Baroni: *Atti accad. naz. Lincei, Classe sci. fis., mat. e nat.*, **23,** 871 (1936).

[192] H. Lecher and G. Joseph: *Ber.*, **59B,** 2603 (1926).

[193] H. P. Kauffman and H. Grosse-Oetringhaus: *Oel Kohle Erdoel Teer*, **14,** 199 (1938).

[194] H. P. Kaufmann and J. Liepe: *Ber.*, **57B,** 923 (1924).

[195] J. Cornog, H. W. Horrabin, and R. A. Karges: *J. Am. Chem. Soc.*, **60,** 429 (1938).

[196] F. Raschig: *Ber.*, **41,** 4194 (1908).

[197] D. A. Spencer: *J. Chem. Soc.*, **127,** 216 (1925).

[198] A. Hantzsch: *Ber.*, **33,** 522 (1900).

[199] W. J. Frierson, J. Kronrad, and A. W. Browne: *J. Am. Chem. Soc.*, **65,** 1696 (1943).

[200] W. J. Frierson and A. W. Browne: *J. Am. Chem. Soc.*, **65,** 1698 (1943).

metals to give azides plus chlorides, with phosphorus explosively according to an undetermined pattern, and with silver azide to give azino silver chloride, N_3AgCl, deep blue and decomposing to silver chloride and nitrogen above −30°C. The halazides are treacherous compounds.

The compounds $ClSCSN_3$ and $BrSCSN_3$ have been obtained as probable products of reactions of azidocarbondisulfide with the appropriate halogen in inert solvents such as chloroform at low temperatures.[201] Silver azidodithiocarbonate reacts with bromine in ether to give a tribromo derivative, Br_3SCSN_3.[201] Reports on the substances IOCN and BrOCN have also appeared.[202]

Interhalogenoids. A series of cyanogen derivatives of other halogenoids has been described, including the compounds cyanogen thiocyanate, CNSCN;[178] cyanogen selenocyanate, CNSeCN;[179] cyanogen azide, CNN_3;[203] and cyanogen azidodithiocarbonate, $CNSCSN_3$.[204] These compounds are low melting, comparatively volatile, crystalline solids which may be obtained by such reactions as those indicated by the equations

$$Hg(CN)_2 + 2(SCN)_2 \rightarrow Hg(SCN)_2 + 2CNSCN$$

$$CNBr + NaN_3 \rightarrow NaBr + CNN_3$$

$$CNBr + NaSCSN_3 \rightarrow NaBr + CNSCSN_3$$

$$Hg(CN)_2 + 2(SCSN_3)_2 \rightarrow Hg(SCSN_3)_2 + 2CNSCSN_3$$

Chemically, these materials undergo hydrolysis much as do the halogens. Cyanogen azidodithiocarbonate decomposes to the products N_2, S, $(SCN)_x$, and $(CNSCN)_x$.[204] Other reactions of this compound are shown by the equations[204]

$$CNSCSN_3 + 2OH^- \rightarrow SCSN_3^- + OCN^- + H_2O$$

$$CNSCSN_3 + 2OH^- \rightarrow CN^- + OSCSN_3^- + H_2O$$

$$CNSCSN_3 + 2NH_3 \rightarrow NH_4SCSN_3 + NH_2CN$$

$$CNSCSN_3 + SCSN_3^- \rightarrow CN(SCSN_3)_2^- \rightarrow CN^- + (SCSN_3)_2$$

[201] W. H. Gardner and A. W. Browne: *J. Am. Chem. Soc.*, **49,** 2759 (1927).
[202] L. Birkenbach and M. Linhard: *Ber.*, **62B,** 2261 (1929); **63B,** 2544 (1930).
[203] G. Darzens: *Compt. rend.*, **154,** 1232 (1912).
[204] L. F. Audrieth and A. W. Browne with C. W. Mason: *J. Am. Chem. Soc.*, **52,** 2799 (1930).

In structure these materials are presumed to be comparable to the interhalogens. For example, cyanogen azidodithiocarbonate is considered to possess the structure

$$N{\equiv}C{-}S{-}\underset{\underset{S}{\|}}{C}{-}N{=}N{\equiv}N$$

A comparable thiocyanogen azidodithiocarbonate, $SCNSCSN_3$, has also been suggested,[164] as resulting from the decomposition of azidocarbondisulfide.

Halogenoid Derivatives of Certain Non-metals. That halogenoid derivatives of certain non-metals can be prepared was indicated by Miquel's[205] observation of metathetical reactions between the anhydrous chlorides of silicon, phosphorous, arsenic, etc., and lead thiocyanate. Although preparations of the thiocyanates of phosphorus(III),[206] silicon,[207] and boron[208] by Miquel's general procedure were reported many years ago, it is largely as a result of studies by Forbes and Anderson[209–227] that information on compounds of this type is available. Compounds studied are all either (iso)cyanates or (iso)thiocyanates. The most stable in each series are believed, particularly on the basis of chemical behaviors and molecular refraction data,[209, 220] to have the *iso* configurations —NCO and —NCS.

[205] P. Miquel: *Ann. chim. phys.* [v], **11,** 289 (1877).
[206] A. E. Dixon: *J. Chem. Soc.*, **79,** 541 (1901).
[207] J. E. Reynolds: *J. Chem. Soc.*, **89,** 397 (1906).
[208] H. E. Cocksedge: *J. Chem. Soc.*, **93,** 2177 (1908).
[209] G. S. Forbes and H. H. Anderson: *J. Am. Chem. Soc.*, **62,** 761 (1940).
[210] H. H. Anderson: *J. Am. Chem. Soc.*, **64,** 1757 (1942).
[211] G. S. Forbes and H. H. Anderson: *J. Am. Chem. Soc.*, **65,** 2271 (1943).
[212] H. H. Anderson: *J. Am. Chem. Soc.*, **66,** 934 (1944).
[213] G. S. Forbes and H. H. Anderson: *J. Am. Chem. Soc.*, **66,** 1703 (1944).
[214] H. H. Anderson: *J. Am. Chem. Soc.*, **67,** 223 (1945).
[215] G. S. Forbes and H. H. Anderson: *J. Am. Chem. Soc.*, **67,** 1911 (1945).
[216] H. H. Anderson: *J. Am. Chem. Soc.*, **67,** 2176 (1945).
[217] G. S. Forbes and H. H. Anderson: *J. Am. Chem. Soc.*, **69,** 1241 (1947).
[218] H. H. Anderson: *J. Am. Chem. Soc.*, **69,** 2495 (1947).
[219] G. S. Forbes and H. H. Anderson: *J. Am. Chem. Soc.*, **69,** 3048 (1947).
[220] H. H. Anderson: *J. Am. Chem. Soc.*, **69,** 3049 (1947).
[221] G. S. Forbes and H. H. Anderson: *J. Am. Chem. Soc.*, **70,** 1043 (1948).
[222] H. H. Anderson: *J. Am. Chem. Soc.*, **70,** 1220 (1948).
[223] G. S. Forbes and H. H. Anderson: *J. Am. Chem. Soc.*, **70,** 1222 (1948).
[224] H. H. Anderson: *J. Am. Chem. Soc.*, **71,** 1799 (1949).
[225] *Ibid.*, 1801.
[226] H. H. Anderson: *J. Am. Chem. Soc.*, **72,** 193 (1950).
[227] *Ibid.*, 196.

TABLE 13·13

PHYSICAL CONSTANTS FOR HALOGENOID DERIVATIVES OF CERTAIN NON-METALS

Compound	Melting Point, °C.	Boiling Point, °C.	Density,* grams/ml.	Refractive Index*	Molecular Refraction, ml.	Vapor Pressure Equation Constants† A	Vapor Pressure Equation Constants† B	Heat of Vaporization, kcal./mole	Trouton's Constant	Ref.
1. Silicon Compounds										
$Si(OCN)_4$	34.5	247.2	1.414 (25°C.)	1.4646 (25°C.)		9.8211	3611	16.5	31.7	209
$Si(NCO)_4$	26.0	185.6	1.434 (25°C.)	1.4610 (25°C.)	37.3	9.0198	2816	12.9	26.5	209
$SiF(NCO)_3$	−29.2	134.3	1.456	1.4161						217
$SiF_2(NCO)_2$	−75	68.6	1.437	1.3536		8.3386	1864.9	10.76	26.4	217
$SiF_3(NCO)$		−6.0								217
$SiCl(NCO)_3$	−35	152.0	1.437 (25°C.)	1.4507						212
$SiCl_2(NCO)_2$	−80	117.8	1.437 (25°C.)	1.4380						212
$SiCl_3(NCO)$	−69	86.8	1.445 (25°C.)	1.4262						212
$Si(OCH_3)(NCO)_3$		168.4	1.313	1.4287						213
$Si(OCH_3)_2(NCO)_2$		152.1	1.208	1.4028						213
$Si(OCH_3)_3(NCO)$		137.6	1.123	1.3839						213
$Si(OC_2H_5)(NCO)_3$		179.6	1.236	1.4251	41.06	8.4374	2515	12.9	26.5	221
$Si(OC_2H_5)_2(NCO)_2$		175.4	1.108	1.4046	44.71	8.2577	2411	11.5	25.4	221
$Si(OC_2H_5)_3(NCO)$		172.9	1.015	1.3922	48.2	8.2179	2380	11.0	24.6	221
$Si(CH_3)(NCO)_3$	2.7	170.8	1.267	1.4430	35.39	8.4150	2457	11.2	25.3	223
$Si(CH_3)_2(NCO)_2$	−31.2	139.2	1.076	1.4221	33.60	8.1540	2174	10.0	24.1	223
$Si(CH_3)_3(NCO)$	−49.0	91.0	0.867	1.3960	31.92	7.8446	1807	8.3	22.7	223
$Si(C_2H_5)(NCO)_3$		183.5	1.2191	1.4468	40.1					227

$Si(C_2H_5)_2(NCO)_2$		176.7	1.0223	1.4348	43.4					227
$Si(C_2H_5)_3(NCO)$		165.1	0.8895	1.4295	45.6					227
$Si(n\text{-}C_3H_7)(NCO)_3$		198.2	1.1726	1.4462	44.9					227
$Si(i\text{-}C_3H_7)(NCO)_3$		192.0	1.1626	1.4444	45.2					227
$Si(n\text{-}C_4H_9)(NCO)_3$	−37	215.5	1.141	1.4479	48.53	8.4830	2737	12.5	25.6	223
$Si(C_6H_5)(NCO)_3$		251.9	1.273	1.5210	55.45	8.6663	3038	13.9	26.4	221
$Si(C_6H_5)_2(NCO)_2$	22.9	319.6	1.188	1.5675	73.3	8.6683	3421	15.7	26.5	221
$Si(C_6H_5)_3(NCO)$	95.0	372.0				8.3234	3511	16.1	24.9	221
$Si(C_6H_5CH_2)(NCO)_3$	−11.0	265	1.225	1.5230	60.2					226
$Si(NCS)_4$	143.8	313.0	ca.1.407		70.4	8.4484	3276	13.9	23.7	220
$SiCl_3(NCS)$	−75	129.5	1.461 (24°C.)	1.5091						214
$Si(OCH_3)_3(NCS)$		170.5	1.134	1.4426		ca.9.48821	ca.2931	ca.13.4	ca.30.2	216
$Si(OC_2H_5)_3(NCS)$		205.8	1.036	1.4431	73.7					226
$Si(CH_3)(NCS)_3$	72.4	266.8	1.304		59.8	8.4273	2995	13.7	25.4	220
$Si(CH_3)_2(NCS)_2$	18.0	217.3	1.142	1.5677	49.92	8.3006	2658	12.15	24.8	220
$Si(CH_3)_3(NCS)$	−32.8	143.1	0.931	1.4820	40.18	7.7899	2043	9.35	22.5	220
$Si(C_2H_5)(NCS)_3$		276	1.264	1.6195	64.25					225
$Si(C_2H_5)_2(NCS)_2$		245.5	1.089	1.5540	59.54					225
$Si(C_2H_5)_3(NCS)$		210.5	0.934	1.4944	54.06					225
$Si(n\text{-}C_3H_7)(NCS)_3$		289.5	1.2248	1.6014	68.7					227
$Si(i\text{-}C_3H_7)(NCS)_3$		279	1.2177	1.6066	69.5					227
$Si(n\text{-}C_4H_9)(NCS)_3$	−0.5	300.6	1.189	1.5928	73.7					226
$Si(C_6H_5)(NCS)_3$	52	339.6	1.291 (31°C.)			8.7676	3607	16.5	26.9	222
$Si(C_6H_5)_2(NCS)_2$	46	376	1.188 (30°C.)			8.9132	3913	17.9	27.6	222
$Si(C_6H_5)_3(NCS)$	76	396				8.2182	3572	16.3	24.4	222
$Si(C_6H_5CH_2)(NCS)_3$	36.0	348.9	1.275							226
$Si_2O(NCO)_6$	44.5	260 (dec.)			57.4					219
$Si_3O_2(NCO)_8$		170 (2mm.)			78.1					219
$Si_2O(NCS)_6$	120–121	347 (?)								219

TABLE 13·13 (*Continued*)

Compound	Melting Point, °C.	Boiling Point, °C.	Density* grams/ml.	Refractive Index*	Molecular Refraction, ml.	Vapor Pressure Equation Constants†		Heat of Vaporization, kcal./mole	Trouton's Constant	Ref.
						A	B			
2. Germanium Compounds										
$Ge(NCO)_4$	−8.0	204.0	1.7714	1.4824	38.77	8.6578	2757	12.6	26.4	211, 228
$Ge(C_2H_5)(NCO)_3$	−31	225.4	1.5344	1.4739	41.70	8.4195	2760	12.7	25.3	224
$Ge(C_2H_5)_2(NCO)_2$	−32	226.0	1.330	1.4619	44.39	8.0861	2597	11.9	23.8	224
$Ge(C_2H_5)_3(NCO)$	−26.4	200.4	1.514	1.4519	47.25	7.9424	2396	11.0	23.1	224
3. Phosphorus Compounds										
$P(NCO)_3$	−2	169.3	1.439 (25°C.)	1.5352 (25°C.)		8.7455	2595	11.9	26.8	209
$PF(NCO)_2$	−55.0	98.7	1.475	1.4678	25.25	8.3210	2022.7	9.25	24.8	218
$PF_2(NCO)$	ca. −108	12.3	ca.1.444	1.3700	ca.17.38					218
$PCl(NCO)_2$	−50	134.6	1.505			8.87981	2445.2	11.2	27.4	216
$PCl_2(NCO)$	−99	104.4	1.513 (31°C.)							214
$PO(NCO)_3$	5.0	193.1	1.570	1.4804		9.1682	2931	13.41	28.8	210
$PF_2(NCS)$	−95	90.3	1.452	1.4978	25.66	7.7045	1752.9	8.08	22.2	218
$PCl_2(NCS)$	−76	148	1.546			9.42681	2756.6	12.6	29.9	216
$PO(NCS)_3$	13.8	300.1	1.484			8.5330	3240	14.82	25.8	210
$POCl_2(NCS)$	−55	173	1.587 (25°C.)	1.5649						214
$PS(NCO)_3$		215	1.538	1.5116		10.032	3492	ca.16.0	ca.33	211
4. Arsenic Compounds										
$As(NCO)_3$	97.1	224.0				8.7638	2924	14.8	26.9	210

* At 20°C., unless otherwise stated.

† $\log p_{mm} = A - B/T$.

In addition to simple halogenoid derivatives of silicon,[209] germanium,[211] phosphorus,[209] and arsenic,[210] halide-halogenoid derivatives of silicon[212, 217] and phosphorus,[214, 216, 218] mixed alkyl-,[220, 221, 225, 227] aryl-,[221, 222] and alkoxy-[213, 226] halogenoid derivatives of silicon in particular, and oxy-halogenoid derivatives of silicon[219] and phosphorus[210] have been characterized. Evidence has been obtained also for the existence of antimony(III),[210] thionyl, sulfur, and chromyl isocyanates[211] and of thionyl, sulfuryl, sulfur, and chromyl isothiocyanates[211] as unstable compounds.

The physical constants for the best characterized of these compounds are summarized in Table 13·13. The compounds are quite generally soluble in non-polar solvents. It is apparent that they are all covalent compounds, although many appear to be associated in the liquid state. Comparison of their properties with those of the corresponding halides, as tabulated in subsequent chapters, shows these compounds to be strictly comparable to the halides. Chemically, these halogenoid derivatives are like the anhydrous halides and substituted halides in the ease with which they undergo hydrolysis. Some of the isocyanates isomerize to the less volatile cyanates on heating.[210, 211] Polymerization reactions also occur.[211] Redistribution of attached groups occurs in certain cases. Thus the compound $PCl(NCO)_2$ rapidly rearranges to a mixture of $P(NCO)_3$ and of $PCl_2(NCO)$,[214] and the substance $SiCl_3(NCS)$ changes to a mixture of $SiCl_4$ and $Si(NCS)_4$.[215]

These compounds are prepared and purified in most cases by reacting the appropriate simple (e.g., $SiCl_4$, PCl_3) or substituted (e.g., R_xSiCl_{4-x}, $POCl_3$) anhydrous chloride with silver (iso)cyanate or silver (iso)-thiocyanate in benzene (under reflux if necessary), filtering off the precipitated silver chloride, evaporating off the solvent, and fractionally distilling.[209–211, 214, 220, 228]

Alternatively, mixed compounds are formed when the anhydrous chloride (e.g., $SiCl_4$) and the simple halogenoid (e.g., $Si(NCO)_4$) are mixed in a hot tube at 600°C.[212] Reaction of silicon tetraisocyanate with methanol yields a mixture of silicon methoxyisocyanates by an alcoholysis reaction.[213] Hydrolysis of silicon tetraisocyanate and tetraisothiocyanate yields, respectively, the oxy compounds Si_nO_{n-1}-$(NCO)_{2n+2}$ and $Si_2O(NCS)_6$.[219] Fluo-halogenoid derivatives are obtained by fluorination of the corresponding halogenoids (e.g., $Si(NCO)_4$,[217] $P(NCO)_3$,[218] $P(NCS)_3$,[218]) with antimony(III) fluoride (p. 428). Triphenylsilyl isocyanate $[Si(C_6H_4)_3(NCO)]$ is also obtainable from the chloride by reaction with urea, thiourea, and sodium

[228] A. W. Laubengayer and L. Reggel: *J. Am. Chem. Soc.*, **65**, 1783 (1943).

urethane,[229] and reaction of triphenylsilyl chloride with lead or ammonium thiocyanate yields triphenylsilyl isothiocyanate.[229] Reactions in which non-metal halides are converted into halogenoids appear to be in accord with Anderson's generalization that atoms connected to one central atom can displace atoms connected to a second central atom only when the atom to be replaced has the larger covalent single bond radius.[230]

SUGGESTED SUPPLEMENTARY REFERENCES

N. V. Sidgwick: *The Chemical Elements and Their Compounds*, pp. 1097–1261. Clarendon Press, Oxford (1950).

A. F. Wells: *Structural Inorganic Chemistry*, 2nd Ed., Ch. VIII. Clarendon Press, Oxford (1950).

W. M. Latimer: *The Oxidation States of the Elements and Their Potentials in Aqueous Solutions*, Ch. V. Prentice-Hall, New York (1938).

Gmelin's *Handbuch der anorganischen Chemie*, 8th Auflage, System Nummern 5, 6, 7, 8. Verlag Chemie, G.m.b.h., Leipzig-Berlin (1926–1933).

J. H. Simons (Ed.): *Fluorine Chemistry*, Vol. I. Academic Press, New York (1950).

---

229 H. Gilman, B. Hofferth, and H. W. Melvin: *J. Am. Chem. Soc.*, **72**, 3045 (1950).

230 H. H. Anderson: *J. Am. Chem. Soc.*, **72**, 2761 (1950).

CHAPTER **14**

Periodic Group VIb
The Oxygen Family

The elements oxygen and sulfur are comparatively common, the quantities in the igneous rocks of the earth being 46.6% and 0.052%, respectively. The other members of the oxygen family, namely, selenium, tellurium, and polonium, are comparatively rare, the percentages in the igneous rocks being roughly 10^{-7}, 10^{-7}, and 10^{-14}, respectively. In this chapter primary stress is placed upon the family as a whole, especially upon those trends, variations, and differences which follow from the considerations offered in Part I of this book. Emphasis upon specific phases of chemistry is restricted to oxygen and sulfur, except where consideration of the other elements is necessary to a more complete understanding of the family as a whole.

FAMILY RELATIONSHIPS AMONG THE ELEMENTS

Numerical data relating to the members of this family are summarized in Table 14·1. Paralleling the addition of more and more electrons are the expected general increases in the sizes of atoms of the element and of ionic species derived from those atoms. Corresponding increases in freezing and boiling points, in heats of fusion and vaporization, and in ionization potentials are apparent, whereas attractions for electrons as measured by electron affinity and electronegativity decrease. The same trends characterize the halogens (p. 419).

Since atoms of these elements are but two electrons short of inert gas atom structures, tendencies to achieve these structures by either the gain or the sharing of electrons would be expected. Comparison of the electronegativities of these elements with those of the corresponding halogens indicates a marked decrease in ability to gain electrons to form true simple anions in going from the halogens to these elements. The electronegativity of oxygen is such that binary ionic compounds will result for essentially all metallic elements (p. 208), but for the other elements only those compounds with the most electropositive metals can be more than 50% ionic (pp. 206–208). It is apparent, too, that but little difference can be expected in the tendencies of sulfur, selenium, and tellurium to form dinegative ions. Bonds which are essentially covalent (less than 50% ionic) result with

TABLE 14·1
NUMERICAL PROPERTIES OF GROUP VIB ELEMENTS

Property	Oxygen	Sulfur	Selenium	Tellurium
Atomic number	8	16	34	52
Outer electronic configuration	$2s^2 2p^4$	$3s^2 3p^4$	$4s^2 4p^4$	$5s^2 5p^4$
Atomic weight	16.0000	32.066	78.96	127.61
Stable isotopes, mass numbers	16, 17, 18	32, 33, 34, 36	74, 76, 77, 78, 80, 82	120, 122, 123, 124, 125, 126, 128, 130
Density of solid, grams/cc.	1.27	2.06* 1.96§	4.80† 4.50§	6.24‡
Atomic volume of solid, cc.	12.6	15.56* 16.35§	16.45† 17.54§	20.24
Melting point, °C.	−218.9	118.95§	217.4†	449.8‡
Boiling point, °C.	−182.96	444.60	684.8	1390
Heat of fusion, kcal./gram atom	0.053	0.35	1.6	4.27
Heat of vaporization, kcal./gram atom	0.814	2.52	4.35	11.0
Covalent radius, A	0.74	1.04*	1.14	1.37
Ionization potential, ev	13.614	10.357	9.750	9.01
Electron affinity, ev‖	−7.28	−3.44	−4.21	....
Electronegativity	3.5	2.5	2.4	2.1
Crystal radii, A				
X^{-2} in X^{-2}	1.40	1.84	1.98	2.21
X^{+6} in XO_4^{-2}	0.09	0.29	0.42	0.56
E^0_{298} for $H_2X \rightleftharpoons X + 2H^+ + 2e^-$, volts	−0.815	−0.14	+0.35	+0.69

* Rhombic. † Hexagonal-rhombohedral, gray.
‡ Hexagonal-rhombohedral, metallic. § Monoclinic. ‖ 2 electrons.

a variety of less electronegative non-metals and metals, and in these the Group VIb elements may be thought of as possessing formal charges of −2.

The tendency to share electron pairs between like atoms is somewhat less pronounced for these elements than for the halogens. For oxygen, the molecules O_2 and O_3 are stable. The paramagnetic character of the diatomic oxygen molecule corresponds to the presence of two unpaired electrons, and it is probable that the structure (p. 212)

$$:\mathrm{O}\overset{\cdot\cdot\cdot}{\underset{\cdot\cdot\cdot}{\text{——}}}\mathrm{O}:$$

containing two 3-electron bonds more closely describes this molecule than does any other.[1] Certainly, structures involving the complete pairing of electrons are ruled out. In terms of this structure, it is not surprising that two such molecules should associate with each other to give diamagnetic O_4 molecules,[2] although it does not appear that true electron pair bonding characterizes the tetratomic molecule. This species and ozone are described in more detail later (pp. 485–487). For sulfur, electron pair sharing results in the formation of polyatomic chains and rings, of which the ring species S_8 is perhaps most common (p. 487). Selenium and tellurium also yield polyatomic molecules in solution and in the gaseous state. The molecules S_2, Se_2, and Te_2 are undoubtedly strictly comparable with the molecule O_2 in structures.[1]

Positive oxidation states are somewhat more common than for the halogens because the reduced electronegativities of elements of the oxygen family permit a greater variety of compounds containing such states and render them somewhat less oxidizing. Oxygen, of course, shows positive oxidation only in compounds containing fluorine (p. 430), but, as one proceeds from sulfur to tellurium (and polonium), such states become increasingly common. Interestingly enough, such states are usually +4 and +6, only a few comparatively unstable compounds having been prepared in which the elements are in +2 states. Among these are the sulfoxylates derived from sulfoxylic acid, H_2SO_2, oxides (SO, SeO, TeO), and a few halides (e.g., SCl_2, $TeCl_2$). A few odd positive oxidation states such as +3 and +5 are reported, but these probably represent more nearly average formal values than true values since they characterize the elements in ions such as $S_2O_4^{-2}$, $S_2O_6^{-2}$, etc., where complete bonding to but a single other type of element is absent.

As is to be expected, the bonding in these positive oxidation states is primarily covalent. Such compounds are normally volatile or anionic. Those most commonly encountered for sulfur, selenium, tellurium, and polonium contain oxygen. In the +4 state, these elements show both oxidizing and reducing properties; in the +6 state, they are only oxidizing. The characteristics of sulfur compounds in these oxidation states are considered in later sections (pp. 518–547), as are a number of comparisons among the sulfur, selenium, and tellurium compounds.

[1] L. Pauling: *The Nature of the Chemical Bond*, 2nd Ed., pp. 272–274. Cornell University Press. Ithaca (1940).

[2] G. N. Lewis: *J. Am. Chem. Soc.*, **46**, 2027 (1924).

MODIFICATIONS OF THE FREE ELEMENTS

All the elements in this family exist in a variety of modifications. These modifications may be true allotropic modifications or they may differ from each other in molecular complexity.

Oxygen

Ordinary oxygen consists essentially of diatomic molecules, the characteristics of which have been described already. Other forms of oxygen contain more or less than two atoms to the molecule.

Atomic Oxygen. Atomic oxygen, like atomic hydrogen (p. 398), has no really stable existence. The heat of dissociation of molecular oxygen is some −117.3 kcal. per mole, from which it is apparent that not only must atomic oxygen be produced under energy-rich conditions, but also, once it is formed, it must revert to molecular oxygen very readily. The latter process is catalyzed by many surfaces, and the amount of energy liberated is sufficient to melt many metals (e.g., platinum). The former process may be effected by passing molecular oxygen through an electric discharge at pressures of about 1 mm.,[3] by passing molecular oxygen at low pressures through a glow discharge as in the production of ozone (p. 486),[4] or by irradiating molecular oxygen at wavelengths below that at which oxygen absorbs continuously (i.e., below 1900 A), using an aluminum spark or a xenon discharge tube.[5] The product is never pure atomic oxygen, but concentrations approaching 80% have been obtained.[3]

Atomic oxygen combines directly with molecular oxygen to yield ozone, the energy of activation of the process being only 4 kcal. per mole. This reaction offers a convenient procedure for the preparation of ozone, and it is probable that it is the governing process in ozone formation in the glow discharge. The oxidizing power of atomic oxygen is apparent from the couple

$$H_2O \rightleftharpoons O(g) + 2H^+ + 2e^- \quad E^0_{298} = -2.2 \text{ volts}$$

Atomic oxygen thus reacts with a variety of reducing agents,[6] among them carbon disulfide, hydrogen sulfide, hydrogen chloride, hydrogen bromide, and a variety of hydrocarbons. Hydrogen is converted ultimately to water, but the reaction is slow, as is also the reaction with carbon monoxide. Many of the reactions appear to involve primary

[3] P. Harteck and U. Kopsch: *Z. physik. Chem.*, **B12**, 327 (1931).

[4] E. Wrede: *Z. Physik*, **54**, 53 (1929).

[5] W. Groth: *Z. Elektrochem.*, **42**, 533 (1936).

[6] K. H. Geib: *Ergeb. exakt. Naturw.*, **15**, 44 (1936).

addition of oxygen, followed by other incompletely understood changes. Thus acetylene at low temperatures adds two oxygen atoms per mole and benzene adds three. Decomposition follows as the temperature is raised. Further studies on the behavior of atomic oxygen should be fruitful.

Ozone. Ozone is a blue gas, the vapor density of which corresponds to the molecular formula O_3. On cooling, it condenses to a diamagnetic blue liquid which boils at −112.4°C. and freezes to a violet-black crystalline solid melting at −249.7°C. The critical temperature and pressure are, respectively, −5°C. and 92.3 atm. Gaseous ozone dissolves to the extent of 0.494 volume in 1 volume of water at 0°C. (1 atm.) and is somewhat more soluble than molecular oxygen. Carbon tetrachloride and chloroform are better solvents for the gas. Liquid ozone and liquid oxygen appear to be miscible only over limited ranges, separation into oxygen- and ozone-rich layers occurring as the ozone concentration increases.

Chemically, ozone is characterized by its oxidizing power, by its ability to add to ethylenic double bonds, and by its tendency to revert to molecular oxygen in terms of the equation

$$O_3 \rightleftharpoons \tfrac{3}{2}O_2 + 34.2 \text{ kcal.}$$

The oxidizing power of ozone is apparent from the couples

$$O_2 + H_2O \rightleftharpoons O_3 + 2H^+ + 2e^- \qquad E^\circ = -2.07 \text{ volts}$$

$$O_2 + 2OH^- \rightleftharpoons O_3 + H_2O + 2e^- \qquad = -1.24$$

from which it is seen that in acidic solutions ozone is exceeded in oxidizing power only by fluorine and materials such as oxygen difluoride, atomic oxygen, and hydroxyl radical, whereas in alkaline solutions it is exceeded only by hydroxyl radical. Many oxidations, among them ammonia to nitrite or nitrate, sulfur (moist) to sulfuric acid, iodine (moist) to iodic acid, and silver(I) to silver(II and III), are thus effected. Because the by-product of such reactions is only molecular oxygen, ozone has been suggested as an analytical oxidizing agent.[7] Addition of ozone to ethylenic linkages is of particular importance in the characterization of organic compounds because hydrolysis of the resulting ozonides to aldehydes causes rupture at the double bond positions. The exothermic reversion of ozone to molecular oxygen often proceeds with explosive violence. Although pure liquid ozone may be distilled without decomposition in the absence of catalysis, reversion to oxygen becomes more rapid as temperature increases and

[7] H. H. Willard and L. L. Merritt: *Ind. Eng. Chem.*, Anal. Ed., **14**, 486 (1942).

is apparently instantaneous at 300°C. or above. Many metals, metal oxides, and other materials (e.g., N_2O_5, Cl_2, Br_2) catalyze the reaction.

The structure of ozone has been the subject of considerable controversy. Early proposals of straight-line or cyclic structures are not compatible with infrared and electron diffraction data. These data indicate clearly that the structure is angular, but considerable disagreement as to the magnitude of the O—O—O angle has resulted. The electron diffraction studies of Shand and Spurr[8] suggest an isosceles triangle arrangement with an angle of 127 ± 3° and an O—O bond distance of 1.26 ± 0.02 A. This structure is assumed to involve resonance among the forms

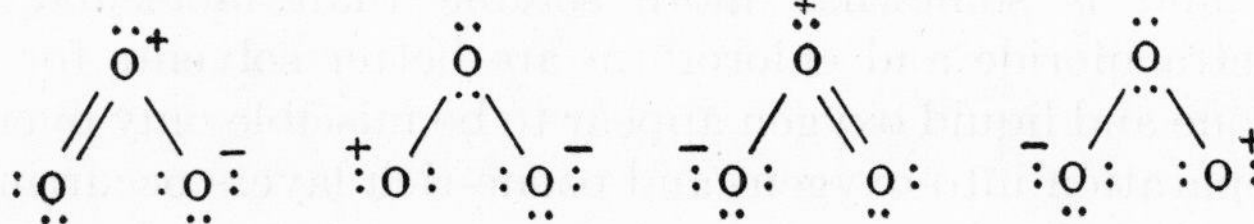

since the measured bond distance is between that for a single bond (1.48 A) and a double bond (1.10 A). This structure appears to be the most satisfactory yet proposed, although it is not in complete agreement with spectroscopic data.[9]

Ozone can be obtained directly from molecular oxygen or indirectly from certain oxygen-containing compounds. The necessary energy for the conversion of molecular oxygen to ozone can be supplied thermally (as in heating a platinum wire in contact with liquid oxygen), radiantly (as when oxygen is irradiated with light of about 2090 A wavelength), electrically (as when oxygen or air is passed through a silent electric discharge), or chemically (as is done for atomic oxygen). Use of the silent electric discharge is the principle upon which most laboratory and large-scale ozonizers depend. Unfortunately, the yields are low (5% using air, 15% using oxygen), and the product is normally contaminated with oxides of nitrogen. Certain chemical reactions, among them reaction of fluorine with water, heating periodic acid, and reaction of ammonium peroxydisulfate with nitric acid, yield ozone as a by-product. More promising for preparative purposes are electrochemical procedures. For instance, anodic oxidation of dilute sulfuric acid at low temperatures gives ozone in good yields.[10] It has been shown that electrolysis of eutectic mixtures of perchloric acid and water at −50°C. or of perchloric acid solutions containing sodium or magnesium perchlorate at somewhat lower temperatures yields ozone

[8] W. Shand and R. A. Spurr: *J. Am. Chem. Soc.*, **65**, 179 (1943).

[9] G. Glockler and G. Matlack: *J. Chem. Phys.*, **14**, 505 (1946).

[10] F. Fischer and K. Massenez: *Z. anorg. Chem.*, **52**, 202, 229 (1907).

smoothly and efficiently by anodic oxidation of water.[11] Concentrations of above 20% are obtained directly, using low overall pressures (0.1 atm.), platinum anodes, and pure lead cathodes. The product is free from impurities beyond hydrogen and oxygen. This process shows considerable promise, especially since the raw material is water. Ozone can be separated from oxygen by liquefaction and fractional distillation.[12]

Tetratomic Oxygen. Although ordinary oxygen is essentially completely diatomic, sufficient tetratomic (O_4) molecules are present to be detectable by spectroscopic means.[13] At lower temperatures, the reaction $2O_2 \rightarrow O_4$ is favored, and at liquid air temperatures the concentration of O_4 molecules becomes appreciable.[2] The species has also been reported in solid oxygen.[14] But little is known about the O_4 molecule, although it appears to be made up of two O_2 molecules bonded together by forces which are weaker than those in electron pair bonds but stronger than those of the pure van der Waals type. The heat of formation of the species O_4 from molecular oxygen is only 0.13 kcal. per mole.

Sulfur

Sulfur exists in a variety of modifications in either the solid, liquid, or gaseous state. The literature describing these modifications is somewhat involved and contradictory.[15] Specific data relative to these forms are given in Table 14·2. Much of the complication arising from the existence of these materials is due to the presence of molecules of varying complexities. Chief among such species are the molecules corresponding in composition to the formula S_8. They are found in all three physical states and represent puckered octagonal rings which may be diagrammed as

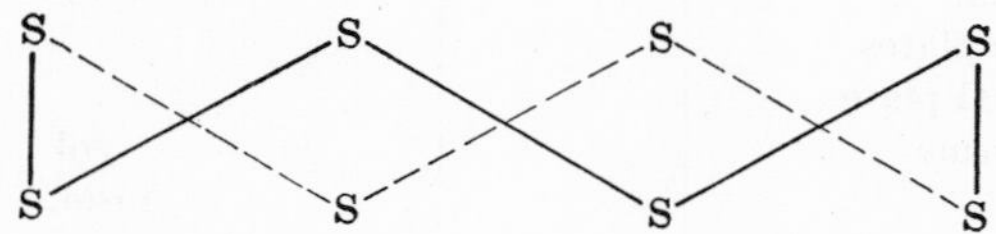

where the S—S bond distance is 2.12 A and the bond angel is 105°.[16]

[11] G. L. Putnam, R. W. Moulton, W. W. Fillmore, and L. H. Clark: *Trans. Electrochem. Soc.*, **93**, 211 (1948).
[12] S. Karrer and O. R. Wulf: *J. Am. Chem. Soc.*, **44**, 239 (1922).
[13] O. R. Wulf: *Proc. Natl. Acad. Sci.*, **14**, 609 (1928).
[14] L. Vegard: *Nature*, **136**, 720 (1935).
[15] H. F. Schaeffer and G. D. Palmer: *J. Chem. Education*, **17**, 473 (1940).
[16] B. E. Warren and J. T. Burwell: *J. Chem. Phys.*, **3**, 6 (1935).

TABLE 14·2
MODIFICATIONS OF SOLID SULFUR

Modification	Designation	Molecular Formula	Crystal Constants, $a:b:c$	Bond Angle, β
1. Crystalline forms				
a. rhombic	S_α or S_I	S_8	0.814:1:1.905	
b. monoclinic				
1. prismatic	S_β or S_{II}	S_8	1.996:1:0.9998	84°14′
2. nacreous	S_γ or S_{III}		1.061:1:0.709	88°13′
3.	S_δ or S_{IV}			
c. rhombohedral	S_ϕ or S_ρ	S_6		
d. miscellaneous				
1. tetragonal	S_θ			
2. rhombic plates	S_ζ			
3. hexagonal plates	S_η			
2. Amorphous forms	S_λ	S_8		
	S_μ			
	S_π	S_4		
3. Plastic form	$S_\mu + S_\lambda$			

TABLE 14·2 (*Continued*)

Modification	Melting Point, °C.	Specific Gravity	Solubility in CS_2	Range of Existence
1. Crystalline forms				
a. rhombic	112.8	2.06	sol	below 95.5°
b. monoclinic				
1. prismatic	118.75	1.96	sol.	95.5–118.75
2. nacreous	106.8		sol.	
3.				unstable
c. rhombohedral		2.135	sol.	?
d. miscellaneous				
1. tetragonal				
2. rhombic plates				
3. hexagonal plates				
2. Amorphous forms			sol.	
			insol.	above 160°
				ca. 200°
3. Plastic form				

Calculations by Pauling[17] give a bond angle of 102°, in excellent agreement with the observed value. Since the angles in this ring are nearly the same as the normal angle (ca. 100°) for S—S bonds,[17] the stability of the S_8 arrangement in comparison with other structures is

[17] L. Pauling: *Proc. Natl. Acad. Sci.*, **35**, 495 (1949).

apparent. Species with compositions S_6 and S_4 are also found in the solid and liquid states. They appear to be chain structures. In the vapor state at temperatures between 500°C. and 850°C., S_2 molecules appear, and they in turn dissociate to some extent at 1900 to 2000°C.

Solid Sulfur. Rhombic sulfur (S_α) and the common monoclinic form (S_β) undergo enantiotropic change at 95.5°C. The transformation from S_α to S_β is endothermic to the extent of 0.105 kcal. per gram atom and is accompanied by an increase in volume. The rates at which these reversible transformations take place are so slow that either form may often be preserved for days at a temperature somewhat removed from the transition value. Freezing point data for solutions in non-polar solvents are in agreement with the formula S_8. The rhombic form is the stable crystalline form at room temperature. If crystals of this form are maintained at around 100°C. for several hours, they become opaque owing to transformation into aggregates of monoclinic crystals. Monoclinic sulfur also forms when molten sulfur is allowed to crystallize slowly or when sulfur is crystallized above the transition temperature from a solvent such as toluene.

The other crystalline forms of sulfur are of less importance. They are prepared by rather specialized techniques[15] and are commonly sufficiently unstable to be difficult to study. It appears that on cooling sulfur the following transformations occur:

$$S_\theta \rightarrow S_\delta \rightarrow S_\eta \rightarrow S_\zeta \rightarrow S_\gamma \rightarrow S_\beta \rightleftharpoons S_\alpha$$

all transitions being monotropic except the last.[18] Another form, S_ρ, is obtained by extracting an acidified thiosulfate solution with toluene. Except for S_α and S_β, it is probably the most important of the crystalline modifications.

A variety of amorphous forms can also be prepared under specific conditions. The commonest form is probably S_μ, which forms when sulfur melts and which increases in quantity as the temperature rises. The relations existing among S_μ, S_λ, and S_π are considered in the next section. The white amorphous material remaining when flowers of sulfur are extracted with carbon disulfide may be S_μ. Milk of sulfur, precipitated by action of acids on polysulfide solutions, appears to be largely S_λ. Colloidal sulfur may be either S_λ or S_μ.

Plastic sulfur, obtained by the sudden cooling of molten sulfur heated above 160°C., is amorphous like rubber, but when stretched it gives an x-ray diagram characteristic of fiber structures. It appears that the stretched material contains chains of sulfur atoms arranged

[18] E. Korinth: *Z. anorg. allgem. Chem.*, **174**, 57 (1928).

parallel to the direction of stretching.[19, 20] Gingrich[21] reports that each sulfur atom has two nearest neighbors 2.08 A removed. Pauling[17] believes each unit in plastic sulfur is made up of sixteen parallel, seven-atom, two-turn spirals. On standing, plastic sulfur reverts slowly to an opaque and brittle material consisting of S_α and S_μ. At temperatures below -29°C., crystallization does not occur. Plastic sulfur can be prepared also by the action of concentrated nitric acid on solid sodium thiosulfate, by the interaction of hydrogen sulfide and sulfur dioxide, or by decomposition of xanthates. In all cases, it appears to result from the rupture of S_8 rings. Plastic sulfur can be preserved by incorporating into it such materials as iodine, arsenic, thallium, the oxides of arsenic or thallium, phosphorus sulfides, and various phenolic products. The combined high elasticity (elongations of 800 to 1000%) and chemical inertness of plastic sulfur suggest that a method imparting permanent stability to the plastic material might well yield a product of technical importance.

Liquid Sulfur. When sulfur is heated rapidly, it melts at 114.5°C. to a pale yellow, mobile liquid. This so-called *natural* melting point is above the true melting point of S_α and below the true melting point of S_β. These true melting points are the temperatures at which crystalline sulfur is in equilibrium with molten S_λ. However, the presence of S_π alters the true melting points, the natural melting point then being the temperature at which crystalline sulfur is in equilibrium with an equilibrium mixture of S_λ and S_π. The presence of S_μ has no effect because at this temperature rapid transformation of S_μ to S_λ and S_π occurs. The normal phase relations involving liquid, solid, and gaseous forms of sulfur are shown in Figure 14·1.

As the temperature of mobile molten sulfur is raised, the liquid becomes dark brown at 160° to 170°C. and very viscous, maximum viscosity resulting in the neighborhood of 200°C. Further increase in temperature is accompanied by decreased viscosity. These phenomena have been attributed to the presence of more than a single species in liquid sulfur formed by a type of dynamic equilibrium. The form S_λ, which results when crystalline sulfur first melts, appears to be converted to S_μ as temperature increases. At the same time, S_π is also formed. Liquid sulfur is therefore a mixture of the three species, S_λ, S_μ, and S_π. The relative percentages of these materials as a function of temperature have been evaluated by Aten.[22] For example,

[19] K. H. Meyer and Y. Go: *Helv. Chim. Acta*, **17**, 1081 (1934).

[20] J. J. Trillat and H. Forestier: *Bull. soc. chim.*, **51**, 248 (1932).

[21] N. S. Gingrich: *J. Chem. Phys.*, **8**, 29 (1940).

[22] A. H. W. Aten: *Z. physik. Chem.*, **88**, 321 (1914).

values at 160°C. are S_μ 4.1%, S_π 6.7%, and S_λ 89.2%. The quantity of S_π reaches a maximum in the region 160° to 200°C., but the quantity of S_μ continues to increase up to the boiling point. The molecular formula for S_π is S_4; that for S_μ is sometimes given as S_6. Dissociation of the cyclic S_8 molecules to produce chains which may become entangled with each other is said to cause the viscosity increase.[16]

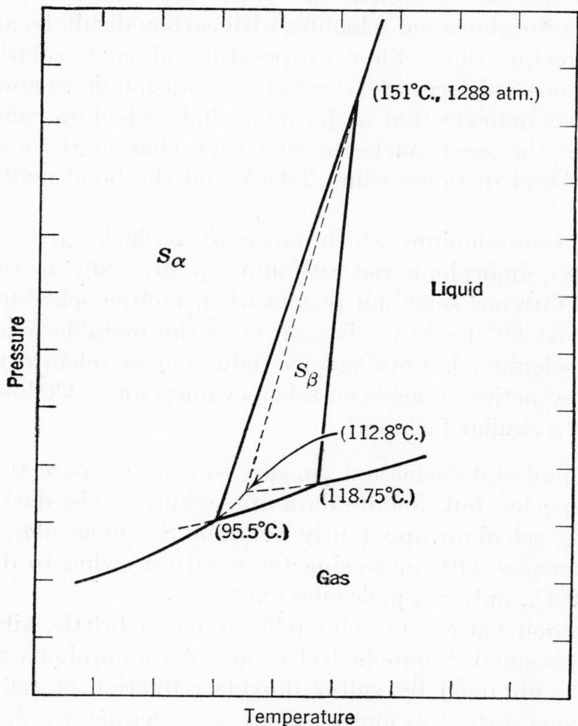

Fig. 14·1. Phase relations for sulfur. (Not drawn to scale.)

Gaseous Sulfur. Sulfur boils at 444.6°C., yielding a red vapor which becomes yellow as the temperature is increased. Vapor density determinations indicate the presence of S_8, S_6, and S_2 molecules, depending on the temperature (p. 489).

Selenium and tellurium

The modifications of selenium appear to be similar to those of sulfur, although they have been studied less extensively. The following solid forms can be distinguished:

1. *Metallic* or *gray* selenium, a hexagonal crystalline form, which is soluble in chloroform but insoluble in carbon disulfide. It is obtained by heating other solid forms of selenium and is the stable form at room temperature. Its electrical conductivity is increased some threefold to 200-fold by exposure to light, a property which is used to advantage in certain photocells.

2. *Monoclinic* or *red* selenium, which is obtained by extracting vitreous or amorphous red selenium with carbon disulfide, and evaporating or precipitating. Slow evaporation of such solutions below 72°C. gives one red form (Se_α); rapid evaporation gives another (Se_β). X-ray studies indicate that alpha monoclinic selenium consists of Se_8 molecules of the same puckered ring type characteristic of rhombic sulfur, the bond distance being 2.34 A and the bond angle 105.3° ± 2.3.[23]

3. *Amorphous* selenium, which may exist as black, vitreous selenium (sp. gr. 4.28), amorphous red selenium (sp. gr. 4.26), or red colloidal selenium. Vitreous selenium results when molten selenium is cooled suddenly. At 60° to 80°C., it reverts to the metallic form. Amorphous red selenium is obtained by reduction of selenite with sulfur dioxide or by action of acids on selenocyanate ion. Colloidal sols are obtained in a similar fashion.

In the liquid state selenium appears to exist as more than a single molecular species, but definite data are lacking. The dark red vapor from boiling selenium apparently contains Se_8 molecules, but vapor density decreases with increasing temperature owing to dissociation. Above 1400°C., only Se_2 molecules exist.

The common variety of solid tellurium is a brittle, silvery-white, metallic, hexagonal-rhombohedral form. An amorphous variety (sp. gr. 6.015) is obtained by sulfur dioxide reduction of tellurium(IV). In the gaseous state, Te_2 molecules are well characterized.

CHEMICAL CHARACTERISTICS OF THE ELEMENTS

The more important aspects of the chemical behavior of the elements in this family are summarized in Table 14·3. The chemical characteristics of these elements are much less amenable to systematic treatment than are those of the halogens (Ch. 13) since alteration from true non-metallic character (with oxygen) to essentially metallic character (with tellurium) is much more profound in this family. The type reactions described in Table 14·3 are more those of sulfur, selenium,

[23] R. D. Burbank: Navy Contract N5ori-07801, Massachusetts Institute of Technology, *Technical Report* 37, June, 1950.

and tellurium than of the family as a whole. As is true of the physical characteristics, the chemical characteristics of oxygen are considerably out of line with those of its congeners. The small size of oxygen imparts enhanced oxidizing power and thus greater reactivity toward a variety of materials. Indeed, oxygen is chemically somewhat more like the halogens than like sulfur, selenium, and tellurium. Certain of these differences are apparent in subsequent sections of this chapter.

TABLE 14·3
CHEMICAL CHARACTERISTICS OF GROUP VIB ELEMENTS

General Equation*	Remarks
$xX + yM \longrightarrow M_yX_x$	With many metals
$zX + M_xX_y \longrightarrow M_xX_{y+z}$	Especially with S, Se
$xX + X^{-2} \longrightarrow X^{-2}{}_{x+1}$	With S, Se
$X + H_2 \longrightarrow H_2X$	With decreasing vigor in the series O_2, S, Se, Te.
$X + 3F_2 \longrightarrow XF_6$	With S, Se, Te, and excess F_2
$2X + 5F_2 \longrightarrow X_2F_{10}$	With S, Se, Te
$2X + Cl_2 \longrightarrow X_2Cl_2$†	With S, Se (Te gives $TeCl_2$)
$X_2Cl_2 + Cl_2 \longrightarrow 2XCl_2$†	With S, Se
$X + 2Cl_2 \longrightarrow XCl_4$†	With S, Se, Te, and excess Cl_2
$X + O_2 \longrightarrow XO_2$	With S (with Se, use $O_2 + NO_2$)
$3X + 4HNO_3 \longrightarrow 3XO_2 + 2H_2O + 4NO$	With S, Se, Te
$3X + 6OH^- \longrightarrow XO_3{}^{-2} + 2X^{-2} + 3H_2O$	With S

* X = S, Se, Te specifically, and O if not otherwise specified.
† Parallel reactions with Br_2.

PREPARATION AND PRODUCTION OF THE FREE ELEMENTS

Oxygen is obtained in the laboratory by the thermal decomposition of oxides of the less active metals (e.g., mercury, silver), peroxides (e.g., hydrogen, barium), certain dioxides (e.g., lead, manganese), or certain oxy salts (e.g., chlorates, perchlorates, nitrates, of the alkali metals); or by the electrolysis of water. Technically, oxygen is obtained most extensively by the fractional distillation of liquid air, although some is produced electrolytically. Sulfur is obtained technically from the large deposits of native sulfur found in the Louisiana-Texas region or in areas of volcanic origin (Sicily, Japan, Mexico). Smaller quantities are obtained by reduction of sulfur dioxide produced in the smelting of sulfidic ores or oxidation of by-product hydrogen sulfide. Crude sulfur is purified by distillation in pure carbon dioxide. Selenium and tellurium are normally recovered as by-products from metallurgical plants which treat selenium- and tellurium-containing sulfide ores.

SOME SPECIAL PHASES OF OXYGEN CHEMISTRY

Special phases of oxygen chemistry to be considered embrace water and its derivatives and hydrogen peroxide and its derivatives.

Water

Commonest of all oxygen-containing compounds is water.* The more important physical constants of water have been summarized in Chapters 10 (p. 341) and 12 (p. 393). Comparisons of some of these values with corresponding ones for other Group VIb hydrides mentioned earlier (pp. 189–191) are summarized in more detail in Table 14·4. In Chapter 10 (pp. 342–344), the solvent properties of water

TABLE 14·4

PHYSICAL CHARACTERISTICS OF SIMPLE HYDRIDES

Property	H_2O	H_2S	H_2Se	H_2Te
Melting point, °C.	0.00	−85.60	−60.4	−51
Boiling point, °C.	100.00	−60.75	−41.5	−1.8
Critical temperature, °C.	374.1	100.4	137	....
Heat of fusion, kcal./mole	1.435	0.568	....	....
Heat of vaporization, kcal./mole	9.719	4.463	4.75	5.7
Density at b.p., grams/ml.	0.958	0.993	2.004	2.650
Heat of formation at 20°C., kcal./mole	68.35	4.80	−18.5	−34.2
Surface tension at b.p., dynes/cm.	58.9	28.7	28.9	30.0
Electrolytic dissociation at 18°C.				
K_1	1.07×10^{-16}	0.91×10^{-7}	1.7×10^{-4}	2.3×10^{-3}
K_2	$< 10^{-36}$	1.2×10^{-15}	ca. 10^{-10}	ca. 10^{-5}
Dipole moment of gas, c.g.s. units $\times 10^{18}$	1.85	1.10	....	0

have been compared with those of a variety of water-like compounds. The relations of water to a system of acids and bases and to acid-base phenomena in general have been treated in Chapter 9 (pp. 308–321). These items should be reviewed in conjunction with the topics considered below.

* The term *water* is ordinarily restricted to the liquid phase of the stoichiometric compound H_2O. In a broad sense, however, it is applied to any of the three physical states of the compound. When so used, it should be qualified by a designation specifying the actual state being considered.

The physical characteristics of water in all its forms have been summarized comprehensively by Dorsey.[24] As already implied (p. 189), many of the characteristics of water which distinguish it from analogous hydrides of sulfur, selenium, and tellurium are associated with its hydrogen bonded structure in the bulk. Individual water molecules have the non-linear structure (p. 186),

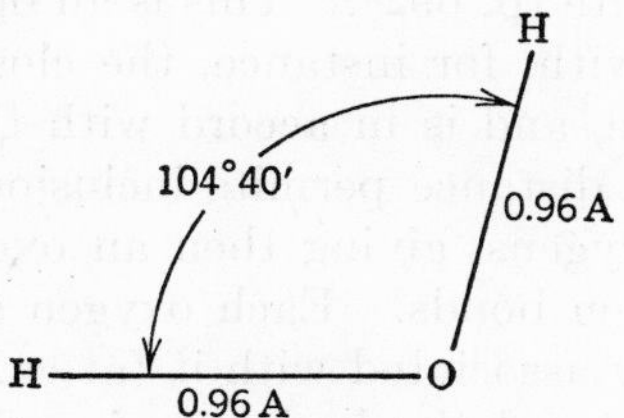

but they are essentially non-existent except in the vapor phase.

The structure of liquid water can best be approached by prior consideration of the solid. Pioneer phase rule studies by Tammann[25] and Bridgman[26, 27] have shown that in addition to the ordinary solid (Ice I), formed by the freezing of liquid water, a number of other solid forms result under pressure. The essential details of the phase diagram (after Bridgman) are included in Figure 14·2. Although

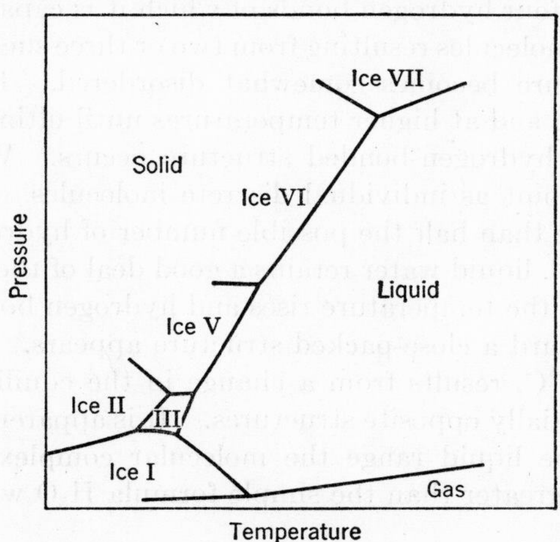

Fig. 14·2. Phase relations for water. (Not drawn to scale.)

[24] N. E. Dorsey: *Properties of Ordinary Water Substance,* American Chemical Society Monograph 81. Reinhold Publishing Corp., New York (1940).

[25] G. Tammann: *Z. physik. Chem.,* **84,** 257 (1913); **88,** 57 (1914).

[26] P. W. Bridgman: *Z. physik. Chem.,* **86,** 513 (1913).

[27] P. W. Bridgman: *J. Chem. Phys.,* **5,** 964 (1937).

x-ray methods are incapable of locating hydrogen atoms in such structures, they do show[28–30] that in Ice I, Ice II, and Ice III each oxygen is surrounded tetrahedrally by four other oxygen atoms, slight distortions in tetrahedral linkages being responsible for the different solid materials. In Ice I, the O—O bond distance is 2.76 A, and the oxygen atoms occupy the positions of Zn and S atoms in wurtzite (p. 133) or of Si atoms in tridymite (p. 692). This is an open structure, particularly in comparison with, for instance, the close-packed structure of solid hydrogen sulfide, and is in accord with the diminished density of Ice I. The O—O distance permits inclusion of a hydrogen atom between each two oxygens, giving then an overall structure of H_2O units held by hydrogen bonds. Each oxygen atom appears to have two hydrogens closely associated with it (at ca. 1 A distance) so that in a given hydrogen bond the hydrogen is unsymmetrically placed. This structure does not seem to be essentially rigid as proposed by Bernal and Fowler[31] but rather to amount to a number of configurations distinguished by different arrangements of hydrogen atoms and resulting either from rotations of water molecules or movements of some hydrogen atoms from positions close to particular oxygen atoms to similar positions close to others.[30]

Only at low temperatures (−183°C.) does each water molecule form completely the four hydrogen bonds of which it is capable.[32] As temperature rises, molecules resulting from two or three such bonds appear, and the structure becomes somewhat disordered. This trend continues on fusion and at higher temperatures until ultimately complete rupture of the hydrogen-bonded structure occurs. Water vaporizes at its boiling point as individual discrete molecules. Even at 40°C. somewhat more than half the possible number of hydrogen bonds still exist.[30] At 0°C. liquid water retains a good deal of the open structure of ice,[31] but, as the temperature rises and hydrogen bonds are broken, a tendency toward a close-packed structure appears. The maximum in density at 4°C. results from a change in the equilibrium between these two essentially opposite structures. It is apparent that throughout most of the liquid range the molecular complexity of water is actually much greater than the simple formula H_2O would predict.

[28] W. H. Barnes: *Proc. Roy. Soc. (London)*, **A125,** 670 (1929).

[29] L. Pauling: *J. Am. Chem. Soc.*, **57,** 2680 (1935).

[30] L. Pauling: *The Nature of the Chemical Bond,* 2nd Ed., pp. 301–304. Cornell University Press, Ithaca (1940).

[31] J. D. Bernal and R. H. Fowler: *J. Chem. Phys.*, **1,** 515 (1933).

[32] P. C. Cross, J. Burnham, and P. A. Leighton: *J. Am. Chem. Soc.*, **59,** 1134 (1937).

The chemical versatility of water is associated with its ability to react as either an oxidizing agent or a reducing agent or as either an acid or a base (p. 310). The oxidizing characteristics of liquid water are summarized by the couples

$$\tfrac{1}{2}H_2 \rightleftharpoons H^+(10^{-7}\,m) + e^- \qquad E^0_{298} = 0.414 \text{ volt}$$

for pure water and

$$\tfrac{1}{2}H_2 + OH^- \rightleftharpoons H_2O + e^- \qquad E^0_{298} = 0.828 \text{ volt}$$

for solutions containing hydroxyl ion at unit activity. From these, it is apparent that any reducing agent characterized by a potential more positive than 0.414 volt will reduce pure water to hydrogen but that reducing agents with potentials more positive than 0.828 volt are required to reduce water in molal hydroxide solutions. The reducing properties of water are summarized by the couples

$$H_2O \rightleftharpoons \tfrac{1}{2}O_2 + 2H^+ + 2e^- \qquad E^0_{298} = -1.229 \text{ volts}$$

in acidic ($a_{H^+} = 1$) solution,

$$H_2O \rightleftharpoons \tfrac{1}{2}O_2 + 2H^+(10^{-7}\,m) + 2e^- \qquad E^0_{298} = -0.815 \text{ volt}$$

in pure water, and

$$2OH^- \rightleftharpoons \tfrac{1}{2}O_2 + H_2O + 2e^- \qquad E^0_{298} = -0.401 \text{ volt}$$

in alkaline ($a_{OH^-} = 1$) solution. From this it is apparent that the oxidation of water, although never easy to effect, becomes decreasingly difficult as the hydrogen ion activity (concentration) decreases. Under any circumstance, a powerful oxidizing agent is required.

The acid-base characteristics of liquid water, as previously discussed (pp. 308–321), are associated with the equilibria

$$H_2O \rightleftharpoons H^+ + OH^- \qquad k_{A_1}' = 10^{-16}$$

$$OH^- \rightleftharpoons H^+ + O^{-2} \qquad k_{A_2}' < 10^{-36}$$

$$H_2O + O^{-2} \rightleftharpoons 2OH^- \qquad k_B' > 10^{+22}$$

Only the first dissociation of water is of importance. Not only is the constant for the second dissociation very small, but hydrolysis of oxide ion in water, as shown by the third equation, is complete for practical purposes, and oxide ions cannot exist in aqueous solutions.

Modes of occurrence of water in inorganic compounds

A variety of inorganic compounds either result from combinations of other materials with water or yield water when heated. Such substances may be regarded as containing chemically bound water, but differences in properties suggest a variety of types of binding. Among the types of bound water, we may distinguish the following.

Water of Constitution. Such water is present as hydroxyl groups, although it can often be removed as such by heating. Strictly speaking, the term *water of constitution* is a misnomer since no actual water molecules can be distinguished in such compounds. Examples are found in the true metal hydroxides (e.g., $NaOH$, $Mg(OH)_2$), in certain basic salts (e.g., $HgOHCl$, $Bi(OH)_2NO_3$), and in the oxy acids (e.g., $SO_2(OH)_2$, O_2NOH).

Coordinated Water. Such water is associated in stoichiometric quantities with cations and is usually said to be held by coordinate linkages. This would imply an exact similarity between all hydrates and such Werner complexes (Ch. VII) as the metal ammines. Actually, the situation is somewhat more complex. There is every reason to believe that, whereas in some instances aquo cations exist as essentially covalent entities, in other cases only electrostatic attractions or the demands of crystal stability govern the presence of water. Not all hydrate water, therefore, can be regarded as coordinated to the cation (see anion water, lattice water, and zeolitic water discussed below). Werner's emphasis upon analogies between hydrates and ammines must be modified in the light of more recent observations. In cases of hydrate isomerism (p. 249), water molecules appear to be covalently bonded to cations; in most other cases, however, bonding is more strictly comparable to that in the reversibly dissociated (normal) complexes (p. 227). Although aquo-cations of definite stoichiometry characterize crystalline salts, the natures of such ions in solution have not been established with certainty (p. 281), for there is little agreement among the results of various experimental methods which are designed to show their compositions.

Anion Water. Such water is present in crystals in stoichiometric quantities but is associated with anions rather than cations, presumably through hydrogen bonding (p. 189). Anion water is not particularly common, but it is found in a number of hydrated sulfates where the number of water molecules present is normally in excess of the coordination number of the metal ion. Copper(II) sulfate 5-hydrate is a typical example. It is well known that dehydration of this salt proceeds in steps, yielding successively $CuSO_4 \cdot 3H_2O$ and $CuSO_4 \cdot H_2O$, but that the removal of the final water molecule is complete only at 200° to 300°C. Four of the water molecules are associated with the copper(II) ion as coordinated water. The fifth molecule is held to the sulfate ion by two hydrogen bonds and is at the same time loosely held by other hydrogen bonds to two of the coordinated waters. The overall structure is then crudely

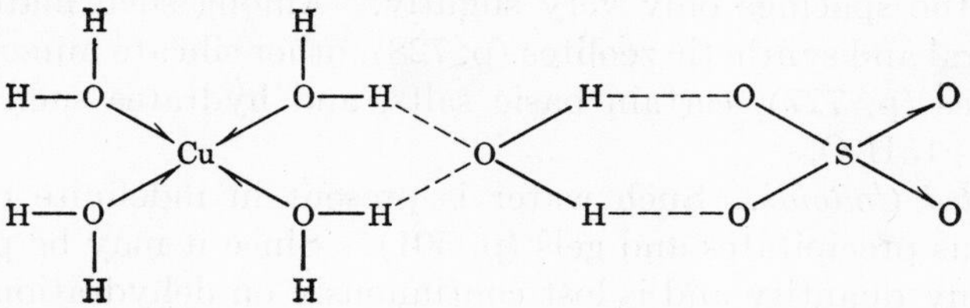

```
    H           H
    |           |
H—O         O—H              H- - - - -O         O
     \      /       \    /         \   /
       Cu             O              S
     /      \       /    \         /   \
H—O         O—H              H- - - - -O         O
    |           |
    H           H
```

Application of heat presumably causes successive loss of the two non-hydrogen-bonded waters, the other two waters coordinated to the cation, and the anion water. It is significant that when copper(II) sulfate reacts with aqueous ammonia the product is $[Cu(NH_3)_4]SO_4 \cdot H_2O$, the anion water having been retained. Other hydrated sulfates such as $NiSO_4 \cdot 7H_2O$, $ZnSO_4 \cdot 7H_2O$, etc., presumably contain a single mole of anion water. The phenomenon may also characterize salts containing other oxy-anions such as oxalate.

Lattice Water. Such water is present in stoichiometric proportions and occupies definite lattice positions, but it is not associated directly with any particular anion or cation. Such a condition might result if neither cation nor anion exhibited a strong tendency to attract water molecules or if water molecules in excess of those with which the ions could associate were present. Thus many simple and complex hydrated halides, e.g., $BaCl_2 \cdot 2H_2O$, $[Coen_3]\,(Cl, Br)_3 \cdot 3H_2O$, $[Cr(H_2O)_5Cl]Cl_2 \cdot H_2O$, $[Cr(H_2O)_4Cl_2]Cl \cdot 2H_2O$, contain water molecules which are not attracted to the halide ions and are presumably of the lattice type. Correspondingly, the extra water present in many excessively highly hydrated compounds is lattice water, and is not present as doubled molecules, $(H_2O)_2$, as Werner originally postulated. This is true in particular of the alums, $M^{I}M^{III}(SO_4)_2 \cdot 12H_2O$, (p. 539) where six water molecules are coordinated octahedrally around the ion M^{+3} whereas the remaining six are arranged octahedrally around the ion M^{+} but at distances too great for definite attachment.[33] Among the poly acids and their salts (pp. 273–277), excessive quantities of water apparently fill in holes in the crystal lattices.

Zeolitic Water. Such water molecules occupy more or less random positions in the crystal lattice and are lost continuously upon dehydration without the appearance of any new solid phases. This behavior is to be contrasted with that of an ordinary hydrate where the water molecules are lost in a stepwise fashion with the production of new

[33] H. Lipson and C. A. Beevers: *Proc. Roy. Soc. (London)*, **A148**, 664 (1935).

solid phases. Zeolitic water is found between layers in a crystal lattice or in the interstices, and its removal either does not alter the lattice or changes the spacings only very slightly. Among such materials are the natural and synthetic zeolites (p. 728), other silicate minerals of the clay types (p. 727), certain basic salts, and hydrates such as green $Cr_2(SO_4)_3 \cdot 15H_2O$.

Hydrated Colloids. Such water is present in indefinite quantities in hydrous precipitates and gels (p. 501). Since it may be present in almost any quantity and is lost continuously on dehydration, there is little likelihood that it is held in any chemical fashion.

The subject of bound water is treated comprehensively by both Emeléus and Anderson[34] and Wells.[35] These references should be consulted for further details.

Derivatives of water

Water may be regarded as the parent of series of oxides, hydroxides, and basic salts containing either O^{-2} or OH^- groups.

Oxides. As already indicated, the binary compounds of oxygen with all but the most electronegative elements show considerable ionic character (p. 208). Inasmuch as those containing the non-metallic elements are discussed in other chapters in connection with those elements, only the metal oxides need be considered here.

Metal oxides may be regarded as containing the O^{-2} ion in their lattices. Because of the marked basic character of this ion, these compounds would be expected to react with acids under a variety of conditions. Acids furnishing high concentrations of protons ordinarily react with most metal oxides, but only those oxides with comparatively small lattice energies react with or dissolve in pure water. This restricts the water-soluble oxides to those of the alkali metals, the alkaline earth metals, and thallium(I). The ionic characteristics of many metal oxides permit their treatment by the Born-Haber cycle (p. 184), and in general many of the properties of oxides can be associated with variations in the magnitudes of the energy quantities in the various steps involved. The structures of metal oxides are described in detail by Wells.[36]

Hydroxides. Strictly speaking, the term hydroxide should be restricted to those compounds which contain actual OH^- groups.

[34] H. J. Emeléus and J. S. Anderson: *Modern Aspects of Inorganic Chemistry*, pp. 154–165. D. Van Nostrand Co., New York (1938).

[35] A. F. Wells: *Structural Inorganic Chemistry*, 2nd ed., pp. 433–453. Clarendon Press, Oxford, (1950)

[36] A. F. Wells: *Quart. Revs.*, **2**, 185 (1948).

Such compounds are derived from both the metallic and the non-metallic elements. Relative to water as a parent solvent, they are basic if they yield OH^- ions or acidic if they yield H^+ (better H_3O^+) ions. As previously shown (pp. 319–321), the dissociation of such materials is related to the charge and size of the central element, with acidic characteristics becoming more pronounced as charge increases and size decreases. Materials of intermediate character are amphoteric.

The insoluble and often gelatinous products which are thrown down when metal salt solutions are treated with hydroxyl ion or hydrolyzed or when hydrogen ion is added to appropriate oxy-anions are commonly called hydroxides. Such usage is careless and often incorrect.

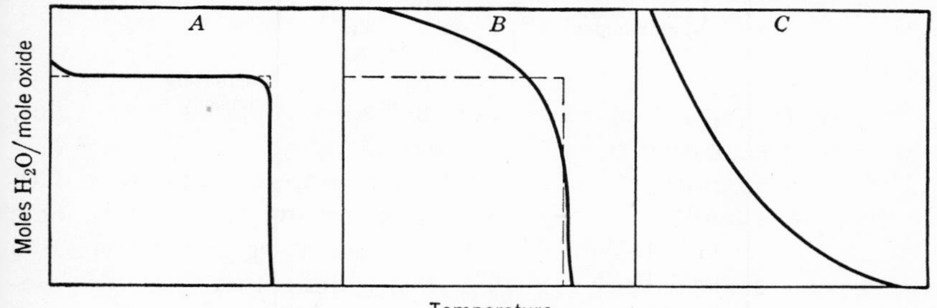

Fig. 14·3. Isobaric dehydration curves for hydrous precipitates. (Adapted from H. B. Weiser: *Inorganic Colloid Chemistry.* Vol. II. *The Hydrous Oxides and Hydroxides*, p. 19. John Wiley and Sons, New York [1935].)

As Weiser points out,[37] such precipitates carry indeterminate quantities of water and are, therefore, properly named *hydrous*, but they are not necessarily hydrous hydroxides. At least three different behaviors, indicating three different types of materials, may be distinguished by isobaric dehydration techniques. This is shown by the schematic curves given in Figure 14·3.

In Figure 14·3, curve *A* indicates loss of water at a definite composition and is characteristic of those compounds in which the water over and above that of the hydrous type is present in the stoichiometric quantity necessary for a true hydroxide, e.g., in $MgO \cdot H_2O$ or $Mg(OH)_2$. Such compounds are then *hydrous hydroxides*. Curve *B* is characteristic of materials which do not rehydrate reversibly and usually contain less water than necessary for a true hydroxide, e.g., $Al_2O_3 \cdot H_2O$. Such compounds are then *hydrous hydrates*. Curve *C* indicates continuous loss of water (p. 499) and the presence of no stoichiometric

[37] H. B. Weiser: *Inorganic Colloid Chemistry.* Vol. II. *The Hydrous Oxides and Hydroxides*, Ch. I. John Wiley and Sons, New York (1935).

combination and is characteristic of materials which precipitate as oxides and trap water in the process, e.g., Fe_2O_3, Cr_2O_3, TiO_2. Such compounds are then *hydrous oxides*. Obviously, decision as to the

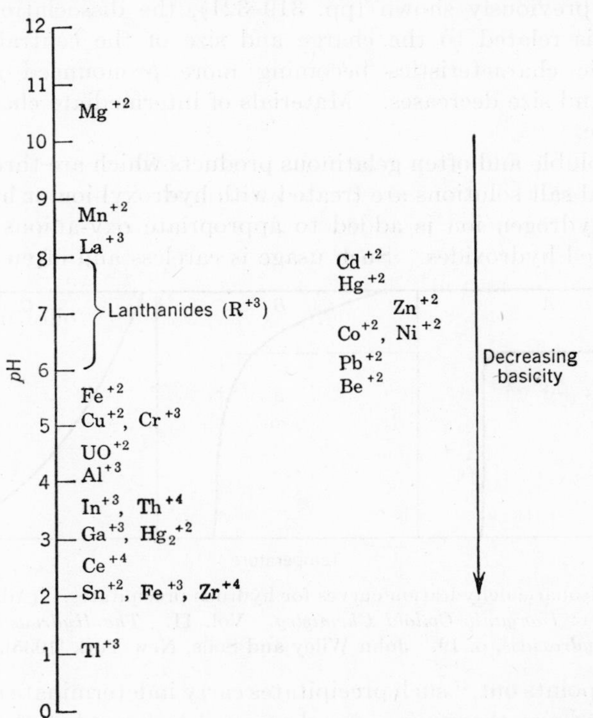

FIG. 14·4. Basicities of metal ions in terms of precipitation pH values for hydrous oxides and hydroxides.

proper term for a particular material can be reached only after experimental study. Since the conditions of formation may alter the nature of the product, the situation is complex.

Useful information on the characteristics of such materials can be obtained by potentiometric studies in which pH changes are followed as a system is titrated with hydroxyl or hydrogen ion. As developed in particular by Britton,[38] this technique permits studies of equilibria such as

$$M^{+n} + nOH^- \rightleftharpoons M(OH)_n(s)$$

$$yM^{+n} + 2nOH^- + (x - n)H_2O \rightleftharpoons M_yO_n{\cdot}xH_2O(s)$$

[38] H. T. S. Britton: *Hydrogen Ions*, 3rd Ed., Vol. II, Ch. XXIII. Chapman and Hall, London (1942).

in terms of the pH at which precipitation begins and the pH region in which precipitation occurs. In fact, Britton has suggested that the basicities of metal ions be measured by the precipitation pH values of their hydroxides or oxides. This leads to an arrangement like that given in Fig. 14·4. It is doubtful that strict comparisons among ions of a variety of charges and types are possible in this fashion, but among closely related ions, such as the tripositive lanthanide ions,[39, 40] they are permitted.

Basic Salts. The term basic salt is normally applied to any compound which is intermediate in composition between a normal salt and a metal oxide or hydroxide. As such, it is applied to oxy- and hydroxyhalides, to other salts containing O^{-2} or OH^- groups, and to materials such as the "basic" beryllium compounds, $Be_4O(RCO_2)_6$ (p. 863).[35] Bassett,[41] in a timely review, cites the following types of basic salts:

1. Salts derived from poly acid bases in which only some of the O^{-2} or OH^- groups have reacted with acid and in which the remainder are covalently attached to the metal, e.g. UO_2X_2, $[Al(OH)(H_2O)_5]SO_4$, $[en_2Co(OH)_2Co\ en_2]X_4$, and $[Co\{(HO)_2Co(NH_3)_4\}_3]Br_6$.
2. Basic salts with infinite three-dimensional lattices of the ionic type, e.g., $LaOF$, $Cu_2(OH)PO_4$, $Zn_2(OH)AsO_4$, $Cu_2(OH)_2CO_3$, $Ca_5(OH)(PO_4)_3$, and $Al_2(F,OH)_2SiO_4$,
3. Basic salts with layer lattices of the ionic type and without hydroxyl, e.g., FeOCl, FeO(OH), and BiOX.
4. Basic salts with layer lattices of the ionic type and containing hydroxyl, e.g., $Mg(OH)Cl$, $Cd(OH)Cl$, $ZnX_2 \cdot Zn(OH)_2$, $ZnX_2 \cdot 4Zn(OH)_2$, $Co_4(OH)_6SO_4$, and $Zn_4(OH)_2(Si_2O_7) \cdot H_2O$.
5. Basic salts containing complex silicate and aluminosilicate anions, e.g., $(OH)_2Ca_2Mg_5(Si_4O_{11})_2$, $[Al_2(OH)_4Si_2O_5)]_n$, and $K_n[Al_2(OH)_2(Si_3AlO_{10})]_n$.
6. Basic salts with discrete molecules, e.g., $Be_4O(RCO_2)_6$, where R = methyl, ethyl, propyl, etc.

The constitutions of basic salts have been considered in detail by Hayek,[42] as well. It is apparent that such a variety of materials possesses too great a complexity of characteristics to warrant a more detailed treatment than this. The references listed should be consulted for other details.

[39] T. Moeller and H. E. Kremers: *J. Phys. Chem.*, **48**, 395 (1944).
[40] T. Moeller and H. E. Kremers: *Chem. Revs.*, **37**, 97 (1945).
[41] H. Bassett: *Quart. Revs.*, **1**, 246 (1947).
[42] E. Hayek: *Monatsh.*, **77**, 58 (1946).

Hydrogen peroxide

The structure of the hydrogen peroxide molecule has been the subject of some controversy. X-ray measurements indicate the O—O bond distance to be 1.46 ± 0.03 A, essentially the same as the calculated single bond O—O distance of 1.48 A. Although the exact positions of the hydrogens are not known, it appears that one is associated with each oxygen at a bond angle of 101.5° and that the two lie at a 106° angle to each other.[43] The structure may thus be diagramed as

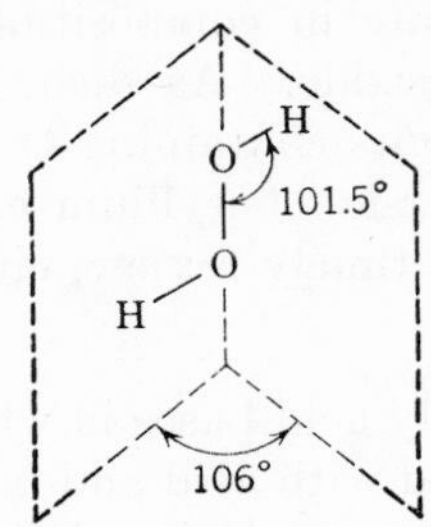

More recent studies are in agreement with this general picture, but indicate an O—O bond distance of 1.49 A, an H—O—O bond angle of ca. 97°, and an angle between the planes containing the hydrogen atoms of 94°.[44]

Reports of the existence of an alternative form $\mathrm{H{-}\overset{\overset{\displaystyle H}{|}}{O}\rightarrow O}$ at temperatures below −115°C. have also appeared[45] but lack confirmation (p. 400). The crystal arrangement is tetragonal, with four molecules to the unit cell, which has the dimensions a = 4.06 A and c = 8.00 A.[44] Individual molecules are held together by hydrogen bonds, each oxygen atom lying at 2.78 A from two oxygen atoms and at 2.90 A from two other oxygen atoms.[44]

Pure hydrogen peroxide is a pale blue, syrupy liquid which decomposes explosively at its normal (760 mm.) boiling point of 151.4°C. but can be distilled at reduced pressures (e.g., b.p. of 69.2°C. at 26 mm.). The liquid has a specific gravity of 1.4694 at 0°C. and freezes at −0.89°C. It is diamagnetic. Pure hydrogen peroxide has a dielectric constant of 93.7, which increases to 97 at 0°C. for the 90% material and to a maximum of 120 for the 65% material. Both the

[43] A. F. Wells. *Structural Inorganic Chemistry*, 2nd Ed., pp. 324–325. Clarendon Press, Oxford (1950).

[44] S. C. Abrahams, R. L. Collin, and W. N. Lipscomb: *Acta Cryst.*, **4,** 15 (1951).

[45] K. H. Geib and P. Harteck: *Ber.*, **65B,** 1551 (1932).

pure compound and its aqueous solutions are, therefore, excellent electrolytic solvents (p. 339). The liquid is more highly associated than water.

Chemically, pure hydrogen peroxide is characterized by extreme instability. As a consequence, chemical characteristics as usually evaluated are for the somewhat more stable aqueous solutions. Such solutions are comparatively stable up to concentrations of some 90% (by weight) in the absence of catalyzing impurities,[46–49] such as metals or metal or hydroxyl ions, or in the presence of stabilizers such as acids, acetanilid, pyrophosphates, stannates, or 8-quinolinol.[50] Decomposition to water and oxygen may be described by the relations

$$H_2O_2(g) \rightleftharpoons H_2O(g) + \tfrac{1}{2}O_2(g)$$

$$\Delta H^0_{298} = 23 \text{ kcal.} \qquad \Delta F^0_{298} = -30 \text{ kcal.}$$

In aqueous solution, hydrogen peroxide is more strongly acidic than water, k_A' for the equilibrium

$$H_2O_2 \rightleftharpoons H^+ + HO_2^-$$

being 1.5×10^{-12} at 20°C. In 50% aqueous solution, however, the ion product is much larger (ca. 10^{-9}). Hydrogen peroxide shows many properties comparable with those of water, e.g., solvate formation, addition to compounds, etc., but its chemistry is complicated by its greater oxidizing and reducing strengths, its ability to add to ethylenic linkages, and its catalytic effect upon certain organic polymerizations.

The oxidizing and reducing properties of hydrogen peroxide are described by the couples

$$2H_2O \rightleftharpoons H_2O_2 + 2H^+ + 2e^- \qquad E^0_{298} = -1.77 \text{ volts}$$

$$H_2O_2 \rightleftharpoons O_2 + 2H^+ + 2e^- \qquad E^0_{298} = -0.68 \text{ volt}$$

in acidic solution and

$$3OH^- \rightleftharpoons HO_2^- + H_2O + 2e^- \qquad E^0_{298} = -0.87 \text{ volt}$$

in alkaline solution. It is apparent that, regardless of pH, hydrogen peroxide is a powerful oxidizing agent but that it can behave as a reducing agent only toward materials which are themselves very strong

[46] J. S. Reichert: *Chem. Eng. News*, **21**, 480 (1943).
[47] E. S. Shanley and F. P. Greenspan: *Ind. Eng. Chem.*, **39**, 1536 (1947).
[48] M. E. Bretschger and E. S. Shanley: *Trans. Electrochem. Soc.*, **92**, 67 (1947).
[49] W. C. Schumb: *Ind. Eng. Chem.*, **41**, 992 (1949).
[50] *Ibid.*

oxidizing agents (e.g., MnO_4^-). In acidic solution, oxidations with hydrogen peroxide are often slow, but in alkaline solution they occur with great rapidity. The instability of hydrogen peroxide with respect to decomposition to water and oxygen is due to its ability simultaneously to oxidize and to reduce itself. This reaction occurs most readily in alkaline medium. It should be pointed out that there is some evidence for the existence of the free hydroxyl group.[51] This material is also strongly oxidizing

$$H_2O \rightleftharpoons OH + H^+ + e^- \qquad E^0_{298} = -2.2 \text{ volts}$$

$$OH^- \rightleftharpoons OH + e^- \qquad E^0_{298} = -1.4 \text{ volts}$$

but likewise possesses reducing properties

$$OH \rightleftharpoons \tfrac{1}{2}O_2 + H^+ + e^- \qquad E^0_{298} = -0.22 \text{ volt}$$

$$OH + OH^- \rightleftharpoons \tfrac{1}{2}O_2 + H_2O + e^- \qquad E^0_{298} = 0.61 \text{ volt}$$

Recent interest in high-concentration (ca. 90%) hydrogen peroxide has centered in its use as both a technical and a military oxidizing agent. In combination with certain organic materials, it yields highly explosive mixtures. At concentrations above 65%, danger of fire on contact with many organic materials exists, but this hazard disappears below concentrations of 35%.

Although hydrogen peroxide results from thermal reaction of hydrogen with oxygen on appropriate surfaces (ice, porcelain) or by action of a glow discharge on water vapor, large-scale production is dependent upon either the action of acids on metal peroxides or the hydrolysis of peroxysulfates. Of these two methods, the former, based upon the formation of barium peroxide by reaction of barium oxide with atmospheric oxygen and its treatment with sulfuric acid, has been largely superseded by the latter. Anodic oxidation of sulfuric acid or ammonium hydrogen sulfate solutions is used to produce peroxydisulfuric acid (p. 512) or its ammonium salt, which is then hydrolyzed to hydrogen peroxide by steam distillation. Alternatively, ammonium peroxydisulfate is converted by metathesis with potassium hydrogen sulfate to the potassium salt before hydrolysis. Hydrogen peroxide so obtained in 30 to 40% aqueous solution is concentrated by vacuum distillation. Formerly, concentrations around 30% were the maximum available. In 1934, high-concentration hydrogen peroxide was

[51] W. H. Rodebush, C. R. Keizer, F. S. McKee, and J. V. Quagliano: *J. Am. Chem. Soc.*, **69**, 538 (1947).

produced in Germany, and after 1939 German production of 80 to 85% material far exceeded that of the rest of the world.[52, 53] Although German efforts were shrouded in secrecy, technical production in the United States reached a high level during the war years and has been maintained. German interest in the material was so great that direct production from hydrogen and oxygen by use of the silent electric discharge and production by reduction of 2-ethylanthraquinone by hydrogen to 2-ethylhydroanthraquinone followed by oxidation to the initial material and hydrogen peroxide were attempted.

Deuterium peroxide, D_2O_2, is obtained by reaction of potassium peroxydisulfate with deuterium oxide and is separated from the deuterium oxide by distillation.[54] Reaction of deuterium peroxide with hydrogen peroxide yields the mixed peroxide, HDO_2.

For further information on hydrogen peroxide, the excellent monograph by Machu[55] and a review by Shanley[56] are recommended.

Derivatives of hydrogen peroxide

Hydrogen peroxide may be regarded as the parent of a series of compounds derived by replacement of or substitution for one or both of its hydrogen atoms. Much of the detailed literature information concerning these compounds has been summarized by Machu[55] and discussed by Emeléus and Anderson.[57] Two classes of such compounds warrant discussion, namely, the peroxides and the peroxy acids and their salts. The peroxyhydrates are treated also.

The Peroxides. Replacement of a single hydrogen atom in the hydrogen peroxide molecule by a metal gives a hydroperoxide (e.g., NaOOH); replacement of both hydrogens yields a peroxide (e.g., Na_2O_2). Both types of compounds are characterized, therefore, by —O—O— groups. Only such compounds should be called *peroxides.* The name *dioxide* should be restricted to those derivatives of tetrapositive metals containing two oxygen atoms (e.g., MnO_2, PbO_2). Unlike the true peroxides, which liberate hydrogen peroxide when treated with acids, the dioxides either yield salts plus water or oxidize the acids. Unfortunately, this distinction has been made consistently only in comparatively recent literature.

[52] Anon.: *Chem. Eng. News,* **23,** 1516 (1945).

[53] L. M. White: *Chem. Eng. News,* **23,** 1626 (1945).

[54] F. Fehér: *Ber.,* **72B,** 1789 (1939).

[55] W. Machu: *Das Wasserstoffperoxyd und die Perverbindungen.* Verlag von J. Springer, Wien (1937).

[56] E. S. Shanley: *J. Chem. Education,* **28,** 260 (1951).

[57] H. J. Emeléus and J. S. Anderson, *Modern Aspects of Inorganic Chemistry,* pp. 338–361. D. Van Nostrand Co., New York (1938).

True peroxides should correspond in formula to M_2O_2, where M is a monopositive cation. Such compounds are known only for ammonium and the elements in Periodic Groups I and II, with the exception of beryllium and gold. Peroxide formation appears to be determined by the size and general electropositive nature of the metal in question. This is exemplified by the fact that although calcium, strontium, and barium yield peroxides, with ease of formation increasing in this order,

TABLE 14·5

TYPICAL PEROXIDES AND RELATED COMPOUNDS

Peroxides	Superoxides	Peroxide-Superoxides	Peroxy Acids and Salts*
H_2O_2	NaO_2	K_2O_3	H_2SO_5
Li_2O_2	KO_2	Rb_2O_3	$H_2S_2O_8$
Na_2O_2	RbO_2	Cs_2O_3	$M_2Cr_2O_{12}\cdot xH_2O$
K_2O_2	CsO_2		$M_6Cr_2O_{16}$
Ag_2O_2(?)	CaO_4		M_2MoO_8
Rb_2O_2	SrO_4		M_4UO_4
Cs_2O_2	BaO_4		M_2UO_6
$(NH_4)_2O_2$			$M_6U_2O_{18}$
$MgO_2\cdot xH_2O$			HNO_4
CaO_2			H_3PO_5
SrO_2			$M_4P_2O_8$
BaO_2			H_3VO_5
ZnO_2			M_3NbO_8
CdO_2			M_3TaO_8
HgO_2			M_2CO_4
			$M_2C_2O_6$
			$M_2Ge_2O_7\cdot 4H_2O$
			M_2GeO_5
			$M_2Sn_2O_7\cdot 3H_2O$
			H_2TiO_4

* M = unipositive metal ion.

magnesium forms only an impure hydrated peroxide, and beryllium forms no peroxide. Comparison of peroxides derived from members of the Ia and IIa families with those from members of the Ib and IIb families shows increases in thermal instability and difficulty of preparation paralleling decreases in electropositive characters of the metals. Known peroxides are summarized in Table 14·5.

Closely related to the true peroxides are compounds of the alkali and alkaline earth metals containing the group O_2^- (Table 14·5). They are called *superoxides*. Best known of these is the potassium compound, which for many years was formulated as K_2O_4. The paramagnetism of this compound, however, corresponds to the presence of one unpaired electron and suggests KO_2 as a better formulation.[58]

[58] E. W. Neuman: *J. Chem. Phys.*, **2**, 31 (1934).

The crystal structure of the compound is comparable with that of calcium carbide and demonstrates clearly the presence of O_2^- ions.[59] The paramagnetism of mixtures containing calcium superoxide is also in agreement with the presence of O_2^- groups,[60] as are data on the recently prepared sodium superoxide.[61] Crystal structure determinations on the latter compound show it to be derived from a sodium chloride structure by substitution of O_2^- ions for Cl^- ions, the O—O distance being 1.33 ± 0.06 A.[62] The nature of the O_2^- ion has been considered already (p. 212).

Superoxide formation occurs most readily with the largest and most electropositive metals (e.g., K, Rb, Cs, Ca, Sr, Ba). Indeed, with the heavy alkali metals, superoxides form more readily than peroxides. Coupled with the observed fact that with lithium the normal oxide forms most readily, this suggests that increasing cation size is essential to promote crystal stability by permitting inclusion of the larger O_2^{-2} and O_2^- ions. That sodium can also form a superoxide has been shown by studies on oxygen absorption by the metal in liquid ammonia and by sodium peroxide under pressure.[61, 63, 64]

Compounds of the type M_2O_3 have also been reported to result when liquid ammonia solutions of potassium, rubidium, and cesium absorb oxygen or when superoxides undergo thermal decomposition.[65] These compounds may be regarded as mixed peroxides-superoxides, probably of composition $2MO_2 \cdot M_2O_2$.[66] The general relations existing among all these peroxidic compounds for the alkali and alkaline earth metals have been reviewed by Schechter and Kleinberg.[67] Some of the physical properties of the alkali metal superoxides are summarized in Table 14·6.

Chemically, the peroxy materials are characterized by their oxidizing properties, by their tendencies to yield oxygen when heated, and by

[59] W. Kassatochkin and W. Kotov: *J. Chem. Phys.*, **4**, 458 (1936).

[60] P. Ehrlich: *Z. anorg. Chem.*, **252**, 370 (1944).

[61] S. E. Stephanou, W. H. Schechter, W. J. Argersinger, Jr., and J. Kleinberg: *J. Am. Chem. Soc.*, **71**, 1819 (1949).

[62] D. H. Templeton and C. H. Dauben: *J. Am. Chem. Soc.*, **72**, 2251 (1950).

[63] W. H. Schechter, H. H. Sisler, and J. Kleinberg: *J. Am. Chem. Soc.*, **70**, 267 (1948).

[64] W. H. Schechter, J. K. Thompson, and J. Kleinberg: *J. Am. Chem. Soc.*, **71**, 1816 (1949).

[65] W. Machu: *Das Wasserstoffperoxyd und die Perverbindungen*, pp. 216–217. Verlag von J. Springer, Wien (1937).

[66] A. Helms and W. Klemm: *Z. anorg. allgem. Chem.*, **241**, 97 (1939); **242**, 201 (1939).

[67] W. H. Schechter and J. Kleinberg: *J. Chem. Education*, **24**, 302 (1947).

their hydrolysis in water or aqueous acids. Peroxides yield hydrogen peroxide by hydrolysis. Superoxides yield hydrogen peroxide and oxygen.

TABLE 14·6
PHYSICAL CONSTANTS FOR SUPEROXIDES

	NaO_2	KO_2	RbO_2	CsO_2
Color of solid (cold)	yellow	yellow	yellow	yellow
Crystalline form	cubic	cubic	plates	needles
Melting point, °C.		380	412	432
Density, grams/cc. (calc.)	2.21	2.14*	3.07*	3.80*
Heat of formation, kcal./mole		133.74	137.6	141.46
Magnetic moment, Bohr magnetons at 20°C.	2.07	1.84	1.89	1.89
Lattice constants, A				
a	5.49	5.71*	6.01*	6.29*
c	....	6.76*	7.04*	7.28*

* As recalculated from data of Helms and Klemm[66] by Templeton and Dauben.[62]

The following general methods of preparation, together with specific examples, can be distinguished:

1. *Direct reaction of metal or metal oxide with oxygen.* The alkali metals yield as combustion products Li_2O, Na_2O_2, KO_2, RbO_2, and CsO_2. The alkaline earth metals give CaO, SrO, and BaO_2(RaO_2?). With strontium, some peroxide results, but the yield is small even under high pressures. Strontium amalgam, however, is converted by oxygen at 60 atm. pressure to the peroxide. The action of ozonized oxygen on silver is said to yield the peroxide, although there is some evidence that the product is silver(II) oxide. The absorption of oxygen by barium oxide and its subsequent desorption at lower pressures is the basis for the Brin process for the technical preparation of oxygen from the atmosphere. Preparation of sodium superoxide has been discussed already (p. 509).

2. *Direct reaction of metal dissolved in liquid ammonia with oxygen.* Alkali and alkaline earth metal peroxides and superoxides are obtained in this manner. With a metal such as potassium, controlled oxidation may be made to yield successively the compounds K_2O_2, K_2O_3, and KO_2. Reaction of the alkaline earth metals with oxygen to give peroxides appears to be fairly easy to effect under these conditions, although, as expected, the yield of the calcium compound is low.

3. *Thermal decomposition of metal superoxides.* Compounds of the type M_2O_3 are formed by thermal decomposition of alkali metal superoxides.

4. *Reactions involving hydrogen peroxide.* Hydrated peroxides are often precipitated by reaction of hydrogen peroxide with metal salt solutions, particularly in the presence of hydroxyl ion. Examples are the compounds $Na_2O_2 \cdot 8H_2O$, $MgO_2 \cdot xH_2O$, $(Sr, Ba)O_2 \cdot 8H_2O$. Preparation of the compounds NH_4O_2H and $(NH_4)_2O_2$ by reaction of hydrogen peroxide with ethereal solutions of ammonia, of the compound HgO_2 by reaction of hydrogen peroxide with alcoholic solutions of mercury(II) chloride or on mercury or mercury(II) oxide, of the compound ZnO_2 (ca. 86% purity) by reaction of ethereal hydrogen peroxide with zinc ethyl or zinc amide, etc., may be cited as typical. Hydrogen peroxide oxidation of peroxides yields superoxides with the alkaline earth elements.

A number of the transition metals, especially those of the titanium, vanadium, and chromium families, yield peroxy compounds which appear to contain normal oxide and hydroxide groups as well and are in effect transition materials between the true peroxides and the peroxy acids (p. 514). Thus salts of the Group IVa elements yield with ammonia and hydrogen peroxide precipitates which are believed[68] to possess structures of the types

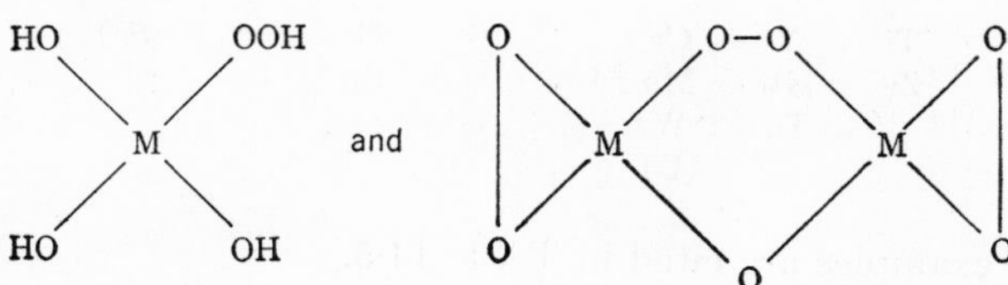

Other examples are cited in Table 14·5.

The Peroxy Acids and Their Salts. Although these compounds were characterized as *per* compounds in the older literature, they are more properly called *peroxy* compounds because of the presence of —O—O— groups.[69] The term *per* is then restricted to materials in which high state of oxidation is shown by the central element, e.g., perchlorate (ClO_4^-), permanganate (MnO_4^-), perrhenate (ReO_4^-), but in which no peroxy linkages are present.

The structure of hydrogen peroxide (p. 504) would indicate the existence of two types of peroxy acids, namely, the *peroxy mono* acids containing the group —O—O—H and the *peroxy di* acids containing the group —O—O—. Definite structural information has been obtained

[68] R. Schwarz and H. Giese: *Z. anorg. allgem. Chem.*, **176**, 209 (1928).

[69] W. P. Jorissen, H. Bassett, A. Damiens, F. Fichter, and H. Rémy: *J. Am. Chem. Soc.*, **63**, 889 (1941).

only for the peroxydisulfate ion in its ammonium and cesium compounds.[70] In this ion, two SO_4 tetrahedra are joined through two oxygen atoms, the S—O and O—O bond distances being 1.50 A and 1.31 A, respectively, and the S—O—O angle being 128°. In the light of these data, the commonly written structures for the peroxysulfuric acids appear correct. They are

```
          ..
        : O :
     ..   ..   ..   ..
  H : O : S : O : O : H
     ..   ..   ..   ..
        : O :
          ..
```

peroxymonosulfuric acid
(Caro's acid)

```
          ..        ..
        : O :     : O :
     ..   ..   ..   ..   ..   ..
  H : O : S : O : O : S : O : H
     ..   ..   ..   ..   ..   ..
        : O :     : O :
          ..        ..
```

peroxydisulfuric acid

In the absence of other data, structures of other peroxy acids may be considered to be analogous. Elements forming peroxy acids or salts are summarized by periodic families in the following tabulation:

IVa	Va	VIa	IIIb	IVb	Vb	VIb
			B	C	N	
					P	S
Ti	V	Cr		Ge		(Se)
Zr	Nb	Mo		Sn		
	Ta	W				
		(U)				

Typical examples are cited in Table 14·5.

Only a few of the peroxy acids have been isolated in the pure form. As such, they are unstable and often explosive compounds. They are better known in either aqueous or non-aqueous solution. In contact with water at ordinary temperatures, all peroxy acids undergo slow hydrolysis, yielding ultimately the normal oxy acids and hydrogen peroxide. Peroxy diacids yield peroxy monoacids as intermediates. Hydrolysis is more rapid at elevated temperatures. A common method of enhancing stability involves extraction into non-aqueous medium. The peroxy salts are more resistant to hydrolysis, but except for the peroxydisulfates and peroxydiphosphates they are still difficult to preserve. Crystalline peroxydisulfates and peroxydiphosphates (e.g., of the alkali metals, barium, lead, etc.) are easy to prepare and keep. Both the peroxy acids and their salts are powerful oxidizing agents. Unfortunately, only limited oxidation potential data are available, namely,

[70] R. C. L. Mooney and W. H. Zachariasen: *Phys. Rev.*, **44**, 327 (1933).

$$2SO_4^{-2} \rightleftharpoons S_2O_8^{-2} + 2e^- \qquad E^0_{298} = -2.05 \text{ volts}$$

$$2H_2CO_3 \rightleftharpoons C_2O_6^{-2} + 4H^+ + 2e^- \qquad E^0_{298} < -1.7 \text{ volts}$$

Peroxydisulfate is a commonly used oxidizing agent. It will effect many important conversions, e.g., $Mn^{+2} \rightarrow MnO_4^-$, $Ce^{+3} \rightarrow Ce^{+4}$, but such reactions are slow at ordinary temperatures unless catalyzed by the silver(I) ion. According to Yost,[71] the catalytic effect of the silver ion is due to the rate-controlling step

$$S_2O_8^{-2} + Ag^+ \rightarrow 2SO_4^{-2} + Ag^{+3}$$

the silver(III) ion then acting as the oxidant. Unlike hydrogen peroxide, the peroxy acids do not show reducing characteristics and thus do not decolorize permanganate.

The following general methods of preparation, given with specific examples, have been employed:

1. *Anodic oxidation.* Early observations that during electrolysis of concentrated sulfuric acid solutions somewhat less than the theoretical quantity of oxygen was obtained at the anode are interpreted in terms of the anode process

$$2HSO_4^- \rightarrow S_2O_8^{-2} + 2H^+ + 2e^-$$

This procedure is employed for the preparation of water solutions of the peroxy acid or, if ammonium or potassium hydrogen sulfates are used, for the preparation of the corresponding salts. It is the basis for the technical procedure for making hydrogen peroxide (p. 506). High current density, low temperature (5° to 10°C.), concentrated solutions, and the presence of fluoride are essential to high efficiency.

In a similar fashion, electrolysis of potassium hydrogen carbonate solutions (at −10° to −15°C.) yields potassium peroxydicarbonate, $K_2C_2O_6$, and electrolysis of potassium hydrogen phosphate solutions containing potassium fluoride yields potassium peroxydiphosphate, $K_4P_2O_8$.

2. *Reactions involving hydrogen peroxide.* Hydrogen peroxide may be used to prepare peroxy acids in the same ways that water is employed to prepare ordinary oxy acids. Thus by reactions analogous to hydrolysis, chlorosulfonic acid is converted by anhydrous hydrogen peroxide to either peroxymonosulfuric acid

$$HSO_3Cl + H_2O_2 \rightarrow H_2SO_5 + HCl$$

[71] D. M. Yost: *J. Am. Chem. Soc.*, **48**, 152 (1926).

or to peroxydisulfuric acid

$$2HSO_3Cl + H_2O_2 \rightarrow H_2S_2O_8 + 2HCl$$

depending upon the quantities of materials employed. By reactions analogous to hydration reactions, phosphorus(V) and nitrogen(V) oxides are converted, respectively, to peroxymonophosphoric acid and to peroxynitric acid

$$P_4O_{10} + 4H_2O_2 + 2H_2O \rightarrow 4H_3PO_5$$

$$N_2O_5 + H_2O_2 \rightarrow HNO_3 + HNO_4$$

Reactions of hydrogen peroxide with certain oxy salts are somewhat different in character and seem to amount to replacement in part of covalently bonded oxygens by peroxy groups. Thus treatment of alkali metal metagermanates and metastannates with hydrogen peroxide yields corresponding peroxygermanates and stannates, $M_2Ge_2O_7 \cdot 4H_2O$ and $M_2Sn_2O_7 \cdot 3H_2O$. Solutions of alkali metal niobates and tantalates, when so treated, give peroxy salts, M_3NbO_8 and M_3TaO_8. With alkali metal molybdates and tungstates, peroxy salts, M_2MoO_8 and M_2WO_8, are formed. Uranate solutions yield hydrated salts of the types M_4UO_8, M_2UO_6, and $M_6U_2O_{13}$, depending upon the quantity of free alkali present. Uranyl salts, on the other hand, give a hydrated peroxide, $UO_4 \cdot 2H_2O$.

Acidified dichromate solutions yield with hydrogen peroxide a blue peroxide, CrO_5, or blue peroxy salts of the type $M_2Cr_2O_{12} \cdot xH_2O$. Alkaline chromate solutions at low temperatures yield red peroxy salts of the type $M_6Cr_2O_{16}$. If such solutions are warmed in the presence of ammonia, a peroxytriammine, $CrO_4 \cdot 3NH_3$, results.

3. *Reactions involving sodium peroxide or hydroperoxide.* Sodium peroxide reacts with one or two moles of carbon dioxide to yield, respectively, sodium peroxymonocarbonate, Na_2CO_4, or sodium peroxydicarbonate, $Na_2C_2O_6$. If sodium hydroperoxide is used, peroxyhydrated peroxycarbonates, $Na_2CO_4 \cdot H_2O_2$ and $Na_2C_2O_6 \cdot H_2O_2$, result. Sodium peroxymonocarbonate is also obtained by the reaction of sodium peroxide with phosgene

$$2Na_2O_2 + COCl_2 \rightarrow Na_2CO_4 + 2NaCl + \frac{1}{2}O_2$$

Boric acid reacts with sodium hydroperoxide to yield a peroxyborate, $NaBO_3$.

4. *Reactions involving fluorine.* Alkali metal peroxydicarbonates result from reaction of fluorine with corresponding carbonates.

$$2Na_2CO_3 + F_2 \rightarrow Na_2C_2O_6 + 2NaF$$

Perchloric acid solutions when treated with fluorine possess many of the properties of peroxy acid solutions and may contain the very unstable acid, $HClO_5$.

The Peroxyhydrates. These are compounds containing hydrogen peroxide of crystallization and are strictly analogous to the ordinary hydrates. Again the literature is somewhat confused, many compounds which are apparently peroxyhydrates being referred to as peroxy salts. Inasmuch as peroxyhydrates contain comparatively loosely bound hydrogen peroxide, they show the reactions of that substance and are thus distinguishable from the true peroxy salts. A true peroxy salt yields hydrogen peroxide slowly by hydrolysis and immediately oxidizes iodide quantitatively to iodine. A true peroxyhydrate yields hydrogen peroxide immediately when in contact with water and does not immediately oxidize iodide.

Peroxyhydrates have been mentioned in conjunction with peroxycarbonates. Alkali metal metasilicates when dissolved in aqueous hydrogen peroxide are converted into peroxyhydrates, e.g., $Na_2SiO_3 \cdot H_2O_2 \cdot H_2O$, but not into peroxy salts. Similarly, treatment of borax with hydrogen peroxide or electrolysis of borate-carbonate solutions, as in the preparation of technical sodium "perborate," gives a peroxyhydrate, $NaBO_2 \cdot H_2O_2 \cdot 3H_2O$, rather than a peroxyborate.

SOME SPECIAL PHASES OF SULFUR CHEMISTRY

The hydrogen, halogen, oxygen, and nitrogen compounds of sulfur are considered as special phases of sulfur chemistry. Where feasible, comparisons with comparable selenium and tellurium materials are included also.

Sulfur-hydrogen compounds and their derivatives

Hydrogen Sulfide. Like oxygen, sulfur forms more than a single binary compound with hydrogen. The simple hydride, H_2S or hydrogen sulfide, is the best known of these. As indicated in Table 14·4, hydrogen sulfide resembles the corresponding selenium and tellurium compounds much more closely in physical properties than it does water. The same resemblance is noted in chemical properties and can probably be traced to the size and electronegativity trends mentioned at the beginning of this chapter. Hydrogen sulfide is a weak acid ($pk_{A_1}' = 7.04$, $pk_{A_2}' = 14.92$), and both its soluble normal and acid salts are, therefore, strongly hydrolyzed. Acid strength in the hydrides increases of course as the size of the sulfur family element increases (p. 318). Hydrogen sulfide is a reducing agent as indicated by the couple

$$H_2S \rightleftharpoons S + 2H^+ + 2e^- \qquad E^0_{298} = -0.141 \text{ volt}$$

in acid solution and the couple

$$S^{-2} \rightleftharpoons S + 2e^- \qquad E^0_{298} = 0.508 \text{ volt}$$

in alkaline solution. Although oxidation commonly yields sulfur as indicated by these couples, strong oxidizing agents may give sulfur(IV) or sulfur(VI) compounds. Reducing strength increases parallel to acid strength with the hydrides of elements in this family (Table 14·4). Many sulfides are water insoluble and are of use in qualitative and quantitative separation schemes.

Hydrogen sulfide is normally obtained by hydrolysis of sulfides, a procedure which follows from both the volatility of the product and the strongly basic character of the sulfide ion. Alkali and alkaline earth metal sulfides, aluminum sulfide, etc., are hydrolyzed by water alone. With more difficultly soluble sulfides stronger protonic acids (e.g., hydrochloric acid) are required. Comparable reactions may be employed for hydrogen selenide and hydrogen telluride. Direct combination of the elements is slow at ordinary temperatures but becomes more rapid at elevated temperatures. The process is reversible, however, and not suitable for preparative purposes.

Hydrogen Persulfide and Polysulfides. In aqueous solutions, alkali metal sulfides dissolve sulfur due to the formation of polysulfide ions, S_x^{-2} (p. 518). Addition of such an aqueous solution to concentrated hydrochloric acid at −15°C. yields a water-insoluble yellow oil which can be fractionally distilled under reduced pressure to give largely H_2S_2 and H_2S_3 and smaller quantities of higher homologs, H_2S_x (x = up to at least 6).[72–74] Electrolytic procedures involving reduction of sulfur(IV) yield mixtures of still higher homologs, H_2S_9 and either H_2S_7 or H_2S_8.[75] Treatment of pure ammonium pentasulfide with anhydrous formic acid gives H_2S_5.[76]

The compound H_2S_2 is called hydrogen persulfide (by analogy with hydrogen peroxide). The others are called hydrogen polysulfides. All these compounds are oily liquids which are soluble in solvents such as benzene, ether, and chloroform. Available data on physical constants are summarized in Table 14.7, comparable values for hydrogen

[72] K. H. Butler and O. Maass: *J. Am. Chem. Soc.*, **52,** 2184 (1930).

[73] J. H. Walton and E. L. Whitford: *J. Am. Chem. Soc.*, **45,** 601 (1923).

[74] F. Fehér and M. Baudler: *Z. anorg. Chem.*, **253,** 170 (1947); **254,** 251, 289 (1947); **258,** 132 (1949).

[75] F. Fehér and E. Heuer: *Angew. Chem.*, **A59,** 237 (1947).

[76] I. Block and F. Höhn: *Ber.*, **41,** 1961, 1971, 1975, 1980 (1908).

TABLE 14·7

PHYSICAL CONSTANTS FOR HYDROGEN PEROXIDE, HYDROGEN PERSULFIDE, AND THE HYDROGEN POLYSULFIDES

Property	H_2O_2	H_2S_2	H_2S_3	H_2S_4	H_2S_5	H_2S_6
Melting point, °C.	−0.89	−89.6	−52	−85 (glassy)	−50 (glassy)	
Boiling point, °C.	151.4 (760 mm.)	70.7 (760 mm.)	50 (4 mm.)			
Vapor pressure, mm. Hg	2.1 (25°C.)					
Heat of fusion, kcal./mole	2.5	1.8				
Heat of vaporization, kcal./mole	11.61	8.54				
Trouton's constant	27.4	24.9				
Density, grams/ml.	1.442 (20°C.)	1.3339 (20°C.)	1.495 (15°C.)	1.588 (15°C.)	1.66 (15°C.)	1.699 (15°C.)
Dipole moment, e.s.u. $\times 10^{18}$	2.1	1.17 (25°C.)				
Dielectric constant	93.7 (0°C.)					
Refractive index	1.4139 (22°C.)		1.7052 (15°C.)			
Surface tension, dynes /cm.	75.94 (18.2°C.)	38.1 (70.7°C.)				
Viscosity, centipoises	1.272 (19.6°C.)					
Specific heat of liquid, cal./gram	0.579 (0–18°C.)					
Magnetic susceptibility, c.g.s. units $\times 10^6$	0.88					
X-X distance, A	1.47	2.05				

peroxide being included for purposes of rigid comparisons between the persulfide and the peroxide. The S—S bond distance of 2.05 A in H_2S_2 is in good agreement with the 2.08 A expected for a single S—S bond, indicating the structure to be $\mathrm{H : \overset{..}{\underset{..}{S}} : \overset{..}{\underset{..}{S}} : H}$, comparable with that of hydrogen peroxide. It is not unlikely, therefore, that the higher members of the series have structures of the type $\mathrm{H : \overset{..}{\underset{..}{S}} : \overset{..}{\underset{..}{(S)}}_{x-2} : \overset{..}{\underset{..}{S}} : H}$

As expected, hydrogen persulfide is much less ionic than the peroxide and is a poorer solvent for ionic materials. It is an excellent physical solvent for a number of covalent compounds and particularly for sulfur. Hydrogen persulfide and the hydrogen polysulfides are all decomposed to hydrogen sulfide and sulfur at elevated temperatures and in the presence of bases. Disproportionation may also occur as shown by the equation

$$2H_2S_3 \rightarrow H_2S_4 + H_2S_2$$

Certain of these compounds form addition compounds with strychnine and brucine and with a few ketones and aldehydes.

The hydrogen compounds just described may be regarded as parent compounds of both inorganic and organic polysulfides. Alkali metal polysulfides result not only from reaction between sulfide ion and sulfur in aqueous solution but also from comparable reactions in liquid ammonia and reaction of liquid ammonia solutions of alkali metals with sulfur. Compounds of the type M_2S_x ($x = 2, 3, 4, 5, 6$) have been isolated. In liquid ammonia, these compounds give highly colored solutions. Many comparable selenium and tellurium compounds can be obtained by analogous reactions. In a sense, these compounds may be regarded as examples of polyanionic aggregation of the type exemplified by the polystannides and polyplumbides (pp. 732–733).

Sulfur-halogen compounds

The halogen compounds of sulfur embrace the halides proper, the oxyhalides, and the halogen-containing oxy acids. Each of these classes may be considered separately. The characteristics of compounds containing sulfur and fluorine have been summarized by Miller and Gall.[77]

Halides of Sulfur. Reported sulfur halides, together with certain of their more important physical constants, are summarized in Table

[77] H. C. Miller and J. F. Gall: *Ind. Eng. Chem.*, **42**, 2223 (1950).

TABLE 14·8
PHYSICAL CONSTANTS FOR SULFUR HALIDES

Compound	Melting Point, °C.	Boiling Point, °C.	Heat of Fusion, kcal./mole	Heat of Vaporization, kcal./mole	Trouton's Constant	Heat of Formation, kcal./mole	Dipole, Moment, e.s.u. × 10^{18}	Dielectric Constant
1. Fluorides								
S_2F_2	−120.5	−38.4						
SF_2(?)								
SF_4	−124	−40		5.18	22.2			
SF_6	−50.8	−63.7 (subl.)	1.201	5.46	26.1	262		
S_2F_{10}	−92	29		7.00	23.2	461		
2. Chlorides								
S_2Cl_2	−80	138				14.3	1.60	4.9 (22°C.)
SCl_2	−78	59 (dec.)				12.0		
SCl_4	−31	dec.				13.7		
S_3Cl_2(?)								
S_4Cl_2(?)								
S_3Cl_4(?)								
3. Bromides								
S_2Br_2	−46	90 (dec.)				4.0		
4. Iodides								
none								

14·8. The absence of sulfur-iodine compounds is noteworthy. Perhaps the outstanding chemical characteristic of these halides is their tendency to hydrolyze in contact with water. This reaction is characteristic of all the halides except the fluorides SF_6 and S_2F_{10} and results in the hydrogen halide and either an oxy acid of sulfur or the free element.

Of the halides, the most unusual is undoubtedly the hexafluoride, SF_6. This compound is insoluble in water and is chemically inert below red heat to free halogens, oxygen, hydrogen, ammonia, silicon, carbon, boron, magnesium, and copper, and even to fused potassium hydroxide or hot copper(II) oxide.[78, 79] It is converted to sulfur and hydrogen fluoride by hydrogen sulfide and to sodium sulfide and fluoride by boiling sodium. Its high-voltage insulation property renders it extremely useful. In it, the fluorine atoms are arranged octahedrally around the sulfur atom, and the bonding is highly covalent in character. In this compound and in the closely comparable compound S_2F_{10},[80] expansion of the normal tetracovalence of sulfur has taken place (p. 177). Selenium and tellurium form hexafluorides with comparable properties and structures, although reactivity increases with increasing size of the non-halogen.

Of the chlorides, the compounds S_2Cl_2 and SCl_2 are perhaps best characterized. Both are of importance in the technical production of rubber. Sulfur monochloride, S_2Cl_2, is an excellent solvent for sulfur, iodine, certain metal halides, and many organic compounds. It is reduced to sulfides and chlorides by metals and undergoes thermal decomposition above 300°C. to sulfur and chlorine. Electron diffraction studies show the S_2Cl_2 molecule to have the arrangement

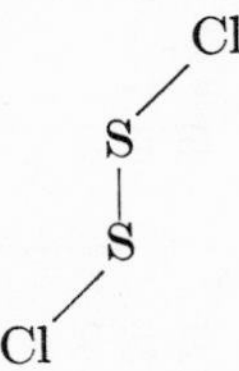

with Cl—S and S—S bond distances of 1.99 A and 2.05 A, respectively, and a Cl—S—S angle of 103°. It has not been determined whether there is free rotation about the S—S bond and, therefore, whether *cis* and *trans* forms exist.[81] The sulfur dichloride molecule has a triangu-

[78] W. C. Schumb and E. L. Gamble: *J. Am. Chem. Soc.*, **52**, 4302 (1930).

[79] W. C. Schumb: *Ind. Eng. Chem.*, **39**, 421 (1947).

[80] K. G. Denbigh and R. Whytlaw-Gray: *J. Chem. Soc.*, **1934**, 1346.

[81] K. J. Palmer: *J. Am. Chem. Soc.*, **60**, 2360 (1938).

lar structure with an S—Cl bond distance of 1.99 A and a Cl—S—Cl angle of 101°. Selenium forms a comparable monochloride, but tellurium does not. Both selenium and tellurium give dichlorides, and each forms a tetrachloride similar to the sulfur compound. Monobromides are known for sulfur and selenium. Di- and tetrabromides are more characteristic of selenium and tellurium. Tetrahalides of selenium and tellurium (except the flourides) decompose thermally to dihalides and free halogen.

The sulfur halides are commonly prepared by direct combination of the elements. With fluorine, the hexafluoride[82] is the primary product, the lower fluorides (especially the decafluoride) forming in smaller quantities. A convenient laboratory preparation of the hexafluoride involves direct reaction of the elements in such fashion that a current of fluorine circulates continuously over the sulfur.[83] Pyrolysis at 400°C. converts the decafluoride to tetra- and hexafluorides; the former, together with any lower fluorides, is removed by scrubbing with water and dilute sodium hydroxide solution. Drying then gives the pure hexafluoride. With chlorine and bromine, the monohalides are the primary products. Continued reaction with chlorine forms, reversibly, the dichloride and possibly the compound S_3Cl_4. Iodine gives no reaction. Reactions with selenium are closely comparable except that the tetrachloride and bromide form with excess halogen, and selenium mono- and tetraiodides form in solution in carbon tetrachloride or ethylenedibromide. The fluorides S_2F_2, SF_2, and SF_4, as well as Se_2F_2, SeF_4, TeF_2, and TeF_4, result from action of hydrogen fluoride on oxides or cobalt(III) fluoride on the free elements.

Oxyhalides of Sulfur. The oxyhalides of sulfur are of three types, namely, SOX_2 [thionyl or sulfur(IV) oxyhalides], SO_2X_2 [sulfuryl or sulfur(VI) oxyhalides], and $S_2O_5X_2$ (pyrosulfuryl halides). Selenium gives oxyhalides, $SeOX_2$ (X = F, Cl, Br), comparable to the thionyl compounds, but tellurium does not. Known compounds and some of their physical constants are summarized in Table 14·9. Except for the fluorides, all these compounds are volatile liquids at ordinary temperatures. They are non-conductors and give many evidences of covalent bonding. The thionyl halides and selenium oxychloride have triangular pyramid molecular structures of the type[81, 84]

[82] D. M. Yost: *Inorganic Syntheses*, Vol. I, p. 121. McGraw-Hill Book Co., New York (1939).

[83] W. C. Schumb: *Inorganic Synthesis*, Vol. III, p. 119. McGraw-Hill Book Co., New York (1950).

[84] D. P. Stevenson and R. A. Cooley: *J. Am. Chem. Soc.*, **62**, 2477 (1940).

TABLE 14·9

PHYSICAL CONSTANTS FOR OXYHALIDES OF SULFUR

Compound	Melting Point, °C.	Boiling Point, °C.	Heat of Vaporization, kcal./mole	Trouton's Constant	Heat of Formation, kcal./mole	Dipole Moment, e.s.u. × 10^{18}	Dielectric Constant	Density of Liquid, grams/ml.	S—X Bond, A	S—O Bond, A	X—S—O Angle, degrees	X—S—X Angle, degrees
1. Thionyl halides												
SOF_2	−110	−43.8	5.18	22.6				3.0	1.6	1.45	114(?)	106(?)
$SOFCl$	−139.5	12.2	5.90	20.7								
$SOCl_2$	−104.5	78.8	7.48	21.2	50.2	1.58 (25°C.)	9.05 (22°C.)	1.656 (14.5°C.)	2.05	1.45	107.5	97.5
$SOBr_2$	−49.5	137	10.40	25.4				2.67 (25°C.)	2.27	1.45	108	96
2. Sulfuryl halides												
SO_2F_2	−136.7	−55.4	4.79	22.0								
SO_2FCl	−124.7	7.1	6.34	22.6				1.623 (0°C.)				
SO_2Cl_2	−54.1	69.1	6.70	19.6	92.9			1.667 (20°C.)	1.99	1.43	106.5	111
3. Pyrosulfuryl halides												
$S_2O_5Cl_2$	−37.5	152.5 (766 mm.)	13.2	31.0	166.5			1.837 (20°C.)				

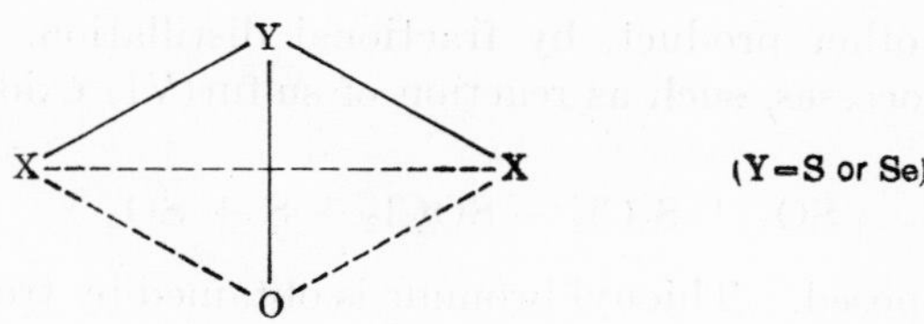

and differ from each other only in the bond distances and angles as shown in Table 14·9. The sulfuryl halides are derived from sulfur trioxide (p. 528) by replacing one oxygen atom by two halogens. Thus the sulfuryl chloride molecule has a tetrahedral structure with the sulfur at the center, available bond data again appearing in Table 14.9. No structural data are available on pyrosulfurylchloride, the only known example of this class of compound.

The thionyl halides hydrolyze to sulfurous acid and hydrogen halide. The analogous selenium compounds react similarly, the fluorides in both cases being hydrolyzed most rapidly. Thionyl chloride is of particular use in organic chemistry for replacing OH groups with Cl. It is also useful in preparing numerous hydrated inorganic chlorides from the hydrates.[85] The acidic properties of thionyl halides in liquid sulfur dioxide and the solvent properties of selenium oxychloride have been covered in earlier chapters (pp. 324–325, 363–365). Sulfuryl fluoride is comparatively inert and undergoes hydrolysis only in warm alkali solutions (ca. 0.5 *N*). Fluosulfonate (p. 524) and fluoride are the primary products, the former undergoing further hydrolysis to sulfate and fluoride. Sulfuryl chloride hydrolyzes readily to sulfuric and hydrochloric acids. With ammonia, both sulfuryl fluoride and chloride yield sulfamide, $SO_2(NH_2)_2$ (p. 553). Sulfuryl chloride undergoes thermal decomposition to sulfur dioxide and chlorine above 280°C., especially in the presence of catalysts. Pyrosulfuryl chloride combines rather slowly with water to form chlorosulfonic acid (p. 524), but it is converted readily to sulfate and chloride by aqueous alkali. Its vapors undergo no thermal decomposition below at least 184°C. Many metals, among them gold and platinum, react with it to form chlorides.

Thionyl fluoride is best obtained by fluorination of liquid thionyl chloride with liquid arsenic(III) fluoride at slightly elevated temperatures. The product is separated from sulfur dioxide and the mixed thionyl halide, SOClF, by low temperature fractional distillation. Thionyl chloride is usually prepared by reacting sulfur dioxide with phosphorus(V) chloride and is separated from phosphorus(V) oxy-

[85] H. Hecht: *Z. anorg. Chem.*, **254**, 37 (1947).

chloride, the other product, by fractional distillation. Other more convenient processes, such as reaction of sulfur(VI) oxide with sulfur monochloride

$$SO_3 + S_2Cl_2 \rightarrow SOCl_2 + S + SO_2$$

have been proposed. Thionyl bromide is obtained by treating thionyl chloride with dry hydrogen bromide at 0°C. and distilling.[86]

Sulfuryl fluoride is prepared by thermal decomposition of dry barium fluosulfonate, the other product being non-volatile barium sulfate. The mixed chlorofluoride, SO_2ClF, results when sulfuryl chloride is fluorinated with antimony(III) fluoride in the presence of antimony(V) chloride (Swartz reaction) and under pressure.[87] Sulfuryl chloride is most readily obtained by direct reaction of chlorine with sulfur dioxide in the presence of either camphor or activated charcoal.[88] As shown above, the reaction is readily reversed. Treatment of solid sulfur monochloride or carbon tetrachloride with sulfur trioxide or of chlorosulfonic acid with phosphorus(V) oxide gives pyrosulfuryl chloride. The reaction between carbon tetrachloride and sulfur trioxide is a convenient one for laboratory preparations.[89]

Halogen-Containing Oxy Acids. Only two such acids, fluosulfonic acid, HSO_3F, and chlorosulfonic acid, HSO_3Cl, are known. The comparable selenium-chlorine acid, $HSeO_3Cl$, has been described also. Fluosulfonic acid is a colorless liquid boiling at 162.6°C. The vapor undergoes no decomposition up to at least 900°C. It does not attack either glass or many metals at ordinary temperatures. In water, it undergoes slow hydrolysis to sulfuric and hydrofluoric acids (p. 523), but the reaction is reversible (p. 525). Chlorosulfonic acid is a colorless liquid (sp. gr. 1.753 at 20°C.) which boils with decomposition at 152°, fumes in moist air, and reacts vigorously with water to form sulfuric and hydrochloric acids. Use of chlorosulfonic acid in forming screening smokes is dependent upon its hydrolysis. Unlike fluosulfonic acid, chlorosulfonic acid is thermally decomposed in the vapor state, giving products such as chlorine, water vapor, and sulfur dioxide. Even at 170° to 180°C. decomposition is appreciable. Chlorosulfonic acid is a useful sulfonating agent toward many organic compounds. The halosulfonic acids and the sulfuryl halides are both acid halides

[86] H. Hibbert and J. C. Pullman: *Inorganic Syntheses*, Vol. I, p. 113. McGraw-Hill Book Co., New York (1939).

[87] H. S. Booth and C. V. Herrmann: *J. Am. Chem. Soc.*, **58**, 63 (1936).

[88] H. R. Allen and R. N. Maxson: *Inorganic Syntheses*, Vol. I, p. 114. McGraw-Hill Book Co., New York (1939).

[89] M. Sveda: *Inorganic Synetheses*. Vol. III, p. 124. McGraw-Hill Book Co., New York (1950).

(p. 426) of sulfuric acid and are related to that acid in terms of the following scheme:

```
        ..                   ..                   ..
       : O :                : O :                : O :
    ..  ..  ..           ..  ..  ..           ..  ..  ..
 H : O : S : O : H    H : O : S : X :      : X : S : X :
    ..  ..  ..           ..  ..  ..           ..  ..  ..
       : O :                : O :                : O :
        ..                   ..                   ..
  sulfuric acid       halosulfonic acid     sulfuryl halide
```

Fluosulfonic acid is prepared either by direct action of concentrated hydrofluoric acid on sulfur trioxide, by distillation from a mixture of calcium fluoride and fuming sulfuric acid (60% SO_3) in an iron retort, or by reaction of potassium hydrogen fluoride with fuming sulfuric acid at low temperatures and subsequent distillation. Chlorosulfonic acid is prepared by direct reaction of dry hydrogen chloride with sulfur trioxide or fuming sulfuric acid or by reaction of a number of covalent chlorides (e.g., PCl_3, PCl_5, CCl_4) with fuming sulfuric acid. It is recovered by distillation. Fluosulfonates result when metal fluorides are added to fuming sulfuric acid or sulfur trioxide. The ammonium salt is readily obtained and is often used for the preparation of other fluosulfonates. Most fluosulfonates are stable to hydrolysis and are water soluble. Chlorosulfonates are more difficult to prepare and preserve because of ready hydrolysis. The sodium salt is obtained when chlorosulfonic acid reacts with dry sodium chloride, the other product being hydrogen chloride.

Oxides of sulfur

Some six oxides of sulfur have been characterized. They have the stoichiometric formulas SO, S_2O_3, SO_2, SO_3, S_2O_7, and SO_4. The monoxide and tetroxide have been known for only a short time; the others have been known for much longer. Only the dioxide and trioxide are of importance.

Sulfur Monoxide (SO). Although emission bands in the 2500 to 3900 A region from discharge tubes containing sulfur dioxide were ascribed to sulfur monoxide by Henri and Wolff,[90] it remained for Schenk and his coworker Cordes[91, 92] to isolate and study the compound. Passage of an electric discharge through a mixture of excess sulfur vapor and sulfur dioxide at low pressures gave a gaseous product

[90] V. Henri and F. Wolff: *J. phys. radium*, **10,** 81 (1929).
[91] P. W. Schenk: *Z. anorg. allgem. Chem.*, **211,** 150 (1933).
[92] H. Cordes and P. W. Schenk: *Z. anorg. allgem. Chem.*, **214,** 33 (1933).

from which an orange-red deposit, probably of the polymeric oxide, could be condensed at liquid air temperatures. Sulfur monoxide also is formed when sulfur is burned in air at 250° to 300°C. and at low pressures,[93] when thionyl chloride reacts with metals such as tin, sodium, or antimony or with tin(II) chloride,[94] and when thionyl chloride is decomposed thermally at 900°C. or thionyl bromide at 520°C.[95] In all cases, the characteristic absorption spectrum of the compound can be used for its detection.

The properties of sulfur monoxide have not been well characterized. The material is normally gaseous and in this state is probably dimeric. It is soluble in thionyl chloride. It is stable only at reduced pressures and decomposes to sulfur and sulfur dioxide at pressures above 40 mm. of mercury. That these products are formed in 1:1 mole ratio indicates the simple composition to be SO,[96] but the general properties of the material suggest that it is a long-chain polymer

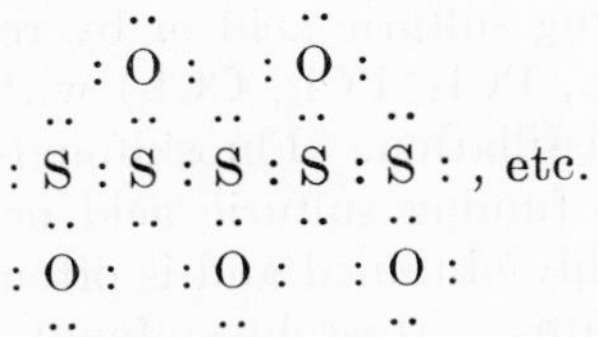

```
             ..      ..
           : O :   : O :
  ..   ..   ..   ..   ..
: S : S : S : S : S : , etc.
  ..   ..   ..   ..   ..
: O :   : O :   : O :
  ..      ..      ..
```

With aqueous potassium hydroxide, sulfur monoxide gives a solution containing sulfide, sulfite, and dithionite,[97] a reaction indicating that the compound is not the anhydride of sulfoxylic acid (p. 533). With water, it gives sulfur, hydrogen sulfide, and sulfur dioxide; with oxygen, it yields sulfur dioxide. Metals yield sulfides,[98] and chlorine and bromine form the corresponding thionyl halides.[96]

It must be pointed out that much of the information on sulfur monoxide is based upon observed absorption bands. Cordes[99] believes these bands to be due to active sulfur molecules, a contention opposed by Schenk[96, 100] on the grounds that they appear only when oxygen is present. Whether sulfur monoxide does exist or not must be decided by further studies.

[93] P. W. Schenk: *Z. anorg. allgem. Chem.*, **220**, 268 (1934).
[94] P. W. Schenk and H. Platz: *Z. anorg. allgem. Chem.*, **215**, 113 (1933).
[95] P. W. Schenk and H. Triebel: *Z. anorg. allgem. Chem.*, **229**, 305 (1936).
[96] P. W. Schenk: *Z. anorg. allgem. Chem.*, **233**, 385 (1937).
[97] P. W. Schenk and H. Platz: *Z. anorg. allgem.*, *Chem.* **222**, 177 (1935).
[98] H. Cordes and P. W. Schenk: *Trans. Faraday Soc.*, **30**, 31 (1934).
[99] H. Cordes: *Z. Physik*, **105**, 251 (1937).
[100] P. W. Schenk: *Z. Physik*, **106**, 271 (1937).

Sulfur Sesquioxide (S_2O_3). This is a blue-green solid oxide which is stable below 15°C. but is decomposed at 40° to 80°C. into sulfur and sulfur trioxide (20%) and into sulfur monoxide and sulfur dioxide (80%).[101] With water, it forms free sulfur plus sulfuric, sulfurous, and various thionic acids (p. 543). It is not the anhydride of dithionous acid, $H_2S_2O_4$ (p. 535). Sulfur sesquioxide is formed by action of sulfur on liquid sulfur trioxide and remains when the excess of the latter is removed.

Sulfur Dioxide (SO_2). Sulfur dioxide [or sulfur(IV) oxide] is a colorless gas which is readily condensed to a liquid. Its physical constants have been summarized in Chapter 10 (Table 10·3). Characteristics of the liquid as a solvent have also been considered in earlier chapters (Ch. 9, 10). The sulfur dioxide molecule is angular, the O—S—O angle being 129°.[81] The S—O bond distance of 1.46 A indicates some double bond character, and the structure probably involves resonance forms such as

$$:\underset{..}{\ddot{O}}:\ddot{S}:\ddot{O}: \quad \text{and} \quad :\ddot{O}::\ddot{S}:\ddot{O}:$$

Selenium dioxide has a comparable structure.

Chemically, sulfur dioxide acts both as an oxidizing agent (e.g., toward hydrogen sulfide) and as a reducing agent (e.g., toward oxygen). The reducing properties are the more important, particularly those involving aqueous solutions of sulfur dioxide. They are considered characteristic of sulfurous acid solutions (p. 537). At low temperatures, sulfur dioxide forms a number of solvates (p. 363), particularly with metal iodides and thiocyanates.

Sulfur dioxide is most commonly obtained by burning sulfur in air or oxygen. Some 3.6% of sulfur trioxide also results under these conditions. Oxidation of sulfides in the roasting of sulfidic minerals accounts for large quantities of sulfur dioxide, much of which is not recovered. Reduction of concentrated sulfuric acid solutions at elevated temperatures by metals such as copper gives relatively pure sulfur dioxide, as does treatment of sulfites or hydrogen sulfites with strong acids. Sulfur dioxide is available in quantity in the liquid form. Its industrial applications and potential applications have expanded tremendously.[102]

Selenium dioxide resembles sulfur dioxide in its water solubility

[101] L. Wöhler and O. Wegwitz: *Z. anorg. allgem. Chem.*, **213**, 129 (1933).
[102] H. F. Johnstone: *Ind. Eng. Chem.*, **34,** 1017 (1942).

and acidic properties, but the tellurium compound is insoluble and more basic in character. Both are better oxidizing agents than sulfur dioxide.

Sulfur Trioxide (SO_3). The physical characteristics of sulfur trioxide [sulfur(VI) oxide] merit special attention. In the vapor state, the material is monomeric, each molecule having a planar, equilateral triangle (120°) arrangement with the sulfur atom at the center and S—O bond lengths of 1.43 A.[81] Although such a structure could be formulated most readily with but a single pair of electrons between each oxygen atom and the sulfur atom, the measured bond distance is less than the single bond distance (see sulfur dioxide), and resonance structures involving double bonds seem reasonable. In the liquid state a slowly established equilibrium involving monomers and trimers apparently exists, the percentage of the monomer increasing with increasing temperature.

In the solid state three apparently distinct modifications exist. They are described, in order of increasing complexity, as:

1. *Gamma* (γ), an ice-like solid in which the molecular group is trimeric and arranged as

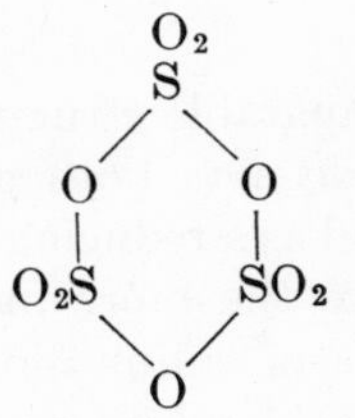

```
        O2
        S
      /   \
     O     O
     |     |
    O2S   SO2
      \   /
        O
```

2. *Beta* (β), an asbestos-like solid in which individual SO_3 groups are linked to each other in long chains as

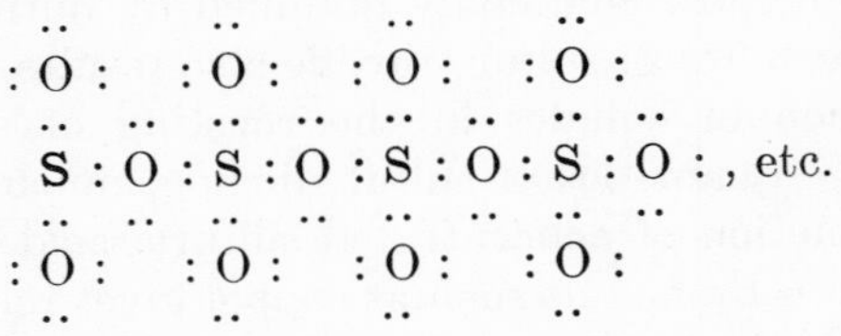

```
 ..      ..      ..      ..
:O:     :O:     :O:     :O:
 ..  ..  ..  ..  ..  ..  ..  ..
 S : O : S : O : S : O : S : O : , etc.
 ..  ..  ..  ..  ..  ..  ..  ..
:O:     :O:     :O:     :O:
 ..      ..      ..      ..
```

3. *Alpha* (α), an asbestos-like solid, like the beta form in structure except that the chains are joined in a layer arrangement.

Physical constants characterizing these modifications are summarized in Table 14·10.*

* The designations employed here are those most commonly used. Some authors reverse the γ and α designations.

TABLE 14·10
PHYSICAL CONSTANTS FOR SULFUR TRIOXIDE

Property	Liquid	Alpha Form	Beta Form	Gamma Form
Equilibrium melting point, °C.		62.3	32.5	16.8
Heat of fusion, kcal./mole		6.2 (62.3°C.)	2.9 (32.5°C.)	1.8 (16.8°C.)
Heat of sublimation, kcal./mole		16.3 (62.3°C.)	13.0 (32.5°C.)	11.9 (16.8°C.)
Heat of vaporization, kcal./mole	10.2	10.1 (62.3°C.)	10.1 (32.5°C.)	10.0 (16.8°C.)
Vapor pressure, mm. Hg at				
0°C.		5.8	32	45
25°C.		73	344	433
50°C.		650	950	950
75°C.		3000	3000	3000
Heat of formation kcal./mole			105.2	106
Density, grams/ml.	1.904			
Surface tension, dynes/cm.	34.17 (19°C.)			
Dielectric constant	3.64 (19°C.)			
Boiling point, °C.	44.5			
Trouton's constant	32.1			

Vapor pressure relations among the forms of sulfur trioxide are summarized in Figure 14·5.[103] Although these data suggest smooth transitions among the three forms, this is not exactly the case, for a number of non-equilibrium solids of varying properties can be obtained, depending upon the mode of preparation, previous treatment, and moisture content.[103] Thus vapor pressures change continuously on vaporization of the solids, and melting points may spread over considerable temperature ranges. The alpha, beta, and gamma modifications of sulfur trioxide cannot be regarded as true allotropic forms. Both gamma and beta forms are metastable with respect to the highly polymerized alpha form. Conversion to the alpha form is catalyzed by moisture. Sulfur, tellurium, carbon tetrachloride, and phosphorus(V) oxychloride all inhibit this polymerization. Preservation of the gamma and beta forms is difficult except in the presence of such inhibitors. However, stabilized sulfur trioxides corresponding roughly to the three forms have been made available technically under the name "Sulfans."[104]

Gamma sulfur trioxide is obtained when highly dried sulfur trioxide is vaporized at room temperatures and the vapors condensed at −80°C. If the same process is carried out using ordinary sulfur trioxide (some water present), the condensed solid is a mixture of the gamma and

[103] A. Smits and P. Schoenmaker: *J. Chem. Soc.*, **125**, 2554 (1925); **1926**, 1108, 1603.

[104] See *Sulfans*, trade publication of General Chemical Co., New York.

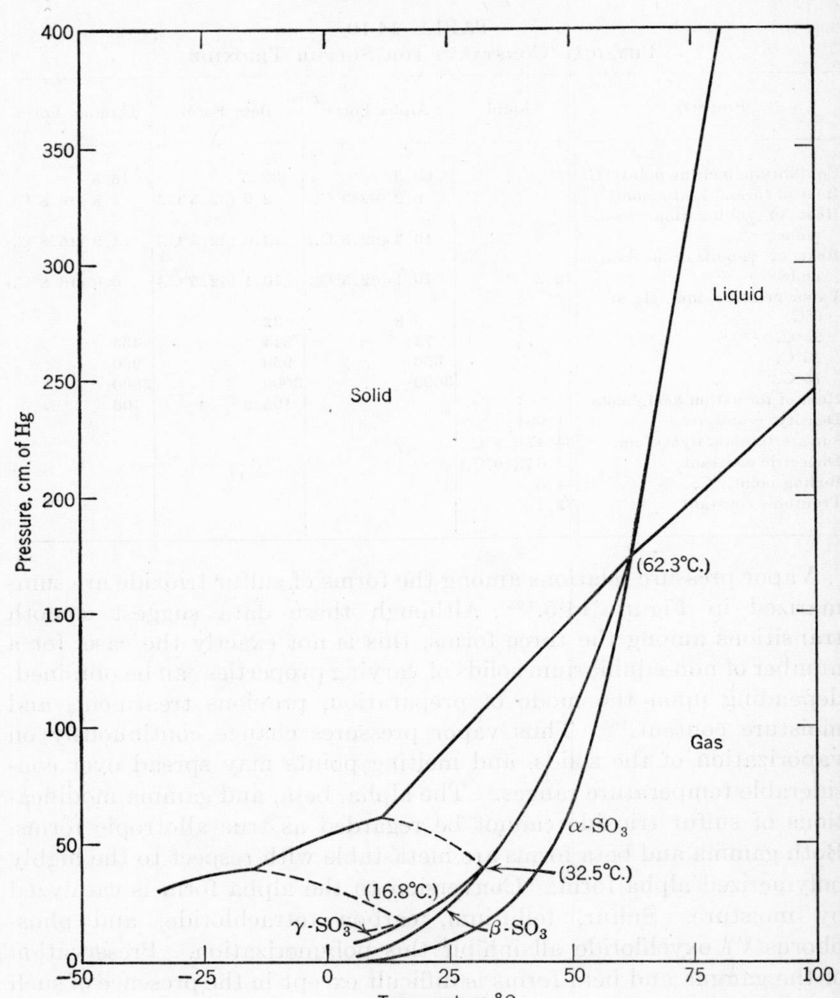

FIG. 14·5. Vapor pressure relations for modifications of sulfur(VI) oxide.

beta forms. Distillation then removes the more volatile gamma form. The alpha form is obtained when sulfur trioxide vapors are condensed at liquid air temperatures.

Chemically, all three forms enter into roughly the same general reactions, but the gamma form is normally the most reactive and the alpha form the least. The reaction with water to yield sulfuric acid or solutions thereof is highly exothermic (21.3 kcal./mole) and difficult to control. Technically, concentrated sulfuric acid (ca. 98%) is commonly employed as a solvent for sulfur trioxide. The system H_2O-SO_3 has been studied extensively and is characterized by a number of hydrates of sulfuric acid. A phase diagram[105] covering the region 0 to 93.7% SO_3 is shown in Figure 14·6. Congruent melting points are obtained for the following materials: $H_2SO_4 \cdot 4H_2O$ (−28.36°C.); $H_2SO_4 \cdot 2H_2O$ (−39.51°C.); $H_2SO_4 \cdot H_2O$ (8.56°C.); H_2SO_4 (10.37°C.); and $H_2S_2O_7$ (35.15°C.). The compounds $H_2SO_4 \cdot 6H_2O$ and $H_2SO_4 \cdot 3H_2O$ melt incongruently and are transformed into the 4-hydrate at −53.73°C. and −36.56°C., respectively.

Sulfur trioxide is a strong acid (p. 327) and readily converts basic oxides to sulfates. It is also an oxidizing agent, giving free halogens (except fluorine) with many metal and non-metal halides. Reactions with organic compounds yield either carbon or sulfonic acids as ultimate products.

Sulfur trioxide is prepared most commonly by oxidation of sulfur dioxide with molecular oxygen in the presence of a catalyst (contact process). Such catalysts as platinum, nickel or cobalt sulfate, and vanadium, tungsten, chromium, molybdenum, and iron oxides are effective. The reaction is exothermic, but the reactants do not combine with measurable velocity at room temperatures. At temperatures where the uncatalyzed reaction velocity becomes appreciable, the yield of product is small. Optimum temperatures of 400° to 665°C. are used technically to permit reasonable yields. Other less important methods of preparation involve dry distillation of certain metal sulfates [notably the iron(III) compound] or pyrosulfates, reaction of sulfur dioxide with ozone at room temperature, and reaction of sulfur dioxide with nitric oxide(NO) under pressure or with nitrogen dioxide(NO_2) at elevated temperatures. The last reaction yields other products besides sulfur trioxide.

The chemistry of sulfur trioxide is becoming increasingly important.[106] Selenium and tellurium trioxides are less important. The selenium compound reacts readily with water to give selenic acid, but the tellurium compound reacts only with hot, concentrated alkali. Indirect methods of preparation are employed.

Sulfur Heptoxide (S_2O_7). This compound has been only very poorly characterized. Berthelot[107] described it as a liquid freezing at around 0°C., decomposing at room temperature to sulfur trioxide and oxygen, and reacting in part with water to give peroxydisulfuric acid. The material was obtained by passing either the dioxide or

[105] C. M. Gable, H. F. Betz, and S. H. Maron: *J. Am. Chem. Soc.*, **72**, 1445 (1950).
[106] H. Baumgarten: *Die Chemie*, **55**, 115 (1942).
[107] M. Berthelot: *Compt. rend.*, **86**, 277, 281 (1878); **90**, 269, 331 (1880).

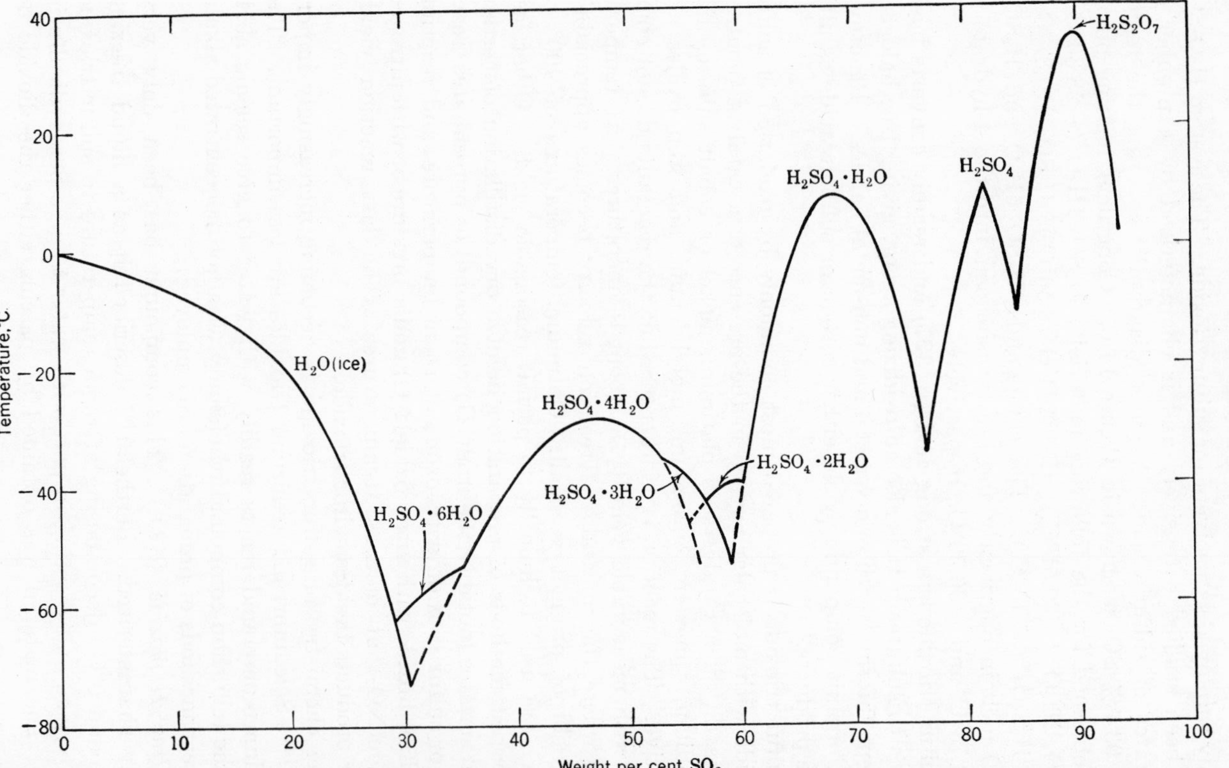

FIG. 14·6. Phase relations in the system SO_3–H_2O.

trioxide mixed with excess oxygen through an electric discharge. Later work has shown, however, that Berthelot's crystalline product contained excess sulfur trioxide, suggesting that it was an equimolar combination of the tri- and tetroxides.[108] Repetition of Berthelot's work by Maisin[109] has given a product of composition S_3O_{11}. The entire problem is in need of re-examination.

Sulfur Tetroxide (SO_4). Sulfur tetroxide is a white solid which melts (with decomposition) at 3°C. to an oily liquid. Cryoscopic determinations in sulfuric acid as a solvent show its molecular weight to be 90 to 95, in agreement with the 96 required by the monomeric formula SO_4.[110] The material is a strong oxidizing agent, converting manganese(II) to manganese(VII), aniline to nitrobenzene, iodide to iodine, etc., and forming sulfate as reduction product. It dissolves with reaction in water but apparently does not give peroxymonosulfuric acid as a product.

Pure sulfur tetroxide was prepared by passing a mixture of dry sulfur dioxide and oxygen ($1SO_2:10O_2$) at 0.5 mm. of mercury pressure through a glow discharge.[110] When the product was condensed in a liquid air trap, solid tetroxide separated. The product was freed of ozone and sulfur dioxide by passage of oxygen at −30°C. and analyzed by precipitation of barium sulfate and oxidation of iodide.

The oxy acids of sulfur

Of the oxides discussed in the preceding section, only the dioxide and the trioxide may be regarded as definite acid anhydrides. The same is true of selenium and tellurium. However, a number of oxy acids of sulfur other than those based upon these oxides are known either in the free condition, in solution, or as salts. The summary in Table 14·11 includes the most important of these.* For selenium and tellurium, only the simple acids based upon the anhydrides are known, although a number of poly acids (pp. 273–276) containing tellurium have been described. Certain of the oxy acids of sulfur merit further discussion. The peroxy acids have been discussed in an earlier section of this chapter (pp. 512–514).

Sulfoxylic Acid (H_2SO_2). This acid is known only in the form of its salts, specifically its sodium, zinc, and cobalt(II) salts, although exist-

[108] F. Meyer, G. Bailleul, and G. Henkel: *Ber.*, **55**, 2923 (1922).
[109] J. Maisin: *Bull. soc. chim. Belg.*, **37**, 326 (1928).
[110] R. Schwarz and H. Achenbach: *Z. anorg. allgem. Chem.*, **219**, 271 (1934).
* The names used in Table 14·11 and throughout subsequent discussions are recommended by the International Union of Chemistry.[69]

TABLE 14·11
Oxy Acids of Sulfur

Formula	Name	Apparent Oxidation State of Sulfur	Probable Structure	Preparation
H_2SO_2	sulfoxylic acid	+2	H : O : S : O : H	salts
$H_2S_2O_4$	dithionous acid (hyposulfurous, hydrosulfurous)	+3	: O : H : O : S : S : O : H : O :	acid, salts
H_2SO_3	sulfurous acid	+4	: O : H : O : S : O : H	acid, salts
$H_2S_2O_5$	pyrosulfurous acid	+5	: O : : O : H : O : S : S : O : H : O :	salts
H_2SO_4	sulfuric acid	+6	: O : H : O : S : O : H : O :	acid, salts
$H_2S_2O_7$	pyrosulfuric acid	+6	: O : : O : H : O : S : O : S : O : H : O : : O :	acid, salts
$H_2S_2O_3$	thiosulfuric acid	+6(−2)	: O : H : O : S : O : H : S :	salts
H_2SO_5	peroxymonosulfuric acid	(+6)	: O : H : O : O : S : O : H : O :	acid, salts
$H_2S_2O_8$	peroxydisulfuric acid	(+6)	: O : : O : H : O : S : O : O : S : O : H : O : : O :	acid, salts
$H_2S_xO_6$ (x = 2–6)	thionic acids	....	: O : : O : H : O : S : $(S)_{x-2}$: S : O : H : O : : O :	salts

ence of the sodium salt is questionable.[111] Vogel and Partington[112] claimed to have obtained the sodium salt by reacting sulfur sesquioxide (p. 527) with sodium ethoxide, allowing the mixture to stand, and precipitating with dilute sulfuric acid. The product was thermally stable, although strongly reducing, and insoluble in alcohol. The zinc salt was believed to have been obtained by the reaction of zinc dust with sulfuryl chloride (p. 523) in ether solution.[113] Data on the cobalt(II) salt are more definite. It is obtained in solution by treating sodium dithionite solution with cobalt(II) acetate and adding aqueous ammonia as

$$CoS_2O_4 + 2NH_3 + H_2O \rightarrow CoSO_2 + (NH_4)_2SO_3$$

and is precipitated as a brown product by saturating with carbon dioxide.[114] Organic sulfones, R_2SO_2, may be regarded as formal derivatives of sulfoxylic acid.

Dithionous Acid ($H_2S_2O_4$). Dithionous (hyposulfurous) acid may be prepared in aqueous solution by reducing sulfurous acid solutions with amalgamated zinc, but such solutions decompose rapidly according to the equation

$$2S_2O_4^{-2} + H_2O \rightarrow S_2O_3^{-2} + 2HSO_3^-$$

or, if acid is added, to sulfurous acid and sulfur. The acid is strong, however, the first hydrogen being lost completely and the ionization constant (k_A') for the second hydrogen being 3.5×10^{-3} (25°C.). Cryoscopic measurements show the dithionite ion to be $S_2O_4^{-2}$.[115] Klemm's observation[116] that the sodium salt is diamagnetic is in accord with the $S_2O_4^{-2}$ formulation as opposed to SO_2^-. Raman data indicate the presence of a single bond sulfur to sulfur link in the dithionite ion.[117] Solutions of the acid are strongly reducing in character.

Dithionites are stable as dry solids and decompose much more slowly in aqueous solution than the acid. However, in the presence of acids, decomposition is rapid. Jellinek's experiments[118] suggest this decomposition to be a second-order process. Dithionites are powerful reduc-

[111] H. Bassett and R. G. Durant: *J. Chem. Soc.*, **1927,** 1401.

[112] I. Vogel and J. R. Partington: *J. Chem. Soc.*, **127,** 1514 (1925).

[113] E. Fromm and J. deS. Palma: *Ber.*, **39,** 3317 (1906).

[114] R. Scholder and G. Denk: *Z. anorg. allgem. Chem.*, **222,** 17 (1935).

[115] K. Jellinek: *Z. anorg. Chem.*, **70,** 93 (1911).

[116] L. Klemm: *Z. anorg. allgem. Chem.*, **231,** 136 (1937).

[117] A. Simon and H. Küchler: *Z. anorg. Chem.*, **260,** 161 (1949).

[118] K. Jellinek and E. Jellinek: *Z. physik. Chem.*, **93,** 325 (1919).

ing agents as indicated by the couples

$$HS_2O_4^- + 2H_2O \rightleftharpoons 2H_2SO_3 + H^+ + 2e^- \qquad E^0_{298} = 0.23 \text{ volt}$$

$$S_2O_4^{-2} + 4OH^- \rightleftharpoons 2SO_3^{-2} + 2H_2O + 2e^- \qquad = 1.4 \text{ volts}$$

Oxidants such as silver(I), iodine, iodate, permanganate, copper(II), hydrogen peroxide, nitrous acid, and molecular oxygen, are all reduced as are a variety of organic dyes. To effect such reductions, sodium dithionite is ordinarily employed. This salt is the most important of the dithionites.

Sodium dithionite is prepared by reducing sodium hydrogen sulfite solution with zinc dust and separated by removing excess sulfite by precipitation with calcium hydroxide and precipitating as the 2-hydrate with a soluble sodium salt, all operations being conducted in the absence of oxygen.[115] The anhydrous salt is obtained by either vacuum dehydration at 60° to 70°C. or alcohol dehydration. Reaction of sodium amalgam with sulfur dioxide[119] or electrolytic reduction of sodium sulfite[116] may be employed also.

Sulfurous Acid (H_2SO_3). Sulfur dioxide dissolves readily in water (ca. 10% by weight at 20°C. and 760 mm. of mercury), giving solutions of sulfurous acid. Such solutions contain largely hydrogen sulfite (HSO_3^-) ions, together with smaller concentrations of sulfite (SO_3^{-2}) ions, the successive dissociation constants of the acid at 25°C. being $pk_{A_1}' = 1.77$ and $pk_{A_2}' = 7.20$. The acid is unknown in the free state, although a hydrate, $SO_2 \cdot 7H_2O$, can be crystallized from concentrated sulfurous acid solutions at low temperatures. The sulfite ion, however, has a pyramidal structure like the chlorate ion, as shown by x-ray data obtained for the sodium salt.[120] Resonance forms seem probable. The existence of organic sulfites and isomeric sulfonates as

suggests the existence of corresponding isomeric forms of sulfurous acid and possibly its inorganic salts. No cases of such isomerism have been found.

Sulfurous acid solutions, like sulfur dioxide (p. 527), are characterized by their reducing properties. The same is true of solutions of

[119] L. Rougeot: *Compt. rend.*, **222**, 1497 (1946).
[120] W. H. Zachariasen and H. E. Buckley: *Phys. Rev.*, **37**, 1295 (1931).

soluble sulfites and hydrogen sulfites. Reactions with molecular oxygen have been studied extensively, especially as regards conditions necessary for quantitative conversion to sulfuric acid or sulfate. Iron(II) and arsenite ions favor such oxidation, whereas it is inhibited by phenol, glycerol, mannitol, tin(II) ion, etc. Oxidation often yields dithionate (p. 535) as well as sulfate. Sulfurous acid solutions are also oxidizing in character (pp. 527, 535) but require strong reducing agents (e.g., iodide, hydrogen sulfide, zinc) for their reduction. The oxidation-reduction characteristics of the acid and its salts are summarized by the couples

$$H_2SO_3 + H_2O \rightleftharpoons SO_4^{-2} + 4H^+ + 2e^- \qquad E^0_{298} = -0.20 \text{ volt}$$

$$H_2SO_2 + H_2O \rightleftharpoons H_2SO_3 + 2H^+ + 2e^- \qquad = > -0.4$$

$$S_2O_3^{-2} + 3H_2O \rightleftharpoons 2H_2SO_3 + 2H^+ + 4e^- \qquad = -0.40$$

$$S + 3H_2O \rightleftharpoons H_2SO_3 + 4H^+ + 4e^- \qquad = -0.45$$

in acidic solution and

$$H_2SO_3 + 4OH^- \rightleftharpoons SO_4^{-2} + 3H_2O + 2e^- \qquad E^0_{298} = 0.90 \text{ volt}$$

$$S_2O_3^{=} + 6OH^- \rightleftharpoons 2SO_3^{-2} + 3H_2O + 4e^- \qquad = 0.58$$

in alkaline solution, together with those considered under dithionous acid (p. 536). Sulfurous acid is both a weaker oxidizing agent and a stronger reducing agent than its selenium and tellurium analogs.

Both normal and hydrogen sulfites are well characterized. Of the former, only the alkali metal compounds are water soluble. Insoluble normal sulfites are often solubilized by sulfur dioxide treatment due to hydrogen sulfite ion formation. Because of the basic character of the sulfite ion, salts with acidic cations [e.g., aluminum, chromium(III)] undergo ready hydrolysis in aqueous solution. Sulfite ion is an excellent coordinating anion (Ch. 7). Addition of acids to normal sulfites gives, successively, hydrogen sulfite ion and sulfur dioxide (p. 527). Sulfites and hydrogen sulfites of the alkali metals are commonly prepared by treating the corresponding carbonates or hydroxides with sulfur dioxide in appropriate proportions.[121]

Pyrosulfurous Acid ($H_2S_2O_5$). Free pyrosulfurous acid is not known but treating alkali metal sulfite or hydrogen sulfite solutions with sulfur dioxide[121] or heating solid alkali metal hydrogen sulfites gives the corresponding pyrosulfites. They do not bear quite the same relation to sulfites as pyrosulfates (p. 534) bear to sulfates because of the

[121] H. F. Johnstone: *Inorganic Synthesis*, Vol. II, p. 162. McGraw-Hill Book Co., New York (1946).

presence of S—S bonds. Thus Zachariasen[122] finds the $S_2O_5^{-2}$ ion to have the arrangement

```
               ..
              : O :
     ..   ..   ..   ..
   : O : S :  S : O :-2
     ..   ..   ..   ..
        : O :  : O :
          ..     ..
```

with S—S and S—O bond distances of 2.18 A and 1.46 A, respectively.

Sulfuric Acid (H_2SO_4). The general chemistries of sulfuric acid and its salts are so well known that no attempt will be made here to cover them in detail. The acid itself is commonly encountered in aqueous solutions of varying concentrations. It is a strong acid (pk_{A_1}' = some negative value), as is also its dissociation product, HSO_4^- ($pk_{A_2}' = 1.70$ at 25°C.). As shown in Figure 14·6, a number of hydrates can be obtained. Treatment of the 98% acid with an appropriate quantity of sulfur trioxide (added as "oleum," $H_2S_2O_7$) gives the pure compound H_2SO_4, a liquid freezing at 10.37°C.[105] This freezing point is sufficiently sharp to be used as a criterion in judging when pure hydrogen sulfate is formed. In the pure compound, each sulfur is surrounded tetrahedrally by four oxygens, the hydrogen atoms serving to bond the various tetrahedra together. The S—O bond distance of 1.51 A, when compared with the radius sum of 1.78 A, suggests resonance involving such structures as

```
     .. -            .. -           .. -              ..
    : O :           : O :          : O :             : O
 -  ..  +  ..   ..   ..  ..    ..   .. -  ..     ..   .. =  ..
: O : S : O :   O : : S : O :  : O : : S : O :  : O : : S : O :
  ..   ..  ..   ..   ..  ..    ..   : :   ..     ..   : :   ..
    : O :           : O :          : O               : O
      .. -            .. -           ..                ..
```

as being more probable than the simple octet arrangement (Table 14·11).[123] Aqueous solutions of sulfuric acid lose water upon evaporation, but at higher temperatures decomposition causes simultaneous evolution of sulfur trioxide. The acid boils at 317°C., where the composition amounts to 98.54% H_2SO_4. This composition is also approached if oleum (p. 541) is heated. The oxidizing properties of sulfuric acid and the sulfate ion have been indicated by oxidation

[122] W. H. Zachariasen: *Phys. Rev.*, **40,** 113, 923 (1932).

[123] L. Pauling: *The Nature of the Chemical Bond*, 2nd Ed., pp. 240–241. Cornell University Press, Ithaca (1940).

potential data (p. 537) as has its conversion to peroxy derivatives (p. 513). The solvent properties of sulfuric acid have been described also (p. 361). The acid is produced technically by the familiar contact and chamber processes.

Normal sulfates characterize most of the metal ions, and hydrogen sulfates are obtainable in the solid state with ammonium and the alkali metals and in solution with many other cations. Sulfates are commonly water soluble (except the lead and alkaline earth metal compounds) and often crystallize as hydrates. In such hydrates, at least a portion of the water appears to be bonded to the sulfate ion (p. 499). Double sulfates are common, these compounds normally being stable as such only in the crystalline state and not coming under strict classification as coordination compounds although coordination by sulfate ion, usually as a monodentate group, may occur (Ch. 7). Two series deserve especial mention, namely, the alums (type formula $M^IM^{III}(SO_4)_2 \cdot 12H_2O$) and the schönites ($M^I_2M^{II}(SO_4)_2 \cdot 6H_2O$).

The alums (p. 499) are a series of commonly isomorphous compounds in which a number of unipositive and tripositive ions may appear and in which selenate (but not tellurate) may often replace sulfate. Examples of the more common alums, together with the crystal radii of their constituent cations, are summarized in Table 14·12. It is immediately apparent that the comparatively large unipositive ions (radii > ca. 1.00 A) and the comparatively small tripositive ions (radii = ca. 0.5–0.7 A) give the largest number of alums. It may be inferred logically, therefore, that such size factors are essential to crystal stability among these compounds. This is supported by the fact that, although larger tripositive ions such as the lanthanide ions give many double sulfates (and selenates), these salts are not alums, and by the fact that sodium alums are most uncommon. With the even smaller lithium ion, doubt may be expressed as to the existence of alums even though evidence for the crystallization of a comparatively unstable phase, $LiAl(SO_4)_2 \cdot 12H_2O$, has been presented.[124,125] In addition to the alums listed in Table 14·12, there are well-known compounds containing the organic groups RNH_3^+, $R_2NH_2^+$, and R_3NH^+. Complete presence of sulfate (or selenate) is not absolutely essential since compounds such as $K_2BeF_4 \cdot Al_2(SO_4)_3 \cdot 24H_2O$ and $K_2ZnCl_4 \cdot Al_2(SO_4)_3 \cdot 24H_2O$ may be classified correctly as alums.[126]

Alums are encountered most commonly as octahedral crystals and are generally considered to be completely isomorphous with each other.

[124] J. F. Spencer and G. T. Oddie: *Nature,* **138,** 169 (1936).
[125] H. A. Horan and A. J. Duane: *J. Am. Chem. Soc.,* **63,** 3533 (1941).
[126] W. R. C. Curjel: *Nature,* **123,** 206 (1929).

TABLE 14·12
COMMON EXAMPLES OF ALUMS

	Li^+ (0.68 A)†	Na^+ (0.98 A)	K^+ (1.33 A)	Rb^+ (1.49 A)	Cs^+ (1.67 A)	Ag^+ (1.13 A)	Tl^+ (1.44 A)	NH_4^+ (1.50 A)	NH_3OH^+	$N_2H_5^+$
Al^{+3} (0.55 A)†	S	S* Se‡	S Se	S Se	S Se	S	S Se	S Se	S	S
Ga^{+3} (0.62 A)			S	S	S Se		S	S		
In^{+3} (0.92 A)				S	S			S		
Ti^{+3} (0.70 A)				S	S					
V^{+3} (0.75 A)		S	S	S	S		S	S		
Cr^{+3} (0.70 A)		S Se	S Se	S Se	S		S Se	S Se	S	S
Mn^{+3}			Se	S	S					
Fe^{+3} (0.67 A)			S Se	S Se	S Se		S	S		
Co^{+3} (0.65 A)			S	S	S		S	S		
Rh^{+3} (0.69 A)			S	S	S		S	S		
Ir^{+3}			S	S	S		S	S		

* Indicates sulfate alum known. † Crystal radii. ‡ Indicates selenate alum known.

Neither of these criteria is absolutely rigid. Crystallization from alkaline medium gives cubic crystals in certain cases,[127, 128] and x-ray studies show the presence of three related but distinct crystal structures, α, β, and γ.[129–131] These structures differ from each other in the distances between the unipositive ions and the sulfate ions and water molecules and consequently in the ways in which these groups are arranged within the crystals. Large unipositive ions give β-alums, small unipositive ions give γ-alums, and ions of intermediate sizes give α-alums. Thus chrome alums containing potassium or ammonium are of the α-type, whereas those containing rubidium, cesium, thallium(I), or methylammonium are of the β-type. Solid solution formation, usually believed to be characteristic of all alums, is limited by these crystal forms and thus by ionic sizes.

The schönites are comparable to the alums in many ways. Just as the compound $KAl(SO_4)_2 \cdot 12H_2O$ is often called "alum" and may be regarded as characteristic of the alums, the compound $K_2Mg(SO_4)_2 \cdot 6H_2O$ is known as "schönite" and is characteristic of this series. Unipositive ions found among the alums are also characteristic of the schönites. Dipositive ions include Zn^{+2}, Ni^{+2}, Co^{+2}, Fe^{+2}, Cu^{+2}, Mn^{+2}, V^{+2}, and Mg^{+2}. The schönites form isomorphous monoclinic crystals. Like the alums, the schönites decompose on dissolution in water, giving solutions containing sulfate, unipositive, and dipositive metal ions.

Selenic acid and the selenates are remarkably similar to sulfuric acid and the sulfates, except that they are stronger oxidizing agents. Telluric acid and the tellurates show not only enhanced oxidizing character but many other differences as well, largely because telluric acid has the composition H_6TeO_6 (compare periodic acid, p. 443). In this acid, tellurium is surrounded octahedrally by six OH groups.[132] The acid is weak, and normally only two hydrogen atoms are removed in salt formation.

Pyrosulfuric Acid ($H_2S_2O_7$). Pyrosulfuric acid results when pure sulfuric acid and sulfur trioxide combine in equimolar proportions. Actually, sulfur trioxide dissolves in sulfuric acid in all proportions to give the so-called fuming sulfuric acids, or oleums, of commerce. Pyrosulfuric acid is the composition of maximum melting point

[127] C. R. von Hauer: *J. prakt. Chem.*, (1), **94**, 241 (1865).
[128] P. A. Paine and W. G. France: *J. Phys. Chem.*, **39**, 425 (1935).
[129] H. Lipson: *Proc. Roy. Soc. (London)*, **A151**, 347 (1935); *Nature*, **135**, 912 (1935); *Phil. Mag.* (vii), **19**, 887 (1935).
[130] H. P. Klug: *J. Am. Chem. Soc.*, **62**, 2992 (1940).
[131] H. P. Klug and L. Alexander: *J. Am. Chem. Soc.*, **62**, 1492, 2993 (1940).
[132] L. Pauling: *Z. Krist.*, **91**, 367 (1935).

(Figure 14·6). The acid itself loses sulfur trioxide, especially on heating, and reacts vigorously with water. It is an excellent sulfonating agent. Heating solid alkali metal hydrogen sulfates causes them to lose water and be converted to pyrosulfates. Normal sulfates also combine directly with sulfur trioxide when heated in closed tubes, and crystallization of alkali metal sulfate or hydrogen sulfate solutions in concentrated sulfuric acid gives pyrosulfates. The alkali metal pyrosulfates behave as excellent high-temperature acids (pp. 333–334). In water they hydrolyze to hydrogen sulfates. Alkaline earth, magnesium, and silver salts are known, but information is lacking about the salts of other metals. Pyrosulfates are simple isopoly sulfates.

Although detailed information is lacking, there are evidences of the existence of higher isopoly sulfates. The nitronium (pp. 609–611) tripoly salt, $(NO_2)_2S_3O_{10}$, a solid melting at 150°C., has been isolated[133] even though attempts to prepare other salts have apparently been fruitless. However, a number of the observed Raman frequencies for oleums may be associated with the tri- and tetrapoly acids, $H_2S_3O_{10}$ and $H_2S_4O_{13}$, and perhaps with higher members of the series.[134] Furthermore, cryoscopic data for oleum solutions of ammonium sulfate can be interpreted best if the formation of such species as $HS_3O_{10}^-$, $S_3O_{10}^{-2}$, $HS_4O_{13}^-$, and $S_4O_{13}^{-2}$ is assumed.[135]

Thiosulfuric Acid ($H_2S_2O_3$). Neither free thiosulfuric acid nor hydrogen thiosulfate salts can be prepared because of reactions between thiosulfate and hydrogen ions. The rates and natures of such reactions are dependent upon the concentration of protonic acid present. At proton concentrations in excess of ca. 10^{-5} *M*, the $HS_2O_3^-$ ion apparently forms but undergoes immediate decomposition to sulfur and sulfurous acid (or sulfur dioxide). This reaction occurs most rapidly at low proton concentrations. At the same time, but more slowly, some pentathionate (p. 544) is also formed. With concentrated hydrochloric acid, even hydrogen sulfide and persulfide apparently result. On the other hand, in neutral or alkaline media, the thiosulfate ion is perfectly stable. The best-known thiosulfates are those of the alkali metals. These are readily soluble in water and are obtained most commonly by direct reactions of the sulfites with sulfur in aqueous solution. Thiosulfates also result from controlled oxidation of sulfides, spontaneous decomposition of dithionites, or reaction between polythionates and alkalies. Some of the heavy metal thiosulfates are water insoluble, although they are commonly soluble in solutions con-

[133] D. R. Goddard, E. D. Hughes, and C. K. Ingold: *J. Chem. Soc.*, **1950**, 2559.
[134] D. J. Millen: *J. Chem. Soc.*, **1950**, 2589.
[135] R. J. Gillespie: *J. Chem. Soc.*, **1950**, 2516.

taining excess thiosulfate ion due to complex ion formation. A case in point is the silver salt, which is readily converted into ions such as $[Ag(S_2O_3)]^-$ and $[Ag(S_2O_3)_2]^{-3}$. Certain heavy metal thiosulfates are readily converted to sulfides with formation of sulfate (and some trithionate) ion when warmed with water.

The thiosulfate ion is a structural analog of the sulfate ion, a sulfur atom having replaced one oxygen atom in the sulfate (Table 14·11). Such a structure is compatible with observations that, when thiosulfate is prepared from sulfite and radioactive sulfur and then decomposed either to sulfur and sulfite (by acids) or to sulfide and sulfate (by decomposition of the silver salt), the radioactivity appears in either the free sulfur or the sulfide.[136, 137] If both sulfur atoms were equivalent in the thiosulfate, partition of the activity between the two products would be expected in both instances. The two sulfurs are linked covalently, but in a formal way the one replacing oxygen may be considered to be negative with respect to the other one. This view is in accord with observations that rapid exchange occurs between radioactive sulfide ion and half the sulfur in the thiosulfate ion.[138]

As indicated by the couples on p. 537 and the couple

$$2S_2O_3^{-2} \rightleftharpoons S_4O_6^{-2} + 2e^- \qquad E^0_{298} = -0.17 \text{ volt}$$

thiosulfate ion is a reducing agent of moderate strength. Conversion to tetrathionate by iodine is perhaps the best known reaction of the thiosulfate. Oxidation to sulfite is complicated by the inherent reducing power of the sulfite. Accordingly, sulfate is the common oxidation product when strong oxidizing agents are employed.

The Thionic Acids ($H_2S_xO_6$, $x = 2$–6). The thionic acids are often classified as dithionic acid ($x = 2$) and polythionic acids ($x > 2$) because of the rather marked differences in properties which set dithionic acid apart from the others. As indicated in Table 14·11, the structures of these acids are assumed to involve sulfur atom chains. This assumption is based upon the appearance of such chains in dithionate[139] and trithionate[140] ions, as revealed by x-ray studies, as well as upon general physical and chemical data.[141] In the dithionate, the S—S bond distance is 2.08 A (single bond) and the S—O distance is 1.50 A (between single and double bond distances). In the tri-

[136] E. B. Andersen: *Z. physik. Chem.*, **B32**, 237 (1936).
[137] H. H. Voge and W. F. Libby: *J. Am. Chem. Soc.*, **59**, 2474 (1937).
[138] H. H. Voge: *J. Am. Chem. Soc.*, **61**, 1032 (1939).
[139] W. H. Barnes and A. V. Wendling: *Z. Krist.*, **99**, 153 (1938).
[140] W. H. Zachariasen: *Z. Krist.*, **89**, 529 (1934).
[141] O. Foss: *Acta Chem. Scand.*, **4**, 404 (1950).

thionate, the S—S—S bond angle is roughly 100°. As an alternative, higher thionates may be considered as derived from trithionate by coordination of sulfur to the central sulfur atom as

$$O_3S{-}S{-}SO_3^{-2} \qquad O_3S{-}\overset{\overset{S}{\uparrow}}{S}{-}SO_3^{-2} \qquad O_3S{-}\underset{\underset{S}{\downarrow}}{\overset{\overset{S}{\uparrow}}{S}}{-}SO_3^{-2}$$

trithionate tetrathionate pentathionate

These structures are supported in some measure by the fact that treatment of the higher thionates ($x > 3$) with alkali removes sulfur atoms successively, but only until the trithionate forms. On the other hand, the ease with which the pentathionate and hexathionate lose thiosulfate when treated with molecules and ions which have affinity for sulfur suggests that these thionates are sulfur-thiosulfate combinations, $S(S_2O_3)_2^{-2}$ and $S_2(S_2O_3)_2^{-2}$, respectively.[142] Such structures are compatible with those proposed by Martin and Metz[143] and supported by both chemical[144] and magnetic[145] data. More work on structures is clearly indicated to be necessary.

DITHIONIC ACID AND THE DITHIONATES. Dithionic acid differs from the other thionic acids in the following ways:

1. Dithionic acid is formed by oxidation of sulfurous acid. The other thionic acids are formed by reduction of sulfurous acid.
2. Dithionic acid is resistant to oxidation. The others are not.
3. Dithionic acid does not combine with sulfur to give the higher acids.

Although comparatively stable in dilute solution at room temperatures, dithionic acid is decomposed to sulfuric acid and sulfur dioxide when such solutions are heated above 50°C. or concentrated. Solutions of the alkali and alkaline earth metal salts undergo no decomposition even on boiling, but solutions of salts of other metals lose sulfur dioxide and give sulfates. Dithionic acid is a strong acid. The acid and its salts are not oxidized by even such strong oxidizing agents as permanganate, hypochlorite, and chlorine at room temperatures. Only powerful reducing agents react with dithionates, sodium amalgam, for example, giving sulfite and dithionite. These processes are probably governed by rate steps since the couples

142 O. Foss: *The Syracuse Chemist*, p. 20, June 1948.
143 F. Martin and L. Metz: *Z. anorg. allgem. Chem.*, **127**, 83 (1923).
144 I. Vogel: *Chem. News*, **128**, 325, 342 (1924); *J. Chem. Soc.*, **127**, 2248 (1925).
145 U. Croatto, V. Scatturin, and A. Fava: *Ricerca sci.*, **19**, 700 (1950).

$$2H_2SO_3 \rightleftharpoons S_2O_6^{-2} + 4H^+ + 2e^- \qquad E^0_{298} = -0.20 \text{ volt}$$

and

$$S_2O_6^{-2} + 2H_2O \rightleftharpoons 2SO_4^{-2} + 4H^+ + 2e^- \qquad = -0.20 \text{ volt}$$

would not predict marked resistance to either oxidation or reduction.

Dithionic acid and its salts are best prepared by oxidation of sulfur dioxide or sulfites. This may be effected electrolytically or by such chemical oxidizing agents as manganese(IV) oxide, permanganate, iron(III) or cobalt(III) hydroxide. A common laboratory preparative procedure[146] utilizes treatment of an aqueous suspension of manganese(IV) oxide with sulfur dioxide below 10°C. to form manganese(II) sulfate and dithionate in solution, removal of manganese and sulfate ions with calcium hydroxide or barium hydroxide, and crystallization of the calcium or barium salt after removal of the excess hydroxide with carbon dioxide. The sodium salt may be obtained in similar fashion by adding sodium carbonate, filtering and crystallizing,[146] or by direct action of sodium hydrogen sulfite solutions on manganese(IV) oxide. Treatment of the barium salt with the calculated quantity of sulfuric acid gives an aqueous solution of the acid.

Dithionates appear to be water soluble regardless of the cation present. Acid salts are unknown.

POLYTHIONIC ACIDS AND THE POLYTHIONATES. Although the free polythionic acids cannot be isolated as such, salts are known for all acids up through hexathionic ($H_2S_6O_6$). Some evidence, although not particularly definite evidence, has been obtained for even higher polythionates in solution. The chemistry of the polythionates is complex and has not been elucidated completely.[147]

The polythionic acids, although unstable, apparently are strong acids. Crystalline normal salts containing a variety of light and heavy metal cations have been prepared. They are uniformly water soluble. Alkali converts the higher polythionates to trithionate, and eventually decomposes the latter to sulfite and thiosulfate. Reactions in acidic solutions are more complex but may be described at least in part by the equations

$$S_nO_6^{-2} \rightarrow (n-2)S + SO_2 + SO_4^{-2} \qquad (n = 3, 4)$$

and

$$2S_nO_6^{-2} + 4H^+ \rightarrow (2n-5)S + 5SO_2 + 2H_2O \qquad (n = 5, 6)$$

[146] R. Pfanstiel: *Inorganic Synthesis*, Vol. II, p. 167. McGraw-Hill Book Co., New York (1946).

[147] A. Kurtenacker: *Abegg's Handbuch der anorganischen Chemie*, Vol. IV, Pt. 1, p. 541. Verlag von S. Hirzel, Leipzig (1927).

In weakly acidic solutions, the tetrathionate decomposes to tri- and pentathionates, the pentathionate to sulfur and tetrathionate, and the hexathionate to sulfur and pentathionate. Cyanides convert polythionates to thiosulfates and sulfates, with formation of thiocyanates. These reactions and others have been combined into an ingenious scheme of analysis applicable to solutions containing not only all the thionates but sulfide, sulfite, sulfate, and thiosulfate as well.[148]

The polythionates are mild reducing agents. However, as indicated by the typical couples,

$$S_3O_6^{-2} + 3H_2O \rightleftharpoons 3H_2SO_3 + 2e^- \qquad E^0_{298} = -0.68 \text{ volt}$$

$$S_5O_6^{-2} + 9H_2O \rightleftharpoons 5H_2SO_3 + 8H^+ + 10e^- \qquad = -0.45 \text{ volt}$$

oxidizing agents capable of attacking them are also capable of oxidizing sulfurous acid to sulfate. Hence sulfate is always the ultimate oxidation product.

The polythionates are formed when thiosulfate solutions containing arsenic(III) oxide react with sulfur dioxide, generated either externally or internally by addition of hydrochloric acid. Although all the polythionates are formed under these circumstances, their relative proportions appear to be closely related to both acid and arsenite concentrations.[149] The role of the arsenic material is obscure. Trithionate, pentathionate, and hexathionate (as sodium salts) are prepared most conveniently by modifications of this general procedure. Tetrathionate, although obtainable by this means, is more conveniently prepared by oxidation of thiosulfate with iodine.[150] Hexathionate is also obtained when nitrate and thiosulfate react in cold 8 *N* hydrochloric acid solution,[151] and an aqueous solution of pentathionic acid apparently results when a dry mixture of hydrogen sulfide (2 moles) and sulfur dioxide (1 mole) is passed into water.[152]

Of some importance in polythionate chemistry is Wackenroder's liquid, the solution (containing colloidal sulfur) which is formed when hydrogen sulfide is passed into sulfurous acid solution. Study of this liquid first revealed the existence of polythionates. Pentathionate and tetrathionate are important components of Wackenroder's liquid, but thiosulfate, sulfite, sulfide, and other polythionates are also present. A similarly complex mixture results from the hydrolysis of sulfur

148 A. Kurtenacker and E. Goldbach: *Z. anorg. allgem. Chem.*, **166,** 187, (1927).

149 A. Kurtenacker and K. Matějka: *Z. anorg. allgem. Chem.*, **229,** 19 (1936).

150 A. Kurtenacker and A. Fritsch: *Z. anorg. allgem. Chem.*, **121,** 335 (1922).

151 E. Weitz and F. Achterberg: *Ber.*, **61B,** 399 (1928).

152 O. von Deines and H. Grassmann: *Z. anorg. allgem. Chem.*, **220,** 337 (1934).

monochloride (p. 520), since hydrogen sulfide and sulfur dioxide are primary hydrolysis products. Although extensively studied, the mechanisms of the reactions involved are only incompletely understood.

Sulfur-nitrogen compounds

The sulfur-nitrogen compounds include the sulfur nitrides, the nitrogen derivatives of sulfuric acid, and the thiocyanates. Certain phases of the chemistry of the thiocyanates are considered in Chapter 13 (pp. 463–480).

Binary Sulfur-Nitrogen Compounds. Although these compounds are properly considered as nitrides because of the greater electronegativity of the nitrogen, they are called sulfides in much of the available literature. To avoid confusion, that terminology will be employed here. Characterized compounds of this type apparently have the compositions N_4S_4, NS_2, and N_2S_5, although the existence of the last two is somewhat questionable.[153] These compounds are not direct analogs of the nitrogen oxides.

TETRANITROGEN TETRASULFIDE, NITROGEN TETRASULFIDE, OR SULFUR NITRIDE (N_4S_4). This compound forms as golden-yellow or orange-red crystals which melt with some decomposition at 178° to 179°C. and sublime under reduced pressures. The boiling point appears to be very close to the melting point, but distillation is often accompanied by explosive decomposition of the compound. The solid has a specific gravity of 2.24 at 18°C. and a refractive index of 2.046 to 1.908 (visible light). It is not wetted by water, but it dissolves readily in a number of organic solvents (e.g., carbon disulfide, benzene, ethanol).[154] It dissolves in liquid ammonia to give bluish-violet solutions, but, on evaporation of the ammonia, the material N_4S_4 is recovered as such. Molecular weight determinations on solutions in naphthalene,[155] benzene,[156, 157] or carbon tetrachloride[156] are in agreement with the tetrameric composition.

The compound is endothermic and explodes when struck or heated strongly, although it is claimed that if the compound is absolutely pure it is explosive only above 195°C.[158] In contact with water, the

[153] M. Goehring and H. W. Kaloumenos: *Z. anorg. allgem. Chem.*, **263,** 137 (1950).

[154] S. A. Voznesenskii: *J. Russ. Phys. Chem. Soc.*, **59,** 221 (1927).

[155] R. Schenck: *Ann.*, **290,** 171 (1896).

[156] A. Andreocci: *Z. anorg. Chem.*, **14,** 246 (1897).

[157] H. B. VanValkenburgh and J. C. Bailar, Jr.; *J. Am. Chem. Soc.*, **47,** 2134 (1925).

[158] M. H. M. Arnold, J. A. C. Hugill, and J. M. Hutson: *J. Chem. Soc.*, **1936,** 1645.

tetrasulfide hydrolyzes slowly to sulfite, pentathionate (23% of sulfur in this form), sulfur, and ammonium ion. In the presence of alkali, rapid hydrolysis gives ammonia, sulfite, and thiosulfate,[159] but, if the solution is only slightly alkaline, trithionate is obtained instead of sulfite.[160] The formation of ammonia is significant in that it indicates strongly the absence of N—N linkages in the compound. The tetrasulfide gives evidences of unsaturated character in many reactions. It adds dry ammonia (gas) to give a material of composition $N_4S_4 \cdot 2NH_3$, which loses ammonia rather readily. Reaction with chlorine in carbon disulfide gives a crystalline yellow tetrachloride, $N_4S_4Cl_4$. With bromine, the compounds $N_4S_4Br_4$ (bronze) and $N_4S_4Br_6$ (red) have been obtained. Treatment with cold sulfur monochloride gives black, crystalline $N_4S_6Cl_2$. Reduction of the tetrasulfide with tin(II) chloride yields a hydrogen compound of analytical composition $(NSH)_x$,[161] which has been shown by molecular weight determinations in acetone[159] to be a tetramer, $N_4S_4H_4$. This compound is a crystalline solid, decomposing at 100° to 148°C., soluble in acetone or pyridine, stable toward acids, but hydrolyzed by alkalies, all of the nitrogen appearing as ammonia. Meuwsen believes the hydrogens to be bonded to the sulfur atoms rather than the nitrogen atoms,[159] but it seems more probable that the compound has a ring structure of alternating —S— and —NH— groups. This view is supported by the observation that the properties of the material are between those of sulfur (S_8 rings) and the compound S_7NH, which has an eight-membered ring structure of seven sulfur atoms and one —NH— group.[162] Both the substance $N_4S_4H_4$ and the substance S_7NH may be regarded as pseudo-sulfurs.

Reaction of the tetrasulfide with acetyl chloride or sulfur monochloride[163, 164] at elevated temperatures gives the yellow thiotrithiazyl chloride, N_3S_4Cl. Use of sulfur monobromide gives the analogous bromide, and other related compounds (e.g., N_3S_4I, $N_3S_4NO_3$, N_3S_4-HSO_4) can be prepared. These compounds are salt-like in their properties. The chloride is stable in dry air but explodes when heated. It is insoluble in many organic solvents (e.g., ether, carbon disulfide).

A number of structural arrangements have been proposed to account for the chemical characteristics of nitrogen tetrasulfide.[155, 158–160]

[159] A. Meuwsen: *Ber.*, **62B**, 1959 (1929).
[160] M. Goehring: *Chem. Ber.*, **80**, 110 (1947).
[161] H. Wöbling: *Z. anorg. Chem.*, **57**, 281 (1908).
[162] M. Goehring, H. Herb, and W. Koch: *Z. anorg. allgem. Chem.*, **264**, 137 (1951).
[163] W. Muthmann and E. Seitter: *Ber.*, **30**, 627 (1897).
[164] A. Meuwsen: *Ber.*, **65B**, 1724 (1932).

However, the problem is better approached by physical means. Early x-ray studies[165] on the compound led to somewhat erroneous conclusions because of the assumption that the crystals are orthorhombic. Actually, they are monoclinic,[166] with constants $a_0 =$ 8.74 A, $b_0 = 7.14$ A, $c_0 = 8.645$ A, $\beta = 92°21'$, and isomorphous with those of realgar (p. 656). Electron diffraction studies[167] on gaseous nitrogen tetrasulfide indicate the molecule to be a cradle-like eight membered ring of alternating nitrogen and sulfur atoms made up of a bisphenoid of sulfur atoms and a square of nitrogen atoms with N—S and S—S bond distances of 1.62 A and 2.69 A, respectively, and S—N—S and N—S—N angles of 112° and 106°, respectively. Resonance among at least the following structures is probable:

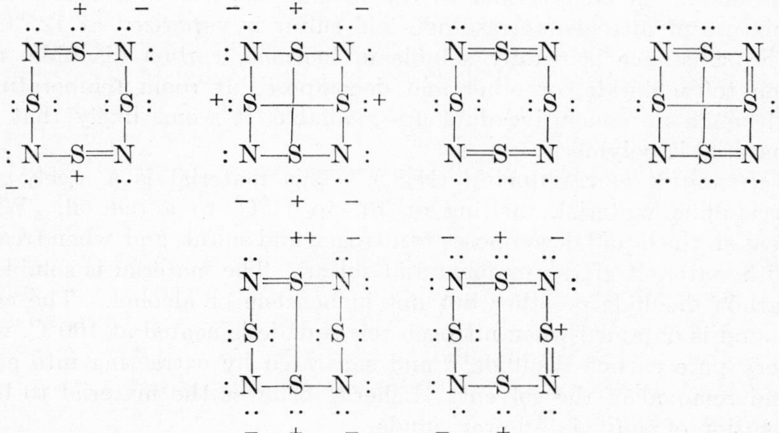

The structure of realgar is exactly similar except that arsenic atoms occupy the sulfur positions and sulfur atoms the nitrogen positions (p. 656).

Nitrogen tetrasulfide can be prepared by either reaction of dry ammonia gas with sulfur dichloride in benzene or with sulfur monochloride in ether[157]

$$6SCl_2 + 16NH_3 \rightarrow N_4S_4 + 12NH_4Cl + 2S$$

$$6S_2Cl_2 + 16NH_3 \rightarrow N_4S_4 + 12NH_4Cl + 8S$$

[165] F. M. Jaeger and J. E. Zanstra: *Proc. Koninkl. Akad. Wetenschap. Amsterdam*, **34,** 782 (1931).

[166] M. J. Buerger: *Am. Mineral.*, **21,** 575 (1936).

[167] C.-S. Lu and J. Donohue: *J. Am. Chem. Soc.*, **66,** 818 (1944).

or reaction of liquid ammonia with dissolved sulfur at −11.5°C. or above

$$10S + 16NH_3 \rightarrow N_4S_4 + 6(NH_4)_2S$$
$$S^{-2} + xS \rightarrow S_{x+1}{}^{-2}$$

In the first general procedure the product is extracted with benzene or carbon disulfide and crystallized. In the second the sulfide and polysulfide ions are removed by adding silver iodide, and then the solution is evaporated to crystallization.[168]

A comparable selenide, N_4Se_4, is obtained by similar means and has similar properties.[157]

NITROGEN DISULFIDE (NS_2). A red, moderately volatile liquid corresponding in composition to the formula NS_2 is obtained when a mixture of nitrogen tetrasulfide and sulfur is vaporized at 125°C.[169] The substance is readily soluble in benzene, carbon disulfide, carbon tetrachloride, or ether and decomposes at room temperatures. Although no conclusive data are available, it seems likely that the material is polymeric.

NITROGEN PENTASULFIDE (N_2S_5). This material is a steely-gray crystalline material, melting at 10° to 11°C. to a red oil. When heated, the liquid decomposes to nitrogen and sulfur, and, when treated with water, it gives ammonia and sulfur. The material is soluble in carbon disulfide or ether but not in benzene or alcohol. The compound is obtained when nitrogen tetrasulfide is heated at 100°C. with very pure carbon disulfide[170] and separated by extracting into ether and removal of the solvent. Usher[169] believes the material to be a solution of sulfur in a lower sulfide.

Nitrogen Derivatives of Sulfuric Acid. A variety of derivatives of sulfuric acid in which nitrogen-to-sulfur bonds are present can be distinguished.[171] Relations existing among a number of these in terms of the nitrogen system of compounds are described in Chapter 15 (p. 572). Here we may consider the amine sulfonic acids, sulfamide, and the hydroxylamine sulfonates. Other pertinent information, particularly on the hydroxylamine sulfonates, is found in Chapter 15.

AMINE SULFONIC ACIDS. The amine sulfonic acids are derived from ammonia by the successive replacement of hydrogens by sulfonic

[168] F. W. Bergstrom: *J. Am. Chem. Soc.*, **48**, 2319 (1926).

[169] F. L. Usher: *J. Chem. Soc.*, **127**, 730 (1925).

[170] W. Muthmann and A. Clever: *Ber.*, **29**, 340 (1896); *Z. anorg. Chem.*, **13**, 200 (1897).

[171] L. F. Audrieth, M. Sveda, H. H. Sisler, and M. J. Butler: *Chem. Revs.*, **26**, 49 (1940).

groups. These materials may be formulated as

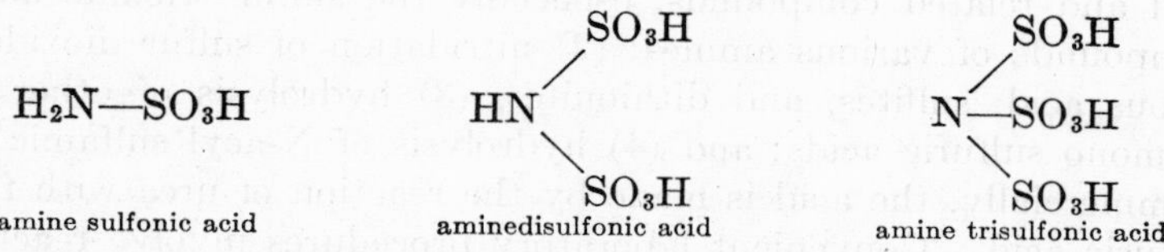

Actually only the first acid is sufficiently stable to be isolated, but salts of all three are well known.

Amine sulfonic acid is more commonly called sulfamic acid. It is a crystalline (rhombic), non-hygroscopic, white solid, melting with decomposition at 205°C. X-ray studies[172] show sulfamic acid to have the zwitterion structure $NH_3^+SO_3^-$, the geometrical arrangement being a distorted tetrahedron. Extensive hydrogen bonding occurs throughout the crystalline material. Interatomic distances are: S—N, 1.73 A; S—O(1), 1.49 A; S—O(2), 1.47 A; and S—O(3), 1.48 A. The compound is soluble in water, but practically insoluble in 70 to 80% sulfuric acid solution. It is also soluble in methanol, ethanol, or liquid ammonia but difficultly soluble in ether. In aqueous solution, sulfamic acid is a strong acid, comparable in strength with hydrochloric acid or nitric acid. Because of this fact and the stability of the compound under ordinary conditions, sulfamic acid is an excellent acidimetric primary standard.[173] Aqueous solutions undergo slow hydrolysis to sulfuric acid and ammonium hydrogen sulfate, but the reaction is rapid at elevated temperatures. The acid is a reducing agent, especially in boiling aqueous solutions. Chlorine, bromine, and chlorates convert it to sulfuric acid, even in the cold, but permanganate and chromic acid are without effect. In the presence of nitrite, sulfamic acid is quantitatively converted to sulfuric acid as

$$HSO_3NH_2 + HNO_2 \rightarrow H_2SO_4 + N_2 + H_2O$$

Nitric acid forms nitrous oxide by a similar reaction. Many of these reactions are also characteristic of the sulfamates. The sulfamates are almost uniformly water soluble. X-ray studies on potassium sulfamate show the structure of the sulfamate ion to be like that of the sulfate ion, with an $—NH_2$ group replacing an oxygen in a slightly distorted tetrahedron and S—N and S—O bond distances of 1.56 A and 1.48 A, respectively.[174] Sulfamic acid may be prepared by any

[172] F. A. Kanda and A. J. King: *J. Am. Chem. Soc.*, **73**, 2315 (1951).

[173] M. J. Butler, G. F. Smith, and L. F. Audrieth: *Ind. Eng. Chem.*, Anal. Ed., **10**, 690 (1938).

[174] J. A. A. Ketelaar and E. L. Heilmann: *Z. Krist.*, **103**, 41 (1940).

one of the following general methods:[171] (1) ammonolysis of sulfuric acid and related compounds, especially the sulfur trioxide addition compounds of various amines; (2) nitridation of sulfur dioxide, sulfurous acid, sulfites, and dithionites, (3) hydrolysis of other aquo-ammono sulfuric acids; and (4) hydrolysis of N-acyl sulfamic acids. Commercially, the acid is made by the reaction of urea with fuming sulfuric acid. Convenient laboratory procedures involve reaction of sulfur dioxide with hydroxylammonium sulfate or acetoxime.[175] Salts are prepared by action of the acid on metals, metal oxides, etc. Sulfamic acid is of importance because of use of its salts as flame-proofing agents, weed killers, electrolytes in metal deposition processes, etc. A number of phases of sulfamic acid chemistry are discussed by Cupery[176] and by Audrieth, Sveda, Sisler, and Butler.[171]

The solid alkali and alkaline earth metal amine disulfonates are stable at room temperature but decompose above room temperature. In aqueous solution, the amine disulfonates hydrolyze to sulfamates as

$$HN(SO_3)_2^{-2} + H_2O \rightarrow H_2NSO_3^- + SO_4^{-2} + H^+$$

They are mild reducing agents but stable toward permanganate in alkaline solution. The potassium salt is the best characterized. It is obtained by careful hydrolysis of potassium amine trisulfonate.

The alkali metal amine trisulfonates (nitrilosulfonates) are well characterized. The potassium salt is only slightly soluble in water but the sodium salt is quite soluble. Aqueous solutions of the alkali metal trisulfonates are neutral and fairly stable. Addition of acid causes rapid hydrolysis to the disulfonate, which in turn hydrolyzes more slowly to the sulfamate. Amine trisulfonate is readily obtained by reaction of nitrite with hydrogen sulfite[177]

$$NO_2^- + 3HSO_3^- \rightarrow N(SO_3)_3^{-3} + H_2O + OH^-$$

the yield of the potassium compound being at a maximum when the ratio of HSO_3^- to NO_2^- is 4 to 1 or greater and the reaction is run at elevated temperatures.[178] Amine trisulfonate is the ultimate product in this reaction, but the general reaction is useful for the preparation of other nitrogen compounds (pp. 581, 616).

[175] H. H. Sisler, M. J. Butler, and L. F. Audrieth: *Inorganic Synthesis*, Vol. II, p. 176. McGraw-Hill Book Co., New York (1946).

[176] M. E. Cupery: *Ind. Eng. Chem.*, **30**, 627 (1938).

[177] A. Claus and S. Koch: *Ann.*, **152**, 336 (1869).

[178] H. Sisler and L. F. Audrieth: *J. Am. Chem. Soc.*, **60**, 1947 (1938). *Inorganic Syntheses*, Vol. II, p. 182. McGraw-Hill Book Co., New York (1946).

SULFAMIDE $[SO_2(NH_2)_2]$. Just as sulfamic acid may be regarded as the monoamide of sulfuric acid, sulfamide is the diamide. The structural relationships among these three materials are thus

```
       ..                   ..
     : O :                : O :                 ..
       ..                   ..               H : O :
  ..        ..         ..        ..           ..    ..   ..
H : O : S : O : H    H : O : S : N : H     H : N : S : N : H
  ..        ..         ..        ..           ..         ..
       ..                   ..    H                ..    H
     : O :                : O :                  : O :
       ..                   ..                     ..
   sulfuric acid        sulfamic acid          sulfamide
```

Sulfamide is a white, crystalline (rhombic) solid which melts sharply at 93°C. and has a density of 1.611 grams per cc. It is readily soluble in water and is ammono-deliquescent. In water solution, sulfamide is only slightly acidic but does form salts of the type $(AgNH)_2SO_2$. In liquid ammonia solution, it is strongly acidic and yields salts of the types $(KNH)_2SO_2$ and $(K_2N)_2SO_2$. Sulfamide decomposes above its melting point to ammonia and sulfimide, $HN = SO_2$. In boiling acidic solution, sulfamide is hydrolyzed to ammonium sulfate. In alkaline solutions, it is converted to amine sulfonates. Like sulfamic acid, nitrous acid converts sulfamide to nitrogen and sulfuric acid. In the presence of sulfuric acid, nitric acid nitrates sulfamide to nitrosulfamide, $H_2NSO_2NHNO_2$. Hypochlorous acid forms monochlorosulfamide, H_2NSO_2NHCl. Sulfamide coordinates to metal ions as a bidentate group after loss of a hydrogen from each nitrogen (p. 238). Sulfamide is prepared by the ammonolysis of sulfuryl chloride

$$SO_2Cl_2 + 4NH_3 \rightarrow SO_2(NH_2)_2 + 2NH_4Cl$$

but with gaseous ammonia and an inert solvent such as benzene or chloroform the reaction is complicated by the formation of sulfimide, imidodisulfamide, $HN(SO_2NH_2)_2$, and higher polymers containing the repeating group $—SO_2NH—$.[179] A better procedure involves addition of sulfuryl chloride to liquid ammonia.[180] The main reaction product is imidodisulfamide, but, if the solid residue remaining after excess ammonia is allowed to evaporate is dissolved in very dilute nitric acid and the solution allowed to stand, hydrolysis to sulfamide occurs. The product is then recovered by evaporation, extraction into ethyl acetate, and crystallization.

A number of nitrogen-substituted sulfamides are also known.[171]

[179] F. Ephraim and F. Michel: *Ber.*, **42,** 3833 (1909).
[180] F. Ephraim and M Gurewitsch: *Ber.*, **43,** 138 (1910).

HYDROXYLAMINE SULFONIC ACIDS. Just as the amine sulfonates are derived from ammonia, a number of hydroxylamine sulfonates are derived from hydroxylamine (pp. 581, 616). Materials of this type may be formulated as

$$HONH{-}SO_3^-$$
hydroxylamine monosulfonate

$$HON(SO_3^-)_2$$
hydroxylamine disulfonate

$$ON(SO_3^-)_2$$
nitrosyl disulfonate

$$H_2N{-}OSO_3^-$$
hydroxylamine isomonosulfonate

$$HN(OSO_3^-)(SO_3^-)$$
hydroxylamine isodisulfonate

$$^-O_3SO{-}N(SO_3^-)_2$$
hydroxylamine trisulfonate

The formation of both N—SO_3 and N—O—SO_3 arrangements is a complicating factor. Certain of these materials are important as intermediates in the synthesis of hydroxylamine (pp. 581–582).

Alkali metal hydroxylamine monosulfonates result from hydrolysis of the disulfonates. The potassium salt is easily recovered by crystallization. Its water solutions are neutral, indicating the parent acid to be strong, but in the presence of acid at 100°C. the hydroxylamine monosulfonate ion is hydrolyzed to hydroxylammonium and sulfate ions. The ion is reducing in character and behaves very much like hydroxylamine (p. 580). The isomeric isomonosulfonates are obtained from the free acid, which precipitates when hydroxylammonium sulfate is warmed with chlorosulfonic acid.[181] The iso compounds also yield hydroxylamine on hydrolysis.

Alkali metal hydroxylamine disulfonates are water-soluble compounds, which give neutral solutions and hydrolyze readily to the monosulfonates and sulfates. They result in the reaction of alkali metal nitrite solutions with sulfur dioxide or alkali metal hydrogen sulfites at low temperatures (pp. 581, 616). The free acid is unknown. The isomeric alkali metal isodisulfonates also give neutral aqueous solutions. In alkaline solutions, they are decomposed to sulfate and sulfamate, whereas the normal disulfonates give nitrite and sulfite. In acidic solutions, sulfate and hydroxylammonium ions result, together with nitric oxide and nitrogen. Sodium amalgam reduces them to sulfamates but does not affect the normal disulfonates. On the other hand, they resist oxidation by lead(IV) oxide in alkaline

[181] F. Sommer, O. F. Schulz, and M. Nassau: *Z. anorg. allgem. Chem.*, **147**, 142 (1925).

solution, whereas the normal disulfonates form nitrosyl disulfonate.[182]

Potassium nitrosyl disulfonate, as obtained by this reaction, is a yellow solid (Fremy's salt, p. 213), which dissolves in water to give a violet-blue solution. Inasmuch as the solid is diamagnetic and its aqueous solutions paramagnetic with measured susceptibilities corresponding to a single unpaired electron,[183] it is believed that the solid is dimeric and the ion in solution monomeric. The solid potassium salt decomposes readily to ammonium sulfate, sulfur dioxide, and nitrous oxide. Solutions of the ion undergo hydrolysis and are good oxidizing agents. Hydrolysis in the presence of alkalies yields hydroxylamine trisulfonates.

The alkali metal hydroxylamine trisulfonates dissolve in water to give neutral solutions. In the presence of alkali, aqueous solutions are stable and resistant to oxidation, but in the presence of acid they undergo rapid hydrolysis to hydroxylamine isodisulfonates and sulfates. The trisulfonates result from oxidation of the disulfonates with lead(IV) oxide in alkaline solution or from reaction of nitrite and hydrogen sulfite solutions, followed by addition of lead(IV) oxide.[184]

SUGGESTED SUPPLEMENTARY REFERENCES

D. M. Yost and H. Russell, Jr.: *Systematic Inorganic Chemistry of the Fifth- and Sixth-Group Non-Metallic Elements*, Ch. 3, 8, 9, 10, 11. Prentice-Hall, New York (1944).

N. V. Sidgwick: *The Chemical Elements and Their Compounds*, pp. 855–997. Clarendon Press, Oxford (1950).

A. F. Wells: *Structural Inorganic Chemistry*, 2nd ed., Ch. X, XI, XII, XIII, XIV. Clarendon Press, Oxford (1950).

---

[182] T. Haga: *J. Chem. Soc.*, **89**, 240 (1906).
[183] R. W. Asmussen: *Z. anorg. allgem. Chem.*, **212**, 317 (1933).
[184] F. Raschig: *Ber.*, **56**, 206 (1923).

CHAPTER 15

Periodic Group Vb
The Nitrogen Family

The elements in this family are all relatively familiar, although their abundance in nature (N 0.0046%, P 0.118%, As 5×10^{-4}%, Sb 1×10^{-4}%, Bi 2×10^{-5}% of the igneous rocks of the earth), except for phosphorus, is not excessively high. Phosphorus ranks tenth in abundance among the elements. Nitrogen is a familiar element because of its rich source, the atmosphere (78.09% nitrogen by volume), and because it is present in such important materials as fertilizers, explosives, and high polymers. Phosphorus is familiar both because it occurs in concentrated deposits and because of the many uses to which the element and its compounds have been put. The other members of the family are familiar because of the comparative ease with which the compounds may be separated, recovered, and reduced to the free elements as well as because of the uses to which some of these materials are put. Nitrogen and phosphorus are undoubtedly among our most versatile and generally useful non-metals. All the elements in this family have been well known for many years.

The nitrogen family is often selected for systematic studies because among its members there is an essentially regular change, with atomic weight and size, from the characteristics of a true non-metal (nitrogen) to an almost true metal (bismuth). This type of trend is of course characteristic of the families in this general region of the periodic system, but the changes in the nitrogen family are often more striking than those in families already discussed. As is expected, the properties of nitrogen are often anomalous, the most regular trends existing among phosphorus, arsenic, antimony, and bismuth. According to the pattern set in preceding chapters, the family is discussed as a whole first, and then some special phases of nitrogen and phosphorus chemistries are considered.

FAMILY RELATIONSHIPS AMONG THE ELEMENTS

Numerical relationships characterizing the members of the nitrogen family are summarized in Table 15·1. Paralleling increases in atomic weight and number are the increases in density, atomic volume, melting point (except for antimony and bismuth), boiling point, and sizes

TABLE 15·1

NUMERICAL PROPERTIES OF NITROGEN FAMILY ELEMENTS

Property	Nitrogen	Phosphorus	Arsenic	Antimony	Bismuth
Atomic number	7	15	33	51	83
Outer electron configuration	$2s^22p^3$	$3s^23p^3$	$4s^24p^3$	$5s^25p^3$	$6s^26p^3$
Molecular formula (gas)	N_2	$P_4 \rightleftharpoons P_2$	$As_4 \rightleftharpoons As_2$	$Sb_4 \rightleftharpoons Sb_2$	$Bi_2 \rightleftharpoons Bi$
Mass numbers, stable isotopes	14, 15	31	75	121, 123	209
Atomic weight	14.008	30.98	74.91	121.76	209.00
Density of solid, grams/cc.	0.8792 (−210°C.)	1.8232* (20°C.) 2.34‡ 2.699‖	5.7† 3.9§	6.58† 5.3§	9.8
Atomic volume of solid, cc.	15.95	16.9*	13.13†	18.50†	21.32
Melting point, °C.	−210.0	44.1* 592.5‡ 587.5‖	814.5 (36 atm.)	630.5	271
Boiling point, °C.	−195.8	280.5*	610 (subl.)	1380	1450
Critical temperature, °C.	−147.1	695			
Critical pressure, atm.	33.5	82.2			
Heat of fusion, kcal./mole	0.1732				
Heat of vaporization, kcal./mole	1.3329				
Covalent radius, A	0.74	1.10	1.21	1.41	1.52
Ionization potential, ev	14.54	11.0	10±	8.64	8±
Electronegativity	3.0	2.1	2.0	1.8	....
Crystal radii, A					
Z^{-3}	1.71	2.12	2.22	2.45	....
Z^{+3}	....	....	0.69	0.90	1.20
Z^{+5} in ZO_3^-	0.11	0.34	0.47	0.62	0.74
E^0_{298} for $ZH_3 \rightleftharpoons Z + 3H^+ + 3e^-$, volts	−0.27	0.03	0.54	0.51	ca. 0.8
E^0_{298} for $Z + 3H_2O \rightleftharpoons H_3ZO_3 + 3H^+ + 3e^-$, volts	−1.44 (HNO_2)	0.49	−0.25 $(HAsO_2)$	−0.21 (SbO^+)	−0.32 (BiO^+)

* White phosphorus. † Metallic arsenic or antimony. ‡ Violet phosphorus. § Yellow arsenic or antimony. ‖ Black phosphorus.

which are characteristic of the families in this part of the periodic arrangement. The striking increase in metallic character with antimony and bismuth makes these trends somewhat less regular than those noted for the Group VIIb and Group VIb elements, where nonmetallic behavior predominates. Reference to Tables 14·1 (p. 482) and 16·1 (p. 662) indicates that the nitrogen family elements are on the average somewhat more volatile than their immediate neighbors. This is a consequence of the five-electron outer arrangements in their atoms. Such arrangements are conducive to the formation of discrete molecules which are comparatively free of attraction for each other.

All the outer electron arrangements are three electrons short of inert gas atom structures. Although some tendency to achieve stable configurations by gain of electrons might be expected, the number of electrons to be gained is so large that the formation of true trinegative ions occurs only with the smallest and most electronegative element, nitrogen. The electronegativities of the other members of the family are so reduced that even in combination with the most electropositive elements they would be bonded in predominantly covalent fashion (p. 207). Covalent structures containing the nitrogen family elements in the formal negative three oxidation state are common, the best characterized examples being the simple hydrides. As is apparent from decreasing values of electronegativities and variations in standard potentials for the Z(−III)–Z(0) couples with atomic weight, the tendency to enter the negative three oxidation state decreases from nitrogen to bismuth. Sharing of electrons among individual atoms to give diatomic and more complex molecular species is a common means of enhancing structural stability.

Data summarized in Table 15·1 give some information relative to positive oxidation states among these elements. Reduced electronegativities among the heavier elements of the family suggest such states in compounds containing more electronegative elements. However, except in combinations involving fluorine, electronegativity differences are too small to permit predominantly ionic character in the bonds. The tendency toward covalence will of course increase as the size of the nitrogen family element decreases. Distribution of valence electrons as ns^2np^3 suggests that positive oxidation states of +3 and +5, corresponding, respectively, to the involvement of the p electrons and both the s and p electrons, should be most common. This is true. In the positive three state, the inert pair (p. 177) is of importance. This oxidation state becomes more characteristic and more resistant to oxidation as one progresses from phosphorus to bismuth. The character of nitrogen is different (p. 559); therefore, comparisons involving nitrogen in this state are not rigorously permissible. Although tripositive bismuth compounds show but little ionic character in the solid state, they do give various ionic species in polar solvents. The tendency decreases through antimony to phosphorus. In the tripositive state, all these materials may act as electron pair donors, but the property is pronounced only with nitrogen. Nitrogen is incapable of accepting electrons because of the octet limitation; the others can behave as acceptors.

In the pentapositive state, all these elements are predominantly non-metallic and acidic in character. This oxidation state becomes less characteristic and more difficult to form as atomic weight increases, the increased stability of the inert pair with increasing size being emphasized again. Nitrogen is again somewhat anomalous in its behavior. In this oxidation state, binding is even more nearly completely covalent than in the positive three state. Compounds of these elements then represent the most striking examples of the comparatively rare pentacovalent materials. The elements (except nitrogen) in this state of oxidation may act as acceptors through expansion of their valency groups. Strictly speaking, such acceptor behavior is limited to small groups because of size factors; but fluoanions of the type $[ZF_6]^-$ are known for phosphorus, arsenic, and antimony, and a hydroxy anion, $[Z(OH)_6]^-$, characterizes at least antimony.

The position of nitrogen is anomalous not only as regards the properties of the tri- and pentapositive compounds but as regards the existence of other oxidation states as well. In combination with oxygen, nitrogen is found in additional positive one, positive two, and positive four states. Well-defined series of such compounds are lacking, however. The characteristics of these compounds are described later.

MODIFICATIONS OF THE FREE ELEMENTS

Like their neighbors in Group VIb, the elements in this family often exist in a variety of modifications in the various physical states. Except with phosphorus, allotropy is not particularly complicated. However, forms differing in molecular complexities are of some importance.

Nitrogen

Elemental nitrogen is diatomic in the gaseous condition. The internuclear distance of 1.095 A[1] for the nitrogen molecule in its normal

[1] F. Rasetti: *Phys. Rev.*, **34**, 367 (1929).

state indicates a triple-bond structure

$$:N:::N:$$

This structure is one of considerable stability as evidenced by the lack of chemical reactivity of nitrogen under any but rather drastic conditions (p. 568) and by the high dissociation energy of some 9.764 ev (225.2 kcal.) per mole[2–4] for the nitrogen molecule. The diatomic condition is presumably characteristic of both liquid and solid nitrogen, van der Waals forces (p. 215) being responsible for the attraction between nitrogen molecules in these states. Two solid forms are known, the low-temperature *alpha* modification (cubic) being transformed at −238.49°C. (35.61°K.) into the *beta* form (hexagonal) with an energy absorption of 0.0547 kcal. per mole. The heat capacity (at constant pressure) is smaller for the beta form.

Active Nitrogen. The large dissociation energy of the nitrogen molecule renders production of atomic nitrogen impossible by available thermal means. The species is observable spectroscopically. Action of an electric discharge upon nitrogen gas at low pressures, however, produces a chemically active material and a comparatively long-lived (several hours) yellow afterglow,[5] the spectrum of which indicates the presence of molecular species. This afterglow is due to the slow release of energy and is of course indicative of the presence of activated (energy-rich) materials. Although it is obtained more readily when traces of oxygen are present,[6] pure nitrogen will give it too.[7] The life of the afterglow is dependent upon the nature of the surface of the containing vessel, suggesting that collision of the activated species with a surface is essential to deactivation. Glass surfaces may be deactivated with metaphosphoric or sulfuric acid[8] and activated by heating in nitrogen[9] or *in vacuo*.[10] Addition of inactive nitrogen[8] or compression stabilizes the afterglow.

Active nitrogen yields nitrides with vapors of sodium, arsenic, or phosphorus and with liquid mercury[11] and reacts with iodine vapor

[2] A. G. Gaydon: *Nature*, **153**, 407 (1944).
[3] A. G. Gaydon and W. G. Penney: *Proc. Roy. Soc.* (*London*), **A183**, 374 (1945).
[4] G. Glockler: *J. Chem. Phys.*, **16**, 602 (1948).
[5] R. J. Strutt (Lord Rayleigh): *Proc. Roy. Soc.* (*London*), **A85**, 219 (1911); **A86**, 262 (1912); **A87**, 179 (1912); **A88**, 539 (1913); **A91**, 303 (1915).
[6] E. Tiede and E. Domcke: *Ber.*, **47**, 420 (1914).
[7] H. B. Baker and R. J. Strutt: *Ber.*, **47**, 801, 1049 (1914).
[8] Lord Rayleigh: *Proc. Roy. Soc.* (*London*), **A151**, 567 (1935).
[9] Lord Rayleigh: *Proc. Roy. Soc.* (*London*), **A180**, 123 (1942).
[10] G. Herzberg: *Z. Physik*, **46**, 878 (1928).
[11] E. Tiede and H.-G. Knoblauch: *Ber.*, **68B**, 1149 (1935).

;iving a blue luminescence. Certain metals, notably copper and gold, ·atalyze conversion to stable molecular nitrogen without giving ıitrides.[12] Nitric oxide (p. 593) reacts to give nitrogen dioxide with a vhite luminescence.

The true nature of active nitrogen is not apparent from presently .vailable data. The chemical behavior of the material and the after- ;low phenomenon appear to be independent of each other, with the nergy associated with the afterglow being comparatively small.[13] Chemical activity persists after destruction of the afterglow.[12,14] At east some dissociation to atomic nitrogen in the activation process eems reasonable in view of observed pressure increases in closed con- ainers,[15] but spectroscopic evidences are contradictory.[16] Debeau[15] elieves that dissociation is responsible for activation and that deac- .vation is due to the formation of a collision complex (NN), followed y either glow or loss of energy as radiation (different from afterglow) r in activating some other material. Further work is indicated.

hosphorus

Phosphorus is comparable to sulfur in the complexity of its modifica- ons, although the solid forms of phosphorus present the most involved roblems. Complexity in the solid state is characteristic of all the ements in the nitrogen family. Two general solid forms are encoun- red, a light non-metallic form and a dense metallic or semi-metallic rm. The first of these is most characteristic of the lighter elements, ıd the second of the heavier elements. Indeed, only the non-metallic rm of nitrogen is noted, whereas only the metallic form of bismuth found. Other modifications of these general forms may exist also. ıosphorus appears to occupy an optimum position as regards .rieties of solid forms. The gaseous and liquid states apparently e not particularly complex.

Gaseous Phosphorus. The vapor density of phosphorus at tempera- res up to 800°C. is in accord with the presence of P_4 molecules. ectron diffraction data[17] show the four phosphorus atoms to be ranged in a tetrahedron (bond angle 60°), the P—P bond distance ing 2.21 ± 0.02 A. This is in excellent agreement with the theo-

[12] E. J. B. Willey: *J. Chem. Soc.*, **1927,** 2188, 2831.

[13] Lord Rayleigh: *Proc. Roy. Soc. (London)*, **A176,** 1, 16 (1940).

[14] R. J. Strutt (Lord Rayleigh): *Proc. Roy. Soc. (London)*, **A92,** 438 (1916).

[15] D. E. Debeau: *Phys. Rev.*, **61,** 668 (1942).

[16] Z. Bay and W. Steiner: *Z. physik. Chem.*, **B3,** 149 (1929).

[17] L. R. Maxwell, S. B. Hendricks, and V. M. Mosley: *J. Chem. Phys.*, **3,** 699 35).

retical single-bond distance of 2.20 A, but the 60° bond angle requires the unusual pd^2 hybridization.[18] This structure is to be contrasted with the structure of the normal diatomic nitrogen molecule. The same contrast is apparent between oxygen and sulfur (pp. 482, 491). It appears reasonable to conclude, therefore, that, although the introductory elements in these two families form molecules by multiple bonding between atoms, this tendency is much reduced in the second members of the families. The same conclusion may be drawn from considerations of compounds of the elements. A comparable situation exists, of course, among the Group IVb elements.

Above 800°C., dissociation occurs. Early conclusions[19] that both the species P_2 and P are present have been shown to be invalid,[20, 21] and it is now well established that the molecule P_2 is the only dissociation product. Even at comparatively high temperatures, equilibrium conditions are unfavorable for the dissociation of the diatomic molecules. In the absence of information to the contrary, it may be assumed that the structure of this molecule is comparable to that of the nitrogen molecule.

Liquid Phosphorus. Comparatively little information is available on the nature and complexity of liquid phosphorus. Fusion of ordinary white phosphorus (p. 563) gives a liquid which x-ray diffraction studies indicate to consist of tetrahedral P_4 molecules (P—P bond distance = 2.25 A).[22] The vapor pressure of this liquid has been measured up to 409.3°C.[23, 24] Fusion of violet phosphorus (p. 563) gives a liquid, the nature of which has not been determined. Vapor pressure data for this liquid are available above 504°C.[23] Although an interval of almost 100°C. exists for which no vapor pressure data are available, there appear to be no discontinuities in this interval, and the two liquids appear thus to be the same. In fact, McRae and Van Voorhis[24] find that where liquid exists in the interval 44° to 634°C vapor pressures may be calculated to ±5% from the equation

$$\log_{10} p_{\text{mm}} = -\frac{2898.1}{T} - 1.2566 \log_{10} T + 11.5694 \qquad (15\cdot 1$$

T being expressed in degrees Kelvin. Spontaneous conversion of the white form into the violet at elevated temperatures and lack of suffi

[18] J. R. Arnold: *J. Chem. Phys.*, **14**, 351 (1946).
[19] G. Preuner and J. Brockmöller: *Z. physik. Chem.*, **81**, 129 (1912).
[20] A. Stock, G. E. Gibson, and E. Stamm: *Ber.*, **45**, 3527 (1912).
[21] D. P. Stevenson and D. M. Yost: *J. Chem. Phys.*, **9**, 403 (1941).
[22] C. D. Thomas and N. S. Gingrich: *J. Chem. Phys.*, **6**, 659 (1938).
[23] A. Smits and S. C. Bokhorst: *Z. physik. Chem.*, **91**, 249 (1916).
[24] D. McRae and C. C. Van Voorhis: *J. Am. Chem. Soc.*, **43**, 547 (1921).

cient supercooling of the liquid violet material account for the uninvestigated region.

It appears, therefore, that in effect molten white phosphorus is supercooled violet phosphorus. It is not unlikely that more than a single polymeric form is present in the liquid and that such polymeric forms are in equilibrium with each other.

Solid Phosphorus. Solid phosphorus is polymorphous,* but the literature contains much confusing information relative to the true natures of the polymorphs. The following forms appear to be well-characterized.

WHITE PHOSPHORUS. White phosphorus is soft and waxy and becomes yellow when exposed to light. Two different crystalline modifications may be distinguished. The ordinary (*alpha* or phosphorus I) material consists of cubic crystals (sp. gr. 1.8232) which are non-conductors and which dissolve readily in a number of organic solvents (especially carbon disulfide). A second variety (*beta* or phosphorus II) is formed from the alpha material below −76.9°C. or at 60°C. under 12,000 atm. pressure.[25] It consists of hexagonal crystals (sp. gr. 2.699) and is apparently similar to the alpha form in other properties.

VIOLET PHOSPHORUS. Heating molten white phosphorus at 240° to 260°C., either alone or particularly in light or in the presence of catalysts such as iodine[26] or sodium, produces a reddish modification which is distinguished from the white form by its reduced chemical reactivity, by its insolubility in solvents such as carbon disulfide, and by its non-poisonous character. The color, vapor pressure, melting point, and other physical constants of this *red* form are dependent upon the temperature and time of heating during the preparation. It is only after the product is heated for some time at about 550°C. that a definite and constant vapor pressure is attained.[23] The color of this material varies from red to violet, but the product is identical in vapor pressure, density, and x-ray diffraction pattern with the violet (Hittorf)[27] modification, which is best obtained[28] by crystallization from molten lead. It appears, therefore, that the true crystalline form is the violet form (phosphorus III) and that the ordinary red phosphorus is essentially violet phosphorus,[29] with perhaps a scarlet

* Allotropic forms of solid materials are referred to as polymorphic forms.

[25] P. W. Bridgman: *J. Am. Chem. Soc.*, **36**, 1344 (1914).

[26] B. C. Brodie: *J. Chem. Soc.*, **5**, 289 (1853).

[27] M. Hittorf: *Phil. Mag.* [4], **31**, 311 (1865).

[28] A. Stock and F. Gomolka: *Ber.*, **42**, 4510 (1909).

[29] R. Hultgren, N. S. Gingrich, and B. E. Warren: *J. Chem. Phys.*, **3**, 351 (1935).

phosphorus impurity. In violet phosphorus each atom has thre nearest neighbors at 2.29 A, the next nearest neighbors being a 3.48 A.[22] Violet phosphorus has a rhombohedral crystal structur and is a non-conductor.

A closely related material, scarlet phosphorus, is obtained as a apparently amorphous, non-poisonous powder of specific gravity 1.8 by exposing a carbon disulfide solution of white phosphorus to sun light,[30] by boiling a phosphorus(III) bromide solution of white phos phorus for several hours,[31] or by reducing phosphorus(III) bromid with mercury at 240°C.[32]

BLACK PHOSPHORUS. Crystalline black phosphorus (phosphorus IV was first prepared by Bridgman[25, 33] by subjecting white phosphoru at 200°C. to pressures of 12,000 to 13,000 kg. per sq. cm. It resem bles graphite in appearance and flakiness, is an electrical conducto and is insoluble in carbon disulfide. Black phosphorus is rhombohe dral in crystal habit. Studies[29] show the crystal to be of the layer typ with each phosphorus atom in a particular layer being 2.18 A. fro its three nearest neighbors and at a bond angle of 102°. Closes neighbors in adjacent layers are 3.68 A removed from each othe Binding between layers is thus weaker than that within a particula layer. Similarities between this structure and the graphite structu (p. 665) are striking. Crystalline black phosphorus is not obtainab from violet phosphorus. Quite the contrary, heating it to 550°C converts it to the violet.

A non-crystalline black modification has been prepared by subjectin white phosphorus to high pressures but at lower temperatures tha those essential to the formation of the crystalline form.[34] This mat rial is transformed to violet phosphorus when heated for a prolonge period at 125°C. Its properties have not been well characterized.

The phase relations among the forms of phosphorus are summarize in a provisional way in Figure 15·1.[23] Although most parts of th diagram are self-explanatory, certain points require emphasis. Alon CC', the influence of pressure on the melting point of α-white pho phorus is shown. The triple point involving violet phosphorus li at D. Hence the region marked violet should also embrace th marked liquid violet supercooled. However, supercooling apparent gives a material the vapor pressure of which is continuous with th

[30] A. Pedler: *J. Chem. Soc.*, **57**, 599 (1890).
[31] R. Schenck and P. Marquart: *J. Soc. Chem. Ind.*, **22**, 1226 (1903).
[32] L. Wolf: *Ber.*, **48**, 1272 (1915).
[33] P. W. Bridgman: *J. Am. Chem. Soc.*, **38**, 609 (1916).
[34] R. B. Jacobs: *J. Chem. Phys.*, **5**, 945 (1937).

f the molten α-white form (p. 562); so the liquid region of white hosphorus is really the anomalous region. In this region white hosphorus is metastable with respect to the solid violet form. It eems probable that much of the difficulty is due to the slowness with which true equilibria are established. The limited range of existence f the black crystalline form is apparent.

A considerable difference of opinion exists as to which solid modification is really the most stable. A variety of evidence suggests that the

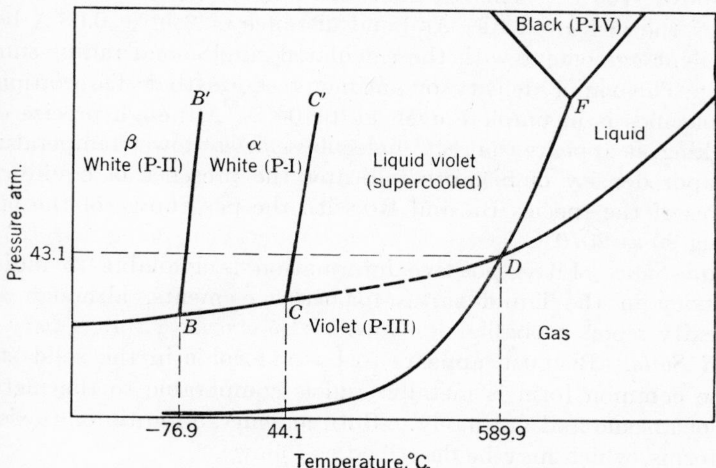

FIG. 15·1. Phase relations for phosphorus. (Not drawn to scale.)

ystalline black form is the most stable. Jacobs[34] has found that the eat evolved per atomic weight of phosphorus when the various forms act with bromine in carbon disulfide increases in this order: crystalne black–commercial red–violet–non–crystalline black–white(α). he vapor pressure of white phosphorus is uniformly higher than that violet phosphorus, and at some temperatures, at least, the vapor essure of the crystalline black form is lower than that of the violet. etastable forms are more soluble in general than stable forms. his is strikingly illustrated by the enhanced solubility of white osphorus, but comparisons between the violet and black forms are fficult to make. White phosphorus is uniformly the most chemically active, and, although differences are not major, it appears that the ack modification is less reactive than the violet. Reactions with ygen are cases in point. All these evidences suggest enhanced stality in the black modification but are admittedly inconclusive.

Arsenic, antimony, and bismuth

Arsenic, antimony, and bismuth are best considered together since differences among their modifications are less striking. As with phosphorus, the greatest complexities are found in the solid materials.

Gaseous State. In the gaseous state, all three elements exist as polyatomic molecules which undergo dissociation at higher temperatures. Arsenic vapor, like the vapor of phosphorus, is tetratomic up to 800°C., with dissociation to the diatomic condition becoming complete above 1700°C. The As_4 molecule, like the P_4 molecule, is tetrahedral,[17] the measured As—As bond distance of 2.44 ± 0.03 A being in excellent agreement with the calculated single-bond radius sum of 2.42 A. The vapor density of antimony shows that dissociation to Sb_2 molecules is incomplete even at 1640°C. Although precise data are lacking, it appears that Sb_4 molecules exist at lower temperatures. The vapor density of bismuth indicates the presence of equilibrium mixtures of the species Bi_2 and Bi, with the percentage of the latter reaching 90 at 2070°C.[35]

Liquid State. Little positive information is available to indicate complexity in the liquid states for these elements, although such complexity seems probable.

Solid State. Bismuth appears to be dimorphic in the solid state but the common form is metallic and is comparable to the metallic forms of arsenic and antimony. Both arsenic and antimony exist in three forms, which may be described as follows.

YELLOW (α). This form is comparable to white phosphorus and is unstable with respect to the others. In this modification, arsenic and antimony are cubic, yellow, transparent solids which are soluble in carbon disulfide. Yellow arsenic is tetratomic in this solvent, and it may be presumed that antimony is too. Yellow arsenic is converted into the gray form by heat, and the reaction is catalyzed by light or by iodine or bromine. Yellow antimony changes to the black form in light at −180°C. and in the dark at −90°C. Yellow arsenic is formed (like white phosphorus) when the heated vapor of the element is cooled suddenly. Yellow antimony is obtained by reaction of oxygen on liquid stibine at −90°C.[36]

BLACK (β). The black forms of arsenic and antimony are comparable with amorphous phosphorus. They are somewhat more stable than the yellow modifications but are metastable with respect to the gray forms. They are insoluble in carbon disulfide. Black arsenic

[35] I. F. Zartman: *Phys. Rev.*, **37**, 383 (1931).
[36] A. Stock and O. Guttmann: *Ber.*, **37**, 885 (1904).

is formed as a deposit on the cooler surfaces when gray arsenic is heated with hydrogen in a glass tube. Black antimony is obtained either by rapidly cooling antimony vapor or by oxidizing stibine with oxygen at −40°C.

GRAY OR METALLIC (γ). These are metallic modifications, comparable to black phosphorus and isomorphous with metallic bismuth. These solids have layer structures, with each atom having three equidistant nearest neighbors and then three more neighbors somewhat farther removed. The interatomic distances are[37]

	Three neighbors at	Three neighbors at
Arsenic	2.51 A	3.15 A
Antimony	2.87	3.37
Bismuth	3.10	3.47

In these modifications the elements have enhanced densities and are electrical conductors. These are the stable forms and result when the others are heated. Their properties are essentially those of metals.

Antimony may be prepared in still another solid form, the so-called *explosive antimony*. This is a black material resembling graphite (sp. gr. 5.25 to 6.3), which is stable under cold water but reverts to the gray or metallic form on being heated to 200°C. or on being scratched. This conversion is exothermic (2.4 kcal. per gram atom) and is commonly explosive in character. Some 10 to 15% of occluded antimony halide is always present,[38] and the antimony is amorphous in character.[39, 40] It is believed that explosive antimony has a gel-like structure involving amorphous antimony and an antimony halide and that explosion is due to the rapid conversion of the antimony into the crystalline form.[41, 42] Explosive antimony is prepared as a cathodic deposit by electrolysis of aqueous antimony(III) halide (chloride preferred, although bromide or iodide works) solutions containing free acid at high current densities, using a platinum cathode and an antimony anode. Electrolysis of solutions of antimony(III) chloride in glacial acetic acid also yields explosive antimony under certain conditions.[43]

[37] A. F. Wells: *Structural Inorganic Chemistry*, 2nd ed., p. 457. Clarendon Press, Oxford (1950).

[38] E. Cohen and C. C. Coffin: *Z. physik. Chem.*, **149**, 417 (1930).

[39] H. von Steinwehr and A. Schulze: *Z. Physik*, **63**, 815 (1930).

[40] J. A. Prins: *Nature*, **131**, 760 (1933).

[41] C. C. Coffin and S. Johnston: *Proc. Roy. Soc.* (*London*), **A146**, 564 (1934).

[42] C. C. Coffin: *Proc. Roy. Soc.* (*London*), **A152**, 47 (1935).

[43] C. W. Stillwell and L. F. Audrieth: *J. Am. Chem. Soc.*, **54**, 472 (1932).

CHEMICAL CHARACTERISTICS OF THE ELEMENTS

The more important aspects of the chemical behaviors of the elements in this family are summarized in Table 15·2. It is apparent

TABLE 15·2

Chemical Characteristics of Group VB Elements

General Equation*	Remarks
$xZ + yM \rightarrow M_yZ_x$	With metals, particularly the highly electropositive ones. Tendency decreases from Z = N to Z = Bi.
$2Z + 3H_2 \rightarrow 2H_3Z$	With N_2.
$4Z + 3O_2 \rightarrow (Z_2O_3)_2$	With P, As, Sb, Bi. P gives P_4O_{10} with excess O_2. N_2 gives NO or NO_2.
$2Z + 3X_2 \rightarrow 2ZX_3$	With P, As, Sb, Bi. ZX_5 forms with excess halogen with P, As, Sb, and F_2, Cl_2, Br_2.
$2Z + 3S \rightarrow Z_2S_3$	Especially with Sb, Bi. Other sulfides also result with P, As.

* Z = P, As, Sb, Bi specifically and N only if mentioned.
X_2 = halogen molecule.

that the situation in this family is strictly comparable to that in the oxygen family (p. 493) as regards systematic trends. Again the reactions listed are probably most characteristic of phosphorus and the heavier members of the family, the behavior of nitrogen being anomalous. The marked stability of the nitrogen molecule (p. 560) renders nitrogen essentially inert under ordinary experimental conditions and necessitates energetic conditions (heat, etc.) for reactions to occur.

PREPARATION AND PRODUCTION OF THE FREE ELEMENTS

Nitrogen is recovered on a large scale by the fractional distillation of liquid air. Commercial nitrogen always contains small quantities of oxygen, which can be removed by passage over hot copper, through chromium(II) salt solutions, etc., as well as traces of the inert gas elements (p. 383). Chemically pure nitrogen is obtained from various nitrogen-containing compounds. For instance, thermal decomposition of sodium or barium azide (p. 588) or oxidation of ammonia in the cold by chlorine, bromine, hypochlorite, or hypobromite or at higher temperatures by copper(II) oxide, nitrite, or dichromate yields nitrogen free from oxygen. Such procedures are useful on a laboratory scale only. Phosphorus is obtained by carbon reduction of rock phosphate (calcium phosphate) in the electric furnace, silica being added to remove residual calcium materials by slag formation. Arsenic, antimony, and bismuth are obtained as metallurgical by-products commonly by carbon reduction of their oxides.

CATENATION AMONG THE GROUP Vb ELEMENTS

Catenation is the phenomenon of self-linkage among the elements. Although it is often regarded as a property peculiar to carbon, it is also characteristic to a much lesser extent of elements placed near carbon in the periodic arrangement. Examples of self-linkages involving the halogens (pp. 445, 455), oxygen (pp. 504–515), and sulfur (pp. 518, 543–544) have been cited already, and other examples are described in this chapter and in Chapters 16 and 17. Catenation can occur only when the atoms involved are electronically unsaturated. Except as it is characteristic of molecules of the free elements, it is *normally* limited to elements the atoms of which contain fewer than seven electrons in their valence shells (for exceptions, see material on the halogens). In general, catenation becomes decreasingly important the farther removed the element is from carbon in the periodic table.

All the elements in the nitrogen family exhibit this phenomenon to some extent, but it is most pronounced in nitrogen. No stable simple compounds of nitrogen containing nitrogen chains with more than two members are known, although certain organic derivatives of the hydronitrogens (pp. 573–574) may contain as many as eight mutually linked nitrogen atoms. The instabilities of these arrangements are associated with the extreme stability of the N≡N arrangement, and simple chain compounds thus tend to revert to elemental nitrogen. Some comparisons among carbon-carbon, nitrogen-nitrogen, phosphorus-phosphorus, and arsenic-arsenic linkages are of interest. From the bond energies tabulated in Table 15·3, it is apparent that,

TABLE 15·3
BOND MULTIPLICITY AMONG THE GROUP VB ELEMENTS AND CARBON

Bond Type	Bond Energy, kcal./mole	Ratio of Bond Energy to That for Single Bond
1. Carbon		
C—C	58.6	1.00
C=C	100	1.71
C≡C	123	2.10
2. Nitrogen		
N—N	20.0	1.00
N=N	.....	.....
N≡N	170	8.50
3. Phosphorus		
P—P	18.9	1.00
P=P	.....	.....
P≡P	.....	.....
4. Arsenic		
As—As	15.1	1.00
As=As	.....	.....
As≡As	.....	.....

although there is a general increase in going from single to triple bonds, the increase is most pronounced with nitrogen. Although multiple linkages (because of strain) are points of weakness in carbon compounds, they are points of strength in nitrogen compounds and are ruptured only by hydrogen reduction. Many instances of nitrogen evolution as preferential to the rupture of such linkages characterize the chemistries of the hydronitrogens, azo compounds, azides, and hyponitrites.

With phosphorus, the commonest examples of catenation are in the hydride P_2H_4 and in hypophosphoric acid ($H_4P_2O_6$) and its salts (p. 643). With the other elements, organic derivatives of the type $R_2Z—ZR_2$ or $RZ = ZR$ (R = alkyl or aryl, Z = As, Sb, Bi) may be cited as examples.

SOME SPECIAL PHASES OF NITROGEN CHEMISTRY

A number of phases of nitrogen chemistry can be treated advantageously as more or less special topics. No claim can be made that the ones here considered are all inclusive, but they are all either important or of general fundamental interest.

The nitrogen system of compounds

It has been shown in the preceding chapter that water may be regarded as a parent for a system of compounds. Such a system, the familiar oxygen system, is the one around which much of our present-day approach to chemistry has been built. The similarities between oxygen chemistry and nitrogen chemistry, and particularly the similarities between water and ammonia which have been pointed out in Chapter 10, indicate clearly that an entirely analogous system of compounds based upon nitrogen may be devised. It is largely to Cady, Kraus, and especially Franklin, whose excellent monograph[44] exploits these concepts so thoroughly, that credit for developing the nitrogen system is due.

The nitrogen system of compounds is based upon equivalent groups containing nitrogen and oxygen (p. 340). Thus the *amide* group ($—NH_2$) is the analog of the hydroxide group (—OH), and the *imide* (=NH) and nitride (≡N) groups are both analogs of the oxide group (=O).* Substitution of nitrogen-containing groups for equivalent

[44] E. C. Franklin: *The Nitrogen System of Compounds.* Reinhold Publishing Corp., New York (1935).

* It is debatable whether the imide group should be regarded as an analog of the hydroxide or oxide. Franklin apparently preferred the former opinion, but the latter appears to be more strikingly borne out by the properties of the materials involved.

oxygen groups gives the nitrogen system analogs of the familiar oxygen system compounds. Compounds derived from water are called *aquo* compounds. Similarly, these derived from ammonia are called *ammono* compounds, and those derived from both hydrides are *aquo-ammono* compounds.

Analogies between the two systems are made more apparent by the summation in Table 15·4.[44] Compounds which fall in a given horizontal line in this table are not only formal analogs but also bear close chemical relationships to each other. These latter are particularly striking in many cases when water solutions of aquo compounds are compared with ammonia solutions of the ammono analogs (pp. 311–

TABLE 15·4
COMPARISON OF OXYGEN SYSTEM AND NITROGEN SYSTEM COMPOUNDS

General Classes	Aquo Compounds	Aquo-Ammono Compounds	Ammono Compounds
1. Inorganic compounds			
Metal hydroxides, oxides vs. amides, imides, nitrides	$LiOH$		$LiNH_2$
	CaO		Ca_3N_2
	$Al_2O_3 \cdot xH_2O$		$AlN \cdot yNH_3$
Acids, acid oxides vs. acids, acid nitrides	$HONO_2$		$HNNN$
	$HONO$		H_2NNNH
	$(HO)_3PO$		$(H_2N)_2PN$
	$HOPO_2$		$HNPN$
	$HOCl$		H_2NCl
	$(HO)_2SO_2$	$HOSO_2NH_2$	..
		$(H_2N)_2SO_2$	
	Cl_2O		Cl_3N
	CO_2		$(C_3N_4)_x$
Salts vs. salts	KNO_3		KN_3
	$HgOHCl$		$HgNH_2Cl$
	$K_2[Zn(OH)_4]$		$(K_2[Zn(NH_2)_4])$
	K_2CO_3		K_2CN_2
Miscellaneous	$HOOH$	$HONH_2$	H_2NNH_2
2. Organic compounds			
Alcohols vs. amines (primary)	CH_3OH		CH_3NH_2
Phenols vs. aromatic amines (primary)	C_6H_5OH		$C_6H_5NH_2$
Ethers vs. amines (secondary, tertiary)	$(C_2H_5)_2O$		$(C_2H_5)_2NH$
Carboxylic acids vs. acid amides, amidines	CH_3COOH	CH_3CONH_2	$CH_3C(NH)NH_2$
Acid anhydrides vs. nitriles	$(CH_3CO)_2O$		CH_3CN
Salts vs. salts	CH_3COOK		$CH_3C(NH)NHK$

312, 344–352). Further analogies may be seen in a comparison of the derivatives of carbonic acid[45] and sulfuric acid[46] summarized in terms of hydration-dehydration, ammonation-deammonation, and hydrolysis-ammonolysis schemes in Tables 15·5 and 15·6. The relations in

TABLE 15·5

NITROGEN DERIVATIVES OF CARBONIC ACID

$$\underset{\text{carbonic acid}}{\mathrm{C(=O)(OH)_2}} \underset{H_2O}{\overset{NH_3}{\rightleftharpoons}} \underset{\text{carbamic acid}}{\mathrm{C(=O)(NH_2)(OH)}} \underset{H_2O}{\overset{NH_3}{\rightleftharpoons}} \underset{\text{urea}}{\mathrm{C(=O)(NH_2)_2}} \underset{H_2O}{\overset{NH_3}{\rightleftharpoons}} \underset{\text{guanidine}}{\mathrm{C(=NH)(NH_2)_2}} \underset{NH_3}{\overset{-NH_3}{\rightleftharpoons}} \underset{\text{cyanamide}}{\mathrm{H_2NC{\equiv}N}}$$

Carbonic acid $\underset{-H_2O}{\overset{H_2O}{\rightleftharpoons}}$ CO_2 (carbon dioxide)

Carbamic acid $\underset{H_2O}{\overset{-H_2O}{\rightleftharpoons}}$ HNCO (isocyanic acid) $\underset{NH_3}{\overset{-NH_3}{\rightleftharpoons}}$ urea

Cyanamide $\underset{-NH_3}{\overset{NH_3}{\rightleftharpoons}}$ $HN(CN)_2$ (dicyanimide) $\underset{-NH_3}{\overset{NH_3}{\rightleftharpoons}}$ $(C_3N_4)_x$ (carbon nitride polymer)

TABLE 15·6

NITROGEN DERIVATIVES OF SULFURIC ACID

$$\underset{\text{sulfuric acid}}{\mathrm{SO_2(OH)_2}} \underset{H_2O}{\overset{NH_3}{\rightleftharpoons}} \underset{\text{sulfamic acid}}{\mathrm{SO_2(NH_2)(OH)}} \underset{H_2O}{\overset{NH_3}{\rightleftharpoons}} \underset{\text{sulfamide}}{\mathrm{SO_2(NH_2)_2}} \underset{NH_3}{\overset{-NH_3}{\rightleftharpoons}} \underset{\text{sulfimide}}{\mathrm{HN{=}SO_2}}$$

Sulfamic acid $\underset{-NH_3}{\overset{NH_3}{\rightleftharpoons}}$ $HN(SO_2OH)_2$ (imidodisulfonic acid) $\underset{-NH_3}{\overset{NH_3}{\rightleftharpoons}}$ $N(SO_2OH)_3$ (aminetrisulfonic or nitrilosulfonic acid)

Sulfamide $\underset{-NH_3}{\overset{NH_3}{\rightleftharpoons}}$ $HN(SO_2NH_2)_2$ (imidodisulfonamide)

Sulfimide $\underset{-NH_3}{\overset{NH_3}{\rightleftharpoons}}$ trisulfimide (cyclic $(HNSO_2)_3$: ring of HN, O_2S, HN, SO_2, NH, SO_2)

these tables are more formal than actual, and it is not implied that the compounds are necessarily preparable from each other by the schemes outlined. It may be pointed out also that the reduction of nitric acid

[45] E. C. Franklin: *The Nitrogen System of Compounds*, Ch. X. Reinhold Publishing Corp., New York (1935).

[46] L. F. Audrieth, M. Sveda, H. H. Sisler, and M. J. Butler: *Chem. Revs.*, **26**, 49 (1940).

(an aquo acid) has a striking parallel in the reduction of hydrazoic acid (an ammono acid). This is apparent in the schemes

$$\underset{\text{nitric acid}}{HNO_3} \xrightarrow{e^-} \underset{\text{nitrous acid}}{HNO_2} \xrightarrow{e^-} \underset{\text{dihydroxylimine}}{((HO)_2NH)} \xrightarrow{e^-} \underset{\text{hydroxylamine}}{HONH_2} \xrightarrow{e^-} \underset{\text{ammonia}}{NH_3}$$

$$\underset{\text{hydrazoic acid}}{HNNN} \xrightarrow{e^-} \underset{\text{triazene}}{H_2NN{=}NH} \xrightarrow{e^-} \underset{\text{triazane}}{(H_2N)_2NH} \xrightarrow{e^-} \underset{\text{hydrazine}}{H_2NNH_2} \xrightarrow{e^-} \underset{\text{ammonia}}{NH_3}$$

Other equally striking analogies suggest themselves.

The nitrogen system of compounds is of particular importance both in inorganic and in organic chemistry. Proper appreciation of the analogies existent between the oxygen and nitrogen systems does much to fit many apparently unrelated materials into a unified picture. Such analogies have often been used to advantage in relating the two systems.

The hydronitrogens

Catenation among nitrogen compounds is most striking in the hydronitrogens. These compounds are nitrogen analogs of the hydrocarbons,[47] but, unlike the hydrocarbons, the hydronitrogens are known largely in the forms of their organic derivatives rather than in the free state. Such derivatives are most commonly considered to be organic compounds, and as such have been discussed largely in terms of the organic substituents rather than in terms of the nitrogen chains which they contain.[47] Consideration of these chains should prove profitable.

The hydronitrogens may be classified into four series analogous to the homologous series of the aliphatic hydrocarbons. The general characteristics and memberships of these series are indicated in Table 15·7.[47] It is at once apparent that no cyclic compounds are involved.

Of the saturated hydronitrogens, only ammonia and hydrazine are of particular importance. These are considered below in some detail. Triazane and tetrazane are known only in the form of their organic derivatives. In the N_nH_n series, all members except the two azides are characterized by the presence of nitrogen chains possessing a single double bond. The two azides really have no place in the classification since they are salts. The simplest member of the series is itself unknown, but its organic derivatives are the familiar azo compounds. Triazene is obtainable in aqueous solution by reduction of

[47] L. F. Audrieth: *J. Chem. Education*, **7**, 2055 (1930).

TABLE 15·7

CLASSIFICATION OF THE HYDRONITROGENS

Compound	Name(s)	Structural Arrangement	Stability
		1. Saturated Hydronitrogens, N_nH_{n+2}	
NH_3	ammonia	H_3N	free
N_2H_4	hydrazine (diamide)	$H_2N—NH_2$	free
N_3H_5	triazane (prozane)	$H_2N—NH—NH_2$	derivatives
N_4H_6	tetrazane (buzane, hydrotetrazine	$H_2N—NH—NH—NH_2$	derivatives
		2. Unsaturated Hydronitrogens, N_nH_n	
N_2H_2	diimide	$HN{=}NH$	derivatives
N_3H_3	triazene (diazoamine)	$HN{=}N—NH_2$	derivatives
N_4H_4	tetrazene (tetrazone, 2-tetrazene)	$H_2N—N{=}N—NH_2$	derivatives
	isotetrazene (buzylene, diazohydrazine, 1-tetrazene)	$HN{=}N—NH—NH_2$	derivatives
	ammonium azide	$NH_4^+N_3^-$	free
N_5H_5	hydrazinium azide	$N_2H_5^+N_3^-$	(free?)
		3. Unsaturated Hydronitrogens, N_nH_{n-2}	
N_3H	hydrogen azide, hydrazoic acid, azoimide, hydronitric acid	$HN{=}N{\equiv}N$	free, salts
N_4H_2(?)	diiminohydrazine	$HN{=}N—N{=}NH$	....
N_5H_3	bisdiazoamine	$HN{=}N—NH—N{=}NH$	derivatives
N_6H_4(?)	bisdiazohydrazine	$HN{=}N—NH—NH—N{=}NH$	....
		4. Unsaturated Hydronitrogens, N_nH_{n-4}	
N_8H_4	octazotriene (octazone)	$HN{=}N—NH—N{=}N—NH—N{=}NH$	derivatives

ammonium azide but cannot be isolated in the pure condition. The tetrazenes are known as organic derivatives. In the N_nH_{n-2} series, hydrazoic acid is the most important member. Its chemistry is also outlined below. Organic bisdiazoamino compounds are well characterized, but no derivatives are known for the other two materials. Unstable organic octazotriene derivatives are the only known examples for materials in the series N_nH_{n-4}.

Ammonia and its derivatives

Certain phases of ammonia chemistry, particularly those relating to solvent systems (Ch. IX, X), have been explored already. In this connection the physical constants of ammonia have been compared with those of water and other water-like solvents (Table 10·3, p. 341), and many of the chemical reactions of ammonia (in the liquid state) have been described (pp. 349–352). Ammonia has been considered also in relation to hydrogen bonding (pp. 188–191) and as an important donor in the formation of Werner complexes (Ch. VII). This information should be reviewed as a supplement to the current discussion. In comparison with the corresponding hydrides of the other members of the nitrogen family (pp. 621–623), ammonia is the most highly associated, the most stable with respect to thermal decomposition into its elements and thus the most readily formed, and the most strongly basic. Alone of these hydrides, ammonia forms stable salts containing ZH_4^+ ions (see p. 622 for comparisons of ammonium and phosphonium compounds). The ammonia molecule is pyramidal in shape (p. 201), with a height of 0.360 A, an N—H bond distance of 1.016 A, an H—H distance of 1.645 A, a bond angle of 109°, and a dipole moment of 1.46×10^{-18} e.s.u. This structure may be regarded as tetrahedral with a pair of electrons occupying one tetrahedral position. In the ammonium ion, the fourth hydrogen then gives the true tetrahedral arrangement.

Ammonia is prepared technically by direct synthesis from the elements at elevated temperatures and high pressures and in the presence of suitable catalysts by a number of variations of the process first used successfully by Haber.[48, 49] Suitable conditions involve equilibration at 400° to 600°C. and 100 to 300 atm. with an iron-iron(II and III) oxide-potassium aluminate catalyst. Because the reaction is exothermic, extremely high temperatures must be avoided, but some optimum temperature is required for necessary activation. Ammonia is also obtained in smaller quantities by hydrolysis of calcium cyanamide*

$$CaNCN + 3H_2O \rightarrow CaCO_3 + 2NH_3$$

with dilute sodium hydroxide solution at 100°C.[49] and as a by-product of the coke industry. In the laboratory, it is made most conveniently by treating an ammonium salt with a strongly basic metal oxide or hydroxide (e.g., CaO, NaOH).

[48] J. E. Crane: *Ind. Eng. Chem.*, **22**, 795 (1930).

[49] H. A. Curtis: *Fixed Nitrogen*. Chemical Catalog Co., New York (1932).

* Calcium cyanamide is made by heating calcium carbide (CaC_2) mixed with 2% or more calcium fluoride in 99.8% (or better) nitrogen at 900° to 1000°C.

Ammonium Compounds. Neutralization of ammonia, either gaseous or aqueous, with protonic acids gives ammonium salts. These compounds are closely comparable with the corresponding alkali metal salts in their solubilities and crystal structures. The resemblance to potassium and rubidium salts is particularly striking, probably because the radius of the ammonium ion (1.43 A) is nearly the same as the radii of these ions. Ammonium salts and potassium or rubidium salts are commonly isomorphous. Ammonium salts are commonly readily soluble in water, important exceptions being the hydrogen tartrate, hexanitrocobaltate(III), hexachloroplatinate(IV), and perchlorate. Soluble ammonium salts usually crystallize anhydrous. The halides, except the fluoride, crystallize in the sodium or cesium chloride lattices. The fluoride has the wurtzite (p. 133) lattice, each nitrogen being surrounded tetrahedrally by four fluorines and each fluorine by four nitrogens, with hydrogen bonds between the two kinds of atoms.[50] This re-emphasizes the limitation of hydrogen bonds to highly electronegative atoms (p. 188). The nitrate is of interest in that five polymorphic solid forms are well characterized.[51]

Ammonium salts are uniformly unstable with respect to heat. The nature of the thermal decomposition is dependent upon the anion present. Ammonium salts containing non-oxidizing anions (e.g., halides, CO_3^{-2} and S^{-2}) yield ammonia as one decomposition product. Ammonium salts containing oxidizing anions (e.g., NO_2^-, NO_3^-, and $Cr_2O_7^{-2}$) yield some oxidation product of ammonia (e.g., nitrogen or one of its oxides) as one decomposition product. Particular attention has been focused upon the thermal decomposition of ammonium nitrate because of several disastrous explosions which have involved this material (e.g., in Oppau, Texas City). The compound decomposes rapidly when heated, and at high temperatures it detonates. The presence of any oxidizable material increases the hazard. Ammonium nitrate is used as an explosive, particularly in admixture with aluminum or trinitrotoluene. As pointed out in an earlier chapter (pp. 332–333), ammonium salts are high-temperature acids.

Amides, Imides, and Nitrides. Amides, imides, and nitrides are related to ammonia via the successive replacement of hydrogen atoms by metal atoms. Of course organic groups may replace the hydrogens in ammonia, but consideration of the resulting compounds has no place in this discussion. The metal amides, imides, and nitrides

[50] W. Zachariasen: *Z. physik. Chem.*, **127**, 218 (1927).

[51] S. B. Hendricks, E. Posnjak, and F. C. Kracek: *J. Am. Chem. Soc.*, **54**, 2766 (1932).

are bases in ammonia and are the ammono analogs (p. 571) of the metal hydroxides and oxides.

The chemistry of the metal amides has been reviewed extensively by Franklin[44] and by Bergstrom and Fernelius.[52] The alkali and alkaline earth metals and a few others (e.g., Ag, Zn) form amides. These compounds are comparatively high-melting, crystalline solids which are ionic in character. The potassium, rubidium, and cesium compounds are readily soluble in liquid ammonia, the sodium compound is less soluble, and the lithium compound is practically insoluble. Liquid ammonia solutions of potassium amide are commonly employed for the preparation of insoluble derivatives of other metals. Just as aqueous potassium hydroxide may precipitate either hydroxides or oxides (the latter because of spontaneous dehydration) so also ammonia solutions of potassium amide may precipitate amides, imides, or nitrides (the last two because of deammonation). Dissolution of these precipitates (e.g., with Zn) in excess potassium amide may occur because of amphoterism. Fused alkali metal amides dissolve metals, attack refractory silicates, and are attacked by sulfur, carbon, etc. In contact with water, they are hydrolyzed to ammonia and the corresponding hydroxides. Of the amides, the sodium compound (often called merely sodamide) is most widely used, particularly in organic syntheses. It is readily obtained either by reaction of gaseous ammonia with molten sodium[53] or by reaction of liquid ammonia with sodium in the presence of an iron catalyst and a sodium peroxide promoter.[54] These methods may be applied to the preparation of other alkali metal amides. Reaction of an alkali metal with ammonia to give an amide and hydrogen is comparable to reaction of the metal with water, but is immeasurably slow except under the special conditions mentioned. With liquid ammonia, iron (formed by reduction of an iron compound by a solution of sodium in liquid ammonia) is most effective as a catalyst, although cobalt, nickel, platinum, or even silver can be employed.

Metal imides are less well characterized than either the amides or the nitrides. Typical imides are those of lithium and lead. Their properties are similar to those of the amides. Nitrides of the majority

[52] F. W. Bergstrom and W. C. Fernelius: *Chem. Revs.*, **12**, 43 (1933); **20**, 413 (1937).

[53] L. M. Dennis and A. W. Browne: *Inorganic Syntheses*, Vol. I, p. 74. McGraw-Hill Book Co., New York (1939).

[54] K. W. Greenlee and A. L. Henne: *Inorganic Syntheses*, Vol. II, p. 128. McGraw-Hill Book Co., New York (1946).

of the elements, both metals and non-metals, are known. Their properties vary widely and are determined very largely by the linkage imposed by the element which is combined with nitrogen. Like the hydrides, the nitrides may be classified as ionic, covalent, or metallic (interstitial).[55]

IONIC NITRIDES. These nitrides are apparently derived from tri-negative nitrogen (N^{-3}) and are characterized by the usual valency formulae. They are formed by lithium, copper(I), all of the Periodic Group II metals except possible mercury, and thorium. These nitrides are crystalline compounds and have high melting points. They are hydrolyzed by water to hydroxides and ammonia. Lithium nitride (Li_3N) has a hexagonal structure with one-third of the lithium ions having two nitrogens at 1.94 A and the others three at 2.11 A. The nitrogens have two lithium neighbors at 1.94 A and six at 2.11 A.[55] Nitrides of the M_3N_2 type are often *anti-isomorphous* with oxides of the type M_2O_3, metal atoms occupying oxygen positions and nitrogen atoms occupying metal positions in the oxide structures. The same is true of metal phosphides and arsenides. Although exact data supporting the presence of ions are lacking, it appears that the N^{-3} ion (radius 1.4 A) is present. No other simple trinegative ion is known, the reduced electronegativity of phosphorus making the existence of P^{-3} ions in corresponding phosphides highly unlikely. The ionic nitrides are obtained either by direct union of the elements or by deammonation of the amides at elevated temperatures (e.g., $Ba(NH_2)_2 \rightarrow Ba_3N_2$).

COVALENT NITRIDES. The covalent nitrides embrace the volatile ones derived from non-metallic elements such as hydrogen, carbon silicon, phosphorus, chlorine, fluorine, etc., and the non-volatile ones derived from such Group III elements as boron and aluminum. The volatile nitrides are discussed individually in other sections of this chapter or in other chapters. They are covalent compounds, the formulas of which follow from usual electronic considerations. The non-volatile nitrides of boron and aluminum (MN) are giant molecules (p. 213), the structures of which are comparable with those of carbon. Thus boron nitride has the graphite structure (p. 665), whereas the nitrides of other Group IIIb elements have the wurtzite structure, which is very much like that of the diamond. This condition arises because of the equivalence of a Group III atom and a Group V atom to two Group IV atoms. Corresponding phosphorus, arsenic, antimony, and bismuth compounds have the zinc blende structure (p. 133).

[55] A. F. Wells: *Structural Inorganic Chemistry*, 2nd Ed., pp. 476–480. Clarendon Press, Oxford (1950).

The nitrides of the Group III elements are discussed in Chapter 17 (pp. 757–758).

INTERSTITIAL OR METALLIC NITRIDES. The transition metals of Periodic Groups IIIa, IVa, and Va form nitrides of the type MN (M=Sc, Ce, La, Pr, Ti, Zr, Hf, V, Nb, Ta), and other nitrides (Mo_2N, W_2N, Mn_4N, Fe_4N) result from closely related metals. These compounds in general crystallize in the cubic system with sodium chloride structures and are often (especially those of Group IV and V metals) characterized by extremely high melting points, extreme hardness (Table 15·8), metallic conductivity, and metallic luster as well as by

TABLE 15·8
CHARACTERISTICS OF INTERSTITIAL NITRIDES

Nitride	Radius Ratio, $R_N:R_M$	Density, grams/cc.	Melting Point, °K	Hardness, Mohs' Scale*	Temperature of Superconductivity, °K
TiN	0.49	5.18	3220 ± 50	8–9	1.2–1.6
ZrN	0.45	6.93	3255 ± 50	8+	9.45
VN	0.53	5.63	2570	9–10	
NbN	0.49	8.40	2570	8+	
TaN			3360 ± 50	8+	

* On Mohs' scale, the following hardness values are used: 10 (diamond), 9 (ruby, sapphire), 8 (topaz), 7 (quartz), 6 (feldspar), 5 (apatite), 4 (fluorite), 3 (calcite), 2 (rock salt), 1 (talc).

chemical inertness. They are true interstitial compounds (p. 221), with nitrogen atoms occupying the interstices in the metal structures. Many are closely comparable in their characteristics to the interstitial carbides (p. 669) and borides (p. 769) and to lesser extent to the interstitial hydrides (p. 411).[56] Metallic nitrides are made by heating the powdered metal in nitrogen or ammonia at 1100° to 1300°C., by heating metal filaments in nitrogen, or by heating a carrier filament (e.g., Pt, W, or C) in a mixture of nitrogen and metal halide vapors and subsequently removing the carrier by high-temperature volatilization. The last procedures yield single crystals. The first yields powders which must be compacted and freed of impurities by vacuum sintering above 2500°C. It must be emphasized that, although the formulas given are stoichiometric, they may deviate slightly from true stoichiometry. Furthermore, certain of the elements form more than a single nitride (e.g., Mn_3N_2, etc.).

[56] K. Becker: *Phys. Z.*, **34**, 185 (1933). Review of nitrides, carbides, borides.

Unfortunately, fitting all known nitrides into these three classes is difficult for lack of detailed structural information. The same trends in properties as are encountered in other binary compounds containing small non-metal ions or atoms are discernible among the nitrides. These are well illustrated by the nitrides of the elements in the first long period,[57] where transition from ionic through metallic to covalent binding parallels increase in atomic number.

Hydroxylamine. The water-like character of hydroxylamine and its characteristics as a solvent and as a parent substance for a system of acids and bases have been discussed in Chapter 10 (pp. 341, 352). Pure hydroxylamine undergoes thermal decomposition above 15°C. to ammonia, water, and a mixture of nitrogen and nitrous oxide. At elevated temperatures, this decomposition is so rapid that it is often explosive. The pure compound must be kept at 0°C. to prevent decomposition. Aqueous solutions of hydroxylamine are more stable, particularly those below 60% concentration. Because of this tendency toward decomposition, hydroxylamine is ordinarily handled as a hydroxylammonium salt, such as the chloride, $NH_3OH^+Cl^-$. Aqueous solutions of hydroxylamine are neutralized readily by strong protonic acids, although the basic strength of hydroxylamine ($k_B' = 6.6 \times 10^{-9}$) is somewhat less than that of ammonia ($k_B' = 1.8 \times 10^{-5}$).

Hydroxylamine is the aquo-ammono analog of hydrogen peroxide. In a sense, therefore, it is not surprising that the compound possesses both oxidizing and reducing properties. These are indicated for acidic solutions by the couples

$$N_2H_5^+ + 2H_2O \rightleftharpoons 2NH_3OH^+ + H^+ + 2e^- \qquad E^0_{298} = -1.46 \text{ volts}$$

$$NH_4^+ + H_2O \rightleftharpoons NH_3OH^+ + 2H^+ + 2e^- \qquad = -1.35$$

$$NH_3OH^+ \rightleftharpoons \tfrac{1}{2}N_2 + 2H^+ + H_2O + e^- \qquad = 1.87$$

$$2NH_3OH^+ \rightleftharpoons N_2O + 6H^+ + H_2O + 4e^- \qquad = 0.05 \text{ volt}$$

$$2NH_3OH^+ \rightleftharpoons H_2N_2O_2 + 6H^+ + 4e^- \qquad = -0.44$$

and for alkaline solution by the couples

$$N_2H_4 + 2OH^- \rightleftharpoons 2NH_2OH + 2e^- \qquad E^0_{298} = -0.74 \text{ volt}$$

$$NH_3 + 2OH^- \rightleftharpoons NH_2OH + H_2O + 2e^- \qquad = -0.42$$

$$2NH_2OH + 2OH^- \rightleftharpoons N_2 + 4H_2O + 2e^- \qquad = 3.04 \text{ volts}$$

$$2NH_2OH + 4OH^- \rightleftharpoons N_2O + 5H_2O + 4e^- \qquad = 1.05$$

$$2NH_2OH + 6OH^- \rightleftharpoons N_2O_2^{-2} + 6H_2O + 4e^- \qquad = 0.73 \text{ volt}$$

[57] R. Juza: *Die Chemie,* **58,** 25 (1945).

Even though these potentials would indicate that hydroxylamine is a powerful oxidizing agent, it is not reduced by many powerful reducing agents, although zinc, titanium(III), chromium(II), etc., will effect reduction to ammonium ion in acidic solutions and iron(II) does the same in alkaline solutions. It appears that the rates of reduction are very slow with many materials. Potential data show further that hydroxylamine is a powerful reducing agent, particularly in alkaline solutions. Many oxidizing agents (noble metal cations, oxygen, permanganate, etc.) react with hydroxylamine in either acidic or alkaline medium, and in the latter hydroxylamine is itself unstable with respect to disproportionation into ammonia and nitrogen. Although thermodynamically favorable, reactions involving direct oxidation of ammonia to hydroxylamine are not practical because the oxidants required continue the oxidation to nitric acid. It is apparent from the equations given above that removal of one electron converts hydroxylamine to nitrogen, and addition of one and two electrons converts it to hydrazine and ammonia, respectively.

Like ammonia and the organic amines, hydroxylamine coordinates with many cations. The resulting complexes are somewhat less stable thermally than the corresponding ammines but differ from them but little in general characteristics. Coordination is apparently through the nitrogen. The reaction of hydroxylamine with carbonyl compounds to give oximes is of importance in organic chemistry.

Hydroxylamine is ordinarily prepared as a hydroxylammonium salt. Two methods may be distinguished. The more important of these is Tafel's[58] electrolytic reduction of nitrate ion in, preferably, 50% sulfuric acid solution. Highest yields result when amalgamated lead electrodes are used. The product is recovered as the chloride by removal of sulfate with barium chloride, evaporation, and extraction with alcohol (in which the chloride is very soluble). The second procedure is based upon reduction of a slightly acidic (5×10^{-5} mole H^+ per liter or less) nitrite solution with sulfur dioxide or alkali metal hydrogen sulfite at $-5°$ to 0°C. to hydroxylamine sulfonates (pp. 554–555) and subsequent hydrolysis of the latter with 0.5 N acid to give hydroxylammonium salts. The reactions involved are complex and are treated to some extent in conjunction with the discussion on nitrous acid (pp. 616–617). According to Rollefson and Oldershaw[59] the reaction is best effected by treating potassium nitrite (1 mole) and potassium acetate (1.2 moles) dissolved in ice water containing undissolved ice with sulfur dioxide. Under these conditions, potassium hydroxylaminedisulfonate, $(KSO_3)_2NOH$, crystallizes out.

[58] J. Tafel: *Z. anorg. Chem.*, **31**, 289 (1902).

[59] G. K. Rollefson and C. F. Oldershaw: *J. Am. Chem. Soc.*, **54**, 977 (1932).

Free hydroxylamine itself is most readily obtained by treating a butanol solution of hydroxylammonium chloride with sodium butoxide in a closed system, removing the precipitated sodium chloride, and crystallizing the hydroxylamine by cooling the filtrate to −10°C.[60, 61]

Hydrazine and its derivatives

Largely because of its unusual characteristics as a fuel, hydrazine has recently attracted considerable attention, and its properties have been explored in great detail.[62, 63] Those phases dealing with the physical and solvent properties of hydrazine and some aspects of the hydrazine system of compounds have been discussed in Chapter 10 (pp. 341, 353–354). Other pertinent information is included here.

Hydrazine is the ammono analog of hydrogen peroxide, and much of its chemistry is closely related to that of hydrogen peroxide. In the vapor state,[64] the N—N bond distance is 1.47 ± 0.02 A, the same as the O—O distance in hydrogen peroxide vapor, the N—H bond distance is roughly 1.04 ± 0.06 A, and the H—N—N bond angle is 108 ± 10°. The N—N bond distance is essentially that given by the radius sum. The vapor is monomeric.[64, 65] Raman data and the high dipole moment of hydrazine indicate an unsymmetrical arrangement,[66]

```
                        H
H\                     /  H
  N ─────────────── N/
H/
```

In the solid state, the N—N bond distance is 1.46 A, the molecules being held together by hydrogen bonds and arranged in zigzag chains.[67] Like the OH groups in hydrogen peroxide, the NH_2 groups do not rotate freely. This structure is supported by a similar unsymmetrical arrangement found for NN′-dimethyl hydrazine, $CH_3NH—NHCH_3$.[68]

Anhydrous hydrazine, unlike hydroxylamine, is thermally stable.

[60] C. D. Hurd and J. H. Brownstein: *J. Am. Chem. Soc.*, **47**, 67 (1925).

[61] C. D. Hurd: *Inorganic Syntheses*, Vol. I, p. 87. McGraw-Hill Book Co., New York (1939).

[62] L. F. Audrieth and P. Mohr: *Chem. Eng. News*, **26**, 3746 (1948).

[63] L. F. Audrieth and Betty A. Ogg: *The Chemistry of Hydrazine.* John Wiley and Sons, New York (1951).

[64] P. A. Giguère and V. Schomaker: *J. Am. Chem. Soc.*, **65**, 2025 (1943).

[65] P. A. Giguère and R. E. Rundle: *J. Am. Chem. Soc.*, **63**, 1135 (1941).

[66] W. G. Penney and G. B. B. M. Sutherland: *Trans. Faraday Soc.*, **30**, 898 (1934); *J. Chem. Phys.*, **2**, 492 (1934).

[67] R. L. Collin and W. N. Lipscomb: *J. Chem. Phys.*, **18**, 566 (1950); *Acta Cryst.*, **4**, 10 (1951).

[68] W. West and R. B. Killingsworth: *J. Chem. Phys.*, **6**, 1 (1938).

It is, however, attacked vigorously by many reagents. It burns in air and reacts vigorously with the halogens, thionyl chloride, sulfur dioxide, sulfur trioxide, and the alkali metals. In the liquid state, it is an excellent solvent for sulfur[69] (54 grams of sulfur per 100 grams of N_2H_4 at room temperature), but slow reaction to liberate nitrogen and give a hydrazinium sulfide ($N_2H_4H_2S$) occurs. Other reactions have been discussed already (p. 353).

Anhydrous hydrazine is seldom encountered, aqueous solutions of the compound being employed in most cases. Aqueous hydrazine is mildly alkaline ($k_{B_1}' = 8.5 \times 10^{-7}$, $k_{B_2}' = 8.9 \times 10^{-16}$) and forms with acids (HA) two series of salts, $N_2H_5^+A^-$ and $N_2H_6^{+2}A_2^-$. The first series is, of course, the more common; it is represented by the chloride, nitrate, etc. Hydrazine gives with water a 1-hydrate, $N_2H_4{\cdot}H_2O$. This material is obtained as a fuming liquid boiling at 118.5°C. and freezing at −40°C. It may be obtained as a solid phase from the hydrazine-water system but, on heating, it dissociates into its components. Hydrazine coordinates with ions such as nickel(II), zinc, silver(I), and cobalt(II). Hydrazine, as phenyl hydrazine, is important in the characterization of organic carbonyl compounds.

Like its aquo and aquo-ammono analogs, aqueous hydrazine shows both oxidizing and reducing properties. This is shown by certain of the couples considered under hydroxylamine (p. 580), together with the couples

$$2NH_4^+ \rightleftharpoons N_2H_5^+ + 3H^+ + 2e^- \qquad E^0_{298} = -1.24 \text{ volts}$$

$$N_2H_5^+ \rightleftharpoons N_2 + 5H^+ + 4e^- \qquad = 0.17 \text{ volt}$$

in acidic solution and the couples

$$2NH_3 + 2OH^- \rightleftharpoons N_2H_4 + 2H_2O + 2e^- \qquad E^0_{298} = -0.1 \text{ volt}$$

$$N_2H_4 + 4OH^- \rightleftharpoons N_2 + 4H_2O + 4e^- \qquad = 1.15 \text{ volts}$$

in alkaline solution. Although potential data show hydrazine to be a powerful oxidizing agent in acidic solutions, reactions with many reducing agents are so slow that only the most powerful ones [e.g., Zn, Ti(III)] reduce it quantitatively to ammonium ion. Obviously, to effect the reverse reaction requires a potent oxidizing agent (e.g., Cl_2). Oxidation of hydrazine is readily effected in either acidic or alkaline solutions, although the reactions are often involved. Nitrogen is the normal oxidation product, although some of the nitrogen often appears as ammonia or hydrazoic acid. Hydroxylamine is not obtained by

[69] F. Ephraim and H. Piotrowski: *Ber.*, **44**, 386 (1911).

oxidation of hydrazine. Bray and Cuy[70] find that one-electron oxidizing agents give as a limit two moles of ammonium ion and one of nitrogen gas in acidic solution and believe the radical N_2H_3 to be a first oxidation product. This then yields ammonium ion and nitrogen as

$$2N_2H_3 + 2H^+ \rightarrow N_2 + 2NH_4^+$$

Two-electron oxidizing agents yield hydrazoic acid as well, and the problem increases in complexity with the more complex oxidants.[71] The four-electron change essential to conversion to nitrogen can be effected quantitatively only under controlled *p*H, temperature, and concentration conditions. Chlorine, bromine, iodine (at *p*H 7 to 7.2), and iodate (in concentrated hydrochloric acid) are useful quantitative oxidizing agents.

Many other oxidants are reduced by hydrazine solutions. Interesting among these is molecular oxygen. Aqueous hydrazine solutions react according to the equation

$$N_2H_4 + O_2 \rightarrow N_2 + 2H_2O$$

Although apparently simple, the reaction actually appears to involve a number of uncharacterized steps. Hydrogen peroxide is formed as one intermediate.[72] Oxidation of aqueous hydrazine by molecular oxygen is catalyzed by metal ions, particularly copper ion. Studies have shown the active copper to be in the positive one state and the catalytic effect to be decreased or destroyed by materials which either precipitate or complex copper(I).[73] Among these are sulfur, thiourea, ethylenediamine, and potassium ethyl xanthate. It should be mentioned also that hydrazine can undergo disproportionation to nitrogen and ammonia, but this does not occur extensively in alkaline medium in the absence of catalysts (e.g., Pt).

Hydrazine can be prepared by three general methods:[62] (1) oxidation of ammonia, (2) reduction of compounds containing N—N linkages, and (3) miscellaneous procedures involving ammonia or its derivatives. Only the first of these is important, but the reduction of nitrates, nitrites, hyponitrites, etc., by chemical or electrochemical means has been studied as have thermal decomposition, electric discharge, etc., procedures involving ammonia. Oxidation of ammonia is effected by

[70] W. C. Bray and E. J. Cuy: *J. Am. Chem. Soc.*, **46**, 858, 1786 (1924). E. J. Cuy, M. E. Rosenberg, and W. C. Bray: *J. Am. Chem. Soc.*, **46**, 1796 (1924). E. J. Cuy: *J. Am. Chem. Soc.*, **46**, 1810 (1924).

[71] R. E. Kirk and A. W. Browne: *J. Am. Chem. Soc.*, **50**, 337 (1928).

[72] E. C. Gilbert: *J. Am. Chem. Soc.*, **51**, 2744 (1929).

[73] P. H. Mohr: Doctoral Dissertation, University of Illinois (1950).

Raschig's procedure,[74] employing sodium hypochlorite and sodium hydroxide in the presence of glue or gelatin. The reactions involved may be described by the equations

$$NH_3 + OCl^- \rightarrow NH_2Cl + OH^-$$

$$NH_2Cl + NH_3 + OH^- \rightarrow N_2H_4 + Cl^- + H_2O$$

The success of the process depends upon use of large excesses of ammonia, thorough mixing of the reactants at low temperatures, and rapid heating to ensure reaction between ammonia and chloramine. A third reaction, shown by the equation

$$N_2H_4 + 2NH_2Cl \rightarrow N_2 + 2NH_4Cl$$

decreases the yield of hydrazine. This reaction is catalyzed by traces of metal ions (especially copper), and glue or gelatin acts as a negative catalyst to inhibit this reaction. A laboratory modification of the commercial procedure[75] converts the hydrazine to a sulfate solution. Technically, the material is recovered by fractional distillation as an 85% solution of the hydrate.

Anhydrous hydrazine may be obtained from the hydrate by dehydration with sodium hydroxide, potassium hydroxide, or barium oxide. Refluxing with barium oxide in an atmosphere of hydrogen and distilling in hydrogen at reduced pressures is effective.[76] The hydrogen sulfate, $N_2H_4 \cdot H_2SO_4$, is converted to the hydrate by distilling with aqueous potassium hydroxide.

Hydrazoic acid and its derivatives

Hydrogen azide or hydrazoic acid is the ammono analog of nitric acid (p. 573) and may be related thus to nitric acid by replacement of =O by =NH and —OH and the other =O together by ≡N to give a structure

$$\text{H—N=N}\equiv\text{N} \qquad \text{or} \qquad \text{H} : \ddot{\text{N}} :: \text{N} ::: \text{N} :$$

Experimental data on both covalent and ionic azides indicate clearly that the three nitrogens do lie in a straight chain, but significant differences in bond lengths are obtained. Thus electron diffraction data[77] on methyl azide (CH_3N_3) give N—N bond distances of 1.26 A

[74] F. Raschig: *Ber.*, **40**, 4580 (1907).

[75] L. F. Audrieth and T. T. Nickles: *Inorganic Syntheses*, Vol. I, p. 90. McGraw-Hill Book Co., New York (1939).

[76] C. F. Hale and F. F. Shetterly: *J. Am. Chem. Soc.*, **33**, 1071 (1911).

[77] L. Pauling and L. O. Brockway: *J. Am. Chem. Soc.*, **59**, 13 (1937).

and 1.10 A, corresponding closely to the 1.20 A and 1.09 A calculated for double and triple bonds, respectively, and are in accord with the arrangement

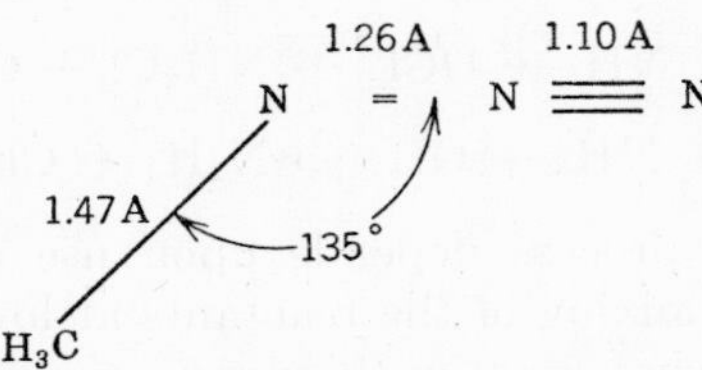

However, in salts, both N—N distances are the same, x-ray data giving values of 1.17 A and 1.15 A for NaN_3,[78, 79] 1.16 A and 1.15 A for KN_3,[78, 79] 1.17 A for NH_4N_3,[80] 1.18 A for AgN_3,[81] and 1.12 A for $Sr(N_3)_2$.[82] Herzberg et al.[83] interpreted the infra-red spectrum of hydrazoic acid as indicating the hydrogen to be outside the straight line of the three nitrogens, and later Eyster[84] showed from infrared data that the structure of this material is best represented as

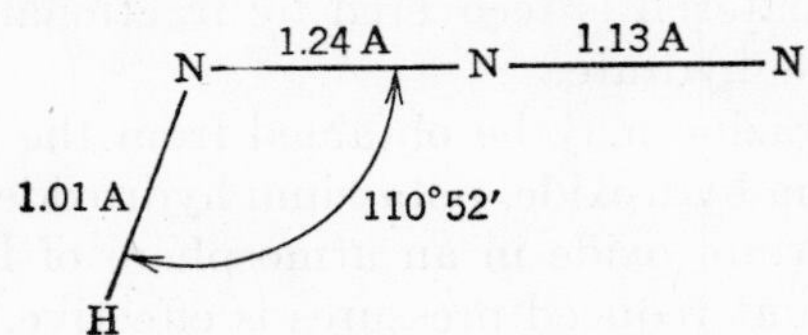

This is in agreement with electron diffraction data.[85] All these data may be correlated best by assuming resonance involving the structures

$$R : \ddot{N} : : \overset{+}{N} : : \ddot{N} :^{-} \qquad \text{and} \qquad R : \underset{\cdot\cdot}{\overset{-}{N}} : \overset{+}{N} : : : N :$$

the predominate form depending upon whether an azide ion or a covalent azide is considered. For the free acid, the second form is the more important. Structural studies have invalidated early postulations of cyclic structures.

The characteristics of hydrazoic acid have been reviewed extensively by Audrieth.[86] The halogenoid character of the azide group has been

[78] S. B. Hendricks and L. Pauling: *J. Am. Chem Soc.*, **47**, 2904 (1925).
[79] L. K. Frevel: *J. Am. Chem. Soc.*, **58**, 779 (1936).
[80] L. K. Frevel: *Z. Krist.*, **94**, 197 (1936).
[81] M. Bassière: *Compt. rend.*, **201**, 735 (1935).
[82] F. J. Llewellyn and F. E. Whitmore: *J. Chem. Soc.*, **1947**, 881.
[83] G. Herzberg, F. Patat, and H. Verleger: *Z. Elektrochem.*, **41**, 522 (1935).
[84] E. H. Eyster: *J. Chem. Phys.*, **8**, 135 (1940).
[85] V. Schomaker and R. Spurr: *J. Am. Chem. Soc.*, **64**, 1184 (1942).
[86] L. F. Audrieth: *Chem. Revs.*, **15**, 169 (1934).

discussed in Chapter 13 (pp. 463–475). Free hydrazoic acid is a colorless liquid boiling at 37°C. and freezing at low temperatures to a solid which melts at −80°C. The volatility of the compound permits its separation from aqueous solutions by distillation. In the vapor condition, the material is monomeric.[87] In the liquid state some association apparently occurs as indicated by the solvent power of the liquid for many salts and the resultant formation of conducting solutions. Chemically, hydrazoic acid is characterized by its tendency to detonate violently when subjected to shock (even when boiling), its poisonous nature, its acidic properties, and its reactions with oxidizing and reducing agents.

In aqueous solution hydrazoic acid is a weak acid ($k_A' = 1.9 \times 10^{-5}$ at 25°C.). The oxidizing and reducing properties are summarized by the couples

$$3NH_4^+ \rightleftharpoons HN_3 + 11H^+ + 8e^- \qquad E^0_{298} = -0.66 \text{ volt}$$

$$NH_4^+ + N_2 \rightleftharpoons HN_3 + 3H^+ + 2e^- \qquad = -1.82 \text{ volts}$$

$$HN_3 \rightleftharpoons \tfrac{3}{2}N_2 + H^+ + e^- \qquad = 2.8$$

in acidic solution and

$$NH_3 + N_2H_4 + 7OH^- \rightleftharpoons N_3^- + 7H_2O + 6e^- \qquad E^0_{298} = 0.62 \text{ volt}$$

$$N_3^- \rightleftharpoons \tfrac{3}{2}N_2 + e^- \qquad = 3.1 \text{ volts}$$

in alkaline solution. Oxidation of the hydrohalogen acids (except hydrofluoric) to free halogens, of many metals, and of many other reducing agents (e.g., Ti^{+3}, Sn^{+2}, etc.), is readily effected, nitrogen, ammonium ion, and hydrazinium ion being formed in various proportions as reduction products. Although the oxidation potential is favorable, oxidation of hydrazoic acid is often slow. Hypochlorous acid, nitrous acid, cerium(IV), and iodine (in the presence of thiosulfate) oxidize the material quantitatively to nitrogen; but permanganate gives a variety of products, and materials such as iron(III) and hydrogen peroxide are not effective.

The azides resemble the halides in solubilities. All azides decompose at elevated temperatures. Explosive decomposition (detonation) occurs when the compounds of lead(II), mercury(II), thallium(I), etc., are struck or heated. These compounds (particularly lead azide) are useful in initiating other explosions. The alkali and alkaline earth metal azides, on the other hand, decompose to the metals

[87] A. O. Beckman and R. G. Dickinson: *J. Am. Chem. Soc.*, **50**, 1870 (1928).

and nitrogen when heated above 300°C. without exploding.[88, 89] Recorded decomposition temperatures and yields of alkali metal are: Cs, 350°C., 90%; Rb, 310°C., 60%; K, 320°C., 80%; Na, 300°C., 100%. Because of the reaction of lithium metal with nitrogen (p. 823), the lithium compound does not behave in this fashion. The differences in thermal behavior among the azides are striking. It is believed[90, 91] that the heavy metal azides owe their detonating property to the presence of crystal imperfections or impurities which provide centers at which decompositions may begin. Azide ion behaves as a donor toward cations such as iron(III) and copper(II) to give complexes.

Azides and hydrazoic acid can be prepared in a variety of fashions, among the more important procedures being the following:

Oxidation of Alkali Metal Amides. Molten sodamide can be oxidized with sodium nitrate at 175°C., the products being sodium azide (65% yield), sodium hydroxide, and ammonia.[92] Heating liquid ammonia solutions of potassium amide and potassium nitrate to 130° to 140°C. in a bomb increases the yield to 75%, but the yield with the sodium salts by this variant is lower.[93] An even better procedure, and one which is useful commercially, involves reaction of molten sodamide (190° ± 4°C.) with nitrous oxide, yields being as high as 90%,[94]

$$2NaNH_2(l) + N_2O(g) \rightarrow NaN_3 + NaOH + NH_3$$

Sodium azide is recovered by dissolving the product in water and recrystallizing.

Oxidation of Hydrazine. Curtius first prepared hydrazoic acid by oxidizing hydrazine with nitrous acid[95]

$$N_2H_5^+ + HNO_2 \rightarrow HN_3 + H^+ + 2H_2O$$

Acidity is important,[96] best results being obtained at high acidities with solutions prepared from hydrazinium chloride, sodium nitrite, and ortho-phosphoric acid. Other oxidizing agents, among them hydrogen peroxide, chlorate, perchlorate, and peroxydisulfate, are

[88] R. Suhrmann and K. Clusius: *Z. anorg. allgem. Chem.*, **152**, 52 (1926).
[89] N. F. Mott: *Proc. Roy. Soc.* (*London*), **A172**, 325 (1939).
[90] W. E. Garner and H. R. Hailes: *Proc. Roy. Soc.* (*London*), **A139**, 576 (1933).
[91] H. W. Melville: *Science Progress*, **33**, 91 (1938).
[92] A. W. Browne and F. Wilcoxon: *J. Am. Chem. Soc.*, **48**, 682 (1926).
[93] E. C. Franklin: *J. Am. Chem. Soc.*, **56**, 568 (1934).
[94] L. M. Dennis and A. W. Browne: *J. Am. Chem. Soc.*, **26**, 577 (1904).
[95] T. Curtius: *Ber.*, **26**, 1263 (1893).
[96] F. Sommer and H. Pincas: *Ber.*, **49**, 259 (1916).

effective,[97] as are also nitric acid, nitrogen trichloride, and ethyl nitrite.

Many other minor procedures have been described. The preparation of pure hydrazoic acid is fraught with danger. The material may be handled better in aqueous or ethereal solutions. Such solutions are obtained by distilling sodium azide–sulfuric acid mixtures, using either water or ether as the original medium.[98]

Binary nitrogen-halogen compounds

Binary halogen compounds embrace the trihalides, NF_3 and NCl_3, and the lower fluorides, NF_2 and N_2F_2. The pure tribromide and triodide are not known, but ammonates, $NBr_3 \cdot 6NH_3$ and $NI_3 \cdot xNH_3$ ($x = 1$ to 12, most commonly 1), have been described. Although all these compounds are referred to quite generally as halides, it is apparent from electronegativity considerations that only the fluorine compounds are true halides. The bromine and iodine compounds are really nitrides, but the chlorine compound is a purely non-polar compound.

Compounds of the Type NX_3. Nitrogen trifluoride is a gas which may be condensed to a liquid boiling at −119°C. and freezing at −216.6°C. The latent heat of vaporization of the liquid is 2.4 kcal. per mole. The vapor density is normal. Electron diffraction data show the molecule to be pyramidal with N—F bond distances of 1.37 A and FNF bond angles of 102.5°.[99] Nitrogen trichloride is a yellow, oily liquid, boiling at around 71°C. and freezing at about −27°C.

Chemically, the trifluoride and the trichloride are distinguished by the extreme thermal stability and lack of reactivity of the former as compared with the instability and general reactivity of the latter. Nitrogen trifluoride is an exothermic compound, whereas the trichloride is endothermic, the molar heats of formation being -26 ± 2 kcal. and 55.4 kcal., respectively. The N—Cl bond is not an inherently weak bond, but the triple bond in the nitrogen molecule is so strong by comparison that nitrogen trichloride is unstable. In nitrogen trifluoride, ionic resonance forms overcome this factor and promote stability. Nitrogen trifluoride does not decompose on heating or sparking, but nitrogen trichloride explodes violently on being heated

[97] A. W. Browne and F. F. Shetterly: *J. Am. Chem. Soc.*, **31**, 221 (1909).
[98] L. F. Audrieth and C. F. Gibbs: *Inorganic Syntheses*, Vol. I, p. 77. McGraw-Hill Book Co., New York (1939).
[99] V. Schomaker and C.-S. Lu: *J. Am. Chem. Soc.*, **72**, 1182 (1950).

above its boiling point or on exposure to ultraviolet radiation. The trifluoride is unaffected (except at elevated temperatures) by water, alkalies, sulfuric acid, silver, ammonia, methane, acetylene, sulfur dioxide, glass (dry), or steel.[100, 101] A reaction

$$2NF_3 + 3H_2O \rightarrow 6HF + NO_2 + NO$$

accompanied by a blue flame, occurs when the trifluoride and water vapor are sparked. The trichloride reacts readily with water (giving ammonia and hypochlorous acid), with alkalies, with hydrogen (giving ammonium chloride and chlorine), and with many organic compounds. The same differences in activity as those noted between the fluorine and chlorine derivatives of oxygen and sulfur are apparent here.

Nitrogen trifluoride was first prepared[100] by electrolysis in a copper cell of molten ammonium hydrogen fluoride (NH_4HF_2) at 125°C. with a current of 10 amp. at 7 to 9 volts. From the product gases (H_2, NF_3, N_2O, N_2, HF, NH_2F, NHF_2, and O_3), nitrogen trifluoride was separated by a system of absorption and low-temperature condensation traps and finally frozen out, together with the substances N_2O, SiF_4, and NH_2F or NHF_2. These were removed with sodium hydroxide. The compound also results from direct fluorination of ammonia, nitrogen being added to reduce the vigor of the reaction.[102] Nitrogen trichloride can be obtained by action of chlorine on ammonia or an ammonium salt, by action of hypochlorous acid on an ammonium salt, by electrolysis of ammonium chloride, or by action of phosphorus(V) chloride on nitrosyl chloride. Noyes[103] recommends its preparation as a 12% solution in carbon tetrachloride by treating aqueous ammonium sulfate solution with chlorine at 10°C. and extracting with carbon tetrachloride. Such a solution is stable.

The compounds NH_2X and NHX_2 (X = F, Cl) are intermediates between ammonia and the trihalides. Only those of the first type have been isolated pure, but the others apparently exist. The fluoride, NH_2F, is a solid subliming at −77°C. (1 atm.).[102] The chloride, NH_2Cl, is a liquid of low vapor pressure, freezing at −66°C. The fluorides are more reactive than nitrogen trifluoride; the chlorides are less reactive than nitrogen trichloride. Chloramine, NH_2Cl, is an intermediate in the Raschig synthesis of hydrazine (p. 585). It decomposes to ammonium chloride and nitrogen on being heated and i

100 O. Ruff, J. Fischer, and F. Luft: *Z. anorg. allgem. Chem.*, **172**, 417 (1928).

101 O. Ruff: *Z. anorg. allgem. Chem.*, **197**, 273 (1931).

102 O. Ruff and E. Hanke: *Z. anorg. allgem. Chem.*, **197**, 395 (1931).

103 W. A. Noyes: *Inorganic Syntheses*, Vol. I, p. 65. McGraw-Hill Book Co New York (1939).

hydrolyzed readily to ammonia and nitrogen. Organic chloramines (e.g., chloramine-T) have been used as germicides. These compounds result in the nitrogen trihalide preparations outlined above. Chapin[104] finds that in the chlorination of ammonia, NH_2Cl forms at pH values above 8.5, $NHCl_2$ at pH 4.5 to 5.0, and NCl_3 at pH values below 4.4.

Reaction of bromine with ammonia at $-95°$C. and 1 to 2 mm. pressure gives the purple ammonate, $NBr_3 \cdot 6NH_3$, but this compound decomposes explosively above $-70°$C. to nitrogen, ammonia, and ammonium bromide.[105] The intermediate bromamines, NH_2Br and $NHBr_2$, are formed apparently by action of bromine on ammonia in ether, but they have not been isolated.[106, 107] Reaction of iodine with ammonia at ordinary temperatures gives the 1-ammonate of nitrogen triiodide,[108] but higher ammonates result at lower temperatures. The compounds have all the reactions expected for nitrogen triiodide —namely, explosive character, hydrolysis by water to hydrogen iodide and nitrogen(III) oxide (N_2O_3), and hydrolysis by alkalies to ammonia and hypoiodite.

Lower Nitrogen Fluorides. Electrolysis of ammonium hydrogen fluoride[100] yields small amounts of a difluoride (NF_2), a gas boiling at about $-125°$C. Decomposition of nitrogen trifluoride gives colorless gaseous N_2F_2, electron diffraction data on which indicate the presence in roughly equal proportions of *cis* and *trans* forms

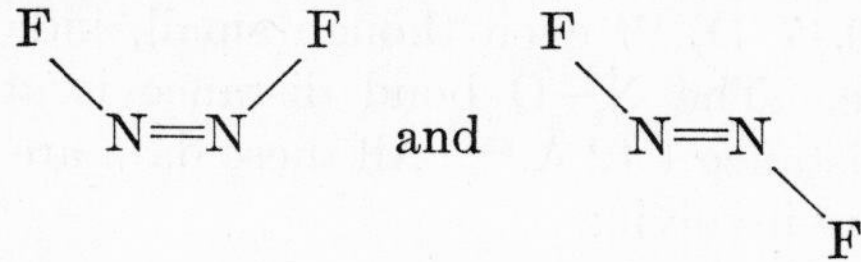

with N—F and N—N bond distances of 1.44 A and 1.25 A, respectively.[109]

Binary oxygen-nitrogen compounds

Some eight oxides of nitrogen have been described. These have the stoichiometric formulas N_2O, NO, N_2O_3, NO_2, N_2O_4, N_2O_5, NO_3, and N_2O_6. Three of these, NO, NO_2, and NO_3, are odd molecules. Technically, only the compounds N_2O, NO, and NO_2 are of any particular importance. The compounds N_2O_3 and N_2O_5 are the anhydrides of

104 R. M. Chapin: *J. Am. Chem. Soc.*, **51**, 2112 (1929); **53**, 912 (1931).
105 M. Schmeisser: *Naturwissenschaften*, **28**, 63 (1940).
106 W. Moldenhauer and M. Burger: *Ber.*, **62B**, 1615 (1929).
107 G. H. Coleman, C. B. Yager, and H. Soroos: *J. Am. Chem. Soc.*, **56**, 965 (1934).
108 F. D. Chattaway and K. J. P. Orton: *Am. Chem. J.*, **24**, 342 (1900).
109 S. H. Bauer: *J. Am. Chem. Soc.*, **69**, 3104 (1947).

nitrous and nitric acids, respectively. Nitrous oxide (N_2O) is the formal anhydride of hyponitrous acid, but although very soluble it does not react with water to form this acid. Available physical constant data for the oxides are summarized in Table 15·9.

TABLE 15·9
PHYSICAL CONSTANTS OF THE NITROGEN OXIDES

Property	N_2O	NO	N_2O_3	$NO_2 \rightleftharpoons N_2O_4$	N_2O_5	NO_3
Melting point, °C.	−90.84	−163.61	−103	−11.2	41	
Boiling point, °C.	−88.51	−151.74	3.5	21.15	32.5(subl.)	
Heat of fusion, kcal./mole	1.563	0.550		3.502	....	
Heat of vaporization, kcal./mole	3.958	3.293		9.110	13.8	
Heat of formation, kcal./mole	19.65	21.50		7.964 (NO_2) 2.239 (N_2O_4)	0.70 (g)	ca. 13.0
Magnetic moment, Bohr magnetons		1.837 (26°C.)				
Trouton constant	21.4	27.1		30.9		

Nitrous Oxide or Nitrogen(I) Oxide (N_2O). The infra-red absorption spectrum of gaseous nitrous oxide[110, 111] and x-ray diffraction data on the solid[112] and liquid[113] are best interpreted in terms of a linear molecule with the two nitrogen atoms bonded to each other, i.e., NNO. Electron diffraction data[85] confirm the linear arrangement, and the dipole moment (0.17 D),[114] even though small, indicates an unsymmetrical structure. The N—O bond distance is about 1.19 A and the N—N bond distance 1.12 A.[85] All these data are in accord with a resonance structure involving

$$\overset{-}{:}\ddot{N}::\overset{+}{N}::\ddot{O}: \quad \text{and} \quad :N:::\overset{+}{N}:\underset{\cdot\cdot}{\overset{\cdot\cdot}{O}}\overset{-}{:}$$

Nitrous oxide is isosteric with carbon dioxide, and the physical properties of the two materials are closely comparable (p. 214). In the solid state, the two compounds are completely isomorphous.

Nitrous oxide is stable and comparatively unreactive at ordinary temperature. Thus it is inert to ozone, hydrogen, the halogens, the alkali metals, etc. At elevated temperatures, decomposition to

[110] E. K. Plyler and E. F. Barker: *Phys. Rev.*, **38**, 1827 (1931); **41**, 369 (1932).

[111] E. F. Barker: *Nature*, **129**, 132 (1932).

[112] J. de Smedt and W. H. Keesom: *Proc. Konink. Akad. Wetenschap. Amsterdam*, **27**, 839 (1924).

[113] P. C. Sharrah: *J. Chem. Phys.*, **11**, 435 (1943).

[114] H. E. Watson, G. G. Rao, and K. L. Ramaswamy: *Proc. Roy. Soc. (London)*, **A143**, 558 (1934).

nitrogen and oxygen occurs, the rate of decomposition becoming appreciable above 565°C. The kinetics of the decomposition are complex.[115] At elevated temperatures, nitrous oxide supports combustion and oxidizes certain organic compounds, the alkali metals, etc. The compound is soluble in alkaline solutions but does not form hyponitrites. A crystalline hydrate, $N_2O{\cdot}6H_2O$, can be obtained at low temperatures. When inhaled, nitrous oxide produces a mild hysteria which is accompanied by anesthetic effects. Its major uses are as an anesthetic and as a dispersing agent in cream whippers.

Nitrous oxide is obtained by controlled reduction of nitrites or nitrates, by the slow decomposition of hyponitrites (p. 614), by the thermal decomposition of hydroxylamine, and by the thermal decomposition of ammonium nitrate (p. 576). The last reaction is the one most commonly employed, the major impurity, aside from water vapor, being nitric oxide. This can be removed with iron(II) sulfate solution.

Nitric Oxide or Nitrogen(II) *Oxide* (NO). Although the nitric oxide molecule contains an odd number of electrons, its properties differ significantly from those of other odd molecules. The material is colorless in the gaseous state, although in both the liquid and solid states it is blue. Under ordinary conditions, it shows no tendency to dimerize, although in the liquid state association is indicated by the high Trouton constant (= 27.1), and in the solid state entropy[116] and magnetic[117, 118] data are consistent with the presence of dimeric molecules (97% dimerization calculated at −163°C.[118]). Infrared and Raman data for the liquid and the solid also indicate the existence of dimers.[119] In comparison with other odd molecules, nitric oxide is chemically rather inactive. These characteristics suggest an unusual structure.

The bond distance of 1.14 A lies between radius sum values of 1.18 A and 1.06 A for double and triple bonds,[120] respectively, suggesting resonance. Two electronic structures may be written,

$$\underset{\text{I}}{:\dot{\text{N}}::\ddot{\text{O}}:} \qquad\qquad \underset{\text{II}}{\overset{-}{:}\ddot{\text{N}}::\dot{\text{O}}\overset{+}{:}}$$

[115] C. N. Hinshelwood and R. E. Burk: *Proc. Roy. Soc.* (*London*), **A106,** 284 (1924).

[116] H. L. Johnston and W. F. Giauque: *J. Am. Chem. Soc.*, **51,** 3194 (1929).

[117] E. Lips: *Helv. Phys. Acta*, **8,** 247 (1935).

[118] H. Bizette and B. Tsai: *Compt. rend.*, **206,** 1288 (1938).

[119] A. L. Smith, W. E. Keller, and H. L. Johnston: *J. Chem. Phys.*, **19,** 189 (1951).

[120] L. Pauling: *The Nature of the Chemical Bond*, 2nd. Ed., pp. 266–271. Cornell University Press, Ithaca (1940).

with structure I being the more probable in view of the unfavorable charge distribution in structure II. However, small stability differences permit resonance between the two structures, imparting an effective three-electron bond structure (p. 212)

$$:\!N\overset{\cdots}{::}O\!:\quad \text{or} \quad :\!N\overset{\cdots}{=\!=}O\!:$$

to the material.[120] This arrangement stabilizes the molecule sufficiently with respect to structure I that the unusual properties mentioned above result. The small dipole moment (0.16 D) and dielectric constant (0.2×10^{-18} e.s.u.) of nitric oxide are also in agreement with this structure.

Nitric oxide is thermally stable. It is an oxidizing agent at elevated temperatures and will support the combustion of materials such as phosphorus. It is also reactive toward oxidizing agents, being converted to nitric acid by permanganate, to nitrogen(IV) oxide by oxygen, and to nitrosyl halides by fluorine, chlorine, and bromine. Reaction with oxygen is important in the technical preparation of nitric acid. This reaction proceeds by a third-order mechanism and is more rapid and complete at low temperatures than at high temperatures. Nitric oxide gives complexes with a number of metal ions and adds to certain metals and metal carbonyls. These reactions are discussed below under the topic *nitrosyl compounds*.

The formation of nitric oxide is essential to the technical production of nitric acid. Direct combination of nitrogen with oxygen is an equilibrium process

$$N_2 + O_2 + \text{energy} \rightleftharpoons 2NO$$

in which even under energy-rich conditions the quantity of nitric oxide formed is unfavorable (2.23% by volume at 2400°C., 4.4% at 3200°C.). The equilibrium is normally established in an electric arc or gas-fired furnace and the mixture cooled rapidly to prevent readjustment to nitrogen and oxygen. A more favorable process involves oxidation of ammonia

$$4NH_3 + 5O_2 \rightarrow 4NO + 6H_2O$$

above 500°C. in the presence of platinum (Ostwald process). In the absence of a catalyst, nitrogen is the oxidation product. In the laboratory pure nitric oxide can be obtained by reducing nitrous acid with iodide[116] or ferrous sulfate[121] and removing impurities by absorption in alkali.

[121] A. A. Blanchard: *Inorganic Syntheses*, Vol. II, p. 126. McGraw-Hill Book Co., New York (1946).

INORGANIC NITROSYL COMPOUNDS. A number of compounds containing the NO group and derivable directly or indirectly from nitric oxide can be distinguished. They are referred to as nitrosyl compounds.[122] Because of its molecular structure, nitric oxide might enter into chemical combination or form nitrosyl compounds as:

1. A positive ion, NO^+, through loss of an electron. Such a nitrosyl (nitrosonium or nitrosylium) cation would probably have the structure

$$(:\mathrm{N}:::\mathrm{O}:)^+ \quad \text{or} \quad (:\mathrm{N}\equiv\mathrm{O}:)^+$$

in view of the presence of a triple bond in the excited molecule.[120]

2. A negative ion, NO^-, through gain of an electron from some electropositive material. Such an anion might be formulated as

$$(:\ddot{\mathrm{N}}::\ddot{\mathrm{O}}:)^- \quad \text{or} \quad (:\ddot{\mathrm{N}}=\ddot{\mathrm{O}}:)^-$$

3. A coordinating group, through donation of an electron pair. Such behavior might involve the neutral molecule or the NO^+ or NO^- group.

It is convenient to classify the inorganic nitrosyl compounds in terms of these considerations.

I. SIMPLE COMPOUNDS CONTAINING THE NO^+ GROUP. In a number of cases the presence of this group has been established by physical measurements; in others its existence may be inferred by analogy.[122] Among compounds of these types are the following: $NOHSO_4$; $(NO)_2S_2O_7$; the nitrosyl halides, NOX (X = F, Cl, Br); $NOClO_4$; $NOBF_4$; $(NO)_2SeO_4$; $NOHSeO_4$; $NOReO_4$; NOSCN; $NOSO_3F$; $NO[Cr(NH_3)_2(SCN)_4]$; $NOPF_6$; $NOAsF_6$; $NOSbF_6$; $NOSbCl_6$; $(NO)_2SnCl_6$; $(NO)_2PtCl_6$; $NOFeCl_4$; $(NO)_2[Fe(CN)_5(NO)]$; $NONO_3$; etc.

Evidence for the presence of the NO^+ group in various of these compounds is varied. The acidic behavior of certain of these substances in liquid dinitrogen tetroxide as described in earlier chapters (pp. 325, 366) indicates the presence of NO^+ ions under these conditions. Angus and Leckie[123] cite the following arguments for the existence of such a radical: (1) The ionization potential of the nitric oxide molecule is low (9.5 ev) in comparison with those of other similar diatomic molecules, making removal of an electron comparatively easy. (2) Both nitrosyl hydrogen sulfate and nitrosyl perchlorate exhibit Raman displacements in the vicinity of 2330 cm.$^{-1}$, these displacements being considered indicative of the presence of the NO^+ group since they are

[122] T. Moeller: *J. Chem. Education*, **23**, 441, 542 (1946); **24**, 149 (1947).
[123] W. R. Angus and A. H. Leckie: *Trans. Faraday Soc.*, **31**, 958 (1935).

comparable with the displacement shown by the isoelectronic N_2 molecule and since other observed Raman displacements for these compounds are characteristic of the HSO_4^- and ClO_4^- ions. (3) Electrolysis of a solution of nitrosyl hydrogen sulfate in concentrated sulfuric acid with an iron cathode causes development of the characteristic brown color of $Fe(NO)^{+2}$ around the cathode, indicating migration of the nitrosyl group to the negative pole. (4) Both nitrosyl hydrogen sulfate and perchlorate give conducting solutions in nitromethane and behave as binary electrolytes. (5) Salts of nitrosyl sulfuric acid cannot be prepared, indicating that the nitrosyl group is the positive one.

To these may be added other pertinent observations. Sulfuric acid solutions of nitrosyl hydrogen sulfate give abnormal molecular weight data which indicate dissociation to $NO^+HSO_4^-$.[124, 125] Both nitrosyl perchlorate and nitrosyl fluoborate have the same crystal structures as the ionic hydronium and ammonium compounds, the NO^+ ion being larger than the NH_4^+ ion but about the same size as the H_3O^+ ion.[126] In non-aqueous solvents such as sulfur dioxide or nitrosyl chloride, metathetical reactions and oxidation-reduction reactions involving the NO^+ group occur.[127] Furthermore, cryoscopic[128] and Raman[129] data show clearly that dissolution of the oxides N_2O_3 and N_2O_4 in sulfuric acid gives the NO^+ ion in terms of the equations

$$N_2O_3 + 3H_2SO_4 \rightarrow 2NO^+ + 3HSO_4^- + H_3O^+$$

and

$$N_2O_4 + 3H_2SO_4 \rightarrow NO^+ + NO_2^+ + 3HSO_4^- + H_3O^+$$

Dinitrogen tetroxide also dissolves in nitric acid to give the positive nitrosyl ion.[130] The ion is solvated by nitrogen dioxide to $NO{\cdot}NO_2^+$.[130, 131]

The nitrosyl halides are essentially covalent compounds as indicated by the data summarized in Table 15·10, but they are definitely polar. Perhaps the best indications of their structures are given by the bond distances and dipole moments listed for the chloride and bromide.[132, 133]

[124] A. Hantzsch: *Z. physik. Chem.*, **65**, 41 (1909).

[125] A. Hantzsch and K. Berger: *Z. anorg. allgem. Chem.*, **190**, 321 (1930).

[126] L. J. Klinkenberg: *Rec. trav. chim.*, **56**, 749 (1937).

[127] F. Seel: *Z. anorg. Chem.*, **261**, 75 (1950).

[128] R. J. Gillespie, J. Graham, E. D. Hughes, C. K. Ingold, and E. R. A. Peeling: *J. Chem. Soc.*, **1950**, 2504.

[129] D. J. Millen: *J. Chem. Soc.*, **1950**, 2600.

[130] J. D. S. Goulden and D. J. Millen: *J. Chem. Soc.*, **1950**, 2620.

[131] J. D. S. Goulden, C. K. Ingold, and D. J. Millen: *Nature*, **165**, 565 (1950).

[132] J. A. A. Ketelaar: *Atti. X° congr. intern. chim.*, **2**, 301 (1938); *Rec. trav. chim.*, **62**, 289 (1943).

[133] J. A. A. Ketelaar and K. J. Palmer: *J. Am. Chem. Soc.*, **59**, 2629 (1937).

The measured N—Cl and N—Br bond distances are somewhat larger than the sums of the covalent single bond radii of 1.73 A (N—Cl) and 1.88 A (N—Br), but less than ionic bonds (e.g., 2.64 A for N—Cl

TABLE 15·10
PHYSICAL PROPERTIES OF THE NITROSYL HALIDES

Property	NOF	NOCl	NOBr
Molecular weight	49.008	65.465	109.924
Melting point, °C.	−132.5	−64.5	−55.5
Boiling point, °C.	−59.5	−6.4	ca. 0
Color (gas)	colorless	orange-yellow	red
Bond distances, A			
X—O		2.65 ± 0.01	2.85 ± 0.02
X—N		1.95 ± 0.01	2.14 ± 0.02
N—O		1.14 ± 0.02	1.15 ± 0.04
Bond angle, degrees		116 ± 2	117 ± 3
Dipole moment, D		1.83	1.87

based upon 1.40 A as the radius of NO^+).[132] Since the N—O bonds are intermediate in lengths between double and triple bonds, as well, such resonance structures as

$$:\ddot{O}::\ddot{N}:\ddot{X}: \quad \text{and} \quad :O:::N:^{+} \quad :\ddot{X}:^{-}$$

undoubtedly characterize the nitrosyl halides. This view is supported by comparison of measured dipole moments with the 0.3 D and 0.4 D as calculated, respectively, for purely covalent nitrosyl chloride and nitrosyl bromide.[133] Both the chloride and bromide are about 50% ionic.[133]

Compounds containing the NO^+ group are generally susceptible to hydrolysis and must be prepared and preserved under anhydrous conditions. Nitrosyl sulfuric acid, $NOHSO_4$, is an intermediate in the chamber process for the manufacture of sulfuric acid. It may be obtained by reaction between fuming nitric acid and sulfur dioxide, reaction between nitrogen(III) or nitrogen(IV) oxide and concentrated sulfuric acid, or reaction between nitrosyl chloride and concentrated sulfuric acid. A general method of preparation for the nitrosyl halides involves direct combination of nitric oxide with the halogen. Nitrosyl fluoride also results from reactions of nitrosyl chloride with silver fluoride, nitrosyl fluoborate with sodium fluoride, and nitrosyl hexafluoantimonate(V) with potassium fluoride. Nitrosyl chloride is obtained by reaction of nitrogen dioxide with moist potassium chloride or reaction of nitrosyl sulfuric acid with sodium or hydrogen chloride.[134] Other nitrosyl compounds of this class are obtained by reactions of nitrogen(II, III, or IV) oxide with the appropriate acids (e.g., $NOClO_4$, $NOBF_4$, $NOReO_4$, $NOHSeO_4$), by metathesis reactions involving nitrosyl chloride or other nitrosyl salt (e.g., $NOClO_4$, NOSCN), or by addition of a nitrosyl halide to a halide (e.g., $NOPF_6$, $NOSbCl_6$, $(NO)_2SnCl_6$).[122] Reactions of nitrosyl chloride with oxides and halides in liquid bromine trifluoride are particularly effective for the preparation of fluorine-containing nitrosyl compounds [e.g., $NOPF_6$, $(NO)_2GeF_6$, and $NOAuF_4$].[135]

II. SIMPLE COMPOUNDS CONTAINING THE NO^- GROUP. The only reported example of a simple compound of this type is sodium nitrosyl, NaNO. This is a white, rather unstable solid which differs distinctly in chemical properties and x-ray diffraction pattern from sodium hyponitrite, which has the same stoichiometric composition.[136] Its diamagnetic properties suggest the presence of the NO^- ion.[137] The compound is obtained by reaction of dry nitric oxide with sodium in liquid ammonia.[136]

III. COORDINATION COMPOUNDS. These are compounds in which the nitrosyl group is directly associated with metal atoms or ions.[122, 138–141] Although the compositions and properties of these materials vary widely, it appears best to consider them together under the broad heading of coordination compounds.

This discussion might be prefaced by a consideration of the coordinating characteristics of the nitrosyl group.[122] Regardless of how the group is attached, attachment to the metal is apparently always through the nitrogen. This is indicated by the fact that reduction of a complex such as $[Fe(CN)_5(NO)]^{-2}$ yields an ammine, $[Fe(CN)_5(NH_3)]^{-3}$, whereas treatment of the same complex with alkali converts it to a nitro derivative, $[Fe(CN)_5(NO_2)]^{-4}$. The existence of volatile nitrosyl carbonyl compounds, such as $Fe(NO)_2(CO)_2$ (p. 600), and the similarities between these compounds and the metal carbonyls

[134] G. H. Coleman, G. A. Lillis, and G. E. Goheen: *Inorganic Syntheses*, Vol. I, p. 55. McGraw-Hill Book Co., New York (1939).

[135] A. A. Woolf: *J. Chem. Soc.*, **1950**, 1053.

[136] E. Zintl and A. Harder: *Ber.*, **66B**, 760 (1933).

[137] J. H. Frazer and N. O. Long: *J. Chem. Phys.*, **6**, 462 (1938).

[138] W. Hieber and R. Nast: *FIAT Reviews of German Science 1939–1946*, *Inorganic Chemistry*, Pt. II, pp. 146–54. Dieterich'sche Verlagsbuchhandlung, Wiesbaden (1948).

[139] F. Seel with W. Hieber: *Z. anorg. allgem. Chem.*, **249**, 308 (1942).

[140] N. V. Sidgwick and R. W. Bailey: *Proc. Roy. Soc. (London)*, **A144**, 521 (1934).

[141] A. J. E. Welch: *Ann. Reports*, **38**, 71 (1941).

(pp. 700–708) suggest coordination by neutral nitric oxide molecules. Such a condition would assume attachment through electron pair bonds and because of preservation of the odd electron in the NO group would render the nitrosyl carbonyls paramagnetic. They are actually diamagnetic. Furthermore, if neutral nitric oxide molecules were involved, they should be replaceable by other neutral molecules without alteration in compound type. Treatment of nitrosyl carbonyls with reagents such as pyridine replaces carbonyl groups rather than nitrosyl groups. Also replacement of neutral carbonyl by nitrosyl alters the oxidation states in complex ions, for example, $[Fe(CN)_5(CO)]^{-3}$ goes to $[Fe(CN)_5(NO)]^{-2}$. Coordination by neutral nitrosyl groups is unlikely in view of experimental evidence.

If the nitrosyl group were to add as NO^-, it would behave as a halide ion. Only in isolated cases are the properties of nitrosyl coordination compounds consistent with such behavior. Positive evidence for addition in this fashion is available only for the diamagnetic pink compounds containing the group $[Co(NH_3)_5(NO)]^{+2}$, where cobalt(II) apparently transfers an electron to the NO group.[142] Such compounds are actually analogous to the halopentammines, $[Co(NH_3)_5X]^{+2}$. The same situation may pertain in the diamagnetic ruthenium complexes, $[Ru(NH_3)_4(H_2O)(NO)]^{+3}$ and $[Ru(NH_3)_4(Cl)(NO)]^{+2}$. In general, however, coordination by the NO^- group is also unlikely.

Evidences for coordination involving NO^+ are more convincing.[139, 140] This cation is isosteric with the carbon monoxide molecule and the cyanide ion, all of which are structurally similar

$$:N:::O:^+ \qquad :C:::O: \qquad :C:::N:^-$$

Corresponding similarities are found among compounds containing these materials, for example, in the series $K_2[Fe(CN)_5(NO)]$, $K_3[Fe(CN)_5(CO)]$, $K_4[Fe(CN)_6]$. In the formation of an NO^+ cation, transfer of the lost electron to the metal atom or ion may occur, producing a decrease of one unit in oxidation state. The overall oxidation states of nitrosyl complexes are consistent with this view. Thus in $[Fe(CN)_5(NO)]^{-2}$ transfer of an electron from NO maintains iron in the +2 state and consideration of NO as +1 gives the overall value of −2. This concept also fits many nitrosyl complexes into Sidgwick's effective atomic number rule (p. 234). The relation

$$G - \frac{xm + 2y + 3z}{x} = x - 1 \qquad (15\cdot2)$$

where G is the atomic number of the next inert gas, m the atomic

[142] D. P. Mellor and D. P. Craig: *J. Proc. Roy. Soc. N. S. Wales*, **78**, 25 (1944).

number of the metal M, and x, y, and z the numbers of groups in compounds of the type $M_x(A)_y(NO)_z$ (A = CO, etc.), applies to many examples.[140]

Although the concept of binding involving three electrons accounts for the compositions of many nitrosyl complexes, it suffers from the general criticism (pp. 232–233) that an unlikely negative charge is accumulated by the metal in question. A suitable alternative involves a four-electron arrangement [120]

$$\overset{+}{\text{M::N::}}\ddot{\text{O}}\text{:}$$

where in a formal way the metal in question acts as both a donor and an acceptor. Although ultimate decision as to the correctness of this view must await evaluation of M—N bond distances in a number of nitrosyl compounds, the concept is a useful one.

A considerable complexity is apparent among coordinated nitrosyl compounds, but the majority of these materials fall into several well-defined classes. The following classification[122] is a useful one:

A. THE NITROSYL CARBONYLS AND RELATED COMPOUNDS. The only definitely established nitrosyl carbonyls are the cobalt and iron compounds, $Co(NO)(CO)_3$ and $Fe(NO)_2(CO)_2$. Acceptance of the view that each nitrosyl group contributes three electrons indicates that these compounds form a graded series with nickel tetracarbonyl (p. 703), in which substitution of a nitrosyl group for a carbonyl accompanies each decrease in atomic number of the metal.[122, 143] Extension of this view would lead to the complete series $Ni(CO)_4$, $Co(NO)(CO)_3$, $Fe(NO)_2(CO)_2$, $Mn(NO)_3(CO)$, $Cr(NO)_4$, each member of which would contain a metal with an effective atomic number of 36.[143] Although the last two members are unknown, the concept is useful. The physical properties of the nitrosyl carbonyls are compared with those of nickel tetracarbonyl in Table 15·11. The enhanced polarity of the nitrosyl group is reflected in the increased melting and boiling points in the series. All three compounds are tetrahedral, but the observed M—C and M—N bond distances[144] are less than the sums of the covalent radii. This and the fact that the observed N—O bond distance is less than the calculated double bond distance suggest that the M—C and M—N bonds are similar and that both two- and four-electron linkages are important.

The nitrosyl carbonyls resemble the carbonyls chemically, although the nitrosyl group is more firmly attached to the metal than the

[143] J. S. Anderson with W. Hieber: *Z. anorg. allgem. Chem.*, **208**, 238 (1932).

[144] L. O. Brockway and J. S. Anderson: *Trans. Faraday Soc.*, **33**, 1233 (1937).

carbonyl group. The cobalt compound is formed when dry nitric oxide reacts with dimeric cobalt tetracarbonyl, $[Co(CO)_4]_2$, when cobalt is treated on pumice with carbon monoxide and nitric oxide, or when an alkaline suspension of cobalt(II) cyanide is treated first with carbon monoxide and then with nitric oxide.[145] Reaction of dry nitric oxide with trimeric iron tetracarbonyl, $[Fe(CO)_4]_3$, gives a mixture of iron nitrosyl carbonyl and iron pentacarbonyl.[143]

Related nitrosyls of iron $[Fe(NO)_4]$ and ruthenium $[Ru(NO)_4$ and $Ru(NO)_5]$ have been reported as products of reactions of nitric oxide

TABLE 15·11

PHYSICAL PROPERTIES OF CARBONYL AND NITROSYL CARBONYL COMPOUNDS

Property	$Ni(CO)_4$	$Co(NO)(CO)_3$	$Fe(NO)_2(CO)_2$
Molecular weight	170.73	172.98	171.89
Melting point, °C.	−23	−1.1	18.4
Boiling point, °C.	43	48.6	110 (extrap.)
Density at 20°C., grams per ml.	1.31	1.47	1.56
Parachor	255.3	249.8	252.5
Mol. susceptibility, $\times 10^6$	−82	−46	....
Bond distances, A			
M—C	1.82 ± 0.02	1.83 ± 0.02	1.84 ± 0.02
C—O	1.15 ± 0.03	1.14 ± 0.03	1.15 ± 0.03
M—N		1.76 ± 0.03	1.77 ± 0.02
N—O		1.10 ± 0.04	1.12 ± 0.03

with the carbonyls $Fe(CO)_5$[146] and $Ru_2(CO)_9$[147] These reactive compounds have not been fully characterized, and structural data are lacking.

B. NITROSYL COMPOUNDS OF THE TYPE $M^I(NO)_xA_y$. Several different types of nitrosyls of monopositive metals may be distinguished:

1. *Metal nitrosyl hydroxides.* Best characterized are the nickel compound, $Ni(NO)OH$, and its alcohol derivatives, $Ni(NO)(OR)(OH)$ and $Ni(OH)OR{\cdot}xROH{\cdot}H_2O$ $[R = CH_3\ (x = 1),\ C_2H_5\ (x = 0)]$. These strongly reducing materials are formed when nickel tetracarbonyl reacts with nitric acid in the presence of water or water and alcohol.[148]

2. *Metal nitrosyl halides.* Compounds such as $Fe_2(NO)_4I_3$, $Fe(NO)_2I$, $Fe(NO)I$, $Fe(NO)_3Cl$, $Co(NO)_2X$ (X = Cl, Br, I), and $Ni(NO)X$ (X = Cl, Br, I) are formed when nitric oxide reacts with

[145] P. Gilmont and A. A. Blanchard: *Inorganic Syntheses,* Vol. II, p. 239. McGraw-Hill Book Co., New York (1946).

[146] W. Manchot and E. Enk: *Ann.,* **470,** 275 (1929).

[147] W. Manchot and W. J. Manchot: *Z. anorg. allgem. Chem.,* **226,** 385 (1936).

[148] J. S. Anderson: *Z. anorg. allgem. Chem.,* **229,** 357 (1936).

appropriate metal halides.[149, 150] Ease of formation decreases in the series Fe-Co-Ni and I-Br-Cl. These compounds are thermally unstable at elevated temperatures, coordinately unsaturated toward donors such as pyridine, and strong reducing agents. Seel suggests[139] a nitrosyl displacement series, comparable with Grimm's hydride displacement series (p. 415), in which addition of n moles of nitric oxide converts a metal atom into a pseudo-atom n groups to the right in the periodic system. Thus in this periodic region one has

Fe	Co	Ni	Cu
	Fe(NO)	Co(NO)	Ni(NO)
		$Fe(NO)_2$	$Co(NO)_2$
			$Fe(NO)_3$

Examples of simple Co(NO) compounds are lacking.

3. *Metal nitrosyl thio compounds.* A bewildering array of such compounds has been described. The true structures of most of these compounds have not been elucidated. Although these substances appear to contain formally unipositive metals, the exact oxidation states of the metals have never been determined with certainty. Iron forms a series of derivatives corresponding in stoichiometry to the general formula $Fe(NO)_2SA$, where A may be hydrogen or a metal, a sulfonic group, or an alkyl or aryl group.[122] These substances appear to be dimeric, and, if iron is assumed to be tetrahedral and 4-coordinate, they may be given the structural formulation

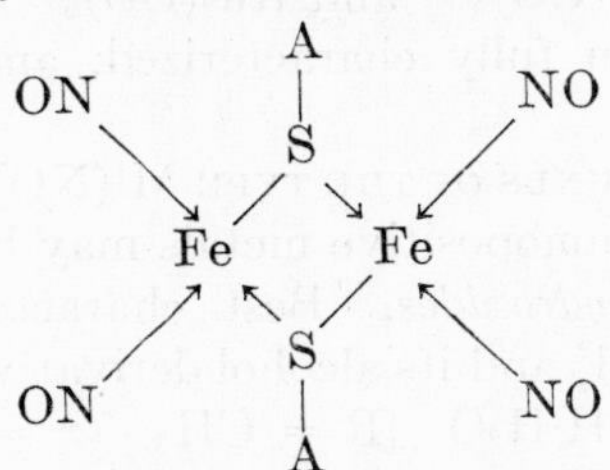

Best known are Roussin's red salts, $M^I[Fe(NO)_2S]$, where $M^I = Na^+$, K^+, NH_4^+, a rather unstable series of compounds obtained in reactions of nitric oxide with freshly precipitated iron(II) sulfide (especially in admixture with polysulfides). Treatment with alkali converts them to the more stable Roussin's black salts (p. 604). Comparable derivatives are $M^I[Fe(NO)SSO_3]$ and ethyl and phenyl compounds, $Fe(NO)_2SR$. Cobalt and nickel yield materials of the types $[Co(NO)_2(SSO_3)_2]^{-3}$, $[Ni(NO)(SSO_3)_2]^{-3}$, $Co(NO)_2SC_2H_5$, and $Ni(NO)SC_2H_5$.[122]

149 W. Hieber and G. Bader: *Z. anorg. allgem. Chem.*, **190**, 193 (1930).
150 W. Hieber and R. Nast: *Z. anorg. allgem. Chem.*, **244**, 23 (1940).

C. NITROSYL COMPOUNDS OF THE TYPE $M^{II}(NO)_xA_y$. Actual assignment of a positive two oxidation state to metals in these compounds is probably more formal than justifiable on the basis of experimental evidence. Absorption of nitric oxide by iron(II) salt solutions up to a limiting ratio of $1NO:1Fe^{+2}$ is well known, especially as a basis for the familiar brown ring test for nitrite or nitrate. The reaction is readily reversed, especially by increased temperature, and loss of nitric oxide regenerates iron(II) salts unchanged. Preparation of solid compounds is difficult, although the crystalline compounds $Fe(NO)HPO_4$ and $Fe(NO)SeO_4 \cdot H_2O$ have been obtained. Stable dithiocarbamate derivatives, $Fe(NO)(R_2NCS_2)_2$, and an ethyl xanthate compound, $Fe(NO)_2(SCSOC_2H_5)_2$, have been prepared.[122] Although iron(II) nitrosyl complexes are normally encountered as brown solutions, green and red species have been described also. Transference studies show the brown to be cationic, the green anionic, and the red neutral in solution. The true nature of such materials is unknown. In the presence of free acids, copper(II) salt solutions absorb nitric oxide up to a limiting mole ratio of $1NO:1Cu^{+2}$. The resulting blue-violet solutions are believed to contain a single anionic nitrosyl species. Palladium(II) compounds, $Pd(NO)_2Cl_2$ and $Pd(NO)_2SO_4$, form by direct absorption of nitric oxide. The nitrosyl dithiocarbamate derivatives of chromium(II), $Cr(NO)_2(R_2NCS_2)_2$, are also representatives of this class.[122]

D. NITROSYL COMPOUNDS OF THE TYPE $M^{III}(NO)_xA_y$. This class is poorly characterized. An iron(III) compound, $Fe_2(NO)_2(SO_4)_3$, has been reported, and it seems probable that the unstable boron halide-nitric oxide compounds, $B(NO)F_3$ and $B(NO)Cl_3$, obtained at low temperatures by direct combination of the components,[151] are examples of the class. So also are the red, diamagnetic substances of formula $Ru(NO)(R_2NCS_2)_3$, where $R = CH_3, C_2H_5$.

E. NITROSYL DERIVATIVES CONTAINING GROUPS OF THE TYPE $[MA_5(NO)]^{\pm n}$. Representative of this class are compounds yielding the ions $[Mn(CN)_5(NO)]^{-3}$, $[Fe(CN)_5(NO)]^{-2}$, $[Mo(CN)_5(NO)]^{-4}$, $[Ru(CN)_5(NO)]^{-2}$, $[Co(NO_2)_5(NO)]^{-3}$, $[Co(NH_3)_5(NO)]^{+2}$, $[Ni(NH_3)_5(NO)]^{+}$, $[Ru(NH_3)_4Cl(NO)]^{+2}$, $[Ru(NH_3)_4(H_2O)(NO)]^{+3}$, $[RuCl_5(NO)]^{-2}$, and $[OsCl_5(NO)]^{-2}$. Best characterized is the series $[M(CN)_5(NO)]^{-n}$, in which the iron compounds, or nitroprussides, are the best-known examples. They are obtained by treating alkali metal hexacyanoferrate(II) salts with nitric acid. They are useful because of the intense violet color developed with sulfide ion (Gmelin reaction), due perhaps to formation of $[Fe(CN)_5(NOS)]^{-4}$, and the red color devel-

[151] G. R. Finlay: *J. Chem. Education*, **24**, 149 (1947).

oped with sulfite ion (Bödecker reaction), due perhaps to formation of $[Fe(CN)_5(NOSO_3)]^{-4}$. The corresponding ruthenium complex is obtained by an analogous reaction involving the $[Ru(CN_6)]^{-4}$ ion, and the manganese compound is prepared by saturating manganese(II) acetate solution containing cyanide with nitric oxide.[122] The disproportionation of hydroxylamine in alkaline solution has been employed for the preparation of the cyano iron, manganese, and molybdenum derivatives as well as a similar nickel complex, $[Ni(CN)_3(NO)]^{-2}$.[152–154] The mixed derivatives $(CH_3)_4N(NO)[Fe(CN)_5(NO)]$ and $(NO)_2[Fe(CN)_5(NO)]$ result from the reaction of tetramethyl ammonium nitroprusside and nitrosyl hexachloroantimonate(V) in liquid sulfur dioxide.[155]

Absorption of nitric oxide by cobalt(II) salt solutions containing ammonia[156, 157] gives black and pink compounds, both series of which contain the group $[Co(NH_3)_5(NO)]^{+2}$. The black compounds are unstable with respect to the pink and evolve nitric oxide on treatment with acids. The pink compounds do not evolve nitric oxide. In the black series, only the chloride and iodate are known, but many examples of the pink compounds have been described. The black compounds are paramagnetic, the pink diamagnetic. The pink compounds are believed to contain tripositive cobalt and the NO^- group.[140, 142] The black compounds are less well understood, but the assumption that they contain dipositive cobalt appears reasonable.[142, 158]

F. MISCELLANEOUS NITROSYL COMPOUNDS. Among these are Roussin's black salts,[140] $M^I[Fe_4(NO)_7S_3)]$, where M^I may be Na^+, K^+, Rb^+, Cs^+, NH_4^+, or Tl^+. Although the exact structures of these compounds are not known, it has been postulated[139] that each iron is 4-coordinate, with sulfurs acting as bridging groups to link the four iron tetrahedra together and nitrosyl groups occupying the remaining positions. These substances are obtained by reaction of nitrite and sulfide ions with iron(II) salt solutions, by reaction of suspensions of iron(II) sulfide or of mixtures of iron(II) chloride and alkali metal polysulfides with nitric oxide, or from the red salts (p. 602).

Alkaline sulfite[159] or dithionite[160] solutions absorb nitric oxide to

152 W. Hieber and R. Nast: *Z. Naturforsch.*, **2b**, 321 (1947).
153 W. Hieber, R. Nast, and E. Proeschel: *Z. anorg. Chem.*, **256**, 159 (1948).
154 W. Hieber, R. Nast, and G. Gehring: *Z. anorg. Chem.*, **256**, 169 (1948).
155 F. Seel and N. H. Walassis: *Z. anorg. Chem.*, **261**, 85 (1950).
156 J. Sand and O. Genssler: *Ber.*, **36**, 2083 (1903).
157 A. Werner and P. Karrer: *Helv. Chim. Acta*, **1**, 54 (1918).
158 S. P. Ghosh and P. Rây: *J. Indian Chem. Soc.*, **20**, 409 (1943).
159 E. Weitz and F. Achterberg: *Ber.*, **66B**, 1718, 1728 (1933).
160 H. Gehlen: *Ber.*, **64B**, 1267 (1931).

give nitrosyls of the type $M_2^ISO_3 \cdot 2NO$. Reduction to amido and hydrazino sulfurous acids shows the presence of the N—S linkage, and conversion of iron(II) sulfide to Roussin's black salts by these substances suggests the presence of individual NO groups.[159] Coordination of both nitrosyl groups to sulfur, $[O_3S(NO)_2]^{-2}$, has been suggested. Analogies between these materials and thiosulfates are explainable on this basis.[159]

Nitrogen Sesquioxide or Nitrogen(III) Oxide (N_2O_3). This oxide probably exists as such only as the solid at very low temperatures. Partial dissociation to nitrogen(II) and nitrogen(IV) oxides occurs in the liquid, and in the vapor state at room temperature the material is largely dissociated as shown by studies[161] on the equilibrium

$$N_2O_3(g) \rightleftharpoons NO(g) + NO_2(g)$$

Condensation of an equimolecular mixture of the compounds NO and NO_2 at $-20°C$. gives the sesquioxide as a blue liquid. Dissolution of an equimolecular mixture of NO and NO_2 gases in alkali gives almost pure nitrite. Treatment of nitrite solutions (especially at low temperatures) with acids gives a blue color which disappears as nitric oxide is evolved. Nitrogen sesquioxide is thus the anhydride of nitrous acid, although when it reacts with water, some nitric acid (due to (NO_2) is formed. Equivalence of the two nitrogens is shown by rapid exchange between ^{14}NO and $^{15}NO_2$ on mixing.[162] The structure

```
   —
  :O:  +      :O:
       N : N
  :O:
```

has been suggested.[163]

Nitrogen Dioxide and Dinitrogen Tetroxide or Nitrogen(IV) Oxides (NO_2 *and* N_2O_4). These two compounds are related to each other in terms of the equilibrium[161]

$$2NO_2 \rightleftharpoons N_2O_4 + \text{energy}$$

and must be discussed together. In the solid state the material is colorless and diamagnetic and is apparently entirely tetroxide. In the liquid and gaseous states brown color and paramagnetism appear and are intensified as temperature increases. These are of course due

[161] F. Verhoek and F. Daniels: *J. Am. Chem. Soc.*, **53**, 1250 (1931).

[162] E. Leifer: *J. Chem. Phys.*, **8**, 301 (1940).

[163] C. K. Ingold and E. H. Ingold: *Nature*, **159**, 743 (1947).

to the odd molecule NO_2. Gas density measurements show that the percentage dissociation of the tetroxide increases from 20 at 27°C. to around 90 at 100°C. It is apparent, therefore, that at ordinary temperatures mixtures are always encountered.

Absorption spectra data show the NO_2 molecules to be angular with an O—N—O bond angle of roughly 110° to 120°.[164] More precise electron diffraction studies[165, 166] give a bond angle of 132 ± 2° and an N—O bond distance of 1.20 A. These are in excellent agreement with Pauling's predictions[120] of ca. 140° and 1.18 A. A resonating system involving the three-electron bond structures (p. 212)

```
      N               N
  :·/   \\         //   \·:
 :O       O:     :O       O:
```

is consistent with these data and accounts for the observed properties of the material. The resonance energy associated with the three-electron bond is insufficient to prevent dimerization here, in contrast with nitric oxide (p. 213).

The tetroxide might be assigned the structure

```
                      :O:⁻
 :O :: N :        +
           :O : N
                    :O:
```

on the basis of its chemical behavior as a mixed anhydride of nitrous and nitric acids, but a symmetrical arrangement

```
  :O:          :O:
     + 	   +
      N : N
 ⁻:O:        :O:⁻
```

is in better accord with spectroscopic data[167] for the gaseous material and x-ray[168] and entropy data[169] for the solid. It must be pointed

[164] G. B. B. M. Sutherland and W. G. Penney: *Nature,* **136,** 146 (1935).
[165] L. R. Maxwell and V. M. Mosley: *J. Chem. Phys.,* **8,** 738 (1940).
[166] S. Claesson, J. Donohue, and V. Schomaker: *J. Chem. Phys.,* **16,** 207 (1948).
[167] G. B. B. M. Sutherland: *Proc. Roy. Soc.* (*London*), **A141,** 342 (1933).
[168] S. B. Hendricks: *Z. Physik,* **70,** 699 (1931).
[169] W. F. Giauque and J. D. Kemp: *J. Chem. Phys.,* **6,** 40 (1938).

out, however, that a planar bridge arrangement

```
             ..
            .O.
   _ ..    .   .+   ..
   :O:N:      .N::O
    ..     .   .    ..
            .O.
             ..
```

is also in agreement with Raman and infrared data.[170] Although an exact decision between these structures has not been made, the critical correlations of Ingold and Ingold[163] support the first (non-bridging). The solid is cubic (a = 7.77 A) with six N_2O_4 molecules to the unit cell.[85] The N—N and N—O bond distances are, respectively, 1.64 ± 0.03 A and 1.17 ± 0.03 A, the O—N—O bond angle being 126 ± 1°.[171] In solution in nitric acid, the compound exists as NO^+ and NO_3^- ions,[130] and in sulfuric acid it gives NO^+ and NO_2^+ ions.[128]

The solvent characteristics of liquid dinitrogen(IV) oxide as already discussed should be reviewed (pp. 366–367). At elevated temperatures, nitrogen dioxide undergoes thermal decomposition

$$NO_2 \rightleftharpoons NO + \tfrac{1}{2}O_2$$

Equilibrium studies show decomposition to be slight at ordinary temperatures but appreciable above 600°C.[169, 172] The nitrogen(IV) oxides react with water, yielding nitrous and nitric acids, the nitrous acid decomposing, especially as the temperature is raised, to nitric acid and nitric oxide. These reactions are important, in conjunction with the catalytic oxidation of ammonia (p. 594), in the technical production of nitric acid. Basic oxides react similarly. The nitrogen(IV) oxides are active oxidizing agents comparable in strength to bromine

$$2HNO_2 \rightleftharpoons N_2O_4 + 2H^+ + 2e^- \qquad E^0_{298} = -1.07 \text{ volts}$$

$$2NO + 2H_2O \rightleftharpoons N_2O_4 + 4H^+ + 4e^- \qquad = -1.03$$

and they often react more rapidly than nitric acid. As such they are useful in the chamber process for producing sulfuric acid (p. 539). They are mild reducing agents

$$N_2O_4 + 2H_2O \rightleftharpoons 2NO_3^- + 4H^+ + 2e^- \qquad E^0_{298} = -0.81 \text{ volt}$$

and are oxidized only by strong oxidants such as permanganate. The nitrogen(IV) oxides corrode metals rapidly and are toxic.

[170] H. C. Longuet-Higgins: *Nature,* **153,** 408 (1944).

[171] J. S. Broadley and J. M. Robertson: *Nature,* **164,** 915 (1949).

[172] M. Bodenstein and Fr. Linder: *Z. physik. Chem.,* **100,** 82 (1922).

Technical production involves oxidation of nitrous acid at moderate temperatures, although the NO_2–N_2O_4 mixture so obtained is seldom prepared except as an intermediate in the production of nitric or sulfuric acids. In the laboratory the material is easily obtained by the thermal decomposition of lead nitrate.

Dinitrogen Pentoxide or Nitrogen(V) Oxide (N_2O_5). In the gaseous state, dinitrogen pentoxide (sometimes called nitrogen pentoxide) exists as N_2O_5 molecules, for which a reasonable structure would be

```
 O             O
    N : O : N
 O             O
```

Electron diffraction data[173] show the N—O—N angle to be 180°. The compound exists in the same molecular condition in solution in phosphorus(V) oxychloride[174] and presumably also in carbon tetrachloride, chloroform, and nitromethane,[175] as judged from Raman data. In solution in sulfuric acid,[176] nitric acid,[176–178] or phosphoric acid,[176] however, the Raman spectra consist of two new lines at 1050 and 1400 cm.$^{-1}$ These lines are ascribed, respectively, to nitrate (NO_3^-) and nitronium (NO_2^+) ions, showing that in these solvents the oxide is dissociated. Inasmuch as the Raman spectrum of the solid oxide[179, 180] shows the same lines, the solid apparently is nitronium nitrate, NO_2^+ NO_3^-. Independent, although admittedly not entirely conclusive, evidence for the existence of this structure in liquid dinitrogen pentoxide is given by the fact that sodium metal reacts with the liquid, liberating nitrogen dioxide and forming sodium nitrate.[181] Crystal structure determinations show the solid oxide to consist of nitronium and nitrate ions, the N—O bond distance being 1.15 A in the NO_2^+ ion and 1.24 A in the NO_3^- ion.[182] Cryoscopic data show

[173] L. R. Maxwell, V. M. Mosley, and L. S. Deming: *J. Chem. Phys.*, **2**, 331 (1934).

[174] P. Walden: *Z. anorg. Chem.*, **68**, 307 (1910).

[175] J. Chédin: *Compt. rend.*, **201**, 552 (1935).

[176] J. Chédin: *Compt. rend.*, **200**, 1397 (1935).

[177] B. Susz and E. Briner: *Helv. Chim. Acta*, **18**, 378 (1935).

[178] C. K. Ingold and D. J. Millen: *J. Chem. Soc.*, **1950**, 2612.

[179] J. Chédin and J. C. Pradier: *Compt. rend.*, **203**, 722 (1936).

[180] D. J. Millen: *J. Chem. Soc.*, **1950**, 2606.

[181] W. R. Angus, R. W. Jones, and G. O. Phillips: *Nature*, **164**, 433 (1949).

[182] E. Grison, K. Eriks, and J. L. de Vries: *Acta Cryst.*, **3**, 290 (1950).

the compound to dissolve in absolute nitric acid as a binary electrolyte, $NO_2^+NO_3^-$.[183]

Dinitrogen pentoxide is characterized by its volatility and by the ease with which it decomposes in the gaseous state according to the equation

$$N_2O_5(g) \rightleftharpoons 2NO_2(g) + \tfrac{1}{2}O_2(g)$$

This reaction is a classic example of a first-order reaction, the rate of decomposition with respect to temperature depending only on the concentration of the pentoxide.[184] Decomposition is appreciable even at room temperature. Dinitrogen pentoxide is converted readily to nitric acid by water. The compound is a strong oxidizing agent, giving iodine(V) oxide with iodine, nitrogen dioxide with nitric oxide, etc.

The compound may be obtained by oxidizing nitric oxide with ozone or by dehydrating 100% nitric acid with phosphorus(V) oxide. A convenient modification of the second procedure[185] involves freezing the nitric acid, allowing the phosphorus oxide to react with the melting acid in the presence of ozone to remove nitrogen(IV) oxides, and distilling in ozone.

THE NITRONIUM ION AND NITRONIUM COMPOUNDS. Existence of the nitronium group in nitrogen pentoxide suggests a further discussion of this radical. Interest in the material arose from the well-known nitrating action of solutions of nitric acid in concentrated sulfuric acid. Such solutions have low nitric acid vapor pressures and are characterized by high electrical conductivity and different Raman and ultraviolet spectra from those of their components. The same is true of solutions of nitric acid in perchloric and selenic acids. On the basis of analytical, cryoscopic, and ultraviolet absorption data, Hantzsch[186, 187] concluded that, in sulfuric acid, reaction between the solvent and nitric acid yielded nitracidium cations such as $H_2NO_3^+$ and $H_3NO_3^{+2}$. This conclusion was supported by isolation from anhydrous perchloric acid–nitric acid mixtures of two crystalline perchlorates, of compositions $[H_2NO_3][ClO_4]$ and $[H_3NO_3](ClO_4)_2$, which behave as salts in nitromethane.[188] The existence of cationic nitrogen in such systems

[183] R. J. Gillespie, E. D. Hughes, and C. K. Ingold: *J. Chem. Soc.*, **1950,** 2552.

[184] F. Daniels and E. H. Johnston: *J. Am. Chem. Soc.*, **43,** 53 (1921).

[185] N. S. Gruenhut, M. Goldfrank, M. L. Cushing, and G. V. Caeser: *Inorganic Syntheses*, Vol. III, p. 78. McGraw-Hill Book Co., New York (1950).

[186] A. Hantzsch: *Z. physik. Chem.*, **65,** 41 (1908).

[187] A. Hantzsch: *Ber.*, **58,** 941 (1925).

[188] A. Hantzsch and K. Berger: *Ber.*, **61B,** 1328 (1928).

has been demonstrated conclusively by electrolysis studies.[189] However, the correctness of Hantzsch's interpretations has been questioned by later studies.[190]

Although nitracidium cations may well occur in the presence of appreciable quantities of water, it appears that in the anhydrous systems the cation is the nitronium (NO_2^+) ion. Much evidence supports this conclusion. Chemically, the tremendous increase in the rate at which nitration reactions occur with nitric–sulfuric acid mixtures as the water content decreases is best explained in terms of this ion.[191] Using a vacuum technique designed to exclude moisture completely, Goddard, Hughes, and Ingold[192] prepared the solid $[H_3NO_3][ClO_4]$, but were able to separate the material into the compounds $[H_3O][ClO_4]$ and $[NO_2][ClO_4]$ by fractional crystallization from nitromethane. A compound $[H_2NO_3][ClO_4]$ could not be prepared. Later the salts $(NO_2)_2S_2O_7$ and $(NO_2)_2S_3O_{10}$ were obtained by reaction of dinitrogen pentoxide with varying quantities of sulfur trioxide in nitromethane.[193] Under similar conditions, nitric acid gives the pyrosulfate, $[NO_2][HS_2O_7]$, with sulfur trioxide, and fluosulfonic acid gives the fluosulfonate, $[NO_2][SO_3F]$, with dinitrogen pentoxide.[193] The Raman spectra of sulfuric acid solutions of nitric acid are characterized by the 1050 $cm.^{-1}$ and 1400 $cm.^{-1}$ lines already mentioned,[176] the second line showing definitely the presence of the NO_2^+ ion.[194, 195] Similarly, Raman data show the presence of the NO_2^+ ion in perchloric,[195] selenic,[195] and pyrosulfuric[196] acid solutions of nitric acid. The 1400 $cm.^{-1}$ line is also characteristic of the Raman spectrum of the solid compound $[NO_2][ClO_4]$.[192] X-ray studies of this solid material also indicate the presence of the NO_2^+ ion.[197] Refined cryoscopic studies on nitric-sulfuric acid solutions.[128, 198] indicate the presence of four ions as demanded by the equation

$$HNO_3 + 2H_2SO_4 \rightarrow NO_2^+ + H_3O^+ + 2HSO_4^-$$

[189] G. M. Bennett, J. C. D. Brand, and G. Williams: *J. Chem. Soc.*, **1946**, 869, 875.

[190] R. J. Gillespie and D. J. Millen: *Quart. Revs.*, **2**, 277 (1948). Excellent review.

[191] F. H. Westheimer and M. S. Kharasch: *J. Am. Chem. Soc.*, **68**, 1871 (1946).

[192] D. R. Goddard, E. D. Hughes, and C. K. Ingold: *Nature*, **158**, 480 (1946).

[193] D. R. Goddard, E. D. Hughes, and C. K. Ingold: *J. Chem. Soc.*, **1950**, 2559.

[194] C. K. Ingold, D. J. Millen, and H. G. Poole: *Nature*, **158**, 480 (1946).

[195] C. K. Ingold, D. J. Millen, and H. G. Poole: *J. Chem. Soc.*, **1950**, 2576.

[196] D. J. Millen: *J. Chem. Soc.*, **1950**, 2589.

[197] E. G. Cox, G. A. Jeffrey, and M. R. Truter: *Nature*, **162**, 259 (1948).

[198] R. J. Gillespie, J. Graham, E. D. Hughes, C. K. Ingold, and E. R. A. Peeling: *Nature*, **158**, 480 (1946).

and do not support Hantzsch's equations

$$HNO_3 + H_2SO_4 \rightarrow H_2NO_3^+ + HSO_4^-$$

$$HNO_3 + 2H_2SO_4 \rightarrow H_3NO_3^{++} + 2HSO_4^-$$

Likewise, when nitric acid is dissolved in oleum (p. 541), the reactions

$$HNO_3 + 2H_2S_2O_7 \rightarrow NO_2^+ + HS_2O_7^- + 2H_2SO_4$$

and

$$HNO_3 + HS_2O_7^- \rightarrow NO_2^+ + 2HSO_4^-$$

apparently take place.[199] Nitronium ions are similarly indicated for solutions of N_2O_5 or N_2O_4 in 100% sulfuric acid (pp. 596, 608).[128, 198] Analysis shows that the white solid obtained when ozone, chlorine dioxide, and nitrogen oxides are mixed is the perchlorate, $[NO_2]$-$[ClO_4]$.[200] Addition of dinitrogen tetroxide to various fluorides, oxides, or free elements in bromine, followed by treatment with bromine trifluoride, gives nitronium fluo salts such as $NO_2[BF_4]$, $(NO_2)_2[SnF_6]$, $NO_2[PF_6]$, $NO_2[AsF_6]$, $NO_2[SbF_6]$, and $NO_2[AuF_4]$.[201] Other evidence is reviewed by Gillespie and Millen.[190]

Although the nitronium ion is in general readily hydrolyzed, the solid perchlorate is fairly stable even in moist air. The nitronium ion is isoelectronic with the species CO_2, N_2O, CNCl, NCO^-, NCS^-, and N_3^-, all of which have linear structures. It seems reasonable to ascribe a similar linear arrangement to it. This structure

```
 ..   +   ..
 O : : N : : O
 ..       ..
```

is in agreement with Raman data.[194]

The nitryl halides, NO_2X (X = F, Cl), bear the same relation to the nitronium salts that the nitrosyl halides (p. 597) bear to the nitrosylium (nitrosyl) salts. The structures of these halides have not been determined experimentally, but of the two proposed.

```
  ..   ..   ..             ..   ..   ..   ..
: O  : N  : X :    and   : O : : N : O  : X :
  ..   ..   ..                       ..   ..
       ..
     : O :
```

the former is perhaps the more consistent with the facts that hydrolysis yields nitric acid and hydrogen halide, that reaction of the chloride

[199] R. J. Gillespie and J. Graham: *J. Chem. Soc.*, **1950,** 2532.
[200] W. E. Gordon and J. W. T. Spinks: *Canadian J. Research,* **18B,** 358 (1940).
[201] A. A. Woolf and H. J. Emeléus; *J. Chem. Soc.*, **1950,** 1050.

with acetic anhydride gives acetyl chloride and acetyl nitrate, that in many ways these halides resemble the nitrosyl halides, and that preparation of the chloride is most readily effected by reaction of nitrosyl chloride with ozone.[202] Certain reactions with organic materials, however, are easier to explain in terms of the second structure.[203] The fluoride, obtained by reaction of fluorine with nitric oxide, is a colorless gas (b.p. −166°C., m.p. −72.4°C.) which reacts with glass.[204] The chloride is a colorless gas (b.p. −145°C., m.p. −15.9°C.) which decomposes to nitrogen dioxide and chlorine at ordinary temperatures[205, 206] at a rate dependent upon total pressure.

Nitrogen Trioxide (NO_3) *and Dinitrogen Hexoxide* (N_2O_6). The status of nitrogen trioxide is comparable to that of sulfur monoxide (p. 525). Although indicated many years ago by the appearance of new absorption bands in the products of reactions of nitrogen oxides with ozone,[207, 208] the material has been studied in detail more recently as a product of the reaction of ozone with the pentoxide[209, 210] or the tetroxide.[211] Claims of production as a condensable white solid by action of a glow discharge on mixtures of the dioxide and oxygen[212] are disputed.[211] The material is apparently a blue gas which decomposes readily at ordinary temperatures. It is said to dissolve in water to give a solution which is strongly oxidizing but shows no peroxy character.[212] Water solutions decompose slowly to nitric acid and oxygen, but, when freshly dissolved in water, nitrogen trioxide can be extracted with ether. With alkali, nitrate, nitrite, and oxygen are formed. The oxide is not the anhydride of peroxynitric acid, and its structure is unknown. It is an odd molecule.

Reaction of fluorine with nitric acid yields an oxide, N_2O_6, which decomposes rapidly with loss of oxygen and appears to be the mixed

202 H.-J. Schumacher and G. Sprenger: *Z. Elektrochem.*, **35,** 653 (1929); *Z. anorg. allgem. Chem.*, **182,** 139 (1929).

203 M. Schmeisser: *Z. anorg. Chem.*, **255,** 33 (1947).

204 O. Ruff, W. Menzel, and W. Neumann: *Z. anorg. allgem. Chem.*, **208,** 293 (1932).

205 H.-J. Schumacher and G. Sprenger: *Z. physik. Chem.*, **12B,** 115 (1931).

206 O. K. Rice and D. V. Sickman: *J. Am. Chem. Soc.*, **56,** 1444 (1934).

207 P. Hautefeuille and J. Chappuis: *Compt. rend.*, **92,** 80 (1881).

208 E. Warburg and G. Leithäuser: *Ann. Physik,* [4], **20,** 743 (1906); [4] **23,** 209 (1907).

209 H.-J. Schumacher and G. Sprenger: *Z. physik. Chem.*, **136A,** 77 (1928); **140A,** 281 (1929); **2B,** 267 (1929).

210 H.-J. Schumacher: *Z. anorg. allgem. Chem.*, **233,** 47 (1937).

211 A. Klemenc and W. Neumann: *Z. anorg. allgem. Chem.*, **232,** 216 (1937).

212 R. Schwarz and H. Achenbach: *Ber.*, **68B,** 343 (1935).

anhydride of nitric and peroxynitric acids.[213] It is not a dimer of the trioxide.

Oxy acids of nitrogen

The oxy acids of nitrogen are listed in Table 15·12. Of these, only

TABLE 15·12
Oxy Acids of Nitrogen

Formula	Name	Apparent Oxidation State of Nitrogen	Probable Structure	Preparation
$H_2N_2O_2$	hyponitrous acid	+1	H : O : N::N : O : H	acid, salts
$H_2N_2O_3$	nitrohydroxylamic acid	+2	H : O : N::N : O : H : O :	salts
H_2NO_2	hydronitrous acid (nitroxylic)	+2	H : O : N : O : H	salts
HNO_2	nitrous acid	+3	H : O : N::O	salts
HNO_3	nitric acid	+5	H : O : N : O : : O :	acid, salts
HNO_4	peroxynitric acid	+5	H : O : O : N : O : : O :	acid, salts

nitric acid is really stable in the free condition. Only hyponitrous, nitrous, and nitric acids need be discussed here. The peroxy acid has been mentioned in the preceding chapter (p. 514).

Hyponitrous Acid ($H_2N_2O_2$). This material is known chiefly in the form of its salts, although the free acid has been obtained as a white crystalline compound by reacting the silver salt with hydrogen chloride in ether and evaporating the resulting ethereal solution.[214] The free acid decomposes readily (often explosively) on heating. Its aqueous

[213] F. Fichter and E. Brunner: *Helv. Chim. Acta*, **12**, 306 (1929).
[214] A. Hantzsch and L. Kaufmann: *Ann.*, **292**, 317 (1896).

solutions are more stable, but lose nitrous oxide slowly. The reverse reaction is thermodynamically impossible, calculations showing that an equilibrium pressure of nitrous oxide of some 10^{27} atm. would be required to give even a 0.001 N solution of the acid. The acid is also soluble in alcohols, ether, chloroform, and benzene. In aqueous solution it is a weak acid ($k_{A_1}' = 9 \times 10^{-8}$, $k_{A_2}' = 1 \times 10^{-11}$ at 25°C.), and its alkali metal salts are extensively hydrolyzed. Freezing point data on aqueous hyponitrite solutions confirm the doubled formula, $N_2O_2^{-2}$.[215] No exact structural data are available, but it appears an arrangement

$$H:\overset{..}{\underset{..}{O}}:\overset{..}{N}::\underset{..}{N}:\overset{..}{\underset{..}{O}}:H$$

is not unlikely. Because of the double bond, *cis-trans* isomerism is possible. Hantzsch believes the acid to have the *trans* configuration.

Hyponitrites possess both reducing and oxidizing properties as indicated by the couples

$$H_2N_2O_2 \rightleftharpoons 2NO + 2H^+ + 2e^- \qquad E^0_{298} = -0.60 \text{ volt}$$

$$H_2N_2O_2 + 2H_2O \rightleftharpoons 2HNO_2 + 4H^+ + 4e^- \qquad = -0.80$$

$$N_2 + 2H_2O \rightleftharpoons H_2N_2O_2 + 2H^+ + 2e^- \qquad = -2.75 \text{ volts}$$

$$2NH_3OH^+ \rightleftharpoons H_2N_2O_2 + 6H^+ + 4e^- \qquad = -0.44 \text{ volt}$$

in acidic solution and the couples

$$N_2O_2^{-2} \rightleftharpoons 2NO + 2e^- \qquad E^0_{298} = -0.10 \text{ volt}$$

$$N_2O_2^{-2} + 4OH^- \rightleftharpoons 2NO_2^- + 2H_2O + 4e^- \qquad = 0.18$$

$$N_2 + 4OH^- \rightleftharpoons N_2O_2^{-2} + 2H_2O + 2e^- \qquad = -1.60 \text{ volts}$$

$$2NH_2OH + 6OH^- \rightleftharpoons N_2O_2^{-2} + 6H_2O + 4e^- \qquad = 0.73 \text{ volt}$$

in alkaline solution. However, the reducing properties predominate. Strong oxidizing agents will convert hyponitrites to nitrates.

Hyponitrites may be prepared by reducing nitrites with sodium amalgam[215, 216] or tin(II) chloride,[217] by hydrolyzing sodium hydroxylamine monosulfonate (p. 554) in the presence of concentrated potassium hydroxide solution, by oxidizing hydroxylamine with nitrous acid or metal oxides (CuO, Ag_2O, HgO), or by reacting hydroxylamine with sodium methoxide or ethoxide and ethyl or amyl nitrite in alcohol

[215] E. Divers: *J. Chem. Soc.*, **75**, 95 (1899).

[216] E. Abel and J. Proisl: *Monatsh.*, **72**, 1 (1938).

[217] F. Raschig: *Z. anorg. allgem. Chem.*, **155**, 225 (1926).

solution.[218, 219] The last method is preferred. Although usually prepared as the sodium salt, hyponitrite is most commonly recovered as the sparingly soluble, yellow silver salt.

Nitrous Acid (HNO_2). Free nitrous acid has not been isolated, although there are indications of its existence in the vapor state, and aqueous solutions are readily obtained by treating soluble nitrites with aqueous protonic acids. Because both organic nitrites, RONO, and nitro compounds, RNO_2, are obtainable from nitrous acid or nitrites, the existence of two corresponding tautomeric forms of the acid

$$H : \ddot{\underset{..}{O}} : \ddot{N} : : \ddot{\underset{..}{O}} \quad \text{and} \quad H : \overset{\overset{..}{:O:}}{\ddot{N}} : : \ddot{\underset{..}{O}}$$

has been postulated. No physical data supporting such tautomerism have been produced, and examples among inorganic derivatives are lacking (refer to discussion of *nitrito* versus *nitro* complexes, pp. 250–251). X-ray and Raman data[220] indicate an angular structure for nitrite ion, the N—O bond distance being 1.13 A and the O—N—O bond angle 120 to 130°. The short bond distance is about that noted for nitrosyl chloride (p. 597), suggesting similarities in the N—O bonds in the two materials. A resonance hybrid involving

$$\left[\ddot{N}\right]^- \text{ (O } \cdot\cdot\text{ N } \cdot\cdot\text{ O)} \quad \text{and} \quad \left[\ddot{N}\right]^-$$

seems likely. In organic nitro compounds, the N—O bond distance is 1.21 A and the O—N—O bond angle 127°.[221]

Nitrogen sesquioxide reacts with water to give nitrous acid, but phase studies show that systems containing two liquid phases are formed at temperatures below 55°C. when the two materials are brought together in equimolecular proportions.[222] Nitrous acid solutions undergo reversible decomposition as described by the equation

$$3HNO_2 \rightleftharpoons H^+ + NO_3^- + 2NO + H_2O$$

[218] L. W. Jones and A. W. Scott: *J. Am. Chem. Soc.*, **46**, 2172 (1924).

[219] A. W. Scott: *J. Am. Chem. Soc.*, **49**, 986 (1927).

[220] A. Langseth and E. Walles: *Z. physik. Chem.*, **27B**, 209 (1934).

[221] L. O. Brockway, J. Y. Beach, and L. Pauling: *J. Am. Chem. Soc.*, **57**, 2693 (1935).

[222] T. M. Lowry and J. T. Lemon: *J. Chem. Soc.*, **1936**, 1.

Because of the weakness of nitrous acid ($k_A' = 6 \times 10^{-4}$ at 30°C.), solutions of alkali metal nitrites are hydrolyzed and yield nitrous acid when treated with strong protonic acids. Simple nitrite salts are limited to those of the alkali metals, alkaline earth metals, and silver. The silver salt is sparingly soluble in water; the others are soluble. Complexes containing the NO_2^- group are much more common (Ch. 7).

Nitrous acid and the nitrites are most commonly employed as oxidizing agents, although strong oxidants (e.g., electric current, MnO_2, and Cl_2) convert nitrous acid to nitric acid and even comparatively weak oxidants (e.g., O_2) convert nitrite to nitrate in alkaline medium. Important couples describing these behaviors are

$$N_2O + 3H_2O \rightleftharpoons 2HNO_2 + 4H^+ + 4e^- \qquad E^0_{298} = -1.29 \text{ volts}$$
$$NO + H_2O \rightleftharpoons HNO_2 + H^+ + e^- \qquad = -0.99 \text{ volt}$$
$$HNO_2 + H_2O \rightleftharpoons NO_3^- + 3H^+ + 2e^- \qquad = -0.94$$

in acidic solutions and

$$N_2O + 6OH^- \rightleftharpoons 2NO_2^- + 3H_2O + 4e^- \qquad E^0_{298} = -0.15 \text{ volt}$$
$$NO + 2OH^- \rightleftharpoons NO_2^- + H_2O + e^- \qquad = 0.46$$
$$NO_2^- + 2OH^- \rightleftharpoons NO_3^- + H_2O + 2e^- \qquad = -0.01$$

in alkaline solutions. The enhanced oxidizing power in acidic media is apparent. The complete behavior of nitrous acid in the presence of reducing agents is not obvious in terms of these couples alone. Other reduction products may result, depending upon the reductant employed, the acidity, and the temperature. Thus hydrogen sulfide gives nitric oxide and sulfur in acidic solution, ammonia and sulfur in sodium hydrogen carbonate buffers, and ammonia, sulfur, and thiosulfate in unbuffered sodium nitrite solutions. Important oxidations are iodide to iodine, ammonium ion to nitrogen, sulfamate ion to nitrogen and sulfate, and urea to nitrogen and carbon dioxide.

Of particular interest is the reduction of nitrous acid with sulfurous acid. This may be formulated, together with useful attendant hydrolysis reactions, as[223]

$$\underset{\text{nitrous acid}}{HNO_2} \xrightarrow{HSO_3^-} \underset{\text{nitrosulfonic acid}}{HO_3SNO} \xrightarrow{HSO_3^-} \underset{\text{hydroxylamine disulfonic acid}}{(HO_3S)_2NOH} \rightarrow \underset{\text{amine trisulfonic acid}}{(HO_3S)_3N}$$

$$HNO_2 \xrightarrow[\text{x's } H^+]{HSO_3^-} \underset{\text{nitrous oxide}}{N_2O} \qquad HO_3SNO \xrightarrow[(H_2O)]{H^+} \underset{\text{hyponitrous acid}}{H_2N_2O_2} \qquad (HO_3S)_2NOH \xrightarrow[(H_2O)]{H^+} \underset{\text{hydroxylammonium salts}}{NH_2OH \cdot H^+} \qquad (HO_3S)_3N \xrightarrow[(H_2O)]{H^+} \underset{\text{ammonium salts}}{NH_4^+}$$

[223] W. M. Latimer: *The Oxidation States of the Elements and Their Potentials in Aqueous Solutions*, Ch. VII. Prentice-Hall, New York (1938).

Certain of the products shown in this scheme have been described in earlier portions of this book (pp. 550–555, 580–581):

Nitrites are prepared either by reduction of nitrates or oxidation (indirectly) of ammonia. Although alkali metal nitrites are formed when the nitrates are heated strongly, a better procedure involves fusion of, say, sodium nitrate, either alone or mixed with sodium hydroxide or sodium carbonate, with a reducing agent (E), the reaction being described by the equation

$$NaNO_3 + E \rightarrow NaNO_2 + EO$$

In the laboratory, lead is useful; technically iron or coke is efficient and cheap. The product is recovered by dissolution in water and crystallization. Oxidation of ammonia to an almost equimolar mixture of nitric oxide and nitrogen dioxide is followed by absorption of the gases in alkaline solutions [e.g., NaOH, $Ca(OH)_2$] and crystallization. Nitric oxide also reacts directly with alkali and alkaline earth metal hydroxides to give nitrites

$$2MOH(s) + 4NO(g) \rightarrow 2MNO_2(s) + N_2O(g) + H_2O(g)$$

$$4MOH(l) + 6NO(g) \rightarrow 4MNO_2(s) + N_2(g) + 2H_2O(g)$$

the rate of the reaction increasing with the basic character of the hydroxide.[224]

Nitric Acid (HNO_3). Absolute (100%) nitric acid is a colorless liquid of comparatively high vapor pressure, boiling at 83°C. and freezing at low temperatures to a colorless crystalline solid melting at −41.59°C. Spectroscopic indications that the oxygen atoms are coplanar with the nitrogen atom and surround the latter at the corners of an equilateral triangle are well supported by electron diffraction data[165] which give the structure

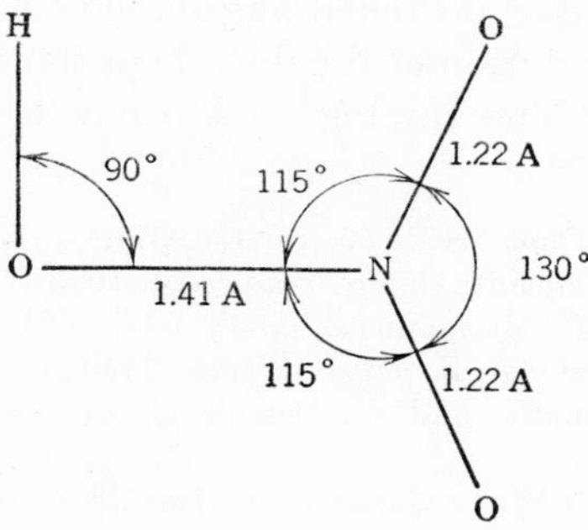

[224] E. Barnes: *J. Chem. Soc.*, **1931**, 2605.

Hydrogen bonding involving other oxygens probably characterizes this structure. In the nitrate ion, resonance involving a basic structure of the type

```
          · · ·–
   ··    +· O ·
   O :: N  ·
   ··      · · –
          · O ·
           · ·
```

$$N\text{–}O = 1.21A$$

doubtless occurs.[225] The Raman spectrum of anhydrous nitric acid is characterized by faint lines at 1050 and 1400 cm.$^{-1}$, showing the existence of small concentrations of nitronium and nitrate ions (p. 610)[226] formed by

$$3HNO_3 \rightleftharpoons NO_2^+ + NO_3^- + HNO_3 \cdot H_2O$$

The 1400 cm.$^{-1}$ line (NO_2^+) disappears when the concentration drops below 94 to 95% HNO_3.

Nitric acid is miscible with water in all proportions. Phase studies[227] indicate the formation of two hydrates, $HNO_3 \cdot H_2O$ (m.p., −37.68°C.) and $HNO_3 \cdot 3H_2O$ (m.p., −18.47°C.). The first of these is probably the ortho acid, H_3NO_4,[228, 229] and the second the 2-hydrate of the ortho acid.[229] The thermodynamic properties of these hydrates have been studied in detail.[230] In aqueous solution nitric acid is completely dissociated. Its salts are uniformly soluble and are hydrolyzed only where the cation is small and highly charged. A few organic nitrates (e.g., nitron nitrate) are sparingly soluble. Although many double nitrates are known, the nitrate ion is a poor coordinating agent and forms few Werner complexes.

Pure nitric acid decomposes, slowly on exposure to light at room temperatures and rapidly on heating, to nitrogen dioxide, oxygen, and water. Concentrated aqueous solutions undergo the same decomposition. Nitrogen dioxide remaining dissolved in the acid imparts a yellow color. Dissolution of the dioxide in the 100% acid gives red, fuming nitric acid. The fuming acid reacts more vigorously than nitric acid alone.

[225] N. Elliott: *J. Am. Chem. Soc.*, **59**, 1380 (1937).

[226] J. Chédin and S. Fénéant: *Compt. rend.*, **224**, 1008 (1947).

[227] F. W. Küster and R. Kremann: *Z. anorg. Chem.*, **41**, 1 (1904).

[228] E. Zintl and W. Haucke: *Z. physik. Chem.*, **174A**, 312 (1935).

[229] W. Biltz, O. Hülsmann, and W. Eicholz: *Nachr. Ges. Wiss. Gött.* [ii], **1**, 95 (1935).

[230] W. R. Forsythe and W. F. Giauque: *J. Am. Chem. Soc.*, **64**, 48 (1942).

Aqueous solutions of nitric acid are among our most common and useful oxidizing agents. Although the reduction products are usually nitric oxide (at low concentrations) and dinitrogen tetroxide (at high concentrations), other reduction products appear when proper reductants and concentration conditions are employed. The relations existing among these reduction products are summarized by the couples in Table 15·13.[223] In spite of favorable potentials, many of the direct reductions listed are seldom achieved in practice. The dioxide catalyzes reduction of the acid. The effect of acid concentration upon the nature of the oxide reduction product is explainable in terms of the equilibrium

$$2NO + 4H^+ + 4NO_3^- \rightleftharpoons 3N_2O_4 + 2H_2O$$

but it is difficult to account for the appearance or lack of appearance of other reduction products.

The data in Table 15·13 indicate clearly the effect of the proton on the oxidizing strength of the nitrate ion. Values summarized for the stepwise reduction of nitrogen(V) to nitrogen(−III) in acidic and alkaline media also demonstrate this clearly. Oxidation processes effected by nitrate are well known and need not be considered in any more detail. Some have been described in earlier sections of this chapter.

The oxidizing powers of mixtures of nitric and hydrochloric acid (aqua regia) are less pronounced than the solvent effects of such mixtures for noble metals (Au, Pt) might suggest. The fact that these metals are converted to chloro complexes increases the ease with which they are oxidized (pp. 300–305), and in the presence of suitable complexing agents nitric acid alone should oxidize them. The reactions are catalyzed by nitrosyl chloride.

As pointed out earlier, nitric acid is prepared most commonly by reaction of nitrogen(IV) oxides with water (p. 607)

$$3N_2O_4 + 2H_2O \rightleftharpoons 4H^+ + 4NO_3^- + 2NO$$

oxygen being added to remove nitric oxide and thereby increase the yield. Distillation of nitrates with sulfuric acid is also employed. Concentration of the acid is best effected by distillation with sulfuric acid since distillation of aqueous solutions gives a constant boiling mixture (68.4% HNO_3, b.p. 121.9°C.).

TABLE 15·13

OXIDATION POTENTIAL DATA FOR REDUCTION OF NITRATE ION

Acidic Solutions			Alkaline Solutions		
$N_2O_4 + 2H_2O$	$\rightleftharpoons 2NO_3^- + 4H^+ + 2e^-$	$E^0_{298} = -0.81$ volt	$N_2O_4 + 4OH^-$	$\rightleftharpoons 2NO_3^- + 2H_2O + 2e^-$	$E^0_{298} = 0.85$ volt
$HNO_2 + H_2O$	$\rightleftharpoons NO_3^- + 3H^+ + 2e^-$	$= -0.94$	$NO_2^- + 2OH^-$	$\rightleftharpoons NO_3^- + H_2O + 2e^-$	$= -0.01$
$NO + 2H_2O$	$\rightleftharpoons NO_3^- + 4H^+ + 3e^-$	$= -0.96$	$NO + 4OH^-$	$\rightleftharpoons NO_3^- + 2H_2O + 3e^-$	$= 0.14$
$N_2O + 5H_2O$	$\rightleftharpoons 2NO_3^- + 10H^+ + 8e^-$	$= -1.11$ volts	$N_2O + 10OH^-$	$\rightleftharpoons 2NO_3^- + 5H_2O + 8e^-$	$= -0.10$
$H_2N_2O_2 + 4H_2O$	$\rightleftharpoons 2NO_3^- + 10H^+ + 8e^-$	$= -0.87$ volt	$N_2O_2^{-2} + 8OH^-$	$\rightleftharpoons 2NO_3^- + 4H_2O + 8e^-$	$= 0.08$
$\frac{1}{2}N_2 + 3H_2O$	$\rightleftharpoons NO_3^- + 6H^+ + 5e^-$	$= -1.24$ volts	$\frac{1}{2}N_2 + 6OH^-$	$\rightleftharpoons NO_3^- + 3H_2O + 5e^-$	$= -0.24$
$NH_3OH^+ + 2H_2O$	$\rightleftharpoons NO_3^- + 8H^+ + 6e^-$	$= -0.73$ volt	$NH_2OH + 7OH^-$	$\rightleftharpoons NO_3^- + 5H_2O + 6e^-$	$= 0.30$
$N_2H_5^+ + 6H_2O$	$\rightleftharpoons 2NO_3^- + 17H^+ + 14e^-$	$= -0.84$	$N_2H_4 + 16OH^-$	$\rightleftharpoons 2NO_3^- + 10H_2O + 14e^-$	$= 0.13$
$NH_4^+ + 3H_2O$	$\rightleftharpoons NO_3^- + 10H^+ + 8e^-$	$= -0.87$	$NH_3 + 9OH^-$	$\rightleftharpoons NO_3^- + 6H_2O + 8e^-$	$= 0.10$

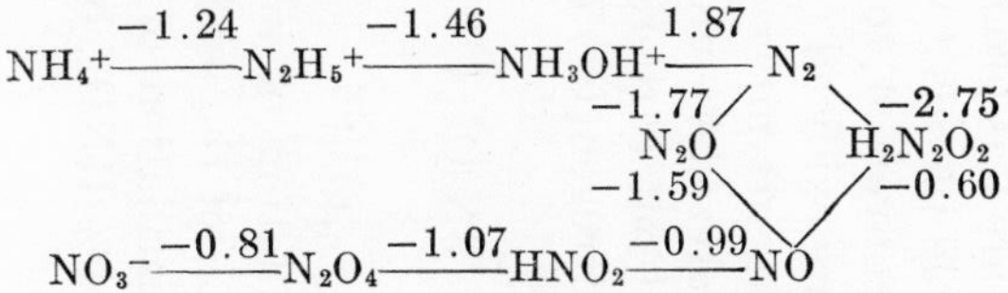

Acidic solutions:

$$NH_4^+ \overset{-1.24}{\text{———}} N_2H_5^+ \overset{-1.46}{\text{———}} NH_3OH^+ \overset{1.87}{\text{———}} N_2$$

$$N_2 \overset{-1.77}{\text{—}} N_2O \overset{-1.59}{\text{—}} NO \qquad N_2 \overset{-2.75}{\text{—}} H_2N_2O_2 \overset{-0.60}{\text{—}} NO$$

$$NO_3^- \overset{-0.81}{\text{———}} N_2O_4 \overset{-1.07}{\text{———}} HNO_2 \overset{-0.99}{\text{———}} NO$$

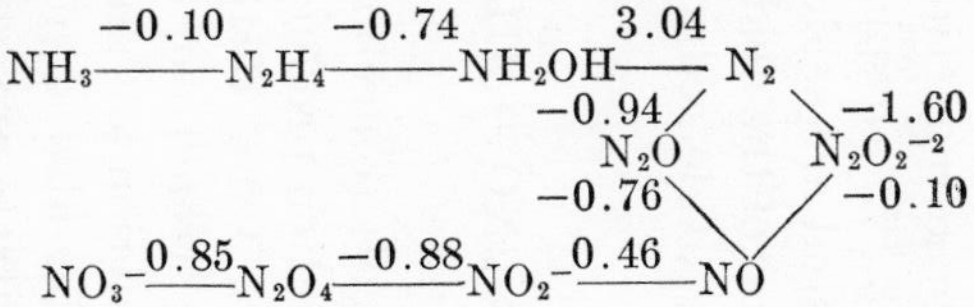

Alkaline solutions:

$$NH_3 \overset{-0.10}{\text{———}} N_2H_4 \overset{-0.74}{\text{———}} NH_2OH \overset{3.04}{\text{———}} N_2$$

$$N_2 \overset{-0.94}{\text{—}} N_2O \overset{-0.76}{\text{—}} NO \qquad N_2 \overset{-1.60}{\text{—}} N_2O_2^{-2} \overset{-0.10}{\text{—}} NO$$

$$NO_3^- \overset{0.85}{\text{———}} N_2O_4 \overset{-0.88}{\text{———}} NO_2^- \overset{0.46}{\text{———}} NO$$

SOME SPECIAL PHASES OF PHOSPHORUS CHEMISTRY

The topics discussed here are of both fundamental and practical importance in an understanding of the chemistry of phosphorus. Analogies between phosphorus compounds and those of the heavier members of the family are often close. Although no attempt is made to discuss the latter specifically, they are referred to where the discussion adds to that on phosphorus.

Phosphorus hydrogen compounds and their derivatives

Two volatile phosphorus hydrides, PH_3 (phosphine) and P_2H_4 (diphosphine), have been characterized. These are formal analogs of ammonia and hydrazine, respectively. A solid hydride, of approximate composition $(P_2H)_x$, has been described also, but its existence is doubtful. With arsenic, antimony, and bismuth, only hydrides of the type ZH_3 are known.

Phosphine (PH_3) *and Its Derivatives.* Phosphine is a colorless gas which can be converted to a liquid boiling at −87.7°C. and a solid melting at −133°C. The heats of vaporization and fusion are, respectively, 3.489 and 0.270 kcal. per mole. These values indicate that, unlike ammonia, but like the corresponding hydrides of arsenic, antimony, and bismuth, phosphine is not associated (p. 189). Spectral studies show the molecule to be pyramidal (like ammonia) with a P—H bond distance of 1.415 A and an H—P—H bond angle of some 93° (as compared with 1.01 A and 109° in ammonia).[231] In the solid state, four modifications of phosphine are known.

Phosphine is a much weaker base than ammonia. This is indicated by its limited water solubility ($\frac{1}{2600}$ that of ammonia at 20°C.) and by the absence of a series of phosphonium salts comparable in characteristics to the ammonium salts. Phosphonium halides, PH_4X (X = Cl, Br, I), are obtainable by direct reaction of phosphine with the appropriate hydrogen halide. Best known is the iodide, which is obtained as a white crystalline sublimate (subl. pt. 62°C.) by reacting phosphorus with iodine in carbon disulfide, evaporating the solvent, and reacting the residue ($P_2I_4 + P$) with water in a carbon dioxide atmosphere.[232] The chloride and bromide are dissociated at room temperature. Unlike the ammonium halides, the phosphonium compounds react completely and rapidly with water

$$PH_4X + H_2O \rightarrow PH_3 + H_3O^+ + X^-$$

[231] D. P. Stevenson: *J. Chem. Phys.*, **8**, 285 (1940).

[232] J. B. Work: *Inorganic Syntheses*, Vol. II, p. 141. McGraw-Hill Book Co., New York (1946).

Indeed, hydrolysis of the iodide, using an alkali, is an excellent means of preparing pure phosphine. The phosphonium halides undergo ready thermal dissociation but at much lower temperatures than the ammonium halides.[233, 234] This is shown in Figure 15·2. The weakly

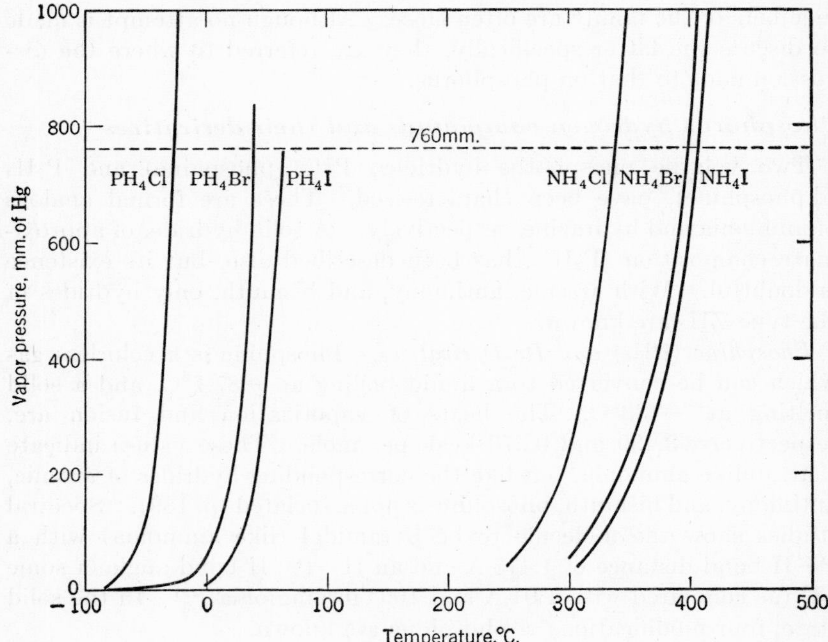

FIG. 15·2. Thermal stabilities of ammonium and phosphonium halides.

basic character of phosphine is also reflected in its poor coordinating ability.

Phosphine is a stronger reducing agent than ammonia (pp. 557, 558). In air, it burns readily, and, with oxygen, it explodes. The apparent spontaneous inflammability of unpurified phosphine is probably due to the presence of small quantities of the higher hydride, P_2H_4. Strong oxidizing agents are reduced by phosphine.

Phosphine is prepared by hydrolysis of phosphides, e.g., of calcium phosphide with water or, better, of aluminum phosphide with dilute acid, by the reaction of white phosphorus with alkali

$$4P + 3OH^- + 3H_2O \rightarrow PH_3 + 3H_2PO_2^-$$

[233] A. Smith and R. P. Calvert: *J. Am. Chem. Soc.*, **36**, 1363 (1914).

[234] F. M. G. Johnson: *J. Am. Chem. Soc.*, **34**, 877 (1912).

by disproportionation of phosphorous or hypophosphorous acid (p. 641) or by direct combination of the elements under pressure.

A variety of alkyl and aryl phosphines have been prepared. These compounds are often highly inflammable. They are more basic than phosphine. The quarternary hydroxides, like their nitrogen analogs, are strong bases and form a variety of salts. The tertiary phosphines, R_3P, yield phosphine oxides, R_3PO, on oxidation. Many Werner complexes containing substituted phosphines have been described.

Arsine, stibine, and bismuthine are comparable with phosphine but decrease in thermal stability, ease of formation, and basicity and increase in reducing power with increasing molecular weight. They are better known as organic derivatives.

Diphosphine (P_2H_4). This compound is a colorless liquid, boiling at 51.7°C. and freezing to a solid which melts at −99°C. The compound is unstable and decomposes, especially in light, to phosphine and the so-called solid hydride, $(P_2H)_x$. The material is a potent reducing agent and burns spontaneously in air. Unlike hydrazine, it shows no basic character. It is formed as a by-product in the preparation of phosphine by hydrolysis and is separated from the phosphine by freezing. Its chemistry has been investigated by Royen and Hill.[235] Although the arsenic and antimony analogs are unknown, a variety of alkyl and aryl derivatives of these hypothetical hydrides have been described.

Solid Phosphorus Hydride [$(P_2H)_x$]. This yellow material is probably better considered as an adsorption complex of phosphine on amorphous phosphorus than as a true compound in the light of x-ray studies.[236]

Phosphorus-halogen compounds

The phosphorus-halogen compounds embrace the binary halides; the oxygen-, sulfur-, and nitrogen-containing halides; and the halogen-containing acids (or their salts).

Binary Phosphorus Halides. Reported phosphorus halides, together with certain of their physical constants, are summarized in Table 15·14. Tri- and penta-halides are most common and important, the tetrahalides being rather unusual compounds. The existence of stable mixed halides is noteworthy. The physical constants are in general those of covalent compounds. These are in accordance with the electronegativity values of phosphorus and the halogens (p. 163).

[235] P. Royen and K. Hill: *Z. anorg. allgem. Chem.*, **229**, 97 (1936).
[236] P. Royen: *Z. anorg. allgem. Chem.*, **229**, 369 (1936).

TABLE 15·14

PHYSICAL CONSTANTS OF PHOSPHORUS HALIDES

Compound	Melting Point, °C.	Boiling Point, °C.	Heat of Vaporization, kcal./mole	Trouton's Constant	Critical Temperature, °C.	Critical Pressure, atm.	Heat of Formation, kcal./mole	Color
1. Trihalides								
PF_3	−151.5	−101.15	3.49	20.3	−2.05	42.69		colorless
PF_2Cl	−164.8	−47.3	4.20	18.6	89.17	44.61		colorless
$PFCl_2$	−144.0	13.85	5.95	20.7	189.84	49.3		colorless
PCl_3	−111.8	74.2	7.28	21.0			76.9(l)	colorless
PF_2Br	−133.8	−16.1	5.72	22.3				colorless
$PFBr_2$	−115.0	78.4	7.62	21.7				colorless
PBr_3	−40	175.3					45.0(l)	colorless
PI_3	61.0						10.9(s)	red
2. Pentahalides								
PF_5	−83	−75						colorless
PF_3Cl_2	−8	10						colorless
PCl_5	148(?)	160 (subl.)	15.5				106.5(s)	colorless
PF_3Br_2	−20	ca. 106						
PBr_5	< 100	dec.					60.6(s)	red-yellow
3. Tetrahalides								
P_2Cl_4	−28	180						colorless
P_2I_4	110	dec.					19.8	red

All halides undergo hydrolysis, forming ultimately hydrogen halides and oxy acids of phosphorus. The fluorides react most slowly. Pseudohalides, e.g., $P(NCO)_3$, and $PCl_2(NCO)$, are known as well (pp. 475–480). The characteristics of these compounds should be compared with those of the corresponding halides.

TRIHALIDES. Electron diffraction data show the trihalides to have pyramidal structures

$$\ddot{P}(X)_3$$

which of course amount to tetrahedra in which an electron pair occupies one position.[237–239] Available data on bond lengths and angles are summarized in Table 15·15. The phosphorus trihalides act as electron

TABLE 15·15
BOND DATA FOR PHOSPHORUS TRIHALIDES

Compound	Bond Distances, A				Bond Angle, degrees
	P—F	P—Cl	P—Br	P—I	X—P—X
PF_3	1.52				104
$PFCl_2$	1.55	2.02			102
PCl_3		2.00			101
PBr_3			2.23		100
PI_3				2.47	98

pair donors and show general unsaturated character. They react readily with oxygen or sulfur to form POX_3 and PSX_3 compounds and with halogens to form pentahalides. The ease of hydrolysis increases as the electronegativities of the halogens decrease. The mixed halides decompose into mixtures of the simple ones, PF_2Br giving PF_3 and PBr_3, for example.[240] The fluochlorides are more resistant to such decomposition than the fluobromides.

The trihalides are most commonly prepared by direct reaction of the elements under controlled conditions to prevent formation of other halides. Procedures for the chloride and bromide[241] illustrate the

[237] L. O. Brockway: *Revs. Mod. Phys.*, **8**, 231 (1936).

[238] A. H. Gregg, G. C. Hampson, G. I. Jenkins, P. L. F. Jones, and L. E. Sutton: *Trans. Faraday Soc.*, **33**, 852 (1937).

[239] O. Hassel and A. Sandbo: *Z. physik. Chem.*, **41B**, 75 (1938).

[240] H. S. Booth and S. G. Frary: *J. Am. Chem. Soc.*, **61**, 2934 (1939).

[241] R. N. Maxson et al.: *Inorganic Syntheses*, Vol. II, pp. 145, 147. McGraw-Hill Book Co., New York (1946).

reactions. With the triiodide, reaction in carbon disulfide as solvent is advantageous. The fluoride is best obtained by reacting the trichloride with arsenic trifluoride. The tribromide and trichloride can be fluorinated, partially, or completely, with antimony trifluoride or calcium fluoride[240, 242] as well (p. 428).

Arsenic, antimony, and bismuth form complete series of trihalides, as indicated in Table 15·16. Those compounds studied have comparable pyramidal structures.[238] Although their properties and modes of preparation are comparable to those of the phosphorus compounds, marked increase in ionic properties characterizes the series P—As—Sb—Bi. This is reflected in increases in melting and boiling points, in decreased hydrolysis, and in the ionic characteristics of aqueous solutions. Thus hydrolysis of PX_3 compounds is complete and gives only phosphorous acid, hydrolysis of AsX_3 compounds is nearly complete, although precipitation of the sulfide from such hydrolyzed solutions suggests the presence of traces (at least) of As^{+3}, and hydrolysis of SbX_3 and BiX_3 compounds gives SbO^+ and BiO^+ as cations. Antimony and bismuth trifluorides are salts.

PENTAHALIDES. The pentahalides are interesting because in their formation one 3*d* orbital must be occupied. This gives bonding of the type *dsp*³, which should lead to (p. 203) trigonal bipyramid structures

```
        X
        |  X
        | /
   X—P<
        | \
        |  X
        X
```

Electron diffraction data show the molecules PF_5, PF_3Cl_2, and PCl_5 to possess this configuration in the vapor states.[243, 244] The P—F bond distances are 1.57 A and 1.59 A in the molecules PF_5 and PF_3Cl_3, respectively, and the P—Cl bond distance is 2.05 A in the molecule PF_3Cl_2. In the molecule PF_3Cl_2, the two chlorines are at the apices of the pyramids. In the molecule PCl_5, the P—Cl bond distances are 2.11 A (those at apices) and 2.04 A (those at the bases). In the liquid state, the molecule PCl_5 retains this structure,[245] but not in the solid state or in solution in solvents of high dielectric constant. X-ray studies of the solid pentachloride show its structure to be $[PCl_4]^+[PCl_6]^-$, the

[242] H. S. Booth and A. R. Bozarth: *J. Am. Chem. Soc.*, **61**, 2927 (1939). Also later papers by Booth et al.

[243] L. O. Brockway and J. Y. Beach: *J. Am. Chem. Soc.*, **60**, 1836 (1938).

[244] M. Rouault: *Compt. rend.*, **207**, 620 (1938).

[245] H. Moureu, M. Magat, and G. Wétroff: *Compt. rend.*, **205**, 276 (1937).

TABLE 15·16
PHYSICAL CONSTANTS OF ARSENIC-, ANTIMONY-, AND BISMUTH-HALOGEN COMPOUNDS

Compound	Melting Point, °C.	Boiling Point, °C.	Specific Conductance, ohm^{-1}	Dipole Moment,* D	Bond Distance, Z—X, A	Bond Angle X—Z—X, degrees
1. Trihalides						
AsF_3	−5.95	63			1.72	
SbF_3	ca. 290	319				
BiF_3						
$AsCl_3$	−13	130	1.24×10^{-6}	3.11	2.16	
$SbCl_3$	72.9	221	0.85×10^{-6} (80°C.)	5.16	2.37	
$BiCl_3$	230	447	0.406 (250°C.)		2.48	100 ± 6
$AsBr_3$	31	220	1.53×10^{-6}	2.90	2.33	
$SbBr_3$	96	288		5.01	2.52	
$BiBr_3$	218	453				
AsI_3	141	ca. 400		1.83	2.54	
SbI_3	170.3	ca. 410			2.75	
BiI_3	439(?)	500 (dec.)				
2. Pentahalides						
AsF_5	−80	−53				
SbF_5	7	150				
$AsCl_5$	ca. −40					
$SbCl_5$	2	140 (dec.)				

* In dioxane at 25°C.

P—Cl bond distance in the tetrahedral cation being 1.98 A and in the octahedral anion 2.06 A.[246] Solutions in nitromethane[247] and liquid bromine[248] are conductors. The solid pentabromide has the ionic structure $[PBr_4]^+Br^-$.[249] Data are lacking for the fluorides. The absence of a pentaiodide is probably due to the steric difficulties which would accompany surrounding the small phosphorus atom with so many large iodine atoms.

The pentahalides, like the trihalides, hydrolyze readily, but the reaction involves two steps

$$PX_5 + H_2O \rightarrow POX_3 + 2HX$$
$$POX_3 + 3H_2O \rightarrow H_3PO_4 + 3HX$$

The pentafluoride appears to be stable thermally, but the pentachloride dissociates (reversibly) to the trichloride and chlorine, the reaction being complete above 300°C. The pentabromide is partially dissociated even in the liquid state. The mixed pentahalides decompose to the simple pentahalides. The pentafluoride yields $[PF_6]^-$ with excess fluoride (pp. 359, 595, 598).

Methods applicable to the preparation of the trihalides, with suitable modifications, can be used for the pentahalides. The pentafluoride also results from action of bromine on the trifluoride because of decomposition of the intermediate compound PF_3Br_2. Fluorinations of the oxide with calcium fluoride and of the chloride with arsenic trifluoride or a metal fluoride are also useful.

Arsenic and antimony both form pentafluorides and pentachlorides (Table 15·16), although the pentachloride of arsenic is poorly characterized. These compounds are analogous to the phosphorus compounds, although somewhat less covalent and more readily reduced. Antimony pentafluoride, obtained by the action of hydrogen fluoride on the pentachloride, is comparatively stable. With fluoride ion, fluo anions, $[AsF_6]^-$ and $[SbF_6]^-$, form. Alkyl and aryl compounds of the types R_3AsX_2, R_3SbX_2, R_2AsX_3, etc., are known. Mixed halides, e.g., SbF_3Cl_2, are known.

TETRAHALIDES. Only two compounds, P_2Cl_4 and P_2I_4, are known. The chloride hydrolyzes readily, oxidizes in air, and decomposes on standing to phosphorus and the trichloride. It is formed by action of an electric discharge on a mixture of phosphorus trichloride and hydro-

[246] D. Clark, H. M. Powell, and A. F. Wells: *J. Chem. Soc.*, **1942,** 642.

[247] G. W. F. Holroyd, H. Chadwick, and J. E. H. Mitchell: *J. Chem. Soc.*, **127,** 2492 (1925).

[248] W. A. Plotnikow and S. Jakubson: *Z. physik. Chem.*, **138A,** 235 (1928).

[249] H. M. Powell and D. Clark: *Nature,* **145,** 971 (1940).

gen.[250] The iodide is a clear red crystalline compound obtained by action of iodine on phosphorus in carbon disulfide.[232, 251] The compound decomposes on heating to iodine and the triiodide. With water it yields a variety of products, among them the substances HI, H_3PO_2, H_3PO_3, H_3PO_4, and PH_3. With alkaline solutions containing hydrogen peroxide, it is converted to hypophosphate (p. 643),[252] suggesting the presence of a P—P link and the possible structure

```
 ..    ..
:I:   :I:
 ..    ..
:P  :  P:
 ..    ..
:I:   :I:
 ..    ..
```

Oxygen-, Sulfur-, and Nitrogen-Containing Halides. All these compounds are derived from pentapositive phosphorus and are of the types POX_3, PSX_3, and $(PNX_2)_x$. Known compounds and their physical constants are summarized in Table 15·17. Comparable compounds of arsenic, antimony, or bismuth are unknown.

PHOSPHORUS(V) OXYHALIDES OR PHOSPHORYL HALIDES (POX_3). The physical constants of these compounds are those of covalent materials. Electron diffraction data[243, 253] for POF_3, POF_2Cl, $POCl_3$, and $POBr_3$ show them to be tetrahedral and characterized by the constants summarized in Table 15·18. The P—O and P—X bond distances are essentially those in the phosphate ion and the trihalides, respectively. Reduction of the tetrahedral bond angle (X—P—X) to 106° to 108° indicates that the P—O bond has some double bond character and involves a 3*d* orbital of the phosphorus.[254] The phosphorus(V) oxyhalides hydrolyze readily to phosphoric acid and hydrogen halides. They are useful (especially $POCl_3$) in replacing organic hydroxyl groups with halogens. The fluoride is obtained by fluorinating the chloride with antimony trifluoride or metal fluorides, by direct action of hydrogen fluoride on phosphorus(V) oxide, or by hydrolysis of the pentafluoride. The chloride and bromide are readily obtained by action of the pentahalide on phosphorus(V) oxide.[255] Partial

[250] A. Besson and L. Fournier: *Compt. rend.*, **150**, 102 (1910).

[251] F. E. E. Germann and R. N. Traxler: *J. Am. Chem. Soc.*, **49**, 307 (1927).

[252] J. H. Kolitowska: *Roczniki Chem.*, **15**, 29 (1935).

[253] J. H. Secrist and L. O. Brockway: *J. Am. Chem. Soc.*, **66**, 1941 (1944).

[254] L. Pauling: *The Nature of the Chemical Bond*, 2nd Ed., pp. 84, 244. Cornell University Press, Ithaca (1940).

[255] H. S. Booth, C. G. Seegmiller, and C. A. Seabright: *Inorganic Syntheses*, Vol. II, pp. 151–155. McGraw-Hill Book Co., New York (1946).

TABLE 15·17

PHYSICAL CONSTANTS OF OXY-, THIO-, AND NITRILOHALIDES

Compound	Melting Point, °C.	Boiling Point, °C.	Heat of Vaporization, kcal./mole	Trouton's Constant	Critical Temperature, °C.	Critical Pressure, atm.	Heat of Formation, kcal./mole	Color
1. Oxyhalides								
POF_3	−39.4	−39.8	5.03	21.6	73.3	41.8		colorless
POF_2Cl	−96.4	3.1	6.09	22.0	150.6	43.4		colorless
$POFCl_2$	−80.1	52.9	7.40	22.7				colorless
$POCl_3$	1.25	105.1	8.20	21.7	77.59		147.1(l)	colorless
POF_2Br	−84.8	30.5	7.09	23.4				colorless
$POCl_2Br$	11	137.6						colorless
$POFBr_2$	−117.2	110.1	7.52	19.6				colorless
$POBr_3$	56	189.5					106.9(s)	colorless
2. Thiohalides								
PSF_3	−148.8	−52.3	4.68	21.1	72.8	37.7		colorless
PSF_2Cl	−155.2	6.3	5.70	20.4	166	40.9		colorless
$PSFCl_2$	−96.0	64.7	6.86	20.3				colorless
$PSCl_3$	−35	125						colorless
PSF_2Br	−136.9	35.5						
$PSFBr_2$	−75.2	125.3						
$PSBr_3$	37.8	212 (dec.)						yellow
3. Nitrilohalides								
$(PNClF)_4$	−25	130.5						
$P_4N_4Cl_2F_6$		105.8						
$(PNCl_2)_3$	114	256						
$(PNCl_2)_4$	123.5	328.5						
$(PNBr_2)_4$								

TABLE 15.18
BOND DATA FOR POX_3, PSX_3, $(PNX_2)_x$ COMPOUNDS

Compound	Bond Distances, A						Bond Angle, degrees
	P—O	P—S	P—N	P—F	P—Cl	P—Br	X—P—X
1. Oxyhalides							
POF_3	1.56			1.52			107
POF_2Cl	1.55			1.51	2.01		106 } (F—P—Cl or Cl—P—Cl or F—P—F)
$POFCl_2$	1.54			1.50	1.94		106 } (F—P—Cl or Cl—P—Cl or F—P—F)
$POCl_3$	1.58				2.02		106
$POBr_3$	1.41					2.06	108
2. Sulfohalides							
PSF_3		1.85		1.51			99.5
$PSCl_3$		1.94			2.01		107
PSF_2Br		1.87		1.45		2.14	106 (F—P—Br)
$PSFBr_2$		1.87		1.50		2.18	100 (Br—P—Br)
$PSBr_3$		1.89				2.13	106
3. Nitrilic halides							
$(PNCl_2)_3$			1.65		1.97		109
$(PNCl_2)_4$			1.67		1.99		105.5

hydrolysis of the pentahalides and reaction of these compounds with oxalic acid are useful preparative procedures, as is reaction of phosphorus trichloride with potassium chlorate. Partial fluorination of the chloride or bromide gives the mixed halides.[256, 257]

PHOSPHORUS(V) SULFOHALIDES OR THIOPHOSPHORYL HALIDES (PSX_3). These compounds have the same structures as their oxygen analogs (Table 15·18).[253, 258, 259] The short P—S bond in the PSF_3 molecule is supposedly due to some triple-bond character as favored by the large ionic character of the P—F bonds.[254] The sulfohalides hydrolyze more slowly than the oxyhalides and yield the acids $HPSOF_2$ and H_3PSO_3 as intermediates. The fluoride is spontaneously inflammable in air. Preparational procedures include fluorination of the chloride with arsenic trifluoride or the pentasulfide with lead fluoride or reaction of the pentasulfide with an appropriate halide.[255] A convenient preparation of phosphorus(V) sulfochloride involves the aluminum chloride-catalyzed reaction of phosphorus trichloride with sulfur.[260] Partial fluorination, using antimony trifluoride, yields mixed sulfofluorides.

PHOSPHONITRILIC HALIDES [$(PNX_2)_x$]. All these compounds are polymeric. Best known are the chlorides,[261] although mixed fluorine-chlorine[262, 263] and bromine[264] derivatives are known. Electron diffraction measurements[265] show the trimeric chloride, $(PNCl_2)_3$, to have a planar ring structure

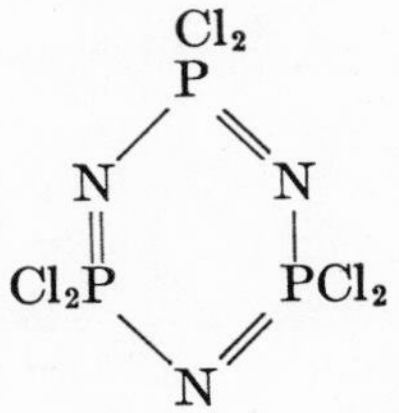

```
           Cl2
            P
          /   \\
         N     N
         ||    |
      Cl2P     PCl2
          \   //
            N
```

in which the P—N bond distance (Table 15·18) is just that calculated for Kekulé resonance such as is found in the benzene ring. The tetra-

[256] H. S. Booth and F. B. Dutton: *J. Am. Chem. Soc.*, **61**, 2937 (1939).

[257] H. S. Booth and C. G. Seegmiller: *J. Am. Chem. Soc.*, **61**, 3120 (1939).

[258] J. Y. Beach and D. P. Stevenson: *J. Chem. Phys.*, **6**, 75 (1938).

[259] D. P. Stevenson and H. Russell: *J. Am. Chem. Soc.*, **61**, 3264 (1939).

[260] F. Knotz: *Österr. Chem.-Ztg.*, **50**, 128 (1949).

[261] L. F. Audrieth, R. Steinman, and A. D. F. Toy: *Chem. Revs.*, **32**, 109 (1943). Excellent review.

[262] O. Schmitz-Dumont and H. Külkens: *Z. anorg. allgem. Chem.*, **238**, 189 (1938).

[263] O. Schmitz-Dumont and A. Braschos: *Z. anorg. allgem. Chem.*, **243**, 113 (1939).

[264] H. Bode: *Z. anorg. allgem. Chem.*, **252**, 113 (1943).

[265] L. O. Brockway and W. M. Bright: *J. Am. Chem. Soc.*, **65**, 1551 (1943).

meric chloride, $(PNCl_2)_4$, has a comparable puckered ring structure[266] of alternate phosphorus and nitrogen atoms, with two chlorines on each phosphorus atom. Its structure apparently involves Kekulé resonance as well. The higher polymers in the chloride series apparently have chain structures[261]

```
       Cl          Cl          Cl
       |           |           |
 ----P  =  N------P  =  N------P  =  N----
       |           |           |
       Cl          Cl          Cl
```

but it is difficult to characterize individual members. Some of the highest polymers are definitely elastomeric in their properties (inorganic rubber) and are amorphous when unstretched but crystalline when stretched.[267] Like rubber, they must consist of zigzag long chains. The fluorine-chlorine compounds resemble the chlorine compounds closely and probably have the same structures. The same is probably true of the bromine compounds.

The phosphonitrilic compounds are irritating and somewhat toxic. Polymerization of the lower members is effected by heating at 250° to 350°C., and is accompanied by successive changes to oils, gums, waxes, rubbers, and an infusible, non-elastic solid as molecular weight increases. Above 350°C., depolymerization occurs. Polymerization is accompanied by decreased solubility in organic solvents and decreased reactivity. Chemically, the phosphonitrilic chlorides undergo hydrolysis, ammonolysis, and aminolysis reactions[261] and also react with a variety of organic compounds containing nitrogen, oxygen, or sulfur functional groups. The chlorines may be replaced by phenyl groups. The fluorine-containing compounds have similar characteristics but yield less stable high polymers.

The phosphonitrilic chlorides can be prepared by ammonolysis of phosphorus pentachloride, by reaction of phosphorus nitrides with chlorine, or by reaction of phosphorus pentachloride with ammonium chloride in an inert solvent.[261] A better procedure involves heating the pentachloride with solid ammonium chloride at 145° to 160°C.

$$x\mathrm{PCl_5} + x\mathrm{NH_4Cl} \rightarrow (\mathrm{PNCl_2})_x + 4x\mathrm{HCl}$$

and extracting the trimer and the tetramer with low-boiling petroleum

[266] J. A. A. Ketelaar and T. A. de Vries: *Rec. trav. chim.*, **58**, 1081 (1939).

[267] K. H. Meyer, W. Lotmar, and G. W. Pankow: *Helv. Chim. Acta*, **19**, 930 (1936).

ether.[268] The trimer is then recovered by distillation under reduced pressure. Reaction of the trimeric chloride with lead fluoride at elevated temperatures gives $P_4N_4Cl_2F_6$ and $(PNClF)_4$.[262, 263]

Halogen-Containing Acids and Salts. Only fluorine-containing compounds of these types have been prepared. Although the free acids are quite generally unstable, salts derived from the acids H_2PO_3F, HPO_2F_2, and HPF_6 are easily prepared. Such acids and phosphorus(V) oxyfluoride may be related to orthophosphoric acid in terms of successive substitution of fluoride for hydroxyl or oxygen as

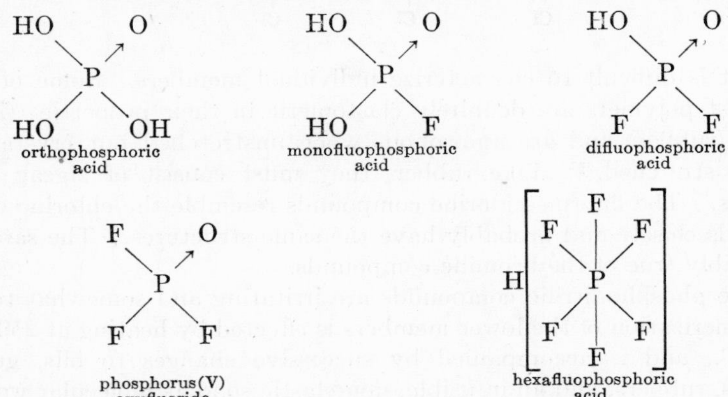

With arsenic and antimony, derivatives of the acids $HAsF_6$, $HSbF_6$, $HSbCl_6$, and $HSbBr_6$ have been described. The inclusion of the larger halogens with the larger Group Vb elements is undoubtedly due to steric factors.

MONOFLUOPHOSPHATES ($M_2^IPO_3F$). Monofluophosphoric acid is an oily liquid which gives a glass at −78°C. and decomposes at 185°C. In water it hydrolyzes slowly to orthophosphoric acid. The silver salt is easily crystallized and is readily converted into other salts by treatment with appropriate chlorides. Monofluophosphates are formed by the hydrolysis of difluophosphates,[269] by the reaction of hydrofluoric acid with orthophosphoric acid,[269] by the fusion of phosphorus(V) oxide with ammonium fluoride,[270] or by the fusion of sodium fluoride with sodium trimetaphosphate.[271] The anhydrous acid can

[268] R. Steinman, F. B. Schirmer, and L. F. Audrieth: *J. Am. Chem. Soc.*, **64**, 2377 (1942).

[269] W. Lange: *Ber.*, **62B**, 793, 1084 (1929).

[270] W. Lange: *Inorganic Syntheses*, Vol. II, pp. 155–158. McGraw-Hill Book Co., New York (1946).

[271] O. F. Hill and L. F. Audrieth: *Inorganic Syntheses*, Vol. III, p. 106. McGraw-Hill Book Co., New York (1950).

be obtained from anhydrous metaphosphoric acid and liquid hydrogen fluoride.[272] A comparable reaction using 100% orthophosphoric acid gives the mono- and di- acids in equi-molar proportions.

DIFLUOPHOSPHATES ($M^IPO_2F_2$). Free difluophosphoric acid has not been prepared. In aqueous solution it hydrolyzes slowly, but hydrolysis is rapid in the presence of acid or alkali. The acid is strong. The difluophosphates resemble the perchlorates, fluoborates, and fluosulfonates closely in solubility, and are often isomorphous with them in the solid state, as might be expected from the similarities in bond lengths. Difluophosphates are readily obtained by alkaline hydrolysis of phosphorus(V) oxyfluoride[269] or by fusion of phosphorus(V) oxide with ammonium fluoride. Both monofluophosphate and difluophosphate are formed in the second reaction, but difluophosphate can be extracted with boiling alcohol.

HEXAFLUOPHOSPHATES (M^IPF_6). Hexafluophosphates have been mentioned in previous discussions (pp. 598, 628). Hexafluophosphoric acid is a strong acid. It is resistant to hydrolysis, but is decomposed by acids and boiling alkali. The salts resemble the perchlorates in solubilities. On being heated, the alkali metal salts lose phosphorus pentafluoride. Reaction of phosphorus pentachloride with alkali metal or ammonium fluorides yields hexafluophosphates,[273] but separation from the by-product metal chlorides is difficult. A better procedure[274] involves reaction in liquid hydrogen fluoride as

$$MCl + PCl_5 + 6HF \rightarrow MPF_6 + 6HCl$$

removal of residual hydrogen fluoride by evaporation, and recrystallization of the products from methanol or water.

Oxides of phosphorus

Well-established oxides of phosphorus have the molecular compositions P_4O_6, $(PO_2)_n$, P_4O_{10}, and PO_3 or P_2O_6. Materials of compositions P_4O and P_2O, although reported as products of the oxidation of phosphorus in ether solution, are probably mixtures. The oxides P_4O_6 and P_4O_{10} are, respectively, the anhydrides of the phosphorous and phosphoric acids. Arsenic and antimony form the compounds As_4O_6, Sb_4O_6, As_2O_5, and Sb_2O_5, which are comparable to the phosphorus oxides but more basic, and also the compounds As_2O_4 and Sb_2O_4, which are salt-like oxides and contain both tri- and

[272] W. Lange and R. Livingston: *J. Am. Chem. Soc.*, **69**, 1073 (1947).

[273] W. Lange and G. von Krueger: *Ber.*, **65B**, 1253 (1932).

[274] M. M. Woyski: *Inorganic Syntheses*, Vol. III, p. 111. McGraw-Hill Book Co., New York (1950).

pentapositive elements, $Z^{III}Z^{V}O_4$.[275] The arsenic and antimony oxides have sufficient acidic strength to yield anionic salts when treated with alkalies. Bismuth gives only the compound Bi_2O_3, although unstable and impure samples approaching Bi_2O_5 in composition have been obtained by treating bismuthates with acids.

Phosphorus(III) Oxide (P_4O_6). Although commonly formulated as a monomer (and called trioxide), this compound is dimeric both in solution in naphthalene[276] and in the vapor state.[277] Electron diffraction data[277, 278] show the four phosphorus atoms to be at the apices of a tetrahedron, with the six oxygen atoms just outside the center points of the six edges as

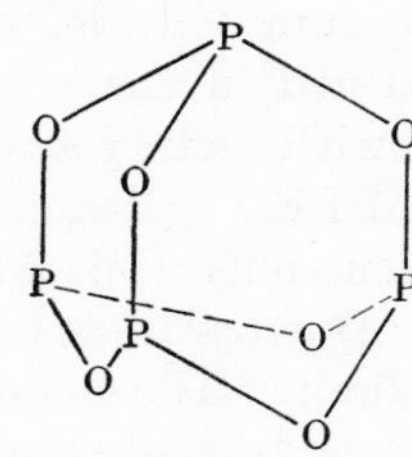

Bond data[277] are: P—O distance 1.65 A, P—O—P angle 127.5°, and O—P—O angle 99°. The oxide melts at 23.8°C. to a nonconducting liquid which boils without decomposition at 175.4°C.

Thermal decomposition is slow below 210°C. but becomes rapid at more elevated temperatures. The products are red phosphorus and the tetroxide, P_2O_4. Phosphorus(III) oxide reacts slowly with oxygen, giving a green glow. With cold water, phosphorous acid, H_3PO_3, is formed, but with hot water phosphorus, phosphine, and phosphoric acid are formed. The compound is obtained by careful oxidation of excess white phosphorus and purified by distillation after conversion of unreacted phosphorus to the red form by exposure to a mercury arc.[279]

Polymeric Phosphorus Dioxide [$(PO_2)_n$]. The true molecular complexity of this compound is not known, although vapor density determinations at 500°C. suggest the compound to be a tetramer, P_4O_8.[280] The compound is commonly called the tetroxide and tacitly assumed

[275] K. Dihlström and A. Westgren: *Z. anorg. allgem. Chem.*, **235**, 153 (1937).
[276] R. Schenck, F. Mihr, and H. Banthien: *Ber.*, **39**, 1506 (1906).
[277] G. C. Hampson and A. J. Stosick: *J. Am. Chem. Soc.*, **60**, 1814 (1938).
[278] L. R. Maxwell, S. B. Hendricks, and L. S. Deming: *J. Chem. Phys.*, **5**, 626 (1937).
[279] L. Wolf and H. Schmager: *Ber.*, **62B**, 771 (1929).
[280] P. H. Emmett and J. F. Schultz: *Ind. Eng. Chem.*, **31**, 105 (1939).

to have the molecular formula P_2O_4. The crystalline compound sublimes above 180°C. Although a formal anhydride of hypophosphoric acid, $H_4P_2O_6$, this oxide neither reacts with water to form the acid nor is obtainable from the latter. With water, it gives metaphosphoric and phosphorous acids, together with some phosphine. The tetroxide is best obtained by heating phosphorus(III) oxide in an evacuated tube at 200° to 250°C. (p. 636).

Phosphorus(V) Oxide (P_4O_{10}). Although usually termed phosphorus pentoxide and formulated as a monomer, this compound has been shown by vapor density determinations to be dimeric.[281] Electron diffraction data[277] show the structure to be the same as that of the P_4O_6 molecule, but with an extra oxygen atom on each phosphorus atom at the very short P—O bond distance 1.39 A. Each phosphorus atom is thus surrounded tetrahedrally by oxygen atoms, three oxygens in each tetrahedron being common to three other tetrahedra.

Phosphorus(V) oxide exhibits polymorphism. Comprehensive studies[282–285] show that three crystalline forms can be distinguished. Certain characteristics of these forms are summarized in Table 15·19. Combustion of phosphorus yields the volatile hexagonal form (H),

TABLE 15·19
POLYMORPHIC FORMS OF P_4O_{10}

Form	Designation	Triple Point		Density	Heat of Vaporization, kcal./mole (P_4O_{10})
		°C.	mm.		
1. Solids					
Hexagonal	H, I, α	420	3600	2.30	22.7
Orthorhombic	O, II	562	437	2.72	36.4
Tetragonal	T, III	580	555	2.89	33.9
2. Liquids					
Metastable (from H)					16.2
Stable (from T)					18.7

in which the structure of the vapor is preserved.[283] Heating the hexagonal form at 400° to 500°C. converts it to an orthorhombic modification (O), which appears to be an infinite sheet type of polymer made up

[281] E. V. Britzkes and E. Hoffmann: *Monatsh.*, **71**, 317 (1938).

[282] W. L. Hill, G. T. Faust, and S. B. Hendricks: *J. Am. Chem. Soc.*, **65**, 794 (1943).

[283] H. C. J. de Decker and C. H. MacGillavry: *Rec. trav. chim.*, **60**, 153 (1941).

[284] H. C. J. de Decker: *Rec. trav. chim.*, **60**, 413 (1941).

[285] C. H. MacGillavry, H. C. J. de Decker, and L. M. Nijland: *Nature*, **164**, 448 (1949).

of interlocking rings but based upon PO_4 tetrahedra.[284] Heating to still higher temperatures gives a tetragonal modification (T) in which corrugated sheets of P_4O_{10} molecules are found.[285] The tetragonal form is the stable form and is remarkable in that it can be heated above its melting point (to 700°C.) without melting.[286] Rapid heating of the hexagonal form gives a liquid which polymerizes rapidly to a glass. A stable liquid is formed when the tetragonal form is melted. The stable liquid is apparently a polymer of the unstable form.[282]

All solid forms of phosphorus(V) oxide react readily with water, forming initially metaphosphoric acid and eventually the pyro and ortho acids (p. 646). On exposure to moist air, all three forms absorb water at the same rate initially, but as time passes the hexagonal form absorbs more rapidly than the others.[282] In contact with liquid water, the hexagonal form reacts with spattering (and with explosive violence if finely divided); the orthorhombic form dissolves slowly even on the steam bath; and the tetragonal form gives first a stiff gel which then liquefies.

Phosphorus(V) oxide is the principal product of the air oxidation of phosphorus when excess oxygen is present, but small quantities of the lower oxides are produced also. These can be removed only by prolonged oxidation at 175° to 200°C. Dehydration of the phosphoric acids is impractical because of the marked affinity of the oxide for water.

Phosphorus Trioxide (PO_3) *or Hexoxide* (P_2O_6). Passage of a mixture of phosphorus(V) oxide and oxygen through an electric discharge at about 1 mm. of mercury pressure has been shown to yield a violet-colored condensate containing 5 to 6% of an oxide P_2O_6.[287, 288] Extraction with chloroform effected concentration up to 11%. On being heated to 130°C., the oxide yielded oxygen and the pentoxide. Treatment with water gave a solution which oxidized iodide to iodine, manganate to permanganate, etc., and had the general properties of peroxydiphosphoric acid solution (p. 512). The oxide, unlike its nitrogen analog (p. 612), appears to be a peroxy material. The dimeric formula is suggested to emphasize the relation to the peroxy acid

$$\begin{array}{ccccccc} HO & & & & O & OH & \\ & \diagdown & & & \uparrow & \diagup & \\ & & P—O—O—P & & & & \\ & \diagup & \downarrow & & & \diagdown & \\ HO & & O & & & & OH \end{array} \quad \text{vs.} \quad \begin{array}{ccccc} O & & & & O \\ & \nwarrow & & \nearrow & \\ & & P—O—O—P & & \\ & \swarrow & & \searrow & \\ O & & & & O \end{array}$$

[286] A. Smits and H. W. Deinum: *Z. physik. Chem.*, **149A**, 337 (1930).

[287] P. W. Schenk and H. Platz: *Naturwissenschaften*, **24**, 651 (1936).

[288] P. W. Schenk and H. Rehaag: *Z. anorg. allgem. Chem.*, **233**, 403 (1937).

but the color of the compound would be in better accord with a monomeric structure. Magnetic data would permit decision as to the correct formulation.

The oxy acids of phosphorus

Like sulfur, phosphorus has a number of oxy acids, in addition to those based directly upon oxides as anhydrides, that are known either in the free condition or in the form of salts. The summary given in Table 15·20 lists the phosphorus oxy acids. Polymers are not included. Certain of these compounds are discussed in detail below. The peroxy acids have been described in Chapter 14 (pp. 511–515). Arsenious (H_3AsO_3) and arsenic (H_3AsO_4, $H_4As_2O_7$, $HAsO_3$) acids (or salts) are comparable to the corresponding phosphorus compounds. Tripositive antimony is amphoteric, and tripositive bismuth is basic in character. Antimonates and bismuthates, containing the pentapositive elements, differ markedly from the phosphates and arsenates and are never polymeric.

Hypophosphorous Acid (H_3PO_2). Free hypophosphorous acid is a colorless, crystalline compound melting at 26.5°C. The compound dissolves readily in water, where it behaves as a monobasic acid. This suggests strongly that only one hydrogen atom is attached to an oxygen atom (Table 15·20), as proposed by Werner, and seems to preclude the existence of a tautomer

$$\begin{array}{cccccc} & & & & \mathrm{H} & \\ & & & & \cdot\cdot & \\ & & & : & \mathrm{O} & : \\ & & \cdot\cdot & & \cdot\cdot & \\ \mathrm{H} & : & \mathrm{O} & : & \mathrm{P} & : \\ & & \cdot\cdot & & \cdot\cdot & \\ & & & & \mathrm{H} & \end{array}$$

That this is the case is proved rather conclusively by Raman data for the acid,[289] by x-ray data obtained for the ammonium salt,[290] by crystal structure determinations on salts $M^{II}(H_2PO_2)_2 \cdot 6H_2O (M^{II} = Zn, Mg)$,[291] and by the lack of exchange when the potassium salt, KH_2PO_2, is dissolved in deuterium oxide (p. 392).[292] The ion $H_2PO_2^-$ is tetrahedral.

In aqueous solution, hypophosphorous acid is moderately strong ($k_A' = 10^{-2}$). The salts are uniformly water soluble. Aqueous solu-

[289] A. Simon and F. Fehér: *Z. anorg. allgem. Chem.*, **230**, 289 (1937).
[290] W. H. Zachariasen and R. C. L. Mooney: *J. Chem. Phys.*, **2**, 34 (1934).
[291] A. Ferrari and C. Colla: *Gazz. chim. ital.*, **67**, 294 (1937).
[292] H. Erlenmeyer and H. Gärtner: *Helv. Chim. Acta*, **17**, 970 (1934).

TABLE 15·20
OXY ACIDS OF PHOSPHORUS

Formula	Name	Apparent Oxidation State of Phosphorus	Probable Structure	Preparation
H_3PO_2	hypophosphorous acid	+1	: Ö : H : Ö : P : H H	acid, salts
HPO_2	metaphosphorous acid	+3	H : Ö : P::Ö :	acid, salts
$H_4P_2O_5$	pyrophosphorous acid	+3	: Ö : H H : Ö : P : Ö : P : Ö : H H : Ö :	acid, salts
H_3PO_3	orthophosphorous acid (phosphorous acid)	+3	H H : Ö : P : Ö : H : Ö :	acid, salts
$H_4P_2O_6$	hypophosphoric acid	+4	: Ö : : Ö : H : Ö : P : P : Ö : H : Ö : : Ö : H H	acid, salts
HPO_3	metaphosphoric acid	+5	H : Ö : P : Ö : : Ö :	salts
$H_5P_3O_{10}$	triphosphoric acid (tripolyphosphoric acid)	+5	H : Ö : : Ö : : Ö : H : Ö : P : Ö : P : Ö : P : Ö : H : Ö : : Ö : : Ö : H H	salts
$H_4P_2O_7$	pyrophosphoric acid	+5	H : Ö : : Ö : H : Ö : P : Ö : P : Ö : H : Ö : : Ö : H	acid, salts
H_3PO_4	orthophosphoric acid	+5	: Ö : H : Ö : P : Ö : H : Ö : H	acid, salts

TABLE 15·20 (*Continued*)

Formula	Name	Apparent Oxidation State of Phosphorus	Probable Structure	Preparation
H_3PO_5	peroxymonophosphoric acid	+5	.. : O : .. .. H : O : P : O : O : H .. .. : O : .. H	salts
$H_4P_2O_8$	peroxydiphosphoric acid	+5	H .. .. : O : : O : .. .. H : O : P : O : O : P : O : H .. .. : O : : O : .. .. H	salts

tions are stable thermally but decompose to hydrogen, phosphine, and orthophosphoric acid above 140°C. The pure acid and its salts decompose similarly at elevated temperatures. As shown by the couples

$$H_3PO_2 + H_2O \rightleftharpoons H_3PO_3 + 2H^+ + 2e^- \qquad E^0_{298} = 0.59 \text{ volt}$$

and

$$P + 2H_2O \rightleftharpoons H_3PO_2 + H^+ + e^- \qquad = 0.29$$

in acidic solution and the couples

$$H_2PO_2^- + 3OH^- \rightleftharpoons HPO_3^{-2} + 2H_2O + 2e^- \qquad E^0_{298} = 1.65 \text{ volts}$$

and

$$P + 2OH^- \rightleftharpoons H_2PO_2^- + e^- \qquad = 1.82$$

in alkaline solution, hypophosphorous acid and its salts are strong reducing agents and weak oxidizing agents. Although oxidation is effected by many oxidizing agents (e.g., halogens and heavy metal ions), many such reactions are very slow,[293, 294] possibly because of the presence of two forms of the acid in slow equilibrium with each other. Because of the reducing power of phosphorous acid (p. 643), strong oxidants convert hypophosphorous acid to phosphoric acid.

Hypophosphites are formed when white phosphorus is dissolved in strongly alkaline [NaOH, $Ba(OH)_2$] solutions

$$4P + 3OH^- + 3H_2O \rightarrow 3H_2PO_2^- + PH_3$$

From a solution of the crystalline barium salt, $Ba(H_2PO_2)_2 \cdot H_2O$, the

[293] A. D. Mitchell: *J. Chem. Soc.*, **117**, 1322 (1920).
[294] R. O. Griffith and A. McKeown: *Trans. Faraday Soc.*, **30**, 530 (1934).

acid can be obtained by precipitation of barium ion with sulfuric acid, evaporation below 130°C., and crystallization at 0°C.

The Phosphorous Acids (HPO_2, $H_4P_2O_5$, H_3PO_3). Although the meta and pyro acids are obtainable either as such or as salts, the ortho acid is the only one which is important. The meta and pyro acids hydrate rapidly to the ortho acid in aqueous solution. The ortho acid is commonly called phosphorous acid. The solid ortho acid melts at 71.7° to 73.6°C., is deliquescent, and dissolves readily in water, where it behaves as a dibasic acid. By analogy to hypophosphorous acid, this behavior suggests that one hydrogen atom is covalently bonded to the phosphorus atom (Table 15·20). No supporting physical data are available. Although the only preparable salts are of the types $M^IH_2PO_3$ and $M_2{}^IHPO_3$, two series of esters with structures

$$\begin{array}{ccccccccc} & & & & \text{R} & & & & \\ & & & : & \text{O} & : & & & \\ \text{R} & : & \ddot{\underset{..}{\text{O}}} & : & \ddot{\underset{..}{\text{P}}} & : & \ddot{\underset{..}{\text{O}}} & : & \text{R} \end{array} \quad \text{and} \quad \begin{array}{ccccccccc} & & & & \text{R} & & & & \\ \text{R} & : & \ddot{\underset{..}{\text{O}}} & : & \ddot{\underset{..}{\text{P}}} & : & \ddot{\underset{..}{\text{O}}} & : & \text{R} \\ & & & : & \underset{..}{\text{O}} & : & & & \end{array}$$

are known. This, plus the fact that the acid itself results from the hydrolysis of phosphorus trichloride, suggests the possibility of a tautomeric equilibrium

$$\begin{array}{ccccccccc} & & & & \text{H} & & & & \\ & & & : & \ddot{\text{O}} & : & & & \\ \text{H} & : & \ddot{\underset{..}{\text{O}}} & : & \underset{..}{\text{P}} & : & \ddot{\underset{..}{\text{O}}} & : & \text{H} \end{array} \rightleftharpoons \begin{array}{ccccccccc} & & & : & \ddot{\text{O}} & : & & & \\ \text{H} & : & \ddot{\underset{..}{\text{O}}} & : & \ddot{\underset{..}{\text{P}}} & : & \ddot{\underset{..}{\text{O}}} & : & \text{H} \\ & & & & \text{H} & & & & \end{array}$$

If such an equilibrium does exist, it must be displaced almost completely toward the dibasic form.

In aqueous solution the acid is moderately strong ($k_{A_1}' = 10^{-2}$, $k_{A_2}' = 2 \times 10^{-7}$ at 18°C.). The alkali metal salts of both series are soluble (the lithium compounds least soluble); the alkaline earth metal salts are less soluble. Both the free acid and its aqueous solutions decompose to phosphine and orthophosphoric acid when heated. As shown by the couples discussed in the preceding section and the following couples

$$H_3PO_3 + H_2O \rightleftharpoons H_3PO_4 + 2H^+ + 2e^- \qquad E^0_{298} = 0.20 \text{ volt}$$

in acidic solution and

$$HPO_3^{-2} + 3OH^- \rightleftharpoons PO_4^{-3} + 2H_2O + 2e^- \qquad E^0_{298} = 1.05 \text{ volts}$$

in alkaline solution, phosphorous acid and the phosphites are strong reducing agents but weak oxidizing agents. As with hypophosphites, reactions with oxidizing agents are often slow, particularly at ordinary temperatures, e.g., those with the halogens,[295–297] dichromate, and peroxydisulfate. Phosphoric acid or phosphate is the oxidation product.

Phosphorous acid is prepared most readily by passing air laden with vapors of phosphorus trichloride through ice water. Crystals of the acid resulting from hydrolysis form readily. Insoluble lead phosphite can be treated with hydrogen sulfide to give a solution from which phosphorous acid can be crystallized. Cation exchange resins operating on the hydrogen cycle could probably be used effectively to convert salts to the acid. Salts are readily obtained by neutralization of the acid. The meta acid forms when phosphine is burned in a limited amount of air. Dehydration of sodium phosphite, $Na_2HPO_3 \cdot 2\frac{1}{2}H_2O$, at 160°C. in a vacuum gives the pyrophosphite, $Na_2H_2P_2O_5$. These materials give orthophosphites in aqueous solution.

Hypophosphoric Acid ($H_4P_2O_6$). That hypophosphoric acid is properly represented as a dimer rather than as the monomer H_2PO_3 follows from cryoscopic data on the acid and its salts,[298] the diamagnetic properties of a number of its salts,[299] the crystal structure of the ammonium salt, $(NH_4)_2H_2P_2O_6$,[300] and Raman data.[301] That the structure involves a P—P bond is indicated by the formation of the acid and its salts only from materials containing P—P links (p. 644), by x-ray absorption edge data,[298] by crystal structure data,[300] and by the remarkable resistance of the hypophosphate to oxidation.

In aqueous solution, hypophosphoric acid is tetrabasic ($pk_{A_1}' = 2.2$, $pk_{A_2}' = 2.81$, $pk_{A_3}' = 7.27$, $pk_{A_4}' = 10.03$). Since the first two hydrogens are about equally easy to remove, it is not surprising that the most common salts are of the type $M_2^IH_2P_2O_6$. Salts of the types $M_3^IHP_2O_6$ and $M_4^IP_2O_6$ are also obtainable. Hypophosphoric and

[295] A. D. Mitchell: *J. Chem. Soc.*, **123**, 2241 (1923).

[296] R. O. Griffith, A. McKeown, and R. P. Taylor: *Trans. Faraday Soc.*, **36**, 752 (1940).

[297] R. O. Griffith and A. McKeown: *Trans. Faraday Soc.*, **29**, 611 (1933); **36**, 766 (1940).

[298] P. Nylén and O. Stelling: *Z. anorg. allgem. Chem.*, **212**, 169 (1933).

[299] F. Bell and S. Sugden: *J. Chem. Soc.*, **1933**, 48.

[300] B. Raistrick and E. Hobbs: *Nature*, **164**, 113 (1949).

[301] J. Gupta and A. K. Majumdar: *J. Indian Chem. Soc.*, **19**, 286 (1942).

pyrophosphoric acids are roughly comparable in strength. Aqueous solutions of the acid disproportionate as

$$H_4P_2O_6 + H_2O \rightleftharpoons H_3PO_3 + H_3PO_4.$$

and this reaction is characteristic of acidified salt solutions as well. In neutral or alkaline solutions, the salts are stable. However, hypophosphate does not exchange radioactive phosphorus with phosphate.[302] The potassium salts are quite soluble, the sodium and lithium salts are only moderately soluble, and the normal thorium and silver salts are quantitatively insoluble, the former even in 6 *N* acid. The couples

$$H_4P_2O_6 + 2H_2O \rightleftharpoons 2H_3PO_4 + 2H^+ + 2e^- \qquad E^0_{298} = \text{ca.} \quad 0.8 \text{ volt}$$

and

$$2H_3PO_3 \rightleftharpoons H_4P_2O_6 + 2H^+ + 2e^- \qquad = \text{ca.} \ -0.4 \text{ volt}$$

emphasize the facts that even powerful reducing agents do not convert phosphoric acid into hypophosphoric acid and that treatment of phosphorous acid with a sufficiently powerful oxidizing agent to give hypophosphoric acid will give phosphoric acid instead. The halogens and dichromate are without effect upon hypophosphates. Permanganate oxidizes them very slowly.

Hypophosphoric acid can be obtained in solution from the lead salt by action of hydrogen sulfide or from water-soluble salts by action of hydrogen-cycle cation exchangers and can be crystallized by vacuum evaporation as a 2-hydrate melting at 70°C. It is more common to prepare the disodium salt, $Na_2H_2P_2O_6 \cdot 6H_2O$. Oxidation of red phosphorus with sodium hypochlorite[303] or sodium chlorite[304] in alkaline media is most convenient, but the yields are low (25 to 42%). Other methods involve hydrolysis of the compound P_2I_4 (p. 629), hydrolysis of phosphorus trihalides in the presence of iodine, air oxidation of white phosphorus in contact with sodium acetate solution, and anodic oxidation of copper phosphide in sulfuric acid solution. Reaction of the polymeric dioxide (p. 636) with water gives phosphorus and orthophosphoric acids rather than hypophosphoric acid.

The Phosphoric Acids (HPO_3, $H_5P_3O_{10}$, $H_4P_2O_7$, H_3PO_4). Few subjects have received more literature attention in the past hundred-odd years than the phosphoric acids and their salts. Yet it is only in the past few years that the true characteristics of these materials have been

[302] G. H. Quinty: Doctoral Dissertation, University of Illinois (1951).
[303] J. Probst: *Z. anorg. allgem. Chem.*, **179**, 155 (1929).
[304] E. Leininger and T. Chulski: *J. Am. Chem. Soc.*, **71**, 2385 (1949).

made apparent and systematic relations among them established. Much of the difficulty has been imposed by the existence of so-called condensed or polyphosphates, the compositions and structures of which have not been well established. These are materials which are derived from more than a single mole of anhydride (taken as P_2O_5) and embrace the metaphosphates, triphosphates, and pyrophosphates. Much work has dealt with the salts themselves rather than with the acids, but conclusions reached for the salts can be extended in certain cases to the acids. A number of important summaries may be consulted with advantage.[305–311]

All structures of the phosphoric acids and their salts are based upon PO_4 tetrahedra. It is only in the orthophosphate, however, that discrete PO_4 groups are found. In the pyro- and triphosphates, two and three such tetrahedra, respectively, are attached by shared oxygens, as shown in Table 15·20. The metaphosphates are even more complex. Although metaphosphoric acid is written as a monomer in Table 15·20, neither the acid nor its salts are ever monomeric. The simplest metaphosphates are the trimer and the tetramer in which the sharing of oxygen atoms between tetrahedra gives the cyclic arrangements

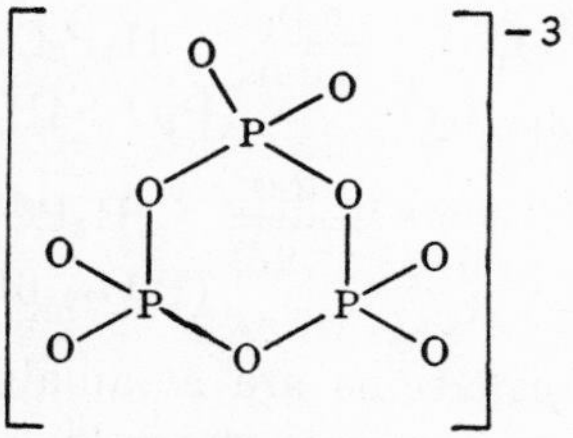

trimetaphosphate 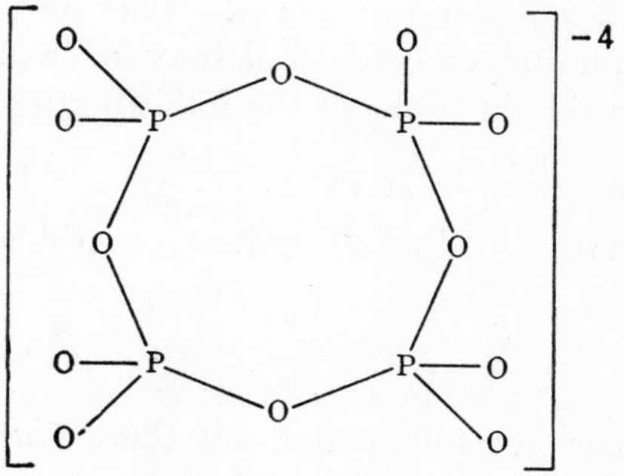 **tetrametaphosphate**

In addition, there appear to be higher polymers, $(PO_3)_x^{-x}$, of indeterminate molecular weights in which linking of PO_4 tetrahedra continues.

[305] H. Terrey: *Ann. Reports,* **34,** 115 (1937).
[306] K. Karbe and G. Jander: *Kolloid-Beihefte,* **54,** 1 (1943).
[307] O. T. Quimby: *Chem. Revs.,* **40,** 141 (1947).
[308] L. F. Audrieth and O. F. Hill: *J. Chem. Education,* **25,** 80 (1948).
[309] E. P. Partridge: *Chem. Eng. News,* **27,** 214 (1949).
[310] B. Topley: *Quart. Revs.,* **3,** 345 (1949).
[311] L. F. Audrieth and R. N. Bell: *Inorganic Syntheses,* Vol. III, p. 85. McGraw-Hill Book Co., New York (1950).

The condensed phosphates are therefore related to each other and to the orthophosphate by processes of polyanionic aggregation[308, 311] which can be summarized by the equations:

$$2HPO_4^{-2} \rightarrow P_2O_7^{-4} + H_2O \qquad H^+:PO_4^{-3} = 1.00$$
$$\text{(i.e., } 2PO_4^{-3} + 2H^+ \rightarrow P_2O_7^{-4} + H_2O)$$
$$H_2PO_4^- + 2HPO_4^{-2} \rightarrow P_3O_{10}^{-5} + 2H_2O \qquad = 1.33$$
$$\text{(i.e., } 3PO_4^{-3} + 4H^+ \rightarrow P_3O_{10}^{-5} + 2H_2O)$$
$$xH_2PO_4^- \rightarrow (PO_3)_x^{-x} + xH_2O \qquad = 2.00$$
$$\text{(i.e., } xPO_4^{-3} + 2xH^+ \rightarrow xPO_3^- + xH_2O)$$

Unlike comparable anionic aggregation with molybdates, tungstates, etc. (pp. 276–277), such reactions do not occur when orthophosphate solutions are acidified, but they certainly take place at elevated temperatures, where they have preparative significance, and probably take place in concentrated phosphoric acid solutions.

As shown in the preceding sections, phosphates (unlike nitrates) are very poor oxidizing agents. A summary of analytical procedures is given by Audrieth and Bell.[311]

THE PHOSPHORIC ACIDS. The phosphoric acids are hydrates of phosphorus(V) oxide and may be related to each other and to the anhydride in terms of the following hydration-dehydration scheme:

$$\underset{(P_4O_{10})}{P_4O_{10}} \underset{-H_2O}{\overset{H_2O}{\rightleftharpoons}} \underset{(P_4O_{10}\cdot 2H_2O)_x}{(HPO_3)_x} \underset{-H_2O}{\overset{H_2O}{\rightleftharpoons}} \underset{(P_4O_{10}\cdot 3.33H_2O)}{H_5P_3O_{10}} \underset{-H_2O}{\overset{H_2O}{\rightleftharpoons}} \underset{(P_4O_{10}\cdot 4H_2O)}{H_4P_2O_7} \underset{-H_2O}{\overset{H_2O}{\rightleftharpoons}} \underset{(P_4O_{10}\cdot 6H_2O)}{H_3PO_4}$$

It does not follow that all these transformations are attainable in practice, but treatment of the anhydride with excess water gives the completely hydrated orthophosphoric acid.

Titrations with alkali show that in aqueous solution all the phosphoric acids, regardless of their compositions, contain one strongly acidic hydrogen atom per phosphorus atom.[312] This hydrogen is neutralized at pH 3.8 to 4.2. Other hydrogen atoms are less strongly acidic, but all may be neutralized in salt formation. Ionization constant data are available for the ortho ($k_{A_1}' = 7.5 \times 10^{-3}$, $k_{A_2}' = 6.2 \times 10^{-8}$, $k_{A_3}' = 10^{-13}$ at 25°C.) and the pyro ($k_{A_1}' = 1.4 \times 10^{-1}$, $k_{A_2}' = 1.1 \times 10^{-2}$, $k_{A_3}' = 2.1 \times 10^{-7}$, $k_{A_4}' = 4.1 \times 10^{-10}$ at 18°C.)

312 J. R. Van Wazer and K. A. Holst: *J. Am. Chem. Soc.*, **72**, 639 (1950).

acids. Triphosphoric acid appears to be somewhat stronger than orthophosphoric acid. It appears that in the highly condensed phosphates there is a single weakly acidic hydrogen atom at each end of a chain of PO_4 groups.[312] These data, in conjunction with the knowledge that PO_4 tetrahedra are present, are indicative that no branched chain materials exist in solution.

The so-called strong phosphoric acids, i.e., those containing more phosphorus(V) oxide than that corresponding to the ortho acid (above 72.4%), are mixtures of the condensed acids. Analysis of such mixtures has shown[313] the relative quantities of ortho-, pyro-, tri-, and

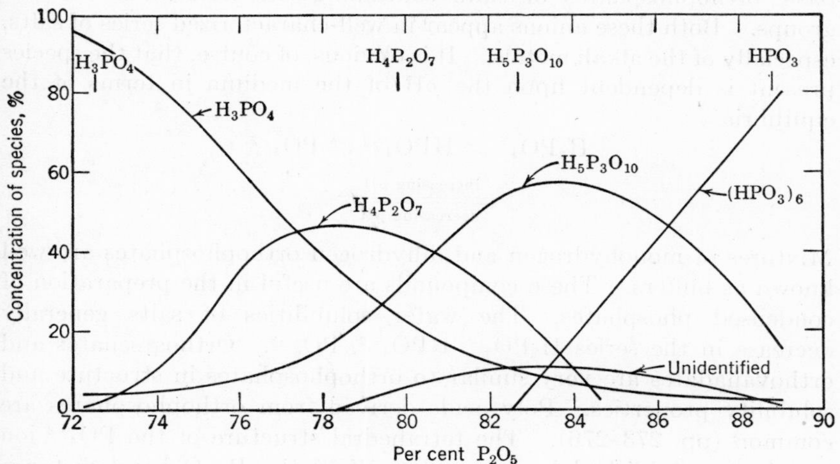

FIG. 15·3. Compositions of the "strong" phosphoric acids. (Adapted from R. N. Bell: *Ind. Eng. Chem.*, **40,** 1464 [1948].)

"hexameta"- phosphoric acids, together with an unknown component, to vary with the anhydride content as indicated in Figure 15·3. It is apparent that, unlike the fuming sulfuric acids or oleums (p. 541), the strong acids of phosphorus cannot be regarded as mixtures of the anhydride and the ortho acid.

The ortho acid may be obtained as a crystalline solid melting at 42.35° to 42.45°C. by removing water from concentrated (syrupy) orthophosphoric acid at reduced pressures and low temperatures.[314] The pyro acid may be prepared as crystalline solid melting at 61°C. by spontaneous crystallization of a polyphosphoric acid mixture contain-

[313] R. N. Bell: *Ind. Eng. Chem.*, **40,** 1464 (1948).

[314] A. G. Weber and G. B. King: *Inorganic Syntheses*, Vol. I, p. 101. McGraw-Hill Book Co., New York (1939).

ing 79.8 ± 0.2% phosphorus(V) oxide.[315] Dehydration of orthophosphoric acid or treatment of the anhydride with an appropriate quantity of water gives the meta acids, but they cannot be isolated as pure substances. Aqueous solutions of the various acids are obtained by treating the appropriate salts with hydrogen-cycle cation exchangers[312] or by action of hydrochloric acid or hydrogen sulfide on suitable heavy metal salts.

THE ORTHOPHOSPHATES. Normal orthophosphates are difficult to obtain because of the low acidity of the third hydrogen atom in the acid. It is probable that precipitation reactions usually yield either basic orthophosphates or salts containing the HPO_4^{-2} or $H_2PO_4^-$ groups. Both these anions appear in well-characterized series of salts, especially of the alkali metals. It is obvious, of course, that the species present is dependent upon the *p*H of the medium in terms of the equilibria

$$H_2PO_4^- \rightleftharpoons HPO_4^{-2} \rightleftharpoons PO_4^{-3}$$

$$\underset{\text{decreasing } p\text{H}}{\overset{\text{increasing } p\text{H}}{\rightleftharpoons}}$$

Mixtures of monohydrogen and dihydrogen orthophosphates are well known as buffers. These compounds are useful in the preparation of condensed phosphates. The water solubilities of salts generally decrease in the series $H_2PO_4^-$, HPO_4^{-2}, PO_4^{-3}. Orthoarsenates and orthovanadates are very similar to orthophosphates in structure and solubility properties. Poly acids derived from orthophosphates are common (pp. 273–276). The tetrahedral structure of the PO_4^{-3} ion has been established by x-ray data,[316, 317] the P—O bond distance being 1.55 A. In the acid anions, e.g., $H_2PO_4^-$, hydrogen bonds link the PO_4 tetrahedra.[316]

THE PYRO- AND TRIPHOSPHATES. These are apparently the only simple linear polyphosphates known, no concrete evidence for tetraphosphates, etc., having appeared. Pyrophosphates in general belong to two series, $M_2^IH_2P_2O_7$ and $M_4^IP_2O_7$. Of the normal salts, only those of the alkali metals are water soluble. Relations between the two series are again *p*H dependent. Normal salts are especially characteristic of tetrapositive metals (e.g., Th, Zr, Hf). The crystal structures of such salts[318] are in agreement with the concept of two PO_4 tetrahedra linked through oxygen. The pyrophosphate ion com-

[315] J. E. Malowan: *Inorganic Syntheses*, Vol. III, p. 96. McGraw-Hill Book Co., New York (1950).

[316] J. West: *Z. Krist.*, **74,** 306 (1930).

[317] L. Helmholz: *J. Chem. Phys.*, **4,** 316 (1936).

[318] G. R. Levi and G. Peyronel: *Z. Krist.*, **92,** 190 (1935).

plexes many metal ions.[319, 320] In solution, pyrophosphates hydrolyze slowly to orthophosphates. Of the pyrophosphates the sodium compounds are most commonly prepared. The disodium salt forms either when sodium dihydrogen orthophosphate (NaH_2PO_4) is heated at 210°C. or when tetrasodium pyrophosphate is treated with acetic acid.[321] The tetrasodium salt is obtained when disodium hydrogen orthophosphate is heated at 500°C.[321]

Triphosphates are of the types, $M_5^IP_3O_{10}$ and $M^IM^{II}_2P_3O_{10}$, no acid salts having been described. The sodium salt, $Na_5P_3O_{10}{\cdot}6H_2O$, is most common. It is employed extensively in detergents. In solution it gives precipitates with many di-, tri-, etc., positive metal ions, but these precipitates are often soluble in excess triphosphate, suggesting complex formation.[320] The hydrated sodium salt is conveniently prepared by hydrolysis of sodium trimetaphosphate with sodium hydroxide. Further hydrolysis to orthophosphate is very slow. The anhydrous sodium salt exists in two forms. The stable phase, $Na_5P_3O_{10}$-I, is formed when a mixture of one mole of sodium dihydrogen orthophosphate and two moles of disodium hydrogen orthophosphate is heated at 540° to 580°C.[321] A metastable phase, $Na_5P_3O_{10}$-II, forms when the same mixture is heated at 850° to 900°C., annealed at 550°C., and cooled rapidly in air.[321] The two forms have different x-ray diffraction patterns.[322]

The phase relations existing among the anhydrous sodium polyphosphates at elevated temperatures are shown in Figure 15·4.[322]

THE METAPHOSPHATES. Inasmuch as the only really systematic studies of metaphosphates deal with the sodium compounds, this discussion is restricted to sodium salts. The multitudinous sodium metaphosphates described in the literature appear to be either simple cyclic trimers or tetramers, insoluble salts, or high-molecular-weight glasses. These compounds have been described by a variety of names, but in the absence of any exact knowledge of the molecular complexities of the materials no systematic nomenclature is possible. That suggested by Partridge[309] and summarized in Table 15·21 is widely accepted. The sodium metaphosphates are the final products in the dehydration (or aggregation) of sodium dihydrogen orthophosphate or disodium dihydrogen pyrophosphate, and their natures are entirely dependent upon the thermal treatment employed. The general rela-

[319] L. B. Rogers and C. A. Reynolds: *J. Am. Chem. Soc.*, **71**, 2081 (1949).

[320] J. R. Van Wazer and D. A. Campanella: *J. Am. Chem. Soc.*, **72**, 655 (1950).

[321] R. N. Bell: *Inorganic Syntheses*, Vol. III, pp. 98–106. McGraw-Hill Book Co., New York (1950).

[322] E. P. Partridge, V. Hicks, and G. W. Smith: *J. Am. Chem. Soc.*, **63**, 454 (1941).

tionships existing among these materials are summarized in Table 15·22.[323]

1. CYCLIC METAPHOSPHATES. Sodium trimetaphosphate exists in three polymorphic forms, $NaPO_3$-I′ and $NaPO_3$-I″ being unstable

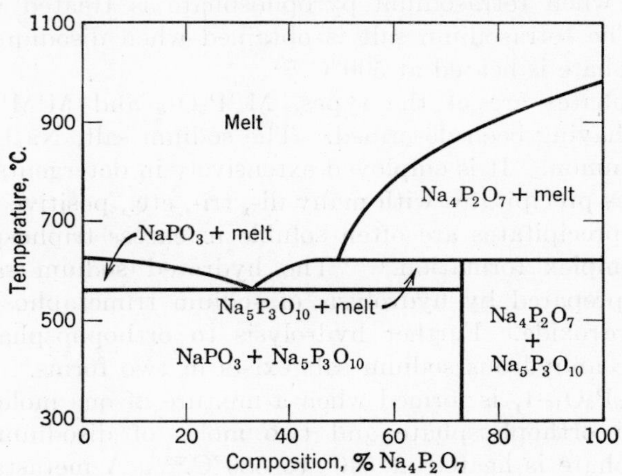

FIG. 15·4. Phase relations in the system $NaPO_3$–$Na_4P_2O_7$. (Adapted from E. P. Partridge, V. Hicks, and G. W. Smith: *J. Am. Chem. Soc.*, **63**, 454 [1941].)

with respect to $NaPO_3$-I (Knorre's salt) as shown in Table 15·22. The stable form is the one commonly prepared.[322] All three forms are readily soluble in water, and the 6-hydrate is readily crystallized from

TABLE 15·21

NOMENCLATURE OF THE SODIUM METAPHOSPHATES

Usual Formula	Common Name	Preferred Name	Preferred Formula
$(NaPO_3)_6$	sodium hexametaphosphate (Graham's salt)	sodium (1:1) phosphate glass	Na_2O (1:1) P_2O_5 glass
$(NaPO_3)_3$	sodium trimetaphosphate	sodium metaphosphate-I	$NaPO_3$-I
		sodium metaphosphate-I′	$NaPO_3$-I′
		sodium metaphosphate-I″	$NaPO_3$-I″
$NaPO_3$	Maddrell's salt	sodium metaphosphate-II	$NaPO_3$-II
		sodium metaphosphate-III	$NaPO_3$-III
$NaPO_3$	Kurrol's salt	sodium metaphosphate-IV	$NaPO_3$-IV

aqueous solution on addition of sodium chloride.[322] Aqueous solutions possess no calcium-sequestering power (p. 653). They undergo slow hydrolysis to orthophosphate *via* triphosphate. Conversion to tri-

[323] R. W. Liddell: *J. Am. Chem. Soc.*, **71**, 207 (1949).

TABLE 15·22

RELATIONS AMONG THE SODIUM METAPHOSPHATES

$Na_2H_2P_2O_7$ —270° C.→ $NaPO_3$—III —400–425° C.→ $NaPO_3$—II —475–500° C.→ $NaPO_3$—I —627.6° C.→ Melt

$Na_2H_2P_2O_7$ —300° C. (Water vapor)→ $NaPO_3$—II

Melt —Cool slowly→ $NaPO_3$—I

Melt —Kurrol seed→ $NaPO_3$—IV → $NaPO_3$—I

Melt —550–600° C. 375–525° C.→ $NaPO_3$—I″ → $NaPO_3$—I

Melt —500–525° C.→ $NaPO_3$—I′ → $NaPO_3$—I

$NaPO_3$—I′ —375° C.→ $NaPO_3$—I″

Melt —Chill→ Glass

Glass —300° C. or above→ $NaPO_3$—II

phosphate is rapid in 1% sodium hydroxide at 100°C. Ions such as zinc, silver, or barium are not precipitated by the trimetaphosphate. Evidence that the material is trimeric is derived from cryoscopic studies,[324] conductance data,[325] titration studies,[312] and the existence of salts of the type $NaM^{II}P_3O_9$. That the structure is cyclic is supported by some crystallographic evidence.[310]

Although not indicated in Tables 15·21 and 15·22 a water-soluble sodium metaphosphate which physical data[324, 325] show to be a tetramer has been prepared by reacting hexagonal phosphorus(V) oxide (p. 637) with sodium carbonate 10-hydrate.[310] The 4- and 10-hydrates are crystalline compounds. The tetrametaphosphate is hydrolyzed in alkaline solutions to pyro- and orthophosphates and possibly to triphosphate as well. It is of interest that crystals of aluminum metaphosphate are made up of Al^{+3} and cyclic $P_4O_{12}^{-4}$ ions.[326] A copper(II) derivative has been described.

2. INSOLUBLE METAPHOSPHATES. The initial dehydration of sodium dihydrogen orthophosphate yields, as temperature is increased, two water-insoluble metaphosphates designated, respectively, as $NaPO_3$–III and $NaPO_3$–II. It is believed that the material referred to in the literature as Maddrell's salt is a mixture of $NaPO_3$–III and $NaPO_3$–II[309] although some prefer restricting Maddrell's salt to $NaPO_3$–II.[310] The two compounds appear to be very similar chemically and physically, but their x-ray diffraction patterns are different.[309] No structural data are available, but the materials are apparently highly polymerized.

The term Kurrol's salt has been applied rather loosely to all the insoluble sodium metaphosphates, although specifically it should be restricted to the fibrous crystalline material ($NaPO_3$–IV) obtained by seeding a metaphosphate melt at 550° to 600°C.[309] (Table 15·22). The existence of this material is now well established, although the fact that its formation occurs only under very limited conditions has prevented its preparation by many investigators. The material swells in contact with water and disperses to a highly viscous sol (or gel). The swelling rate is markedly catalyzed by metal ions, possibly because of ion exchange.[310] Gel character is lost on standing or boiling because of hydrolysis.

3. METAPHOSPHATE GLASSES. Rapid cooling of sodium metaphosphate melts (e.g., by pouring on a steel plate),[321] prevents devitrifica-

[324] P. Bonneman-Bémia; *Ann. chim.* [11], **16,** 395 (1941).
[325] C. W. Davies and C. B. Monk: *J. Chem. Soc.*, **1949,** 413.
[326] L. Pauling and J. Sherman: *Z. Krist.*, **96,** 481 (1937).

tion, and produces transparent, water-soluble glasses which crystallize on being reheated to 300°C. or above largely to $NaPO_3$–I but to a lesser extent to $NaPO_3$–II (Table 15·22). Glasses form whenever the $Na_2O:P_2O_5$ ratio is in the range 1:1 to 5:3, from which it is apparent that the composition is not necessarily exactly that of a metaphosphate. True sodium metaphosphate glass is sometimes called Graham's salt, and for many years the term hexametaphosphate was applied. It has been shown that discrete $(PO_3)_6^{-6}$ units are not present, indicating the inaccuracy of such a term. It is better to describe all the glasses in terms of the $Na_2O:P_2O_5$ ratio,[309] Graham's salt then becoming sodium (1:1) phosphate glass (Table 15·21).

The degree of aggregation is dependent upon the exact conditions of preparation and upon the exact composition. Dialysis measurements upon aqueous "solutions" of sodium metaphosphate glasses[306] indicate molecular weights in the range of 1000 to 8000. Values up to 13,000 are indicated by sedimentation studies,[327] and end-group titration data[328] and viscosity data[329] are consistent with highly polymeric conditions. Solubility fractionation by the addition of organic solvents such as acetone[328] effects separation into materials of a variety of ionic weights. In glasses approaching the $5Na_2O{\cdot}3P_2O_5$ composition, there is definite evidence for the presence of crystalline pyro- and triphosphates.[328] The glasses are apparently made up of PO_4 tetrahedra and amount to condensation polymers.[330] In the composition range from vitreous P_4O_{10} to the 1:1 glass, the materials have three-dimensional structures which vanish on dissolution. When the $Na_2O:P_2O_5$ ratio exceeds one, the polymers are straight chain.[330]

The 1:1 glasses behave as high-temperature acids in reactions with metal oxides,[331] sulfides,[331] and fluorides[332] (pp. 333–334). Another striking characteristic of Graham's salt is the ability of its aqueous solutions to complex ("sequester") metal ions. This is of particular importance with the ordinarily difficultly complexed calcium ion and is of course responsible for the widespread use of the metaphosphate as a water-softening agent. Although no complexes have been isolated as such and the true natures of the species present in solution have not

[327] O. Lamm and H. Malmgren: *Z. anorg. allgem. Chem.*, **245**, 103 (1940); **252**, 256 (1944).

[328] J. R. Van Wazer: *J. Am. Chem. Soc.*, **72**, 647 (1950).

[329] *Ibid.*, 906.

[330] *Ibid.*, 644.

[331] L. F. Audrieth and T. Moeller: *J. Chem. Education*, **20**, 219 (1943).

[332] O. F. Hill and L. F. Audrieth: *J. Phys. Colloid Chem.*, **54**, 690 (1950).

been established with absolute certainty, polarographic and pH titration data[320] indicate chelation as represented by the structure

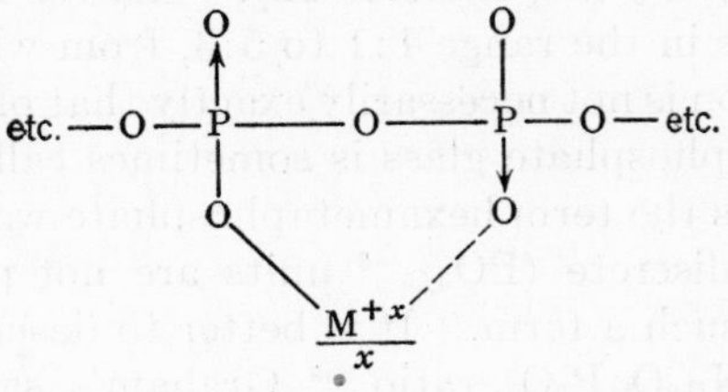

etc.—O—P(→O)(—O)—O—P(O)(→O)—O—etc., with both lower O atoms coordinated to $\frac{M^{+x}}{x}$

Dissociation constants for a number of such complexes, including those of the alkali metals, have been evaluated for a particular glass.[320] It is of interest that the other non-cyclic polymeric sodium metaphosphates ($NaPO_3$–II, $NaPO_3$–III, $NaPO_3$–IV) also complex metal ions. The physical properties of aqueous solutions of sodium metaphosphate glass are described by Van Wazer.[333]

Phosphorus-sulfur compounds

Phosphorus-sulfur compounds include the phosphorus sulfides, phosphorus oxysulfide, the phosphorus(V) sulfohalides (pp. 630–632), the thiophosphoric acids, and the ammonothiophosphoric acids (p. 660).

Phosphorus Sulfides. The older literature notwithstanding, there appear to be only four phosphorus sulfides.[334] They are the materials P_4S_3, P_4S_5, P_4S_7, and P_4S_{10}, the physical properties of which are summarized in Table 15·23. Except for the last (P_4S_{10}), these compounds are obviously not the analogs of the oxides (p. 635). Although data are lacking on the structures of these compounds, Pernert and Brown[334] believe the following structures to be consistent with the general properties of the compounds P_4S_3, P_4S_7, and P_4S_{10}:

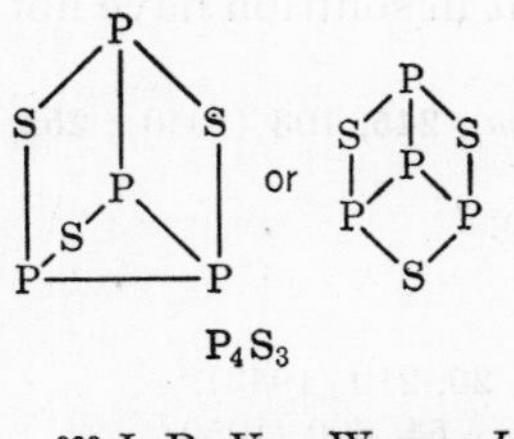

[Structures: P_4S_3 (two alternative forms, "or"), P_4S_7, P_4S_{10}]

P_4S_3 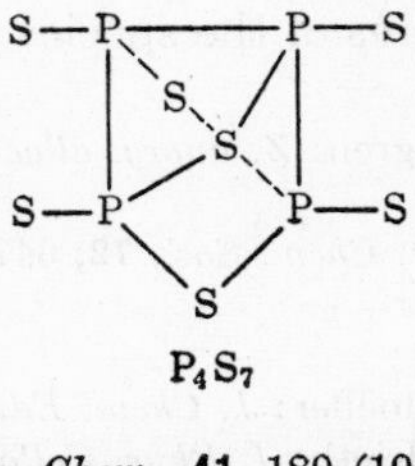 P_4S_7 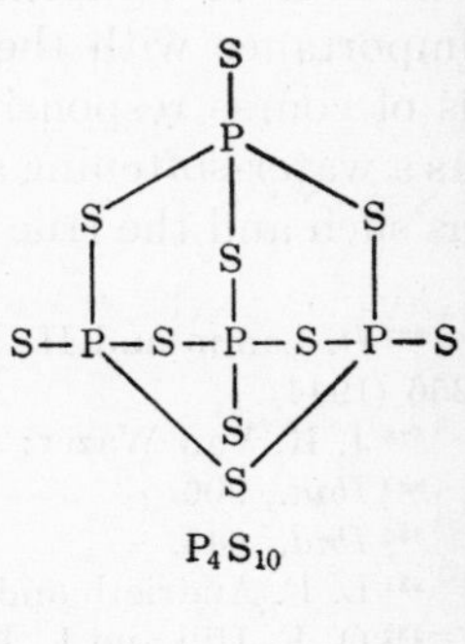 P_4S_{10}

[333] J. R. Van Wazer: *Ind. Eng. Chem.*, **41**, 189 (1949).
[334] J. C. Pernert and J. H. Brown: *Chem. Eng. News*, **27**, 2143 (1949).

The P_4S_{10} structure is analogous to those of P_4O_{10} (p. 637) and $P_4S_4O_6$ (p. 657). These structures are based upon tetrahedral phosphorus atoms. Except for the compound P_4S_{10}, they should be regarded as no more than provisional. The presence of four phosphorus atoms to the molecule in each is probably significant.

All the phosphorus sulfides are yellow crystalline compounds. The formulas given are consistent with molecular weights as determined from vapor densities or the properties of benzene or carbon disulfide

TABLE 15·23
PHYSICAL CHARACTERISTICS OF PHOSPHORUS SULFIDES

Property	P_4S_3	P_4S_5	P_4S_7	P_4S_{10}
Color				
solid	yellow	yellow	nearly white	yellow
liquid (300°C.)	brownish-yellow	(dec.)	yellow	red-brown
Melting point, °C.	173–174.5	170–220 (dec.)	305–310	286–290
Boiling point, °C.	407–408	(dec.)	523	513–515
Density, grams/cc. at 17°C.	2.03	2.17 (25°C.)	2.19	2.09
Solubility, grams/100 grams solvent	....	....	....	....
CS_2 (0°C.)	27.0	....	0.005	0.182
CS_2 (17°C.)	100	~10	0.029	0.222
C_6H_6 (17°C.)	2.5	....	....	....
C_6H_6 (80°C.)	11.1	....	....	....

solutions. Vapor density data indicate decomposition at elevated temperatures. All the sulfides are soluble in aqueous alkalies with reaction to form hydrogen, phosphine, hypophosphite, phosphite, orthophosphate, and sulfide in varying proportions.[334, 335] The phosphorus sulfides are useful in converting organic oxy compounds (e.g., alcohols, ketones, etc.) into the corresponding sulfur analogs. Phosphorus sesquisulfide or tetraphosphorus trisulfide (P_4S_3) is a universal component of "strike-anywhere" matches. It oxidizes readily at elevated temperatures and in solution in carbon disulfide. Sulfur converts it to the higher sulfides P_4S_7 and P_4S_{10}. Tetraphosphorus pentasulfide (P_4S_5) is poorly characterized. Tetraphosphorus heptasulfide (P_4S_7) is the most readily hydrolyzed of the four compounds and is particularly effective in the preparation of organic sulfur compounds.[334] Phosphorus(V) sulfide or phosphorus pentasulfide (P_4S_{10}) is readily hydrolyzed by water to orthophosphoric acid and hydrogen sulfide. It is useful chiefly in the preparation of flotation agents and organic

[335] W. D. Treadwell and C. Beeli: *Helv. Chim. Acta,* **18,** 1161 (1935).

sulfur compounds. Its conversion to phosphorus(V) sulfohalides has been mentioned (p. 632).

The phosphorus sulfides are prepared in general by direct reaction of the elements or from the sesquisulfide. Direct reaction of excess red phosphorus with sulfur in an atmosphere of carbon dioxide or in a vacuum at elevated temperatures, followed by extraction with carbon disulfide or distillation, yields the sesquisulfide. The compound P_4S_5 results when a carbon disulfide solution of the sesquisulfide and iodine is exposed to light. It is also formed together with P_4S_7 when a molten mixture of phosphorus and sulfur (2P:3S) is cooled slowly.[335] The compound P_4S_7 may be separated from this reaction mixture by extracting the more soluble compound P_4S_5 with carbon disulfide. It also forms when the sesquisulfide is reacted with iodine in carbon disulfide and, together with the compounds P_4S_3, when P_4S_5 undergoes thermal decomposition. Technical production of this compound in the pure state is quite recent.[334] The "pentasulfide" (P_4S_{10}) is obtained by the same procedure as the sesquisulfide, except that excess sulfur is employed. It is purified by recrystallization from carbon disulfide.

Arsenic forms three sulfides, As_4S_4 (realgar), As_4S_6 (orpiment), and As_2S_5 (perhaps As_4S_{10}). In the vapor state, the first of these has a "cradle" structure (p. 549)

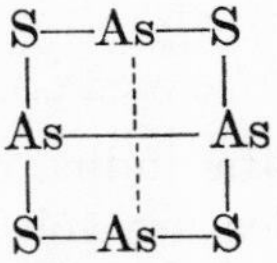

$$\begin{array}{ccccc} \mathrm{S} & - & \mathrm{As} & - & \mathrm{S} \\ | & & \vdots & & | \\ \mathrm{As} & - & - & - & \mathrm{As} \\ | & & \vdots & & | \\ \mathrm{S} & - & \mathrm{As} & - & \mathrm{S} \end{array}$$

with two arsenic atoms above and two below the plane of the four sulfur atoms (As—S = 2.23 A, As—As = 2.49 A, ∠As—S—As = 101°, ∠S—As—S = 93°).[336] The vapor of the compound As_4S_6 has the P_4O_6 (As_4O_6) structure[336] with As—S = 2.25 A, ∠As—S—As = 100°, ∠S—As—S = 114°. These sulfides give thioarsenites or thioarsenates with alkalies or soluble sulfides. Antimony gives the sulfides Sb_2S_3 (orange or black) and Sb_2S_5, which are soluble in sulfide ion but more metallic than the arsenic compounds. The only bismuth sulfide, Bi_2S_3, is definitely a metal sulfide.

Phosphorus Oxysulfide ($P_4S_4O_6$). Although an amorphous oxysulfide, $P_4S_3O_4$, results from oxidation of the sesquisulfide in an organic solvent, the only oxysulfide of phosphorus about which much is known

[336] C.-S. Lu and J. Donohue: *J. Am. Chem. Soc.*, **66**, 818 (1944).

is the compound $P_4S_4O_6$. This is a colorless compound (yellow when impure) melting at ca. 102°C. to a viscous liquid which boils at 295°C. The vapor is thermally stable, and its density corresponds closely to the formula given. Electron diffraction data[337] show the molecular structure of the vapor to be the same as that of the compound P_4O_{10}, oxygen atoms acting as bridges between phosphorus atoms. Pertinent bond distances are P—O 1.61 A, P—S 1.85 A, and P—P 2.85 A, and bond angles are O—P—O 101.5°, P—O—P 123.5°, and O—P—S 116.5°. Resonance accounts for shortening of the P—O and P—S bonds below single and double bond distances, respectively. The tetragonal crystals of the compound dissolve readily in organic solvents (e.g., CS_2, C_6H_6). The compound is deliquescent and hydrolyzes readily to metaphosphoric acid and hydrogen sulfide. The original method of preparation[338] by the violent reaction of phosphorus(III) oxide and sulfur in a sealed tube at 160°C. is much less convenient than a newer procedure[334] involving direct reaction of the oxide P_4O_{10} with the sulfide P_4S_{10} at 400° to 500°C. The product distills from the reaction mixture and is purified by subsequent distillations.

Thiophosphoric Acids and Their Salts. Fusion of sodium metaphosphate glass with sodium sulfide yields the monothioorthophosphate Na_3PO_3S by an acid-base reaction.[339] From solution, this material yields salts of the type $NaM^{II}PO_3S \cdot 8H_2O$ (M^{II} = Ca, Sr, Ba),[340] but addition of hydrochloric acid does not give the free acid. The acid H_3PO_3S, obtained by decomposition of aqueous solutions of the acid $H_3PO_2S_2$, is fairly stable (10% decomposition at −2°C. in 18 weeks) and may be concentrated to an oily liquid (84% H_3PO_3S) by vacuum evaporation at 0°C.[340] Reaction of phosphorus pentasulfide with sodium hydroxide solution saturated with hydrogen sulfide yields a mixture of thiophosphates from which the pure salt Na_3PO_3S can be separated by dissolution in 10% sodium sulfide solution at 20°C. and crystallization at 4°C.[340] This reaction also yields dithio-, trithio-, and tetrathioorthophosphates, all of which can be recovered by appropriate fractionation.[340] The salts $Na_3PO_2S_2 \cdot 11H_2O$, $Na_3POS_3 \cdot 11H_2O$, $Ba_3(POS_3)_2 \cdot 6H_2O$, and $Ba_3(PS_4)_2 \cdot 12H_2O$ have been characterized. Heavy metal thiophosphates appear to be water insoluble. Treatment of the compound $Ba_3(PS_4)_2$ with sulfuric acid, removal of barium sulfate, and evacuation to remove hydrogen sulfide give a 2% solu-

[337] A. J. Stosick: *J. Am. Chem. Soc.*, **61**, 1130 (1939).
[338] T. E. Thorpe and A. E. Tutton: *J. Chem. Soc.*, **59**, 1023 (1891).
[339] E. Zintl and A. Bertram: *Z. anorg. allgem. Chem.*, **245**, 16 (1940).
[340] R. Klement: *Z. anorg. Chem.*, **253**, 237 (1947).

tion of the acid $H_3PO_2S_2$, which then hydrolyzes. Hydrolysis proceeds according to the scheme

$$PO_xS_y^{-3} + nH_2O \rightarrow PO_{x-n}S_{y-n}^{-3} + nH_2S$$

the ease of hydrolysis increasing with sulfur content. Monothioorthophosphates are stable in solution even above 80°C., but tetrathioorthophosphates hydrolyze above 10°C. The paper by Klement[340] summarizes other work on these compounds.

Arsenic and antimony sulfides form analogous compounds by reaction with aqueous sulfides and hydroxides.

Phosphorus-nitrogen compounds

Phosphorus-nitrogen compounds include the phosphorus nitrides, the phosphonitrilic halides (pp. 632–634), and the ammono derivatives of the various oxy and thio acids of phosphorus.

Phosphorus Nitrides. Reported phosphorus nitrides are those with compositions P_3N_5, P_2N_3 (or P_4N_6), and PN. The structures of these compounds have not been determined. The nitride P_3N_5 is a white solid which is hydrolyzed by water at 100°C. (or above) to ammonium phosphate and is converted by oxygen at 800°C. to nitrogen and phosphorus(V) oxide. It is resistant to attack by aqueous hydrochloric acid. This compound results when the addition compound $P_2S_5 \cdot 6NH_3$ is heated to red heat in ammonia.[341] The nitride $P_2N_3(P_4N_6)$ is a solid which decomposes thermally to nitrogen and the substance PN at 750°C. and hydrolyzes when heated with water to ammonium phosphite and phosphate. It is obtained by heating the imide $P_2(NH)_3$.[342] The nitride PN exists in two amorphous forms, α (red, stable, resistant to cold sulfuric acid) and β (yellow, decomposed by cold sulfuric acid). Dissociation occurs above 750°C., and at 800°C. it is converted to the nitride P_3N_5 by ammonia. In a closed heated tube, water converts the compound to ammonium phosphite, ammonium phosphate, and hydrogen. This nitride forms when the compound P_3N_5 is heated in a vacuum at 750°C.[343] or by combination of nitrogen with phosphorus on a tungsten filament at 1500° to 1800°C.[344]

Ammono- and Aquo-Ammono Derivatives of Oxy Acids of Phosphorus. Application of the concepts of the nitrogen system of compounds to the phosphorous and phosphoric acids yields a variety of ammono- and aquo-ammono derivatives some of which are summarized in

[341] A. Stock and B. Hoffmann: *Ber.*, **36**, 314 (1903).
[342] H. Moureu and G. Wetroff: *Bull. soc. chim.* [v], **4**, 918, 1839, 1850 (1937).
[343] H. Moureu and P. Rocquet: *Bull. soc. chim.* [v], **3**, 1801 (1936).
[344] H. Moureu and G. Wetroff: *Compt. rend.*, **207**, 915 (1938).

Tables 15·24, 15·25.[345, 346] Of these materials, only a few of the phosphoric acid derivatives need be discussed.

A number contain the PN^{+2} grouping and are referred to as phosphonitrilic compounds. These are hydrolysis or ammonolysis products of the phosphonitrilic halides (pp. 632–634). Similar aminolysis

TABLE 15·24

Nitrogen Derivatives of Phosphoric Acid

1. Aquo-Ammono Derivatives

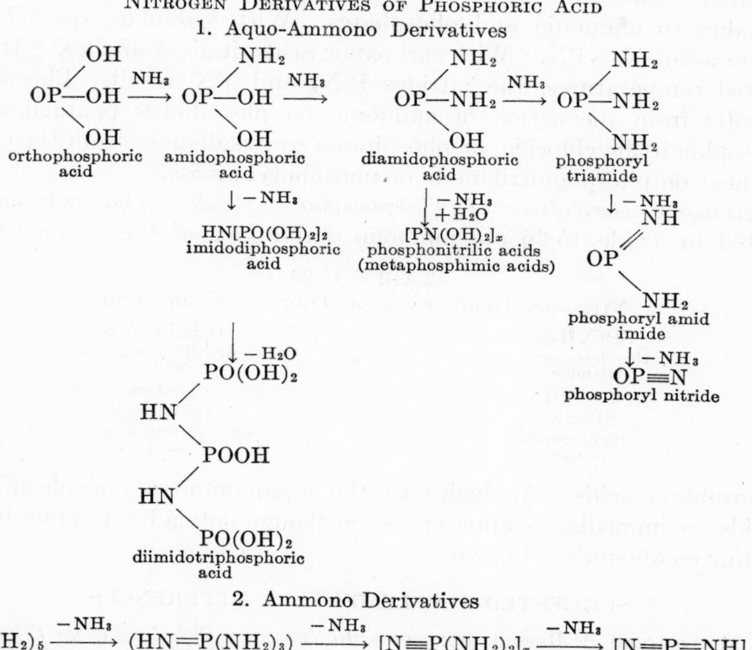

2. Ammono Derivatives

$$P(NH_2)_5 \xrightarrow{-NH_3} (HN{=}P(NH_2)_3) \xrightarrow{-NH_3} [N{\equiv}P(NH_2)_2]_x \xrightarrow{-NH_3} [N{\equiv}P{=}NH]_x$$

phosphorus pentamide; phosphorus(V) amide imide; phosphonitrilamide; phospham

TABLE 15·25

Nitrogen Derivatives of Phosphorous Acid

$$HOP(OH)_2 \xrightarrow{NH_3} H_2NP(OH)_2 \xrightarrow{NH_3} (H_2N)_2POH \xrightarrow{NH_3} P(NH_2)_3$$

phosphorous acid; amidophosphorous acid; diamidophosphorous acid; phosphorous triamide

$$P(NH_2)_3 \xrightarrow{-NH_3} HN{=}P(NH_2)_2 \xrightarrow{-NH_3} P_2(NH)_3$$

phosphorous(III) amide imide; diphosphorus triimide

products, $[PN(NHR)_2]_x$, are known also. In keeping with the polymeric characters of the phosphonitrilic halides, the phosphonitrilic acids and amides are polymers and probably possess structures com-

[345] L. F. Audrieth, R. Steinman, and A. D. F. Toy: *Chem. Revs.*, **32**, 99 (1943).

[346] L. F. Audrieth: *Chem. Eng. News*, **25**, 2552 (1947).

parable to those of the halides. The hydrogens in the phosphonitrilamides are only very weakly acidic. Aquo-ammono compounds containing the OP^{+3} group are in turn hydrolysis and ammonolysis products of the phosphoryl halides (pp. 629–632). Aminolysis products are known also.

Phospham, $[NPNH]_x$, is of some interest. It is a white, infusible powder, insoluble in water and dilute acids but decomposed by fused alkalies to ammonia and phosphates. With sodamide (p. 577), it gives a salt NaNPN. With carboxylic acids, it gives nitriles. At elevated temperatures, the nitrides P_3N_5 and PN result. Phospham results from the action of ammonia on phosphorus pentachloride, phosphonitrilic chloride, or phosphorus pentasulfide or from the effect of heat on phosphonitrilamide or phosphoryl amide.

Ammono Derivatives of Thiophosphoric Acids. The compounds listed in Table 15·26 are ammono derivatives of the various thiophosphoric acids. Analogies to the aquo-ammono phosphosphoric acids are immediately apparent, even though only a limited number of sulfur compounds is known.

TABLE 15·26

NITROGEN DERIVATIVES OF THIOPHOSPHORIC ACID

$SP(NH_2)_3$ thiophosphoryl triamide	$(HS)_3P{=}NH$ imidotrithiophosphoric acid
$\downarrow -NH_3$	$\downarrow -H_2S$
$SP{\equiv}N$ thiophosphoryl nitride	$(HS)_2P{\equiv}N$ dithiophosphonitrilic acid

SUGGESTED SUPPLEMENTARY REFERENCES

D. M. Yost and H. Russell, Jr.: *Systematic Inorganic Chemistry of the Fifth- and Sixth-Group Non-Metallic Elements*, Ch. 1–7, incl. Prentice-Hall, New York (1944).

N. V. Sidgwick: *The Chemical Elements and Their Compounds*, pp. 654–803. Clarendon Press, Oxford (1950).

A. F. Wells: *Structural Inorganic Chemistry*, 2nd Ed., Ch. XV, XVI. Clarendon Press, Oxford (1950).

W. M. Latimer: *The Oxidation States of the Elements and Their Potentials in Aqueous Solutions*, Ch. VII. Prentice-Hall, New York (1938).

CHAPTER 16

Periodic Group IVb
The Carbon Family

Except for germanium, all the elements in this family are comparatively familiar, although their abundances in the crust of the earth (C 0.032%, Si 27.72%, Ge 7×10^{-4}%, Sn 4×10^{-3}%, Pb 1.6×10^{-3}%) indicate that all but silicon are comparatively uncommon. Inasmuch as carbon is found in more compounds than all the other elements combined, the situation with carbon might appear anomalous if one failed to remember that the quantities of carbon present in the plant and animal kingdoms are tremendous. Tin and lead are less abundant than many of the so-called rare elements; yet the facts that they are found in concentrated natural deposits, that they are easily obtained in the metallic state, and that they have widespread uses both as such and in alloys and compounds make them familiar. Silicon, especially as the dioxide and its derivatives, is as important to the mineral world as carbon to the plant and animal worlds.

In this family, the trends in changes from non-metallic to metallic behaviors which so strikingly characterized the nitrogen family are even more pronounced. Carbon is definitely a non-metal; silicon is usually considered non-metallic although it possesses some metallic properties; germanium is more metallic than non-metallic; and tin and lead are true metals. These trends are associated, of course, with the reduced numbers of electrons in the outer shells and the reduced nuclear charges and increased sizes of the atoms. The properties of carbon are unique and impart to that element a chemistry which has no parallel. Silicon differs somewhat from germanium, tin, and lead, but the differences are much less striking. In keeping with the procedure adopted in the preceding three chapters, the family is discussed as a whole first, and then some specific phases of carbon and silicon chemistries are treated in detail. Material on tin and lead is included where appropriate.

FAMILY RELATIONSHIPS AMONG THE ELEMENTS

Numerical properties characterizing the members of the carbon family are summarized in Table 16·1. Increases in atomic weight and

TABLE 16·1
NUMERICAL PROPERTIES OF CARBON FAMILY ELEMENTS

Property	Carbon	Silicon	Germanium	Tin	Lead
Atomic number	6	14	32	50	82
Outer electron configuration	$2s^2 2p^2$	$3s^2 3p^2$	$4s^2 4p^2$	$5s^2 5p^2$	$6s^2 6p^2$
Mass numbers, stable isotopes	12, 13	28, 29, 30	70, 72, 73, 74, 76	112, 114, 115, 116, 117, 118, 119, 120, 122, 124	204, 206 207, 208
Atomic weight	12.010	28.06	72.60	118.70	207.21
Density of solid at 20°C., grams/cc.	3.51* 2.22‡	2.33	5.36	7.31† 5.75§	11.34
Atomic volume of solid, cc.	3.42*	12.04	13.55	16.23†	18.27
Melting point, °C.	ca. 3570	1414	958.5	231.8	327.5
Boiling point, °C.	3470 (subl.)	2355	....	2362	1755
Heat of sublimation, kcal./gram atom	ca. 170	85	....	78	47.5
Covalent radius, A	0.77	1.17	1.22	1.40	1.46
Ionization potential, ev	11.264	8.149	8.13	7.32	7.415
Electronegativity	2.5	1.8	1.7	1.7	
Crystal radii, A					
M^{-4}	2.60	2.71	2.72	2.94	
M^{+2}					1.32
M^{+4}	0.15	0.41	0.53	0.71	0.84
Standard potential, E^0_{298}, volts					
$M + 2H_2O \rightleftharpoons MO_2 + 4H^+ + 4e^-$	....	0.84	ca. 0.3	....	....
$M \rightleftharpoons M^{+2} + 2e^-$	....	....	....	0.136	0.126

* Diamond. † White tin. ‡ Graphite. § Gray tin.

atomic number are again paralleled by increases in density, atomic volume, and atomic and ionic sizes. The decreasing melting points apparent among the heaviest members of the nitrogen family (Table 15·1) characterize the entire carbon family and are paralleled by decreasing boiling points and heats of sublimation. These factors indicate that the strength of binding in the elemental solids decreases with increasing atomic weight or size, a characteristic which is not uncommon among the metals. Three-dimensional covalent bonding is at a maximum with carbon and decreases with increasing atomic weight. Fusion or vaporization would require rupture of some or all of these bonds and would thus be most difficult with carbon. The melting and boiling points of the elements of the carbon family are notably higher than those of either the boron (Table 17·1) or nitrogen (Table 15·1) families because of the tendencies of the elements in the last two families to form discrete molecules rather than giant molecules.

That the outermost electronic levels in the atoms of these elements are effectively half filled imparts certain unique properties. The stable inert gas atom configurations are still of importance in this family in governing the behavior of its members. However, gain of sufficient electrons to achieve such structures is energetically impossible for all the elements except possibly carbon. Even with carbon, only an extremely electropositive element could form a bond with any appreciable ionic character (p. 208). Although certain of the metal carbides are classified as salt-like or ionic (pp. 697–698), the bonding present is almost invariably predominantly covalent. Even covalent structures containing these elements in the formally -4 oxidation state essential to the inert gas arrangement are uncommon except for carbon, where the simple hydride (CH_4) is perhaps the best-characterized example. Because of decreasing electronegativities, such an oxidation state would become increasingly difficult to attain as atomic weight increases in the family. Indeed, it is doubtful that the state really exists with lead or even tin. Supporting numerical data are lacking, but general observations show this to be true. The reluctance of these elements to assume negative oxidation states is merely a continuation of the general trend already noted in the VIIb, VIb, and Vb families and is another evidence of increase in metallic character as the outer electron population decreases.

As regards positive oxidation states, the reduced electronegativities, particularly of the heaviest members of the family, indicate this possibility clearly. Bonds between the heavier elements and the more electronegative elements show considerable ionic character (p. 208). For carbon, however, the most ionic bond, the C—F bond, is only 44% ionic in terms of Pauling's treatment (p. 206). Arrangement of the outermost electrons as ns^2np^2 suggests the existence of both $+2$ and $+4$ oxidation states, corresponding respectively to the involvement of the two p electrons and all the electrons. The positive two state occurs because of the presence of the inert pair (p. 177). This condition is seldom found in carbon because of the tendency of the small atoms of that element to saturate themselves covalently, but it becomes increasingly important with increasing atomic size. Although uncommon in silicon and strongly reducing in character in germanium, the state is important in tin and common in lead. Dipositive tin and lead are both known as ionic species in polar solvents. The donor characteristics of the elements in this oxidation state are unimportant, but they do behave as acceptors.

In the tetrapositive state, all these elements give predominantly covalent compounds and are necessarily more acidic than in any lower oxidation state. As was true in the oxygen and nitrogen families, attainment of this state becomes increasingly difficult as atomic weight increases, probably because of the enhanced stability of the inert pair. This is reflected not only in the oxidation potentials for the M(0)–M(IV) couples listed in Table 16·1 but also in the potentials for the M(II)–M(IV) couples as given in Table 16·2. Because of

TABLE 16·2
RELATIONS BETWEEN THE +2 AND +4 OXIDATION STATES

Couple	E^0_{298}, volts Ge	Sn	Pb
1. Acidic solutions			
$M^{+2} + 2H_2O \rightleftharpoons MO_2 + 4H^+ + 2e^-$	ca. 0.2	......	−1.456
$M^{+2} \rightleftharpoons M^{+4} + 2e^-$	......	−0.15	....
2. Alkaline solutions			
$HMO_2^- + 2OH^- \rightleftharpoons HMO_3^- + H_2O + 2e^-$	ca. 1.4	0.96 ($Sn(OH)_6^{-2}$)	....
$MO + 2OH^- \rightleftharpoons MO_2 + H_2O + 2e^-$	.....	....	−0.250

octet limitations, carbon has no acceptor properties in this oxidation state. However, the other elements do behave as weak acceptors, particularly toward halide or oxy ions.

Covalent structures in which atoms of these elements are bonded simultaneously to more and less electronegative atoms are not uncommon. This is particularly true of carbon, where bonding to fluorine, chlorine, bromine, oxygen, or nitrogen and to hydrogen commonly occurs in the same molecule. Under such circumstances, use of any formal oxidation number for the central element is not only impractical but also definitely misleading. Such structures are dictated not by any demands of electron excess or deficiency but rather by the demands of the covalency rules. Carbon is most stable when 4-covalent, and it appears to matter but little what groups are present to meet this demand. In the 4-covalent state, all the elements in this family are characterized by sp^3 bonding and are thus tetrahedral (p. 201).

MODIFICATIONS OF THE FREE ELEMENTS

Unlike the non-metallic elements discussed thus far, the elements in this group do not appear to form polyatomic gaseous molecules. In the solid state, however, allotropy is encountered, but it is much less involved than corresponding phenomena with the oxygen and nitrogen family elements.

Carbon

Carbon exists in two crystalline forms, diamond and graphite. In an early application of the x-ray technique, the Braggs[1] demonstrated

[1] W. H. Bragg and W. L. Bragg: *Proc. Roy. Soc. (London)*, **A89**, 277 (1913).

clearly that in the diamond each carbon atom is covalently bonded to four other carbon atoms arranged tetrahedrally (Fig. 16·1). The C—C bond distance is 1.54 A. The structure is thus that of an atomic crystal or giant molecule (p. 213). The extreme hardness of the diamond is the direct result of such a structure since rupture of the structure would require the breaking of many bonds, and the lack of electrical conductivity is the result of the complete pairing of all electrons. It is of interest, however, that a few diamonds (ca. 1%) have

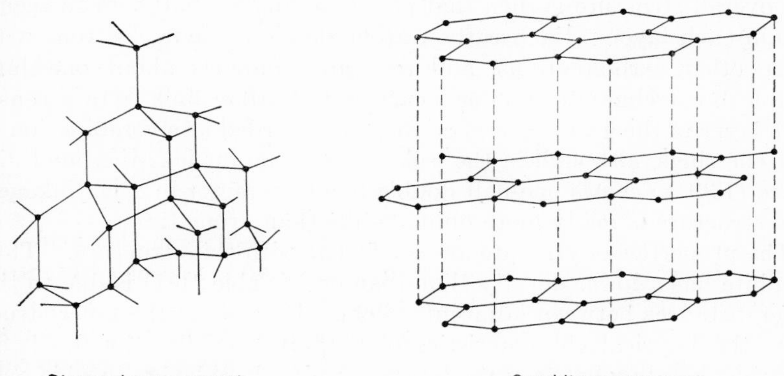

FIG. 16·1. Crystal arrangements in diamond and graphite.

no absorption band at 8 μ and are transparent to ultraviolet light up to some 2250 A.[2] These diamonds have the same dielectric constant and lattice constants[3] as ordinary diamonds, and the differences are not due to impurities. Raman[4] has pointed out that, because of both sense and direction in the tetrahedral axis, carbon atoms in the diamond may be oriented in four ways in space and that four diamond structures must thus exist. Two of these are tetrahedral (TdI and TdII) and identical in characteristics (referred to as positive and negative). These structures are the common ones. The other two have full octahedral symmetry (OhI and OhII) and are physically different from each other. They are comparatively rare, but, where they do occur, interpenetration of the two octahedral forms imparts laminar characteristics to the diamonds. The existence of all four types has been confirmed by x-ray and spectroscopic studies.[5] The physical characteristics of the diamond have been explored very thor-

[2] R. Robertson, J. J. Fox, and A. E. Martin: *Phil. Trans.*, **A232**, 463 (1934).

[3] K. Lonsdale: *Nature*, **153**, 22 (1944).

[4] C. V. Raman: *Proc. Indian Acad. Sci.*, **19A**, 189 (1944); *Nature*, **155**, 69, 144, 171, 234, 572 (1945).

[5] R. S. Krishnan: *Proc. Indian Acad. Sci.*, **19A**, 298 (1944).

oughly because of the fundamental importance of the diamond structure.[6] Gem character is due to a combination of hardness, transparency, and extremely high refractive index (2.417 for D-line of sodium).

In the graphite crystal, the carbon atoms are arranged in sheets of regular hexagons (Fig. 16·1), the C—C bond distance being 1.42 A.[7] The distance between these layers is sufficiently large (3.40 A) to preclude covalent bonds between them. The layers are thus held together by comparatively weak van der Waals forces (p. 215), and the overall structure is then that of a two-dimensional giant molecule within each layer. Each carbon atom shares its four electrons with three other carbon atoms, and resonance imparts about one-third double bond character to each carbon to carbon link.[7] In a sense, each layer in the graphite crystal may be regarded as a combination of benzene rings, although in the isolated benzene nucleus the bond distance (1.39 A) shows one-half double bond character in each linkage.[7] The structure is really more quinone-like than aromatic.

The properties of graphite are consistent with this structure. That graphite has a lower density than diamond (Table 16·1) is due to the large distances between adjacent sheets. Because of the layer structure, the physical characteristics of graphite are directional. Lack of strong bonding between the layers permits these layers to slide over each other and imparts greasy feel and lubricating character to graphite. These structural factors also permit the insertion of a variety of materials between the layers. Thus treatment of graphite with gaseous or molten potassium (or rubidium) causes separation of the layers due to the insertion of the metal atoms between them and yields two apparently stoichiometric materials, KC_8 (copper or bronze colored) and KC_{16} (steel-blue colored).[8, 9] The potassium may be removed by extraction with mercury. X-ray data indicate the existence of layers of metal atoms between the layers of carbon hexagons,[10] and in the KC_8 material potassium atoms are between all successive layers whereas in the KC_{16} material they are between alternate pairs of layers.

Treatment of graphite with strong oxidizing agents such as nitric acid or potassium chlorate causes swelling and yields green-to-brown,

[6] For detailed information, consult papers contributed in a symposium on the diamond and published in *Proc. Indian Acad. Sci.*, **19A**, 189–342 (1944).

[7] L. Pauling: *The Nature of the Chemical Bond*, 2nd Ed., pp. 172–175. Cornell University Press, Ithaca (1940).

[8] K. Fredenhagen and G. Cadenbach: *Z. anorg. allgem. Chem.*, **158,** 249 (1926).

[9] K. Fredenhagen and H. Suck: *Z. anorg. allgem. Chem.*, **178,** 353 (1929).

[10] A. Schleede and M. Wellmann: *Z. physik., Chem.*, **18B,** 1 (1932).

non-conducting oxygenated derivatives known variously as *graphitic acid* (Brodie, 1860) and *graphitic oxide* (Berthelot, 1869).[11] In these materials, the carbon sheets remain unchanged, but the sheets are separated to distances of 6 to 11 A, the degree of separation increasing with increasing oxygen content. Oxygen atoms appear to be attached to both sides of the sheets, presumably as —C—C— groups,[12] but

$$\begin{array}{c}—\text{C}—\text{C}— \\ \diagdown\;\diagup \\ \text{O}\end{array}$$

they are present in C:O ratios varying between 3.5:1 and 2.2:1.[13] True formulas cannot be written, therefore. It is of interest that the heat of combustion of carbon (per gram) is the same for both graphite and graphitic oxide.[14] Water and alcohol molecules can be absorbed between the separated layers,[15] and treatment with alkali causes complete separation and the formation of colloidal carbon. Complete oxidation of graphite gives mellitic acid, $C_6(COOH)_6$, a benzene derivative.

Treatment of graphite with oxidizing agents in the presence of strong acids gives so-called *graphitic salts*,[16] of which the sulfate, $C_{24}HSO_4{\cdot}2H_2SO_4$, is typical. Similar materials result in the presence of nitric, phosphoric, arsenic, selenic, and perchloric acids. These compounds are stable in the presence of concentrated acids but are decomposed by water to graphite, which retains some oxygen. For sulfuric acid, maximum separation of adjacent carbon layers is 4.55 A. For nitric and selenic acids, separations of 4.44 A and 4.85 A, respectively, are noted. Maximum expansion occurs when the acid molecules are between adjacent layers. If less acid is used or oxidation is incomplete, the acid molecules are inserted between sheets which are farther removed. Detailed structures have not been worked out for these materials. Treatment of certain natural graphites with nitric and sulfuric acids, followed by heating, causes enormous expansions along one axis due to penetration between layers,[17, 18] but not all samples behave in this fashion.

Graphite which has been degassed (or norite) absorbs fluorine at elevated temperatures[19] to give a monofluoride, CF, which possesses

[11] U. Hofmann and E. König: *Z. anorg. allgem. Chem.*, **234,** 311 (1937).
[12] U. Hofmann and R. Holst: *Ber.*, **72B,** 754 (1939).
[13] L. Meyer: *Trans. Faraday Soc.*, **34,** 1056 (1938).
[14] U. Hofmann, A. Frenzel, and E. Osalán: *Ann.*, **510,** 1 (1934).
[15] U. Hofmann and W. Rüdorff: *Trans. Faraday Soc.*, **34,** 1017 (1938).
[16] W. Rüdorff and U. Hofmann: *Z. anorg. allgem. Chem.*, **238,** 1 (1938).
[17] H. Thiele: *Z. anorg. allgem. Chem.*, **207,** 340 (1932).
[18] H. Boersch and L. Meyer: *Z. physik. Chem.*, **29B,** 59 (1935).
[19] O. Ruff and O. Bretschneider: *Z. anorg. allgem. Chem.*, **217,** 1 (1934).

neither the luster nor the electrical conductivity of graphite. The interlayer distance of 8.17 A indicates that the fluorine has entered between the carbon layers. Bromine vapor is also absorbed (up to a composition $CBr_{0.77}$),[20] the interplanar separation being 7.05 A. Iron(III) chloride can also be inserted up to a composition $C_9(FeCl_3)$ without alteration of the magnetic moment of iron.[21]

The many forms[22] of so-called amorphous carbon (e.g., charcoal, lampblack, etc.) are all micro-crystalline in character and are made up of crystallites with the graphite structure[10, 23, 24] oriented in random fashion. In general, particle size increases as the temperature at which the material forms increases. The variety of physical properties associated with such forms of carbon are largely determined by differences in surface area.

The relations existing between diamond and graphite are of considerable interest.[25] Inasmuch as the heat of combustion of graphite (−94.052 kcal. per gram atom) is less than that for diamond (−94.505 kcal. per gram atom) at 25°C.,[26] it is apparent that at ordinary temperatures graphite is the stable form (heat of transformation 0.453 kcal. per gram atom). This also appears to be the case up to at least 2300°C. at ordinary pressures.[27] At higher pressures, however, conversion of graphite to diamond seems to be more feasible. Calculations by Rossini and Jessup[28] show that whereas at ca. 13,000 atm. there is no temperature at which diamond is stable with respect to graphite, at ca. 16,000 atm. equilibrium should result at 300°K., and at ca. 20,000 atm. it should be established at 470°K. Bridgman[29] found that at 2000°C. diamond was transformed to graphite at some 15,000 kg. per sq. cm. pressure, but that this transformation became less rapid at increasing pressures and ceased at 30,000 kg. per sq. cm. However, no conversion of graphite to diamond could be effected. Negative results for this conversion have been reported for studies at higher temperatures and pressures.[27] Inasmuch as diamond does not form under

[20] W. Rüdorff and H. Schulz: *Z. anorg. allgem. Chem.*, **245**, 121 (1940).

[21] W. Rüdorff: *Z. anorg. allgem. Chem.*, **245**, 383 (1940).

[22] C. L. Mantell: *Industrial Carbon.* D. Van Nostrand Co., New York (1928).

[23] U. Hofmann and D. Wilm: *Z. physik., Chem.* **18B**, 401 (1932).

[24] A. H. White and L. H. Germer: *J. Chem. Phys.*, **9**, 492 (1941).

[25] D. P. Mellor: *Research*, **2**, 314 (1949).

[26] E. J. Prosen, R. S. Jessup, and F. D. Rossini: *J. Research Natl. Bur. Standards*, **33**, 447 (1944).

[27] P. L. Günther, P. Geselle, and W. Rebentisch: *Z. anorg. allgem. Chem.*, **250**, 357 (1943).

[28] F. D. Rossini and R. S. Jessup: *J. Research Natl. Bur. Standards*, **21**, 491 (1938).

[29] P. W. Bridgman: *J. Chem. Phys.*, **15**, 92 (1947).

conditions much more drastic than those theoretically calculated,[28] it is possible that the controlling factor is the speed of conversion. The mechanism by means of which diamonds were formed in nature remains a mystery, although it seems obvious that excessively high pressures were essential.

The synthetic production of diamonds has been singularly unsuccessful.[25, 30, 31] Hannay[32] heated mixtures of various oils and lithium to high temperatures in welded iron tubes and isolated crystals which have been shown by x-ray diffraction data[33] to be diamonds of the rare octahedral type (p. 665). Some question has been raised as to whether the crystals examined were so obtained.[34] Moissan[35] claimed to have obtained tiny diamonds by suddenly cooling molten iron containing dissolved carbon by quenching in cold water and then dissolving away the iron in acid, but no really definite confirmatory evidence was presented. Ruff[36] claimed success with Moissan's method, and offered experimental evidence supporting his statements. Parsons[37] has also claimed to have produced synthetic diamonds. The thermodynamic evidence cited renders all these claims questionable. Repetition and extension of these studies would seem necessary to the ultimate solution of the problem.[25] Under ordinarily available conditions, all forms of carbon normally revert to graphite.

Silicon, germanium, tin, and lead

Silicon is known in only one crystalline form, namely, the octahedral form in which the silicon atoms have the diamond arrangement. So-called *amorphous* silicon consists of minute octahedral crystals which are the same as the large crystals characterizing ordinary metallic silicon. Germanium also crystallizes in the diamond form as does gray tin. Tin exists in two other solid forms, the relations among its allotropes being indicated schematically as[38, 39]

$$\underset{\text{(diamond type)}}{\text{gray tin}} \overset{13.2°\text{C.}}{\rightleftharpoons} \underset{\text{(tetragonal)}}{\text{white tin}} \overset{161°\text{C.}}{\rightleftharpoons} \underset{\text{(rhombic)}}{\text{brittle tin}} \overset{231.8°\text{C.}}{\rightleftharpoons} \text{liquid}$$

[30] C. H. Desch: *Nature,* **152,** 148 (1943).

[31] D. P. Mellor: *J. Chem. Phys.,* **15,** 525 (1947).

[32] J. B. Hannay: *Proc. Roy. Soc.* (*London*), **30,** 188, 450 (1880).

[33] F. A. Bannister and K. Lonsdale: *Nature,* **151,** 334 (1943); *Mineralog. Mag.,* **26,** 309 (1943).

[34] Lord Rayleigh: *Nature,* **152,** 597 (1943).

[35] H. Moissan: *Compt. rend.,* **116,** 218 (1893); *Ann. chim.* [vii], **8,** 466 (1896).

[36] O. Ruff: *Z. anorg. allgem. Chem.,* **99,** 73 (1917).

[37] C. A. Parsons: *Phil. Trans.,* **A220,** 67 (1920).

[38] E. Cohen and A. K. W. A. van Lieshout: *Z. physik. Chem.,* **173A,** 32 (1935).

[39] P. Saldau: *Z. anorg. allgem. Chem.,* **194,** 1 (1930).

Although transition of white tin to the gray, less dense form should occur at any temperature below 13.2°C. it becomes rapid only at −50°C. unless a catalyst [e.g., gray tin, tin(IV)] is present. This conversion is known popularly as *tin pest* or *tin disease.* The lattice in white tin is metallic in nature. For lead, only the cubic metallic lattice is known. The trend from non-metal to metal with increasing atomic weight is thus emphasized by changes in the physical structures of the solid elements.

CHEMICAL CHARACTERISTICS OF THE ELEMENTS

The most important aspects of the chemical behaviors of the elements in this family are summarized in Table 16·3. The situation

TABLE 16·3
CHEMICAL CHARACTERISTICS OF GROUP IVB ELEMENTS

General Equation*	Remarks
$M + 2X_2 \rightarrow MX_4$	With halogens. Lead gives PbI_2 and unstable $PbBr_4$, $PbCl_4$.
$M + O_2 \rightarrow MO_2$	With C, Si, Ge, Sn. Lead gives PbO, Pb_3O_4.
$M + 2S \rightarrow MS_2$	Lead gives PbS.
$M + 2H^+ \rightarrow M^{+2} + H_2$	With Sn and Pb only.
$3M + 4HNO_3 \rightarrow 3MO_2 + 4NO + 2H_2O$	With C, Si, Ge, Sn, especially Ge and Sn. Lead gives Pb^{+2}.
$M + 2OH^- + H_2O \rightarrow MO_3^{-2} + 2H_2$	With Si, Ge. Tin and lead give MO_2^{-2} slowly.

* M = Si, Ge, Sn, and Pb; and C only where specifically indicated.

here is again quite comparable with the situations discussed in the preceding three chapters in that the lightest element shows anomalous behavior. Carbon (and to lesser extents silicon and germanium) reacts with a variety of metals to form carbides and in general shows more of the characteristics of the non-metals already described than of the more metallic members in its own family. The allotropy of carbon has but little influence upon its reactivity, although diamond is slightly easier to oxidize than graphite. Because of increased surface, the "amorphous" varieties are somewhat more reactive.

PREPARATION AND PRODUCTION OF THE FREE ELEMENTS

Graphite occurs naturally in various places (e.g., Ceylon, Bohemia, Siberia, United States), but the major portion of that used technically is prepared electrothermally by passing an electric current through a mass of powdered coke covered with sand and containing carbon rods as conductors (Acheson process). The "amorphous" forms of carbon are prepared in a variety of fashions. Thus *charcoal* is obtained by the thermal decomposition of cane sugar or wood; the various *carbon blacks* are obtained by the incomplete combustion of natural gases; *coke* is obtained by heating coal; etc. So-called *activated* charcoal results when charcoal is prepared in the presence of air or steam or various inorganic compounds (which are dissolved out), the function of these foreign materials being to remove obstructions from the pores in the material.

Elemental silicon is obtained technically by reduction of the dioxide with carbon or calcium carbide in the electric furnace. In the laboratory, it is obtained most conveniently by reducing the dioxide with aluminum in the presence of sulfur in a thermite type reaction, but yields are low. Reduction of the tetrachloride with zinc vapor has been suggested also. Reduction of the dioxide with magnesium or of alkali metal fluosilicates with zinc or aluminum is also useful. Crystallization from zinc or aluminum gives a highly crystalline product. Germanium is obtained by reducing the dioxide with hydrogen or carbon at elevated temperatures. Tin is obtained technically by reducing the refined native dioxide with carbon, and lead is prepared from the native sulfide either by an ingenious process in which partial oxidation to oxide and sulfate is followed by reduction of these materials at higher temperatures by the remaining sulfide or by roasting and reduction with coke. Electrolytic methods are useful for purification of tin and lead. Further details may be found in standard textbooks on elementary chemistry or metallurgy.

COMPOUNDS OF THE GROUP IVb ELEMENTS

It is manifestly impossible in a book of this type to consider completely or comprehensively all the compounds which carbon forms. Nor does it seem wise to attempt complete coverage of all the compounds of the other elements in the family. However, consideration of a number of classes of compounds serves not only to emphasize trends and differences among the elements but also to place carbon logically with the others as far as its inorganic chemistry is concerned. Some special phases of carbon and silicon chemistries can then be discussed to complete the picture.

Catenation among the Group IVb elements

The phenomenon of self-linkage among the elements is most characteristic of carbon. This is probably the result of a number of factors, among them the 4-electron outer arrangement in the carbon atom, the almost invariable 4-covalent nature of carbon which is most readily satisfied by other carbon and hydrogen atoms, the ease with which an inert gas arrangement can be obtained in this fashion, and the lack of donor or acceptor properties in the 4-covalent carbon. These factors, however, cannot account for the fact that the tendency toward catenation decreases so markedly from carbon to silicon and practically disappears among the heavier members of the family. Bond energy data provide at least a partial answer to this problem. From the data in Table 16·4, it is apparent that the carbon to carbon single

TABLE 16·4
BOND ENERGY DATA FOR CARBON AND SILICON BONDS

Linkage	Bond Energy, kcal./mole M = C	M = Si	Difference
M—M	58.6	42.5	16.1
M—H	87.3	75.1	12.2
M—F	107.0	143.0	−36.0
M—Cl	66.5	85.8	−19.3
M—Br	54.0	69.3	−15.3
M—I	45.5	51.1	− 5.6
M—O	70.0	89.3	−19.3
M—S	54.5	60.9	− 6.4
C—Si	57.6 kcal./mole		
Ge—Ge	42.5		

bond is much more stable than the silicon to silicon single bond, and it may be assumed logically that further decreases characterize the heavier elements. Comparison of values for these linkages with those for linkages of carbon or silicon to other elements indicates further that the carbon to carbon bond is either more stable than or almost as stable as many such linkages whereas bonds between silicon and other elements are uniformly more stable than the silicon to silicon bond. This indicates that silicon will form bonds to other elements preferentially and that in the presence of other elements silicon to silicon bonds are readily broken. The reverse is commonly true for carbon.

Furthermore, the carbon to hydrogen bond has a higher bond energy than any other single carbon bond except the carbon to fluorine link. The preponderance of carbon to hydrogen linkages in chained carbon compounds is thus reasonable. For silicon, the linkage to hydrogen is again less stable than linkages to certain other elements (especially fluorine, oxygen) and is thus more readily ruptured. As shown in Table 15·3, multiple carbon to carbon bonds are easily obtained. Comparable data are not available for silicon or the other members of this family, but the fact that no compounds of any of these elements are known in which there are definite multiple bonds indicates the inherent instabilities of such linkages.

Hydrides

Of the elements in this family, all except carbon are less electronegative than hydrogen. Strictly speaking, therefore, reference to all the binary hydrogen compounds as hydrides is not entirely correct. Usage of the term, however, is nearly universal and is well established.

TABLE 16·5
HYDRIDES OF THE GROUP IVB ELEMENTS

Type and Property	M = C	Si	Ge	Sn	Pb
1. MH_4					
Melting point, °C.	−182.7	−185	−165	−150	
Boiling point, °C.	−161.3	−111.9	−88.1	−52	ca. −13
Density of liquid, gram/ml.	0.415 (−164°C.)	0.68 (−185°C.)			
Decomposition temperature, °C.	800	450	285	150	0
2. M_2H_6					
Melting point, °C.	−172	−132.5	−109		
Boiling point, °C.	−88.7	−14.5	29		
Density of liquid, gram/ml.	0.546 (−88°C.)	0.686 (−25°C.)			
3. M_3H_8					
Melting point, °C.	−189.9	−117.4	−105.6		
Boiling point, °C.	−44.5	52.9	110.5		
Density of liquid, gram/ml.	0.585 (−44°C.)	0.743 (0°C.)			
4. M_4H_{10}					
Melting point, °C.	−135	−84.3			
Boiling point, °C.	−0.5	107.4			
Density of liquid, gram/ml.	0.602 (−0.8°C.)	0.825 (0°C.)			
5. M_5H_{12}					
Boiling point, °C.	36.2	> 100			
6. M_6H_{14}					
Boiling point, °C.	69.0	> 100			

As alternatives, one might employ hydrosilicons, hydrogermaniums, etc., as analogs of hydrocarbons. Because of the impossibility of discussing the hydrocarbons in detail, they are referred to only where comparisons with corresponding compounds of the other elements are instructive.

Known binary hydrogen compounds are listed in Table 16·5, together with certain physical constants and comparative values for the analogous carbon compounds. It is apparent that all these compounds are covalent in character and that volatility and melting point are quite generally functions of molecular weight. Where multiple hydrides are known, they are of the type M_nH_{2n+2}, i.e., formal analogs of the members of the methane series. These materials are known as silanes, germanes, stannanes, and plumbanes, with prefixes (di-, tri-, etc.) being employed to show the numbers of atoms of silicon, germanium, etc., present per molecule. Members of unsaturated series are unknown, although apparently polymeric but uncharacterized compounds of compositions $(SiH_2)_x$ and $(GeH_2)_y$ have been prepared. Numerous halogenated, oxygenated, and organic derivatives of these hydrides have been studied. Certain of them are considered below. It is of interest that substitution of alkyl or aryl groups for hydrogens gives general increases in the stabilities of catenated compounds. Because of the marked strength of the silicon to oxygen bond (Table 16·4), the silicon hydrides react vigorously with oxygen, water, and alkalies. The germanium hydrides are somewhat less reactive. General methods of preparation have been described in Chapter 12 (pp. 409–410), but specific details are considered below.

Silicon Hydrides. The classic research on the silicon hydrides was carried out by Stock and his students,[40, 41] and the major portion of present-day knowledge stems from their studies. Mono- and disilane are colorless gases at ordinary temperatures; the higher homologs colorless liquids (Table 16·5). All the hydrides burn spontaneously in contact with air or oxygen, the kindling temperatures being thus considerably below those for the corresponding hydrocarbons and decreasing with increasing molecular weight. Although the silanes are not affected by pure water in silica vessels, they do react with water in glass vessels or when glass is added to water in silica. This is due to their extreme sensitivities toward alkalies to give silicates and hydrogen. The hydrides are strong reducing agents, reducing, e.g., permanganate to manganese(IV) oxide, mercury(II) to mercury(I or 0), iron(III) to iron (II), copper(II) to copper hydride, etc. Halogenation reactions with chlorine or bromine are explosively violent at room temperatures. However, treatment of monosilane, for example, with hydrogen chloride or bromide at 100°C. in the presence of the corresponding aluminum halide as catalyst, effects successive replacement of hydrogens by halogens. The higher silanes yield chlorine-substituted products by violent reactions with chloroform or carbon tetrachloride in the presence of oxygen, but these reactions are moderated by exclusion of oxygen and use of aluminum chloride catalysts at low

[40] A. Stock: *Z. Elektrochem.*, **32**, 341 (1926).

[41] A. Stock: *Hydrides of Boron and Silicon*, Cornell University Press, Ithaca (1933).

temperatures. The silanes undergo thermal decomposition, the ease of decomposition increasing with increasing molecular weight. Mono- and disilane appear to be stable indefinitely at room temperatures, but the higher homologs decompose slowly. Studies on tetrasilane,[42] however, suggest that this instability may be due to impurities since decomposition (by an auto-catalytic reaction) occurred only with impure samples. Although silicon and hydrogen are the ultimate decomposition products at red heat, the higher silanes undergo *cracking* reactions at lower temperatures to give other hydrides.

In the classic procedure[40, 41] for the preparation of the silanes 20% hydrochloric acid is added to magnesium silicide (prepared by heating magnesium and silicon together in the absence of air) in a current of hydrogen. Although hydrogen is apparently the major product, some 25% of the silicon is converted to a mixture of hydrides which can then be separated by fractional distillation. The hydride mixture contains roughly 40% SiH_4, 30% Si_2H_6, 15% Si_3H_8, 10% Si_4H_{10}, 5% higher silanes. It appears that an intermediate, $H_2Si(MgOH)_2$, is formed first,[43] and this then reacts with the acid as

$$H_2Si(MgOH)_2 + 4HCl \rightarrow 2MgCl_2 + 2H_2O + H_2 + SiH_2$$

the SiH_2 undergoing polymerization immediately. Reaction of these polymers with water then gives silanes as, for example,

$$(SiH_2)_2 + H_2O \rightarrow SiH_2O + SiH_4$$

$$(SiH_2)_3 + H_2O \rightarrow SiH_2O + Si_2H_6, \text{ etc.}$$

The material SiH_2O undergoes polymerization as formed. The temperature and general conditions attending formation of the magnesium silicide influence both the yield and the relative proportions of the various silanes.[42] For a product obtained by use of 10% excess magnesium and ignition in hydrogen at 650°C. for 24 hours, 35% yields result.[42] It is believed that silicides other than the material Mg_2Si, which may result at elevated temperatures, are responsible for formation of increased quantities of the higher silanes. The lower silanes (SiH_4, Si_2H_6) can be prepared in 70 to 80% yields by reaction of magnesium silicide with ammonium bromide (an acid) in liquid ammonia in a current of hydrogen.[44, 45] Although monosilane is normally the major product, use of specially prepared magnesium silicides gives

[42] H. J. Emeléus and A. G. Maddock: *J. Chem. Soc.*, **1946**, 1131.
[43] R. Schwarz and E. Konrad: *Ber.*, **55**, 3242 (1922).
[44] W. C. Johnson and T. R. Hogness: *J. Am. Chem. Soc.*, **56**, 1252 (1934).
[45] W. C. Johnson and S. Isenberg: *J. Am. Chem. Soc.*, **57**, 1349 (1935).

mixtures containing up to 60% disilane.[45] Compounds other than the substance Mg_2Si are believed to be of importance in formation of anything but monosilane.[45] Improved yields are doubtless due to absence of reaction between the silanes and ammonia. Almost complete conversion of silicon tetrachloride and hexachlorodisilane to monosilane (99%) and disilane (87%), respectively, can be effected by treatment with lithium aluminum hydride in diethyl ether at 0°C.[46] Uncharacterized mixtures of silanes are formed when magnesium silicide is added to molten ethylenediamine hydrochloride or trimethylamine hydrochloride or is heated with dry ammonium bromide.[47]

DERIVATIVES OF THE SILANES. Among the silicon compounds which may be considered derivatives of the silanes are the halosilanes (e.g., $SiHCl_3$, SiH_2Cl_2), the alkyl and aryl silanes (e.g., R_3SiH, R_4Si), the alkyl and aryl halosilanes (e.g., R_2SiCl_2, R_3SiCl), a variety of oxygen and nitrogen derivatives (e.g., $(R_3Si)_2O$, $(SiH_3)_3N$, etc.), and certain metal silicides. Some of these materials are discussed in later sections of this chapter. Alkyl and aryl chlorosilanes result from reactions of appropriate Grignard reagents with silicon tetrachloride but are more conveniently prepared by direct reaction at elevated temperatures of alkyl or aryl chlorides with silicon in the presence of copper or silver as catalyst.[48–50]

NON-VOLATILE SILICON HYDRIDES. A hydride $(SiH_2)_x$ is formed when calcium monosilicide (CaSi) is treated with either absolute ethanol saturated with hydrogen chloride or with glacial acetic acid.[51] It is a brown amorphous solid which is spontaneously inflammable in air and reacts with aqueous acids to give silica and hydrogen. Cracking at 380°C. gives a mixture of silanes. Monosilane is decomposed in an electric discharge to a solid material of composition $SiH_{1.2-1.4}$, and a similar material is formed when monosilane is irradiated with mercury resonance radiation.[52] No structural data are available for any of these materials. They are all non-volatile, insoluble in inert solvents, and decomposed by alkali solutions.

Hydrides of Germanium, Tin, and Lead. The three germanes (Table 16·5) are quite similar to the corresponding silanes. All are oxidzed by oxygen to the dioxide and water, ease of oxidation increasing with

[46] A. E. Finholt, C. A. Bond, Jr., K. E. Wilzbach, and H. I. Schlesinger: *J. Am. Chem. Soc.*, **69**, 2692 (1947).

[47] D. T. Hurd: *J. Am. Chem. Soc.*, **69**, 1647 (1947).

[48] E. G. Rochow: *J. Am. Chem. Soc.*, **67**, 963 (1945).

[49] D. T. Hurd and E. G. Rochow: *J. Am. Chem. Soc.*, **67**, 1057 (1945).

[50] E. G. Rochow and W. F. Gilliam: *J. Am. Chem. Soc.*, **67**, 1772 (1945).

[51] R. Schwarz and F. Heinrich: *Z. anorg. allgem. Chem.*, **221**, 277 (1935).

[52] H. J. Emeléus and K. Stewart: *Trans. Faraday Soc.*, **32**, 1577 (1936).

molecular weight, but they are not as inflammable as the silanes. Unlike the silanes, they do not react with water, and monogermane is resistant to even 33% alkali. Digermane evolves hydrogen under comparable conditions. At elevated temperatures, the germanes decompose to germanium and hydrogen, although cracking reactions may occur at intermediate temperatures. Treatment of magnesium germanide with dilute hydrochloric acid yields a mixture of the germanes (mostly monogermane), the overall conversion of germanium being only some 22.7%.[53] The individual compounds are separated by fractional distillation as is done with the silanes. Monogermane is obtained in greater yield by reaction of magnesum germanide with ammonium bromide in liquid ammonia[54] or by reaction of lithium aluminum hydride with germanium tetrachloride.[46] A variety of halo and organo derivatives of monogermane have been prepared. These are quite generally comparable with the analogous silicon compounds in properties and modes of preparation.

A non-volatile hydride, $(GeH_2)_y$, is formed as a yellow solid when calcium germanide is treated with aqueous hydrogen chloride.[55] It reacts with oxygen (explosively when dry) and is converted to germanium tetrabromide and hydrogen bromide by bromine. With aqueous alkali, it gives monogermane, hydrogen, and germanite ion. Thermal decomposition at 120° to 220°C. gives hydrogen mixed with the three germanes.[56]

For tin and lead, only the simple hydrides, MH_4, are known. Monostannane, SnH_4, is resistant to attack by 15% sodium hydroxide, dilute sulfuric acid, dilute or concentrated nitric acid, copper(II) ion, and iron(III) ion. It reacts, however, with silver nitrate and mercury(II) chloride solutions. Above 145° to 150°C., it undergoes rapid thermal decomposition, but at lower temperatures decomposition is slow. The lead compound has not been well characterized. Monostannane results in very small quantities when a tin-magnesium alloy is dissolved in dilute acids or when tin(II) sulfate solution containing dextrine or glucose and sulfuric acid is reduced cathodically.[57–59] The compound results in much better yields (20.4%) from the reaction of tin(IV) chloride with lithium aluminum hydride in diethyl ether at

[53] L. M. Dennis, R. B. Corey, and R. W. Moore: *J. Am. Chem. Soc.*, **46**, 657 (1924).

[54] C. A. Kraus and E. S. Carney: *J. Am. Chem. Soc.*, **56**, 765 (1934).

[55] P. Royen and R. Schwarz: *Z. anorg. allgem. Chem.*, **211**, 412 (1933).

[56] P. Royen and R. Schwarz: *Z. anorg. allgem. Chem.*, **215**, 295 (1933).

[57] F. Paneth and K. Fürth: *Ber.*, **52**, 2020 (1919).

[58] F. Paneth, A. Johannsen, and M. Matthies: *Ber.*, **55**, 769 (1922).

[59] F. Paneth and E. Rabinowitsch: *Ber.*, **57**, 1877 (1924).

$-30°C$.[46] Lead hydride apparently results in minute quantities as a gaseous product upon dissolution of a lead-magnesium alloy in dilute acids or cathodic reduction of lead salts.[60] Atomic hydrogen reacts with lead to give a volatile compound only if carbon is present.[61] Tin and lead tetralkyls and tetraryls are well-known and comparatively stable compounds. Alkyl and aryl lead hydrides and halides are also well characterized. Although tin to tin and lead to lead linkages are unknown in the hydrides, they do exist in alkyl and aryl compounds. Best known are the distannanes ($R_3Sn{-}SnR_3$) and diplumbanes ($R_3Pb{-}PbR_3$), although polystannanes up to a composition of $Sn_5(CH_3)_{12}$ have been prepared. Free SnR_3 and PbR_3 radicals result from dissociation of the hexa-substituted distannanes and diplumbanes.

Halides

Both simple and substituted halides and oxyhalides of these elements are known. The simple halides are most commonly of the types MX_2 and MX_4, but with carbon and silicon catenated halides also are formed. The tetrahalides are most characteristic and form with all the elements. The dihalides are not noted with carbon and silicon. As is expected, the tetrahalides are predominantly covalent, whereas the dihalides are more ionic in character. Mixed tetrahalides (e.g., $SiCl_3Br$, $SiFCl_3$, etc.) have been described (especially for silicon) as well, and many comparable halogenoid derivatives are known (pp. 475–480).

Tetrahalides. Available melting and boiling point data for the simple tetrahalides as summarized in Table 16·6 indicate ionic bonding only in tin tetrafluoride. It may be presumed that lead(IV) fluoride would be ionic also. It is rather remarkable that silicon tetrachloride is more volatile than carbon tetrachloride, especially since this effect does not appear in any other series of halides or substituted halides. Hildebrand ascribes this phenomenon to the comparatively large increase in molecular volume in going from the carbon compound to the silicon compound.[62] The melting points of carbon tetrachloride, tetrabromide, and tetraiodide are anomalously high.

The thermal instabilities of carbon tetrabromide and iodide may be due to the crowding of the large halogen atoms around the small carbon atom. The absence of a tetrabromide and a tetraiodide of lead is due to the enhanced reducing powers of bromide and iodide and the

[60] F. Paneth and O. Nörring: *Ber.*, **53**, 1693 (1920).

[61] T. G. Pearson, P. L. Robinson, and E. M. Stoddart: *Proc. Roy. Soc.* (*London*), **A142**, 275 (1933).

[62] J. H. Hildebrand: *J. Chem. Phys.*, **15**, 727 (1947).

resulting ease of their conversion to free halogens by lead(IV). Even lead tetrachloride reverts to the dichloride and chlorine unless maintained at low temperatures. All the tetrahalides are tetrahedral. The bond distances (Table 16·6)[63–65] are less than those calculated by radius sums in most cases.

TABLE 16·6
PHYSICAL CONSTANTS OF GROUP IVB TETRAHALIDES

Compound Type and Property	C	Si	Ge	Sn	Pb
1. Tetrafluorides					
Melting point, °C.	−185	−90.2	−15	....	....
Boiling point, °C.	−128	−95.7 (subl.)	−37.4 (subl.)	705 (subl.)	....
2. Tetrachlorides					
Melting point, °C.	−22.9	−70.4	−49.5	−36.2	−15
Boiling point, °C.	76.4	57.0	86.5	114.1	ca. 150
Molecular volume at 25°C., ml.*	97.1	115.4	114.5	117.6	....
M—Cl distance, A	1.76	2.00	2.08	2.30	2.43
3. Tetrabromides					
Melting point, °C.	93.7	5.2	26.1	33.0	....
Boiling point, °C.	dec.	154.6	186.5	203.3	....
Molecular volume at 25°C., ml.*	....	126.5	126.0	130.6	....
M—Br distance, A	1.94	2.14	2.29	2.44	....
4. Tetraiodides					
Melting point, °C.	171.0	123.8	144	144.5	....
Boiling point, °C.	dec.	290	ca. 348	346	....
M—I distance, A	2.15	2.43	2.50	2.64	....

* Reference 62.

Except for the carbon compounds, the tetrahalides hydrolyze, largely as indicated by the general equation

$$MX_4 + 2H_2O \rightarrow MO_2 \text{ (or hydrate thereof)} + 4HX$$

Resistance of the carbon tetrahalides to hydrolysis is probably due to the fact that they are covalently saturated. In the other instances, acceptance of water molecules by coordination may occur, and the resulting structures may then undergo decomposition to give the dioxides and hydrogen halides. The silicon compounds undergo complete hydrolysis, but, as the ionic characters of the tetrahalides increase with the other elements, hydrolysis is less complete and may be suppressed by addition of acids. Thus aqueous hydrochloric acid solutions of tin tetrachloride can be prepared, and hydrolysis of tin

[63] L. O. Brockway and F. T. Wall: *J. Am. Chem. Soc.*, **56**, 2373 (1934).
[64] L. O. Brockway: *Revs. Mod. Phys.*, **8**, 231 (1936).
[65] M. W. Lister and L. E. Sutton: *Trans. Faraday Soc.*, **37**, 393 (1941).

tetrafluoride is even less pronounced. Hydrolysis of silicon tetrafluoride is complicated by the fact that this compound reacts with its hydrolysis product hydrogen fluoride to give soluble and stable fluosilicic acid. Hydrolysis thus proceeds approximately as

$$2SiF_4(g) + 2H_2O \rightarrow SiO_2(s) + 2H^+ + SiF_6^{-2} + 2HF(g)$$

silica precipitating from the solution.

Except for the carbon compounds, the tetrahalides show tendencies to form haloanions of the general type $[MX_6]^{-2}$. Reaction of carbon halides with halide ions is precluded by the octet limitation. For the other materials, stabilities of haloanions decrease as the size of the halide ion increases, presumably because of steric factors, but as the size of the central atom increases the larger halides can be accommodated more readily. For silicon only the $[SiF_6]^{-2}$ species is known, but for tin and lead $[SnCl_6]^{-2}$, $[SnBr_6]^{-2}$, $[SnI_6]^{-2}$, and $[PbCl_6]^{-2}$ species have been described. Of these, the fluosilicates and fluogermanates are most common.

Fluosilicic acid, the parent of the fluosilicates, is a strong acid as indicated by an apparent degree of dissociation of 0.76 at 25°C. in 0.1 N solution (H_2SO_4: 0.61 under same conditions) and the slight hydrolysis of many of its salts in cold aqueous solutions.[66] The production of solutions approximately $H_2SiF_6 \cdot SiF_4$ has been described.[67] Although the anhydrous acid cannot be isolated and is not formed when anhydrous silicon tetrafluoride and hydrogen fluoride are mixed, a 4-hydrate can be prepared below 0°C. and a 2-hydrate above 0°C. Addition of sulfuric acid causes decomposition to silicon and hydrogen fluorides. Of the many known fluosilicates, the majority are extremely soluble in water, notable exceptions being those of the alkali metals (Na, K, Rb, Cs), barium, yttrium, and the lanthanides. This property has rendered many heavy metal fluosilicates especially useful in the electrodeposition of metals (e.g., lead). Fluosilicates are also useful as insecticides. The fluosilicate ion is octahedral,[68, 69] but slightly distorted. Many of the reactions of silicon tetrafluoride and fluosilicates are described by Caillot.[70]

Silicon tetrafluoride is obtained ordinarily by treating a mixture of a fluoride and silica with sulfuric acid or heating barium fluosilicate. Germanium tetrafluoride is formed when barium fluogermanate is

[66] P. Kubelka and V. Přistoupil: *Z. anorg. allgem. Chem.*, **197**, 391 (1931).
[67] S. M. Thomsen: *J. Am. Chem. Soc.*, **72**, 2798 (1950).
[68] J. A. A. Ketelaar: Z. Krist., **92**, 155 (1935).
[69] J. L. Hoard and W. B. Vincent: *J. Am. Chem. Soc.*, **62**, 3126 (1940).
[70] R. Caillot: *Ann. chim.* [11], **20**, 367 (1945).

heated. Reaction of tin tetrachloride with hydrogen fluoride gives tin tetrafluoride. Direct reactions between the elements are useful for preparations of the other tetrahalides.

Dihalides. Complete series of dihalides are known for germanium, tin, and lead. Comparison of physical constants of these compounds (Table 16·7) with those of the tetrahalides (Table 16·6) indicates

TABLE 16·7
PHYSICAL CONSTANTS OF GROUP IVB DIHALIDES

Compound Type and Property	Ge	Sn	Pb
1. Difluorides			
Melting point, °C.			818
Boiling point, °C.			1285
2. Dichlorides			
Melting point, °C.		247	298
Boiling point, °C.	subl.	603	954
M—Cl distance, A		2.42	
3. Dibromides			
Melting point, °C.	122	215	373
Boiling point, °C.		619	916
M—Br distance, A		2.55	
4. Diiodides			
Melting point, °C.		320	412
Boiling point, °C.		720	
M—I distance, A	2.94	2.73	

clearly enhanced ionic bonding in these materials. Reducing power decreases, and ease of preservation increases from germanium to lead for each series. The germanium dihalides combine with halide ion to give anionic species (e.g., $[GeCl_3]^-$), but this tendency decreases through tin to lead. Water solubilities decrease with increasing size of either the metallic ion or the halide ion. The germanium halides may have bridged structures as

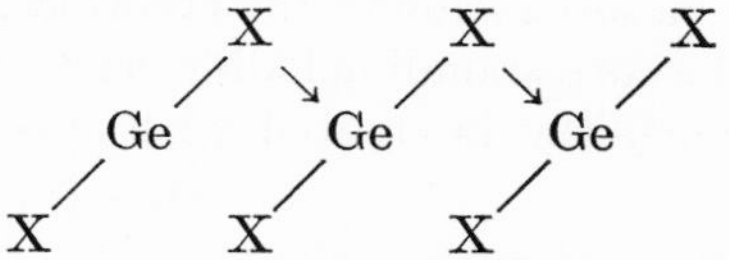

```
        X       X       X
       / ↘     / ↘     /
     Ge      Ge      Ge        , etc.
    /       /       /
   X       X       X
```

but this is unlikely for the tin compounds, in view of observations that the chloride is monomeric in both the vapor state[71] and in solution in urethane.[72] Electron diffraction data show the molecules $SnCl_2$, $SnBr_2$, and SnI_2 to be angular.[73] Germanium dihalides are commonly obtained by heating the tetrahalides with germanium. The others

[71] H. Biltz and V. Meyer: *Z. physik. Chem.*, **2**, 184 (1888).

[72] J. F. Eykman: *Z. physik. Chem.*, **4**, 497 (1889).

[73] M. W. Lister and L. E. Sutton: *Trans. Faraday Soc.*, **37**, 406 (1941).

result from metathesis reactions involving hydrogen or alkali metal halides.

Additional Silicon-Halogen Compounds. A variety of mixed tetrahalides, catenated halides, and oxyhalides of silicon have been characterized as well as a number of halomonosilanes. Many of these compounds have been described by Schumb.[74] Physical constants of certain of these compounds are summarized in Table 16·8.

The mixed tetrahalides have properties intermediate between those of the pure tetrahalides. These compounds have been obtained by a variety of reactions, among them reaction of a free halogen with another halosilane,[75, 76] fluorination of the tetrachloride with antimony trifluoride (p. 428),[77] and interaction of two tetrahalides,[78] followed by fractional distillation to separate the products. The completely mixed halide, SiFClBrI, although not reported, would be of especial interest because it should exhibit optical isomerism. Mixed tetrahalides become less common as the atomic weight of the central element increases.

Only a limited number of catenated halo silanes is known, since the silicon to halogen bond energies (Table 16·4) are such that in the presence of halogens the silicon to silicon bond is readily ruptured. These compounds are members of the series Si_nX_{2n+2}. Chlorine compounds up to Si_6Cl_{14} are known, but only Si_2X_6 compounds have been described for the other halogens. All these materials are covalent. In contact with water, they all hydrolyze. An important hydrolysis product of the materials Si_2X_6 is *silico-oxalic* acid, $H_2Si_2O_4$. The higher chlorides burn when heated in air. The fluoride, Si_2F_6, is obtained by fluorinating the corresponding chloride with zinc fluoride.[79] The higher chlorides and the tetrachloride are obtained as mixtures when a calcium-silicon alloy is chlorinated at 150°C.[80] Fractional distillation permits successive separation of the chlorides. The bromide, Si_2Br_6, is formed when the corresponding iodide is treated with bromine or when a calcium-silicon alloy is treated with bromine at 180° to

[74] W. C. Schumb: *Chem. Revs.*, **31**, 587 (1942).

[75] W. C. Schumb and H. H. Anderson: *J. Am. Chem. Soc.*, **58**, 994 (1936); **59**, 651 (1937).

[76] W. C. Schumb and E. L. Gamble: *J. Am. Chem. Soc.*, **54**, 3943 (1932).

[77] H. S. Booth and C. Swinehart: *J. Am. Chem. Soc.*, **54**, 4750 (1932).

[78] H. H. Anderson: *J. Am. Chem. Soc.*, **67**, 859 (1945); **72**, 2091 (1950).

[79] W. C. Schumb and E. L. Gamble: *J. Am. Chem. Soc.*, **54**, 583 (1932).

[80] W. C. Schumb and E. L. Gamble: *Inorganic Syntheses*, Vol. I, p. 42, McGraw-Hill Book Co., New York (1939).

TABLE 16·8

PHYSICAL CONSTANTS OF VARIOUS SILICON-HALOGEN COMPOUNDS

Compound	Melting Point, °C.	Boiling Point, °C.
1. Mixed Halides		
SiF_3Cl	−138	−70
SiF_2Cl_2	−144	−31.7
$SiFCl_3$		12.2
SiF_3Br	−70.5	−41.7
SiF_2Br_2	−66.9	13.7
$SiFBr_3$	−82.5	83.8
SiF_3I		−24
SiF_2I_2		84.5
$SiFI_3$		188
$SiCl_3Br$	−62	80.3
$SiCl_2Br_2$	−45.5	104.4
$SiClBr_3$	−20.8	128
$SiFCl_2Br$		35.4
$SiFClBr_2$		59.5
2. Catenated Halides		
Si_2F_6	−19.0	−19.1
Si_2Cl_6	2.5	147
Si_3Cl_8		216
Si_4Cl_{10}		150 (15 mm.)
Si_5Cl_{12}		190 (15 mm.)
Si_6Cl_{14}		subl. 200 (vac.)
Si_2Br_6	95	265
Si_2I_6	250 (dec.)	
3. Oxyhalides		
Si_2OF_6	−47.8	−23.3
$Si_2OF_4Cl_2$	−60.0	16.8
$Si_2OF_3Cl_3$	−100.0	42.9
Si_2OCl_6		137
$Si_3O_2Cl_8$		76 (15 mm.)
$Si_4O_3Cl_{10}$		109–110 (15 mm.)
$Si_5O_4Cl_{12}$		130–131 (15 mm.)
$Si_6O_5Cl_{14}$		139–141 (15 mm.)
$Si_7O_6Cl_{16}$		145–147 (15 mm.)
Si_2OBr_6		118 (15 mm.)
$Si_3O_2Br_8$		159 (12 mm.)
$Si_4O_3Br_{10}$		122 ($<$ 0.5 mm.)
$Si_5O_4Br_{12}$		150 ($<$ 0.5 mm.)
$(SiOCl_2)_4$		91 (15 mm.)
$(SiOBr_2)_4$		155 (7 mm.)
4. Halo-Monosilanes		
$SiHF_3$	−131.2	−97.5
SiH_2F_2		
SiH_3F		
$SiHCl_3$	−128.2	31.5
SiH_2Cl_2	−122	8.3
SiH_3Cl	−118.1	−30.4
$SiHBr_3$	−73.5	111.8
SiH_2Br_2	−70.1	64
SiH_3Br	−94	1.9
$SiHI_3$	ca. 8	ca. 185
$SiHF_2Cl$	−144	−50
$SiHFCl_2$	−149.1	−18.4

200°C.[81] The iodide, Si_2I_6, is obtained by heating the tetraiodide with silver at 280°C.[82]

Oxyhalides of the type $Si_nO_{n-1}X_{2n+2}$ (X = Cl, Br) are the most common. In the chloride series, compounds up to $n = 7$ have been prepared,[83] whereas in the bromide series materials up to $n = 6$ have been characterized.[84] All the chlorine compounds are colorless oils which hydrolyze in the presence of moisture and are converted by absolute ethanol into ethyl esters. They are miscible with carbon tetrachloride, silicon tetrachloride, chloroform, or carbon disulfide. Members of these series are obtained when silica is heated with a mixture of oxygen and halogen, when a silicon tetrahalide is oxidized, or when silicon tetrachloride is partially hydrolyzed with moist ether.[85] They are separated by fractional distillation. The tetramers, $(SiOBr_2)_4$ and $(SiOCl_2)_4$, which are not members of these series, result in the first two reactions but not in the third one. They have the same types of properties but presumably possess cyclic structures, whereas the other materials have chain structures like

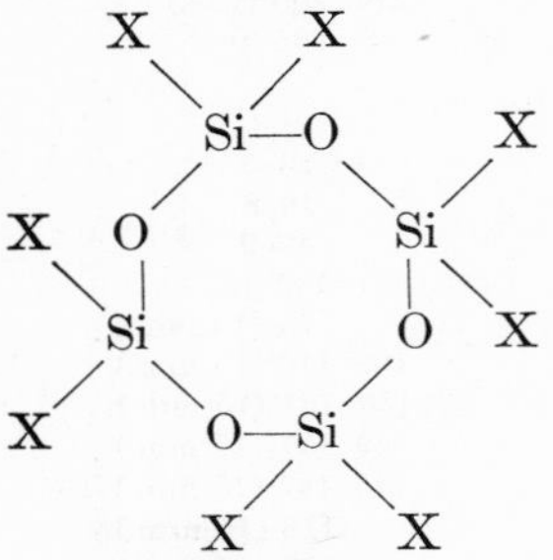

$(SiOX_2)_4$

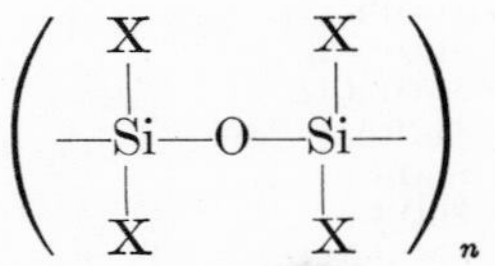

$Si_nO_{n-1}X_{2n+2}$

Terminal groups in the chain structures are then $—SiX_3$. Because of the presence of Si—O—Si arrangements, these materials are called halosiloxanes. Fluorination of chlorodisiloxane (Si_2OCl_6) with antimony trifluoride in the presence of antimony pentachloride[86] gave the various fluorine-containing siloxanes, $Si_2OF_3Cl_3$, $Si_2OF_4Cl_2$, and Si_2OF_6, as well as silicon tetrafluoride. All these compounds hydrolyze to silica and hydrogen halides and are comparable in general characteristics to the simple chlorine and bromine compounds. Monomeric

[81] W. C. Schumb: *Inorganic Syntheses*, Vol. II, p. 98. McGraw-Hill Book Co., New York (1946).

[82] C. Friedel and A. Ladenburg: *Ann.*, **203**, 241 (1880).

[83] W. C. Schumb and D. F. Halloway: *J. Am. Chem. Soc.*, **63**, 2753 (1941).

[84] W. C. Schumb and C. H. Klein: *J. Am. Chem. Soc.*, **59**, 261 (1937).

[85] W. C. Schumb and A. J. Stevens: *J. Am. Chem. Soc.*, **72**, 3178 (1950).

[86] H. S. Booth and R. A. Osten: *J. Am. Chem. Soc.*, **67**, 1092 (1945).

analogs of the carbonyl halides (COX_2) are unknown with silicon. Oxyhalides of tin and lead are poorly characterized.

The halomonosilanes are covalent compounds, the properties of which (Table 16·8) are intermediate between those of monosilane and the corresponding tetrahalides. As a group, they resemble the tetrahalides in general properties, but they are somewhat less stable thermally. General methods of preparation have been outlined previously (p. 676). Compounds of the type $SiHX_3$ (analogs of chloroform, etc.) are of particular interest. The chlorine compound is obtained in 75 to 80% yields by reaction of hydrogen chloride with silica at 380°C., followed by distillation.[87] A comparable reaction involving hydrogen bromide at 360° to 400°C. gives tribromosilane (silicobromoform).[88] Fluorination of trichlorosilane gives a mixture of the fluorine derivatives, $SiHF_3$, $SiHF_2Cl$, and $SiHFCl_2$, which mixture can be fractionally distilled to effect separations.[89] Germanium forms comparable compounds.

Oxygen compounds

The Group IVb elements form monoxides (MO) derived from the dipositive elements, and dioxides (MO_2) derived from the tetrapositive elements. Like the lower halides, the lower oxides are most stable and characteristic with the heavier elements. With these elements they are but slightly amphoteric and predominantly basic. The dioxides are predominantly acidic with all the elements, acid properties again decreasing with increasing atomic weight of the Group IVb element. Carbon forms a suboxide, C_3O_2, and some other minor oxides (e.g., C_5O_2) containing carbon to carbon bonds and possessing linear structures (pp. 694–695).[90] Lead gives oxides of compositions Pb_2O_3 and Pb_3O_4, which are really salt-like (p. 635) and more nearly correctly designated as plumbous plumbates, $Pb^{II}Pb^{IV}O_3$ and $Pb_2^{II}Pb^{IV}O_4$.

Monoxides. Carbon and silicon monoxides are sufficiently different from the monoxides of the other elements to merit special treatment.

CARBON MONOXIDE. The physical characteristics of carbon monoxide have been compared with those of the isosteric nitrogen in Chapter 6 (Table 6·14), and some comparisons between the CO, NO^+, and CN^- groups have been discussed in Chapter 15 (p. 599).

[87] H. S. Booth and W. D. Stillwell: *J. Am. Chem. Soc.*, **56**, 1529 (1934).

[88] W. C. Schumb and R. C. Young: *J. Am. Chem. Soc.*, **52**, 1464 (1930). See also W. C. Schumb: *Inorganic Syntheses*, Vol. I, p. 38. McGraw-Hill Book Co., New York (1939).

[89] H. S. Booth and W. D. Stillwell: *J. Am. Chem. Soc.*, **56**, 1531 (1934).

[90] L. Pauling: *The Nature of the Chemical Bond*, 2nd Ed., Ch. VI. Cornell University Press, Ithaca (1940).

A triple bond in the carbon monoxide molecule was first suggested by Langmuir[91] as being more compatible with the properties of the substance than a double bond. It is more probable, however, that the actual structure is a resonance hybrid involving the three structures[90, 92]

$$\underset{\text{I}}{:\overset{+}{\text{C}}:\overset{\cdot\cdot\,-}{\underset{\cdot\cdot}{\text{O}}}:} \qquad \underset{\text{II}}{:\text{C}::\overset{\cdot\cdot}{\text{O}}:} \qquad \underset{\text{III}}{:\overset{-}{\text{C}}:::\overset{+}{\text{O}}:}$$

All three structures make about equal contributions, structures I and II because of stabilization of structure I by the high electronegativity of oxygen and structure III because of the counteracting effects of the triple bond on the unfavorable charge distribution. Although these structures are markedly different, they are rendered about equally important because of the opposing effects of number of covalent bonds and charge separation. The presence of structure III is indicated by the small dipole moment (= 0.1 D) observed for carbon monoxide,[93] since a structure to balance the dipole effect of structure I is essential. The bond distance of 1.13 A,[94] when compared with values of 1.51 A, 1.22 A, and 1.10 A for structures I, II, and III, respectively, indicates only that the triple bond arrangement is not incompatible.

Carbon monoxide is combustible and is often a component of fuel gases (e.g., producer gas, water gas). Its reducing power toward metal oxides at elevated temperatures makes it useful in metallurgy. At elevated temperatures and in the presence of a suitable catalyst (e.g., Pd, Fe, Ni) it disproportionates to carbon and carbon dioxide,

$$2CO \rightleftharpoons C + CO_2$$

but as temperature increases the equilibrium percentage of the dioxide decreases. Although a formal anhydride of formic acid, carbon monoxide is insoluble in and unreactive with water. When heated with alkali, it is converted to formate. In the presence of suitable catalysts, carbon monoxide can be hydrogenated to methanol and a variety of other organic compounds. Reaction of carbon monoxide with halogens, sulfur, etc., gives carbonyl compounds of the type COX_2 (pp. 689–690). Perhaps the most interesting reactions of carbon monoxide, however, are those with certain metals and metal compounds to give

[91] I. Langmuir: *J. Am. Chem. Soc.*, **41**, 1543 (1919).

[92] L. Pauling: *The Nature of the Chemical Bond*, 2nd Ed., pp. 135–136. Cornell University Press, Ithaca (1940).

[93] H. E. Watson, G. G. Rao, and K. L. Ramaswamy: *Proc. Roy. Soc.* (*London*), **A143**, 558 (1934).

[94] L. Gerö, G. Herzberg, and R. Schmid: *Phys. Rev.*, **52**, 467 (1937).

the metal carbonyls and their derivatives. These will be discussed later (pp. 700–717). The poisonous character of carbon monoxide is associated with the strength of the bond which it forms with iron in the hemoglobin.

Carbon monoxide is formed when carbon or combustible carbon compounds are burned in limited quantities of air. It is a product of the reduction of the dioxide by carbon (see above equilibrium). On a large scale, it is obtained (mixed with hydrogen) by reduction of water vapor with hot coke (p. 403). In the laboratory, it is prepared by the dehydration of formic or oxalic acids with concentrated sulfuric acid, by reaction of formic acid with chlorosulfonic acid, by reduction of the dioxide with zinc or iron at elevated temperatures, by reaction of ferrocyanide with sulfuric acid, or by thermal decomposition of nickel carbonyl. The last reaction gives a pure product.[95]

SILICON MONOXIDE. Some confusion exists as to the nature and identity of this material. Products of this stoichiometry are obtained as brown amorphous powders (sold as a pigment under the name "Monox") by heating silica with carbon[96] or as brown powders[97] or glassy black solids[98, 99] by heating silica or silicates with silicon or silicides and condensing the vapors slowly or rapidly, respectively. X-ray diffraction studies show the brown products produced by either carbon reduction[100] or slow cooling of the gaseous material[98, 99] to be finely divided mixtures of silicon and silica. The black glassy products give no diffraction patterns and are apparently amorphous, polymeric samples of the true monoxide.[98, 99] Existence of the compound in the solid state is thus dependent upon the conditions under which the vapor is condensed. The presence of the monoxide in the vapor is indicated clearly by absorption spectra studies.[101]

Solid silicon monoxide is friable and resinous in character. It has a specific gravity of 2.18 to 2.2,[98, 102] is as hard as silicon, is a non-conductor (the brown material conducts), and does not fluoresce in ultraviolet light. On being heated, it reverts to silicon and silica. It forms no salts with acid but is soluble in hydrofluoric acid. The molar heat of formation of the gas is estimated to be −32 kcal. at 1600°K. and

[95] G. Meyer, R. A. Henkes, and A. Slooff: *Rec. trav. chim.*, **54**, 797 (1935).

[96] H. N. Potter: *Trans. Am. Electrochem. Soc.*, **12**, 191 (1907).

[97] E. Zintl, W. Bräuning, H. L. Grube, W. Krings, and W. Morawietz: *Z. anorg. allgem. Chem.*, **245**, 1 (1940).

[98] H. deW. Erasmus and J. A. Persson: *J. Electrochem. Soc.*, **95**, 316 (1949).

[99] G. Grube and H. Speidel: *Z. Elektrochem.*, **53**, 339 (1949).

[100] H. N. Baumann: *Trans. Electrochem. Soc.*, **80**, 95 (1941).

[101] K. F. Bonhoeffer: *Z. physik. Chem.*, **131**, 363 (1928).

[102] H. von Wartenberg: *Z. Elektrochem.*, **53**, 343 (1949).

−29 kcal. at room temperatures;[103] that of the solid is −103 kcal.,[102] the molar heat of vaporization being −70 kcal.[102] Solid silicon monoxide is useful as an abrasion and tarnish-resistant coating on mirrors and optical glass.[98]

MONOXIDES OF GERMANIUM, TIN, AND LEAD. All these compounds show both acidic and basic properties, the latter becoming increasingly important with increasing atomic weight of the metal. All may be regarded as parents of both cationic compounds (halides, sulfides, etc.) and anionic compounds (germanites, stannites, plumbites). Treatment of tin(II) and lead(II) salt solutions with alkali precipitates gelatinous hydrous oxide hemihydrates, $MO \cdot 0.5H_2O$. Lead monoxide (plumbous oxide) exists in two enantiotropic forms, *alpha* (red, tetragonal, low-temperature modification) and *beta* (yellow, orthorhombic, high-temperature modification), but the transitions are slow and the transition temperature is not known. The alpha lead monoxide and tin monoxide (stannous oxide) are in effect giant molecules in which each oxygen atom is surrounded tetrahedrally by four metal atoms, each of which in turn has four oxygens associated to one side of it in a square, the Sn—O and Pb—O bond distances being 2.21 A and 2.30 A, respectively.[104] Reducing power decreases with increasing atomic weight of the metal. Stannous and plumbous oxides are obtained by dehydration of the hydrous oxides. Oxidation of lead above 550°C. also yields plumbous oxide, other lead oxides being unstable with respect to this compound above that temperature.

Dioxides. Carbon dioxide is a gas at ordinary temperatures. The other dioxides are solids. The difference arises from the fact that carbon dioxide exists as discrete CO_2 molecules formed by complete sharing of electrons between carbon and oxygen, whereas in the others metal atoms are linked by oxygen bridges due to the instabilities of multiple links. Attractions between individual CO_2 molecules are small, but disrupting the structures of the other dioxides requires breaking a number of bonds and the consequent expenditure of considerable energy.

CARBON DIOXIDE AND ITS DERIVATIVES. Rapid expansion of carbon dioxide has a sufficient cooling effect to convert part of the material into solid. The solid has a sublimation pressure of 1 atm. at −78.5°C. The liquid is obtained either when the solid is heated under pressure or when the gas is compressed, the triple point being −56.6°C. at 5.01 atm. The critical temperature is 31.0°C., the critical pressure being 73 atm. Liquid carbon dioxide is available in cylinders. The

[103] G. Grube and H. Speidel: *Z. Elektrochem.*, **53**, 341 (1949).

[104] W. J. Moore and L. Pauling: *J. Am. Chem. Soc.*, **63**, 1392 (1941).

solid exists as cubic crystals at −190°C. The resonance forms of the carbon dioxide molecule have been discussed earlier (p. 195). The observed C—O bond distance of 1.15 A is in agreement with the presence of $:\overset{-\,..}{\underset{..}{O}}:\overset{+}{C}:::O:$ structures. The molecule is linear (p. 186).

Carbon dioxide is a comparatively weak oxidizing agent and will not support the combustion of carbonaceous compounds, sulfur, or phosphorus. On the other hand, previously ignited sodium, potassium, or magnesium burn in carbon dioxide, with the formation of carbonates, oxalates, or oxides and carbon, and at elevated temperatures carbon reduces carbon dioxide to the monoxide. At temperatures above 1000°C., carbon dioxide is dissociated appreciably to the monoxide and oxygen, the degree of dissociation increasing with increasing temperature.

In contact with water, carbon dioxide dissolves. The resulting solutions are faintly acidic due to the formation of carbonic acid, H_2CO_3 ($pk_{A_1}{}' = 6.46$, $pk_{A_2}{}' = 10.22$). Only a small proportion (ca. 1%) of the dissolved carbon dioxide appears to react with the water. Both normal and hydrogen carbonates are known for the alkali metals, but for the heavier elements the hydrogen carbonates exist only in solution and decompose to normal carbonates and carbon dioxide upon evaporation of the solutions. Most carbonates are difficultly soluble in water, but precipitation from solution, using an alkali metal carbonate, commonly gives basic salts because of extensive hydrolysis of the carbonate ion. The carbonate and nitrate ions are isosteric (p. 215). Peroxycarbonates have been described in Chapter 14 (pp. 513–514).

A variety of ammono and aquo-ammono derivatives of carbonic acid have been described. Certain of these are related to each other in the preceding chapter (pp. 571–572). A number of so-called carbonyl derivatives of type formula COX_2 (X = uninegative radical) are known. The melting points and boiling points of the more common of these are listed in Table 16·9. The halides, obtained by direct

TABLE 16·9

Physical Constants of Carbonyl Compounds

Compound	Melting Point, °C.	Boiling Point, °C.
COF_2	−114	−83
$COCl_2$	−118	8.2
$COBr_2$	....	64.5
$CO(CN)_2$		
COS	−138.8	−50.2
COSe	−122.2	−20
$CO(NH_2)_2$	132.7	dec

reactions of carbon monoxide with the free halogens in the presence of light, undergo ready hydrolysis to carbon dioxide and hydrogen halide or ammonolysis to urea and ammonium halide. The intensely poisonous chloride (phosgene) is the parent solvent in a system of acids and bases (pp. 323–324, 365). The fluoride attacks glass and many metals. Alternative methods of preparation involve reaction of carbon tetrachloride with sulfur trioxide (p. 524), reaction of carbon tetrabromide with concentrated sulfuric acid, and reaction of carbon monoxide with silver(II) fluoride.[105] The structures of the chloride and the amide (urea) are comparable:[106]

$COCl_2$	Urea
Cl–C(=O)–Cl; ∠Cl–C–Cl 117°, ∠Cl–C=O 121.5°	H_2N–C(=O)–NH_2; ∠N–C–N 110°, ∠N–C=O 125°
C–Cl = 1.68A	C–N = 1.37A
C–O = 1.28A	C–O = 1.25A

The cyanide results from reaction of carbon monoxide with cyanogen in the presence of light. The sulfide is intermediate between carbon dioxide and carbon disulfide. The molecule is linear,[107] and the bond distances[108] of 1.16 A and 1.56 A for C—O and C—S, respectively, are in accord with equal contributions by the resonance structures[90]

$$\ddot{\underset{\cdot\cdot}{O}}::C::\ddot{\underset{\cdot\cdot}{S}} \qquad :\overset{+}{O}:::C:\overset{\cdot\cdot\,-}{\underset{\cdot\cdot}{S}}: \qquad \overset{-\,\cdot\cdot}{:\underset{\cdot\cdot}{O}}:C:::\overset{+}{S}:$$

It is obtained by direct reaction of carbon monoxide with sulfur in a hot tube, by reaction of water vapor with carbon disulfide below 400°C., by controlled reduction of sulfur dioxide with charcoal, by oxidation of carbon disulfide with sulfur trioxide, by hydrolysis of thiocyanic acid, or by decomposition of certain thiocarbonates and thiocarbamates with acid. These carbonyl compounds are of considerable use in organic reactions.

Carbon dioxide, a combustion product of all carbonaceous fuels, is obtained by thermal decomposition or acid decomposition of carbonates.

[105] O. Ruff and G. Miltschitzky; *Z. anorg. allgem. Chem.*, **221**, 154 (1934).

[106] A. F. Wells: *Structural Inorganic Chemistry*, 2nd Ed.. p. 518. Clarendon Press, Oxford (1950).

[107] A. Eucken and K. Schäfer: *Z. physik. Chem.*, **B51**, 60, 126 (1941).

[108] P. C. Cross and L. O. Brockway: *J. Chem. Phys.*, **3**, 821 (1935).

SILICON DIOXIDE AND ITS DERIVATIVES. The name silicon dioxide is a misnomer to the extent that it implies the presence of discrete SiO_2 molecules. In all forms of silica, each silicon atom is surrounded tetrahedrally by four oxygen atoms, each oxygen being shared with another tetrahedron. The resulting giant molecule has the average stoichiometry SiO_2. Silica exists in three different crystalline forms, each of which has a low-temperature and a high-temperature modification. The relations among these forms as indicated by the scheme

$$\underset{\text{(hemihedral hexagonal)}}{\beta\text{-quartz}} \xrightleftharpoons{870°\text{C}} \underset{\text{(holohedral hexagonal)}}{\beta\text{-tridymite}} \xrightleftharpoons{1470°\text{C}} \underset{\text{(cubic)}}{\beta\text{-cristobalite}} \xrightleftharpoons{1710°\text{C}} \text{liquid}$$

$$\updownarrow 573°\text{C.} \qquad \updownarrow 120°\text{–}160°\text{C.} \qquad \updownarrow 200°\text{–}275°\text{C.}$$

$$\underset{\text{(tetartohedral hexagonal)}}{\alpha\text{-quartz}} \qquad \underset{\text{(biaxial, rhombic?)}}{\alpha\text{-tridymite}} \qquad \underset{\text{(biaxial)}}{\alpha\text{-cristobalite}}$$

are summarized in Figure 16·2. Many of these transitions are slow, and crystallization of the liquid is difficult to effect. As a consequence,

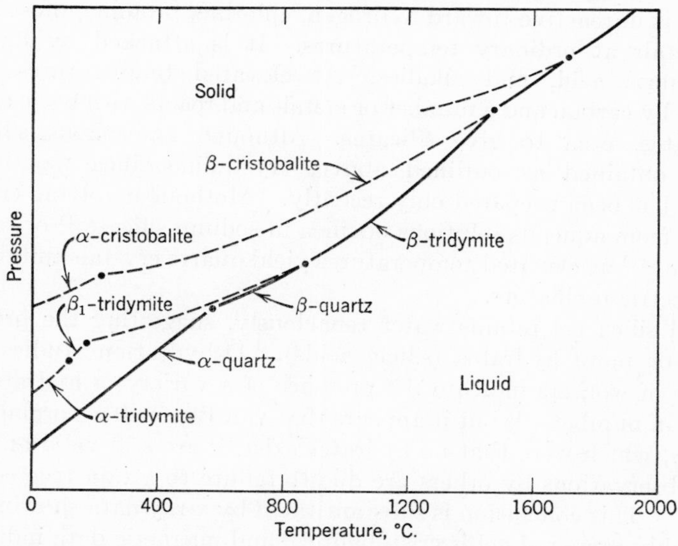

FIG. 16·2. Phase relations for silica. (Vertical axis not drawn to scale.)

all three polymorphic forms are found in nature, quartz being most common, even though they may be metastable.

In the forms quartz, tridymite, and cristobalite, the arrangements of linked SiO_4 tetrahedra are different. Cristobalite has the diamond structure (p. 665), with a silicon atom in the position of each carbon atom and an oxygen atom at the midpoint of each bond, the bond angle of oxygen being distorted to 180°. In tridymite and quartz a screw-like arrangement of the atoms imparts optical activity. Differences among these three forms are somewhat comparable with those existing among the diamond, zinc blende, and wurtzite structures. Conversions among these structures require bond rupture and are sluggish. The $\alpha \rightleftharpoons \beta$ transformations, however, involve only minor structural distortions and are both easy to effect and readily reversible.[109]

Slow cooling of molten silica or heating any form of silica to the softening temperature (below fusion) gives a vitreous, glassy material which is amorphous. It has a low coefficient of expansion and is transparent to ultraviolet. Hydrolysis of silicon tetrachloride or tetraethyl silicate or addition of mineral acids to alkali metal silicate solutions gives hydrous silica, which can be washed and dried to an apparently amorphous powder. Silica containing water may set to an amorphous gel. The extensive colloid chemistry of silica is based upon the amorphous material.[110]

Silica is unreactive toward hydrogen, chlorine, bromine, most acids, and metals at ordinary temperatures. It is attacked by fluorine, hydrofluoric acid, and alkalies. At elevated temperatures, it is reduced by carbon and a number of metals and reacts with basic oxides, carbonates, etc., to give silicates. Although amorphous silica is readily obtained as outlined above, crystalline silica (specifically quartz) has been prepared only recently. Methods involving crystallization from aqueous solutions of silica in sodium silicate[111] or sodium carbonate[112] at elevated temperatures yield quartz crystals suitable for peizoelectric oscillators.

Dried silica gel retains water tenaciously, suggesting the presence of one or more hydrates (silicic acids). Dehydration studies by a number of workers indicate the presence of a variety of hydrates (up to nine in number),[110] but it appears that van Bemmelen's orginal conclusions, which were that no hydrates exist,[113] are still valid and contrary observations by others are due to failure to attain true equilibrium.[110] This conclusion is substantitated by x-ray data showing that the freshly prepared gel is cristobalite[114] and magnetic data indicating

[109] A. F. Wells: *Structural Inorganic Chemistry*, 2nd Ed., pp. 567–569. Clarendon Press, Oxford (1950).

[110] H. B. Weiser: *Inorganic Colloid Chemistry*, Vol. II, Ch. VII. John Wiley and Sons, New York (1935).

[111] N. Wooster and W. A. Wooster: *Nature*, **157**, 297 (1946).

[112] A. C. Walker and E. Buehler: *Ind. Eng. Chem.*, **42**, 1369 (1950).

[113] J. M. van Bemmelen: *Die Absorption*, pp. 196, 214, 232 (1910).

[114] L. Krejci and E. Ott: *J. Phys. Chem.*, **35**, 2061 (1931).

the presence of only silica and water.[115] The preparation of the hydrates $SiO_2 \cdot H_2O$ (i.e., H_2SiO_3) and $2SiO_2 \cdot H_2O$ (i.e., $H_2Si_2O_5$) as reported by Schwarz and Richter[116] has not been substantiated. On the other hand, soluble silicic acids may exist metastably in solution before undergoing aggregation to insoluble silica. Thus when sodium silicate solution is treated with hydrochloric acid, much of the material first formed is ionic in nature,[117] and when silicon tetrachloride is hydrolyzed in the presence of silver oxide at *p*H 2 to 2.5, a liquid containing up to 80% silicic acid is obtained.[118]

Although silicic acid is unknown, a variety of esters of the type $Si(OR)_4$ and silicates containing SiO_3^{-2} and SiO_4^{-2} groups have been studied. The chemistry of the silicates is complicated, however, by the existence of many other silicon-oxygen radicals and bears no relation to the chemistry of the carbonates. It is best considered on a structural basis, and, as such, it is taken up in detail in a later section of this chapter (pp. 722–729).

THE DIOXIDES OF GERMANIUM, TIN, AND LEAD. Germanium dioxide exists in two forms, one with a cristobalite type lattice and the other with a rutile (TiO_2) type lattice, the latter form being metastable with respect to the former and less soluble in water. The transition temperature is 1033°C.[119] Tin dioxide exists in three polymorphic forms, but only the rutile form (as cassiterite) is important. Lead dioxide has only the rutile form. There is no evidence that any of these dioxides gives a hydrate corresponding to $M(OH)_4$.

It is of interest that treatment of tin(IV) solutions with alkali or carbonate or careful low-temperature hydrolysis of tin(IV) compounds gives a hydrous product (α-oxide) which is distinguished from the product obtained by oxidation of tin with nitric acid (β-oxide) by being readily soluble in acids or excess hydroxyl ion. High-temperature hydrolysis also gives the β-oxide. X-ray studies have shown that both oxides are cassiterite, containing adsorbed water.[120–122] The difference in properties is thus due to differences in particle size and the extent of coalescence of primary particles into others rather than to isomerism as formerly postulated.

Meta and ortho germanates, GeO_3^{-2} and GeO_4^{-4}, have been de-

[115] P. Pascal: *Compt. rend.*, **175**, 814 (1922).
[116] R. Schwarz and H. Richter: *Ber.*, **60B**, 2263 (1927); **62B**, 31 (1929).
[117] F. Mylius and E. Groschuff: *Ber.*, **39**, 116 (1906).
[118] R. Willstätter, H. Kraut, and K. Lobinger: *Ber.*, **61B**, 2280 (1928).
[119] A. W. Laubengayer and D. S. Morton: *J. Am. Chem. Soc.*, **54**, 2303 (1932).
[120] E. Posnjak: *J. Phys. Chem.*, **30**, 1073 (1926).
[121] R. Förster: *Phys. Z.*, **28**, 151 (1927).
[122] G. F. Hüttig and H. Döbling: *Ber.*, **60B**, 1029 (1927).

scribed. Alkali metal stannate and plumbate 3-hydrates are isomorphous with each other and with the platinates, $[Pt(OH)_6]^{-2}$.[123] This suggests species of the type $[M(OH)_6]^{-2}$ (M = Sn, Pb). This is confirmed by observations of structural similarities between $K_2[Sn(OH)_6]$ and $K_2[PtCl_6]$ and proof of an octahedral arrangement of six groups around the central tin(IV).[124] Further evidence that the water is actually water of constitution (p. 498) is provided by the fact that dehydration alters the properties of these materials profoundly. Plumbates (including the compound Pb_3O_4) are more stable with respect to loss of oxygen at elevated temperatures than the dioxide itself. Germanium and tin dioxide dissolve in acids (except nitric, in which they are insoluble) by metathesis, but lead dioxide normally dissolves by oxidizing the anion of the acid.

MISCELLANEOUS OXIDES OF CARBON. Carbon suboxide, C_3O_2, is a gas which condenses to a liquid boiling at −6.8°C. It combines with water to give malonic acid and is thus the anhydride of that acid. The carbon suboxide molecule is linear with bond distances of C—C = 1.29 A and C—O = 1.20 A[125] and exists in the resonance forms

$$:\ddot{O}::C::C::C::\ddot{O}: \qquad \overset{+}{:}O:::C:C:::C:\underset{\cdot\cdot}{\ddot{O}}:^{-}$$

I II

$$\overset{-}{:}\underset{\cdot\cdot}{\ddot{O}}:C:::C:C:::O\overset{+}{:}$$

III

with structure I contributing around 60% and II and III around 20% each.[90] Carbon suboxide is obtained by dehydrating malonic acid with phosphorus(V) oxide in a vacuum at 140° to 150°C.

Pentacarbon dioxide, C_5O_2, is reported to be a comparatively stable liquid boiling at ca. 105°C. and freezing below −100°C. It is obtained by passing carbon suboxide through a glass tube at 200°C.[126] Its existence seems questionable, however.[127] If it is a true compound, its molecular arrangement is undoubtedly similar to that of the suboxide, with less double bond character because of greater charge separation.[90]

The type of resonance characterizing the dioxide (p. 195) and suboxide is possible in molecules of the type C_nO_2 only when an odd num-

[123] F. Reiff and S.-M. Toussaint: *Z. anorg. allgem. Chem.*, **241**, 372 (1939).
[124] R. W. G. Wyckoff: *Am. J. Sci.* [v], **15**, 297 (1928).
[125] L. O. Brockway and L. Pauling: *Proc. Natl. Acad. Sci.*, **19**, 860 (1933).
[126] A. Klemenc and G. Wagner: *Ber.*, **70B**, 1880 (1937).
[127] O. Diels: *Ber.*, **71B**, 1197 (1938).

ber of carbon atoms is present. That materials with even n (e.g., C_2O_2, C_4O_2) are unknown is probably related to this fact.

Sulfur compounds

Both monosulfides (MS) and disulfides (MS_2) are known for these elements. Like the oxides, the disulfides become less stable and the monosulfides more stable as atomic weight of the metallic element increases. Thus carbon monosulfide is very short lived, and lead disulfide does not exist. The disulfides are of course more acidic than the monosulfides; in fact they behave as acids toward sulfide ion.

Monosulfides (MS). Carbon monosulfide apparently forms as a gas of short life when an electric discharge is passed through carbon disulfide vapor.[128–130] It is of no importance. Silicon monosulfide has not been characterized. The monosulfides of germanium, tin, and lead are precipitated from weakly acidic salt solutions by hydrogen sulfide. The tin and lead compounds are of analytical importance.

Disulfides (MS_2). Carbon disulfide is a liquid boiling at 46.2°C. and freezing to a solid melting at −111.6°C. It has a low kindling temperature and undergoes hydrolysis to hydrogen sulfide when treated with alkali or water (400° to 500°C.). With sulfide ion it forms thiocarbonate, CS_3^{-2}, the barium salt of which is easily obtained. Carbon disulfide is endothermic to the extent of 22 kcal. per mole. Electron diffraction data[108] show the gaseous molecules to be linear with C—S bond distances of 1.54 A. The measured bond distance is in agreement with equal contributions by the resonance structures

```
 ..     ..           +     .. −            − ..       +
 S: :C: :S         : S: : :C : S :         : S : C: : :S :
 ..     ..                 ..                ..
```

Similarities among the molecules CO_2, COS, and CS_2 are striking.

Silicon disulfide is much more poorly characterized, but in the solid state it appears to be made up of infinite chains of SiS_4 tetrahedra which share opposite edges.[131] The material is obtained as colorless needles, which hydrolyze readily, by heating silicon with sulfur.[132]

Germanium and tin disulfides are quite insoluble in 6 M acids. In the germanium disulfide crystal, each germanium atom is surrounded tetrahedrally by four sulfur atoms, and every sulfur atom is shared between two germanium atoms, the S—Ge—S bond angle being 103°

[128] A. Klemenc with E. Hayek: *Z. Elektrochem.*, **36**, 722 (1930).
[129] K. Mayer and J. B. Wibaut: *Rec. trav. chim.*, **56**, 359 (1937).
[130] V. Kondrat'ev and E. Magaziner: *J. Phys. Chem.* (*U.S.S.R.*), **14**, 6 (1940).
[131] E. Zintl and K. Loosen: *Z. physik. Chem.*, **174A**, 301 (1935).
[132] W. Büssem, H. Fisher, and E. Gruner: *Naturwissenschaften*, **23**, 740 (1935).

and the Ge—S bond distance 2.19 A.[133] The tin disulfide lattice is of the cadmium iodide type, with six sulfur atoms surrounding each tin atom. Both disulfides react with sulfide ion to give thioanions ($Ge_2S_7^{-6}$, SnS_3^{-2}, SnS_4^{-4}). These disulfides are obtained by direct combination of the elements, by precipitation of chloride solutions with hydrogen sulfide, or by precipitation of thio-anion solutions with acid.

Nitrogen compounds

In previous chapters, the binary compounds polymeric carbon nitride (p. 572) and cyanogen (pp. 466–467) have been discussed. A number of other binary carbon-nitrogen compounds are known (e.g., C_4N_2 and C_3N_{12}), but they are essentially organic in properties. The cyanides are discussed both as pseudohalides in Chapter 13 (pp. 463–475) and as such in a subsequent section in this chapter (pp. 717–721). Silicon, germanium, and tin form covalent nitrides of the type M_3N_4. The silicon and germanium compounds are chemically very stable, but the tin compound decomposes appreciably into the elements even at 360°C. In the germanium compound, each germanium atom is surrounded tetrahedrally by four nitrogens, one nitrogen being common to three tetrahedra.[134] These nitrides result as ultimate products when the ammonolysis products of the tetrachlorides are heated. No comparable lead compound has been prepared.

SOME SPECIAL PHASES OF CARBON CHEMISTRY

As special phases of carbon chemistry, the carbides, the metal carbonyls, and the cyanides and related compounds are discussed.

Carbides

The binary compounds of carbon with the other elements are called carbides, although in the sense that carbon is present in combination with more electronegative elements as well as less electronegative ones the term is not always completely accurate. Compounds with more electronegative elements (e.g., CX_4, CO_2, CS_2) are better considered as halides, oxides, etc., since their properties are better described in this fashion. Compounds with more electropositive elements (i.e., the true carbides) vary widely in properties, depending upon the type of linkage present. On this basis they may be classified as ionic, covalent, or metallic (interstitial),[135] as was done with the hydrides

[133] W. H. Zacharaisen: *J. Chem. Phys.*, **4,** 618 (1936).

[134] R. Juza and H. Hahn: *Naturwissenschaften*, **27,** 32 (1939).

[135] A. F. Wells: *Structural Inorganic Chemistry*, 2nd Ed., pp. 550–553. Clarendon Press, Oxford (1950).

(p. 404) and the nitrides (p. 578). The discussion which follows may be supplemented by reference to available reviews.[135–137]

Ionic Carbides. Ionic or salt-like carbides are formed by the metals in Periodic Groups I, II, and III. In general, these compounds exist as transparent crystals, and in the solid state they are non-conductors of the electric current. When treated with water or acids, they evolve hydrocarbons because of hydrolysis of the negative ions.[137] In general, they may be further classified on the basis of the type of anion (C_x^{-n}) present in the crystal as those containing (*a*) discrete C^{-4} groups (methanides), (*b*) diatomic C_2^{-2} groups (acetylides), and (*c*) triatomic C_3^{-4} groups (allylides).[135, 137]

METHANIDES. Carbides of this type yield methane on hydrolysis and are thus derived from methane. Examples are the beryllium and aluminum compounds, Be_2C and Al_4C_3. Beryllium carbide has an antifluorite structure (i.e., Be in place of F and C in place of Ca in the CaF_2 structure), each carbon atom being surrounded cubically by eight beryllium atoms. In aluminum carbide, each carbon atom is surrounded by aluminum atoms at distances of 1.90 to 2.22 A, the shortest carbon-to-carbon distance being 3.16 A.[138] In carbides of this type, the carbon-to-carbon distances are sufficiently large to permit the presence of discrete C^{-4} groups, and methane is the primary hydrolysis product (some hydrogen also results). In the series Be_2C, Al_4C_3, SiC, there is a regular change from ionic to covalent character paralleling decrease in electropositive nature of the metal. The absence of methanides of the larger cations (alkali metals, calcium, etc.) is apparently due to lattice limitations. For the alkali metals, too many cations are needed for compounds of the type M_4C to be accommodated by the available two tetrahedral holes per anion. For the alkaline earth metals, the large cations so deform the anion lattice that rupture to discrete C_2^{-2} anions occurs, giving acetylides rather than methanides.

ACETYLIDES. Carbides of this type yield acetylene (completely or predominantly) on hydrolysis and are believed to contain $:C:::C:^{-2}$ groups. Examples embrace the alkali metal and coinage metal compounds M_2C_2 (M = Li. . . .Cs; Cu. . . .Au); the periodic group II metal compounds, MC_2 (M = Be. . . .Ba; Zn, Cd); the periodic group III metal compounds, M_2C_6 (M = Al, Ce) and MC_2 (M = Y, La, Ce, Pr, Nd, Sm); and a few miscellaneous compounds, e.g., ThC_2, VC_2, and UC_2. Two types of crystal structures characterize

[136] G. T. Morgan and F. H. Burstall: *Inorganic Chemistry. A Survey of Modern Developments*, Ch. XVI. W. Heffer and Sons, Ltd., Cambridge (1936).

[137] G. L. Putnam and K. A. Kobe: *Chem. Revs.*, **20**, 131 (1937).

[138] M. von Stackelberg and E. Schnorrenberg: *Z. physik. Chem.*, **B27**, 37 (1934).

these carbides.[135, 139] Both are tetragonal and derived from the sodium chloride structure (p. 137) by replacement of Cl^- ions by C_2^{-2} ions. However, in the more common type (the CaC_2 type) the axial ratio is greater than one, whereas in the other (the ThC_2 type) it is less than unity. It is of interest that the normally tripositive lanthanide elements and tetrapositive thorium yield carbides of this type. The presence of a dipositive condition is suggested. Some support of this view is given by the fact that whereas calcium carbide gives only acetylene on hydrolysis, the lanthanide and thorium carbides give ethylene and methane as well, and thorium carbide also yields hydrogen. It is thus conceivable that the dipositive metals in the carbides release hydrogen from water in being oxidized to their normal oxidation states and that this hydrogen converts acetylene into other hydrocarbons. The carbides Al_2C_6 and Ce_2C_6 behave normally, liberating only acetylene. Hydrolysis of alkaline earth carbides is paralled by hydrolysis of the corresponding peroxides (p. 506).

ALLYLIDES. The only carbide of this class is the magnesium compound, Mg_2C_3. On hydrolysis, it yields allylene (methylacetylene), and its properties are consistent with the presence of a three-membered carbon chain in its crystal structure.[140] This peculiar carbide is formed when the acetylide (MgC_2) is heated.

The ionic carbides are normally prepared by heating either the metals or their oxides with carbon or by treating compounds of the metals with acetylene (e.g., with Cu, Ag, Au, Zn, Cd).

Covalent Carbides. The simplest covalent carbide is undoubtedly methane, and other carbon-hydrogen compounds may also be called carbides. However, they are usually classed as hydrides and have been considered as such in earlier discussions (pp. 673–674). The only truly covalent carbides which need be described here are those of silicon and boron to which complete three-dimensional covalent bonding imparts giant molecule characteristics. Silicon carbide or Carborundum (SiC) exists in three crystalline forms related to each other as the diamond, zinc blende, and wurtzite structures (pp. 133, 692).[141] In every case, carbon and silicon atoms alternate and are each surrounded tetrahedrally. In rupturing the structure, one must break a number of bonds. The high decomposition temperature (above 2200°C.), chemical inertness, and extreme hardness (9.15 on Mohs' scale) are thus reasonable. Boron carbide (B_4C) has a peculiar struc-

[139] M. von Stackelberg: *Z. physik., Chem.* **B9**, 437 (1930).

[140] W. H. C. Rueggeberg: *J. Am. Chem. Soc.*, **65**, 602 (1943).

[141] A. F. Wells: *Structural Inorganic Chemistry*, 2nd Ed., pp. 556–557. Clarendon Press, Oxford (1950).

ture in which the structural units are linear chains of three carbon atoms and groups of twelve boron atoms arranged at the vertices of a regular icosahedron.[142, 143] These are present in a sodium chloride type structure, with the center of the icosahedron substituting for the Na^+ ion and the central carbon for the Cl^- ion. Each boron atom is bonded to five other boron atoms in the same B_{12} group and to either a carbon or a boron atom in the adjacent B_{12} group, producing a continuous three-dimensional boron network. The bond distances are[143] B—B, 1.74 to 1.80 A; B—C, 1.64 A; and C—C, 1.39 A. The extreme hardness (9.32 on Mohs' scale), chemical inertness, and appreciable electrical conductivity of the compound are consistent with this structure. Observed B:C ratios above four are accounted for by spaces in the lattice which can accommodate extra boron atoms. Silicon and boron carbides are obtained by reducing the oxides with carbon in the electric furnace.

Interstitial Carbides. The transition metals of Periodic Groups IVa, Va, and VIa form carbides of the types MC (M = Ti, Zr, Hf, V, Nb, Ta, Mo, W) and M_2C (M = V, Mo, W) in which the small carbon atoms occupy interstitial positions in the crystal lattices of the metals. These compounds, like the corresponding hydrides (pp. 411–415), nitrides (pp. 579–580) and borides (pp. 770–773) are characterized by opacity, metallic luster, and high electrical conductivity, and like the nitrides and borides they are hard, high melting, and chemically inert.[144] As is true of metals, electrical conductivities decrease with increasing temperatures, and some carbides show superconductivity at low temperatures. Some of the physical characteristics of these carbides are summarized in Table 16·10. The MC type carbides have cubic close-packed structures, whereas those of the M_2C type have hexagonal close-packed structures. Interstitial carbides are obtained with metals having atomic radii greater than about 1.3 A, since the radius ratio $R_C:R_M$ must be less than 0.59. With metals having larger atomic radii, carbides of other types result.

The closely related (but smaller) transition metals chromium, manganese, iron, cobalt, and nickel give the carbides Cr_3C_2 and M_3C (M = Mn, Fe, Co, Ni). These carbides, although formally similar to the true interstitial carbides, are distinguished from the latter by their ready reactions with water or dilute acids to give either simple hydrocarbons (e.g., Mn_3C gives methane and hydrogen) or mixtures

[142] G. S. Zhdanov and N. G. Sevast'yanov: *Compt. rend. acad. sci. U.R.S.S.*, **32**, 432 (1941).

[143] H. K. Clark and J. L. Hoard: *J. Am. Chem. Soc.*, **65**, 2115 (1943).

[144] K. Becker: *Phys. Z.*, **34**, 185 (1933).

of methane, ethylene, ethane, and even liquid and solid hydrocarbons and free carbon (e.g., Fe_3C). These compounds may perhaps represent transitions between interstitial and ionic carbides, but their radius ratios (0.60 to 0.61) place them closer to the interstitial than to the ionic. The structures are incompletely known, although the M_3C compounds appear to contain discrete C anions, and the carbon atoms in the chromium compound are present as chains.

TABLE 16·10
PROPERTIES OF INTERSTITIAL OR METALLIC CARBIDES

Carbide	Radius Ratio, $R_C:R_M$	Resistivity, microhm/cm.	Melting Point, °K.	Hardness, Mohs' Scale	Temperature of Superconductivity, °K.
TiC	0.53	105	3410 ± 90	8+	< 1.15
ZrC	0.48	75	3805 ± 125	8–9	2.1–4.1
HfC			4160 ± 150	....	none to 1.28
VC	0.58			9–10	
NbC	0.53	74	3770 ± 125	9+	10.1
TaC	0.53	30	4150 ± 150	9+	7.6–9.5
MoC	0.56		2965 ± 150	7–8	
Mo_2C			2960 ± 50	7–9	
WC	0.55		3140 ± 50	9+	
W_2C			3130 ± 50	9–10	
4TaC:1ZrC			4205		
4TaC:1HfC			4215		

Interstitial carbides are obtained by the same general procedures useful for the preparation of interstitial nitrides (p. 579) except that in direct reactions of the elements higher temperatures (2200°C.) are required. Powdered carbides are compacted by powder metallurgical methods. The sintered compacts are often bonded with metals (e.g., with cobalt) into forms suitable for high-speed tools.

Metal carbonyls and their derivatives

Since the characterization of the reaction product of nickel with carbon monoxide as a carbonyl of composition $Ni(CO)_4$ by Mond, Langer, and Quincke,[145] interest in compounds of this type has increased, and the literature has expanded tremendously, particularly as a result of the studies of Hieber and his school. The metal carbonyls, $M_x(CO)_y$, may be regarded as parents of a number of related

[145] L. Mond, C. Langer, and F. Quincke: *J. Chem. Soc.*, **57**, 749 (1890).

compounds embracing the metal nitrosyl carbonyls, $M(NO)_y(CO)_z$ (discussed on pp. 600–601); the metal carbonyl hydrides, $H_xM(CO)_y$; the metal carbonyl halides, $M_x(CO)_yX_z$, and their derivatives; the carbonyl-cyano complex ions, e.g., $[Fe(CN)_5CO]^{-3}$; and a number of metal carbonyls containing other coordinated groups such as amines, e.g., $M_x(CO)_y(py)_z$. The many available reviews[146–154] may be consulted as supplements to the discussion which follows.

Compounds of these types are formed most commonly by the metals in Periodic Group VIII, less commonly by the neighboring transition elements in Groups VIIa and VIa, and still less commonly by certain of the neighboring elements in Group Ib. They are formed by reactions involving carbon monoxide and either free metals or metal salts and are characterized by having CO groups bonded directly to metal atoms. Their properties, although dependent of course upon the class of compound, are those of covalent materials. Unlike the other compounds of many of the metals which they contain, they are uniformly diamagnetic.

It is appropriate that the structures of these compounds and the nature of the bonding present be examined before the compound types are described in detail. Inasmuch as the CO groups can often be replaced successively by neutral molecules, it is apparent that they exist as such in the metal carbonyls. Since one-to-one replacement is effected by groups such as pyridine or cyanide, each CO group must occupy the equivalent of one coordination position. That the linkage to the metal is through carbon rather than oxygen is indicated by the enhanced tendency of carbon to be 4-covalent as well as by x-ray and electron diffraction studies, particularly of the iron compounds.[155, 156] Furthermore, these CO groups appear to retain without material alteration the general bond character of the carbon monoxide molecule.

[146] W. E. Trout: *J. Chem. Education*, **14**, 453, 575 (1937); **15**, 77, 113 (1938).

[147] A. A. Blanchard: *Chem. Revs.*, **21**, 3 (1937); **26**, 409 (1940).

[148] H. J. Emeléus and J. S. Anderson: *Modern Aspects of Inorganic Chemistry*, Ch. XII. D. Van Nostrand Co., New York (1938).

[149] A. A. Blanchard: *Science*, **94**, 311 (1941).

[150] A. J. E. Welch: *Ann. Reports*, **38**, 71 (1941).

[151] W. Hieber: *Die Chemie*, **55**, 7, 24 (1942).

[152] W. C. Fernelius: *Inorganic Syntheses*, Vol. II, pp. 229–233. McGraw-Hill Book Co., New York (1946).

[153] J. S. Anderson: *Quart. Revs.*, **1**, 331 (1947).

[154] W. Hieber: *F I A T Reviews of German Science* 1939–1946, *Inorganic Chemistry*, Pt. II, pp. 108–145 Dieterich'sche Verlagsbuchhandlung, Wiesbaden (1948).

[155] H. M. Powell and R. V. G. Ewens: *J. Chem. Soc.*, **1939**, 286.

[156] R. V. G. Ewens and M. W. Lister: *Trans. Faraday Soc.*, **35**, 681 (1939).

Thus the dipole moment of nickel carbonyl is zero,[157] indicating that the Ni—C—O bonds are linear and that, because of covalency limitations, the C—O bond must be comparable to that in carbon monoxide. This is supported by electron diffraction data,[156, 158, 159] indicating the C—O bond distances in the carbonyls and their derivatives to be 1.14 to 1.16 A as compared with 1.13 A in carbon monoxide (p. 686). Further support is given by Raman data which show the presence of a triple bond in nickel carbonyl.[160]

The most acceptable picture then involves coordination of carbon monoxide molecules to a central neutral atom, a situation which is most unusual but apparently paralleled in certain nitrosyls (pp. 598–601) and in cyanides of the type $K_4[M(CN)_4]$ (M = Ni, Pd).[161] The nature of the bond, however, is open to some question. The measured Ni—C bond distance of 1.82 A in nickel carbonyl[158] is some 0.18 A shorter than an expected single covalent bond distance,[162] even though the C—O distance (see above) shows clearly that the structure : C: : :O : is present. A structure

$$
\begin{array}{c} | \\ \text{—Ni::C::}\ddot{\text{O}}\text{ :} \\ | \end{array}
$$

would correspond to an Ni—C distance of 1.79 A.[162] It has the added advantage of rendering the nickel neutral, whereas the structure

$$
\begin{array}{c} | \\ \text{—Ni : C:::O :} \\ | \end{array}
$$

imposes an unlikely negative charge on the nickel. In the light of these data, a resonance hybrid involving both structures appears likely for nickel carbonyl. Although this type of resonance apparently characterizes other carbonyls as well, the observed shortening of the M—C bonds is less pronounced (Table 16·11), and the triple-bonded structure must be of enhanced importance. The isosterism among the CO, CN^-, and NO^+ groups (p. 599) is of some importance in this connection as well because it would predict observed similarities among isoelectronic materials such as $Cr^{\circ}(CO)_6$, $[Fe^{II}(CN)_6]^{-4}$,

[157] L. E. Sutton, R. G. A. New, and J. B. Bentley: *J. Chem. Soc.*, **1933**, 652.

[158] L. O. Brockway and P. C. Cross: *J. Chem. Phys.*, **3**, 828 (1935).

[159] L. O. Brockway, R. V. G. Ewens, and M. W. Lister: *Trans. Faraday Soc.*, **34**, 1350 (1938).

[160] J. S. Anderson: *Nature*, **130**, 1002 (1932).

[161] C. L. Deasy: *J. Am. Chem. Soc.*, **67**, 152 (1945).

[162] L. Pauling: *The Nature of the Chemical Bond*, 2nd Ed., pp. 251–254. Cornell University Press, Ithaca (1940).

and $[Co^{III}(CN)_6]^{-3}$ or $[Fe^{II}(CN)_6]^{-4}$, $[Fe^{II}(CN)_5(CO)]^{-3}$, and $[Fe^{II}(CN)_5(NO)]^{-2}$, and those mentioned in Chapter 15 (p. 599).

Metal-to-carbon bonds such as these must result from orbital hybridization (pp. 200–204). The nickel carbonyl molecule is tetrahedral,[158] suggesting sp^3 bonding. The electronic configuration of the nickel atom ($1s^22s^22p^63s^23p^63d^84s^2$) very probably reverts to the energetically similar $3d^{10}$ outer arrangement permitting the hybridization $4s4p^3$. Molecules of the isoelectronic nitrosyl carbonyls and the carbonyl hydrides of cobalt and iron are also tetrahedral[158] and

TABLE 16·11

BOND DISTANCES IN METAL CARBONYL COMPOUNDS

Compound	Measured Bond Distances				Calculated M—C Distance, A	Shortening of M—C Bond, A
	C—O, A	M—C, A	N—O, A	M—N, A		
$Ni(CO)_4$	1.15	1.82			2.00	−0.18
$Fe(CO)_5$	1.15	1.84			2.00	−0.16
$Cr(CO)_6$	1.15	1.92			2.02	−0.10
$Mo(CO)_6$	1.15	2.08				ca. −0.10
$W(CO)_6$	1.13	2.06				ca. −0.10
$Co(CO)_3(NO)$	1.14	1.83	1.10	1.76	1.99	−0.16
$Fe(CO)_2(NO)_2$	1.15	1.84	1.12	1.77	2.00	−0.16
$Co(CO)_4H$	1.16	1.83			1.99	−0.16
$Fe(CO)_4H_2$	1.15	1.82			2.00	−0.18

undoubtedly possess the same bonding. Molecules of the hexacarbonyls of chromium, molybdenum, and tungsten are characterized by octahedral arrangements of CO groups around the central metal atoms.[159, 163] These are consistent with the d^2sp^3 bonding permitted by the electronic configurations of the neutral atoms. Iron pentacarbonyl, $Fe(CO)_5$, has the trigonal bipyramidal molecular structure[156] consistent with required dsp^3 bonding.

The existence of polynuclear metal carbonyls (e.g., $Fe_2(CO)_9$ and $Co_2(CO)_8$) introduces a complication. Sidgwick and Bailey's contention[164] that CO groups may bridge metal atoms by bonds through both carbon and oxygen appears unlikely in view of the resultant necessary accumulation of positive charge upon the adjacent carbon and oxygen atoms. Crystallographic studies[155] show the carbonyl $Fe_2(CO)_9$ to have three CO groups bonded to each iron in the usual

[163] W. Rüdorff and U. Hofmann: *Z. physik. Chem.*, **B28**, 351 (1935).

[164] N. V. Sidgwick and R. W. Bailey: *Proc. Roy. Soc. (London)*, **A144**, 521 (1934).

fashion, the other three CO groups being bonded to both iron atoms in a ketone-like fashion. Each iron is thus tripositive. Pictorially this structure amounts to

The direct bond between the two iron atoms is suggested by the fact that the diamagnetic character of the material must be due to opposed spins of the odd electrons in the two iron atoms.[162] The measured Fe—Fe distance of 2.46 A[155] is only slightly greater than that required for a covalent bond. This structure confirms Brill's views[165] and is consistent with infrared data.[166] However, such an arrangement is difficult to apply to other polynuclear carbonyls (e.g., $Fe_3(CO)_{12}$, $Co_4(CO)_{12}$) because of the appearance of unlikely oxidation states and coordination numbers. Furthermore, the assignment of two types of linkages to the Fe—C bonds does not agree with the properties of all the compounds. A resonance of bridging groups involving the forms

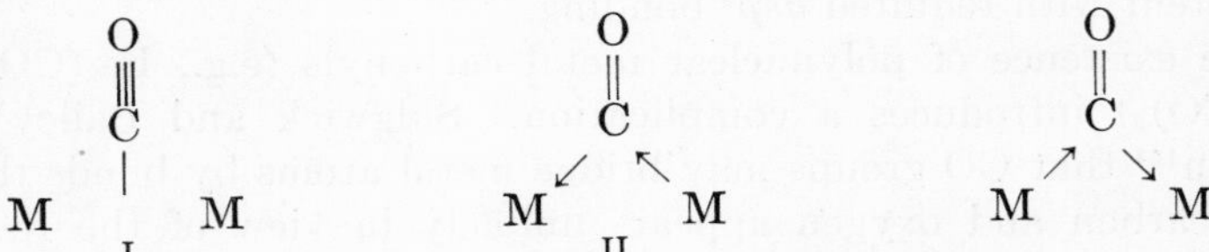

has been suggested as a solution to this dilemma,[167] but structures involving covalent M—M bonds are to be preferred on the bases of

[165] R. Brill: *Z. Krist.*, **65**, 85 (1927).
[166] R. K. Sheline and K. S. Pitzer: *J. Am. Chem. Soc.*, **72**, 1107 (1950).
[167] K. A. Jensen and R. W. Asmussen: *Z. anorg. Chem.*, **252**, 234 (1944).

x-ray, magnetic, and color data.[168] It is obvious that further studies are essential to complete elucidation of this problem. A promising beginning has been made by Sheline,[169] who suggests that the diamagnetic susceptibility, x-ray diffraction, and infrared data for trimeric iron tetracarbonyl are best explained by the bridge structure

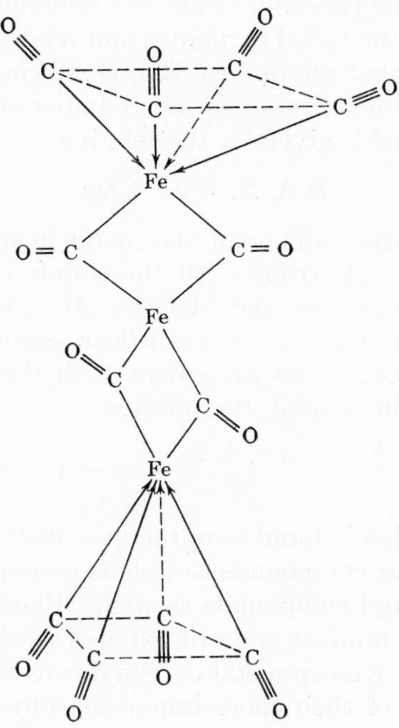

Evidences for ketone-like character in the bridging CO groups and for only slightly modified carbon monoxide character in the end CO groups are given.

The nitrosyl carbonyls have the same types of structures as the metal carbonyls (pp. 600–601). The metal carbonyl hydrides of cobalt and iron have the nickel carbonyl structure, and it has been suggested that for each hydrogen present an electron is transferred to the metal, the proton then attaching to an electron pair on an oxygen to give the arrangement[156]

$$
\begin{array}{c}| \\ -\text{M} : \text{C}:::\text{O} : \text{H}^+ \\ | \end{array}
$$

[168] R. V. G. Ewens: *Nature,* **161,** 530 (1948).
[169] R. K. Sheline: *J. Am. Chem. Soc.,* **73,** 1615 (1951).

The : C : : : O : H$^+$ group is isoelectronic with the : N : : : O :$^+$ group, making the carbonyl hydrides the analogs of the nitrosyl carbonyls. The carbonyl halides and related compounds presumably contain halide, etc., groups attached directly to metal atoms, and in the various amine derivatives amine molecules are coordinated to the metal atoms, with the carbonyl structures remaining unchanged.

The adherence of the metal carbonyls and related compounds to the effective atomic number relation (p. 233) is striking.[164] In the simple carbonyls, $M(CO)_y$, the effective atomic number of metal M is that of the next inert gas and is given by the relation

$$\text{E.A.N.} = m + 2y \tag{16·1}$$

where m is the atomic number of the metal in question. Each CO group thus adds two electrons. All the simple carbonyls, $Ni(CO)_4$, $M(CO)_5$ (M = Fe, Ru, Os), and $M(CO)_6$ (M = Cr, Mo, W), fit this picture, and the absence of mononuclear carbonyls with cobalt, rhodium, rhenium, etc., is in agreement with the concept. For the carbonyls $M_x(CO)_y$ in general, the relation

$$G - \frac{xm + 2y}{x} = x - 1 \tag{16·2}$$

holds, G being the atomic number of the next inert gas. This relation applies to polynuclear compounds as well as mononuclear and to most of the related carbonyl compounds as well. Blanchard has exploited the effective atomic number concept extensively for the carbonyls.[147]

Metal Carbonyls. Known metal carbonyls are listed in Table 16·12, together with some of their more important physical properties. A report made in 1949[170] gives mass spectrographic data suggesting the presence of a dinuclear manganese carbonyl in the products isolated from the reaction of manganese(II) iodide with carbon monoxide in the presence of a Grignard reagent. Later work has led to the preparation of the compound as a crystalline material.[171] Inasmuch as rhenium also forms a carbonyl, there appears to be no reason why technetium should not. However, it should be pointed out also that no palladium or platinum analogs of nickel carbonyl have been isolated. The volatility of copper when heated in carbon monoxide[172] suggests the formation of a copper carbonyl, as does the separation of yellow copper-containing precipitates in methanol prepared from

[170] D. T. Hurd, G. W. Santell, and F. J. Norton: *J. Am. Chem. Soc.*, **71**, 1899 (1949).

[171] E. O. Brimm: Private communication.

[172] H. Bloom: *Nature*, **159**, 539 (1947).

TABLE 16·12

THE METAL CARBONYLS

Group VIa	Group VIIa	Group VIII		
$Cr(CO)_6$ rhombic; colorless; sublimes		$Fe(CO)_5$ yellow; m.p. −20°C.; b.p. 103°C.		$Ni(CO)_4$ colorless; m.p. −25°C.; b.p. 43°C.
	$[Mn(CO)_5]_2$ brownish; sublimes (?)	$Fe_2(CO)_9$ triclinic; yellow; dec. 100°C.	$[Co(CO)_4]_2$ orange-red; m.p. 51°C.	
		$[Fe(CO)_4]_3$ monoclinic; green; dec. 140°C.	$[Co(CO)_3]_4$ crystalline; black; dec. 60°C.	
$Mo(CO)_6$ rhombic; colorless; sublimes		$Ru(CO)_5$ colorless; m.p. −22°C.		
		$Ru_2(CO)_9$ monoclinic; orange	$[Rh(CO)_4]_2$ crystalline; orange; m.p. 76°C. (dec.)	
		$[Ru(CO)_4]_3$ needles; green	$[Rh(CO)_3]_n$ crystalline; red	
			$[Rh_4(CO)_{11}]_m$ black	
$W(CO)_6$ rhombic; colorless; sublimes		$Os(CO)_5$ colorless; m.p. −15°C.		
	$[Re(CO)_5]_2$ monoclinic; colorless; m.p. 177°C.; sublimes	$Os_2(CO)_9$ yellow; m.p. 224°C.; sublimes	$[Ir(CO)_4]_2$ crystalline; yellow-green; sublimes	
			$[Ir(CO)_3]_n$ rhombohedral; yellow; dec. 210°C.	

carbon monoxide and hydrogen in the presence of a copper catalyst.[173] However, there is no concrete evidence that either the Group Ib or Group IIb elements give simple or polymeric metal carbonyls.

The covalent characteristics of the metal carbonyls are indicated not only by the data on volatility given in Table 16·12 but also by the fact that these compounds are insoluble in polar solvents but soluble in many non-polar solvents. The metal carbonyls decompose to the metals and carbon monoxide when heated, although polynuclear carbonyls may form as intermediates. In many reactions, their properties are those of the metals and carbon monoxide. Thus nickel carbonyl yields nickel bromide (and carbon monoxide) with bromine, but with Grignard reagents its reactions are those of carbon monoxide. In other reactions, the characteristics of the compound predominate. Examples are reactions in which varying numbers of CO groups are replaced by NO groups or amine groups (pp. 601, 716). Certain of the metal carbonyls give solutions with alkalies which yield metal carbonyl hydrides when acidified (pp. 711–714), and in some instances they react directly with free halogens to give metal carbonyl halides (pp. 714–716). The metal carbonyls are easily oxidized (some spontaneously) by atmospheric oxygen. Many are extremely toxic. Carbonyls of the Periodic Group VIa elements are more stable and less reactive than those of the Group VIII elements.

The metal carbonyls are obtained by a variety of procedures, among which the following can be distinguished.[153]

DIRECT SYNTHESES FROM METALS AND CARBON MONOXIDE. In practice, this procedure is limited to carbonyls of those metals which can be obtained in active form by low-temperature reduction procedures. Nickel absorbs carbon monoxide at room temperature and normal pressures. With reduced iron [prepared from iron(III) oxide at 500°C.], the pentacarbonyl is formed at 180° to 200°C. and pressures of 50 to 200 atm., although Mittasch[174] maintains that absolutely pure iron is as reactive as nickel. The presence of impurities sometimes has a beneficiary effect, however, for traces of sulfur favor the formation of nickel and iron carbonyls, and, in the presence of sulfides and iron or copper, molybdenum and tungsten form carbonyls readily.[153, 174] Because of the marked volume reduction occurring during carbonyl formation, high carbon monoxide pressures are beneficial. Because of enhanced sorption of the product carbonyl by the reaction metal and resultant decrease in activity, continuous circulation of the gaseous materials is practiced, particularly in the technical synthesis

[173] D. A. Pospekhov: *J. Applied Chem.* (*U.S.S.R.*), **19,** 848 (1946).

[174] A. Mittasch: *Angew. Chem.*, **41,** 827 (1928).

of iron pentacarbonyl. Rhenium, osmium, and iridium carbonyls have not been prepared by direct reactions. Convenient directions are available for the direct preparation of nickel tetracarbonyl.[175]

INDIRECT SYNTHESES INVOLVING THE GRIGNARD REAGENT. In studying the accelerating effects of anhydrous chromium(III) chloride on the reaction between carbon monoxide and the Grignard reagent, Job and his coworkers[176] isolated chromium hexacarbonyl, $Cr(CO)_6$. Similar reactions in the presence of molybdenum(V) and tungsten(VI) chlorides gave the corresponding hexacarbonyls.[177] The low yields characterizing these reactions can be improved by using high carbon monoxide pressures, a 60% yield of the chromium compound resulting, for example, at pressures of 35 to 70 atm.[178] The exact mechanisms of such reactions are unknown. However, with chromium it has been shown that no carbonyl is formed prior to hydrolysis of the Grignard,[179] indicating a probable organo-chromium carbonyl intermediate, which on decomposition with acid yields chromium hexacarbonyl as one product as

$$3Cr(CO)_2R_4 + 6H^+ \rightarrow Cr(CO)_6 + 2Cr^{+3} + 12R + 3H_2$$

That organo-chromium compounds do form under such circumstances and undergo comparable disproportionation reactions is indicated by Hein's work,[180] although syntheses of organo-chromium compounds may be questioned. Comparable reactions may be assumed to occur in syntheses of molybdenum and tungsten carbonyls by this procedure. It is significant that only the covalent halides mentioned are reactive under these conditions.

INDIRECT SYNTHESES INVOLVING METAL COMPOUNDS. Reaction of carbon monoxide with certain metal compounds, either alone or in the presence of supplementary reducing agents, often yields metal carbonyls. Although it may be concluded that reduction to the metal precedes carbonyl formation in general, the formation of carbonyl complexes which undergo decomposition to the carbonyls cannot be overlooked as a possible mechanism. Nickel tetracarbonyl is obtained when aqueous solutions of the complex cyanide, $K_2[Ni(CN)_3]$, are

[175] W. L. Gilliland and A. A. Blanchard: *Inorganic Syntheses*, Vol. II, p. 234. McGraw-Hill Book Co., New York (1946).

[176] A. Job and A. Cassal: *Bull. soc. chim.* [4], **41,** 1041 (1927).

[177] A. Job and J. Rouvillois: *Compt. rend.*, **187,** 564 (1928).

[178] B. B. Owen, J. English, H. G. Cassidy, and C. V. Dundon: *J. Am. Chem. Soc.*, **69,** 1723 (1947).

[179] W. Hieber and E. Romberg: *Z. anorg. allgem. Chem.*, **221,** 321 (1935).

[180] Fr. Hein: *J. prakt. Chem.*, **132,** 59 (1931).

allowed to absorb carbon monoxide and are then acidified,[181] when nickel(II) cyanide,[182] sulfide,[182] or mercaptide[183] suspended in sodium hydroxide solution is treated with carbon monoxide, or in general when nickel salts of inorganic or organic thio acids[151] are treated with carbon monoxide. According to Manchot and Gall[181], reaction proceeds by two steps, namely,

$$2NiX_2 + 2nCO \rightarrow 2Ni(CO)_nX + X_2$$

$$2Ni(CO)_nX + (4 - 2n)CO \rightarrow Ni(CO)_4 + NiX_2$$

absorption of the group X_2 by —OH, —SH, etc., occurring as it is formed in the first reaction.

Although ruthenium does react with carbon monoxide, the iodide, RuI_3, gives the carbonyl iodide, $Ru(CO)_2I_2$, even at ordinary pressures, and in the presence of an iodine acceptor (e.g., finely divided silver or copper) and at high pressures this compound is converted to the pentacarbonyl, $Ru(CO)_5$.[184] It appears that the process is stepwise and may be represented by the equilibria

$$RuI_3 \rightleftharpoons Ru(CO)_2I_2 \rightleftharpoons Ru(CO)_nI \rightleftharpoons Ru(CO)_5$$

A similar mechanism describes the conversion of iridium halides to polynuclear carbonyls, $[Ir(CO)_4]_2$ and $[Ir(CO)_4]_x$,[185, 186] but little or no carbonyl is formed if reduction to iridium metal occurs prior to introduction of carbon monoxide. Ease of conversion increases in the series chloride-bromide-iodide. Comparable reactions of carbon monoxide with osmium halides under pressure (120°C., 200 atm.) yield carbonyl halides of the type $Os(CO)_4X_2$, which undergo conversion to the pentacarbonyl, $Os(CO)_5$, in the presence of copper or silver.[187] Reaction of carbon monoxide with osmium tetroxide, OsO_4, to give the pentacarbonyl occurs under milder conditions (100°, 50 atm.).[187] Rhodium halides, RhX_3, react as do iridium halides, although somewhat more readily, to give the carbonyls $[Rh(CO)_4]_2$ and $[Rh(CO)_4]_x$.[188]

Comparable reactions of carbon monoxide with the rhenium compounds $ReCl_5$, $K_2[ReCl_6]$, and $K_2[ReBr_6]$ in the presence of copper and

181 W. Manchot and H. Gall: *Ber.*, **59,** 1060 (1926).

182 A. A. Blanchard, J. R. Rafter, and W. B. Adams, *J. Am. Chem. Soc.*, **56,** 16 (1934).

183 W. Manchot and H. Gall: *Ber.*, **62B,** 678 (1929).

184 W. Manchot and W. J. Manchot: *Z. anorg. allgem. Chem.*, **226,** 385 (1936).

185 W. Hieber and H. Lagally: *Z. anorg. allgem. Chem.*, **245,** 321 (1940).

186 W. Hieber, H. Lagally, and A. Mayr: *Z. anorg. allgem. Chem.*, **246,** 138 (1941).

187 W. Hieber and H. Stallmann: *Z. Elektrochem.*, **49,** 288 (1943).

188 W. Hieber and H. Lagally: *Z. anorg. allgem. Chem.*, **251,** 96 (1943).

under pressure give the carbonyl halides $Re(CO)_5Cl$ and $Re(CO)_5Br$, whereas the carbonyl iodide is formed from the compound $K_2[ReI_6]$ even at ordinary pressures.[189] These carbonyl halides, unlike the corresponding platinum metal compounds, are of sufficient stability so that they are not converted into rhenium carbonyl. This carbonyl, $[Re(CO)_5]_2$, is formed from reaction of carbon monoxide with such rhenium compounds as Re_2S_7, Re_2O_7, ReO_3, etc., at 250°C. and 200 atm.[190]

It is of interest that the high-pressure technique is also useful in conversion of iron, cobalt, and nickel compounds derived from highly polarizable non-metals (sulfur, iodine, etc.) into the corresponding carbonyls[191, 192] and is of technical importance.

SYNTHESES FROM OTHER CARBONYLS. Under influence of ultraviolet light, iron pentacarbonyl loses some carbon monoxide and yields the enneacarbonyl, $Fe_2(CO)_9$.[193] This compound undergoes thermal decomposition to the pentacarbonyl and a trimeric tetracarbonyl, $[Fe(CO)_4]_3$. Osmium pentacarbonyl undergoes comparable decomposition, yielding the compound $Os_2(CO)_9$.[187]

SYNTHESES FROM CARBONYL HYDRIDES. Oxidation of iron carbonyl hydride, $H_2Fe(CO)_4$, with manganese dioxide or hydrogen peroxide forms the trimeric tetracarbonyl.[194] Thermal decomposition of cobalt carbonyl hydride, $HCo(CO)_4$, is a convenient method of preparing the dimeric tetracarbonyl.[195]

The metal carbonyls are useful for the preparation of metal powders containing spherical particles (e.g., Fe), for the preparation of pure metals (especially nickel by the Mond process), and for the preparation of metal mirrors and plates (e.g., Ni, Cr). Iron pentacarbonyl is useful as an anti-knock additive to motor fuels.

The Metal Carbonyl Hydrides. Known metal carbonyl hydrides are $HRe(CO)_5$, $H_2Fe(CO)_4$, $H_2Os(CO)_4$, $HCo(CO)_4$, $HRh(CO)_4$, and $HIr(CO)_4$. Of these, only the iron and cobalt compounds have been studied in detail, the existence of some of the others being inferred rather than proved by isolation of the compounds. There is some

[189] W. Hieber, R. Schuh, and H. Fuchs: *Z. anorg. allgem. Chem.*, **248**, 243 (1941).

[190] W. Hieber and H. Fuchs: *Z. anorg. allgem. Chem.*, **248**, 256 (1941).

[191] W. Hieber, H. Schulten, and R. Marin: *Z. anorg. allgem. Chem.*, **240**, 261 (1939).

[192] W. Hieber, H. Behrens, and U. Teller: *Z. anorg. allgem. Chem.*, **249**, 26 (1942).

[193] J. Dewar and H. O. Jones: *Proc. Roy. Soc. (London)*, **A79**, 66 (1906).

[194] W. Hieber: *Z. anorg. allgem. Chem.*, **204**, 165 (1932).

[195] P. Gilmont and A. A. Blanchard. *Inorganic Syntheses*, Vol. II, p. 238, McGraw-Hill Book Co., New York (1946).

evidence also for the existence of a manganese compound.[170] As mentioned previously (p. 705), the metal carbonyl hydrides have the same structures as the metal carbonyls and nitrosyl carbonyls, COH groups being equivalent to CO groups.

Iron carbonyl hydride is a pale yellow, volatile liquid (m. p. −70°C.), which decomposes rapidly above −10°C. to the pentacarbonyl, a polymeric tricarbonyl, and hydrogen. It is strongly reducing in character and is readily converted to iron carbonyl iodide, $Fe(CO)_4I_2$, by iodine. Cobalt carbonyl hydride is obtained as a white to light yellow solid, melting at −33°C. to a yellow liquid. The liquid darkens as temperature increases because of decomposition to dimeric cobalt tetracarbonyl and hydrogen. On the other hand, the compound is stable in the vapor state in the presence of excess carbon monoxide. Like the iron compound, it is reducing in character. Preparation of polynuclear carbonyls from these carbonyl hydrides has been described.

An outstanding characteristic of the carbonyl hydrides is their behavior as weak acids and consequently their ability to form metal derivatives. The successive dissociation constants (k_A') of the iron compound are 4×10^{-5} and 4×10^{-14} at 17.5°C.[196] Two series of metal derivatives are thus obtained for the iron compound, but only one series is possible for the cobalt material. Derivatives of the alkali metals and large amine or ammine cations are salt-like in character, but those of other metals are not. Iron carbonyl hydride forms compounds of the types $(pyH)_2[Fe(CO)_4]$, $(pyH)H[Fe(CO)_4]$, $(o\text{-phenH}_2)[Fe(CO)_4]$ with pyridine and orthophenanthroline[197] and yields crystalline compounds of the type $[M^{II}(NH_3)_6][HFe(CO)_4]_2$ (M = Fe, Co, Ni) with many ammines.[198] These ammine derivatives and corresponding compounds containing metal ions with coordinated amines give highly conducting solutions in acetone or methanol.[198] Comparable compounds are formed by cobalt carbonyl hydride,[199] and it is of interest that dimeric cobalt tetracarbonyl reacts directly with ammonia to give the ammine salt $[Co(NH_3)_6][Co(CO)_4]_2$ and carbon monoxide.

Many heavy metal derivatives of the metal carbonyl hydrides are difficultly soluble and comparatively stable. The formation of the mercury compound, $Hg[Fe(CO)_4]$, as a product of the reaction of iron pentacarbonyl with mercuric salts was noted even before discovery of iron carbonyl hydride.[200] The same compound is precipitated from mercury(II) salt solutions by iron carbonyl hydride. It is a yellow

[196] R. Krumholz and H. M. A. Stettiner: *J. Am. Chem. Soc.*, **71**, 3035 (1949).
[197] W. Hieber and H. Vetter: *Z. anorg. allgem. Chem.*, **212**, 145 (1933).
[198] W. Hieber and E. Fack: *Z. anorg. allgem. Chem.*, **236**, 83 (1938).
[199] W. Hieber and H. Schulten: *Z. anorg. allgem. Chem.*, **232**, 17 (1937).
[200] H. Hock and H. Stuhlmann: *Ber.*, **61B**, 2097 (1928); **62B**, 431, 2690 (1929).

solid, stable in air, decomposed at 150°C. into iron, mercury, and carbon monoxide, and converted to the carbonyl iodide by iodine. Other heavy metal derivatives of both the iron and cobalt compounds are similar.

Iron and cobalt carbonyl hydrides are formed when certain carbonyls ($Fe(CO)_5$, $[Co(CO)_4]_2$) are absorbed in strongly alkaline solutions [KOH, $Ba(OH)_2$] and are liberated when acid is added.[201, 202] Hydrolysis reactions involved may be summarized by the equations

$$Fe(CO)_5 + 2OH^- \rightarrow H_2[Fe(CO)_4] + CO_3^{-2}$$
$$3[Co(CO)_4]_2 + 4OH^- \rightarrow H[Co(CO)_4] + 2CO_3^{-2} + 2[Co(CO)_3]_n$$

Cobalt carbonyl hydride, rather than a cobalt carbonyl, is the product obtained when an alkaline cobalt(II) salt solution containing cyanide is treated with carbon monoxide.[175] In other reactions comparable to those used for the preparation of nickel tetracarbonyl, cobalt carbonyl hydride also is formed. This is particularly true of reactions in the presence of cysteine,[203] xanthates,[151] and other thio compounds.[151] Alcohol or amine substituted metal carbonyls are sometimes decomposed by acids to carbonyl hydrides, iron carbonyl hydride being formed, for example, in the reaction of the compound $Fe_2(CO)_4en_3$ with acid.[204]

High-pressure reactions of the types employed in the preparation of the metal carbonyls (pp. 708–711) have been particularly useful for the preparation of the carbonyl hydrides. In the presence of copper, moist cobalt sulfide is readily converted into the carbonyl hydride by carbon monoxide under pressure,[191] and comparable reactions are useful for the preparation of other metal carbonyl hydrides. The cobalt compound is also formed at 165°C., in what amounts to a total synthesis, by the action of hydrogen (120 atm.) on the dimeric tetracarbonyl under high carbon monoxide pressure (150 atm.),[191] and partial conversions are effected, starting with cobalt metal or sulfide. The iron compound is not formed under comparable conditions.[205] High-pressure reactions involving carbon monoxide, metals more basic than copper, and either cobalt salts, cobalt, or dimeric cobalt tetracarbonyl yield metal derivatives of cobalt carbonyl hydride of the types $M^I[Co(CO)_4]$ (M^I = Tl), $M^{II}[Co(CO)_4]_2$ (M^{II} = Zn, Cd, Hg, Sn,

[201] W. Hieber and F. Leutert: *Naturwissenschaften*, **19**, 360 (1931); *Z. anorg. allgem. Chem.*, **204**, 145 (1932).

[202] W. Hieber and H. Schulten: *Z. anorg. allgem. Chem.*, **232**, 29 (1937).

[203] M. P. Schubert: *J. Am. Chem. Soc.*, **55**, 4563 (1933).

[204] W. Hieber and H. Leutert: *Ber.*, **64B**, 2832 (1931).

[205] W. Hieber and U. Teller: *Z. anorg. allgem. Chem.*, **249**, 58 (1942).

Pb), and $M^{III}[Co(CO)_4]_3$ (M^{III} = Ga?, In, Tl.).[206] The volatilities of these compounds and their solubilities in organic solvents suggest that they are polynuclear compounds.[206]

Metal Carbonyl Halides. Compounds of this type are formed by all the metals which yield carbonyls except chromium, molybdenum, tungsten, and nickel and by palladium, platinum, copper, silver, and gold as well. Examples of carbonyl halides (and closely related compounds) are summarized in Table 16·13. Of these compounds, those

TABLE 16·13
METAL CARBONYL HALIDES

Group VIIa	Group VIII			Group Ib
	$Fe(CO)_5X_2$ $Fe(CO)_4X_2$ $[Fe(CO)_3Br_2]_3$ $Fe(CO)_2X_2$ $Fe(CO)_2I$	$Co(CO)I_2$		$Cu(CO)X$
	$Ru(CO)_2X_2$ $Ru(CO)Br$	$[Rh(CO)_2X]_2$	$[Pd(CO)Cl_2]_n$ $H[Pd(CO)Cl_3]$	$Ag_2SO_4{\cdot}CO$
$Re(CO)_5X$	$Os(CO)_4X_2$ $Os(CO)_3X_2$ $Os(CO)_2X_2$ $[Os(CO)_4X]_2$	$Ir(CO)_3X$ $Ir(CO)_2X_2$	$Pt(CO)_2Cl_2$ $[Pt(CO)X_2]_2$ $H[Pt(CO)X_3]$	$Au(CO)Cl$

X = Cl, Br, I.

derived from iron have been studied most extensively. They resemble the iron carbonyls in being volatile and in being able to lose carbon monoxide by stepwise substitution by amines. Like the iron carbonyls, they are soluble in non-polar solvents and are photosensitive. Their thermal stabilities increase from chloride to iodide. A number of the more important reactions of the iron carbonyl iodides are summarized in Table 16·14.[153] The iron carbonyl halides are formed from direct reactions of the halogens with iron pentacarbonyl[207] or with iron carbonyl hydride or of carbon monoxide with iron halides under pressure.[208] Reaction of iron pentacarbonyl with iodine monochloride or bromide yields mixed carbonyl halides, $Fe(CO)_4XY$ (X = I, Y = Cl or Br.)[209]

[206] *Ibid.*, 43.

[207] W. Hieber and G. Bader: *Ber.*, **61B**, 1717 (1928); *Z. anorg. allgem. Chem.*, **190**, 193 (1930); **201**, 329 (1931).

[208] W. Hieber: *Z. Elektrochem.*, **43**, 390 (1937).

[209] W. Hieber and A. Wirsching: *Z. anorg. allgem. Chem.*, **245**, 35 (1940).

The carbonyl halides of ruthenium,[184] osmium,[187] rhodium,[188] iridium,[185, 186] and rhenium[189] are quite comparable with those of iron. However, the carbonyl halides of palladium, platinum, and the coinage metals are somewhat different. The platinum compounds, $Pt(CO)Cl_2$, $Pt(CO)_2Cl_2$, and $Pt_2(CO)_3Cl_4$, were first isolated by reaction of platinum with chlorine and carbon monoxide at 250°C.[210] but are also

TABLE 16·14

SOME IMPORTANT REACTIONS INVOLVING IRON CARBONYL IODIDES

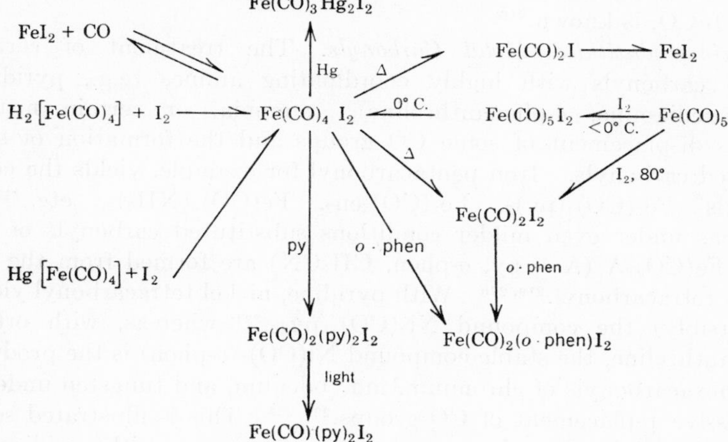

obtained by action of carbon monoxide on platinum(II) chloride at 250°C. or platinum(IV) chloride at 140°C. The first two compounds add ammonia to give the ammines $[Pt(NH_3)_2(CO)Cl]Cl$ and $[Pt(NH_3)_2(CO)_2]Cl_2$ and lose carbon monoxide in contact with strongly coordinating groups. Although decomposed to platinum by water, they dissolve in hydrochloric acid to give the complex acid $H[Pt(CO)Cl_3]$, of which many salts are known.[211] The compounds $Pt(CO)Cl_2$ and $Pt(CO)_2Cl_2$ are non-electrolytes, and the former is undoubtedly dimeric with a bridge structure (p. 273) such as

```
┌ Cl        Cl        CO ┐        ┌ Cl        Cl        CO ┐
     \     ↙   \     ↙                 \     ↙   \     ↙
       Pt         Pt          or         Pt         Pt
     ↗     \    ↗    \                 /     ↖   /     ↖
└ OC        Cl        Cl ┘        └ Cl        Cl        CO ┘
```

The bromide and iodide, $Pt(CO)X_2$ (X = Br, I), are comparable but

[210] P. Schützenberger: *Ann. chim.* [iv], **15**, 100 (1868); [iv], **21**, 350 (1870).

[211] A. D. Gel'man: *Ann. secteur platine, Inst. chim. gén.* (*U.R.S.S.*), **18**, 50 (1945).

of lower thermal and higher chemical stabilities. Palladium(II) chloride gives the compound $Pd(CO)Cl_2$ with carbon monoxide in the presence of methanol vapor.[212] This compound is comparable to its platinum analog in properties. Formation of copper(I) carbonyl halides as ammines or hydrates by action of carbon monoxide on copper(I) salt solutions is well known.[213] A stable gold compound, Au(CO)Cl, is formed from direct reaction of carbon monoxide with either gold(I) chloride at room temperature or gold(III) chloride in tetrachloroethylene at 140°C.,[214, 215] but with silver only the sulfate, $Ag_2SO_4 \cdot CO$, is known.[216]

Amine-Substituted Metal Carbonyls. The treatment of certain metal carbonyls with highly coordinating amines (e.g., pyridine, ethylenediamine, *o*-phenanthroline), ammonia, or certain nitriles effects displacement of some CO groups and the formation of substituted carbonyls. Iron pentacarbonyl for example, yields the compounds $Fe_2(CO)_4(py)_3$, $Fe_2(CO)_5en_2$, $Fe(CO)_3(NH_3)_2$, etc.,[217, 218] whereas under even milder conditions substituted carbonyls of the type $Fe(CO)_3A$ (A = py, *o*-phen, CH_3CN) are formed from the trimeric tetracarbonyl.[219, 220] With pyridine, nickel tetracarbonyl yields (reversibly) the compound $Ni_2(CO)_3(py)_2$,[221] whereas, with ortho-phenanthroline, the stable compound $Ni(CO)_2(o\text{-phen})$ is the product. The hexacarbonyls of chromium, molybdenum, and tungsten undergo successive replacement of CO groups.[222, 223] This is illustrated schematically for the chromium compound on treatment with pyridine as

$$\underset{\text{colorless}}{Cr(CO)_6} \xrightarrow{py} \underset{\text{yellow}}{Cr(CO)_4(py)_2} \xrightarrow{py} \underset{\text{yellow-red}}{Cr_2(CO)_7(py)_5} \xrightarrow{py} \underset{\text{red}}{Cr(CO)_3(py)_3}$$

$$Cr(CO)_3(py)_3 \underset{\text{heat}}{\overset{\text{py}}{\rightleftharpoons}} Cr_2(CO)_6(py)_3$$

The amine-substituted metal carbonyls have the properties of covalent compounds. Amine-substituted carbonyl halides [e.g., $Fe(CO)_2(py)_2X_2$] are known also.

[212] W. Manchot and J. König: *Ber.*, **59**, 883 (1926).
[213] O. H. Wagner: *Z. anorg. allgem. Chem.*, **196**, 364 (1931).
[214] W. Manchot and H. Gall: *Ber.*, **58**, 2175 (1925).
[215] M. S. Kharasch and H. S. Isbell: *J. Am. Chem. Soc.*, **52**, 2918 (1930).
[216] W. Manchot and J. König: *Ber.*, **60**, 2183 (1927).
[217] W. Hieber and F. Sonnekalb: *Ber.*, **61B**, 2421 (1928).
[218] W. Hieber, F. Sonnekalb, and E. Becker: *Ber.*, **63B**, 973 (1930).
[219] W. Hieber and E. Becker: *Ber.*, **63B**, 1405 (1930).
[220] W. Hieber and H. Vetter: *Ber.*, **64B**, 2340 (1931).
[221] W. Hieber, F. Mühlbauer, and E. A. Ehmann: *Ber.*, **65B**, 1090 (1932).
[222] W. Hieber and F. Mühlbauer: *Z. anorg. allgem. Chem.*, **221**, 337 (1935).
[223] W. Hieber and E. Romberg: *Z. anorg. allgem. Chem.*, **221**, 349 (1935).

Miscellaneous Metal Carbonyl Derivatives. Commonest of these are cyano derivatives such as $K_3[Fe(CN)_5(CO)]$, $K_3[Co(CN)_5(CO)]$, and $K_2[Ni(CN)_3(CO)]$.[181] Of particular interest are the nickel(0) derivatives, $K[Ni(CN)(CO)_3]$, $K_2[Ni(CN)_2(CO)_2]$, and possibly $K_3[Ni(CN)_3(CO)]$, formed either by reaction of nickel tetracarbonyl with potassium cyanide or by reaction of potassium tetracyanonickelate(0) (p. 719) with carbon monoxide.[224] Of some interest also are the mercaptide derivatives of iron and cobalt carbonyls, $Fe(CO)_3SR$ and $Co(CO)_3SR$.[225] These may be regarded as formal analogs of Roussin's salts (pp. 602, 604), with three CO groups being equivalent to two NO groups. The compounds $Fe_3(CO)_8Y_2$ ($Y = S$, Se), obtained by reaction of carbon monoxide (200 atm.) and hydrogen sulfide or selenide with iron powder,[226] are apparently analogs of the iron carbonyl halides.

Cyanides

The cyanides are derived from hydrogen cyanide, many of the properties of which have been described in Chapter 10 (pp. 341, 361) in conjunction with discussion of its solvent character. Hydrogen cyanide might be thought of as existing in two tautomeric forms, HCN and HNC, corresponding, respectively, to the well-known organic nitriles and isonitriles. However, all attempts to effect separations into two such forms have been unsuccessful, and their existence in actual fact must be regarded as questionable. Dadieu's[227] Raman data suggesting the presence of 0.5% HNC are better interpreted in terms of the 1% $H^{13}CN$ present.[228] If any HNC molecules are present, their numbers must be negligibly small.

The halogenoid character of the cyanide radical has been discussed in Chapter 13 (pp. 463–475), and the nature of cyanogen and a number of its derivatives has been described there. The present discussion should be supplemented by reference to these items. Only the metal cyanides are treated here. These have been discussed in detail by Wells[229] and are described in a useful summary by Callis.[230] They may be classed conveniently as ionic cyanides, covalent cyanides, complex cyanides containing discrete $[M^{+x}(CN)_n]^{+x-n}$ groups, and metal derivatives of these complexes.[229]

[224] A. B. Burg and J. C. Dayton: *J. Am. Chem. Soc.*, **71,** 3233 (1949).
[225] W. Hieber and P. Spacu: *Z. anorg. allgem. Chem.*, **233,** 353 (1937).
[226] W. Hieber and O. Geisenberger: *Z. anorg. Chem.*, **262,** 15 (1950).
[227] A. Dadieu: *Naturwissenschaften*, **18,** 895 (1930).
[228] G. Herzberg: *J. Chem. Phys.*, **8,** 847 (1940).
[229] A. F. Wells: *Structural Inorganic Chemistry*, 2nd Ed., pp. 536–544. Clarendon Press, Oxford (1950).
[230] C. F. Callis: *J. Chem. Education*, **25,** 150 (1948).

Ionic Cyanides. Ionic cyanides are formed by the alkali metals (except Li), thallium(I), and possibly by the alkaline earth metals. Their existence in many other cases appears to be precluded by extensive hydrolysis of the strongly basic cyanide ion and resultant precipitation of hydrous metal oxides or hydroxides. At ordinary temperatures, the sodium, potassium, and rubidium compounds have the sodium chloride lattice arrangement (p. 137), whereas the cesium and thallium(I) compounds have the cesium chloride structure (p. 183). It may be assumed that freely rotating CN^- groups occupy Cl^- positions in the lattices. It is of interest that at lower temperatures this free rotation is no longer present, and in sodium cyanide crystals at −10°C. or below all the CN^- groups are parallel,[229] the structure resembling the sodium chloride structure in the same fashion as does the CaC_2 structure (p. 698). In the cyanide ion, the C—N bond distance is 1.05 A, the bond being about 57% ionic and involving the resonance forms[231]

$$:C:::N: \quad \text{and} \quad :\overset{+}{C}::\overset{\cdot\cdot}{N}\overset{-}{:}$$

Covalent Cyanides. The covalent metal cyanides embrace the silver compound (AgCN), cyano-organo-gold compounds such as $[R_2AuCN]_4$ and possibly the cyanides of metal ions which form four planar covalent bonds (Pd^{+2}, Pt^{+2}, Ni^{+2}, Cu^{+2}). X-ray diffraction data on the silver compound indicate the presence of infinite chains of alternating silver and cyanide groups, the silver atoms being joined by cyanide groups bonding both through carbon and nitrogen.[232] These chains are arranged into a hexagonal lattice, with the silver atoms at the apices of rhombohedra.[233] The Ag—Ag distance of 5.26 A is constant with an —Ag—C≡N—Ag— arrangement.[229] Cyanide bridges have been shown to be characteristic of the cyano-organo-gold compounds as well (p. 843),[234] and may characterize materials such as palladium(II) cyanide.

Complex Cyanides. Complex cyanides containing discrete $[M^{+x}(CN)_n]^{+x-n}$ groups are characteristic of a number of the transition metals and the metals immediately following the transition series. They are usually characterized by their remarkable stabilities (often unaffected by acids) and by the complete difference in their properties

[231] L. Pauling: *The Nature of the Chemical Bond*, 2nd Ed., p. 75. Cornell University Press, Ithaca (1940).

[232] H. Braekken: *Kgl. Norske Videnskab. Selskabs. Forh.* II, **1929**, Medd. No. 48, 169 (1930).

[233] C. D. West: *Z. Krist.*, **88**, 173 (1934).

[234] A. Burawoy, C. S. Gibson, and S. Holt: *J. Chem. Soc.*, **1935**, 1024.

from those of the simple cations from which they are derived. Formation of such complexes is usually attended by profound alterations in oxidation potentials (pp. 300–305) and often results in the stabilization of unusual oxidation states. In such complex ions, the metals present are most commonly 2-, 4-, 6-, or 8-covalent (Table 16·15).

TABLE 16·15

COMMON CYANO COMPLEX IONS

Type	Stereochemistry	x	Examples of Metals
$[M(CN)_2]^{+x-2}$	linear	1	Cu, Ag, Au
$[M(CN)_4]^{+x-4}$	square planar or tetrahedral	0	Ni, Pd
		1	Cu
		2	Ni, Zn, Cd, Hg, Pd, Pt
$[M(CN)_6]^{+x-6}$	octahedral	1	Mn
		2	Mn, Fe, Co, Ru, Os
		3	V, Cr, Mn, Fe, Co, Rh, Ir
$[M(CN)_8]^{+x-8}$	dodecahedral	4	Mo, W

The spatial arrangements in such complex cyanides as have been studied are in accord with the predictions of orbital hybridization (pp. 200–204). Thus in the 4-covalent complexes $[Ni(CN)_4]^{-2}$, $[Pd(CN)_4]^{-2}$, and $[Pt(CN)_4]^{-2}$, the arrangement is planar (dsp^2 bonding);[235] in the 6-covalent complexes $[Cr(CN)_6]^{-3}$, $[Fe(CN)_6]^{-3}$, and $[Co(CN)_6]^{-3}$, the arrangement is octahedral (d^2sp^3 bonding)[236]; and in the 8-covalent complex $[Mo(CN)_8]^{-4}$ the arrangement is dodecahedral (d^4sp^3 bonding).[237]

As is true of the carbonyl group, binding of the cyanide group to the metal is apparently through carbon. Because of similarity in size of carbon and nitrogen, only the most accurate x-ray measurements can establish the orientation of the cyanide group. Data on the cyanide complexes of silver,[238] iron(II),[239] and molybdenum(IV)[237] are consistent with metal to carbon linkages. Chemical data on the splitting off of methyl isocyanide from methylated ferrocyanides and on hydrolysis of the cobalt complex $[Co(CN)_6]^{-3}$ to $[Co(CN)_5(COO)]^{-3}$ also indicate this type of bonding. Although the absence of metal-to-nitrogen linkages cannot be ruled out on the basis of these observations alone, they seem unlikely in view of the general similarities in properties characterizing the complex cyanides as a whole.

[235] H. Brasseur, A. de Rassenfosse, and J. Piérard: *Z. Krist.*, **88**, **210** **(1934)**; *Compt. rend.*, **198**, 1048 (1934).

[236] H. Steinmetz: *Z. Krist.*, **57**, 233 (1922).

[237] J. L. Hoard and H. H. Nordsieck: *J. Am. Chem. Soc.*, **61**, 2853 (1939).

[238] J. L. Hoard: *Z. Krist.*, **84**, 231 (1933).

[239] H. M. Powell and G. W. R. Bartindale: *J. Chem. Soc.*, **1945**, 799.

Bonding of the cyanide group to a metal incurs the same difficulties discussed in connection with the metal carbonyls (pp. 701–703). Pauling considers resonance involving the ionic structure

$$M^+(:C:::N:)^-$$

and the covalent structures

$$\overset{-}{M}:C:::N: \quad \text{and} \quad \overset{-}{M::C::N:}$$

to be important with the double bond structure contributing extensively.[240]

Metal Derivatives of Complex Cyanides. Although the alkali metal and alkaline earth metal salts of many of the complex cyanides just described are water soluble, many of the transition metal ions and copper(II) ion yield highly insoluble, often gelatinous, precipitates with them. These compounds are characterized by their stabilities toward acids and by the fact that they commonly contain alkali metal ions. Such ions may be held by chemical or adsorption forces.

The blue materials obtained by reaction of iron(III) salts with hexacyanoferrate(II) or by reaction of iron(II) salts with hexacyanoferrate(III) are of especial interest. Although these compounds are described as soluble or insoluble, they are all water insoluble, and the so-called soluble substances are merely those which can be peptized readily. All such materials have the stoichiometric composition $M^IFeFe(CN)_6$ (M^I = K, most commonly), but the true distribution of oxidation states is difficult to establish. Formulation of the materials as $KFe^{II}[Fe^{III}(CN)_6]$ (Turnbull's blue) and $KFe^{III}[Fe^{II}(CN)_6]$ (Prussian blue) is based only upon metathetical relationships and is not supported by sound chemical evidence. Thus Prussian blue is converted by sodium hydroxide to iron(III) hydroxide and hexacyanoferrate(II) but by ammonium carbonate to hexacyanoferrate(III). Furthermore, Prussian blue is formed from reduction of iron(III) hexacyanoferrate(III) (Berlin green) with either hydrogen peroxide [which reduces $Fe(CN)_6^{-3}$ ion but not Fe^{+3} ion] or sulfur dioxide [which reduces Fe^{+3} ion but not $Fe(CN)_6^{-3}$ ion]. However, the bulk of the evidence favors presence of iron(III) and hexacyanoferrate(II) in all the blue materials, even though in solution the equilibrium

$$Fe^{+3} + Fe(CN)_6^{-4} \rightleftharpoons Fe^{+2} + Fe(CN)_6^{-3}$$

is displaced largely to the right as written.[241]

[240] L. Pauling: *The Nature of the Chemical Bond*, 2nd Ed., pp. 254–256. Cornell University Press, Ithaca (1940).

[241] D. Davidson: *J. Chem. Education*, **14**, 238, 277 (1937).

X-ray studies[242] indicate definite similarities between the structures of Prussian blue and Berlin green. The latter has a cubic lattice. This is preserved with Prussian blue, but alternate iron atoms are reduced to the dipositive state and unipositive ions are inserted in alternate unit cells to preserve the charge balance. Although no distinction between iron(II) and iron(III) can be made, it is probable that the two are equivalent in the lattice. The same types of structures characterize the materials $M^{I}CuFe(CN)_6$ and $M^{I}FeRu(CN)_6$ (ruthenium purple), substitution for iron(II) occurring atom for atom. If it is assumed that the cyanide group can coordinate through the nitrogen as well as through the carbon, each $Fe(CN)_6$ group can then be surrounded by six metal ions and each metal ion by six $Fe(CN)_6$ groups. This gives a supercomplex of the type demanded by the Keggin structure. Such anions may contain the group $[Fe^{III}\{Fe(CN)_6\}]^-$, which Davidson calls *berlinate*.[241] Alkali metal, iron(II), iron(III), etc., berlinates then become possible.

The heavy metal hexacyanoferrate(II) compounds are also supercomplexes (e.g. $M_2[Cu\{Fe(CN)_6\}]$, $Zn[Zn_3\{Fe(CN)_6\}_2]$), as are the metal derivatives of cyano complexes containing no iron (e.g., $K_2[Mn\{Mn(CN)_6\}]$).

SOME SPECIAL PHASES OF SILICON CHEMISTRY

Special topics of silicon chemistry covered in this discussion embrace the silicates, some phases of the organic chemistry of silicon, and cationic silicon compounds. Some suggestions on nomenclature are included also.

The silicates

The silicates may be divided roughly into soluble and insoluble materials. The soluble silicates are derived only from the alkali metals and have compositions commonly expressed in terms of varying amounts of metal oxide, silica, and (usually) water.[243] The insoluble silicates are the naturally occurring mineral materials, together with certain synthetic zeolite-like compounds useful as ion exchangers. The two series of materials bear but little formal relation to each other, although they are structurally similar. Much of the difficulty in systematizing the chemistry of the silicates is traceable to early attempts to consider them as derivatives of a series of polysilicic acids derived from the inter- and intramolecular dehydration of the equally hypothetical orthosilicic acid, H_4SiO_4.

[242] J. F. Keggin and F. D. Miles: *Nature*, **137**, 577 (1936).
[243] R. C. Merrill: *J. Chem. Education*, **24**, 262 (1947).

The Soluble Silicates. Commonest of these are the sodium compounds, obtained most generally by fusion in varying proportions of silica sand with sodium carbonate at around 1300°C. Products in which the silica-to-alkali weight ratio is around 2 are water soluble, whereas those in which this ratio is above 2.5 must be dissolved by steam under pressure. The resulting viscous aqueous solutions are often sold as such. A variety of crystalline compounds has been isolated and studied. Among these compounds are anhydrous Na_2SiO_3 (metasilicate), $Na_2Si_2O_5$ (disilicate), Na_4SiO_4 (orthosilicate), and $Na_6Si_2O_7$ (pyrosilicate) and the hydrates $Na_2SiO_3 \cdot nH_2O$ (n = 5, 6, 8, 9), $Na_2Si_4O_9 \cdot 7H_2O$, and $Na_3HSiO_4 \cdot 5H_2O$. The phase diagram for the Na_2O–SiO_2 system shows the anhydrous meta and ortho compounds as congruent melting substances.[244] Closely comparable potassium compounds have been described as well. Soluble silicates characterized by silica-to-alkali ratios up to 2 dissolve to true solutions, but those with higher ratios give colloidal suspensions containing dispersed silica. Metal salt solutions are precipitated by soluble silicates, but the precipitates so obtained are commonly mixtures of silica, basic salts, and hydrous oxides or hydroxides rather than silicates.

The Naturally Occurring Silicates. The naturally occurring silicates, when considered from the point of view of chemical composition alone, are an amazingly complex series of materials. Early attempts at systematization of these substances as based upon analytical compositions were notably unsuccessful, for the materials can be fitted into no logical scheme of salts and are derived from no series of silicic acids. It is only since the application of x-ray crystallographic methods to the study of these materials[245, 246] that the sources of these difficulties have become apparent and that systematic classification has been shown to be possible only in terms of structural arrangements.

The essential difficulties associated with silicate classification are these. Analytical data alone are insufficient since a given set of data for a material of such complexity may be consistent with a number of different molecular formulations. Furthermore, the homogeneity of the sample in question may be in doubt, and the assignment of any particular formula based upon analysis alone may thus be entirely fortuitous. Another factor involves isomorphous replacement. Ions such as Mg^{+2}, Ca^{+2}, Fe^{+2}, etc., may replace each other, and similar replacements involving Al^{+3} and Fe^{+3}, Na^+ and K^+, or OH^- and F^-

244 F. C. Kracek: *J. Phys. Chem.*, **34**, 1583 (1930).

245 W. L. Bragg: *Atomic Structure of Minerals*, Ch. IX–XVI. Cornell University Press, Ithaca, N. Y. (1937).

246 L. Pauling: *The Nature of the Chemical Bond*, 2nd Ed., pp. 385–400. Cornell University Press, Ithaca (1940).

may occur in almost endless variety. Such replacements involve no changes in oxidation states or general compositions, but they do impose analytical difficulties. A more significant type of replacement, however, is that of silicon by aluminum. This is possible because of size similarities ($r_{Si^{+4}} = 0.50$ A, $r_{Al^{+3}} = 0.55$ A) and is extremely common. Because of the difference in oxidation number, replacement of silicon by aluminum raises the anion oxidation state by one unit and requires the presence of either a balancing cation (e.g., Na^+) or a further isomorphous replacement of one cation by another of higher positive charge (e.g., Na^+ by Ca^{+2}). A further complication is introduced in such circumstances by the fact that whereas silicon is always 4-coordinate toward oxygen, aluminum may be either 4-coordinate or 6-coordinate. An AlO_4 group would be the structural analog of an SiO_4 group, but an AlO_6 group would not. It is apparent, therefore, that the only logical classification of the silicates is that based upon structures.

The silicates are in effect coordinate structures based upon large anions arranged about small cations. The dimensions of the lattice are in general controlled by the anions rather than the cations because of the larger sizes of the former. Most important are the Si^{+4} and O^{-2} ions.* In all silicates the basic structural unit is the SiO_4 tetrahedron. This appears to remain essentially unaltered regardless of the other materials present, the Si—O and O—O bond distances remaining constant at 1.62 A and 2.7 A, respectively. For convenience such tetrahedra may be represented variously as

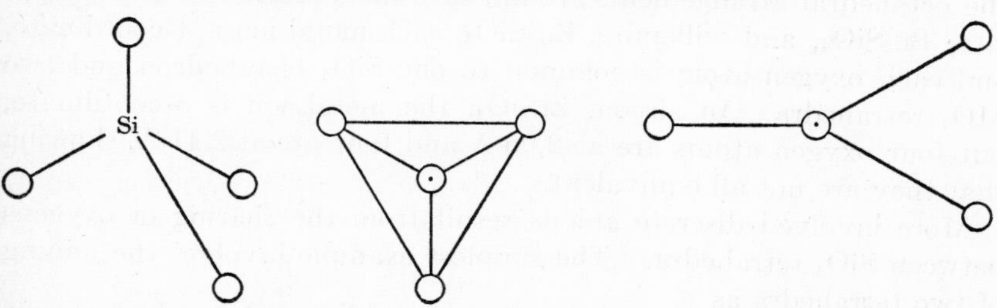

the first representation being self-explanatory and the other two being tetrahedra as viewed from above, with the central silicon designated as a dot. Linking of tetrahedra then occurs by the sharing of oxygens at apices.

According to such tetrahedral arrangements (plus substitution of aluminum for silicon), the following types of structures can be distinguished:

* The term *ions* is used advisedly here. Actually, there are no discrete Si^{+4} and O^{-2} ions present, but each Si—O linkage is predominantly ionic in character.

Discrete anions, in which either individual tetrahedra are present (SiO_4^{-4} as in orthosilicates) or a limited number of tetrahedra are combined into ionic groups ($Si_2O_7^{-6}$, $Si_3O_9^{-6}$, $Si_6O_{18}^{-12}$).

Extended anions, in which tetrahedra are linked into chains of indefinite length (SiO_3^{-2}, $Si_4O_{11}^{-6}$) or into sheets of indeterminate area ($Si_2O_5^{-2}$).

Three-dimensional networks, in which tetrahedra are completely linked in all three directions (SiO_2).

Each of these may be discussed briefly.

DISCRETE ANIONS. In the orthosilicates, individual SiO_4 tetrahedra are present, and there is no sharing of oxygen atoms between adjacent tetrahedra. However, the oxygens present are coordinated to the metal cations, and, because of the variety of fashions in which this can occur, a variety of orthosilicate structures can be distinguished. Among silicates of this type are olivine and related minerals, the chondrodites, phenacite, willemite, and zircon. Olivine, $9Mg_2SiO_4 \cdot Fe_2SiO_4$, and its related compounds may be formulated as $M_2^{II}SiO_4$ (M^{II} = Mg, Fe, Mn, alone or mixed). In this structure each dipositive metal (normally magnesium) is so arranged that it is surrounded octahedrally by six oxygens, each oxygen atom present being linked, therefore, to one silicon and coordinated to three magnesiums. This type of structure is similar to that of magnesium hydroxide (brucite), and these two structures are combined in the chrondrodite minerals, $mMg_2SiO_4 \cdot nMg(OH, F)_2$, where sheets of the olivine structure are separated by layers of OH^- or F^- ions. These ions are then part of the octahedral arrangements around each magnesium ion. In phenacite, Be_2SiO_4, and willemite, Zn_2SiO_4, each metal ion is 4-coordinate, and each oxygen atom is common to one SiO_4 tetrahedron and two MO_4 tetrahedra. In zircon, $ZrSiO_4$, the metal ion is 8-coordinate, but four oxygen atoms are at 2.05 A and four are at 2.41 A, showing that they are not all equivalent.

More involved discrete anions result from the sharing of oxygens between SiO_4 tetrahedra. The simplest example involves the joining of two tetrahedra as

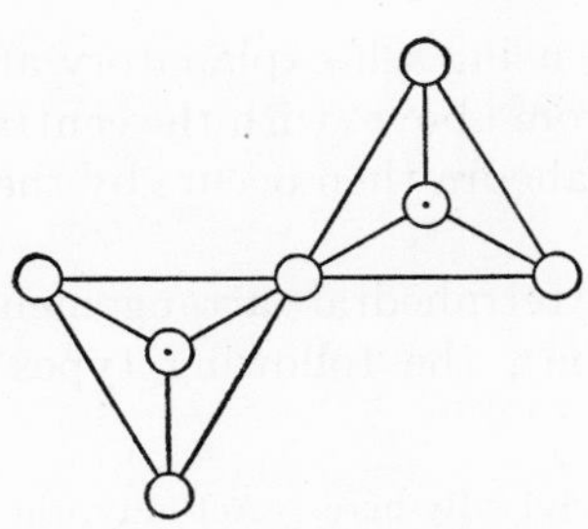

$Si_2O_7^{-6}$

to give the ion $Si_2O_7^{-6}$. Such an arrangement is characteristic of thortveitite, $Sc_2Si_2O_7$, and hemimorphite, $Zn_4(OH)_2Si_2O_7 \cdot H_2O$. In thortveitite, each scandium ion is surrounded octahedrally by oxide ions, whereas in hemimorphite the crystal contains OH^- ions as well as $Si_2O_7^{-6}$ ions. The discrete anions $Si_3O_9^{-6}$ and $Si_6O_{18}^{-12}$ involve cyclic arrangements of tetrahedra as

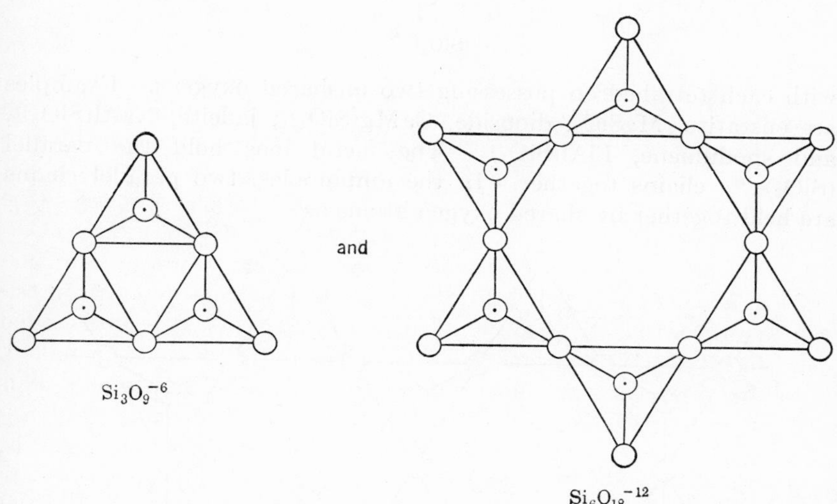

The $Si_3O_9^{-6}$ group is characteristic of benitoite, $BaTiSi_3O_9$, and wollastonite, $Ca_3Si_3O_9$, whereas the $Si_6O_{18}^{-12}$ group is found in beryl (emerald, aquamarine), $Be_3Al_2Si_6O_{18}$. In both the benitoite and beryl structures the rings are arranged in sheets (but not layer structures), with the metal ions between the sheets and binding them together. In benitoite the Ti^{+4} and Ba^{+2} ions are 6-coordinate, but in beryl the Be^{+2} ions are 4-coordinate and the Al^{+3} ions 6-coordinate. In beryl the layers are so arranged that channels exist through the centers of superimposed hexagons, thus rendering beryl permeable to gases with small molecules (e.g., helium).

EXTENDED ANIONS. The indefinite linking of SiO_4 tetrahedra into chains gives the composition $(SiO_3)_n^{-2n}$ (metasilicate) where the chains are single and the composition $(Si_4O_{11})_n^{-6n}$ (metatetrasilicate) where the chains are double. These are characteristic, respectively, of the pyroxenes and the amphiboles. In the pyroxenes, the single chains amount to

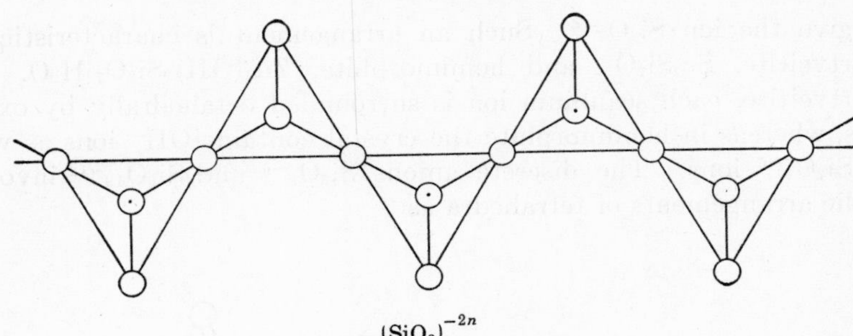

$(SiO_3)_n^{-2n}$

with each tetrahedron possessing two unshared oxygens. Examples are enstatite, $MgSiO_3$, diopside, $CaMg(SiO_3)_2$, jadeite, $NaAl(SiO_3)_2$, and spodumene, $LiAl(SiO_3)_2$. The metal ions hold the parallel $(SiO_3)_n^{-2n}$ chains together. In the amphiboles, two parallel chains are held together by shared oxygen atoms as

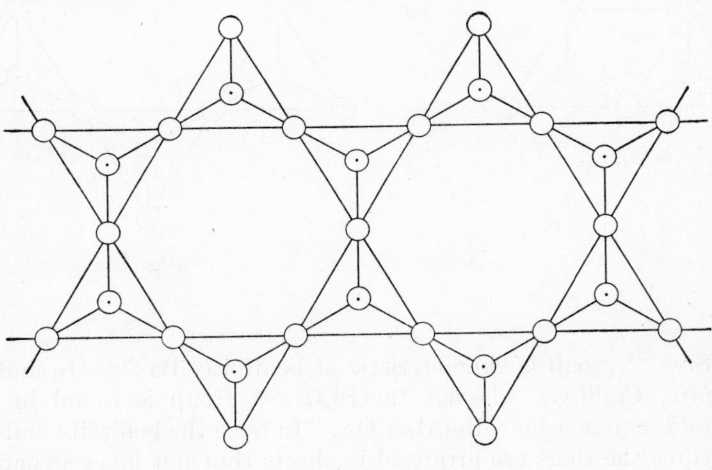

$(Si_4O_{11})_n^{-6n}$

Examples are tremolite, $(HO)_2Ca_2Mg_5(Si_4O_{11})_2$, and the various materials derived from tremolite by isomorphous replacement of either the metal ions or silicon. The metal ions again hold the chains together. It is of interest that the structures of these minerals are related to the ease with which cleavage occurs between chains and to their fibrous natures. The asbestos minerals are amphiboles and the closely related chrysotile, $(HO)_6Mg_6Si_4O_{11}\cdot H_2O$.

The complete two-dimensional cross-linking of chains gives sheet structures of composition $(Si_2O_5)_n^{-2n}$ as indicated by the arrangement

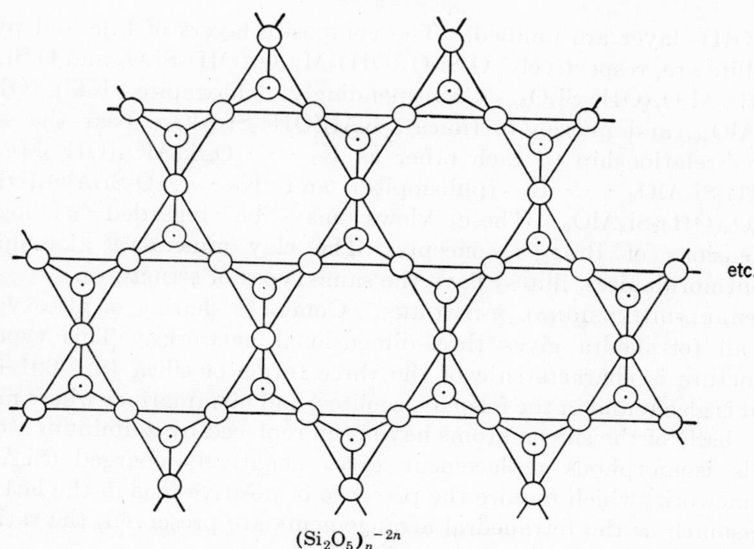

$(Si_2O_5)_n^{-2n}$

The repeating unit of Si_6O_{18} rings is thus characteristic of each sheet. Three oxygen atoms in each SiO_4 tetrahedra are shared with other tetrahedra, one oxygen atom being unshared and behaving as if it possessed a free valency. Individual layers are bonded to each other by electrostatic forces involving the cations present. These forces are small compared with the forces within each sheet and are exerted over much longer distances (ca. 20 A between sheets) so that minerals characterized by this type of arrangement are easily cleaved into thin sheets. The micas and clay minerals have this general structure.

Unfortunately, the minerals of this group are often aluminosilicates rather than the simple silicates, and AlO_4 tetrahedra are also important. The net result is that composite layers are built up of silicon-oxygen sheets combined with layers of hydroxyl groups bonded to the silicon-oxygen sheets by aluminum or magnesium ions. Pauling has suggested that such minerals are built up of superimposed layers of $Si_2O_5^{-2}$ sheets, $Mg(OH)_2$ (brucite), and $Al(OH)_3$ (hydrargillite or gibbsite),[247] each layer being somewhat modified by isomorphous replacement. Aluminum may thus replace a portion of the silicon, or four atoms of aluminum may be replaced by six atoms of magnesium. Thus talc, $Mg_3Si_4O_{11}\cdot H_2O$, has layers of brucite between silicon-oxygen layers, whereas in pyrophillite, $Al_2Si_4O_{11}\cdot H_2O$, where aluminum has replaced magnesium in talc, one-third of the positions in the central

[247] L. Pauling: *Proc. Natl. Acad. Sci.*, **16**, 123 (1930).

$Al(OH)_3$ layer are unfilled. The composite layers of talc and pyrophillite are, respectively, $O_6Si_4O_4(OH)_2Mg_6O_4(OH)_2Si_4O_6$ and $O_6Si_4O_4(OH)_2Al_4O_4(OH)_2Si_4O_6$. Correspondingly, phlogopite, $KMg_3(OH)_2Si_3AlO_{10}$, and muscovite (mica), $KAl_2(OH)_2Si_3AlO_{10}$, bear the same layer relationship to each other as $K_2 \cdots O_6Si_3AlO_4(OH)_2Mg_6O_4(OH)_2Si_3AlO_6 \cdots K_2$ (phlogopite) and $K_2 \cdots O_6Si_3AlO_4(OH)_2Al_4O_4(OH)_2Si_3AlO_6$. These views may be regarded as logical extensions of Bragg's concepts. The clay minerals[248] (kaolinites, montmorillonites, illites) have the same types of structures.

THREE-DIMENSIONAL NETWORKS. Complete sharing of all oxygens in all tetrahedra gives three-dimensional networks. This type of structure is characteristic of the three forms of silica (pp. 691–692) and is also found in the felspars, zeolites, and ultramarines where many (ca. half) of the silicon atoms have been replaced by aluminum atoms. This isomorphous replacement gives negatively charged $(Si,Al)O_2$ frameworks which require the presence of positive ions in the lattices. Inasmuch as the tetrahedral arrangements are preserved, the ratio of Al + Si to O must always be 1:2.

The felspars constitute some two-thirds of the igneous rocks. They are divided between two groups: (1) orthoclase, $KAlSi_3O_8$, and celsian, $BaAl_2Si_2O_8$, and (2) the plagioclase felspars albite, $NaAlSi_3O_8$, and anorthite, $CaAl_2Si_2O_8$. In orthoclase and albite one-fourth of the normal silicon positions are occupied by aluminum ions, whereas in celsian and anorthite further replacements of silicon necessitate the presence of more highly charged cations. The essential differences between the two types of felspars stem from differences in the sizes of the cations (large K^+ and Ba^{+2} versus smaller Na^+ and Ca^{+2}), which alter the symmetry but not the general arrangements.

The zeolites are also made up of $(Si,Al)_nO_{2n}$ networks, with balancing cations, but unlike the felspars they have comparatively open structures which permit them to take up water rather loosely (pp. 499–500) as well as gases, alcohol, or mercury.[249] A further characteristic of these materials is their ability to exchange their cations for other cations on contact with salt solutions. These reversible exchange properties render the zeolites (and their synthetic analogs) useful as water softeners and for effecting ion separations. The zeolites are of three important types: (1) tetrahedra linked into four- and six-membered rings which are joined together into a three-dimensional network as in analcite, $NaAlSi_2O_6 \cdot H_2O$; (2) lamellar types consisting of closely knit sheets of tetrahedra and cleaving into plates as in heulandite, $Ca_2Al_4Si_{14}O_{36} \cdot 12H_2O$; and (3) fibrous types in which chains

[248] C. E. Marshall: *Sci. Progress*, **119**, 422 (1936).

[249] R. M. Barrer: *Ann. Reports*, **41**, 31 (1944).

can be distinguished as in natrolite, $Na_2Al_2Si_3O_{10}\cdot 2H_2O$, or thomsonite, $NaCa_2Al_5Si_5O_{20}\cdot 6H_2O$. The synthetic zeolites (e.g. "Permutit") appear to be entirely similar in structures to the natural materials.

The ultramarines are synthetically produced colored silicates. The mineral lapis lazuli and certain colorless minerals such as sodalite have closely related structures and may be considered with the ultramarines. In addition to the $(Si,Al)_nO_{2n}$ frameworks characteristic of the three-dimensional silicates and balancing cations, these materials also contain negative ions such as Cl^-, SO_4^{-2}, or S^{-2}. Typical compositions are $Na_8Al_6Si_6O_{24}S_2$ (ultramarine), $Na_8Al_6Si_6O_{24}Cl_2$ (sodalite), and $Na_8Al_6Si_6O_{24}SO_4$ (noselite). Structurally, these materials are basket-like, all "baskets" being joined to each other. The cations and anions are found in the various cavities in the networks. As with the zeolites, the cations are exchangeable,[250] and the anions may also be exchanged. Variation of the cation content produces variation in color. The color of ultramarine is still a point for contention. It is destroyed when ultramarine is heated with sodium formate or chlorine, operations which increase and decrease, respectively, the alkali metal content. The sulfur content is also critical, and it appears that the sulfur is present as both sulfide and polysulfide. It seems likely that the polysulfide is in some fashion responsible for the color, but no positive statements can be made. Jaeger's excellent summaries[250, 251] should be consulted for further information on the ultramarines.

The entire glass, ceramic, and cement industries are based upon silicate chemistry. In addition, the metallurgical industries are concerned with it not only because many minerals are themselves silicates but also because of the presence of silicates in practically all slags. The silicates are by far the most important of the silicon compounds.

Organic chemistry of silicon

The organic chemistry of silicon is based upon the classic researches of Frederick S. Kipping as described in a series of fifty-odd papers appearing chiefly in the Journal of the Chemical Society over the period 1901–1944. Advances in recent years have been particularly rapid, and the literature on this phase of silicon chemistry has grown tremendously.[252, 253] Much of this interest has been stimulated by

[250] F. M. Jaeger: *Trans. Faraday Soc.*, **25**, 320 (1929).

[251] F. M. Jaeger: *Optical Activity and High Temperature Measurements*, Pt. III, pp. 403–441. McGraw-Hill Book Co., New York (1930).

[252] E. G. Rochow: *An Introduction to the Chemistry of the Silicones*, 2nd Ed. John Wiley and Sons, New York (1951).

[253] H. W. Post: *Silicones and Others Organic Silicon Compounds.* Reinhold Publishing Corp., New York (1949).

development of the silicones as industrial products of unusual and highly desirable properties.

It is beyond the scope of this book to treat the organic chemistry of silicon in detail, but a brief consideration of the silicones is in order because these materials may be regarded as being both inorganic and organic in character. The silicones are polymeric organosilicon compounds containing silicon-oxygen-silicon linkages.[254, 255] They are derived from siloxane, $H_3Si{-}O{-}SiH_3$, and may be regarded as being built up of substituted siloxane groups. The silicones may be linear polymers of the type

```
     R         R         R         R
     |    O    |    O    |    O    |    O
  \  |  /   \  |  /   \  |  /   \  |  /   \    etc.
     Si        Si        Si        Si
     |         |         |         |
     R         R         R         R
```

or they may be cross-linked polymers of the types

```
                                                    |
   R        R        R                       R      O       R
   |   O    |   O    |   O                   |  O   |   O   |
  \|  / \   |  / \   |  / \                  | / \  |  / \  |/
   Si       Si       Si                      Si     Si      Si
   |        |        |                       |      |       |
   R        O        R                       R      O       R
            |        R          and          R      |       R
        O   |   O    |                       |  O   |   O   |
      /  \  |  / \   |  /                   \| / \  |  / \  |/
            Si       Si                      Si     Si      Si
            |        |                       |      |       |
            R        R                       R      O       R
                                                    |
```

The amount of cross-linking, as well as the nature of the R group, determines the properties of the polymer. Materials ranging from oils which remain fluid at very low temperatures to rubber-like solids are known. Properties generally characteristic of the silicones are water-repellent character, high dielectric strength, resistance to oxidation and thermal decomposition, and resistance to attack by many organic reagents. The silicones are obtained by the hydrolysis of alkyl or aryl chlorosilanes (p. 676), followed by dehydration of the resultant *ol* compounds, e.g., as

$$(CH_3)_2SiCl_2 \xrightarrow{H_2O} (CH_3)_2Si(OH)_2 \xrightarrow{-H_2O} [(CH_3)_2SiO]_n$$

[254] E. G. Rochow: *Chem. Eng. News*, **23**, 612 (1945).
[255] D. V. N. Hardy and N. J. L. Megson: *Quart. Revs.*, **2**, 25 (1948).

Cationic silicon compounds

Ions containing silicon are almost uniformly negatively charged. It is of interest to speculate as to the existence of cationic species containing silicon. Simple cations are ruled out as previously indicated (p. 663), but complex species may exist. Although silicon has but little tendency to complex in this fashion, it does combine with acetylacetone (and perhaps other β-diketones). Since the coordination number of silicon is six, three acetylacetone molecules react, but because the oxidation number of silicon is positive four, one positive charge remains unneutralized. This must of necessity be satisfied by an ionic group outside the coordination sphere. A number of salt-like compounds, among them the tetrachloraurate(III) of composition

$$\left[\mathrm{Si}\left(\begin{array}{c} \mathrm{O{-}C(CH_3)} \\ \mathrm{CH} \\ \mathrm{O{=}C(CH_3)} \end{array}\right)_3\right]\mathrm{AuCl_4}$$

have been described.[256] It appears that other such compounds may exist also.

Nomenclature of silicon compounds

The increasingly large number of complicated silicon compounds has produced a number of confusing and not necessarily logical systems of nomenclature. The situation is not particularly complex with regard to inorganic compounds, but it is involved with organic derivatives. Systematic recommendations[257, 258] should do much to clarify

TABLE 16·16

NOMENCLATURE OF SILICON COMPOUNDS

Material	Name	Material	Name
SiH_4	silane	$H_3Si{-}O{-}SiH_3$	siloxane
Si_2H_6	disilane	$H_3Si{-}O{-}SiH_2{-}$	disiloxanyl radical
Si_3H_8	trisilane	$H_3Si{-}O{-}$	siloxy radical
$SiH_3{-}$	silyl radical	$H_3Si{-}NH{-}$	silylamino radical
$SiH_2{=}$	silylene radical	$H_2Si{=}O$	oxosilane
$SiH{\equiv}$	silylidyne radical	SiH_3OH	silanol
$Si_2H_5{-}$	disilanyl radical	SiH_3X	halosilane
$Si_3H_7{-}$	trisilanyl radical	SiH_2X_2	dihalosilane
$Si(OR)_4$	tetra-alkyl(aryl) silicate	$SiHX_3$	trihalosilane

[256] W. Dilthey: *Ber.*, **36**, 923, 1595 (1903).
[257] R. O. Sauer: *J. Chem. Education*, **21**, 303 (1944).
[258] E. J. Crane: *Chem. Eng. News*, **24**, 1233 (1946).

the matter. Items particularly useful to the inorganic chemist are summarized in Table 16·16. These conventions have been employed in previous sections of this chapter.

POLYANIONIC COMPOUNDS OF THE GROUP IVb ELEMENTS

The polysulfides, and to a lesser extent the polyselenides and polytellurides, have been described in Chapter 14 (pp. 516–518). Comparable series of compounds $M_3^IZ_n$ (M^I = Na; Z = As, Sb, Bi; n = 3, 5, 7) are known for the heavier members of the nitrogen family. In the carbon family, the compounds Na_4Sn_9, Na_4Pb_7, and Na_4Pb_9 have been described.[259–261] These materials are salt-like, rather than alloy-like, and contain polyanions. Since all components of the anions are the same, the term homoatomic anions is sometimes used. It is important that a few words be devoted to these substances because they are essential intermediates between true valency compounds and intermediate phases. The metals of Groups IIIb, IIb, etc., form only intermediate phases. These relations are shown in Table 16·17.[259]

TABLE 16·17

INTERMEDIATE PHASES VS. POLYANIONS

Group Ib	Group IIb	Group IIIb	Group IVb	Groub Vb	Group VIb
					Na_2S_{2-7}
	Na—Zn			$Na_3As_{3,5,7}$	Na_2Se_{2-6}
	Na—Cd		Na_4Sn_9	$Na_3Sb_{3,7}$	Na_2Te_{2-4}
Na—Au	Na—Hg	Na—Tl	Na_4Pb_7	$Na_3Bi_{3,5}$	
			Na_4Pb_9		
Intermediate Phases			Polyanions		

Inasmuch as the major experimental work has dealt with the polyanionic lead compounds, these are discussed in detail. However, what is said about the lead materials may be transferred, with some necessary modifications, to the tin, bismuth, antimony, etc., compounds as well. Although early observations[262] of the solubility of elemental lead in solutions of sodium in liquid ammonia were believed to indicate polyplumbide formation, this view was actually confirmed by electrometric titration of liquid ammonia solutions of lead(II) iodide with sodium.[259] The compounds Na_4Pb_9 and Na_4Pb_7 are "soluble" in liquid ammonia to give highly colored "solutions." Electrolysis of such "solutions" liberates sodium at the cathode. At the anode the

259 E. Zintl, J. Goubeau, and W. Dullenkopf: *Z. physik. Chem.*, **A154,** 1 (1931).
260 E. Zintl and A. Harder: *Z. physik. Chem.*, **A154,** 47 (1931).
261 E. Zintl and H. Kaiser: *Z. anorg. allgem. Chem.*, **211,** 113 (1933).
262 A. Joannis: *Compt. rend.*, **114,** 585 (1892); *Ann. chim.* (8), **7,** 5 (1906).

ion $[Pb_7]^{-4}$ is oxidized to the ion $[Pb_9]^{-4}$, which in turn deposits lead. Treatment of such "solutions" with lead salts effects aggregation as

$$[Pb_7]^{-4} + 2Pb^{+2} \rightarrow 9Pb$$
$$[Pb_9]^{-4} + 2Pb^{+2} \rightarrow 11Pb$$

Evaporation yields ammoniated products, e.g., $[Na(NH_3)_x]_4[Pb_9]$, which lose ammonia to give the polyplumbides as pyrophoric products. Ammonia "solutions" appear to contain the anions $[Pb_7]^{-4}$ and $[Pb_9]^{-4}$, but these are so large as to be colloidal in character. Zintl[259] regards the species as $[Pb(Pb)_6]^{-4}$ and $[Pb(Pb)_8]^{-4}$ and thus assigns coordination numbers of six and eight to the plumbide ion.

Homoatomic lead materials are obtained by action of solutions of sodium in liquid ammonia upon lead or soluble lead salts. For preparative purposes, however, it is better to extract these materials from lead-sodium alloys with liquid ammonia. When the lead to sodium ratio is less than 9:4 both the compounds Na_4Pb_9 and Na_4Pb_7 are extracted; when it exceeds 9:4, only the compound Na_4Pb_9 is extracted, and lead remains behind.

SUGGESTED SUPPLEMENTARY REFERENCES

N. V. Sidgwick: *The Chemical Elements and Their Compounds*, pp. 488–627. Clarendon Press, Oxford (1950).

W. M. Latimer: *The Oxidation States of the Elements and Their Potentials in Aqueous Solutions*, pp. 117–146. Prentice-Hall, New York (1938).

A. F. Wells: *Structural Inorganic Chemistry*, 2nd Ed., Ch. XVII, XVIII, XIX. Clarendon Press, Oxford (1950).

CHAPTER 17

Periodic Group IIIb
The Boron Family

Boron and aluminum are usually considered familiar elements and gallium, indium, and thallium unfamiliar, although only aluminum is particularly abundant in nature (B, $3 \times 10^{-4}\%$; Al, 8.13%; Ga, $1.5 \times 10^{-3}\%$; In, $1 \times 10^{-5}\%$; Tl, $10^{-4} - 10^{-5}\%$ of the crust of the earth). Aluminum is, of course, the most abundant of all the metals and the third most abundant of all the elements. The comparative scarcity of boron may be due in part to the ease with which the nuclei of its atoms are transmuted by natural bombardment processes. Boron is well known, however, because of the existence of concentrated deposits of its compounds, particularly in arid regions such as the southwestern part of the United States, and because of the desirable properties of many of its compounds which have necessitated large-scale recovery of boron materials. Gallium, indium, and thallium are never found in concentrated deposits, and until recently they were never recovered in sizable quantities. Recent interest in some of their unusual properties will undoubtedly make their chemistries more familiar, but large-scale production of the metals and their compounds and nominal prices probably cannot be expected.

The general trends in properties noted in the nitrogen and carbon families also characterize the boron family, but approach to the electronic configurations of the purely metallic elements produce some significant differences. Small size and high concentration of nuclear charge give boron strictly non-metallic characteristics. The other elements of the family are all metals, with aluminum being particularly highly electropositive in nature. Thus between boron and aluminum there is a discontinuity in properties which is without parallel in the families discussed thus far. The chemistries of aluminum, gallium, indium, and thallium are closely related. Boron chemistry resembles silicon chemistry more closely than the chemistries of the other members of its own family.

FAMILY RELATIONSHIPS AMONG THE ELEMENTS

Numerical properties characterizing the members of the boron family are summarized in Table 17·1. Increases in atomic weight

TABLE 17·1
NUMERICAL PROPERTIES OF BORON FAMILY ELEMENTS

Property	Boron	Aluminum	Gallium	Indium	Thallium
Atomic number	5	13	31	49	81
Outer electron configuration	$2s^22p^1$	$3s^23p^1$	$4s^24p^1$	$5s^25p^1$	$6s^26p^1$
Mass numbers, stable isotopes	10, 11	27	69, 71	113, 115	203, 205
Atomic weight	10.82	26.97	69.72	114.76	204.39
Density of solid at 20°C, grams/cc.	2.33* 2.45†	2.70	5.927	7.293	11.85
Atomic volume of solid, cc.	4.64* 4.42†	9.99	11.76	15.74	17.25
Melting point, °C.	2300	659.8	29.780	155	303.5
Boiling point, °C.	2550(?)	2270	2070	1450	1457
Covalent radius, A.	0.80	1.248	1.245	1.497	1.549
Ionization potential ev	8.296	5.984	6.00	5.785	6.106
Electronegativity	2.0	1.5	......	......	......
Crystal radius M^{+3}, A	0.20	0.50	0.62	0.81	0.95
Standard potential, E^0_{298}, volts $M \rightleftharpoons M^{+3} + 3e^-$	0.73 (H_3BO_3)	1.67	0.52	0.34	−0.719
$M + 4OH^- \rightleftharpoons H_2MO_3^- + H_2O + 3e^-$	2.5	2.35	1.22	1.18 (In_2O_3)	......

* Crystalline. † Amorphous.

and number are paralleled by increases in density, atomic volume, and atomic and ionic sizes. The melting point of boron is extremely high, indicating very strong bonding between individual atoms in the solid state. The metallic lattices of the other elements are much more readily ruptured, and melting points are significantly lower. The very low value noted for gallium is most unusual, although the appearance of a minimum in the family is not unique (e.g., Table 16·1). The structures of solid gallium, indium, and thallium are apparently particularly weak. Boiling points are generally high and decrease in general with increasing atomic weight. Except for boron, the elements of this family are characterized by long liquid ranges. This property is most pronounced with gallium. In fact, no other element has as long a useful liquid range. Ionization potential values are high, but the removal of only one electron requires less energy for any element in this family than for its neighboring elements (p. 155). The highly electropositive natures of all the elements (except thallium) must be due in large measure to high energies of hydration of the gaseous ions.

Inasmuch as the outer electronic arrangements in the atoms of these elements contain three more electrons than the stable inert gas (with B, Al) or pseudo-inert gas (with Ga, In, Tl) structures, a uniform +3 oxidation state is expected. This state is characteristic of all the elements. As indicated by the potential data in Table 17·1, tendencies to enter this state decrease from aluminum to thallium. The +3 state is a strictly covalent oxidation state with boron and is largely covalent with the other elements as well. Tripositive cations are known in aqueous solutions for all the elements except boron, but such species are normally highly complexed (by water, etc.) and extensively hydrolyzed.

The electronic arrangements ns^2np^1 also suggest +1 oxidation states. This state is well known with thallium where oxidation potential data (Table 17·2) indicate it to be quite generally more stable in aqueous

TABLE 17·2

Relations among the Oxidation States of the Group IIIb Elements

Couple	Equation	E^0_{298}, volts
Ga(O)–Ga(II)	$Ga \rightleftharpoons Ga^{+3} + 2e^-$	ca. 0.45
Ga(II)–Ga(III)	$Ga^{+2} \rightleftharpoons Ga^{+3} + e^-$	ca. 0.65
In(O)–In(I)	$In \rightleftharpoons In^+ + e^-$	ca. 0.25
	$In + Cl^- \rightleftharpoons InCl + e^-$	0.34
In(I)–In(II)	$In^+ \rightleftharpoons In^{+2} + e^-$	ca. 0.35
In(II)–In(III)	$In^{+2} \rightleftharpoons In^{+3} + e^-$	ca. 0.45
Tl(O)–Tl(I)	$Tl \rightleftharpoons Tl^+ + e^-$	0.3363
	$Tl + OH^- \rightleftharpoons TlOH(s) + e^-$	0.3445
	$Tl + Cl^- \rightleftharpoons TlCl + e^-$	0.557
	$Tl + Br^- \rightleftharpoons TlBr + e^-$	0.658
	$Tl + I^- \rightleftharpoons TlI + e^-$	0.765
	$2Tl + S^{-2} \rightleftharpoons Tl_2S + 2e^-$	1.04
Tl(I)–Tl(III)	$Tl^+ \rightleftharpoons Tl^{+3} + 2e^-$	−1.25
	$TlOH(s) + 2OH^- \rightleftharpoons Tl(OH)_3 + 2e^-$	0.05
	$TlCl \rightleftharpoons Tl^{+3} + Cl^- + 2e^-$	−1.36

systems than the +3 state. A few unipositive indium compounds (mostly halides) are known in the solid state, and a unipositive gallium sulfide has been reported. Reductions of aluminum(III) halides, sulfide, and selenide with aluminum at elevated temperatures yield unstable unipositive compounds.[1–4] Anodic oxidations of

[1] W. Klemm and E. Voss: *Z. anorg. allgem. Chem.*, **251**, 233 (1943).

[2] W. Klemm, K. Geiersberger, B. Schaeler, and H. Mindt: *Z. anorg. Chem.*, **255**, 287 (1948).

[3] W. Klemm, E. Voss, and K. Geiersberger: *Z. anorg. Chem.*, **256**, 15 (1948).

[4] L. M. Foster, A. S. Russell, and C. N. Cochran: *J. Am. Chem. Soc.*, **72**, 2580 (1950).

aluminum, gallium, indium, and thallium in acetic acid solutions indicate clearly the formation of unipositive species.[5] Theoretical evaluation of heats of formation for the halides of unipositive aluminum[6] indicates that these compounds are only slightly less stable than the corresponding trihalides in the solid state, but somewhat less stable in the gaseous state. For boron, however, there are no evidences for a +1 state. Stability of the +1 state increases regularly with increasing atomic weight, the influence of the inert pair (p. 177) thus becoming increasingly important with the heavier elements. The situation parallels those discussed for the Group IVb (p. 664) and Group Vb (p. 558) elements. Only for thallium are the unipositive compounds stable in contact with aqueous media. For the other elements, stability is achieved by disproportionation as

$$3M^+ \rightarrow M^{+3} + 2M$$

For thallium, stabilization of the +1 state through insolubility (Table 17·2) bears much resemblance to the situation characterizing silver (p. 304).

In terms of electronic configurations, existence of a +2 oxidation state seems most unlikely. No real evidence for such a state has been offered for boron or aluminum, and theoretical calculations[6] show that any aluminum(II) halides would be more unstable thermally than either the corresponding aluminum(I) or aluminum(III) compounds For gallium, however, solid halides, a sulfide, and an oxide of the requisite stoichiometry have been prepared. These might well be regarded as appropriate mixtures of unipositive and tripositive gallium compounds, particularly since at least the chloride is diamagnetic,[7] were it not for the fact that vapor density studies on the chloride show the existence of considerable numbers of $GaCl_2$ molecules along with some polymeric species.[8] These observations are incompatible and indicate the necessity for additional fundamental study The possibility of gallium-gallium linkages cannot be overlooked. With indium, the apparently +2 halides have properties not inconsistent with formulation as $In^{I}[In^{III}X_4]$. The same situation pertains with thallium.

Only boron is sufficiently electronegative to show any tendencies toward a negative oxidation state. In the borides of the most highly electropositive elements, boron presumably exists in the −3 state. However few borides have structures entirely consistent with this simple situation (pp. 769–773).

[5] A. W. Davidson and F. Jirik: *J. Am. Chem. Soc.*, **72**, 1700 (1950).
[6] B. Irmann: *Helv. Chim. Acta*, **33**, 1449 (1950).
[7] W. Klemm and W. Tilk: *Z. anorg. allgem. Chem.*, **207**, 175 (1932).
[8] A. W. Laubengayer and F. B. Schirmer: *J. Am. Chem. Soc.*, **62**, 1578 (1940).

MODIFICATIONS OF THE FREE ELEMENTS

Unlike many of the elements discussed in preceding chapters, the elements of Group IIIb do not exist in a variety of modifications. Little information is available about the gaseous state, but, in the light of the general properties of the individual elements of the family, it seems highly unlikely that marked molecular complexity is characteristic of any of the elements, except possibly boron. Data are also lacking for the liquid state. In the solid state, boron apparently exists in both amorphous and crystalline forms. The other elements are crystalline, but polymorphism is well established only with thallium.

So-called amorphous boron was first obtained by Moissan[9] by reduction of boric oxide with magnesium in a thermite-type reaction. This is the best preparational procedure at the present time,[10–13] although electrolysis of fused oxide and borate baths[14] also gives amorphous products, as do thermal reductions of fluoborates (pp. 760–763) with alkali metals or magnesium. Pure amorphous boron has not been obtained, but vigorous treatment of the products of magnesium reduction with alkali, hydrochloric acid, and hydrofluoric acid, followed by fusion with boric oxide, has given purities as high as 98.3%.[9] Complete removal of magnesium has not been effected, and traces of oxygen apparently always remain. The final product is a dark-colored powder which is largely amorphous to x-rays but which apparently contains small quantities of crystalline boron as well as borides and oxides.

Fusion of amorphous boron, followed by crystallization, or reduction of boron tribromide or trichloride vapors with hydrogen in an electric arc[10] or in contact with an electrically heated filament[15] yields crystalline boron. With boron tribromide as starting material, reduction on tungsten or tantalum filaments at temperatures of 1300°C. or above has yielded crystals of pure boron.[15] Crystalline boron is a black material which is characterized by extreme hardness (ca. 9.3 on Mohs' scale, between silicon carbide, 9.15, and boron carbide, 9.32), opacity,

[9] H. Moissan: *Compt. rend.*, **114**, 392 (1892); *Ann. chim. phys.* [7], **6**, 296 (1895).

[10] E. Weintraub: *Trans. Am. Electrochem. Soc.*, **16**, 165 (1909); *J. Ind. Eng. Chem.*, **3**, 299 (1911); **5**, 106 (1913).

[11] H. E. Kremers: *School Sci. Math.*, **42**, 221 (1942).

[12] A. W. Laubengayer, A. E. Newkirk, and R. L. Brandaur: *J. Chem. Education*, **19**, 382 (1942).

[13] J. Cueilleron: *Ann. chim.* [11], **19**, 459 (1944).

[14] L. Andrieux: *Ann. chim. phys.* [10], **12**, 423 (1929).

[15] A. W. Laubengayer, D. T. Hurd, A. E. Newkirk, and J. L. Hoard: *J. Am. Chem. Soc.*, **65**, 1924 (1943).

metallic luster, and rather poor electrical conductivity. Conductivity increases with increasing temperature, but the change between 20° and 600°C. is actually only about a hundredfold,[15] as opposed to the millionfold increase usually indicated.[10] Both needle-like and hexagonal plate-like crystals are obtained, but it appears that both are monoclinic and not fundamentally different from each other in structure.[15] The complete structure of the material has not been determined. However, it appears that each boron atom has six nearest neighbors at an average distance of 1.89 A.[16]

Pure crystalline boron is not to be confused with the "crystalline boron" obtained by aluminothermic reduction of boric oxide in the presence of sulfur. This material is a metallic, lustrous solid, which was regarded by early workers as elemental boron. It is actually a boride of stoichiometric composition AlB_{12}.[17, 18]

CHEMICAL CHARACTERISTICS OF THE ELEMENTS

The more important aspects of the chemical behaviors of the elements in this family are summarized in Table 17·3. Trends in properties are strictly comparable with those noted for the Group IVb elements (p. 670). The reactions of boron are those of a nonmetal and are, therefore, markedly different from those of the other elements in several respects. Thus, boron is resistant to attack by non-oxidizing acids, even though the potential for conversion of the element into boric acid is favorable (Table 17·1). Boron reacts with many metals to give borides, whereas the other Group IIIb elements are unreactive. It is also more susceptible to attack by alkaline

TABLE 17·3

CHEMICAL CHARACTERISTICS OF GROUP IIIB ELEMENTS

General Equation*	Remarks
$2M + 3X_2 \rightarrow 2MX_3$	With halogens. Tl gives TlX also.
$4M + 3O_2 \rightarrow 2M_2O_3$	At elevated temperatures. Tl gives Tl_2O.
$2M + 3S \rightarrow M_2S_3$	At elevated temperatures. Also with Se, Te. Tl gives Tl_2S.
$2M + N_2 \rightarrow 2MN$	With B, Al at elevated temperatures.
$2M + 6H^+ \rightarrow 2M^{+3} + 3H_2$	With Al, Ga, In. Tl gives Tl^+.
$2M + 2OH^- + 2H_2O \rightarrow 2MO_2^- + 3H_2$	With Al, Ga. B gives $H_2BO_3^-$.
$nM + M' \rightarrow M'M_n$	With B only.

* M = B, Al, Ga, In, or Tl.

[16] T. N. Godfrey and B. E. Warren: *J. Chem. Phys.*, **18,** 1121 (1950).
[17] L. Wöhler: *Ann.*, **141,** 268 (1867).
[18] W. Hampe: *Ann.*, **183,** 75 (1876).

reagents. The nature of the boron preparation used has a profound effect upon its reactivity. The crystalline material is notably inert even to concentrated nitric acid, hot concentrated sulfuric acid, chromic acid, caustic alkali, or oxygen at elevated temperatures.[15] Amorphous boron, on the other hand, reacts fairly readily with these reagents. Particle size is undoubtedly a factor of some importance in accounting for these differences.

The observed chemical reactivity of aluminum is commonly less than that indicated by potential data because of the ready formation of adherent and unreactive oxide films. Aluminum is essentially passive toward concentrated nitric acid for this reason. Its permanence in air even at elevated temperatures is due to the same effect. However, the ready solubility of the oxide in hydrochloric acid or in excess hydroxyl ion promotes rapid reaction in the presence of these reagents. Oxide coatings do not adhere to amalgamated aluminum surfaces. Amalgamated aluminum is thus oxidized rapidly at room temperatures by atmospheric oxygen, water, etc. The other metals in the family react slowly at ordinary temperatures.

PREPARATION AND PRODUCTION OF THE FREE ELEMENTS

Amorphous boron is produced in small quantities by magnesium reduction (p. 738) for use in preparation of impact resistant alloy steels and other special-purpose alloys. The crystalline form is not produced technically.

Aluminum is obtained universally by electrolysis of the purified oxide dissolved in a mixture of fused sodium, calcium, and aluminum fluorides at temperatures of the order of 875° to 950°C., using carbon anodes and carbon-lined vessels as cathodes (Hall and Héroult processes.)[19] This process is complicated by the need for pure (especially iron-free) aluminum oxide. Treatment of natural bauxites with caustic soda, followed by hydrolytic precipitation of the hydrous hydroxide from the resulting aluminate solution (Bayer process), requires low-silica ($< 7\%$ SiO_2) ores because of aluminum losses due to formation of an insoluble sodium aluminum silicate in the initial reaction.[20–22] Alumina recovery from the red muds remaining after digestion with alkali is effected by sintering with sodium and calcium carbonates and extracting sodium aluminate with water.[20–22] Prior

[19] J. D. Edwards, F. C. Frary, and Z. Jeffries: *The Aluminum Industry. Vol. I. Aluminum and Its Production.* McGraw-Hill Book Co., New York (1930).

[20] Anon.: *Chem. Eng. News*, **23**, 41 (1945).

[21] F. C. Frary: *Chem. Eng. News*, **23**, 1324 (1945).

[22] R. F. Gould: *Ind. Eng. Chem.*, **37**, 797 (1945).

to the second World War, recovery of alumina from clay was too costly to be economically feasible. War-instigated projects, however, showed that ammonium hydrogen sulfate fusion, hydrochloric acid treatment, sulfur dioxide treatment, and fusion with calcium carbonate can all be used to decompose clays and render aluminum recoverable ultimately as the oxide.[23–28] It appears that, except under wartime economy or with depletion of bauxite reserves, clay cannot serve as a competitive source of alumina.

Preparation of aluminum metal by other means is difficult and often costly. Electrodeposition from aqueous media is impossible because of preferential hydrogen discharge. Although electrodeposition from solutions of aluminum compounds in various non-aqueous solvents is feasible, experimental and cost difficulties have proved insurmountable thus far. Thermal reduction of the anhydrous chloride or double sodium chloride with sodium, although of historical importance, is not competitive. Carbothermic reduction of the oxide normally yields the carbide, although some success has been reported for a German process employing a centrifugal furnace.[25, 27] Hydrogen is not effective as a reducing agent.

Gallium, indium, and thallium are readily obtained as metals by thermal reduction procedures involving carbon or hydrogen or by electrodeposition. Difficulties with these elements embrace the production of concentrates from low-grade ores rather than the ultimate reduction procedures.

COMPOUNDS OF THE GROUP IIIb ELEMENTS

As already indicated, the compounds of boron have properties which are materially different from those of aluminum and the other elements in this family. Tripositive aluminum, gallium, indium, and thallium give compounds which are generally similar in characteristics, the trends in properties being the same as those distinguishable among compounds of the Group IVb (pp. 671–696) or Group IIb (pp. 852–867) elements. It seems reasonable to point out a number of family relations among the compounds in general and then to discuss several of the distinguishing special phases of boron chemistry. No attempt is made to cover the entire family completely or comprehensively.

[23] F. C. Frary: *Chem. Eng. News*, **21,** 2018 (1943).

[24] J. R. Callahan: *Chem. Met. Eng.*, **52,** (No. 12), 108 (1945).

[25] Anon: *J. Chem. Education*, **23,** 291, 617 (1946); **25,** 159 (1948).

[26] O. Redlich, C. C. March, M. F. Adams, F. H. Sharp, E. K. Holt, and J. E. Taylor: *Ind. Eng. Chem.*, **38,** 1181 (1946).

[27] Anon.: *Chem. Eng. News*, **25,** 929, 1590 (1947).

[28] T. P. Hignett: *Ind. Eng. Chem.*, **39,** 1052 (1947).

Catenation among the Group IIIb elements

Except in a few boron compounds, catenation is probably non-existent among the members of this family in the sense that it is encountered among the more non-metallic elements of the oxygen, nitrogen, and carbon families. Simple electron pair bonds between like atoms characterize boron halides of the type B_2X_4 (p. 749), a few oxy-boron compounds (pp. 753, 812–816), and probably certain of the linkages in the boron hydrides (pp. 793–795). However, among the hydrides, which are formal analogs of well-known catenated compounds of other elements, electron deficiency precludes existence of complete series of electron pair bonds and requires the existence of hydrogen bridges (pp. 789–793). Similar situations characterize the aluminum and gallium hydrides. No data are available for the energies of B—B bonds or similar bonds for the other members of the family. Catenation is not a characteristic or important property of these elements.

Electron-deficient compounds

Electron-deficient compounds are more characteristic of the elements of this family than of those of any other family because each Group IIIb atom possesses but three valence electrons but has a tendency to be 4-covalent. This does not produce electron deficiency in all types of compounds, since strong donor groups can impart 4-covalence by formation of coordinate linkages (pp. 759–768). However, in the hydrides and certain of their derivatives, the compositions of the only preparable compounds require electron-deficient bonding. Thus no simple hydrides of the expected composition MH_3 ($M = B$, Al, Ga) have been prepared. Instead, dimers, such as B_2H_6 (pp. 773–774) and Ga_2H_6,[29, 30] or polymers, such as $(AlH_3)_x$,[31] are obtained as the simplest compounds. Similarly, among the higher hydrides (e.g., B_4H_{10}) or among alkyl compounds such as $[AlR_3]_2$ ($R = CH_3$, C_2H_5, n-C_3H_7), $B_2H_2R_4$, $B_2H_3R_3$, $Al_2H_2(CH_3)_4$,[31] $Al_2H_3(CH_3)_3$,[31] and $Ga_2H_2(CH_3)_4$[29] complete electron pair bonding in the usual sense is impossible. On the other hand, formally similar halogen compounds such as Al_2X_6 or $Al_2(CH_3)_4X_2$ ($X = Cl$, Br) are different in that halogen bridges (p. 272) are present[32] as

[29] E. Wiberg and T. Johannsen: *Naturwissenschaften*, **29**, 320 (1941).
[30] E. Wiberg and T. Johannsen: *Die Chemie*, **55**, 38 (1942).
[31] O. Stecher and E. Wiberg: *Ber.*, **75B**, 2003 (1942).
[32] L. O. Brockway and N. R. Davidson: *J. Am. Chem. Soc.*, **63**, 3287 (1941).

X X X CH_3 X CH_3
Al Al and Al Al
X X X CH_3 X CH_3

Bridge structures involving coordinate oxygen to aluminum linkages undoubtedly explain similar associations among the aluminum alkoxides, $[Al(OR)_3]_x$.[33]

The structures of the electron-deficient hydrides and their derivatives are considered in a later section of this chapter (pp. 787–795). The aluminum alkyls present problems which are somewhat different. These compounds are liquids at ordinary temperatures but are readily vaporized. Existence of dimeric molecular species is well established by vapor density measurements[34] and cryoscopic studies in ethylene dibromide[35] and benzene.[36] Extent of dimerization decreases from complete for the methyl compound through the ethyl and *n*-propyl compounds to nil for the isopropyl compound.[36] Early electron diffraction studies[32, 37] on the dimeric trimethyl compound suggested an ethane-like structure comparable to that for hexamethyl disilane, with Al—Al and Al—C bond distances of 2.02 A and 2.05 A, respectively, and an Al—Al—C bond angle of $105 \pm 10°$. However, the covalent radius of aluminum would predict an Al—Al bond distance of 2.496 A, assuming electron pair bonding, and a somewhat longer bond might be expected for an electron-deficient structure. Such an arrangement seems improbable. Electron diffraction data are not consistent with a carbon bridge structure. On the other hand, Raman data suggest a bridged structure of some type.[38] Burawoy[39] resolves the difficulty in terms of the arrangement

H
CH_3 C—H CH_3
H
Al Al
H
CH_3 H—C CH_3
H

[33] H. Ulich and W. Nespital: *Z. physik. Chem.*, **A165**, 294 (1933).

[34] A. W. Laubengayer and W. F. Gilliam: *J. Am. Chem. Soc.*, **63**, 477 (1941).

[35] E. Louïse and L. Roux: *Compt. rend.*, **107**, 600 (1888).

[36] K. S. Pitzer and H. S. Gutowsky: *J. Am. Chem. Soc.*, **68**, 2204 (1946).

[37] N. R. Davidson, J. A. C. Hugill, H. A. Skinner, and L. E. Sutton: *Trans. Faraday Soc.*, **36**, 1212 (1940).

[38] K. W. F. Kohlrausch and J. Wagner: *Z. physik. Chem.*, **52B**, 185 (1942).

[39] A. Burawoy: *Nature*, **155**, 269 (1945).

for which calculated bond distances are in reasonable agreement with measured values. Longuet-Higgins,[40] on the other hand, prefers a "methylated double bond" comparable in character to Pitzer's "protonated double bond" in boron hydride structures[41] (pp. 790–795). Pitzer and Gutowsky,[36] however, believe all published data to be explained best in terms of polar attractions between positive aluminum atoms and negative alpha carbon atoms. This view is consistent with decreasing tendencies toward dimerization with increasing complexity of the alkyl group (see above) and derives added support from the fact that, whereas alkyls of all elements more electropositive than aluminum are highly polymeric, those of less electropositive elements are monomeric.[36] Thus analogous boron, gallium, and indium compounds are monomeric. The mixed alkyl hydrides of boron, aluminum, and gallium probably have structures comparable to those of the hydrides, since at least two hydrogen atoms per molecule are always present.

Halides

All the Group IIIb elements form halides of the type MX_3. In addition, boron gives peculiar lower halides of the type B_2X_4 (X = Cl, Br, I), and the heavier elements form compounds of stoichiometric compositions MX and MX_2. Of these lower valent materials, only the thallium(I) compounds are important. The major portion of the current discussion is limited to the trihalides, some of the physical constants for which are summarized in Table 17.4. A few mixed halides, e.g., BBr_2I (b.p. 125°C.) and $BBrI_2$ (b.p. 180°C.), have been reported also, and boron forms a few pseudo-halides (p. 475). The marked differences in properties noted between the boron compounds and those of the heavier elements suggest separate discussions.

Boron Trihalides (BX_3). The physical properties of the boron trihalides are those of essentially covalent compounds. As in many materials of this type, volatility decreases with increasing molecular weight. Vapor density studies show boron trifluoride to be monomeric to temperatures as low as −75°C.[42] Boron trichloride and tribromide also have normal vapor densities, and the latter compound gives a normal cryoscopic molecular weight in benzene.[43] Absence of polymerization may be assumed logically for the iodide. Electron

[40] H. C. Longuet-Higgins: *J. Chem. Soc.*, **1946**, 139.

[41] K. S. Pitzer: *J. Am. Chem. Soc.*, **67**, 1126 (1945).

[42] W. Fischer and W. Weidemann: *Z. anorg. allgem. Chem.*, **213**, 106 (1933).

[43] A Stock and E. Kuss: *Ber.*, **47**, 3113 (1914).

TABLE 17·4
PHYSICAL PROPERTIES OF GROUP IIIB TRIHALIDES

Compound	Melting Point, °C.	Boiling Point, °C.	Heat of Formation, kcal./mole	Equivalent Conductance of Liquid at m.p., $ohm^{-1} \times 10^6$
1. Fluorides				
BF_3	−127.1	−101	258.1	
AlF_3	1290	1291 (subl.)		
GaF_3	950 (subl.)			
InF_3	1170	1200		
TlF_3	550			
2. Chlorides				
BCl_3	−107	12.5		
$AlCl_3$*	192.6 (1700 mm.)	180 (subl.)	167	
$GaCl_3$	77.9	201.3		0.1
$InCl_3$	586	subl.		14.7
$TlCl_3$	25(?)	subl.		
3. Bromides				
BBr_3	−46	90.8		
$AlBr_3$*	97.5	255	121	
$GaBr_3$	121.5	279		5
$InBr_3$	436	subl.		6.4
$TlBr_3$				
4. Iodides				
BI_3	43	210		
AlI_3	179.5	381	71	
GaI_3	212	346		0.02
InI_3	210			2.3

* Dimers.

diffraction studies[44] show the gaseous trifluoride, trichloride, and tribromide molecules to be planar with X—B—X bond angles of 120° and B—X bond distances of 1.30 A (X = F), 1.73 A (X = Cl), and 1.87 A (X = Br). All these bond distances are somewhat less than calculated single bond distances as demanded by the structure

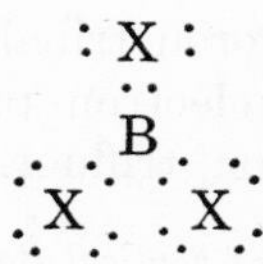

[44] H. A. Lévy and L. O. Brockway: *J. Am. Chem. Soc.*, **59,** 2085 (1937).

However, the presence of a fourth available bond orbital permits major contributions by the resonance structures

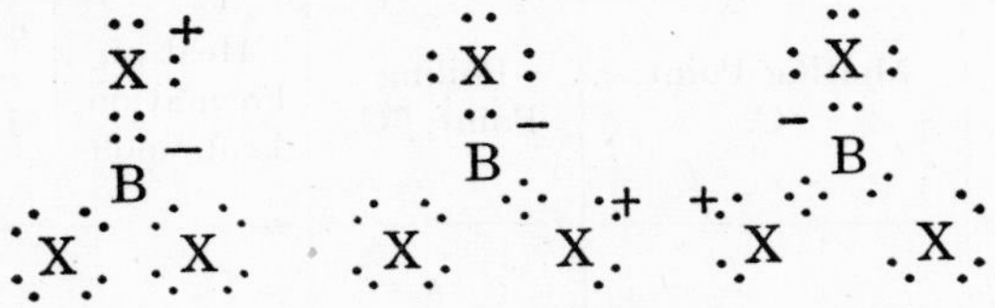

in spite of unfavorable charge distributions, as well as by such ionic structures as[45]

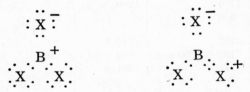

The net effect for the chloride and bromide (and presumably the iodide) is one-third double bond character and two-thirds single bond character in each bond, or an effective resonating structure

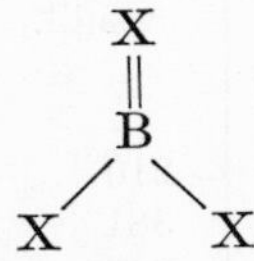

Bond distances calculated on this basis (1.74 A for X = Cl and 1.89 A for X = Br) agree with observed values. For the fluoride, the greater ionic character of the B—F bond must render contributions by ionic structures more important since the calculated B—F distance (on above basis) of 1.39 A is still too large.[45]

The boron trihalides are soluble in a variety of organic solvents. With water, the chloride, bromide, and iodide undergo rapid and complete hydrolysis to boric acid and the corresponding hydrogen halide. The fluoride, however, gives fluoboric acids (p. 760) as well as boric acid (compare silicon tetrafluoride, p. 679). Many of the chemical behaviors of the boron trihalides are associated with their acceptor properties toward electron pair donors. This property is most pronounced with boron trifluoride[46] and decreases markedly

[45] L. Pauling: *The Nature of the Chemical Bond*, 2nd Ed., pp. 237–239. Cornell University Press, Ithaca (1940).

[46] H. S. Booth and D. R. Martin: *Boron Trifluoride and Its Derivatives*, Ch. 4. John Wiley and Sons, New York (1949).

through the chloride[47] to the bromide and iodide,[48] probably because of increasing size and decreasing electronegativity of the acceptor. Differences between the fluoride and chloride are most striking. Thus, although the non-metals fluorine, chlorine, oxygen, sulfur, nitrogen, and phosphorus, serve as donors toward both boron trifluoride and boron trichloride, the number of the boron trifluoride derivatives and their thermal stabilities far exceed those of boron trichloride. Comparatively few such compounds are derived from the tribromide and triiodide. Many compounds which act as donors toward the trifluoride rupture boron-halogen bonds in the other trihalides. Typical donors toward the various boron trihalides are summarized in Table 17·5. The strong acceptor ability of boron trifluoride toward many functional groups in organic compounds renders the material a catalyst of virtually unparalleled versatility and importance.[49] The acidic properties of boron trifluoride (pp. 327, 335) and its behavior with the inert gas elements (pp. 379–380) have been discussed previously. Fluoboric acids and the fluoborates are described in a later section of this chapter (pp. 760–763).

Boron trifluoride is formed when boron is reacted with elemental fluorine; when other boron trihalides are reacted with fluorine, with antimony(III) fluoride in the presence of antimony(V) chloride, or with calcium fluoride; when fluoborates such as the potassium compound are heated; or when boric oxide is heated with calcium fluoride or a fluoborate and sulfuric acid.[50] A more convenient procedure, which gives larger yields of a product containing but little silicon tetrafluoride, involves warming a mixture of sodium or ammonium fluoborate and boric oxide with sulfuric acid.[51] The product is purified by distillation. Boron trichloride is formed when boron or a boride is burned in chlorine; when a mixture of boric oxide and carbon is heated with chlorine; or when boric oxide is reacted with phosphorus(V) chloride in a closed tube. A much better procedure involves heating boron trifluoride with anhydrous aluminum chloride,[52, 53] the driving force for the reaction being the formation of ionic, non-volatile

[47] D. R. Martin: *Chem. Revs.*, **34**, 461 (1944).

[48] D. R. Martin: *Chem. Revs.*, **42**, 581 (1948).

[49] H. S. Booth and D. R. Martin: *Boron Trifluoride and Its Derivatives*, Ch. 6. John Wiley and Sons, New York (1949).

[50] *Ibid.*, Ch. 1.

[51] H. S. Booth and K. S. Willson: *Inorganic Syntheses*, Vol. I, p. 21. McGraw-Hill Book Co., New York (1939).

[52] E. L. Gamble, P. Gilmont, and J. F. Stiff: *J. Am. Chem. Soc.*, **62**, 1257 (1940).

[53] E. L. Gamble: *Inorganic Syntheses*, Vol. III, p. 27. McGraw-Hill Book Co., New York (1950).

TABLE 17·5
DONOR GROUPS TOWARD BORON TRIHALIDES

Donor Atom	Typical Examples of Donors			
	BF_3	BCl_3	BBr_3	BI_3
F	HF MF_x NOF CH_3COF	$(C_6H_5)_3CF$	none	none
Cl	HCl MCl_x	SCl_4 $FeCl_2$ $(C_6H_5)_3CCl$ C_2H_5Cl	PCl_5	none
O	H_2O $M_2{}^{I}SO_4$ NO $M_3{}^{III}PO_4$ POF_3 ROH RCHO R_2CO RCOOH R_2O $(RCO)_2O$ RCOOR′	$POCl_3$ SO_3 SO_2 R_2O	$POCl_3$	none
S	H_2S RSH R_2S	H_2S B_2S_3	B_2S_3	none
N	NH_3 RNH_2 R_2NH R_3N $C_6H_5NR_2$(or H_2) C_5H_5N $RCONH_2$ HCN RCN	NH_3 RNH_2 R_2NH R_3N $C_6H_5NR_2$(or H_2) RCN NOCl CNCl	NH_3 RNH_2 R_2NH R_3N $C_6H_5NR_2$(or H_2) C_5H_5N RCN AgCN	NH_3
P	PH_3	PH_3 PCl_3	PCl_3 PBr_3	none
As	none	AsH_3	AsH_3	none
C	RHC=CHR(?)	none	none	none

aluminum fluoride. Boron tribromide is prepared by the same types of reactions, the boron trifluoride-anhydrous aluminum bromide reaction[53] being favored. Boron triiodide is obtained when either boron tribromide or boron trichloride vapor mixed with hydrogen iodide is passed through a heated tube or when solid sodium or lithium borohydride (p. 782) is reacted with iodine at 200° or 120°C., respectively.[54]

Boron Subhalides (B_2X_4). Boron subchloride or tetrachlorodiborine, B_2Cl_4, is a liquid boiling at 55°C. (extrapolated) and freezing to a solid with melting point −98°C. The vapor density of the compound agrees with the formulation B_2Cl_4.[55] The compound undergoes slow decomposition in the absence of air to boron and boron trichloride. It is soluble in water, with the evolution of only small quantities of hydrogen to give a solution of subboric acid (p. 813).[56] Alcohols give esters of composition $B_2(OR)_4$.[55] It follows that the compound is the acid chloride of subboric acid and has the structure

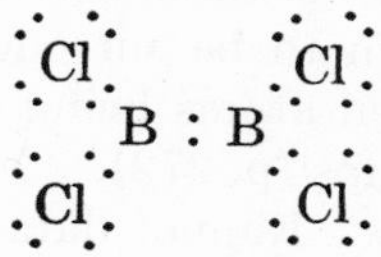

```
 ..        ..
:Cl:      :Cl:
 ..  B : B ..
 ..        ..
:Cl:      :Cl:
 ..        ..
```

The compound is not reduced by lithium aluminum hydride, but lithium borohydride converts it largely to diborane (p. 774).[55] Hydrogen gives decaborane, and ethers form addition compounds such as $B_2Cl_4{\cdot}R_2O$ and $B_2Cl_4{\cdot}2R_2O$. The subchloride is obtained by subjecting boron trichloride to an electric arc struck with a zinc anode,[56] but passing boron trichloride vapors (1 to 2 mm.) through a glow discharge established between mercury electrodes gives better yields.[55] Allowing a mixture of boron subchloride and boron tribromide to stand at room temperature gives the subbromide, B_2Br_4.[55] Boron subiodide, or tetraiododiborine, is obtained as a pale-yellow crystalline solid by the action of an electrodeless discharge on boron triiodide vapors at 1 to 3 mm. pressure.[54] A lower iodide, B_xI_y ($x > y$), also forms, and decomposition of the subiodide at room temperatures yields a mixture of the triiodide and a polymer $(BI)_n$.[54]

Trihalides of Aluminum and Its Heavier Congeners (MX_3). All the possible compounds except thallium(III) iodide have been characterized. A compound of composition TlI_3 can be prepared, but its properties are essentially those of a thallium(I) triiodide, $Tl^+I_3^-$. This is in keeping with the enhanced oxidizing power of thallium(III). Indeed, both the tribromide and trichloride of thallium show marked tendencies to revert to the thallium(I) compounds. The data in

[54] W. C. Schumb, E. L. Gamble, and M. D. Banus: *J. Am. Chem. Soc.*, **71**, 3225 (1949).

[55] T. Wartik, R. Moore, and H. I. Schlesinger: *J. Am. Chem. Soc.*, **71**, 3265 (1949).

[56] A. Stock, A. Brandt, and H. Fischer: *Ber.*, **58**, 643 (1925).

Table 17·4 show the trifluorides to be ionic and the other trihalides to be largely covalent, decreased covalent character paralleling increased size of the cation. The differences are most striking for aluminum, where the change from a salt to covalent materials is particularly abrupt.

Except for the fluoride, the aluminum trihalides vaporize largely as dimers. This tendency is most pronounced for the chloride. The percentages of the monomeric species near the boiling points have been determined[57] to be: $AlCl_3$, 0.02% (180°C.); $AlBr_3$, 0.7% (255°C.); AlI_3, 24% (380°C.). Dimeric structures persist in solvents such as benzene but not in coordinating solvents such as pyridine or ether.[58] Electron diffraction studies[59] of these three halides in the gaseous state show each aluminum atom to be surrounded tetrahedrally by four halogen atoms, two halogen atoms being common to two tetrahedra and acting as bridging groups (p. 272). Measured bond distances are summarized in Table 17·6. Raman data show that such structures

TABLE 17·6

Bond Distances in Group IIIb Trihalide Molecules

Metal	M—X Bond Distance, A Cl	Br	I
Al	2.06*	2.21*	2.53*
	2.21†	2.33†	2.58*
Ga	2.22	2.34	2.50
In	2.46	2.58	2.76

* Non-bridging halogen. † Bridging halogen.

persist in the fused state.[60] The trichlorides, tribromides, and triiodides of gallium and indium are also dimeric in the vapor state,[61, 62] bond distances being given in Table 17·6. In the absence of conflicting data, bridge structures may be assumed for these compounds as well.

The anhydrous trifluorides are only slightly soluble in water, but the other trihalides dissolve readily. Aqueous solutions are ionic although extensively hydrolyzed (p. 736). In non-polar solvents, the compounds are non-conductors. All the trihalide molecules are electron pair acceptors (Lewis acids). As such they combine with

[57] W. Fischer and O. Rahlfs: *Z. anorg. allgem. Chem.*, **205**, 1 (1932).
[58] A. Werner: *Z. anorg. Chem.*, **15**, 1 (1897).
[59] K. J. Palmer and N. Elliott: *J. Am. Chem. Soc.*, **60**, 1852 (1938).
[60] H. Gerding and E. Smit: *Z. physik. Chem.*, **B51**, 217 (1942).
[61] D. P. Stevenson and V. Schomaker: *J. Am. Chem. Soc.*, **64**, 2514 (1942).
[62] H. Brode: *Ann. Physik*, **37**, 344 (1940).

halide ions (p. 765), amines, and a variety of organic compounds containing donor groups. Anhydrous aluminum(III) chloride resembles boron trifluoride in its catalytic power. There is some evidence that anhydrous gallium(III) chloride is an even better acid catalyst than its aluminum analog.[63]

The anhydrous trihalides are best made by direct reaction of the elements at elevated temperatures. Sublimation is a common method of purification. Directions for aluminum tribromide are typical.[64] The thallium compounds can be made also by reaction of the thallium(I) compounds with the appropriate halogens. Aqueous solutions of the trihalides may be obtained by reaction of solutions of the hydrohalogen acids upon the oxides or, except with thallium, upon the free metals. Concentration of such solutions gives either hydrates or basic salts.

Oxyhalides (MOX). Reaction of boron trifluoride with boric oxide yields a volatile compound $(BOF)_x$,[65] which is apparently a trimer with the cyclic structure

```
              ..
             : F :
              ..
              B
           . .   .
        : O : : O :
   ..     ..     ..   ..
 : F : B  . . .  B : F :
   ..     .   .       ..
              O
              ..
```

The compound is also formed when alumina and boron trifluoride are heated at 450°C. An analogous oxychloride has not been characterized completely, although heat is said to convert alkoxychloroboron compounds such as CH_3OBCl_2 into at least a small quantity of the oxychloride.[66, 67] A number of these alkoxyhaloboron compounds are known. Aluminum oxyhalides, AlOX (X = Cl, Br), are formed when ether addition compounds of the trihalides are heated.[68] The heavier elements probably form similar compounds.

[63] H. Ulich: *Die Chemie*, **55**, 37 (1942).

[64] D. G. Nicholson, P. K. Winter, and H. Fineberg: *Inorganic Syntheses*, Vol. III, p. 30. McGraw-Hill Book Co., New York (1950).

[65] P. Baumgarten and W. Bruns: *Ber.*, **72B**, 1753 (1939); **74B**, 1232 (1941).

[66] H. Ramser and E. Wiberg: *Ber.*, **63B**, 1136 (1930).

[67] E. Wiberg and W. Sütterlin: *Z. anorg. allgem. Chem.*, **202**, 1 (1931).

[68] W. Menzel and M. Froehlich: *Ber.*, **75B**, 1055 (1942).

Compounds derived from oxygen family elements

Complete series of oxides and sulfides of the types M_2O_3 and M_2S_3 are known for the Group IIIb elements. All but thallium form analogous selenides and tellurides (B_2Te_3 not known). Boron forms poorly characterized lower oxides of compositions B_2O, B_4O_3, B_4O_5, and B_2O_2. There is spectroscopic evidence for a lower aluminum oxide, AlO, as well as a sulfide and a selenide (p. 736). For gallium and indium, lower oxides, sulfides, and selenides are known but comparatively unstable compounds. However, the unipositive thallium compounds are stable and well characterized (pp. 736, 769). It seems appropriate again to discuss the boron compounds separately.

Boron Compounds. Boric oxide, B_2O_3, exists in both crystalline and glassy forms, the conversion of the crystalline to the glassy being characterized by a heat of reaction of 4.360 kcal. per gram formula weight and a free energy change of 2.600 kcal. per gram formula weight, both at 298.1°K.[69] The transition temperature is not known. The crystalline material has a specific gravity of 1.805, the glass a specific gravity of 1.795. The crystalline material melts at 450 ± 2°C.,[70] whereas the glassy material softens over a long temperature range and becomes fluid at red heat (compare silica, pp. 691–692). The boiling point probably lies above 1500°C., but there is noticeable volatility at 1000°C. Boric oxide is reduced only by the most active reducing agents (p. 738). The compound is a high-temperature acid (p. 333)[71, 72] and behaves as an acid at ordinary temperatures toward hydroxides, etc. Its slightly basic properties are evident in the formation of compounds such as the phosphate, BPO_4 (p. 816). Boric oxide is not particularly soluble in water, but it hydrates readily to the meta (HBO_2) and ortho (H_3BO_3) acids. It is also the anhydride of the various hypothetical polyboric acids. These acids and their derivatives are discussed as a special topic in a later section of this chapter (pp. 808–811).

Glassy boric oxide is obtained by either fusing the crystalline form or dehydrating orthoboric acid at red heat. The crystalline form is obtained by dehydrating orthoboric acid at lower temperatures.[70, 73] The procedure of Kracek, Morey, and Merwin,[70] one version of which amounts to heating the acid for a week at 120°C., followed by daily

[69] J. C. Southard: *J. Am. Chem. Soc.*, **63,** 3147 (1941).

[70] F. C. Kracek, G. W. Morey, and H. E. Merwin: *Am. J. Sci.* [5], **35A,** 143 (1938).

[71] W. E. Gürtler: *Z. anorg. Chem.*, **40,** 225 (1904).

[72] M. Foex: *Compt. rend.*, **206,** 349 (1938).

[73] L. McCulloch: *J. Am. Chem. Soc.*, **59,** 2650 (1937).

temperature increases of 10°C. until heating for a day at 200°C., addition of more acid, and final heating at 400°C. for two days, gives excellent results.[69, 74] A porous variety is obtained by heating orthoboric acid at 200°C. in a vacuum over phosphorus(V) oxide.[75, 76]

The oxide B_2O has not been prepared as such, but an apparent hydrate, $B_2(OH)_2$, has been reported[77] as a product of the reaction of the salt $H_4B_2(OK)_2$ with sulfuric acid. This compound is readily oxidized by iodine to the oxide B_2O_2. Repeated extraction of magnesium boride (p. 776) with water, followed by treatment with aqueous ammonia, evaporation, and heating *in vacuo*, gives the oxides B_2O_2 and B_4O_5.[78, 79] The oxide B_4O_5 is contaminated with some 5% of a material $B_4O_3{\cdot}2H_2O$. Of these, the compound B_2O_2 is most important. It is obtained also by hydrolysis of boron subchloride (p. 749)[56] or of the potassium compound $K_2B_2H_6$ (p. 781).[80] It is a water-soluble material which is readily oxidized to boric acid by nitric acid. Molecular weight determinations support the dimeric composition, and properties of the compound are in accord with the structure[81]

$$\overset{\cdot\cdot}{\underset{\cdot\cdot}{O}}::B:B::\overset{\cdot\cdot}{\underset{\cdot\cdot}{O}}$$

Whether this compound is identical with the oxide BO obtained by heating boron with zirconium(IV) oxide *in vacuo* at 1800°C.[82] has not been determined.

Boron sesquisulfide, B_2S_3, is a colorless, crystalline compound, which melts at 310°C. but sublimes completely at 200°C. It is readily hydrolyzed by water to boric acid and hydrogen sulfide and burns in oxygen or chlorine. The compound results from direct combination of the elements at elevated temperatures[83] or from the thermal decomposition of the compound $B_2S_3{\cdot}H_2S$ or $H_2B_2S_4$. The latter compound is obtained by reaction of hydrogen sulfide with boron tribromide dis-

[74] K. K. Kelley: *J. Am. Chem. Soc.*, **63**, 1137 (1941).

[75] E. Tiede and A. Ragoss: *Ber.*, **56**, 656 (1923).

[76] W. Lange: *Inorganic Syntheses*, Vol. II, p. 22. McGraw-Hill Book Co., New York (1946).

[77] R. C. Ray: *J. Chem. Soc.*, **121**, 1088 (1922).

[78] M. W. Travers, R. C. Ray, and N. M. Gupta: *J. Indian Inst. Sci.*, **1**, 1 (1914).

[79] R. C. Ray and P. C. Sinha: *J. Chem. Soc.*, **1941**, 742.

[80] A. Stock, W. Sütterlin, and F. Kurzen: *Z. anorg. allgem. Chem.*, **225**, 225 (1935).

[81] E. Wiberg and W. Ruschmann: *Ber.*, **70B**, 1393 (1937).

[82] E. Zintl, W. Morawietz, and E. Gastinger: *Z. anorg. allgem. Chem.*, **245**, 8 (1940).

[83] H. Moissan: *Ann. chim. phys.* [7], **6**, 312 (1895).

solved in carbon disulfide or benzene.[84, 85] Its structure appears to be

```
               ..
               S
     ..     .: ..   ..
H : S : B .:.. B : S : H
     ..     ..:.    ..
               S
               ..
```

A selenide, B_2Se_3, is obtained by direct combination of the elements.[83]

Compounds of Aluminum and the Heavier Elements. Aluminum oxide, Al_2O_3, is encountered most commonly as corundum (α-Al_2O_3). In this structure each aluminum atom is surrounded octahedrally by six oxygen atoms, and each oxygen atom is surrounded by four aluminum atoms, giving in effect a close-packed lattice of oxygen atoms in which aluminum atoms occupy tetrahedral holes. A less common variety, γ-Al_2O_3, has a spinel structure (p. 756). Surface oxidation yields another oxide, γ'-Al_2O_3, which has a defect rock-salt structure in which a random distribution of 21⅔ aluminum atoms over 32 lattice positions is found. So-called β-Al_2O_3 is really a material of composition $Na_2O{\cdot}11Al_2O_3$.[86] Corundum is a high-temperature modification; γ-Al_2O_3 a low-temperature modification. Corundum melts at 2030°C. and boils at ca. 2980°C. Its specific gravity is 3.99, whereas that of γ-Al_2O_3 is 3.42 to 3.64. Corundum ranks next to silicon carbide in hardness (ca. 9 on Mohs' scale).

Aluminum oxide has a high thermal stability, its heat of formation (−402.9 kcal. per mole) being very large. The alpha form is insoluble in and unreactive toward water and is very resistant to attack by aqueous acids. The gamma form is hygroscopic and dissolves in acids.

Crystalline aluminum oxide is found in nature as ruby and sapphire and in an impure form as emery. Various hydrates are also found (e.g., bauxite, diaspore, gibbsite). Alundum is an artificial aluminum oxide made by fusing bauxite. It is useful as an abrasive and as a refractory. Synthetic aluminum oxide is made by dehydrating the hydroxide, giving the gamma form below 950°C. and the alpha form at higher temperatures. Careful dehydration at low temperatures gives a product with highly developed surfaces which is useful as a catalyst and as an adsorbing agent. The beauty and hardness of ruby and sapphire (and related colored species such as oriental

[84] A. Stock and O. Poppenberg: *Ber.*, **34,** 399 (1901).

[85] A. Stock and M. Blix: *Ber.*, **34,** 3039 (1901).

[86] A. F. Wells: *Structural Inorganic Chemistry*, 2nd Ed., p. 383. Clarendon Press, Oxford (1950).

amethyst, oriental emerald, oriental topaz) have long been prized. Synthetic rubies were first produced by Verneuil[87] by an ingenious process in which powdered alumina mixed with a small proportion of chromium(III) oxide was fused in an oxyhydrogen flame, the fused mass being allowed to crystallize as a *boule* on an alumina rod. Both ruby and sapphire are now produced in sizable quantities by essentially the same process,[88–90] various color effects being obtained by the addition of suitable substances (e.g., Cr_2O_3 for ruby, Fe_3O_4 and TiO_2 for blue sapphire). Even gems exhibiting asterism (star gems) are obtained by appropriate treatment of materials containing titanium(IV) oxide.[91] Synthetic ruby and sapphire are used for jewel bearings, thread guides in textile mills, jewelry, etc.

Hydration of alumina, hydrolysis of aluminate solutions, or treatment of aluminum salt solutions with alkalies (soluble hydroxides, carbonates, sulfides) gives materials usually referred to as aluminum hydroxide. Careful study has shown that the following hydrates of aluminum oxide exist:[92–94]

1. α-$Al_2O_3 \cdot 3H_2O$ (bayerite), metastable with respect to gibbsite but stable with respect to böhmite. This is obtained by aging böhmite gel under dilute alkali, by reaction of amalgamated aluminum with water at 40°C. for several days, or by slow hydrolysis of an aluminate solution or reaction with carbon dioxide at room temperature.

2. γ-$Al_2O_3 \cdot 3H_2O$ (gibbsite or hydrargillite), the stable 3-hydrate or hydroxide. This form is found as a mineral and is obtained by rapid hydrolysis of an aluminate solution or reaction with carbon dioxide at 100°C. or by digesting bayerite with dilute alkali at 60°C.

3. α-$Al_2O_3 \cdot H_2O$ (diaspore), a naturally occurring material. This is formed by heating γ-Al_2O_3 with water under pressure at 430°C. and seeding. On being heated in steam at 400°C., it gives α-Al_2O_3.

4. γ-$Al_2O_3 \cdot H_2O$ (böhmite), a material stable in steam at 400°C. This is precipitated from boiling aluminum salt solutions by ammonia.

[87] A. Verneuil: *Ann. chim. phys.* [8], **3**, 20 (1904).

[88] Anon.: *J. Chem. Education*, **20**, 2 (1943).

[89] Anon.: *Synthetic Sapphire, Ruby, and Spinel.* Bulletin of the Linde Air Products Company, New York (1946).

[90] A. E. Alexander: *J. Chem. Education*, **23**, 418 (1946).

[91] J. M. Burdick and J. W. Glenn: U. S. Patent 2,488,507, Nov. 15, 1949. Assigned to the Linde Air Products Company.

[92] H. B. Weiser: *Inorganic Colloid Chemistry. Vol. II. The Hydrous Oxides and Hydroxides*, Ch. III. John Wiley and Sons, New York (1935).

[93] R. Fricke and G. F. Hüttig: *Hydroxyde and Oxydhydrate*, pp. 57–113. Akademische Verlagsgesellschaft m. b. H., Leipzig (1937).

[94] R. Fricke and J. Jockers: *Z. anorg. Chem.*, **262**, 3 (1950).

It is also obtained as the first product of the aging of the amorphous gel thrown down by alkalies at room temperature, by reaction of amalgamated aluminum with water at 60°C., or by aging gibbsite at 350°C. in a hydrothermal bomb.

Studies by Laubengayer and Weisz[95] indicate the following ranges of stability: bayerite, below 155°C.; gibbsite, 155° to 280°C.; böhmite, 155° to 280°C.; diaspore, 280° to 450 ± 5°C.; γ-Al_2O_3, metastable in range 100° to 500°C.; α-Al_2O_3, above 450 ± 5°C. Even below 155°C., bayerite is less stable than gibbsite.

Freshly precipitated aluminum hydroxide is amorphous, but aging gives crystals. It is readily peptized to a hydrosol. The crystalline material (γ-$Al_2O_3 \cdot 3H_2O$) is built up of double layers of hydroxyl groups, with aluminum atoms occupying two-thirds of the octahedral holes between the layers.[96] Hydroxyl bonds (p. 192) hold adjacent layers of OH groups together.

Aluminum hydroxide is predominantly basic and forms salts by reaction with a variety of acids. In solution, of course, these salts are extensively hydrolyzed. Complete hydrolysis occurs with very strongly basic anions (e.g., S^{-2}, CO_3^{-2}, CN^-, HCO_3^-). Aluminum hydroxide is also weakly acidic ($pk_A' = 12.2$, compared with 9.24 for boric acid). Reactions with alkali metal hydroxide solutions give aluminate solutions, which, because of the weakness of the acid, are strongly hydrolyzed. Even carbon dioxide causes complete hydrolysis with precipitation of the hydrous hydroxide. Solid meta-aluminates, $NaAlO_2 \cdot \frac{5}{4}H_2O$, $NaAlO_2 \cdot 3H_2O$, and $KAlO_2 \cdot \frac{3}{2}H_2O$, have been prepared,[97, 98] but ortho-aluminates are not known. The composition of the aluminate ion in solution remains undetermined. In view of the tendency of aluminum(III) to add donor groups, compositions such as $[Al(OH)_4]^-$ or $[Al(H_2O)_2(OH)_4]^-$ are not improbable.

A number of naturally occurring aluminates of composition $M^{II}(AlO_2)_2$ (M^{II} = Mg, Zn, Fe, Be) are known. These are referred to as spinels, the name spinel being given specifically to the magnesium compound. In crystals of these materials, the oxygen atoms (or ions) are arranged in a cubic close-packed fashion, with aluminum atoms occupying octahedral holes and atoms of the dipositive elements tetrahedral holes.[99] The spinel structure is characteristic of a variety

[95] A. W. Laubengayer and R. S. Weisz: *J. Am. Chem. Soc.*, **65**, 247 (1943).

[96] A. F. Wells: *Structural Inorganic Chemistry*, 2nd Ed., pp. 417–419. Clarendon Press, Oxford (1950).

[97] R. Fricke and P. Jucaitis: *Z. anorg. allgem. Chem.*, **191**, 129 (1930).

[98] P. Jucaitis: *Z. anorg. allgem. Chem.*, **220, 257** (1934).

[99] A. F. Wells: *Structural Inorganic Chemistry*, 2nd Ed., pp. 379–383. Clarendon Press, Oxford (1950).

of natural and synthetic compounds of type formula $M^{II}(M^{III}O_2)_2$ (M^{II} = Be, Mg, Zn, Cd, Mn, Fe, Co, Ni; M^{III} = Al, Ga, In, Fe, Co, Cr). Thus the chromites (p. 882) and the ferrites (p. 887) are typical spinels. Closely related are compounds such as $Fe^{III}MgFe^{III}O_4$, or $B(AB)O_4$ as compared with $A(BO_2)_2$ for spinels. In crystals of these compounds, half the B atoms occupy tetrahedral positions, and the remaining B atoms together with all the A atoms occupy octahedral positions.[99] Crystalline beryllium aluminate, $Be(AlO_2)_2$, of gem quality is known as chrysoberyl. Magnesium aluminate containing excess aluminum oxide (ca. $MgO \cdot 3.5Al_2O_3$) is produced synthetically by the Verneuil procedure (p. 755) for use as gem material, abrasion-resistant bearings, etc. (hardness = 8 on Mohs' scale).[88] It is referred to technically as spinel. The solubility of γ-Al_2O_3 in spinel is due to the fact that both crystallize in the same structure.

The sesquioxides of gallium, indium, and thallium are quite generally comparable with the aluminum compound. Gallium(III) oxide exists as a low-temperature alpha form and a high-temperature beta form, the latter being insoluble in acids. The indium and thallium compounds are not polymorphic. Two hydrated gallium(III) oxides are known, $Ga_2O_3 \cdot H_2O$ (comparable with diaspore) and $Ga_2O_3 \cdot 3H_2O$ (metastable like bayerite). Indium gives only $In_2O_2 \cdot 3H_2O$, and thallium(III) oxide is anhydrous. These compounds are all water insoluble. Only the gallium compounds are acidic enough to dissolve in aqueous alkali.

Aluminum sulfide, Al_2S_3, is a yellow crystalline material which sublimes at elevated temperatures. It is completely hydrolyzed in contact with water. It is obtained by reaction of sulfur with molten aluminum or with a mixture of alumina and carbon. The selenide is comparable in properties and mode of preparation. The gallium compounds are similar, but, by contrast, the sulfides, selenides, and tellurides of indium(III) are stable, water-insoluble compounds. The thallium(III) compounds are unstable with respect to the thallium(I) compounds.

Nitrides

All the elements in this family except thallium form nitrides of the type MN. Boron also forms a number of compounds containing characteristic B—N linkages. These are considered separately in a later section of this chapter (pp. 795–807). Aluminum, gallium, and indium also form comparable binary phosphides, arsenides, and antimonides.

All the simple nitrides are covalent materials (p. 578). In solid boron nitride, the unit cell is a hexagonal unit of alternating boron and nitrogen atoms, B_3N_3, the constants of which are $a = 2.5038 \pm 0.0001$ A and $c = 6.660 \pm 0.001$ A.[100] The structure has been considered to be that of graphite (p. 666),[101, 102] the B—N bond distance of 1.45 A being comparable to the C—C bond distance of 1.42 A in that substance and lying between the theoretical single and double B—N bond distances of 1.54 A and 1.36 A, respectively. Indeed, the compound has been called "inorganic graphite." According to Pease,[100] however, the hexagonal rings are packed directly on top of each other, with the positions of the boron and nitrogen atoms being interchanged in adjacent layers. The structure is thus basically the same as that of graphite, but with slight displacements of adjacent layers. Within each layer, a giant molecule arrangement pertains. An apparently amorphous material is known also. Aluminum, gallium, and indium nitrides crystallize in wurtzite-type lattices (p. 133),[103, 104] in which M and N alternate. These materials are thus giant molecules. In aluminum nitride, the Al—N bond distance is 1.87 A.

Crystalline boron nitride is a white refractory solid which sublimes below 3000°C. and melts under pressure at that temperature. It is inert even at elevated temperatures to oxygen, hydrogen, iodine, etc. At red heat, it is hydrolyzed by water vapor to ammonia and boric oxide. Aqueous acids or alkalies cause no decomposition, but fusion with alkali metal hydroxides or carbonates forms borates. Amorphous boron nitride is somewhat more reactive. Aluminum nitride melts at ca. 2200°C. under pressure, but undergoes thermal decomposition at lower temperatures. It is readily hydrolyzed by cold water to hydrated alumina and ammonia. The gallium and indium compounds are comparable to aluminum nitride.

Boron nitride is the ultimate product of the thermal decompositions of many boron-nitrogen compounds, e.g., $B(NH_2)_3$ and $BF_3{\cdot}NH_3$. It is also obtained by heating boron with nitrogen or ammonia or by heating borax with ammonium chloride. Aluminum nitride is formed when the metal is heated in nitrogen or ammonia or when the oxide is heated with carbon and nitrogen. Gallium nitride is also obtained by heating the metal in ammonia gas, but the indium compound is better formed by thermal decomposition of the compound $(NH_4)_3[InF_6]$.[104]

[100] R. S. Pease: *Nature,* **165,** 722 (1950).
[101] O. Hassel: *Norsk. Geol. Tids.,* **9,** 266 (1926).
[102] A. Brager: *Acta Physicochim. U. R. S. S.,* **7,** 699 (1937).
[103] H. Ott: *Z. Physik,* **22,** 201 (1924).
[104] R. Juza and H. Hahn: *Z. anorg. allgem. Chem.,* **239,** 282 (1938).

Carbides

The structures and general characteristics of the carbides of boron and aluminum have been discussed in Chapter 16 (pp. 697–699). Both boron carbide, B_4C, and aluminum carbide, Al_4C_3, are obtained by direct combination of the elements at elevated temperatures or by thermal reduction of the oxides with carbon. The ready hydrolysis of the aluminum compound by water or acids is to be contrasted with the chemical inertness of the boron derivative. The yellow aluminum carbide crystals melt at 2200°C. and sublime *in vacuo* at 1800°C.

Salts of the tripositive elements

Although most of the anhydrous compounds of these elements with non-metals and acid radicals are highly covalent, certain of the hydrated compounds possess salt-like character. Thus the anhydrous chloride, Al_2Cl_6, is a covalent substance (p. 750), but the hydrate, $AlCl_3{\cdot}6H_2O$, behaves as a salt. Coordination of water molecules to the tripositive metal ions overcomes covalent tendencies. This situation is common with aluminum, gallium, and indium. For boron, no salts are known as such, although a number of compounds containing effectively cationic boron are known. These are described later (pp. 816–817). For thallium, the strong oxidizing power of the uncomplexed tripositive ion sharply limits the number of characterizable salts.

Common water-soluble salts embrace the halides (except fluorides), perchlorates, sulfates, selenates, and nitrates. All these materials are extensively hydrolyzed in aqueous solutions (p. 736), particularly the thallium compounds. The sulfates and selenates are particularly prone to form double salts (cf., the alums, pp. 539–541). Double halides also form quite readily. These often have the general properties of complexes. Few complete series of insoluble salts have been characterized. Fluorides, phosphates, iodates, borates, etc., appear to be insoluble.

Complexes derived from the tripositive elements

Differences already pointed out between the simple compounds of boron and of the other elements are also apparent among the complex compounds. Boron resembles silicon (Ch. 16) quite closely in its ability to form complexes and in the nature of such complexes, whereas aluminum and the heavier members of the family give complexes which are comparable to those of tin, lead, zinc, cadmium, etc. Because of octet limitations, the coordination number of boron is invariably *four*.

The coordination number of aluminum is either *four* or *six*. The heavier members are most commonly 6-coordinate.

Complexes of Boron. Because of the acceptor strength of the boron atom, a variety of molecular addition compounds are known. These are formed most commonly between boron trihalides (especially boron trifluoride), boron alkyls, or boron aryls and compounds containing donor nitrogen or donor oxygen. Some of these materials have been described already (pp. 746–748); others are discussed in conjunction with the material on the hydrides of boron (pp. 780–781). Materials which are complexes in the more usual sense are the fluoborates, the chelated oxy derivatives, and perhaps the borohydrides. The borohydrides are discussed in connection with the boron hydrides (pp. 782–786) because of close chemical relations. In all these compounds, sp^3 hybridizations confer a tetrahedral geometry upon boron.

FLUOBORIC ACIDS AND FLUOBORATES. The only stable halo-complexes of boron are those containing fluorine. A variety of fluoboric acids and derived salts have been described.[105] These are either completely fluo compounds (e.g., HBF_4, H_2BF_5, $H_2B_2F_6$) or mixed aquo-fluo compounds [e.g., $(HO)_2BF$, HOB(F)O(F)BOH, etc.]. Many of these compounds are poorly characterized or have unconfirmed compositions. Important fluoboric acids are the compound HBF_4 and those materials which are related to it by successive substitution of hydroxyl groups for fluorides. These are related to each other as

$$H\left[\begin{array}{ccc} F & & F \\ & B & \\ F & & F \end{array}\right] \quad H\left[\begin{array}{ccc} F & & OH \\ & B & \\ F & & F \end{array}\right] \quad H\left[\begin{array}{ccc} F & & OH \\ & B & \\ F & & OH \end{array}\right] \quad H\left[\begin{array}{ccc} HO & & OH \\ & B & \\ F & & OH \end{array}\right]$$

all but the last compound being known. Substitution for the last fluoride would give the substance $H[B(OH)_4]$, which is also unknown as such. The name *fluoboric acid* is properly restricted to the first material, HBF_4. The other two materials are then hydroxy-fluoboric acids. Since all the compounds are referred to collectively as fluoboric acids, use of the more restrictive term *tetrafluoboric acid* for HBF_4 is even more desirable.

Tetrafluoboric acid has not been obtained in the free condition, although aqueous solutions containing 80 to 85% of the material have been prepared. The acid is strong, although accurate evaluations of its strength are difficult because of its hydrolysis. The ultimate

[105] H. S. Booth and D. R. Martin: *Boron Trifluoride and Its Derivatives*, Ch. 5. John Wiley and Sons, New York (1949).

hydrolytic reaction is given by the equation

$$BF_4^- + 3H_2O \rightleftharpoons H_3BO_3 + 4F^- + 3H^+$$

However, stepwise reactions in which the hydroxy acids $H[BF_3OH]$, $H[BF_2(OH)_2]$, and perhaps $H[BF(OH)_3]$ are formed successively give a better picture of the true hydrolytic process.[106] At 25°C., the degree of hydrolysis to $H[BF_3OH]$ varies from 0.777 for a 0.001018 *M* solution to 0.0550 for a 5.41 *M* solution,[106] the hydrolysis reaction being characterized by a hydrolysis constant of 2.3×10^{-3}. Hydrolysis is slow at room temperatures but rapid at elevated temperatures. Freshly prepared tetrafluoboric acid solutions do not attack glass, but on standing or being heated they do. Aqueous solutions of tetrafluoboric acid are formed by hydrolysis of boron trifluoride (p. 746). A better procedure involves treating cold concentrated aqueous hydrofluoric acid with boric acid in the mole ratio $4HF:1H_3BO_3$.[107] The reaction involves two steps:[106]

$$H_3BO_3 + 3HF \rightarrow H[BF_3OH] + 2H_2O \text{ (rapid)}$$

$$H[BF_3OH] + HF \rightleftharpoons H[BF_4] + H_2O \text{ (slow)}$$

Crystal structure studies on salts show the tetrafluoborate ion, $[BF_4]^-$, to be tetrahedral.[108–110] The tetrafluoborates are remarkably similar to the perchlorates in crystal structures[108] and in solubilities.[111] Many instances of isomorphism are noted. Salts of many of the heavy metal ions are water soluble, whereas the potassium, hexammine-nickel(II), and hexammine-cobalt(III) compounds, like the corresponding perchlorates, are much less soluble. Similarities of these types arise from similarities in size, in bond lengths (B—F, 1.53 A; Cl—O, 1.63 A), in tetrahedral character, and in the deformation-resisting fluorine and oxygen atoms surrounding the central atoms. Similarities to permanganates (p. 884) and fluosulfonates (p. 525) are also discernible.[111] Many tetrafluoborates have been characterized.[105, 111] The nitrosyl compound has been mentioned earlier (p. 595). An acetyl derivative, $(CH_3CO)[BF_4]$, is also of interest. The salts are usually prepared by metathesis reactions involving the acid or a soluble salt. The potassium salt is easily prepared by direct

[106] C. A. Wamser: *J. Am. Chem. Soc.*, **70,** 1209 (1948); **73,** 409 (1951).

[107] P. A. van der Meulen and H. L. Van Mater: *Inorganic Syntheses*, Vol. **I,** p. 24. McGraw-Hill Book Co., New York (1939).

[108] J. L. Hoard and V. Blair: *J. Am. Chem. Soc.*, **57,** 1985 (1935).

[109] L. J. Klinkenberg: *Rec. trav. chim.*, **56,** 36 (1937).

[110] L. J. Klinkenberg: Dissertation, University of Leyden (1937).

[111] E. Wilke-Dörfurt and G. Balz: *Z. anorg. allgem. Chem.*, **159,** 197 (1927).

precipitation.[107] The ammonium salt, which is a convenient source of boron trifluoride (p. 747), is obtained by reaction of boric acid with ammonium hydrogen fluoride as

$$H_3BO_3 + 2NH_4HF_2 \rightarrow NH_4[BF_4] + 3H_2O + NH_3$$

either in aqueous solution or by fusion.[112] Tetrafluoboric acid and its salts are often employed in the electrodeposition of metals.

Boron trifluoride forms a 2-hydrate, $BF_3 \cdot 2H_2O$, when treated with water at low temperatures.[113] The compound is a non-fuming liquid, which boils at 58.5° to 60°C. (1.2 mm.) and freezes to a crystalline solid melting at 5.9° to 6.1°C. In the crystalline state, the structure is similar to those of ammonium perchlorate and ammonium tetrafluoborate, and the compound is believed, therefore, to be hydronium monohydroxyfluoborate, $H_3O^+[BF_3OH]^-$.[114] The compound is only slightly soluble in benzene but dissolves in polar solvents such as dioxane and water In aqueous solution, the acid is about as strong as sulfuric acid.[110] Formation of the acid in solution as a hydrolysis product of tetrafluoboric acid has been discussed (p. 761). Aqueous solutions of the 1-hydrate of boron trifluoride undoubtedly contain this acid.[110] The only well-characterized salt is the potassium compound, which has been prepared by reaction of boric acid with potassium hydrogen fluoride in aqueous solution.[106, 115] The monohydroxyfluoborate ion is distinguished from the tetrafluoborate ion by its lack of precipitation by potassium ion or nitron acetate and by it ease of hydrolysis in alkaline solution.

Dihydroxyfluoboric acid is a colorless, syrupy liquid which boils at 159° to 160°C. and freezes to a solid melting between 4.0°C. and 4.5°C. It is insoluble in carbon tetrachloride, carbon disulfide, or benzene. Solvents such as water, methanol, or ethanol react to give uncharacterized fluorine-containing solids. Sulfuric acid converts it into boron trifluoride and boric oxide. Active metals liberate hydrogen. Salts are formed when dihydroxyfluoboric acid reacts with metal hydroxides or carbonates. The acid fumes in moist air. The compound is obtained as a decomposition product during distillation of boron trifluoride 2-hydrate.[113] It is also obtained by reaction of hydrogen fluoride with boric oxide or boric acid, or by reaction of

[112] H. S. Booth and S. Rehmar: *Inorganic Syntheses*, Vol. II, p. 23. McGraw-Hill Book Co., New York (1946).

[113] J. S. McGrath, G. G. Stack, and P. A. McCusker: *J. Am. Chem. Soc.*, **66**, 1263 (1944).

[114] L. J. Klinkenberg and J. A. A. Ketelaar: *Rec. trav. chim.*, **54**, 959 (1935).

[115] I. G. Ryss: *Compt. rend. acad. sci. U.R.S.S.*, **54**, 325 (1946).

sulfuric acid with a mixture of boric oxide and calcium fluoride.[116, 117] The hydroxyfluoboric acids are useful catalysts. Acid strength decreases markedly in the series $H[BF_4]$–$H[BF_3OH]$–$H[BF_2(OH)_2]$–($H[BF(OH)_3]$)–H_3BO_3.[106]

CHELATED OXY DERIVATIVES. All known chelate rings containing boron involve oxygen to boron bonds. Either one (monochelate) or two (dichelate) rings may be present, giving the fundamental structures

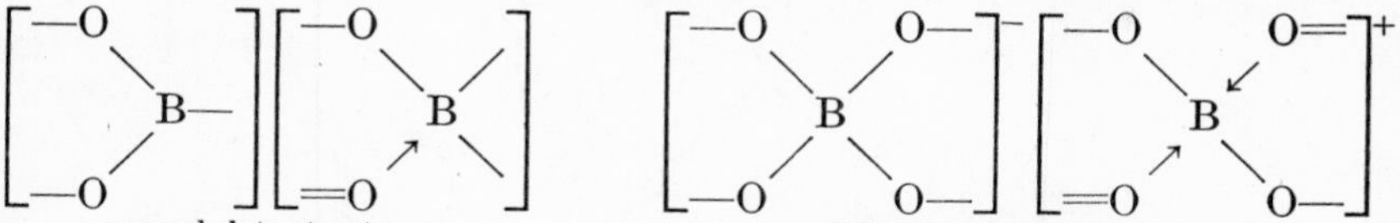

```
┌—O        ┐┌—O        ┐     ┌—O      O—┐⁻ ┌—O      O=┐⁺
│   \      ││   \   /  │     │   \   /   │  │   \   ↙   │
│    B—    ││    B     │     │     B     │  │     B     │
│   /      ││   ↗   \  │     │   /   \   │  │   ↗   \   │
└—O        ┘└=O        ┘     └—O      O—┘  └=O      O—┘
```

monochelate structures dichelate structures

The conversion of the weak orthoboric acid to comparatively strong monobasic acids by addition of polyhydroxy compounds such as glycerol or mannitol has been recognized for many years and is of considerable analytical importance. Only polyhydric alcohols are effective, and then only when the hydroxy groups on adjacent carbon atoms are *cis* to each other rather than *trans*. Thus ethanol is without effect, nor is ethylene glycol effective where mutual repulsions of the two hydroxy groups apparently impart considerable *trans* character. These observations are consistent with the formation of chelate structures of the types

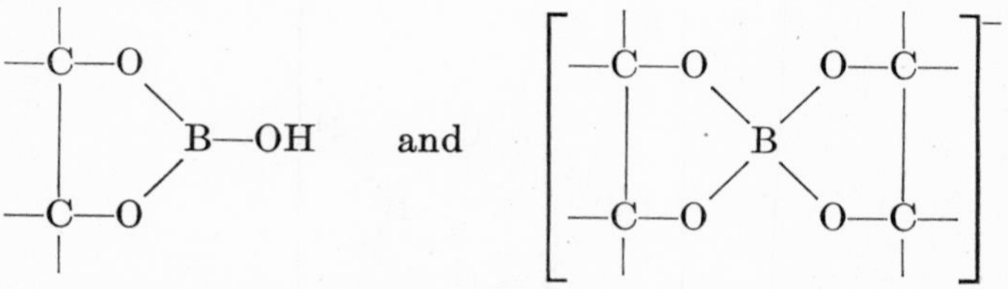

```
   |                        ┌  |                   |   ┐⁻
  —C—O                      │ —C—O           O—C—    │
   |   \                    │  |   \       /   |     │
   |    B—OH      and       │  |     B         |     │
   |   /                    │  |   /   \       |     │
  —C—O                      │ —C—O           O—C—    │
   |                        └  |                 |   ┘
```

with consequent decrease in the firmness of the bonding of the acidic hydrogen.[118, 119] Physical data confirm the existence of such species.[120, 121] Indeed, formation of such compounds is useful in determination of the configurations of various diols.[122] Catechol and sali-

[116] F. J. Sowa, J. W. Kroeger, and J. A. Nieuwland: *J. Am. Chem. Soc.*, **57**, 454 (1935).

[117] J. W. Kroeger, F. J. Sowa, and J. A. Nieuwland: *J. Am. Chem. Soc.*, **59**, 965 (1937).

[118] J. Böeseken, N. Vermaas, and A. T. Küchlin: *Rec. trav. chim.*, **49**, 711 (1930).

[119] J. Böeseken and N. Vermaas: *J. Phys. Chem.*, **35**, 1477 (1931).

[120] H. Schäfer: *Z. anorg. allgem. Chem.*, **247**, 96 (1941).

[121] R. E. Rippere and V. K. LaMer: *J. Phys. Chem.*, **47**, 204 (1943).

[122] J. Böeseken: *Rec. trav. chim.*, **47**, 683 (1928).

cyclic acid (and other related compounds) form similar chelates which can be isolated as salts of the types

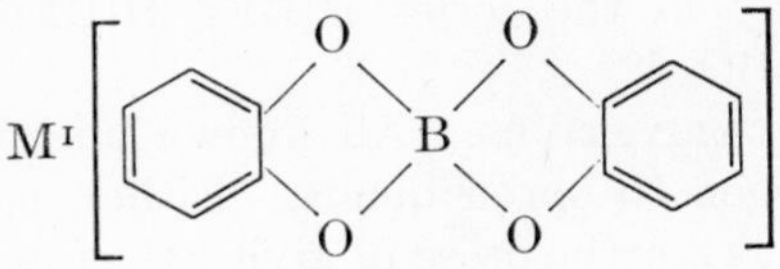

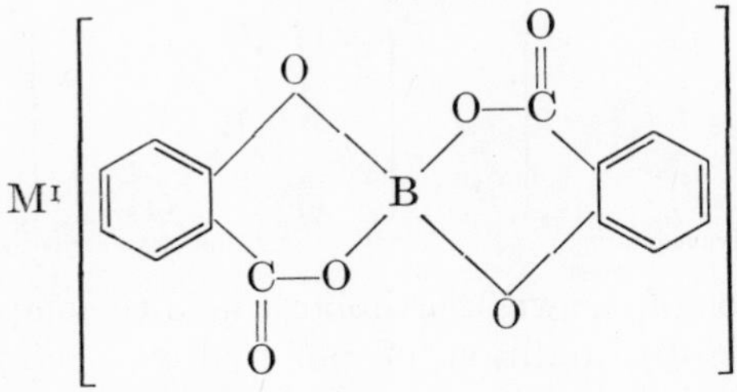

In these, direct attachment of four oxygens to each boron requires the presence of a balancing cation.[123] The brucine and strychnine salts of the 4-chlorocatechol[124] and salicylic acid[125] derivatives have been resolved, showing the distribution of bonds around the central boron to be tetrahedral.

Boron trifluoride reacts with various β-diketones in benzene solution to give chelates of the type[126]

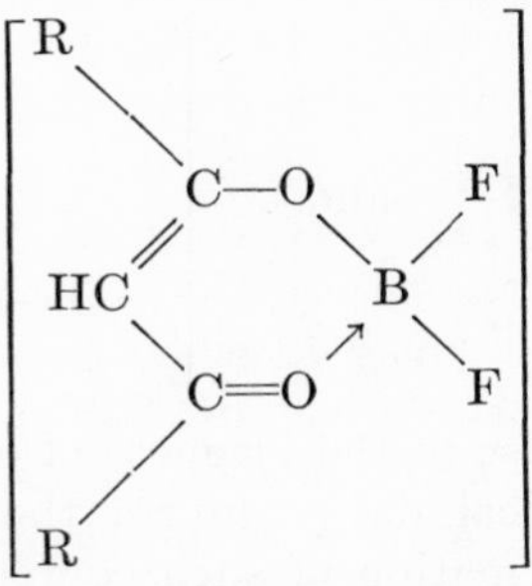

These compounds are essentially monomeric in benzene and are characterized by the low-melting points and lack of conductivity common to covalent materials. Certain hydroxy-anthraquinones give similar compounds with boron triacetate.[127]

[123] H. Schäfer: *Z. anorg. allgem. Chem.*, **250,** 82 (1942).
[124] J. Böeseken and J. A. Mijs: *Rec. trav. chim.*, **44,** 758 (1925).
[125] J. Meulenhoff: *Z. anorg. allgem. Chem.*, **142,** 373 (1925).
[126] G. T. Morgan and R. B. Tunstall: *J. Chem. Soc.*, **125,** 1963 (1924).
[127] O. Dimroth and T. Faust: *Ber.*, **54,** 3020 (1921).

Reaction of boron trichloride with various β-diketones gives materials in which two chelate rings are present,[128] i.e., $[B(AA)_2]X$ or

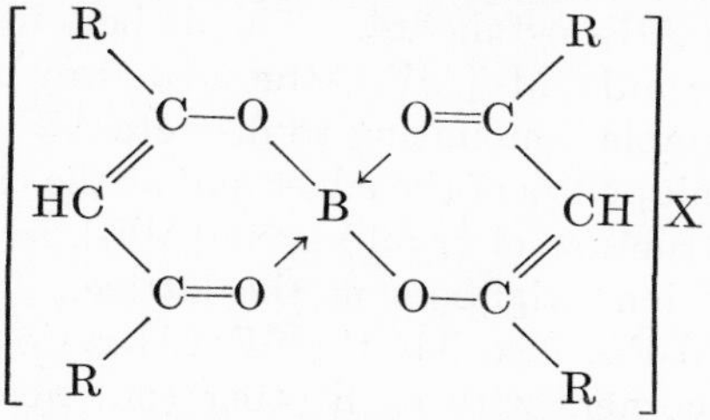

```
 ┌ R                         R ┐
 │  \                       /  │
 │   C—O           O=C         │
 │  //    \      ↙     \       │
 │ HC        B           CH    │X
 │  \     ↗     \      //      │
 │   C=O           O—C         │
 │  /                    \     │
 └ R                         R ┘
```

Although the covalency of boron is satisfied in the chelate structure, one of its primary valencies is not, and a negative group (X^-) is necessary. Compounds where $X^- = Cl^-, I^-$, etc., are difficult to purify, but those where $X^- = FeCl_4^-$, $AuCl_4^-$, $ZnCl_3^-$, $SnCl_6^{-2}$, $PtCl_6^{-2}$, etc., can be obtained. These "boronium" compounds are strictly comparable to the corresponding "siliconium" compounds, $[Si(AA)_3]X$ (p. 731).

Complexes of Aluminum and the Heavier Elements. Comparatively few molecular addition compounds are known for these elements, those which are known being definitely less stable than their boron analogs. Stability also decreases with increasing atomic weight and size of the Group IIIb element. As is true of boron, the anhydrous halides have the greatest tendency toward formation of compounds of this type. Oxygen and nitrogen are again the best donors. For the aluminum halides, addition compounds with ammonia, the amines, a few cyanides, water, alcohols, ethers, aldehydes, and ketones are known. Their compositions are in general $X_3Al \leftarrow NR_3$ or $X_3Al \leftarrow OR_2$ (R = hydrogen or other substituent). These compounds are often unstable in contact with water or when heated. Comparable phosphine and hydrogen sulfide compounds, $X_3Al \leftarrow PH_3$ and $X_3Al \leftarrow SH_2$, are also obtainable as are addition compounds of the aluminum alkyls, e.g., $R_3Al \leftarrow OR'_2$. The number of preparable addition compounds of the heavier elements is sharply reduced, the most stable being the ammines and etherates of the gallium alkyls. Best characterized of the ordinary type complexes are the halo complexes and the chelated oxy complexes. Among the latter, nitrogen may also act as a donor. Stable ammine or amine complexes have not been characterized.

HALO COMPLEXES. Fluo complexes are most characteristic of aluminum and gallium. Chloro and bromo complexes are better characterized with the heavier elements. Iodo complexes are almost unknown.

[128] W. Dilthey and F. J. Schumacher: *Ann.*, **344**, 300 (1906).

A number of fluoaluminates can be distinguished, but all may be described by the general formula $M_x{}^{I}[Al_yF_z]$.[129] Structurally, these are all based upon AlF_6 octahedra. This is best illustrated for compounds of type formula $M_3{}^{I}[AlF_6]$, the structure of the ammonium compound, for example, amounting to discrete $AlF_6{}^{-3}$ octahedra with $NH_4{}^+$ ions at the midpoints of the edges and at the centers of the cubic unit cells. The structure of cryolite, $Na_3[AlF_6]$, is similar, each Na^+ ion having six F^- ion neighbors in the lattice. The mineral cryolithionite, $Na_3Li_3Al_2F_{12}$, also has the 6F:1Al ratio. The AlF_6 octahedra may share corners with each other (but not edges because of the highly charged central Al^{+3} ions) to give compounds of other stoichiometries. Thus if two opposite corners of each octahedron are shared, a chain structure of composition $(AlF_5)_n{}^{-2n}$ is formed. This is characteristic of compounds such as Tl_2AlF_5. Sharing of all four equatorial fluorine atoms of each octahedron gives a layer structure of composition AlF_4, which is characteristic of the thallium(I), ammonium, and alkali metal salts, $M_2{}^{I}AlF_4$. Combination of these two situations gives even more complex structures. For example, in the mineral chiolite, $Na_5Al_3F_{14}$, layers of composition Al_3F_{14} are built up of AlF_6 octahedra, one-third of which share four corners and two-thirds of which share two corners. The majority of the known fluoaluminates are of the type $M_3{}^{I}[AlF_6]$. An x-ray study has shown that the only sodium fluoaluminates precipitated from aqueous solution are cryolite and chiolite,[130] the sodium ion being too small to give tetra- or penta-fluo structures. Fluogallates of the types $M_3{}^{I}[GaF_6]\cdot xH_2O$ and $M^{II}[GaF_5(H_2O)]\cdot 6H_2O$ have been described.

Chloroaluminates of the type $M^{I}[AlCl_4]$ are obtainable from fused melts or from solutions of the chlorides in benzene but not from aqueous solutions. Gallium forms similar compounds, but indium gives 6-coordinate compounds, $M_3{}^{I}[InCl_6]\cdot xH_2O$. Thallium gives compounds of the types $M^{I}[TlCl_4]$, $M_2{}^{I}[TlCl_5]$, $M_3{}^{I}[TlCl_6]$, and $M_3{}^{I}[Tl_2Cl_9]$, all of which are hydrated. The $TlCl_6{}^{-3}$ group is octahedral.[131] The $Tl_2Cl_9{}^{-3}$ group is of particular interest in that it is formed of two $TlCl_6$ octahedra, with the three chlorine atoms of one face held in common.[132, 133] The structure is like that of the $W_2Cl_9{}^{-3}$ ion (p. 272) and probably involves thallium to thallium bonding.

[129] A. F. Wells: *Structural Inorganic Chemistry*, 2nd Ed., pp. 304–306. Clarendon Press, Oxford (1950).

[130] J. M. Cowley and T. R. Scott: *J. Am. Chem. Soc.*, **69**, 2596 (1947).

[131] J. L. Hoard and L. Goldstein: *J. Chem. Phys.*, **3**, 645 (1935).

[132] *Ibid.*, 199.

[133] H. M. Powell and A. F. Wells: *J. Chem. Soc.*, **1935**, 1008.

Solid bromoaluminates, $M^I[AlBr_4]$, are obtainable by crystallization from benzene or toluene or by direct reaction of the component halides in the absence of water. Bromo complexes of the heavier Group IIIb elements are comparable to the chloro compounds. A few iodo complexes are known with thallium. Thallium halides of compositions TlX_2 and Tl_2X_3 are really thallium(I) salts of halothallate(III) ions, e.g., $Tl[TlX_4]$, $Tl_3[TlX_6]$.

CHELATED OXY COMPOUNDS. These are almost all 6-coordinate complexes. The β-diketones yield stable inner complexes (p. 270) with aluminum, gallium, and indium

$$\left[\left(\begin{array}{c} R \\ \quad\diagdown \\ \quad C{-}O \\ \;/\!\!/ \qquad \diagdown \\ HC \qquad\qquad M \\ \;\diagdown \qquad \nearrow \\ \quad C{=}O \\ \;/ \\ R \end{array}\right)_3\right]$$

These are crystalline compounds which melt at comparatively low temperatures (192°C., 194°C., 186°C., respectively, for M = Al, Ga, In) and vaporize without decomposition. They are difficultly soluble in water but dissolve in alcohol, benzene, and other organic solvents. The compounds are monomeric both in the vapor state and in solution. Three different crystal forms (α, β, and γ) are distinguishable, α for M = Al, Ga; β for M = Ga, In; and γ for M = In.[134] Thallium dialkyls give compounds of the type[135]

$$\left[\begin{array}{c} R \\ \quad\diagdown \\ \quad C{-}O \qquad\quad R' \\ \;/\!\!/ \qquad \diagdown \quad / \\ HC \qquad\qquad Tl \\ \;\diagdown \qquad \nearrow \quad \diagdown \\ \quad C{=}O \qquad\quad R' \\ \;/ \\ R \end{array}\right]$$

(compare gold, p. 843). Acetoacetic ester, diethylmalonate, etc., give similar, but less stable, compounds with these elements.

Polyhydric alcohols do not yield compounds comparable to those

[134] G. T. Morgan and H. D. K. Drew: *J. Chem. Soc.*, **119,** 1058 (1921).
[135] R. C. Menzies and E. R. Wiltshire: *J. Chem. Soc.*, **1932,** 2604.

formed by boron. However, the diphenol catechol gives an aluminum complex

$$\left[\left(C_6H_4O_2\right)_3Al\right]^{-3}$$

which is said to have been resolved with strychnine.[136]

A variety of aluminum lakes of comparable structures are known. Better characterized are the complexes derived from the lower dicarboxylic acids. Thus trioxalato salts, $M_3^I[M^{III}(C_2O_4)_3]\cdot xH_2O$ (M^{III} = Al, Ga, Tl), and dioxalato salts, $M^I[In(C_2O_4)_2(H_2O)_2]\cdot yH_2O$, are particularly common. The trioxalato salts are very similar to those of iron(III), cobalt(III), and chromium(III) in crystallographic properties and modes of preparation.[137] Reports of the resolution of the aluminum[138] and gallium[139] derivatives must be regarded with some skepticism in view of the probable ionic characters of the bonds and particularly in view of the isotopic carbon exchange studies of Long[140] (p. 266).

Chelate rings involving oxygen and donor nitrogen characterize the 8-quinolinol and substituted 8-quinolinol chelates of these elements, the fundamental structures being

$$\left[\left(C_9H_6NO\right)_3M\right]$$

M = Al, Ga, In, Tl. These are yellow crystalline compounds, which are insoluble in water but dissolve in chloroform to give solutions useful for the colorimetric determination of the metals.[141–143]

136 W. D. Treadwell with G. Szabados and E. Haimann: *Helv. Chim. Acta*, **15**, 1049 (1932).

137 J. C. Bailar, Jr., and E. M. Jones: *Inorganic Syntheses*, Vol. I, p. 35. McGraw-Hill Book Co., New York (1939).

138 W. Wahl: *Ber.*, **60**, 399 (1927).

139 P. Neogi and N. K. Dutt: *J. Indian Chem. Soc.*, **15**, 83 (1938).

140 F. A. Long: *J. Am. Chem. Soc.*, **63**, 1353 (1941).

141 T. Moeller: *Ind. Eng. Chem.*, Anal. Ed., **15**, 270, 346 (1943).

142 T. Moeller and A. J. Cohen: *Anal. Chem.*, **22**, 686 (1950).

143 T. Moeller and A. J. Cohen: *J. Am. Chem. Soc.*, **72**, 3546 (1950).

Thallium(I) Compounds

The only well-characterized series of compounds of unipositive elements in this family are those of thallium. These are commonly more stable than the thallium(III) materials (Table 17·2), particularly in the ionic condition The thallium(I) ion resembles both the alkali metal ions and the silver ion in its properties. Thus, like the alkali metal ions, it forms a soluble, strongly basic hydroxide, and a soluble carbonate, oxide, and cyanide. On the other hand, like the silver ion, it gives a very soluble fluoride but difficultly soluble other halides and a difficultly soluble bromate, iodate, and sulfide. The nitrate, sulfate, chlorate, and perchlorate are all isomorphous with the corresponding potassium compounds.

SOME SPECIAL PHASES OF BORON CHEMISTRY

Although many of the peculiarities of boron chemistry are apparent from the foregoing discussions, there are certain other phases which are best considered as special topics. Those chosen for discussion here embrace the borides, the boron hydrides and their derivatives, compounds containing boron-nitrogen linkages, the oxy acids of boron and their salts, and cationic boron. In conjunction with the discussion of boron hydrides, pertinent information about analogous aluminum and gallium compounds is given also.

Borides

The name boride is properly restricted to a binary compound of boron with a less electronegative element (i.e., a metal most commonly). Binary compounds with hydrogen (pp. 774–778), the halogens (pp. 744–749), oxygen and sulfur (pp. 752–754), nitrogen (pp. 757–758), and carbon (pp. 697–699) are thus not considered borides. As shown by the summary in Table 17·7, the majority of the known borides are those of the transition metals. Except in isolated cases, the compositions depart from the required stoichiometries for compounds containing trinegative boron and are apparently determined more by the requirements of metal and boron lattices than by valency relationships. Most of the borides have metallic properties regardless of the metals from which they are derived. It appears, therefore, that systematic classifications such as were used for the metal hydrides (pp. 404–406), nitrides (pp. 578–580), and carbides (pp. 696–697) cannot be made on the basis of existing information. It seems reasonable, however, to regard the majority of the borides as interstitial materials. On the basis of compositions, they may be classed as MB, MB_2, MB_4, MB_6, M_2B, M_3B_2, and M_3B_4 types. Such a classification has some basis in structural arrangements as well. Borides are useful as abrasives, refractories, and electron emitters.

Structures of the Metal Borides. Detailed structural information is available for specific borides of the types MB, MB_2, MB_4, and MB_6. In the boride FeB, the boron atoms lie at the centers of trigonal prisms, each formed by six iron atoms, the Fe—B distance being ca. 2.15 A.[144] However, each boron atom is close enough to two other boron atoms (1.77 A) to be bonded to them covalently, and the boron atoms are

TABLE 17·7

COMPOSITIONS OF REPORTED METAL BORIDES

Group I	Group II	Group III	Group IV	Group V	Group VI	Group VII	Group VIII
Cu_3B_2	Mg_3B_2	AlB_2	SiB_3	VB	CrB	MnB	Fe_2B
	CaB_6	AlB_{12}	SiB_6	VB_2	CrB_2	MnB_2	FeB
	SrB_6	YB_6	TiB	NbB_2	Cr_3B_2		Co_2B
	BaB_6	LaB_6	TiB_2	TaB_2	MoB_2		CoB
		CeB_4	ZrB		Mo_3B_4		CoB_2
		CeB_6	ZrB_2		WB		Ni_2B
		PrB_6	Zr_3B_4		WB_2		Ni_3B_2
		NdB_6	HfB		UB_2*		NiB
		SmB_6	HfB_2		UB_4*		NiB_2
		GdB_6	ThB_4*		UB_{12}*		Pt_2B
		ErB_6	ThB_6*				
		YbB_6					

* Inclusion in these periodic groups for convenience only.

thus arranged in zigzag chains throughout the solid material. It is not improbable that other compounds of the same composition have the same type of structure.

The structures of a number of borides of the type MB_2 have been determined.[145–148] The lattice of the aluminum compound consists of hexagonal layers of the boron atoms (like the layers of carbon atoms in graphite) between which the aluminum atoms are interspersed in a simple hexagonal structure.[145] Each boron atom is associated with three other boron atoms (at 1.73 A) and six aluminum atoms. Likewise crystals of the isomorphous diborides of titanium, zirconium, vanadium, niobium, and tantalum consist of alternate layers of metal and boron atoms, the metal atoms lying in simple hexagonal lattices.[148]

144 C. Gottfried and F. Schossberger (Ed.): *Strukturbericht*, Vol. III, p. 12. Akademische Verlagsgesellschaft M.b.h., Leipzig (1937).

145 W. Hofmann and W. Jäniche: *Z. physik. Chem.*, **B31**, 214 (1936).

146 P. McKenna: *Ind. Eng. Chem.*, **28**, 767 (1936).

147 R. Kiessling: *Acta Chem. Scand.*, **3**, 90, 603 (1949).

148 J. T. Norton, H. Blumenthal, and S. J. Sindeband: *J. Metals*, **1** (No. 10), *Trans.*, 749 (1949).

The tetraborides, CeB_4, ThB_4, and UB_4 crystallize in the same type of lattice.[149] The metal atoms are coplanar, each having five neighbors in its plane, with two neighbors in adjacent planes. Holes between the layers of metal atoms are filled with boron atoms, part of the boron atoms being bounded by six metal atoms at the corners of a trigonal prism (the MB_2 structure) and the others being grouped together as octahedra, each bounded by metal atoms at the corners of square prisms (the MB_6 structure).

Borides of the type MB_6 are quite generally isomorphous. These materials have cubic structures of the cesium chloride type,[150, 151] the boron atoms lying as octahedral B_6 groups in the centers of cubes of metal atoms. It appears also that the B_6 octahedra are arranged cubically in the crystals of at least the lanthanide compounds.[152] The metal atoms are not bonded to the boron lattices, making the structures completely interstitial. The metallic conductances shown by the compounds must thus be due to the presence of mobile valence electrons as in the metal lattices themselves. Magnetic studies of the lanthanide element hexaborides[153] show the metals to be effectively tripositive.

Data on borides of other types are apparently lacking, but the general similarities between the properties of these compounds and those of the MB_2, MB_4 and MB_6 types suggest similarities in structures. A possible exception may lie in the M_3B_2 type borides since these compounds could contain B^{-3} groups. That the magnesium compound Mg_3B_2 reacts readily with water and acids, whereas borides of other types are notably unreactive (p. 813), may be cited as evidence in indirect support of this possibility. According to Kiessling,[154] metal boride structures are characterized by the following boron atom arrangements: isolated boron atoms (M_2B type); zigzag boron chains (MB type); double boron chains or fragments of nets (M_3B_4 type); hexagonal boron nets (MB_2 type); and three-dimensional boron frameworks (MB_6 and UB_{12} types). In any event, available data are in general accord with Hägg's contention that simple interstitial boride structures can be formed only from metals with dense crystal structures

[149] A. Zalkin and D. H. Templeton: *J. Chem. Phys.*, **18**, 391 (1950).
[150] G. Allard: *Bull. soc. chim.* [4], **51**, 1213 (1932).
[151] M. von Stackelberg and F. Neumann: *Z. physik. Chem.*, **B19**, 314 (1932).
[152] Anon.: *Chem. Eng. News*, **28**, 3771 (1950). J. M. Lafferty: *J. Applied Phys.*, **22**, 299 (1951).
[153] W. Klemm, W. Schüth, and M. von Stackelberg: *Z. physik. Chem.*, **B19**, 321 (1932).
[154] R. Kiessling: *J. Electrochem. Soc.*, **98**, 166 (1951).

(cubic or hexagonal close-packed).[155] For such cases, the radius ratio ($R_B:R_M$) is less than 0.59.

Properties of the Metal Borides. As a class, the metal borides have the high melting points, extreme hardnesses, and high electrical conductivities characteristic of the interstitial nitrides (pp. 579–580) and

TABLE 17·8

PROPERTIES OF CERTAIN METAL BORIDES

Boride	Density, grams/cc.	Melting Point, °K.	Hardness, Mohs' Scale
CaB_6	2.43 (15°C.)		ca. 9+
SrB_6	3.28 (15°C.)		
BaB_6	4.36 (15°C.)		ca. 9+
YB_6	3.72 (15°C.)		
LaB_6	4.61 (15°C.)		
CeB_6	4.69 (15°C.)		ca. 9+
NdB_6	4.68 (15°C.)		
GdB_6	4.65 (15°C.)		
ErB_6	4.61 (15°C.)		
YbB_6	4.37 (15°C.)		
ThB_6	6.27 (15°C.)		ca. 8–9
CeB_4	5.74		
ThB_4	8.45		
UB_4	9.38		ca. 8+
TiB_2	4.0 (15°C.)		9+
ZrB_2	5.64		
VB_2	5.28 (15°C.)		8
CbB_2	6.4 (15°C.)		9+
TaB_2	11.0 (15°C.)		9+
WB_2	10.77		9+
ZrB		3265 ± 50	9+
HfB		3335	
CrB	6.1 (15°C.)		
WB		3195 ± 50	
MnB	6.12 (15°C.)		8
FeB	7.15 (18°C.)		
CoB	7.25 (18°C.)		ca. 7–8
Cr_3B_2	6.14 (15°C.)		ca. 8+
Zr_3B_4	5.97 (15°C.)		8
Mo_3B_4	7.1		9+

carbides (pp. 699–700). Although these properties are particularly characteristic of the refractory borides of the metals of Periodic Groups IVa, Va, and VIa,[156] they are also found among the MB_6 compounds of the metals of Groups II and III.[152] This is apparent from the data summarized in Table 17·8. In hardness, many borides approach the diamond quite closely.

[155] G. Hägg: *Z. physik. Chem.*, **B6**, 221 (1930); **B12**, 33 (1931).

[156] K. Becker: *Phys. Z.*, **34**, 185 (1933).

The metal borides are characterized by general chemical inertness toward non-oxidizing acids (Mg_3B_2, MnB are exceptions). Many are stable in air even to comparatively high temperatures. Strong oxidizing agents such as chlorine, fluorine, nitric acid, or hydrogen peroxide cause decompositions in most cases. The compounds are particularly susceptible to attack by alkaline materials, especially by fused alkalies under oxdizing conditions (e.g., with Na_2O_2, PbO_2). The inertness of the MB_6-type borides is striking, particularly in comparison with the ease with which nitrides and carbides of these same elements are hydrolyzed. Thus these compounds are not attacked by acids such as hydrochloric, hydrofluoric, or dilute sulfuric, although they are decomposed by hot concentrated sulfuric acid or nitric acid.

Preparation of the Metal Borides. Borides have been obtained by direct combination at elevated temperatures (1800 to 2200°C.) and preferably *in vacuo*, by reaction of metals with the vapors of boron-containing compounds at elevated temperatures, by thermal reduction of mixed boric and metal oxides with carbon, by reduction of mixed metal and boron halide vapors with hydrogen on heated metal filaments, or by electrolysis of fused borates. The last procedure, that of Andrieux,[157, 158] has been the most generally successful. It involves electrolytic decomposition of a fused bath prepared either from a borate of the metal in question or from a mixture of boric and metal oxides and containing the fluoride or chloride of the metal to enhance fluidity and conductivity. Magnesium compounds are sometimes included also. According to Andrieux, electrolysis liberates the metal, part of the metal then reducing the boron compounds to elemental boron and the remainder combining with the liberated boron. When magnesium compounds are present, it is assumed that liberated magnesium reduces the boron materials. Purifications are effected by leaching with acids or by strong heating *in vacuo*.

Boron hydrides and their derivatives

As perhaps the classic examples of compounds of the electron deficient type, the boron hydrides have been studied extensively both from the point of view of their structures and with regard to their physical and chemical characteristics. The pioneering researches of Stock[159] have, to a very great extent, governed subsequent investiga-

[157] J. L. Andrieux: *Ann. chim.* [10], **12,** 463 (1929).

[158] J. L. Andrieux and P. Blum: *Compt. rend.,* **229,** 210 (1949).

[159] A. Stock: *Hydrides of Boron and Silicon.* Cornell University Press, Ithaca (1933).

tions, and many of the elegant techniques developed by Stock are still employed essentially without change. Later studies have been concerned largely with problems of structure, development of better preparative techniques, and evaluation of the properties of derivatives of the boron hydrides. Some concept of the tremendous interest in this general field is given by the volume of available literature. Of the many pertinent papers, a number may be consulted with particular profit.[160–166] The preparation of formally similar electron-deficient aluminum[31,164] and gallium[29,30,164] compounds (p. 742) has provided added interest.

The Boron Hydrides. Characterized volatile boron hydrides, together with certain of their physical constants, are summarized in Table 17·9. Other volatile hydrides have been reported, e.g., B_6H_{12}

TABLE 17·9

PHYSICAL PROPERTIES OF VOLATILE BORON HYDRIDES

Molecular Formula	Melting Point, °C.	Boiling Point °C.	Density grams/ml.	Viscosity of Liquid, millipoises	Surface Tension, dynes/cm.	Common Name
B_2H_6	−165.5	−92.5	0.4698* (−120.4°C.)	2.10* (−120.4°C.)	18.6* (−121.6°C.)	diborane
B_4H_{10}	−120	18	0.56 (−35°C.)			tetraborane
B_5H_9	− 46.6	48	0.6468* (−4.1°C.)	4.17* (−4.1°C.)	24.5* (−3.6°C.)	stable pentaborane
B_5H_{11}	−123	63				unstable pentaborane
B_6H_{10}	− 65		0.69 (0°C.)			hexaborane
$B_{10}H_{14}$	99.7	213	0.78 (100°C.)			decaborane

* More extensive data are available from S. H. Smith and R. R. Miller: *J. Am. Chem. Soc.*, **72**, 1452 (1950).

(p. 794),[159] and B_9H_{13} on the basis of mass spectographic data for a sample of the hydride B_5H_{11} which had been stored for some time at −78°C.[167] However, no hydride other than those listed in Table 17·9 has been definitely characterized. Known compounds may be classified as *boranes*, type formula B_nH_{n+4}, or *dihydroboranes*, type

[160] A. J. E. Welch: *J. Soc. Chem. Ind.*, **58**, 969, 937 (1939).
[161] H. J. Emeléus: *Ann. Reports*, **37**, 138 (1940).
[162] H. I. Schlesinger and A. B. Burg: *Chem. Revs.*, **31**, 1 (1942).
[163] S. H. Bauer: *Chem. Revs.*, **31**, 43 (1942).
[164] E. Wiberg: *Ber.*, **77A**, 75 (1944).
[165] R. P. Bell and H. J. Emeléus: *Quart. Revs.*, **2**, 132 (1948).
[166] E. Wiberg: *Ber.*, **69B**, 2816 (1936).
[167] F. J. Norton: *J. Am. Chem. Soc.*, **72**, 1849 (1950).

formula B_nH_{n+6}. No examples of type formula B_nH_{n+2} are known. Decompositions of the lower molecular weight volatile boron hydrides yield non-volatile colorless or yellow solid boron hydrides which range from $(BH_{1.5})_x$ to $(BH)_x$ in stoichiometries[159,168] With aluminum, the polymeric hydride, $(AlH_3)_x$, has been obtained in ether solution.[169] and as a solid,[31] but no simple hydrides are known. For gallium, only the hydride Ga_2H_6 (m.p. −21.4°C., extrapolated b.p., 139°C.) is known.[29,30]

The chemical behavior of diborane is commonly considered to be representative of those of the other boron hydrides, and many discussions and studies have thereby been limited to that compound. Although the characteristics of the higher hydrides are markedly like those of diborane, there are some significant differences. The chemical behaviors of the gallium and aluminum hydrides have not been elucidated completely, but these compounds decompose to the free elements at elevated temperatures and appear to resemble the boron hydrides in general. At red heat, all the boron hydrides decompose to boron and hydrogen. At lower temperatures, decomposition gives other boron hydrides. The most stable of the hydrides are stable pentaborane (B_5H_9), which undergoes only very slow decomposition even at 150°C., and decaborane ($B_{10}H_{14}$), which is stable at 150°C. but decomposes appreciably at 170°C. Unstable pentaborane (B_5H_{11}) decomposes rapidly at room temperature, and, even at −78°C., it is slowly transformed into higher homologs.[168] Tetraborane is somewhat more stable toward thermal decomposition, but hexaborane decomposes quite rapidly at room temperatures. Diborane gives stable pentaborane and decaborane at 100° to 150°C., but it can be stored at room temperatures for prolonged periods without undergoing extensive decomposition (ca. 10% in a year).

All the boron hydrides react with oxygen, usually to give dark-colored products of undetermined compositions, but the rates and vigors of the reactions differ widely. Diborane and tetraborane may remain for some days in contact with air or oxygen at room temperatures without inflaming, but their kindling temperatures are only slightly above room temperature. The pentaboranes are spontaneously inflammable in air at ordinary temperatures. Hexaborane reacts slowly at room temperatures, and decaborane inflames only at elevated temperatures. Traces of the silicon hydrides or boron alkyls increase the reactivities of the boron hydrides toward oxygen. Reac-

[168] A. Stock and W. Mathing: *Ber.*, **69B**, 1469 (1936).

[169] A. E. Finholt, A. C. Bond, and H. I. Schlesinger: *J. Am. Chem. Soc.*, **69**, 1199 (1947).

tions with halogens parallel those with oxygen rather closely as regards rates. Halogenated boranes are formed (e.g., B_2H_5X from B_2H_6). Reactions of the hydrides with hydrogen halides or, in some cases, boron trihalides give the same products. Stable pentaborane and decaborane are unaffected by hydrogen chloride or boron trichloride. Reactions with hydrogen give other boron hydrides.

The boron hydrides are hydrolyzed by water, the ultimate products being hydrogen and boric acid. With diborane, the reaction is instantaneous; with tetraborane and unstable pentaborane, it is slower at room temperatures; and, with the others, it is complete only at elevated temperatures. Room temperature hydrolyses of stable pentaborane and hexaborane yield reducing solutions of subboric acid (p. 813). Reactions with alkaline solutions often yield hypoborates (p. 812), as, for example,

$$B_4H_{10} + 4KOH \rightarrow 4KOBH_3 + H_2$$

Ammonia yields stoichiometric compounds with most of the boron hydrides (e.g., $B_2H_6{\cdot}2NH_3$). These are discussed in a subsequent section (pp. 779–780).

Other important reactions of diborane are (1) formation of alkyl and aryl boron compounds by reaction with hydrocarbons or organoboron compounds, (2) formation of a series of borine (BH_3) addition compounds by reaction with strong electron pair donors, (3) formation of metal derivatives (e.g., $Na_2B_2H_6$) by reaction with amalgams, and (4) formation of borohydrides by reactions with metal alkyls. Additional information on some of these reactions is given below.

Although general procedures for the preparation of the boron hydrides have been outlined in conjunction with the discussion of hydrides (pp. 409–410), some additional and more specific details are essential. The classic procedure of Stock[159] involves dropping powdered magnesium boride into 10% hydrochloric acid in a container through which hydrogen is circulated. Better results are obtained with 8 *N* phosphoric acid at 70°C.[170] The gaseous mixture, consisting largely of hydrogen with small quantities of boron hydrides, silicon hydrides, phosphine, etc., is condensed in a liquid nitrogen trap and then fractionated. By a series of fractional distillation and fractional condensation processes, the individual boron hydrides are separated. Unfortunately, yields are low (never above 11%), and the procedure is cumbersome and time consuming. Even the preparation of suitably active magnesium boride samples (from boric oxide and magnesium) is troublesome. The mechanism of the hydrolysis reaction is complicated, and probably a variety of side reactions reduces the

[170] B. D. Steele and J. E. Mills: *J. Chem. Soc.*, **1930**, 74.

overall yield. Because of its reactivity with aqueous solutions, diborane is not a product of this process.

Although diborane was obtained originally by thermal decomposition of tetraborane, a number of direct procedures for its preparation are now available. Passage of mixture of boron trichloride vapor and hydrogen (H_2:BCl_3 mole ratio = 10:1) at a total pressure of 5 to 10 mm. through an electric discharge gives a mixture of hydrogen chloride, the monochloro derivative of diborane, and traces of diborane together with unchanged boron trichloride and hydrogen.[171] Fractionation at −120°C. gives a mixture of the chlorides BCl_3 and B_2H_5Cl. At 0°C. and 2 atm. pressure, rapid decomposition

$$6B_2H_5Cl \rightleftharpoons 5B_2H_6 + 2BCl_3$$

occurs, the diborane then being removed readily by fractionation. The yield is some 55%. Substitution of boron tribromide improves the process because the decomposition of the compound B_2H_5Br is more nearly complete.[172] Treatment of lithium aluminum hydride (p. 786) with boron trichloride in anhydrous diethyl ether gives diborane in quantitative (99.4%) yield[169] in terms of the equation

$$3LiAlH_4 + 4BCl_3 \rightarrow 3LiCl + 3AlCl_3 + 2B_2H_6$$

Other reactions which have been found useful for the preparation of diborane in high yields are indicated by the equations[173]

$$3LiH + BF_3 \rightarrow 3LiF + \tfrac{1}{2}B_2H_6 \ (40\text{–}70\%)$$

$$3Na[HB(OCH_3)_3] + 4BF_3 \rightarrow 3NaBF_4 + 3B(OCH_3)_3 + \tfrac{1}{2}B_2H_6$$

$$3NaBH_4 + 4BF_3 \rightarrow 3NaBF_4 + 2B_2H_6 \ (99\%)$$

All these reactions are run in diethyl ether solution and probably depend upon the acidic properties of boron trifluoride. The last reaction is particularly rapid and useful. The compound $Na[HB(OCH_3)_3]$ is formed as a stable product when trimethyl borate and sodium hydride are refluxed in ether. Reduction of boron trihalides with hydrogen over metals such as aluminum, magnesium, zinc, or sodium at elevated temperatures gives both diborane and its monohalo derivatives.[174] Diborane also is obtained when gaseous boron trihalides are reduced with sodium or calcium hydride.[174]

[171] H. I. Schlesinger and A. B. Burg: *J. Am. Chem. Soc.*, **53**, 4321 (1931).

[172] A. Stock and W. Sütterlin: *Ber.*, **67B**, 407 (1934).

[173] H. C. Brown, H. I. Schlesinger, et al.: Paper presented as a portion of the Symposium on Hydrides, 110th National Meeting of the American Society, September 1946.

[174] D. T. Hurd: *J. Am. Chem. Soc.*, **71**, 20 (1949).

Higher boron hydrides are obtained by thermal decomposition of diborane. Thus unstable pentaborane is formed when diborane is heated in a U-tube at 115°C., whereas mixtures of stable and unstable pentaboranes are obtained when diborane at an initial pressure of 120 mm. is passed through a tube at 250° to 300°C. by means of a circulating pump.[175, 176] Increasing the temperature decreases the quantity of unstable pentaborane present. Although small quantities of hexaborane are produced in these hot tube procedures, this hydride is better obtained by acid hydrolysis of magnesium boride. Heating diborane in a sealed bulb at around 160°C. gives decaborane, as do thermal decompositions of tetraborane and unstable pentaborane. Tetraborane is obtained by reaction of hydrogen with unstable pentaborane at 100°C. as[174]

$$B_5H_{11} + H_2 \rightarrow B_4H_{10} + \tfrac{1}{2}B_2H_6$$

The mechanisms of these interconversion reactions should be interesting.

Passage of mixtures of aluminum trimethyl dimer (p. 743) and hydrogen (1:150 to 1:400 mole ratio) through a glow discharge gives the volatile compound $Al_2H_2(CH_3)_4$, which on treatment with trimethylamine and subsequent heating yields polymeric aluminum hydride as a white solid.[31] The polymeric hydride can be obtained in ether solution by reaction of aluminum chloride with either lithium hydride or lithium aluminum hydride in that solvent.[169] Spontaneous precipitation or evaporation gives the solid polymer. Reaction of gallium trimethyl with hydrogen in a glow discharge gives the liquid compound $Ga_2H_2(CH_3)_4$, which reacts with triethylamine at room temperature to form the hydride Ga_2H_6 plus an addition compound of gallium trimethyl.[29, 30]

Derivatives of the Boron Hydrides. Among the derivatives of the boron hydrides which can be discussed to advantage are the alkyl diboranes, the ammonia "addition" compounds, the borine coordination compounds, the borane salts, and the metal borohydrides.

ALKYL DIBORANES. Reaction of diborane with boron trimethyl at room temperature yields four methyl derivatives of diborane, which have been shown by hydrolysis studies to be $CH_3B_2H_5$, 1,1-$(CH_3)_2B_2H_4$, 1,1,2-$(CH_3)_3B_2H_3$, and 1,1,2,2-$(CH_3)_4B_2H_2$.[177] Four analogous ethyl

[175] A. B. Burg and H. I. Schlesinger: *J. Am. Chem. Soc.*, **55**, 4009 (1933).

[176] A. Stock and W. Mathing: *Ber.*, **69B**, 1456 (1936).

[177] H. I. Schlesinger and A. O. Walker: *J. Am. Chem. Soc.*, **57**, 621 (1935).

derivatives have been prepared also as have the mono-*n*-propyl and the 1,1-di-*n*-propyl compounds. Symmetrical 1,2-$(CH_3)_2B_2H_4$ forms in the reaction of the monomethyl compound with dimethyl ether.[178] These compounds are similar to diborane in their reactions with air and moisture but are more stable toward decomposition by loss of hydrogen. Those with two alkyl groups attached to one boron appear to be more stable than those with but a single alkyl group so attached, and are formed at the expense of the latter. It is more significant, however, that no alkyl derivative with three groups attached to one boron has been obtained. This suggests that two hydrogen atoms in diborane are different from the others and are essential to the stability of the boron-boron bond (see pp. 786–793).

AMMONIA "ADDITION" COMPOUNDS. Reactions of boron hydrides with ammonia at low temperatures yield a series of so-called addition compounds, of which the materials $B_2H_6 \cdot 2NH_3$ and $B_5H_9 \cdot 4NH_3$ are the most stable and the most important.[159] The diborane derivative forms only under carefully controlled conditions (reaction of diborane with solid ammonia at −120°C., followed by removal of excess ammonia by sublimation at −100°C.). It is apparently but one of a series of ammoniated products because studies[179] on solutions of diborane in ammonia show the presence of materials of compositions $B_2H_6 \cdot xNH_3$.

These compounds are salt-like solids. The "diammoniate" of diborane gives conducting solutions in liquid ammonia which, upon electrolysis, evolve hydrogen at the cathode. The ionic structure $(NH_4)_2^+[B_2H_4]^{-2}$ has been suggested as compatible with observed behavior.[166] However, one equivalent of sodium liberates but one equivalent of hydrogen from one mole of the compound dissolved in liquid ammonia.[180] Furthermore, the compound is readily converted into compounds containing B—N linkages (pp. 795–807). These behaviors are consistent with formulation of the compound as a monoammonium salt,

$$(NH_4)^+ \left[H_3B : \overset{\displaystyle H}{\underset{\displaystyle H}{\overset{\cdot\cdot}{\underset{\cdot\cdot}{N}}}} : BH_3 \right]^-$$

[178] H. I. Schlesinger, N. W. Flodin, and A. B. Burg: *J. Am. Chem. Soc.*, **61**, 1078 (1939).

[179] G. W. Rathjens and K. S. Pitzer: *J. Am. Chem. Soc.*, **71**, 2783 (1949).

[180] H. I. Schlesinger and A. B. Burg: *J. Am. Chem. Soc.*, **60**, 290 (1938).

the extra electron essential to this structure being provided by the proton forming the ammonium ion. Existence of the radical

$$\left[\begin{array}{c} \quad\quad H \\ \quad\quad \cdot\cdot \\ H_3B : N : \\ \quad\quad \cdot\cdot \\ \quad\quad H \end{array} \right]^-,$$

which may be regarded as an intermediate in the formation of the "diammoniate," is well established.[180] The observation that only *six* hydrogen atoms per mole (i.e., those linked to nitrogen) undergo exchange when the compound is treated with deuteroammonia (ND_3) offers independent support for such a structure.[181] Other "ammoniates" probably have similar structures.

BORINE COORDINATION COMPOUNDS. Although the borine radical (BH_3) is not obtainable by thermal dissociation of diborane, its acidic characteristics are so pronounced that treatment of diborane with many compounds which contain strong electron-pair donor atoms ruptures the boron to boron link and gives borine coordination compounds of the general composition $A{:}BH_3$ (A = donor molecule).[162] Thus trimethylamine, even at −110°C., converts diborane quantitatively into trimethylamine borine, $(CH_3)_3N{:}BH_3$, a white solid (m.p. 94°C., b.p. 171°C.) which is stable in dry air but is hydrolyzed by hydrochloric acid into boric acid, hydrogen, and trimethylammonium chloride.[182] Some of the higher boron hydrides yield the same compound with trimethylamine.[162] Pyridine yields at 0°C. a compound which apparently has the structure $C_5H_5N{:}BH_3$.[162] Methyl cyanide gives the compound $CH_3CN{:}BH_3$ at −80°C.[162] Phosphine gives a material of formal composition $B_2H_6{\cdot}2PH_3$ at −110°C.,[183] but this compound does not behave as an analog of the "diammoniate" (p. 779). Its ready conversion to trimethylamineborine and phosphine suggests the structure to be $H_3P{:}BH_3$. Dimethyl ether forms the etherate $(CH_3)_2O{:}BH_3$ as a solid which dissociates reversibly to the reactants even at very low temperatures (e.g., dissociation pressure of 18 mm. at −78 5°C.).[182] Borine carbonyl, $OC{:}BH_3$, forms when diborane is heated with carbon monoxide at 100°C. under some 20 atm. pressure.[182] The compound decomposes to the reactants at room temperatures but is stable at low temperatures (m.p. −137.0°C., extrapolated b.p. −64°C.). Carbon monoxide is replaced by trimethylamine, and the compound is hydrolyzed by water to hydrogen, carbon monoxide, and boric acid. Similarities to the metal carbonyls (pp. 700–711) are formal rather than actual. Electron diffraction

[181] A. B. Burg: *J. Am. Chem. Soc.*, **69**, 747 (1947).

[182] A. B. Burg and H. I. Schlesinger: *J. Am. Chem. Soc.*, **59**, 780 (1937).

[183] E. L. Gamble and P. Gilmont: *J. Am. Chem. Soc.*, **62**, 717 (1940).

data for borine carbonyl have been interpreted in terms of resonance structures of the types[184]

```
      H                       H
      ..  _        +          ..  _ +    ..
  H : B : C: : :O :       H : B : C: :O :
      ..                      ..
      H                       H

      H                       H
      ..          ..          ..    +    .. _
  H : B_: :C: :O :        H : B_: :C : O :
      H+                      H+         ..
```

BORANE SALTS. Reaction of diborane with amalgams of metals such as sodium, potassium, or calcium yields so-called borane salts of general composition $M_2{}^IB_2H_6$.[80, 185] The diamagnetic properties of these compounds[186] preclude use of the simple formulation M^IBH_3. These are non-volatile solid compounds, which are insoluble in liquid ammonia and organic solvents but are decomposed by water to hypoborates (p. 812). They are sufficiently stable thermally to be freed of residual mercury by distillation, and the sodium and potassium compounds can be sublimed *in vacuo* (with some decomposition) at 400°C. Reaction with hydrogen bromide yields hydrogen and tetrabromo compounds, e.g., $K_2B_2H_2Br_4$. The properties of these compounds are consistent with ionic structures, i.e., $M_2{}^+[B_2H_6]^{-2}$, the stability of the $[B_2H_6]^{-2}$ ion being expected because of its structural similarity to ethane. Tetraborane and stable pentaborane yield, respectively, the rather similar but less stable compounds $M_2{}^IB_4H_{10}$ and $M_2{}^IB_5H_9$.[187, 188] The existence of these materials as a separate class of compounds is somewhat questioned, however, by an observation[189] that the sodium compound[188] gives the same x-ray diffraction pattern as sodium borohydride.[190] It seems probable, therefore, that these materials are really borohydrides, although previously obtained data are difficult to reconcile with this conclusion. Further investigations are indicated.

[184] S. H. Bauer: *J. Am. Chem. Soc.*, **59**, 1804 (1937).

[185] A. Stock and E. Pohland: *Ber.*, **59**, 2210 (1926).

[186] L. Klemm and W. Klemm: *Z. anorg. allgem. Chem.*, **225**, 258 (1935).

[187] A. Stock, F. Kurzen, and H. Laudenklos: *Z. anorg. allgem. Chem.*, **225**, 243 (1935).

[188] A Stock and H. Laudenklos: *Z. anorg. allgem. Chem.*, **228**, 178 (1936).

[189] J. S. Kaspar, L. V. McCarty, and A. E. Newkirk: *J. Am. Chem. Soc.*, **71**, 2583 (1949).

[190] A. M. Soldate: *J. Am. Chem. Soc.*, **69**, 987 (1947).

METAL BOROHYDRIDES AND RELATED COMPOUNDS. Compounds of the type $M^{+n}(BH_4)_n$ (M^{+n} = Li,[191] Na,[192] K,[192] Be,[193] Mg,[194] Al,[195, 196] $(CH_3)_2Ga$,[197] Ti(III),[198] Zr,[198] Hf,[198] Th,[198] U(IV),[199]) are called borohydrides. The numerical properties of certain of these compounds are summarized in Table 17·10. The alkali metal compounds are salt-like in character, but the others are not, covalent character increasing in general with increasing electronegativity of the metal present. The thorium compound is more salt-like than those of the other heavy metals. An outstanding characteristic of all but the alkali metal compounds is extreme volatility. No other known compounds of these metals compare in volatilities.

The alkali metal compounds are stable in dry air. The more covalent borohydrides of beryllium, aluminum, hafnium, and zirconium, however, burn spontaneously in contact with air. The borohydrides are strong reducing agents, reducing strength apparently increasing as electronegativity of the metal increases. This is ascribed to an increasing tendency toward $BH_3 + H^-$ character as opposed to BH_4^- character in the more salt-like compounds.[198] Sodium borohydride shows excellent promise as an analytical reducing agent, and the lithium compound is useful for organic reductions. In contact with water, the borohydrides undergo general conversions to borates and hydrogen. These reactions are commonly vigorous. However, the sodium compound may be recrystallized from cold water, although it is decomposed by hot water. It is one of the better solid sources of hydrogen, particularly when it is pelleted with cobalt(II) chloride. In contact with water, this combination gives a black cobalt boride (Co_2B) which then catalyzes reaction of the remaining borohydride with water. Hydrogen chloride converts the borohydrides

[191] H. I. Schlesinger and H. C. Brown: *J. Am. Chem. Soc.*, **62**, 3429 (1940).

[192] H. I. Schlesinger, H. R. Hoekstra, and H. C. Brown: Abstracts of Papers, 115th Meeting of the American Chemical Society, March 1949, p. 9–0.

[193] A. B. Burg and H. I. Schlesinger: *J. Am. Chem. Soc.*, **62**, 3425 (1940).

[194] H. I. Schlesinger et al.: U. S. Navy Report, Contract Nos. N173 s-9058, s-9820 (1945).

[195] H. I. Schlesinger, R. T. Sanderson, and A. B. Burg: *J. Am. Chem. Soc.*, **61**, 536 (1939).

[196] H. I. Schlesinger, R. T. Sanderson, and A. B. Burg: *J. Am. Chem. Soc.*, **62**, 3421 (1940).

[197] H. I. Schlesinger, H. C. Brown, and G. W. Schaeffer: *J. Am. Chem. Soc.*, **65**, 1786 (1943).

[198] H. R. Hoekstra and J. J. Katz: *J. Am. Chem. Soc.*, **71**, 2488 (1949).

[199] H. I. Schlesinger and H. C. Brown: *Chemistry of Uranium*, Pt. II. Vol. 6, pp. 550–557. Div. VIII, National Nuclear Energy Series. McGraw-Hill Book Co., New York (1951).

TABLE 17·10

NUMERICAL CONSTANTS FOR METAL BOROHYDRIDES

Compound	Melting Point, °C.	Boiling Point, °C.	Vapor Pressure, mm.	Vapor Pressure*		Heat of Fusion, kcal./mole	Heat of Sublimation, kcal./mole	Heat of Vaporization kcal./mole	Heat of Formation, kcal./mole
				A	B				
$LiBH_4$	275 (dec.)		10^{-4} (0°C.)						−44.15
$NaBH_4$									−43.83
$Be(BH_4)_2$	> 123	91.3 (subl.)	5.4 (20.4°C.)	3240	11.772			14.81	
$Al(BH_4)_3$	−64.5	44.5	257 (16.9°C)	1565	7.808			7.16	
$Ga(CH_3)_2(BH_4)$	1.5	92†	51 (24°C.)						
$Zr(BH_4)_4$	28.7	123†	15.0 (25°C.)	2039‡	8.032‡	4.3	13.6	9.3	
$Hf(BH_4)_4$	29.0	118†	14.9 (25°C.)	2097‡	8.247‡	3.4	13.0	9.6	
$Th(BH_4)_4$	203		0.05 (130°C.)	2844§	10.719§		(21)		
$U(BH_4)_4$	126 (dec.)	subl.	0.19 (30°C.)	4265§	13.354§				

* Constants in equation $\log p_{mm} = -\frac{A}{T} + B$. † Extrapolated. ‡ Liquid. § Solid.

into chlorides, with liberation of hydrogen (one mole per gram atom of boron present) and diborane. Acids such as boron trifluoride also give diborane (p. 777). Lithium boromethoxide, $Li[B(OCH_3)_4]$, is obtained as an intermediate in the reaction of lithium borohydride with methanol. This compound is related to sodium trimethoxyborohydride, $Na[HB(OCH_3)_3]$ (p. 777) which is chemically very similar to the borohydride itself.[173] In benzene solution, the reaction

$$6LiC_2H_5 + 2Al(BH_4)_3 \rightarrow 6LiBH_4 + Al_2(C_2H_5)_6$$

occurs, showing the inherently greater stability of the lithium compound. Alkali metal borohydrides are unreactive toward trimethylamine, but the beryllium compound and (especially) the aluminum compound add the base and then undergo decomposition to give trimethylamine borine (pp. 795–800). Changes in stabilities among the borohydrides are again apparent.

X-ray diffraction data show a slightly distorted tetrahedral arrangement of hydrogen atoms about each boron atom in lithium borohydride.[200] Sodium borohydride exists as ionic crystals in which the unit cells each contain four boron atoms and four sodium ions, the arrangement in each BH_4^- ion being tetrahedral.[190] Some question has been raised as to the structures of the more volatile borohydrides. The rather regular transitions in properties in series such as

$$B_2H_6 - Al(BH_4)_3 - Be(BH_4)_2 - LiBH_4 - NaBH_4$$

suggest similarities to boron hydride structures for such materials. Best evidence would then support hydrogen bridge structures (pp. 789–791) such as

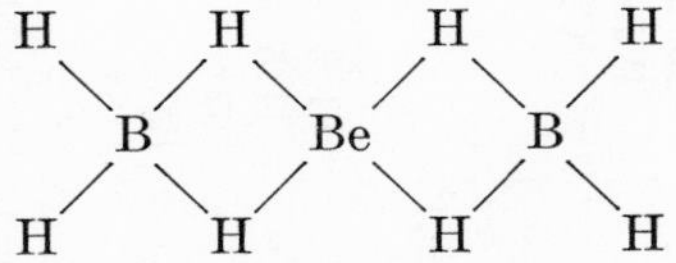

```
H       H       H       H
  \   /   \   /   \   /
    B       Be      B
  /   \   /   \   /   \
H       H       H       H
```

for the beryllium compound.

The electron diffraction data of Bauer and his colleagues have seemed to contradict such an hypothesis. Thus the aluminum borohydride molecule was found to be planar with three BH_4 groups bonded to the aluminum atom at 120° angles.[201] Each boron atom was reported to be the center of a trigonal bipyramid formed by four hydrogen atoms and the central aluminum atom. Similarly, the

[200] P. M. Harris and E. P. Meibohm: *J. Am. Chem. Soc.*, **69,** 1231 (1947).
[201] J. Y. Beach and S. H. Bauer: *J. Am. Chem. Soc.*, **62,** 3440 (1940).

beryllium borohydride molecule was reported to have the chain structure

$$H—B—Be—B—H$$

with three other hydrogen atoms uniformly spaced in a girdle about each boron atom and at slightly greater distances than the hydrogen atoms shown.[202] These structures were considered to eliminate proton bridges completely. However, reexamination of the data, particularly in the light of positive evidence for the presence of BH_4 tetrahedra in other compounds, has convinced Bauer that, although symmetrical hydrogen bridges are unlikely, unsymmetrical ones are not inconsistent with electron diffraction data.[203] These would involve tetrahedral BH_4 arrangements and might be diagramed as

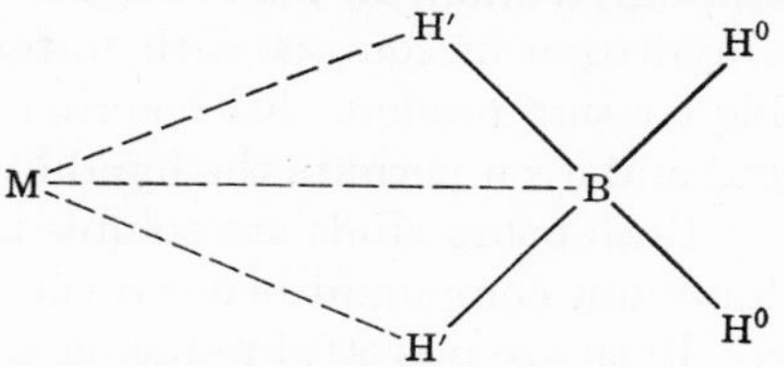

Further work appears necessary before the problem can be settled. Structural data for the beryllium and aluminum compounds are:[203] $Be(BH_4)_2$: B—H′, 1.28 A; B—H°, 1.22 A; Be—B. 1.74 A; Be—H′, 1.63 A; ∠BeBH′, 65°; $Al(BH_4)_3$: B—H′, 1.28 A; B—H°, 1.21 A; Al—B, 2.15 A; Al—H′, 2.1 A; ∠AlBH′, 60°.

Lithium, beryllium, and aluminum borohydrides are prepared by reactions of the corresponding metal alkyls with diborane

$$3LiC_2H_5 + 2B_2H_6 \rightarrow 3LiBH_4 + B(C_2H_5)_3$$

Lithium and aluminum methoxides or ethoxides react similarly, the corresponding esters of boric acid being the other products. Lithium borohydride is formed when lithium hydride is reacted directly with diborane in diethyl ether solution. Sodium borohydride is obtained in 95% yield by reaction of sodium hydride with trimethyl borate at 250°C.[173, 192]

$$4NaH + B(OCH_3)_3 \xrightarrow{250^\circ C.} NaBH_4 + 3NaOCH_3$$

Thorium and uranium(IV) borohydrides are prepared by reaction of the tetrafluorides with aluminum borohydride[198]

$$MF_4 + 2Al(BH_4)_3 \rightarrow M(BH_4)_4 + 2AlF_2BH_4$$

[202] G. Silbiger and S. H. Bauer: *J. Am. Chem. Soc.*, **68,** 312 (1946).
[203] S. H. Bauer: *J. Am. Chem. Soc.*, **72,** 622 (1950).

Similar reactions with the fluo compounds $NaM^{IV}F_5$ give the hafnium and zirconium compounds. Titanium(III) borohydride is obtained by reaction of the tetrachloride with lithium borohydride:

$$2TiCl_4 + 8LiBH_4 \rightarrow 2Ti(BH_4)_3 + 8LiCl + B_2H_6 + H_2$$

Lithium aluminum hydride, $LiAlH_4$, and lithium gallium hydride, $LiGaH_4$, are the formal analogs of lithium borohydride[169] but are apparently somewhat less ionic in character. Both are white solids which undergo thermal decomposition to the metals, hydrogen, and lithium hydride. The decomposition temperature of lithium aluminum hydride (125° to 150°C.) is somewhat lower than that of lithium borohydride (250° to 275°C.). Lithium aluminum hydride and lithium borohydride are strikingly similar in many ways. Both are stable in dry air but release hydrogen in contact with water. Formation of a protective hydroxide coating renders this reaction less rapid with the aluminum compound and even permits the handling of this compound in rather moist air. Both compounds are soluble in diethyl ether, the solubility of the aluminum compound being seven to eight times that of the borohydride. Both are powerful reducing agents and owe most of their uses to this property. Since its introduction, lithium aluminum hydride has become increasingly important as a selective reducing agent in organic syntheses. Unlike the borohydride, the aluminum compound reacts with ammonia and amines. A number of the chemical characteristics of lithium aluminum hydride have been mentioned previously (e.g., pp. 409, 777). Various equations describing its more important behavior with inorganic materials are summarized in Table 17·11.[169, 204] The heat of formation of the compound is −24.08 kcal. per mole (compare Table 17·10).[205]

Both lithium aluminum hydride and lithium gallium hydride are prepared by reactions of the anhydrous chlorides with lithium hydride in anhydrous diethyl ether[169]

$$MCl_3 + 4LiH \rightarrow LiMH_4 + 3LiCl$$

The compounds are recovered from the filtered solutions by evaporation of the solvent. Sodium and calcium aluminum hydrides have been prepared also.[169]

Structural Considerations. The proposal of structures which are compatible with both the unusual properties of the boron hydrides

[204] A. E. Finholt, A. C. Bond, K. E. Wilzbach, and H. I. Schlesinger: *J. Am. Chem. Soc.*, **69**, 2692 (1947).

[205] W. D. Davis, L. S. Mason, and G. Stegeman: *J. Am. Chem. Soc.*, **71, 2775** (1949).

and their electron-deficient natures has been a challenge to many investigators, and a voluminous literature is devoted to the subject. In addition to certain papers already cited,[40, 41, 160, 163, 165, 166] a number of others may be consulted with profit as general references.[206–213] Many other references to specific phases of the problem are also important. Most published information is concerned with the structure of diborane, the assumption that elucidation of its structure would provide a key to the structures of the higher hydrides being quite reasonable.

TABLE 17·11

SOME REACTIONS OF LITHIUM ALUMINUM HYDRIDE

Reactant	Equation
H_2O	$LiAlH_4 + 4H_2O \longrightarrow LiOH + Al(OH)_3 + 4H_2$
NH_3	$2LiAlH_4 + 5NH_3 \longrightarrow [LiAlH(NH_2)_2]_2NH + 6H_2$
RNH_2	$LiAlH_4 + 4RNH_2 \longrightarrow LiAl(RNH)_4 + 4H_2$
R_2NH	$LiAlH_4 + 4R_2NH \longrightarrow LiAl(R_2N)_4 + 4H_2$
B_2H_6	$LiAlH_4 + 2B_2H_6 \longrightarrow LiBH_4 + Al(BH_4)_3$
$Al_2(CH_3)_6$	$LiAlH_4 + Al_2(CH_3)_6 \xrightarrow{\text{ether}} 2AlH(CH_3)_2 + LiAlH_2(CH_3)_2$
$Zn(CH_3)_2$	$LiAlH_4 + Zn(CH_3)_2 \xrightarrow{\text{ether}} ZnH_2 + LiAlH_2(CH_3)_2$
MR_xX_{4-x}*	$(4 - x)LiAlH_4 + 4MR_xX_{4-x} \xrightarrow{\text{ether}} 4MR_xH_{4-x} + (4 - x)LiX + (4 - x)AlX_3$
$SiCl_4$	$LiAlH_4 + SiCl_4 \xrightarrow{\text{ether}} SiH_4 + LiCl + AlCl_3$
$SnCl_4$	$LiAlH_4 + SnCl_4 \xrightarrow{\text{ether}} SnH_4 + LiCl + AlCl_3$
BCl_3	$3LiAlH_4 + 4BCl_3 \xrightarrow{\text{ether}} 2B_2H_6 + 3LiCl + 3AlCl_3$
$AlCl_3$	$3LiAlH_4 + AlCl_3 \xrightarrow{\text{ether}} 4AlH_3 + 3LiCl$

* M = Si, Ge, Sn; X = halogen; R = alkyl or aryl group.

STRUCTURE OF DIBORANE. Early concepts, as reviewed by Wiberg,[166] had no basis other than molecular compositions and need not be considered. Real progress in elucidation of the diborane structure can be traced to the introduction of physical methods of structure determination. The chemical characteristics of diborane are too varied to provide positive information. It must be pointed out that the tendency of diborane to yield borine derivatives with strong donors (p.

[206] H. C. Longuet-Higgins and R. P. Bell: *J. Chem. Soc.*, 207 **1943**, 250.

[207] A. Burawoy: *Nature*, **155**, 328 (1945).

[208] R. P. Bell and H. C. Longuet-Higgins: *Nature*, **155**, 328 (1945).

[209] R. P. Bell and H. C. Longuet-Higgins: *Proc. Roy. Soc.* (*London*), **A183**, 357 (1945).

[210] F. Seel: *Z. Naturforsch.*, **1**, 146 (1946).

[211] A. D. Walsh: *J. Chem. Soc.*, **1947**, 89.

[212] R. S. Mulliken: *Chem. Revs.*, **41**, 207 (1947).

[213] R. E. Rundle: *J. Am. Chem. Soc.*, **69**, 1327, 2075 (1947).

780) and that the impossibility of substitution of alkyl groups for more than four of the hydrogen atoms in diborane (p. 779) are significant to the structure of the compound. Of the many structures proposed, consideration may be given to (1) *ionic* structures, (2) *ethane-like* structures, and (3) *hydrogen-bridge* structures.

Ionic structures were based upon the faulty assumption that reaction of diborane with ammonia (pp. 779–780) depended upon the presence of acidic hydrogens in diborane.[166] Formulations both as a dibasic acid

$$\begin{array}{ccccccc} & & \mathrm{H} & & \mathrm{H} & & \\ & & \cdot\cdot & & \cdot\cdot & & \\ \mathrm{H_2^+[H} & : & \mathrm{B} & :: & \mathrm{B} & : & \mathrm{H]^{-2}} \end{array}$$

and as a monobasic acid

$$\begin{array}{ccccccc} & & \mathrm{H} & & \mathrm{H} & & \\ & & \cdot\cdot & & \cdot\cdot & & \\ \mathrm{H^+[H} & : & \mathrm{B} & : & \mathrm{B} & : & \mathrm{H]^-} \\ & & \cdot\cdot & & & & \\ & & \mathrm{H} & & & & \end{array}$$

cannot be supported by experimental data. Indeed, the exchange studies by Burg[181] preclude the existence of acidic hydrogens. In a sense, the *protonated double bond* arrangement proposed by Pitzer[41] is an ionic structure, but it is better considered as a variation of the hydrogen bridge concept. As such, ionic structures are highly unlikely.

Ethane-like structures have been assumed by many investigators, with or without supporting evidences. These structures owe their origin to Sidgwick's suggestion[214] that two of the hydrogen atoms in diborane are held by one-electron bonds as

$$\begin{array}{ccccccc} & & \mathrm{H} & & \mathrm{H} & & \\ & & \cdot\cdot & & \cdot\cdot & & \\ \mathrm{H} & \cdot & \mathrm{B} & : & \mathrm{B} & \cdot & \mathrm{H} \\ & & \cdot\cdot & & \cdot\cdot & & \\ & & \mathrm{H} & & \mathrm{H} & & \end{array}$$

That the electronegativities of hydrogen and boron are nearly the same may be regarded as supporting the possibility of existence of such one-electron bonds. Development of the concept of resonance suggested further stabilization of the diborane molecule by resonance of the one-electron hydrogen-boron bonds among all six positions.[215, 216]

[214] N. V. Sidgwick: *The Electronic Theory of Valency*, p. 103. Clarendon Press, Oxford (1927).

[215] L. Pauling: *J. Am. Chem. Soc.*, **53**, 3225 (1931).

[216] R. S. Mulliken: *J. Chem. Phys.*, **3**, 635 (1935).

Further resonance might also involve structures containing zero-electron bonds[217] as

```
     H   H                  H+  H
     ..  ..                     ..  –
 H : B   B : H     or   H : B : B : H
     ..  ..                 ..  ..
     H   H                  H   H
```

The overall ethane-like structure would then involve all the one-electron and zero-electron types of resonance structures.[218] Such structures were stongly supported by Bauer's early interpretations of electron diffraction data.[159, 219]

Hydrogen bridge structures were first suggested by Dilthey[220] and by Core[221] and were exploited somewhat by Nekrasov.[222] However, modern views and definite support of this type of structure are traceable to the excellent work of Longuet-Higgins and Bell.[206] In simple form, this structure may be written

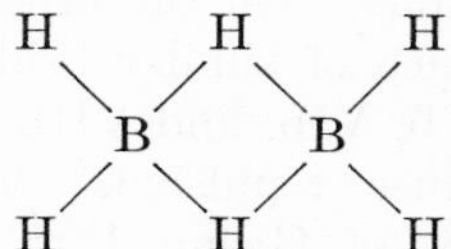

with no committment as to the exact nature of the hydrogen bridge. Several interpretations of such a bridge are conceivable.

1. Burawoy's concept[207] of the hydrogen bridge as an example of hydrogen bonding of the conventional type (pp. 187–191) seems most unlikely in view of the steadily decreasing tendency toward this type of linkage in the series FH—OH_2—NH_3—CH_4.[208] The low electronegativity of boron and the absence of negative groups which might enhance the attraction of boron for hydrogen also mitigate against this possibility. Furthermore, normal hydrogen bonding would imply unsymmetrical positioning of the bridging hydrogen atoms with respect to the boron atoms. However, spectroscopic data preclude such lack of symmetry.[223]

[217] G. N. Lewis: *J. Chem. Phys.*, **1**, 17 (1933).

[218] L. Pauling: *The Nature of the Chemical Board*, 2nd Ed., pp. 259–264. Cornell University Press, Ithaca (1940).

[219] S. H. Bauer: *J. Am. Chem. Soc.*, **59**, 1096 (1937).

[220] W. Dilthey: *Z. angew. Chem.*, **34**, 596 (1921).

[221] A. F. Core: *J. Soc. Chem. Ind.*, **46**, 642 (1927).

[222] B. V. Nekrasov: *J. Gen. Chem.* (*U.S.S.R.*), **10**, 1021, 1156 (1940).

[223] W. C. Price: *J. Chem. Phys.*, **15**, 614 (1947).

2. Resonance formulations involving covalent and ionic structures of the types

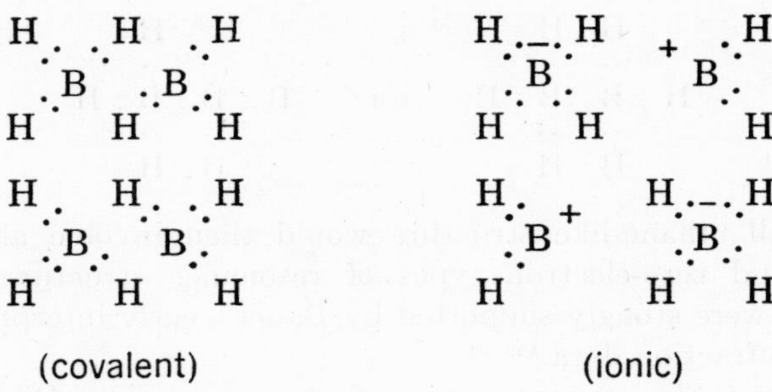

are perhaps more likely as explanations.[206, 222, 224] Since only paired electrons are present, these arrangements are consistent with the observed diamagnetic behavior of diborane. However, it seems somewhat unlikely that two parts of a molecule can be held together by resonance stabilization alone. On the other hand, such a picture is consistent with the absence of similar bridge structures among the hydrides of the Groups Vb, VIb, and VIIb elements where unshared electron pairs would cause repulsion. Similar bridges might be expected among hydrides of Group I to III elements. Longuet-Higgins and Bell[206] prefer the term *resonance link* for such a bond.

3. Pitzer's concept[41] of a *protonated double bond* between the two boron atoms represents a modified hydrogen bridge structure

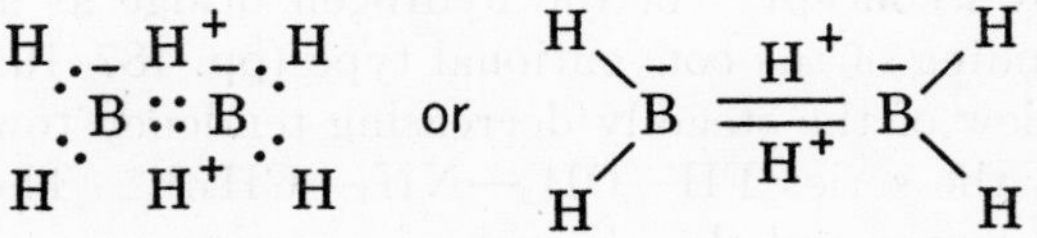

or

in which the two protons are imbedded in the electron cloud of the double bond in a plane at right angles to the remainder of the molecule. Such an arrangement is not consistent with the observed somewhat longer boron to boron distance than that predicted for a double bond nor with the absence of acidic properties in diborane,[181] but it does suggest a useful analogy to ethylene rather than ethane. Spectroscopic[222] and magnetic[163] similarities to ethylene are striking. That the double bond in ethylene readily associates with cations (pp. 237, 840–841) is also of interest in this connection. A number of other arguments in favor of such a concept have been offered.

[224] Ya. K. Syrkin and M. E. Dyatkina: *Acta Physicochim. U.R.S.S.*, **14**, 547 (1941).

4. Coordination by bonding electrons may also be regarded as a possibility.[211] This would reduce the hydrogen bridge to

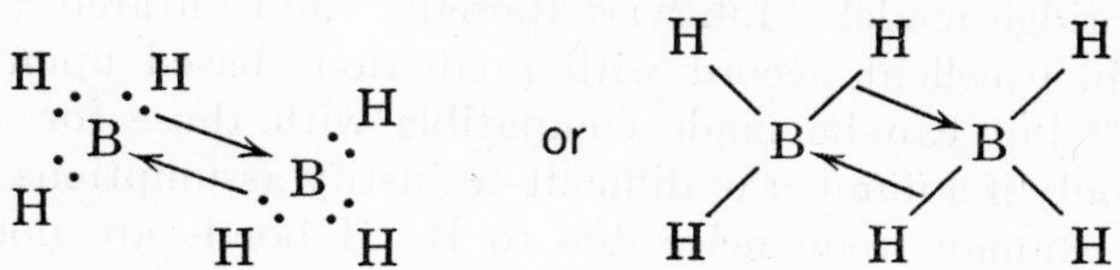

Such a type of bonding is normally highly unlikely because of the strength of the existing electron pair bonds. However, boron-hydrogen bonds are somewhat weaker than similar bonds in other hydrides,[211] and such arrangements may conceivably exist. In a sense, this concept lies in the middle ground between the resonance link and protonated bond views.

5. A molecular orbital (pp. 197–198) picture as worked out by Mulliken[212] emphasizes similarities to ethylene and is not inconsistent with the double bond concept of the hydrogen bridge.

6. That the hydrogen bridge amounts to a "half-bond" (p. 214) type of structure in which each of the two hydrogens, using one electron pair and its 1*s* orbital, bonds the two borons together[213] may be regarded as a version of the protonated double bond concept without the thought of direct protonation. This would permit the two bridging hydrogen atoms to lie, respectively, above and below the plane of the rest of the molecule and impose a general tetrahedral arrangement about each boron, but repulsions between the two hydrogens would make the B—H—B angle less than 180°.

Which (if any) of these interpretations is the correct one cannot be determined from existing data. However, it does appear that, regardless of its exact constitution, the bridge structure is a better representation of the diborane molecule than the ethane-like structure. The basic differences between these two structures, regardless of binding, involve (1) equivalence of all hydrogen atoms in the ethane structure but difference of two from the other four in the bridge arrangement and (2) free rotation of the two ends of the molecule in the ethane structure as opposed to hindered rotation in the other.

The first of these differences is readily reconciled by a bridge structure since two hydrogen atoms in diborane are apparently different from the others (p. 779) and since, although the molecule $B(CH_3)_3$ shows no tendency to dimerize, the material $HB(CH_3)_2$ is known only in the dimeric form. The second of the differences can probably be approached only through physical data since the *cis-trans* isomerism predicted for the bridge structure may not exist in fact because of the labilities of the compounds. Specific heat data[225] are compatible with the ethane structure only if hindered rotation is assumed but agree well with the bridge model. Likewise Raman[226] and infrared[223, 225, 227, 228] data are in excellent accord with predictions based upon a bridge structure[209] but can be made compatible with those for an ethane structure only if a number of difficult-to-justify assumptions are made. Thus two Raman frequencies due to B—H bonds are noted. The ethane structure would permit only one since all hydrogens would be equivalent. Furthermore, the infrared spectra are markedly like those for ethylene and bear little resemblance to those for ethane. Calculated moments of inertia from infrared data are in agreement with a bridge structure but not an ethane arrangement.

The ethane structure has received its greatest support from electron diffraction data.[163, 219] However, the two models differ mainly in the hydrogen to hydrogen distances, and these cannot be determined with certainty by electron diffraction. Bauer reported bond distances of B—B = 1.86 A and B—H = 1.27 A. However, the electron diffraction data are equally consistent with the structure

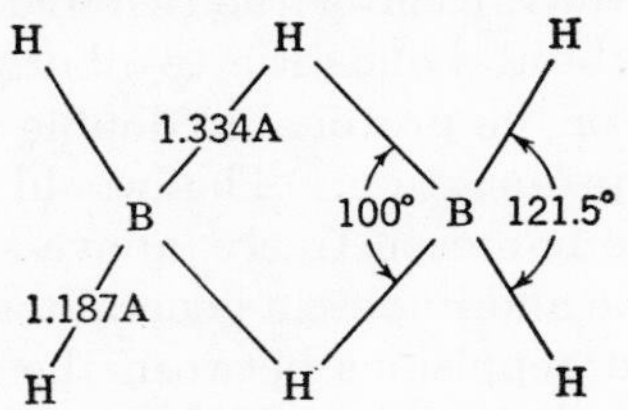

with the bridging hydrogens lying in a plane at right angles to a plane containing the remaining atoms,[206, 229] although Bauer does not agree.[163] However, electron diffraction studies on tetramethyl diborane (p. 778) indicate the four methyl groups and the two boron atoms to be coplanar,[230] strongly supporting the bridge arrangement, and comparative electron diffraction studies on diborane and ethane definitely eliminate the ethane structure for the former and support the bridge arrangement.[231] Crystal structure determinations by

[225] F. Stitt: *J. Chem. Phys.*, **8**, 981 (1940); **9**, 780 (1941).
[226] T. F. Anderson and A. B. Burg: *J. Chem. Phys.*, **6**, 586 (1938).
[227] W. E. Anderson and E. F. Barker: *J. Chem. Phys.*, **18**, 698 (1950).
[228] R. C. Lord and E. Nielsen: *J. Chem. Phys.*, **19**, 1 (1951).
[229] M. E. Dyatkina and Ya. K. Syrkin: *Compt. rend. acad. sci. U.R.S.S.*, **35**, 180 (1942).
[230] L. Pauling: *Chem. Eng. News*, **25**, 2970 (1947).
[231] K. Hedberg and V. Schomaker: *J. Am. Chem. Soc.*, **73**, 1482 (1951).

x-ray[232] locate the boron atoms but do not permit decision as to the correct model.

STRUCTURES OF THE HIGHER HYDRIDES. Detailed evidence for the structures of all of the higher hydrides is lacking, although it may be assumed logically that whatever type of electron-deficient bonding is characteristic of diborane must also be characteristic of the other materials. In the light of the foregoing discussion, this must involve hydrogen bridges. However, there is insufficient electron deficiency to permit such bridges between all boron pairs, and as a consequence some normal covalent boron to boron linkages must also exist.

In extending his concept of the protonated double bond, Pitzer[41] has outlined the following principles of higher boron hydride structures:

1. In addition to simple boron to boron and boron to hydrogen bonds, the structures will contain protonated double bonds between boron atoms if each such atom has both a vacant orbital and a singly bonded hydrogen attached. This is equivalent to saying that the hydrides are built up through hydrogen bridges of hypothetical borine groups such as BH_3, $H_2B{\cdot}BH_2$, and $H_2B{\cdot}BH{\cdot}BH_2$.

2. Protonated double bonds will form until all vacant orbitals are occupied. However, orbitals conjugated with two or more protonated double bonds must be regarded as occupied. Thus any BH group between two boron atoms which are themselves bridged to others cannot be involved in such a bridge.

3. Rings with less than five boron atoms are not stable because of strain.

Based upon these principles, the known higher hydrides may be formulated as:

$$B_4H_{10} = H_2B{\cdot}BH_2 + 2BH_3$$

```
H          H              H
  \        |             /
   B(H2)B—B(H2)B
  /           |          \
H             H            H
```

$$B_5H_9 = H_2B{\cdot}BH{\cdot}BH_2 + H_2B{\cdot}BH_2$$

```
              H
              |
              B
            /   \
          /       \
      H—B           B—H
       (H2)        (H2)
      H—B———————B—H
```

[232] H. Mark and E. Pohland: *Z. Kryst.*, **62**, 103 (1925).

$$B_5H_{11} = H_2B{\cdot}BH{\cdot}BH_2 + 2BH_3$$

```
H          H     H          H
  \        |     |        /
   B(H2)B—B—B(H2)B
  /        |              \
H          H               H
```

$$B_6H_{10} = 2H_2B{\cdot}BH{\cdot}BH_2$$

```
        H     H
        |     |
        B(H2)B
       /      \
   H—B          B—H
       \      /
        B(H2)B
        |     |
        H     H
```

$$B_{10}H_{14} = 2B_5H_7 \text{ (rings)}$$

```
        H              H
        |              |
   H—B—B              B—B—H
        \            /
   (H2)    B(H2)B      (H2)
        /            \
   H—B—B              B—B—H
        |              |
        H              H
```

the symbol (H_2) being used to indicate hydrogen bridges or protonated double bonds. In addition, a six-membered ring with alternate bridges is suggested for the hydride B_6H_{12}, a compound not yet characterized but considered by Stock to exist.[159] In the range up to B_6, no unknown compounds are predicted by these principles. Above B_6, many presently unknown materials are of course predicted. That these have not been isolated does not preclude their existence, however.

Structures of this type find their greatest opposition in interpretations of electron diffraction data. Thus values for tetraborane,[233] stable pentaborane (B_5H_9),[234] and unstable pentaborane (B_5H_{11})[233] have been considered to be compatible, respectively, with butane-, methylcyclobutane-, and pentane- or isopentane-like arrangements. Later data[235] are considered to rule out Pitzer's structure for stable pentaborane and to be in agreement with a structure for decaborane in which two symmetrical pentagons are joined by a normal boron to boron link but in which no hydrogen bridges are present. However, such interpretations are open to the same questions raised in the con-

[233] S. H. Bauer: *J. Am. Chem. Soc.*, **60**, 805 (1938).
[234] S. H. Bauer and L. Pauling: *J. Am. Chem. Soc.*, **58**, 2403 (1936).
[235] G. Silbiger and S. H. Bauer: *J. Am. Chem. Soc.*, **70**, 115 (1948).

sideration of diborane (pp. 792–793). Schomaker[236] has stated that neither proposed structure for stable pentaborane is entirely correct, but his early view that a non-planar five-membered ring of boron atoms with hydrogen bridges located as in Pitzer's model is more probable seems questionable.[237] More recent electron diffraction data for stable pentaborane[237] and decaborane[238] are consistent with the assumption that part of the hydrogen is present in bridges. Both electron diffraction[237] and x-ray[239] data indicate that the structure of the stable pentaborane molecule amounts to a tetragonal pyramid of boron atoms with a hydrogen atom on each boron atom and the other four hydrogen atoms in bridges linking the boron atoms in the base of the pyramid. More comprehensive studies are needed.

Compounds containing boron-nitrogen linkages

Compounds containing boron-nitrogen linkages are of a number of types. In previous sections of this chapter boron nitride (pp. 757–758), addition compounds of borine such as $(CH_3)_3N:BH_3$ and $CH_3CN:BH_3$ (pp. 780–781), and ammonia "addition" compounds of the boron hydrides, especially of diborane (pp. 779–780), have been discussed. Structural analogies between boron nitride and graphite (p. 758) suggest similarities between carbon to carbon and boron to nitrogen bonds. This is not unexpected since such bonds are isoelectronic and since the BN and CC arrangements should have nearly the same size. It is not surprising, therefore, to find series of boron-nitrogen compounds which are in effect direct analogs of both aliphatic and aromatic organic substances. These are discussed below. In addition, some data on the rather peculiar compound B_2H_7N and its derivatives are given. These latter compounds are rather closely related to diborane and its ammonia "addition" product and to borine addition compounds, but are not related to other boron-nitrogen compounds.

The Compound B_2H_7N *and Its Derivatives.* The compound B_2H_7N (or $B_2H_5NH_2$) melts at −66.4°C. and boils at 76.2°C.[162] Its vapor is monomeric. It is stable for several days at room temperatures in the absence of air or moisture. Slow decomposition, however, gives diborane and a polymeric residue, $(BH_4N)_x$. Aqueous hydrochloric acid causes decomposition to ammonium chloride, hydrogen, and

[236] V. Schomaker: *J. Chim. phys.*, **46**, 262 (1949).

[237] K. Hedberg, M. E. Jones, and V. Schomaker: *J. Am. Chem. Soc.*, **73**, 3538 (1951).

[238] C. M. Lucht: *J. Am. Chem. Soc.*, **73**, 2373 (1951).

[239] W. J. Dulmage and W. N. Lipscomb: *J. Am. Chem. Soc.*, **73**, 3539 (1951).

boric acid, whereas hydrogen chloride apparently causes substitution of chlorine for some of the hydrogen. At −80°C., it forms the compound $B_2H_7N \cdot N(CH_3)_3$ with trimethylamine. Ammonia converts it to borazole (p. 800) at 200°C., but at low temperatures an ammonia addition compound is formed. This compound liberates one gram atom of hydrogen per mole when treated with sodium in liquid ammonia at −60°C. The compound B_2H_7N is obtained when ammonia reacts with diborane at elevated temperatures or better when diborane is passed over its "diammoniate."[240]

The N-methyl derivative, $B_2H_5NHCH_3$, and the N-dimethyl derivative, $B_2H_5N(CH_3)_2$, are obtained, respectively, by reaction of diborane with methylamine and with dimethylamine.[241] The methyl derivative has an extrapolated boiling point of 66.8°C and an estimated heat of vaporization of 6.666 kcal. per mole. The dimethyl compound boils at ca. 50.3°C. with a heat of vaporization of 6.670 kcal. per mole and melts at ca. −54.6°C. Thermal stability increases as methyl groups are added, the dimethyl derivative being stable even at 90°C. for prolonged periods. Both methyl compounds add trimethylamine as does the parent compound. Rather similar N-silyl derivatives, $B_2H_5(CH_3NSiH_3)$ and $B_2H_5N(SiH_3)_2$, are formed, respectively, in reactions of the amines $CH_3N(SiH_3)_2$ and $(SiH_3)_3N$ with the compound B_2H_5Br.[242]

Electron diffraction data indicate the presence of an angular B/N\B (B–N–B) linkage in the compound B_2H_7N. Early interpretations[243] gave a bond angle of 109° and a B—N bond distance of 1.56 A as required by the formulation $H_3B—NH—BH_3$. However, later interpretations[244] of electron diffraction data for the compound B_2H_7N and its dimethyl derivative lead to bridge structures of the types

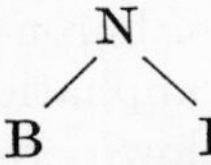

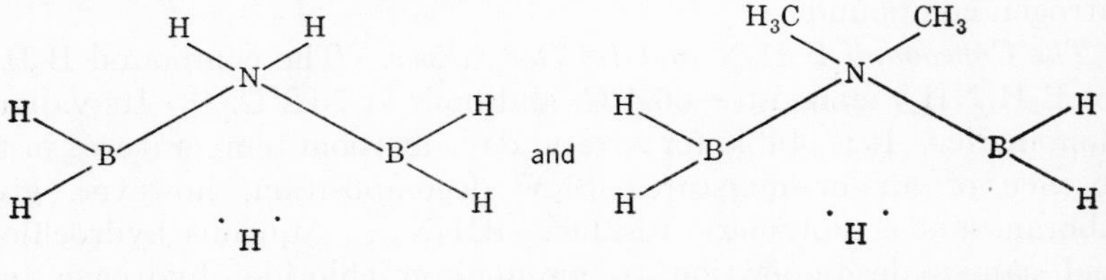

```
      H     H                          H3C     CH3
        \  /                              \   /
         N                                  N
H      /   \      H               H       /   \      H
  \   /     \    /                  \    /     \    /
   B         B          and           B         B
  /    . H .   \                     /   . H .   \
H               H                  H               H
```

[240] H. I. Schlesinger, D. M. Ritter, and A. B. Burg: *J. Am. Chem. Soc.*, **60,** 2297 (1938).

[241] A. B. Burg and C. L. Randolph: *J. Am. Chem. Soc.*, **71,** 3451 (1949).

[242] A. B. Burg and E. S. Kuljian: *J. Am. Chem. Soc.*, **72,** 3103 (1950).

[243] S. H. Bauer: *J. Am. Chem. Soc.*, **60,** 524 (1938).

[244] A. J. Stosick: Abstracts of Papers, 115th Meeting of the American Chemical Society, March 1949, p. 26–0.

where the bridging hydrogen atom employs one pair of electrons to form two bonds. Bond angles obtained are 96° and 89° for $B_2H_5NH_2$ and $B_2H_5N(CH_3)_2$, respectively, with corresponding boron to boron distances of 2.32 A and 2.19 A. The properties of these compounds are consistent with such structures.[241] It is probable that the N-silyl derivatives have similar bridge structures.[242]

Boron-Nitrogen Analogs of the Aliphatic Hydrocarbons. Excellent evidence exists that in the preparation of hexamethyltriborinetriamine or hexamethylborazole (p. 803) by reaction of boron trimethyl with methylamine (400°C., 20 atm.) a number of intermediates result according to the scheme[245]

$$\begin{array}{l} B(CH_3)_3 + CH_3NH_2 \rightarrow (CH_3)_3B \leftarrow NH_2CH_3 \\ \qquad\qquad\qquad\qquad\qquad \downarrow \text{I} \\ \qquad\qquad\qquad\qquad (CH_3)_2B \leftleftarrows NHCH_3 \\ \qquad\qquad\qquad\qquad\qquad \downarrow \text{II} \\ \qquad\qquad\qquad\qquad (CH_3)B \Lleftarrow NCH_3 \\ \qquad\qquad\qquad\qquad\qquad \downarrow \text{III} \\ \qquad\qquad\qquad [-B(CH_3) \leftleftarrows N(CH_3)-]_3 \end{array}$$

Similarly, condensation of boron trimethyl with phenylamine gives an addition compound which decomposes when heated (300°C., 20 atm.) to similar materials, the scheme for the reaction series being[246]

$$\begin{array}{l} B(CH_3)_3 + C_6H_5NH_2 \rightarrow (CH_3)_3B \leftarrow NH_2C_6H_5 \\ \qquad\qquad\qquad\qquad\qquad \text{I} \quad \downarrow \\ \qquad\qquad\qquad\qquad (CH_3)_2B \leftleftarrows NHC_6H_5 \\ \qquad\qquad\qquad\qquad\qquad \downarrow \quad \text{II} \\ \qquad\qquad\qquad\qquad CH_3B \underset{\text{III}}{\Lleftarrow} NC_6H_5 \end{array}$$

Also, in the preparation of B, B′, B″—trimethylborazole (p. 805) from the addition compound $(CH_3)_3B \leftarrow NH_3$ (Type I, above), the material $(CH_3)_2B \leftleftarrows NH_2$ (Type II, above) is obtained as an intermediate.[247] It is apparent that compounds of Types I, II, and III are, respectively, formal analogs of ethane, ethylene, and acetylene type hydrocarbons. These relations are shown more clearly in Table 17·12, the proposed names[245, 248] for materials of these types

[245] E. Wiberg and K. Hertwig: *Z. anorg. Chem.*, **255,** 141 (1947).
[246] E. Wiberg and K. Hertwig: *Z. anorg. Chem.*, **257,** 138 (1948).
[247] E. Wiberg, K. Hertwig, and A. Bolz: *Z. anorg. Chem.*, **256,** 177 (1948).
[248] E. Wiberg: *Naturwissenschaften*, **35,** 182 (1948).

being chosen to emphasize such similarities. A significant difference lies of course in the formation of the B—N bond. All C—C bonds, regardless of multiplicity, are of the normal covalent type. The B—N bonds, however, involve donation of an electron pair by the nitrogen atom in addition to any electron sharing of the normal covalent type which may be present. It might be expected, therefore, that on the average the B—N linkages would be more readily ruptured than their C—C counterparts. It follows, of course, that addition compounds of boron trihalides with ammonia and the amines (pp. 746–748) are corresponding analogs of halogenated ethanes. Wiberg's excellent review[248] should be consulted for more complete details.

TABLE 17·12

Boron-Nitrogen Analogs of Aliphatic Hydrocarbons

Boron-Nitrogen Compounds		Hydrocarbons	
Name	Structure	Structure	Name
Borazanes	$R_3B : NH_2R$	$R_3C : CH_2R$	Alkanes (ethanes)
Borazenes	$R_2B::NHR$	$R_2C::CHR$	Alkenes (ethylenes)
Borazynes	$RB:::NR$	$RC:::CR$	Alkynes (acetylenes)

That the relationships among these compounds are more than merely formal ones is apparent from comparisons of the properties of the isosteric compounds. Such melting point and boiling point data as are available (Table 17.13) bear out this conclusion for alkene analogs in particular, although comparisons with the alkanes are less striking. Of course substitution on the nitrogen gives somewhat different effects from substitution on the boron. Furthermore, the borazenes and borazynes show unsaturation and undergo addition reactions just as do the corresponding hydrocarbons. The borazynes polymerize in fashions comparable to the acetylenic hydrocarbons and are actually known only in the trimeric forms (i.e., as borazole and its derivatives, pp. 800–806).

A number of formally similar borine derivatives such as H_2BNR_2 ($R = CH_3, C_2H_5$),[249] H_2BNH_2,[249] and Br_2BNR_2[249] and the silyl compounds $H_2BN(SiH_3)_2$ and $(CH_3)_2BN(SiH_2Br)_2$[242] are known. These are isosteric with the corresponding alkenes and undoubtedly have unsaturated structures of the general type

$$\begin{array}{c} \ \ \ \ R\ \ \ R \\ \ \ \ \ \cdot\cdot\ \ \ \cdot\cdot \\ R : B::N : R \end{array}$$

That they tend to dimerize at low temperatures and compare in

[249] E. Wiberg, A. Bolz, and P. Buchheit: *Z. anorg. Chem.*, **256**, 285 (1948).

general physical characteristics with the alkenes lends support to this view. The dimers are notably less reactive than the monomers. The monomers form as temperature rises. With hydrogen bromide, the N-dimethyl compound gives the B-dibromo compound, $Br_2BN(CH_3)_2$, and hydrogen. With water, boric acid, dimethylamine, and hydrogen form. N-dimethylaminoborine, $H_2BN(CH_3)_2$, is obtained by heating dimethylamine with diborane at 180° to 200°C., hydrogen

TABLE 17·13

SOME COMPARISONS BETWEEN BORON-NITROGEN COMPOUNDS AND THEIR ALIPHATIC ANALOGS

Boron-Nitrogen Compound			Aliphatic Analog		
Formula	Melting Point, °C.	Boiling Point, °C.	Formula	Melting Point, °C.	Boiling Point, °C.
$H_3B \leftarrow NH_3$	ca. 90		$H_3C—CH_3$	−172	− 88.3
$H_3B \leftarrow NH_2CH_3$	5–10		$H_3C—CH_2CH_3$	−189.9	− 42.2
$H_3B \leftarrow NH(CH_3)_2$	10–12		$H_3C—CH(CH_3)_2$	−145	− 10.2
$H_3B \leftarrow N(CH_3)_3$	94	171	$H_3C—C(CH_3)_3$	− 20	9.5
$(CH_3)H_2B \leftarrow N(CH_3)_3$	1	176	$(CH_3)H_2C—C(CH_3)_3$	− 98.2	49.7
$(CH_3)_2HB \leftarrow N(CH_3)_3$	−18	171	$(CH_3)_2HC—C(CH_3)_3$	− 25.0	80.9
$(CH_3)_3B \leftarrow N(CH_3)_3$	128	110 (subl.)	$(CH_3)_3C—C(CH_3)_3$	104	106.8
$(CH_3)_3B \leftarrow NH(CH_3)_2$	35	143	$(CH_3)_3C—CH(CH_3)_2$	− 25.0	80.9
$(CH_3)_3B \leftarrow NH_2CH_3$	27	147	$(CH_3)_3C—CH_2CH_3$	− 98.2	49.7
$(CH_3)_3B \leftarrow NH_3$	74	> 98	$(CH_3)_3C—CH_3$	− 20	9.5
$H_2B \leftrightharpoons NH_2$		(gas)	$H_2C{=}CH_2$	−169.4	−103.9
$H_2B \leftrightharpoons N(CH_3)_2$		(gas)	$H_2C{=}C(CH_3)_2$		− 6
$(CH_3)_2B \leftrightharpoons N(CH_3)_2$		ca. 80	$(CH_3)_2C{=}C(CH_3)_2$		73
$(CH_3)_2B \leftrightharpoons NHCH_3$		ca. 38	$(CH_3)_2C{=}CHCH_3$	−124	38.4
$(CH_3)_2B \leftrightharpoons NH_2$		ca. 4	$(CH_3)_2C{=}CH_2$		− 6
$F_3B \leftarrow NH_3$	180		$F_3C—CH_3$	−107	− 46.8
$F_3B \leftarrow N(CH_3)_3$	138	233	$F_3C—C(CH_3)_3$		
$Cl_3B \leftarrow N(CH_3)_3$	243		$Cl_3C—C(CH_3)_3$		

being the other product.[249] Alternatively, the addition product formed by condensing diborane and dimethylamine can be heated at 130°C. in nitrogen[241] or dimethylammonium chloride can be reacted with lithium borohydride in diethyl ether to give the product, lithium chloride, and hydrogen.[250] Reaction of diborane with ammonia above 100°C. gives the material H_2BNH_2, which in contrast to the other materials, exists as a high polymer.[249] Silyl derivatives are obtained by reaction of trisilylamine, $(SiH_3)_3N$, with the compounds B_2H_5Br and $(CH_3)_2BBr$.[242]

[250] G. W. Schaeffer and E. R. Anderson: *J. Am. Chem. Soc.*, **71**, 2143 (1949).

Somewhat different are the borine derivatives of the types HB-$(NR_2)_2$.[251] Compounds of this type apparently have the structure (resonance possible)

```
        R   H   R
        ··  ··  ··
    R : N : : B : N : R
                  ··
```

and are not isosteric with any types of hydrocarbons. The methyl compound (m.p. −45°C.) dimerizes readily but is monomolecular in the vapor state. On standing with N-dimethylaminoborine, it forms a high polymer. With water, it gives hydrogen and the compound $HOB[N(CH_3)_2]_2$. The compound, together with hydrogen, is formed when N-dimethylaminoborine and dimethylamine are heated together at 200°C.[251]

Boron-Nitrogen Analogs of the Aromatic Hydrocarbons. Perhaps the most remarkable of the boron nitrogen compounds are triborinetriamine or borazole, $B_3N_3H_6$, and its N-methyl and B-methyl derivatives. The discoverers of borazole believed its properties to be consistent with a six-membered ring structure of alternating boron and nitrogen atoms.[252] Such a structure is supported by electron diffraction data which indicate a planar arrangement exactly comparable to that found in benzene,[163, 253] the bond angle being 120° and the B—N bond distance 1.44 A. That this bond distance lies between those expected for single (1.54 A) and double (1.36 A) boron-nitrogen bonds suggests resonance of the Kekulé type. Such a structure may be formulated as

```
              H
              |
              B
            /   \
      H — N:     :N — H
          |       |
      H — B       B — H
            \   /
             :N
              |
              H
```

the extra electron pair on each nitrogen atom being capable of contributing to either of two boron-nitrogen linkages. As with the ali-

[251] E. Wiberg and A. Bolz: *Z. anorg. Chem.*, **257**, 131 (1948).
[252] A. Stock and E. Pohland: *Ber.*, **59**, 2215 (1926).
[253] A. Stock and R. Wierl: *Z. anorg. allgem. Chem.*, **203**, 228 (1931).

TABLE 17·14
COMPARISON OF PHYSICAL PROPERTIES OF BORAZOLE AND BENZENE

Property	Borazole, $B_3N_3H_6$	Benzene, C_6H_6
Molecular weight	80.532	78.108
Melting point, °K.	215	279
Boiling point, °K.	328	353
Critical temperature, °K.	525	561
Liquid density at boiling point, grams/ml.	0.81	0.81
Molecular volume at boiling point, ml.	99.42	96.42
Heat of vaporization at boiling point, kcal./mole	7.0	7.4
Trouton's constant	21.3	21.0
Surface tension at melting point, dynes/cm.	31.1	31.0
Parachor	208	206
Molar polarization, cm.^{3}	24	27
Dipole moment, D	0	0
Bond distances, A		
B—N	1.44	
B—H	1.20	
N—H	1.02	
C—C		1.42
C—H		1.08

TABLE 17·15
COMPARISON OF PHYSICAL CONSTANTS OF METHYL BORAZOLES AND METHYL BENZENES

Property	B,B′,B″-Trimethylborazole	1,3,5-Trimethylbenzene	Hexamethylborazole	Hexamethylbenzene
Molecular weight	122.610	120.186	164.688	162.264
Melting point, °K.	305	221	370	439
Boiling point, °K.	400	438	494	537
Heat of vaporization at boiling point, kcal./mole	10.1	10.0	11.5	12.9
Trouton's constant	25.2	22.8	23.3	24.0
Solubility in				
benzene	soluble	soluble	very soluble	very soluble
diethyl ether	soluble	soluble	soluble	soluble
ethanol	soluble	soluble	difficultly soluble	sparingly soluble
water	insoluble	insoluble	insoluble	insoluble

TABLE 17·16
COMPARISON OF MELTING AND BOILING POINTS OF BORAZOLE AND BENZENE ANALOGS

Compound	Melting Point, °K.	Boiling Point, °K.	Ratio of Absolute Boiling Points, $T_{BN}:T_C$
1. Benzenes			
borazole	215	328	0.93
benzene	279	353	....
2. Toluenes			
B-methylborazole	214	360	0.94
N-methylborazole	....	357	0.93
toluene	178	383.8	....
3. Xylenes			
B,B′-dimethylborazole	225	380	0.92
N, N′-dimethylborazole	....	381	0.92
m-xylene	219.4	411.8	....
B, N-dimethylborazole*	....	397	0.95 or 0.97
o-xylene	244	417	....
p-xylene	286.2	411.5	....
4. Mesitylenes			
B,B′,B″-trimethylborazole	305	400	0.91
N,N′,N″-trimethylborazole	264	405	0.92
mesitylene	220.3	437.6	....
5. Hemimellitenes or Pseudocumenes			
N,B,B′-trimethylborazole*	....	412	0.92 or 0.93
hemimellitene	<258	449.5	....
pseudocumene	....	442.8	....
6. Isodurenes			
N,B,B′,B″-tetramethylborazole	....	431	0.92
isodurene	249	470	....
7. Mellitenes			
hexamethylborazole	370	494	0.92
mellitene	439	537	....

* Relative positions of methyl groups not determined with certainty.

phatic analogs, the linkages are combinations of normal and coordinate covalences and should be formulated B ⇆ N. Infrared and Raman data also support such a resonating structure.[254] Wiberg has suggested the term "inorganic benzene" for the compound.[255]

Because of such structural similarities, one would expect marked

[254] B. L. Crawford and J. T. Edsall: *J. Chem. Phys.*, **7**, 223 (1939).
[255] E. Wiberg and A. Bolz: *Ber.*, **73B**, 209 (1940).

similarities in properties between borazole and benzene and between corresponding derivatives of the two compounds. The facts are in accord with such expectations.[159, 162, 245, 248, 252, 255, 256] This is shown particularly well by the comparison of physical constants in Table 17·14 and Table 17·15. Data which are essentially dependent upon structures are almost identical in many instances. Further comparison of structurally similar compounds is made in Table 17·16. It is significant that, although the hydrocarbon is the higher boiling compound in each instance, the ratio of the absolute boiling points ($T_{BN} : T_C$) is constant at 0.93 for the entire series.

Borazole and its derivatives are also quite comparable with their isosteric aromatic analogs in chemical behavior, although they are in general somewhat more reactive. Among the more important reactions are addition and substitution reactions involving, in particular, halogen and oxygen materials. Thus one mole of borazole adds three moles of hydrogen halides (X = Cl, Br), water, methanol, or methyl iodide. Additions that are slower and more difficult to effect occur with ammonia, trimethylamine, and diethyl ether. Substituted borazoles show similar behavior. In such reactions, the more negative group in the adding molecule normally goes to the boron atom.

Reactions with hydrogen chloride and hydrogen bromide have been investigated in detail.[255, 256] With borazole, cyclic trihalo analogs of symmetrical trihalocyclohexanes are formed initially, but these lose hydrogen at 50° to 100°C. to give symmetrical trihalo-borazoles. Such reactions may be formulated as

$$\text{borazole} \xrightarrow{+3HX} \text{addition compound} \xrightarrow{-3H_2} \text{trihaloborazole}$$

With hexamethylborazole, the reactions are somewhat more complicated and may be formulated as[245, 256]

[256] E. Wiberg: *Naturwissenschaften*, **35**, 212 (1948).

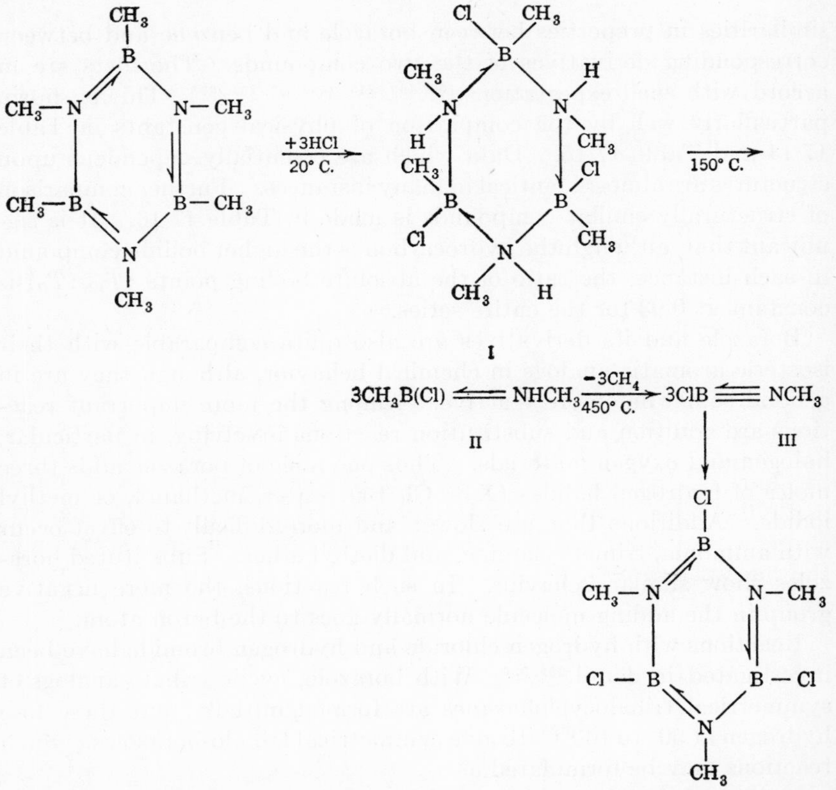

$\xrightarrow[20^\circ\text{ C.}]{+3\text{HCl}}$ I $\xrightarrow{150^\circ\text{ C.}}$

$$3CH_3B(Cl) \Longleftarrow NHCH_3 \xrightarrow[450^\circ\text{ C.}]{-3CH_4} 3ClB \equiv NCH_3$$

II III

The intermediates I and II can be isolated, but the acetylenic analog III trimerizes immediately and cannot be recovered (p. 798). Excess hydrogen chloride ruptures all boron-nitrogen bonds and gives the compounds CH_3BCl_2 and $CH_3NH_2 \cdot HCl$ as products. Borazole adds two moles of bromine at 0°C., the addition compound decomposing to a dibromoborazole at 60°C.[255] These reactions may be formulated as

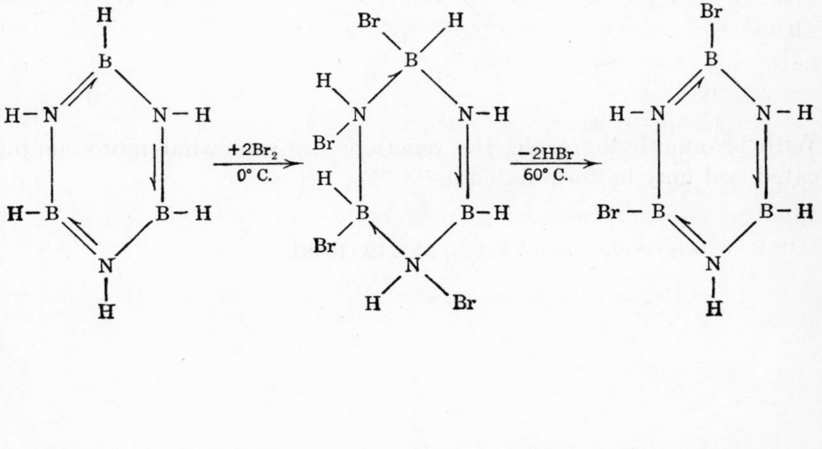

$\xrightarrow[0^\circ\text{ C.}]{+2\text{Br}_2}$ $\xrightarrow[60^\circ\text{ C.}]{-2\text{HBr}}$

The product is readily hydrolyzed by water to an analog of resorcinol.

Borazole and N,N′,N″-trimethylborazole react with water in a 1:3 stoichiometry to yield hydroxyborazoles

OH B H − N N − H HO− B B − OH N H

and

OH B CH_3− N N − CH_3 HO− B B − OH N CH_3

by loss of hydrogen.[247, 255] B,B′,B″-trimethylborazole and hexamethylborazole, however, are hydrolyzed to ammonia or methylamine with decomposition of the boron-nitrogen ring and formation of the ring structure[247, 255]

CH_3 B O O CH_3——B B——CH_3 O

With excess water vapor at 150°C. or above, complete hydrolyses to boric acid or methylboric acid, $CH_3B(OH)_2$, and ammonia or methylamine occur.

Reactions with methanol are quite comparable to those with water. Ammonia and amines add to borazole, but these reactions have not been investigated comprehensively. It is of especial interest that, although benzene is hydrogenated in the presence of palladium catalysts, borazole is actually dehydrogenated under comparable conditions.[255]

Simple substitution reactions are somewhat less common. It is apparent, of course, that the products obtained in some of the reactions discussed above are substitution products, but in most cases intermediate addition compounds can be isolated. However, borazole reacts with boron trimethyl to give B,B′,B″-trimethylborazole[257]

[257] H. I. Schlesinger, D. M. Ritter, and A. B. Burg: *J. Am. Chem. Soc.*, **60**, 1296 (1938).

in some 60% yield as

$$\text{(H}_3\text{B}_3\text{N}_3\text{H}_3\text{)} + \tfrac{3}{n}\,B(CH_3)_3 \longrightarrow \text{(CH}_3)_3\text{B}_3\text{N}_3\text{H}_3 + \tfrac{3}{n}\,BH_n(CH_3)_{3-n}$$

small quantities (ca. 5%) of the mono- and dimethyl derivatives being produced together with a non-volatile product of composition BNH. With excess borazole, larger quantities of the mono- and disubstituted compounds are formed. The various N-methylborazoles give B,N-methyl derivatives.[257] Treatment of borazole with boron trichloride or boron tribromide gives B-mono-, di-, and trihaloborazoles.[258] An unstable material, presumably a mono-fluo derivative, forms in a comparable reaction involving boron trifluoride. These reactions presumably involve substitution, although hydrogen, diborane, and various solid materials are formed also.

Borazole is formed when the "ammoniates" of the boron hydrides (p. 779) are heated at 180° to 200°C., hydrogen being the other product.[252] Although the diborane compound is commonly used, somewhat better yields are obtained with the tetraborane compound.[259] Direct reaction of diborane with ammonia at 250° to 300°C. and under 1 atm. pressure gives borazole in 50% yields.[252, 255] It is presumed that such a reaction involves the formation of the borine complex, $H_3B \leftarrow NH_3$, which loses hydrogen and polymerizes according to the scheme[255]

$$3B_2H_6 \xrightarrow{+6NH_3} 6H_3B \leftarrow NH_3 \xrightarrow{-H_2} 6H_2B \leftrightharpoons NH_2 \xrightarrow{-H_2} 6HB \equiv NH \longrightarrow 2B_3N_3H_6$$

Borazole is obtained in 35% yields by reaction of lithium borohydride with ammonium chloride at 275°C., diborane being produced as a by-product.[258] B-methylborazoles are formed when borazole is

[258] G. W. Schaeffer, R. Schaeffer, and H. I. Schlesinger: *J. Am. Chem. Soc.*, **73,** 1612 (1951).

[259] A. Stock, E. Wiberg, and H. Martini: *Ber.*, **63B,** 2927 (1930).

treated with boron trimethyl[257] or better when the "ammoniates" of the mono-, di-, or trimethyl diboranes (p. 778) are heated at 200°C. in closed tubes.[260] The N-methyl compounds are obtained when diborane is heated with methylamine or with mixtures of ammonia and methylamine.[257] Thus, N,N′,N″-trimethylborazole is formed in 90% yield by reaction of diborane with methylamine at 190°C.[247] Reaction of boron trimethyl with ammonia, followed by heating the addition compound $(CH_3)_3B \leftarrow NH_3$ at 330°C. and 20 atm. pressure, gives B,B′,B″-trimethylborazole.[247] Also, the hexamethyl derivative is obtained when the addition compound $(CH_3)_3B \leftarrow NH_2CH_3$ is heated at 450°C. and 20 atm. pressure.[245] N,N′,N″-trimethylborazole is obtained also by reaction of monomethylammonium chloride with lithium borohydride[250] as

$$3CH_3NH_3Cl + 3LiBH_4 \rightarrow B_3N_3H_3(CH_3)_3 + 3LiCl + 9H_2$$

It is interesting to speculate upon the possible existence of analogous compounds in which boron and nitrogen have been replaced, respectively, by their congeners aluminum and phosphorus. Such compounds might be formulated tentatively as[256]

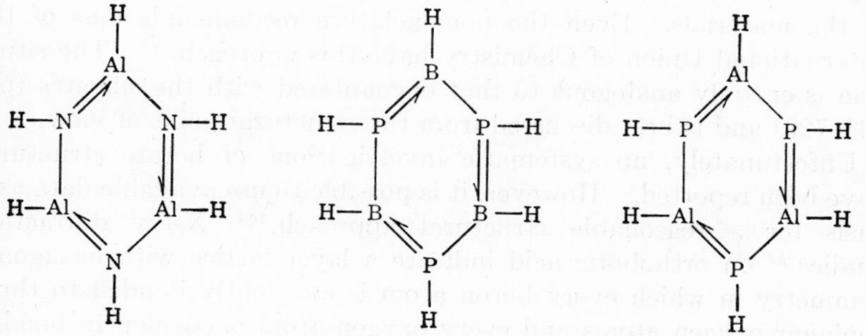

```
          H                    H                     H
          |                    |                     |
          Al                   B                     Al
        //  \                //  \                 //  \
  H—N        N—H       H—P        P—H        H—P        P—H
    |        ||          |        ||           |        ||
  H—Al       Al—H      H—B        B—H        H—Al       Al—H
       \\  /                \\  /                 \\  /
          N                    P                     P
          |                    |                     |
          H                    H                     H
```

However, very little evidence indicating that such substances or their derivatives can be prepared has been offered. Although some polymeric substances such as $(HAlNH)_x$, $(RAlNH)_y$, $(RAlNR)_z$, and $(R_2Al—PR_2)_3$ have been mentioned,[256] they do not have the aromatic characteristics of the borazoles. A fortuitous combination of donor-acceptor properties and size relationships apparently renders the borazole arrangement unique.[256]

[260] H. I. Schlesinger, L. Horvitz, and A. B. Burg: *J. Am. Chem. Soc.*, **58**, 409 (1936).

Oxy acids of boron and their salts

The oxy acids of boron are of essentially two types: (1) the boric acids, which are based upon the anhydride boric oxide, and (2) the lower oxy acids, which are quite generally related to the boron hydrides and are presumably based upon boron to boron structural linkages. It is convenient to discuss these types separately.

The Boric Acids and Their Salts. Phase studies of the system boric oxide–water[70, 261] show the only stable hydrates of the oxide to be the 1-hydrate or HBO_2 (metaboric acid) and the 3-hydrate or H_3BO_3 (orthoboric acid). The hemi-hydrate or $H_2B_4O_7$ (tetraboric acid), although often reported in the older literature, apparently has no stable existence. There exist, however, many compounds (especially minerals) which appear to be derived from a series of polyboric acids, all of which are based upon boric oxide as the anhydride. Such acids cannot be isolated and are non-existent. Furthermore, there is no evidence that anionic aggregation (p. 276) occurs when orthoborate solutions are treated with progressively increasing quantities of acid. Characterization of these compounds as polyborates based upon a series of isopolyboric acids is, therefore, unwarranted, although it must be recognized that such a system has been followed in the naming of the materials. Even the nomenclature recommendations of the International Union of Chemistry have this approach.[262] The situation is entirely analogous to that encountered with the silicates (pp. 722–729) and is best discussed from the structural point of view.

Unfortunately, no systematic investigations of borate structures have been reported. However, it is possible to use available data as a basis for a reasonable structural approach.[263] X-ray diffraction studies[264] on orthoboric acid indicate a layer lattice with hexagonal symmetry in which every boron atom is covalently bonded to three coplanar oxygen atoms and every oxygen atom is covalently bonded to one boron atom and by hydrogen bonds to two other oxygen atoms. The B—O and O—H . . . O bond distances are, respectively, 1.36 A and 2.71 A, individual layers or sheets being 3.18 A apart. The elements of the structure within each layer may be represented pictorially as

[261] H. Menzel, H. Schulz, and H. Deckert: *Z. anorg. allgem. Chem.*, **220**, 49 (1934).

[262] W. P. Jorissen H. Bassett, A. Damiens, F. Fichter, and H. Rémy: *J. Am. Chem. Soc.*, **63**, 889 (1941).

[263] A. F. Wells: *Structural Inorganic Chemistry*, 2nd Ed., pp. 598–600. Clarendon Press, Oxford (1950).

[264] W. H. Zachariasen: *Z. Krist.*, **88**, 150 (1934).

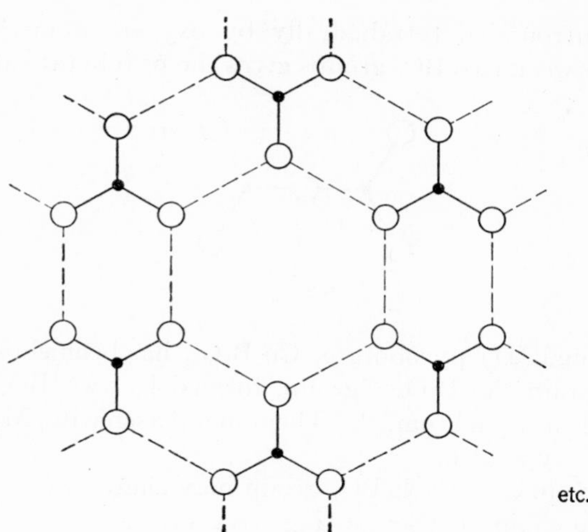

solid circles representing boron atoms, open circles oxygen atoms, and dotted lines hydrogen bonds. The unit of borate structures may thus be considered to be the planar BO_3 group, and structures dependent upon this group may be derived in the same fashion as was done for the tetrahedral SiO_4 group with the silicates.

Based upon such arrangements, the following types of structures might be distinguished:

1. *Discrete anions* in which either individual BO_3 groups are present (BO_3^{-3} or orthoborate) or a limited number of BO_3 groups are combined by sharing oxygen atoms ($B_2O_5^{-4}$ or pyroborate).
2. *Extended anions* in which individual BO_3 groups are linked into chains or rings (e.g., $B_3O_6^{-3}$, $B_2O_4^{-2}$, or metaborate).
3. *Two-dimensional sheets* in which all the oxygen atoms of each BO_3 group are shared with other BO_3 groups (e.g., B_2O_3; $B_5O_{10}^{-5}$, or pentaborate).

Each of these may be discussed briefly.

DISCRETE ANIONS. Orthoborates, containing discrete BO_3^{-3} groups, are limited in number, but they are formed by a number of tripositive metals. The structures of the compounds $ScBO_3$, YBO_3, and $InBO_3$ are all similar to those of compounds of the types $M^{II}CO_3$ and $M^{I}NO_3$.[265] Each contains planar BO_3 groups. The mineral hambergite, $Be_2(BO_3)OH$, contains OH and BO_3 groups so arranged that each beryl-

[265] V. M. Goldschmidt: *Nachr. Ges. Wiss. Gött.*, **1932**, 53.

lium ion is surrounded tetrahedrally by oxygen atoms.[263] Sharing one oxygen between two BO_3 groups gives the pyroborate arrangement

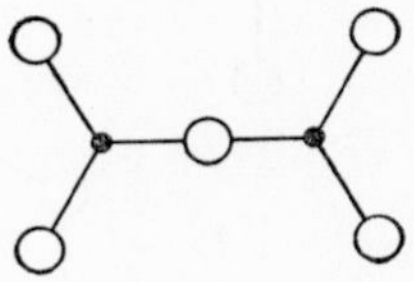

$B_2O_5^{-4}$

Crystalline cobalt(II) pyroborate, $Co_2B_2O_5$, has been shown by x-ray studies to contain the $B_2O_5^{-4}$ group, formed by two BO_3^{-3} triangles sharing a single oxygen atom.[266] The mineral ascharite, $Mg_2B_2O_5 \cdot H_2O$ may be of this type also.

EXTENDED ANIONS. Each BO_3 group may share two oxygen atoms to give infinite chain or discrete ring structures as

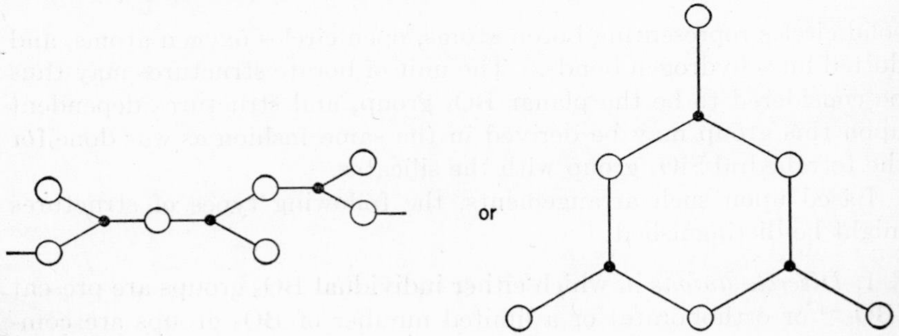

or

In each instance the empirical composition would be $(BO_2)_n^{-n}$, i.e., the metaborate composition. An infinite chain arrangement is characteristic of calcium metaborate, $Ca(BO_2)_2$,[267, 268] the boron-oxygen chains being held together by calcium ions. An analogy to the pyroxene structure (p. 725) is apparent. Amphibole (p. 726) analogs, however, have not been characterized with certainty although such an arrangement may characterize borax, $Na_2B_4O_7 \cdot 10H_2O$, or kernite, $Na_2B_4O_7 \cdot 4H_2O$, since they have the requisite $B_4O_7^{-2}$ empirical stoichiometry. Six-membered B_3O_3 rings are characteristic of sodium and potassium metaborates,[269] the B—O distances being 1.38 A in the ring and 1.33 A outside. These compounds should be assigned trimeric formulas, $M_3^IB_3O_6$. The same ring system has been encoun-

[266] S. V. Berger: *Acta Chem. Scand.*, **4**, 1054 (1950).
[267] W. H. Zachariasen: *Proc. Natl. Acad. Sci.*, **17**, 617 (1931).
[268] W. H. Zachariasen and G. E. Ziegler: *Z. Krist.*, **83**, 354 (1932).
[269] W. H. Zachariasen: *J. Chem. Phys.*, **5**, 919 (1937).

tered with other boron-oxygen compounds (pp. 751, 805). The metaborates are common derivatives of the heavy metals.

TWO-DIMENSIONAL SHEETS. Such an arrangement is presumably found in crystalline boric oxide (p. 752). In combination with BO_4 tetrahedra, it may be characteristic of borates such as the pentaborate $KH_4B_5O_{10}\cdot 2H_2O$ for which one might write[263]

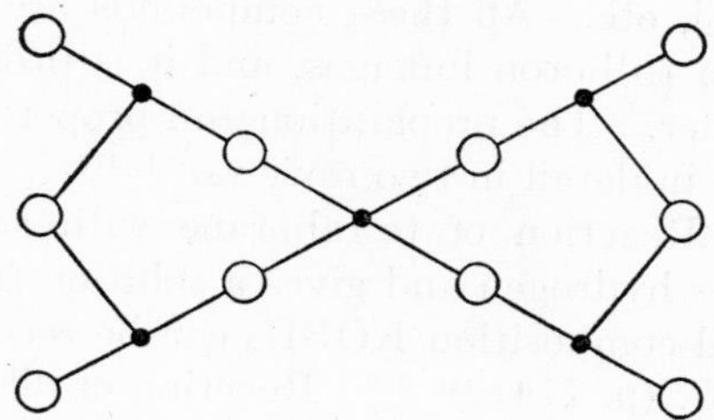

Such considerations may provide a key to borate structures. It must be admitted, however, that our present state of knowledge does not permit systematic classification of such substances as colemanite, $Ca_2B_6O_{11}\cdot 5H_2O$; boracite, $2Mg_3B_8O_{15}\cdot MgCl_2$; or boronatrocalcite, $Na_2B_4O_7\cdot Ca_2B_6O_{11}\cdot 16H_2O$, The same may be said of the so-called boron ultramarines, which are obtained by fusing borax with sodium sulfide or sulfur,[270] and many of the borosilicates.

Orthoboric acid is a flaky crystalline compound, which occurs in but a single crystalline form.[261] It is moderately soluble in cold water and quite soluble in hot water. It decomposes to metaboric acid and then to boric oxide (p. 752) when heated, but volatilizes in steam. Steams from certain natural fumaroles (especially in Tuscany, Italy) contain appreciable quantities of boric acid. Solid metaboric acid exists in three crystalline forms, one of which is stable (m.p. 236°C.) and the others of which are metastable (m.p. 201° and 176°C.). The extreme weakness of boric acid in aqueous solutions ($k'_{A_1} = 5.8 \times 10^{-10}$, $k'_{A_2} = 1.8 \times 10^{-13}$, $k'_{A_3} = 3 \times 10^{-14}$) indicates extensive hydrolysis of soluble (alkali metal) borates. The enhanced strength of boric acid in the presence of polyhydroxy compounds has been discussed (pp. 763–764). Orthoboric acid is obtained by treating a concentrated alkali metal borate solution with hydrochloric acid and is purified by crystallization from water. All borates are decomposed to orthoboric acid by strong acid.

Boric acid readily forms a variety of heteropoly acids and salts with molybic and tungstic acids and their derivatives (pp. 274–276). Peroxyborates are also known as well as peroxyhydrated borates (pp. 511–515).

[270] J. Hofmann: *Z. anorg. allgem. Chem.*, **183**, 37 (1929).

Lower Oxy Acids of Boron and Their Salts. Certain compounds of these types have been mentioned in discussions of the lower halides (p. 749), the lower oxides (p. 753), and the hydrides (pp. 776, 781) of boron. Several types of compounds have been described, namely, *hypoborates,* derived from $H_2[H_6B_2O_2]$; *sub-borates,* derived from $H_4[B_2O_4]$; and *borohydrates,* derived from α- and β-$H_2[H_4B_2O_2]$, $H_2[B_4O_2]$, $H_2[B_2O_2]$, etc. All these compounds are apparently characterized by boron to boron linkages, and it is probable that all are related to each other. The preparation and properties of these materials are described in detail in two reviews.[271, 272]

HYPOBORATES. Reaction of tetraborane with aqueous potassium hydroxide liberates hydrogen and gives a solution from which a compound of empirical composition $KOBH_3$ can be recovered by vacuum evaporation at 0°C. (p. 776).[159, 273] Reaction of diborane with potassium hydroxide gives the same compound but in smaller yields. The compound is stable in dry air at ordinary temperatures. When heated *in vacuo* it loses some water and hydrogen at 110°C. and is said to decompose at 400° to 450°C. according to the equation

$$5KOBH_3 \rightarrow K_3B_5O_3 + 2K + 2H_2O + \tfrac{11}{2}H_2$$

It dissolves in water to give alkaline solutions which slowly decompose to borate and hydrogen. The rate of this decomposition is increased by addition of acids, but addition of alkalies effects stabilization. Aqueous solutions are strongly reducing,[80] converting silver, mercury, arsenic, antimony, and bismuth compounds to the free metals, copper compounds to copper hydride, and nickel compounds to black nickel boride, Ni_2B (p. 770). The last reaction is a sensitive test for hypoborate. In its reducing character, the hypoborate is comparable to the hypophosphite.

The diamagnetic character of the potassium compound[186] suggests that the formula be doubled, thus giving the anion $[H_6B_2O_2]^{-2}$. A possible electronic formula for such an anion might be

$$\left[\begin{array}{ccccccc} & & H & & & & \\ & & \cdot\cdot & & \cdot\cdot & & \\ H & : & B & : & O & : & H \\ & & \cdot\cdot & & \vdots & & \\ H & : & B & : & O & : & H \\ & & \cdot\cdot & & \cdot\cdot & & \\ & & H & & & & \end{array}\right]^{-2}$$

although no supporting data are available.

[271] H. Terrey: *Ann. Reports,* **34,** 132 (1937).
[272] R. C. Ray: *Chem. & Ind.,* **1946,** 322.
[273] A. Stock and E. Kuss: *Ber.,* **47,** 810 (1914).

SUBBORATES. Reactions of boron subchloride with water[56] and alcohols[57] to give, respectively, subboric acid, $H_4[B_2O_4]$, and its esters, $R_4[B_2O_4]$, have been described (p. 749). The free acid is formed as a white, comparatively stable solid when the esters are hydrolyzed *in vacuo*.[81] Aqueous solutions of the acid decompose as

$$H_4[B_2O_4] + 2H_2O \rightarrow 2H_3BO_3 + H_2$$

but are somewhat stabilized by either acid or alkali. The acid is a strong reducing agent in aqueous solution, converting copper and silver salts to the free metals, mercury(II) compounds to mercury(I), and manganese(VII) to manganese(II). Unlike hypoborate, it does not form nickel boride, and, unlike the various borohydrates, it does not reduce iodine.

The acid is derived from the oxide B_2O_2 (p. 753). Proof of the presence of a boron to boron linkage in the molecule lies in synthesis of the esters from alkoxyboron halides by a "Wurtz reaction" as[81]

$$(RO)_2B\text{—}\boxed{Cl + 2Na + Cl}\text{—}B(OR)_2 \rightarrow (RO)_2B\text{—}B(OR)_2 + 2NaCl$$

The acid must then have the structure

$$(HO)_2B:B(OH)_2$$

BOROHYDRATES. This name had its origin in fancied resemblances of these compounds to the carbohydrates.[272] However, there is justification for its retention because these materials are closely related to the boron hydrides and borohydrides in properties and presumably in structures.

Although acid hydrolysis of magnesium boride is useful in the preparation of boron hydrides (pp. 776–777), it was early observed that hydrolysis with water alone yields a variety of oxygenated compounds, the borohydrates.[78, 272, 274, 275] Thus reaction of a specially prepared

[274] M. W. Travers and R. C. Ray: *Proc. Royal Soc.* (*London*), **A87**, 163 (1912).

[275] M. W. Travers, R. C. Ray, and N. M. Gupta: *Some Compounds of Boron, Oxygen, and Hydrogen.* H. K. Lewis and Co., London (1917).

magnesium boride (from heating to redness in hydrogen an intimate mixture of 1 part of boric oxide and 2¼ parts of magnesium) with water gave only traces of hydrogen and boron hydrides but formed a solution which evolved hydrogen on treatment with acids and reduced iodine.[274] Solutions with similar properties but yielding only half as much hydrogen when acidified were obtained by similar hydrolysis of a boride containing boric acid and magnesium.[275] From the characteristics of these solutions, the presence of two isomeric compounds of composition $H_6B_2O_2$ was deduced.

Magnesium salts of such acids cannot be isolated, but two isomeric potassium compounds have been prepared. Treatment of pure magnesium boride with $N/100$ potassium hydroxide, followed by fractional crystallization after removal of precipitated magnesium hydroxide, yielded a water-soluble, crystalline compound of composition $K_2[H_4B_2O_2]$, the so-called alpha salt.[77] A comparable procedure, using magnesium boride containing 2% magnesium powder and 15% boric acid, gave isomeric β-$K_2[H_4B_2O_2]$ and another salt $K_2[H_2B_2O_2]$.[276] The compound β-$K_2[H_4B_2O_2]$ was converted to a tetra-potassium salt, β-$K_4[H_2B_2O_2]$, by potassium hydroxide, but no such conversion is reported for α-$K_2[H_4B_2O_2]$. All these salts are crystalline compounds which, in solution, give copper hydride with copper salts, the free metals with gold and silver compounds, and green precipitates containing nickel and boron with nickel salts. With the exception of β-$K_2[H_4B_2O_2]$ they are reported to be stable *in vacuo* or in dry, carbon dioxide-free air.

Hydrolysis of magnesium boride normally yields the substance $Mg_3B_2(OH)_6$ as an intermediate, and presumably subsequent reactions convert this material to boron hydrides. However, at temperatures below −10°C., the primary hydrolysis product is $H_3B_2(MgOH)_3$,[277] an analog of the compound $H_2Si(MgOH)_2$ formed in the hydrolysis of magnesium silicide (p. 675). Although this compound is largely converted to the compound $Mg_3B_2(OH)_6$ at more elevated temperatures as

$$H_3B_2(MgOH)_3 + 3H_2O \rightarrow Mg_3B_2(OH)_6 + 3H_2$$

a small portion (ca. 10%) is converted to the borohydrates α-$H_2[H_4B_2O_2]$ and β-$H_2[H_4B_2O_2]$. The residue, $Mg_3B_2(OH)_6$, when extracted with aqueous ammonia in an atmosphere of hydrogen, yields

[276] R. C. Ray: *Trans. Faraday Soc.*, **33**, 1260 (1937).
[277] R. C. Ray and P. C. Sinha: *J. Chem. Soc.*, **1935**, 1694.

a solution from which the compounds $(NH_4)_2[H_2B_2O_2]$ and $(NH_4)_2$-$[B_4O_6]$ can be crystallized.[79] A material $H_{12}B_4O_6$ apparently forms as an hydrolysis product of $Mg_3B_2(OH)_6$,[275] but its derivatives have not been isolated. The relationships existing among all these compounds are summarized in Table 17·17.[272] In the presence of acids, the hydrolytic decomposition

$$2H_3B_2(MgOH)_3 + 6H_2O \rightarrow B_4H_{10} + 6Mg(OH)_2 + H_2$$

is favored.

TABLE 17·17

RELATIONSHIPS AMONG THE BOROHYDRATES

$$Mg_3B_2 \xrightarrow{+3H_2O} H_3B_2(MgOH)_3 \xrightarrow{+H_2O} \begin{cases} Mg_3B_2(OH)_6 \xrightarrow{+6H_2O} H_{12}B_4O_6 \xrightarrow[\text{(vac.)}]{\Delta} B_4O_5 \xrightarrow{+H_2O} H_2B_4O_6 \\ \beta\text{-}H_6B_2O_2 \xrightarrow{+H^+} H_4B_2O_2 \xrightarrow{+I_2} B_2O_2 \\ \alpha\text{-}H_6B_2O_2 \xrightarrow{+H^+} H_2B_2O_2 \xrightarrow{+I_2} B_2O_2 \end{cases}$$

$$B_2O_2 \xrightarrow{+2H_2O} H_4B_2O_4$$

Physical data which might indicate the structures of these compounds are lacking. It has been suggested[272] that isomeric forms of the material $H_6B_2O_2$ are due to *cis-trans* isomerism based upon double-bonded structures as

$$H_2^+\left[\begin{array}{c} H : B : \ddot{\underset{..}{O}} : H \\ :: \\ H : B : \ddot{\underset{..}{O}} : H \end{array}\right]^{-2} \qquad H_2^+\left[\begin{array}{c} H : \ddot{\underset{..}{O}} : B : H \\ :: \\ H : B : \ddot{\underset{..}{O}} : H \end{array}\right]^{-2}$$

α-form (*cis*) β-form (*trans*)

Loss of more hydrogen atoms by the α-form then occurs readily to give $H_2B_2O_2$

$$\begin{array}{c} \ddot{B} : \ddot{\underset{..}{O}} : H \\ :: \\ B : \ddot{\underset{..}{O}} : H \end{array}$$

but with the β- form the compound $H_4B_2O_2$

$$\begin{array}{l} H : \overset{\cdot\cdot}{\underset{\cdot\cdot}{O}} : \underset{\cdot\cdot}{B} : H \\ \quad\;\; H : B : \overset{\cdot\cdot}{\underset{\cdot\cdot}{O}} : H \end{array}$$

is produced. However, the possibility of bridging structures must not be discounted since these compounds are intimately related to the boron hydrides.

All the lower oxy acids of boron can be considered as hydrolysis products of tetraborane in terms of the equations[274]

$$B_4H_{10} + 4H_2O \rightarrow 2H_2[H_6B_2O_2] + H_2$$
$$B_4H_{10} + 8H_2O \rightarrow 2H_4[B_2O_4] + 9H_2$$
$$B_4H_{10} + 4H_2O \rightarrow 2H_2[H_4B_2O_2](\alpha \text{ and } \beta) + 3H_2$$
$$B_4H_{10} + 4H_2O \rightarrow 2H_2[B_2O_2] + 7H_2$$
$$B_4H_{10} + 4H_2O \rightarrow 2H_2[H_2B_2O_2] + 5H_2$$
$$B_4H_{10} + 6H_2O \rightarrow H_{12}B_4O_6 + 5H_2$$
$$B_4H_{10} + 6H_2O \rightarrow H_2[B_4O_6] + 10H_2$$

although only the first two reactions have been carried out experimentally (B_2O_2 is formed in the second).[80] Only $H_4[B_2O_4]$ is sufficiently stable to be isolated in the free condition.

Compounds containing cationic boron

Although boron is electropositive in the majority of its compounds, simple cationic boron is non-existent (p. 736). Cationic boron compounds are formed when chelating groups (e.g., β-diketones) which satisfy all four coordination positions around the boron atom, but have only two primary valencies, are present (p. 765). There exist also a number of boron derivatives of oxy acids which have the formal compositions of boron salts. These are sometimes called *boryl* compounds.

Perhaps best characterized are the orthophosphate, BPO_4, and the orthoarsenate, $BAsO_4$. Both these compounds have crystal structures of the distorted high cristobalite type (p. 691), with both the boron and phosphorus or arsenic atoms surrounded tetrahedrally by oxygens, each oxygen belonging to both a boron tetrahedron and a phosphorus or arsenic tetrahedron.[278, 279] The calculated (x-ray) specific gravities are 2.802 and 3.660 for the phosphate and the arsenate, respectively. The corresponding aluminum compounds have quartz structures. Boron phosphate and arsenate are somewhat soluble in water when prepared at low temperatures and are hydrolyzed, giving acidic solutions. Hydrates, $BPO_4 \cdot xH_2O$ ($x = 6, 5, 4, 3$) and $BAsO_4 \cdot yH_2O$ ($y = 6, 3$), form,[280] and the 3-hydrates give monoammines with ammonia.[280] When heated, the anhydrous compounds become insoluble and resist hydrolysis. Crystallization occurs at elevated temperatures.[279] Boron phsophate begins to vaporize only at ca. 1450°C.[281] Boron phosphate is prepared by evaporating mixtures of boric and phosphoric acids and heating the residues[282–284] or by heating boric oxide with diammonium hydrogen orthophosphate.[279] Boron arsenate is obtained by comparable procedures. Boric acid and boron phosphate are the only stable solid phases in the system B_2O_3–P_4O_{10}–H_2O.[285]

From the system B_2O_3–SO_3–H_2O, the materials $B_2O_3 \cdot SO_3 \cdot 4H_2O$ and $2B_2O_3 \cdot SO_3 \cdot 3H_2O$ can be isolated[285] as crystalline, hygroscopic solids. In anhydrous systems, the solids $B_2O_3 \cdot SO_3$ and $B_2O_3 \cdot 2SO_3$ form.[286] Little concrete evidence exists for the hydrogen sulfate, $B(HSO_4)_3$. Reaction of boric oxide with anhydrides of various carboxylic acids gives compounds of the type $B(O \cdot CO \cdot R)_3$,[287] the best-characterized material being the acetate, $B(O \cdot CO \cdot CH_3)_3$. It is a solid, m.p. 147° to 148°C.,[288] which dissolves in chloroform or acetone but decomposes when vaporized.

SUGGESTED SUPPLEMENTARY REFERENCES

N. V. Sidgwick: *The Chemical Elements and Their Compounds.* pp. 334–438, 458–487. Clarendon Press, Oxford (1950).

A. F. Wells: *Structural Inorganic Chemistry,* 2nd Ed. Ch. XX. Clarendon Press, Oxford (1950).

W. M. Latimer: *The Oxidation States of the Elements and Their Potentials in Aqueous Solutions,* pp. 147–154, 258–264. Prentice-Hall, New York (1938).

---

[278] G. E. R. Schulze: *Naturwissenschaften,* **21,** 562 (1933).
[279] G. E. R. Schulze: *Z. physik. Chem.,* **B24,** 215 (1934).
[280] E. Gruner: *Z. anorg. allgem. Chem.,* **219,** 181 (1934).
[281] F. A. Hummel and T. A. Kupinski: *J. Am. Chem. Soc.,* **72,** 5318 (1950).
[282] A. Vogel: *Z. anal. Chem.,* **9,** 376 (1870).
[283] G. Meyer: *Ber.,* **22,** 2919 (1889).
[284] F. Mylius and A. Meusser: *Ber.,* **37,** 397 (1904).
[285] M. Levi and L. F. Gilbert: *J. Chem. Soc.,* **1927,** 2117.
[286] A. Pictet and G. Karl: *Bull. soc. chim.* [4], **3,** 1114 (1908).
[287] A. Pictet and A. Geleznoff: *Ber.,* **36,** 2219 (1903).
[288] L. Kahovec: *Z. physik. Chem.,* **B43,** 109 (1939).

CHAPTER 18

Periodic Group I
The Alkali and Coinage Metals

All the remaining representative elements, those in Periodic Groups I and II, are metals. A number of the compounds of these elements have been considered in previous chapters (Ch. 13–17), where various anionic species derived from the non-metals have been discussed. It seems reasonable, therefore, to restrict the current discussion somewhat and to describe specifically only those phases of the chemistries of these metals which are strictly characteristic of the free elements themselves and of the ions which they form. This approach is followed in both this chapter and Chapter 19. The approach adopted seems to be handled best by discussions on comparative bases. To this end, not only are the members of a given family described, but also both families in each periodic group are included in the same discussion. The advantages of such a presentation are apparent.

Of the Periodic Group Ia elements (the alkali metals), only sodium and potassium are really familiar and abundant (Li $6.5 \times 10^{-3}\%$, Na 2.83%, K 2.59%, Rb $3.1 \times 10^{-2}\%$, Cs $7 \times 10^{-4}\%$, Fr ca. 0% of the igneous rocks of the earth). The heaviest alkali metal, francium, occurs in nature only in minute quantities as a short-lived radioisotope formed by the branching alpha decay of actinium (Appendix II, p. 918).[1, 2, 3] Of the coinage metals, none is particularly abundant (Cu $1 \times 10^{-4}\%$, Ag $10^{-8}\%$, Au $10^{-9}\%$ of the crust of the earth), but all have become familiar either because of occurrence in concentrated deposits or because of possession of desirable properties which has promoted production for many centuries.

GROUP AND FAMILY RELATIONSHIPS AMONG THE ELEMENTS

Numerical properties characterizing the alkali and coinage metals are summarized, respectively, in Table 18·1 and Table 18·2. Among

[1] M. Perey: *Compt. rend.*, **208**, 97 (1939).
[2] M. Perey: Dissertation, University of Paris (1946).
[3] M. Perey: *J. chim. Phys.*, **43**, 155, 262, 269 (1946).

TABLE 18·1

NUMERICAL PROPERTIES OF THE ALKALI METALS

Property	Lithium	Sodium	Potassium	Rubidium	Cesium	Francium
Atomic number	3	11	19	37	55	87
Outer electronic configuration	$1s^2 2s^1$	$2s^2 2p^6 3s^1$	$3s^2 3p^6 4s^1$	$4s^2 4p^6 5s^1$	$5s^2 5p^6 6s^1$	$6s^2 6p^6 7s^1$
Mass numbers, natural isotopes	6, 7	23	39, 40,* 41	85, 87*	133	223*
Atomic weight	6.940	22.997	39.096	85.48	132.91	
Density of solid at 20°C., grams/cc.	0.535	0.971	0.862	1.532	1.90	
Atomic volume of solid, cc.	12.97	23.68	45.36	55.80	69.95	
Melting point, °C.	179	97.9	63.5	39.0	28.45	
Boiling point, °C.	1336	882.9	757.5	700	670	
Heat of sublimation at 25°C., kcal./gram atom	36.44	25.95	21.52	20.50	18.83	
Ionization potential, ev	5.390	5.138	4.339	4.176	3.893	
Heat of hydration of gaseous ion, kcal./mole	123	97	77	70	63	
E_{298}^0 for $M \rightleftharpoons M^+ + e^-$, volts	3.02	2.71	2.92	2.99	3.02	
Electronegativity	1.0	0.9	0.8	0.8	0.7	
Radii, A						
M	1.225	1.572	2.025	2.16	2.35	
M^+	0.60	0.95	1.33	1.48	1.69	
Gas molecules, M_2						
Bond energy, kcal./mole	27.2	17.5	11.8	11.3	10.4	
Bond distance, obs., A	2.67	3.08	3.91	.....	4.55	
Bond distance, calc., A	2.66	3.14	4.06	4.32	4.70	

* Radioactive.

TABLE 18·2

NUMERICAL PROPERTIES OF THE COINAGE METALS

Property	Copper	Silver	Gold
Atomic number	29	47	79
Outer electronic configuration	$3d^{10}4s^1$	$4d^{10}5s^1$	$5d^{10}6s^1$
Mass numbers, natural isotopes	63, 65	107, 109	197
Atomic weight	63.54	107.880	197.2
Density of solid at 20°C., grams/cc.	8.92	10.5	19.3
Atomic volume of solid, cc.	7.12	10.27	10.22
Melting point, °C.	1083	960.5	1063
Boiling point, °C.	2310	1950	2600
Ionization potential, ev	7.723	7.574	9.223
E_{298}^0 for			
$M \rightleftharpoons M^+ + e^-$	−0.522	−0.799	−1.68
$M \rightleftharpoons M^{+2} + 2e^-$	−0.3448	−1.389	
Radii, A			
M	1.173	1.339	1.336
M^+	0.96	1.26	1.37

the alkali metals, observed trends in properties are strictly in accord with those predicted on the bases of electronic configurations and nuclear charges of the component atoms. Thus, paralleling addition of electrons to higher and higher energy levels, there is a regular and marked increase in atomic size with increasing atomic number. This is reflected in values for atomic volumes and atomic radii and is implicit in values for crystal radii of the unipositive ions. The electronic configurations of atoms of the alkali metals are not conducive to large attractions between adjacent atoms. As a consequence, the members of the family are characterized by softness, by low melting points, by low sublimation energies, and by low boiling points. That all these decrease with increasing atomic numbers is consistent with parallel increases in atomic sizes. Atoms of the alkali metals are comparatively large. This factor combines with the presence of but single valence electrons outside inert gas atom arrangements to permit ready loss of electrons and consequent ease of oxidation. This characteristic is reflected not only in the ionization potential, standard potential, and electronegativity values summarized in Table 18·1, but also in the excellent electrical conductivities of these metals and in their ready solubilities in liquid ammonia (pp. 217–218, 347–349). In fact, the chemical behaviors of the alkali metals are almost entirely dependent upon electron loss. Ease of electron loss of course increases with increasing atomic size, the apparent anomaly in standard potential values resulting from hydration effects as previously described (pp. 295–296).

Among the coinage metals, trends in properties are somewhat less regular and less subject to ready interpretation. Thus, although the silver atom is somewhat larger than the copper atom, delayed effects of the lanthanide contraction (pp. 146–150) so reduce the size of the gold atom that its radius is essentially the same as that of the silver atom. The increased electron populations of the immediately underlying shells promote attractions between atoms of these elements, and as a consequence the hardnesses, melting points, and boiling points are greater than those of the alkali metals. Increased densities result from enhanced packing in the solid state. Addition of electrons to inner shells (*nd* in general) combine with increased nuclear charges to render the coinage metal atoms (and derived cations) significantly smaller than those of the alkali metals (p. 146). These factors reduce the ease with which electrons are lost, but the differences between the two families are more profound than one might expect on this basis alone. In terms of the Born-Haber type treatment already described (pp. 184–186), it is apparent that the higher boiling points of the coinage metals contribute significantly to their nobilities. As evidence of their enhanced resistance to oxidation, ionization potential and oxidation potential values may be cited (Table 18·2). It is particularly striking that among the coinage metals ease of electron loss actually decreases with increasing atomic size. The same phenomenon is of course characteristic also of the members of succeeding periodic families (e.g., IIb, IIIb, etc.). This is due, of course, to the fact that size increases are insufficient to counterbalance the opposing nuclear charge increases.

The alkali metals exist in a uniform positive one state of oxidation in all their compounds. Such compounds are inherently ionic, and the chemistries of the alkali metals are largely the chemistries of their unipositive ions. Numerous references to this state of oxidation and to these ions have appeared in earlier sections of this book. Actually, the chemistry of the alkali metals is simpler by far than that of any other family of metallic elements.

The electronic arrangements $(n-1)d^{10}ns^1$ characteristic of the coinage metal atoms permit the removal of more than a single electron since energy differences between the ns and $(n-1)d$ electrons are not major (p. 96). Oxidation states of +1, +2, and +3 are quite generally encountered with all these elements. Although the +1 state might be regarded as most characteristic, the +2 state with copper and the +3 state with gold are more common and more resistant to reduction than the +1 states. For silver, the reverse is true. That the 18-electron underlying arrangement is more easily deformed than the 8-electron arrangement renders even the +1 state more covalent in character for these elements than for the alkalies. Covalent complexes involving all these oxidation states are common and are often representative of stabilizations of the various states (pp. 303–304, 825–826). Negative oxidation states are precluded for all elements in this group.

It is of interest that, although the alkali metals give vapors which are predominantly monatomic, appreciable numbers (ca. 1% of the whole) of diatomic molecules can be detected by band spectra measurements. Bond energies and internuclear distances[4–6] characterizing these molecules are summarized in Table 18·1. Such molecules are apparently covalent in character and result from the sharing of the ns^1 electrons characterizing the alkali metal atoms.[7] The small bind-

[4] J. H. Bartlett and W. H. Furry: *Phys. Rev.*, **38,** 1615 (1931).
[5] N. Rosen and S. Ikehara: *Phys. Rev.*, **43,** 5 (1933).
[6] F. W. Loomis and P. Kusch: *Phys. Rev.*, **46,** 292 (1934).
[7] L. Pauling: *The Nature of the Chemical Bond*, 2nd Ed., p. 50. Cornell Univeristy Press, Ithaca (1940).

ing energies of these valence electrons and the necessary large spatial extensions of the orbitals combine to render these molecules comparatively unstable.

CHEMICAL CHARACTERISTICS OF THE ELEMENTS

The more important aspects of the chemical behaviors of the elements in the two families of this group are summarized in Table 18·3. Save for differences in oxidation states, the essential differences in the reactions of the alkali and coinage metals are compatible with the differences in ease of electron loss as discussed above. Much greater regularity can be distinguished in the reactions of the alkali metals than in those of the coinage metals. This stems again from simplicity in electronic structure combined with the stability of the inert gas atom arrangement. Although among the alkali metals activity increases regularly with most reagents (e.g., with dry oxygen, dry bromine) with increasing size, it is significant that with the very small non-metals (e.g., hydrogen, nitrogen, carbon) the reverse is true, lithium being the most reactive. This is associated with the fact that combination of small gaseous cations with small gaseous anions releases proportionately large amounts of energy and thus imparts to compounds of such types comparatively large heats of formation (pp. 184–185). The alkali metals are our most reactive metals; the coinage metals, except copper, are among our least reactive. It is important to remember that the reducing powers of the coinage metals are influenced tremendously by the presence of groups which can precipitate or complex the oxidation products (pp. 303–304, 825–826).

PREPARATION AND PRODUCTION OF THE FREE METALS

Because of their strong reducing powers, the alkali metals are best prepared by electrolytic means. Electrolytic reduction of aqueous salt solutions of course yields hydrogen, but, if a cathode (e.g., mercury) on which hydrogen has a high overvoltage is employed, the alkali metal may be deposited as an alloy (e.g., an amalgam). However, recovery of the free metals from such alloys is difficult. Electrolytic reduction of fused salts (e.g., chlorides, hydroxides, cyanides) gives pure alkali metals. Thus commercial sodium is produced annually to the extent of many thousands of tons in the United States alone by electrolysis of the fused chloride (Downs process). Among useful small-scale preparative procedures one might list thermal decomposition of the azides (p. 588). The volatilities of the alkali metals combine with the comparatively small heats of formation of certain of their compounds (e.g., oxides, sulfides) to permit preparations by

TABLE 18·3

CHEMICAL CHARACTERISTICS OF GROUP I METALS

Alkali Metals*		Reagent	Coinage Metals*	
General Equation	Remarks		General Equation	Remarks
$M + \frac{1}{2}X_2 \rightarrow MX$	With all halogens.	X_2	$M + \frac{n}{2}X_2 \rightarrow MX_n$	With halogens. With Cu, $n = 2$ for F_2, Cl_2, Br_2; $n = 1$ for I_2. With Ag, $n = 1$. With Au, $n = 3$ for Cl_2, Br_2; $n = 1$ for I_2.
$2M + \frac{1}{2}O_2 \rightarrow M_2O$	With Li only.	O_2	$M + O_2 \rightarrow M_2O$	With Cu above 1000°. With Ag under pressure.
$2M + O_2 \rightarrow M_2O_2$	With Na, K, Rb, Cs.			
$M + O_2 \rightarrow MO_2$	Especially with K, Rb, Cs.		$M + O_2 \rightarrow MO$	With Cu below 1000°.
$2M + S \rightarrow M_2S$	Also with Se, Te.	S	$2M + S \rightarrow M_2S$	With Cu, Ag. Also with Se, Te. Au gives $AuTe_2$.
$3M + \frac{1}{2}N_2 \rightarrow M_3N$	With Li only.	N_2		Unreactive.
$3M + P \rightarrow M_3P$	Also with As, Sb.	P	$3M + P \rightarrow M_3P$	With Cu.
$M + \frac{1}{2}H_2 \rightarrow MH$	Vigorous.	H_2		Unreactive.
$M + H^+ \rightarrow M^+ + \frac{1}{2}H_2$	Very vigorous.	H^+	$M + 2H^+ + \frac{1}{2}O_2 \rightarrow M^{+2} + H_2O$	With Cu. No reaction in absence of O_2.
$M + H_2O \rightarrow MOH + \frac{1}{2}H_2$	Vigorous.	H_2O		Unreactive.
$M + ROH \rightarrow MOR + \frac{1}{2}H_2$	R = alkyl or aryl.	ROH		Unreactive.
$M + NH_3 \rightarrow MNH_2 + \frac{1}{2}H_2$	Especially in presence of Fe, etc. Liquid or gaseous NH_3.	NH_3	$M + 4NH_3 + \frac{1}{2}O_2 + H_2O \rightarrow [M(NH_3)_4]^{+2} + 2OH^-$	With Cu and aqueous NH_3.
$M + H^+ \rightarrow M^+ + \frac{1}{2}H_2$	Some reduction products of NO_3^- also.	HNO_3	$3M + 4H^+ + NO_3^- \rightarrow 3M^+ + NO + 2H_2O$	With Ag. Cu gives Cu^{+2}.
$M + H^+ \rightarrow M^+ + \frac{1}{2}H_2$	Vigorous.	H_2SO_4	$2M + 4H^+ + SO_4^{-2} \rightarrow 2M^+ + SO_2 + 2H_2O$	With Ag. Cu gives Cu^{+2}.
$M + H^+ \rightarrow M^+ + \frac{1}{2}H_2$		$HNO_3 + HCl$	$M + 5H^+ + 4Cl^- + NO_3^- \rightarrow HMCl_4 + NO + 2H_2O$	With Au. Cu gives Cu^{+2}, Ag gives AgCl.
$M + H_2O \rightarrow MOH + \frac{1}{2}H_2$		$CN^- + H_2O + O_2$	$2M + 4CN^- + \frac{1}{2}O_2 + H_2O \rightarrow 2[M(CN)_2]^- + 2OH^-$	Especially with Ag, Au.

* M = any metal of Group I.

thermal reduction procedures. Thus reduction of carbonates with carbon, of chlorides with calcium or even sodium, of hydroxides or sulfides with iron, aluminum, or magnesium, etc., are all feasible small-scale procedures in which the metals are produced in the gaseous state. Production of potassium is on a relatively small scale since this metal offers no technical advantages over sodium.[8] The rarer members of the family are recovered only in minor quantities for special purposes.

Decreases in the reducing powers of the coinage metals render their preparations much simpler. Oxygenated compounds of all these elements are readily reduced at elevated temperatures, and in fact with silver and gold compounds addition of auxiliary reducing agents is seldom necessary since direct decompositions to the metals occur readily. Similarly, electrolytic reductions, even in aqueous media, are easy to effect, purification of all these elements being brought about commonly in this way. Although conversions of pure compounds to the free elements present no difficulties, the technical recoveries of the metals from natural sources are somewhat more involved. Native copper, because of its occurrence in massive or near massive forms, is easily recovered by gravity classification and fusion. However, because native silver and gold are often found in trace quantities, rather involved procedures are essential. Most effective is extraction with aqueous cyanide, followed by precipitation with zinc. In these reactions, complexing with cyanide ion so alters the oxidation potentials of these metals that they can be oxidized by atmospheric oxygen or peroxide. Of course, any naturally occurring compounds of these elements are also soluble under these conditions and can be extracted. The lead, copper, and nickel industries contribute major quantities of by-product silver. Most technical copper comes from sulfide ores, which are treated by a complicated process of roasting and reduction to yield the metal. The utilities of these metals are familiar to everyone.

COMPOUNDS OF THE GROUP I ELEMENTS

In view of the coverage of compound types in a general way in preceding chapters, it seems reasonable to limit discussion of the individual compound types of these elements to comparisons rather than to detailed descriptions of preparations, properties, uses, etc. Factual information of this type is contained in many freshman textbooks and should be reviewed. It is valuable to include also some data on the various oxidation states of the coinage metals and to discuss in some detail instances of covalent bonding in both families.

[8] H. N. Gilbert: *Chem. Eng. News*, **26**, 2604 (1948).

Oxidation states among the coinage metals

As previously indicated (p. 821), the coinage metals are distinguished from the alkali metals by their abilities to exist in +2 and +3 oxidation states as well as in the +1 state. Not all these states are completely characterized for all the coinage metals, nor can it be said that

TABLE 18·4

TYPICAL OXIDATION POTENTIALS FOR COINAGE METALS

Couple	Half-Reaction	E^0_{298} volts
Cu(O)–Cu(I)	$Cu + xH_2O \rightleftharpoons Cu^+(aq) + e^-$	−0.522
	$2Cu + 2OH^- \rightleftharpoons Cu_2O + H_2O + 2e^-$	0.361
Cu(O)–Cu(II)	$Cu + xH_2O \rightleftharpoons Cu^{+2}(aq) + 2e^-$	−0.3448
	$Cu + 2OH^- \rightleftharpoons Cu(OH)_2 + 2e^-$	0.258
Cu(I)–Cu(II)	$Cu^+ \rightleftharpoons Cu^{+2} + e^-$	−0.167
	$Cu_2O + H_2O + 2OH^- \rightleftharpoons 2Cu(OH)_2 + 2e^-$	0.087
Cu(II)–Cu(III)	$Cu^{+2} \rightleftharpoons Cu^{+3} + e^-$	< −1.8
	$Cu(OH)_2 + 2OH^- \rightleftharpoons CuO_2^- + 2H_2O + e^-$	< −0.8
Ag(O)–Ag(I)	$Ag + xH_2O \rightleftharpoons Ag^+(aq) + e^-$	−0.7995
	$2Ag + 2OH^- \rightleftharpoons Ag_2O + H_2O + 2e^-$	−0.344
Ag(I)–Ag(II)	$Ag^+ \rightleftharpoons Ag^{+2} + e^-$	−1.98
	$Ag_2O + 2OH^- \rightleftharpoons 2AgO + H_2O + 2e^-$	−0.57
Ag(I)–Ag(III)	$Ag^+ + H_2O \rightleftharpoons AgO^+ + 2H^+ + 2e^-$	ca. −2.0
Ag(II)–Ag(III)	$Ag^{+2} + H_2O \rightleftharpoons AgO^+ + 2H^+ + e^-$	ca. −2.1
	$2AgO + 2OH \rightleftharpoons Ag_2O_3 + H_2O + 2e^-$	−0.74
Au(O)–Au(I)	$Au + xH_2O \rightleftharpoons Au^+(aq) + e^-$	ca. −1.68
	$Au + 2Br^- \rightleftharpoons [AuBr_2]^- + e^-$	−0.96
	$Au + 2SCN^- \rightleftharpoons [Au(SCN)_2]^- + e^-$	−0.69
	$Au + I^- \rightleftharpoons AuI + e^-$	−0.50
	$Au + 2CN^- \rightleftharpoons [Au(CN)_2]^- + e^-$	0.60
Au(O)–Au(III)	$Au + xH_2O \rightleftharpoons Au^{+3}(aq) + 3e^-$	−1.42
	$Au + 4Cl^- \rightleftharpoons [AuCl_4]^- + 3e^-$	−1.00
	$Au + 4Br \rightleftharpoons [AuBr_4]^- + 3e^-$	−0.87
	$Au + 4OH^- \rightleftharpoons AuO_2^- + 2H_2O + 3e^-$	ca. −0.5
Au(I)–Au(II)	$Au^+ \rightleftharpoons Au^{+2} + e^-$	< −1.29(?)
Au(I)–Au(III)	$Au^+ \rightleftharpoons Au^{+3} + 2e^-$	ca. −1.29
	$[AuBr_2]^- + 2Br^- \rightleftharpoons [AuBr_4]^- + 2e^-$	−0.82
	$[Au(SCN)_2]^- + 2SCN^- \rightleftharpoons [Au(SCN)_4]^- + 2e^-$	−0.69
Au(II)–Au(III)	$Au^{+2} \rightleftharpoons Au^{+3} + e^-$	> −1.29(?)

even where all are known for a given metal are all the relationships among them understood completely. There appears to be no particular regularity in characteristic oxidation states among these metals. This is apparent in the fundamental potential values summarized for copper, silver, and gold in Table 18·4. It is immediately apparent also that data on the simple aquated ions are incomplete. This arises, of course, from the fact that oxidizing and reducing powers are at general maximum values for these species, making the formation and study of such species exceedingly difficult. Stabilization of these oxidation states either through insolubility or complex formation is common. In this connection, additional potentials on copper and silver couples discussed in Chapter 8 (pp. 303–304) should be consulted.

Oxidation State +1. Although characteristic of all three metals, this oxidation state is common and essentially stable only for silver. For copper, potential values show that, although it is easy to oxidize the metal to the +1 state in the presence of various precipitating and complexing agents, the +2 state is the more stable in aqueous solutions. In the absence of such agents, then, oxidation in solution gives the +2 state, and unipositive copper compounds are unstable with respect to the transformation

$$2Cu^+ \rightarrow Cu^0 + Cu^{+2}$$

Furthermore, reduction of dipositive copper normally yields the metal, the +1 state being produced only if suitable precipitants or complexing groups are present. This is perhaps more apparent if the equation just given is expressed as an equilibrium. Calculations from potential data (pp. 299–300) then show the equilibrium constant at 25°C. to be

$$K_{298} = C_{Cu^{+2}}/C^2_{Cu^+} = 1.2 \times 10^6 \qquad (18\cdot1)$$

a value in general agreement with experimental data on the quantities of copper(I) in equilibrium with copper(II) solutions containing copper.[9, 10] Thus the equilibrium concentration of Cu^{+2} ion is always ca. 10^6 times the square of that of Cu^+ ion and copper(I) materials can be stable only so long as they produce a limited concentration of Cu^+ ions In practice, this means that, although insoluble copper(I) compounds are reasonably common (e.g., chloride, bromide, iodide, oxide, sulfide), water-soluble materials exist only in the presence of complexing groups (e.g., chloride ion, cyanide ion, ammonia, acetonitrile). Indeed, in the presence of complexing groups (ethylenediamine is a notable exception), copper(I) is commonly more stable than copper(II).[11]

The differences between the copper and silver systems are again obvious in terms of potential data. It is apparent that, although disproportionation of silver(I) may occur as

$$2Ag^+ \rightleftharpoons Ag^0 + Ag^{+2}$$

[9] F. Fenwick: *J. Am. Chem. Soc.*, **48**, 860 (1926).
[10] E. Heinerth: *Z. Elektrochem.*, **37**, 61 (1931).
[11] J. E. B. Randles: *J. Chem. Soc.*, **1941**, 802.

the equilibrium is so far displaced toward silver(I) (K_{298} = ca. 10^{-17}) that in practice disproportionation never does occur. Silver(I) is thus the stable state in aqueous solution. For gold, the situation is similar to that for copper except that the +1 state reverts to the metal and the +3 state as

$$3Au^+ \rightleftharpoons 2Au^0 + Au^{+3}$$

(K_{298} = ca. 10^{13}). Indeed, it appears that the only really stable gold(I) materials are the dicyanoaurate(I) ion, $[Au(CN)_2]^-$, and possibly the iodide, AuI. It is significant in this respect that, although silver(I) fluoride is perfectly stable, the corresponding copper(I) and gold(I) compounds have not been well characterized. It is presumed that these compounds are sufficiently ionic to permit disproportionations to occur.

These remarks upon the stabilities of oxidation states are strictly applicable only for room temperature conditions. At elevated temperatures, there is every evidence that binary copper(I) compounds, for example, can be formed at the expense of the copper(II) materials. Thus copper(II) oxide loses oxygen and gives the copper(I) compound above 900°C. For the sulfide, an analogous decomposition occurs at red heat. Among the halides, decomposition temperatures for similar reactions decrease with increasing atomic weight of the halogen until for the iodide only the copper(I) compound can be prepared. The effects of temperature upon the oxidation state of copper are significant since it is well known that many igneous minerals contain only unipositive copper. For gold, the situation is similar to the extent that gold(III) halides lose halogens when heated gently to form the gold(I) compounds prior to reduction to the metals.

Simple copper(I) and gold(I) compounds are water insoluble but do dissolve in the presence of complexing groups. For silver, almost all compounds (except notably the fluoride, perchlorate, nitrate) are also water insoluble. The solubility of silver(I) fluoride (saturated solution 14 N at the 25°C.) is remarkable when compared with the remarkably low solubilities of the other silver halides. Silver perchlorate is even more remarkable in that it is soluble not only in water and other polar solvents but also in non-polar materials such as benzene and toluene. For all cations, solubilities of the halides decrease with increasing atomic weights of the halogens.

Evidences for covalence among a number of compounds in this oxidation state are presented later in this chapter. For the silver(I) compounds, in particular, colors may be used as criteria of covalency. Thus the increasing colors in the series chloride-bromide-iodide are in direct agreement with the prediction of Pitzer and Hildebrand[12] that increasing color is associated with increasing covalency (p. 211). That the same is true among oxy compounds is shown by the data in Table 18·5.[13, 14]

The nature of the species copper(I) has received considerable attention, probably because its halides are associated in the vapor state (p. 832). However, it appears from potentiometric and solubility studies[15] that the ionic species is Cu^+ and that there is no justification for using the formulation Cu_2^{+2}.

TABLE 18·5

COLOR AND COVALENCY AMONG SILVER(I) COMPOUNDS

Compound	Color of Crystals	Silver-Halogen or Silver-Oxygen Bond Distance, A: Measured	Ionic Radius Sum	Covalent Radius Sum	Bond Type
AgF	Colorless	2.46	2.62	2.25	Ionic
AgCl	Colorless	2.77	3.07	2.52	↓
AgBr	Pale yellow	2.88	3.21	2.64	
AgI	Yellow	3.05	3.42	2.81	Covalent
$AgClO_3$	Colorless	2.51	2.66	2.27	Ionic
Ag_2SO_4	Colorless	2.50	2.66	2.27	↓
$KAgCO_3$	Colorless	2.42	2.66	2.27	
Ag_3PO_4	Yellow	2.34	2.66	2.27	
Ag_3AsO_4	Red brown	2.34	2.66	2.27	
Ag_2CO_3	Yellow	2.30	2.66	2.27	
Ag_2O	Black	2.06	2.66	2.02*	Covalent

* Coordination number 2.

Oxidation State +2. As shown by the data in Table 18·4, this state is common and stable in solution in the absence of complexing species only with copper. In addition to simple copper(II) compounds, many complex compounds are known. Although not a real problem here, it is apparent from potential data (pp. 303, 825) that the dipositive state in copper is stabilized in certain instances by either insolubility or complex formation.

For silver,[16] the only stable simple compounds are the oxide and the fluoride, although a number of complex compounds are well characterized in the solid state. Silver(II) oxide dissolves in oxidizing acids to give solutions with strong oxidizing powers. These solutions

[12] K. S. Pitzer and J. H. Hildebrand: *J. Am. Chem. Soc.*, **63**, 2472 (1941).
[13] L. Helmholz and R. Levine: *J. Am. Chem. Soc.*, **64**, 354 (1942).
[14] J. Donohue and L. Helmholz: *J. Am. Chem. Soc.*, **66**, 295 (1944).
[15] G. Bodländer and O. Storbeck: *Z. anorg. Chem.*, **31**, 1, 458 (1902).
[16] J. C. Bailar, Jr.: *J. Chem. Education*, **21**, 523 (1944).

normally decompose quite rapidly, but solutions in concentrated nitric acid are reasonably stable. None of these solutions exhibits peroxide character. It may be assumed, therefore, that they contain Ag^{+2} species. Silver(II) compounds are prepared either by electrolytic oxidation or by chemical oxidation with materials such as peroxydisulfate. They are useful oxidants.

The classic studies of high valent silver compounds were made by A. A. Noyes and his students.[17–21] The reaction between silver(I) nitrate and ozone in concentrated nitric acid was shown to proceed at a rate proportional to the concentration of each reactant but to yield solutions containing only dipositive silver. Two successive steps described by the equations

$$Ag^+ + O_3 \rightarrow AgO^+ + O_2 \qquad \text{(slow)}$$

$$AgO^+ + Ag^+ + 2H^+ \rightarrow 2Ag^{+2} + H_2O \qquad \text{(fast)}$$

were believed responsible for the process. The chemical and magnetic characteristics of the resulting solutions were consistent with the presence of dipositive silver, although the ionic species present were not established positively. The listed oxidation potential (Table 18·4) is a measure of the oxidizing power of silver(II) in nitric acid solution. This potential is of course considerably modified in the presence of reagents such as pyridine, dipyridyl, and *o*-phenanthroline, which yield comparatively stable silver(II) complexes (p. 301).

Instances of dipositive character are somewhat more limited with gold. Although materials of stoichiometric compositions, $AuSO_4$, AuO, $3AuO{\cdot}H_2O$, etc., have been reported, the only apparently gold(II) compound which is stable in contact with water appears to be the black, insoluble sulfide, AuS. The existence of even this compound seems questionable, however, since the very exhaustive studies of Gutbier and Dürrwächter[22] show that reaction of hydrogen sulfide with chlorauric acid gives either gold metal, gold(III) sulfide, or mixtures of the two as precipitates and no other materials. In the absence of structural and molecular weight data, it is of course difficult to determine with certainty that these materials are true gold(II) com-

[17] A. A. Noyes, J. L. Hoard, and K. S. Pitzer: *J. Am. Chem. Soc.*, **57**, 1221 (1935).

[18] A. A. Noyes, K. S. Pitzer, and C. L. Dunn: *J. Am. Chem. Soc.*, **57**, 1229 (1935).

[19] A. A. Noyes and A. Kossiakoff: *J. Am. Chem. Soc.*, **57**, 1238 (1935).

[20] A. A. Noyes, C. D. Coryell, F. Stitt, and A. Kossiakoff: *J. Am. Chem. Soc.*, **59**, 1316 (1937).

[21] A. A. Noyes, D. DeVault, C. D. Coryell, and T. J. Deahl: *J. Am. Chem. Soc.*, **59**, 1326 (1937).

[22] A. Gutbier and E. Dürrwächter: *Z. anorg. allgem. Chem.*, **121**, 266 (1932).

pounds. Equimolecular combinations of unipositive and tripositive materials would have the same stoichiometry. That such a possibility cannot be overlooked is indicated by the fact that formally gold(II) compounds of the type M^IAuCl_3 (M^I usually Cs) are actually diamagnetic,[23] precluding the existence of dipositive gold, and have crystal structures[24] containing linear $[AuCl_2]^-$ and square planar $[AuCl_4]^-$ ions. These black compounds are thus written more properly $M_2{}^IAu^IAu^{III}Cl_6$. Potential values recorded in Table 18·4 for the Au(I)–Au(II) and Au(II)–Au(III) couples are only approximations as given by Latimer[25] and can give no accurate indication of the concentration of gold(II) ions (if such do exist) in such systems. In any event, dipositive gold would doubtless disproportionate to the unipositive and tripositive materials in aqueous solution.

Oxidation State +3. This oxidation state is common and stable only with gold. Information on tripositive copper is fragmentary. Basing his conclusions upon observations that copper(II) hydroxide is soluble in alkaline solutions containing hypochlorite, probably as CuO_2^-, and that such solutions are precipitated by calcium ion and decomposed by acids with evolution of oxygen, Latimer[25] has arrived at the approximate potentials given in Table 18·4. Malatesta[26] has prepared a series of periodates of general composition $M_7{}^ICu^{III}(IO_6)_2 \cdot nH_2O$ and tellurates of general composition $M_9{}^ICu^{III}(TeO_6)_2 \cdot nH_2O$. ($M^I$ = Na, K, H, or combination thereof) by peroxysulfate oxidation of copper(II) in alkaline solution. Analogous silver(III) and gold(III) compounds also are formed. The diamagnetic properties of these compounds[26] suggest the presence of the tripositive elements. In the absence of stabilization of this type, copper(III) is too strongly oxidizing to be preserved.

The formation of an unstable silver(III) species in solution when silver(I) compounds are added as catalysts in certain oxidation reactions, notably those involving peroxydisulfate, appears to be well established (p. 829).[17,27,28] Anodic, fluorine, or peroxydisulfate oxidation of silver(I) salt solutions also gives analyzable but unstable silver(III) compounds.[16] The instability of this oxidation state is indicated by oxidation potential data (Table 18·4). Complexing,

[23] N. Elliott: *J. Chem. Phys.*, **2**, 419 (1934).

[24] N. Elliott and L. Pauling: *J. Am. Chem. Soc.*, **60**, 1846 (1938).

[25] W. M. Latimer: *The Oxidation States of the Elements and Their Potentials in Aqueous Solutions*, Ch. XI. Prentice-Hall, New York (1938).

[26] L. Malatesta: *Gazz. chim. ital.*, **71**, 467, 580 (1941).

[27] D. M. Yost: *J. Am. Chem. Soc.*, **48**, 374 (1926).

[28] D. M. Yost and W. H. Claussen: *J. Am. Chem. Soc.*, **53**, 3349 (1931).

especially with ethylenebiguanide,[29] is effective in stabilizing the oxidation state. Such complexes are 4-coordinate and diamagnetic.

Tripositive gold is common in both simple and complex compounds. Thus an amphoteric oxide and a similar hydroxide, salts containing the anions $[AuO_2]^-$, $[AuCl_4]^-$, $[AuBr_4]^-$, etc., trihalides (except iodide), and numerous aryls, alkyls, and complex derivatives are comparatively easy to prepare. Oxidation potential data indicate this state to be formed preferentially from the metal by direct oxidation. Naturally, the reverse process is easy to effect.

Comparisons among compound types

Certain of the more important compound types of the alkali and coinage metals can now be compared to advantage.

Halides. Except for lithium iodide (p. 208), the halides of the alkali metals are predominantly ionic, in fact for practical purposes

TABLE 18·6
HEATS OF FORMATION OF ALKALI METAL HALIDES

Metal	Heat of Formation, kcal./mole			
	Fluoride	Chloride	Bromide	Iodide
Li	144.7	97.5	83.7	65.0
Na	136.6	98.2	86.3	69.5
K	134.5	104.9	94.2	78.9
Rb	132.8	104.9	96.1	80.8
Cs	131.5	106.6	97.5	83.9

essentially completely so. For this reason and because of the simplicity of their compositions, crystal structures, and charge arrangements, these compounds are commonly used as examples in all discussions of pure ionic character (pp. 137–138, 178–181, 183–186). They are of course more amenable to theoretical treatment than other more involved compound types. All these compounds, except lithium fluoride, are water soluble. The insolubility of lithium fluoride is associated with the high lattice energy of the compound resulting from combination of the very small lithium and fluoride ions. Among the fluorides of the alkali metals, the heats of formation decrease with increasing atomic weight or size of the alkali metal, whereas among the other halides the reverse is true (Table 18·6). This apparently anomalous situation with the fluorides is due again to their comparatively large lattice energies as is apparent from the Born-Haber treatment (pp. 183–186). The same trends are noted with other comparatively small anions (notably hydride, oxide, nitride,

[29] P. Rây: *Nature*, **151**, 643 (1943).

carbide). Polyhalides have been discussed in Chapter 13 (pp. 453–460).

As expected and previously indicated, the analogous coinage metal halides are considerably less ionic in character. This is apparent from the melting and boiling point data summarized in Table 18·7.

TABLE 18·7
MELTING AND BOILING POINTS OF ANHYDROUS GROUP I HALIDES

Metal	Fluoride		Chloride		Bromide		Iodide	
	Melting Point, °C.	Boiling Point, °C.	Melting Point, °C.	Boiling Point, °C.	Melting Point, °C.	Boiling Point, °C.	Melting Point, °C.	Boiling Point, °C.
Li	870	1676	613	1353	547	1265	446	1190
Na	992	1705	801	1430	755	1390	651	1300
K	880	1500	776	1500	730	1376	723	1330
Rb	760	1410	715	1390	682	1340	642	1300
Cs	684	1250	646	1290	636	1300	621	1280
Cu(I)	908?	1100 (subl.)	422	1366	504	1345	605	1290
Cu(II)			498	993 (dec.)	498			
Ag(I)	435		455	1550	434	700 (dec.)	552 (dec.)	
Au(I)			170 (dec.)		115 (dec.)		120 (dec.)	
Au(III)			254 (dec.)	265 (subl.)	160 (dec.)			

The situation with the silver compounds is indicative of that existing with the copper and gold compounds. Pauling[30] estimates the ionic characters of the silver halides to be AgF 70%, AgCl 30%, AgBr 23%, AgI 11%. That the coinage metal(I) halides are uniformly much less soluble (except silver fluoride) in polar solvents than their alkali metal analogs, are sometimes colored, are much poorer conductors, and give evidences of association are associated with their enhanced covalent characteristics. The alkali metal halides vaporize as ion pairs, the coinage metal(I) halides as simple or polymeric molecules. Thus extensive studies on copper(I) chloride, bromide, and iodide vapors show the presence of associated molecules. Early reports on the existence of Cu_2Cl_2 molecules[31] are to be questioned in the light of later data[32] indicating the vapor of copper(I) chloride to contain only trimeric and monomeric species. Of the halides of the uniposi-

[30] L. Pauling: *The Nature of the Chemical Bond*, 2nd Ed., p. 73. Cornell University Press, Ithaca (1940).

[31] H. Biltz and V. Meyer: *Z. physik. Chem.*, **4**, 249 (1889).

[32] L. Brewer and N. L. Lofgren: *J. Am. Chem. Soc.*, **72**, 3038 (1950).

tive coinage metals, only the copper[33] and gold[34] fluorides remain as uncharacterized compounds. The rather unique photosensitivities of solid silver chloride, bromide, and iodide appear to be due to defect lattices (pp. 224–225).

Of the higher halides of the coinage metals, the copper(II) compounds, silver(II) fluoride, and the gold(III) compounds may be mentioned. Anhydrous copper(II) fluoride crystallizes in the fluorite lattice with a Cu-F bond distance of 2.34 A[35] and is ionic. Both anhydrous copper(II) chloride and bromide, however, have chain structures involving halogen bridges (p. 272)[36]

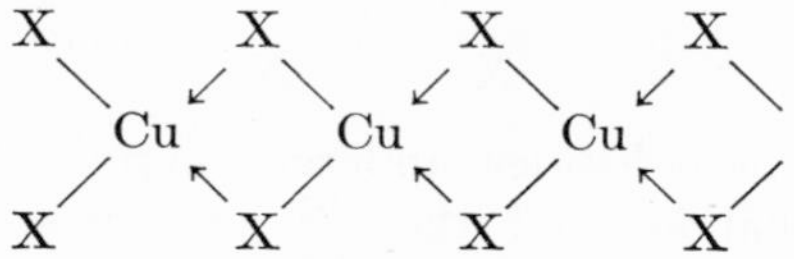

```
X       X       X       X
 \    ↙  \    ↙  \    ↙  \
  Cu      Cu      Cu      etc.
 /    ↖  /    ↖  /    ↖  /
X       X       X       X
```

and are largely covalent. In the bromide, each copper atom is associated with four bromine atoms in a particular chain at 2.40 A distance, the two bromine atoms in the next chain being 3.18 A removed from the copper atom. The hydrates are more salt-like. Copper(II) fluoride is difficultly soluble in water, but the chloride and bromide are readily soluble. In concentrated solutions, the chloride and bromide apparently exist in part at least as halo complexes (e.g., $[CuX_3]^-$, $[CuX_4]^{-2}$), but these revert to aquo complexes on dilution (p. 841). Corresponding complexes are formed on addition of chloride or bromide ion. The familiar dark brown color which appears when copper(II) chloride is reduced with elemental copper in the presence of concentrated hydrochloric acid is due to the presence of both unipositive and dipositive copper as chloro complexes.

Silver(II) fluoride is a dark brown, paramagnetic solid which is formed by reaction of fluorine with silver(I) halides or elemental silver at slightly elevated temperatures.[37] Although its dissociation pressure was originally reported[37] to be one atmosphere at 435° to 450°C., later studies[38] indicate greater stability (m.p. 690°C., stable at 700°C. under one-tenth of an atmosphere of fluorine). The heat of formation is given as -84.5 ± 1.2 kcal. per mole. The compound, a

[33] H. von Wartenberg: *Z. anorg. allgem. Chem.*, **241,** 381 (1939).
[34] V. Lenher: *J. Am. Chem. Soc.*, **25,** 1136 (1903).
[35] F. Ebert and H. Woitinek: *Z. anorg. allgem. Chem.*, **210,** 269 (1933).
[36] L. Helmholz: *J. Am. Chem. Soc.*, **69,** 886 (1947).
[37] O. Ruff and M. Giese: *Z. anorg. allgem. Chem.*, **219,** 143 (1934).
[38] H. von Wartenberg: *Z. anorg. allgem. Chem.*, **242,** 406 (1939).

strong oxidizing agent, is useful as an excellent fluorinating agent. Other silver(II) halides are unknown.

Tripositive gold yields a chloride, a bromide, and an iodide. No fluoride is known. These compounds are covalent materials, as shown by their volatilities. Vapor density determinations show the chloride to be dimeric,[39] and boiling point studies indicate the bromide to be dimeric in solution in liquid bromine.[40] Halogen bridge structures (p. 272) of the type

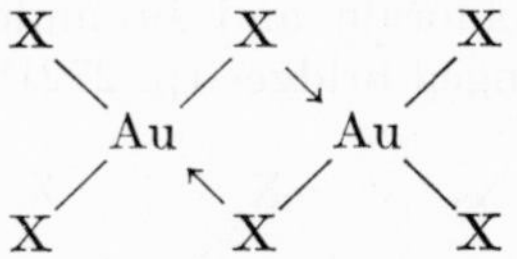

```
X       X       X
  \   /   ↘   /
   Au       Au
  /   ↖   /   \
X       X       X
```

are thus probable. These halides undergo thermal decomposition, first to the gold(I) halides and then to elemental gold, ease of decomposition increasing of course from chloride through bromide to iodide. The tendency of gold in this state of oxidation to complex is so pronounced that the chloride and bromide react with water to give species of the type $[AuX_3OH]^-$, and all three react with halide ion to give species of the type $[AuX_4]^-$.

Numerous reports concerning a group of silver subhalides, Ag_2X, have appeared. Although no conclusive evidence for existence of the chloride[41,42], the bromide,[43] and the iodide[44] has been found, the fluoride is well characterized. It is a bronze-colored compound, the crystal structure of which[45] shows the complete absence of elemental silver and silver(I) fluoride. Successive layers of silver, silver, and fluorine are present, the silver-silver distance being 2.86 A (nearly twice the metallic radius of 1.53 A) and the silver-fluoride distance being 2.46 A (as in ionic AgF). The compound is thus intermediate between a salt and a metal, the bonds between the silver layers being metallic and those between the silver and fluorine layers being predominantly ionic.[46] The excellent electrical conductivity of the material is in accord with this structure. Decomposition to silver and silver(I) fluoride begins at 100°C. and is complete at 200°C. Water

[39] W. Fischer: *Z. anorg. allgem. Chem.*, **184**, 333 (1929).

[40] A. Burawoy and C. S. Gibson: *J. Chem. Soc.*, **1935**, 217.

[41] H. Weisz: *Z. physik. Chem.*, **54**, 305 (1906).

[42] E. J. Hartung: *J. Chem. Soc.*, **127**, 2691 (1925).

[43] E. J. Hartung: *J. Chem. Soc.*, **125**, 2198 (1924).

[44] E. J. Hartung: *J. Chem. Soc.*, **1926**, 1349.

[45] H. Terrey and H. Diamond: *J. Chem. Soc.*, **1928**, 2820.

[46] L. Pauling: *The Nature of the Chemical Bond*, 2nd Ed., p. 421. Cornell University Press, Ithaca (1940).

effects the same decomposition. The compound results from reaction of silver with silver(I) fluoride at 50° to 90°C.[47] or from cathodic reduction of aqueous silver(I) fluoride solutions at low current densities.[48]

Binary Compounds with Oxygen Family Elements. Oxides, peroxides, and superoxides of the alkali metals have been discussed in some detail in Chapter 14 (pp. 507–511). Like the halides, all these compounds are essentially ionic. Unlike the halides, however, all these materials contain readily hydrolyzable anions and are converted to hydroxides by water (p. 510). Of the simple oxides (M_2O), only the lithium compound is stable with respect to reaction with molecular oxygen. Although lithium and sodium oxides are always white, the potassium compound changes from white to yellow on heating, the rubidium compound changes from light yellow to golden yellow, and the cesium compound changes from orange through purple to black. The simple oxides are obtainable by direct combination in the presence of excess metal (followed by distillation to remove the metal) or (except with lithium) reaction of the metal with its nitrate at elevated temperatures as

$$5M + MNO_3 \rightarrow 3M_2O + \tfrac{1}{2}N_2$$

They crystallize in fluorite-type lattices. The hydroxides are salts (p. 309). They are most commonly obtained in water solution either by electrolysis of the chlorides or by metathesis of the carbonates with calcium hydroxide. Aqueous hydroxide solutions are strongly alkaline.

Coinage metal oxides of the types M_2O (M = Cu, Ag, Au), MO (M = Cu, Ag, Au), and M_2O_3 (M = Au) have been characterized. Peroxides are known also (pp. 507–511). The same general differences in properties which set the alkali metal halides apart from the coinage metal(I) halides are also characteristic of the corresponding oxides. Thus coinage metal oxides of the type M_2O are uniformly less soluble, less ionic, and more highly colored than the simple alkali metal oxides. Copper(I) oxide is a diamagnetic compound, melting at ca. 1230°C., which is insoluble in water or alkaline solutions but is converted by acids such as nitric or sulfuric to copper and the copper(II) salt. Depending upon the method of preparation, the oxide may vary in color from yellow to red. This is apparently due to differences in particle size rather than to differences in crystal structure.[49, 50] Silver(I) oxide crystallizes in the same lattice as its copper

[47] A. Guntz: *Compt. rend.*, **110,** 1337 (1890); **112,** 861 (1891).
[48] A. Hettich: *Z. anorg. allgem. Chem.*, **167,** 67 (1927).
[49] M. Straumanis and A. Cirulis: *Z. anorg. allgem. Chem.*, **224,** 107 (1935).
[50] P. Bévillard: *Bull. soc. chim.*, **1950,** 561.

analog and is also covalent (Table 18.5). It is distinguished from the copper compound, however, by its ease of thermal decomposition and its enhanced basicity. Although difficultly soluble, its aqueous suspensions give alkaline reactions and absorb carbon dioxide. The enhanced solubility of the compound in alkaline solutions is indicative of some acidic properties, however, and an acid dissociation constant of 7.9×10^{-13} has been recorded.[51] Gold(I) oxide is even less stable toward heat than the silver compound and is somewhat more acidic in character. All these oxides are obtainable by precipitation, using alkali metal hydroxide solutions.

Copper(II) oxide is a common source of dipositive copper compounds. It is a perfectly stable black substance with a crystal lattice in which each copper atom is surrounded in a square-planar fashion by four oxygen atoms at Cu—O bond distances of 1.95 A and is covalent.[52] The compound is difficultly soluble in water but dissolves in acids. Precipitation of aqueous copper(II) salt solutions with alkali gives a blue hydrate which is converted to the oxide when the suspension is boiled. As expected, copper(II) oxide is more acidic than the copper(I) compound. Information on silver(II) oxide is somewhat controversial since a material of the necessary 1:1 stoichiometry might be either $Ag^{II}O$ or $Ag_2{}^{I}O_2$. A material of this composition is obtainable either by anodic oxidation of silver or peroxydisulfate oxidation of aqueous silver nitrate. The observations of Noyes et al.[17–21] indicate quite conclusively that the compound contains dipositive silver, but magnetic data are inconclusive.[53, 54] The ease with which the black compound can be converted into silver(II) compounds certainly supports the view that it is a true silver(II) compound. Gold(II) oxide and its hydrate, $3AuO \cdot H_2O$, are dark-colored, unstable compounds of indeterminate structures.

Gold(III) oxide is obtained as a brown powder by dehydration of its hydrate after precipitation from, for instance, tetrachloraurate(III) solutions with alkali. On being warmed, it reverts to gold(I) oxide. Both the oxide and its hydrate are soluble in alkali and are weakly acidic, successive acidic dissociation constants (k_A') of 1.8×10^{-12}, 4.4×10^{-14}, and 5×10^{-16} being given for $Au(OH)_3$.[55] Although pure silver(III) oxide has not been prepared, continued anodic oxidation of silver (p. 830) gives a product intermediate in composition between

[51] H. L. Johnston, F. Cuta, and A. B. Garrett: *J. Am. Chem. Soc.*, **55**, 2311 (1933).

[52] G. Tunell, E. Posnjak, and C. J. Ksanda: *Z. Krist.*, **90**, 120 (1935).

[53] S. Sugden: *J. Chem. Soc.*, **1932**, 161.

[54] W. Klemm: *Z. anorg. allgem. Chem.*, **201**, 32 (1931).

[55] H. L. Johnston and H. L. Leland: *J. Am. Chem. Soc.*, **60**, 1439 (1938).

AgO and Ag_2O_3, which is probably a solid solution of the latter in the former. This evolves oxygen on warming, leaving AgO.

The alkali metals form water-soluble sulfide, selenide, and telluride salts, but because of the strongly basic natures of these anions, such salts undergo extensive hydrolysis. Reaction with the free non-metal to give poly compounds is characteristic (pp. 493, 518). Copper and silver form sulfides, selenides, and probably tellurides of the type M_2Z, and copper gives compounds of the type MZ. Gold has been reported to form sulfides of both these types and also the compound Au_2S_3 (p. 829). Both silver and gold alloy with tellurium to give various intermetallic compounds, some of which (especially those of gold) are important minerals. All coinage metal compounds of these types are water insoluble, although gold(III) sulfide undergoes complete decomposition in contact with water. The compounds Cu_2S, Ag_2S, and CuS are all difficultly soluble in non-oxidizing acids and are thus of analytical importance. Precipitation or direct combination reactions may be used in their preparation. All three occur in nature. It is of interest that cyaniding is effective with silver sulfide only when oxidizing agents are present to remove sulfide ion. This is apparent from oxidation potential data.

Binary Compounds with Nitrogen Family Elements. The generally reduced electronegativities of the nitrogen family elements decrease the number of true compounds which they can form with the Periodic Group I elements. Of the alkali metals, only lithium forms a nitride (p. 578). Little information is available on arsenides, etc. Azides are well characterized (p. 587). The coinage metals, however, form a number of compounds with the elements of this family. Among these are the explosive azides [MN_3 and $Cu(N_3)_2$], the nitrides (M_3N), and some copper phosphides (Cu_3P, CuP_2). These compounds are unimportant.

Ternary, etc., Compounds. Almost every ternary, etc., inorganic (or organic) acid, whether stable or unstable in the pure state, is known in the form of its alkali metal salts. As such, many of these compounds have been described in preceding chapters since their properties are most commonly those of the anions which they contain. It is characteristic that these salts are almost all water soluble. Even in instances of reduced solubilities, the compounds are ordinarily quantitatively insoluble only under highly specialized conditions. Sodium and potassium salts are the normal articles of commerce, in most instances the potassium compounds being the more nearly pure because of generally slightly reduced solubilities.

It is manifestly impractical to attempt any comprehensive listing of all the coinage metal salts. Only a few general remarks seem essential. Salts of these types are normally the silver(I) or copper(II) materials for the reasons outlined previously (pp. 825–831). Certain of the characteristics of the silver(I) compounds have been described (pp. 827–828). Of the copper(II) compounds, the sulfate is most important. Other salts, with the exception in particular of the nitrate, acetate, chlorate, and perchlorate, are water insoluble.

Coordination compounds and complex ions

Periodic Group I is essentially unique in that the members of one family form almost no complexes whereas those of the other family form a wide variety of such materials.

The Alkali Metals. The ions of these metals possess none of the characteristics ordinarily regarded as those of acceptor cations. They are too large, their charges are too small, and, most important, their electronic arrangements are such that orbital hybridizations essential to covalent linkages are highly unlikely if not completely impossible. In those instances where apparent complexes do form, the bonding is necessarily ionic.

In the solid state many alkali metal compounds are hydrated, and it is reasonable to assume that at least a portion of this hydrate water is associated in each instance with the alkali metal ion. Hydration decreases in general for each type of salt as size of the alkali metal ion increases. In aqueous solution, of course, the ions are hydrated but to indeterminate extents. The small lithium ion apparently carries more such water than the others. The solid ammoniates, investigated by Biltz,[56, 57] are somewhat similar to the hydrates. Among such compounds, thermal stabilities decrease in the order Li $>$ Na $>$ K, etc., and I $>$ Br $>$ Cl, the most stable compound being $LiI \cdot 4NH_3$. In contact with water, ammonia is removed completely. Comparable amine derivatives and alcoholates have the same characteristics. It would be difficult to consider any of these compounds as true complexes.

Chelating groups often impose acceptor properties on cations and might thus be useful in forming complexes of the alkali metals. Alkali metal derivatives of β-diketones and β-keto esters are normally salt-like and are insoluble in hydrocarbon solvents. However, addition of sufficient neutral molecules to bring the apparent coordination number of the alkali metal ion up to *four* or *six* imparts some complex character.[58, 59] Thus anhydrous sodium benzoylacetonate is insoluble

[56] W. Biltz and W. Hansen: *Z. anorg. allgem. Chem.*, **127,** 1 (1923).

[57] W. Biltz: *Z. anorg. allgem. Chem.*, **130,** 93 (1923).

[58] N. V. Sidgwick and F. M. Brewer: *J. Chem. Soc.*, **127,** 2379 (1925).

[59] F. M. Brewer: *J. Chem. Soc.*, **1931,** 361.

in toluene, but the 2-hydrate dissolves in that solvent and is presumed therefore, to be covalent. The structural differences may be indicated as

```
    C6H5                      ┌ C6H5                    ┐
        \                     │     \                   │
         C—O⁻ Na⁺             │      C—O        OH2     │
        //                    │     //    \    ↙        │
   H—C                        │ H—C         Na          │
        \                     │     \     ↗    ↖        │
         C=O                  │      C=O        OH2     │
        /                     │     /                   │
    CH3                       └ CH3                     ┘
```

Similarly, the sodium salt of salicylaldehyde (p. 240) adds a mole of salicylaldehyde and becomes non-salt-like in properties.[60] Comparable alkali metal derivatives of reagents such as acetylacetone, acetoacetic ester, methyl salicylaldehyde, *o*-nitrophenol, *o*-nitrocresol, etc., containing water or one or two additional moles of the reagent have covalent properties.[58, 59] It must be pointed out, however, that decision as to covalence in these materials is based largely upon solubility in materials such as benzene or toluene. This approach is doubtless quite valid, but independent supporting evidence would appear desirable. After all, the salt silver perchlorate is also soluble in benzene and toluene (p. 827).

The Coinage Metals. With the coinage metals, all factors favoring true complex formation involving covalent bonds are present. As a consequence a wide variety of coordination materials of all types can be distinguished. Principal coordination numbers exhibited are two and four. A few types of complexes may be mentioned to advantage.

COMPLEXES CONTAINING UNIPOSITIVE METALS. Halo complex ions of the types $[MX_2]^-$ and $[MX_3]^{-2}$ (X = Cl, Br, I) are characteristic of copper and silver in this state of oxidation. Gold gives comparable $[AuCl_2]^-$ ions. Complexes involving oxygen as donor are uncommon. Thiosulfato complexes of the types $[M(S_2O_3)]^{-1}$ (M = Cu, Ag, Au), $[M(S_2O_3)_2]^{-3}$ (M = Ag, Au), and $[M_3(S_2O_3)_4]^{-5}$ (M = Ag) are reported, the silver materials being important in the photographic fixing process. Sulfur compounds such as thioethers and thiourea add readily. Most common of the resulting materials are the thiourea (tu) copper compounds of the type $[Cu(tu)_3]X$. Ammonia forms ammines of the type $[M(NH_3)_n]^+$ ($n = 2$ usually but also 1 or 3) with all three elements. Pyridine and other substituted ammonias form similar compounds. The diamminesilver(I) complex is particularly common. Nitriles and azo groups also act as donors toward these metals. Of

[60] A. Hantzsch: *Ber.*, **39**, 3072 (1906).

particular interest also is the tendency of phosphine and arsine and their substituted derivatives to add to the coinage metal(I) halides to produce compounds of considerable thermal stability. Although the gold compounds (e.g., $R_3P \rightarrow AuX$) are apparently monomeric, the copper and silver analogs are tetrameric in solvents such as acetone, benzene, and ethylenedibromide.[61] This is confirmed by x-ray analysis of the compound $[(C_2H_5)_3As \rightarrow CuI]_4$, which shows the four copper atoms to lie at the apices of a regular tetrahedron, the iodine atoms to be at the centers of but above the tetrahedral faces, and the arsenic atoms to be tetrahedral as well.[62] Cyano complexes, $[M(CN)_n]^{1-n}$ ($n = 2$ most commonly, but also 3 and 4 for copper), are particularly stable with respect to dissociation into their components as previously mentioned. Carbon monoxide is readily absorbed by solutions of copper(I) chloride in ammonia or hydrochloric acid, probably because of the formation of the carbonyl derivative Cu(CO)Cl since the 1-hydrate, $Cu(CO)Cl \cdot H_2O$, can be isolated as a colorless, unstable, crystalline compound (p. 716). Comparable silver compounds are unknown, but a gold analog, Au(CO)Cl, can be prepared. Ethylene and certain substituted ethylenes react with copper(I) chloride (or bromide) to give compounds of the type CuCl·Un (Un = C_2H_4, etc.) which readily lose hydrocarbons even at 0°C. Aqueous solutions of unsaturated organic acids (H_2Un = maleic, fumaric, etc., acid) react with copper(I) chloride not only to give comparable complexes, $CuCl \cdot H_2Un$, but also soluble species such as $Cu \cdot H_2Un^+$, $CuCl \cdot HUn^-$, and Cu·HUn.[63–65] The absorption of ethylenic hydrocarbons by aqueous silver salt solutions gives soluble complexes of the type $Ag \cdot Un^+$, the relative stabilities of which appear to decrease as the hydrogen atoms in ethylene are replaced by alkyl groups.[66, 67] Complexes of this type are regarded as arising from argentation of double bonds. Winstein and Lucas[67] regard the true structure of, for instance, the ethylene complex, to be a resonance hybrid based upon the equilibrium arrangements

[61] F. G. Mann, D. Purdie, and A. F. Wells: *J. Chem. Soc.*, **1936**, 1503.

[62] A. F. Wells: *Z. Krist.*, **94**, 447 (1936).

[63] L. J. Andrews and R. M. Keefer: *J. Am. Chem. Soc.*, **70**, 3261 (1948).

[64] L. J. Andrews and R. M. Keefer: *J. Am. Chem. Soc.*, **71**, 2379 (1949).

[65] R. M. Keefer, L. J. Andrews, and R. E. Kepner: *J. Am. Chem. Soc.*, **71**, 2381 (1949).

[66] W. F. Eberz, H. J. Welge, D. M. Yost, and H. J. Lucas: *J. Am. Chem. Soc.*, **59**, 45 (1937).

[67] S. Winstein and H. J. Lucas: *J. Am. Chem. Soc.*, **60**, 836 (1938).

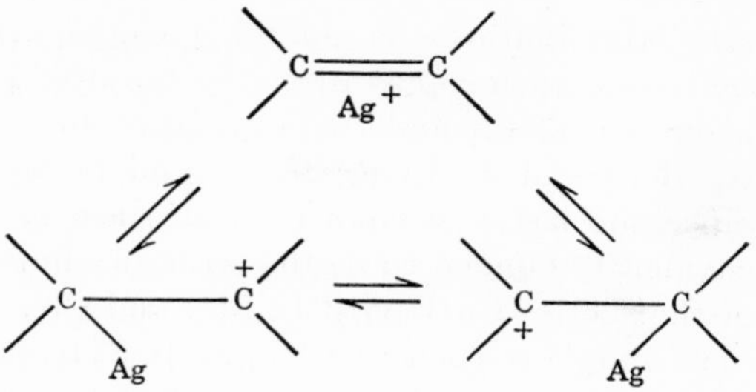

$$\gt C{=}C\lt \;\; Ag^{+}$$

$$\gt C(Ag){-}\overset{+}{C}\lt \;\rightleftharpoons\; \gt\overset{+}{C}{-}C(Ag)\lt$$

Raman data are in accord with such a proposal.[68] Certain aromatic hydrocarbons also give complexes of the types $Ag{\cdot}Un^{+}$ and $Ag_2{\cdot}Un^{+2}$,[69] but no gold derivatives are known.

COMPLEXES CONTAINING DIPOSITIVE METALS. Such derivatives are of importance only with copper, since the only others characterized are a few silver(II) complexes (pp. 301, 829). Copper(II) is normally 4-covalent in its coordination compounds, but a few 6-covalent derivatives have been reported. The stereochemistry of copper(II) has been discussed in a previous chapter (pp. 256–257).

Halo complexes of copper(II) are of the types $[MX_3]^-$ and $[MX_4]^{-2}$ (X = F, Cl, Br), the fourth coordination position in the first type probably being filled with water. These anions apparently are most common in the solid alkali metal salts, but upon dissolution in water these anions undergo dissociation which becomes essentially complete at high dilutions. These changes are accompanied by significant color changes. Treatment of aqueous copper(II) halide solutions with large excesses of halide ions reverses these color changes, apparently because of complex formation. It is probable that equilibria of the type

$$[CuX_4]^{-2} \underset{X^-}{\overset{H_2O}{\rightleftharpoons}} [CuX_3(H_2O)]^- \underset{X^-}{\overset{H_2O}{\rightleftharpoons}} [CuX_2(H_2O)_2] \underset{X^-}{\overset{H_2O}{\rightleftharpoons}} [CuX(H_2O)_3]^+ \underset{X^-}{\overset{H_2O}{\rightleftharpoons}} [Cu(H_2O)_4]^{+2}$$

(coordination number = 4 being assumed in all cases) are involved, with the $[CuX_4]^{-2}$ species being the most stable in the chloride system at least.[70, 71] However, the problem is far from solved, and the compositions of the solid salts as written above may even be misleading

[68] H. J. Taufen, M. J. Murray, and F. F. Cleveland: *J. Am. Chem. Soc.*, **63**, 3500 (1941).

[69] L. J. Andrews and R. M. Keefer: *J. Am. Chem. Soc.*, **71**, 3644 (1949).

[70] H. Remy and G. Laves: *Ber.*, **66B**, 401 (1933).

[71] T. Moeller: *J. Phys. Chem.*, **48**, 111 (1944).

since structural determinations on solid $M_2^I[CuCl_4]\cdot 2H_2O$ (M^I = K, Rb, NH_4) indicate that each copper atom is associated in a plane with two chlorine atoms at 2.32 A and two oxygen atoms at 1.97 A, with the other two chlorine atoms lying above and below the plane at 2.95 A.[72, 73] Since the last two chlorine atoms are too far from the copper to be covalently bonded to it, the structure must amount to a combination of the species $Cu(H_2O)_2Cl_2$, M^+, and Cl^-.

Although a few simple oxygen (e.g., aquo, p. 841) and sulfur (e.g., thiourea) complexes of copper(II) are known, most materials containing Cu—O or Cu—S bonds possess chelate structures. Among these may be mentioned the β-diketone chelates, oxalato derivatives, tartrato derivatives, catechol chelates, and organic disulfide chelates. Many complexes containing nitrogen donors are well known. The simple ammines, $[Cu(NH_3)_n]^{+2}$ (n = 2, 4, 5, 6) are familiar, particularly the tetrammines, as are the derivatives of substituted amines (e.g., pyridine). Especially important are chelate complexes of this type, particularly the ethylenediammine chelates, $[Cu(en)_2]^{+2}$ and more rarely $[Cu(en)_3]^{+2}$, the amino acid chelates (p. 241), the azoamine chelates which are important as metallated dyes, and the phthalocyanin derivative (p. 278). Less common examples of donor nitrogen are found in azide complexes (e.g., $[Cu(N_3)_4]^{-2}$, $[Cu_2(N_3)_5]^{-1}$), nitro complexes (e.g., $[Cu(NO_2)_5]^{-3}$), and nitrosyl complexes (p. 603). Although cyanide normally reduces copper(II), a few cyano derivatives of the type $[Cu(CN)_4]^{-2}$ have been described.

COMPLEXES CONTAINING TRIPOSITIVE METALS. These are important only with gold (pp. 831, 834). Although a few simple gold(III) compounds are known as previously indicated, the chemistry of this state of oxidation of the element is very largely the chemistry of its complexes.

The halo complexes, $[AuX_4]^-$ (X = Cl, Br, I), are of particular interest because of their stabilities. Not only do these anionic arrangements exist in solid salts, but they persist in solution and even in such solid acids as $H[AuBr_4]\cdot 2H_2O$. The expected square planar arrangement in such complexes is confirmed by structural studies on Cs_2Au^I–$Au^{III}Cl_6$[23, 24] (p. 830) and $K[AuBr_4]\cdot 2H_2O$.[74] It seems reasonable that many so-called double gold(III) halides, such as $PCl_5\cdot AuCl_3$, $NOCl\cdot AuCl_3$, etc., are really tetrahaloaurate(III) salts. Substitution for halogen in $[AuX_4]^-$ groups gives a variety of other complexes, among them $[AuCl_3OH]^-$, $[AuBr_3\cdot(py)]$, $[AuBr_2(py)_2]Br$. The aurate and thioaurate ions may be regarded as simple oxygen- and sulfur-contain-

[72] S. B. Hendricks and R. G. Dickinson: *J. Am. Chem. Soc.*, **49**, 2149 (1927).
[73] L. Chrobak: *Z. Krist.*, **88**, 35 (1934).
[74] E. G. Cox and K. C. Webster: *J. Chem. Soc.*, **1936**, 1635.

ing complexes. Simple β-diketone, oxalato, etc., complexes are not known, but those containing dialkyl gold are characterized by their stabilities. Typical formulations are

```
[                 CH3 ]   [                                                ]
[                /    ]   [                                                ]
[ CH3     O—C        ]   [ C2H5      O—C=O          C2H5                  ]
[    \   /    \\      ]   [     \   /    |   ↘      /                      ]
[     Au        CH    ]   [      Au      |     Au                          ]
[    /   ↖    /       ]   [     /   ↖    |   /      \                      ]
[ CH3     O=C         ]   [ C2H5      O=C—O          C2H5                  ]
[            \        ]   [                                                ]
[             CH3     ]   [                                                ]
```

acetylacetonate oxalate

It is interesting that dialkyl gold compounds readily add a variety of other donor groups as well (e.g., ethylenediamine, organic sulfides), this tendency being so pronounced that they even dimerize when pure as

```
R        Br        R
 \      /  ↘      /
   Au          Au
 /      ↖  /      \
R        Br        R
```

Simple amine and ammine complexes (e.g., $[Au(NH_3)_4]^{+3}$) are limited in number. Phosphorus acts as a donor in compounds of the type $[(CH_3)_3P \rightarrow AuBr_3]$. These are planar as regards gold.[75] Simple cyano complexes revert to the gold(I) material, but the dialkyl cyano compounds are stable. These are tetrameric, e.g., $[R_2AuCN]_4$, the arrangement being planar around each gold, with the cyano groups acting as bridges between the gold atoms (p. 718). The required arrangement

```
[    R                 R     ]
[    |                 |     ]
[ R—Au—C≡N→Au—R              ]
[    ↑                 |     ]
[    N                 C     ]
[    |||               |||   ]
[    C                 N     ]
[    |                 ↓     ]
[ R—Au←N≡C—Au—R              ]
[    |                 |     ]
[    R                 R     ]
```

has been confirmed for the propyl compound by x-ray methods.[76]

[75] M. F. Perutz and O. Weisz: *J. Chem. Soc.*, **1946,** 438.

[76] R. F. Phillips and H. M. Powell: *Proc. Roy. Soc.* (*London*), **A173,** 147 (1939).

SUGGESTED SUPPLEMENTARY REFERENCES

N. V. Sidgwick: *The Chemical Elements and Their Compounds*, pp. 59–192. Clarendon Press, Oxford (1950).

A. F. Wells: *Structural Inorganic Chemistry*, 2nd Ed., pp. 612–627. Clarendon Press, Oxford (1950).

W. M. Latimer: *The Oxidation States of the Elements and Their Potentials in Aqueous Solutions*, Ch. XI, XXI. Prentice-Hall, New York (1938).

CHAPTER 19

Periodic Group II The Alkaline Earth and Zinc Family Elements

Of the Periodic Group IIa elements, only magnesium and calcium are really abundant (Be $6 \times 10^{-4}\%$, Mg 2.09%, Ca 3.63%, Sr 0.03%, Ba 0.025%, Ra $1.3 \times 10^{-10}\%$ of the igneous rocks of the earth). Strontium and barium, although comparatively uncommon, are usually classified as a familiar elements, largely because of the existence of concentrated and readily available natural sources. Beryllium, on the other hand, is called unfamiliar, not so much because of the absence of beryllium minerals in reasonable concentrations as because of the difficulties which for many years attended the recovery of beryllium materials from such minerals. The scarcity of radium is an obvious reason for its unfamiliar character. Of the Periodic Group IIb elements, none is particularly abundant (Zn 0.013%, Cd $1.5 \times 10^{-5}\%$, Hg ca. $10^{-5} - 10^{-6}\%$ of the igneous rocks of the earth), yet like the coinage metals possession of desirable properties and general ease of recovery have combined to render all comparatively familiar. The Group IIa metals are often called the alkaline earth metals, although in a strict sense this term should be limited to calcium, strontium, and barium. The Group IIb metals bear no really distinguishing family name.

GROUP AND FAMILY RELATIONSHIPS AMONG THE ELEMENTS

Numerical properties characterizing the Group IIa and the Group IIb elements are summarized, respectively, in Table 19·1 and Table 19·2. Trends discernible among the Group IIa elements are strictly comparable to those noted for the alkali metals (pp. 819–820) and need not be discussed as such because they arise from the same causes. However, the atoms of these elements are smaller than those of the comparable alkali metals because of enhanced nuclear charges. This difference is reflected in the greater densities, in the enhanced ionization potentials, in the higher melting and boiling points, in the increased hardness, etc., which distinguish the members of this family from the alkali metals. However, the atoms are still comparatively large (except for the beryllium atom). Because of this factor and the presence of but two electrons outside the inert gas arrangements, the elements are still comparatively easily oxidized, as indicated by their standard oxidation potentials. Even though ionization potential data

TABLE 19·1

NUMERICAL PROPERTIES OF THE GROUP IIA ELEMENTS

Property	Beryllium	Magnesium	Calcium	Strontium	Barium	Radium
Atomic number	4	12	20	38	56	88
Outer electronic configuration	$1s^22s^2$	$2s^22p^63s^2$	$3s^23p^64s^2$	$4s^24p^65s^2$	$5s^25p^66s^2$	$6s^26p^67s^2$
Mass numbers, natural isotopes	9	24, 25, 26	40, 42, 43, 44, 46, 48	84, 86, 87, 88	130, 132, 134, 135, 136, 137, 138	226*
Atomic weight	9.013	24.32	40.08	87.63	137.36	226.05
Density of solid at 20°C. grams/cc.	1.86	1.75	1.55	2.6	3.59	(5.0)
Atomic volume of solid, cc.	4.85	14.00	26.08	34.01	38.26	(45.21)
Melting point, °C.†	1280	651	851	800	850	(960)
Boiling point, °C.†	1500	1107	1487	1366	1537	(1140)
Ionization potential, ev						
First	9.320	7.644	6.111	5.692	5.210	5.277
Second	18.206	15.03	11.87	10.98	9.95	(10.10)
Heat of hydration of gaseous ion, kcal./mole		460	395	355	305	
E_{298}^0 for						
$M \rightleftharpoons M^{+2} + 2e^-$, volts	1.70	2.34	2.87	2.89	2.90	
Electronegativity	1.5	1.2	1.0	1.0	0.9	
Radii, A						
M	0.889	1.364	1.736	1.914	1.981	
M^{+2}	0.31	0.65	0.99	1.13	1.35	

* Radioactive. † Not accurately determined in many instances.

(at least with the lighter elements) might suggest the removal of two electrons to be too difficult to achieve by chemical oxidation alone, no stable unipositive derivatives of these elements are known. Any oxidizing agent capable of removing one electron is also capable of removing another, probably because the energies recovered in crystal formation or by solvation are sufficient to counterbalance the unfavorable ionization potential effects.

The position of beryllium is even more unusual in this family than is that of lithium in the alkali metal family. For beryllium, the combination of small size and comparatively high nuclear charge are much more pronounced than for lithium and reduce the chemical reactivity of the metal considerably. Beryllium compounds also appear anomalous because of the combined effects of small size and high cationic charge. These effects cannot be overcome even by the hydration energy of the beryllium ion, and as a consequence the standard oxidation potential for beryllium is less positive than that for magnesium by a considerable factor. That the standard potentials for the other elements approach those of the comparable alkali metals so

TABLE 19·2

NUMERICAL PROPERTIES OF THE GROUP IIB ELEMENTS

Property	Zinc	Cadmium	Mercury
Atomic number	30	48	80
Outer electronic configuration	$3d^{10}4s^2$	$4d^{10}5s^2$	$5d^{10}6s^2$
Mass numbers, natural isotopes	64, 66, 67, 68, 70	106, 108, 110, 111, 112, 113, 114, 116	196, 198, 199, 200, 201, 202, 204
Atomic weight	65.38	112.41	200.61
Density of solid at 20°C., grams/cc.	7.14	8.64	13.546 (l)
Atomic volume of solid, cc.	9.17	13.01	14.82 (l)
Melting point, °C.	419.4	320.9	−38.89
Boiling point, °C.	907	767.3	356.95
Ionization potential, ev			
First	9.391	8.991	10.434
Second	17.89	16.84	18.65
E°_{298} for			
$M \rightleftharpoons M^{+2} + 2e^-$, volts	0.762	0.402	−0.854
Radii, A			
M	1.249	1.413	1.440
M^{+2}	0.74	0.97	1.10

closely in spite of the requirements of the loss of an extra electron is doubtless due to the enhanced hydration energies of the dipositive gaseous ions.

The uniform positive two state of oxidation of the Group IIa elements is predominantly an ionic state for the heavier members but becomes increasingly covalent as cation size decreases until for beryllium it is predominantly covalent in most instances. The chemistries of these elements are thus less completely the chemistries of their cations than was true of the alkali metals. More complexities in behavior can thus be expected, although the fundamental chemistries of the materials derived from these elements are generally simple.

Trends in numerical properties among the Group IIb elements, though considerably less regular than those among the Group IIa elements and less susceptible to simple interpretation, are much more regular than those noted for the coinage metals (pp. 819–821). Although the general remarks describing the coinage metals may be extended to the members of this family, there are significant differences. The effects of the lanthanide contraction (pp. 146–151) are sufficiently diminished that resemblances between mercury and cadmium are much less pronounced than those between silver and gold. Indeed, the similarities in this family are more between zinc and cadmium, and mercury stands apart. These metals are markedly less noble than the coinage metals, their much lower boiling points being important contributing factors. Increase in nobility with increasing atomic weight (size) is characteristic of the family (p. 821), as is greater nobility than with the Group IIa elements.

The electronic arrangements $(n-1)d^{10}ns^2$ characteristic of the Group IIb elements might conceivably permit removal of more than two electrons. However, it appears that the $(n-1)d$ arrangements. are more nearly stabilized among these elements than among the coinage metals, and it seems to be energetically impossible to remove more than the two ns electrons in compound formation. Differences between the first and second ionization potentials (Table 19·2) suggest the existence of both +1 and +2 oxidation states. Although evidence for unipositive zinc and cadmium compounds is probably unreliable, unipositive mercury compounds are well known. The enhanced deformability of the underlying 18-electron arrangement renders all compounds of the Group IIb elements more covalent than those of the Group IIa elements. Complexes are very characteristic, but the transition element characteristics of the coinage metals in their compounds are much reduced in the derivatives of the elements in this family.

Although the Group IIa elements appear to yield monatomic vapors, sufficient diatomic molecules are present in the vapors of the Group IIb elements to give characteristic absorption bands. That the vapor densities are normal shows the concentrations of such species to be small. Bond energies in such molecules are very low.

CHEMICAL CHARACTERISTICS OF THE ELEMENTS

The more important aspects of the chemical behaviors of the elements in the two families of this group are summarized in Table 19·3. Except for the decreased reducing powers of the Group IIb metals, the reactions of the members of both families are closely comparable. Because of the absence of a variety of oxidation states, greater regularities are apparent in the behavior of the Group IIb elements than were noted for their coinage metal analogs. The chemical charac-

TABLE 19·3

CHEMICAL CHARACTERISTICS OF GROUP II METALS

Group IIa Metals*		Reagent	Group IIb Metals*	
General Equation	Remarks		General Equation	Remarks
$M + X_2 \rightarrow MX_2$	With all halogens.	X_2	$M + X_2 \rightarrow MX_2$	With all halogens.
$M + \frac{1}{2}O_2 \rightarrow MO$	With all members.	O_2	$M + \frac{1}{2}O_2 \rightarrow MO$	On heating. Very slowly with Hg.
$M + O_2 \rightarrow MO_2$	With Ba, Ra(?). Sr under pressure.			
$M + S \rightarrow MS$	With all members. Also with Se, Te.	S	$M + S \rightarrow MS$	On heating. Also with Se, Te.
$3M + N_2 \rightarrow M_3N_2$	On heating.	N_2		Unreactive.
$M + H_2 \rightarrow MH_2$	With Ca, Sr, Ba, Ra(?) on heating.	H_2		Unreactive.
$M + 2H^+ \rightarrow M^{+2} + H_2$	Vigorous, except with Be.	H^+	$M + 2H^+ \rightarrow M^{+2} + H_2$	With Zn, Cd.
$M + 2H_2O \rightarrow M(OH)_2 + H_2$	With cold water with Ca, Sr, Ba, Ra. Mg, Be give oxides with steam.	H_2O	$M + H_2O \rightarrow MO + H_2$	With Zn and high-temperature steam.
$M + OH^- + H_2O \rightarrow HMO_2^- + H_2$	With Be only.	$OH^- + H_2O$	$M + OH^- + H_2O \rightarrow HMO_2^- + H_2$	With Zn only.
$M + 6NH_3 \rightarrow M(NH_3)_6$	With Ca, Sr, Ba.	$NH_3(l)$		Unreactive.
$3M + 8H^+ + 2NO_3^- \rightarrow 3M^{+2} + 2NO + 4H_2O$	With all but Be. Vigorous.	HNO_3	$3M + 8H^+ + 2NO_3^- \rightarrow 3M^{+2} + 2NO + 4H_2O$	With Zn, Cd, Hg. Excess Hg gives Hg_2^{+2}.
$M + 2H^+ \rightarrow M^{+2} + H_2$	Slow with Ca, Sr, Ba because of insoluble MSO_4.	H_2SO_4 (dil.)	$M + 2H^+ \rightarrow M^{+2} + H_2$	With Zn, Cd. Hot conc. H_2SO_4 gives $Hg^{+2} + SO_2$.

* M = any Group II metal.

TABLE 19·4

TYPICAL OXIDATION POTENTIALS FOR GROUP IIB METALS

Couple	Half-Reaction	E^0_{298}, volts
Zn(O)–Zn(II)	$Zn + xH_2O \rightleftharpoons Zn^{+2}(aq) + 2e^-$	0.762
	$Zn + 3C_2O_4^{=} \rightleftharpoons [Zn(C_2O_4)_3]^{-4} + 2e^-$	ca. 1.02
	$Zn + 4NH_3 \rightleftharpoons [Zn(NH_3)_4]^{+2} + 2e^-$	1.03
	$Zn + CO_3^{-2} \rightleftharpoons ZnCO_3 + 2e^-$	1.07
	$Zn + 4OH^- \rightleftharpoons ZnO_2^{-2} + 2H_2O + 2e^-$	1.216
	$Zn + 4CN^- \rightleftharpoons [Zn(CN)_4]^{-2} + 2e^-$	1.26
	$Zn + S^{-2} \rightleftharpoons ZnS + 2e^-$	1.44
Cd(O)–Cd(II)	$Cd + xH_2O \rightleftharpoons Cd^{+2}(aq) + 2e^-$	0.402
	$Cd + 4NH_3 \rightleftharpoons [Cd(NH_3)_4]^{+2} + 2e^-$	0.597
	$Cd + CO_3^{=} \rightleftharpoons CdCO_3 + 2e^-$	0.80
	$Cd + 2OH^- \rightleftharpoons Cd(OH)_2 + 2e^-$	0.815
	$Cd + 4CN^- \rightleftharpoons [Cd(CN)_4]^{-2} + 2e^-$	0.90
	$Cd + S^{-2} \rightleftharpoons CdS + 2e^-$	1.23
Hg(O)–Hg(II)	$Hg + xH_2O \rightleftharpoons Hg^{+2}(aq) + 2e^-$	−0.854
	$Hg + 2IO_3^- \rightleftharpoons Hg(IO_3)_2 + 2e^-$	−0.40
	$Hg + 4Cl^- \rightleftharpoons [HgCl_4]^{-2} + 2e^-$	−0.38
	$Hg + 4Br^- \rightleftharpoons [HgBr_4]^{-2} + 2e^-$	−0.21
	$Hg + 2OH^- \rightleftharpoons HgO + H_2O + 2e^-$	−0.0984
	$Hg + 4I^- \rightleftharpoons [HgI_4]^{-2} + 2e^-$	0.04
	$Hg + 4CN^- \rightleftharpoons [Hg(CN)_4]^{-2} + 2e^-$	0.37
	$Hg + S^{-2} \rightleftharpoons HgS + 2e^-$	0.70
Hg(O)–Hg(I)	$2Hg + xH_2O \rightleftharpoons Hg_2^{+2}(aq) + 2e^-$	−0.7986
	$2Hg + SO_4^{-2} \rightleftharpoons Hg_2SO_4 + 2e^-$	−0.615
	$2Hg + CrO_4^{-2} \rightleftharpoons Hg_2CrO_4 + 2e^-$	−0.54
	$2Hg + C_2O_4^{-2} \rightleftharpoons Hg_2C_2O_4 + 2e^-$	−0.41
	$2Hg + CO_3^{-2} \rightleftharpoons Hg_2CO_3 + 2e^-$	−0.32
	$2Hg + 2IO_3^- \rightleftharpoons Hg_2(IO_3)_2 + 2e^-$	−0.27
	$2Hg + 2Cl^- \rightleftharpoons Hg_2Cl_2 + 2e^-$	−0.2676
	$2Hg + 2SCN^- \rightleftharpoons Hg_2(SCN)_2 + 2e^-$	−0.22
	$2Hg + 2Br^- \rightleftharpoons Hg_2Br_2 + 2e^-$	−0.1397
	$2Hg + 2OH^- \rightleftharpoons Hg_2O + H_2O + 2e^-$	−0.123
	$2Hg + 2I^- \rightleftharpoons Hg_2I_2 + 2e^-$	0.0405
	$2Hg + 2CN^- \rightleftharpoons Hg_2(CN)_2 + 2e^-$	0.36
	$2Hg + S^{-2} \rightleftharpoons Hg_2S + 2e^-$	0.53
Hg(I)–Hg(II)	$Hg_2^{+2} \rightleftharpoons 2Hg^{+2} + 2e^-$	−0.910

teristics of magnesium and of zinc and cadmium are rather closely parallel. Beryllium and zinc are unique in being oxidized by water in alkaline solutions. This is due, of course, to the amphoterism of their hydroxides. The reactions and reactivities of calcium, strontium, barium, and radium are closely comparable to those of the alkali metals and are sometimes even more vigorous. Trends distinguishable among the alkali metals (pp. 822–823) are also noted here.

The reducing powers of the Group. IIb metals are influenced by the presence of precipitating or complexing groups, although except for mercury less detailed potential data are available than for the coinage metals. These effects are apparent in the potentials summarized in Table 19.4. The enhanced reducing powers of these metals in the presence of hydroxyl, cyanide, and sulfide ions are of particular importance, as are corresponding increases with mercury in the presence of the halides (Cl^-, Br^-, I^-).

PREPARATION AND PRODUCTION OF THE FREE ELEMENTS

Because of their extensive reducing powers, the Group IIa metals are prepared either by electrolytic or by thermal means in the absence of moisture. Calcium and the heavier members of the family can be deposited from aqueous solutions into mercury cathodes, but such procedures are not used for commercial production. Removal of mercury is difficult. Electrolysis of the fused chlorides is useful for the large-scale production of beryllium, magnesium, and calcium. For beryllium and magnesium, the addition of sodium chloride to improve bath conductivity is necessary. Wartime production of magnesium by this means was based upon anhydrous magnesium chloride obtained from salt wells, sea water, or minerals such as magnesite ($MgCO_3$) or brucite ($Mg(OH)_2$). Beryl (p. 725) is the only useful source of beryllium chloride. Calcium chloride is a by-product in the Solvay process for the manufacture of sodium carbonate. Electrolyses of fused double beryllium fluorides and magnesium fluoride mixtures are also useful.

Thermal reductions of the oxides with carbon are complicated by carbide formation in all cases except magnesium. Carbothermic reduction of magnesium oxide at elevated temperatures is a useful commercial process (Hansgirg process) if the equilibrium gaseous mixture is cooled rapidly to prevent reversal of the reaction.

Carbon reduction of beryllium oxide–copper(II) oxide mixtures is useful in the preparation of beryllium-copper master alloys. Thermal reductions of the oxides with aluminum (King process) are employed for preparation of elemental strontium and barium. Ferrosilicon is used to reduce magnesium oxide to the metal (Pidgeon process). In these instances, reactions are run under high vacuum conditions and rendered complete by sublimation of the metal products. Magnesium, along with aluminum, is very important as a light structural metal. Beryllium is used chiefly in alloys (especially with copper). Calcium has many potential applications.[1, 2] The other metals are used to more limited extents.

[1] Anon.: *J. Chem. Education*, **19,** 504 (1942).

[2] A. B. Klingel: *Mining and Met.*, **22,** 488 (1941).

The Group IIb metals are obtained more readily. Electrolytic reduction of aqueous salt solutions is feasible in all cases and is employed on a particularly large scale for the production of pure commercial zinc. It is of interest that the high overvoltage of hydrogen on zinc permits electrodeposition of the metal even from reasonably acidic solutions. Inasmuch as all these metals occur in nature in sulfidic minerals, technical procedures often entail roasting to the oxides and thermal reduction with carbon. With mercury, addition of carbon is unnecessary since any intermediate oxide decomposes directly to the metal at elevated temperatures. Oxidized zinc minerals are calcined and reduced. Cadmium is recovered as a by-product from the zinc industry. Separation from zinc by volatilization of the metal or by selective electrodeposition is feasible. Zinc and cadmium are of particular importance as plating metals. Elemental mercury is employed in various electrochemical industries. Many alloys are important.

COMPOUNDS OF THE GROUP II ELEMENTS

The discussion of compound types in this chapter parallels closely that given for the Group I materials in the preceding chapter for the same reasons outlined there (p. 824). As is true of the compounds of the Group I elements, those of the B elements are distinguished from the corresponding ones of the A elements by being more covalent and less basic in character.

Oxidation states among the Group IIb elements

This section can be comparatively brief because, except for the unipositive mercury compounds, all well-established compounds contain dipositive metals.

Oxidation State +1. Although cadmium(I) compounds such as the oxide and the chloride have been described, magnetic data indicate that they are mixtures of cadmium(II) compounds and the finely divided metal.[3,4] Latimer's estimates[5] for the couples

$$2Cd \rightleftharpoons Cd_2^{+2} + 2e^- \qquad E^0_{298} < 0.2 \text{ volt}$$

and

$$Cd_2^{+2} \rightleftharpoons 2Cd^{+2} + 2e^- \qquad E^0_{298} > 0.6 \text{ volt}$$

are, therefore, without any real significance.

[3] W. R. A. Hollens and J. F. Spencer: *J. Chem. Soc.*, **1934**, 1062.

[4] W. R. A. Hollens and J. F. Spencer: *J. Chem. Soc.*, **1935**, 495.

[5] W. M. Latimer: *The Oxidation States of the Elements and Their Potentials in Aqueous Solutions*, p. 161. Prentice-Hall, New York (1938).

Numerous mercury compounds, however, are known for this state of oxidation. From the oxidation potential data given in Table 19·4 it is apparent that oxidation of the metal gives the +1 state preferentially, but the difference in potential values between the Hg(O)–Hg(I) and Hg(O)–Hg(II) couples is so small that oxidizing agents can ordinarily effect either oxidation. Inasmuch as mercury(II) ion is a better oxidizing agent toward free mercury, it follows that treatment of mercury(II) compounds with reducing agents will give mercury(I). However, the difference is again so small that reduction normally continues down to the metal. In any event, powerful oxidizing agents are essential, but even comparatively weak reducing agents can be employed. It is obvious also that in the presence of excess mercury such oxidizing agents will give mercury(I) compounds since mercury(II) ion is reduced by mercury to mercury(I) ion. In view of the variations in potential values given in Table 19·4, the absence of precipitants or complexing agents which will affect the activities (concentrations) of the unipositive and dipositive ions unequally is essential to the foregoing conclusions.

Although the simple mercury(I) ion is stable with respect to disproportionation into mercury(II) ion and mercury, it has been shown in a previous chapter (p. 300) that because the equilibrium concentration of mercury(I) ion in the system

$$Hg^{+2} + Hg \rightleftharpoons Hg_2^{+2}$$

is at 25°C. only some 79 times* that of mercury(II) ion, treatment of mercury(I) salt solutions with many reagents which yield mercury(II) derivatives that are more insoluble or more highly complexed than the corresponding mercury(I) derivatives permits such disproportionation. Reagents which are typical are sulfide ion, hydroxyl ion, cyanide ion, ammonia in the presence of chloride ion, ammines, acetylacetone, alkyl sulfides, etc. Such behavior doubtless accounts for early views that mercury(I) compounds were in effect mercury(II) compounds plus mercury. The foregoing equilibrium is temperature dependent and is somewhat more displaced toward mercury(II) at elevated temperatures.

The mercury(I) ion is a most unusual species. Evidences that the group is actually Hg_2^{+2} rather than Hg^+ are multiple. Among them are the following:

* This value is a thermodynamic value based upon potential data. Direct experimental determinations by Ogg[6] and by Abel[7] gave values of 112 (18°C.) and 120, respectively, for the concentration ratio $Hg^{+2}:Hg_2^{+2}$.

1. When the concentrations of the mercury(II) and mercury(I) ions in mercury(II) nitrate solution treated with mercury are determined, the direct ratio of these values, $C_{Hg(II)}:C_{Hg(I)}$, is constant as required by the above equation, but the ratio $C_{Hg(II)}:C^2_{Hg(I)}$, as required by

$$Hg^{+2} + Hg \rightleftharpoons 2Hg^{+}$$

is not constant.[6,7]

2. When silver nitrate solution is equilibrated with liquid mercury, the concentrations of silver ion, mercury(I) ion, and silver in the liquid amalgam formed give[6] constant values for the expression

$$\frac{C_{Hg(I)} \times C_{Ag}^2}{C_{Ag^+}^2} = K \tag{19·1}$$

suggesting the equation for the reaction to be

$$2Ag^{+} + Hg \rightleftharpoons Hg_2^{+2} + 2Ag \text{ (amalg.)}$$

rather than

$$Ag^{+} + Hg \rightleftharpoons Hg^{+} + Ag \text{ (amalg.)}$$

3. The measured potential (0.029 volt at 17°C.) of the concentration cell*

Hg,	0.05 *N* mercury(I) nitrate in 0.1 *N* nitric acid	0.5 *N* mercury(I) nitrate in 0.1 *N* nitric acid	,Hg

requires a 2-electron change ($n = 2$) in the equation (p. 291)

$$E = \frac{RT}{n} \ln \frac{C_2}{C_1} = \frac{0.058}{n} \log \frac{C_2}{C_1} \tag{19·2}$$

since the concentration ratio is ten to one.[6]

4. The measured conductances of mercury(I) nitrate solutions containing nitric acid to repress hydrolysis are those of solutions of an $M(NO_3)_2$ type electrolyte rather than an MNO_3 type,[6] suggesting that the cation is Hg_2^{+2}.

5. The Raman spectra of aqueous mercury(I) nitrate solutions give characteristic lines in addition to the nitrate lines.[8] Since solutions of other metal nitrates give only nitrate lines, showing that monoatomic cations are not effective, the presence of a polyatomic cationic species in mercury(I) solutions is indicated.

[6] A. Ogg: *Z. physik. Chem.*, **27**, 285 (1898).

[7] E. Abel: *Z. anorg. Chem.*, **26**, 376 (1901).

* That a cell containing the same reactants but at different concentrations will develop a potential follows from consideration of concentration effects as outlined previously (pp. 291–292).

[8] L. A. Woodward: *Phil. Mag.* [7], **18**, 823 (1934).

6. The crystal structure of mercury(I) chloride is based upon linear Cl–Hg–Hg–Cl units,[9, 10] whereas in crystals of other compounds of the type MCl, M^+ and Cl^- ions alternate. This is more convincing evidence for the existence of discrete Hg_2^{+2} groups than the fact that the molecular weights of the mercury(I) halides as determined cryoscopically in mercury(II) halides as solvents[11] indicate dimeric molecules Hg_2X_2 (X = Cl, Br, I).

Inasmuch as the mercury(I) ion has two ionic valencies, sharing of an electron pair between the two mercuries to give an arrangement

$$(Hg{:}Hg)^{+2}$$

must occur Although this type of metal to metal bonding is not common, it is by no means unique to mercury(I).[12] Other examples are found in the ion $[W_2Cl_9]^{-3}$ (p. 272), where the two tungsten atoms are closer to each other (2.46 A) than are adjacent atoms in tungsten metal (2.60 A),[13] and the carbonyl $Fe_2(CO)_9$, the structure of which has been described in Chapter 16 (pp. 703–704).

Few mercury(I) compounds are water soluble (e.g., nitrate, chlorate, perchlorate). The halides, sulfate, and salts of various organic acids are less soluble than the mercury(II) compounds. Where the reverse is true, only the mercury(II) compounds can be characterized (p. 853). In its solubility relations, the mercury(I) ion bears certain resemblances to the silver(I) ion. Unlike mercury(II), mercury(I) has no measurable tendency to form the covalent bonds essential to true complexes. Addition of coordinating agents causes disproportionation (p. 853). Solutions of its soluble salts are those of strong electrolytes, although they do undergo measurable hydrolysis.

Oxidation State +2. Fundamental considerations relative to this oxidation state have been offered above (pp. 847–848). Specific details as to actual trends and behaviors appear in subsequent discussion of individual compound types. Among the Group IIa elements, comparable barium and radium compounds are often isomorphous (e.g., Cl^-, SO_4^{-2}), permitting one to use barium to carry the much less abundant radium in recovery processes.

[9] R. J. Havighurst: *Am. J. Sci.*, **10**, 15 (1925).
[10] R. J. Havighurst: *J. Am. Chem. Soc.*, **48**, 2113 (1926).
[11] E. Beckmann: *Z. anorg. Chem.*, **55**, 175 (1907).
[12] L. Pauling: Chem. Eng. News, **25**, 2970 (1947).
[13] C. Brosset: *Ark. Kem. Mineral. Geol.*, **12A**, No. 4 (1935).

Comparisons among compound types

Only a few of the compound types require detailed discussion.

1. *Halides.* Variations in ionic character among the Group. IIa halides are significant and are dependent, of course, upon both cation and anion (pp. 209–210). As the size of the cation increases, changes from essentialy complete covalent behavior for the beryllium compounds to complete ionic character for the barium and radium analogs are noted. Thus the anhydrous beryllium halides are comparatively

TABLE 19·5
MELTING AND BOILING POINTS OF ANHYDROUS HALIDES

Metal	Fluoride		Chloride		Bromide		Iodide	
	Melting Point, °C.	Boiling Point, °C.	Melting Point, °C.	Boiling Point, °C.	Melting Point, °C.	Boiling Point, °C.	Melting Point, °C.	Boiling Point, °C.
Be	800 (subl.)		405	488	490	520	510	590
Mg	1396	2239	708	1412	700		ca. 700	
Ca	1360		772	> 1600	765	810	575	718
Sr	1450	2489	873		643		402	
Ba	1285	2137	962	1560	847		740 (dec.)	
Ra			1000		728			
Zn	872		275	732	394	650	446	624
Cd	1110	1758	568	960	583	863	388 (α)	796 (α)
Hg(I)	570		302	383.7	345 (subl.)		140 (subl.)	310 (dec.)
Hg(II)	645	650	280	302.5	238	318	257	351

low-melting, relatively volatile (Table 19·5), nonconducting[14] compounds. The fluoride is a glass-like, randomly arranged solid,[15] but the others are crystalline. Both the chloride and bromide are somewhat dimeric in the gaseous state (23% Be_2Cl_4 and 34% Be_2Br_4 at 566°C.).[16] The beryllium halides are all water soluble (with considerable hydrolysis), and the chloride, bromide, and iodide dissolve in many organic solvents as well. There is strong evidence of covalent unsaturation, e.g., in catalytic effects in organic syntheses and formation of a variety of complexes especially of the type $BeX_2 \cdot 2A$, etc. Indeed, the beryllium halides closely resemble the analogous aluminum halides in many of their characteristics.

The magnesium halides are transitory in character between those of beryllium and those of the heavier members of the family, but

[14] G. von Hevesy: *Z. physik. Chem.*, **127**, 401 (1927).
[15] B. E. Warren and C. F. Hill: *Z. Krist.*, **89**, 481 (1934).
[16] O. Rahlfs and W. Fischer: *Z. anorg. allgem. Chem.*, **211**, 349 (1933).

resemblances to those of the latter elements are more pronounced. Magnesium bromide and iodide resemble the beryllium compounds in their solubilities in organic solvents and tendencies to add various oxygenated compounds. As a group, however, the halides of magnesium and the other metals in the family are largely ionic. The fluorides are only slightly soluble in water; the other halides are readily soluble. High lattice energies favor insolubility among the fluorides. With beryllium fluoride, this factor is probably counterbalanced by high hydration energy of the cation.

The analogous dihalides of the Group IIb elements are much less ionic in character as indicated by melting point, boiling point, and conductance data (Table 19·5). Where vapor density data are available (e.g., for $ZnCl_2$, $CdBr_2$), there are no evidences of association in the gaseous state. In the vapor state, mercury(II) chloride, bromide, and iodide molecules are linear with bond distances Hg—Cl 2.20 A, Hg—Br 2.40 A, and Hg—I 2.55 A.[17,18] Solid mercury(II) fluoride has an ionic lattice of the fluorite type. The solid chloride and bromide have layer lattices in which each mercury atom is surrounded by six halogen atoms in distorted octahedral arrangements, with two halogen atoms much closer (2.25 A for the chloride, 2.48 A for the bromide) to the mercury atom than the others (two at 3.63 A and two at 3.34 A for the chloride, four at 3.23 A for the bromide). Mercury(II) is thus essentially 2-covalent in its chloride and bromide. In the solid iodide, each mercury atom is surrounded tetrahedrally by four iodine atoms at 2.78 A.

The zinc and cadmium halides are all water soluble, but with mercury(II) the bromide and iodide (especially) are insoluble. Aqueous solutions of these halides (except fluorides) show abnormalities in conductances and transference numbers which indicate the presence of undissociated molecules and auto-complex ions. For the zinc halides, these effects are noted only in concentrated solutions; for the cadmium halides they are apparent at much lower concentrations; and for mercury(II) chloride and bromide they are found regardless of concentration. Electromotive force measurements[19,20] and conductance studies[21] of cadmium halide solutions show the following

[17] H. Braune and S. Knoke: *Z. physik. Chem.*, **B23**, 163 (1933).

[18] A. H. Gregg, G. C. Hampson G. I. Jenkins, P. L. F. Jones, and L. E. Sutton: *Trans. Faraday Soc.*, **33**, 852 (1937).

[19] H. L. Riley and V. Gallafent: *J. Chem. Soc.*, **1932**, 514.

[20] R. G. Bates and W. C. Vosburgh: *J. Am. Chem. Soc.*, **59**, 1583 (1937); **60**, 137 (1938).

[21] E. L. Righellato and C. W. Davies: *Trans. Faraday Soc.*, **26**, 592 (1930).

species to be present in quantities decreasing in this order: CdX^+, Cd^{+2}, CdX_2, CdX_3^-, and CdX_4^{-2}. The percentage of simple Cd^{+2} decreases from chloride to iodide, with the percentages of the other species increasing accordingly. In mercury(II) chloride and bromide solutions, neutral molecules, HgX_2, predominate, with HgX^+ ions being present in very small quantities. Chloride ions are so firmly bound that species of the type $[HgX_3]^-$ or $[HgX_4]^{-2}$ cannot form. In the presence of added halide ions (except fluoride), species of the types $[MX_3]^-$ and $[MX_4]^{-2}$ become very important (p. 865). The mercury(II) halides are much less hydrolyzed in solution than are those of zinc and cadmium. Mercury(II) iodide exists in two common crystalline forms, the ordinary red form being converted to a less stable yellow one at 126°C.

Of the mercury(I) halides, the fluoride is water soluble and the others insoluble, with solubility decreasing as the size of the halogen increases. The fluoride undergoes complete hydrolysis upon dissolution in water. The chloride and bromide are both easily volatilized and give diamagnetic vapors[22] which correspond in densities to the simple formulation HgX.[23, 24] Inasmuch as HgX vapors should be paramagnetic, it is suggested that the mercury(I) halides dissociate to mercury and mercury(II) halides on heating. The presence of mercury in the vapors[23] confirms this view. Heat converts the iodide to mercury and mercury(II) iodide. The mercury(I) halides are better conductors than their mercury(II) analogs.

Oxides and Hydroxides. Some information on the oxides, peroxides, and superoxides of the Group II elements has been summarized in Chapter 14 (pp. 500, 508). The same general differences in properties are found between the oxides of the members of the two families as between the halides, and variations within each family are similar. All the simple oxides of the Group IIa elements except beryllium have the ionic sodium chloride type crystal structure. Beryllium oxide has the wurtzite lattice characteristic of covalent linkages. The heats of formation of these oxides (BeO −136 kcal. per mole, MgO −146, CaO −151.7, SrO −141, BaO −133) indicate compounds of considerable stability. The apparently anomalously high value for the calcium compound arises from the high lattice energy of this material (Table 6·5). The oxides of calcium and the heavier metals hydrate (slake) readily to ionic hydroxides. Magnesium oxide hydrates only if not prepared at an elevated temperature, whereas beryllium oxide is unreactive toward water. Behaviors with aqueous acids are similar.

[22] P. W. Selwood and R. Preckel: *J. Am. Chem. Soc.*, **62**, 3055 (1940).
[23] F. T. Gucker, Jr., and R. H. Munch: *J. Am. Chem. Soc.*, **59**, 1275 (1937).
[24] G. Jung and W. Ziegler: *Z. physik. Chem.*, **150**, 139 (1930).

Basicity of course increases with increasing radius of the cation. Only the oxides of barium and (presumably) radium react directly with oxygen to give peroxides.

Zinc and cadmium oxides sublime at elevated temperatures and do not undergo thermal decomposition. Mercury(II) oxide decomposes to the metal and oxygen above 300°C. Zinc oxide has a wurtzite lattice and cadmium oxide a sodium chloride lattice. Zinc oxide is a semiconductor, probably because of the presence of zinc atoms in the crystal lattice. The colors of these oxides (ZnO yellow when hot, CdO brown, HgO red or yellow) are doubtless due to ion deformation (p. 211) since the components are all colorless. The red and yellow forms of mercury(II) oxide apparently differ from each other only in particle size since energy differences between them are minute.[25] None of these oxides hydrates appreciably in water, and all are much less reactive toward aqueous acids (because of reduced basicities) than the oxides of the Group IIa elements. The compounds $Zn(OH)_2$ and $Cd(OH)_2$ are crystalline substances obtainable by precipitation. The mercury(II) analog does not exist. Mercury(I) oxide is also non-existent, all attempts to prepare it by precipitation yielding a mixture of mercury and mercury(II) oxide.[26]

Sulfides, Selenides, and Tellurides. Sulfides of these elements are comparable to the oxides but are more highly covalent. The sulfides of the Group IIb elements are water insoluble. Indeed, equilibrium concentrations of sulfide ion are so small that acids are required to effect dissolution, the required proton concentration increasing with increasing atomic weight of the metal. With mercury(II) sulfide an oxidant is normally required as well. The sulfides of the Group IIa elements are much more soluble and, except for the beryllium compound, undergo hydrolysis in contact with water to $M(SH)_2$ and H_2S. All react readily with aqueous acids. Polysulfides are formed with the calcium, strontium, and barium compounds. Mercury(II) sulfide is sufficiently amphoteric to dissolve in excess sulfide ion (p. 866). Selenides and tellurides are comparable in character in all cases. Mercury(I) compounds are again unknown. The effects of cation and anion size in determining crystal lattices are pronounced. The following structure types are distinguishable: zinc blende (covalent) with BeS, MgTe, ZnS, ZnSe, ZnTe, CdTe, HgS, HgSe, HgTe; wurtzite (covalent) with BeSe, BeTe, ZnS, CdS, CdSe; and sodium chloride (ionic) with MgS, MgSe, CaS, SrS, BaS, CaSe, SrSe, BaSe, CaTe, SrTe, BaTe, HgS. Certain of the materials are obviously dimorphous.

[25] A. B. Garrett and A. E. Hirschler: *J. Am. Chem. Soc.*, **60**, 299 (1938).
[26] R. Fricke and P. Ackermann: *Z. anorg. allgem. Chem.*, **211**, 233 (1933).

Compounds with Nitrogen Family Elements. The Group IIA elements form (usually by direct combination) nitrides of the type M_3N_2, which are colorless, crystalline compounds. The beryllium compound is somewhat volatile; the others are not. All decompose to the elements when heated excessively, and all are hydrolyzed to ammonia and the metal oxide or hydroxide in contact with water. The Group IIb metals give analogous, but poorly characterized, compounds by indirect reactions involving amides. These compounds are definitely less stable than the more ionic nitrides of the IIa elements. Phosphides, arsenides, etc., form with decreasing ease. Azides are obtainable with the Group IIa elements.

A variety of mercury(II)-nitrogen compounds has been described. All these compounds are ammonia derivatives and may be classified into three general types as (1) ammines, (2) ammonobasic compounds, and (3) mixed aquo-ammonobasic compounds.

AMMINES. Examples of the series $[Hg(NH_3)_2]X_2$ and $[Hg(NH_3)_4]X_2$ are known. These may be true ammines or ammoniates. They are mentioned in more detail in a later section of this chapter (p. 866).

AMMONOBASIC COMPOUNDS. Most familiar of these is the compound $Hg(NH_2)Cl$, which is formed when ammonia reacts with mercury(II) chloride or, along with mercury, when ammonia reacts with mercury(I) chloride. Ethylamine gives an analogous compound, $Hg(NHC_2H_5)Cl$, but oxy compounds or mercury give mixed aquo-ammonobasic derivatives instead. Derivatives containing $=NH$ or $\equiv N$ are possible also (p. 570).

MIXED AQUO-AMMONOBASIC COMPOUNDS. Parent compound in this series is Millon's base, $(HOHg)_2NH_2OH$, a yellow powder which is formed when aqueous ammonia reacts with yellow mercury(II) oxide. The crystal structure of this compound amounts to HgN groups in a three-dimensional framework of the idealized cristobalite (p. 691) type.[27] The mercury atoms have linear bonds of the *sp* type and the nitrogen atoms tetrahedral bonds of the sp^3 type. The structure is face-centered cubic with a = 9.58 A, and the Hg—N bond distance is 2.07 A. The following formulations are both in accord with the stoichiometry of the compound:

```
H—O—Hg                              Hg
       \                           /  \
        NH·H2O                    O    NH2OH·H2O
       /                           \  /
H—O—Hg                              Hg
       I                                  II
```

When treated with acids, the compound is neutralized and yields a series of salts of composition OHg_2NH_2X (X = Cl, Br, NO_3^-).

[27] W. N. Lipscomb: *Acta Cryst.*, **4**, 156 (1951).

Dehydration of the original base yields, successively, OHg_2NH_2OH and explosive OHg_2NH. These behaviors would seem to favor structure II, although structure I is often written. The chloride of Millon's base, OHg_2NH_2Cl, is formed when ammonobasic mercury(II) chloride is hydrolyzed by heating with water. The iodide is precipitated when Nessler's reagent (p. 865) reacts with ammonia.

Compounds Containing Metal-Carbon Linkages. Carbides formed by the Group II elements have been described in Chapter 16 (pp. 696–698). Also well characterized are the cyanides, which are known for all metals in the family. All cyanides except the mercury(II) compound are comparatively stable toward heat and salt-like in character. Mercury(II) cyanide gives cyanogen when heated (p. 467). Its aqueous solutions are those of a non-electrolyte and apparently contain the species $Hg(CN)_2$ since there are present insufficient cyanide ions to give auto complexes. The absence of ions is indicated by the very low electrical conductivities of such solutions, by the fact that they are not precipitated by hydroxyl or iodide ions, and by the formation of the compound from mercury compounds and normally stable cyanides such as Prussian blue (p. 720). Mercury(I) cyanide does not exist, again because of disproportionation.

Alkyl and aryl derivatives are common for beryllium, magnesium, and the Group IIb elements. The alkaline earth metals proper do not give many compounds of this type. Of particular interest to the organic chemist are the magnesium compounds of the type RMgX ($X = Cl, Br, I$), the Grignard reagents. All these compounds are considered in textbooks on organic chemistry.

Ternary, etc., Compounds. Almost all ternary, etc., acids are known in the form of their salts with the Group IIa elements and, to lesser extents, the Group IIb elements. It is somewhat beyond the scope of this book to detail all the characteristics of all these salts. In a general way, however, salts of the Group IIa elements are somewhat less soluble than corresponding ones of the Group Ia elements, whereas in a comparison of salts of the Groups IIb and Ib elements the reverse is commonly true. Water solubility is limited in general in both families to nitrates, chlorates, perchlorates, acetates, etc. Significant differences lie in the sulfates where the calcium, strontium, barium, and radium compounds have limited solubilities. Hydrolysis effects give many basic salts with beryllium.

Coordination compounds and complex ions

The situation in this group, although comparable to that in Group I, is different to the extent that the enhanced charges and reduced sizes of the ions of the members of the A family do promote covalence to a greater extent. For beryllium, conditions are particularly favorable, and many complexes are known.

The Group IIa Metals. It would appear advisable to discuss this topic under the headings beryllium complexes and complexes of the other members of the family. This is dictated by the fact that, although conditions for complex formation are nearly as unfavorable for the heavier members of the family as for the alkali metals, they are very favorable for beryllium indeed.

BERYLLIUM COMPLEXES. The concentration of positive charge which makes the beryllium ion prone to accept electron pairs confers considerable stabilities upon the resulting complexes, Covalent binding in such species is of the sp^3 type and is tetrahedral (p. 257).

Although freezing point data in binary systems of beryllium chloride with various metal chlorides (e.g., LiCl, TlCl, $BaCl_2$) indicate double salts which might be formulated as $M_2^I[BeCl_4]$ or M^{II} $[BeCl_4]$[28, 29] such a chloro anion has no stability in aqueous solution. Tetrafluoberyllate(II) ion, $[BeF_4]^{-2}$ is well known, however, both in solution and in the form of solid salts. These salts are recoverable by crystallization from aqueous solutions, although the reactions of such solutions indicate some dissociation of the $[BeF_4]^{-2}$ ion. The tetrafluoberyllates resemble the sulfates in their solubilities and in the formation of double salts such as $M_2^IM^{II}(BeF_4)_2{\cdot}6H_2O$ because of similarities in size and structure.[30] The compound $K_2BeF_4{\cdot}Al_2(SO_4)_3{\cdot}24H_2O$ is of the alum type (pp. 539–541.) The crystal structure of the ammonium salt, $(NH_4)_2[BeF_4]$, shows the arrangement to be the same as that in K_2SO_4, indicating the BeF_4^{-2} and SO_4^{-2} groups to have essentially the same size and shape. Each beryllium atom is surrounded tetrahedrally by four fluorine atoms at 1.61 A.[31] The tetrafluoberyllates are formed from reaction of beryllium oxide with acid fluorides. In the presence of excess beryllium fluoride, materials of the type $M^I[BeF_3]$ can be obtained, but these revert to tetrafluoberyllates in water.

Complexes containing beryllium to oxygen bonds are very numerous. In a sense, the simplest of these are aquo complexes. Most beryllium salts are hydrated, often with four moles of water per beryllium atom, and it may be assumed, as a reasonable hypothesis, that these water molecules are associated with the beryllium ion as $[Be(H_2O)_4]^{+2}$. The situation in aqueous solutions of beryllium salts is, of course, quite indeterminate (p. 281), but the properties of such solutions (high

[28] J.-M. Schmidt: *Ann. chim.* (x), **11,** 351 (1929).

[29] H. O'Daniel and L. Tscheischwili: *Z. Krist.,* **104,** 124 (1942).

[30] N. N. Rây: *Z. anorg. allgem. Chem.,* **205,** 257 (1932).

[31] R. Hultgren: *Z. Krist.,* **88,** 233 (1934).

viscosity, low cation mobility, abnormal freezing point depressions) indicate the beryllium ion to be more highly hydrated than any other dipositive species.[32] Ethers, aldehydes, ketones, and other oxygenated compounds add readily to anhydrous beryllium compounds such as the chloride, giving compounds of the general type $Be(OR)_2X_2$ (OR = organic oxy compound).

Beryllium salt solutions dissolve several moles of beryllium oxide, hydroxide, or basic carbonate per mole of beryllium ion present to give systems with only slightly diminished electrical conductivities and slightly enhanced freezing point depressions. The conclusion of Sidgwick and Lewis[33] that such solutions contain complexes of the type $[Be(OBe)_x(H_2O)_{4-x}]^{+2}$ accounts for their properties and also explains such observations as the enhanced solubilities of beryllium salts (e.g., the sulfate) in the presence of the oxide. Beryllate ion, BeO_2^{-2} or $HBeO_2^-$, is also an oxy complex.

Many chelated species are known also. Of particular interest among these are chelates of the β-diketones[34] and β-keto esters (p. 241) and a series of so-called basic beryllium derivatives of the type $Be_4O(RCO_2)_6$ (R = CH_3, C_2H_5, C_6H_5, etc.)[35] These "basic" compounds are characterized by volatility, solubility in non-polar solvents, and complete lack of ionic properties. Structural studies[36–38] indicate the presence of a central oxygen surrounded tetrahedrally by four beryllium atoms, the acetate, etc., groups being arranged along the six edges of the tetrahedron. This gives a series of chelate rings

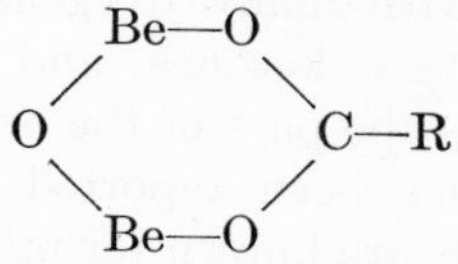

```
      Be—O
     /    \
    O      C—R
     \    /
      Be—O
```

The arrangement around each beryllium atom is also tetrahedral, and the structure amounts then to four BeO_4 tetrahedra with one oxygen atom common to all four, the remaining oxygen atoms being supplied by the organic groups. Other oxy complexes embrace those derived from phenols, aromatic *o*-hydroxy acids, and dicarboxylic acids.

[32] R. Fricke and H. Schützdeller: *Z. anorg. allgem. Chem.*, **131**, 130 (1923).

[33] N. V. Sidgwick and N. B. Lewis: *J. Chem. Soc.*, **1926**, 1287.

[34] A. Arch and R. C. Young: *Inorganic Syntheses*, Vol. II, pp. 17–20. McGraw-Hill Book Co., New York (1946).

[35] T. Moeller: *Inorganic Syntheses*, Vol. III, pp. 4–9. McGraw-Hill Book Co., New York (1950).

[36] W. H. Bragg and G. T. Morgan: *Proc. Roy. Soc.* (*London*), **A104**, 437 (1923).

[37] G. T. Morgan and W. T. Astbury: *Proc. Roy. Soc.* (*London*), **A112**, 441 (1926).

[38] L. Pauling and J. Sherman: *Proc. Natl. Acad. Sci.*, **20**, 340 (1934).

Beryllium complexes containing donor nitrogens are less common. The anhydrous halides give ammines, $BeX_2 \cdot nNH_3$ (n = 4, 6, 12 if X = Cl, Br, I), but because of the strength of the Be—O bond, these compounds are decomposed by water. Various amines, diamines, and nitriles give similar compounds, although usually only two or four groups are present.

COMPLEXES OF MAGNESIUM, CALCIUM, STRONTIUM, BARIUM, AND RADIUM. The only derivatives of calcium and the heavier members of the group which could be called complexes are a few poorly characterized β-diketone and β-keto ester compounds, some alcoholates, and a few relatively unstable ammines (e.g., $MX_2 \cdot nNH_3$). To this list one might add hydrates. In all cases, the thermal stabilities of such materials decrease markedly as cation size increases. Indeed, even hydration is limited among the heavier members. The situation is of course essentially the same as that characterizing the alkali metals. In solution, however, hydroxy anions such as tartrate and citrate do tie up these cations, species such as Sr(tar) and $Sr(cit)^-$ having been reported and characterized by pk' values of 1.69 and 2.81, respectively, at 25°C.[39, 40] The sequestering of calcium, etc., ions with polymetaphosphate (p. 653) and reagents such as ethylenediaminetetraacetate or nitriloacetate probably involves complex formation also.

As expected, the behavior of magnesium is intermediate between the behavior of these elements and of beryllium. Magnesium compounds hydrate quite readily, and the anhydrous magnesium halides in particular combine readily with many oxygenated organic compounds (e.g., ethers, alcohols, esters, ketones, and aldehydes), presumably through donor behavior as the part of the oxygen. A poorly characterized acetylacetonate has been reported. Various ammines and amine addition compounds are known for many magnesium salts, but these are generally unstable in contact with water. The species $M^I[MgF_3]$ and $M_2^I[MgF_4]$ apparently exist in systems such as $KF–MgF_2$ and $RbF–MgF_2$,[41] but fluo anions are non-existent in aqueous solutions. It is probable that none of these species possesses predominant covalent character.

The Group IIb Metals. For these elements, conditions for the formation of complexes are generally more favorable but, on the average, probably less favorable than for the coinage metals (pp. 839–843). Coordination numbers of *four* (in particular) and *six* (occasionally) are noted. In the common 4-coordinate complexes, sp^3 hybridization imparts tetrahedral geometry, wherever the bonding is truly covalent.

[39] J. Schubert: *J. Phys. Colloid Chem.*, **52**, 340 (1948).
[40] J. Schubert and J. W. Richter: *J. Phys. Colloid Chem.*, **52**, 350 (1948).
[41] H. Remy and W. Seemann: *Rec. trav. chim.*, **59**, 516 (1940).

The hybridization $nsnp^3nd^2$ may be assumed for the 6-coordinate complexes. In their complexes, the elements of this family are in a uniform +2 state of oxidation.

HALO COMPLEXES. A number of solid double halides of compositions $M^IM^{II}X_3$, $M_2{}^IM^{II}X_4$, and $M_3{}^IM^{II}X_5$ (M^I = Na, K, etc.; M^{II} = Zn, Cd; X = Cl, Br, I) can be distinguished. Included also are a few fluorides of the first two types and with cadmium a few materials of type $M_4{}^I[CdX_6]$ (X = Cl, Br). The $[MX_5]^{-3}$ group is a combination of $[MX_4]^{-2}$ and X^- (p. 258). The same is probably true of the $[MX_6]^{-2}$ arrangement. Mercury gives no fluo derivatives but chloro, bromo, and iodo compounds of the types $M^I[HgX_3]$ and $M_2{}^{II}[HgX_4]$ are reported. In solution, there is some evidence for the existence of halozincate ions, and very excellent evidence for halo anions containing cadmium and mercury is available (pp. 857–858). Of all the species which may be present in solution, the $[MX_4]^{-2}$ type of halo complex is most important. Stability of these species increases regularly with increasing weight or size of either cation or anion, maximum stability being achieved with the $[HgI_4]^{-2}$ ion. This is shown rather vividly by the fact that the *p*H values at which cadmium hydroxide[42] and mercury(II) oxide[43] precipitate from aqueous solutions increase markedly as the excess anion present is changed from chloride to bromide to iodide. Indeed, cadmium oxide is quite soluble in alkali metal iodide solutions,[42] and mercury(II) oxide dissolves quantitatively in chloride, bromide, or iodide solutions as

$$HgO + 4X^- + H_2O \rightarrow [HgX_4]^{-2} + 2OH^-$$

the reaction being most pronounced with iodides.[44] The stability of the tetraiodomercurate(II) complex is also indicated by the ease with which normally insoluble mercury(II) iodide dissolves in solutions containing iodide ion and by the fact that solutions containing this species can be made strongly alkaline without precipitating (Nessler's reagent). The tetrahedral nature of the $[HgX_4]^{-2}$ group has been confirmed.[45] Of the salts of these halo complexes, the tetraiodomercurates are the most important. The silver(I) and copper(I) compounds containing this anion are highly colored and insoluble. They undergo striking color changes when heated because of dimorphism.

COMPLEXES CONTAINING OXYGEN FAMILY DONORS. The donor ability of oxygen toward cations in this family decreases rapidly from zinc to cadmium to mercury. This is indicated by decreases in ten-

[42] T. Moeller and P. W. Rhymer: *J. Phys. Chem.*, **46,** 477 (1942).

[43] H. T. S. Britton and B. M. Wilson: *J. Chem. Soc.*, **1932,** 2550.

[44] H. T. S. Britton and B. M. Wilson: *J. Chem. Soc.*, **1933,** 9.

[45] J. A. A. Ketelaar: *Z. Krist.*, **80,** 190 (1931).

dency toward hydrate, alcoholate, etherate, etc., formation, the zinc compounds being the most numerous and the most stable. Zinc alone forms oxyanions with alkali, i.e., the zincates. Chelate complexes embrace acetylacetonates, dioxalato compounds, and a few others. Zinc forms a "basic" acetate, $Zn_4O(CH_3CO_2)_6$, which is volatile like its beryllium analog but more readily hydrolyzed.[46]

Sulfur appears to be a better donor than oxygen. Important sulfur complexes are the dialkyl sulfide addition products of the halides, $(R_2S)_2 \cdot MX_2$ (M = Zn, Cd, Hg). With mercury, $R_2S \cdot 2HgX_2$ and $R_2S \cdot HgX_2$ form also, the last being the most common. Thiourea (tu) gives a zinc complex, $[Zn(tu)_2]Br_2$, and mercury(II) sulfide dissolves in alkali metal polysulfide solutions because of formation of the thio anion, $[HgS_2]^{-2}$.

COMPLEXES CONTAINING NITROGEN FAMILY DONORS. Salts of these metals absorb ammonia readily to give a number of ammoniates. Certain of these are true ammines $[M(NH_3)_x]^{+2}$, which retain their identities in solution. Commonest are the tetrammines, although diammines are well-characterized with mercury and hexammines with zinc and cadmium. With mercury, formation of ammonobasic derivatives (p. 860) is a competitive process but can be reduced in importance by the presence of ammonium ion. It is of interest that the mercury(II) halides add only two moles of ammonia, presumably because two coordination positions are already filled with covalently bonded halogens, whereas more ionic mercury(II) compounds (e.g., nitrate, perchlorate) add four moles. Organic amines and diamines also give complex cations. Ethylenediamine gives complexes of the type $[M(en)_3]^{+2}$ (M = Zn, Cd, Hg), thereby rendering these materials 6-coordinate. A few nitrile and nitro complexes have been reported.

Tertiary phosphines (R_3P) and arsines (R_3As) form a number of different types of compounds with cadmium and mercury. These are formulated by Mann and his co-workers,[47, 48] using the phosphines as typical, as

```
┌R3P       X┐┌ X         X        PR3┐┌          X          PR3┐
│   ↘    ╱  ││   ╲     ↙   ╲     ↙    ││       ╱   ↘     ↙      │
│     M     ││     M         M        ││ R3P→M←—X—M—X           │
│   ↗    ╲  ││   ↗     ╲   ↗     ╲    ││       ╲   ↗     ↖      │
└R3P       X┘└R3P        X         X  ┘└          X          PR3┘
      I                  II                       III
```

[46] V. Augur and I. Robin: *Compt. rend.*, **178**, 1546 (1924).

[47] R. C. Evans, F. G. Mann, H. S. Peiser, and D. Purdie: *J. Chem. Soc.*, **1940**, 1209.

[48] F. G. Mann and D. Purdie: *J. Chem. Soc.*, **1940**, 1230.

```
|  X          X          X          X  |    |X         X         PR3|
|    \      ↙   \      ↙   \      /    |    |  \     ↙   \     ↙    |
|      Hg         Hg         Hg        |    |    Hg         Hg      |
|    ↗    \    ↗    \    ↗    ↖        |    |  /     ↖   ↗    \     |
|R3P        X          X         PR3   |    |X         X         X  |
                                            |            \    ↙     |
                                            |              Hg       |
                                            |            ↗    \     |
                                            |       R3P         X   |
                  IV                                    V
```

Types I, II, and III are common to both cadmium and mercury, but Types IV and V are perculiar to mercury. The proposed structure of the Type V material is most unusual. That of Type III is not well established.

COMPLEXES CONTAINING CARBON FAMILY DONORS. The most important complexes of this kind are the cyanides $[M(CN)_3]^-$ and $[M(CN_4)]^{-2}$ (M = Zn, Cd, Hg), the second type being the more important. In the tetracyano complexes, the arrangement around the central cation has been proved to be tetrahedral.[49] The stabilities of these species are indicated by the oxidation potential data in Table 19·4. Instability constants for the zinc and cadmium tetracyano ions are estimated to be 1.3×10^{-17} and 1.4×10^{-17}, respectively.[50] Zinc forms a few peculiar alkyl complexes, especially ethyl complexes of the types $M^I[Zn(C_2H_5)_3]$ and $M_2^I[Zn(C_2H_5)_4]$ (M^I = alkali metal). These materials are conductors of the electric current[51, 52] in solution in diethyl zinc and are electrolyzed to zinc and various hydrocarbons. Zinc chloride adds hydrocarbons such as 2-methylbutene-2, a behavior similar to that noted for silver in Group I.

SUGGESTED SUPPLEMENTARY REFERENCES

N. V. Sidgwick: *The Chemical Elements and Their Compounds*, pp. 193–333. Clarendon Press, Oxford (1950).

W. M. Latimer: *The Oxidation States of the Elements and Their Potentials in Aqueous Solutions*, Ch. X, XX. Prentice-Hall, New York (1938).

[49] R. G. Dickinson: *J. Am. Chem. Soc.*, **44,** 774 (1922).

[50] H. von Euler: *Ber.*, **36,** 3400 (1903).

[51] F. Hein: *Z. Elektrochem.*, **28,** 469 (1922).

[52] F. Hein with E. Petschner, K. Wagler, and A. Segitz: *Z. anorg. allgem. Chem.*, **141,** 161 (1924).

CHAPTER 20

The Transition Elements

As previously indicated (pp. 103–106), the transition series arise because of preferential occupancy of $(n - 1)$ d orbitals, the ns arrangements remaining constant or nearly constant. By this definition, one includes as transition elements all those in the series Sc-Ni, Y-Pd, La-Pd, and Ac on. However, because of the filling of $4f$ and $5f$ orbitals, certain of the elements in the latter two series (the inner transition elements) possess properties which are sufficiently distinctive to warrant separate consideration of these elements. This is done in Chapter 21. Remarks in the current chapter are restricted, therefore, to the transition elements proper.

All the transition elements are metals. They vary widely in abundance, some (e.g., Fe, Ti) being plentiful, others (e.g., Sc, Re) being rare. Many of the elements are distinctly unfamiliar in general practice either because of inherent scarcity or difficulty of recovery, yet the transition series also contain a number of metals (e.g., Fe, Ni, Cr, W, Mo, Ti) about which world technical economy is built. The characteristics of the transition metals vary tremendously from family to family, yet as a group these elements are characterized by high densities, low atomic volumes, high melting points, high boiling points, and abilities to form alloys both with each other and with some of the representative elements. Within any particular transition series there is a well-defined similarity among the members which is not encountered to any particular extent among representative elements of gradually changing atomic numbers. Such similarities reside in similarities in electronic arrangements and sizes and are, of course, even more pronounced with the inner transition elements. As their name implies, the transition metals really serve as transition elements between the most highly electropositive and the least highly electropositive representative elements.

It is manifestly impossible to discuss the transition elements comprehensively within the space of a single chapter. However, it is practical to give an overall summary which may be useful in relating these elements to the other elements of the periodic classification. Accordingly, some of the general characteristics of the elements and those properties of the elements and their compounds which are most closely dependent upon electronic configurations are discussed. This information is then supplemented by brief consideration of the members of the individual families.

PHYSICAL AND CHEMICAL CHARACTERISTICS OF THE ELEMENTS

Numerical properties characteristic of the members of the first, second, and third transition series are summarized, respectively, in Tables 20·1, 20·2, and 20·3. Similarities and differences within each series are thus readily apparent. The trends within each family are shown by comparison of the three tables. These trends are in general those already discussed for the other metallic elements and are due to the same underlying causes. The effects of the lanthanide contraction are shown quite clearly. The values in these three tables may be compared to advantage with corresponding data for the Group I (Tables 18·1 and 18·2), Group II (Tables 19·1 and 19·2), and lanthanide (Table 21·1) elements.

It is impossible to distinguish any regularity in the chemical characteristics of the transition metals. The metals vary from highly electropositive (e.g., Sc, Y, La, Ac) to essentially inert (e.g., platinum metals) character. Even within individual families significant differences appear. These become most apparent toward the ends of the transition series and are least pronounced among the beginning members. Individual properties are discussed in conjunction with members of the individual families.

CHARACTERISTICS RELATED TO ELECTRONIC ARRANGEMENTS

Addition of electrons to $(n-1)d$ orbitals without significant alteration of the "outermost" arrangements renders the transition metals and their derived ions significantly different from the representative elements. Such differences appear in oxidation states, magnetic properties, colors of ionic and complex species, and formation of complex materials and interstitial compounds. However, the distinguishing $(n-1)d$ electrons readily become the "outermost" electrons and are not particularly shielded even in the neutral atoms. As a consequence, they are involved completely or in part when the elements enter into chemical combination and never contribute to unusual characteristics to the extent that f electrons do (pp. 895–901). Size decreases with increasing atomic numbers are significantly less than

TABLE 20·1
NUMERICAL PROPERTIES OF ELEMENTS OF FIRST TRANSITION SERIES

Property	Sc	Ti	V	Cr	Mn	Fe	Co	Ni
Atomic number	21	22	23	24	25	26	27	28
Outer electron configuration	$3d^14s^2$	$3d^24s^2$	$3d^34s^2$	$3d^54s^1$	$3d^54s^2$	$3d^64s^2$	$3d^74s^2$	$3d^84s^2$
Mass numbers, stable isotopes	45	46, 47, 48, 49, 50	51	50, 52, 53, 54	55	54, 56, 57, 58	59	58, 60, 61, 62, 64
Atomic weight	45.10	47.90	50.95	52.01	54.93	55.85	58.94	58.69
Density of solid at 20°C., grams/cc.	3.1	4.43	6.07	7.188	7.21	7.869	8.70	8.902
Atomic volume, cc.	14.55	10.81	8.39	7.24	7.62	7.10	6.77	6.59
Melting point, °C.		1725	1710	1550	1260	1535	1490	1452
Boiling point, °C.		> 3000	3000(?)	2475	1900	2735	2900	2730
Covalent radius, A	1.439	1.324	1.224	1.172	1.168	1.165	1.157	1.149
Ionization potential, ev	6.56	6.83	6.74	6.76	7.432	7.896	7.86	7.633
Electronegativity	1.3	1.6						

TABLE 20·2

NUMERICAL PROPERTIES OF ELEMENTS OF SECOND TRANSITION SERIES

Property	Y	Zr	Nb	Mo	Tc	Ru	Rh	Pd
Atomic number	39	40	41	42	43	44	45	46
Outer electron configuration	$4d^15s^2$	$4d^25s^2$	$4d^45s^1$	$4d^55s^1$	$4d^65s^1$	$4d^75s^1$	$4d^85s^1$	$4d^{10}$
Mass numbers, stable isotopes	89	90, 91, 92, 94, 96	93	92, 94, 95, 96, 97, 98, 100	......	96, 98, 99, 100, 101, 102, 104	103	102, 104, 105, 106, 108, 110
Atomic weight	88.92	91.22	92.91	95.95	(99)*	101.7	102.91	106.7
Density of solid at 20°C., grams/cc.	4.34	6.49	8.569	10.218	11.487†	12.43	12.42	12.03
Atomic volume, cc.	20.49	14.06	10.84	9.39		8.18	8.29	8.87
Melting point, °C.	1450–1500	1860	1950	2620		1950	1966	1555
Boiling point, °C.		> 2900	3300	4800(?)		> 2700	> 2500	2200
Covalent radius, A	1.616	1.454	1.342	1.291		1.241	1.247	1.278
Ionization potential, ev	6.6	6.95	6.77	7.18		7.5	7.7	8.33
Electronegativity	1.3	1.6						

* Longest-lived isotope. † Calculated from x-ray data.

TABLE 20·3

NUMERICAL PROPERTIES OF ELEMENTS OF THIRD TRANSITION SERIES

Property	La	Hf	Ta	W	Re	Os	Ir	Pt
Atomic number	57	72	73	74	75	76	77	78
Outer electron configuration	$5d^1 6s^2$	$5d^2 6s^2$	$5d^3 6s^2$	$5d^4 6s^2$	$5d^5 6s^2$	$5d^6 6s^2$	$5d^9$	$5d^9 6s^1$
Mass numbers, stable isotopes	138, 139	174, 176, 177, 178, 179, 180	181	180, 182, 183, 184, 186	185 187*	184, 186, 187, 188, 189, 190, 192	191, 193	192, 194, 195, 196, 198
Atomic weight	138.92	178.6	180.88	183.92	186.31	190.2	193.1	195.23
Density of solid at 20°C., grams/cc.	6.194	13.30	16.654	19.262	20.996	22.70	22.64	21.45
Atomic volume, cc.	22.43	13.43	10.86	9.55	8.87	8.38	8.53	9.11
Melting point, °C.	885	2227	3030	3370	3140	2500	2454	1774
Boiling point, °C.		> 3200	5300(?)	5930(?)		> 5300	4800	4130
Covalent radius, A	1.690	1.442	1.343	1.299	1.278	1.255	1.260	1.290
Ionization potential, ev	5.61	5.5 ±	6 ±	7.98	7.87	8.7	9.2	8.96

* Radioactive.

among the representative elements because of the constancy of outer electron arrangements. It is important to point out again (p. 93) that the principle of maximum multiplicity promotes lack of electron pairing in the *d* orbitals.

Oxidation states

Known oxidation states for the various transition metals are summarized in Table 20·4. Constancy of oxidation state is character-

TABLE 20·4
OXIDATION STATES OF THE TRANSITION METALS

Sc	Ti	V	Cr	Mn	Fe	Co	Ni
+3	+2	+2	+2	+2	(+1)*	(+1)	(+1)
	+3	+3	+3	+3	+2	+2	+2
	+4	+4	+6	+4	+3	+3	(+3)
		+5		+6	+6	+4	+4
				+7			
Y	**Zr**	**Nb**	**Mo**	**Tc**	**Ru**	**Rh**	**Pd**
+3	(+3)	(+2)	+2	+7	+2	+2	+2
	+4	+3	+3		+3	+3	(+3)
		(+4)	+4		+4	+4	+4
		+5	+5		(+5)	(+6)	
			+6		+6		
					(+7)		
					+8		
La	**Hf**	**Ta**	**W**	**Re**	**Os**	**Ir**	**Pt**
+3	(+3)	(+2)	+2	(−1)	+2	+2	+2
	+4	(+3)	+3	(+1)	+3	+3	(+3)
		(+4)	+4	(+2)	+4	+4	+4
		+5	+5	+3	+6	(+6)	(+6)
			+6	+4	+8		
				+5			
				+6			
				+7			

* Oxidation states given in parentheses have been reported but are either extremely unstable or poorly characterized.

istic of the Group IIIa elements and, with the exception of titanium, of the Group IVa elements, but among the other materials variability is the rule. The lowest common positive oxidation state is +2, corresponding to the removal of the ns^2 electrons generally characteristic of the transition metal atoms. If other oxidation states exist, they commonly differ from each other by unity, corresponding to the lack of pairing of *d* electrons. For a given element, increases in covalent character, acidity, ease of hydrolysis, etc., of course parallel increases in oxidation number.

Striking similarities in solubilities and crystallographic properties are found among compounds of adjacent transition metals, provided the oxidation state remains constant. These are due to essential constancy in crystal radii with changing atomic number. Thus, for members of the first transition series (taken as typical), the following empirical radii (in angstroms) are given:

	V	Cr	Mn	Fe	Co	Ni
+2			0.91	0.83	0.82	0.78
+3	0.75	0.65		0.67	0.65	

Except for such regularities, the general characteristics of the various oxidation states, particularly the oxidizing and reducing properties, vary from family to family and often from element to element.

Magnetic properties

Previous discussions have been devoted to the magnetic properties of both the simple transition metal ions (pp. 169–170) and certain of the complexes derived from them (pp. 227–278). In almost all instances, the observed magnetic moment is related directly to the number of unpaired electrons present in the *d* orbitals.

Color and absorption spectra

Transition metal ions containing unpaired *d* electrons are colored both in solid salts and in solution. This is indicated for the members of the first transition series and related materials in Table 20.5. Such

TABLE 20·5

COLORS OF SIMPLE IONS OF MEMBERS OF FIRST TRANSITION SERIES AND RELATED METALS

Number of Unpaired Electrons	Ionic Species and Color
0	K^+, Ca^{+2}, Sc^{+3}, Ti^{+4}, Cu^+, Zn^{+2}, Ga^{+3} (colorless)
1	Ti^{+3} (purple), V^{+4} (blue)
2	V^{+3} (green), Ni^{+2} (green)
3	V^{+2} (violet), Cr^{+3} (violet), Co^{+2} (pink)
4	Cr^{+2} (blue), Mn^{+3} (violet), Fe^{+2} (green)
5	Mn^{+2} (pink), Fe^{+3} (yellow)

colors are reasonably intense, but they are readily modified by the presence of a variety of complexing agents. This indicates further that transitions involving the *d* electrons present are responsible for the colors since these are the electrons which are involved in complex formation. The absorption spectra of most colored transition series species consist of rather broad absorption bands, the positions of which are characteristic of the ionic or complex species present.

Complex formation

The ability to form complex species is at a maximum among the transition metal ions,[1] doubtless because of a combination of such favorable acceptor factors as small cation size, comparatively large nuclear or ionic charges, and appropriate electronic arrangements. This is apparent from the discussions in Chapter 7, where most of the examples considered are derived from transition metal ions. It must not be assumed, however, that all transition metal ions form complexes with equal ease. Not only are there marked variations from family to family and within each family but also significant differences among the various oxidation states of particular metals as well. However, there are very readily distinguishable trends toward enhanced stabilities of complex species with increasing atomic number in each particular transition series, with decreasing size in a particular state of oxidation in each particular family, and with increasing oxidation number for each particular element. Of course, exceptions to these trends can be found without difficulty.

Cobalt(III) and closely related cations form a variety of truly covalent complex species, the chemistries of which have been described to some extent in Chapter 7. Among these, sp^3, dsp^2, and d^2sp^3 hybridizations (pp. 256–261) are readily obtained. Much of the chemistry of the platinum metals is that of the complexes which they form. These tendencies of course carry over into certain oxidation states of the coinage metals (pp. 839–843). At the other extreme among the Group IIIa cations, tendencies toward the formation of stable complex species are practically indistinguishable except for scandium ion. Such species as exist only in solution are presumably predominantly ionic in character (pp. 902–903) and normally have no stable existence in the solid state. All instances between these extremes characterize cations of the intermediate elements.

The effect of oxidation state is often striking. The classic example, of course, is again cobalt where in the dipositive state only comparatively unstable ionic complexes form whereas in the tripositive state stable covalent species form (p. 227). Similar situations are found for chromium, vanadium, and a number of other metals. In some instances, for example among the carbonyls (pp. 700–717) and certain cyano derivatives (pp. 718–719), even the neutral metals yield com-

[1] J. C. Bailar, Jr.: *Chem. Revs.*, **23**, 65 (1938).

plex species. The appearance of otherwise unknown oxidation states is not uncommon (pp. 300–301).

Interstitial compound formation

The transition metals appear to be unique in their ability to react with small non-metal atoms to give interstitial compounds. The characteristics of hydrides (pp. 411–415), nitrides (pp. 579–580), carbides (pp. 699–700), and borides (pp. 769–773) of this type should be reviewed. It should be pointed out also that formation of non-stoichiometric compounds (pp. 224–225) is also a striking characteristic of the transition metals.

CHARACTERISTICS OF INDIVIDUAL TRANSITION METAL FAMILIES

Periodic Group IIIa (Sc, Y, La, Lu, Ac)

The chemistries of all these elements except scandium are intimately related to the chemistries of the inner transition elements as described in Chapter 21. As such they need not be covered at this point. All these elements are highly electropositive and in general have the properties which one would predict by an extension of the trends noted between the alkali metals (Ch. 18) and the alkaline earth metals (Ch. 19). They are all comparatively rare and distinctly unfamiliar. Scandium is somewhat different from the others because of the smaller size of its cation. Such differences appear largely in mode of occurrence in nature (scandium usually not associated with the others) and ease of complex formation.

Periodic Group IVa (Ti, Zr, Hf)

Except for hafnium, these elements are reasonably abundant, in nature (Ti, 0.44%; Zr, 0.022%; Hf, 4.5×10^{-4}% of the igneous rocks of the earth). Yet the difficulties of separation and particularly of preparation of the free metals have rendered them comparatively unfamiliar for many years. The widespread use of titanium(IV) oxide as a white pigment[2] and realization of the excellent physical and chemical properties (like those of stainless steel) of elemental titanium[3–5] have given titanium materials technical status. A similar situation

[2] J. Barksdale: *Titanium. Its Occurrence, Chemistry, and Technology,* Ch. 10–20. The Ronald Press Co., New York (1949).

[3] W. H. Waggaman and E. A. Gee: *Chem. Eng. News,* **26,** 377 (1948).

[4] O. C. Ralston and F. J. Cservenyak: *Ind. Eng. Chem.,* **42,** 214 (1950).

[5] E. A. Gee, W. H. Van Derhoef, and C. H. Winter: *J. Electrochem. Soc.,* **97,** 49 (1950).

may be expected for zirconium.[3, 6–8] Hafnium differs so slightly from zirconium because of lanthanide contraction effects that its development appears to offer no immediate advantages. Its separation from the much more abundant zirconium is so difficult that it is seldom carried out technically.

TABLE 20.6
Oxidation Potentials Characteristic of Group IVa Elements

Couple	Equation	E^0_{298}, volts		
		Ti	Zr	Hf
M(O)–M(IV)*	$M + 2H_2O \rightleftharpoons MO_2 + 4H^+ + 4e^-$	0.95	1.43	1.57
	$M + H_2O \rightleftharpoons MO^{++} + 2H^+ + 4e^-$	ca. 0.95	1.53	1.68
	$M + 4OH^- \rightleftharpoons MO(OH)_2 + H_2O + 4e^-$		2.32	2.60
M(O)–M(II)	$Ti \rightleftharpoons Ti^{+2} + 2e^-$	1.75		
M(II)–M(III)	$Ti^{+2} \rightleftharpoons Ti^{+3} + e^-$	0.37		
M(III)–M(IV)	$Ti^{+3} + H_2O \rightleftharpoons TiO^+ + 2H^+ + e^-$	ca. −0.1		

* Comparative values for thorium:

$$Th \rightleftharpoons Th^{+4} + 4e^- \qquad E^0_{298} = \text{ca. } 2.06 \text{ volts}$$
$$Th + 2H_2O \rightleftharpoons ThO_2 + 4H^+ + 4e^- \qquad = 1.80$$
$$Th + 4OH^- \rightleftharpoons ThO_2 + 2H_2O + 4e^- \qquad = 2.64$$

The metals react readily with the halogens, oxygen, sulfur, nitrogen, hydrogen, water vapor, etc., at elevated temperatures but are comparatively unreactive at ordinary temperatures. Pertinent oxidation potential data for the free elements and various ionic species with titanium are summarized in Table 20.6. The +4 oxidation state is most characteristic and is weakly oxidizing. For titanium the lower states are well characterized and strongly reducing. The tetrapositive compounds are quite readily hydrolyzed. In this state, there is a fair resemblance to thorium. The free metals are obtained in ductile form by thermal reduction of the anhydrous tetrachlorides with magnesium,[3, 5, 8] followed by sintering and mechanical working or fusion.

Periodic Group Va (V, Nb, Ta)

These elements are reasonably rare (V, $1.5 \times 10^{-2}\%$; Nb, $2.4 \times 10^{-3}\%$; and Ta, $2.1 \times 10^{-4}\%$ of the igneous rocks of the earth) and generally lacking in familiarity. Vanadium is widely used in the pro-

[6] Anon: *Chem. Eng. News,* **27,** 3198 (1949).
[7] Anon: *J. Chem. Education,* **27,** 24 (1950).
[8] W. J. Kroll and W. W. Stephens: *Ind. Eng. Chem.,* **42,** 395 (1950).

duction of ferrous alloys both as a scavenger and as a strengthening and toughening agent. The marked improvement in the properties of alloy steels produced by even small quantities of the metal (added as ferrovanadium, an iron-vanadium alloy) has contributed to technical use of the metal. Development of niobium and tantalum has been slowed by uncertain mineral supplies and processing difficulties. However, the marked resistance of both metals, particularly of tantalum, to acid corrosion has made them useful in the production of chemical process equipment. Technically, tantalum is the more important,[9–11] and its future is assured. Niobium is more difficult to recover than tantalum. It appears to offer advantages over the other metal in ferrous alloys and high temperature resisting alloys.

TABLE 20.7

OXIDATION POTENTIALS CHARACTERISTIC OF GROUP VA ELEMENTS

Couple	Equation	E^0_{298}, volts		
		V	Nb	Ta
M(O)–M(V)	$2M + 5H_2O \rightleftharpoons M_2O_5 + 10H^+ + 10e^-$		0.62	0.71
M(O)–M(III)	$M \rightleftharpoons M^{+3} + 3e^-$		ca. 1.1	
M(O)–M(II)	$M \rightleftharpoons M^{+2} + 2e^-$	ca. 1.5		
M(II)–M(III)	$M^{+2} \rightleftharpoons M^{+3} + e^-$	0.20		
M(III)–M(IV)	$M^{+3} + H_2O \rightleftharpoons MO^{+2} + 2H^+ + e^-$	−0.314		
M(IV)–M(V)	$MO^{+2} + 3H_2O \rightleftharpoons M(OH)_4^+ + 2H^+ + e^-$	−1.00		

The metals are somewhat less reactive than the Group IVa metals, but they do react at elevated temperatures with the halogens, oxygen, sulfur, nitrogen, carbon, etc. A variety of products is formed. Vanadium dissolves in nitric acid. The others are resistant to all acids except to mixtures of nitric and hydrofluoric acids. Oxidation potentials characteristic of the metals and various ionic species are summarized in Table 20·7. Tantalum is well known in only the +5 state. Niobium forms well-characterized compounds in the +3 state as well. For vanadium, a number of oxidation states are known, the most important species being V^{+2} (vanadous), V^{+3} (vanadic), VO^{+2} (vanadyl), VO^{+3} or $V(OH)_4^+$ (pervanadyl), and VO_3^- (metavanadate). The lower oxidation states of vanadium are strongly reducing, the higher moderately oxidizing (Table 20.7). Niobium(III) is reducing. In the +5 state, all three elements are readily hydrolyzed and readily

[9] K. Rose: *Materials and Methods*, October 1947.

[10] C. W. Balke: *Chemistry and Industry*, **1948**, 83.

[11] Anon.: *J. Chem. Education*, **27**, 24 (1950).

converted into anionic species. The vanadates are somewhat similar to the phosphates (pp. 644–654). In addition to simple ortho- and meta-vanadates, a simple pyrovanadate ($V_2O_7^{-4}$) and a variety of more complex isopoly- and heteropoly-vanadates (pp. 273–277) can be distinguished. A number of similarities between tantalum and protactinium chemistries are known.

Pure elemental vanadium is seldom prepared, ferrovanadium as obtained by the reduction of mixed iron and vanadium oxides being suited to the needs of the steel industry. Reduction of vanadium(V) oxide with calcium in the presence of iodine yields the ductile metal in a high state of purity.[12] Tantalum is obtained in powder form by electrolysis of the fused double fluoride, $K_2[TaF_7]$. Niobium is obtained similarly or by reaction of the pentapositive oxide with the carbide at elevated temperatures. The powdered metals are compacted by sintering and rendered ductile by working *in vacuo*.

Periodic Group VIa (Cr, Mo, W)

Except for chromium, these elements are not particularly abundant (Cr, 0.02%; Mo, ca. 10^{-3} to 10^{-4}%; W, ca. 10^{-3} to 10^{-4}% of the igneous rocks of the earth). Chromium is generally regarded as a familiar element and the others as unfamiliar, although it must be admitted that both molybdenum and tungsten are very widely used as such as alloying elements in the steel industry to impart hardness and toughness and that tungsten is used in sizable quantities for filaments in the electronics industry. These uses, together with those of a number of compounds, combine to make total production of molybdenum and tungsten materials very large. Yet the fundamental chemistries of their compounds still remain distinctly unfamiliar. The widespread use of chromium as a decorative and protective metal, in alloys, and as compounds is well known. Chromium-containing steels are important because of their hardness and resistance to corrosion.

The metals are stable in air at ordinary temperatures but react with oxygen at elevated temperatures. Reactions with the halogens, carbon, sulfur, boron, etc., also take place at elevated temperatures. Chromium is oxidized by hydronium ion, but molybdenum and tungsten are not. Nitric acid dissolves chromium but converts the other two metals to oxides of the type MO_3. Chromium becomes passive in contact with concentrated nitric acid and other strong oxidizing agents. The reaction products of the various elements differ widely and are difficult to systematize. Important oxidation potential data are summarized in Table 20·8. Because of the widely different half-

[12] R. K. McKechnie and A. U. Seybolt: *J. Electrochem. Soc.*, **97**, 311 (1950).

reactions involved, potentials are given by elements rather than by type reactions. Many of the values for molybdenum and tungsten couples are provisional only. Ionic species of importance are Cr^{+2}, Cr^{+3}, $Cr_2O_7{}^{-2}$, $CrO_4{}^{-2}$, Mo^{+3}, $MoO_2{}^+$, $MoO_4{}^{-2}$, and $WO_4{}^{-2}$. In addition, many complex ions derived in particular from chromium(III), molybdenum(II, III, IV, V), and tungsten(II, III, IV, V) are known.

TABLE 20·8

OXIDATION POTENTIALS CHARACTERISTIC OF GROUP VIA ELEMENTS

Couple	Equation	E^0_{298}, volts
Cr(O)–Cr(II)	$Cr \rightleftharpoons Cr^{+2} + 2e^-$	0.86
Cr(O)–Cr(III)	$Cr \rightleftharpoons Cr^{+3} + 3e^-$	0.71
	$Cr + 3OH^- \rightleftharpoons Cr(OH)_3 + 3e^-$	1.3
Cr(II)–Cr(III)	$Cr^{+2} \rightleftharpoons Cr^{+3} + e^-$	0.41
Cr(III)–Cr(VI)	$2Cr^{+3} + 7H_2O \rightleftharpoons Cr_2O_7{}^{-2} + 14H^+ + 6e^-$	−1.36
	$Cr(OH)_3 + 5OH^- \rightleftharpoons CrO_4{}^{-2} + 4H_2O + 3e^-$	0.12
Mo(O)–Mo(III)	$Mo \rightleftharpoons Mo^{+3} + 3e^-$	ca. 0.2
Mo(O)–Mo(VI)	$Mo + 3H_2O \rightleftharpoons MoO_3 + 6H^+ + 6e^-$	−0.1
	$Mo + 8OH^- \rightleftharpoons MoO_4{}^{-2} + 4H_2O + 6e^-$	0.97
Mo(III)–Mo(V)	$Mo^{+3} + 2H_2O \rightleftharpoons MoO_2{}^+ + 4H^+ + 2e^-$	ca. 0.0
Mo(V)–Mo(VI)	$MoO_2{}^+ + 2H_2O \rightleftharpoons H_2MoO_4(aq) + 2H^+ + e^-$	ca. −0.4
W(O)–W(IV)	$W + 2H_2O \rightleftharpoons WO_2 + 4H^+ + 4e^-$	0.05
W(O)–W(VI)	$W + 8OH^- \rightleftharpoons WO_4{}^{-2} + 4H_2O + 6e^-$	ca. 1.1
W(IV)–W(V)	$2WO_2 + H_2O \rightleftharpoons W_2O_5 + 2H^+ + 2e^-$	ca. 0.0
W(V)–W(VI)	$W_2O_5 + H_2O \rightleftharpoons 2WO_3 + 2H^+ + 2e^-$	−0.15

Chromium(II) or chromous compounds are somewhat similar to iron(II) compounds but are more strongly reducing. Chromium(II) ion can be prepared in acid solution either by direct action of acid (*e.g.*, hydrochloric) on the metal or by zinc reduction of chromium(III), but it is readily oxidized either by hydrogen ion or atmospheric oxygen. Such solutions are excellent for quantitative removal of oxygen from gas mixtures. Solid chromium(II) compounds oxidize in moist air and should be preserved under nitrogen or *in vacuo*. Chromium(II) acetate is more readily prepared than most other chromium(II) compounds because of its water insolubility.[13, 14] It is a red crystalline compound useful as a reducing agent. Chromium(II) ion is basic, only slightly hydrolyzed, and not readily complexed. Chromium(III) or chromic compounds resemble those of iron(III) but are less strongly oxidizing and more readily oxidized. This is the most generally stable oxidation state of chromium in aqueous solution.

[13] J. H. Balthis and J. C. Bailar, Jr.: *Inorganic Syntheses*, Vol. I, p. 122. McGraw-Hill Book Co., New York (1939).

[14] M. R. Hatfield: *Inorganic Syntheses*, Vol. III, p. 148. McGraw-Hill Book Co., New York (1950).

Chromium(III) ion is readily complexed, and the simple aquated ion presumably can exist only in contact with a limited number of anions (e.g., NO_3^-, ClO_4^-). In the absence of strongly complexing groups, chromium(III) is amphoteric toward hydroxyl ion and is strongly hydrolyzed. Chromium(VI) is most commonly encountered as chromate (CrO_4^{-2}) or dichromate ($Cr_2O_7^{-2}$). The anionic aggregation responsible for conversion of chromate to dichromate on addition of acid is continued in the further conversion to trichromate ($Cr_3O_{10}^{-2}$) at extremely high acidities (p. 273). Stable dichromates are known for the alkali metals and ammonium, but the heavy metals yield chromates preferentially. These are commonly insoluble. Free chromic acid is unknown. The acid chlorides, CrO_2Cl_2 (chromyl chloride), and CrO_3Cl^- (chlorochromate) ion, are readily prepared but undergo rapid hydrolysis to chromate. Chromium(VI) is strongly oxidizing in acidic solution, the potential being markedly dependent upon the proton concentration (Table 20·8), but only weakly oxidizing in alkaline media. Conversion of chromium(III) to chromium(VI) is readily effected (e.g., by peroxides) in alkaline solution or by fusion under alkaline conditions (e.g., by nitrates or chlorates or even atmospheric oxygen). Peroxy chromium compounds are described in Chapter 14 (pp. 508, 514), and a number of chromium(II) complexes are discussed in Chapter 7.

The lower oxidation states of both molybdenum and tungsten are quite generally reducing in character and undergo fairly ready conversion to the +6 state. For molybdenum, the uncomplexed tripositive ion appears to be capable of existence in aqueous solution. However, all the lower oxidation states of both elements are best characterized in various complex ions and compounds. Information on these materials is at best incomplete and requires considerable systematization. Molybdenum(VI) and tungsten(VI) are the most stable and best-characterized oxidation states. The simple molybdates and tungstates resemble the chromates in solubilities, but the chemistry of this oxidation state is more complicated by isopoly and heteropoly anion formation (pp. 273–277). Reduction of molybdates and tungstates is markedly different from reduction of chromates. A variety of reducing agents [including molybdenum(III)] convert molybdates into colloidal *molybdenum blues*, the compositions of which approach $Mo_8O_{23}{\cdot}xH_2O$.[15] Comparable *tungsten blues* are obtained by reduction of tungstates in aqueous solution. At elevated temperatures, however, alkali and alkaline earth metal tungstates are reduced

[15] F. B. Schirmer, L. F. Audrieth, S. T. Gross, D. S. McClellan, and L. J. Seppi: *J. Am. Chem. Soc.*, **64**, 2543 (1942).

by hydrogen, zinc, electrolysis, etc., to metallic appearing, highly colored, conducting solids called *tungsten bronzes* (p. 225). These compounds have compositions approaching $M_x^IWO_3$ ($x < 1$) and apparently have defect structures (pp. 224–225) in which omission of sodium ions is compensated for by oxidation of equivalent quantities of tungsten(V) to tungsten(VI). Their colors are apparently due to the presence of two oxidation states and their metallic conductivities to statistical distribution of the extra valency electron in tungsten(V) throughout the lattice. Further information on these materials is given in several papers.[16–19]

Elemental chromium is obtained by aluminothermic reduction of the tripositive oxide or by electrodeposition from acidified chromium(VI) solutions. For use in the steel industry, it is obtained as ferrochrome by direct carbon reduction of the mineral chromite, $Fe(CrO_2)_2$. Molybdenum and tungsten are obtained as powders by hydrogen reduction of the +6 oxides, MO_3. The powders are compacted by pressure and sintering and cold-worked to give the ductile metals.

Periodic Group VIIa (Mn, Tc, Re)

Manganese is abundant (0.1% of the igneous rocks of the earth), rhenium is exceedingly rare (10^{-7}% of the igneous rocks of the earth), and technetium apparently does not occur in nature (p. 26). Manganese is of technical importance both as the metal and in the form of its compounds (especially the dioxide). Manganese is indispensable to the steel industry because of its excellent scavenging and toughening characteristics. Rhenium has few, if any, technical applications. Technetium was first characterized in the decay products resulting from the bombardment of molybdenum with neutrons or deuterons (p. 77).[20, 21] It is also an important product of the fission of uranium-235. Only manganese is a familiar element.

Elemental manganese is a rather powerful reducing agent and is oxidized by hydrogen ion, water, the halogens, sulfur, etc. to the dipositive state. Oxygen yields the salt-like oxide Mn_3O_4; carbon gives the carbide Mn_3C; and nitrogen yields a nitride Mn_5N_3. Rhenium is much less electropositive and is attacked only by rather power-

[16] M. E. Straumanis: *J. Am. Chem. Soc.*, **71**, 679 (1949).

[17] M. E. Straumanis and A. Dravnieks: *J. Am. Chem. Soc.*, **71**, 683 (1949).

[18] P. M. Stubbin and D. P. Mellor: *J. Proc. Roy. Soc. N. S. Wales*, **82**, 225 (1948).

[19] E. O. Brimm, J. C. Brantley, J. H. Lorenz, and M. H. Jellinek: *J. Am. Chem. Soc.*, **73**, 5427 (1951).

[20] C. Perrier and E. Segrè: *J. Chem. Phys.*, **5**, 712 (1937); **7**, 155 (1939).

[21] J. C. Hackney: *J. Chem. Education*, **28**, 186 (1951).

ful oxidizing agents or at more elevated temperatures to give most commonly +4 and +7 compounds. In general characteristics, rhenium metal is much more like tungsten and the platinum metals than like manganese. Technetium presumably occupies an intermediate position. Important potentials characteristic of the free elements and their compounds are summarized in Table 20·9. Most important of the oxidation states are manganese(II, IV, VII) and rhenium(IV, VI, VII).

TABLE 20·9

OXIDATION POTENTIALS CHARACTERISTICS OF GROUP VIIA ELEMENTS

Couple	Equation	E^0_{298}, volts
Mn(O)–Mn(II)	$Mn \rightleftharpoons Mn^{+2} + 2e^-$	1.05
	$Mn + 2OH^- \rightleftharpoons Mn(OH)_2 + 2e^-$	1.47
Mn(II)–Mn(III)	$Mn^{+2} \rightleftharpoons Mn^{+3} + e^-$	−1.51
	$Mn(OH)_2 + OH^- \rightleftharpoons Mn(OH)_3 + e^-$	0.4
Mn(II)–Mn(IV)	$Mn^{+2} + 2H_2O \rightleftharpoons MnO_2 + 4H^+ + 2e^-$	−1.28
Mn(II)–Mn(VII)	$Mn^{+2} + 4H_2O \rightleftharpoons MnO_4^- + 8H^+ + 5e^-$	−1.52
Mn(III)–Mn(IV)	$Mn^{+3} + 2H_2O \rightleftharpoons MnO_2 + 4H^+ + e^-$	−1.1
	$Mn(OH)_3 + OH^- \rightleftharpoons MnO_2 + 2H_2O + e^-$	−0.5
Mn(IV)–Mn(VI)	$MnO_2 + 2H_2O \rightleftharpoons MnO_4^{-2} + 4H^+ + 2e^-$	−2.23
	$MnO_2 + 4OH^- \rightleftharpoons MnO_4^{-2} + 2H_2O + 2e^-$	−0.58
Mn(IV)–Mn(VII)	$MnO_2 + 2H_2O \rightleftharpoons MnO_4^- + 4H^+ + 3e^-$	−1.67
	$MnO_2 + 4OH^- \rightleftharpoons MnO_4^- + 2H_2O + 3e^-$	−0.57
Mn(VI)–Mn(VII)	$MnO_4^{-2} \rightleftharpoons MnO_4^- + e^-$	−0.54
Re(O)–Re(IV)	$Re + 2H_2O \rightleftharpoons ReO_2 + 4H^+ + 4e^-$	ca. 0.0
	$Re + 4OH^- \rightleftharpoons ReO_2 + 2H_2O + 4e^-$	ca. 0.8
	$Re + 6Cl^- \rightleftharpoons [ReCl_6]^{-2} + 4e^-$	ca. 0.1
Re(O)–Re(VII)	$Re + 4H_2O \rightleftharpoons ReO_4^- + 8H^+ + 7e^-$	−0.15
	$Re + 8OH^- \rightleftharpoons ReO_4^- + 4H_2O + 7e^-$	0.81
Re(IV)–Re(VII)	$ReO_2 + 2H_2O \rightleftharpoons ReO_4^- + 4H^+ + 3e^-$	ca. −0.3

Manganese(II) or manganous compounds are rather strongly basic and resemble the corresponding chromium(II) and iron(II) compounds as to solubilities and crystal structures but are less easily oxidized in either acidic or alkaline medium. Oxidation in acidic solution gives manganese(IV) (as MnO_2) preferentially, although strong oxidants [e.g., lead(IV) oxide, bismuthate(V)] give manganese(VII) (as MnO_4^-). In alkaline medium, however, tripositive manganese is obtained even by atmospheric oxidation. More powerful oxidants (e.g., peroxide) then give manganese(IV). Manganese(III) or manganic ion is unstable in aqueous solution with respect to the disproportionation

$$2Mn^{+3} + 2H_2O \rightarrow MnO_2 + Mn^{+2} + 4H^+$$

but the "hydroxide" (often given as MnOOH) is stable. Tripositive manganese is also stabilized as the insoluble orthophosphate or the cyano complex, $[Mn(CN)_6]^{-3}$ (p. 301) and to a somewhat lesser extent as an alum (p. 540). Oxidation of manganese(II) in concentrated hydrochloric acid apparently gives a colored manganese(III) chloro complex of indeterminate composition.[22]

Manganese(IV) is usually encountered as the dioxide, formed either by oxidation of manganese(II) in acidic (e.g., with chlorate) or alkaline (e.g., with peroxide) medium or by reduction of manganese(VII) in alkaline medium [e.g., with tin(II)]. It is a powerful oxidant in its own right and is readily reduced to manganese(II). No manganese(IV) salts have been characterized, but the somewhat acidic character of the dioxide is shown by the existence of compounds such as $CaMnO_3$, the manganites. Manganese(VI), or manganate, resembles chromate (CrO_4^{-2}) and ferrate (FeO_4^{-2}) in the solubilities of its compounds, but is intermediate in stability. Manganese(VI) undergoes disproportionation in terms of the equilibrium

$$3MnO_4^{-2} + 2H_2O \rightleftharpoons 2MnO_4^- + MnO_2 + 4OH^-$$

The reaction is favored by acids (even carbon dioxide). As a consequence, manganese(VI) is stable only in strongly alkaline solutions or in difficultly soluble compounds such as the barium salt. Manganese(VI) compounds are usually obtained by fusion of the dioxide with an alkali such as sodium carbonate and an oxidizing agent such as a chlorate. The ion MnO_4^{-2} is bright green in color.

Manganese(VII) is best known as the ion MnO_4^- (permanganate), an intensely purple-colored species. The free acid is known only in solution, and the properties of aqueous solutions of its salts indicate it to be very strong. In solubilities and crystal structures, the permanganates are closely comparable to the perchlorates (pp. 442–443). Manganese(VII) is one of our best-characterized strong oxidants in acidic solution, and as such it can be formed from manganese(II or IV) compounds only by very powerful oxidants (see above). Its oxidizing power in alkaline solutions is materially reduced. Most reductants convert manganese(VII) to the dipositive state in acidic solution. In strongly acidic solution, water is slowly oxidized with evolution of oxygen.

The lower oxidation states of rhenium remain poorly characterized although studies have provided potentially useful data for their systematization.[23, 24] Most intriguing is the −1 state which apparently results when rhenium(VII) is reduced by zinc in sulfuric acid

[22] J. A. Ibers and N. Davidson: *J. Am. Chem. Soc.*, **72**, 4744 (1950).
[23] J. J. Lingane: *J. Am. Chem. Soc.*, **64**, 1001, 2182 (1942).
[24] E. K. Maun and N. Davidson: *J. Am. Chem. Soc.*, **72**, 2254, 3509 (1950).

solution[25] but which remains essentially uncharacterized. Rhenium(IV) is known in such compounds as oxide, sulfide, halides, and halocomplexes, $[ReX_6]^{-2}$. It differs from manganese(IV) in being a mildly reducing state rather than oxidizing and is quite stable. Rhenium(VI) is known as a stable oxide and as salts containing the ion ReO_4^{-2}. Rhenium(VII) is the commonest and most stable oxidation state. The oxide, Re_2O_7, is stable, unlike the highly explosive manganese analog. The acid, $HReO_4$, cannot be isolated as such but is apparently strong. Its salts, the perrhenates, are comparable to permanganates and perchlorates in general properties, but the perrhenate ion is a very weak oxidizing agent. Unlike the permanganate, it is colorless. Rhenium compounds undergo disproportionation very readily. Technetium compounds appear to be somewhat closer in properties to rhenium compounds than to manganese compounds.

Pure elemental manganese is obtained by aluminothermic reduction of the salt-like oxide Mn_3O_4 or by electrodeposition from a manganese(II) sulfate solution. Rhenium is obtained in powder form by hydrogen reduction of various oxygenated compounds. The ductile metal is prepared by powder metallurgical procedures.

Periodic Group VIII

Periodic Group VIII consists of three triads of metals, members of the first triad being referred to as the ferrous metals and those of the other two collectively as the platinum metals. Resemblances between the ferrous and platinum metals are slight. Resemblances among the ferrous metals and among the platinum metals are much more pronounced.

The Ferrous Metals (Fe, Co, Ni). The abundances of these metals in the igneous rocks of the earth are Fe, 5.0%; Co, 2.3×10^{-3}%; and Ni, 8.0×10^{-3}%. It appears, however, that the core of the earth is largely iron together with a considerable quantity of nickel. Iron is in all probability, therefore, the most abundant element. Maximum abundance in this region is expected in terms of nuclear stabilities (pp. 38, 61). Although cobalt is the rarest of the three, desirable properties of both the element and its alloys, existence of concentrated and accessible natural deposits, and long-standing interest in its coordinaion compounds have combined to render its chemistry comparatively familiar.

Iron, cobalt, and nickel are all moderately strong reducing agents. They are converted by hydrogen ion to the dipositive ions. Stronger

[25] G. E. F. Lundell and H. B. Knowles: *J. Research Natl. Bur. Standards,* **18,** 629 (1937).

oxidizing agents (e.g., oxygen, the halogens except iodine, nitric acid) give the tripositive state with iron, but with the other two the dipositive state results. Cobalt does give a mixed oxide, Co_3O_4, with oxygen and a higher fluoride, CoF_3, with fluorine, but these are isolated reactions. The metals, particularly iron, become passive in contact with strong oxidizing agents (e.g., concentrated nitric acid, dichromates). The most important oxidation states are iron(II, III), cobalt(II, III), and nickel(II). Other oxidation states are rare. Important oxidation potentials characteristic of the elements and their compounds are given in Table 20·10. Additional values illustrating the stabilization of various oxidation states are given in Table 8·4.

TABLE 20·10
OXIDATION POTENTIALS CHARACTERISTIC OF THE FERROUS METALS

Couple	Equation	E^0_{298}, volts		
		Fe	Co	Ni
M(O)–M(II)	$M \rightleftharpoons M^{+2} + 2e^-$	0.440	0.277	0.250
	$M + 2OH^- \rightleftharpoons M(OH)_2 + 2e^-$	0.877	0.73	0.66
M(II)–M(III)	$M^{+2} \rightleftharpoons M^{+3} + e^-$	−0.771	−1.82	
	$M(OH)_2 + OH^- \rightleftharpoons M(OH)_3 + e^-$	0.56	−0.2	
M(II)–M(IV)	$M^{+2} + 2H_2O \rightleftharpoons MO_2 + 4H^+ + 2e^-$			−1.75
	$M(OH)_2 + 2OH^- \rightleftharpoons MO_2 + 2H_2O + 2e^-$			−0.49
M(II)–M(VI)	$M^{+2} + 4H_2O \rightleftharpoons MO_4^{-2} + 8H^+ + 4e^-$			< −1.8
M(III)–M(IV)	$M^{+3} + 2H_2O \rightleftharpoons MO_2 + 4H^+ + e^-$		< −1.8	
M(III)–M(VI)	$M^{+3} + 4H_2O \rightleftharpoons MO_4^{-2} + 8H^+ + 3e^-$	< −1.9		
	$M(OH)_3 + 5OH^- \rightleftharpoons MO_4^{-2} + 4H_2O + 3e^-$	< −0.9		

Compounds of the dipositive elements resemble those of chromium(II) and manganese(II) but are somewhat less basic and more strongly hydrolyzed because of smaller cation radii. Resemblances between cobalt(II) and nickel(II) are so close as to render difficult separation of these species. The dipositive ions form a variety of complex species, many of which have been discussed in Part I of this book (e.g., Chapter 7).

From oxidation potential data (Table 20·10), it is apparent that these ions resist oxidation in acidic solutions, but are reasonably readily oxidized in neutral or alkaline media. In the presence of many complexing groups, cobalt(II) is very readily oxidized (pp. 301–302). A simple (i.e., aquated) tripositive ion is characteristic only of iron. Iron(III) or ferric compounds resemble those of chromium(III), vanadium(III), and aluminum(III) quite closely. Decreased basicity, increased hydrolysis, and increased covalence characterize the transition from iron(II) to iron(III). Many compounds containing the FeO_2^- group, i.e., the ferrites, have been prepared. Those derived from a number of dipositive elements, $M^{II}(FeO_2)_2$, are isomorphous with corresponding chromites and aluminates and are spinels (pp. 756–757). The magnetic oxide, Fe_3O_4, is an iron(II) ferrite, $Fe(FeO_2)_2$. The chemistry of cobalt(III) is almost entirely that of its complexes.

Cobalt(IV) is poorly characterized, but there are evidences for its existence in certain coordination compounds and in an unstable oxide. Nickel(IV) is well known as the oxide, a compound which has been employed for many years as the oxidizing agent in the alkaline Edison storage cell. The tetrapositive materials are strongly oxidizing, and no simple +4 ions are known. The +6 state of oxidation is well characterized only in the ferrates, FeO_4^{-2}, the corresponding nickel compounds being but little known. The ferrates are comparable to the chromates and manganates in solubilities and the permanganates in color. Iron(VI) is strongly oxidizing, particularly in acidic solution, and has been suggested as an analytical oxidizing agent.[26] Ferrates are commonly obtained by hypochlorite oxidation of iron(III) in alkaline solution. A convenient procedure for preparation of the potassium salt involves oxidation of iron(III) hydroxide with hypochlorite in concentrated sodium hydroxide solution as

$$2Fe(OH)_3 + 3ClO^- + 4OH^- \rightarrow 2FeO_4^{-2} + 3Cl^- + 5H_2O$$

followed by removal of insoluble sodium chloride and ultimate precipitation with potassium hydroxide.[27,28] The washed and dried salt is said to be stable. Its effective magnetic moment of 3.06 ± 0.02 Bohr magnetons, as compared with a theoretical value of 2.83, indicates the presence of two unpaired $3d$ electrons in the FeO_4^{-2} ion.[27] The barium salt is stable also, presumably because of its low solubility.

Iron is obtained technically by carbon monoxide reduction of the oxides by the blast furnace technique. Iron free from carbon is exceedingly difficult to prepare. High purity products are obtained by hydrogen reduction of the oxides, thermal decomposition of the pentacarbonyl, or electrodeposition. The presence of even minute quantities of carbon markedly alters the properties of the product. A comprehensive discussion of the iron-carbon system and of iron products and steels is beyond the scope of this volume. Cobalt and

[26] J. M. Schreyer, G. W. Thompson, and L. T. Ockerman: *Anal. Chem.*, **22**, 691 (1950).

[27] J. Hrostowski and A. B. Scott: *J. Chem. Phys.*, **18**, 105 (1950).

[28] G. W. Thompson, L. T. Ockerman, and J. M. Schreyer: *J. Am. Chem. Soc.*, **73**, 1379 (1951).

nickel are obtained by carbon reduction of their oxides, separation of the two metals being effected through volatilization of nickel as the tetracarbonyl (pp. 700, 711). Because of the complexities of most cobalt and nickel ores, recovery processes are involved and costly.

The Platinum Metals (Ru, Rh, Pd *and* Os, Ir, Pt). The platinum metals are all quite rare (Ru, present; Rh, 10^{-7}%; Pd, 10^{-6}%; Os, present %; Ir, 10^{-7}%; Pt, 5×10^{-7}% of the igneous rocks of the earth). However, a number of comparatively concentrated deposits both of the native metals and of the few known naturally occurring compounds exist in the Ural Mountains, Colombia, Ontario, Transvaal, etc. The metals all occur together but in varying quantities, depending upon the mineral source. Thus native platinum is largely platinum with small quantities of the others, whereas osmiridium is largely osmium and iridium, and platiniridium is chiefly platinum and iridium. The permanency and decorative appearance of the metals and their excellent catalytic properties have made the platinum metals articles of commerce, although prices are necessarily high.

The commonly considered distinguishing characteristic of the platinum metals is their nobility. In this respect they are often compared with gold. In terms of the Born-Haber treatment (pp. 184–186), this nobility must be due in large measure to high melting and boiling points and resultant high sublimation energies. Passivity is also an important factor. Although noble to a degree exceeding any other family of elements, the platinum metals differ markedly from each other in their resistance to attack by various reagents. Thus platinum, osmium, and palladium are soluble in aqua regia, but the others resist its attack. Palladium dissolves in nitric acid, but the others do not. Osmium and ruthenium give compounds $M_2{}^IOsO_4$ and $M_2{}^IRuO_4$ when fused with alkali and an oxidant, but the others are unreactive. Platinum shows no reaction with oxygen, but iridium and palladium give oxides at red heat, and osmium and ruthenium form the volatile MO_4 type oxides. A few important oxidation potentials are summarized in Table 20·11. Many of these values are provisional only. Oxidation states of particular importance are ruthenium(III, IV, VI, VIII), rhodium(III), palladium(II, IV), osmium(III, IV, VI, VIII), iridium(III, IV), and platinum(II, IV).

The characteristics of the various oxidation states of the platinum metals are difficult to systematize, and a comprehensive discussion of them is beyond the scope of this treatment. Few compounds containing uncomplexed species are known, the only real exceptions being oxides, sulfides, and a few halides and sulfates. Distinct parallels may be drawn among the complexes of iron, ruthenium, and osmium,

TABLE 20·11
OXIDATION POTENTIALS CHARACTERISTIC OF THE PLATINUM METALS

Couple	Equation	E^0_{298}, volts
Ru(O)–Ru(III)	$Ru + 5Cl^- \rightleftharpoons [RuCl_5]^{-2} + 3e^-$	ca. −0.4
Ru(O)–Ru(IV)	$Ru + 5Cl^- + H_2O \rightleftharpoons [RuCl_5(OH)]^{-2} + H^+ + 4e^-$	ca. −0.6
Ru(O)–Ru(VIII)	$Ru + 8OH^- \rightleftharpoons RuO_4 + 4H_2O + 8e^-$	−0.3
Os(O)–Os(VIII)	$Os + 4H_2O \rightleftharpoons OsO_4 + 8H^+ + 8e^-$	−0.85
	$Os + 9OH^- \rightleftharpoons HOsO_5^- + 4H_2O + 8e^-$	−0.02
Os(IV)–Os(VIII)	$OsO_2 + 5OH^- \rightleftharpoons HOsO_5^- + 2H_2O + 4e^-$	−0.2
Rh(O)–Rh(II)	$Rh \rightleftharpoons Rh^{+2} + 2e^-$	ca. −0.6
Rh(O)–Rh(III)	$Rh \rightleftharpoons Rh^{+3} + 3e^-$	ca. −0.7
Rh(III)–Rh(IV)	$Rh^{+3} + H_2O \rightleftharpoons RhO^{+2} + 2H^+ + e^-$	−1.40
	$Rh_2O_3 + 2OH^- \rightleftharpoons 2RhO_2 + H_2O + 2e^-$	> −0.9
	$[RhCl_6]^{-3} + 2H_2O \rightleftharpoons RhO_2 + 4H^+ + 6Cl^- + e^-$	< −1.4
Rh(IV)–Rh(VI)	$RhO^{+2} + 3H_2O \rightleftharpoons RhO_4^{-2} + 6H^+ + 2e^-$	−1.46
	$RhO_2 + 4OH^- \rightleftharpoons RhO_4^{-2} + 2H_2O + 2e^-$	> −0.9
Ir(O)–Ir(III)	$Ir \rightleftharpoons Ir^{+3} + 3e^-$	ca. −1.0
	$2Ir + 6OH^- \rightleftharpoons Ir_2O_3 + 3H_2O + 6e^-$	−0.1
	$Ir + 6Cl^- \rightleftharpoons [IrCl_6]^{-3} + 3e^-$	−0.72
Ir(III)–Ir(IV)	$Ir^{+3} + 2H_2O \rightleftharpoons IrO_2 + 4H^+ + e^-$	ca. −0.7
	$Ir_2O_3 + 2OH^- \rightleftharpoons 2IrO_2 + H_2O + 2e^-$	−0.1
	$[IrCl_6]^{-3} \rightleftharpoons [IrCl_6]^{-2} + e^-$	−1.021
Ir(IV)–Ir(VI)	$IrO_2 + 4OH^- \rightleftharpoons IrO_4^{-2} + 2H_2O + 2e^-$	> −0.4
Pd(O)–Pd(II)	$Pd \rightleftharpoons Pd^{+2} + 2e^-$	−0.83
	$Pd + 2OH^- \rightleftharpoons Pd(OH)_2 + 2e^-$	−0.1
	$Pd + 4Cl^- \rightleftharpoons [PdCl_4]^{-2} + 2e^-$	−0.64
Pd(II)–Pd(IV)	$Pd^{+2} \rightleftharpoons Pd^{+4} + 2e^-$	< −1.6
	$Pd(OH)_2 + 2OH^- \rightleftharpoons Pd(OH)_4 + 2e^-$	ca. −0.8
	$[PdCl_4]^{-2} + 2Cl^- \rightleftharpoons [PdCl_6]^{-2} + 2e^-$	−1.288
Pt(O)–Pt(II)	$Pt \rightleftharpoons Pt^{+2} + 2e^-$	ca. −1.2
	$Pt + 2OH^- \rightleftharpoons Pt(OH)_2 + 2e^-$	−0.16
	$Pt + S^{-2} \rightleftharpoons PtS + 2e^-$	0.83
	$Pt + 4Cl^- \rightleftharpoons [PtCl_4]^{-2} + 2e^-$	−0.73
	$Pt + 4Br^- \rightleftharpoons [PtBr_4]^{-2} + 2e^-$	−0.68
Pt(II)–Pt(IV)	$Pt(OH)_2 \rightleftharpoons PtO_2 + 2H^+ + 2e^-$	ca. −1.1
	$Pt(OH)_2 + 4OH^- \rightleftharpoons [Pt(OH)_6]^{-2} + 2e^-$	−0.1 to −0.4
	$[PtCl_4]^{-2} + 2Cl^- \rightleftharpoons [PtCl_6]^{-2} + 2e^-$	−0.72
	$[PtBr_4]^{-2} + 2Br^- \rightleftharpoons [PtBr_6]^{-2} + 2e^-$	−0.63
	$PtS + S^{-2} \rightleftharpoons PtS_2 + 2e^-$	0.64

of cobalt, rhodium, and iridium, and of nickel, palladium, and platinum; but complications are introduced by the multiplicity of oxidation states among the platinum metal derivatives. Delayed effects of the lanthanide contraction are also apparent. Material presented in earlier sections on coordination compounds in general (pp. 227–270), on polynuclear halides (pp. 272–273), on nitrosyls (pp. 598–604), and on carbonyls (pp. 700–717) should be reviewed in this connection. In general, reduction of any oxidation state to the free metal is rather readily effected.

Preparation of an individual platinum metal from its purified compounds is easily accomplished, often by heat alone. However, separation of the various metals from each other is complicated by marked similarities in the reactions of either the metals or their compounds and is, therefore, tedious and involved.[29, 30] No details can be given here.

SUGGESTED SUPPLEMENTARY REFERENCES

W. M. Latimer: *The Oxidation States of the Elements and Their Potentials in Aqueous Solutions,* Ch. XII–XIX. Prentice-Hall, New York (1938).

N. V. Sidgwick: *The Chemical Elements and Their Compounds,* pp. 628–653 (Group IVa); 804–853 (Group Va); 998–1068 (Group VIa); 1262–1315 (Group VIIa); 1316–1628 (Group VIII). Clarendon Press, Oxford (1950).

B S. Hopkins: *Chapters in the Chemistry of the Less Familiar Elements,* Ch. 11–17, 21. Stipes Publishing Co., Champaign, Illinois (1938–1940).

A. E. van Arkel (Ed.): *Reine Metalle,* Ch. IV–VIII. Verlag von J. Springer, Berlin (1939).

W. Klemm: "Chemistry of the Transition Elements," *Naturwissenschaften,* **37**, 150, 172 (1950).

A. F. Wells: *Structural Inorganic Chemistry,* 2nd Ed. Ch. XXII. Clarendon Press, Oxford (1950).

---

[29] H. J. Emeléus and J. S. Anderson: *Modern Aspects of Inorganic Chemistry,* pp. 378–389. D. Van Nostrand Co., New York (1939).

[30] R. Gilchrist: *Chem. Revs.,* **32,** 277 (1943).

CHAPTER 21

The Inner Transition Elements

The two inner transition series arise, respectively, because of preferential filling of the 4*f* and 5*f* orbitals (pp. 103–106). Although it is quite generally agreed that the first 4*f* electron appears with cerium (Z = 58),[1] it is not known with certainty that 5*f* electrons appear before uranium (Z = 92). That they are present in uranium and in the transuranium elements is undeniable, and it is well established that the characteristics of the elements in the transuranic region are remarkably like those of elements in the Z = 57–71 region of the periodic system as a consequence of basic similarities in electronic arrangements. Although there are many undeniable similarities between the transuranium elements on the one hand and those which immediately precede uranium in atomic number (i.e., Ac, Th, Pa) on the other hand, there are also many instances of dissimilarity and many instances of close resemblance of these latter elements to lanthanum, hafnium, and tantalum, respectively.[2] It is debatable, therefore, whether one can consider the second inner transition series to be the exact analog of the first. However, there are many points of close resemblance.

Classically, the first inner transition series is called the rare earth series, probably because compounds of the elements which make it up were separated from two rare and complex oxide (earth) mixtures, yttria and ceria, which were first isolated around 1800. Although not real members of the series by strict electronic definition (p. 104), lanthanum and lutetium are so similar in properties as to be given membership in common parlance. They are so considered here. Yttrium is also included as a member of this series, not because of electronic similarities, but rather because lanthanide contraction effects render yttrium very similar to the heaviest members of the series (p. 151). Modern terminology refers to this series as the *lanthanide* series and to the individual members as *lanthanide* elements or *lanthanons*.[3] By analogy, the second inner transition series is then

[1] W. F. Meggars: *Science,* **105,** 514 (1947).

[2] M. Haïssinsky: *J. Chem. Soc.,* **1949** (Supp. Issue No. 2), S241.

[3] J. K. Marsh: *Quart. Revs.,* **1,** 126 (1947).

the *actinide* series,[4] although in view of the dissimilarities pointed out above, some would prefer to ignore a direct periodic system analogy and call the series a *uranide* series.[2] This is an academic question. In this discussion, actinium and the heavier elements are included.

It is interesting that, although the chemistry of uranium had been quite thoroughly understood for many years, its recognition as an essentially "rare earth-like" element came only after elucidation of the characteristics of the transuranium elements. Even taking into account the differences mentioned above, there are many points of similarity between the chemistries of the heaviest elements and those of the rare earth elements.[5] As a key to an understanding of the chemistries of these synthetic elements, prior information on the rare earth elements, as accumulated over a period of many years and often as a result of exceedingly painstaking work, was invaluable.

The members of the inner transition series are quite generally rare and, with a few notable exceptions (e.g., La, Ce, Nd, Th, U, Pu), of somewhat limited technical use. It must be pointed out, however, that many of the members of the rare earth series are sufficiently abundant (Table 2·1) to permit production in technical quantities should important uses be developed. As a family, the rare earth metals account for some $1.0 \times 10^{-2}\%$ of the igneous rocks of the crust of the earth. It is beyond the scope of this book to discuss all these elements comprehensively. No attempt is made, therefore, to give more than the overall discussion essential to an understanding of their place in the family of elements as a whole. Supplemental information is to be found in the general references cited at the end of this chapter (p. 910). Because the sum total of information is greater for the first series and because characteristics dependent upon the presence of f electrons are perhaps better defined in this series, major emphasis is placed upon the rare earth elements. Analogies and differences between the series are mentioned in turn. Prior review of sections dealing with electronic configurations (pp. 103–106), the lanthanide and actinide contractions (pp. 146–151), and magnetic behavior (pp. 168–170) is recommended as is reference to the general characteristics of the transition metals as a whole as described in Chapter 20.

PHYSICAL AND CHEMICAL CHARACTERISTICS OF THE ELEMENTS

Numerical constants, insofar as they are known, are summarized for the lanthanide and the actinide elements in Table 21·1 and Table

[4] G. T. Seaborg *Chem. Eng. News,* **23,** 2190 (1945).
[5] G. T. Seaborg: *Nucleonics,* **5** (No. 5), 16 (1949).

TABLE 21·1

NUMERICAL PROPERTIES OF YTTRIUM AND THE LANTHANIDE ELEMENTS

Symbol	Atomic Number	Outer Electron Configuration	Atomic Weight	Density of Solid at 20°C. grams/cc.	Melting Point, °C.	Ionization Potential, ev	E_{298} for $M \rightleftharpoons M^{+3} + 3e^-$, volts*
Y	39	$4d^15s^2$	88.92	4.34	1450–1500	6.6	2.1
La	57	$5d^16s^2$	138.92	6.194	885	5.61	2.37
Ce	58	$4f^26s^2$	140.13	6.78	815	(6.91)	2.3
Pr	59	$4f^36s^2$	140.92	6.776	932	(5.76)	2.2
Nd	60	$4f^46s^2$	144.27	7.004	840	(6.31)	2.2
	61	$4f^56s^2$	(147)†				
Sm	62	$4f^66s^2$	150.43	6.93	1350	5.6	2.2
Eu	63	$4f^76s^2$	152.0	5.244‡	1100–1200	5.67	2.2
Gd	64	$4f^75d^16s^2$	156.9	7.948		6.16	2.2
Tb	65	$4f^96s^2$	159.2	8.332		(6.74)	2.2
Dy	66	$4f^{10}6s^2$	162.46	8.562		(6.82)	2.2
Ho	67	$4f^{11}6s^2$	164.94	8.764			2.1
Er	68	$4f^{12}6s^2$	167.2	9.164	1250 (?)		2.1
Tm	69	$4f^{13}6s^2$	169.4	9.346			2.1
Yb	70	$4f^{14}6s^2$	173.04	7.010‡	ca. 1800	6.2	2.1
Lu	71	$4f^{14}5d^16s^2$	174.99	9.740		5.0	2.1

* Rough values only.
† Most stable isotope.
‡ Cubic close packed lattice; others hexagonal close packed.

TABLE 21·2

NUMERICAL PROPERTIES OF THE ACTINIDE ELEMENTS

Symbol	Atomic Number	Outer Electron Configuration	Atomic Weight	Density of Solid at 20°C., grams/cc.	Melting Point, °C.	Covalent Radius, A	Crystal Radii,* A	
							M^{+4}	M^{+3}
Ac	89	$6d^17s^2$	227					1.11
Th	90	$6d^27s^2$	232.12	11.7	1730	1.652	0.95	(1.08)
Pa	91	$5f^26d^17s^2$	231				(0.91)	(1.06)
U	92	$5f^36d^17s^2$	238.07	19.05	1133	1.421	0.89	1.04
Np	93	$5f^46d^17s^2$	(237)†	19.5	640		0.88	1.02
Pu	94	$5f^56d^17s^2$	(239)†				0.86	1.01
Am	95	$5f^66d^17s^2$	(241)†	11.7			0.85	1.00
Cm	96	$5f^76d^17s^2$	(242)†	7(?)				
Bk	97	$5f^86d^17s^2$	(243?)†					
Cf	98	$5f^96d^17s^2$	(244?)†					

* Values from W. H. Zachariasen: *Phys. Rev.*, **73**, 1104 (1948). † Most stable isotope.

21·2, respectively. Some additional values for the lanthanide elements are given in Table 5·5. The paucity of reliable data for these metals is due largely to the fact that preparations of pure samples have been exceedingly difficult. Although some similarities are discernible between the two series, the greatest similarities are of course within each series. It is probable that evaluation of the properties of elements in the transplutonium region will provide more analogies between the two series.

The rare earth metals (and yttrium) are remarkably close to the alkaline earth metals in general characteristics. The same is true of actinium, thorium, and the transplutonium elements in particular, but to a much lesser extent of the other actinide elements. Trends in properties noted between the Group Ia and Group IIa elements extend quite generally to all these metals. Within the lanthanide family, trends are quite regular. Similarities in characteristics are of course associated with repetition of outermost electronic arrangements and only slight differences within inner shells. Differences in properties are quite generally due to changes in nuclear charges as reflected in the lanthanide contraction (Table 5.5). Among the actinides, similar conditions pertain but are less regular.

TABLE 21·3

Chemical Characteristics of the Lanthanide Elements

General Equation*	Remarks
$2M + 3X_2 \rightarrow 2MX_3$	With halogens. Cerium gives CeF_4.
$4M + 3O_2 \rightarrow 2M_2O_3$	Cerium gives CeO_2.
$2M + 3S \rightarrow M_2S_3$	On heating. Also with Se, Te (?).
$2M + N_2 \rightarrow 2MN$	On heating. Probably also with P, As(?).
$M + 2C \rightarrow MC_2$	On heating.
$2M + 3H_2 \rightarrow 2MH_3$	On heating moderately. Number of hydrogen atoms slightly less than 3.
$2M + 3H_2O \rightarrow 2M(OH)_3 + 3H_2$	Slowly when cold. Vigorously when heated.
$M + 3H^+ \rightarrow M^{+3} + \frac{3}{2}H_2$	Vigorously.
$2M + 3H_2O + 3CO_2 \rightarrow M_2(CO_3)_3 + 3H_2$	In air.

* M = any lanthanide metal.

The elemental lanthanides are reducing agents which are nearly comparable in strength, as indicated by oxidation potential data, with the alkaline earth metals. High heats of formation of many of their compounds render these elements powerful reducing agents even under anhydrous conditions. They cannot be preserved in contact with oxygen, moisture, carbon dioxide, etc. The more important reactions of yttrium and the rare earth metals are summarized in Table 21·3. These behaviors are to be contrasted with those of the Periodic Group IIIb elements (pp. 739–740). The reactions of actinium are very similar as apparently are those of the heaviest actinides. Thorium also behaves similarly but is tetrapositive in the resulting compounds. In this respect, the behaviors of cerium and thorium are analogous. Although uranium, neptunium, and plutonium enter into many comparable reactions, greater variability in oxidation states is noted among the product materials. The reactions of elemental protactinium are probably closer to those of tantalum.

CHARACTERISTICS RELATED TO ELECTRONIC ARRANGEMENTS

Addition of electrons to well-shielded lower orbitals without material alteration of the "outermost" arrangements confers upon the inner transition elements a number of properties which might be regarded as unusual. Among these are constancy in oxidation states, predominantly ionic behavior, marked color and unusual light absorption characteristics, and distinctive magnetic behaviors. Size decreases with increasing atomic number are not unusual but are of singular importance (pp. 146–151).

Oxidation states

The lanthanide elements are characterized by the uniform +3 oxidation state which would be expected of members of Periodic Group IIIa. In terms of the idealized electronic arrangements $4f^n5s^25p^65d^16s^2$ as suggested by Hund,[6] such an oxidation state is reasonable in all cases, but its appearance is not necessarily expected in terms of the general $4f^m5s^25p^66s^2$ $(m = n + 1)$ structures which are regarded as more probable for most of the elements[1] (pp. 100, 104). Except with lanthanum, gadolinium, and lutetium, removal of a $4f$ electron is essential to the formation of the +3 state. It is apparent in the light of the general stability of this oxidation state that the removal of this $4f$ electron requires essentially no more energy than would the removal of a $5d$ electron. According to Connick,[7] ionization potential data and hydration energies for the resulting gaseous ions are such that the +3 state is stable in aqueous solution.

The concept of a +3 oxidation state as characteristic of the lanthanide elements has become so deep seated that other oxidation states have often been termed "anomalous."[8, 9] Such states are really expected rather than anomalous. Spectroscopic evidence indicates particular stabilities for the electronic configurations of the ions La^{+3} $(4f^05s^25p^6)$, Gd^{+3} $(4f^75s^25p^6)$, and Lu^{+3} $(4f^{14}5s^25p^6)$, where the $4f$ orbitals are, respectively, empty, half-filled, and completely filled.

[6] F. Hund: *Linienspektern und periodisches System der Elements*, pp. 54–5, Verlag von J. Springer, Berlin (1927).

[7] R. E. Connick: *J. Chem. Soc.*, **1949** (Suppl. Issue No. 2), S235.

[8] D. W. Pearce: *Chem. Revs.*, **16**, 121 (1935).

[9] D. W. Pearce and P. W. Selwood: *J. Chem. Education*, **13**, 224 (1936).

The "anomalous" oxidation states may be regarded as arising, therefore, from tendencies to approach these configurations through the loss of more or less than three electrons. Thus, the lanthanum(III) configuration is achieved with cerium ($Z = 58$) by the loss of four electrons and the formation of cerium(IV). With praseodymium ($Z = 59$), only four electrons are lost, and the stable lanthanum configuration is approached but not completely achieved. Existence of the praseodymium(V) essential to such achievement is very doubtful. Europium(II) and terbium(IV) have the gadolinium(III) configuration. Samarium(II) approaches but does not achieve this arrangement. Correspondingly, ytterbium(II) has the lutetium(III) structure. That these arrangements are correct is indicated by similarities among magnetic susceptibilities for isoelectronic ions.[9] The relationships among the oxidation states of the lanthanides are summarized in Table 21·4. The characteristics of these oxidation states are discussed in a later section of this chapter (pp. 902–905).

TABLE 21·4
OXIDATION STATES AMONG THE LANTHANIDE ELEMENTS

Symbol	Atomic Number, Z	Probable Electronic Configurations* M(II)	M(III)	M(IV)	Known Oxidation States
La	57		$4f^0$ ←		+3
Ce	58		$4f^1$ ←	$4f^0$	+3, +4
Pr	59		$4f^2$	$4f^1$	+3, +4
Nd	60		$4f^3$		+3
	61		$4f^4$		+3
Sm	62	$4f^6$	$4f^5$		+2, +3
Eu	63	$4f^7$	→ $4f^6$		+2, +3
Gd	64		→ $4f^7$ ←		+3
Tb	65		$4f^8$	$4f^7$	+3, +4
Dy	66		$4f^9$		+3
Ho	67		$4f^{10}$		+3
Er	68		$4f^{11}$		+3
Tm	69		$4f^{12}$		+3
Yb	70	$4f^{14}$	$4f^{13}$		+2, +3
Lu	71		→ $4f^{14}$		+3

* Arrangement of other electrons constant.

With the actinides, the situation is much more complex. There is no oxidation state which may be regarded as characteristic of all members, although there appears to be a greater general preference for the +4 state than for any other.[5] The increasing stability of the +3 state with increasing atomic number[5] is an indication of the rare-earth-like character of the heaviest actinide elements. Known oxidation states for the actinide elements are given in Table 21·5. It is apparent that the regularity characteristic of the lanthanide series is absent. The difficulties of relating oxidation states to electronic configurations in any simple fashion are also immediately obvious. Connick points out[7] that the absence of a uniformly stable +3 state results from differences in ionization potentials and hydration energies between the two inner transition series. The enhanced stabilities of the +5 and +6 states (e.g., with U, Np, Pu) are ascribed to their occurrence in oxy cations, MO_2^+ and MO_2^{+2}. With thorium and with protactinium, states other than +4 and +5, respectively, are highly

TABLE 21·5

OXIDATION STATES AMONG THE ACTINIDE ELEMENTS

Symbol	Atomic Number, *Z*	Reported Oxidation States
Ac	89	+3
Th	90	+4 (+3, +2)*
Pa	91	+5 (+4)
U	92	+3, +4, +5, +6
Np	93	+3, +4, +5, +6
Pu	94	+3, +4, +5, +6
Am	95	+3, +4, +5, +6 (+2)
Cm	96	+3
Bk	97	+3, +4
Cf	98	+3

* States given in parentheses have been reported but are exceedingly unstable.

unstable and subject to ready oxidation (e.g., by water). Comparisons with the lanthanide series are not generally warranted.

Magnetic properties

Except for lanthanum(III) and lutetium(III) which are diamagnetic, the tripositive lanthanide ions are strongly paramagnetic. Because of significant orbital contributions, it is impossible to account for observed moments in terms of the number of unpaired electrons alone. This was made apparent in Chapter 5 (pp. 168–170), where it was shown that two maxima exist, one in the Pr^{+3}–Nd^{+3} region and the other in the Dy^{+3}–Ho^{+3} region. Although it is reasonable to associate the paramagnetic characteristics of these ions with the 4*f* orbitals, an exact interpretation of observed behaviors requires an involved mathematical approach which has no place in this discussion.[10, 11] The

[10] J. H. Van Vleck: *The Theory of Electric and Magnetic Susceptibilities.* Oxford University Press, London (1932).

[11] D. M. Yost, H. Russell, and C. S. Garner: *The Rare-Earth Elements and Their Compounds,* Ch. 2. John Wiley and Sons, New York (1947).

magnetic characteristics of the non-tripositive lanthanide ions are quite generally comparable to those of isoelectronic tripositive ions (p. 896).

Among the actinides, quantitative interpretations are lacking, but observed paramagnetic behaviors among ions in a variety of oxidation states are qualitatively similar to those among the lanthanides.[12] This is apparent from data given in Figure 21·1.[12] The similarity

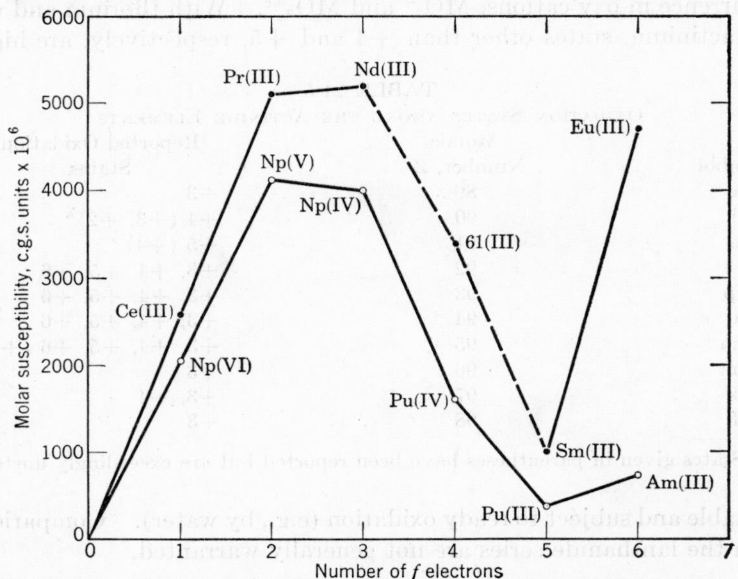

FIG. 21·1. Magnetic properties of certain lanthanide and actinide ions.

stems, in all probability, from similarities in electronic arrangements and offers more or less independent confirmation of the presence of *f* electrons in atoms of the heaviest elements.

Color and absorption spectra

Many of the tripositive lanthanide ions are strikingly colored both in crystalline compounds and in aqueous salt solutions. The remarkable periodicity in color which results when the ions are arranged in order of atomic numbers, which is shown in Table 21·6, was first noted by Main Smith.[13] It is apparent that an ion having n more electrons than lanthanum has very nearly the same color as an ion having $14 - n$ electrons more. This suggests the 4*f* orbitals as the source of

[12] J. J. Howland and M. Calvin: *J. Chem. Phys.*, **18**, 239 (1950).
[13] J. D. Main Smith: *Nature*, **120**, 583 (1927).

color, but the problem is complicated by the fact that the non-tripositive ions are differently colored from isoelectronic tripositive species. Thus, among the non-tripositive species, the following ionic colors are noted: Ce(IV), orange-red; Sm(II), red-brown; Eu(II), straw; Yb(II), green.

Color is, of course, a manifestation of light absorption and is more correctly described, therefore, in terms of absorption spectra. Lanthanum(III) and lutetium(III) have no absorption bands in either the

TABLE 21·6

COLORS OF TRIPOSITIVE LANTHANIDE IONS

Ion	Atomic Number, *Z*	Number of 4*f* Electrons	Color	Color	Number of 4*f* Electrons	Atomic Number, *Z*	Ion
La^{+3}	57	0	colorless	colorless	14	71	Lu^{+3}
Ce^{+3}	58	1	colorless	colorless	13	70	Yb^{+3}
Pr^{+3}	59	2	yellowish-green	pale green	12	69	Tm^{+3}
Nd^{+3}	60	3	reddish-violet	reddish	11	68	Er^{+3}
	61	4	pink (?)	yellowish	10	67	Ho^{+3}
Sm^{+3}	62	5	pale yellow	yellowish	9	66	Dy^{+3}
Eu^{+3}	63	6	colorless*	colorless*	8	65	Tb^{+3}
Gd^{+3}	64	7	colorless	colorless	7	64	Gd^{+3}

* As commonly observed. Some authors report very pale pink.

ultraviolet, visible, or near infrared regions. The absorption spectra of all the other tripositive lanthanide ions are characterized by bands in these regions,[14–16] bands in the visible being found for the colored species (e.g., with Pr^{+3}, Nd^{+3}, Er^{+3}) and those in either the ultraviolet (e.g., with Ce^{+3}, Eu^{+3}, Gd^{+3}) or near infrared (e.g., with Yb^{+3}) for the colorless species. These spectra vary in complexity, but for given ions they are characteristic whether those ions are found in solid salts or in solution. The spectrum of neodymium chloride given in Figure 21·2[16] is among the most complex observed, but it may be regarded as essentially typical. Measurements show the spectra of chloride and nitrate solutions of synthetic element 61 to be exactly comparable with those of the other lanthanide ions.[17] Absorption spectra are useful not only for the qualitative detection of the lanthanide ions but also for their quantitative determination in complex mixtures.[15, 16]

[14] W. Prandtl and K. Scheiner: *Z. anorg. allgem. Chem.*, **220,** 112 (1934).
[15] C. J. Rodden: *J. Research Natl. Bur. Standards,* **26,** 557 (1941); **28,** 265 (1942).
[16] T. Moeller and J. C. Brantley: *Anal. Chem.,* **22,** 433 (1950).
[17] G. W. Parker and P. M. Lantz: *J. Am. Chem. Soc.,* **72,** 2834 (1950).

An outstanding characteristic of these spectra is the sharpness of the individual absorption bands. Many such bands are almost line-like in nature, and in general the bands become even narrower as temperature is decreased. By contrast, it should be mentioned that absorption bands characterizing other colored inorganic species (e.g., transition metal ions, complex ions and molecules) except the actinide

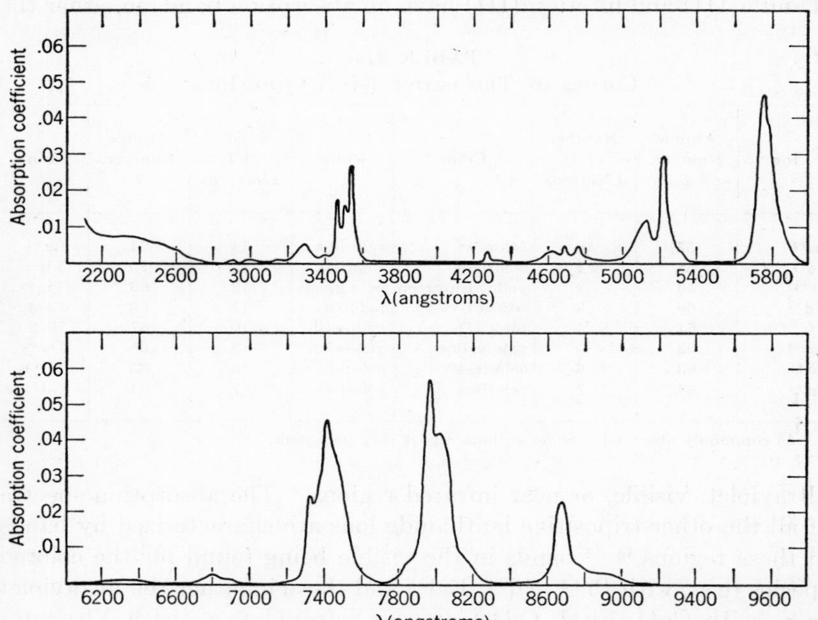

FIG. 21·2. Absorption spectrum of aqueous neodymium chloride solution. (Adapted from T. Moeller and J. C. Brantley: *Anal. Chem.*, **22**, 433 [1950].)

ions are broad and often diffuse. A difference in the source of absorption is apparent. It is quite generally agreed that the absorption bands of the tripositive lanthanides arise from electronic transitions (p. 82) within the $4f$ level. Furthermore, it appears that these transitions involve two energy states of the same $4f^n$ configuration. They are, therefore, transitions which are normally of a forbidden type. Inasmuch as the $4f$ electrons are responsible for the absorption bands, environmental factors which affect the outermost orbitals are without material effect upon the wavelengths of these bands. For example, spectra in the presence of complexing groups are strikingly similar to those of the simple (aquated) cations. Among compounds of the transition metals, the reverse is commonly true (p. 874).

It is striking that for the non-tripositive states characteristic absorption bands are broad and more like those of the ions of the transition metals. Our present state of knowledge does not permit anything but a fragmentary explanation of the origins of the rare earth absorption spectra and of the differences among them. As for paramagnetic behaviors, much available explanatory information lies beyond the scope of this book.[18]

Where measured, the absorption spectra of the compounds of uranium and the heavier actinide elements have been found to be remarkably like those of the tripositive lanthanides both in their complexities and in the sharpnesses of the characteristic absorption bands.[5, 19, 20] In some cases, e.g., americium(III),[21] the bands are particularly sharp (1 to 5 A wide). A major difference from the lanthanides lies in the fact that oxidation state has little or no effect upon the sharpness of the spectrum. It is logical to associate the absorption bands characteristic of the actinide ions with electronic transitions within the 5*f* level.[5]

Contraction effects

Review of the nature and origins of the lanthanide and actinide contractions, as discussed in Chapter 5 (pp. 146–151), indicates clearly the importance of size differences in accounting for observed differences in properties within a given oxidation state as atomic number is varied. Thus paralleling increase in atomic number, increase in ease of complex formation, decrease in basicity, etc., are found to be characteristic. Were it not for the lanthanide and actinide contractions, characterization of these elements in a particular state of oxidation would be a task of extreme difficulty. This is particularly true of the lanthanide elements because of the general absence of a variety of available oxidation states and the consequent restriction of most operations to a single state.

SOME SPECIFIC PHASES OF THE CHEMISTRY OF THE LANTHANIDE ELEMENTS

The chemistries of the lanthanide elements are sufficiently different from those of the elements thus far considered to merit special atten-

[18] D. M. Yost, H. Russell, and C. S. Garner: *The Rare-Earth Elements and Their Compounds*, Ch. 3. John Wiley and Sons, New York (1947).

[19] J. C. Hindman, L. B. Magnusson, T. J. LaChapelle: *J. Am. Chem. Soc.*, **71**, 687 (1949).

[20] R. E. Connick, M. Kasha, W. H. McVey, and G. E. Sheline: Paper 4.20 in *The Transuranium Elements*, Vol I, p. 559. McGraw-Hill Book Co., New York (1949).

[21] S. Freed and F. J. Leitz: *J. Chem. Phys.*, **17**, 540 (1949).

tion. Topics chosen for discussion relate to chemical characteristics in various states of oxidation and to separation techniques. No attempt is made to discuss the chemistries of the actinide elements. However, it is apparent that in the lower oxidation states (e.g., +3, +4) distinct parallels exist between the two series.

Chemical characteristics in the various oxidation states

Essentially similar electronic arrangements with but small changes in size impose distinct similarities upon all these elements in a particular state of oxidation (i.e., +3). Among different oxidation states, however, the expected significant differences appear. Because the +3 state is most important, it is discussed first.

Oxidation State +3. This is the generally stable oxidation state in aqueous solutions. It is a quite generally highly basic state as indicated by the rather slight hydrolysis of salts containing weakly basic anions (e.g., Cl^-, ClO_4^-, NO_3^-, SO_4^{-2}),[22, 23] basicity decreasing with increasing atomic number.[22] As regards solubilities, the chlorides, bromides, iodides, nitrates, perchlorates, bromates, and acetates are uniformly and usually quite readily soluble in water, but the oxides, hydroxides, oxalates, carbonates, phosphates, fluorides, and many double carbonates, sulfates, etc. are insoluble. The simple sulfates vary widely, but all are less soluble in hot solutions than in cold. As expected, the behaviors of yttrium compounds are comparable with those of dysprosium and holmium. Except for samarium, europium, and ytterbium, the tripositive ions are uniformly resistant to reduction to lower states, and, except for cerium, they resist oxidation in solution.

Salts of the tripositive ions readily combine with other simple salts to produce double salts. Important among these are double ammonium nitrates $M^{III}(NO_3)_3 \cdot 2NH_4NO_3 \cdot 4H_2O$; double nitrates with dipositive metals, $M_2^{III}M_3^{II}(NO_3)_{12} \cdot 24H_2O$($M^{II}$ = Mg, Mn, Ni, Co, Zn); double alkali metal sulfates, $M^{III}M^I_3(SO_4)_3 \cdot xH_2O$ (M^I = Na, K, Tl^+); etc. Many simple salts are known as hydrates. These compounds are not complex compounds. Indeed, it is exceedingly difficult to prepare true complexes from the tripositive ions. This is probably due not only to the large sizes of these ions but also to the absence of orbitals which might be used for hybridization in the usual sense. Acetylacetone and other β-diketones do yield inner complexes which are soluble in solvents such as benzene or chloroform, but which decompose rather than volatilize upon being heated. 8-Quinolinol and some of its derivatives form comparable compounds. Hydroxy

[22] T. Moeller and H. E. Kremers: *Chem. Revs.*, **37**, 97 (1945).

[23] T. Moeller: *J. Phys. Chem.*, **50**, 242 (1946).

acids (e.g., tartaric, citric) form complexes in aqueous solutions, but these have not been isolated in the solid state. Nitriloacetate and ethylenediaminetetraacetate complexes are known. A few amines such as pyramidone and antipyrine are said to form complex cations with the tripositive lanthanides. A few ammoniates are also known in the solid state but not in solution. However, the majority of the familiar donor groups show no tendency to combine with these cations. Although such complexes as can be made agree in compositions with a coordination number of six, it is probable that the binding is always ionic and that the octahedral configuration is non-existent as a stable entity.

As indicated by the potential values in Table 21·1 and in Table 21·7, the tripositive ions resist reduction both to the free metals and to the dipositive state and resist oxidation to the tetrapositive state.

TABLE 21·7

Important Lanthanide Ion Couples

Couple	Equation	E^0_{298}, volts
M(II)–M(III)	$Sm^{+2} \rightleftharpoons Sm^{+3} + e^-$	ca. 0.8*
	$Eu^{+2} \rightleftharpoons Eu^{+3} + e^-$	0.43
	$Yb^{+2} \rightleftharpoons Yb^{+3} + e^-$	1.15
M(III)–M(IV)	$Ce^{+3} \rightleftharpoons Ce^{+4} + e^-$	−1.28 (2*f* HCl)
		−1.44 (1*f* H_2SO_4)
		−1.61 (1*f* HNO_3)
		−1.70 (1*f* $HClO_4$)
	$Pr^{+3} \rightleftharpoons Pr^{+4} + e^-$	ca. −2.94*

* Rough estimates.

Oxidation State +2. Although actually known only with samarium, europium, and ytterbium, the more general existence of this oxidation state has been suggested from time to time. Thus the isolation of a series of carbides of composition MC_2 (p. 698) is difficult to reconcile by any postulation other than the presence of a +2 state. On the other hand, indications that polarographic reductions of the tripositive ions in aqueous solutions lead first to the dipositive ions and then to the metals[24] are probably in error in all cases except with europium and are better accounted for in terms of catalytic hydrogen discharge.

Europium(II), ytterbium(II), and samarium(II) are well-characterized species, however. In ease of formation and in resistance to oxidation, they decrease in this order. It is probable, therefore, that the estimated potential for the Sm(II)–Sm(III) couple (Table 21·7) is considerably in error. All the dipositive ions are readily oxidized to the tripositive state by elemental oxygen or by water. They are

[24] W. Noddack and A. Brukl: *Angew. Chem.*, **50**, 352 (1937).

thus unstable in aqueous solution and function as powerful reducing agents. In their solubility characteristics and in the crystalline properties of their compounds, they are remarkably similar to strontium. Such similarities arise from size similarities, the crystal radii of Eu^{+2} and Yb^{+2} being 1.17 A and 1.06 A, respectively, as compared with 1.13 A for Sr^{+2}. The dipositive ions are commonly recovered as the difficultly soluble sulfates (p. 908).

Europium(II) is readily obtained in solution by amalgamated zinc or electrolytic reduction of europium(III). Ytterbium(II) results from electrolytic reduction of ytterbium(III) salt solutions, but samarium(II) cannot be obtained in these fashions in aqueous systems. More vigorous reducing agents such as sodium amalgam give amalgams rather than the dipositive ions. Magnesium reduction in ethanol, however, does give samarium(II). Solid compounds containing the dipositive metals may be obtained by high-temperature hydrogen, ammonia, or aluminum reduction of the anhydrous trihalides or by thermal decomposition of the anhydrous triiodides, e.g., as

$$SmI_3 \rightarrow SmI_2 + \tfrac{1}{2}I_2$$

The preparation of dipositive europium compounds is an excellent exercise in synthetic chemistry.[25]

Oxidation State +4. Cerium(IV) is probably more common and more important than cerium(III). It is well known both in solid compounds and in aqueous salt solutions such as the nitrate, perchlorate, or sulfate. Praseodymium(IV) and terbium(IV) are known only in solid compounds. The oxides Pr_6O_{11} (black) and Tb_4O_7 (brown) are obtained as final oxidation products in the ignition in air of the oxides, carbonates, oxalates, etc., of the tripositive elements. It is probable that both tri- and tetrapositive materials are present in these oxides. A pure compound, PrO_2, is said to form in the presence of oxygen under pressure. Terbium dioxide, TbO_2, has been obtained by action of atomic oxygen. Treatment of these praseodymium and terbium compounds with acids gives the tripositive ions in solution.

Cerium(IV) compounds, as expected, are more acidic, more highly hydrolyzed, and more susceptible to complex formation than the corresponding cerium(III) compounds. In their solubilities they are more closely comparable with the thorium compounds than with those of the tripositive lanthanides. This is in accord with size similarities (radii: Ce^{+4} = 1.02 A, Th^{+4} = 1.10 A) as well as with equality in charge. Cerium(IV) forms double salts readily, best characterized

[25] R. A. Cooley and D. M. Yost: *Inorganic Syntheses*, Vol. II, pages 69–73. McGraw-Hill Book Co., New York (1946).

being the double ammonium nitrate, $Ce(NO_3)_4 \cdot 2NH_4NO_3$, a material which crystallizes readily from nitric acid solutions and is useful in the purification of cerium. Although such compounds may exist as cerates (e.g., $(NH_4)_2[Ce(NO_3)_6]$) in the solid state, there is little positive proof of the existence of species such as $[Ce(NO_3)_6]^{-2}$ in aqueous solution. The outstanding characteristic of cerium(IV) is its oxidizing power. As indicated in Table 21·7, this is a function of the acid present, suggesting interactions between cerium(IV) and the various anionic species. Because of its oxidizing power and the inherent simplicity of the couple involved, cerium(IV) has become an extremely important analytical oxidant.[26]

Cerium(IV) compounds are obtained in acidic solution by peroxydisulfate or electrolytic oxidation. Bromate effects the oxidation in solutions buffered with calcium carbonate. Permanganate or iodate may be used also. In alkaline medium, chlorine, peroxide, or even atmospheric oxygen is effective. Cerium(IV) is commonly recovered by hydrolytic precipitation or precipitation of the double ammonium nitrate.

Recovery and separation techniques

Of the many known minerals containing the lanthanide elements, the only one of widespread commercial importance is monazite sand, which is essentially a mixture of phosphates, RPO_4, containing up to some 10 to 12% thorium (probably as silicate), together with small amounts of zirconium (as silicate) and iron and titanium (as ilmenite). The classic and still most widely employed procedure for cracking this mineral involves digestion with concentrated sulfuric acid at elevated temperatures. Treatment of the resulting mass with a controlled quantity of cold water effects dissolution of the mixed sulfates and permits removal of insoluble silica, zircon, etc. Thorium is most commonly removed by precipitation as pyrophosphate after further dilution to a predetermined acidity. The remaining tripositive lanthanide elements may then be recovered by precipitation with oxalic acid prior to separation, although a cheaper and more common procedure involves treatment with sodium sulfate. This divides the lanthanide elements roughly into two groups, namely the cerium earths (roughly La through Eu), the double sodium sulfates of which are insoluble in sodium sulfate solution, and the yttrium earths (Y and roughly Gd through Lu), the double sodium sulfates of which are soluble. With monazite as raw material, the cerium earths predominate in quantity.

[26] G. F. Smith: *Cerate Oxidimetry*. G. Frederick Smith Chemical Co., Columbus, Ohio (1942).

The double sulfates may be converted to acid-soluble hydrous oxides and hydroxides with caustic soda. Cerium is commonly removed by oxidation (p. 908) before separation of the cerium earths. Useful details of extraction and recovery procedures are given by Pearce et al.[27]

Separation of the lanthanide elements from each other has long been a classic problem in inorganic chemistry. Because of inherent similarities within a given oxidation state, techniques not based upon oxidation or reduction are commonly slow, tedious, and fractional in character. Preparation of pure materials is difficult, especially if those materials are comparatively rare. Even division of the elements into cerium and yttrium groups is not clean-cut, since gradations in solubilities rather than marked differences are encountered. Techniques involving more than a single oxidation state are rapid and yield pure products, but they are limited to a few members of the series. For many years, separation of any but the most abundant elements (e.g., La, Ce, Nd, Sm) in quantity was well nigh impossible, but new methods which operate continuously and automatically have aided materially in solving the problem. Important reported procedures may be classified under the broad headings:

1. Fractional crystallization procedures.
2. Procedures involving basicity differences.
3. Oxidation-reduction procedures.
4. Liquid-liquid extraction procedures.

More comprehensive references[3, 28, 29] are suggested for additional details.

Fractional Crystallization Procedures. Separation by fractional crystallization is dependent upon the formation of isomorphous compounds which not only differ significantly from each other in solubilities but also have solubilities that change fairly markedly with temperature changes. Fractional crystallization procedures were the first applied to the lanthanide elements as a group. At present, however, they are most useful for the separation of specific materials rather than for working up the entire family of elements. Among the useful fractional crystallization procedures are the following: double magnesium or manganese(II) nitrates for separation of the cerium earths; double ammonium nitrates for separation of lanthanum from

[27] D. W. Pearce, R. A. Hanson, J. C. Butler, and R. G. Russell: *Inorganic Syntheses*, Vol. II, pp. 38–65. McGraw-Hill Book Co., New York (1946).

[28] D. M. Yost, H. Russell, and C. S. Garner: *The Rare-Earth Elements and Their Compounds*, Ch. 5. John Wiley and Sons, New York (1947).

[29] R. Bock: *Angew. Chem.*, **62**, 375 (1950).

praseodymium; and bromates or ethyl sulfates for separation of the yttrium earths. Bismuth(III) acts as a useful separating ion in double magnesium nitrate crystallizations involving samarium, europium, and gadolinium and in simple nitrate crystallizations of gadolinium, terbium, and dysprosium because of the intermediate solubilities of the isomorphous bismuth compounds.

Procedures Involving Basicity Differences. The gradual decrease in basicity with increasing atomic number which is characteristic of the tripositive ions[22] may be used as a basis for separation by a variety of means. Since basicity increases sharply when dipositive materials are formed and decreases sharply when tetrapositive materials are produced, basicity procedures may be combined with oxidation procedures to advantage in certain cases.

FRACTIONAL PRECIPITATION. Since the insolubility of a compound is measured by the extent to which the cation attracts the anion, separation by the fractional precipitation of any type of compound of a series of closely related elements may be regarded as a procedure dependent upon differences in basicity. Precipitation of hydrous hydroxides or oxides by gradually increasing the *p*H of an aqueous solution by addition of ammonia, amines, or alkali, by hydrolysis of urea or hexamethylenetetramine, by hydrolysis of anions (e.g., nitrites, azides) of the lanthanide element salts themselves, or by electrolysis effects separations, the least basic materials being precipitated first. Precipitations by chromate, hexacyanoferrate(II or III), oxalate, etc., are also effective. However, since basicity differences are slight within the +3 state, blanket separations are not obtained, and the separation of adjacent members by simple precipitation procedures is seldom particularly effective. Yttrium is removed rather effectively by this means, however.

COMPLEX FORMATION. The stabilities of complex ions containing the tripositive lanthanides increase with increasing atomic number (p. 901). Differences in stabilities of complex species of a given type can be taken advantage of in separational procedures because they cause differences in the rates and extents of particular reactions. Thus precipitation of oxalates from solutions containing nitriloacetate[30] or ethylenediaminetetraacetate[31] leads to separations because the cations forming the least stable complexes precipitate first.

More striking results are obtained by ion exchange procedures.[32]

[30] G. Beck: *Mikrochem. ver. Mikrochim. Acta*, **33**, 344 (1948).

[31] J. K. Marsh: *J. Chem. Soc.*, **1950**, 1819; **1951**, 1461.

[32] A comprehensive series of papers on ion-exchange, many of them covering the behaviors of the lanthanide ions, is found in *J. Am. Chem. Soc.*, **69**, 2769–2881 (1947).

In brief, these procedures depend upon adsorption of the mixed tripositive lanthanides upon a small portion of a column of cation exchanger, followed by elution at controlled *p*H with a complexing agent such as ammonium citrate. Although the tendency of a cation in solution to exchange with, for instance, hydrogen ion on the exchange resin increases with cation size, the opposing tendency to form complex ions with citrate increases much more rapidly with decreasing cation size. As the solution passes through the exchange column, a series of competitive equilibria between ions on the exchanger and in complex form in solution are established. These lead to progressive enrichment of the smallest (most highly complexed) lanthanides in the material passing down the column. If the column is sufficiently long, separation into bands ultimately occurs, and, if the eluate from the column is collected in fractions, the various lanthanide ions appear separately in reverse order of atomic numbers (i.e., lutetium first, lanthanum last). Although first adapted to separation of tracer quantities, ion exchange procedures are also effective for macroscopic separations.[32–34] Cost of reagents may mitigate somewhat against use of such techniques on commercial scales, but, for the preparation of small samples of highly purified materials, they are invaluable.

MISCELLANEOUS BASICITY PROCEDURES. Among such procedures which have been applied in individual separations are thermal decompositions of oxy compounds and reactions of oxides, etc., with acids. These are all fractional in character.

Oxidation-Reduction Procedures. Oxidation in aqueous solution is effected only with cerium (p. 904). Separation of cerium(IV) from the tripositive lanthanide ions is easily effected because of marked basicity differences (pp. 904, 907). Concentrations of praseodymium and terbium have been effected by either chemical (e.g., with fused nitrates, chlorates, etc.) or electrolytic (e.g., of oxides dissolved in fused potassium hydroxide) oxidation in the absence of water, followed by removal of the more basic tripositive materials by leaching with water or weakly acidic mixtures.[35–38]

Reduction to the dipositive state followed by sulfate precipitation

[33] F. H. Spedding, E. I. Fulmer, T. A. Butler, and J. E. Powell: *J. Am. Chem. Soc.*, **72**, 2349 (1950).

[34] F. H. Spedding, E. I. Fulmer, J. E. Powell, and T. A. Butler: *J. Am. Chem. Soc.*, **72**, 2354 (1950).

[35] B. Brauner: *Collection Czechoslov. Chem. Communications*, **5**, 279 (1933).

[36] G. Beck: *Angew. Chem.*, **52**, 536 (1939).

[37] J. K. Marsh: *J. Chem. Soc.*, **1946**, 17, 20.

[38] C. R. Hough and D. W. Pearce: Abstracts of Papers, 111th Meeting of the American Chemical Society, April 1947, p. 10P.

is effective in removing and thereby concentrating europium and ytterbium. For europium, either electrolytic reduction[39] or amalgamated zinc reduction[25, 40] is effective. For ytterbium, only electrolytic reduction can be used.[41] For samarium, reduction with magnesium in ethanol and subsequent precipitation of samarium(II) chloride offer promise.[42] Direct reduction to the metals (as amalgams) is excellent for the removal of europium, ytterbium, and samarium. This is best accomplished by extracting aqueous acetate solutions with liquid sodium amalgams in the presence of acetic acid.[43, 44] Products obtained by oxidation or reduction procedures are usually essentially free from other lanthanide materials.

Liquid-Liquid Extraction Procedures. Such procedures are attractive because they can be operated continuously. Although significant solubility differences are noted among salts of the tripositive lanthanide ions in certain non-aqueous solvents,[45] separation procedures have shown but little promise except among ions of widely differing basicities. Formation of complex species, e.g., β-diketone chelates, may improve such separations. However, removal of cerium(IV)[46, 47] and thorium[48–51] from the tripositive materials is readily effected by such procedures.

PERIODIC RELATIONS AND THE INNER TRANSITION ELEMENTS

Accommodation of the inner transition elements by any but the most extended electronic forms of the periodic system (Ch. 4) is geometrically difficult. It seems best to regard the lanthanide elements as members of the A family of the third periodic group but to list them separately for convenience. A separate listing is almost

[39] L. F. Yntema: *J. Am. Chem. Soc.*, **52**, 2782 (1930).

[40] H. N. McCoy: *J. Am. Chem. Soc.*, **57**, 1756 (1935); **58**, 1577, 2279 (1936).

[41] R. W. Ball with L. F. Yntema: *J. Am. Chem. Soc.*, **52**, 4264 (1930).

[42] A. F. Clifford and H. C. Beachell: *J. Am. Chem. Soc.*, **70**, 2730 (1948).

[43] J. K. Marsh: *J. Chem. Soc.*, **1942**, 398, 523; **1943**, 8, 531.

[44] T. Moeller and H. E. Kremers: *Ind. Eng. Chem.*, Anal. Ed., **17**, 798 (1945).

[45] C. C. Templeton: *J. Am. Chem. Soc.*, **71**, 2187, 4167 (1949).

[46] R. Bock and E. Bock: *Naturwissenschaften*, **36**, 344 (1949).

[47] J. C. Warf: *J. Am. Chem. Soc.*, **71**, 3257 (1949).

[48] C. C. Templeton and N. F. Hall: *J. Phys. Colloid Chem.*, **51**, 1441 (1947); **54**, 954, 958 (1950).

[49] B. F. Rothschild, C. C. Templeton, and N. F. Hall: *J. Phys. Colloid Chem.*, **52**, 1006 (1948).

[50] C. C. Templeton, B. F. Rothschild, and N. F. Hall: *J. Phys. Colloid Chem.*, **53**, 838 (1949).

[51] G. F. Asselin, L. F. Audrieth, and E. W. Comings: *J. Phys. Colloid Chem.*, **54**, 640 (1950).

completely essential for the actinide elements because of the diversity of exhibited properties. Placing the two series together as

La	Ce	Pr	Nd	61	Sm	Eu	Gd	Tb	Dy	Ho	Er	Tm	Yb	Lu
Ac	Th	Pa	U		Np	Pu	Am	Cm	Bk	Cf				

has the advantage of pointing out similarities but does not allow for the striking differences which characterize the Pa-Pu region. It may be pointed out, however, that similarities between terbium and berkelium and between dysprosium and californium as suggested by such an arrangement are found in practice and are of use in characterizing these new synthetic elements.[52, 53]

Certain degrees of periodicity are distinguishable among the members of each inner transition series. A number of physical and chemical characteristics of the lanthanide elements show detectable changes at the midpoint of the series (gadolinium) and are in general agreement with the arrangement

La	Ce	Pr	Nd	61	Sm	Eu
Gd	Tb	Dy	Ho	Er	Tm	Yb
Lu						

Among these are colors, absorption spectra, and oxidation states.

SUGGESTED SUPPLEMENTARY REFERENCES

G. von Hevesy: *Die seltenen Erden vom Standpunkte des Atombaues.* Verlag von J. Springer, Berlin (1927).

D. M. Yost, H. Russell, and C. S. Garner: *The Rare-Earth Elements and Their Compounds.* John Wiley and Sons, New York (1947).

D. W. Pearce: *Inorganic Syntheses,* Vol II, pp. 29–38. McGraw-Hill Book Co., New York (1946).

H. F. V. Little: J. N. Friend's *A Textbook of Inorganic Chemistry,* Vol. IV. Charles Griffin and Co., London (1917).

G. T. Seaborg, J. J. Katz, and W. M. Manning (Editors): *The Transuranium Elements, Research Papers,* Vol I and II. McGraw-Hill Book Co., New York (1949).

M. W. Lister: "Chemistry of the Transuranic Elements," *Quart. Revs.,* **4,** 20 (1950).

A. F. Wells: *Structural Inorganic Chemistry,* 2nd. Ed., Ch. XXIII. Clarendon Press, Oxford (1950).

---

[52] S. G. Thompson, B. B. Cunningham, and G. T Seaborg: *J. Am. Chem. Soc.,* **72,** 2798 (1950).

[53] K. Street, S. G. Thompson, and G. T. Seaborg: *J. Am. Chem. Soc.,* **72,** 4832 (1950).

APPENDIX I

CHARACTERISTICS OF THE NATURALLY OCCURRING ISOTOPES[1]

Symbol	Nuclear Charge Z	Mass Number, A	Isotopic Mass, M	Mass Defect, $\Delta = M - A$	Packing Fraction, $f = \Delta/A$ $\times 10^4$	Binding Energy per Nucleon, Mev	Relative Abundance, %	Neutron to Proton Ratio, N/Z
n	0	1	1.00893	+0.00893	+89.3	...		
H	1	1	1.008123	+0.008123	+81.2	...	99.9844	0
		2	2.014708	+0.014708	+73.5	1.1	0.0156	1.000
		3*	3.01707	+0.01707	+56.9	2.8	ca. 0	2.000
He	2	3	3.01700	+0.01700	+56.7	2.5	1.3×10^{-4}	0.500
		4	4.00390	+0.00390	+ 9.8	7.0	99.9999	1.000
Li	3	6	6.01697	+0.01697	+28.3	5.3	7.39	1.000
		7	7.01822	+0.01822	+26.0	5.6	92.61	1.333
Be	4	9	9.01503	+0.01503	+16.7	6.4	100	1.250
B	5	10	10.01618	+0.01618	+16.2	6.4	18.83	1.000
		11	11.01284	+0.01284	+11.7	6.9	81.17	1.200
C	6	12	12.00382	+0.00382	+ 3.2	7.6	98.9	1.000
		13	13.00751	+0.00751	+ 5.8	7.4	1.1	1.167
		14*	14.007741	+0.007741	+ 5.5	7.5	ca. 10^{-10}	1.333
N	7	14	14.00751	+0.00751	+ 5.3	7.4	99.62	1.000
		15	15.00489	+0.00489	+ 3.3	7.6	0.38	1.143
O	8	16	16.00000	+0.00000	0.0	7.9	99.757	1.000
		17	17.00450	+0.00450	+ 2.7	7.7	0.039	1.125
		18	18.00490	+0.00490	+ 2.7	7.7	0.204	1.250
F	9	19	19.00450	+0.00450	+ 2.4	7.7	100	1.111
Ne	10	20	19.99877	−0.00123	− 0.6	8.0	90.51	1.000
		21	20.99963	−0.00037	− 0.2	8.0	0.28	1.100
		22	21.99844	−0.00156	− 0.7	8.0	9.21	1.200
Na	11	23	22.99618	−0.00382	− 1.7	8.1	100	1.090
Mg	12	24	23.9925	−0.0075	− 3.1	8.2	78.60	1.000
		25	24.9938	−0.0062	− 2.5	8.1	10.11	1.083
		26	25.9898	−0.0102	− 3.9	8.3	11.29	1.167
Al	13	27	26.9899	−0.0101	− 3.7	8.3	100	1.078
Si	14	28	27.9866	−0.0134	− 4.8	8.4	92.28	1.000
		29	28.9866	−0.0134	− 4.6	8.4	4.67	1.071
		30	29.9832	−0.0168	− 5.6	8.5	3.05	1.143
P	15	31	30.9843	−0.0157	− 5.1	8.4	100	1.067
S	16	32	31.98089	−0.01911	− 6.0	8.5	95.06	1.000
		33	32.9800	−0.0200	− 6.1	8.5	0.74	1.063
		34	33.97710	−0.02290	− 6.7	8.6	4.18	1.125
		36	35.978	−0.022	− 6.1	8.5	0.016	1.250
Cl	17	35	34.97867	−0.02133	− 6.1	8.5	75.4	1.059
		37	36.97750	−0.02250	− 6.1	8.5	24.6	1.177
A	18	36	35.9780	−0.0220	− 6.1	8.5	0.307	1.000
		38	37.974	−0.026	− 6.8	8.6	0.060	1.111
		40	39.9756	−0.0244	− 6.1	8.5	99.633	1.222
K	19	39	38.9747	−0.0253	− 6.5	8.5	93.3	1.053
		40*	39.9760	−0.0240	− 6.0	8.5	0.011	1.105
		41	40.974	−0.026	− 6.3	8.5	6.7	1.158
Ca	20	40	39.9753	−0.0247	− 6.2	8.5	96.96	1.000
		42	41.9711	−0.0289	− 6.9	8.6	0.64	1.100

CHARACTERISTICS OF THE NATURALLY OCCURRING ISOTOPES[1]

(*Continued*)

Symbol	Nuclear Charge Z	Mass Number, A	Isotopic Mass, M	Mass Defect, $\Delta = M - A$	Packing Fraction, $f = \Delta/A \times 10^4$	Binding Energy per Nucleon, Mev	Relative Abundance, %	Neutron to Proton Ratio, N/Z
		43	42.9723	−0.0277	− 6.4	8.6	0.15	1.150
		44					2.06	1.200
		46					0.0033	1.300
		48					0.19	1.400
Sc	21	45	44.9669	−0.0331	− 7.4	8.6	100	1.143
Ti	22	46	45.9661	−0.0339	− 7.3	8.6	7.95	1.091
		47	46.9647	−0.0353	− 7.5	8.6	7.75	1.136
		48	47.9631	−0.0369	− 7.7	8.7	73.45	1.182
		49	48.9646	−0.0354	− 7.2	8.6	5.51	1.227
		50	49.9621	−0.0379	− 7.6	8.7	5.34	1.273
V	23	51	50.9577	−0.0423	− 8.3	8.7	100	1.217
Cr	24	50	49.9642	−0.0358	− 7.2	8.6	4.49	1.083
		52	51.9557	−0.0443	− 8.5	8.7	83.78	1.167
		53	52.9550	−0.0450	− 8.5	8.7	9.43	1.208
		54	53.9540	−0.0460	− 8.5	8.8	2.30	1.250
Mn	25	55	54.957	−0.043	− 7.8	8.7	100	1.200
Fe	26	54	53.9575	−0.0425	− 7.9	8.7	5.81	1.078
		56	55.9531	−0.0469	− 8.4	8.7	91.64	1.154
		57	56.9546	−0.0454	− 8.0	8.7	2.21	1.192
		58	57.9506	−0.0494	− 8.5	8.8	0.34	1.231
Co	27	59					100	1.185
Ni	28	58	57.9594	−0.0406	− 7.0	8.6	67.76	1.071
		60	59.9495	−0.0505	− 8.4	8.7	26.16	1.143
		61	60.9537	−0.0463	− 7.6	8.7	1.25	1.179
		62	61.9493	−0.0507	− 8.2	8.7	3.66	1.214
		64	63.9471	−0.0529	− 8.3	8.8	1.16	1.286
Cu	29	63	62.957	−0.043	− 6.8	8.6	69.09	1.172
		65	64.955	−0.045	− 7.0	8.7	30.91	1.241
Zn	30	64	63.9534	−0.0466	− 7.3	8.6	48.89	1.133
		66	65.9465	−0.0535	− 8.1	8.7	27.81	1.200
		67	66.9479	−0.0521	− 7.8	8.7	4.07	1.233
		68	67.9485	−0.0515	− 7.6	8.7	18.61	1.267
		70	69.946	−0.054	− 7.7	8.7	0.620	1.333
Ga	31	69	68.952	−0.048	− 7.0	8.6	60.2	1.226
		71	70.952	−0.048	− 6.8	8.6	39.8	1.290
Ge	32	70					20.55	1.188
		72					27.37	1.250
		73					7.61	1.281
		74					36.74	1.313
		76					7.67	1.375
As	33	75	74.934	−0.066	− 8.9	8.8	100	1.273
Se	34	74					0.87	1.176
		76					9.02	1.235
		77					7.58	1.265
		78	77.938	−0.062	− 8.0	8.7	23.52	1.294
		80	79.942	−0.058	− 7.3	8.7	49.82	1.353
		82					9.19	1.412
Br	35	79	78.9440	−0.0560	− 7.1	8.6	50.5	1.257
		81	80.9419	−0.0581	− 7.2	8.7	49.5	1.314
Kr	36	78	77.945	−0.055	− 7.1	8.5	0.342	1.167
		80					2.223	1.222
		82	81.939	−0.061	− 7.4	8.6	11.50	1.278
		83					11.48	1.306

CHARACTERISTICS OF THE NATURALLY OCCURRING ISOTOPES[1]
(*Continued*)

Symbol	Nuclear Charge, Z	Mass Number, A	Isotopic Mass, M	Mass Defect, $\Delta = M - A$	Packing Fraction, $f = \Delta/A \times 10^4$	Binding Energy per Nucleon, Mev	Relative Abundance, %	Neutron to Proton Ratio, N/Z
		84	83.938	−0.062	− 7.4	8.7	57.02	1.333
		86	85.939	−0.061	− 7.1	8.7	17.43	1.389
Rb	37	85					72.8	1.297
		87*					27.2	1.351
Sr	38	84					0.56	1.211
		86					9.86	1.263
		87					7.02	1.289
		88					82.56	1.316
Y	39	89					100	1.281
Zr	40	90					51.46	1.250
		91					11.23	1.275
		92					17.11	1.300
		94					17.40	1.350
		96					2.80	1.400
Nb	41	93	92.926	−0.074	− 8.0	8.7	100	1.268
Mo	42	92					15.86	1.190
		94	93.945	−0.055	− 5.8	8.5	9.12	1.238
		95	94.946	−0.054	− 5.7	8.5	15.7	1.262
		96	95.944	−0.056	− 5.8	8.5	16.5	1.286
		97	96.945	−0.055	− 5.7	8.5	9.45	1.310
		98	97.943	−0.057	− 5.6	8.5	23.75	1.333
		100	99.945	−0.055	− 5.5	8.5	9.62	1.381
Tc	43							
Ru	44	96	95.945	−0.055	− 5.7	8.5	5.68	1.182
		98	97.943	−0.057	− 5.8	8.5	2.22	1.227
		99	98.944	−0.056	− 5.7	8.5	12.81	1.250
		100	99.942	−0.058	− 5.8	8.5	12.70	1.273
		101	100.946	−0.054	− 5.3	8.5	16.98	1.295
		102	101.941	−0.059	− 5.8	8.5	31.34	1.318
		104					18.27	1.364
Rh	45	103	102.941	−0.059	− 5.7	8.5	100	1.289
Pd	46	102	101.941	−0.059	− 5.8	8.5	0.8	1.217
		104	103.941	−0.059	− 5.7	8.5	9.3	1.261
		105	104.942	−0.058	− 5.5	8.5	22.6	1.283
		106	105.941	−0.059	− 5.6	8.5	27.2	1.303
		108	107.941	−0.059	− 5.5	8.4	26.8	1.348
		110	109.941	−0.059	− 5.4	8.5	13.5	1.391
Ag	47	107	106.945	−0.055	− 5.1	8.4	51.35	1.276
		109	108.944	−0.056	− 5.1	8.5	48.65	1.319
Cd	48	106					1.215	1.208
		108					0.875	1.250
		110					12.39	1.292
		111					12.75	1.313
		112					24.07	1.333
		113					12.26	1.354
		114					28.86	1.375
		116					7.58	1.417
In	49	113					4.23	1.306
		115*					95.77	1.346
Sn	50	112					0.90	1.240
		114					0.61	1.280
		115	114.940	−0.060	− 5.2	8.5	0.35	1.300
		116	115.939	−0.061	− 5.3	8.5	14.07	1.320

CHARACTERISTICS OF THE NATURALLY OCCURRING ISOTOPES[1]
(*Continued*)

Symbol	Nuclear Charge, Z	Mass Number, A	Isotopic Mass, M	Mass Defect, $\Delta = M - A$	Packing Fraction, $f = \Delta/A \times 10^4$	Binding Energy per Nucleon, Mev	Relative Abundance, %	Neutron to Proton Ratio, N/Z
		117	116.937	−0.063	− 5.4	8.5	7.54	1.340
		118	117.937	−0.063	− 5.3	8.5	23.98	1.360
		119	118.938	−0.062	− 5.2	8.5	8.68	1.380
		120	119.937	−0.063	− 5.3	8.5	33.03	1.400
		122	121.945	−0.055	− 4.5	8.4	4.78	1.440
		124	123.944	−0.056	− 4.5	8.4	6.11	1.480
Sb	51	121					57.25	1.373
		123					42.75	1.404
Te	52	120					0.091	1.308
		122					2.49	1.346
		123					0.89	1.365
		124					4.63	1.385
		125					7.01	1.408
		126					18.72	1.423
		128					31.72	1.462
		130					34.46	1.500
I	53	127					100	1.396
Xe	54	124					0.094	1.296
		126					0.088	1.333
		128					1.90	1.370
		129	128.946	−0.054	− 4.2	8.4	26.23	1.389
		130					4.07	1.407
		131					21.17	1.426
		132	131.946	−0.054	− 4.1	8.4	26.96	1.443
		134					10.54	1.481
		136					8.95	1.519
Cs	55	133					100	1.419
Ba	56	130					0.101	1.321
		132					0.097	1.357
		134					2.42	1.393
		135					6.59	1.411
		136					7.81	1.428
		137					11.32	1.446
		138					71.66	1.463
La	57	138					0.089	1.421
		139	138.953	−0.047	− 3.4	8.3	99.911	1.438
Ce	58	136					0.193	1.345
		138					0.250	1.379
		140					88.48	1.413
		142					11.07	1.448
Pr	59	141					100	1.390
Nd	60	142					27.13	1.366
		143					12.20	1.383
		144					23.87	1.400
		145	144.962	−0.038	− 2.6	8.2	8.30	1.417
		146	145.962	−0.038	− 2.6	8.2	17.18	1.433
		148	147.962	−0.038	− 2.6	8.2	5.72	1.467
		150	149.964	−0.036	− 2.4	8.2	5.60	1.500
	61							
Sm	62	144					3.16	1.323
		147					15.07	1.371
		148					11.27	1.387
		149					13.84	1.403

CHARACTERISTICS OF THE NATURALLY OCCURRING ISOTOPES[1]
(Continued)

Symbol	Nuclear Charge, Z	Mass Number, A	Isotopic Mass, M	Mass Defect, $\Delta = M - A$	Packing Fraction, $f = \Delta/A \times 10^4$	Binding Energy per Nucleon, Mev	Relative Abundance, %	Neutron to Proton Ratio, N/Z
		150					7.47	1.419
		152*					26.63	1.450
		154					22.53	1.484
Eu	63	151					47.77	1.397
		153					52.23	1.428
Gd	64	152					0.20	1.375
		154	153.971	−0.029	− 1.9	8.2	2.15	1.406
		155	154.971	−0.029	− 1.9	8.2	14.78	1.422
		156	155.972	−0.028	− 1.8	8.2	20.59	1.437
		157	156.973	−0.027	− 1.7	8.2	15.71	1.453
		158	157.973	−0.027	− 1.7	8.2	24.78	1.468
		160	159.974	−0.026	− 1.6	8.2	21.79	1.500
Tb	65	159					100	1.445
Dy	66	156					0.0524	1.364
		158					0.0902	1.394
		160					2.294	1.424
		161					18.88	1.439
		162					25.53	1.455
		163					24.97	1.470
		164					28.18	1.485
Ho	67	165					100	1.463
Er	68	162					0.1	1.382
		164					1.5	1.412
		166					32.9	1.441
		167					24.4	1.456
		168					26.9	1.471
		170					14.2	1.500
Tm	69	169					100	1.448
Yb	70	168					0.06	1.400
		170					4.21	1.429
		171					14.26	1.443
		172					21.49	1.457
		173					17.02	1.471
		174					29.58	1.486
		176					13.38	1.514
Lu	71	175					97.5	1.464
		176*					2.5	1.479
Hf	72	174					0.18	1.417
		176					5.30	1.444
		177					18.47	1.458
		178					27.10	1.472
		179					13.84	1.486
		180					35.11	1.500
Ta	73	181					100	1.480
W	74	180					0.122	1.432
		182					25.77	1.460
		183					14.24	1.473
		184					30.68	1.487
		186					29.17	1.513
Re	75	185					37.07	1.467
		187*					62.93	1.493
Os	76	184					0.018	1.421
		186					1.59	1.447

CHARACTERISTICS OF THE NATURALLY OCCURRING ISOTOPES[1]

(Continued)

Symbol	Nuclear Charge, Z	Mass Number, A	Isotopic Mass, M	Mass Defect, $\Delta = M - A$	Packing Fraction, $f = \Delta/A \times 10^4$	Binding Energy per Nucleon, Mev	Relative Abundance, %	Neutron to Proton Ratio, N/Z
		187					1.64	1.461
		188					13.3	1.474
		189	189.04	+0.04	+ 2.1	7.8	16.1	1.487
		190	190.03	+0.03	+ 1.6	7.8	26.4	1.500
		192	192.04	+0.04	+ 2.1	7.8	41.0	1.527
Ir	**77**	191	191.04	+0.04	+ 2.1	7.8	38.5	1.481
		193	193.04	+0.04	+ 2.1	7.8	61.5	1.507
Pt	**78**	192					0.78	1.461
		194	194.039	+0.039	+ 2.0	7.8	32.8	1.487
		195	195.039	+0.039	+ 2.0	7.8	33.7	1.500
		196	196.039	+0.039	+ 2.0	7.8	25.4	1.513
		198	198.05	+0.05	+ 2.5	7.8	7.23	1.538
Au	**79**	197	197.04	+0.04	+ 2.0	7.8	100	1.493
Hg	**80**	196					0.15	1.450
		198					10.1	1.475
		199					17.0	1.488
		200	200.028	+0.028	+ 1.4	7.9	23.3	1.500
		201					13.2	1.512
		202					29.6	1.525
		204					6.7	1.550
Tl†	**81**	203	203.05	+0.05	+ 2.5	7.8	29.1	1.506
		205	205.05	+0.05	+ 2.4	7.8	70.9	1.530
Pb†	**82**	204	204.05	+0.05	+ 2.5	7.8	1.5	1.488
		206	206.05	+0.05	+ 2.4	7.8	23.6	1.512
		207	207.05	+0.05	+ 2.4	7.8	22.6	1.524
		208	208.05	+0.05	+ 2.4	7.8	52.3	1.537
Bi†	83	209	209.05	+0.05	+ 2.4	7.8	100	1.518
Po†	84	210*						1.500
At†	85	218*						1.565
Rn†	86	222*						1.581
Fr†	87	223*						1.563
Ra†	88	226*						1.567
Ac†	89	227*						1.550
Th†	90	232*	232.11	+0.11	+ 4.7	7.5	100	1.577
Pa†	91	231*						1.538
U†	92	234*					0.0051	1.543
		235*	235.12	+0.12	+ 5.1	7.6	0.71	1.554
		238*	238.12	+0.12	+ 5.0	7.5	99.28	1.587
Np	93							
Pu	94	239*						1.543

* Radioactive.

† Short-lived, naturally occurring isotopes not included.

[1] Data compiled from following sources:

G. T. Seaborg and I. Perlman: *Rev. Modern Phys.*, **20,** 585 (1948).

H. A. Bethe: *Elementary Nuclear Theory*, pp. 123–140. John Wiley and Sons, New York (1947).

G. Friedlander and J. W. Kennedy: *Introduction to Radiochemistry*, pp. 299–389. John Wiley and Sons, New York (1949).

J. Mattauch: *Nuclear Physics Tables*, pp. 110–120. Interscience Publishers, New York (1946).

APPENDIX II

MEMBERS OF THE DISINTEGRATION SERIES

Isotope	Symbol	Z	A	Decay	Half-life	Energy, Mev
				$4n$ (Thorium) Series		
Thorium	Th	90	232	α	1.39×10^{10} y.	4.20
Mesothorium 1	$MsTh_1$	88	228	β^-	6.7 y.	0.053
Mesothorium 2	$MsTh_2$	89	228	β^-, γ	6.13 h.	1.55 (β^-)
Radiothorium	RdTh	90	228	α, γ	1.90 y.	5.42 (α)
Thorium X	ThX	88	224	α	3.64 d.	5.68
Thoron	Tn	86	220	α	54.5 s.	6.28
Thorium A	ThA	84	216	α (ca. 100%) β^- (0.013%)	0.158 s.	6.77 (α) ....
Astatine-216	At	85	216	α	3×10^{-4} s.	7.64
Thorium B	ThB	82	212	β^-, γ	10.6 h.	0.36 (β^-)
Thorium C	ThC	83	212	β^- (66.3%), γ α (33.7%)	60.5 m.	2.20 (β^-) 6.04 (α)
Thorium C′	ThC′	84	212	α	3×10^{-7} s.	8.78
Thorium C″	ThC″	81	208	β^-, γ	3.1 m.	1.72 (β^-)
Thorium D	ThD	82	208	none	stable	....
				$4n + 1$ (Neptunium) Series		
Plutonium-241	Pu	94	241	β^-	2.5×10^4 y.	0.02
Americium-241	Am	95	241	α, γ	500 y.	5.48 (α)
Neptunium-237	Np	93	237	α	2.25×10^6 y.	4.73
Protactinium-233	Pa	91	233	β^-, γ, e^-	27.4 d.	0.23 (β^-)
Uranium-233	U	92	233	α, γ, e^-	1.63×10^5 y.	4.82 (α)
Thorium-229	Th	90	229	α	7×10^3 y.	4.85
Radium-225	Ra	88	225	β^-	14.8 d.	0.2
Actinium-225	Ac	89	225	α	10.0 d.	5.80
Francium-221	Fr	87	221	α	4.8 m.	6.30
Astatine-217	At	85	217	α	0.020 s.	7.02
Bismuth-213	Bi	83	213	α (2%) β^- (98%)	47 m.	5.86 (α) 1.2 (β^-)
Polonium-213	Po	84	213	α	10^{-6} s.	8.34
Thallium-209	Tl	81	209	β^-	2.2 m.	1.8
Lead-209	Pb	82	209	β^-	3.3 h.	0.68
Bismuth	Bi	83	209	none	stable	....

MEMBERS OF THE DISINTEGRATION SERIES (*Continued*)

Isotope	Symbol	Z	A	Decay	Half-life	Energy, Mev
				$4n + 2$ (Uranium) Series		
Uranium I	UI	92	238	α	4.51×10^9 y.	4.2
Uranium X_1	UX_1	90	234	β^-, γ	24.5 d.	0.190 (β^-)
Uranium X_2	UX_2	91	234	β^-, γ, I.T.	1.14 m.	2.32 (β^-)
Uranium Z	UZ	91	234	β^-, γ	6.7 h.	0.45 (β^-)
Uranium II	UII	92	234	α	2.33×10^5 y.	4.76
Ionium	Io	90	230	α, γ	8.3×10^4 y.	4.66 (α)
Radium	Ra	88	226	α, γ	1590 y.	4.29 (α)
Radon	Rn	86	222	α	3.825 d.	5.49
Radium A	RaA	84	218	α (99.97%)	3.05 m.	6.00 (α)
				β^- (0.03%)		....
Astatine-218	At	85	218	α	few s.	6.72
Radium B	RaB	82	214	β^-, γ	26.8 m.	0.65 (β^-)
Radium C	RaC	83	214	β^- (99.96%), γ	19.7 m.	3.15 (β^-)
				α (0.04%)		5.50 (α)
Radium C′	RaC′	84	214	α	1.5×10^{-4} s.	7.68
Radium C″	RaC″	81	210	β^-	1.32 m.	1.80
Radium D	RaD	82	210	β^-, γ	22 y.	0.025 (β^-)
Radium E	RaE	83	210	β^- (ca. 100%)	5.0 d.	1.17 (β^-)
				α (5×10^{-5}%)		4.87 (α)
Radium F	RaF	84	210	α, γ	140 d.	5.30 (α)
Radium E″	RaE″	81	206	β^-	4.23 m.	1.7
Radium G	RaG	82	206	none	stable	....
				$4n + 3$ (Actinium) Series		
Actinouranium	AcU	92	235	α, γ	7.07×10^8 y.	4.4 (α)
Uranium Y	UY	90	231	β^-, γ, e^-	24.6 h.	0.2 (β^-)
Protactinium	Pa	91	231	α, γ	3.2×10^4 y.	5.0 (α)
Actinium	Ac	89	227	β^-(98.8%),	13.5 y.	0.01
				α (1.2%)		5.0
Radioactinium	RdAc	90	227	α, γ	18.9 d.	6.05 (α)
Actinium K	AcK	87	223	β^-, γ	21 m.	1.20 (β^-)
Actinium X	AcX	88	223	α, γ	11.2 d.	5.72 (α)
Actinon	An	86	219	α	3.92 s.	6.82
Actinium A	AcA	84	215	α (ca. 100%)	1.83×10^{-3} s.	7.36
				β^- (5×10^{-4}%)		....
Astatine-215	At	85	215	α	ca. 10^{-4} s.	8.00
Actinium B	AcB	82	211	β^-, γ	36.1 m.	0.5 (β^-)
Actinium C	AcC	83	211	α (99.68%)	2.16 m.	6.62
				β^- (0.32%),		
Actinium C′	AcC′	84	211	α	5×10^{-3} s.	7.43
Actinium C″	AcC″	81	207	β^-, γ	4.76 m.	1.47 (β^-)
Actinium D	AcD	82	207	none	stable	

Abbreviations: y. = year; d. = day; h. = hour; m. = minute; s. = second.

Author Index

Abegg, R., 172, 173, 274
Abel, E., 614, 854
Abelson, P. H., 77
Abrahams, S. C., 504
Achenbach, H., 533, 612
Achterberg, F., 546, 604
Ackermann, P., 859
Adams, M. F., 741
Adams, W. B., 710
Addison, C. C., 325, 366, 367
Adell, B., 251
Aldrich, L. T., 45, 49
Alexander, A. E., 755
Alexander, J., 24
Alexander, L., 258, 541
Allard, G., 771
Allen, H. R., 524
Allen, J., 367
Allison, F., 387
Alrich, F. R., 458
Amaldi, E., 72
Andersen, E. B., 543
Anderson, C. D., 8
Anderson, C. O., 422
Anderson, E. R., 799
Anderson, H. H., 475, 480, 682
Anderson, J. S., 219, 225, 279, 301, 363, 404, 500, 507, 600, 601, 701, 702, 890
Anderson, T. F., 449, 792
Anderson, W. E., 792
Andreocci, A., 547
Andrews, L. J., 840, 841
Andrieux, L., 738, 773
Angus, W. R., 325, 367, 595, 608
Arch, A., 863
Argersinger, W. J., Jr., 509
Argo, W. L., 422
Argument, C., 435
Arnold, J. R., 562
Arnold, M. H. M., 547
Arrhenius, S., 172, 308, 337
Ascher, E., 446
Asmussen, R. W., 555, 704
Asselin, G. F., 909
Astbury, W. T., 863
Aston, F. W., 22, 23, 24, 32, 33, 36, 38, 39, 42, 46
Aten, A. H. W., 490
Audrieth, L. F., 191, 332, 336, 338, 353, 354, 368, 369, 464, 474, 550, 551, 552, 567, 572, 573, 582, 585, 586, 589, 632, 634, 645, 646, 653, 659, 881, 909
Augur, V., 866
Auten, R. W., 267

Babor, J. A., 106, 123, 125
Bader, G., 602, 714
Bahl, R. K., 436
Bailar, J. C., Jr., 236, 247, 265, 266, 267, 301, 547, 768, 828, 875, 880
Bailey, R. W., 598, 703
Bailleul, G., 533
Bainbridge, K. T., 24
Baker, H. B., 560
Balke, C. W., 878
Ball, R. W., 909
Ballard, K. H., 457, 458, 459
Balthis, J. H., 880
Balz, G., 761
Bancroft, W. D., 458
Banks, A. A., 326
Bannister, F. A., 669
Banthien, H., 636
Banus, M. D., 749
Bardwell, D. C., 407
Barker, E. F., 592, 792
Barksdale, J., 876
Barnes, E., 617
Barnes, M. D., 415
Barnes, W. H., 496, 543
Baroni, A., 473
Barratt, S., 449
Barrer, R. M., 728
Bartholomay, H., Jr., 334
Bartindale, G. W. R., 719
Bartlett, J. H., 821
Bass, L. W., 229, 279
Bassett, H., 243, 503, 511, 535, 808
Bassière, M., 586
Bates, R. G., 857
Baudler, M., 516
Bauer, H., 364
Bauer, S. H., 428, 591, 774, 781, 784, 785, 789, 794, 796

Baumann, H. N., 687
Baumgärtel, H., 50
Baumgarten, H., 531
Baumgarten, P., 751
Baxter, G. P., 34
Bay, Z., 561
Beach, J. Y., 428, 472, 615, 626, 632, 784
Beachell, H. C., 909
Beams, J. W., 46
Beck, G., 907, 908
Becker, E., 716
Becker, E. W., 50
Becker, H., 8
Becker, K., 579, 699, 772
Beckman, A. O., 587
Beckmann, E., 855
Becquerel, H., 61
Beeli, C., 655
Beerbower, A., 463
Beevers, C. A., 499
Behrens, H., 711
Bell, F., 643
Bell, R. N., 645, 646, 647, 649
Bell, R. P., 335, 336, 774, 787, 789, 790
Bémont, G., 61
Benedict, M., 44
Bennett, G. M., 610
Bennett, W. E., 345
Bentley, J. B., 702
Berga, J., 361
Berger, E., 215
Berger, K., 596, 609
Berger, S. V., 810
Bergstrom, F. W., 550, 577
Bernal, J. D., 192, 217, 496
Bernstein, R. B., 51
Berraz, G., 379
Berthelot, M., 531, 533, 667
Bertram, A., 657
Berzelius, J. J., 172, 307
Besson, A., 629
Bethe, H. A., 77, 916
Betz, H. F., 531
Bévillard, P., 835
Bhatnagar, S. S., 467
Biggers, E. D., 400
Bigorgne, M., 432
Biltz, H., 681, 832
Biltz, W., 227, 618, 838
Birch, A. J., 349
Birckenbach, L., 48, 463, 464, 470, 474
Birr, E. J., 339
Bishop, E. R., 387
Bizette, H., 593
Bjerrum, J., 279, 328
Bjerrum, N., 335
Blair, V., 761
Blanchard, A. A., 234, 301, 594, 601, 701, 709, 710, 711
Bleakney, W., 394
Blix, M., 754
Block, I., 516
Blohm, C., 357
Bloom, H., 706
Blum, P., 773
Blumenthal, H., 770
Bock, E., 909
Bock, R., 906, 909
Bode, H., 632
Bodenstein, M., 433, 607
Bodländer, G., 828
Böeseken, J., 763, 764
Boersch, H., 667
Bohr, N., 15, 67, 73, 79, 81, 82, 83, 84, 85, 86, 87, 88, 89, 90, 106, 107, 121
Bokhorst, S. C., 562
Bolton, H. C., 367
Boltwood, B. B., 20
Bolz, A., 797, 798, 800, 802
Boncyk, L., 346
Bond, A. C., 410, 676, 775, 786
Bonhoeffer, K. F., 395, 399, 687
Bonneman-Bémia, P., 652
Bonner, N. A., 78
Boomer, E. H., 378
Booth, H., 434
Booth, H. S., 123, 379, 380, 428, 446, 451, 460, 524, 625, 626, 629, 632, 682, 684, 685, 746, 747, 760, 762
Born, M., 184
Bothe, W., 8
Bowen, E. J., 108, 434
Bowman, G. B., 349
Boyle, R., 307
Bozarth, A. R., 626
Bozarth, R. M., 455
Bradley, A. J., 222
Bradley, R. S., 336
Bradlow, H. L., 215
Bradt, P., 48
Braekken, H., 718
Bräuning, W., 687
Brager, A., 758
Bragg, W. H., 664, 863
Bragg, W. L., 136, 137, 664, 722
Braida, A., 448, 451, 452
Brand, J. C. D., 610
Brandaur, R. L., 738
Brandt, A., 749
Brandt, R. L., 364
Brantley, J. C., 882, 899, 900
Braschos, A., 632

Brasseur, H., 719
Braune, H., 857
Brauner, B., 908
Bray, W. C., 584
Brenschede, W., 435
Bretschger, M. E., 505
Bretschneider, O., 667
Brewer, A. K., 48
Brewer, F. M., 838
Brewer, L., 832
Brickwedde, F. G., 387
Bridgman, P. W., 495, 563, 564, 668
Briggs, T. R., 457, 458, 459
Bright, W. M., 632
Brightsen, R. A., 19
Brill, R., 704
Brimm, E. O., 706, 882
Briner, E., 608
Briscoe, H. T., 15, 126
Briscoe, H. V. A., 35
Britten, R. J., 48
Britton, H. T. S., 502, 865
Britzkes, E. V., 637
Broadley, J. S., 607
Brockmöller, J., 562
Brockway, L. O., 430, 463, 466, 467, 585, 600, 615, 625, 626, 629, 632, 679, 690, 694, 702, 742, 745
Brode, H., 750
Broderson, H. J., 353
Broderson, K., 367
Brodie, B. C., 563, 667
Brodkorb, F., 414
Brønsted, J. N., 47, 309, 311, 317
Brosset, C., 855
Brown, H. C., 334, 777, 782
Brown, J. H., 654
Browne, A. W., 463, 469, 473, 474, 577, 584, 588, 589
Brownstein, J. H., 582
Brukl, A., 903
Brunner, E., 613
Bruns, W., 751
Buchheit, P., 798
Buckley, H. E., 536
Buehler, E., 692
Buerger, M. J., 549
Büssem, W., 695
Burawoy, A., 718, 743, 787, 789, 834
Burbank, R. D., 492
Burdick, J. M., 755
Burg, A. B., 366, 717, 774, 777, 778, 779, 780, 782, 792, 796, 805, 807
Burger, M., 591
Burgess, W. M., 349
Burk, R. E., 247, 279, 593
Burnham, J., 496
Burstall, F. H., 278, 279, 697
Burton, E. F., 377
Burwell, J. T., 487
Bury, C. R., 87
Butler, J. C., 906
Butler, K. H., 516
Butler, M. J., 550, 551, 552, 572
Butler, T. A., 908

Cadenbach, G., 666
Cady, G. H., 423, 430, 437, 439, 463
Cady, H. P., 323, 338, 374, 570
Caeser, G. V., 609
Caillot, R., 680
Calas, R., 381
Callahan, J. R., 741
Callis, C., 717
Calvert, R. P., 622
Calvin, M., 279, 898
Campanella, D. A., 649
Campbell, G. W., Jr., 366
Campbell, J. A., 129, 136
Cappel, N. O., 344
Cario, G., 399
Carlisle, P. J., 406
Carlsohn, H., 461
Carlson, C. A., 423
Carney, E. S., 677
Carroll, B., 96
Carter, S. R., 422
Cartledge, G. H., 210
Cassal, A., 709
Cassidy, H. G., 709
Cauquil, G., 381
Cavendish, H., 373, 374
Chadwick, H., 628
Chadwick, J., 8, 66
Chapin, R. M., 591
Chapman, S., 44
Chappell, W., 356
Chappuis, J., 612
Chattaway, F. D., 591
Chédin, J., 608, 618
Cheesman, G. H., 459
Chernaev, I. I., *see* Tscherniaev, I. I.
Chiang, M.-C., 119
Chittum, J. F., 349
Chrétien, P., 437
Christer, C., 379
Chrobak, L., 842
Chulski, T., 644
Cirulis, A., 835
Clack, K. D. G., 459
Claesson, S., 606
Clark, C. H. D., 108, 170

Clark, D., 628
Clark, G. L., 455
Clark, H. K., 699
Clark, L. H., 487
Clarke, F. W., 29
Clarke, J. T., 398
Claus, A., 552
Claussen, W. H., 830
Cleveland, F. F., 841
Clever, A., 550
Clifford, A. F., 359, 909
Clusius, K., 44, 45, 398, 588
Cochran, C. N., 736
Cocksedge, H. E., 475
Coffin, C. C., 567
Coggeshall, N. D., 24
Cohen, A. J., 768
Cohen, E., 567, 669
Cohen, K., 40
Coleman, G. H., 591, 598
Colla, C., 639
Collin, R. L., 504, 582
Comings, E. W., 909
Conant, J. B., 312
Condon, E. U., 78
Connick, R. E., 895, 901
Cook, R. P., 466
Cooke, J. P., 111
Cooley, R. A., 521, 904
Copaux, H., 276
Copley, M. J., 301
Cordes, H., 525, 526
Core, A. F., 789
Corey, R. B., 677
Cornog, J., 449, 473
Corson, D. R., 77, 417, 418
Corte, H., 398
Coryell, C. D., 77, 78, 829
Coslett, V. E., 473
Coster, D., 87
Coulson, C. A., 198
Cowley, J. M., 766
Cox, E. G., 257, 610, 842
Craig, D. P., 599
Crane, E. J., 731
Crane, J. E., 575
Cranshaw, T. E., 62
Crawford, B. L., 802
Cremer, H. W., 456, 457, 458, 459
Crittenden, E. D., 49
Croatto, U., 544
Crookes, W., 6, 19, 20
Cross, P. C., 496, 690, 702
Crouthamel, C. E., 443
Cservenyak, F. J., 876
Cueilleron, J., 738
Cunningham, B. B., 910
Cupery, M. E., 552
Curie, I., 66, 72
Curie, M., 61
Curie, P., 61
Curjel, W. R. C., 539
Curtis, H. A., 575
Curtius, T., 588
Cushing, M. L., 609
Cuta, F., 836
Cuy, E. J., 584

Dadieu, A., 717
D'Agostino, O., 72
Dalton, J., 5, 110
Damianovich, H., 379
Damiens, A., 243, 423, 430, 511, 808
Daniels, F., 15, 76, 108, 605, 609
Darrow, K. K., 73
Darzens, G., 474
Dauben, C. H., 509, 510
Daunt, J. G., 49
Davidson, A. W., 280, 345, 356, 420, 737
Davidson, D., 335, 720, 721
Davidson, N., 884
Davidson, N. R., 742, 743
Davidson, W. L., 71, 78
Davies, C. W., 652, 857
Davies, M., 191
Davis, W. D., 786
Davy, H., 307
Dawson, J. A. T., 385
Deahl, T. J., 829
Deasy, C. L., 702
Debeau, D. E., 561
de Boisbaudran, L., 115
de Broglie, L., 7
de Bruyn, C. A. L., 352, 353
de Chancourtois, A. E. B., 111, 112
de Decker, H. C. J., 637
Deckert, H., 808
de Forcrand, R., 381
Deinum, H. W., 638
Delahay, P., 305
Demers, P., 62
Deming, L. S., 608, 636
Dempster, A. J., 22, 23, 24
Denbigh, K. G., 520
Denk, G., 535
Dennis, L. M., 423, 437, 577, 588, 677
de Rassenfosse, A., 719
Derbyshire, D. H., 462
Desch, C. H., 669
de Smedt, J., 592
DeVault, D., 95, 108, 829

de Vries, J. L., 608
de Vries, T. A., 633
Dewar, J., 711
Deyrup, A. J., 361
Diamond, H., 834
Dibeler, V. H., 48
Dickel, G., 44, 45, 398
Dickinson, R. G., 587, 842, 867
Diehl, H., 237
Diels, O., 694
Dietz, N., 312, 356
Dihlström, K., 636
Dilthey, W., 731, 765, 789
Dimroth, O., 764
Divers, E., 614
Dix, W. M., 166
Dixon, A. E., 475
Döbereiner, J. W., 110
Döbling, H., 693
Domange, L., 448
Domcke, E., 560
Donohue, J., 549, 606, 656, 828
Dootson, F. W., 44
Dorsey, N. E., 495
Downes, H. C., 317
Downs, W. R., 414
Dravnieks, A., 882
Drew, H. D. K., 237, 767
Drude, P., 173, 218
Duane, A. J., 539
Duckworth, H. E., 38
Dürrwächter, E., 829
Dullenkopf, W., 732
Dulmage, W. J., 795
Duncan, D. R., 456, 457, 458, 459
Dundon, C. V., 709
Dunitz, J. D., 431
Dunn, C. L., 829
Durant, R. G., 535
Dutt, N. K., 768
Dutton, F. B., 632
Duval, C., 251
Dyatkina, M. E., 226, 700, 792

Ebert, F., 833
Ebert, L., 336
Eberz, W. F., 840
Edsall, J. T., 802
Edwards, J. D., 740
Ehmann, E. A., 716
Ehrlich, P., 509
Eicholz, W., 618
Eidinoff, M. L., 387
Elliott, N., 618, 750, 830
Elsey, H. M., 323
Emeléus, H. J., 219, 279, 301, 326, 338, 363, 404, 421, 446, 451, 452, 500, 507, 611, 675, 676, 701, 774, 890
Emmett, P. H., 636
English, A. C., 62
English, J., 709
Enk, E., 601
Enskog, D., 44
Ephraim, F., 425, 459, 553, 583
Erasmus, H. deW., 687
Eriks, K., 608
Erlenmeyer, H., 215, 639
Essen, L. N., 255
Eucken, A., 690
Evans, R. C., 179, 866
Ewens, R. V. G., 701, 702, 705
Ewing, F. J., 223
Eykman, J. F., 681
Eyring, H., 388, 389
Eyster, E. H., 586

Fack, E., 712
Fajans, K., 63, 208
Fano, L., 78
Faraday, M., 5, 172
Farkas, A., 388, 389, 391, 396, 397, 398, 416
Farmer, R. C., 366
Farquharson, J., 433, 472
Faust, G. T., 637
Faust, T., 764
Fava, A., 544
Fehér, F., 507, 516, 639
Fénéant, S., 618
Fenrich, E. G., 432, 440
Fenwick, F., 826
Fermi, E., 72
Fernelius, W. C., 216, 243, 245, 247, 270, 279, 347, 349, 350, 577, 701
Ferrari, A., 639
Fichter, F., 243, 436, 460, 511, 613, 808
Fillmore, W. W., 487
Fineberg, H., 751
Finholt, A. E., 410, 676, 775, 786
Finkelstein, W., 462
Finlay, G. R., 603
Fischer, F., 486
Fischer, H., 749
Fischer, J., 590
Fischer, W., 744, 750, 834, 856
Fisher, H., 695
Fleischer, M., 458
Flodin, N. W., 779
Flood, H., 322
Fluegge, S., 29, 55, 78
Förland, T., 322

Förster, R., 693
Foex, M., 752
Foote, H. W., 457, 458
Forbes, G. S., 34, 475
Forestier, H., 490
Forrester, A. T., 41
Forsythe, W. R., 618
Foss, O., 543, 544
Foster, L. M., 736
Foster, L. S., 121, 176, 177, 301
Fouque, G., 461
Fournier, L., 629
Fowler, R. H., 496
Fox, J. J., 665
Fox, M., 50
France, W. G., 541
Franck, J., 399
Frankland, E., 374
Frankland, P. F., 366
Franklin, E. C., 322, 323, 338, 570, 572, 577, 588
Frary, F. C., 740, 741
Frary, S. G., 428, 625
Frazer, J. H., 598
Fred, M., 104
Fredenhagen, H., 358
Fredenhagen, K., 448, 666
Freed, S., 901
French, S. J., 206
Frenzel, A., 667
Freudenberg, K., 247
Frevel, L. K., 586
Fricke, R., 755, 756, 859, 863
Friedel, C., 684
Friedel, R. A., 395
Friedlander, G., 77, 916
Friend, J. N., 247, 279, 910
Frierson, W. J., 473
Frisch, O. R., 73
Frisch, P., 431
Fritsch, A., 546
Froehlich, M., 751
Fromm, E., 535
Frost, A. A., 305, 388
Fuchs, H., 711
Fürth, K., 677
Fulmer, E. I., 908
Furry, W. H., 45, 821

Gable, C. M., 531
Gärtner, H., 639
Gaertner, P., 468
Gall, H., 710, 716
Gall, J. F., 518
Gallafent, V., 857
Gallais, F., 319, 320
Galstaun, L. S., 413
Gamble, E. L., 423, 520, 682, 747, 749, 780
Gardner, R., 106
Gardner, W. H., 469, 474
Garner, C. S., 897, 901, 906, 910
Garner, W. E., 588
Garrett, A. B., 836, 859
Gastinger, E., 753
Gaydon, A. G., 560
Gay-Lussac, J., 307
Gebhert, A. I., 364
Gee, E. A., 876
Gehlen, H., 604
Gehring, G., 604
Geib, K. H., 400, 484, 504
Geiersberger, K., 736
Geiger, H., 12
Geigle, W. F., 459
Geisenberger, O., 717
Geleznoff, A., 817
Gel'man, A. D., 255, 715
Genssler, O., 604
Gerding, H., 750
Germann, A. F. O., 323, 365
Germann, F. E. E., 629
Germer, L. H., 668
Gerö, L., 686
Gershinowitz, H., 467
Gerstein, M., 334
Geselle, P., 668
Ghiorso, A., 62
Ghosh, S. P., 604
Giauque, W. F., 593, 606, 618
Gibb, T. R. P., 404, 415
Gibbs, C. F., 589
Gibbs, H. D., 354
Gibson, C. S., 718, 834
Gibson, D. T., 29
Gibson, G. E., 562
Giese, H., 511
Giese, M., 833
Giguère, P. A., 582
Gilbert, E. C., 584
Gilbert, F. L., 456
Gilbert, H. N., 824
Gilbert, L. F., 817
Gilchrist, R., 279, 890
Gillespie, L. J., 413, 414
Gillespie, R. J., 362, 542, 596, 609, 610, 611
Gilliam, W. F., 676, 743
Gilliland, W. L., 709
Gilman, H., 480
Gilmont, P., 601, 711, 747, 780
Gingrich, N. S., 490, 562, 563

Glasstone, S., 15, 39, 78, 108, 305
Glendenin, L. E., 77
Glenn, J. W., 755
Glockler, G., 486, 560
Gmelin, L., 247, 385, 416, 454, 480
Go, Y., 490
Godchot, M., 381
Goddard, D. R., 542, 610
Godfrey, T. N., 739
Goebel, A., 467
Goehring, M., 547, 548
Goheen, G. E., 598
Goldbach, E., 546
Goldfrank, M., 609
Goldhaber, M., 394
Goldschmidt, V. M., 29, 137, 143, 144, 152, 809
Goldstein, E., 21
Goldstein, L., 766
Goldstein, R. R., 456
Gomberg, M., 434
Gomolka, F., 563
Gonda-Hunwald, K., 462
Goodeve, C. F., 431, 433, 434
Gordon, W. E., 611
Gore, G., 452
Gorushkina, E., 255
Gotta, A., 407, 414
Gottfried, C., 770
Goubeau, J., 732
Gould, L. P., 458
Gould, R. F., 740
Goulden, J. D. S., 596
Grace, N. S., 454, 458
Gráf, G., 462
Graham, J., 362, 596, 611
Grassmann, H., 546
Gray, L. T. M., 449
Greenlee, K. W., 577
Greenspan, F. P., 505
Gregg, A. H., 625, 857
Greiff, L. J., 49
Griffith, R. O., 641, 643
Grilly, E. R., 395
Grimm, H. G., 215, 415
Grison, E., 608
Groschuff, E., 693
Gross, F. P., 373
Gross, S. T., 881
Grosse, A. V., 387
Grosse-Oetringhaus, H., 473
Groth, W., 39, 484
Grube, G., 687, 688
Grube, H. L., 687
Gruenhut, N. S., 609
Grüttner, B., 361
Grummitt, O., 247, 279
Gruner, E., 695, 817
Gucker, F. T., Jr., 858
Günther, P. L., 668
Gürtler, W. E., 752
Guntz, A., 835
Gupta, J., 643
Gupta, N. M., 753, 813
Gurewitsch, M., 553
Gutbier, A., 829
Guter, M., 383
Gutmann, V., 451
Gutowsky, H. S., 213, 743, 744
Guttmann, O., 566

Haber, F., 184, 575
Hackney, J. C., 882
Hägg, G., 221, 772
Haga, T., 555
Hagemann, F., 62
Hahn, H., 696, 758
Hahn, O., 72, 73
Hailes, H. R., 588
Haimann, E., 768
Haïssinsky, M., 891
Hale, C. F., 585
Hall, F. P., 413
Hall, N. F., 308, 311, 312, 317, 335, 356, 909
Hall, R. E., 118
Halloway, D. F., 684
Hammel, E. F., 395
Hammett, L. P., 312, 318, 356, 361
Hampe, W., 739
Hampson, G. C., 267, 625, 636, 857
Hanke, E., 590
Hannay, J. B., 669
Hannay, N. B., 207, 208
Hansen, W., 838
Hansley, V. L., 406
Hanson, N. W., 449
Hanson, R. A., 906
Hantzsch, A., 315, 317, 361, 473, 596, 609, 610, 611, 613, 839
Harder, A., 598, 732
Hardy, D. V. N., 730
Harker, D., 320
Harkins, W. D., 17, 26, 36, 42, 48, 118
Harris, I. W. H., 459
Harris, P. M., 784
Harteck, P., 394, 395, 400, 433, 484, 504
Hartung, E. J., 834
Harvey, J. A., 62
Hassel, O., 625, 758
Hatfield, M. R., 880
Haucke, W., 618

Hautefeuille, P., 612
Havighurst, R. J., 129, 855
Hayek, E., 503, 695
Hayes, A., 42
Hayes, A. M., 443
Hazelhurst, T. H., 93, 94
Hecht, H., 364, 522
Hedberg, K., 431, 792, 795
Helferich, B., 204
Heilmann, E. L., 551
Hein, F., 709, 867
Heinerth, E., 826
Heinrich, F., 676
Heisenberg, W., 395
Heitler, W., 195, 196
Helmholz, L., 648, 828, 833
Helms, A., 509, 510
Hendricks, S. B., 561, 576, 586, 606, 636, 637, 842
Henkel, G., 533
Henkes, R. A., 687
Henkeshoven, W., 277
Henne, A. L., 577
Henri, V., 525
Herb, H., 548
Herrmann, C. V., 524
Hertwig, K., 797
Hertz, G., 42, 43
Herzberg, G., 95, 560, 586, 686, 717
Hettich, A., 835
Heuer, E., 516
Hewlett, C. W., 377
Heyrovsky, J., 285
Hibbert, H., 524
Hicks, V., 649, 650
Hieber, W., 598, 600, 602, 604, 700, 701, 709, 710, 711, 712, 713, 714, 716, 717
Hignett, T. P., 741
Hildebrand, J. H., 211, 345, 347, 428, 678, 828
Hilgert, H., 353
Hill, C. F., 856
Hill, K., 623
Hill, O. F., 634, 645, 653
Hill, W. L., 637
Hillebrand, W. F., 374
Hincks, E. P., 62
Hindman, J. C., 901
Hinshelwood, C. N., 593
Hintenberger, H., 48
Hipple, J. A., 24
Hirschler, A. E., 859
Hittorf, M., 563
Hixon, A. W., 424
Hoard, J. L., 268, 680, 699, 719, 738, 761, 766, 829
Hobbs, E., 643
Hock, H., 712
Höhn, F., 516
Hoekstra, H. R., 782
Hoel, A. B., 463
Hönigschmid, O., 34, 35, 48, 78
Hoernes, P., 48
Hofferth, B., 480
Hoffmann, B., 658
Hoffmann, E., 637
Hoffmann, R., 471
Hofmann, J., 811
Hofmann, K. A., 352
Hofmann, U., 667, 668, 703
Hofmann, W., 770
Hogerton, J. F., 44
Hogness, T. R., 410, 675
Hollens, W. R. A., 852
Holroyd, G. W. F., 628
Holst, K. A., 646
Holst, R., 667
Holt, E. K., 741
Holt, S., 718
Hopkins, B. S., 110, 126, 368, 373, 385, 890
Horan, H. A., 539
Horrabin, H. W., 473
Horvitz, L., 807
Hoselitz, K., 382
Hough, C. R., 908
Howland, J. J., 898
Hrostowski, J., 887
Hsueh, C.-F., 119
Hückel, W., 226
Hülsmann, O., 618
Hüttig, G. F., 413, 414, 693, 755
Huffman, E. H., 266
Huffman, J. R., 50
Huggins, M. L., 133
Hughes, E. D., 362, 542, 596, 609, 610
Hugill, J. A. C., 547, 743
Hultgren, R., 563, 862
Hume-Rothery, W., 222
Humiston, B., 422
Hummel, F. A., 817
Humphreys, C. J., 104
Humphreys, R. F., 46
Hund, F., 195, 197, 895
Hunt, H., 346, 349, 464
Hunter, L., 191
Hunter, R. M., 424
Hurd, C. D., 582
Hurd, D. T., 410, 676, 706, 738, 777

Hurley, F. H., 368
Hutson, J. M., 547

Ibers, J. A., 884
Ikehara, S., 821
Ingold, C. K., 362, 542, 596, 605, 607, 608, 609, 610
Ingold, E. H., 605, 607
Irmann, B., 737
Isbell, H. S., 716
Isenberg, S., 675

Jacobs, R. B., 564, 565
Jaeger, F. M., 267, 549, 729
Jäniche, W., 770
Jahr, K. F., 277
Jakubson, S., 628
James, T. C., 449
Jander, G., 277, 324, 338, 357, 361, 362 363, 364, 367, 369, 645
Janssen, P. J. C., 374
Jeffrey, G. A., 610
Jeffries, Z., 740
Jelley, J. V., 62
Jellinek, E., 535
Jellinek, K., 535
Jellinek, M. H., 882
Jenkins, F. A., 42
Jenkins, G. I., 625, 857
Jensen, K. A., 704
Jessup, R. S., 668
Jirik, F., 737
Joannis, A., 732
Job, A., 709
Jockers, J., 755
Jörgensen, S. M., 250
Joffe, E. M., 382
Johannsen, A., 677
Johannsen, T., 742
Johnson, F. M. G., 622
Johnson, R. P., 219
Johnson, W. C., 347, 410, 675
Johnston, E. H., 609
Johnston, H. L., 49, 398, 593, 836
Johnston, S., 567
Johnston, W. M., 387
Johnstone, H. F., 527, 537
Joliot, F., 66
Jonassen, H. B., 266
Jones, E. M., 768
Jones, G., 453
Jones, H., 222
Jones, H. O., 711
Jones, L. W., 615
Jones, M. E., 795
Jones, P. L. F., 625, 857
Jones, R. C., 45
Jones, R. W., 325, 367, 608
Joos, G., 208
Jordan, D. O., 226
Jordan, E. B., 24
Jorissen, W. P., 243, 511, 808
Joseph, G., 473
Jost, W., 449
Jucaitis, P., 756
Jukkola, E. E., 368
Jung, G., 858
Juza, R., 580, 696, 758

Kahovec, L., 817
Kaiser, H., 732
Kaloumenos, H. W., 547
Kanda, F. A., 551
Kappeler, H., 436
Kapur, P. L., 467
Karandashova, E. F., 255
Karbe, K., 380, 382, 645
Karges, R. A., 449, 473
Karl, G., 817
Karrer, P., 604
Karrer, S., 487
Karsten, B. J., 448
Kasha, M., 901
Kaspar, J. S., 781
Kassatochkin, W., 509
Katz, J. J., 782, 910
Katzin, L. I., 62
Kaufmann, H. P., 468, 473
Kaufmann, L., 613
Keefer, R. M., 840, 841
Keesom, W. H., 47, 377, 592
Keggin, J. F., 276, 721
Keim, C. P., 41
Keim, R., 452
Keizer, C. R., 506
Keller, J. M., 9
Keller, R. N., 237, 279
Keller, W. E., 593
Kellermann, K., 463, 464, 470
Kelley, K. K., 753
Kellogg, K. B., 437
Kemp, J. D., 606
Kendall, J., 49
Kennedy, J. W., 77, 916
Kepner, R. E., 840
Kerr, E. C., 398
Kerstein, H., 471
Ketelaar, J. A. A., 472, 551, 596, 633, 680, 762, 865
Kharasch, M. S., 610, 716
Khosla, B. D., 467
Kiess, C. C., 104

Kiessling, R., 770, 771
Killingsworth, R. B., 582
Kimball, A. H., 393
Kimball, G. E., 108, 203
King, A. J., 551
King, F. E., 433
King, G. B., 647
Kipping, F. S., 729
Kirk, R. E., 584
Kistiakowsky, G. B., 467
Klein, C. H., 684
Kleinberg, J., 215, 345, 420, 460, 461, 509
Klemenc, A., 612, 694, 695
Klement, R., 657, 658
Klemm, A., 48
Klemm, L., 535, 781
Klemm, W., 369, 509, 510, 736, 737, 771, 781, 836, 890
Klingel, A. B., 851
Klinkenberg, L. J., 596, 761, 762
Klug, H. P., 258, 541
Knoblauch, H.-G., 560
Knoke, S., 857
Knotz, F., 632
Knowles, H. B., 885
Kobayashi, M., 265
Kobe, K. A., 355, 697
Koch, S., 552
Koch, W., 548
Kögler, F., 468
König, E., 667
König, J., 716
Körösy, F., 462
Kohlrausch, K. W. F., 743
Kohlschütter, V., 352
Kolitowska, J. H., 629
Kolthoff, I. M., 285, 336
Kondrat'ev, V., 695
Konopik, N., 336, 361
Konrad, E., 675
Kopsch, U., 484
Korinth, E., 489
Kossel, W., 86, 173, 174, 175
Kossiakoff, A., 320, 829
Kotov, W., 509
Kracek, F. C., 576, 722, 752
Kraus, C. A., 218, 338, 348, 349, 354, 570, 677
Kraut, H., 693
Krefft, H., 379
Krefft, O T., 448
Krejci, L., 692
Kremann, R., 618
Kremers, H. E., 150, 503, 738, 902, 909
Krings, W., 687
Krishnan, R. S., 665
Kroeger, J. W., 763
Kroll, W. J., 877
Kronig, R. deL., 198
Kronrad, J., 473
Krug, H., 451
Krumholz, R., 712
Ksanda, C. J., 836
Kubelka, P., 680
Küchler, H., 535
Küchlin, A. T., 763
Külkens, H., 632
Küster, F. W., 618
Kuljian, E. S., 796
Kummer, E., 258
Kupinski, T. A., 817
Kurbatov, J. D., 19
Kusch, P., 821
Kurtenacker, A., 545, 546
Kurzen, F., 753, 781
Kuss, E., 744, 812
Kwasnik, W., 463

La Chapelle, T. J., 901
Ladenburg, A., 684
Lafferty, J. M., 771
Lagally, H., 710
Laitinen, H. A., 349
La Mer, V. K., 317, 763
Lamm, O., 653
Landé, A., 136
Lange, J., 361
Lange, W., 634, 635, 753
Langer, C., 700
Langmuir, I., 86, 174, 175, 214, 215, 398, 399, 686
Langseth, A., 615
Lantz, P. M., 899
Larsen, E. M., 243
Latimer, W. M., 188, 285, 296, 305, 408, 480, 616, 660, 733, 817, 830, 844, 852, 867, 890
Laubengayer, A. W., 479, 693, 737, 738, 743, 756
Laudenklos, H., 781
Laun, D. D., 104
Laves, G., 841
Lavoisier, A., 307
Lebeau, P., 423, 430, 451
Lecher, H., 467, 473
Leckie, A. H., 595
Lecomte, J., 251
Leech, H. R., 422
Lehrman, A., 96
Leifer, E., 605
Leighton, P. A., 496

Leininger, E., 644
Leithäuser, G., 612
Leitz, F. J., 901
Leland, H. L., 836
Lemon, J. T., 615
Lenher, V., 365, 833
Leo, M., 215
Leslie, W. B., 344
Leutert, F., 713
Levi, G. R., 648
Levi, M., 817
Levine, R., 828
Lévy, H. A., 745
Lewis, B., 435
Lewis, G. N., 51, 86, 173, 174, 175, 193, 195, 306, 326, 328, 387, 388, 406, 483, 789
Lewis, J., 367
Lewis, N. B., 863
Li, S.-T., 145
Libby, W. F., 387, 543
Liddell, R. W., 650
Lidov, A. P., 464, 470
Liebhafsky, H. A., 271
Leibig, J., 307, 308
Liepe, J., 473
Lillis, G. A., 598
Lindemann, F. A., 46, 47, 48
Linder, Fr., 607
Lindqvist, I., 258, 279
Lingane, J. J., 884
Linhard, M., 474
Lips, E., 593
Lipscomb, W. N., 504, 582, 795, 860
Lipson, H., 499, 541
Lister, M. W., 679, 681, 701, 702, 910
Little, H. F. V., 910
Livingston, R., 635
Llewellyn, F. J., 586
Lobinger, K., 693
Lockyer, J. N., 374
Lofgren, N. L., 832
London, F., 195, 196
Long, F. A., 266, 768
Long, L. H., 226
Long, N. O., 598
Longuet-Higgins, H. C., 213, 607, 744, 787, 789, 790
Lonsdale, K., 665, 669
Loomis, F. W., 821
Loosen, K., 695
Lord, R. C., 446, 792
Lorentz, H. A., 219
Lorenz, J. H., 882
Lotmar, W., 633
Louïse, E., 743
Lowenheim, F. A., 361
Lowry, T. M., 193, 232, 309, 456, 615
Lozier, W. W., 394
Lu, C.-S., 549, 589, 656
Lucas, H. J., 840
Lucasse, W. W., 218
Lucht, C. M., 795
Luder, W. F., 93, 106, 120, 123, 177, 326, 328, 331, 335, 336
Luft, F., 590
Lundell, G. E. F., 885
Lux, H., 321
Lynch, M. A., 446, 453

McCarty, L. V., 781
McClellan, D. S., 881
McCoy, H. N., 909
McCulloch, L., 752
McCusker, P. A., 762
MacDonald, R. T., 51, 388
McElroy, A. D., 345
McFarland, D. F., 374
MacGillavry, C. H., 637
McGrath, J. S., 762
McGuire, W. S., 328
McInteer, B. B., 45
McKechnie, R. K., 879
McKee, F. S., 506
McKenna, P., 770
MacKenzie, K. R., 77, 417, 418
McKeown, A., 641, 643
McMillan, E., 77
McMorris, J., 446
McRae, D., 562
McReynolds, J. P., 270, 323, 324
McVey, W. H., 901
Maass, O., 516
Machu, W., 507, 509
Maddock, A. G., 657
Madorsky, S. L., 48
Magat, M., 626
Magaziner, E., 695
Magnusson, L. B., 901
Maisin, J., 533
Majumdar, A. K., 643
Malatesta, L., 830
Malmgren, H., 653
Malowan, J. E., 648
Manchot, W., 601, 710, 716
Manchot, W. J., 601, 710
Manley, J. J., 378
Mann, F. G., 265, 272, 840, 866
Manning, W. M., 910
Mantell, C. L., 668
March, C. C., 741
Marchi, L. E., 241, 243, 270

Marin, R., 711
Marinsky, J. A., 77
Mark, H., 793
Maron, S. H., 531
Marquart, P., 564
Marsden, E., 12
Marsh, J. K., 891, 907, 908, 909
Marshall, C. E., 728
Martell, A. E., 279
Martin, A. E., 665
Martin, D. R., 746, 747, 760
Martin, D. S., 443
Martin, F., 544
Martini, H., 806
Mason, C. W., 474
Mason, L. S., 786
Massenez, K., 486
Masson, I., 435, 437
Matějka, K., 546
Mathers, F. C., 422, 442
Mathewson, C., 471
Mathing, W., 775, 778
Matlack, G., 486
Mattauch, J., 24, 29, 55, 916
Matthies, M., 677
Maun, E. K., 884
Maxson, R. N., 524, 625
Maxted, E. B., 389, 400
Maxwell, L. R., 561, 606, 608, 636
May, A. N., 62
Mayer, K., 695
Mayer, M. G., 19
Mayr, A., 710
Megaw, H. D., 192
Meggars, W. F., 101, 103, 891
Megson, N. J. L., 730
Meibohm, E. P., 784
Meints, R. E., 368
Meitner, L., 72, 73
Mellor, D. P., 257, 599, 668, 669, 882
Melville, H. W., 588
Melvin, H. W., 480
Mendeléeff, D., 112, 113, 115, 116, 126, 172, 374
Menzel, H., 808
Menzel, W., 430, 431, 452, 612, 751
Menzies, R. C., 767
Merrill, R. C., 721
Merritt, L. L., 485
Merwin, H. E., 752
Metz, L., 544
Meulenhoff, J., 764
Meusser, A., 817
Meuwsen, A., 548
Meyer, A. W., 347
Meyer, F., 533
Meyer, G., 687, 817
Meyer, K. H., 490, 633
Meyer, L., 112, 113, 114, 126, 132, 667
Meyer, V., 681, 832
Michel, F., 553
Middleton, A. R., 273
Mihr, F., 636
Miles, F. D., 721
Millen, D. J., 542, 596, 608, 610
Miller, H. C., 518
Miller, R. R., 774
Millikan, R. A., 7
Mills, J. E., 776
Mills, W. H., 255
Miltschitzky, G., 690
Mindt, H., 736
Miolati, A., 274, 276
Miquel, P., 475
Mitchell, A. D., 641, 643
Mitchell, J. E., 364
Mitchell, J. E. H., 628
Mittasch, A., 708
Moeller, T., 146, 148, 150, 251, 332, 503, 595, 653, 768, 841, 863, 865, 899, 900, 902, 909
Moers, K., 406
Mohr, P. H., 354, 582, 584
Moissan, H., 421, 422, 452, 669, 738, 753
Moldenhauer, W., 591
Mond, L., 700
Monk, C. B., 652
Mooney, R. C. L., 455, 456, 512, 639
Moore, C. E., 154, 157
Moore, R., 749
Moore, R. W., 677
Moore, T. S., 188
Moore, W. J., 688
Morawietz, W., 687, 753
Morey, G. W., 752
Morgan, G. T., 237, 278, 279, 697, 764, 767, 863
Morris, W. C., 451, 460
Mortimer, B., 48
Morton, D. S., 693
Moseley, H. G. J., 12, 13, 14, 117, 173
Mosley, V. M., 561, 606, 608
Mott, N. F., 222, 588
Moulton, R. W., 487
Moureu, H., 626, 658
Mühlbauer, F., 716
Muir, M. M. P., 436
Mulliken, R. S., 46, 164, 195, 197, 787, 788, 791
Munch, R. H., 858
Munson, R. J., 382

Murphy, E. J., 387
Murphy, G. M., 387
Murray, M. J., 841
Muthmann, W., 548, 550
Mylius, F., 693, 817

Nakamura, A., 265
Nassau, M., 554
Nast, R., 598, 602, 604
Naumann, A., 356
Nekrasov, B. V., 789
Nelson, H. W., 368
Neogi, P., 768
Nespital, W., 743
Neudorffer, J., 448
Neuman, E. W., 508
Neumann, F., 771
Neumann, W., 612
Neumark, H. R., 423
New, R. G. A., 702
Newkirk, A. E., 738, 781
Newlands, J. A. R., 112
Newman, K. C., 442
Newton, A. S., 415
Nicholson, D. G., 751
Nickles, T. T., 585
Nielsen, E., 792
Nier, A. O., 24, 45, 49
Nieuwland, J. A., 763
Nijland, L. M., 637
Nikitin, B. A., 382
Nilson, L. F., 115
Noddack, W., 903
Nörring, O., 678
Nordsieck, H. H., 719
Norton, F. J., 395, 706, 774
Norton, J. T., 770
Noyes, A. A., 829
Noyes, W. A., 590
Nyholm, R. S., 279
Nylén, P., 643
Nyman, C. J., 349

Ockerman, L. T., 887
O'Daniel, H., 862
Oddie, G. T., 539
Odling, W., 111
Ogburn, S. C., 421
Ogg, A., 854
Ogg, B. A., 354, 582
Ogg, R. A., 349
Oldershaw, C. F., 581
Oliphant, M. L. E., 394
O'Neal, R. D., 394
Oppenheimer, J. R., 71
Orchin, M., 395
Orton, K. J. P., 591
Osalán, E., 667
Osten, R. A., 684
Ostwald, W., 308, 337
Ott, E., 692
Ott, H., 758
Owen, B. B., 709

Padelt, E., 433
Paine, P. A., 541
Palma, J. deS., 535
Palmer, G. D., 487
Palmer, K. J., 467, 520, 596, 750
Palmer, W. G., 171, 198
Paneth, F., 404, 410, 677, 678
Pankow, G. W., 633
Parham, O. L., 48
Parker, G. W., 899
Parkins, W. E., 41
Parsons, C. A., 669
Partington, J. R., 433, 436, 535
Partridge, E. P., 645, 649, 650
Partridge, M. A., 226
Pascal, P., 693
Patat, F., 586
Pauling, L., 93, 107, 108, 133, 134, 136, 137, 138, 143, 144, 145, 146, 147, 162, 163, 191, 194, 195, 199, 200, 201, 206, 207, 208, 212, 219, 223, 226, 233, 267, 275, 320, 455, 463, 467, 483, 488, 496, 538, 541, 585, 586, 593, 615, 629, 652, 666, 685, 686, 688, 694, 702, 718, 720, 722, 727, 746, 788, 789, 792, 794, 821, 830, 832, 834, 855, 863
Pearce, D. W., 895, 906, 908, 910
Pearson, T. G., 678
Pease, R. S., 758
Pedler, A., 564
Peeling, E. R. A., 362, 596, 610
Peiser, H. S., 866
Penfield, S. L., 453
Penney, W. G., 560, 582, 606
Percy, J. H., 364
Perey, M., 818
Perlman, I., 25, 78, 417, 916
Pernert, J. C., 654
Perrier, C., 77, 882
Persson, J. A., 687
Perutz, M. F., 843
Peters, K., 407
Petschner, E., 867
Peyronel, G., 648
Pfanstiel, R., 545
Pfeiffer, P., 188, 247, 275
Phillips, G. O., 325, 367, 608
Phillips, M., 71

Phillips, R. F., 843
Phragmén, G., 222
Piazzo, J., 379
Pictet, A., 817
Piérard, J., 719
Pincas, H., 588
Pinkston, J. T., 446
Piotrowski, H., 583
Pitzer, K. S., 211, 213, 704, 743, 744, 779, 788, 790, 793, 794, 828, 829
Planck, M., 79, 80
Platz, H., 526, 638
Plotnikow, W. A., 628
Plyler, E. K., 592
Pohland, E., 781, 793, 800
Pollack, H. C., 46
Pollard, E. C., 71, 78
Poole, H. G., 610
Poppenberg, O., 754
Posnjak, E., 576, 693, 836
Pospekhov, D. A., 708
Post, H. W., 729
Potter, H. N., 687
Pourbaix, M., 305
Powell, H. M., 224, 258, 383, 628, 701, 719, 766, 843
Powell, J. E., 908
Powney, J., 434
Pradier, J. C., 608
Prandtl, W., 899
Preckel, R., 858
Preuner, G., 562
Price, W. C., 789
Prins, J. A., 567
Přistoupil, V., 680
Probst, J., 644
Probst, R. E., 49
Proeschel, E., 604
Proisl, J., 614
Prosen, E. J., 668
Prout, W., 5
Pullman, J. C., 524
Purdie, D., 840, 866
Putnam, G. L., 355, 487, 697

Quagliano, J. V., 506
Quam, G. N., 110, 120, 126
Quam, M. B., 110, 120, 126
Quibell, T. H. H., 255
Quill, L. L., 104
Quimby, O. T., 645
Quincke, F., 700
Quinty, G. H., 644

Rabinowitsch, E., 410, 677
Rafter, J. R., 710
Ragoss, A., 753
Rahlfs, O., 750, 856
Raistrick, B., 643
Ralston, O. C., 876
Raman, C. V., 665
Ramaswamy, K. L., 592, 686
Ramsay, W., 374
Ramser, H., 751
Randles, J. E. B., 826
Randolph, C. L., 796
Rang, F., 121
Rankama, K., 29
Rao, G. G., 592, 686
Raschig, F., 473, 555, 585, 614
Rasetti, F., 72, 559
Rathjens, G. W., 779
Rây, H. N., 862
Rây, P., 198, 604, 831
Ray, R. C., 753, 812, 813, 814
Ray, W. L., 365
Rayleigh, Lord, 42, 374, 560, 561, 669
Read, J. G., Jr., 48
Rebentisch, W., 668
Redlich, O., 741
Reedy, J. H., 400
Rees, A. L. G., 52
Reggel, L., 479
Rehaag, H., 638
Rehmar, S., 762
Reichert, J. S., 505
Reiff, F., 694
Rémy, H., 243, 511, 808, 841, 864
Reynolds, C. A., 649
Reynolds, J. E., 475
Rhymer, P. W., 865
Ricci, J. E., 320
Rice, F. O., 170
Rice, O. K., 136, 144, 226, 612
Richards, T. W., 34
Richardson, F. D., 431, 433
Richter, H., 693
Richter, J. W., 864
Rienäcker, G., 435
Rifkin, E. B., 398
Righellato, E. L., 857
Riley, H. L., 857
Rippere, R. E., 763
Ritter, D. M., 796, 805
Roald, B., 322
Roberts, E. R., 425
Robertson, G. R., 425
Robertson, J. M., 607
Robertson, R., 665
Robey, R. F., 166, 216
Robin, I., 866
Robinson, P. L., 466, 678

Rochow, E. G., 423, 437, 676, 729, 730
Rocquet, P., 658
Rodden, C. J., 899
Rodebush, W. H., 146, 188, 191, 506
Röhler, H., 368
Roell, E., 407
Röntgen, W. C., 12
Rogers, D. A., 423
Rogers, L. B., 649
Rohner, F., 436
Rohrback, G. H., 430, 463
Rollefson, G. K., 581
Rollinson, C. L., 243
Romberg, E., 709, 716
Rompe, R., 378
Rose, K., 878
Rosen, N., 821
Rosenberg, M. E., 584
Rosenheim, A., 274
Ross, J., 364
Rossi, R., 20
ini, F. D., 668
ild, B. F., 909
M., 626
., 536
J., 709
743
623, 677
V., 667, 668, 703
g, W. H. C., 698
., 357
21, 430, 431, 446, 448, 451,
590, 612, 667, 669, 690, 833
E., 213, 214, 415, 582, 787
, W., 753
S., 20, 736
555, 632, 660, 897, 901, 906,
. G., 906
rd, E., 11, 14, 17, 63, 66, 394
G., 762
en, R., 35
T. G., 29
P., 669
., 604
A., 625
on, R. T., 782
G. W., 706
, W. A., 459
O., 731
., 72
V., 544
., 763, 764
., 398, 445, 690
G. W., 782, 799, 806
Schaeffer, H. F., 487
Schaeffer, R., 806
Schaeler, B., 736
Schechter, W. H., 509
Scheiner, K., 899
Schenck, R., 547, 564, 636
Schenk, P. W., 525, 526, 638
Scherrer, G. A., 458
Schirmer, F. B., 634, 737, 881
Schlee, R., 35
Schleede, A., 666
Schlegelmilch, F., 459
Schlesinger, H. I., 410, 676, 749, 774, 775, 777, 778, 779, 780, 782, 786, 796, 805, 806, 807
Schmager, H., 636
Schmeisser, M., 435, 591, 612
Schmid, R., 686
Schmidt, H., 357
Schmidt, J.-M., 862
Schmidt, M. T., 332
Schmitz-Dumont, O., 632
Schnorrenberg, E., 697
Schoenmaker, P., 529
Schofield, M., 373
Scholder, R., 535
Scholz, G., 361
Schomaker, V., 582, 586, 589, 606, 750, 792, 795
Schossberger, F., 770
Schreyer, J. M., 887
Schubert, J., 864
Schubert, M. P., 713
Schüth, W., 771
Schützdeller, H., 863
Schützenberger, P., 715
Schuh, R., 711
Schulten, H., 711, 712, 713
Schultz, J. F., 636
Schulz, H., 668, 808
Schulz, O. F., 554
Schulze, A., 567
Schulze, G. E. R., 817
Schumacher, F. J., 765
Schumacher, H.-J., 431, 433, 435, 612
Schumb, W. C., 423, 446, 453, 505, 520, 521, 682, 684, 685, 749
Schwarz, R., 229, 279, 434, 435, 511, 533, 612, 675, 676, 677, 693
Scott, A. B., 887
Scott, A. W., 615
Scott, M. R., 78
Scott, T. R., 766
Seaborg, G. T., 25, 62, 77, 78, 104, 106, 417, 892, 910, 916
Seabright, C. A., 428, 629

Secoy, C. H., 439
Secrist, J. H., 629
Seegmiller, C. G., 629, 632
Seel, F., 364, 596, 598, 602, 604, 787
Seemann, W., 864
Segitz, A., 867
Segrè, E., 72, 77, 417, 418, 882
Seitter, E., 548
Seitz, F., 219
Selwood, P. W., 168, 170, 389, 394, 858, 895
Seppi, L. J., 881
Serber, R., 18
Seubert, K., 126
Sevast'yanov, N. G., 699
Seybolt, A. U., 879
Shand, W., 486
Shanley, E. S., 505, 507
Sharp, F. H., 741
Sharpe, A. G., 446, 451, 452
Sharrah, P. C., 592
Sheline, G. E., 901
Sheline, R. K., 704, 705
Sherman, A., 198
Sherman, J., 153, 157, 183, 652, 863
Sherr, R., 394
Shetterly, F. F., 585, 589
Sickman, D. V., 612
Sidgwick, N. V., 171, 177, 193, 194, 195, 200, 232, 233, 234, 327, 385, 416, 445, 446, 480, 555, 598, 660, 703, 733, 788, 817, 838, 844, 863, 867, 890
Siegel, J. M., 74
Sieverts, A., 407, 413, 414
Silbiger, G., 785, 794
Simmons, L. M., 96, 124, 125
Simon, A., 535, 639
Simons, J. H., 312, 358, 428, 451, 480
Sindeband, S. J., 770
Sinha, P. C., 753, 814
Sisler, H. H., 153, 226, 280, 509, 550, 552, 572
Skarstrom, C., 46
Skinner, H. A., 743
Skoog, F., 449
Slater, J. C., 195, 199, 219
Slooff, A., 687
Slowinski, E. J., 446
Smit, E., 750
Smith, A., 622
Smith, A. L., 598
Smith, G. B. L., 325, 365, 463, 470
Smith, G. F., 442, 443, 551, 905
Smith, G. W., 649, 650
Smith, H. G., 377
Smith, J. D. Main, 88, 109, 126, 898
Smith, L. G., 394
Smith, L. P., 41
Smith, P. T., 394
Smith, S. H., 774
Smits, A., 529, 562, 638
Smoker, E. H., 349
Smyth, C. P., 207, 208
Smyth, H. D., 39, 41, 78
Soddy, F., 20, 63, 374
Söderback, E., 468
Soldate, A. M., 781
Sommer, A. L., 387
Sommer, F., 470, 554, 588
Sommerfeld, A., 15, 84, 88
Sonnekalb, F., 716
Soper, F. G., 439
Soroos, H., 591
Southard, J. C., 752
Sowa, F. J., 763
Spacu, P., 469, 717
Spedding, F. H., 415, 908
Speidel, H., 687, 688
Spencer, D. A., 473
Spencer, J. F., 539, 852
Spindel, W., 51
Spinks, J. W. T., 611
Sprenger, G., 612
Springall, H. D., 467
Spurr, R. A., 486, 586
Squires, A. M., 39
Stack, G. G., 762
Stafford, O. F., 354
Stallmann, H., 710
Stamm, E., 562
Stas, J. S., 34, 110
Stecher, O., 742
Steele, B. D., 776
Stegeman, G., 786
Stein, C. P., 449
Steiner, W., 561
Steinman, R., 191, 632, 634
Steinmetz, H., 719
Stelling, O., 643
Stephanou, S. E., 509
Stephans, W. W., 877
Stern, S., 460
Stettiner, H. M. A., 712
Stevens, A. J., 684
Stevenson, D. P., 472, 632, 750
Stewart, A., 384
Stewart, A. W., 15, 77
Stewart, D. W., 39
Stewart, K., 676
Stewart, L. C., 424
Stieger, G., 433

Stiff, J. F., 747
Stillwell, C. W., 136, 144, 179, 219, 368, 567
Stillwell, W. D., 685
Stitt, F., 792, 829
Stock, A., 404, 562, 563, 566, 658, 674, 744, 749, 753, 754, 773, 774, 775, 776, 777, 778, 781, 794, 800, 806, 812
Stoddart, E. M., 678
Stoner, E. C., 88
Stoney, G. J., 6
Stoops, R., 78
Storbeck, O., 828
Stosick, A. J., 636, 657, 796
Strada, M., 468
Stranathan, J. D., 6, 14, 15, 24, 39, 77
Strassmann, F., 72, 73
Straumanis, M. E., 835, 882
Straus, S., 48
Street, K., 910
Strutt, R. J., *see* Lord Rayleigh
Stubbin, P. M., 882
Studier, M. H., 62
Stuhlmann, H., 712
Sturdivant, J. H., 277
Style, D. W. G., 449
Suck, H., 666
Sütterlin, W., 751, 753, 777
Sugden, S., 643, 836
Suhrmann, R., 588
Sun, C. E., 145
Susz, B., 608
Sutherland, G. B. B. M., 582, 606
Sutherland, M. M. J., 247, 279
Sutton, L. E., 195, 430, 579, 625, 681, 702, 743, 857
Sveda, M., 524, 550, 552, 572
Swezey, F. H., 463
Swinehart, C. F., 460, 682
Synan, J. F., 432, 440
Syrkin, Ya. K., 226, 790, 792
Szabados, G., 768
Szabó, Z., 104
Szper, J., 467

Ta, Y., 96
Tafel, J., 581
Tammann, G., 495
Taufen, H. J., 841
Taylor, H. S., 39, 108, 388, 394
Taylor, J. E., 741
Taylor, J. K., 48
Taylor, M. C., 432, 440
Taylor, M. D., 334
Taylor, R. P., 643
Taylor, T. I., 51
Taylor, W. H., 112
Teller, E., 170
Teller, U., 711, 713
Templeton, C. C., 909
Templeton, D. H., 509, 510, 771
Tenney, A. H., 424
Terrey, H., 645, 812, 834
Thew, K., 78
Thewlis, J., 222
Thiele, H., 667
Thode, H. G., 50
Thomas, C. D., 562
Thompson, G. W., 887
Thompson, J. K., 509
Thompson, R., 325, 366
Thompson, S. G., 910
Thomsen, S. M., 680
Thomson, J. J., 7, 11, 20, 21, 172
Thorne, P. C. L., 425
Thorpe, T. E., 657
Tiede, E., 560, 753
Tilk, W., 737
Timpany, C. R., 323
Tomkins, F. S., 104
Topley, B., 389, 645
Toussaint, S. M., 694
Toy, A. D. F., 632, 659
Travers, M. W., 374, 753, 813
Traxler, R. N., 629
Treadwell, W. D., 655, 768
Treffers, H. P., 361
Triebel, H., 526
Trillat, J. J., 490
Trout, W. E., 701
Truter, M. R., 610
Tsai, B., 593
Tscheischwili, L., 862
Tscherniaev, I. I., 254, 256
Tschistow, W. O., 462
Tsuchida, R., 265
Tunell, G., 836
Tunstall, R. B., 764
Turkevich, A., 472
Turner, L. A., 73
Tutton, A. E., 657
Tzentnershrer, M., 467

Ulich, H., 743, 751
Ullman, R., 470
Urey, H. C., 39, 47, 49, 50, 51, 387
Usanovich, M., 329, 357
Uschakow, M. I., 462
Usher, F. L., 550

van Arkel, A. E., 179, 890
van Bemmelen, J. M., 692

Van Derhoef, W. H., 876
van der Meulen, P. A., 761
Vander Werf, C. A., 153, 215, 280, 461
van Dijk, H., 47
van Lieshout, A. K. W. A., 669
Van Mater, H. L., 761
van Rysselberghe, P., 305
Van Valkenburgh, H. B., 547
Van Vleck, J. H., 168, 198, 897
Van Voorhis, C. C., 562
Van Wazer, J. R., 646, 649, 653, 654
Veeder, J. M., 423
Vegard, L., 487
Venable, F. P., 109, 126
Verhoek, F., 605
Verleger, H., 586
Vermaas, N., 763
Verneuil, A., 755
Vetter, H., 712, 716
Villard, P., 381
Vincent, G. P., 432, 440
Vincent, W. B., 680
Voge, H. H., 543
Vogel, A., 817
Vogel, I., 535, 544
Voigt, W., 317
Volkoff, G., 78
Volmer, M., 442
von Deines, O., 546
von Euler, H., 867
von Hauer, C. R., 541
von Hevesy, G., 47, 87, 856, 910
von Krueger, G., 635
von Pettenkofer, M., 110
von Stackelberg, M., 697, 698, 771
von Steinwehr, H., 567
von Wartenberg, H., 687, 833
Vosburgh, W. C., 857
Voss, E., 736
Voznesenskii, S. A., 547

Waggaman, W. H., 876
Wagler, K., 867
Wagner, G., 694
Wagner, H. A., 123
Wagner, J., 743
Wagner, O. H., 716
Wahl, A. C., 78
Wahl, W., 768
Walassis, N. H., 604
Walden, P., 307, 338, 339, 353, 354, 356, 363, 369, 464, 608
Walker, A. C., 692
Walker, A. O., 778
Walker, O. J., 39
Wall, F. T., 679
Walles, E., 615
Walsh, A. D., 237, 787
Walton, J. H., 516
Wamser, C. A., 761
Warburg, E., 612
Wardlaw, W., 257, 422
Warf, J. C., 415, 909
Warren, B. E., 487, 563, 739, 856
Wartik, T., 749
Wasastjerna, J. A., 137
Washburn, E. W., 49, 387
Washington, H. S., 29
Waters, W. A., 462
Watson, H. E., 592, 686
Watt, G. W., 344, 347, 349, 350
Way, K., 78
Weber, A. G., 647
Webster, K. C., 257, 842
Weeks, M. E., 110, 126
Wegwitz, O., 527
Weichselfelder, T., 415
Weidemann, W., 744
Weinberger, H., 469
Weinland, R. F., 279, 459
Weintraub, E., 738
Weiser, H. B., 501, 692, 755
Weissberger, A., 315
Weissman, S. A., 377
Weisz, H., 834
Weisz, O., 843
Weisz, R. S., 756
Weitz, E., 546, 604
Welch, A. J. E., 39, 45, 598, 701, 774
Welge, H. J., 840
Wellmann, M., 666
Wells, A. F., 179, 191, 226, 258, 445, 480, 500, 504, 555, 567, 578, 628, 660, 690, 692, 696, 698, 717, 733, 754, 756, 766, 808, 817, 840, 844, 890, 910
Wells, H. L., 453, 458, 459, 471
Welsh, T. W. B., 353
Wender, I., 395
Wendling, A. V., 543
Wendt, H., 362, 364
Werner, A., 121, 172, 229, 230, 242, 247, 251, 255, 259, 265, 266, 278, 604, 639, 750
Werner, T. H., 312
West, C. D., 718
West, J., 648
West, W., 582
Westgren, A. F., 222, 636
Westhaver, J. W., 48
Westheimer, F. H., 610
Wétroff, G., 626, 658
Wheeler, H. L., 453

Wheeler, J. A., 73
White, A. H., 668
White, J. F., 432, 440
White, L. M., 507
Whitford, E. L., 516
Whitmore, F. E., 586
Whytlaw-Gray, R., 35, 520
Wibaut, J. B., 695
Wiberg, E., 380, 382, 742, 751, 753, 774, 787, 797, 798, 800, 802, 803, 806
Wicke, E., 445
Wickert, K., 324, 336
Wiele, H., 434
Wier, T. P., 368
Wierl, R., 800
Wikswo, J. P., 458
Wilcoxon, F., 588
Wilhelm, J. O., 377
Wilke-Dörfurt, E., 761
Wilkinson, J. A., 360
Willard, H. H., 442, 444, 485
Willey, E. J. B., 561
Williams, C., 44
Williams, G., 610
Williams, J. W., 355
Williams, M. B., 268
Williams, R. R., Jr., 71
Willson, K. S., 379, 380, 747
Willstätter, R., 693
Wilm, D., 668
Wilson, B. M., 865
Wilson, C. L., 15, 77
Wilson, C. T. R., 9
Wiltshire, E. R., 767
Wilzbach, K. E., 410, 676, 786
Winkler, C., 115
Winmill, T. F., 188
Winstein, S., 840
Winter, C. H., 876
Winter, P. K., 751
Wirsching, A., 714
Wiswesser, W. J., 96, 108, 125
Wittkopf, I., 357
Wöbling, H., 548
Wöhler, L., 527, 739
Woitinek, H., 833
Wolf, L., 564, 636
Wolff, F., 525
Wolfgang, R. L., 387
Woodhead, M., 35
Woodward, E. R., 432, 440
Woodward, L. A., 854
Woolf, A. A., 326, 451, 452, 598, 611
Wooster, N., 692
Wooster, W. A., 692
Work, J. B., 621
Woyski, M. M., 428, 635
Wrede, E., 484
Wulf, O. R., 487
Wyckoff, R. W. G., 142, 455, 694

Yager, C. B., 591
Yatsimirskii, K., 357
Yi, P.-F., 96
Yntema, L. F., 368, 909
Yolles, S., 364
Yost, D. M., 446, 449, 463, 513, 521, 555, 562, 660, 830, 840, 897, 901, 904, 906, 910
Young, L. B., 24
Young, R. C., 685, 863
Yukawa, H., 9

Zachariasen, W. H., 142, 143, 144, 150, 512, 536, 538, 543, 576, 639, 696, 808, 810, 893
Zalkin, A., 771
Zanstra, J. E., 549
Zartman, I. F., 566
Zhdanov, G. G., 699
Ziegler, G. E., 810
Ziegler, W., 858
Zingaro, R. A., 461
Zintl, E., 435, 598, 618, 657, 687, 695, 732, 733, 753
Zmaczynski, E. W., 120, 123
Zuffanti, S., 326, 328, 335, 336
Zwartsenberg, J. W., 472

Subject Index

Abundances of elements, crustal, 30–32
Abundances of isotopes, 28–29
Acetic acid, physical constants, 341
Acetic anhydride, physical constants, 341
Acid-base behavior, characteristics, 306
  in gas phase, 334
  at high temperatures, 332–334
    Brønsted-Lowry approach, 333
    examples, 332–334
    Lewis approach, 333–334
  phenomenological criteria, 306
  relationship to oxidation-reduction, 331–332
Acid-base catalysis, 334–335
Acid-base concept, applications, 331–335
  Bjerrum's correlation, 328
  Brønsted-Lowry concept (protonic concept), 309–321
  historical development, 307–308
  Lewis electronic theory, 326–329
    advantages and disadvantages, 328–329
    definitions, 326–327
    examples, 327
    and the phenomenological criteria, 328
  Lux-Flood concept, 321–322
  modern approaches, 308–330
  protonic concept, 309–321
    in aqueous solutions, 310–311
    conjugate acid, 310
    conjugate base, 310
    definitions, 309–310
    equilibria, 310
    limitations, 321
    in non-aqueous solutions, 311–312
    relationship to salt hydrolysis, 311
    strengths of acids and bases, 312–321; *see also* Acid-base strength
    types of acids and bases, 310–311
  recapitulation, 330
  solvent systems theory, 322–326
    advantages and disadvantages, 326
    auto-ionization of solvents, 322–323
    definitions, 323
    neutralization reactions, 323, 324
    non-protonic solvents, 323–326
Acid-base concept, Usanovich concept, 329–330
    advantages and disadvantages, 330
    definitions, 329
    examples, 330
  water-ion (Arrhenius) concept, 308–309
Acid-base strength, 312–321
  in aprotic solvents, 316–318
  in aqueous solutions, 313–316
  equilibrium considerations, 313
  evaluation, numerical, 313–315
  of hydrated cations, 321
  of hydro acids, 318–319
  indicators, use of, 316–318
  numerical values, aqueous solutions, 314–315
  of oxy acids, 319–321
    calculation of constants, 320–321
    rules, 320
  relationship to dielectric constant, 318
  relationship to electronegativity, 319–321
  relationship to solvent type, 315–318
  strong acids, 315–318
  trends, aqueous solution, 318–321
Acids and bases, 306–336
Actinide contraction, 150, 191
  effects of, 150, 901
  numerical data, 150
Actinide elements, *see also* Inner transition elements
  absorption spectra, 901
  electronic configurations, 104, 106
  magnetic properties, 898
  oxidation states, 896–897
  periodic relationships, 910
  properties, physical and chemical, 892–895
Actinium, *see* Actinide elements
Actinium ($4n + 3$) decay series, 62, 65, 918
Actinon, 374
Activity, definition, 285
Activity coefficient, 285
Albite, structure, 728

Alkali metal compounds, 831–843
amides, 577
azides, 837
borohydrides, 782–786
carbides, 697
complexes, 838–839
cyanides, 718
halides, 831–832
hydrides, 406–408
hydroxides, 835
nitrides, 837
oxides, 835
peroxides, 508–511
selenides, 837
silicates, 722
sulfides, 837
superoxides, 508–510
tellurides, 837
ternary salts, 837
Alkali metals, 818–844
abundances, 818
chemical characteristics, 822, 823
family relationships, 818–822
oxidation potentials, 296
physical constants, 819
preparation and production, 822, 824
vapors, complexity, 821–822
Alkaline earth metal compounds, 856–864
borides, 770–773
carbides, 697–698
hydrides, 406–408
peroxides, 508–511
superoxides, 508–509
Alkaline earth metals, 845–867
abundances, 845
chemical characteristics, 848–850
family relationships, 845–848
physical constants, 846
preparation and production, 851
vapors, complexity, 848
Alloys, natures of, 220–223
Alpha particle, characteristics, 10
emission, 57
scattering, 11–12
Alumina, *see also* Aluminum, oxide
technical recovery, 740–741
Aluminates, 756–757
fluo-, *see* Fluoaluminates
Alumino silicates, structures, 727–729
Aluminum, chemical characteristics, 739–740
oxidation states, 736–737
physical constants, 735
preparation and production, 740–741
Aluminum compounds, alkoxides, structures, 743
alkyls, structures, 742–744
antimonide, 757
arsenide, 757
carbides, 697, 698, 759
complexes, 765–768
halides, tri-, physical constants, 745
properties, 750–751
structures, 742–743
bond distances, 750
dimerization, 750
hydride, 742, 775, 778
hydroxides, 756
lakes, 768
nitride, 578, 758
oxide, 754–756
forms, 754
gem quality, 754–755
hydrates, 755–756
oxyhalides, 751
phosphide, 757
selenide, 757
sulfide, 757
Aluminum coordination number, 760
Alums, 539–541
crystalline forms, 539, 541
examples, 540
formation, 539
non-sulfate, 539
structure, 499
Americium, *see* Actinide elements
Amide group, 570
Amides, metal, 576–577
Amine sulfonic acids (salts), 550–552
disulfonic acid, 552
monosulfonic acid, *see* Sulfamic acid
trisulfonic acid, 552
Ammonia, 575–582; *see also* Hydronitrogens, Metallic state, Nitrogen system, Solvents (non-aqueous)
catalytic oxidation, 594
liquid, 349–352
physical constants, 341
preparation, 575
structure, 201, 575
hydrogen bond, 188–191
Ammonium compounds, 576
Ammonium halides, thermal stabilities, 622
Ammono compounds, 571
Amphibole, structure, 726
Analcite, structure, 728
Antibase, 328
Anti-isomorphous materials, 578
Antimonates, 639

Antimonites, 639
Antimony, *see also* Nitrogen family
  chemical characteristics, 568
  physical constants, 557
  preparation, 568
Antimony compounds, halides, 626–628
  oxides, 635–636
  oxy acids (salts), 639
  sulfides, 656
Antimony modifications, 566–567
  gas, 566
  liquid, 566
  solid, 566–567
Anti-neutrino, 9, 10
Aquamarine, 725
Aquation, 235
Aquo-ammono compounds, 571
Aquo cations, 498
  acid strengths, 321
Aquo compounds, 571
Argon, chemical characteristics, -boron trifluoride system, 379–380
    hydrate, 381
    -quinol clathrate, 382
  discovery, 374
  physical constants, 375
Arsenates, 639
Arsenic, *see also* Nitrogen family
  chemical characteristics, 568
  physical constants, 557
  preparation, 568
Arsenic compounds, halides, 626–628
  oxides, 635
  oxy acids (salts), 639
  sulfides, 656
Arsenic modifications, 566–567
  gas, 566
  liquid, 566
  solid, 566–567
Arsenites, 639
Asbestos minerals, structure, 726
Ascharite, structure, 810
Astatine, 417–418
Asterism, 755
Atmophilic elements, 29
Atmosphere, composition, 383
Atomic crystals, 213
Atomic number, 14
Atomic structure, Bury's views, 87
  Langmuir's views, 86, 87
  valence models, 86
Atomic theory, modern, 10–15
Atomic volumes, 129–132
  applications, 132
  curve, 130–131
Atomic volumes, relationship to periodic classification, 113
Atomic weights, chemical, 33
    evaluation, 33–35
  constancy in nature, 35
  from gas densities, 35
  physical, 33
    evaluation, 33
  relationship between scales, 34
Atoms, complexity, 5
  components, 6–10
  jelly-like (Thomson), 11
  nuclear (Rutherford), 11
Aurates, 842
Azides, 585–588
Azidocarbondisulfide, 469–470
Azidodithiocarbonate, *see* Halogenoids
Azino silver chloride, 474

Barium, *see also* Alkaline earth metals
  chemical characteristics, 849, 850
  physical constants, 846
  preparation, 851
Barium compounds, azide, 860
  complexes, 861
  halides, 856, 857
  nitride, 860
  oxide, 858
  peroxide, 859
  salts, 861
  selenide, 859
  sulfide, 859
  telluride, 859
Basic salts, 498, 503
  classification, 503
Basicity, oxides and hydroxides, 502–503
Bauxite, 754
Bayer process, 740
Bayerite, 755, 756
Benitoite, 725
Berkelium, *see* Actinide elements
Berlin green, 720, 721
Berlinate ion, 721
Beryl, structure, 725
Beryllium, *see also* Alkaline earth metals
  chemical characteristics, 848–850
  physical characteristics, 846–847
  preparation, 851
Beryllium compounds, azide, 860
  beryllates, fluo- , *see* Fluoberyllates
  borohydride, 782, 783, 784, 785
  carbide, 697, 861
  complexes, 862–864
    "basic" compounds, 863
    beryllated species, 863

Beryllium compounds, complexes, halo, 862
halides, 856
nitride, 860
oxide, 858
salts, 861
selenide, 859
sulfide, 859
Beta emission, 54, 55, 57
Bidentate groups, 237
Binding energies, nuclear, 59–61
numerical values, 911–916
Bismuth, *see also* Nitrogen family
chemical characteristics, 568
physical constants, 557
preparation, 568
Bismuth compounds, halides, 626, 627
oxides, 636
oxy acids (salts), 639
sulfide, 656
Bismuth modifications, 566–567
gas, 566
liquid, 566
solid, 566–567
Bödecker reaction, 604
Böhmite, 755, 756
Bohr magneton, 168
Bohr theory, 81–84
Bonds, chemical, *see also* Covalent bond, Ionic bond, Metallic bond
classification, 175, 225–226
definition, 171
Boracite, structure, 811
Boranes, 774; *see also* Boron hydrides
Borates, fluo- +, *see* Fluoboric acids
hypo- +, 812, 816
oxy,- 808–811
meta, structures, 810–811
ortho, structure, 809
penta, structure, 811
pyro, structure, 810
structures, 809–811
tetra, structure, 810
types, 809
peroxy, *see* Peroxyborates
peroxyhydrated, 515
sub- , 813, 816
Borax, structure, 810
Borazanes, 798
Borazenes, 798
Borazole, 800–807
comparison with benzene, 801, 802
physical constants, 801
preparation, 806–807
properties, 803–806
structure, 800, 802
Borazole analogs, 807
Borazole derivatives, halo, 803–804
methyl, 801, 802, 803–807
Borazynes, 798
Borides, metal, 769–773
classification, 769–770
compositions, 770
preparation, 773
properties, 772–773
structures, 770–772
Borines, amino, 799–800
borine carbonyl, 780–781
triborinetriamine, *see* Borazole
Born-Haber cycle, 184–186
applications, 185–186
to alkali metal compounds, 831
to coinage metal compounds, 820–821
to electron affinity evaluation, 162
to oxidation potential data, 294–297
to oxides, 500
to platinum metal nobility, 888
to solubility, 342–343
Borohydrates, 813–816
isomeric forms, 814–816
relationships among, 815
structures, 815–816
Borohydrides (metal), 782–786
examples, 782
preparation, 785–786
properties, 782–784
structures, 784–785
Boron, chemical characteristics, 739–740
oxidation states, 736–737
physical constants, 735
preparation, 738, 740
Boron compounds, acetate, 817
arsenate, ortho- , 816–817
carbide, 698–699, 759
cationic compounds, 816–817
complexes, 760–765
fluo, *see* Fluoboric acids
oxy, 763–765
halides, sub- , 749
tri- , 744–749
acceptor properties, 747, 748
chemical characteristics, 746–747
physical properties, 744, 745
preparation, 747–749
structure, 745–746
trifluoride 2-hydrate, 762
hydrides, 773–795
chemical characteristics, 775–776
derivatives, 786–795
physical constants, 774

Boron compounds, hydrides, preparation, 776–778
structures, 786–795
hydrides (specific compounds), diborane, alkyl derivatives, 778–779
ammonia "addition" compounds, 779–780
borane salts, 781
borine coordination compounds, 780–781
borohydrides, *see* Borohydrides, metal
chemical characteristics, 775–776
physical constants, 774
preparation, 776–777
structure, 778–793
pentaborane (stable), structure, 795
nitride, 578, 757–758
nitrogen compounds, 795–807
aliphatic analogs, 797–800
aromatic analogs, 800–807; *see also* Borazole
compound B_2H_7N, 795–797
silyl derivatives, 796, 798, 799
oxides, 752–753
boric oxide, forms, 752–753
hydrates, 808
structure, 811
miscellaneous oxides, 753
oxy acids (salts), 808–816; *see also* Borates
boric acids (salts), 808–811
poly, 808, 811
preparation, 811
properties, 811
structure, 808–809
types, 808–810
lower acids (salts), 812–816
oxyhalides, 751
phosphate, ortho- , 816–817
selenide, 754
sulfates, 817
sulfide, 753–754
Boron coordination number, 759
Boron family, 734–817
abundances, 734
chemical characteristics, 739–740
family relationships, 735–737
modifications, free elements, 738–739
oxidation states, 736–737
physical constants, 735
preparation and production, 740–741
Boron family compounds, 741–769
carbides, 759
Born family compounds, catenation, 742
complexes, 759–768
electron-deficient, 742–744
halides, 744–751
oxygen family derivatives, 752–757
nitrides, 757–758
salts, 759
Boron modifications, 738–739
amorphous, 738
crystalline, 738–739
Boronatrocalcite, structure, 811
Boronium compounds, 765
Borosilicates, 811
Boryl compounds, 816–817
Boule, 755
Bragg's substitutional procedure, 136
Brillouin zones, 219
relationships to Hume-Rothery ratios, 222–223
Bromamines, 591
Bromates, 441
Bromazide, 473
Bromides, 426; *see also* Halides
Bromine, *see also* Halogens
abundance, 417
chemical characteristics, 420–421
physical constants, 419
preparation and production, 424–425
Bromine compounds, *see also* Halogen compounds
cationic, 462, 463
chloride, mono- , 447, 448–449
fluorides, mono- , 447, 448
penta- , 447, 452, 453
tri- , 447, 450–451, 453; *see also* Solvents (non-aqueous)
oxides, 434–435
oxy acids, *see* Halogen compounds, Oxy acids
Bromine isotopes, concentration, 46
Brucite, structure, 724

Cadmium, chemical characteristics, 849–851
oxidation potentials, 850
oxidation states, 852
physical constants, 847
preparation and production, 852
Cadmium compounds, complexes, 864–867
halides, 856, 857–858
oxide, 859
salts, 861
selenide, 859
sulfide, 859

Cadmium compounds, telluride, 859
Calcium, *see also* Alkaline earth metals
  chemical characteristics, 849, 850
  physical constants, 846
  preparation, 851
Calcium compounds, azide, 860
  carbide structure, 698
  complexes, 864
  halides, 856, 857
  hydride, 406, 407, 408, 412
  nitride, 860
  oxide, 858
  salts, 861
  selenide, 859
  sulfide, 859
  telluride, 859
Calcium ion, sequestration, 650, 653
Californium, *see* Actinide elements
Calutron, 40
Canal rays, 8
Carbides (metal), 696–700
  covalent, 698–699
  interstitial, 699–700
  ionic, 697–698
    acetylides, 697–698
    allylides, 698
    methanides, 697
Carbon, bond energies, 672
  chemical characteristics, 670
  physical constants, 662
  preparation, 670–671
Carbon blacks, 668, 671
Carbon compounds, *see also* Carbon family compounds
  halides, monofluoride, 667–668
    tetrahalides, 678–679
  oxides, dioxide, 668–690
      physical constants, 214
      preparation, 690
      properties, 688–689
      structure, 195, 689
    monoxide, 685–687; *see also* Carbonyls (metal)
      chemical characteristics, 686–687
      physical constants, 214
      preparation, 687
      structure, 686
    pentacarbon dioxide, 694
    suboxide, 694
  oxy acids (salts), nitrogen derivatives, 572
    peroxy, 508, 513–514
  sulfides, 695
  thiocarbonates, 695
Carbon family compounds, 671–696
  catenation, 671–673
Carbon family compounds, halides, 678–685
  hydrides, 673–678
  nitrogen compounds, 696
  oxygen compounds, 685–695
  sulfur compounds, 695–696
Carbon family elements, 661–733
  abundances, 661
  chemical characteristics, 670
  family relationships, 662–664
  modifications, 664–670
  oxidation potentials, 664
  oxidation states, 663–664
  physical constants, 662
  preparation and production, 670–671
Carbon isotopes, concentration, by exchange reactions, 50, 51
  by thermal diffusion, 45
Carbon modifications, 664–669; *see also* Diamond, Graphite
  "amorphous," 668, 670
  microcrystalline, 668
Carbonyl compounds, amide, *see* Urea
  cyanide, 689, 690
  halides, 689–690; *see also* Solvents (non-aqueous)
  selenide, 689
  sulfide, 689–690
Carbonyl halides (metal), 714–716
  examples, 714
  preparation, 714
  properties, 714–716
Carbonyl hydrides (metal), 711–714
  bond distances, 703
  examples, 711
  preparation, 713–714
  properties, 712–713, 714
  structures, 705–706
Carbonyls (metal), 599, 700–717
  bond distances, 703
  chemical characteristics, 708
  derivatives, amine-substituted, 716
    cyano derivatives, 717
    examples, 706, 707
    polynuclear, 703–705
    preparation, 708–711
    selenium derivatives, 717
    structures, 701–706
    sulfur derivatives, 717
Carborundum, 698
Castner-Kellner cell, 424
Catenation, 569
Cathode rays, 6–7
Celsian, structure, 728
Ceria, 891

Cerium, *see* Lanthanide elements
Cesium, *see also* Alkali metals
  chemical characteristics, 822, 823
  physical constants, 819
Chalcophilic elements, 29
Charcoal, 668, 671
Charge to mass ratios, 7, 8
Chelate structures, 237–242
  examples, 238–240
  importance, 240–242
Chiolite, structure, 766
Chloramines, 590–591
Chlorates, 441; *see also* Chlorine, Oxy acids
Chlorazide, 473
Chlorides, *see also* Halides
  in preparation of chlorine, 423–424
  properties, 182, 426
Chlorine, *see also* Halogens
  abundance, 417
  chemical characteristics, 420–421
  oxidation states, 418–419
  physical constants, 419
  preparation and production, 423–424
Chlorine compounds, cationic, 462
  halides, monofluoride, 447, 448
    trifluoride, 447, 450–451
  oxides, 431–434
    dioxide, 432–433, 440–441
    heptoxide, 434
    hexoxide, 433–434
    monoxide, 431–432
    physical constants, 431
    tetroxide, 434
  oxy acids, 437–438; *see also* Halogens, Oxy acids, Chlorates, Chlorites, Hypochlorous acid (salts), Perchloric acid (salts)
    oxidation potential data, 438
    properties, 438
Chlorine isotopes, concentration, 42, 45, 46, 48, 52
Chlorites, 440–441; *see also* Halogens, Oxy acids
Chromium, *see* Transition elements (periodic group VIa)
Chromium compounds, carbide, 699
  carbonyl (hexa-), 703, 707, 708, 709
  carbonyl amines, 716
  peroxy acids (salts), 508, 514
Chromium family borides, 770, 772
Chrondrodite, structure, 724
Chrysoberyl, 757
Chrysotile, structure, 726
Clathrate compounds, 223–224
  of inert gas elements, 382–383
Clay minerals, structure, 728
Cobalt, *see also* Transition elements (periodic group VIII)
  oxidation potential data, 302
Cobalt compounds, carbide, 699
  carbonyl hydride, 711–714
  carbonyls, 707
  complexes, tripositive cobalt, *see also* Chapter 7
    chloroammines, 228–229
    isomerism, 247–269
    nomenclature, 244
    stabilization, 301–302
Coinage metal compounds, azides, 837
  carbides, 697
  complexes, 839–843
  halides, 832–835
  nitrides, 837
  oxidation states, characteristics, of +1, 826–828
    of +2, 828–830
    of +3, 830–831
  oxygen family compounds, 835–837
  phosphides, 837
  salts, 837–838
Coinage metals, 818–844
  abundances, 818
  chemical characteristics, 822, 823
  family relationships, 818–822
  oxidation potential data, 825
  oxidation states, 821, 825–831
  physical constants, 819
  preparation and production, 824
Coke, 671
Colemanite, structure, 811
Color, relationship to covalence, 211
Complex compounds, *see* Coordination compounds
Complex ions, detection in solution, 277–278
  factors affecting formation, 234–242
Complexes, normal, 227
  penetration, 227
Coordinate covalent bond, 193, 232
  nature, 232–233
  orbital hybridization, 233
Coordination, in diborane structure, 791
Coordination compounds, 227–279
  applications, 278
  electronic interpretations, 232–234
  factors affecting formation, 234–242
  isomerism, 247–270; *see also* Isomerism, coordination compounds
  nomenclature, 242–246
  systematic approach to, 228–232
  Werner's theory, 229–230

Coordination number, chemical, 143, 230
crystallographic, 143
Coordination sphere, 231
Copper, *see also* Coinage metals
chemical characteristics, 822, 823
oxidation potential data, 303, 825
oxidation states, 821, 825–830
physical constants, 819
preparation and production, 824
Copper compounds, carbonyl compounds, 706, 708, 716, 840
complexes, 833, 839, 841–842
halides, copper(I), 832–833
copper(II), 833
hydride, 414–415
oxidation states, characteristics, of +1, 826, 827, 828
of +2, 828
of +3, 830
oxides, 835, 836
selenides, 837
sulfate, structure of 5-hydrate, 498–499
sulfides, 837
tellurides, 837
Copper isotopes, concentration, 48
Copper(II) stereochemistry, 257
Corundum, 754
Covalence, definition, 175
maximum values, 200
Covalent bond, 192–215
atomic orbitals, 200–201
directional characteristics, 200–205
electron pair, 193–194
electronic formulation, 192–193
Helferich's rules, 204–205
from hybrid orbitals, 202–203
nature of, 195–200
oxidation numbers in, 211–212
partial ionic character, 205–208
relationship to electronegativity, 206–208
summary, 208
values, 206–207
polarization, 208–210; *see also* Fajans's rules
from pure orbitals, 201–202
strength, 203–204
theoretical approaches, 196–200
Heitler-London theory, 196–197
Hund-Mulliken theory, 197–198
Pauling-Slater theory, 199–200
unpaired electrons, 196
Cristobalite, 691, 692
Cross section, nuclear, 67
Cryolite, structure, 766
Cryolithionite, structure, 766
Crystal structures, 178–180
Crystal systems, 179, 180
Curie law, 168
Curie-Weiss law, 168
Curium, *see* Actinide elements
Cyanamide process, 575
Cyanides (metal), 717–721
complex, 718–721
covalent, 718
heavy metal, 720–721
ionic, 718
Cyanogen, 466–467; *see also* Halogenoids
Cyanogen halides, 471–473
Cyanuric compounds, 472

Dalton's atomic theory, 5, 110
Deacon process, 424
Defect lattices, 225
Degenerate gas, 377
Deuterides, 393; *see also* Hydrides
Deuterium, 387–394; *see also* Hydrogen isotopes
chemical characteristics, 390–391
discovery, 387
exchange reactions involving, 390–391, 392
ortho-para equilibrium, 396–397
ortho-para forms, 391
ortho, physical constants, 397–398
physical characteristics, 389, 390
separation, by diffusion, 43
by electrolysis, 387–389
Deuterium compounds, *see also* Hydrogen compounds
oxide, 391–394
peroxide, 507
Deuteron, characteristics, 10
Diamagnetic behavior, 165–166; *see also* Magnetic behavior
definition, 165
examples, 166
source, 165–166
Diamond, 664–666, 668–689
properties, 665–666
relationship to graphite, 668–669
structure, 133, 665
synthetic, 669
Diaspore, 754, 755, 756
Diastereoisomers, 266
Dielectric constant, definition, 339
relationship to solubility, 343
relationship to solute behavior, 339, 340

Dihydroboranes, 774–775; *see also* Boron hydrides
Diopside, structure, 736
Dipole attractions, 187
Dipole moment, origin, 186
relationship to bond character, 206
relationship to electronegativity, 186
Dipoles, definition, 186
in inert gas atoms, 376
in inert gas compounds, 381
relationship to paramagnetism, 166
Döbereiner's triads, 110
Dulong and Petit law, 34
Dysprosium, *see* Lanthanide elements

Earth, age of, 63
Effective atomic number concept, 233–234
applied to carbonyls, 706
applied to nitrosyls, 599–600
Einstein equation, 59
Electrodeposition, non-aqueous solvents, 367–368
Electrodotic character, 332
Electron(s), anti-bonding, 198
bonding, 198
characteristics of, 6–7, 10
designations in atoms, 90
designations in molecules, 198
momentum, angular, 81, 82
non-bonding, 198
solvated, 348
wave properties, 7
Electron affinity, 161–162
definition, 161
numerical magnitude, 162
Electron-deficient compounds, 213–214; *see also* Aluminum, Boron, Gallium compounds
Electron orbits, Bohr (circular), 81
Sommerfeld (elliptical), 84–85
Electronegativity, 162–164
applications, 164
evaluation, 162–163
numerical magnitude, 163
periodic variations, 164
relationship to acid-base strength, 319–321
relationship to hydride type, 405–406
relationship to ionic character, 206–208
relationship to oxidation number, 281
trends, 163–164
Electronic configurations, atoms, 92–102
occupancy of quantum levels, 91–92
quantum designations, 88–108
Electronic configurations (ionic), 176–177
Electronic configurations (non-ionic), 177
Electrophilic character, 332
Electrostatic attractions, miscellaneous, 186–187
Electrostatic bonds, 178–192
Electrovalence, 175
Electrovalent bond, *see* Ionic bond
Elements, types of, 102–106
Emerald, 725
Energy, radiant, 80, 82
Energy equivalent of mass, 59
Energy levels, electronic, 81, 88
diagrammatic representation, 94, 95
in hydrogen atom, 153
molecular, 197–198
nuclear, 55–56
Enstatite, structure, 726
Entropy, 295
Equivalent groups, 340, 570
Erbium, *see* Lanthanide elements
Europium, *see* Lanthanide elements
Exchange reactions, isotope separations, 49–52
equilibrium constants, 49–50
Exclusion principle (Pauli), 91

Fajans's rules, 209–210
Felspars, structure, 728
Ferromagnetic behavior, 165
Ferrous metal borides, 770, 772
Ferrous metals, *see* Transition elements (periodic group VIII)
Fluoaluminates, 776
Fluoberyllate, tetra-, 862
Fluoboric acids (salts), 760–763
dihydroxy, 762–763
monohydroxy, 762
tetra, 760–761
Fluophosphoric acids (salts), 634–635
di-, 635
hexa-, 635
mono-, 634–635
Fluosilicic acid (salts), 680
Fluosulfonic acid (salts), 524–525
Fluoramines, 590
Fluorides, 426; *see also* Halides
acid, 189, 422–423, 428
Fluorination of covalent halides, 428, 524
Fluorine, *see also* Halogens
chemical characteristics, 420, 421
physical constants, 419
preparation and production, 422–423

Fluorine compounds, *see also* Halogen compounds
nitrate, 463
oxy acids, 437
perchlorate, 463
Formulas, electronic, 175
Francium, 818; *see also* Alkali metals
Free energy, 284
Free energy change, 298, 299
Fremy's salt, 213, 555
Frenkel defects, 225

Gadolinium, *see* Lanthanide elements
Gallium, chemical characteristics, 739–740
oxidation potential data, 736
oxidation states, 736–737
physical constants, 735
preparation, 741
Gallium compounds, antimonide, 757
arsenide, 757
complexes, 765–769
halides, physical constants, 745
preparation, 751
properties, 750, 751
structures, 750
hydride, 742, 775, 778
nitride, 758
oxide, 757
phosphide, 757
selenide, 757
sulfide, 757
Gamma radiation, 57
Geochemistry, 29
Germanates, 693–694
Germanes, *see* Germanium compounds, hydrides
Germanium, chemical characteristics, 670
physical constants, 662
preparation, 671
Germanium compounds, *see also* Carbon family compounds
halides, 679, 681
hydrides, 673, 676–677
nitride, 696
oxides, 688, 693, 694
peroxy acid (salts), 508, 514
sulfides, 695–696
thiogermanates, 696
Germanium modifications, 669
Giant molecules, 213, 578
Gibbsite, 754, 755, 756
Gmelin reaction, 603

Gold, *see also* Coinage metals
chemical characteristics, 822, 823
oxidation potential data, 825
oxidation states, 821, 825–831
physical constants, 819
preparation, 824
Gold compounds, *see also* Coinage metal compounds
carbonyl compounds, 716, 840
complexes, 718, 830, 842, 843
halides, 832, 833, 834
oxidation states characteristics, of +1, 827
of +2, 829–830
of +3, 831
oxides, 836
sulfides, 829, 837
tellurides, 837
Graham's salt, 650, 652
Graphite, 665, 666–669
properties, 666–668
reactions, layer separation, 666–668
with acids, 667
with halogens, 667–668
with iron(III) chloride, 668
with oxidizing agents, 666–667
with potassium, 666
relationship to diamond, 668–669
structure, 665, 666
in covalent nitrides, 578
Graphitic acid, 667
Graphitic oxide, 667
Graphitic salts, 667
Grignard reagent, 861
Grimm's hydride displacement law, 415–416

Haber process, 575
Hafnium, *see* Transition elements (periodic group IVa)
Hafnium carbide, 699, 700
Halamines, 590–591
Halazides, 473–474
Half-bond, in diborane structure, 791
Half-life period, 58
Halides, 425–429
complex, 428–429
covalent (acid), 426–428
ionic (salt-like), 425–426
Hall process, 740
Halogen compounds, 425–480
bond types, 418–419
interhalogens (interhalogen compounds), 444–453
oxy acids (salts), 437–444
halic acids (halates), 441

Halogen compounds, oxy acids (salts),
halous acids (halites), 440–441
hypohalous acids (hypohalites), 439–440
perhalic acids (perhalates), 441–444
oxygen compounds, 429–437
polyhalides, 453–460
Halogenoids, 463–480
comparisons with halogens, 464–465
definitions, 464
free halogenoids, 464, 466–470
ions, 464, 465
non-metal derivatives, 475–480
oxidizing-reducing powers, 465
Halogens, 417–463
abundances, 417
in aqueous solutions, 421
chemical characteristics, 420–421
colors, 419–420
electropositive characteristics, 460–463
family relationships, 418–420
oxidation potential data, 296, 421
oxidation states, 418–419
physical constants, 419
preparation, 422–425
trends, 418–420
Hambergite, structure, 809–810
Harkins's rules, 26–28
Heat of formation, 184–186
Heitler-London theory, 196–197
Helferich's rules, 204–205
Helides, 378–379
Helium, *see also* Inert gas elements
discovery, 374
liquid forms, 376–377; *see also* Helium I and Helium II
phase relationships, 377
property changes, 376
transition, 376, 377
occurrence in nature, 374, 383
physical constants, 375
preparation and production, 384
Helium I, 376, 377
Helium II, 376–377
limitation to 4-isotope, 377
physical characteristics, 376–377
structure, 377
theory, 377
Helium isotopes, concentration by superfluid flow, 49
Helium molecule-ion, 378
Hemimorphite, structure, 725
Héroult process, 740
Heteropoly acids (salts), 274–276
compositions, 274
definition, 273
theories, Miolati-Rosenheim, 274–275
structural, 275–276
types, 274
x-ray studies, 275–276
Heulandite, structure, 728
Holmium, *see* Lanthanide elements
Homoatomic anions, 732–733
Hooker cell, 424
Hume-Rothery ratios, 222–223
relationship to Brillouin zones, 222–223
Hund-Mulliken theory, 197–198
Hydrates, hydrous, 501
Hydrazine, 582–585; *see also* Solvents (non-aqueous)
oxidation, 583–584, 588–589
physical constants, 341
preparation, 584–585
properties, 353, 354, 582–584
structure, 582
Hydrazine hydrate, 585
Hydrazine salts, 583, 585
Hydrazinium compounds, 583
Hydrazoic acid (salts), 585–589; *see also* Azides
preparation, 588–589
properties, 586–587
reduction, 573
structure, 585–586
Hydride ion, oxidation, 408
Hydrides, 403–416; *see also* specific hydrides
association, 189
classification, 404–406
covalent (molecular), 404–405, 409–411
examples, 409
preparation, 409–410
properties, 404–405, 410–411
structures, 410
densities, 407
Grimm's displacement law, 415–416
heats of formation, 407
metallic (interstitial), 404, 405, 411–415
compositions, 411, 412, 413
stabilities, thermal, 413
structures, 411
physical properties, 190, 191
saline (salt-like), 404, 406–409
applications, 408
ionic characteristics, 406–407
preparation, 406

Hydrides, saline (salt-like), properties, 404, 407–408
  structures, 406
Hydrogen, 386–416
  absorption by metals (occlusion), 411
  applications, 403
  chemical characteristics, 401, 402
  general chemistry, 400–403
  periodic classification, 386
  physical constants, 390, 401
  preparation, 401–403
  varieties, 386–400
Hydrogen (anionic), 400
Hydrogen (atomic), 398–400
  chemical characteristics, 399–400
  formation, 398–399
  stability, 399
Hydrogen (cationic), 400
Hydrogen (combined), 400
Hydrogen (covalent), 400
Hydrogen (molecular), 395–398
  ortho and para forms, 395–398
  ortho-para equilibrium, 396–397
  ortho-para separation, 396, 398
  para, characteristics, 397–398
Hydrogen (nascent), 400
Hydrogen bond, 187–191
  in diborane, 789
  directional characteristics, 191
  examples, 189–191
  experimental approaches, 191
  limitations, 188
  nature, 189
  origin and recognition, 187–188
  relationship to electronegativity, 188
  relationship to size, 189
  strength, 188
  in water structure, 496
Hydrogen bridge, in diborane, 789–793
  in higher boron hydrides, 793–795
Hydrogen compounds, association, 189
  azide, *see* Hydrazoic acid
  bromide, *see* Hydrogen compounds, halides
  chloride, *see* Hydrogen compounds, halides
  cyanide, physical constants, 341
    structure, 717
  fluoride, *see also* Hydrogen compounds, halides; Solvents (non-aqueous)
    physical constants, 341
    structure, 428
  halides, 427–428
    preparations, 427–428
    properties, 427–428
Hydrogen compounds, iodide *see* Hydrogen compounds, halides
  peroxide, 504–507
    chemical characteristics, 505–506
    derivatives, 507–515
    physical properties, 504
    preparation, 506–507
    structure, 504
  selenide, 494
  sulfide, physical constants, 341
  telluride, 494
Hydrogen ion, characteristics, 403
Hydrogen isotopes, *see also* Deuterium, Tritium
  characteristics, 386–387
  concentration and separation, 43, 47, 49, 50–51, 52, 387–389
Hydrogen molecule-ion, 212
Hydronitrogens, 573–574; *see also* Ammonia, Hydrazine, Hydrazoic acid
  saturated, 573–574
  unsaturated, 573–574
Hydroperoxides, 507
Hydroxides, 498, 500–503
  acid-base characteristics, 501
  hydrous, 501
Hydroxylamine, 580–582; *see also* Solvents (non-aqueous)
  physical constants, 341
  preparation, 581–582
  properties, 352, 580–581
Hydroxylamine sulfonic acids (salts), 554–555, 581–582
  nomenclature, 554
  properties, 554–555
  structures, 554
Hydroxyl bond, 192
Hydroxyl radical, 506
Hypochlorous acid (salts), 439–440
Hyponitrous acid (salts), 613–615
Hypophosphoric acid (salts), 640, 643–644
  preparation, 644
  properties, 643–644
  structure, 643
Hypophosphorous acid (salts), 639, 640, 641–642
  preparation, 641–642
  properties, 639, 641
  structure, 639

Illites, structure, 728
Imide group, 570
Imides (metal), 576, 577
Indium, chemical characteristics, 739–740

Indium, oxidation potential data, 736
  oxidation states, 736–737
  physical constants, 735
  preparation, 741
Indium compounds, antimonide, 757
  arsenide, 757
  borate, ortho- , 809
  complexes, 765–768
  halides, physical constants, 745
    preparation, 751
    properties, 750–751
    structures, 750
  nitride, 758
  oxide, 757
  phosphide, 757
  selenide, 757
  sulfide, 757
  telluride, 757
Inert gas atoms, electronic arrangements, 86, 88, 102
Inert gas configurations, stabilities, 155, 176
Inert gas element compounds, 378–383
  aluminum(III) halide derivatives, 382
  clathrate compounds, 382–383
  coordination compounds, 379–380
  deuterohydrates, 381–382
  under excited conditions, 378–379
  hydrates, 381–382
  induced dipole attractions, 381–382
  interstitial penetration, 379
  phenol derivatives, 382
Inert gas elements, 373–385
  applications, 385
  chemical behaviors, 378–383
  history, 373–374
  occurrence, 383–384
  periodic classification, 374
  physical characteristics, 375–377
  recovery from atmosphere, 384
  structures, 376
Inert pair, 177
Inner complexes, 270–272
Inner transition elements, 891–910; *see also* Actinide elements, Lanthanide elements
  abundances, 892
  electronic arrangements, 103–106
  electronic arrangements, characteristics related to, 895–901
    color and absorption spectra, 898–901
    contraction effects, 146–151, 901
    magnetic properties, 168–170, 897–898
Inner transition elements, electronic arrangements, oxidation states, 895–897
  physical and chemical characteristics, 892–895
  physical constants, 893
Inorganic benzene, 802; *see also* Borazole
Inorganic chemistry, nature and scope, 3–4
Inorganic graphite, 758; *see also* Boron compounds, nitride
Inorganic rubber, 633; *see also* Phosphorus compounds, phosphonitrilic halides
Interhalogen compounds, 444–453
  compositions, 444–445
  formation, 445
  nomenclature, 446
  physical constants, 447
  structures, 445–446
  type XX′, 446–449
  type XX'_3, 449–451
  type XX'_5, 452
  type XX'_7, 452–453
Interhalogen-halogenoids, 471–474
Interhalogenoids, 474–475
Intermediate phases, 221–223
  Hume-Rothery ratios, 222–223
Intermetallic compounds, 221
Interstitial compounds, 221
  borides, 769–773
  carbides, 699–700
  hydrides, 411–415
  nitrides, 579
Iodates, 441
Iodazide, 473
Iodides, 426; *see also* Halides
Iodine, *see also* Halogens
  chemical characteristics, 420–421
  oxidation states, 418–419
  physical constants, 419
  preparation and production, 424–425
  solutions, properties, 420
Iodine compounds, cationic, 435–437, 460–462
    iodine(I) compounds, 461–462
    iodine(III) compounds, 436–437, 460–461
  halides, heptafluoride, 452–453
    iodine-chlorine system, 450
    monobromide, 447, 449
    monochloride, 447, 449, 450
    pentafluoride, 452
    trichloride, 445, 447, 450, 451
  oxides, 435–437

Iodine compounds, oxides, pentoxide, 436
salt-like oxides, 436–437
oxy acids (salts), 441,443–444; *see also* Halogens, oxy acids, Iodates, Periodic acids (salts)
oxidation potential data, 438
Iodyl compounds, 436–437
Ion aggregation, high temperature, 334
solution, 266–267
Ion deformation, *see* Ion polarization
Ion-electron half-reactions, 281–284
conventions, 283–284
formulation, 282–284
relationship to electrode processes, 282
use in oxidation-reduction, 283–284
Ion exchange, in isotope separations, 51
in lanthanide separations, 907–908
Ion polarization, 208–210; *see also* Fajans's rules
factors affecting, 209–210
relationship to bond character, 209
Ionic bond, 178–186
characteristics, 181–182
formation, 178
nature, 178
thermochemical relationships, 184–185
Ionic potential, 210–211
Ionium, identity with thorium, 20
Ionization potential, 152–161
applications, 161
definition, 152–153
factors affecting, 153–154
numerical magnitudes, 156–159
periodic variations, 160
Iridium, *see* Transition elements (periodic group VIII)
Iridium carbonyls, 707, 710
Iron, *see also* Transition elements (periodic group VIII)
oxidation potential data, 302
Iron compounds, carbide, 699, 700
carbonyl amines, 716
carbonyl halides, 714, 715
carbonyl hydride, 711–713
carbonyls, enneacarbonyl, 703–704, 707, 711
pentacarbonyl, 703, 707, 708
tetracarbonyl trimer, 704–705, 707, 710
hexacyanoferrates, 720–721
Isobars, 25, 55; *see also* Mattauch's rule
Isomeric transition, 56, 57
Isomerism, coordination compounds, 247–270
cis-trans, coordination number 4, 254
coordination number 6, 261–264
coordination, 248–249
coordination position, 251–252
geometrical, 253–270; *see also* Stereoisomerism
hydrate, 249
ionization, 250
miscellaneous types, 252
optical, coordination number 4, 255
optical coordination number 6, 264–267
origin, 264
in polynuclear complexes, 266–267
relationship to covalence, 266
resolution of enantiomorphs, 265–266
rotary powers of complexes, 265
Walden inversion, 267
polymerization, 247–248
stereo, 253–270
structural (salt), 250–251
valence, 252
Isomerism (nuclear), 55–57
Isopoly acids (salts), 276–277
anion aggregation, 276–277
definition, 273
structural data, 277
theories, Copaux-Miolati, 276
Jander, 277
Isosteric groups, 214–215, 599
Isotopes, 19–52; *see also* individual elements
abundances, 26–28, 911–916
concentration and separation, 38–52
centrifugal methods, 45–47
chemical methods, 49–52
diffusion methods, 41–45
distillation methods, 47–48
electrolysis methods, 49
electromagnetic methods, 40–41
exchange methods, 49–52
ion migration methods, 48
thermal diffusion methods, 44–45
definition, 20
detection and study, 21–25
enrichment factor, 40
existence of, 19–20
generalizations concerning, 25–29
numerical properties, 911–916
separation factor, 39
Isotopic masses, from nuclear rections, 68–69
numerical values, 911–916

Isotopic weight, 32

Jadeite, structure, 726

Kaolinites, structure, 728
K-electron capture, 54, 55, 57
Kernite, structure, 810
Knorre's salt, 650
Krypton, *see also* Inert gas elements
  chemical characteristics, -boron trifluoride system, 380
    deuterohydrate, 381
    hydrate, 381
    phenol derivative, 382
    -quinol clathrate, 382
  discovery, 374
  physical constants, 375
Kurrol's salt, 650, 651, 652

Lambda(λ)-point, 49, 376, 377
Langevin law, 168
Lanthanide contraction, 146–151, 901
  effects of, 150–151, 901
  numerical data, 147
  origin, 146
Lanthanide elements, *see also* Inner transition elements
  abundances, 28, 31
  chemical characteristics, 894–895
  color and absorption spectra, 898–901
  contraction effects, 150–151, 901
  oxidation states, 895–896, 902–905
    "anomalous," 895
    systematization, 896
  periodic relationships, 909–910
  physical constants, 893
  recovery from monazite, 905–906
  separation procedures, 906–909
    basicity procedures, 907–908
      complex formation, 907–908
      ion exchange, 907–908
      precipitation, 907
    crystallization procedures, 906–907
    extraction procedures, 909
    miscellaneous procedures, 908
    oxidation-reduction procedures, 908–909
Lanthanide elements (electronic configurations), 103–104
Lanthanide elements (isotopic compositions), 28
Lanthanide metal borides, 770, 771, 772
Lanthanide metal carbides, 697–698
Lanthanide metal hydrides, 407
Lanthanide metal ions, magnetic moments, 170
Lanthanons, *see* Lanthanide elements
Lanthanum, *see* Inner transition elements; Lanthanide elements; Transition elements (periodic group IIIa)
Lattice energy, application to solubility, 342
  calculation of, 183
  definition, 181
  factors affecting, 183
  in polyhalide formation, 455
Lead, chemical characteristics, 670
  physical constants, 662
  preparation, 671
Lead compounds, *see also* Carbon family compounds
  halides, 681–682
  hydrides, 673, 678
  oxides, 688, 693, 694
  polyplumbides, 732–733
  sulfide, 695
Lead modifications, 670
Lithium, *see also* Alkali metals
  chemical characteristics, 822, 823
  physical constants, 819
Lithium compounds, *see also* Alkali metal compounds
  aluminum hydride, 777, 786, 787
  borohydride, *see* Borohydrides, metal
  boromethoxide, 784
  fluoride, 831
  gallium hydride, 786
  hydride, 406, 407, 408, 412
  nitride, 578, 837
Lithium isotopes, concentration, 48, 51
Lithophilic elements, 29
Lutetium, *see* Lanthanide elements

Madelung constant, 183
Maddrell's salt, 650, 652
"Magic numbers," 19
Magnesium, *see also* Alkaline earth metals
  chemical characteristics, 849
  physical constants, 846
  preparation and production, 851
Magnesium compounds, *see also* Alkaline earth metal compounds
  azide, 860
  boride, 770, 773
    hydrolysis, 776, 813–815
  carbide, 698
  complexes, 864
  halides, 856–857
  nitride, 860
  oxide, 858

Magnesium compounds, salts, 861
 selenide, 859
 sulfide, 859
 telluride, 859
Magnetic behavior, relationship to unpaired electrons, 166
 types of, 165
Magnetic fields, effects on materials, 165
Magnetic moment, calculation, 168
 definition, 165
 orbital contribution, 167
 relationship to electron motion, 165
 relationship to unpaired electrons, 168–169
 spin contribution, 167
Magnetic permeability, calculation, 167
 definition, 167
Magnetic properties, 165–170
 relationship to stereochemistry, 256–257
Magnetic susceptibility, calculation, 167
 definition, 167
 temperature, 168
Manganese, *see* Transition elements (periodic group VIIa)
Manganese compounds, boride, 770, 772, 773
 carbide, 699
 carbonyl, 706, 707
Manhattan District (Project), 74
Mass defect, 36–38
 definition, 36
 numerical values, 911–916
Mass number, 17
Mass spectra, isotopic abundances from, 22–24
 photographic record, 23–24
 positive ion current record, 22–23
 typical, 24
Mass spectrograph, Aston type, 23–24
 characteristics, 25
Mass spectrometer, characteristics, 25
 Dempster type, 22
Mattauch's rule, 55, 62
Maximum multiplicity, principle of, 93
 relationship to paramagnetic behavior, 166
Mecke-Childs factor, 33
Mellitic acid, 667
Mendeléeff's periodic system, 112–117
 postulations, 113, 115
 predictions, 117
Mercurous ion, 853–855
Mercury, 845
 chemical characteristics, 849–851
 oxidation potential data, 850
 oxidation states, 853–855
 physical constants, 847
 preparation and production, 852, 858
Mercury cells, in chlorine production, 424
Mercury compounds, complexes, 864–867
 cyanide, 861
 halides, 856, 858
 nitrogen compounds, 860–861
 oxidation states, characteristics of, 853–855
  equilibrium between, 853
 oxides, 859
 salts, 861
 selenide, 859
 sulfide, 859
 telluride, 859
Mercury isotopes, concentration, 47–48
Mesons, discovery, 9
 role in nuclear forces, 18, 52
 synthesis, 9
 types, 9, 10
Metallic bond, characteristics, 217
 electronic concept, 217–220
 relationship to other bonds, 220
 species possessing, 220
Metallic state, 216–223
 physical characteristics, 216–217
Metals, *see also* Alloys, Metallic state, individual elements
 basicities of, 331
 liquid ammonia solutions, 217–218
Methanol, physical constants, 341
Methylamine, physical constants, 341
Meyer's periodic system, 112–113, 114
Mica, structure, 727, 728
Millon's base, 860
Mohs's hardness scale, 579
Molecular compounds, 227
Molecular orbitals, 197–198
 in diborane structure, 791
Molecular volumes, 129–132
Molybdenum, *see* Transition elements (periodic group VIa)
Molybdenum compounds, blues, 881
 carbides, 699, 700
 carbonyl (hexa-), 703, 707, 708, 709
 peroxy acids (salts), 508, 514
Monazite, treatment for lanthanide elements, 905–906
Monox, 687

Montmorillonite, structure, 728
Muscovite, structure, 728

Natrolite, structure, 729
Negatron, *see* Electron
Nelson cell, 424
Neodymium, *see* Inner transition elements, Lanthanide elements
Neon, *see also* Inert gas elements
  discovery, 374
  physical constants, 375
Neon isotopes, concentration, 42, 43, 47
Neptunium, *see* Actinide elements
Neptunium ($4n + 1$) decay series, 62, 64, 917
Nessler's reagent, 861, 865
Neutrino, 9, 10
Neutron, *see also* Nuclear fission
  characteristics, 8, 10
  discovery, 8
  nuclear forces involving, 52
  role in nucleus, 17, 18
  thermal, 72, 73
Neutron capture, 72
Neutron emission, 54
Neutron moderators, 72
Neutron-proton ratios, 52, 54
Newlands's law of octaves, 112
Nickel, *see* Transition elements (periodic group VIII)
Nickel compounds, carbide, 699
  carbonyl (tetra-), 601, 700, 702, 703, 707, 708, 709–710
  carbonyl amines, 716
  stereochemistry, 256–257
Niobium, *see* Transition element (speriodic group Va)
Niobium compounds, carbide, 699, 700
  peroxy acids (salts), 508, 514
Nitracidium cations, 609, 610
Nitrates, 613, 617–620
Nitration reactions, 610
Nitric acid (salts), 613, 617–620; *see also* Solvents (non-aqueous)
  oxidation potential data,620
  preparation, 594, 619
  properties, 618–619
  reduction, 573
  structure, 617–618
Nitride group, 570
Nitrides (metal), 577–580
  covalent, 578–579
  interstitial (metallic), 579
  ionic, 578
Nitrogen, 556
  chemical characteristics, 568
Nitrogen, physical constants, 214, 557
  preparation and production, 568
Nitrogen compounds, *see also* specific compounds, e.g., ammonia
  halides, 589–591
    bromide ammoniate, 591
    chloride, 589–590
    flourides, 589–590, 591
    iodide ammoniate, 591
  hydrides, *see* Hydronitrogens
  oxides, 591–613
    dinitrogen hexoxide, 612–613
    dinitrogen pentoxide, 592, 608–609; *see also* Nitronium compounds
    dinitrogen tetroxide, 592, 605–608; *see also* Solvents (non-aqueous)
    dioxide, 592, 605–608
    examples, 591
    nitric oxide, 592, 593–605; *see also* Nitrosyl compounds
    nitrous oxide, 214, 592–593
    physical constants, 592
    sesquioxide, 592, 605
    trioxide, 612, 613
  oxy acids (salts), 613–620
    examples, 613
    hyponitrous (salts), 613–615
    nitric (salts), 573, 594, 613, 617–620
    nitrous (salts), 613, 615–617
    peroxy (salts), 508, 612–613
  selenide (tetra), 550
  sulfides, 547–550
    disulfide, 550
    pentasulfide, 550
    tetrasulfide, 547–550
Nitrogen family, 556–660
  abundances, 556
  catenation, 569–570
  chemical characteristics, 568
  electronic arrangements, 558
  family relationships, 557–559
  modifications, 559–567
  oxidation states, 558–559
  physical constants, 557
  preparation, 568
Nitrogen isotopes, concentration, 50, 51
Nitrogen modifications, 559–561
  active, 560–561
  molecular, 559–560
Nitrogen system of compounds, 570–573
Nitronium compounds, 609–612
  examples, 610–611
  preparation, 611, 612
  properties, 609–612

Nitronium ion, 596, 608, 609–611, 618
  in dinitrogen pentoxide, 608–609
  evidences for, 609–611
  Raman frequencies for, 608, 609, 610
  structure, 611
Nitroprussides, 603
Nitrosyl anion, 595, 598, 599, 604
Nitrosyl cation, 595–598, 599–600
  evidences for, 595–596
  solvation, 596
Nitrosyl compounds, 595–605
  anionic, 598
  carbonyls, 598, 599, 600–601, 703, 705
    physical constants, 601
    preparation, 601
    structure, 600, 601, 703, 705
  cationic, 595–598
    examples, 595
    preparation, 597–598
    properties, 597–598
  coordination, 598–605
    classification, 600–605
      type $M^{I}(NO)_xA_y$, 601–602
      type $M^{II}(NO)_xA_y$, 603
      type $M^{III}(NO)_xA_y$, 603
      type $[MA_5(NO)]^{\pm n}$, 603–604
    miscellaneous, 604–605
    structures, 598–600
  halides, 595, 596–597
    physical constants, 597
    structures, 597
  salts, 595, 598
  thio, 602, 603
Nitrosyl displacement series, 602
Nitrosyl group, 598–600
Nitrosylium ion, *see* Nitrosyl cation
Nitrosyls, metal, 601
    halides, 601–602
    hydroxides, 601
    thio compounds, 602
Nitrous acid (salts), 613, 615–617
  preparation, 615, 617
  properties, 616–617
Nitryl halides, 611–612
Non-aqueous solvents, *see* Solvents (non-aqueous)
Non-electrostatic bonds, 192–215
Non-polar linkages, 206
Non-stoichiometric compounds, 224–225
Norite, 667
Noselite, structure, 729
Nuclear compositions, 17–19
Nuclear decay processes, 54–55, 57
Nuclear fission, 72–76
  chain reaction, 75–76
Nuclear fission, critical mass, 75
  energy release, 74–75
  history, 72, 73
  "liquid drop" approach, 73
  natural, 74
  yields, 74
Nuclear forces, 18
Nuclear fusion, 68, 69
Nuclear reactions, 66–77
  alpha-induced, 70, 71
  bombarding particles, 67
  capture type, 69
  deuteron-induced, 70, 71
  energetics, 68
  fission type, 69
  fusion type, 69
  gamma-induced, 70, 71
  history, 66
  neutron-induced, 70, 71
  notation, 67–68
  particle-particle type, 69
  proton-induced, 70, 71
  spallation type, 69
  theory, 67
  types, 69, 70, 71
Nuclear stability, 52–77; *see also* Radioactivity
Nucleonics, 76
Nucleons, 18
Nuclides, 26

Odd molecules, 212–213
Oleum, 538, 541–542
Olivine structure, 724
One-electron bonds, 212
"Onium" salts, high temperature acids, 332–333
Oppenheimer-Phillips reaction, 71
Optical activity, *see also* Isomerism, optical
  dependence upon wavelength, 267, 268
  molecular rotation, 265
  rotatory dispersion, 267, 268
  specific rotation, 265
Orbital electron capture, 54
Orbital hybridization, 201–203
  in 4-coordinate complexes, 256–257
  in 6-coordinate complexes, 259–261
Orbitals (atomic), 90
  dependence upon n and l, 96
  directional characteristics, 106–108
  order of occupancy, 93–97
Orbitals (molecular), 197–198
Orpiment, 656
Orthoclase, structure, 728

Osmium, *see* Transition elements, periodic group VIII
Osmium carbonyls, 707, 710, 711
Ostwald process, 594
Oxidation, 280–281
Oxidation number, definition, 179
  magnitude, 179–180
Oxidation potentials, 284–305
  of alkali metals, 296
  applications, 297–305
  Born-Haber treatment, 294–297
  combinations of half-reactions, 297–299
  concentration effects, 291–292
  conventions, 285
  evaluation of equilibrium constants, 299–300
  of halogens, 296
  hydrogen ion concentration effects, 292–293
  magnitudes, 290–297
  numerical values, 286–290
  origin, 284–285
  reaction predictions, 297
  relationship to electronegativity, 293
  signs, 285, 290
  stabilization of oxidation state, 300–305
  standard values, 285
Oxidation states, in covalent compounds, 281
  definition, 179
  stabilization, 300–305
    by coordination, 301–305
    examples, 301
    oxidation potential data, 302–304
    by precipitation, 301–305
Oxides, 500
  hydrous, 502
Oxy acids, 498
Oxycyanogen, 470
Oxygen, chemical characteristics, 492–493
  physical constants, 482
  preparation, 493
Oxygen family, 481–555
  abundances, 481
  chemical characteristics, 492–493
  family relationships, 481–484
  modifications, free elements, 484–492
  physical constants, 482
  polymerization, free elements, 482–483
  preparation and production, 493
Oxygen family hydrides, physical constants, 494
Oxygen fluorides, 430–431
  difluoride, 430
  monofluoride, 431
Oxygen isotopes, concentration, 47, 52
Oxygen modifications, 484–487
  atomic, 484–485
  diatomic, 482
  tetratomic, 483, 487
Ozone, 485–487
  preparation, 486–487
  properties, 485
  structure, 486

Packing fraction, 36–38
  definition, 36
  in evaluation of atomic weights, 38
  numerical values, 37, 911–916
  significance, 38
Palladium, *see* Transition elements (periodic group VIII)
Palladium carbonyl halides, 716
Palladium hydride, 413–414
Paracyanogen, 466
Paramagnetic behavior, definition, 165
  examples, 166–167
  source, 166
  temperature dependence, 166
Parathiocyanogen, 467
Particles, atomic, 6–10
Pauling-Slater theory, 199–200
Perbromic acid, non-existence, 444
Perchloric acid (salts), 441–443
  preparation, 442
  properties, 442–443
Periodic acids (salts), 443–444
  dimeso- , 443
  meso- , 443
  meta- , 443
  para- , 443
  preparation, 444
  properties, 443–444
Periodic classification, *see also* Mendeléeff's periodic system, Meyer's periodic system
  bases for, 117–119
  conventions in, 125–126
  electronic forms, 123–125
  essentials of, 120
  families in, 125
  geometrical forms, 121
  historical development, 110–117
  long form, 121–123
  modern trends, 120–125
  periods in, 126
  series in, 126
Permutit, structure, 729

Peroxides, 507–511
examples, 508
nomenclature, 507
preparation, 510–511
properties, 509–510
Peroxy acids (salts), 511–515
examples, 508, 512
nomenclature, 511
preparation, 513–515
properties, 512–513
structures, 511–512
Peroxyboric acid (salts), 514
Peroxycarbonic acids (salts), 508, 514
Peroxychromic acids (salts), 508, 514
Peroxyhydrates, 515
Peroxynitric acid (salts), 612, 613
Peroxyphosphoric acids (salts), 508, 512–514, 641
Peroxysulfuric acids (salts), 508, 512–514
Phenacite, structure, 724
Phlogopite, structure, 728
Phospham, 660
Phosphates, *see also* Phosphoric acids
condensed, 640, 645, 646, 648–654
meta-, 640, 645–646, 649–654
cyclic, 650–652
glasses, 652–654
acidic properties, 653
hexameta-, 653
insoluble, 652
nomenclature, 649–650
phase relationships, 650
relationships among types, 651
ortho-, 640, 648
poly-, 640, 645, 646, 648–654
pyro-, 640, 645–646, 648–649
phase relationships, 650
tri-, 640, 645–646, 648–649
phase relationships, 650
Phosphites, *see* Phosphorous acids
Phosphoric acids, 640, 645, 646–648; *see also* Phosphates
hydration-dehydration relationships, 646
pure acids, 647–648
strengths, 646–647
strong, compositions, 647
structures, 645
Phosphorous acids (salts), 640, 642–643
preparation, 643
properties, 642–643
structures, 642
Phosphorus, chemical characteristics, 568
physical constants, 557
Phosphorus, preparation, 568
Phosphorus compounds, halides, 623–629
numerical constants, 624
penta-, 624, 626, 628
structures, 626, 628
tetra-, 624, 628–629
tri-, 624, 625–626
structure, 625
halogen-containing acids, 634–635
hydrides, 621–623
diphosphine, 623
phosphine, 621–623
solid hydride, 623
nitrides, 658
nitrogen compounds, 658–660
oxides, 635–639
dioxide, polymeric, 636–637
hexoxide, 638–639
phosphorus(III) oxide, 636
phosphorus(V) oxide, 637–638
polymorphic forms, 637
structure, 637
trioxide, 638–639
oxy acids (salts), 639–654; *see also* Hypophosphoric acid, Peroxyphosphoric acids, Phosphoric acids, Phosphorous acids
ammono, 658–660
types, 640–641
oxy halides, 629–632
physical constants, 630
preparation, 629, 632
structures, 629, 631
oxy sulfide, 656–657
phosphonitrilic halides, 629, 630, 631, 632–634
physical constants, 630
polymerization, 632–633
preparation, 633–634
structures, 632–633
phosphonium halides, 621–622
thermal stabilities, 622
pseudo halides, 625
sulfides, 654–656
physical constants, 655
preparation, 656
properties, 655
structures, 654–655
sulfo halides, 629, 630, 631, 632
sulfur compounds, 654–658
thio acids (salts), 657–658, 660
Phosphorus modifications, 561–565
gaseous, 561–562
liquid, 562–563
vapor pressure relationships, 562

Phosphorus modifications, phase relationships, 564–565
  solid, 563–564
    black, 564
    red, 563
    scarlet, 564
    violet, 563–564
    white, 563
Pile, chain reacting, 76
Plagioclase felspars, structure, 728
Platinum, *see* Transition elements (periodic group VIII)
Platinum compounds, carbonyl halides, 715–716
  dipositive, stereochemistry, 254–256
  helide, 379
Platinum metals, *see* Transition elements (periodic group VIII)
Plumbanes, *see* Lead compounds, hydrides
Plumbates, 694
Plutonium, *see also* Actinide elements
  production, 76
Polar linkages, 206
Polonium, *see* Oxygen family
  discovery, 61
Poly acids (salts), 273–277; *see also* Heteropoly acids, Isopoly acids
Polyanionic aggregation, 276–277, 518
  among group IVb elements, 732–733
  among phosphates, 646
Polyanions, vs. intermediate phases, 732
Polydentate groups, 237
Polyhalide-halogenoids, 470–471
Polyhalides, 453–460
  examples, 454
  formation, 453–454
  phase rule studies, 457–458
  properties, 456–457
  structures, 455–456
  theory, 454–455
  thermal stabilities, 455, 456
  type X_n^-, 458–459
  type $XX'_n{}^-$, 459–460
  type $XX'X''_n{}^-$, 460
Polyhalogenoids, 470–471
Polymolybdates, 273–277
Polynuclear complexes, 272–273
  nomenclature, 243
  optical isomerism, 266–267
Polyplumbanes, 678
Polyplumbides, 732–733
Polystannanes, 678
Polystannides, 732–733
Polysulfides, 518
Polysulfuric acids (salts), 542
Polytungstates, 273–277
Polyvanadates, 273, 274, 277
Positive rays, analysis, 21–25
  generation, 8
  parabolic recording, 21
Positron, characteristics, 9, 10
  discovery, 8
  emission, 54, 55, 57
  role in nucleus, 18
Potassium, *see also* Alkali metals
  chemical characteristics, 822, 823
  physical constants, 819
  preparation, 824
Potassium isotopes, concentration, 48
Praseodymium, *see* Lanthanide elements
Precipitates, hydrous, 501–502
  isobaric dehydration, 501
  precipitation *p*H, 502–503
Properties, non-periodic, 118
  periodic, 118
    theoretical evaluation, 119
Protactinium, *see* Actinide elements
Proton, characteristics, 7–8, 10
  emission, 55
  nuclear forces, 52
  role in nucleus, 17, 18
Protonated double bond, 213
  in boron hydrides, 790, 793–794
Prout's hypothesis, 5, 110
Prussian blue, 720–721
Pseudo-halogens, *see* Halogenoids
Pseudo inert gas structures, stabilities, 155
Pyrophillite, structure, 727, 728
Pyroxene, structure, 725–726

Quanta, 80
Quantum numbers, 89–91
  azimuthal, 84, 89–90
  magnetic, 90
  principal, 84, 89
  spin, 91
  subsidiary, 89–90
Quantum theory, 79, 80–81
Quartz, 691, 692

Radial distribution curves, 128, 129
Radiation, discontinuous nature, 79–80
Radii (atomic), 132–136
Radii (covalent), 132–136
  bond multiplicity and, 133
  constancy, 133
  determination, 132–133
  effect on ionization potentials, 154
  factors affecting, 133–134

Radii (covalent), magnitudes, 135
normal valence, 134
octahedral, 134
square, 134
tetrahedral, 134
Radii (crystal), 138
Radii (ionic), 136–145
calculated, 137–139
determination, 136–137
empirical, 137
factors affecting, 143–144
graphic representation, 148–149
magnitudes, 139, 140–142
relationship to charge, 151
theoretical evaluation, 145
univalent, 138
Radii (metallic), 134
Radii (van der Waals), 145–146
Radioactive decay, 58–59
Radioactive decay chains, 58
Radioactive decay series, 62–66, 917–918
characteristics, 63
memberships, 917–918
periodic relationships, 64–65
Radioactive displacement laws, 63, 66
Radioactive equilibrium, 58–59
Radioactivity (artificial), 66–77
applications, 77
discovery, 66
Radioactivity (natural), 61–66
discovery, 61
Radioisotopes, naturally occurring, 62
Radium, *see also* Alkaline earth elements
chemical characteristics, 849, 850
discovery, 61
physical constants, 846
Radium halides, 856
Radium peroxide, 859
Radius ratio, 137
effect on crystal radii, 143–144
Radon, *see also* Actinon, Thoron
chemical characteristics, aluminum-(III) halide derivatives, 382
hydrate, 381
phenol derivative, 382
history, 374
physical constants, 375
recovery from radium, 384–385
Rare earth elements, *see also* Lanthanide elements
electronic configurations, 103–104
Realgar, structure, 549, 656
Reduction, 280–281
Representative elements, electronic configurations, 102–103
Representative elements, general characteristics, 417
Resonance, covalent bonds, 194–195
nature of, 194
origin of, 194
relationship to bond distances, 195
relationship to bond strengths, 194
nucleus, 18
Resonance energy, 194
Resonance link, in diborane, 790
Resonance structures, 195
Rhenium, *see* Transition elements (periodic group VIIa)
Rhenium carbonyl, 707, 710–711
Rhodium, *see* Transition elements(periodic group VIII)
Rhodium carbonyls, 707, 710
Rollin film, 376
Roussin's black salts, 602, 604, 605
Roussin's red salts, 602
Rubidium, *see also* Alkali metals
chemical characteristics, 822, 823
physical constants, 819
Ruby, 754
synthetic, 755
Rule of eight, 86, 172
limitations, 175–178
Rule of two, 178
Ruthenium, *see* Transition elements (periodic group VIII)
Ruthenium carbonyls, 707, 710
Ruthenium purple, 721
Rydberg constant, 81

Samarium, *see* Lanthanide elements
Sapphire, 754
synthetic, 755
Scandium, *see* Transition elements (periodic group IIIa)
Schönites, 539, 541
Schottky defects, 225
Selenic acid (salts), 540, 541
Selenium, *see also* Oxygen family
chemical characteristics, 493
oxidation states, 483
physical constants, 482
preparation, 493
Selenium compounds, halides, 520, 521
oxides, 527–528, 531
oxy acids, 540, 541
Selenium modifications, 491–492
Selenocyanogen, 469
Semi-polar bond, 193, 232
Siderophilic elements, 29
Silanes, *see* Silicon compounds, hydrides

Silica, *see also* Silicon compounds, oxides, dioxide
gel, 692–693
structure, 728
Silicates, 721–729
applications, 729
meta-, 725
naturally occurring, 722–729
classification, 722–723
isomorphous replacement, 722–723
structures, 723–729
soluble, 722
structures, 723–729
discrete anions, 724–725
extended anions, 725–728
three-dimensional networks, 728–729
tetrameta-, 725
Silicic acid, 693, 721
Silicon, chemical characteristics, 670
organic chemistry, 729–730
physical constants, 662
preparation, 671
Silicon compounds, bond energies, 672
carbide, 698
cationic compounds, 731
halogen compounds, 678–681, 682–685
halides, 678–681, 682
halosilanes, 730, 682–684, 685
oxy halides, 683–685
hydrides, 673, 674–676
chemical characteristics, 674–675
derivatives, 676
physical constants, 673
preparation, 675–676
nitride, 696
nomenclature, 731–732
oxides, dioxide, 691–693; *see also* Silica
chemical characteristics, 692
modifications, 691, 692
phase relationships, 691
structures, 691, 692
monoxide, 687–688
silico-oxalic acid, 682
sulfide, 695
Silicon modifications, 669
Silicones, 730
Siliconium compounds, 731, 765
Silicon-oxygen tetrahedra, 723
Siloxane, 730
halo, 684
Silver, *see also* Coinage metals
chemical characteristics, 822, 823
oxidation potential data, 304, 825
oxidation states, 821, 825–831
Silver, physical constants, 819
preparation, 824
Silver compounds, carbonyl sulfate, 716
complexes, with ethylenic materials, 840–841
cyanide, 718
halides, silver(I), 832
silver(II) fluoride, 833–834
sub-, 834–835
oxidation states, characteristics of,
+1, 826, 827–828
+2, 828–829
+3, 829, 830–831
oxides, silver(I), 835–836
silver(II), 836
silver(III), 836–837
selenide, 837
sulfide, 837
telluride, 837
Silver isotopes, concentration, 48
Size-charge relationships, 152
Size relationships, 127–152; *see also* Radii
applications, 151–152
factors determining, 129
among transition elements, 146
trends, 146–151
Sodalite, structure, 729
Sodium, *see also* Alkali metals
chemical characteristics, 822, 823
physical constants, 819
preparation and production, 822, 824
Sodium compounds, *see also* Alkali metal compounds
borates, structures, 810
borohydride, *see* Borohydrides (metal)
chloride, structure, 137
hydride, 406, 407, 408
nitrosyl, 598
phosphates, meta-, 649–654
Solid solutions, interstitial, 221
substitutional, 220
Solubility, in polar solvents, 342–344
relationship to hydrogen bonding, 190–191
Solvation, of anions, 189
of ions in equations, 281–282
or proton, 309
Solvation energy, relationship to oxidation potentials, 294–296
relationships to solubility, 342–343
Solvents, acidic, 312
amphiprotic, 312
aprotic, 312
basic, 312

Solvents, classification, 338–342
  differentiating, 316, 339–340
  electrolytic, 339
  equivalent groups, 340, 342
  historical development, 337–338
  leveling, 315, 339–340
  non-aqueous, 337–369
  polar, solubility relationships, 342–344
  protonic, 312
  water-like, 341–342
    physical constants, 341
Solvents (non-aqueous), 337–369
  acetonitrile, 357
  acid amides, 354
  acid anhydrides, 357
  acids, aliphatic, 356–357
  alcohols, 355
  amines, 354–355
  ammonia, 344–352
    acid-base behaviors, 350
    ammonation reactions, 351
    ammonolysis reactions, 351–352
    metal solutions, 217–218, 347–349
    metathesis reactions, 351
    reactions, 349–352
    reduction reactions, 349–350
    solubilities, 344–347
  ammonias, substituted, 352–355
  bromine trifluoride, 325–326, 366
  carbonyl chloride, 323–324, 365
  dinitrogen(IV) oxide, 325, 366–367
  electrodeposition from, 367–368
  ethanolamines, 354
  ethers, 355
  ethylenediamine, 355
  hydrazine, 353–354
  hydrogen cyanide, 361
  hydrogen fluoride, 357–360
    dissolution processes, 358–360
    ions in, 358–359
    solubilities, 358
  hydrogen sulfide, 360
    thiohydrolysis reactions, 360
  hydroxylamine, 352–353
  ketones, 356
  mercury(II) bromide, 367
  nitric acid, 362, 596
  nitromethane, 357
  nitrosyl chloride, 366
  organic liquids, 355–357
  selenium oxychloride, 325, 365
  sulfuric acid, 361–362
    cryoscopic studies, 596, 610–611
Sommerfeld theory, 84–86
Spectra, atomic, 79–80
  hydrogen, 81–83
Spectra, x-ray, 12–14
Sphalerite, structure, 133
Spinels, 756–757
Spodumene, structure, 726
Stannanes, *see* Tin compounds, hydrides
Stationary states, electronic, 81, 82, 85
Stereochemistry, various elements, 269
Stereoisomerism, coordination number 2, 253
  coordination number 3, 253
  coordination number 4, 253–257
    optical activity, 255
    orbital hybridization, 256–257
    square planar arrangement, 253–257
      in platinum(II) complexes, 254–256
      trans effect, 256
    tetrahedral arrangement, 254
  coordination number 5, 258
  coordination number 6, 258–267
    octahedral arrangement, 259
    optical isomerism, 264–267
    orbital hybridization, 259–261
    possible arrangements, 258–259
  coordination number 7, 267–268
  coordination number 8, 268, 270
    orbital hybridization, 270
Strontium, *see also* Alkaline earth metals
  chemical characteristics, 849, 850
  physical constants, 846
  preparation, 851
Strontium compounds, azide, 860
  complexes, 861
  halides, 856, 857
  hydride, 407, 408, 412
  nitride, 860
  oxide, 858
  salts, 861
  selenide, 859
  sulfide, 859
  telluride, 859
Sulfamic acid (salts), 551–552
Sulfamide, 522, 553
Sulfites, *see* Sulfurous acid
Sulfite vs. sulfonate, 536
Sulfoxylic acid (salts), 533–534
Sulfur, chemical characteristics, 492, 493
  oxidation states, 482, 483
  physical constants, 482
  preparation and production, 493
Sulfur compounds, halides, 518–521

Sulfur compounds, bromides, 519, 521
chlorides, 519, 520–521
fluorides, 519–521
physical constants, 519
hydrogen compounds, 515–518
persulfide, 516–518
polysulfides, 516–518
sulfide, 341, 494, 515–516
nitrides, *see* Nitrogen compounds, sulfides
nitrogen compounds, 547–555
oxides, 525–533
dioxide, 527–528; *see also* Solvents (non-aqueous)
hydrate, 382
physical constants, 341
preparations, 527
properties, 527
heptoxide, 531, 533
monoxide, 525–526
sesquioxide, 527
tetroxide, 533
trioxide, 528–531, 532
chemical characteristics, 530–531
hydrates, 531, 532
modifications, solid, 528–530
physical constants, 529
preparation, 529–531
vapor pressure relationships, 529–530
oxy acids (salts), 533–547
compositions, 534
dithionous, 535–536
halogen-containing, 524–525
chlorosulfonic, 524–525
fluosulfonic, 522, 524–525
hyposulfurous, *see* Sulfur compounds, oxy acids, dithionous
peroxy, 508, 512–514
pyrosulfuric, 541–542
pyrosulfurous, 537–538
sulfuric, *see* Sulfuric acid (salts)
sulfurous, *see* Sulfurous acid (salts)
thionic, *see* Thionic acids (salts)
thiosulfuric, 542–543
structure, 543
oxy halides, 521–524
chemical characteristics, 523
physical constants, 522
preparation, 523, 524
pyrosulfuryl, 521, 522, 524
structures, 521, 523
sulfuryl halides, 521–524
thionyl halides, 521–524
Sulfur modifications, 487–491
gas, 491
Sulfur modifications, liquid, 490–491
effects upon properties, 490–491
transformations, 490–491
phase relationships, 491
plastic, 489–490
solid, 488, 489–490
monoclinic, 489
physical constants, 488
rhombic, 489
transformations, 489
Sulfur molecular species, 487–489
structures, 487–488
Sulfuric acid (salts), 538–542; *see also* Solvents (non-aqueous)
nitrogen derivatives, 550–555, 572
poly, 610
properties, 538–539
structure, 538
Sulfurous acid (salts), 536–537
isomerism, 536
preparation, 536
properties, 536–537
structure, 536
Superfluid flow, 49, 376, 377
Superoxides, 508–511
examples, 508
formation, 509, 510
properties, 509–510
structure, 509

Talc, structure, 727, 728
Tantalum, *see* Transition elements (periodic group Va)
Tantalum compounds, carbide, 699, 700
peroxy acids (salts), 508, 514
Technetium, *see* Transition elements (periodic group VIIa)
Telluric acids (salts), 541
Telluric screw, 111–112
Tellurium chemical characteristics, 493
physical constants, 482
preparation, 493
Tellurium compounds, halides, 520–521
oxides, 528, 531
Tellurium modifications, 491–492
Terbium, *see* Lanthanide elements
Thallium, chemical characteristics, 739–740
oxidation potential data, 736
oxidation states, 736–737
physical constants, 735
preparation, 741
Thallium(I) compounds, 769
Thallium(III) compounds, complexes, 765–768
halides, 745, 749, 751

Thallium(III) compounds, oxide, 757
Thermal diffusion, 44–45
Thiocyanogen, 467–469; *see also* Parathiocyanogen
Thiocyanogen halides, 473
Thionic acids (salts), 543–547
  dithionic acid (salts), 544–545
  polythionic acids (salts), 545–547
  structures, 543–544
Thomsonite, structure, 729
Thorium, *see also* Actinide elements
  oxidation potential data, 877
  recovery from monazite, 905
Thorium compounds, boride, 771, 772
  borohydride, 782, 783, 785
  carbide, 697, 698
Thorium (4*n*) decay series, 62, 64, 917
Thoron, 374
Thorteveitite, structure, 725
Three-electron bonds, 212–213
Thulium, *see* Lanthanide elements
Tin, chemical characteristics, 670
  physical constants, 662
  preparation and production, 671
Tin compounds, halides, 679–680, 681–682
  hydrides, 673, 677
  nitride, 696
  oxides, 688, 693, 694
  peroxy acid (salts), 508, 514
  stannates, 694
  sulfides, 695, 696
  thiostannates, 696
Tin disease, 670
Tin modifications, 669–670
Titanium, *see* Transition elements (periodic group IVa)
Titanium compounds, carbide, 699, 700
  peroxy acids (salts), 508
Titanium family borides, 770, 772
Titanium family borohydrides, 782, 783, 786
Trans effect, 256
Transition elements, 868–890
  characteristics of families, 876–890
  characteristics related to electronic configurations, 869–876
    color and absorption spectra, 874–875
    complex formation, 875–876
    interstitial compounds, 876
    magnetic properties, 169–170, 874
    oxidation states, 873–874
  electronic arrangements, 103–106
  physical constants, 870–872
Transition elements (periodic group IIIa), 876
  physical constants, 870–872
Transition elements (periodic group IVa), 876–877
  abundances, 876
  applications, 876
  oxidation potential data, 877
  oxidation states, 873–874
  physical constants, 870–872
  preparation, 877
  properties, 877
Transition elements (periodic group Va), 877–879
  abundances, 877
  applications, 878
  oxidation potential data, 878
  oxidation states, 873–874, 878–879
  physical constants, 870–872
  preparation, 879
  properties, 878
Transition elements (periodic group VIa), 879–882
  abundances, 879
  applications, 879
  oxidation potential data, 880
  oxidation states, 873–874, 880–882
  physical constants, 870–872
  preparation, 882
  properties, 879–880
Transition elements (periodic group VIIa), 882–885
  abundances, 882
  applications, 882
  oxidation potential data, 883
  oxidation states, 873–874, 883–885
  physical constants, 870–872
  preparation, 885
  properties, 882–883
Transition elements (periodic group VIII), 885–890
  ferrous metals, 885–888
    abundances, 885
    applications, 885
    oxidation potential data, 886
    oxidation states, 873–874, 886–887
    physical constants, 870–872
    preparation, 887–888
    properties, 885–886
  platinum metals, 888–890
    abundances, 888
    applications, 888
    oxidation potential data, 889
    oxidation states, 873–874, 888–890
    preparation, 890
    properties, 888

Transition metal carbides, 699–700
Transition metal ions, magnetic moments, 169
Transition metal peroxy compounds, 511, 512, 514
Transuranium elements, 76–77; *see also* Actinide elements
electronic configurations, 104, 106
Tremolite, structure, 726
Tridymite, 691, 692
Triiodide ion, 453, 454, 458
Tritium, 394–395; *see also* Hydrogen isotopes
occurrence in nature, 394
physical constants, 395
radioactivity, 395
synthesis, 394–395
Trouton's constant, 449
Tungsten, *see* Transition elements (periodic group VIa)
Tungsten compounds, blues, 881
bronzes, 882–883
carbides, 699–700
carbonyl, hexa-, 703, 707, 708, 709
peroxy acids (salts), 508, 514
Turnbull's blue, 720–721

Ultramarines, 729
boron, 811
Uncertainty principle, 84
Uranide elements, 892
Uranium, *see* Actinide elements
Uranium compounds, boride, 771, 772
borohydride, 782, 783, 785
carbide, 697
deuteride, 415
fluoride, hexa-, 46
hydride, 415
peroxy acids (salts), 508, 514
Uranium ($4n + 2$) decay series, 62, 65, 918
Uranium isotopes, separation, 40–41, 43–44, 45, 46
Urea, 689, 690

Valency, definition, 171
development of electronic theory, 171–175
electrostatic concept, 172
Kossel's approach, 173, 174
Lewis's approach, 174–175
primary, 230
relationship to electrons, 173
relationship to stable configurations, 173–175
secondary, 230
Valency, structural concept, 172
Vanadium, *see* Transition elements (periodic group Va)
Vanadium compounds, carbides, 697, 699, 700
peroxy acids (salts), 508
Vanadium family borides, 770, 772
van der Waals forces, 215
liquefaction of inert gas elements, 376
liquefaction of nitrogen, 560
Verneuil process, 755
Vorce cell, 424

Wackenroder's liquid, 546
Walden inversion, 267
Water, 494–500
acid-base character, 497
association, 496
chemical characteristics, 497
derivatives, 500–503
modes of occurrence, 497–500
anion, 498–499
of constitution, 498
coordinated, 498
hydrated colloids, 500
lattice, 499
zeolitic, 499–500
oxidation-reduction characteristics, 497
phase relationships, 495
physical constants, 341, 494
solid forms, 495–496
structure, liquid, 496
solid, 496
Water molecule, structure, 186, 200, 207–208, 495
Werner complexes, 227
Werner's theory, 229–230
applications, 230–232
Willemite, structure, 724
Wollastonite, structure, 725
Wurtzite structure, 133

Xenon, *see also* Inert gas elements
chemical characteristics, deuterohydrate, 381
hydrate, 381
phenol derivative, 382
-quinol clathrate, 382
discovery, 374
physical constants, 375

Ytterbium, *see* Lanthanide elements
Yttria, 891
Yttrium, *see* Lanthanide elements; Transition elements, periodic group IIIa

Zeolites, in exchange reactions, 51
  structure, 728–729
Zero point energy, 49, 390
Zinc, chemical characteristics, 849–851
  oxidation potential data, 850
  physical constants, 847
  preparation and production, 852
Zinc blende structure, 133
Zinc compounds, "basic" acetate, 866
  complexes, 864–867
  halides, 856, 857
  oxide, 859
  salts, 861
  selenide, 859
  sulfide, 859
Zinc compounds, telluride, 859
Zinc family elements, 845–867
  abundances, 845
  chemical characteristics, 848–851
  compounds, 852–867
  family relationships, 845–848
  oxidation potential data, 850
  oxidation states, 848, 852–855
  physical constants, 847
  preparation and production, 852
Zinc family peroxides, 508, 511
Zircon, structure, 724
Zirconium, *see* Transition elements (periodic group IVa)
Zirconium carbide, 699, 700